Supreme Court Cases on Political Representation
1787-2001

SUPREME COURT

CASES ON POLITICAL

REPRESENTATION

1787-2001

CHRISTOPHER A. ANZALONE

EDITOR

M.E.Sharpe
Armonk, New York
London, England

Library of Congress Cataloging-in-Publication Data

Supreme Court cases on political representation, 1787–2001 / Christopher A. Anzalone, editor
    p. cm.
Includes bibliographical references and index.
ISBN 0-7656-0710-7 (hardcover : alk paper)
  1. Election law—United States—Digests. 2. Representative government and
representation—United States—Digests. 3. Proportional representation—United
States—History. I. Anzalone, Christopher A., 1963–

KF4885.A75 S87 2002
342.73′053—dc21   2001031154

Printed in the United States of America

The paper used in this publication meets the minimum requirements of
American National Standard for Information Sciences
Permanence of Paper for Printed Library Materials,
ANSI Z 39.48-1984.

∞

To Michael, Toni, Kathryn, and Damien

Contents

Preface

It is certain in Theory, that the only moral Founation of Government is the consent of the People. But to what an Extent Shall We carry this Principle?

John Adams (1776)

If the notion that political rights are relegated to some arcane domain of the legal specialist, that they fail to merit the attention or passions of the American public, that all the major issues have been resolved, and all that remain are the minute tinkering of details, then how does one explain the compelling drama leading to *Bush v. Gore* (page 478) decided by the U.S. Supreme Court in December 2000? Charges and counter-charges of voting irregularities, stolen elections, and partisan courts were rampant. Meanwhile, a myriad of issues during this millennial period indicate that the quest for political rights is alive and well and worthy of more than just prosaic attention and debate. Term limits, referenda and initiatives, instructions to legislators, accuracy of the census, legislative redistricting, and campaign finance reform are, and will continue to be, front-burner issues with Americans. And as Alexis de Tocqueville reminds us, most controversies in the United States ultimately find some sort of resolution in court.

Political rights are about fairness in voting; the right to vote; the right to seek office; the access to the tools to exercise while seeking office; quali-fications for political office; the right to speech, press, and association related to the political process; protections for those testifying in front of congressional committees, and the like. When one considers whether Americans have political rights, it is not really about how the constitution addresses political rights nor is it what laws were crafted to address political rights; rather it is how the laws are played out daily, one case at a time.

Between the covers of this one volume there are over 400 Supreme Court cases, the first one, *Anderson v. Dunn* (page 508), was decided in 1821; the last, in 2001. Although the Supreme Court is obviously a creation of the U.S. Constitution, which was drafted in 1787, the Court did not decide its first political rights case until 1821. Since there were no earlier cases, this book is, in fact, the complete history of the Supreme Court for political rights and representation.

The cases have been edited—often substantially—to keep the focus on political rights. Only the opinions for the Court are included. This is in recognition of the indisputable impact the majority opinion has on governing; concurring and dissenting opinions have inherent value in legal discourse, but by definition they offer only alternatives.

As mentioned above, this book includes several hundred cases, some of which are landmark events in American constitutional and political history; others are far less newsworthy. But in the aggregate, these cases demonstrate a more thoughtful and steady (and at times glacial) approach to judicial decision-making and constitutional interpretation. It is the reality of the Court.

This book is divided into sixteen chapters. Chapter 1 is about suffrage, voter fraud, voter qualifications, and relevant judicial review of the Voting Rights Act of 1965. Chapter 2 concerns poll taxes and literacy tests as prequalifications to voting, which the Court eventually declared unconstitutional. Chapter 3 is about the states' responsibility to draw federal legislative districts. This responsibility has been tempered by the Voting Rights Act of 1965 and in particular the Act's preclearance provision. The census is the subject of Chapter 4. The Supreme Court in recent decades has ruled on the regulations, execution, and implementation of the census. Chapter 5 is about the rights and legal procedures candidates encounter when seeking elective office. Political parties are the subjects of Chapter 6. Candidate support, independent third parties, the Communist Party, and racial policies are common issues the Court has reviewed. Campaign finance laws and regulations and their impact on political rights, free speech, and associational rights are included in Chapter 7. Chapter 8 is about the Court's review of the Electoral College. Chapter 9 demonstrates that although these election officials have considerable authority, it is not absolute. Chapter 10 is about the rights and re-

strictions of federal, state, and local legislators, including qualifications of legislators, the Speech and Debate Clause, and the extent of a legislative body's authority over the discipline of its members. Cases involving political libel, the use and restrictions of the media in campaigns, and the requirements in the media for fairness in political races are in Chapter 11. Chapter 12 involves the role of the right of citizens to preserve political self-destination. Chapter 13 includes a myriad of cases involving congressional testimony and congressional investigations of internal security. Oaths of allegiance and loyalty statements for purposes of employment, receipt of governmental benefits, and education are the subjects of Chapter 14. The Constitution guarantees a republican form of government. This guarantee vis-à-vis government organization and the Voting Rights Act's preclearance requirements are the subjects of Chapter 15. Finally, Chapter 16 includes the Supreme Court decisions that do not neatly fit into the other chapters; for example, there are political rights decisions within the criminal justice, patronage, and judicial orders to a legislative branch.

Lastly, the bibliography points readers to useful scholarly resources to facilitate additional research, and the table of cases and index allow quick referencing within the book.

Acknowledgments

I would like to thank my invaluable team at M.E. Sharpe: Peter Labella, Esther Clark, and Henrietta Toth. I share with them all the great things about this book. I would also like to recognize the excellent resources at the law libraries at Washington College of Law (American University) and Albany Law School.

SUPREME COURT CASES ON POLITICAL REPRESENTATION 1787-2001

1
Voters and Voting

This chapter looks at suffrage for minorities and women, laws against obstruction of voting or voting fraudulently, registration and qualifications of voters, and the Court's decisions on various provisions of the Voting Rights Act of 1965.

Minor v. Happerset
88 U.S. 162 (1874)

The question is . . . whether, since the adoption of the Fourteenth Amendment, a woman, who is a citizen of the United States and of the State of Missouri, is a voter in that State, notwithstanding the provision of the constitution and laws of the State, which confine the right of suffrage to men alone. . . .

. . .

There is no doubt that women may be citizens. They are persons, and by the Fourteenth Amendment "all persons born or naturalized in the United States and subject to the jurisdiction thereof" are expressly declared to be "citizens of the United States and of the State wherein they reside." But, in our opinion, it did not need this amendment to give them that position. . . .

. . .

Other proof of like character might be found, but certainly more cannot be necessary to establish the fact that sex has never been made one of the elements of citizenship in the United States. In this respect men have never had an advantage over women. The same laws precisely apply to both. The Fourteenth Amendment did not affect the citizenship of women any more than it did of men. In this particular, therefore, the rights of Mrs. Minor do not depend upon the amendment. She has always been a citizen from her birth, and entitled to all the privileges and immunities of citizenship. The amendment prohibited the State, of which she is a citizen, from abridging any of her privileges and immunities as a citizen of the United States; but it did not confer citizenship on her. That she had before its adoption.

If the right of suffrage is one of the necessary privileges of a citizen of the United States, then the constitution and laws of Missouri confining it to men are in violation of the Constitution of the United States, as amended, and consequently void. The direct question is, therefore, presented whether all citizens are necessarily voters.

The Constitution does not define the privileges and immunities of citizens. For that definition we must look elsewhere. In this case we need not determine what they are, but only whether suffrage is necessarily one of them.

It certainly is nowhere made so in express terms. The United States has no voters in the States of its own creation. The elective officers of the United States are all elected directly or indirectly by State voters. The members of the House of Representatives are to be chosen by the people of the States, and the electors in each State must have the qualifications requisite for electors of the most numerous branch of the State legislature. Senators are to be chosen by the legislatures

3

of the States, and necessarily the members of the legislature required to make the choice are elected by the voters of the State. Each State must appoint in such manner, as the legislature thereof may direct, the electors to elect the President and Vice President. The times, places, and manner of holding elections for Senators and Representatives are to be prescribed in each State by the legislature thereof; but Congress may at any time, by law, make or alter such regulations, except as to the place of choosing Senators. It is not necessary to inquire whether this power of supervision thus given to Congress is sufficient to authorize any interference with the State laws prescribing the qualifications of voters, for no such interference has ever been attempted. The power of the State in this particular is certainly supreme until Congress acts.

The amendment did not add to the privileges and immunities of a citizen. It simply furnished an additional guaranty for the protection of such as he already had. No new voters were necessarily made by it. Indirectly it may have had that effect, because it may have increased the number of citizens entitled to suffrage under the constitution and laws of the States, but it operates for this purpose, if at all, through the States and the State laws, and not directly upon the citizen.

It is clear, therefore, we think, that the Constitution has not added the right of suffrage to the privileges and immunities of citizenship as they existed at the time it was adopted. This makes it proper to inquire whether suffrage was coextensive with the citizenship of the States at the time of its adoption. If it was, then it may with force be argued that suffrage was one of the rights which belonged to citizenship, and in the enjoyment of which every citizen must be protected. But if it was not, the contrary may with propriety be assumed.

When the Federal Constitution was adopted, all the States, with the exception of Rhode Island and Connecticut, had constitutions of their own. These two continued to act under their charters from the Crown. Upon an examination of those constitutions we find that in no State were all citizens permitted to vote. Each State determined for itself who should have that power. . . .

In this condition of the law in respect to suffrage in the several States it cannot for a moment be doubted that if it had been intended to make all citizens of the United States voters, the framers of the Constitution would not have left it to implication. . . . But if further proof is necessary to show that no such change was intended, it can easily be found both in and out of the Constitution. . . . If suffrage is necessarily a part of citizenship, then the citizens of each State must be entitled to vote in the several States precisely as their citizens are. This is more than asserting that they may change their residence and become citizens of the State and thus be voters. It goes to the extent of insisting that while retaining their original citizenship they may vote in any State. This, we think, has never been claimed. . . . And if suffrage was necessarily one of the absolute rights of citizenship, why confine the operation of the limitation to male inhabitants? Women and children are, as we have seen, "persons." They are counted in the enumeration upon which the apportionment is to be made, but if they were necessarily voters because of their citizenship unless clearly excluded, why inflict the penalty for the exclusion of males alone? Clearly, no such form of words would have been selected to express the idea here indicated if suffrage was the absolute right of all citizens.

And still again, after the adoption of the Fourteenth Amendment, it was deemed necessary to adopt a fifteenth, as follows: "The right of citizens of the United States to vote shall not be denied or abridged by the United States, or by any State, on account of race, color, or previous condition of servitude." The Fourteenth Amendment had already provided that no State should make or enforce any law which should abridge the privileges or immunities of citizens of the United States. If suffrage was one of these privileges or immunities, why amend the Constitution to prevent its being denied on account of race, etc.? Nothing is more evident than that the greater must include the less, and if all were already protected why go through with the form of amending the Constitution to protect a part?

. . .

. . . No new State has ever been admitted to the Union which has conferred the right of suffrage upon women, and this has never been considered a valid objection to her admission. On the contrary, as is claimed in the argument, the right of suffrage was withdrawn from women as early as 1807 in the State of New Jersey, without any attempt to obtain the interference of the United States to prevent it. Since then the governments of the insurgent States have been reorganized under a requirement that before their representatives could be admitted to seats in Congress they must have adopted new constitutions, republican in form. In no one of these constitutions was suffrage conferred upon women, and yet the States have all been restored to their original position as States in the Union.

Besides this, citizenship has not in all cases been made a condition precedent to the enjoyment of the right of suffrage. . . .

. . .

We have given this case the careful consideration its importance demands. If the law is wrong, it ought to be changed; but the power for that is not with us. . . .

Being unanimously of the opinion that the Constitution of the United States does not confer the right of suffrage upon any one, and that the constitutions and laws of the several States which commit that important trust to men alone are not necessarily void, we affirm the judgment.

United States v. Cruikshank
92 U.S. 542 (1875)

The first and ninth counts state the intent of the defendants to have been to hinder and prevent the citizens named in the free exercise and enjoyment of their

> lawful right and privilege to peaceably assemble together with each other and with other citizens of the United States for a peaceful and lawful purpose.

The right of the people peaceably to assemble for lawful purposes existed long before the adoption of the Constitution of the United States. In fact, it is, and always has been, one of the attributes of citizenship under a free government. . . .

. . .

The right of the people peaceably to assemble for the purpose of petitioning Congress for a redress of grievances, or for anything else connected with the powers or the duties of the national government, is an attribute of national citizenship, and, as such, under the protection of, and guaranteed by, the United States. The very idea of a government republican in form implies a right on the part of its citizens to meet peaceably for consultation in respect to public affairs and to petition for a redress of grievances. If it had been alleged in these counts that the object of the defendants was to prevent a meeting for such a purpose, the case would have been within the statute, and within the scope of the sovereignty of the United States. Such, however, is not the case. . . .

. . .

The sixth and fourteenth counts state the intent of the defendants to have been to hinder and prevent the citizens named, being of African descent, and colored,

> in the free exercise and enjoyment of their several and respective right and privilege to vote at any election to be thereafter by law had and held by the people in and of the said State of Louisiana, or by the people of and in the parish of Grant aforesaid.

. . . the right of suffrage is not a necessary attribute of national citizenship, but that exemption from discrimination in the exercise of that right on account of race, etc., is. The right to vote in the States comes from the States, but the right of exemption from the prohibited discrimination comes from the United States. The first has not been granted or secured by the Constitution of the United States, but the last has been.

Inasmuch, therefore, as it does not appear in these counts that the intent of the defendants was to prevent these parties from exercising their right to vote on account of their race, etc., it does not appear that it was their intent to interfere with any right granted or secured by the Constitution or laws of the United States. We may suspect that race was the cause of the hostility, but it is not so averred. . . .

The seventh and fifteenth counts are no better than the sixth and fourteenth. The intent here charged is to put the parties named in great fear of bodily harm, and to injure and oppress them, because, being and having been in all things qualified, they had voted

> at an election before that time had and held according to law by the people of the said State of Louisiana, in said State, to-wit, on the fourth day

of November, 1872, and at divers other elections by the people of the State, also before that time had and held according to law.

There is nothing to show that the elections voted at were any other than State elections, or that the conspiracy was formed on account of the race of the parties against whom the conspirators were to act. The charge as made is really of nothing more than a conspiracy to commit a breach of the peace within a State. Certainly it will not be claimed that the United States have the power or are required to do mere police duly in the States. If a State cannot protect itself against domestic violence, the United States may, upon the call of the executive, when the legislature cannot be convened, lend their assistance for that purpose. . . .

. . .

The order of the Circuit Court arresting the judgment upon the verdict is, therefore, affirmed; and the cause remanded, with instructions to discharge the defendants.

Ex parte Yarbrough
110 U.S. 651 (1884)

Though several different sections of the Revised Statutes are brought into the discussion as the foundation of the indictments found in the record, we think only two of them demand our attention here, namely, sections 5508 and 5520. They are in the following language:

> SEC. 5508. If two or more persons conspire to injure, oppress, threaten, or intimidate any citizen in the free exercise or enjoyment of any right or privilege secured to him by the Constitution or laws of the United States, or because of his having so exercised the same, or if two or more persons go in disguise on the highway, or on the premises of another, with intent to prevent or hinder his free

exercise or enjoyment of any right or privilege so secured, they shall be fined not more than five thousand dollars and imprisoned not more than ten years; and shall, moreover, be thereafter ineligible to any office or place of honor, profit, or trust created by the Constitution or laws of the United States.

SEC. 5520. If two or more persons in any State or territory conspire to prevent, by force, intimidation, or threat, any citizen who is lawfully entitled to vote from giving his support or advocacy, in a legal manner, towards or in favor of the election of any lawfully qualified person as an elector for President or Vice-President, or as a member of the Congress of the United States, or to injure any citizen in person or property on account of such support or advocacy, each of such persons shall be punished by a fine of not less than five hundred nor more than five thousand dollars, or by imprisonment, with or without hard labor, not less than six months nor more than six years, or by both such fine and imprisonment.

The indictments, four in number, on which petitioners were tried, charge in each one all of the defendants with a conspiracy under these sections, directed against a different person in each indictment. On the trial, the cases were consolidated, and as each indictment is in the identical language of all the others. . .

. . .

. . . [T]he offense charged in this indictment as that the defendants conspired to intimidate Berry Saunders, a citizen of African descent, in the exercise of his right to vote for a member of the Congress of the United States, and, in the execution of that conspiracy, they beat, bruised, wounded, and otherwise maltreated him; and, in the second count, that they did this on account of his race, color, and previous condition of servitude, by going in disguise and assaulting him on the public highway and on his own premises.

If the question were not concluded in this Court, as we have already seen that it is by the decision of the Circuit Court, we entertain no doubt that the conspiracy here described is one which is embraced within the provisions of the Revised Statutes which we have cited.

That a government whose essential character is republican, whose executive head and legislative body are both elective, whose numerous and powerful branch of the legislature is elected by the people directly, has no power by appropriate laws to secure this election from the influence of violence, of corruption, and of fraud, is a proposition so startling as to arrest attention and demand the gravest consideration. If this government is anything more than a mere aggregation of delegated agents of other States and governments, each of which is superior to the general government, it must have the power to protect the elections on which its existence depends from violence and corruption.

If it has not this power, it is left helpless before the two great natural and historical enemies of all republics, open violence and insidious corruption.

. . . [T]here is no express power to provide for preventing violence exercised on the voter as a means of controlling his vote, no such law can be enacted. . . .

. . .

So, also, has the Congress been slow to exercise the powers expressly conferred upon it in relation to elections by the fourth section of the first article of the Constitution.

. . .

Will it be denied that it is in the power of that body to provide laws for the proper conduct of those elections? To provide, if necessary, the officers who shall conduct them and make return of the result? And especially to provide, in an election held under its own authority, for security of life and limb to the voter while in the exercise of this function? Can it be doubted that Congress can, by law, protect the act of voting, the place where it is done, and the man who votes from personal violence or intimidation, and the election itself from corruption or fraud?

If this be so, and it is not doubted, are such powers annulled because an election for state officers is held at the same time and place? Is it any less important that the election of members of Congress should be the free choice of all the electors, because state officers are to be elected at the same time?

. . .

. . . [I]t is not correct to say that the right to vote for a member of Congress does not depend on the Constitution of the United States.

The office, if it be properly called an office, is created by that Constitution, and by that alone. It also declares how it shall be filled—namely, by election. . . .

. . .

The States, in prescribing the qualifications of voters for the most numerous branch of their own legislatures, do not do this with reference to the election for members of Congress. Nor can they prescribe the qualification for voters. . . . They define who are to vote for the popular branch of their own legislature, and the Constitution of the United States says the same persons shall vote for members of Congress in that State. . . .

It is not true, therefore, that electors for members of Congress owe their right to vote to the state law, in any sense which makes the exercise of the right to depend exclusively on the law of the State.

. . .

It is as essential to the successful working of this government that the great organisms of its executive and legislative branches should be the free choice of the people as that the original form of it should be so. In absolute governments, where

the monarch is the source of all power, it is still held to be important that the exercise of that power shall be free from the influence of extraneous violence and internal corruption.

In a republican government like ours, where political power is reposed in representatives of the entire body of the people, chosen at short intervals by popular elections, the temptations to control these elections by violence and by corruption is a constant source of danger.

Such has been the history of all republics, and, though ours has been comparatively free from both these evils in the past, no lover of his country can shut his eyes to the fear of future danger from both sources.

If the recurrence of such acts as these prisoners stand convicted of are too common in one quarter of the country, and give omen of danger from lawless violence, the free use of money in elections, arising from the vast growth of recent wealth in other quarters, presents equal cause for anxiety.

If the government of the United States has within its constitutional domain no authority to provide against these evils—if the very sources of power may be poisoned by corruption or controlled by violence and outrage, without legal restraint— then indeed is the country in danger, and its best powers, its highest purposes, the hopes which it inspires, and the love which enshrines it are at the mercy of the combinations of those who respect no right but brute force on the one hand, and unprincipled corruptionists on the other.

The rule to show cause in this case is discharged, and the writ of habeas corpus denied.

Murphy v. Ramsey
114 U.S. 15 (1885)

The wrong complained of in each case by the respective plaintiffs is "that the defendants, and each of them, intending to wrongfully deprive the plaintiff of the elective franchise in said territory, willfully and maliciously, by the acts and in the manner aforesaid, refused the plaintiff registration, as a voter, at the said registration commenced on the second Monday of September, 1882, and deprived the plaintiff of the right to vote at the election held in said territory on the seventh day of November, 1882, and at all elections under said registration."

The acts which, it is alleged, were done by the five defendants, as a board of commissioners or canvassers, under the law of March 22, 1882, and which contributed to the wrong, and constituted part of it, are that they prescribed as a condition of registration an unauthorized oath, set out in the complaint, in a rule promulgated by them for the government of the registration officers; and that the deputy registration officer having, in obedience to such rule, "acting under the directions of the other defendants," willfully and maliciously refused to receive the affidavit tendered by the plaintiff, in lieu of that prescribed by the rule of the board, and to register the plaintiff; and that the county registration officer, on appeal, having refused to order otherwise, the board of commissioners also refused to reverse and correct these rulings, and to direct the registration of the plaintiffs, respectively, but affirmed and approved the same.

But an examination of the ninth section of the act of March 22, 1882, providing for the appointment and prescribing the duties and powers of that board, shows that they have no functions whatever in respect to the registration of voters, except the appointment of officers in place of those previously authorized, whose offices are by that section of the law declared to be vacant; and the persons appointed to succeed them are not subject to the direction and control of the board, but are required, until other provision be made by the legislative assembly of the territory, to perform all the duties relating to the registration of voters, "under the existing laws of the United States and of said territory." The board are not authorized to prescribe rules for governing them in the performance of these duties, much less to prescribe any qualifications for voters as a condition of registration. The statutory powers of the board are limited to the appointment of the registration and election officers, authorized to act in the first instance under the law until provision is made by the territorial legislature for the appointment of their successors, and to the canvass of the returns and the issue of certificates of election "to those persons who, being eligible for such election, shall appear to have been lawfully elected." The proviso in the section does, indeed, declare "that said board of five persons shall not exclude any person otherwise eligible to vote from the polls on account of any opinion such person may entertain but, in the absence of any general and express power over the subject of declaring the qualification of voters," it is not a just inference, from the words of this proviso, that it was intended to admit by implication the existence of any authority in the board to exclude from registration, or the right to vote, any person whatever, or in any manner to define and declare what the qualifications of a voter shall be. The prohibition against excluding any person from the polls, for the reason assigned, must be construed, with the additional injunction, "nor shall they refuse to count any such vote on account of the opinion of the person casting it on the subject of bigamy or polygamy," to apply to the action of the board in canvassing the returns of elections, made to them by the officers holding such elections; or, if it includes more, it is to be taken as the announcement of a general principle to govern all officers concerned in the registration of in canvassing the returns of elections.

It follows that the rules promulgated by the board, prescribing the form of oath to be exacted of persons offering to register as voters, and which constitute the directions under which it is alleged the registration officers acted, were without force, and no effect can be given to them. It cannot be alleged that they had the effect in law of preventing the registration of the plaintiffs, for the registration officers were not bound to obey them; and if they did so, they did it in their own wrong. There was no relation between the board and the officers appointed by them of principal and agent, so as to make the members of the former liable for what the latter may have illegally done under their instructions, and therefore no connection in law between the acts of the board as charged and the wrongs complained of. The judgment in favor of the defendants, composing the board of commissioners, upon their demurrer, therefore, was rightly rendered.

The cases, as the other defendants, the registration officers, stand on different principles. If they were merely ministerial officers, and if they have deprived the respective plaintiffs of their right to be registered as voters, in violation of law, they may be responsible in an action for damages. Whether they are so must depend, in the first instance, not upon what they have done or omitted, but upon the question whether the plaintiffs have severally shown themselves entitled to the right of which, it is alleged, they were illegally deprived. And in entering upon the consideration of this point it is to be observed, in the first place, that the pleader has not in any of the complaints alleged, as matter of fact, that the plaintiff was a legally qualified voter, entitled to be registered as such. He has preferred, in each case, with variations to suit the circumstances, to aver the exist-

ence of specific enumerated qualifications, and the absence of specific and enumerated disqualifications, leaving it to be inferred, as a matter of law, that the plaintiff was a legally qualified voter and entitled to be registered as such. That legal inference is necessary to complete the case as stated; and the sufficiency of the statement must depend on whether all the positive qualifications required by law are alleged to have existed, and all the disqualifications affixed by law have been negatived. To ascertain this we have to compare the allegations of the complaint in each case with the requisitions of the law, and, by construction, to determine whether they conform. So far as the requirements of the law existing at the time of the passage of the act of March 22, 1882, and which continued in force concurrently with that, are concerned, there is no difficulty. Each of the plaintiffs is shown to have been a qualified voter, unless disqualified by the latter act. The only question is whether they have brought themselves within the meaning of that act. The language on which the questions arise occurs in the eighth section, and is: "That no polygamist, bigamist, or any person cohabiting with more than one woman, and no woman cohabiting with any of the persons described as aforesaid in this section," etc.—that is, with any polygamist, bigamist, or person cohabiting with more than one woman— shall be entitled to vote at any election held in the territory.

In the case in which Mary Ann M. Pratt is plaintiff, she clearly excludes herself from the disqualifications of the act. She alleges in her complaint "that she is not, and never has been, a bigamist or a polygamist; that she is the widow of Orson Pratt, Sr., who died prior to the twenty-second day of March, 1882, after a continuous residence in said territory of more than thirty years, and that since the death of her said husband she has not cohabited with any man." The same is true in reference to the allegations of the complaint in the case in which Mildred E. Randall and her husband are plaintiffs. They are, "that the plaintiff Mildred E. Randall, for more than three years last past, has been and is the wife of the plaintiff Alfred Randall, who is, and prior to March 22, 1882, was, a native-born citizen of the United States of America; that she has not, on or since March 22, 1882, cohabited with any bigamist, polygamist, or with any man cohabiting with more than one woman; that she is not a bigamist or polygamist, and never has been a bigamist or polygamist, and has not in any way violated the act of congress entitled 'An act to amend section 5352 of the Revised Statutes of the United States in reference to bigamy, and for other purposes,' approved March 22, 1882." The requirements of the eighth section of the act, in reference to a woman claiming the right to vote, are that she does not, at the time she offers to register, cohabit with a polygamist, bigamist, or person cohabiting with more than one woman; and it is sufficient if the complaint denies the disqualification in the language of the act. These requirements are fully met in the two cases just refered to.

The case of Ellen C. Clawson is different. In the complaint, filed by herself and her husband, it is alleged that she "is not, and never has been, a bigamist or polygamist, and is not cohabiting, and never has cohabited, with any man except her husband, the co-plaintiff herein, to whom she was lawfully married more than fifteen years ago, and of whom she is the first and lawful wife; that the plaintiff Hiram B. Clawson has not married, or entered into any marriage contract or relation with any woman within the last six years, and has continuously and openly resided in the city of Salt Lake, in said territory of Utah, for more than twenty years last past." It is quite consistent with these statements that the husband of the female plaintiff was, at the time she claimed registration, a bigamist or a polygamist, or that he was then cohabiting with more than one woman; and that she was cohabiting with him at the same time. She would be, on either supposition, expressly disqualified from voting by the eighth section of the act of March 22, 1882, and she does not negative the fact. It cannot, therefore, be inferred that she was a lawfully qualified voter.

The cases of Murphy and Barlow are alike in substance. In Murphy's case the allegations are "that he has not, since more than three years prior to March 22, 1882, married or entered into any marriage contract or relation with any woman, or in anywise violated the act of congress, approved July 1, 1862, defining and providing for the punishment of bigamy in the territories . . . and has not violated any of the provisions of the act of congress, approved March 22, 1882 . . . and that he has not, on or since the twenty-second day of March, 1882, cohabited with more than one woman, and has never been charged with or accused or convicted of bigamy or polygamy, or cohabiting with more than one woman, in any court or before any officer or tribunal." In Barlow's case, the statement on one point is stronger. It is "that he has not, on or since the first day of July, 1862, married or entered into any marriage contract or relation with any woman, or in anywise violate the act of congress, approved July 1, 1862, defining and providing for the punishment of bigamy in the territories." That is to say, that, although he may have married a second wife, it was before any law existed in the territory prohibiting it, and therefore it could not have been a criminal offense when committed.

But in both cases the complaints omit the allegation, that, at the time the plaintiffs respectively claimed to be registered as voters, they were not each either a bigamist or a polygamist. It is admitted that the use of these very terms in the complaint is not necessary, if the disqualifications lawfully implied by them are otherwise substantially denied. That such is their case is maintained by the appellants. The words "bigamist" and "polygamist" evidently are not used in this statute in the sense of describing those who entertain the opinion that bigamy and polygamy ought to be tolerated as a practice, not inconsistent with the good order of society, the welfare of the race, and a true code of morality, if such there be; because, in the proviso in the ninth section of the act, it is expressly declared that no person shall be excluded from the polls, or be denied his vote, on account of any opinion on the subject. It is argued that they cannot be understood as meaning those who, prior to the passage of the act of March 22, 1882, had contracted a bigamous or polygamous marriage, either in violation of an existing law, such as that of July 1, 1862, or before the enactment of any law forbidding it; for to do so would give to the statute a retrospective effect, and by thus depriving citizens of civil rights merely on account of past offenses, or on account of acts which, when committed, were not offenses, would make it an ex post facto law, and therefore void. And the conclusion is declared to be necessary, that the words polygamist and bigamist, as used in the eighth section of the act, can mean only such persons as, having violated the first section of the act, are guilty of polygamy; that is, "every person who has a husband or wife living, who, in a territory or other place over which the United States have exclusive jurisdiction, hereafter marries another, whether married or single, and any man who hereafter simultaneously or on the same day marries more than one woman, in a territory or other place over which the United States have exclusive jurisdiction."

But there is another meaning which may be given to these words, which, we think, is the one intended by congress. In our opinion, any man is a polygamist or bigamist, in the sense of this section of the act, who, having previously married one wife, still living, and having another at the time when he presents himself to claim registration as a voter, still maintains that relation to a plurality of wives, although from the date of the passage of the act of March 22, 1882, until the day he offers to register and to vote, he may not in fact have cohabited with more than one woman. . . . It is not, therefore, because the person has committed the offense of bigamy or polygamy, at some previous time, in violation of some existing statute, and as an additional punishment for its commission, that he is disfranchised by the act of congress of March 22, 1882; nor because he is guilty of the offense, as defined and punished by the terms of that act; but because, having at some time entered into a bigamous or polygamous relation, by a marriage with a second or third wife, while the first was living, he still maintains it, and has not dissolved it, although for the time being he restricts actual cohabitation to but one. He might in fact abstain from actual cohabitation with all, and be still as much as ever a bigamist or a polygamist. He can only cease to be such when he has finally and fully dissolved in some effective manner, which we are not called on here to point out, the very relation of husband to several wives, which constitutes the forbidden status he has previously assumed. Cohabitation is but one of many incidents to the marriage relation. It is not essential to it. . . . The statute makes an express distinction between bigamists and polygamists on the one hand, and those who cohabit with more than one woman on the other; whereas, if cohabitation with several wives was essential to the description of those who are bigamists or polygamists, those words in the statute would be superfluous and unnecessary. It follows, therefore, that any person having several wives is a bigamist or polygamist in the sense of the act of March 22, 1882, although since the date of its passage he may not have cohabited with more than one of them.

Upon this construction the statute is not open to the objection that it is an ex post facto law. It does not seek in this section and by the penalty of disfranchisement to operate as a punishment upon any offense at all. The crime of bigamy or polygamy consists in entering into a bigamous or polygamous marriage, and is complete when the relation begins. That of actual cohabitation with more than one woman is defined and the punishment prescribed in the third section. The disfranchisement operates upon the existing state and condition of the person, and not upon a past offense. It is, therefore, not retrospective. He alone is deprived of his vote who, when he offers to register, is then in the state and condition of a bigamist or a polygamist, or is then actually cohabiting with more than one woman. Disfranchisement is not prescribed as a penalty for being guilty of the crime and offense of bigamy or polygamy; for, as has been said, that offense consists in the fact of unlawful marriage, and a prosecution against the offender is barred by the lapse of three years, by section 1044 of the Revised Statutes. Continuing to live in that state afterwards is not an offense, although co-habitation with more than one woman is. But as one may be living in a bigamous or polygamous state without cohabitation with more than one woman, he is in that sense a bigamist or a polygamist, and yet guilty of no criminal offense. So that, in respect to those disqualifications of a voter under the act of March 22, 1882, the objection is not well taken that rep-

resents the inquiry into the fact by the officers of registration as an unlawful mode of prosecution for crime. In respect to the fact of actual cohabitation with more than one woman the objection is equally groundless, for the inquiry into the fact, so far as the registration officers are authorized to make it, or the judges of election, on challenge of the right of the voter if registered, are required to determine it, is not in view of its character as a crime, nor for the purpose of punishment, but for the sole purpose of determining, as in case of every other condition attached to the right of suffrage, the qualification of one who alleges his right to vote. It is precisely similar to an inquiry into the fact of nativity, of age, or of any other status made necessary by law as a condition of the elective franchise. It would be quite competent for the sovereign power to declare that no one but a married person shall be entitled to vote; and in that event the election officers would be authorized to determine for that occasion, in case of question in any instance, upon the fact of marriage as a continuing status. There is no greater objection, in point of law, to a similar inquiry for the like purpose into the fact of a subsisting and continuing bigamous or polygamous relation, when it is made, as by the statute under consideration, a disqualification to vote.

The counsel for the appellants in argument seem to question the constitutional power of congress to pass the act of March 22, 1882, so far as it abridges the rights of electors in the territory under previous laws. But that question is, we think, no longer open to discussion. . . . It rests with congress to say whether, in a given case, any of the people resident in the territory shall participate in the election of its officers or the making of its laws; and it may, therefore, take from them any right of suffrage it may previously have conferred, or at any time modify or abridge it, as it may deem expedient. . . . For, certainly, no legislation can be supposed more wholesome and necessary in the founding of a free, self-governing commonwealth, fit to take rank as one of the coordinate states of the Union, than that which seeks to establish it on the basis of the idea of the family, as consisting in and springing from the union for life of one man and one woman in the holy estate of matrimony; the sure foundation of all that is stable and noble in our civilization; the best guaranty of that reverent morality which is the source of all beneficent progress in social and political improvement. And to this end no means are more directly and immediately suitable than those provided by this act, which endeavors to withdraw all political influence from those who are practically hostile to its attainment.

It remains to be considered whether, in the two cases in which Mary Ann M. Pratt and Mildred E. Randall and husband are respectively the plaintiffs, and in which the plaintiffs have shown a title to vote, the defendants, who were registration officers, are sufficiently charged with a legal liability. As we have pointed out, they were bound, by virtue of their appointment under the ninth section of the act of March 22, 1882, to perform their duties under the existing laws of the United States and of the territory. The law of the territory then in force, being "An act providing for the registration of voters, and to further regulate the manner of conducting elections in this territory," approved February 22, 1878, made it the duty of the registration officers and their deputies "to make careful inquiry as to any or all persons entitled to vote," and ascertain in all cases upon what ground the person claims to be a voter; and it is provided that "he shall require each person entitled to vote and desiring to be registered to take and subscribe in substance the following oath," etc. The form of the oath is then set out,

containing a statement of all the particulars which, according to the laws then in force, were necessary to show the qualifications of a voter. It was then provided that, upon the receipt of such affidavit, the officer "shall place the name of such voter upon the register list of the voters of the county."

The act of March 22, 1882, created the additional disqualifications which have been mentioned, and which, of course, are not met by the oath as prescribed by the territorial act of 1878, and it is not consistent with the express provisions of the act of congress that every person willing to take the oath in the form prescribed by the territorial act shall be permitted to register as a voter. Either the oath itself must be regarded merely as a model, to be modified by the operation of the act of congress, so as to meet by appropriate denials the several new disqualifications created by it, and then to be taken with the prescribed effect of entitling the person subscribing it to register as a voter without other proof; or else the effect of the act of congress is to limit the class entitled to take the oath in the form prescribed by the territorial act, with the effect thereby given to it, to those who are not subject to the disqualifications which the act of congress imposes. The existing laws of the United States and of the territory, under which the election officers are bound to perform their duties, must include the act itself, which provides for their appointment and defines their duties, and if they have not the right to exact on oath different from that, the form of which is given in the territorial act, they must otherwise satisfy themselves that persons offering to register are free from the disqualifications defined in the act of congress. In doing so, they are of course required to exercise diligence and good faith in their inquiries, and are responsible in damages for rejections made without reasonable cause, or maliciously.

In the two cases last referred to, the allegations of the complaint show, not only that the several plaintiffs were legally entitled to be registered as voters, but declare that the refusal of the registration officers to admit them to the list was wrongful and malicious. The demurrers admit the plaintiffs' case, as thus stated, and therefore ought to have been overruled. It follows that the judgments in the three cases in which Jessie J. Murphy, Ellen C. Clawson, and Hiram B. Clawson, her husband, and James M. Barlow are the respective plaintiffs, are affirmed as to all the defendants; in the two cases in which Mary Ann M. Pratt and Mildred E. Randall, and Alfred Randall, her husband, are the plaintiffs, respectively, the judgments in favor of the five defendants, Alexander Ramsey, A. S. Paddock, G. L. Godfrey, A. B. Carleton, and J. R. Pettigrew are affirmed; and as to the defendants, E. D. Hoge, John S. Lindsay, and Harmel Pratt, the judgments are reversed, and as to them the cases are remanded, with instructions to overrule the demurrers, and for further proceedings.

Blitz v. United States
153 U.S. 308 (1894)

. . . The statute makes it an offense for any person to knowingly personate and vote, or attempt to vote, in the name of another person, whether living, dead, or fictitious, at an election for representative or delegate in Congress. It appears in this case—and, if it did not appear, the court would judicially know—that the election referred to in the introductory part of the indictment was a general one, at which voters were at liberty to vote at the same poll, by printed ballot, not only for a representative in Congress, but for state officers, including presidential electors. It was one

election for all such officers, and the exercise of the privilege of voting was manifested by one act upon the part of the voter, namely, depositing in the ballot box a general ballot, showing, upon its face, for what officers he voted.

The first count charged that the defendant knowingly personated and voted, and attempted to vote, in the name of another person, to the grand jurors unknown, at an election had and held for choice of representative in the Congress of the United States. But that was not, except by inference, a charge that the defendant in fact voted for representative in Congress. He may have voted only for state officers, and yet it could be said, not unreasonably, that he voted at an election had and held for representative in Congress. If, in voting for a state officer at such election, he knowingly personated and voted in the name of another, it was an offense against the state, punishable alone by the state, although the general election at which he voted was one at which a representative in Congress was chosen. The object of section 5511 was to prevent frauds that would affect the vote for representatives in Congress, and not to bring elections for state officers under the control of the general government. It was consequently held . . . that a conspiracy by unlawful means to induce the officers of election appointed by the state to omit the duty imposed upon them by the state law in respect to the custody and safe keeping of sealed returns showing the results of an election held for both state officers and for representatives in Congress, was an offense against the United States, although the only purpose of the conspirators may have been to obtain the custody of such returns for the purpose of fraudulently changing them so far as they applied to certain state officers. . . .

It is not to be inferred from the decision in that case that section 5511 is applicable to any act or omission of duty upon the part of an officer of election, or of a voter or other person, except such act or omission of duty as affected or might affect the integrity of the election for a representative in Congress. The conspiracy charged in that case did imperil the integrity of the vote for representative in Congress, because the returns of the election related to representative in Congress as well as to state officers, and were liable to be falsified if they passed, before certificates of election were issued, into the hands of unauthorized persons. But this reasoning has no application to the present case. Voting, in the name of another, for a state officer, cannot possibly affect the integrity of an election for representative in Congress. With frauds of that character the national government has no concern, and therefore an indictment under section 5511, for knowingly personating and voting under the name of another, should clearly show that the accused actually voted for a representative in Congress, and not simply that in voting he falsely personated another at a general election at which such representative was or could have been chosen. In cases like the present one it should not be left in doubt, or to mere inference, from the words of the indictment, whether the offense charged was one within federal cognizance. The general rule that an indictment for an offense purely statutory is sufficient if it pursues substantially the words of the statute is subject to the qualification, fundamental in the law of criminal procedure, "that the accused must be apprised by the indictment, with reasonable certainty, of the nature of the accusation against him, to the end that he may prepare his defense, and plead the judgment as a bar to any subsequent prosecution for the same offense." . . .

The want of care in framing the first count is further shown by the fact that, although voting, and attempting to vote, knowingly, in the name of another, for representative in Congress, may be distinct offenses under the statute, the indictment charges that the defendant did knowingly "personate and vote and attempt to vote" in the name of another person. If the attempt to so vote was immediately followed by voting, then the allegation that the accused attempted to vote was unnecessary. The first count leaves it in doubt whether it was intended to charge two distinct offenses, or only the offense of voting in the name of another person. This defect alone might not have been sufficient, after verdict, as ground for arresting the judgment on that count; but it is referred to as supporting of illustrating the rule that enjoins such certainty in an indictment as will inform the accused of the precise nature of the charge against him.

. . .

The judgment upon the first count must be reversed, and the cause remanded, with directions to arrest judgment upon that count. The judgment below, so far as it relates to the third count, is affirmed.

Connors v. United States
158 U.S. 408 (1895)

This was an indictment in the district court of the United States for the district of Colorado under section 5511 of the Revised Statutes, providing:

> If, at any election for representative or delegate in congress, any person knowingly personates and votes, or attempts to vote, in the name of any other person, whether living, dead, or fictitious; or votes more than once at the same election for any candidate for the same office; or votes at a place where he may not be lawfully entitled to vote; or votes without having a lawful right to vote; or does any unlawful act to secure an opportunity to vote for

himself, or any other person; or by force, threat, intimidation, bribery, reward, or offer thereof, unlawfully prevents any qualified voter of any state, or of any territory, from freely exercising the right of suffrage, or by any such means induces any voter to refuse to exercise such right, or compels, or induces, by any such means, any officer of an election in such state or territory to receive a vote from a person not legally qualified or entitled to vote; or interferes in any manner with any officer of such election in the discharge of his duties; or by any such means, or other unlawful means, induces any officer of an election or officer whose duty it is to ascertain, announce, or declare the result of any such election, or give or make any certificate, document, or evidence in relation thereto, to violate or refuse to comply with his duty or any law regulating the same; or knowingly receives the vote of any person not entitled to vote, or refuses to receive the vote of any person entitled to vote; or aids, counsels, procures, or advises any such voter, person, or officer to do any act hereby made a crime, or attempts to do so, he shall be punished by a fine of not more than five hundred dollars, or by imprisonment not more than three years, or by both, and shall pay the costs of the prosecution.

The indictment charged that on the fourth day of November, 1890, at the county of Arapahoe, state of Colorado, the accused, James Connors,

did unlawfully interfere with the judges of election of the Eighteenth voting precinct in said county of Arapahoe, in the discharge of their duties, which said judges of election were then and there officers of the election for representative in the Fifty-Second congress of the United States, in accordance with the laws of the state of Colorado and of the United States, and did then and there unlawfully and with force and arms seize, carry away, and secrete the ballot box containing the ballots of said Eighteenth voting precinct, which on said 4th day of November, in the year aforesaid, at said election, had been cast for said representative in congress, and did then and there knowingly aid and assist in the forcible and unlawful seizure, carrying away, and secreting of said ballot box, and did then and there counsel, advise, and procure divers

other persons, whose names are to the grand jurors unknown, so to seize, carry away, and secrete said ballot box, thereby, as aforesaid, interfering with said judges of election of said Eighteenth voting precinct, and hindering and preventing them, the said judges of election, from counting the votes which had been cast at said election, and from declaring and certifying the result thereof.

. . .

. . . The offense charged was that of unlawfully interfering with the officers of the election in the discharge of their duties. Their duty was to ascertain and disclose the result of the election. That duty could not be performed without inspection of the ballots. Seizing, carrying away, and secreting the ballot box containing the ballots cast for representative in Congress necessarily interfered with the discharge of that duty. The indictment describes—perhaps with unnecessary particularity—the mode in which the crime charged was committed. If the accused himself unlawfully seized, carried away, and secreted the ballot box, or if he knowingly aided and assisted others in doing so, or if he counseled, advised, and procured others to do so, in either case he was guilty of the crime of having unlawfully interfered with the officers of election in the discharge of their duties. The verdict of guilty had reference to that crime, whether committed in one or the other of the modes specified in the indictment. Undoubtedly, it was in the discretion of the court to compel the prosecutor to state whether he would proceed against the accused for having himself seized, carried away, and secreted the ballot box, or for having assisted or procured others to do so. But there was no motion to require the prosecutor to make such a statement. If the objection now urged could have been taken by motion to quash the indictment, it is sufficient to say that, although the record shows that there was such a motion, the grounds of it are not stated.

So far as the record discloses, the specific objection now urged was made for the first time after verdict by a motion in arrest of judgment. But such an objection, not made until after verdict, would not justify an arrest of judgment, and is not available on writ of error. Nor, if made by demurrer or by motion, and overruled, would it avail on error unless it appeared that the substantial rights of the accused were prejudiced by the refusal of the court to require a more restricted or specific statement of the particular mode in which the offense charged was committed. There is no ground whatever to suppose that the accused was taken by surprise in the progress of the trial, or that he was in doubt as to what was the precise offense with which he was charged.

. . .

. . . The law assumes that every citizen is equally interested in the enforcement of the statute enacted to guard the integrity of national elections, and that his political opinions or affiliations will not stand in the way of an honest discharge of his duty as a juror in cases arising under that statute. So, also, active participation in politics cannot be said, as matter of law, to imply either unwillingness to enforce the statutes designed to insure honest elections and due returns of the votes cast, or inability to do justice to those charged with violating the provisions of those statutes. Strong political convictions are by no means inconsistent with a desire to protect the freedom and purity of elections.

. . . If an inquiry of a juror as to his political opinions and associations could ever be appropriate in any case arising under the statute in question, it could only be when it is made otherwise to appear that the particular juror has himself, by his conduct or declarations, given reason to believe that he will regard the case as one involving the interests of political parties rather than

the enforcement of a law designed for the protection of the public against frauds in elections.

. . .

We perceive no reason to doubt that the accused was fairly tried. . . . the judgment is affirmed.

Mills v. Green
159 U.S. 651 (1895)

The bill alleged that by a statute of South Carolina of December 24, 1894, a convention was called to revise the constitution of the state, the delegates to be elected on the third Tuesday of August, 1895, and the convention to assemble on the second Tuesday of September, 1895; that the same and other statutes of South Carolina contained regulations as to the registration of voters, and as to certificates of registration, which were in violation of the constitution of South Carolina and of the Constitution of the United States in various particulars, pointed out, as abridging, impeding, and destroying the suffrage of citizens of the state and of the United States; that the defendant was exercising the duties prescribed by those statutes, and intended to continue to do so, and specifically intended to furnish and deliver to the boards of managers appointed to hold the election of delegates to the constitutional convention the registration books of the several precincts, to be used by the managers at that election; that the plaintiff had failed to register as a voter because, notwithstanding repeated efforts to become registered, he found himself unable to comply with the unreasonable and burdensome regulations prescribed by the unconstitutional registration laws; that he was desirous of voting for delegates to the constitutional convention at the election prescribed by the statute of 1894 for that purpose; that the registration books in the defendant's hands did not and would not contain the plaintiff's name; that he, and others under like circumstances, would not be permitted by the managers to vote at that election, unless their names were found upon the books, and unless they could produce registration certificates; and that, if the defendant were permitted to continue the illegal, partial, and void registration, and were allowed to turn over the books to the managers, the plaintiff would be deprived of his right to vote at that election, and grievous and irreparable wrong would be done to him, and to other citizens under like circumstances.

. . .

In the case at bar the whole object of the bill was to secure a right to vote at the election, to be held, as the bill alleged, on the third Tuesday of August, 1895, of delegates to the constitutional convention of South Carolina. Before this appeal was taken by the plaintiff from the decree of the circuit court of appeals dismissing his bill, that date had passed; and, before the entry of the appeal in this court, the convention had assembled, pursuant to the statute of South Carolina of 1894, by which the convention had been called. The election of the delegates and the assembling of the convention are public matters, to be taken notice of by the court, without formal plea or proof. The lower courts of the United States, and this court of appeal from their decisions, take judicial notice of the constitution and public laws of each state of the Union. Taking judicial notice of the constitution and laws of the state, this court must take judicial notice of the days of public general elections of members of the legislature, or of a convention to revise the fundamental law of the state, as well as of the times of the commencement of the sitting of those bodies, and of the dates when their acts take effect.

It is obvious, therefore, that, even if the bill could properly be held to present a case within the jurisdiction of the circuit court, no relief within the scope of the bill could now be granted.

Appeal dismissed. . . .

Williams v. State of Mississippi
170 U.S. 213 (1898)

. . . There is an allegation of the purpose of the convention to disfranchise citizens of the colored race; but with this we have no concern, unless the purpose is executed by the constitution or laws or by those who administer them. If it is done in the latter way, how or by what means should be sworn. We gather from the statements of the motion that certain officers are invested with discretion in making up lists of electors, and that this discretion can be and has been exercised against the colored race, and from these lists jurors are selected. The supreme court of Mississippi, however, decided, in a case presenting the same questions as the one at bar, "that jurors are not selected from or with reference to any lists furnished by such election officers."

. . .

This comment is not applicable to the constitution of Mississippi and its statutes. They do not on their face discriminate between the races, and it has not been shown that their actual administration was evil; only that evil was possible under them.

If follows, therefore, that the judgment must be affirmed.

Wiley v. Sinkler
179 U.S. 58 (1900)

This action is brought against election officers to recover damages for their rejection of the plaintiff's vote for a member of the House of

Representatives of the United States. The complaint, by alleging that the plaintiff was at the time, under the constitution and laws of the state of South Carolina and the Constitution and laws of the United States, a duly qualified elector of the state, shows that the action is brought under the Constitution and laws of the United States.

. . .

By the constitution of South Carolina, every male citizen of the age of twenty-one years and upwards, who has resided in the state for one year, and in the county where he offers to vote for sixty days, next preceding any election, and is not disqualified by the Constitution of the United States, nor a lunatic or a prisoner, nor been convicted of an infamous crime or of dueling, is entitled to vote for all officers elected by the people. That Constitution also makes it the duty of the legislature to provide from time to time for the registration of all electors.

The Revised Statutes of South Carolina of 1893 provide that every man not laboring under the disabilities named in the constitution of the state . . . shall be entitled to vote; and further provide that all electors of the state shall be registered, and that no person shall be allowed to vote at any election unless theretofore registered as required by those statutes or by previous laws.

The constitution and the laws of the state thus require that, in order to entitle anyone to have his vote received at any election, he must not only have the requisite qualifications of an elector, but he must have been registered. By elementary rules of pleading, both these essential requisites must be distinctly alleged by the plaintiff in any action against the managers of an election for refusing his vote.

The complaint in this case alleges that the plaintiff was a duly qualified elector; but it contains no allegation that he was ever registered as such. Because of this omission the complaint does not state facts sufficient to constitute a cause of action.

It was argued, in behalf of the plaintiff, that the registration act of South Carolina was unconstitutional because it allowed for registration only one day in each month between the day of a general election in November and the first day of July before the next general election; required the registration books to be closed from such first day of July for four months, until the ensuing election day; and thus in effect required each voter to reside in the county for one hundred and twenty days (whereas the Constitution required only sixty days) before the election, and otherwise unreasonably impeded the exercise of the constitutional right of voting; that the only exception allowed was in the case of voters coming of age during those four months, and there was no exception in the case of electors who, by reason of sickness or absence or other good and sufficient cause, did not or could not have registered before the first day of July.

. . .

. . . It is only on the day when his vote was refused, that he alleges that he had resided in the state for a year and in the county for sixty days, and was of age and otherwise a qualified elector. He does not allege when he first became qualified. So far as appears, he may have become of age and otherwise qualified but a few days before the election day on which he tendered his vote, in which case he would confessedly . . . have been entitled to apply for registration. Yet he does not allege that he ever was registered, or made any application to be registered.

. . .

Judgment affirmed.

Mason v. State of Missouri ex rel Mccaffery
179 U.S. 328 (1900)

The . . . Nesbit law, in addition to prescribing certain qualifications as necessary to the right to vote, empowered the general assembly of the state to "provide by law for the registration of voters in cities and counties having a population of more than 100,000 inhabitants"; and further directed that the general assembly "may provide for such a registration in cities having a population exceeding 25,000 inhabitants and not exceeding 100,000, but not otherwise." A law approved May 13, 1895, applied to all cities having a population in excess of 100,000 inhabitants, and before the adoption of the Nesbit law the act of 1895 was operative in the city of St. Louis. The Nesbit law, which applied to cities having a population of over 300,000 inhabitants, necessarily withdrew the city of St. Louis from the operation of the earlier statute.

The contention that the Nesbit law denied to citizens of St. Louis the equal protection of the laws, in violation of the first section of the Fourteenth Amendment. . . .

. . .

. . . [T]he obvious answer is that the law in question has been declared to be valid under the constitution of the state. The general right to vote in the state of Missouri is primarily derived from the state, and the elective franchise, if one of the fundamental privileges and immunities of the citizens of St. Louis, as citizens of Missouri and of the United States, is clearly such franchise "as regulated and established by the laws or Constitution of the state in which it is to be exercised." The power to classify cities with reference to their population having been exercised in conformity with the constitution of the

state, the circumstance that the registration law in force in the city of St. Louis was made to differ in essential particulars from that which regulates the conduct of elections in other cities in the state of Missouri does not in itself deny to the citizens of St. Louis the equal protection of the laws. Nor did the exercise by the general assembly of Missouri of the discretion vested in it by law give rise to a violation of the Fourteenth Amendment to the Constitution of the United States.

Judgment affirmed.

Swafford v. Templeton
185 U.S. 487 (1902)

The sole question is, Did the circuit court err in dismissing the action, on the ground that it was not one within the jurisdiction of the court? An affirmative answer to this question is rendered necessary by the decision in *Wiley v. Sinkler.* . . .

It is manifest from the context of the opinion in the case just referred to that the conclusion that the cause was one arising under the Constitution of the United States was predicated on the conception that the action sought the vindication or protection of the right to vote for a member of Congress, a right, as declared in *Ex parte Yarbrough*, "fundamentally based upon the Constitution . . . which created the office of member of Congress, and declared it should be elective, and pointed to the means of ascertaining who should be electors." That is to say, the ruling was that the case was equally one arising under the Constitution or laws of the United States, whether the illegal act complained of arose from a charged violation of some specific provision of the Constitution or laws of the

United States, or from the violation of a state law which affected the exercise of the right to vote for a member of Congress, since the Constitution of the United States had adopted, as the qualifications of electors for members of Congress, those prescribed by the state for electors of the most numerous branch of the legislature of the state.

. . .

. . . The distinction between the cases referred to and the one at bar is that which must necessarily exist between controversies concerning rights which are created by the Constitution or laws of the United States, and which consequently are in their essence federal, and controversies concerning rights not conferred by the Constitution or laws of the United States, the contention respecting which may or may not involve a federal question depending upon what is the real issue to be decided or the substantiality of the averments as to the existence of the rights which it is claimed are federal in character. The distinction finds apt illustration in the decisions of this court holding that suits brought by or against corporations chartered by acts of Congress are cases per se of federal cognizance. It may not be doubted that if an action be brought in a circuit court of the United States by such a corporation, there would be jurisdiction to entertain it, although the averments set out to establish the wrong complained of or the defense interposed were unsubstantial in character. . . .

It follows that the court below erred in dismissing the action for want of jurisdiction. Of course, in reaching this conclusion we must not be understood as expressing any opinion as to the sufficiency of the declaration.

The judgment of the circuit court is reversed, and the action is remanded for further proceedings, in conformity with this opinion.

Giles v. Harris
189 U.S. 475 (1903)

The allegations of the bill may be summed up as follows: The plaintiff is subject to none of the disqualifications set forth in the constitution of Alabama and is entitled to vote—entitled, as the bill plainly means, under the constitution as it is. He applied in March, 1902, for registration as a voter, and was refused arbitrarily on the ground of his color, together with large numbers of other duly qualified negroes, while all white men were registered. The same thing was done all over the state. Under 187 of article 8 of the Alabama Constitution, persons registered before January 1, 1903, remain electors for life unless they become disqualified by certain crimes, etc., while after that date severer tests come into play which would exclude, perhaps, a large part of the black race. Therefore by the refusal the plaintiff and the other negroes excluded were deprived, not only of their vote at an election which has taken place since the bill was filed, but of the permanent advantage incident to registration before 1903. The white men generally are registered for good under the easy test, and the black men are likely to be kept out in the future as in the past. This refusal to register the blacks was part of a general scheme to disfranchise them, to which the defendants and the state itself, according to the bill, were parties. The defendants accepted their office for the purpose of carrying out the scheme. The part taken by the state, that is, by the white population which framed the constitution, consisted in shaping that instrument so as to give opportunity and effect to the wholesale fraud which has been practised.

The bill sets forth the material sections of the state constitution, the general plan of which, leaving out details, is as follows: By 178 of article 8, to entitle a person to vote he must have resided in the state at least two years, in the county one year, and in the precinct or ward three months, immediately preceding the election, have paid his poll taxes, and have been duly registered as an elector. By 182 idiots, insane persons, and those convicted of certain crimes are disqualified. Subject to the foregoing, by 180, before 1903 the following male citizens of the state, who are citizens of the United States, were entitled to register, viz.: First. All who had served honorably in the enumerated wars of the United States, including those on either side in the "war between the states." Second. All lawful descendants of persons who served honorably in the enumerated wars or in the war of the Revolution. Third. "All persons who are of good character and who understand the duties and obligations of citizenship under a republican form of government." As we have said, according to the allegations of the bill, this part of the Constitution, as practically administered and as intended to be administered, let in all whites and kept out a large part, if not all, of the blacks, and those who were let in retained their right to vote after 1903, when tests which might be too severe for many of the whites as well as the blacks went into effect. By 181, after January 1, 1903, only the following persons are entitled to register: First. Those who can read and write any article of the Constitution of the United States in the English language, and who either are physically unable to work or have been regularly engaged in some lawful business for the greater part of the last twelve months, and those who are unable to read and write solely because physically disabled. Second. Owners or husbands of owners of 40 acres of land in the state, upon which they reside, and owners or husbands of owners of real or personal estate in the state assessed for taxation at $300 or more, if the taxes have been

paid, unless under contest. By 183 only persons qualified as electors can take part in any method of party action. By 184 persons not registered are disqualified from voting. By 185 an elector whose vote is challenged shall be required to swear that the matter of the challenge is untrue before his vote shall be received. By 186 the legislature is to provide for registration after January 1, 1903, the qualification and oath of the registrars are prescribed, the duties of registrars before that date are laid down, and an appeal is given to the county court and supreme court if registration is denied. There are further executive details in 187, together with the above-mentioned continuance of the effect of registration before January 1, 1903. By 188, after the last mentioned date, applicants for registration may be examined under oath as to where they have lived for the last five years, the names by which they have been known, and the names of their employers. This, in brief, is the system which the plaintiff asks to have declared void.

. . .

. . . We have recognized . . . that the deprivation of a man's political and social rights properly may be alleged to involve damage to that amount, capable of estimation in money. But, assuming that the allegation should have been made in a case like this, the objection to its omission was not raised in the circuit court, and, as it could have been remedied by amendment, we think it unavailing. . . . There is no pecuniary limit on appeals to this court under 5 of the act of 1891; and we do not feel called upon to send the case back to the circuit court in order that it might permit the amendment. . . .

We assume further, for the purposes of decision, that 1979 extends to a deprivation of rights under color of a state constitution, although it might be argued with some force that the enumeration of "statute, ordinance, regulation, custom, or usage" purposely is confined to inferior sources of law. On these assumptions we are not prepared to say that an action at law could not be maintained on the facts alleged in the bill. Therefore, we are not prepared to say that the decree should be affirmed on the ground that the subject-matter is wholly beyond the jurisdiction of the circuit court.

. . .

The other difficulty is of a different sort, and strikingly reinforces the argument that equity cannot undertake now, any more than it has in the past, to enforce political rights, and also the suggestion that state constitutions were not left unmentioned in 1979 by accident. In determining whether a court of equity can take jurisdiction, one of the first questions is what it can do to enforce any order that it may make. This is alleged to be the conspiracy of a state, although the state is not and could not be made a party to the bill. The circuit court has no constitutional power to control its action by any direct means. And if we leave the state out of consideration, the court has as little practical power to deal with the people of the state in a body. The bill imports that the great mass of the white population intends to keep the blacks from voting. To meet such an intent something more than ordering the plaintiff's name to be inscribed upon the lists of 1902 will be needed. If the conspiracy and the intent exist, a name on a piece of paper will not defeat them. Unless we are prepared to supervise the voting in that state by officers of the court, it seems to us that all that the plaintiff could get from equity would be an empty form. Apart from damages to the individual, relief from a great political wrong, if done, as alleged, by the people of a state and the state itself, must be given by them or by the legislative and po-

litical department of the government of the United States.

Decree affirmed.

James v. Bowman
190 U.S. 127 (1903)

The single question presented for our consideration is whether 5507 can be upheld as a valid enactment. . . . On its face the section purports to be an exercise of the power granted to Congress by the Fifteenth Amendment, for it declares a punishment upon anyone who, by means of bribery, prevents another to whom the right of suffrage is guaranteed by such amendment from exercising that right. But that amendment relates solely to action "by the United States or by any state," and does not contemplate wrongful individual acts. . . .

. . .

But the contention most earnestly pressed is that Congress has ample power in respect to elections of representative in Congress; that the election which was held, and at which this bribery took place, was such an election; and that therefore under such general power this statute and this indictment can be sustained. The difficulty with this contention is that Congress has not by this section acted in the exercise of such power. It is not legislation in respect to elections of federal officers, but is leveled at all elections, state or federal, and it does not purport to punish bribery of any voter, but simply of those named in the Fifteenth Amendment. On its face it is clearly an attempt to exercise power supposed to be conferred by the Fifteenth Amendment in respect to all elections, and not in pursuance of the general control by Congress over particular elections. To change this statute, enacted to punish bribery of persons named in the Fifteenth Amendment at all elections, to a statute punishing bribery of any voter at certain elections would be in effect judicial legislation. It would be wresting the statute from the purpose with which it was enacted and making it serve another purpose. Doubtless even a criminal statute may be good in part and bad in part, providing the two can be clearly separated, and it is apparent that the legislative body would have enacted the one without the other, but there are no two parts to this statute. If the contention be sustained, it is simply a transformation of the statute in its single purpose and scope. . . .

. . .

We deem it unnecessary to add anything to the views expressed in these opinions. We are fully sensible of the great wrong which results from bribery at elections, and do not question the power of Congress to punish such offenses when committed in respect to the election of federal officials. At the same time it is all-important that a criminal statute should define clearly the offense which it purports to punish, and that when so defined it should be within the limits of the power of the legislative body enacting it. Congress has no power to punish bribery at all elections. The limits of its power are in respect to elections in which the nation is directly interested, or in which some mandate of the national Constitution is disobeyed; and courts are not at liberty to take a criminal statute, broad and comprehensive in its terms and in these terms beyond the power of Congress, and change it to fit some particular transaction which Congress might have legislated for if it had seen fit.

The judgment of the district court is affirmed.

Giles v. Teasley
193 U.S. 146 (1904)

A consideration of the plaintiff's petition shows that it attacked the provisions of the Alabama Constitution regulating the qualifications and registration of the electors of the state as an attempt to disregard the provisions of the Fourteenth and Fifteenth Amendments to the Constitution of the United States, by qualifying the whites to exercise the elective franchise and denying the same rights to the negroes of the state. . . .

. . .

It is apparent that paragraph 3 of 180, permitting the registration of electors before 1903, of "all persons who are of good character and who understand the duties and obligations of citizenship under a republican form of government," opened a wide door to the exercise of discretionary power by the registrars. It is charged that this section, in connection with 181, permitting the registration of certain persons after January, 1903, was intended to be so carried into operation and effect that the negroes of Alabama should be excluded from the elective franchise, and to permit the white men to register before January 1, 1903, and thus become electors, compelling the colored men to wait until after January 1, 1903, and then to apply under conditions which were especially framed and would have the effect to exclude the colored man from voting. It is charged that the registrars well knew the scheme and purpose set forth in the complaint to work the disfranchisement of negro voters and to qualify the white voters to exercise the elective franchise, and it is charged that the defendants were appointed by the state under sections of the state constitution adopted for the purpose of denying the colored man the right to vote and under which the defendants are undertaking to carry out the scheme and were so acting when they denied the right of the plaintiff to register, thus depriving him of the right guaranteed to him by the first section of the Fifteenth Amendment to the Constitution of the United States. A consideration of the allegations of this complaint, to which the demurrer was sustained, makes apparent that the federal right for which the plaintiff sought protection and the recovery of damages was that secured by the amendment to the federal Constitution which prohibits a state from denying to the citizen the right of suffrage because of race, color, or previous condition of servitude. But in the present case the state court has not sustained the right of the state to thus abridge the constitutional rights of the plaintiff. It has planted its decision upon a ground independent of the alleged state action seeking to nullify the force and effect of the constitutional amendments protecting the right of suffrage. The first ground of sustaining the demurrer is, in effect, that, conceding the allegations of the petition to be true, and the registrars to have been appointed and qualified under a constitution which has for its purpose to prevent negroes from voting and to exclude them from registration for that purpose, no damage has been suffered by the plaintiff, because no refusal to register by a board thus constituted in defiance of the Federal Constitution could have the effect to disqualify a legal voter, otherwise entitled to exercise the elective franchise. In such a decision no right, immunity, or privilege, the creation of federal authority, has been set up by the plaintiff in error, and denied in such wise as to give this court the right to review the state court decision. This view renders it unnecessary to consider whether, where a proper case was made for the denial of the right of suffrage, it would be a defense for the election officers to say that they were acting in a judicial capacity where the denial of the right was solely because of the race, color, or previous condition of servitude of the plaintiff. In the ground first stated we are of opinion that the state court decided the case for reasons independent of the federal right claimed, and hence its action is not reviewable here.

. . .

. . . It is apparent that the thing complained of, so far as it involves rights secured under the Federal Constitution, is the action of the state of Alabama in the adoption and enforcing of a constitution with the purpose of excluding from the exercise of the right of suffrage the negro voters of the state, in violation of the Fifteenth Amendment to the Constitution of the United States. The great difficulty of reaching the political action of a state through remedies afforded in the courts, state or federal, was suggested by this court. . . .

In reaching the conclusion that the present writs of error must be dismissed the court is not unmindful of the gravity of the statements of the complainant charging violation of a constitutional amendment which is a part of the supreme law of the land; but the right of this court to review the decisions of the highest court of a state has long been well settled, and is circumscribed by the rules established by law. We are of opinion that plaintiffs in error have not brought the cases within the statute giving to this court the right of review.

The writs of error in both cases will be dismissed.

Pope v. Williams
193 U.S. 621 (1904)

We are of opinion that the statute does not violate any federal right of the plaintiff in error which he seeks to assert in this proceeding. The statute, so far as it concerns him and the right which he urges, is one making regulations and conditions for the registry of persons for the purpose of voting. It was only for the purpose of thereafter voting that the plaintiff in error sought to be registered, and it was the denial of that right only which he can now review. His application for registry as a voter was denied by the board of registry solely because of his failure to comply with the statute. Whatever other right he may have as a citizen of Maryland by reason of his removal there with an intent to become such citizen is not now in question. So far as appears no other right, if any he may have, has been infringed by the statute. The simple matter to be herein determined is whether, with reference to the exercise of the privilege of voting in Maryland, the legislature of that state had the legal right to provide that a person coming into the state to reside should make the declaration of intent a year before he should have the right to be registered as a voter of the state.

The privilege to vote in any state is not given by the Federal Constitution, or by any of its amendments. It is not a privilege springing from citizenship of the United States. It may not be refused on account of race, color, or previous condition of servitude, but it does not follow from mere citizenship of the United States. In other words, the privilege to vote in a state is within the jurisdiction of the state itself, to be exercised as the state may direct, and upon such terms as to it may seem proper, provided, of course, no discrimination is made between individuals, in violation of the Federal Constitution. The state might provide that persons of foreign birth could vote without being naturalized, and . . . such persons were allowed to vote in several of the states upon having declared their intentions to become citizens of the United States. Some states permit women to vote; others refuse them that privilege. A state, so far as the Federal Constitution is concerned, might provide by its own constitution and laws that none but native-born citizens should be permitted to vote, as the Federal Constitution does not confer the right of suffrage upon any one, and the conditions under which that right is to be exercised are matters for the states alone to pre-

scribe, subject to the conditions of the Federal Constitution, already stated; although it may be observed that the right to vote for a member of Congress is not derived exclusively from the state law. But the elector must be one entitled to vote under the state statute. In this case no question arises as to the right to vote for electors of President and Vice President, and no decision is made thereon. The question whether the conditions prescribed by the state might be regarded by others as reasonable or unreasonable is not a federal one. We do not wish to be understood, however, as intimating that the condition in this statute is unreasonable or in any way improper.

We are unable to see any violation of the Federal Constitution in the provision of the state statute for the declaration of the intent of a person coming into the state before he can claim the right to be registered as a voter. The statute, so far as it provides conditions precedent to the exercise of the elective franchise within the state, by persons coming therein to reside . . . is neither an unlawful discrimination against any one in the situation of the plaintiff in error nor does it deny to him the equal protection of the laws, nor is it repugnant to any fundamental or inalienable rights of citizens of the United States, nor a violation of any implied guaranties of the Federal Constitution. The right of a state to legislate upon the subject of the elective franchise as to it may seem good, subject to the conditions already stated, being, as we believe, unassailable, we think it plain that the statute in question violates no right protected by the Federal Constitution.

. . .

It is unnecessary in this case to assert that under no conceivable state of facts could a state statute in regard to voting be regarded as an infringement upon or a discrimination against, the individual rights of a citizen of the United

States removing into the state, and excluded from voting therein by state legislation. The question might arise if an exclusion from the privilege of voting were founded upon the particular state from which the person came, excluding from that privilege, for instance, a citizen of the United States coming from Georgia and allowing it to a citizen of the United States coming from New York or any other state. In such case an argument might be urged that, under the Fourteenth Amendment of the Federal Constitution, the citizen from Georgia was, by the state statute, deprived of the equal protection of the laws. Other of the equal protection of the laws. Other extreme cases might be suggested. We neither assert nor deny that, in the case supposed, the claim would be well founded that a federal right of a citizen of the United States was violated by such legislation, for the question does not arise herein. We do, however, hold that there is nothing in the statute in question which violated the federal rights of the plaintiff in error by virtue of the provision for making a declaration of his intention to become a citizen before he can have the right to be registered as a voter and to vote in the state.

The plaintiff in error has no ground for complaint in regard to the decision of the courts below, and the judgment of the Court of Appeals of Maryland is therefore affirmed.

Jones v. Montague
194 U.S. 147 (1904)

. . . The facts alleged in respect to the Constitution, the purpose of the dominant party, the action of the convention, the refusal to submit the proposed Constitution to the vote of the people, and the registration ordinance, were all stated for the purpose of showing that the election on No-

vember 4, 1902, was illegal, and that there ought to be no canvass of the returns cast at that election. The prayer of the petitioners specifically is to restrain such canvass. Even the general clause at the close of the prayer is "for such other and further orders in the premises as shall and may make the prayer of your petitioners effectual." But—as shown by the affidavit, and as, indeed, we might, perhaps, take judicial notice by the presence in the House of Representatives of the individuals elected at that election from the various congressional districts of Virginia— the thing sought to be prohibited has been done, and cannot be undone by any order of court. The canvass has been made, certificates of election have been issued, the House of Representatives (which is the sole judge of the qualifications of its members) has admitted the parties holding the certificates to seats in that body, and any adjudication which this court might make would be only an ineffectual decision of the question whether or not these petitioners were wronged by what has been fully accomplished. Under those circumstances there is nothing but a moot case remaining, and the motion to dismiss must be sustained.

Guinn & Beal v. United States
238 U.S. 347 (1915)

This case is before us on a certificate drawn by the court below as the basis of two questions which are submitted for our solution. . . . Those issues arose from an indictment and conviction of certain election officers of the state of Oklahoma (the plaintiffs in error) of the crime of having conspired unlawfully, wilfully, and fraudulently to deprive certain negro citizens, on account of their race and color, of a right to vote at a general election held in that state in 1910, they being entitled to vote under the state law, and which right was se-cured to them by the Fifteenth Amendment to the Constitution of the United States. . . .

. . .

Suffrage in Oklahoma was regulated by 4a, article 3, of the constitution under which the state was admitted into the Union. Shortly after the admission there was submitted an amendment to the constitution making a radical change in that article, which was adopted prior to November 8, 1910. At an election for members of Congress which followed the adoption of this amendment, certain election officers, in enforcing its provi-sions, refused to allow certain negro citizens to vote who were clearly entitled to vote under the provision of the constitution under which the state was admitted; that is, before the amendment; and who, it is equally clear, were not entitled to vote under the provision of the suffrage amendment if that amendment governed. The persons so ex-cluded based their claim of right to vote upon the original constitution and upon the assertion that the suffrage amendment was void because in con-flict with the prohibitions of the Fifteenth Amend-ment, and therefore afforded no basis for denying them the right guaranteed and protected by that amendment. And upon the assumption that this claim was justified and that the election officers had violated the Fifteenth Amendment in deny-ing the right to vote, this prosecution, as we have said, was commenced. At the trial the court in-structed that by the Fifteenth Amendment the states were prohibited from discriminating as to suffrage because of race, color, or previous con-dition of servitude, and that Congress, in pursu-ance of the authority which was conferred upon it by the very terms of the amendment. . .

. . .

The questions which the court below asks are these:

1. Was the amendment to the constitution of Okla-homa, heretofore set forth, valid?
2. Was that amendment void in so far as it attempted to debar from the right or privilege of voting for a qualified candidate for a member of Congress in Oklahoma unless they were able to read and write any section of the constitution of Oklahoma, negro citizens of the United States who were otherwise qualified to vote for a qualified candidate for a member of Congress in that state, but who were not, and none of whose lineal ancesters was, en-titled to vote under any form of government on January 1, 1866, or at any time prior thereto, be-cause they were then slaves?

As these questions obviously relate to the pro-visions concerning suffrage in the original Con-stitution and the amendment to those provisions which form the basis of the controversy, we state the text of both. . . .

. . .

Considering the questions in the light of the text of the suffrage amendment if is apparent that they are twofold because of the twofold charac-ter of the provisions as to suffrage which the amendment contains. The first question is con-cerned with that provision of the amendment which fixes a standard by which the right to vote is given upon conditions existing on January 1, 1866, and relieves those coming within that stan-dard from the standard based on a literacy test which is established by the other provision of the amendment. The second question asks as to the validity of the literacy test and how far, if intrin-sically valid, it would continue to exist and be operative in the event the standard based upon January 1, 1866, should be held to be illegal as violative of the Fifteenth Amendment.

. . .

The questions then are: (1) Giving to the propo-sitions of the government the interpretation which the government puts upon them, and assuming that the suffrage provision has the significance which the government assumes it to have, is that provision as a matter of law repugnant to the Fifteenth Amendment? which leads us, of course, to consider the operation and effect of the Fifteenth Amendment. (2) If yes, has the assailed amendment insofar as it fixes a standard for voting as of January 1, 1866, the meaning which the government attributes to it?; which leads us to analyze and interpret that provision of the amendment. (3) If the investigation as to the two prior subjects establishes that the standard fixed as of January 1, 1866, is void, what, if any, effect does that conclusion have upon the literacy standard otherwise established by the amendment?; which involves determining whether that standard, if legal, may survive the recognition of the fact that the other, or 1866, standard, has not and never had any legal existence. Let us consider these subjects under separate headings.

1. The operation and effect of the Fifteenth Amendment . . .

. . .

(a) Beyond doubt the Amendment does not take away from the state governments in a general sense the power over suffrage which has belonged to those governments from the beginning, and without the possession of which power the whole fabric upon which the division of state and national authority under the Constitution and the organization of both governments rest would be without support, and both the authority of the nation and the state would fall to the ground. In fact, the very command of the amendment recognizes the possession of the general power by the state, since the amendment seeks to regulate its exercise as to the particular subject with which it deals.

(b) But it is equally beyond the possibility of question that the amendment in express terms restricts the power of the United States or the states to abridge or deny the right of a citizen of the United States to vote on account of race, color, or previous condition of servitude. The restriction is coincident with the power and prevents its exertion in disregard to the command of the amendment. But while this is true, it is true also that the amendment does not change, modify, or deprive the states of their full power as to suffrage except, of course, as to the subject with which the amendment deals and to the extent that obedience to its command is necessary. Thus the authority over suffrage which the states possess and the limitation which the amendment imposes are co-ordinate and one may not destroy the other without bringing about the destruction of both.

(c) While in the true sense, therefore, the amendment gives no right of suffrage, it was long ago recognized that in operation its prohibition might measurably have that effect; that is to say, that as the command of the amendment was self-executing and reached without legislative action the conditions of discrimination against which it was aimed, the result might arise that, as a consequence of the striking down of a discrimination clause, a right of suffrage would be enjoyed by reason of the generic character of the provision which would remain after the discrimination was stricken out. A familiar illustration of this doctrine resulted from the effect of the adoption of the amendment on state constitutions in which, at the time of the adoption of the amendment, the right of suffrage was conferred on all white male citizens, since by the inherent power of the amendment the word "white" disappeared and therefore all male citizens, without discrimination on account of race, color, or previous condition of servitude, came under the generic grant of suffrage made by the state.

With these principles before us how can there be room for any serious dispute concerning the repugnancy of the standard based upon January 1, 1866 (a date which preceded the adoption of the Fifteenth Amendment), if the suffrage provision fixing that standard is susceptible of the significance which the government attributes to it? Indeed, there seems no escape from the conclusion that to hold that there was even possibility for dispute on the subject would be but to declare that the Fifteenth Amendment not only had not the self-executing power which it has been recognized to have from the beginning, but that its provisions were wholly inoperative because susceptible of being rendered inapplicable by mere forms of expression embodying no exercise of judgment and resting upon no discernible reason other than the purpose to disregard the prohibitions of the amendment by creating a standard of voting which, on its face, was in substance but a revitalization of conditions which, when they prevailed in the past, had been destroyed by the self-operative force of the amendment.

2. The standard of January 1, 1866, fixed in the suffrage amendment and its significance.

The inquiry, of course, here is, Does the amendment as to the particular standard which this heading embraces involve the mere refusal to comply with the commands of the Fifteenth Amendment as previously stated? This leads us, for the purpose of the analysis, to recur to the text of the suffrage amendment. Its opening sentence fixes the literacy standard which is all inclusive, since it is general in its expression and contains no word of discrimination on account of race or color or any other reason. This, however, is immediately followed by the provisions creating the standard based upon the condition existing on January 1, 1866, and carving out those coming under that standard from the inclusion in the literacy test which would have controlled them but for the exclusion thus expressly provided for . . .

We have difficulty in finding words to more clearly demonstrate the conviction we entertain that this standard has the characteristics which the government attributes to it than does the mere statement of the text. It is true it contains no express words of an exclusion from the standard which it establishes of any person on account of race, color, or previous condition of servitude, prohibited by the Fifteenth Amendment, but the standard itself inherently brings that result into existence since it is based purely upon a period of time before the enactment of the Fifteenth Amendment, and makes that period the controlling and dominant test of the right of suffrage. In other words, we seek in vain for any ground which would sustain any other interpretation but that the provision, recurring to the conditions existing before the Fifteenth Amendment was adopted and the continuance of which the Fifteenth Amendment prohibited, proposed by in substance and effect lifting those conditions over to a period of time after the amendment, to make them the basis of the right to suffrage conferred in direct and positive disregard of the Fifteenth Amendment. And the same result, we are of opinion, is demonstrated by considering whether it is possible to discover any basis of reason for the standard thus fixed other than the purpose above stated. We say this because we are unable to discover how, unless the prohibitions of the Fifteenth Amendment were considered, the slightest reason was afforded for basing the classification upon a period of time prior to the Fifteenth Amendment. Certainly it cannot be said that there was any peculiar necromancy in the time named which engendered attributes affecting the qualification to vote which would not exist at another and different period unless the Fifteenth Amendment was in view.

While these considerations establish that the

standard fixed on the basis of the 1866 test is void, they do not enable us to reply even to the first question asked by the court below, since to do so we must consider the literacy standard established by the suffrage amendment and the possibility of its surviving the determination of the fact that the 1866 standard never took life, since it was void from the beginning because of the operation upon it of the prohibitions of the Fifteenth Amendment. And this brings us to the last heading:

3. The determination of the validity of the literacy test and the possibility of its surviving the disappearance of the 1866 standard with which it is associated in the suffrage amendment.

No time need be spent on the question of the validity of the literacy test, considered alone, since, as we have seen, its establishment was but the exercise by the state of a lawful power vested in it, not subject to our supervision, and, indeed, its validity is admitted. Whether this test is so connected with the other one relating to the situation on January 1, 1866, that the invalidity of the latter requires the rejection of the former, is really a question of state law; but, in the absence of any decision on the subject by the supreme court of the state, we must determine it for ourselves. We are of opinion that neither forms of classification nor methods of enumeration should be made the basis of striking down a provision which was independently legal, and therefore was lawfully enacted, because of the removal of an illegal provision with which the legal provision or provisions may have been associated. We state what we hold to be the rule thus strongly because we are of opinion that on a subject like the one under consideration, involving the establishment of a right whose exercise lies at the very basis of government, a much more exacting standard is required than would ordinarily obtain where the influence of the declared unconstitutionality of one provision of a statute upon another and constitutional provision is required to be fixed. Of course, rigorous as is this rule and imperative as is the duty not to violate it, it does not mean that it applies in a case where it expressly appears that a contrary conclusion must be reached if the plain letter and necessary intendment of the provision under consideration so compels, or where such a result is rendered necessary because to follow the contrary course would give rise to such an extreme and anomalous situation as would cause it to be impossible to conclude that it could have been, upon any hypothesis whatever, within the mind of the law making power. Does the general rule here govern, or is the case controlled by one or the other of the exceptional conditions which we have just stated, is, then, the remaining question to be decided. Coming to solve it we are of opinion that by a consideration of the text of the suffrage amendment in so far as it deals with the literacy test, and to the extent that it creates the standard based upon conditions existing on January 1, 1866, the case is taken out of the general rule and brought under the first of the exceptions stated. We say this because, in our opinion, the very language of the suffrage amendment expresses, not by implication nor by forms of classification nor by the order in which they are made, but by direct and positive language the command that the persons embraced in the 1866 standard should not be, under any conditions, subjected to the literacy test—a command which would be virtually set at naught if, on the obliteration of the one standard by the force of the Fifteenth Amendment, the other standard should be held to continue in force.

The reasons previously stated dispose of the case and make it plain that it is our duty to answer the first question, No, and the second, Yes;

but before we direct the entry of an order to that effect, we come briefly to dispose of an issue the consideration of which we have hitherto postponed from a desire not to break the continuity of discussion as to the general and important subject before us.

In various forms of statement not challenging the instructions given by the trial court concretely considered, concerning the liability of the election officers for their official conduct, it is insisted that, as in connection with the instructions the jury was charged that the suffrage amendment was unconstitutional because of its repugnancy to the Fifteenth Amendment, therefore, taken as a whole, the charge was erroneous. But we are of opinion that this contention is without merit, especially in view of the doctrine long since settled concerning the self-executing power of the Fifteenth Amendment, and of what we have held to be the nature and character of the suffrage amendment in question. . . .

We answer the first question, No, and the second question, Yes.

Myers v. Anderson
238 U.S. 368 (1915)

Prior to the adoption of the Fifteenth Amendment the privilege of suffrage was conferred by the constitution of Maryland of 1867 upon "every white male citizen," but the Fifteenth Amendment by its self-operative force obliterated the word "white," and caused the qualification therefore to be "every male citizen," and this came to be recognized by the court of appeals of the state of Maryland. Without recurring to the establishment of the city of Annapolis as a municipality in earlier days, or following the development of its government, it suffices to say that before 1877 the right to vote for the governing municipal body was vested in persons entitled to vote for members of the general assembly of Maryland, which standard, by the elimination of the word "white" from the Constitution by the Fifteenth Amendment embraced "every male citizen." In 1896 a general election law comprising many sections was enacted in Maryland. Laws of 1896. It is sufficient to say that it provided for a board of supervisors of elections in each county to be appointed by the governor, and that this board was given the power to appoint two persons as registering officers and two as judges of election for each election precinct or ward in the county. Under this law each ward or voting precinct in Annapolis became entitled to two registering officers. While the law made these changes in the election machinery it did not change the qualification of voters.

In 1908 an act was passed "to fix the qualifications of voters at municipal elections in the city of Annapolis and to provide for the registration of said voters." This law authorized the appointment of three persons as registers, instead of two, in each election ward or precinct in Annapolis, and provided for the mode in which they should perform their duties, and conferred the right of registration and consequently the right to vote on all male citizens above the age of twenty-one years who had resided one year in the municipality and had not been convicted of crime, and who came within any one of the three following classes:

> 1. All taxpayers of the city of Annapolis assessed on the city books for at least $500. 2. And duly naturalized citizens. 2½. And male children of naturalized citizens who have reached the age of twenty-one years. 3. All citizens who prior to January 1, 1868, were entitled to vote in the state of Maryland or any other state of the United States at a state election, and the lawful male descendants of any person who prior to January 1, 1868, was

entitled to vote in this state or in any other state of the United States at a state election, and no person not coming within one of the three enumerated classes shall be registered as a legal voter of the city of Annapolis or qualified to vote at the municipal elections held therein, and any person so duly registered shall, while so registered, be qualified to vote at any municipal election held in said city; said registration shall in all other respects conform to the laws of the state of Maryland relating to and providing for registration in the state of Maryland.

The three persons who are defendants in error in these cases applied in Annapolis to the board of registration to be registered as a prerequisite to the enjoyment of their right to vote at an election to be held in July, 1909, and they were denied the right by a vote of two out of the three members of the board. They consequently were unable to vote. Anderson, the defendant in error in No. 8, was a negro citizen who possessed all the qualifications required to vote exacted by the law in existence prior to the one we have just quoted, and who on January 1, 1868, the date fixed in the third class in the act in question, would have been entitled to vote in Maryland but for the fact that he was a negro, albeit he possessed none of the particular qualifications enumerated by the statute in question. Howard, the defendant in error in No. 9, was a negro citizen possessing all the qualifications to vote required before the passage of the act in question, whose grandfather resided in Maryland and would have been entitled to vote on January 1, 1868, but for the fact that he was a negro. Brown, the defendant in error in No. 10, also had all the qualifications to vote under the law previously existing, and his father was a negro residing in Maryland who would have been able to vote on the date named but for the fact that he was a negro. The three parties thereupon began these separate suits

to recover damages against the two registering officers who had refused to register them on the ground that thereby they had been deprived of a right to vote secured by the Fifteenth Amendment, and that there was liability for damages under 1979 . . .

The complaints were demurred. . . . The cases were then tried to the court without a jury, and to the judgments in favor of the plaintiffs which resulted these three separate writs of error were prosecuted.

The nonliability in any event of the election officers for their official conduct is seriously pressed in argument, and it is also urged that in any event there could not be liability under the Fifteenth Amendment for having deprived of the right to vote at a municipal election. . . .

This brings us to consider the statute in order to determine whether its standards for registering and voting are repugnant to the Fifteenth Amendment. There are three general criteria. We test them by beginning at the third, as it is obviously the most comprehensive, and, as we shall ultimately see, the keystone of the arch upon which all the others rest. In coming to do so it is at once manifest that, barring some negligible changes in phraseology . . . we pass from its consideration and approach the first and a subdivision numbered 2½. The first confers the rights to register and vote free from any distinction on account of race or color upon all taxpayers assessed for at least $500. We put all question of the constitutionality of this standard out of view as it contains no express discrimination repugnant to the Fifteenth Amendment, and it is not susceptible of being assailed on account of an alleged wrongful motive on the part of the lawmaker or the mere possibilities of its future operation in practice, and because, as there is a reason other than discrimination on account of race or color discernible upon which the standard may rest, there is no room for the conclusion that it must be assumed, because of the impossibility of finding any other reason for its enactment, to rest alone upon a purpose to violate the Fifteenth Amendment. And as, in order to dispose of the case, as we shall see, it is not necessary to examine the constitutionality of the other standards, that is, numbers 2 and 2½ relating to naturalized citizens and their descendants, merely for the sake of argument we assume those two standards, without so deciding, to be also free from constitutional objection, and come to consider the case under that hypothesis.

The result, then, is this: that the third standard is void because it amounts to a mere denial of the operative effect of the Fifteenth Amendment, and, based upon that conception, proceeds to re-create and re-establish a condition which the amendment prohibits and the existence of which had been previously stricken down in consequence of the self-operative force of its prohibitions; and the other standards separately considered are valid or are assumed to be such and therefore are not violative of the Fifteenth Amendment. On its face, therefore, this situation would establish that the request made by all the plaintiffs for registration was rightfully refused since, even if the void standard be put wholly out of view, none of the parties had the qualifications necessary to entitle them to register and vote under any of the others. This requires us therefore to determine whether the two first standards which we have held were valid or have assumed to be so must nevertheless be treated as nonexisting as the necessary result of the elimination of the third standard because of its repugnancy to the prohibition of the Fifteenth Amendment. And by this we are brought therefore to determine the interrelation of the provisions and the dependency of the two first, in-

cluding the substandard under the second, upon the third; in other words, to decide whether or not such a unity existed between the standards that the destruction of one necessarily leaves no possible reason for recognizing the continued existence and operative force of the others.

. . .

. . . First, because, looking at the context of the provision, we think that the obvious purpose was not to subject to the exactions of the first standard (the property qualification) any person who was included in the other standards; and second, because the result of holding that the other standards survived the striking down of the third would be to bring about such an abnormal result as would bring the case within the second exception, since it would come to pass that every American-born citizen would be deprived of his right to vote unless he was able to comply with the property qualification, and all naturalized citizens and their descendants would be entitled to vote without being submitted to any property qualification whatever. If the clauses as to naturalization were assumed to be invalid, the incongruous result just stated would, of course, not arise, but the legal situation would be unchanged, since that view would not weaken the conclusion as to the unity of the provisions of the statute, but, on the contrary, would fortify it.

But it is argued even although this result be conceded, there nevertheless was no right to recover, and there must be a reversal since, if the whole statute fell, all the clauses providing for suffrage fell, and no right to suffrage remained, and hence no deprivation or abridgment of the right to vote resulted. . . . The qualification of voters under the constitution of Maryland existed and the statute which previously provided for the registration and election in Annapolis was unaffected by the void provisions of the statute which we are considering. The mere change in some respects of the administrative machinery by the new statute did not relieve the new officers of their duty, nor did it interpose a shield to prevent the operation upon them of the provisions of the Constitution of the United States and the statutes passed in pursuance thereof. The conclusive effect of this view will become apparent when it is considered that if the argument were accepted, it would follow that although the Fifteenth Amendment by its self-operative force, without any action of the state, changed the clause in the Constitution of the state of Maryland conferring suffrage upon "every white male citizen" so as to cause it to read "every male citizen," nevertheless the amendment was so supine, so devoid of effect, as to leave it open for the legislature to write back by statute the discriminating provision by a mere changed form of expression into the laws of the state, and for the state officers to make the result of such action successfully operative.

There is a contention pressed concerning the application of the statute upon which the suits were based to the acts in question. But we think, in view of the nature and character of the acts, of the self-operative force of the Fifteenth Amendment, and of the legislation of Congress on the subject, that there is no ground for such contention. Affirmed.

United States v. Mosley
238 U.S. 383 (1915)

The indictment contains four counts. The first charges a conspiracy of the two defendants, who were officers and a majority of the county election board of Blaine County, Oklahoma, to injure and oppress certain legally qualified electors of the United States, being all the voters of eleven precincts in the county, in the free exercise and enjoyment of their right and privilege, under the Constitution and laws of the United States, of voting for a member of Congress for their district. To that end, it is alleged, the defendants agreed that, irrespective of the precinct returns being lawful and regular, they would omit them from their count and from their returns to the state election board. The second count charges the same conspiracy, a secret meeting of the defendants without the knowledge of the third member of their board, for the purpose of carrying it out, and the overt act of making a false return, as agreed, omitting the returns from the named precincts, although regular and entitled to be counted. The third count is like the first with the addition of some details of the plan, intended to deceive the third member of their board. The fourth charges the same conspiracy, but states the object as being to injure and oppress the same citizens for and on account of their having exercised the right described.

. . . It is not open to question that this statute is constitutional, and constitutionally extends some protection, at least, to the right to vote for members of Congress. We regard it as equally unquestionable that the right to have one's vote counted is as open to protection by Congress as the right to put a ballot in a box.

The only matter that needs argument is that upon which the district court expressed its view-whether, properly construed, the statute purports to deal with such conduct as that of the defendants, assuming that there is no lack of power if such be its intent. Manifestly the words are broad enough to cover the case, but the argument that they have a different scope is drawn from the fact that originally this section was part of the enforcement act of May 31, 1870, and that by an earlier section of the same statute every person who, by any unlawful means, hindered or combined with others to hinder any citizen from voting at any election in any state, etc., was subjected to a much milder penalty than that under 6. It may be thought that the act of 1870 cannot have meant to deal a second time and in a much severer way in 6 with what it had disposed of a few sentences before. The other sections have been repealed, but 19, it may be said, must mean what it meant in 1870 when the enforcement act was passed, and what it did mean will be seen more clearly from its original words.

In its original form the section began: "If two or more persons shall band or conspire together or go in disguise upon the public highway, or upon the premises of another, with intent to violate any provision of this act, or to injure, oppress," etc. The source of this section in the doings of the Ku Klux and the like is obvious, and acts of violence obviously were in the mind of Congress. Naturally Congress put forth all its powers. But this section dealt with federal rights, and with all federal rights, and protected them in the lump, whereas 4, dealt only with elections, and although it dealt with them generally and might be held to cover elections of federal officers, it extended to all elections. It referred to conspiracies only as incident to its main purpose of punishing any obstruction to voting at any election in any state. The power was doubtful and soon was held to have been exceeded. The subject was not one that called for the most striking exercise of such power as might exist. Any overlapping that there may have been well might have escaped attention, or, if noticed, have been approved, when we consider what must have been the respective emphasis in the mind to Congress when the two sections were passed.

But 6 being devoted, as we have said, to the protection of all federal rights from conspiracies against them, naturally did not confine itself to conspiracies contemplating violence, although, under the influence of the conditions then existing, it put that class in the front. Just as the Fourteenth Amendment . . . was adopted with a view to the protection of the colored race, but has been found to be equally important in its application to the rights of all, 6 had a general scope and used general words that have become the most important now that the Ku Klux have passed away. The clause as to going in disguise upon the highway has dropped into a subordinate place, and even there has a somewhat anomalous sound. The section now begins with sweeping general words. Those words always were in the act, and the present form gives them a congressional interpretation. Even if that interpretation would not have been held correct in an indictment under 6, which we are far from intimating, and if we cannot interpret the past by the present, we cannot allow the past so far to affect the present as to deprive citizens of the United States of the general protection which, on its face, 19 most reasonably affords.

Judgment reversed.

Mackenzie v. Hare
239 U.S. 299 (1915)

> The plaintiff was born and ever since has resided in the state of California. On August 14, 1909, being then a resident and citizen of this state and of the United States, she was lawfully married to Gordon Mackenzie, a native and subject of the kingdom of Great Britain. He had resided in California prior to that time, still resides here, and it is his intention to make this state his permanent residence. He has not become naturalized as a citizen of the United States and it does not appear that he intends to do so. Ever since their marriage the plain-

tiff and her husband have lived together as husband and wife. On January 22, 1913, she applied to the defendants to be registered as a voter. She was then over the age of twenty-one years and had resided in San Francisco for more than ninety days. Registration was refused to her on the ground that, by reason of her marriage to Gordon Mackenzie, a subject of Great Britain, she thereupon took the nationality of her husband and ceased to be a citizen of the United States.

Plaintiff in error claims a right as a voter of the state under its constitution and the Constitution of the United States.

The constitution of the state gives the privilege of suffrage to "every native citizen of the United States," and it is contended that under the Constitution of the United States every person born in the United States is a citizen thereof. The latter must be conceded, and if plaintiff has not lost her citizenship by her marriage, she has the qualification of a voter prescribed by the constitution of the state of California. The question then is. Did she cease to be a citizen by her marriage?

On March 2, 1907, that is, prior to the marriage of plaintiff in error, Congress enacted a statute the third section of which provides: "That any American woman who marries a foreigner shall take the nationality of her husband. At the termination of the marital relation she may resume her American citizenship, if abroad, by registering as an American citizen within one year with a consul of the United States, or by returning to reside in the United States, or, if residing in the United States at the termination of the marital relation, by continuing to reside therein."

Plaintiff contends that "such legislation, if intended to apply to her, is beyond the authority of Congress."

Questions of construction and power are, therefore, presented. Upon the construction of the act it is urged that it was not the intention to deprive

an American-born woman, remaining within the jurisdiction of the United States, of her citizenship by reason of her marriage to a resident foreigner. The contention is attempted to be based upon the history of the act and upon the report of the committee, upon which, it is said, the legislation was enacted. Both history and report show, it is asserted, "that the intention of Congress was solely to legislate concerning the status of citizens abroad and the questions arising by reason thereof."

Does the act invite or permit such assistance? Its declaration is general, "that any American woman who marries a foreigner shall take the nationality of her husband." There is no limitation of place; there is no limitation of effect, the marital relation having been constituted and continuing. For its termination there is provision, and explicit provision. At its termination she may resume her American citizenship if in the United States by simply remaining therein; if abroad, by returning to the United States, or, within one year, registering as an American citizen. The act is therefore explicit and circumstantial. It would transcend judicial power to insert limitations or conditions upon disputable considerations of reasons which impelled the law, or of conditions to which it might be conjectured it was addressed and intended to accommodate.

. . .

It will thus be seen that plaintiff's contention is in exact antagonism to the statute. Only voluntary expatriation, as she defines it, can devest a woman of her citizenship, she declares; the statute provides that, by marriage with a foreigner, she takes his nationality.

. . .

. . . It may be conceded that a change of citizenship cannot be arbitrarily imposed, that is, imposed without the concurrence of the citizen.

The law in controversy does not have that feature. It deals with a condition voluntarily entered into, with notice of the consequences. We concur with counsel that citizenship is of tangible worth, and we sympathize with plaintiff in her desire to retain it and in her earnest assertion of it. But there is involved more than personal considerations. As we have seen, the legislation was urged by conditions of national moment. And this is an answer to the apprehension of counsel that our construction of the legislation will make every act, though lawful, as marriage, of course, is, a renunciation of citizenship. The marriage of an American woman with a foreigner has consequences of like kind, may involve national complications of like kind, as her physical expatriation may involve. Therefore, as long as the relation lasts, it is made tantamount to expatriation. This is no arbitrary exercise of government. It is one which, regarding the international aspects, judicial opinion has taken for granted would not only be valid, but demanded. It is the conception of the legislation under review that such an act may bring the government into embarrassments, and, it may be, into controversies. It is as voluntary and distinctive as expatriation and its consequence must be considered as elected.

Judgment affirmed.

United States v. Gradwell
243 U.S. 476 (1917)

In the *Gradwell* case and in the *Hambly* case the fourteen defendants are charged in the indictments with having conspired together "to defraud the United States," and to commit a wilful fraud upon the laws of the state of Rhode Island, by corrupting and debauching, by bribery of voters, the general election held on the third of Novem-

ber, 1914, at which a Representative in Congress was voted for and elected in the second congressional district of Rhode Island in the *Gradwell* case, and in the first congressional district in the *Hambly* case, thereby preventing "a fair and clean" election.

No. 775 relates to the conduct of a primary election held in the state of West Virginia on the sixth of June, 1916, under a law of that state providing for a state-wide nomination of candidates for the United States Senate. In the indictment twenty defendants are charged with conspiring "to defraud the United States in the matter of its governmental right to have a candidate of the true choice and preference of the Republican and Democratic parties nominated for said office and one of them elected," by causing and procuring a large number of persons who had not resided in the state a sufficient length of time to entitle them to vote under the state law, to vote at the primary for a candidate named, and also to procure four hundred of such persons to vote more than once at such primary election.

The indictment in No. 776 charges that the same defendants named in No. 775 conspired together to "injure and oppress" . . . three candidates for the Republican nomination for United States Senator who were voted for at the primary election held in West Virginia on June sixth, 1916, under a law of that state, by depriving them of the "right and privilege of having each Republican voter vote, and vote once only, for some one" of the Republican candidates for such nomination, and of not having any votes counted at such election except such as were cast by Republican voters duly qualified under the West Virginia law. The charge is that the defendants conspired to accomplish this result by procuring a thousand persons, who were not qualified to vote under the state law, because they had not resided in that state a sufficient length of time, to vote for an opposing candidate, William F. Hite, and many of them to vote more than once, and to have their votes cast, counted, and returned as cast in favor of such candidate.

A demurrer to the indictment by each of the defendants in each case, on the ground that it fails to set forth any offense under the laws of the United States, was sustained by the district court of the district of Rhode Island in the first two cases and of the southern district of West Virginia in the third. The cases are here on error.

. . .

The applicable portions of 37 and 19 are as follows:

> Section 37. If two or more persons conspire either to commit any offense against the United States, or to defraud the United States in any manner for any purpose, . . . each of the parties to such conspiracy shall be fined not more than ten thousand dollars, or imprisoned not more than two years, or both.
>   Section 19. If two or more persons conspire to injure, oppress, threaten, or intimidate any citizen in the free exercise of enjoyment of any right or privilege secured to him by the Constitution or laws of the United States, or because of his having so exercised the same . . . they shall be fined not more than five thousand dollars and imprisoned not more than ten years, and shall, moreover, be thereafter ineligible to any office, or place of honor, profit, or trust created by the Constitution or laws of the United States.

. . . This presents for decision the questions:

Is 37 of the Criminal Code applicable to congressional elections, and, if it is, has the United States such an interest or right in the result of such elections that to bribe electors constitutes a fraud upon the government within the meaning of this section?

To admit, as it must be admitted, that the people of the United States, and so their gov-

ernment, considered as a political entity, have an interest in and a right to honest and fair elections, advances us but little toward determining whether 37 was enacted to protect that right, and whether a conspiracy to bribe voters is a violation of it. Obviously the government may have this right and yet not have enacted this law to protect it. It may be, as is claimed, that Congress intended to rely upon state laws and the administration of them by state officials to secure honest elections, and that this section was enacted for purposes wholly apart from those here claimed for it.

To answer the questions presented requires that we look to the origin and history of 37, and that we consider what has been, and is now, the policy of Congress in dealing with the regulation of elections of Representatives in Congress. . . .

. . . [T]his is the first time that it has been attempted to extend its application to the conduct of elections . . . suggest strongly that it was not intended by Congress for such a purpose.

Further aid in determining the application and construction of the section may be derived from the history of the conduct and policy of the government in dealing with congressional elections.

. . .

Whatever doubt may at one time have existed as to the extent of the power which Congress may exercise under this constitutional sanction in the prescribing of regulations for the conduct of elections for Representatives in Congress, or in adopting regulations which states have prescribed for that purpose, has been settled by repeated decisions of this court. . . .

Although Congress has had this power of regulating the conduct of congressional elections from the organization of the government, our legislative history upon the subject shows that . . . it has been its policy to leave such regulations almost entirely to the states, whose representatives Congressmen are. . . .

. . . [I]n 1870 . . . for the first time, a comprehensive system for dealing with congressional elections was enacted.

These laws provided extensive regulations for the conduct of congressional elections. They made unlawful false registration, bribery, voting without legal right, making false returns of votes cast, interfering in any manner with officers of election, and the neglect by any such officer of any duty required of him by state or federal law; they provided for appointment by circuit judges of the United States of persons to attend at places of registration and at elections, with authority to challenge any person proposing to register or vote unlawfully, to witness the counting of votes, and to identify by their signatures the registration of voters and election tally sheets; and they made it lawful for the marshals of the United States to appoint special deputies to preserve order at such elections, with authority to arrest for any breach of the peace committed in their view.

It will be seen from this statement of the important features of these enactments that Congress by them committed to federal officers a very full participation in the process of the election of Congressmen, from the registration of voters to the final certifying of the results, and that the control thus established over such elections was comprehensive and complete. It is a matter of general as of legal history that Congress, after twenty-four years of experience, returned to its former attitude toward such elections, and repealed all of these laws with the exception of a few sections not relevant here. This repealing act left in effect, as apparently relating to the elective franchise, only the provisions contained in the eight sections of chapter 3 of the Criminal Code, 19 to 26, inclusive, which have not been added to or substantially modified during the twenty-three years which have since elapsed.

. . .

With it thus clearly established that the policy of Congress for so great a part of our constitutional life has been, and now is, to leave the conduct of the election of its members to state laws, administered by state officers, and that whenever it has assumed to regulate such elections it has done so by positive and clear statutes, such as were enacted in 1870, it would be a strained and unreasonable construction to apply to such elections this 37, originally a law for the protection of the revenue, and for now fifty years confined in its application to "Offenses against the Operations of the Government," as distinguished from the processes by which men are selected to conduct such operations.

When to all this we add that there are no common-law offenses against the United States, that before a man can be punished as a criminal under the federal law his case must be "plainly and unmistakably" within the provisions of some statute, and that Congress has always under its control the means of defeating frauds in the election of its members by enacting appropriate legislation and by resort to the constitutional grant of power to judge of the elections, returns, and qualifications of its own members, we cannot doubt that the district court was right in holding that the section was never intended to apply to elections, and that to bribe voters to vote at such an election is not such a fraud upon the United States or upon candidates or the laws of Rhode Island as falls within either the terms or purposes of the section.

There remains to be considered the second West Virginia case. The indictment in this case charges that the defendants conspired to procure and did procure a large number of persons, not legal voters of West Virginia, to vote, and a number of them to vote more than once, in favor of one of the four candidates for the Republican nomination for United States Senator at a state primary. The claim is that such illegal voting "injured and oppressed" the three other party candidates, within the meaning of 19 of the Criminal Code of the United States, by depriving them of a right which it is argued they had "by the Constitution and laws of the United States," to have only qualified Republican voters of the state vote, not more than once, for some one of the candidates of that party for Senator at such election.

Here again, confessedly, an attempt is being made to make a new application of an old law to an old type of crime; for 19 has been in force, in substance, since 1870, but has never before been resorted to as applicable to the punishment of offenses committed in the conduct of primary elections or nominating caucuses or conventions, and the question presented for decision is:

Did the candidates named in the indictment have such a right under the applicable West Virginia law that a conspiracy to corrupt the primary election held under that law on the sixth day of last June "injured and oppressed" them within the meaning of 19 of the Federal Criminal Code?

That this 19 of the Criminal Code is applicable to certain conspiracies against the elective franchise is decided by this court in *Mosley*, but that decision falls far short of making the section applicable to the conduct of a state nominating primary, and does not advance us far toward the claimed conclusion that illegal voting for one candidate at such a primary so violates a right secured to the other candidates by the United States Constitution and laws as to constitute an offense within the meaning and purpose of the section.

The constitutional warrant under which regulations relating to congressional elections may be provided by Congress is in terms applicable to the "times, places, and manner of holding elections (not nominating primaries) for Senators and Representatives." Primary elections, such as it is claimed the defendants corrupted, were not only unknown when the Constitution was adopted, but they were equally unknown for many years after the law, now 19, was first enacted. They are a development of comparatively recent years, designed to take the place of the nominating caucus or convention, as these existed before the change, and even yet the new system must be considered in an experimental stage of development, under a variety of state laws.

The claim that such a nominating primary, as distinguished from a final election, is included within the provision of the Constitution of the United States, applicable to the election of Senators and Representatives, is by no means indisputable. Many state supreme courts have held that similar provisions of state constitutions relating to elections do not include a nominating primary.

But even if it be admitted that, in general, a primary should be treated as an election within the meaning of the constitution, which we need not and do not decide, such admission would not be of value in determining the case before us, because of some strikingly unusual features of the West Virginia law under which the primary was held, out of which this prosecution grows. By its terms this law provided that only candidates for Congress belonging to a political party which polled 3 percent of the vote of the entire state at the last preceding general election could be voted for at this primary, and thereby . . . only Democratic and Republican candidates could be and were voted for, while candidates of the Prohibition and Socialist parties were excluded, as were also independent voters who declined to make oath that they were "regular and qualified members and voters" of one of the greater parties. Even more notable is the provision of the law that, after the nominating primary, candidates, even persons who have failed at the primary, may be nominated by certificate signed by not less than 5 percent of the entire vote polled at the last preceding election.

Such provisions as these, adapted though they may be to the selection of party candidates for office, obviously could not be lawfully applied to a final election at which officers are chosen, and it cannot reasonably be said that rights which candidates for the nomination for Senator of the United States may have in such a primary under such a law are derived from the Constitution and laws of the United States. They are derived wholly from the state law, and nothing of the kind can be found in any federal statute. Even when Congress assumed . . . to provide an elaborate system of supervision over congressional elections, no action was taken looking to the regulation of nominating caucuses or conventions, which were the nominating agencies in use at the time such laws were enacted.

What power Congress would have to make regulations for nominating primaries, or to alter such regulations when made by a state, we need not inquire. It is sufficient to say that as yet it has shown no disposition to assume control of such primaries or to participate in them in any way, and that it is not for the courts, in the absence of such legislation, to attempt to supply it by stretching old statutes to new uses, to which they are not adapted and for which they were not intended. In this case, as in the others, we conclude that the section of the Criminal Code relied upon, originally enacted for the protection of the civil rights of the then lately enfranchised negro, cannot be extended so as to make it an agency for enforcing a state primary law, such as this one of West Virginia.

The claim that the effect of the Federal Corrupt Practices Act, recognizing primary elections and limiting the expenditures of candidates for senator in connection with them, is, in effect, an adoption by Congress of all state primary laws, is too unsubstantial for discussion; and the like claim that the temporary measure, enacted by Congress for the conduct of the nomination and election of Senators until other provisions should be made by state legislation cannot be entertained, because this act was superseded by the West Virginia primary election law, passed February 20, 1914, effective ninety days after its passage.

It results that the judgments of the District Court in each of these cases must be affirmed.

United States v. Bathgate
246 U.S. 220 (1918)

Except as to parties, the indictments in these six cases are alike. Each contains three counts; the first and second undertake to allege a conspiracy to injure and oppress in violation of section 19, Criminal Code, and the third a conspiracy to defraud the United States, contrary to section 37. Demurrers were sustained upon the ground that, rightly construed, neither section applies to the specified acts.

. . .

And the two counts based thereon charge defendants with conspiring to injure candidates for presidential electors, the United States Senate and representative in Congress at the regular election in Ohio, November 7, 1916, also qualified electors who might properly vote thereat, in the free exercise and enjoyment of certain rights and privileges secured by Constitution and laws of the United States, namely, the right (a) of being a candidate; (b) that only those duly qualified should vote; (c) that the results should be determined by voters who had not been bribed; and (d) that the election board should make a true and accurate count of votes legally cast by qualified electors and no others. The indictment further alleged the conspiracy was carried into effect as intended by purchasing votes of certain electors and causing election boards to receive them and make inaccurate returns.

The real point involved is whether section 19 denounces as criminal a conspiracy to bribe voters at a general election within a state where presidential electors, a United States Senator and a representative in Congress are to be chosen. Our concern is not with the power of Congress, but with the proper interpretation of action taken by it. This must be ascertained in view of the settled rule that "there can be no constructive offenses, and before a man can be punished his case must be plainly and unmistakably within the statute"; and the policy of Congress to leave the conduct of elections at which its members are chosen to state law alone, except where it may have expressed a clear purpose to establish some further or definite regulation.

Departing from the course long observed, Congress undertook to prescribe a comprehensive system intended to secure freedom and integrity of elections. . . .

. . .

The government in effect maintains that lawful voters at an election for presidential electors, senator and member of Congress and also the candidates for those places have secured to them by Constitution or laws of the United States the right and privilege that it shall be fairly and honestly conducted; and that Congress intended by section 6, Act of 1870, to punish interference with such right and privilege through conspiracy to influence voters by bribery.

Section 19, Criminal Code, of course, now has the same meaning as when first enacted as section 6, Act of 1870; and considering the policy of Congress not to interfere with elections within a state except by clear and specific provisions, together with the rule respecting construction of criminal statutes, we cannot think it was intended to apply to conspiracies to bribe voters. Bribery, expressly denounced in another section of the original act, is not clearly within the words used; and the reasoning relied on to extend them thereto would apply in respect of almost any act reprehensible in itself, or forbidden by state statutes, and supposed injuriously to affect freedom, honesty, or integrity of an election. This conclusion is strengthened by express repeal of the section applicable in terms to bribery and we think is rendered entirely clear by considering the nature of the rights or privileges fairly within intendment of original section 6.

The right or privilege to be guarded, as indicated both by the language employed and context, was a definite, personal one, capable of enforcement by a court, and not the political, non-judicable one common to all that the public shall be protected against harmful acts, which is here relied on. The right to vote is personal and we have held it is shielded by the section in question. . . .

The court below properly construed the statute and its judgments are affirmed.

Leser v. Garnett
258 U.S. 130 (1922)

On October 12, 1920, Cecilia Streett Waters and Mary D. Randolph, citizens of Maryland, applied for and were granted registration as qualified voters in Baltimore City. To have their names stricken from the list Oscar Leser and others brought this suit in the court of common pleas. The only ground of disqualification alleged was that the applicants for registration were women, whereas the constitution of Maryland limits the suffrage to men. Ratification of the proposed amendment to the federal Constitution, now known as the Nineteenth, had been proclaimed on August 26, 1920. The Legislature of Maryland had refused to ratify it. The petitioners contended, on several grounds, that the amendment had not become part of the federal Constitution. The trial court overruled the contentions and dismissed the petition. Its judgment was affirmed by the Court of Appeals of the state; and the case comes here on writ of error. . . .

. . .

. . . Affirmed.

Grovey v. Townsend
295 U.S. 45 (1935)

The petitioner, by complaint filed in the justice court of Harris county, Texas, alleged that although he is a citizen of the United States and of the state and county, and a member of and believer in the tenets of the Democratic Party, the respondent, the county clerk, a state officer, having as such only public functions to perform, refused him a ballot for a Democratic Party primary election, because he is of the negro race. He demanded ten dollars damages. The pleading quotes articles of the Revised Civil Statutes of Texas which require the nomination of candidates at primary elections by any organized political party whose nominees received 100,000 votes or more at the preceding general election, and recites that agreeably to these enactments a Democratic primary election was held on July 28, 1934, at which petitioner had the right to vote. Referring to statutes which regulate absentee voting at primary

elections, the complaint states the petitioner expected to be absent from the county on the date of the primary election, and demanded of the respondent an absentee ballot, which was refused him in virtue of a resolution of the state Democratic Convention of Texas, adopted May 24, 1932. . . .

The complaint charges that the respondent acted without legal excuse and his wrongful and unlawful acts constituted a violation of the Fourteenth and Fifteenth Amendments of the Federal Constitution.

A demurrer, assigning as reasons that the complaint was insufficient in law and stated no cause of action, was sustained; and a motion for a new trial, reasserting violation of the federal rights mentioned in the complaint, was overruled. . . . The charge is that respondent, a state officer, in refusing to furnish petitioner a ballot, obeyed the law of Texas, and the consequent denial of petitioner's right to vote in the primary election because of his race and color was state action forbidden by the Federal Constitution; and it is claimed that former decisions require us so to hold. The cited cases are, however, not in point. . . . It is that the primary election was held under statutory compulsion; is wholly statutory in origin and incidents; those charged with its management have been deprived by statute and judicial decision of all power to establish qualifications for participation therein inconsistent with those laid down by the laws of the state, save only that the managers of such elections have been given the power to deny negroes the vote. It is further urged that while the election is designated that of the Democratic Party, the statutes not only require this method of selecting party nominees, but define the powers and duties of the party's representatives and of those who are to conduct the election so completely, and make them so thoroughly officers of the state, that any action taken by them in connection with the qualifications of members of the party is in fact state action and not party action.

. . .

While it is true that Texas has by its laws elaborately provided for the expression of party preference as to nominees, has required that preference to be expressed in a certain form of voting, and has attempted in minute detail to protect the suffrage of the members of the organization against fraud, it is equally true that the primary is a party primary; the expenses of it are not borne by the state, but by members of the party seeking nomination; the ballots are furnished not by the state, but by the agencies of the party; the votes are counted and the returns made by instrumentalities created by the party; and the state recognizes the state convention as the organ of the party for the declaration of principles and the formulation of policies.

. . .

. . . The Supreme Court of the state has decided, in a case definitely involving the point, that the Legislature of Texas has not essayed to interfere, and indeed may not interfere, with the constitutional liberty of citizens to organize a party and to determine the qualifications of its members. If in the past the Legislature has attempted to infringe that right and such infringement has not been gainsaid by the courts, the fact constitutes no reason for our disregarding the considered decision of the state's highest court. The legislative assembly of the state, so far as we are advised, has never attempted to prescribe or to limit the membership of a political party, and it is now settled that it has no power so to do. The state, as its highest tribunal holds, though it has guaranteed the liberty to organize political parties, may legislate for their governance when formed, and for the method whereby they may

nominate candidates, but must do so with full recognition of the right of the party to exist, to define its membership, and to adopt such policies as to it shall seem wise. In the light of the principles so announced, we are unable to characterize the managers of the primary election as state officers in such sense that any action taken by them in obedience to the mandate of the state convention respecting eligibility to participate in the organization's deliberations is state action.

. . .

We find no ground for holding that the respondent has in obedience to the mandate of the law of Texas discriminated against the petitioner or denied him any right guaranteed by the Fourteenth and Fifteenth Amendments.

Judgment affirmed.

United States v. Saylor
322 U.S. 385 (1944)

As the cases present identical questions it will suffice to state No. 716. The indictment charged that a general election was held November 3, 1942, in Harlan County, Kentucky, for the purpose of electing a Senator of the United States, at which election the defendants served as the duly qualified officers of election; that they conspired to injure and oppress divers citizens of the United States who were legally entitled to vote at the polling places where the defendants officiated, in the free exercise and enjoyment of the rights and privileges guaranteed to the citizens by the Constitution and laws of the United States, namely, the right and privilege to express by their votes their choice of a candidate for Senator and their right to have their expressions of choice given full value and effect by not having their votes impaired, lessened, diminished, diluted and destroyed by fictitious ballots fraudulently cast and counted, recorded, returned, and certified. The indictment charged that the defendants, pursuant to their plan, tore from the official ballot book and stub book furnished them, blank unvoted ballots and marked, forged, and voted the same for the candidate of a given party, opposing the candidate for whom the injured voters had voted, in order to deprive the latter of their rights to have their votes cast, counted, certified and recorded and given full value and effect; that the defendants inserted the false ballots they had so prepared into the ballot box, and returned them, together with the other ballots lawfully cast, so as to create a false and fictitious return respecting the votes lawfully cast. The appellees demurred to the indictment, as failing to state facts sufficient to constitute a crime against the United States. The demurrer attacked the indictment on other grounds raising questions which, if decided, would not be reviewable here under the Criminal Appeals Act. The District Court decided only that the indictment charged no offense against the laws of the United States. This ruling presents the question for decision.

. . . The inquiry is whether the provision of 19 embraces a conspiracy by election officers to stuff a ballot box in an election at which a member of the Congress of the United States is to be elected.

. . .

. . . For election officers knowingly to prepare false ballots, place them in the box, and return them, is certainly to prevent an honest count by the return board of the votes lawfully cast. The mathematical result may not be the same as would ensue throwing out or frustrating the count of votes lawfully cast. But the action pursuant to the conspiracy here charged constitutes the rendering of a return which, to some extent, falsifies the count of votes legally cast. We are unable to distinguish a conspiracy so to act from that which was held a violation of 19 in the *Mosley* case.

It is urged that any attempted distinction between the conduct described in the *Bathgate* case and that referred to in the *Mosley* case is illogical and insubstantial; that bribery of voters as badly distorts the result of an election and as effectively denies a free and fair choice by the voters as does ballot box stuffing or refusal to return or count the ballots. Much is to be said for this view. The legislative history does not clearly disclose the Congressional purpose in the repeal of the other sections of the Enforcement Act, while leaving 6 (now 19) in force. Section 19 can hardly have been inadvertently left on the statute books. Perhaps Congress thought it had an application other than that given it by this court in the *Mosley* case. On the other hand, Congress may have intended the result this court reached in the *Mosley* decision. We think it unprofitable to speculate upon the matter for Congress has not spoken since the decisions in question were announced, and the distinction taken by those decisions has stood for over a quarter of a century. Observance of that distinction places the instant case within the ruling in the *Mosley* case and outside that in the *Bathgate* case.

Our conclusion is contrary to that of the court below and requires that the judgments be reversed.

South v. Peters
339 U.S. 276 (1950)

The Georgia statute which appellants attack as violative of the Fourteenth and Seventeenth Amendments provides that county unit votes shall determine the outcome of a primary election. Each county is allotted a number of unit votes, ranging from six for the eight most populous counties, to two for most of the counties. The candidate who receives the highest popular vote in the county is awarded the appropriate number of unit votes. Appellants, residents of the most populous county in the State, contend that their votes and those of all other voters in that county have on the average but one-tenth the weight of those in the other counties. Urging that this amounts to an unconstitutional discrimination against them, appellants brought this suit to restrain adherence to the statute in the forthcoming Democratic Party primary for United States Senator, Governor and other state offices.

The court below dismissed appellants' petition. We affirm. Federal courts consistently refuse to exercise their equity powers in cases posing political issues arising from a state's geographical distribution of electoral strength among its political subdivisions.

Affirmed.

Day-Brite Lighting, Inc. v. Missouri
342 U.S. 421 (1952)

Missouri has a statute, first enacted in 1897, which was designed to end the coercion of employees by employers in the exercise of the franchise. It provides that an employee may absent himself from his employment for four hours between the opening and closing of the polls without penalty, and that any employer who among other things deducts wages for that absence is guilty of a misdemeanor.

Appellant is a Missouri corporation doing business in St. Louis. November 5, 1946, was a day for general elections in Missouri, the polls being open from 6 A.M. to 7 P.M. One Grotemeyer, an employee of appellant, was on a shift that worked from 8 A.M. to 4:30 P.M. each day, with thirty minutes for lunch. His rate of pay was $1.60 an hour. He requested four hours from the scheduled work day to vote on November 5, 1946. That request was refused; but Grotemeyer and all other employees on his shift were allowed to leave at 3 P.M. that day, which gave them four consecutive hours to vote before the polls closed.

Grotemeyer left this work at 3 P.M. in order to vote and did not return to work that day. He was not paid for the hour and a half between 3 P.M. and 4:30 P.M. Appellant was found guilty and fined for penalizing Grotemeyer in violation of the statute. The judgment was affirmed by the Missouri Supreme Court, over the objection that the statute violated the Due Process and the Equal Protection Clauses of the Fourteenth Amendment and the Contract Clause of Art. I, 10.

. . . Our recent decisions make plain that we do not sit as a super-legislature to weigh the wisdom of legislation nor to decide whether the policy which it expresses offends the public welfare. The legislative power has limits. . . . But the state legislatures have constitutional authority to experiment with new techniques; they are entitled to their own standard of the public welfare; they may within extremely broad limits control practices in the business-labor filed, so long as specific constitutional prohibitions are not violated and so long as conflicts with valid and controlling federal laws are avoided. . . .

. . .

The only semblance of substance in the constitutional objection to Missouri's law is that the employer must pay wages for a period in which the employee performs no services. Of course many forms of regulation reduce the net return of the enterprise; yet that gives rise to no constitutional infirmity. Most regulations of business necessarily impose financial burdens on the enterprise for which no compensation is paid. Those are part of the costs of our civilization. Extreme cases are conjured up where an employer is required to pay wages for a period that has no relation to the legitimate end. Those cases can await decision as and when they arise. The present law has no such infirmity. It is designed to eliminate any penalty for exercising the right of suffrage and to remove a practical obstacle to getting out the vote. The public welfare is a broad and inclusive concept. The moral, social, economic, and physical well-being of the community is one part of it; the political well-being, another. The police power which is adequate to fix the financial burden for one is adequate for the other. The judgment of the legislature that time out for voting should cost the employee nothing may be a debatable one. It is indeed conceded by the opposition to be such. . . .

The classification of voters so as to free employees from the domination of employers is an attempt to deal with an evil to which the one group has been exposed. The need for that classification is a matter for legislative judgment, and does not amount to a denial of equal protection under the laws.

Affirmed.

Perez v. Brownell
356 U.S. 44 (1958)

Petitioner, a national of the United States by birth, has been declared to have lost his American citizenship by operation of the Nationality Act of 1940. Section 401 of that Act provided that

> A person who is a national of the United States, whether by birth or naturalization, shall lose his nationality by:
> (e) Voting in a political election in a foreign state or participating in an election or plebiscite to determine the sovereignty over foreign territory; or

> (j) Departing from or remaining outside of the jurisdiction of the United States in time of war or during a period declared by the President to be a period of national emergency for the purpose of evading or avoiding training and service in the land or naval forces of the United States.

He seeks a reversal of the judgment against him on the ground that these provisions were beyond the power of Congress to enact.

Petitioner was born in Texas in 1909. He resided in the United States until 1919 or 1920, when he moved with his parents to Mexico, where he lived, apparently without interruption, until 1943. In 1928 he was informed that he had been born in Texas. At the outbreak of World War II, petitioner knew of the duty of male United States citizens to register for the draft, but he failed to do so. In 1943 he applied for admission to the United States as an alien railroad laborer, stating that he was a native-born citizen of Mexico, and was granted permission to enter on a temporary basis. He returned to Mexico in 1944 and shortly thereafter applied for and was granted permission, again as a native-born Mexican citizen, to enter the United States temporarily to continue his employment as a railroad laborer. Later in 1944 he returned to Mexico once more. In 1947 petitioner applied for admission to the United States at El Paso, Texas, as a citizen of the United States. At a Board of Special Inquiry hearing (and in his subsequent appeals . . .), he admitted having remained outside of the United States to avoid military service and having voted in political elections in Mexico. He was ordered excluded on the ground that he had expatriated himself; this order was affirmed on appeal. In 1952 petitioner, claiming to be a native-born citizen of Mexico, was permitted to enter the United States as an alien agricultural laborer. He surrendered in 1953 to immigration authorities in San Francisco as an alien unlawfully in the United States but claimed the right to remain by virtue of his American citizenship. After a hearing before a Special Inquiry Officer, he was ordered deported as an alien not in possession of a valid immigration visa; this order was affirmed on appeal to the Board of Immigration Appeals.

Petitioner brought suit in 1954 in a United States District Court for a judgment declaring him to be a national of the United States. The Court, sitting without a jury, found (in addition to the undisputed facts set forth above) that petitioner had remained outside of the United States from November 1944 to July 1947 for the purpose of avoiding service in the armed forces of the United States and that he had voted in a "political election" in Mexico in 1946. The court, concluding that he had thereby expatriated himself, denied the relief sought by the petitioner. The United States Court of Appeals for the Ninth Circuit affirmed. . . .

. . .

The inference is fairly to be drawn from the congressional history of the Nationality Act of 1940, read in light of the historical background of expatriation in this country, that, in making voting in foreign elections (among other behavior) an act of expatriation, Congress was seeking to effectuate its power to regulate foreign affairs. . . .

. . .

Our starting point is to ascertain whether the power of Congress to deal with foreign relations may reasonably be deemed to include a power to deal generally with the active participation, by way of voting, of American citizens in foreign political elections. . . . We cannot deny to Congress the reasonable belief that these difficulties might well become acute, to the point of jeopardizing the successful conduct of international relations, when a citizen of one country

chooses to participate in the political or governmental affairs of another country. The citizen may by his action unwittingly promote or encourage a course of conduct contrary to the interests of his own government; moreover, the people or government of the foreign country may regard his action to be the action of his government, or at least as a reflection if not an expression of its policy.

It follows that such activity is regulable by Congress under its power to deal with foreign affairs. And it must be regulable on more than an ad hoc basis. The subtle influences and repercussions with which the Government must deal make it reasonable for the generalized, although clearly limited, category of "political election" to be used in defining the area of regulation. That description carries with it the scope and meaning of its context and purpose; classes of elections—nonpolitical in the colloquial sense—as to which participation by Americans could not possibly have any effect on the relations of the United States with another country are excluded by any rational construction of the phrase. The classification that Congress has adopted cannot be said to be inappropriate to the difficulties to be dealt with. Specific applications are of course open to judicial challenge, as are other general categories in the law, by a "gradual process of judicial inclusion and exclusion."

The question must finally be faced whether, given the power to attach some sort of consequence to voting in a foreign political election, Congress . . . could attach loss of nationality to it. Is the means, withdrawal of citizenship, reasonably calculated to effect the end that is within the power of Congress to achieve, the avoidance of embarrassment in the conduct of our foreign relations attributable to voting by

American citizens in foreign political elections? The importance and extreme delicacy of the matters here sought to be regulated demand that Congress be permitted ample scope in selecting appropriate modes for accomplishing its purpose. The critical connection between this conduct and loss of citizenship is the fact that it is the possession of American citizenship by a person committing the act that makes the act potentially embarrassing to the American Government and pregnant with the possibility of embroiling this country in disputes with other nations. The termination of citizenship terminates the problem. Moreover, the fact is not without significance that Congress has interpreted this conduct, not irrationally, as importing not only something less than complete and unswerving allegiance to the United States but also elements of an allegiance to another country in some measure, at least, inconsistent with American citizenship.

Of course, Congress can attach loss of citizenship only as a consequence of conduct engaged in voluntarily. But it would be a mockery of this Court's decisions to suggest that a person, in order to lose his citizenship, must intend or desire to do so. . . .

It cannot be said, then, that Congress acted without warrant when, pursuant to its power to regulate the relations of the United States with foreign countries, it provided that anyone who votes in a foreign election of significance politically in the life of another country shall lose his American citizenship. To deny the power of Congress to enact the legislation challenged here would be to disregard the constitutional allocation of governmental functions that it is this Court's solemn duty to guard.

. . .

Judgment affirmed.

Gray v. Sanders
372 U.S. 368 (1963)

This suit was instituted by appellee, who is qualified to vote in primary and general elections in Fulton County, Georgia, to restrain appellants from using Georgia's county unit system as a basis for counting votes in a Democratic primary for the nomination of a United States Senator and statewide officers, and for declaratory relief. Appellants are the Chairman and Secretary of the Georgia State Democratic Executive Committee, and the Secretary of State of Georgia. Appellee alleges that the use of the county unit system in counting, tabulating, consolidating, and certifying votes cast in primary elections for statewide offices violates the Equal Protection Clause and the Due Process Clause of the Fourteenth Amendment and the Seventeenth Amendment. As the constitutionality of state statute was involved and the question was a substantial one, a three-judge court was properly convened.

Appellants moved to dismiss; and they also filed an answer denying that the county unit system was unconstitutional and alleging that it was designed "to achieve a reasonable balance as between urban and rural electoral power."

Under Georgia law each county is given a specified number of representatives in the lower House of the General Assembly. This county unit system at the time this suit was filed was employed as follows in statewide primaries: (1) Candidates for nominations who received the highest number of popular votes in a county were considered to have carried the county and to be entitled to two votes for each representative to which the county is entitled in the lower House of the General Assembly; (2) the majority of the county unit vote nominated a United States Senator and Governor; the plurality of the county unit vote nominated the others.

Appellee asserted that the total population of Georgia in 1960 was 3,943,116; that the population of Fulton County, where he resides, was 556,326; that the residents of Fulton County comprised 14.11 percent of Georgia's total population; but that, under the county unit system, the six unit votes of Fulton County constituted 1.46 percent of the total of 410 unit votes, or one-tenth of Fulton County's percentage of statewide population. The complaint further alleged that Echols County, the least populous county in Georgia, had a population in 1960 of 1,876, or .05 percent of the State's population, but the unit vote of Echols County was .48 percent of the total unit vote of all counties in Georgia, or 10 times Echols County's statewide percentage of population. One unit vote in Echols County represented 938 residents, whereas one unit vote in Fulton County represented 92,721 residents. Thus, one resident in Echols County had an influence in the nomination of candidates equivalent to 99 residents of Fulton County.

On the same day as the hearing in the District Court, Georgia amended the statutes challenged in the complaint. This amendment modified the county unit system by allocating units to counties in accordance with a "bracket system" instead of doubling the number of representatives of each county in the lower House of the Georgia Assembly. Counties with from 0 to 15,000 people were allotted two units; an additional one unit was allotted for the next 5,000 persons; an additional unit for the next 10,000 persons; another unit for each of the next two brackets of 15,000 persons; and, thereafter, two more units for each increase of 30,000 persons. Under the amended Act, all candidates for statewide office (not merely for Senator and Governor as under the earlier Act) are required to receive a majority of the county unit votes to be entitled to nominated in the first primary. In addition, in order to be nominated in the first primary, a candidate has to receive a majority of the popular votes unless there are only two candidates for the nomination and each receives an equal number of unit votes, in which event the candidate with the popular majority wins. If no candidate receives both a majority of the unit votes and a majority of the popular votes, a second run-off primary is required between the candidate receiving the highest number of unit votes and the candidate receiving the highest number of popular votes. In the second primary, the candidate receiving the highest number of unit votes is to prevail. But again, if there is a tie in unit votes, the candidate with the popular majority wins.

Appellee was allowed to amend his complaint so as to challenge the amended Act. The District Court held that the amended Act had some of the vices of the prior Act. It stated that under the amended Act "the vote of each citizen counts for less and less as the population of the county of his residence increases." . . .

The District Court held that . . . the county unit system as applied violates the Equal Protection Clause, and it issued an injunction, not against conducting any party primary election under the county unit system, but against conducting such an election under a county unit system that does not meet the requirements specified by the court. In other words, the District Court did not proceed on the basis that in a statewide election every qualified person was entitled to one vote and that all weighted voting was outlawed. Rather, it allowed a county unit system to be used in weighting the votes if the system showed no greater disparity against a county than exists against any state in the conduct of national elections. Thereafter the Democratic Committee voted to hold the 1962 primary election for the statewide offices mentioned on a popular vote basis. . . .

. . .

This case, unlike *Baker v. Carr*, does not involve a question of the degree to which the Equal Protection Clause of the Fourteenth Amendment limits the authority of a state legislature in designing the geographical districts from which representatives are chosen either for the state legislature or for the federal House of Representatives. Nor does it include the related problems of *Gomillion v. Lightfoot*, where "gerrymandering" was used to exclude a minority group from participation in municipal affairs. Nor does it present the question, inherent in the bicameral form of our federal government, whether a state may have one house chosen without regard to population. The District Court, however, analogized Georgia's use of the county unit system in determining the results of a statewide election to phases of our federal system. It pointed out that under the electoral college, required by Art. II, 1, of the Constitution and the Twelfth Amendment in the election of the President, voting strength "is not in exact proportion to population. . . . Recognizing that the electoral college was set up as a compromise to enable the formation of the Union among the several sovereign states, it still could hardly be said that such a system used in a state among its counties, assuming rationality and absence of arbitrariness in end result, could be termed invidious."

Accordingly the District Court as already noted held that use of the county unit system in counting the votes in a statewide election was permissible "if the disparity against any county is not in excess of the disparity that exists against any state in the most recent electoral college allocation." Moreover the District Court held that use of the county unit system in counting the votes in a state-

wide election was permissible "if the disparity against any county is not in excess of the disparity that exists . . . under the equal proportions formula for representation of the several states in the Congress." The assumption implicit in these conclusions is that since equality is not inherent in the electoral college and since precise equality among blocs of votes in one state or in the several states when it comes to the election of members of the House of Representatives is never possible, precise equality is not necessary in statewide elections.

We think the analogies to the electoral college, to districting and redistricting, and to other phases of the problems of representation in state or federal legislatures or conventions are inapposite. . . . Nor does the question here have anything to do with the composition of the state or federal legislature. . . . The present case is only a voting case. Georgia gives every qualified voter one vote in a statewide election; but in counting those votes she employs the county unit system which in end result weights the rural vote more heavily than the urban vote and weights some small rural counties heavier than other larger rural counties.

States can within limits specify the qualifications of voters in both state and federal elections; the Constitution indeed makes voters' qualifications rest on state law even in federal elections. . . . we need not determine all the limitations that are placed on this power of a state to determine the qualifications of voters, for appellee is a qualified voter.

The Fifteenth Amendment prohibits a state from denying or abridging a Negro's right to vote. The Nineteenth Amendment does the same for women. If a state in a statewide election weighted the male vote more heavily than the female vote or the white vote more heavily than the Negro vote; none could successfully contend that that discrimination was allowable. How then can one person be given twice or ten times the voting power of another person in a statewide election merely because he lives in a rural area or because he lives in the smallest rural county? Once the geographical unit for which a representative is to be chosen is designated, all who participate in the election are to have an equal vote—whatever their race, whatever their sex, whatever their occupation, whatever their income, and wherever their home may be in that geographical unit. This is required by the Equal Protection Clause of the Fourteenth Amendment. The concept of "we the people" under the Constitution visualizes no preferred class of voters but equality among those who meet the basic qualifications. The idea that every voter is equal to every other voter in his state, when he casts his ballot in favor of one of several competing candidates, underlies many of our decisions.

The Court has consistently recognized that all qualified voters have a constitutionally protected right "to cast their ballots and have them counted at Congressional elections." Every voter's vote is entitled to be counted once. It must be correctly counted and reported. . . . And these rights must be recognized in any preliminary election that in fact determines the true weight a vote will have. The concept of political equality in the voting booth contained in the Fifteenth Amendment extends to all phases of state elections . . . ; and, as previously noted, there is no indication in the Constitution that homesite or occupation affords a permissible basis for distinguishing between qualified voters within the state.

The only weighting of votes sanctioned by the Constitution concerns matters of representation, such as the allocation of Senators irrespective of population and the use of the electoral college in the choice of a President.

Yet when Senators are chosen, the Seventeenth Amendment states the choice must be made "by the people." . . . [O]nce the class of voters is chosen and their qualifications specified, we see no constitutional way by which equality of voting power may be evaded. . . .

. . .

While we agree with the District Court on most phases of the case and think it was right in enjoining the use of the county unit system in tabulating the votes, we vacate its judgment and remand the case so that a decree in conformity with our opinion may be entered.

Carrington v. Rash
380 U.S. 89 (1965)

A provision of the Texas Constitution prohibits "[a]ny member of the Armed Forces of the United States" who moves his home to Texas during the course of his military duty from ever voting in any election in that state "so long as he or she is a member of the Armed Forces." The question presented is whether this provision, as construed by the Supreme Court of Texas in the present case, deprives the petitioner of a right secured by the Equal Protection Clause of the Fourteenth Amendment. The Supreme Court of Texas decided that it does not and refused to issue a writ of mandamus ordering petitioner's local election officials to permit him to vote. . . .

The petitioner, a sergeant in the United States Army, entered the service from Alabama in 1946 at the age of 18. The State concedes that he has been domiciled in Texas since 1962, and that he intends to make his home there permanently. He has purchased a house in El Paso, where he lives with his wife and two children. He is also the proprietor of a small business there. The petitioner's post of military duty is not in Texas, but at White Sands, New Mexico. He regularly commutes from his home in El Paso to his Army job at White Sands. He pays property taxes in Texas, and has his automobile registered there. But for his uniform, the State concedes that the petitioner would be eligible to vote in El Paso County, Texas.

Texas has unquestioned power to impose reasonable residence restrictions of the availability of the ballot. There can be no doubt either of the historic function of the states to establish, on a nondiscriminatory basis, and in accordance with the Constitution, other qualifications for the exercise of the franchise. Indeed, "[t]he States have long been held to have broad powers to determine the conditions under which the right of suffrage may be exercised."

. . .

This Texas constitutional provision, however, is unique. Texas has said that no serviceman may ever acquire a voting residence in the state so long as he remains in service. It is true that the State has treated all members of the military with an equal hand. And mere classification, as this Court has often said, does not of itself deprive a group of equal protection. But the fact that a State is dealing with a distinct class and treats the members of that class equally does not end the judicial inquiry.

. . .

The theory underlying the State's first contention is that the Texas constitutional provision is necessary to prevent the danger of a "takeover" of the civilian community resulting from concentrated voting by large numbers of military personnel in bases placed near Texas towns and cities. . . . But if they are in fact residents, with the intention of making Texas their home indefinitely, they, as all other qualified residents, have a right to an equal opportunity for political representation. "Fencing out" from the franchise a sector of the population because of the way they may vote is constitutionally impermissible. "[T]he exercise of rights so vital to the maintenance of democratic institutions," cannot constitutionally be obliterated because of a fear of the political views of a particular group of bona fide residents. Yet that is what Texas claims to have done here.

The State's second argument is that its voting ban is justified because of the transient nature of service in the Armed Forces. . . .

. . .

But only where military personnel are involved has Texas been unwilling to develop more precise tests to determine the bona fides of an individual claiming to have actually made his home in the state long enough to vote. The state's law reports disclose that there have been many cases where the local election officials have determined the issue of bona fide residence. These officials and the courts reviewing their actions have required a "freely exercised intention" of remaining within the state. The declarations of voters concerning their intent to reside in the state and in a particular county is often not conclusive; the election officials may look to the actual facts and circumstances. Texas deals with particular categories of citizens who, like soldiers, present specialized problems in determining residence. Students at colleges and universities in Texas, patients in hospitals and other institutions within the state, and civilian employees of the United States government may be as transient as military personnel. But all of them are given at least an opportunity to show the election officials that they are bona fide residents.

. . .

We deal here with matters close to the core of our constitutional system. "The right . . . to choose," that this Court has been so zealous to protect means, at the least, that states may not casually deprive a class of individuals of the vote because of some remote administrative benefit to the state. By forbidding a soldier ever to controvert the presumption of nonresidence, the Texas Constitution imposes an invidious discrimination in violation of the Fourteenth Amendment.

. . .

We recognize that special problems may be involved in determining whether servicemen have actually acquired a new domicile in a state for franchise purposes. We emphasize that Texas is free to take reasonable and adequate steps, as have other states, to see that all applicants for the vote actually fulfill the requirements of bona fide residence. But this constitutional provision goes beyond such rules. "[T]he presumption here created is . . . definitely conclusive—incapable of being overcome by proof of the most positive character." All servicemen not residents of Texas before induction come within the provision's sweep. Not one of them can ever vote in Texas, no matter how long Texas may have been his true home. "[T]he uniform of our country . . . [must not] be the badge of disfranchisement for the man or woman who wears it."

Reversed.

United States v. Mississippi
380 U.S. 128 (1965)

The United States, by the Attorney General, brought this action in the United States District Court for the Southern District of Mississippi, Jackson Division, against the State of Mississippi, the three members of the Mississippi State Board of Election Commissioners, and six county Registrars of Voters. The complaint charged that the defendants and their agents had engaged, and, unless restrained, would continue to engage, in

acts and practices hampering and destroying the right of Negro citizens of Mississippi to vote, in violation of 42 U.S.C. §1971(a) and of the Fourteenth and Fifteenth Amendments and Article I of the United States Constitution. Jurisdiction of the Court was invoked . . . and, because the complaint charged that provisions of the state constitution and statutes pertaining to voter registration violated the United States Constitution, the case was heard by three judges. . . . All the defendants moved to dismiss on the ground that the complaint failed to state a claim on which relief could be granted. In addition, the State moved separately to dismiss on the ground that the United States had no power to make it a defendant in such a suit, and the three Election Commissioners answered that the complaint failed to show that they had enforced, or that they had a duty to enforce, the provisions of state law alleged to be unconstitutional. Five of the registrars moved for a severance and separate trials, and the four who were not residents of the Southern District of Mississippi, Jackson Division, moved for changes of venue to the respective districts and divisions where they lived. The District Court . . . dismissed the complaint on all the grounds which the defendants had assigned, and also ruled that the registrars could not be sued jointly, and that venue was improper as to the registrars who did not live in the district and division in which the court was sitting. . . .

The basic issue before us in this case is whether the dismissal for failure to state a claim upon which relief could be granted was proper. The United States alleges that, in 1890, a majority of the qualified voters in Mississippi were Negroes, but that, in that year, a constitutional convention adopted a new state constitution one of the chief purposes of which was, in the words of the complaint, to "restrict the Negro franchise and to establish and perpetuate white political supremacy and racial segregation in Mississippi." Section 244 of that constitution established a new prerequisite for voting: that a person otherwise qualified be able to read any section of the Mississippi Constitution, or understand the same when read to him, or give a reasonable interpretation thereof. This new requirement, coupled with the fact that, until about 1952, Negroes were not eligible to vote in the primary election of the Democratic Party, victory in which was "tantamount to election," worked so well in keeping Negroes from voting, the complaint charges, that, by 1899, the percentage of qualified voters in the state who were Negroes had declined from over 50 percent to about 9 percent, and, by 1954, only about 5 percent of the Negroes of voting age in Mississippi were registered.

By the 1950s, a much higher proportion of Negroes of voting age in Mississippi was literate than had been the case in 1890, and, since a decision of the Fifth Circuit in 1951 had pointed out that the 1890 requirement allowed persons to vote if they met any one of the three alternative requirements, the State took steps to multiply the barriers keeping its Negro citizens from voting. In 1954, the state constitution was amended to provide that, thereafter, an applicant for registration had to be able to read and copy in writing any section of the Mississippi Constitution, and give a reasonable interpretation of that section to the county registrar, and, in addition, demonstrate to the registrar "a reasonable understanding of the duties and obligations of citizenship under a constitutional form of government." The complaint charges that these provisions lend themselves to misuse and to discriminatory administration because they leave the registrars completely at large, free to be as demanding or as lenient as they choose in judging an applicant's understanding

of the "duties and obligations of citizenship," and that, since the adoption of this amendment, the registrars have in fact applied standards which varied in difficulty according to whether an applicant was white or colored.

In 1960, the state constitution was amended to add a new voting qualification of "good moral character," an addition which it is charged was to serve as yet another device to give a registrar power to permit an applicant to vote or not, depending solely on the registrar's own whim or caprice, ungoverned by any legal standard. A statute also passed in 1960 repealed a prior Mississippi statute which had provided that application forms be retained as permanent public records, and adopted a new rule that, unless appeal is taken from an adverse ruling and no new application is made prior to final judgment on that appeal, registrars no longer need keep any record made in connection with the application of anyone to register to vote. This law is alleged to be in direct violation of Title III of the Civil Rights Act of 1960, which requires that records of voting registration be kept. The complaint alleged further that the defendants had destroyed and, unless restrained by the court, would continue to destroy, these records. Finally, it was alleged that, in 1962, the Mississippi Legislature adopted a package of legislation affecting registration, the purpose and effect of which was to

> deter, hinder, prevent, delay and harass Negroes and to make it more difficult for Negroes in their efforts to become registered voters, to facilitate discrimination against Negroes, and to make it more difficult for the United States to protect the right of all its citizens to vote without distinction of race or color.

These 1962 laws provide, among other things, that application forms must be filled out "properly and responsively" by the applicant without any assistance, and that a registrar may not tell an applicant why he failed the test because to do might constitute assistance, and they allegedly give registrars even greater discretion to deny Negroes the right to register on formal, technical, inconsequential errors.

By way of relief the court was asked (1) to declare the challenged state laws unconstitutional as violations of federal constitutional provisions and statutes; (2) to find that by these laws Negroes had been denied the right to vote pursuant to a "pattern and practice" of racial discrimination; (3) to enjoin the defendants from enforcing any of these state laws or in any other way acting to

> delay, prevent, hinder, discourage, or harass Negro citizens, on account of their race or color, from applying for registration and becoming registered voters in the State of Mississippi,

or using any other interpretation or understanding test which "bears a direct relationship to the quality of public education afforded Negro applicants"; and (4) to order the defendants to register any Negro applicant who is over age 21, able to read, a resident for the period of time prescribed by state law, and not disqualified by state laws disfranchising the insane and certain convicted criminals.

It is apparent that the complaint which the majority of the District Court dismissed charged a longstanding, carefully prepared, and faithfully observed plan to bar Negroes from voting in the state of Mississippi, a plan which the registration statistics included in the complaint would seem to show had been remarkably successful. . . .

One ground upon which the majority of the District Court dismissed the government's complaint was that the United States is without authority, absent the clearest possible congressional

authorization, to bring an action like this one which challenges the validity of state laws allegedly used as devices to keep Negroes from voting on account of their race. . . . Section 1971(a) guarantees the right of citizens "who are otherwise qualified by law to vote at any election" to be allowed to vote. . . . The District Court's holding that . . . the United States still was not authorized to file this suit seems to rest on the emphasis it places on the phrase "otherwise qualified by law" in §1971(a). By stressing these words, the majority below reached the conclusion that, if Negroes were kept from voting by state laws, even though those laws were unconstitutional, instead of being barred by unlawful discriminatory application of laws otherwise valid, then they were not "otherwise qualified," and so §1971 did not apply to them. In other words, while private persons might file suits under §1971 against individual registrars who discriminated in applying otherwise valid laws, and while such suits might even be filed by the government, the statute did not authorize the United States to bring suits challenging the validity of the state's voting laws as such, however discriminatory they might be. We can find no possible justification for such a construction. . . . Subsection (a) explicitly stated the legislative purpose of protecting the rights of colored citizens to vote notwithstanding "any constitution, law, custom, usage, or regulation of any state." The phrase "otherwise qualified by law to vote" obviously meant that Negroes must possess the qualifications required of all voters by valid state or federal laws. It is difficult to take seriously the argument that Congress intended to dilute its guarantee of the right to vote regardless of race by saying at the same time that a state was free to disqualify its Negro citizens by laws which violated the United States Constitution. The Fifteenth Amendment protects the right to vote regardless of race against any denial or abridgment by the United States or by any state. Section 1971 was passed by Congress under the authority of the Fifteenth Amendment to enforce that amendment's guarantee, which protects against any discrimination by a state, its laws, its customs, or its officials in any way. . . .

The District Court held, and it is contended here, that even if the Attorney General did have power to file this suit on behalf of the United States . . . nevertheless he was without power to make the State a party defendant. The District Court gave great weight to Mississippi's argument that the Fifteenth Amendment "is directed to persons through whom a state may act, and not to the sovereign entity of the state itself." Largely to avoid what it called this "substantial constitutional claim," the District Court proceeded to construe the language of §1971 as not granting the Attorney General authority to make the state a defendant. We do not agree with that construction.

Section 1971(c) says that, whenever the Attorney General institutes a suit under this section against a state official who has deprived a citizen of his right to vote because of race or color, the act or practice shall also be deemed that of the state, and the state may be joined as a party defendant and, if, prior to the institution of such proceeding, such official has resigned or has been relieved of his office and no successor has assumed such office, the proceeding may be instituted against the state. The District Court accepted the State's argument that this meant that a state can be made a defendant in such a case only when the office of registrar is vacant, so that there is no registrar against whom to file suit. This argument relies on the fact that, in a case pending in this Court when the statutory language was changed, registrars had resigned their offices in order to keep

from being sued under § 1971. Congress, the State says, passed the provision authorizing suit against a state solely to provide a party defendant when registrars resigned, as they had in the Alabama case. But whatever the reasons Congress had for amending §1971(c) . . . the language Congress adopted leaves no room for the construction which the District Court put on these provisions. . . .

The State argues also that, even if Congress has authorized making the state a defendant here . . . Congress had no constitutional power to do so. The Fifteenth Amendment, in plain, unambiguous language, provides that no "state" shall deny or abridge the right of citizens to vote because of their color. In authorizing the United States to make a state a defendant in a suit under §1971, Congress was acting under its power, given in §2 of the Fifteenth Amendment, to enforce that Amendment by appropriate legislation. . . . The Eleventh Amendment . . . forbids suits against states only when "commenced or prosecuted . . . by Citizens of another State, or by Citizens or Subjects of any Foreign State." While this has been read to bar a suit by a state's own citizen as well, nothing in this or any other provision of the Constitution prevents or has ever been seriously supposed to prevent a state's being sued by the United States. The United States in the past has in many cases been allowed to file suits in this and other courts against states, with or without specific authorization from Congress. In light of this history, it seems rather surprising that the District Court entertained seriously the argument that the United States could not constitutionally sue a state. . . . We hold that the state was properly made a defendant in this case.

. . . Under state law, the Election Commissioners have power, authority, and responsibility to help administer the voter registration laws by formulating rules for the various tests applied to applicants for registration. . . . These "interpretation" and "duties and obligations of citizenship" tests . . . are vitally important elements of the Mississippi laws challenged as unconstitutional in this suit. Should the government prove its case and obtain an injunction, it would be natural to assume that such an order should run against the Board of Election Commissioners with reference to these two tests. Therefore, the Election Commissioners should not have been stricken as defendants.

The District Court said that the complaint improperly attempted to hold the six county registrars jointly liable for what amounted to nothing more than individual torts committed by them separately with reference to separate applicants. For this reason, apparently it would have held the venue improper as to the three registrars who lived outside the Southern District of Mississippi and a fourth who lived in a different division of the Southern District, and it would have ordered that each of the other two registrars be sued alone. But the complaint charged that the registrars had acted and were continuing to act as part of a statewide system designed to enforce the registration laws in a way that would inevitably deprive colored people of the right to vote solely because of their color. On such an allegation, the joinder of all the registrars as defendants in a single suit is authorized by Rule 20(a) of the Federal Rules of Civil Procedure. . . .

These registrars were alleged to be carrying on activities which were part of a series of transactions or occurrences the validity of which depended to a large extent upon "question[s] of law or fact common to all of them." Since joinder of the registrars in one suit was proper, the argument that venue as to some of them was not properly laid is also without merit.

As a general ground for dismissal, the District Court held that the complaint failed to state a claim upon which relief could be granted. . . . In this situation, we have decided that it is the more appropriate course to pass only upon the sufficiency of the complaint's allegations to justify relief if proved.

We have no doubt whatsoever that it was error to dismiss the complaint without a trial. . . . The allegations of this complaint were too serious, the right to vote in this country is too precious, and the necessity of settling grievances peacefully in the courts is too important, for this complaint to have been dismissed. The case should have been tried. It should now be tried without delay.

Reversed and remanded.

Louisiana v. United States
380 U.S. 145 (1965)

. . . [T]he Attorney General brought this action on behalf of the United States in the United States District Court for the Eastern District of Louisiana against the State of Louisiana, the three members of the State Board of Registration, and the Director-Secretary of the Board. The complaint charged that the defendants, by following and enforcing unconstitutional state laws, had been denying and, unless restrained by the court, would continue to deny, Negro citizens of Louisiana the right to vote, in violation of 42 U.S.C. §1971(a) and the Fourteenth and Fifteenth Amendments to the United States Constitution. The case was tried, and, after submission of evidence, the three-judge District Court . . . gave judgment for the United States. The State and the other defendants appealed. . . .

The complaint alleged, and the District Court

found, that, beginning with the adoption of the Louisiana Constitution of 1898, when approximately 44 percent of all the registered voters in the State were Negroes, the State had put into effect a successful policy of denying Negro citizens the right to vote because of their race. The 1898 constitution adopted what was known as a "grandfather clause," which imposed burdensome requirements for registration thereafter, but exempted from these future requirements any person who had been entitled to vote before January 1, 1867, or who was the son or grandson of such a person. Such a transparent expedient for disfranchising Negroes whose ancestors had been slaves until 1863 and not entitled to vote in Louisiana before 1867 was held unconstitutional in 1915 as a violation of the Fifteenth Amendment in a case involving a similar Oklahoma constitutional provision. Soon after that decision, Louisiana, in 1921, adopted a new constitution replacing the repudiated "grandfather clause" with what the complaint calls an "interpretation test," which required that an applicant for registration be able to "give a reasonable interpretation" of any clause in the Louisiana Constitution or the Constitution of the United States. From the adoption of the 1921 interpretation test until 1944, the District Court's opinion stated, the percentage of registered voters in Louisiana who were Negroes never exceeded one percent. Prior to 1944, Negro interest in voting in Louisiana had been slight, largely because the State's white primary law kept Negroes from voting in the Democratic Party primary election, the only election that mattered in the political climate of that state. In 1944, however, this Court invalidated the substantially identical white primary law of Texas, and, with the explicit statutory bar to their voting in the primary removed, and because of a generally heightened political interest, Negroes in in-

creasing numbers began to register in Louisiana. The white primary system had been so effective in barring Negroes from voting that the "interpretation test," as a disfranching devise, had been ignored over the years. Many registrars continued to ignore it after 1944, and, in the next dozen years, the proportion of registered votes who were Negroes rose from two-tenths of one percent to approximately 15 percent by March, 1956. This fact, coupled with this Court's 1954 invalidation of laws requiring school segregation, prompted the State to try new devices to keep the white citizens in control. The Louisiana Legislature created a committee, which became known as the "Segregation Committee," to seek means of accomplishing this goal. The chairman of this committee also helped to organize a semi-private group called the Association of Citizens Councils, which thereafter acted in close cooperation with the legislative committee to preserve white supremacy. The legislative committee and the Citizens Councils set up programs, which parish voting registrars were required to attend, to instruct the registrars on how to promote white political control. The committee and the Citizens Councils also began a wholesale challenging of Negro names already on the voting rolls, with the result that thousands of Negroes, but virtually no whites, were purged from the rolls of voters. Beginning in the middle 1950s, registrars of at least 21 parishes began to apply the interpretation test. In 1960, the state constitution was amended to require every applicant thereafter to "be able to understand," as well as "give a reasonable interpretation" of, any section of the state or federal constitution "when read to him by the registrar." The State Board of Registration in cooperation with the Segregation Committee issued orders that all parish registrars must strictly comply with the new provisions.

The interpretation test, the court found, vested in the voting registrars a virtually uncontrolled discretion as to who should vote and who should not. Under the state's statutes and constitutional provisions, the registrars, without any objective standard to guide them, determine the manner in which the interpretation test is to be given, whether it is to be oral or written, the length and complexity of the sections of the state or federal constitution to be understood and interpreted, and what interpretation is to be considered correct. There was ample evidence to support the District Court's finding that registrars in the 21 parishes where the test was found to have been used had exercised their broad powers to deprive otherwise qualified Negro citizens of their right to vote; and that the existence of the test as a hurdle to voter qualification has, in itself, deterred, and will continue to deter, Negroes from attempting to register in Louisiana.

Because of the virtually unlimited discretion vested by the Louisiana laws in the registrars of voters, and because in the 21 parishes where the interpretation test was applied that discretion had been exercised to keep Negroes from voting because of their race, the District Court held the interpretation test invalid on its face and as applied, as a violation of the Fourteenth and Fifteenth Amendments to the United States Constitution and of 42 U.S.C. §1971(a). The District Court enjoined future use of the test in the state, and, with respect to the 21 parishes where the invalid interpretation test was found to have been applied, the District Court also enjoined use of a newly enacted "citizenship" test, which did not repeal the interpretation test and the validity of which was not challenged in this suit, unless a reregistration of all voters in those parishes is ordered, so that there would be no voters in those parishes who had not passed the same test.

. . . There can be no doubt from the evidence in this case that the District Court was amply justified in finding that Louisiana's interpretation test, as written and as applied, was part of a successful plan to deprive Louisiana Negroes of their right to vote. This device for accomplishing unconstitutional discrimination has been little, if any, less successful than was the "grandfather clause" invalidated by this Court's decision in *Guinn v. United States*. . . . The Governor of Louisiana stated in 1898 that he believed that the "grandfather clause" solved the problem of keeping Negroes from voting "in a much more upright and manly fashion" than the method adopted previously by the states of Mississippi and South Carolina, which left the qualification of applicants to vote "largely to the arbitrary discretion of the officers administering the law." . . .

But Louisianans of a later generation did place just such arbitrary power in the hands of election officers who have used it with phenomenal success to keep Negroes from voting in the state. The State admits that the statutes and provisions of the state constitution establishing the interpretation test "vest discretion in the registrars of voters to determine the qualifications of applicants for registration," while imposing "no definite and objective standards upon registrars of voters for the administration of the interpretation test." . . . The applicant facing a registrar in Louisiana thus has been compelled to leave his voting fate to that official's uncontrolled power to determine whether the applicant's understanding of the federal or state constitution is satisfactory. As the evidence showed, colored people, even some with the most advanced education and scholarship, were declared by voting registrars with less education to have an unsatisfactory understanding of the constitution of Louisiana or of the United States. This is not a test, but a trap, sufficient to stop even the most brilliant man on his way to the voting booth. The cherished right of people in a country like ours to vote cannot be obliterated by the use of laws like this, which leave the voting fate of a citizen to the passing whim or impulse of an individual registrar. Many of our cases have pointed out the invalidity of laws so completely devoid of standards and restraints.... We ... affirm here the District Court's holding that the provisions of the Louisiana Constitution and statutes which require voters to satisfy registrars of their ability to "understand and give a reasonable interpretation of any section" of the federal or Louisiana Constitution violate the Constitution. And we agree with the District Court that it specifically conflicts with the prohibitions against discrimination in voting because of race found both in the Fifteenth Amendment and 42 U.S.C. §1971(a) to subject citizens to such an arbitrary power as Louisiana has given its registrars under these laws.

This leaves for consideration the District Court's decree. We bear in mind that the court has not merely the power, but the duty, to render a decree which will, so far as possible, eliminate the discriminatory effects of the past as well as bar like discrimination in the future. Little if any objection is raised to the propriety of the injunction against further use of the interpretation test as it stood at the time this action was begun, and, without further discussion, we affirm that part of the decree.

... Confining itself to the allegations of the complaint, the District Court did not pass upon the validity of the new test, but did take it into consideration in formulating the decree. The court found that past discrimination against Negro applicants in the 21 parishes where the interpretation test had been applied had greatly reduced the proportion of potential Negro voters who were registered as compared with the proportion of whites. Most if not all of those white voters had been permitted to register on far less rigorous terms than colored applicants whose applications were rejected. Since the new "citizenship" test does not provide for a reregistration of voters already accepted by the registrars, it would affect only applicants not already registered, and would not disturb the eligibility of the white voters who had been allowed to register while discriminatory practices kept Negroes from doing so. In these 21 parishes, while the registration of white persons was increasing, the number of Negroes registered decreased from 25,361 to 10,351. Under these circumstances, we think that the court was quite right to decree that, as to persons who met age and residence requirements during the years in which the interpretation test was used, use of the new "citizenship" test should be postponed in those 21 parishes where registrars used the old interpretation test until those parishes have ordered a complete reregistration of voters, so that the new test will apply alike to all or to none.

It also was certainly an appropriate exercise of the District Court's discretion to order reports to be made every month concerning the registration of voters in these 21 parishes in order that the court might be informed as to whether the old discriminatory practices really had been abandoned in good faith. The need to eradicate past evil effects and to prevent the continuation or repetition in the future of the discriminatory practices shown to be so deeply engrained in the laws, policies, and traditions of the state of Louisiana completely justified the District Court in entering the decree it did and in retaining jurisdiction of the entire case to hear any evidence of discrimination in other parishes, and to enter such orders as justice from time to time might require.

Affirmed.

South Carolina v. Katzenbach
383 U.S. 301 (1966)

. . . South Carolina has filed a bill of complaint, seeking a declaration that selected provisions of the Voting Rights Act of 1965 violate the Federal Constitution, and asking for an injunction against enforcement of these provisions by the Attorney General. . . . Because no issues of fact were raised in the complaint, and because of South Carolina's desire to obtain a ruling prior to its primary elections in June 1966, we dispensed with appointment of a special master and expedited our hearing of the case.

Recognizing that the questions presented were of urgent concern to the entire country, we invited all of the states to participate in this proceeding as friends of the Court. A majority responded by submitting or joining in briefs on the merits, some supporting South Carolina and others the Attorney General. Seven of these states also requested and received permission to argue the case orally at our hearing. . . . All viewpoints on the issues have been fully developed, and this additional assistance has been most helpful to the Court.

The Voting Rights Act was designed by Congress to banish the blight of racial discrimination in voting, which has infected the electoral process in parts of our country for nearly a century. The Act creates stringent new remedies for voting discrimination where it persists on a pervasive scale, and, in addition, the statute strengthens existing remedies for pockets of voting discrimination elsewhere in the country. Congress assumed the power to prescribe these remedies from §2 of the Fifteenth Amendment, which authorizes the National Legislature to effectuate by "appropriate" measures the constitutional prohibition against racial discrimination in voting.

We hold that the sections of the Act which are properly before us, are an appropriate means for carrying out Congress' constitutional responsibilities, and are consonant with all other provisions of the Constitution. . . .

The constitutional propriety of the Voting Rights Act of 1965 must be judged with reference to the historical experience which it reflects. Before enacting the measure, Congress explored with great care the problem of racial discrimination in voting. . . . The House approved the bill . . . and the measure passed the Senate. . . .

. . .

The Voting Rights Act of 1965 reflects Congress's firm intention to rid the country of racial discrimination in voting. The heart of the Act is a complex scheme of stringent remedies aimed at areas where voting discrimination has been most flagrant. Section 4(a)-(d) lays down a formula defining the states and political subdivisions to which these new remedies apply. The first of the remedies, contained in §4(a), is the suspension of literacy tests and similar voting qualifications for a period of five years from the last occurrence of substantial voting discrimination. Section 5 prescribes a second remedy, the suspension of all new voting regulations pending review by federal authorities to determine whether their use would perpetuate voting discrimination. The third remedy, covered in §§6(b), 7, 9, and 13(a), is the assignment of federal examiners on certification by the Attorney General to list qualified applicants who are thereafter entitled to vote in all elections.

. . .

At the outset, we emphasize that only some of the many portions of the Act are properly before us. South Carolina has not challenged §§2, 3, 4(e), 6(a), 8, 10, 12(d) and (e), 13(b), and other miscellaneous provisions having nothing to do with this lawsuit. Judicial review of these sections must await subsequent litigation. In addition, we find that South Carolina's attack on §§11 and 12(a)–(c) is premature. . . . Consequently, the only sections of the Act to be reviewed at this time are §§4(a)–(d), 5, 6(b), 7, 9, 13(a), and certain procedural portions of §14, all of which are presently in actual operation in South Carolina. . . .

. . .

These provisions of the Voting Rights Act of 1965 are challenged on the fundamental ground that they exceed the powers of Congress and encroach on an area reserved to the states by the Constitution. South Carolina and certain of the amici curiae also attack specific sections of the Act for more particular reasons. They argue that the coverage formula prescribed in §4(a)-(d) violates the principle of the equality of states, denies due process by employing an invalid presumption and by barring judicial review of administrative findings, constitutes a forbidden bill of attainder, and impairs the separation of powers by adjudicating guilt through legislation. They claim that the review of new voting rules required in §5 infringes Article III by directing the District Court to issue advisory opinions. They contend that the assignment of federal examiners authorized in §6(b) abridges due process by precluding judicial review of administrative findings, and impairs the separation of powers by giving the Attorney General judicial functions; also that the challenge procedure prescribed in §9 denies due process on account of its speed. Finally, South Carolina and certain of the amici curiae maintain that §§4(a) and 5, buttressed by §14(b) of the Act, abridge due process by limiting litigation to a distant forum.

Some of these contentions may be dismissed at the outset. The word "person" in the context of the Due Process Clause of the Fifth Amend-ment cannot, by any reasonable mode of interpretation, be expanded to encompass the states of the Union, and, to our knowledge, this has never been done by any court. Likewise, courts have consistently regarded the Bill of Attainder Clause of Article I and the principle of the separation of powers only as protections for individual persons and private groups, those who are peculiarly vulnerable to nonjudicial determinations of guilt. Nor does a state have standing as the parent of its citizens to invoke these constitutional provisions against the federal government, the ultimate parens patriae of every American citizen. The objections to the Act which are raised under these provisions may therefore be considered only as additional aspects of the basic question presented by the case: has Congress exercised its powers under the Fifteenth Amendment in an appropriate manner with relation to the states?

The ground rules for resolving this question are clear. The language and purpose of the Fifteenth Amendment, the prior decisions construing its several provisions, and the general doctrines of constitutional interpretation all point to one fundamental principle. As against the reserved powers of the states, Congress may use any rational means to effectuate the constitutional prohibition of racial discrimination in voting. . . .

. . .

. . . [D]ecisions have been rendered with full respect for the general rule . . . that States "have broad powers to determine the conditions under which the right of suffrage may be exercised." The gist of the matter is that the Fifteenth Amendment supersedes contrary exertions of state power.

. . .

South Carolina contends that the cases cited . . . are precedents only for the authority of the judiciary to strike down state statutes and procedures—that to allow an exercise of this authority by Congress would be to rob the courts of their rightful constitutional role. On the contrary, §2 of the Fifteenth Amendment expressly declares that "Congress shall have power to enforce this article by appropriate legislation." By adding this authorization, the Framers indicated that Congress was to be chiefly responsible for implementing the rights created in §1. . . . Accordingly, in addition to the courts, Congress has full remedial powers to effectuate the constitutional prohibition against racial discrimination in voting.

Congress has repeatedly exercised these powers in the past, and its enactments have repeatedly been upheld. . . . On the rare occasions when the Court has found an unconstitutional exercise of these powers, in its opinion Congress had attacked evils not comprehended by the Fifteenth Amendment.

The basic test to be applied in a case involving §2 of the Fifteenth Amendment is the same as in all cases concerning the express powers of Congress with relation to the reserved powers of the states. . . .

We therefore reject South Carolina's argument that Congress may appropriately do no more than to forbid violations of the Fifteenth Amendment in general terms—that the task of fashioning specific remedies or of applying them to particular localities must necessarily be left entirely to the courts. Congress is not circumscribed by any such artificial rules under §2 of the Fifteenth Amendment. . . .

Congress exercised its authority under the Fifteenth Amendment in an inventive manner when it enacted the Voting Rights Act of 1965. First: the measure prescribes remedies for voting discrimination which go into effect without any need for prior adjudication. This was clearly a legitimate response to the problem, for which there is ample precedent under other constitutional provisions. Congress had found that case-by-case litigation was inadequate to combat widespread and persistent discrimination in voting, because of the inordinate amount of time and energy required to overcome the obstructionist tactics invariably encountered in these lawsuits. After enduring nearly a century of systematic resistance to the Fifteenth Amendment, Congress might well decide to shift the advantage of time and inertia from the perpetrators of the evil to its victims. The question remains, of course, whether the specific remedies prescribed in the Act were an appropriate means of combating the evil, and to this question we shall presently address ourselves.

Second: the Act intentionally confines these remedies to a small number of states and political subdivisions which, in most instances, were familiar to Congress by name. This, too, was a permissible method of dealing with the problem. Congress had learned that substantial voting discrimination presently occurs in certain sections of the country, and it knew no way of accurately forecasting whether the evil might spread elsewhere in the future. In acceptable legislative fashion, Congress chose to limit its attention to the geographic areas where immediate action seemed necessary. The doctrine of the equality of states, invoked by South Carolina, does not bar this approach, for that doctrine applies only to the terms upon which states are admitted to the Union, and not to the remedies for local evils which have subsequently appeared.

We now consider the related question of whether the specific states and political subdivisions within §4(b) of the Act were an appropriate target for the new remedies. South Carolina contends that the coverage formula is awkwardly designed in a number of respects, and that it disregards various local conditions which have nothing to do with racial discrimination. These arguments, however, are largely beside the point. Congress began work with reliable evidence of actual voting discrimination in a great majority of the states and political subdivisions affected by the new remedies of the Act. The formula eventually evolved to describe these areas was relevant to the problem of voting discrimination, and Congress was therefore entitled to infer a significant danger of the evil in the few remaining states and political subdivisions covered by §4(b) of the Act. No more was required to justify the application to these areas of Congress' express powers under the Fifteenth Amendment.

. . . In identifying past evils, Congress obviously may avail itself of information from any probative source.

The areas listed above, for which there was evidence of actual voting discrimination, share two characteristics incorporated by Congress into the coverage formula: the use of tests and devices for voter registration, and a voting rate in the 1964 presidential election at least 12 points below the national average. Tests and devices are relevant to voting discrimination because of their long history as a tool for perpetrating the evil; a low voting rate is pertinent for the obvious reason that widespread disenfranchisement must inevitably affect the number of actual voters. Accordingly, the coverage formula is rational in both practice and theory. It was therefore permissible to impose the new remedies on the few remaining states and political subdivisions covered by the formula, at least in the absence of proof that they have been free of substantial voting discrimination in recent years. Congress is clearly not bound by the rules relating to statutory presumptions in criminal cases when it prescribes civil remedies against other organs of government under §2 of the Fifteenth Amendment.

It is irrelevant that the coverage formula excludes certain localities which do not employ voting tests and devices but for which there is evidence of voting discrimination by other means. Congress had learned that widespread and persistent discrimination in voting during recent years has typically entailed the misuse of tests and devices, and this was the evil for which the new remedies were specifically designed. . . . Legislation need not deal with all phases of a problem in the same way, so long as the distinctions drawn have some basis in practical experience. There are no states or political subdivisions exempted from coverage under §4(b) in which the record reveals recent racial discrimination involving tests and devices. This fact confirms the rationality of the formula.

Acknowledging the possibility of overbreadth, the Act provides for termination of special statutory coverage at the behest of states and political subdivisions in which the danger of substantial voting discrimination has not materialized during the preceding five years. Despite South Carolina's argument to the contrary, Congress might appropriately limit litigation under this provision to a single court in the District of Columbia, pursuant to its constitutional power under Art. III, §1, to "ordain and establish" inferior federal tribunals. . . . We have discovered no suggestion that Congress exceeded constitutional bounds in imposing these limitations on litigation against the federal government, and the Act is no less reasonable in this respect.

South Carolina contends that these termination procedures are a nullity because they impose an impossible burden of proof upon states and political subdivisions entitled to relief. As the Attorney General pointed out during hearings on the Act, however, an area need do no more than submit affidavits from voting officials, asserting that they have not been guilty of racial discrimination through the use of tests and devices during the past five years, and then refute whatever evidence to the contrary may be adduced by the federal government. Section 4(d) further assures that an area need not disprove each isolated instance of voting discrimination in order to obtain relief in the termination proceedings. The burden of proof is therefore quite bearable, particularly since the relevant facts relating to the conduct of voting officials are peculiarly within the knowledge of the states and political subdivisions themselves.

The Act bars direct judicial review of the findings by the Attorney General and the Director of the Census which trigger application of the coverage formula. . . . The Court has already permitted Congress to withdraw judicial review of administrative determinations in numerous cases involving the statutory rights of private parties. . . . In the event that the formula is improperly applied, the area affected can always go into court and obtain termination of coverage under §4(b), provided, of course, that it has not been guilty of voting discrimination in recent years. This procedure serves as a partial substitute for direct judicial review.

We now arrive at consideration of the specific remedies prescribed by the Act for areas included within the coverage formula. South Carolina assails the temporary suspension of existing voting qualifications, reciting the rule laid down by *Lassiter* . . . that literacy tests and related devices are not in themselves contrary to the Fifteenth Amendment. . . . The record shows that, in most of the states covered by the Act, including South Carolina, various tests and devices have been instituted with the purpose of disenfranchising Negroes, have been framed in such a way as to facilitate this aim, and have' been administered in a discriminatory fashion for many years. Under these circumstances, the Fifteenth Amendment has clearly been violated.

The Act suspends literacy tests and similar devices for a period of five years from the last occurrence of substantial voting discrimination. This was a legitimate response to the problem, for which there is ample precedent in Fifteenth Amendment cases. Underlying the response was the feeling that states and political subdivisions which had been allowing white illiterates to vote for years could not sincerely complain about "dilution" of their electorates through the registration of Negro illiterates. Congress knew that continuance of the tests and devices in use at the present time, no matter how fairly administered in the future, would freeze the effect of past discrimination in favor of unqualified white registrants. . . .

The Act suspends new voting regulations pending scrutiny by federal authorities to determine whether their use would violate the Fifteenth Amendment. This may have been an uncommon exercise of congressional power, as South Carolina contends, but the Court has recognized that exceptional conditions can justify legislative measures not otherwise appropriate. Congress knew that some of the states covered by §4(b) of the Act had resorted to the extraordinary stratagem of contriving new rules of various kinds for the sole purpose of perpetuating voting discrimination in the face of adverse federal court decrees. Congress had reason to suppose that these states might try similar maneuvers in the future in order to evade the remedies for voting discrimination contained in the Act itself. Under the compulsion of these unique circumstances, Congress responded in a permissibly decisive manner.

For reasons already stated, there was nothing inappropriate about limiting litigation under this provision to the District Court for the District of Columbia, and in putting the burden of proof on the areas seeking relief. Nor has Congress authorized the District Court to issue advisory opinions, in violation of the principles of Article III invoked by Georgia as amicus curiae. The Act automatically suspends the operation of voting regulations enacted after November 1, 1964, and furnishes mechanisms for enforcing the suspension. A state or political subdivision wishing to make use of a recent amendment to its voting laws therefore has a concrete and immediate "controversy" with the federal government. An appropriate remedy is a judicial determination that continued suspension of the new rule is unnecessary to vindicate rights guaranteed by the Fifteenth Amendment.

The Act authorizes the appointment of federal examiners to list qualified applicants who are thereafter entitled to vote, subject to an expeditious challenge procedure. This was clearly an appropriate response to the problem, closely related to remedies authorized in prior cases. . . . Congress realized that merely to suspend voting rules which have been misused or are subject to misuse might leave this localized evil undisturbed. As for the briskness of the challenge procedure, Congress knew that, in some of the areas affected, challenges had been persistently employed to harass registered Negroes. It chose to forestall this abuse, at the same time providing alternative ways for removing persons listed through error or fraud. . . .

. . .

After enduring nearly a century of widespread resistance to the Fifteenth Amendment, Congress has marshalled an array of potent weapons against the evil, with authority in the Attorney General to employ them effectively. Many of the areas directly affected by this development have indicated their willingness to abide by any restraints legitimately imposed upon them. We here hold that the portions of the Voting Rights Act properly before us are a valid means for carrying out the commands of the Fifteenth Amendment. Hopefully, millions of non-white Americans will now be able to participate for the first time on an equal basis in the government under which they live. . . .

The bill of complaint is dismissed.

Afroyim v. Rusk
387 U.S. 253 (1967)

Petitioner, born in Poland in 1893, immigrated to this country in 1912 and became a naturalized American citizen in 1926. He went to Israel in 1950, and in 1951, he voluntarily voted in an election for the Israeli Knesset, the legislative body of Israel. In 1960, when he applied for renewal of his United States passport, the Department of State refused to grant it on the sole ground that he had lost his American citizenship by virtue of §401(e) of the Nationality Act of 1940, which provides that a United States citizen shall "lose" his citizenship if he votes "in a political election in a foreign state." Petitioner then brought this declaratory judgment action in federal district court alleging that §401(e) violates both the Due Process Clause of the Fifth Amendment and §1, cl. 1, of the Fourteenth Amendment, which grants American citizenship to persons like petitioner. Because neither the Fourteenth Amendment nor any other provision of the Constitution expressly grants Congress the power to take away that citizenship once it has been acquired, petitioner contended that the only way he could lose his citizenship was by his own voluntary renunciation of it. Since the Government took the position that §401(e) empowers it to terminate citizenship without the citizen's voluntary renunciation, petitioner argued that this section is prohibited by the Constitution. The District Court and the Court of Appeals, rejecting this argument, held that Congress has constitutional authority forcibly to take away citizenship for voting in a foreign country based on its implied power to regulate foreign affairs. Consequently, petitioner was held to have lost his American citizenship regardless of his intention not to give it up. . . .

. . .

To uphold Congress's power to take away a man's citizenship because he voted in a foreign election in violation of §401(e) would be equivalent to holding that Congress has the power to "abridge," "affect," "restrict the effect of," and "take . . . away" citizenship. Because the Fourteenth Amendment prevents Congress from doing any of these things, we agree with the Chief Justice's dissent in the *Perez* case that the government is without power to rob a citizen of his citizenship under §401(e).

. . . Citizenship in this nation is a part of a cooperative affair. Its citizenry is the country, and the country is its citizenry. The very nature of our free government makes it completely incongruous to have a rule of law under which a group of citizens temporarily in office can deprive another group of citizens of their citizenship. We hold that the Fourteenth Amendment was designed to, and does, protect every citizen of this nation against a congressional forcible destruction of his citizenship, whatever his creed, color, or race. Our holding does no more than to give to this citizen that which is his own, a constitutional right to remain a citizen in a free country unless he voluntarily relinquishes that citizenship.

Perez v. Brownell is overruled. The judgment is reversed.

Allen v. State Board of Elections
393 U.S. 544 (1969)

These four cases, three from Mississippi and one from Virginia, involve the application of the Voting Rights Act of 1965 to state election laws and regulations. The Mississippi cases were consolidated on appeal and argued together in this Court. Because of the grounds on which we decide all four cases, the appeal in the Virginia case is also disposed of by this opinion.

. . .

. . . [I]n states covered by the Act, literacy tests and similar voting qualifications were suspended for a period of five years from the last occurrence of substantial voting discrimination. However, Congress apparently feared that the mere suspension of existing tests would not completely solve the problem, given the history some states had of simply enacting new and slightly different requirements with the same discriminatory effect. Not underestimating the ingenuity of those bent on preventing Negroes from voting, Congress therefore enacted §5, the focal point of these cases.

Under §5, if a state covered by the Act passes any "voting qualification or prerequisite to voting, or standard, practice, or procedure with respect to voting different from that in force or effect on November 1, 1964," no person can be deprived of his right to vote "for failure to comply with" the new enactment "unless and until" the State seeks and receives a declaratory judgment in the United States District Court for the District of Columbia that the new enactment "does not have the purpose and will not have the effect of denying or abridging the right to vote on account of race or color."

However, §5 does not necessitate that a covered State obtain a declaratory judgment action before it can enforce any change in its election laws. It provides that a State may enforce a new enactment if the State submits the new provision to the Attorney General of the United States and, within 30 days of the submission, the Attorney General does not formally object to the new statute or regulation. The Attorney General does not act as a court in approving or disapproving the state legislation. If the Attorney General objects to the new enactment, the State may still enforce the legislation upon securing a declaratory judgment in the District Court for the District of Columbia. Also, the State is not required to first submit the new enactment to the Attorney General, as it may go directly to the District Court for the District of Columbia. . . . Once the State has successfully complied with the §5 approval requirements, private parties may enjoin the enforcement of the new enactment only in traditional suits attacking its constitutionality; there is no further remedy provided by §5.

In these four cases, the States have passed new laws or issued new regulations. The central issue is whether these provisions fall within the prohibition of §5 that prevents the enforcement of "any voting qualification or prerequisite to voting, or standard, practice, or procedure with respect to voting" unless the State first complies with one of the section's approval procedures.

No. 25, involves a 1966 amendment to §2870 of the Mississippi Code of 1942. The amendment provides that the board of supervisors of each county may adopt an order providing that board members be elected at large by all qualified electors of the county. Prior to the 1966 amendment, all counties, by law, were divided into five districts; each district elected one member of the board of supervisors. After the amendment, Adams and Forrest Counties adopted the authorized orders, specifying that each candidate must

run at large, but also requiring that each candidate be a resident of the county district he seeks to represent.

The appellants are qualified electors and potential candidates in the two counties. They sought a declaratory judgment in the United States District Court for the Southern District of Mississippi that the amendment to §2870 was subject to the provisions of §5 of the Act, and hence could not be enforced until the State complied with the approval requirements of §5.

No. 26, concerns a 1966 amendment to §6271-08 of the Mississippi Code. The amendment provides that, in 11 specified counties, the county superintendent of education shall be appointed by the board of education. Before the enactment of this amendment, all these counties had the option of electing or appointing the superintendent. Appellants are qualified electors and potential candidates for the position of county superintendent of education in three of the counties covered by the 1966 amendment. They sought a declaratory judgment that the amendment was subject to §6, and thus unenforceable unless the State complied with the §5 approval requirements.

No. 36, involves a 1966 amendment to §3260 of the Mississippi Code, which changed the requirements for independent candidates running in general elections. The amendment makes four revisions: (1) it establishes a new rule that no person who has voted in a primary election may thereafter be placed on the ballot as an independent candidate in the general election; (2) the time for filing a petition as an independent candidate is changed to 60 days before the primary election from the previous 40 days before the general election; (3) the number of signatures of qualified electors needed for the independent qualifying petition is increased substantially; and

(4) a new provision is added that each qualified elector who signs the independent qualifying petition must personally sign the petition and must include his polling precinct and county. Appellants are potential candidates whose nominating petitions for independent listing on the ballot were rejected for failure to comply with one or more of the amended provisions.

In all three of these cases, the three-judge District Court ruled that the amendments to the Mississippi Code did not come within the purview of and are not covered by §5, and dismissed the complaints. Appellants brought direct appeals to this Court. We consolidated the cases and postponed consideration of jurisdiction to a hearing on the merits.

No. 3, concerns a bulletin issued by the Virginia Board of Elections to all election judges. The bulletin was an attempt to modify the provisions of §24–252 of the Code of Virginia of 1950 which provides . . . that "any voter [may] place on the official ballot the name of any person in his own handwriting. . . ." The Virginia Code further provides that voters with a physical incapacity may be assisted in preparing their ballots. . . . However, no statutory provision is made for assistance to those who wish to write in a name, but who are unable to do so because of illiteracy. When Virginia was brought under the coverage of the Voting Rights Act of 1965, Virginia election officials apparently thought that the provision in §24–252, requiring a voter to cast a write-in vote in the voter's own handwriting, was incompatible with the provisions of §4(a) of the Act suspending the enforcement of any test or device as a prerequisite to voting. Therefore, the Board of Elections issued a bulletin to all election judges, instructing that the election judge could aid any qualified voter in the preparation of his ballot, if the voter so requests and if the

voter is unable to mark his ballot due to illiteracy.

Appellants are functionally illiterate registered voters from the Fourth Congressional District of Virginia. They brought a declaratory judgment action in the United States District Court for the Eastern District of Virginia, claiming that §24–252 and the modifying bulletin violate the Equal Protection Clause of the Fourteenth Amendment and the Voting Rights Act of 1965. A three-judge court was convened and the complaint dismissed. A direct appeal was brought to this Court and we postponed consideration of jurisdiction to a hearing on the merits.

In the 1966 elections, appellants attempted to vote for a write-in candidate by sticking labels, printed with the name of their candidate, on the ballot. The election officials refused to count appellants' ballots, claiming that the Virginia election law did not authorize marking ballots with labels. As the election outcome would not have been changed had the disputed ballots been counted, appellants sought only prospective relief. In the District Court, appellants did not assert that §5 precluded enforcement of the procedure prescribed by the bulletin. Rather, they argued §4 suspended altogether the requirement of §24–252 that the voter write the name of his choice in the voter's own handwriting. Appellants first raised the applicability of §5 in their jurisdictional statement filed with this Court. We are not precluded from considering the applicability of §5, however. The Virginia legislation was generally attacked on the ground that it was inconsistent with the Voting Rights Act. Where all the facts are undisputed, this Court may, in the interests of judicial economy, determine the applicability of the provisions of that Act even though some specific sections were not argued below.

. . .

The Act was drafted to make the guarantees

of the Fifteenth Amendment finally a reality for all citizens. Congress realized that existing remedies were inadequate to accomplish this purpose, and drafted an unusual, and in some aspects a severe, procedure for insuring that States would not discriminate on the basis of race in the enforcement of their voting laws.

The achievement of the Act's laudable goal could be severely hampered, however, if each citizen were required to depend solely on litigation instituted at the discretion of the Attorney General. For example, the provisions of the Act extend to states and the subdivisions thereof. The Attorney General has a limited staff, and often might be unable to uncover quickly new regulations and enactments passed at the varying levels of state government. It is consistent with the broad purpose of the Act to allow the individual citizen standing to insure that his city or county government complies with the §5 approval requirements.

. . .

We hold that the restriction of §14(b) does not apply to suits brought by private litigants seeking a declaratory judgment that a new state enactment is subject to the approval requirements of §5, and that these actions may be brought in the local district court. . . .

. . .

We conclude that, in light of the extraordinary nature of the Act in general, and the unique approval requirements of §5, Congress intended that disputes involving the coverage of §5 be determined by a district court of three judges.

Finding that these cases are properly before us, we turn to a consideration of whether these state enactments are subject to the approval requirements of §5. These requirements apply to "any voting qualification or prerequisite to voting, or standard, practice, or procedure with re-

spect to voting. . . ." The Act further provides that the term "voting"

> shall include all action necessary to make a vote effective in any primary, special, or general election, including, but not limited to, registration, listing . . . or other action required by law prerequisite to voting, casting a ballot, and having such ballot counted properly and included in the appropriate totals of votes cast with respect to candidates for public or party office and propositions for which votes are received in an election.

. . .

We must reject a narrow construction that appellees would give to §5. The Voting Rights Act was aimed at the subtle, as well as the obvious, state regulations which have the effect of denying citizens their right to vote because of their race. Moreover, compatible with the decisions of this Court, the Act gives a broad interpretation to the right to vote, recognizing that voting includes "all action necessary to make a vote effective." We are convinced that, in passing the Voting Rights Act, Congress intended that state enactments such as those involved in the instant cases be subject to the §5 approval requirements.

. . .

The weight of the legislative history and an analysis of the basic purposes of the Act indicate that the enactment in each of these cases constitutes a "voting qualification or prerequisite to voting, or standard, practice, or procedure with respect to voting" within the meaning of §5.

No. 25 involves a change from district to at-large voting for county supervisors. The right to vote can be affected by a dilution of voting power, as well as by an absolute prohibition on casting a ballot. Voters who are members of a racial minority might well be in the majority in one district, but in a decided minority in the county as a whole. This type of change could therefore nullify their ability to elect the candidate of their choice, just as would prohibiting some of them from voting.

In No. 26, an important county officer in certain counties was made appointive, instead of elective. The power of a citizen's vote is affected by this amendment; after the change, he is prohibited from electing an officer formerly subject to the approval of the voters. Such a change could be made either with or without a discriminatory purpose or effect; however, the purpose of §5 was to submit such changes to scrutiny.

The changes in No. 36 appear aimed at increasing the difficulty for an independent candidate to gain a position on the general election ballot. These changes might also undermine the effectiveness of voters who wish to elect independent candidates. One change involved in No. 36 deserves special note. The amendment provides that no person who has voted in a primary election may thereafter be placed on the ballot as an independent candidate in the general election. This is a "procedure with respect to voting" with substantial impact. One must forgo his right to vote in his party primary if he thinks he might later wish to become an independent candidate.

The bulletin in No. 3 outlines new procedures for casting write-in votes. As in all these cases, we do not consider whether this change has a discriminatory purpose or effect. It is clear, however, that the new procedure with respect to voting is different from the procedure in effect when the state became subject to the Act; therefore, the enactment must meet the approval requirements of §5 in order to be enforceable.

In these cases, as in so many others that come before us, we are called upon to determine the applicability of a statute where the language of the statute does not make crystal clear its intended

scope. In all such cases, we are compelled to resort to the legislative history to determine whether, in light of the articulated purposes of the legislation, Congress intended that the statute apply to the particular cases in question. We are of the opinion that . . . the balance of legislative history . . . indicates that §5 applies to these cases. In saying this, we, of course, express no view on the merit of these enactments; we also emphasize that our decision indicates no opinion concerning their constitutionality.

. . .

In No. 3, the judgment of the District Court is vacated; in Nos. 25, 26, and 36, the judgments of the District Court are reversed. All four cases are remanded to the District Courts with instructions to issue injunctions restraining the further enforcement of the enactments until such time as the States adequately demonstrate compliance with §5.

McDonald v. Board of Election Commissioners
394 U.S. 802 (1969)

Appellants and the class they represent are unsentenced inmates awaiting trial in the Cook County jail who, though they are qualified Cook County electors, cannot readily appear at the polls either because they are charged with nonbailable offenses or because they have been unable to post the bail imposed by the courts of Illinois. They cannot obtain absentee ballots, for they constitute one of a number of classes for whom no provision for absentee voting has yet been made by the Illinois Legislature. The constitutionality of Illinois's failure to include them with those who are entitled to vote absentee is the primary issue in this direct appeal. . . .

The specific provisions attacked here, have made absentee balloting available to four classes of persons: (1) those who are absent from the county of their residence for any reason whatever; (2) those who are "physically incapacitated," so long as they present an affidavit to that effect from a licensed physician; (3) those whose observance of a religious holiday precludes attendance at the polls, and (4) those who are serving as poll watchers in precincts other than their own on election day. The availability of the absentee ballot in Illinois has been extended to its present coverage by various amendments over the last 50 years. Prior to 1917, Illinois had no provision for absentee voting, requiring personal attendance at the polls, and in that year the legislature made absentee voting available to those who would be absent from the county on business or other duties. In 1944, absentee voting was made available to all those absent from the county for any reason. The provisions for those remaining in the county but unable to appear at the polls because of physical incapacity, religious holidays, or election duties were added in 1955, 1961, and 1967, respectively.

. . . [A]ppellants made timely application for absentee ballots for the . . . primary because of their physical inability to appear at the polls on that election day. The applications were accompanied by an affidavit from the warden of the Cook County jail attesting to that inability. These applications were refused by the appellee Board of Election Commissioners on the ground that appellants were not "physically incapacitated" within the meaning of §§ 19-1 and 19-2 of the Illinois Election Code. On the same day, appellants filed a complaint, alleging that they were unconstitutionally excluded from the coverage of the absentee provisions. . . . The District Court granted appellants' request for temporary relief . . . and

ordered the Board to issue ballots to qualified Illinois electors awaiting trial in the Cook County jail. Both parties then filed motions for summary judgment, the Board asserting that to honor the applications would subject its members to criminal liability under Illinois law.

. . . [T]he District Court granted summary judgment for the Board, holding that the Illinois provisions extending absentee voting privileges to those physically incapacitated because of medical reasons from appearing at the polls constituted a proper and reasonable legislative classification not violative of equal protection. The case was brought here by appellants on direct appeal. . . .

Appellants argue that Illinois' absentee ballot provisions violate the Equal Protection Clause of the Fourteenth Amendment for two reasons. First, they contend that, since the distinction between those medically incapacitated and those "judicially" incapacitated bears no reasonable relationship to any legitimate state objective, the classifications are arbitrary and therefore in violation of equal protection. Secondly, they argue that, since pretrial detainees imprisoned in other states or in counties within the state other than those of their own residence can vote absentee as Illinois citizens absent from the county for any reason, it is clearly arbitrary to deny the absentee ballot to other unsentenced inmates simply because they happen to be incarcerated within their own resident counties. . . .

Before confronting appellants' challenge to Illinois's absentee provisions, we must determine initially how stringent a standard to use in evaluating the classifications made thereunder and whether the distinctions must be justified by a compelling state interest. . . . Thus, while the "States have long been held to have broad powers to determine the conditions under which the right of suffrage may be exercised," we have held that, once the States grant the franchise, they must not do so in a discriminatory manner. More importantly, however, we have held that, because of the overriding importance of voting rights, classifications "which might invade or restrain them must be closely scrutinized and carefully confined" where those rights are asserted under the Equal Protection Clause. . . . And a careful examination on our part is especially warranted where lines are drawn on the basis of wealth or race . . . two factors which would independently render a classification highly suspect and thereby demand a more exacting judicial scrutiny.

Such an exacting approach is not necessary here, however, for two readily apparent reasons. First, the distinctions made by Illinois's absentee provisions are not drawn on the basis of wealth or race. Secondly, there is nothing in the record to indicate that the Illinois statutory scheme has an impact on appellants' ability to exercise the fundamental right to vote. It is thus not the right to vote that is at stake here, but a claimed right to receive absentee ballots. . . . Faced as we are with a constitutional question, we cannot lightly assume, with nothing in the record to support such an assumption, that Illinois has, in fact, precluded appellants from voting. We are then left with the more traditional standards for evaluating appellants' equal protection claims. . . .

Since there is nothing to show that a judicially incapacitated, pretrial detainee is absolutely prohibited from exercising the franchise, it seems quite reasonable for Illinois's legislature to treat differently the physically handicapped, who must, after all, present affidavits from their physicians attesting to an absolute inability to appear personally at the polls in order to qualify for an absentee ballot. Illinois could, of course, make voting easier for all concerned by extending absentee voting privileges to those in appellants' class. Its failure to do so, however, hardly seems arbitrary, particularly in view of the many other classes of Illinois citizens not covered by the absentee provisions, for whom voting may be extremely difficult, if not practically impossible.

Similarly, the different treatment accorded unsentenced inmates incarcerated within and those incarcerated without their resident counties may reflect a legislative determination that, without the protection of the voting booth, local officials might be too tempted to try to influence the local vote of in-county inmates. Such a temptation, with its attendant risks to prison discipline would, of course, be much less urgent with prisoners incarcerated out of state or outside their resident counties. Constitutional safeguards are not thereby offended simply because some prisoners, as a result, find voting more convenient than appellants.

We are satisfied then that appellants' challenge to the allegedly unconstitutional incompleteness of Illinois' absentee voting provisions cannot be sustained. Ironically, it is Illinois's willingness to go further than many states in extending the absentee voting privileges so as to include even those attending to election duties that has provided appellants with a basis for arguing that the provisions operate in an invidiously discriminatory fashion to deny them a more convenient method of exercising the franchise. . . . That Illinois has not gone still further, as perhaps it might, should not render void its remedial legislation, which need not, as we have stated before, "strike at all evils at the same time."

Accordingly, the judgment of the District Court is affirmed.

Kramer v. Union Free School District No. 15
395 U.S. 621 (1969)

In this case, we are called on to determine whether §2012 of the New York Education Law is constitutional. The legislation provides that, in certain New York school districts, residents who are otherwise eligible to vote in state and federal elections may vote in the school district election only if they (1) own (or lease) taxable real property within the district, or (2) are parents (or have custody of) children enrolled in the local public schools. . . .

. . .

The challenged statute is applicable only in the districts which hold annual meetings. . . .

. . . Generally, the board of education has the basic responsibility for local school operation, including prescribing the courses of study, determining the textbooks to be used, and even altering and equipping a former schoolhouse for use as a public library. Additionally, in districts selecting members of the board of education at annual meetings, the local voters also pass directly on other district matters. . . .

Appellant is a 31-year-old college-educated stockbroker who lives in his parents' home in the Union Free School District No. 15, a district to which §2012 applies. He is a citizen of the United States, and has voted in federal and state elections since 1959. However, since he has no children and neither owns nor leases taxable real property, appellant's attempts to register for and vote in the local school district elections have been unsuccessful. After the school district rejected his 1965 application, appellant instituted the present class action challenging the constitutionality of the voter eligibility requirements.

The United States District Court for the East-

ern District of New York denied appellant's request that a three-judge district court be convened, and granted appellees' motion to dismiss appellant's complaint. On appeal, the Court of Appeals for the Second Circuit reversed, ruling appellant's complaint warranted convening a three-judge court. On remand, the three-judge court ruled that §2012 is constitutional, and dismissed appellant's complaint. . . .

. . . The sole issue in this case is whether the additional requirements of §2012—requirements which prohibit some district residents who are otherwise qualified by age and citizenship from participating in district meetings and school board elections—violate the Fourteenth Amendment's command that no State shall deny persons equal protection of the laws. . . .

. . . Statutes granting the franchise to residents on a selective basis always pose the danger of denying some citizens any effective voice in the governmental affairs which substantially affect their lives. Therefore, if a challenged state statute grants the right to vote to some bona fide residents of requisite age and citizenship and denies the franchise to others, the Court must determine whether the exclusions are necessary to promote a compelling state interest.

. . . [W]hen we are reviewing statutes which deny some residents the right to vote, the general presumption of constitutionality afforded state statutes and the traditional approval given state classifications if the Court can conceive of a "rational basis" for the distinctions made are not applicable. The presumption of constitutionality and the approval given "rational" classifications in other types of enactments are based on an assumption that the institutions of state government are structured so as to represent fairly all the people. However, when the challenge to the statute is, in effect, a challenge of this basic assumption, the assumption can no longer serve as the basis for presuming constitutionality. And the assumption is no less under attack because the legislature which decides who may participate at the various levels of political choice is fairly elected. Legislation which delegates decisionmaking to bodies elected by only a portion of those eligible to vote for the legislature can cause unfair representation. Such legislation can exclude a minority of voters from any voice in the decisions just as effectively as if the decisions were made by legislators the minority had no voice in selecting.

. . . States do have latitude in determining whether certain public officials shall be selected by election or chosen by appointment and whether various questions shall be submitted to the voters. In fact, we have held that, where a county school board is an administrative, not legislative, body, its members need not be elected. . . .

. . . Our exacting examination is not necessitated by the subject of the election; rather, it is required because some resident citizens are permitted to participate and some are not. . . .

. . .

Appellant . . . contends that he and others of his class are substantially interested in and significantly affected by the school meeting decisions. All members of the community have an interest in the quality and structure of public education, appellant says, and he urges that "the decisions taken by local boards . . . may have grave consequences to the entire population." Appellant also argues that the level of property taxation affects him, even though he does not own property, as property tax levels affect the price of goods and services in the community.

We turn therefore to question whether the exclusion is necessary to promote a compelling state interest. First, appellees argue that the State has

a legitimate interest in limiting the franchise in school district elections to "members of the community of interest"—those "primarily interested in such elections." Second, appellees urge that the State may reasonably and permissibly conclude that "property taxpayers" (including lessees of taxable property who share the tax burden through rent payments) and parents of the children enrolled in the district's schools are those "primarily interested" in school affairs.

. . .

We need express no opinion as to whether the State in some circumstances might limit the exercise of the franchise to those "primarily interested" or "primarily affected." Of course, we therefore do not reach the issue of whether these particular elections are of the type in which the franchise may be so limited. For, assuming, arguendo, that New York legitimately might limit the franchise in these school district elections to those "primarily interested in school affairs," close scrutiny of the §2012 classifications demonstrates that they do not accomplish this purpose with sufficient precision to justify denying appellant the franchise.

. . . Section 2012 does not meet the exacting standard of precision we require of statutes which selectively distribute the franchise. The classifications in §2012 permit inclusion of many persons who have, at best, a remote and indirect interest in school affairs and, on the other hand, exclude others who have a distinct and direct interest in the school meeting decisions.

Nor do appellees offer any justification for the exclusion of seemingly interested and informed residents—other than to argue that the §2012 classifications include those "whom the State could understandably deem to be the most intimately interested in actions taken by the school board," and urge that the task of . . . balancing the interest of the community in the maintenance of orderly school district elections against the interest of any individual in voting in such elections should clearly remain with the Legislature.

But the issue is not whether the legislative judgments are rational. . . . The issue is whether the §2012 requirements do, in fact, sufficiently further a compelling state interest to justify denying the franchise to appellant and members of his class. The requirements of §2012 are not sufficiently tailored to limiting the franchise to those "primarily interested" in school affairs to justify the denial of the franchise to appellant and members of his class.

The judgment of the United States District Court for the Eastern District of New York is therefore reversed. The case is remanded for further proceedings consistent with this opinion.

Cipriano v. City of Houma
395 U.S. 701 (1969)

In this case, we must determine whether provisions of Louisiana law which give only "property taxpayers" the right to vote in elections called to approve the issuance of revenue bonds by a municipal utility are constitutional. . . . [A] three-judge District Court determined that the Louisiana provisions were constitutional. . . .

The Louisiana Constitution provides that the legislature may authorize municipalities to issue bonds "[f]or the purpose of constructing, acquiring, extending or improving any revenue-producing public utility." Pursuant to this provision, the legislature enacted legislation authorizing Louisiana municipalities to issue revenue bonds. The legislature further provided, however, that the municipalities could issue the bonds only if they were approved by

a "majority in number and amount of the property taxpayers qualified to vote . . . [who vote at the bond election]."

Appellee City of Houma owns and operates gas, water, and electric utility systems. In September 1967, the city officials scheduled a special election to obtain voter approval for the issuance of $10,000,000 of utility revenue bonds. The city planned to finance extension and improvement of the municipally owned utility systems with the bond proceeds. At the special election, a majority "in number and amount" of the property taxpayers approved the bond issue. However, within the period provided by Louisiana law for contesting the result of the election, this suit was instituted in the United States District Court for the Eastern District of Louisiana.

Appellant alleged that he was a duly qualified voter of the City of Houma, and that he had been prevented from voting in the revenue bond election solely because he was not a property owner. He sued for himself and for a class of 6,926 nonproperty taxpayers otherwise qualified as City of Houma voters. Appellant sought to enjoin the issuance of the bonds approved at the special election and to obtain a declaratory judgment that the limitation of the franchise to property taxpayers is unconstitutional. . . . The court then dismissed the suit, finding the Louisiana provisions constitutional. Appellant brought a direct appeal to this Court. . . .

. . .

At the time of the election, only about 40 percent of the city's registered voters were property taxpayers. Of percent course, the operation of the utility systems—gas, water, and electric—affects virtually every resident of the city, nonproperty owners as well as property owners. All users pay utility bills, and the rates may be affected substantially by the amount of revenue bonds outstanding. Certainly property owners are not alone in feeling the impact of bad utility service or high rates, or in reaping the benefits of good service and low rates.

. . .

The challenged statute contains a classification which excludes otherwise qualified voters who are as substantially affected and directly interested in the matter voted upon as are those who are permitted to vote. When, as in this case, the State's sole justification for the statute is that the classification provides a "rational basis" for limiting the franchise to those voters with a "special interest," the statute clearly does not meet the "exacting standard of precision we require of statutes which selectively distribute the franchise." . . .

. . . [W]e will apply our decision in this case prospectively. That is, we will apply it only where, under state law, the time for challenging the election result has not expired, or in cases brought within the time specified by state law for challenging the election and which are not yet final. Thus, the decision will not apply where the authorization to issue the securities is legally complete on the date of this decision. . . .

The judgment of the District Court is reversed. The case is remanded for further proceedings consistent with this opinion.

Hall v. Beals
396 U.S. 45 (1969)

The appellants moved from California to Colorado in June 1968. They sought to register to vote in the ensuing November presidential election, but were refused permission because they would not, on election day, have satisfied the six-month residency requirement that Colorado then impose for eligibility to vote in such an election. The appellants then commenced the present class action against the appellees, electoral officials of El Paso County, Colorado. Their complaint challenged the six-month residency requirement as a violation of the Equal Protection, Due Process, and Privilege and Immunities Clauses of the Constitution. For relief, they sought (1) a writ of mandamus compelling the appellees to register them for the upcoming presidential election; (2) an injunction restraining the enforcement and operation of the Colorado residency laws insofar as they applied to the presidential election, and (3) a direction that the appellees register the appellants and allow them to vote. . . .

On October 30, the . . . District Court entered judgment for the appellees and dismissed the complaint, holding that the six-month requirement was not unconstitutional. As a result, the appellants did not vote in the 1968 presidential election. They took a direct appeal to this Court. . . . Thereafter, the Colorado Legislature reduced the residency requirement for a presidential election from six months to two months.

The 1968 election is history, and it is now impossible to grant the appellants the relief they sought in the District Court. Further, the appellants have now satisfied the six-month residency requirement of which they complained. But apart from these considerations, the recent amendatory action of the Colorado Legislature has surely operated to render this case moot. We review the judgment below in light of the Colorado statute as it now stands, not as it once did. And, under the statute as currently written, the appellants could have voted in the 1968 presidential election. The case has therefore lost its character as a present, live controversy of the kind that must exist if we are to avoid advisory opinions on abstract propositions of law. The appellants object now to the two-month residency requirement as vigorously as they did to the six-month rule in effect when they brought suit. . . . The appellants "cannot represent a class of [which] they are not a part"—that is, the class of voters disqualified in Colorado by virtue of the new two-month requirement, a class of which the appellants have never been members.

. . .

The judgment of the District Court is vacated, and the case is remanded with directions to dismiss the cause as moot.

Evans v. Cornman
398 U.S. 419 (1970)

Appellees live on the grounds of the National Institutes of Health (NIH), a federal reservation or enclave located within the geographical boundaries of Montgomery County in the state of Maryland. In October 1968, the Permanent Board of Registry of Montgomery County announced that persons living on NIH grounds did not meet the residency requirement of Art. 1, §1, of the Maryland Constitution. Accordingly, such persons were not qualified to vote in Maryland elections, and the names of those previously registered would be removed from the county's voter rolls. Appellees then instituted the present suit against the members of the Permanent Board, requesting that a . . . federal District Court be convened to enjoin as unconstitutional this application of the Maryland voter residency law.

After the District Court issued a temporary restraining order so that appellees who had previously registered could vote in the November 1968 general election, the case was considered on the pleadings and stipulations of fact. The

District Court issued the requested permanent injunction, holding that to deny appellees the right to vote was to deny them the equal protection of the laws. Thereafter, a motion by the present appellants to intervene as additional defendants was granted, and a direct appeal was prosecuted to this Court. . . .

. . . NIH, a medical research facility owned and operated by the United States government, is one of the places subject to . . . congressional power. The facility commenced operation more than 30 years ago, when land was purchased and residential buildings were built to allow scientists and doctors to live near their work. It did not become a federal reservation, however, until 1953 when the state of Maryland ceded jurisdiction over the property to the United States.

Before that time, persons who resided on NIH grounds could register and vote in Montgomery County; they continued to do so, apparently without question, for another 15 years. In 1963, however, in a case involving residents of another federal enclave, the Maryland Court of Appeals ruled that a resident of a federal reservation is not "a resident of the State" within the meaning of that term in Art. 1, §1, of the Maryland Constitution, the provision that governs voter qualifications.

. . .

Appellants argue that, even if appellees are residents of Maryland, the State may constitutionally structure its election laws so as to deny them the right to vote. . . .

The sole interest or purpose asserted by appellants to justify the limitation on the vote in the present case is essentially to insure that only those citizens who are primarily or substantially interested in or affected by electoral decisions have a voice in making them. Without deciding the question, we have assumed that such an interest could be sufficiently compelling to justify limitations on the suffrage, at least with regard to some elections. However, it is clear that such a claim cannot lightly be accepted. This Court has held that a State may not dilute a person's vote to give weight to other interests, and a lesser rule could hardly be applicable to a complete denial of the vote. All too often, lack of a "substantial interest" might mean no more than a different interest, and "'[f]encing out' from the franchise a sector of the population because of the way they may vote is constitutionally impermissible."

. . . As the District Court noted, Congress has now permitted the States to extend important aspects of state powers over federal areas. While it is true that federal enclaves are still subject to exclusive federal jurisdiction and Congress could restrict as well as extend the powers of the States within their bounds, whether appellees are sufficiently disinterested in electoral decisions that they may be denied the vote depends on their actual interest today, not on what it may be sometime in the future.

. . .

In their day-to-day affairs, residents of the NIH grounds are just as interested in and connected with electoral decisions as they were prior to 1953, when the area came under federal jurisdiction, and as are their neighbors who live off the enclave. In nearly every election, federal, state, and local, for offices from the Presidency to the school board, and on the entire variety of other ballot propositions, appellees have a stake equal to that of other Maryland residents. As the District Court concluded, they are entitled under the Fourteenth Amendment to protect that stake by exercising the equal right to vote.

The judgment is affirmed.

City of Phoenix v. Kolodziejski
399 U.S. 204 (1970)

. . . [O]n June 10, 1969, the City of Phoenix, Arizona, held an election to authorize the issuance of $60,450,000 in general obligation bonds, as well as certain revenue bonds. Under Arizona law, property taxes were to be levied to service this indebtedness, although the city was legally privileged to use other revenues for this purpose. . . . Pursuant to Arizona constitutional and statutory provisions, only otherwise qualified voters who were also real property taxpayers were permitted to vote on these bond issues. All of the bond issues submitted to the voters were approved by a majority of those voting.

On June 16, 1969, six days after the election in Phoenix, this Court held, in *Cipriano v. City of Houma*, that restricting the franchise to property taxpayers in elections on revenue bonds violated the Equal Protection Clause of the Fourteenth Amendment. That ruling was applied to the case before the Court, in which, under local law, the authorization of the revenue bonds was not yet final when the challenge to the election was raised in the District Court. On August 1, 1969, appellee Kolodziejski, a Phoenix resident who was otherwise qualified to vote but who owned no real property, filed her complaint in the United States District Court for the District of Arizona challenging the constitutionality of the restriction on the franchise in Arizona bond elections and attacking the validity of the June, 1969, election approving the Phoenix bond issues. . . . In the District Court, appellants conceded that, under this Court's decisions in *Cipriano* and *Kramer*, the bond election was invalid with regard to the revenue bonds that had been approved. The District Court perceived no significant difference between revenue bonds and general obligation bonds, and therefore held that the exclusion of nonproperty-owning voters from the election on the general obligation bonds was unconstitutional. . . . [T]he court held the *Cipriano* rule applicable and declared the June 10, 1969, bond election invalid. The appellants were enjoined from taking further action to issue the bonds approved in that election. The City of Phoenix and the members of the City Council appealed . . . with respect to the general obligation bonds. . . .

. . . It is . . . argued that the rationale of *Cipriano* does not render unconstitutional the exclusion of nonproperty owners from voting in elections on general obligation bonds.

. . .

Concededly, the case of elections to approve general obligation bonds was not decided in *Cipriano*. But we have concluded that the principles of that case, and of *Kramer*, dictate a like result where a State excludes nonproperty taxpayers from voting in elections for the approval of general obligation bonds. The differences between the interests of property owners and the interests of nonproperty owners are not sufficiently substantial to justify excluding the latter from the franchise. This is so for several reasons.

. . .

. . . We . . . affirm the District Court's declaratory judgment that the challenged provisions of the Arizona Constitution and statutes, as applied to exclude nonproperty owners from elections for the approval of the issuance of general obligation bonds, violate the Equal Protection Clause of the United States Constitution.

In view of the fact that, over the years, many general obligation bonds have been issued on the good faith assumption that restriction of the franchise in bond elections was not prohibited by the Federal Constitution, it would be unjustifiably

disruptive to give our decision in this case full retroactive effect. We therefore adopt a rule similar to that employed with respect to the applicability of the *Cipriano* decision: our decision in this case will apply only to authorizations for general obligation bonds that are not final as of June 23, 1970, the date of this decision. . . .

Affirmed.

Oregon v. Mitchell
400 U.S. 112 (1970)

In these suits, certain States resist compliance with the Voting Rights Act Amendments of 1970, because they believe that the Act takes away from them powers reserved to the States by the Constitution to control their own elections. By its terms, the Act does three things. First: it lowers the minimum age of voters in both state and federal elections from 21 to 18. Second: based upon a finding by Congress that literacy tests have been used to discriminate against voters on account of their color, the Act enforces the Fourteenth and Fifteenth Amendments by barring the use of such tests in all elections, state and national, for a five-year period. Third: the Act forbids States from disqualifying voters in national elections for presidential and vice-presidential electors because they have not met state residency requirements.

. . . In summary, it is the judgment of the Court that the 18–year-old vote provisions of the Voting Rights Act Amendments of 1970 are constitutional and enforceable insofar as they pertain to federal elections, and unconstitutional and unenforceable insofar as they pertain to state and local elections.

. . .

The Framers of our Constitution provided in

Art. I, §2, that members of the House of Representatives should be elected by the people and that the voters for Representatives should have "the Qualifications requisite for Electors of the most numerous Branch of the State Legislature." Senators were originally to be elected by the state legislatures, but, under the Seventeenth Amendment, Senators are also elected by the people, and voters for Senators have the same qualifications as voters for Representatives. In the very beginning, the responsibility of the States for setting the qualifications of voters in congressional elections was made subject to the power of Congress to make or alter such regulations if it deemed it advisable to do so. . . . Moreover, the power of Congress to make election regulations in national elections is augmented by the Necessary and Proper Clause. . . .

The breadth of power granted to Congress to make or alter election regulations in national elections, including the qualifications of voters, is demonstrated by the fact that the Framers of the Constitution and the state legislatures which ratified it intended to grant to Congress the power to lay out or alter the boundaries of the congressional districts. . . . And in *Colegrove*, no Justice of this Court doubted Congress's power to rearrange the congressional districts according to population; the fight in that case revolved about the judicial power to compel redistricting.

Surely no voter qualification was more important to the Framers than the geographical qualification embodied in the concept of congressional districts. The Framers expected Congress to use this power to eradicate "rotten boroughs," and Congress has, in fact, used its power to prevent states from electing all Congressmen at large. There can be no doubt that the power to alter congressional district lines is vastly more significant in its effect than the power to permit 18-year-old citizens to go to the polls and vote in all federal elections.

. . .

In short, the Constitution allotted to the States the power to make laws regarding national elections, but provided that, if Congress became dissatisfied with the state laws, Congress could alter them. A newly created national government could hardly have been expected to survive without the ultimate power to rule itself and to fill its offices under its own laws. The Voting Rights Act Amendments of 1970, now before this Court, evidence dissatisfaction of Congress with the voting age set by many of the States for national elections. I would hold, as have a long line of decisions in this Court, that Congress has ultimate supervisory power over congressional elections. Similarly, it is the prerogative of Congress to oversee the conduct of presidential and vice-presidential elections and to set the qualifications for voters for electors for those offices. It cannot be seriously contended that Congress has less power over the conduct of presidential elections than it has over congressional elections.

On the other hand, the Constitution was also intended to preserve to the States the power that even the Colonies had to establish and maintain their own separate and independent governments, except insofar as the Constitution itself commands otherwise. . . . No function is more essential to the separate and independent existence of the States and their governments than the power to determine, within the limits of the Constitution, the qualifications of their own voters for state, county, and municipal offices and the nature of their own machinery for filling local public offices. Moreover, Art. I, §2, is a clear indication that the Framers intended the States to determine the qualifications of their own voters for state offices, because those qualifications were adopted for federal offices unless Congress directs otherwise under Art. I, §4. It is a plain fact of history that the Framers never imagined that the national Congress would set the qualifications for voters in every election from President to local constable or village alderman. It is obvious that the whole Constitution reserves to the States the power to set voter qualifications in state and local elections, except to the limited extent that the people, through constitutional amendments, have specifically narrowed the powers of the States. Amendments Fourteen, Fifteen, Nineteen, and Twenty-four, each of which has assumed that the States had general supervisory power over state elections, are examples of express limitations on the power of the States to govern themselves. And the Equal Protection Clause of the Fourteenth Amendment was never intended to destroy the States' power to govern themselves, making the Nineteenth and Twenty-fourth Amendments superfluous. . . . In interpreting what the Fourteenth Amendment means, the Equal Protection Clause should not be stretched to nullify the States' powers over elections which they had before the Constitution was adopted and which they have retained throughout our history.

. . .

In enacting the 18-year-old vote provisions of the Act now before the Court, Congress made no legislative findings that the 21-year-old vote requirement was used by the States to disenfranchise voters on account of race. I seriously doubt that such a finding, if made, could be supported by substantial evidence. Since Congress has attempted to invade an area preserved to the States by the Constitution without a foundation for enforcing the Civil War Amendments' ban on racial discrimination, I would hold that Congress has exceeded its powers in attempting to lower the voting age in state and local elections. On the other hand, where Congress legislates in a do-

main not exclusively reserved by the Constitution to the States, its enforcement power need not be tied so closely to the goal of eliminating discrimination on account of race.

To invalidate part of the Voting Rights Act Amendments of 1970, however, does not mean that the entire Act must fall, or that the constitutional part of the 18-year-old vote provision cannot be given effect. . . . In this case, it is the judgment of the Court that Title III, lowering the voting age to 18, is invalid as applied to voters in state and local elections. It is also the judgment of the Court that Title III is valid with respect to national elections. We would fail to follow the express will of Congress in interpreting its own statute if we refused to sever these two distinct aspects of Title III. Moreover, it is a longstanding canon of statutory construction that legislative enactments are to be enforced to the extent that they are not inconsistent with the Constitution, particularly where the valid portion of the statute does not depend upon the invalid part. Here, of course, the enforcement of the 18–year-old vote in national elections is in no way dependent upon its enforcement in state and local elections.

. . .

Our judgments today give the federal government the power the Framers conferred upon it, that is, the final control of the elections of its own officers. Our judgments also save for the States the power to control state and local elections which the Constitution originally reserved to them and which no subsequent amendment has taken from them. The generalities of the Equal Protection Clause of the Fourteenth Amendment were not designed or adopted to render the States impotent to set voter qualifications in elections for their own local officials and agents in the absence of some specific constitutional limitations.

Perkins v. Matthews
400 U.S. 379 (1971)

Appellants, voters and candidates for mayor or alderman, sought to enjoin the 1969 elections in this action brought in the United States District Court for the Southern District of Mississippi. They alleged that the requirements at the 1969 elections differed from those in effect on November 1, 1964, and at the last mayoral and aldermanic elections in 1965 because of (1) changes in locations of the polling places, (2) changes in the municipal boundaries through annexations of adjacent areas which enlarged the number of eligible voters, and (3) a change from ward to at-large election of aldermen. The city of Canton, they alleged, sought to enforce these changes without first submitting them to the Attorney General or obtaining a declaratory judgment under §5. Pending the convening of the court of three judges required by §5, a single judge temporarily restrained the elections, which were originally scheduled for the spring of 1969. The three-judge court . . . dissolved the temporary injunction and dismissed the complaint. The elections were then held in October 1969, with the challenged changes in effect. . . .

. . .

. . . [W]e think it clear that the location of polling places constitutes a "standard, practice, or procedure with respect to voting." The abstract right to vote means little unless the right becomes a reality at the polling place on election day. The accessibility, prominence, facilities, and prior notice of the polling place's location all have an effect on a person's ability to exercise his franchise. Given §5's explicit concern with both the purpose and the effect of a voting "standard, practice, or procedure," the location of polling places comes within the section's coverage. Moreover, the legislative history provides ample support for the conclusion that Congress intended §5 to cover a change in polling places. Before the Senate Judiciary Committee, the Attorney General explicitly testified that a change in "the place of registration" and a change "from a paper ballot to a machine" were changes of the kind that § 5 was designed to reach. Plainly the relocation of the polling places is precisely the same kind of change. Moreover, there inheres in the determination of the location of polling places an obvious potential for "denying or abridging the right to vote on account of race or color." Locations at distances remote from black communities or at places calculated to intimidate blacks from entering, or failure to publicize changes adequately might well have that effect. Consequently, we think it clear that §5 requires prior submission of any changes in the location of polling places.

Changing boundary lines by annexations which enlarge the city's number of eligible voters also constitutes the change of a "standard, practice, or procedure with respect to voting." Clearly, revision of boundary lines has an effect on voting in two ways: (1) by including certain voters within the city and leaving others outside, it determines who may vote in the municipal election and who may not; (2) it dilutes the weight of the votes of the voters to whom the franchise was limited before the annexation, and

> the right of suffrage can be denied by a debasement or dilution of the weight of a citizen's vote just as effectively as by wholly prohibiting the free exercise of the franchise.

. . .

. . . Since the District Court is more familiar with the nuances of the local situation than are we, and has heard the evidence in this case, we think the question of the appropriate remedy is for that court to determine, in the first instance, after hearing the views of both parties.

The judgment of the District Court is reversed, and the case is remanded to that court with instructions to issue injunctions restraining the further enforcement of the changes until such time as the appellees adequately demonstrate compliance with §5, and for further proceedings consistent with this opinion.

Dunn v. Blumstein
405 U.S. 330 (1972)

Various Tennessee public officials (hereinafter Tennessee) appeal from a decision by a three-judge federal court holding that Tennessee's durational residence requirements for voting violate the Equal Protection Clause of the United States Constitution. The issue arises in a class action for declaratory and injunctive relief brought by appellee James Blumstein. Blumstein moved to Tennessee on June 12, 1970, to begin employment as an assistant professor of law at Vanderbilt University in Nashville. With an eye toward voting in the upcoming August and November elections, he attempted to register to vote on July 1, 1970. The county registrar refused to register him, on the ground that Tennessee law authorizes the registration of only those persons who, at the time of the next election, will have been residents of the state for a year and residents of the county for three months.

After exhausting state administrative remedies, Blumstein brought this action challenging these residence requirements on federal constitutional grounds. A three-judge court . . . concluded that Tennessee's durational residence requirements were unconstitutional (1) because they impermissibly interfered with the right to vote and (2) because they created a "suspect" classification penalizing some Tennessee residents because of recent interstate movement. . . .

The subject of this lawsuit is the durational residence requirement. Appellee does not challenge Tennessee's power to restrict the vote to bona fide Tennessee residents. Nor has Tennessee ever disputed that appellee was a bona fide resident of the state and county when he attempted to register. But Tennessee insists that, in addition to being a resident, a would-be voter must have been a resident for a year in the state and three months in the county. It is this additional durational residence requirement that appellee challenges.

Durational residence laws penalize those persons who have traveled from one place to another to establish a new residence during the qualifying period. Such laws divide residents into two classes, old residents and new residents, and discriminate against the latter to the extent of totally denying them the opportunity to vote. The constitutional question presented is whether the Equal Protection Clause of the Fourteenth Amendment permits a State to discriminate in this way among its citizens.

To decide whether a law violates the Equal Protection Clause, we look, in essence, to three things: the character of the classification in question; the individual interests affected by the classification; and the governmental interests asserted in support of the classification. In considering laws challenged under the Equal Protection Clause, this Court has evolved more than one test, depending upon the interest affected or the classification involved. First, then, we must determine what standard of review is appropriate. In the present case, whether we look to the benefit withheld by the classification (the opportunity to vote) or the basis for the classification (recent interstate travel), we conclude that the State must show a substantial and compelling reason for imposing durational residence requirements.

. . .

. . . [D]urational residence laws must be measured by a strict equal protection test: they are unconstitutional unless the State can demonstrate that such laws are "necessary to promote a compelling governmental interest." Thus phrased, the constitutional question may sound like a mathematical formula. But legal "tests" do not have the precision of mathematical formulas. The key words emphasize a matter of degree: that a heavy burden of justification is on the State, and that the statute will be closely scrutinized in light of its asserted purposes.

It is not sufficient for the State to show that durational residence requirements further a very substantial state interest. In pursuing that important interest, the State cannot choose means that unnecessarily burden or restrict constitutionally protected activity. Statutes affecting constitutional rights must be drawn with "precision," and must be "tailored" to serve their legitimate objectives. And if there are other, reasonable ways to achieve those goals with a lesser burden on constitutionally protected activity, a State may not choose the way of greater interference. If it acts at all, it must choose "less drastic means."

We turn, then, to the question of whether the State has shown that durational residence requirements are needed to further a sufficiently substantial state interest. We emphasize again the difference between bona fide residence requirements and durational residence requirements. We have in the past noted approvingly that the states have the power to require that voters be bona fide residents of the relevant political subdivision. An appropriately defined and uniformly applied requirement of bona fide residence may be necessary to preserve the basic conception of a political community, and therefore could withstand close constitutional scrutiny. But durational residence requirements, representing a separate voting qualification imposed on bona fide residents, must be separately tested by the stringent standard.

It is worth noting at the outset that Congress has, in a somewhat different context, addressed the question whether durational residence laws further compelling state interests. In §202 of the Voting Rights Act of 1965, added by the Voting Rights Act Amendments of 1970, Congress outlawed state durational residence requirements for presidential and vice-presidential elections, and prohibited the States from closing registration more than 30 days before such elections. In doing so, it made a specific finding that durational residence requirements and more restrictive registration practices do "not bear a reasonable relationship to any compelling State interest in the conduct of presidential elections." . . . In our present case, of course, we deal with congressional, state, and local elections, in which the State's interests are arguably somewhat different; and, in addition, our function is not merely to determine whether there was a reasonable basis for Congress' findings. . . .

. . .

Preservation of the "purity of the ballot box" is a formidable-sounding state interest. The impurities feared, variously called "dual voting" and "colonization," all involve voting by nonresidents, either singly or in groups. The main concern is that nonresidents will temporarily invade the state or county, falsely swear that they are residents to become eligible to vote, and, by voting, allow a candidate to win by fraud. Surely the prevention of such fraud is a legitimate and compelling government goal. But it is impossible to view durational residence requirements as necessary to achieve that state interest.

Preventing fraud, the asserted evil that justifies state lawmaking, means keeping nonresidents from voting. But, by definition, a durational residence law bars newly arrived residents from the franchise along with nonresidents. The State argues that such sweeping laws are necessary to prevent fraud because they are needed to identify bona fide residents. This contention is particularly unconvincing in light of Tennessee's total statutory scheme for regulating the franchise.

Durational residence laws may once have been necessary to prevent a fraudulent evasion of state voter standards, but today in Tennessee, as in most other states, this purpose is served by a system of voter registration. Given this system, the record is totally devoid of any evidence that durational residence requirements are, in fact, necessary to identify bona fide residents. The qualifications of the would-be voter in Tennessee are determined when he registers to vote, which he may do until 30 days before the election. His qualifications—including bona fide residence—are established then by oath. There is no indication in the record that Tennessee routinely goes behind the would-be voter's oath to determine his qualifications. Since false swearing is no obstacle to one intent on fraud, the existence of burdensome voting qualifications like durational residence requirements cannot prevent corrupt nonresidents from fraudulently registering and voting. As long as the State relies on the oath-swearing system to establish qualifications, a durational residence requirement adds nothing to a simple residence requirement in the effort to stop fraud. The nonresident intent on committing election fraud will as quickly and effectively swear that he has been a resident for the requisite period of time as he would swear that he was simply a resident. Indeed, the durational residence requirement becomes an effective voting obstacle only to residents who tell the truth and have no fraudulent purposes.

Moreover, to the extent that the State makes an enforcement effort after the oath is sworn, it is not clear what role the durational residence requirement could play in protecting against fraud. The State closes the registration books 30 days before an election to give officials an opportunity to prepare for the election. Before the books close, anyone may register who claims that he will meet the durational residence requirement at the time of the next election. Although Tennessee argues that this 30-day period between registration and election does not give the State enough time to verify this claim of bona fide residence, we do not see the relevance of that position to this case. As long as the State permits registration up to 30 days before an election, a lengthy durational residence requirement does not increase the amount of time the State has in which to carry out an investigation into the sworn claim by the would-be voter that he is in fact, a resident.

Even if durational residence requirements imposed, in practice, a pre-election waiting period that gave voting officials three months or a year in which to confirm the bona fides of residence, Tennessee would not have demonstrated that these waiting periods were necessary. At the outset, the State is faced with the fact that it must defend two separate waiting periods of different lengths. It is impossible to see how both could be "necessary" to fulfill the pertinent state objective. If the state itself has determined that a three-month period is enough time in which to confirm bona fide residence in the state and county, obviously a one-year period cannot also be justified as "necessary" to achieve the same purpose. Beyond that, the job of detecting nonresidents from among persons who have registered is a relatively simple one. It hardly justifies prohibiting all newcomers from voting for even three months. To prevent dual voting, state voting officials simply have to cross-check lists of new registrants with their former jurisdictions. Objective information tendered as relevant to the question of bona fide residence under Tennessee law—places of dwelling, occupation, car registration, driver's license, property owned, etc.—is easy to double-check, especially in light of modern communications. Tennessee itself concedes that "[i]t might well be that these purposes can be achieved under requirements of shorter duration than that imposed by the State of Tennessee. . . ." Fixing a constitutionally acceptable period is surely a matter of degree. It is sufficient to note here that 30 days appears to be an ample period of time for the State to complete whatever administrative tasks are necessary to prevent fraud—and a year, or three months, too much. This was the judgment of Congress in the context of presidential elections. And, on the basis of the statutory scheme before us, it is almost surely the judgment of the Tennessee lawmakers as well. . . .

It has been argued that durational residence requirements are permissible because a person who has satisfied the waiting period requirements is conclusively presumed to be a bona fide resident. In other words, durational residence requirements are justified because they create an administratively useful conclusive presumption that recent arrivals are not residents, and are therefore properly barred from the franchise. This presumption, so the argument runs, also prevents fraud, for few candidates will be able to induce migration for the purpose of voting if fraudulent voters are required to remain in the false locale for three months or a year in order to vote on election day.

In *Carrington v. Rash*, this Court considered and rejected a similar kind of argument in support of a similar kind of conclusive presumption. . . .

. . . The State's legitimate purpose is to determine whether certain persons in the community are bona fide residents. A durational residence requirement creates a classification that may, in a crude way, exclude nonresidents from that group. But it also excludes many residents. Given the State's legitimate purpose and the individual interests that are affected, the classification is all too imprecise. In general, it is not very difficult for Tennessee to determine on an individualized basis whether one recently arrived in the community is in fact, a resident, although of course there will always be difficult cases. Tennessee has defined a test for bona fide residence, and appears prepared to apply it on an individualized basis in various legal contexts. That test could easily be applied to new arrivals. Furthermore, if it is unlikely that would-be fraudulent voters would remain in a false locale for the lengthy period imposed by durational residence requirements, it is just as unlikely that they would collect such objective indicia of bona fide residence as a dwelling, car registration, or driver's license. In spite of these things, the question of bona fide residence is settled for new arrivals by conclusive presumption, not by individualized inquiry. Thus, it has always been undisputed that appellee Blumstein is himself a bona fide resident of Tennessee within the ordinary state definition of residence. But since Tennessee's presumption from failure to meet the durational residence requirements is conclusive, a showing of actual bona fide residence is irrelevant, even though such a showing would fully serve the State's purposes embodied in the presumption and would achieve those purposes with far less drastic impact on constitutionally protected interests. The Equal Protection Clause places a limit on government by classification, and that limit has been exceeded here.

Our conclusion that the waiting period is not

the least restrictive means necessary for preventing fraud is bolstered by the recognition that Tennessee has at its disposal a variety of criminal laws that are more than adequate to detect and deter whatever fraud may be feared. At least six separate sections of the Tennessee Code define offenses to deal with voter fraud. . . . In addition . . . Tennessee permits the bona fides of a voter to be challenged on election day. Where a State has available such remedial action to supplement its voter registration system, it can hardly argue that broadly imposed political disabilities such as durational residence requirements are needed to deal with the evils of fraud. Now that the Federal Voting Rights Act abolishes those residence requirements as a precondition for voting in presidential and vice-presidential elections, it is clear that the States will have to resort to other devices available to prevent nonresidents from voting. Especially since every State must live with this new federal statute, it is impossible to believe that durational residence requirements are necessary to meet the State's goal of stopping fraud.

The argument that durational residence requirements further the goal of having "knowledgeable voters" appears to involve three separate claims. The first is that such requirements "afford some surety that the voter has, in fact, become a member of the community." But here the State appears to confuse a bona fide residence requirement with a durational residence requirement. As already noted, a State does have an interest in limiting the franchise to bona fide members of the community. But this does not justify or explain the exclusion from the franchise of persons not because their bona fide residence is questioned, but because they are recent, rather than long-time, residents.

The second branch of the "knowledgeable voters" justification is that durational residence

requirements assure that the voter "has a common interest in all matters pertaining to [the community's] government. . . ." By this, presumably, the State means that it may require a period of residence sufficiently lengthy to impress upon its voters the local viewpoint. This is precisely the sort of argument this Court has repeatedly rejected. . . .

. . .

Finally, the State urges that a long-time resident is "more likely to exercise his right [to vote] more intelligently." To the extent that this is different from the previous argument, the state is apparently asserting an interest in limiting the franchise to voters who are knowledgeable about the issues. In this case, Tennessee argues that people who have been in the state less than a year and the county less than three months are likely to be unaware of the issues involved in the congressional, state, and local elections, and therefore can be barred from the franchise. We note that the criterion of "intelligent" voting is an elusive one, and susceptible of abuse. But without deciding as a general matter the extent to which a State can bar less knowledgeable or intelligent citizens from the franchise, we conclude that durational residence requirements cannot be justified on this basis.

. . .

Similarly, the durational residence requirements in this case founder because of their crudeness as a device for achieving the articulated state goal of assuring the knowledgeable exercise of the franchise. The classifications created by durational residence requirements obviously permit any long-time resident to vote regardless of his knowledge of the issues—and obviously many long-time residents do not have any. On the other hand, the classifications bar from the franchise many other, admittedly new, residents who have become at least minimally, and often fully, informed about the issues. Indeed, recent migrants who take the time to register and vote shortly after moving are likely to be those citizens, such as appellee, who make it a point to be informed and knowledgeable about the issues. Given modern communications, and given the clear indication that campaign spending and voter education occur largely during the month before an election, the State cannot seriously maintain that it is "necessary" to reside for a year in the state and three months in the county in order to be knowledgeable about congressional, state, or even purely local elections. There is simply nothing in the record to support the conclusive presumption that residents who have lived in the state for less than a year and their county for less than three months are uninformed about elections. These durational residence requirements crudely exclude large numbers of fully qualified people. Especially since Tennessee creates a waiting period by closing registration books 30 days before an election, there can be no basis for arguing that any durational residence requirement is also needed to assure knowledgeability. It is pertinent to note that Tennessee has never made an attempt to further its alleged interest in an informed electorate in a universally applicable way. Knowledge or competence has never been a criterion for participation in Tennessee's electoral process for long-time residents. Indeed, the State specifically provides for voting by various types of absentee persons. These provisions permit many long-time residents who leave the county or state to participate in a constituency in which they have only the slightest political interest, and from whose political debates they are likely to be cut off. That the State specifically permits such voting is not consistent with its claimed compelling interest in intelligent, informed use of the ballot. If the

State seeks to assure intelligent use of the ballot, it may not try to serve this interest only with respect to new arrivals.

It may well be true that new residents as a group know less about state and local issues than older residents; and it is surely true that durational residence requirements will exclude some people from voting who are totally uninformed about election matters. But as devices to limit the franchise to knowledgeable residents, the conclusive presumptions of durational residence requirements are much too crude. They exclude too many people who should not, and need not, be excluded. They represent a requirement of knowledge unfairly imposed on only some citizens. We are aware that classifications are always imprecise. By requiring classifications to be tailored to their purpose, we do not secretly require the impossible. Here, there is simply too attenuated a relationship between the state interest in an informed electorate and the fixed requirement that voters must have been residents in the state for a year and the county for three months. Given the exacting standard of precision we require of statutes affecting constitutional rights, we cannot say that durational residence requirements are necessary to further a compelling state interest.

Concluding that Tennessee has not offered an adequate justification for its durational residence laws, we affirm the judgment of the court below.

Goosby v. Osser
409 U.S. 512 (1973)

. . . It is a class action brought by and on behalf of persons awaiting trial and confined in Philadelphia County prisons because either unable to afford bail or because charged with nonbailable offenses. The complaint alleges that provisions of the Pennsylvania Election Code, in violation of the Equal Protection and Due Process Clauses of the Fourteenth Amendment, absolutely deny petitioners' class the right to vote in that they neither permit members of the class to leave prison to register and vote nor provide facilities for the purpose at the prisons, and in that they expressly prohibit persons "confined in penal institutions" from voting by absentee ballot. . . .

. . . The single judge . . . ruled that the concession on behalf of the Commonwealth officials meant there was no case or controversy before the court as required by Art. III of the Constitution, and dismissed the complaint. On petitioners' appeal, the Court of Appeals for the Third Circuit affirmed. . . . A petition for rehearing en banc was denied. . . .

The single judge clearly erred in holding that the concession of the Commonwealth officials foreclosed the existence of a case or controversy. All parties are in accord that Pennsylvania law did not oblige the municipal officials to defer to the concession of the Commonwealth officials, or otherwise give the Commonwealth officials a special status as "principal defendants." . . .

. . .

The Court of Appeals also erred. We disagree with its holding that *McDonald v. Board of Election Commissioners*, rendered petitioners' constitutional claims wholly insubstantial.

. . .

. . . We neither decide nor intimate any view upon the merits. It suffices that we hold that *McDonald* does not "foreclose the subject" of petitioners' challenge to the Pennsylvania statutory scheme. The significant differences between that scheme and the Illinois scheme leave ample "room for the inference that the questions sought to be raised [by petitioners] can be the subject of controversy."

We therefore conclude that this case must be "heard and determined by a district court of three judges. . . ." The judgment of the Court of Appeals is therefore reversed, and the case is remanded with direction to enter an appropriate order pursuant to that section for the convening of a three-judge court to hear and determine the merits of petitioners' constitutional claims or, if deemed appropriate, to abstain from such determination pending state court proceedings.

Marston v. Lewis
410 U.S. 679 (1973)

Fourteen county recorders and other public officials of Arizona appeal from a judgment of a three-judge district court holding the state's 50-day durational voter residency requirement and its 50-day voter registration requirement unconstitutional under the decision in *Dunn v. Blumstein*. A permanent injunction was entered against enforcement of these or any other greater than 30-day residency and registration requirements in any election held after November 1972. Appellants do not seek review of the District Court's judgment insofar as it enjoins application of the 50-day requirements in presidential elections. Appellants assert, however, that the requirements, as applied to special, primary, or general elections involving state and local officials, are supported by sufficiently strong local interests to pass constitutional muster. . . .

In *Dunn*, we struck down Tennessee's durational voter residency requirement of one year in the state and three months in the county. . . . The Arizona scheme, however, stands in a different light. The durational residency requirement is only 50 days, not a year or even three months. Moreover . . . the Arizona requirement is tied to the closing of the State's registration process at 50 days prior to elections, and reflects a state legislative judgment that the period is necessary to achieve the State's legitimate goals.

We accept that judgment, particularly in light of the realities of Arizona's registration and voting procedures. . . .

An additional complicating factor in Arizona registration procedures is the State's fall primary system. The uncontradicted testimony demonstrates that, in the weeks preceding the deadline for registration in general elections—a period marked by a curve toward the "peak" in terms of the registration affidavits received—county recorders and their staffs are unable to process the incoming affidavits because of their work in the fall primaries. It is only after the primaries are over that the officials can return to the accumulated backlog of registration affidavits and undertake to process them in accordance with applicable statutory requirements.

On the basis of the evidence before the District Court, it is clear that the State has demonstrated that the 50-day voter registration cutoff (for election of state and local officials) is necessary to permit preparation of accurate voter lists. . . . In the present case, we are confronted with a recent and amply justifiable legislative judgment that 50 days, rather than 30, is necessary to promote the State's important interest in accurate voter lists. The Constitution is not so rigid that that determination and others like it may not stand.

The judgment of the District Court, insofar as it has been appealed from, is reversed.

Burns v. Fortson
410 U.S. 686 (1973)

By statute, Georgia registrars are required to close their voter registration books 50 days

prior to November general elections, except for those persons who seek to register to vote for President or Vice President. The District Court upheld the registration cutoff against appellants' constitutional attack based upon this Court's decision in *Dunn v. Blumstein.* This appeal followed.

The State offered extensive evidence to establish "the need for a 50-day registration cut-off point, given the vagaries and numerous requirements of the Georgia election laws." Plaintiffs introduced no evidence. On the basis of the record before it, the District Court concluded that the State had demonstrated

> that the 50-day period is necessary to promote . . . the orderly, accurate, and efficient administration of state and local elections, free from fraud.

Although the 50-day registration period approaches the outer constitutional limits in this area, we affirm the judgment of the District Court. . . .

Rosario v. Rockefeller
410 U.S. 752 (1973)

For more than 60 years, New York has had a closed system of primary elections, whereby only enrolled members of a political party may vote in that party's primary. Under the State's Election Law, a registered voter enrolls as a party member by depositing an enrollment blank in a locked enrollment box. The last day for enrollment is 30 days before the general election each year. Section 186 of the Election Law provides that the enrollment boxes shall not be opened until the Tuesday following the general election, and party affiliations are then entered on the State's official registration books. The voter is then duly enrolled as a member of his party and may vote in a subsequent primary election.

The effect of §186 is to require a voter to enroll in the party of his choice at least 30 days before the general election in November in order to vote in the next subsequent party primary. If a voter fails to meet this deadline, he cannot participate in a party primary until after the following general election. Section 187 provides an exemption from this waiting period for certain classes of voters, including persons who have attained voting age after the last general election, persons too ill to enroll during the previous enrollment period, and persons who moved from one place to another within a single county. Under §187, these classes of voters may be specially enrolled as members of a party even after the general election has taken place.

The petitioners are New York residents who became eligible to vote when they came of age in 1971. Although they could have registered and enrolled in a political party before the cutoff date in 1971 . . . they failed to do so. Instead, they waited until early December 1971, to register and to deposit their enrollment blanks. At that time, they could not be specially and immediately enrolled in a party under §187, since they had attained the voting age before, rather than after, the 1971 general election. Hence, pursuant to §186, their party enrollment could not become effective until after the November 1972, general election. Because of New York's enrollment scheme, then, the petitioners were not eligible to vote in the presidential primary election held in June 1972.

The petitioners filed these complaints for declaratory relief . . . alleging that §186 unconstitutionally deprived them of their right to vote in the June primary and abridged their freedom to associate with the political party of their choice. The District Court, in an unreported opinion, granted them the declaratory relief sought. The Court of Appeals for the Second Circuit reversed, holding §186 constitutional. . . .

The petitioners argue that, through §186, New York disenfranchised them by refusing to permit them to vote in the June 1972, primary election on the ground that they had not enrolled in a political party at least 30 days prior to the preceding general election. More specifically, they contend that §186 has operated to preclude newly registered voters, such as themselves, from participating in the primary election of the party of their choice. According to the petitioners, New York has no "compelling state interest" in its delayed-enrollment scheme so as to justify such disenfranchisement, and hence the scheme must fall. In support of this argument, the petitioners rely on several cases in which this Court has struck down, as violative of the Equal Protection Clause, state statutes that disenfranchised certain groups of people.

. . .

Section 186 . . . did not absolutely disenfranchise the class to which the petitioners belong— newly registered voters who were eligible to enroll in a party before the previous general election. Rather, the statute merely imposed a time deadline on their enrollment, which they had to meet in order to participate in the next primary. Since the petitioners attained voting age before the October 2, 1971, deadline, they clearly could have registered and enrolled in the party of their choice before that date and been eligible to vote in the June 1972 primary. Indeed, if the petitioners had not been able to enroll by the October 2, 1971, deadline because they did not attain the requisite age until after the 1971 general election, they would have been eligible for special enrollment under §187. The petitioners do not say why they did not enroll prior to the cutoff date;

however, it is clear that they could have done so, but chose not to. Hence, if their plight can be characterized as disenfranchisement at all, it was not caused by §186, but by their own failure to take timely steps to effect their enrollment.

For the same reason, we reject the petitioners' argument that §186 violated their First and Fourteenth Amendment right of free association with the political party of their choice. Since they could have enrolled in a party in time to participate in the June 1972 primary, §186 did not constitute a ban on their freedom of association, but merely a time limitation on when they had to act in order to participate in their chosen party's next primary.

. . .

The only remaining question, then, is whether the time limitation imposed by §186 is so severe as itself to constitute an unconstitutionally onerous burden on the petitioners' exercise of the franchise or on their freedom of political association. . . . [T]he State is certainly justified in imposing some reasonable cut-off point for registration or party enrollment, which citizens must meet in order to participate in the next election. Hence, our inquiry must be whether the particular deadline before us here is so justified.

The cutoff date for enrollment prescribed by §186 occurs approximately eight months prior to a presidential primary (held in June) and 11 months prior to a nonpresidential primary (held in September). The petitioners argue that this period is unreasonably long, and that it therefore unduly burdens the exercise of their constitutional rights. . . .

It is true that the period between the enrollment deadline and the next primary election is lengthy. But that period is not an arbitrary time limit unconnected to any important state goal. The purpose of New York's delayed-enrollment scheme, we are told, is to inhibit party "raid-ing," whereby voters in sympathy with one party designate themselves as voters of another party so as to influence or determine the results of the other party's primary. This purpose is accomplished, the Court of Appeals found, not only by requiring party enrollment several months in advance of the primary, on the theory that "long-range planning in politics is quite difficult," but also by requiring enrollment prior to a general election. . . .

It is clear that preservation of the integrity of the electoral process is a legitimate and valid state goal. In the service of that goal, New York has adopted its delayed-enrollment scheme, and an integral part of that scheme is that, in order to participate in a primary election, a person must enroll before the preceding general election. . . . For this reason, New York's scheme requires an insulating general election between enrollment and the next party primary. The resulting time limitation for enrollment is thus tied to a particularized legitimate purpose, and is in no sense invidious or arbitrary.

New York did not prohibit the petitioners from voting in the 1972 primary election or from associating with the political party of their choice. It merely imposed a legitimate time limitation on their enrollment, which they chose to disregard.

Accordingly, the judgment below is affirmed.

***National Association for the
Advancement of Colored People
v. New York
413 U.S. 345 (1973)***

This appeal from a three-judge district court for the District of Columbia comes to us pursuant to the direct review provisions of §4(a) of the

Voting Rights Act of 1965. The appellants seek review of an order dated April 13, 1972, unaccompanied by any opinion, denying their motion to intervene in a suit that had been instituted against the United States by the State of New York, on behalf of its counties of New York, Bronx, and Kings. New York's action was one for a judgment declaring that, during the 10 years preceding the filing of the suit, voter qualifications prescribed by the State had not been used by the three named counties "for the purpose or with the effect of denying or abridging the right to vote on account of race or color," within the language and meaning of §4(a), and that the provisions of §§4 and 5 of the Act are, therefore, inapplicable to the three counties.

In addition to denying the appellants' motion to intervene, the District Court, by the same order, granted New York's motion for summary judgment. This was based upon a formal consent by the Assistant Attorney General in charge of the Civil Rights Division, on behalf of the United States, consistent with the government's answer theretofore filed, "to the entry of a declaratory judgment under Section 4(a) of the Voting Rights Act of 1965." . . .

. . .

The three New York counties that the present litigation concerns were not covered by §§4 and 5 of the original 1965 Act. They became subject thereto because of the provisions of the 1970 Act and the respective published determinations, hereinabove described, of the Attorney General and the Director of the Bureau of the Census. Indeed, it is clear that the three counties were a definite target of the 1970 amendments.

It was in December 1971, during the pendency of state legislative proceedings for the redrafting of congressional and state senate and assembly district lines, that the State of New York filed its

complaint in the present action. The amended complaint . . . alleged that certain of the State's qualifications for registration and voting, prescribed by New York's Constitution . . . and by its Election Law (the ability to read and write English, the administration of a literacy test, and the presentation of evidence of literacy in lieu of the test), had not been used during the preceding 10 years "for the purpose or with the effect of denying or abridging the right to vote on account of race or color," that the State's literacy requirements were suspended in 1970 and remained suspended; that, after enactment of the 1965 Act, the New York City Board of Elections provided English-Spanish affidavits to be executed in lieu of a diploma or certificate in conformity with the requirements of the Act; and that, beginning in 1964 and continuing through 1971, with the exception of 1967, there were voter registration drives every summer designed to increase the number of registered voters in the three named counties. New York and the United States stipulated that the government could file its answer or other pleading by March 10, 1972. The answer was filed on that day. The government therein admitted that English-Spanish affidavits were provided by the City Board of Elections but averred, on information and belief, that such affidavits were not so provided prior to 1967. The answer also alleged that the United States was without knowledge or information sufficient to form a belief as to the truth of the plaintiff's allegation that the literacy tests were administered with no intention or effect to abridge or deny the right to vote on the basis of race or color.

On March 17, New York filed its motion for summary judgment. . . .

Two and one-half weeks later, on April 3, the United States filed its formal consent . . . to the entry of the declaratory judgment for which New York had moved. . . .

. . . . Appellants asserted that, if New York were successful in the present action, the appellants would be deprived of the protections afforded by §§4 and 5; that they "would be legally bound" thereby in their simultaneously filed §5 action in the Southern District of New York; and that the latter action "would necessarily fail." The appellants also alleged that the §5 suit asserted that New York

> has gerrymandered Assembly, Senatorial and Congressional districts in Kings, Bronx and New York counties so that, on purpose and in effect, the right to vote will be denied on account of race or color.

Thus, it was said, the disposition of the present suit might impair or impede the appellants' ability to protect their interests in registering to vote, voting, and seeking public office. It was further claimed that . . . attorneys in the Department of Justice thrice had represented to appellants' counsel that the United States would oppose New York's motion for summary judgment. . . .

. . .

The United States took no position with respect to the appellants' motion to intervene. New York opposed the motion on six grounds. The first was untimeliness, in that the suit had been pending for more than four months, an article about it had appeared in early February in the New York Times, and the appellants did not deny that they had knowledge of the pendency of the action. The second was failure to allege appropriate supporting facts. The third was the lack of a requisite interest, in that none of the appellants asserted he was a victim of discriminatory application of the literacy test; rather, the motion to intervene was subordinate to the appellants' real interest in invalidating New York's reapportionment of its assembly, senate, and congressional districts, as evidenced by the institution of their action in the Southern District of New York. The fourth was

adequate representation of the appellants' interest by the United States. The fifth was that delay in the granting of the motion for summary judgment would prejudice New York and jeopardize the impending primary elections for offices of Assembly, Senate, and Congress, as well as for delegates to the upcoming Democratic National Convention. The sixth was that the appellants and others who claimed discrimination still could raise those issues in the state and federal courts of New York.

On April 13, the three-judge court entered its order denying the appellants' motion to intervene and granting summary judgment for New York.

On April 24, the appellants filed a motion to alter judgment on the ground. . . .

. . .

The District Court promptly denied the Motion to Alter Judgment.

. . .

. . . [W]e readily conclude that the District Court's denial of the appellants' motion to intervene was proper because of the motion's untimeliness, and that the denial was not an abuse of the court's discretion. . . .

. . .

We . . . conclude that the motion to intervene was untimely and that the District Court did not abuse its discretion in denying the appellants' motion. This makes it unnecessary for us to consider whether other conditions for intervention under Rule 24 were satisfied.

Affirmed.

Kusper v. Pontikes
414 U.S. 51 (1973)

Under §73(d) of the Illinois Election Code, a person is prohibited from voting in the primary election of a political party if he has voted in the primary of any other party within the preceding 23 months. Appellee, Harriet G. Pontikes, is a qualified Chicago voter who voted in a Republican primary in February 1971; she wanted to vote in a March 1972 Democratic primary, but was barred from doing so by this 23-month rule. She filed a complaint for declaratory and injunctive relief in the United States District Court for the Northern District of Illinois, alleging that §7-43(d) unconstitutionally abridged her freedom to associate with the political party of her choice by depriving her of the opportunity to vote in the Democratic primary. A statutory three-judge court was convened, and held . . . that the 23-month rule is unconstitutional. . . .

. . .

There can be little doubt that §7-43(d) substantially restricts an Illinois voter's freedom to change his political party affiliation. One who wishes to change his party registration must wait almost two years before his choice will be given effect. Moreover, he is forced to forgo participation in any primary elections occurring within the statutory 23-month hiatus. The effect of the Illinois statute is thus to "lock" the voter into his preexisting party affiliation for a substantial period of time following participation in any primary election, and each succeeding primary vote extends this period of confinement.

The 23-month rule does not, of course, deprive those in the appellee's position of all opportunities to associate with the political party of their choice. . . .

. . . A prime objective of most voters in associating themselves with a particular party must surely be to gain a voice in that selection process. By preventing the appellee from participating at all in Democratic primary elections during the statutory period, the Illinois statute deprived her of any voice in choosing the party's candidates, and thus substantially abridged her ability to associate effectively with the party of her choice.

As our past decisions have made clear, a significant encroachment upon associational freedom cannot be justified upon a mere showing of a legitimate state interest. . . .

The appellants here urge that the 23-month rule serves the purpose of preventing "raiding"—the practice whereby voters in sympathy with one party vote in another's primary in order to distort that primary's results. It is said that our decision in *Rosario v. Rockefeller*, recognized the state interest in inhibiting "raiding," and upheld the constitutional validity of legislation restricting a voter's freedom to change parties, enacted as a means of serving that interest.

. . . [I]t does not follow from *Rosario* that the Illinois statutory procedures also pass muster under the Fourteenth Amendment, for the Illinois Election Code differs from the New York delayed enrollment law in a number of important respects.

. . .

The basic difference in the Illinois law is obvious. Since the appellee here voted in the 1971 Republican primary, the state law absolutely precluded her from participating in the 1972 Democratic primary. Unlike the petitioners in *Rosario*, whose disenfranchisement was caused by their own failure to take timely measures to enroll, there was no action that Mrs. Pontikes could have taken to make herself eligible to vote in the 1972 Democratic primary. The Illinois law . . . "locks" voters into a preexisting party affiliation from one primary to the next, and the only way to break the "lock" is to forgo voting in any primary for a period of almost two years.

. . .

We conclude, therefore, that §73(d) of the

Illinois Election Code unconstitutionally infringes upon the right of free political association protected by the First and Fourteenth Amendments. The judgment of the District Court is accordingly affirmed.

O'Brien v. Skinner
414 U.S. 524 (1974)

This is an appeal from the judgment of the Court of Appeals of New York taken by 72 persons who were, at the time of the trial of the original action, detained in confinement. Some are simply detained awaiting trial, others are confined pursuant to misdemeanor convictions; none is subject to any voting disability under the laws of New York.

The Court of Appeals of New York . . . held that failure of the State to provide appellants with any means of registering and voting was not a violation of the New York statutes and not a denial of any federal or state constitutional right.

Before the November 1972 general elections in New York, the appellants applied to the authorities of Monroe County, including the Board of Elections, to establish a mobile voters registration unit in the county jail in compliance with a mobile registration procedure which had been employed in some county jails in New York State. This request was denied, and appellants then requested that they be either transported to polling places under appropriate restrictions or, in the alternative, that they be permitted to register and vote under New York's absentee voting provisions which, essentially, provide that qualified voters are allowed to register and vote by absentee measures if they are unable to appear personally because of illness or physical disability, or because of their "duties, occupation or

business." The statutes also allow absentee voting, but not registration, if the voter is away from his residence on election day because he is confined in a veterans' hospital or is away on vacation. The election authorities denied the request, taking the position that they were under no obligation to permit the appellants to register or to vote in person, and that inmates did not qualify for absentee voting under the provisions of the New York statutes.

The Supreme Court for Monroe County in New York considered the claims presented by the appellants and treated them as a proceeding in the nature of mandamus. The conclusion reached by that court was that the legislature of New York had provided for absentee registration and voting by any voter unable to appear personally because of confinement in an institution (other than a mental institution). The court concluded that the election laws should be construed to apply to an inmate confined in jail and not otherwise disenfranchised, since this constituted a "physical disability" in the sense that he was physically disabled from leaving his confinement to go to the polls to vote, and that the statute therefore entitled such persons to vote by absentee ballot. However, the court noted that there was no showing that any of the persons claiming these rights had timely filed all the necessary forms, but that this could yet be accomplished in time for voting by absentee ballot in November 1972. The Appellate Division of the Fourth Judicial Department of the Supreme Court of New York, on review, gave a similar construction to the election laws. . . .

On appeal to the New York Court of Appeals . . . these holdings were reversed. . . .

. . .

It is important to note at the outset that the New York election laws here in question do not raise any question of disenfranchisement of a person because of conviction for criminal conduct. As we noted earlier, these appellants are not disabled from voting except by reason of not being able physically—in the very literal sense— to go to the polls on election day or to make the appropriate registration in advance by mail. The New York statutes are silent concerning registration or voting facilities in jails and penal institutions, except as they provide for absentee balloting. If a New York resident eligible to vote is confined in a county jail in a county in which he does not reside, paradoxically, he may secure an absentee ballot and vote, and he may also register by mail, presumably because he is "unavoidably absent from the county of his residence."

Thus, under the New York statutes, two citizens awaiting trial—or even awaiting a decision whether they are to be charged—sitting side by side in the same cell, may receive different treatment as to voting rights. As we have noted, if the citizen is confined in the county of his legal residence, he cannot vote by absentee ballot, as can his cellmate whose residence is in the adjoining county. Although neither is under any legal bar to voting, one of them can vote by absentee ballot and the other cannot.

. . .

New York's election statutes, as construed by its highest court, discriminate between categories of qualified voters in a way that, as applied to pretrial detainees and misdemeanants, is wholly arbitrary. . . . The New York statutes, as construed, operate as a restriction which is "so severe as itself to constitute an unconstitutionally onerous burden on the . . . exercise of the franchise." Appellants and others similarly situated are . . . under no legal disability impeding their legal right to register or to vote; they are simply not allowed to use the absentee ballot, and

are denied any alternative means of casting their vote although they are legally qualified to vote.

The construction given the New York statutes by its trial court and the Appellate Division may well have been a reasonable interpretation of New York law, but the highest court of the State has concluded otherwise, and it is not our function to construe a state statute contrary to the construction given it by the highest court of a State. We have no choice, therefore, but to hold that, as construed, the New York statutes deny appellants the equal protection of the laws guaranteed by the Fourteenth Amendment.

Reversed and remanded for further proceedings not inconsistent with this opinion.

Anderson v. United States
417 U.S. 211 (1974)

Petitioners were convicted of violating 18 U.S.C. §241, which . . . makes it unlawful for two or more persons to

> conspire to injure, oppress, threaten, or intimidate any citizen in the free exercise or enjoyment of any right or privilege secured to him by the Constitution or laws of the United States. . . .

Specifically, the government proved that petitioners engaged in a conspiracy to cast fictitious votes for candidates for federal, state, and local offices in a primary election in Logan County, West Virginia. . . . [T]he Court of Appeals thought it necessary to resolve the question whether a conspiracy to cast false votes in a state or local election, as opposed to a conspiracy to cast false votes in a federal election, is unlawful under §241. The Court of Appeals affirmed petitioners' convictions. . . .

The underlying facts are not in dispute. On

May 12, 1970, a primary election was held in West Virginia for the purpose of nominating candidates for the United States Senate, United States House of Representatives, and various state and local offices. One of the nominations most actively contested in Logan County was the Democratic nomination for County Commissioner, an office vested with a wide variety of legislative, executive, and judicial powers. Among the several candidates for the Democratic nomination for this office were the incumbent, Okey Hager, and his major opponent, Neal Scaggs.

Petitioners are state or county officials, including the Clerk of the Logan County Court, the Clerk of the County Circuit Court, the Sheriff and Deputy Sheriff of the County, and a State Senator. The evidence at trial showed that, by using the power of their office, the petitioners convinced three election officials in charge of the Mount Gay precinct in Logan County to cast false and fictitious votes on the voting machines and then to destroy poll slips so that the number of persons who had actually voted could not be determined except from the machine tally. While it is apparent from the record that the primary purpose behind the casting of false votes was to secure the nomination of Hager for the office of County Commissioner, it is equally clear that about 100 false votes were, in fact, cast not only for Hager, but also for Senator Robert Byrd and Representative Ken Hechler, who appeared on the ballot for renomination to their respective chambers of the United States Congress, as well as for other state and local candidates considered part of the Hager slate.

The conspiracy achieved its primary objective, the countywide vote totals showing Hager the winner by 21 votes, counting the Mount Gay precinct returns. About two weeks after the election, on May 27, 1970, the election results were certi-

fied. After that date, Scaggs filed an election contest challenging certain returns, including the Mount Gay County Commissioner votes. No challenge was made, however, to the Mount Gay votes for either of the federal offices, and they became final on May 27.

. . .

. . . [P]etitioners argued that §241 was limited to conspiracies to cast false votes in federal elections, and did not apply to local elections. Accordingly, they contended that the conspiracy in the present case, so far as federal jurisdiction was concerned, ended on May 27, 1970, the date on which the election returns were certified and the federal returns became final. Statements made after this date by one alleged conspirator, the argument continued, could not, as a matter of law, have been made in furtherance of the conspiracy charged under §241, and therefore should not have been considered by the jury in determining the guilt or innocence of the other defendants.

. . .

This case is therefore an inappropriate vehicle for us to decide whether a conspiracy to cast false votes for candidates for state or local office, as opposed to candidates for federal office, is unlawful under §241, and we intimate no views on that question.

Affirmed.

Richardson v. Ramirez
418 U.S. 24 (1974)

The three individual respondents in this case were convicted of felonies and have completed the service of their respective sentences and paroles. They filed a petition for a writ of mandate in the Supreme Court of California to compel California county election officials to register them as voters. They claimed, on behalf of themselves and others similarly situated, that application to them of the provisions of the California Constitution and implementing statutes which disenfranchised persons convicted of an "infamous crime" denied them the right to equal protection of the laws under the Federal Constitution. The Supreme Court of California held that,

> as applied to all ex-felons whose terms of incarceration and parole have expired, the provisions of article II and article XX, section 11, of the California Constitution denying the right of suffrage to persons convicted of crime, together with the several sections of the Elections Code implementing that disqualification . . . , violate the equal protection clause of the Fourteenth Amendment.

. . .

Despite . . . settled historical and judicial understanding of the Fourteenth Amendment's effect on state laws disenfranchising convicted felons, respondents argue that our recent decisions invalidating other state-imposed restrictions on the franchise as violative of the Equal Protection Clause require us to invalidate the disenfranchisement of felons as well. They rely on such cases as *Dunn, Bullock, Kramer,* and *Cipriano,* to support the conclusions of the Supreme Court of California that a State must show a "compelling state interest" to justify exclusion of ex-felons from the franchise and that California has not done so here.

As we have seen, however, the exclusion of felons from the vote has an affirmative sanction in §2 of the Fourteenth Amendment, a sanction which was not present in the case of the other restrictions on the franchise which were invalidated in the cases on which respondents rely. We hold that the understanding of those who adopted the Fourteenth Amendment, as reflected in the express language of §2 and in the historical and judicial interpretation of the amendment's applicability to state laws disenfranchising felons, is of controlling significance in distinguishing such laws from those other state limitations on the franchise which have been held invalid under the Equal Protection Clause by this Court. . . .

Pressed upon us by the respondents, and by amici curiae, are contentions that these notions are outmoded, and that the more modern view is that it is essential to the process of rehabilitating the ex-felon that he be returned to his role in society as a fully participating citizen when he has completed the serving of his term. We would by no means discount these arguments if addressed to the legislative forum which may properly weigh and balance them against those advanced in support of California's present constitutional provisions. But it is not for us to choose one set of values over the other. If respondents are correct, and the view which they advocate is indeed the more enlightened and sensible one, presumably the people of the State of California will ultimately come around to that view. And if they do not do so, their failure is some evidence, at least, of the fact that there are two sides to the argument.

We therefore hold that the Supreme Court of California erred in concluding that California may no longer, consistent with the Equal Protection Clause of the Fourteenth Amendment, exclude from the franchise convicted felons who have completed their sentences and paroles. The California court did not reach respondents' alternative contention that there was such a total lack of uniformity in county election officials' enforcement of the challenged state laws as to work a separate denial of equal protection, and we believe that it should have an opportunity to consider the claim before we address ourselves to it.

Accordingly, we reverse and remand for further proceedings not inconsistent with this opinion.

Hill v. Stone
421 U.S. 289 (1975)

Appellees, residents of Fort Worth, Texas, brought this action to challenge the state and city laws limiting the franchise in city bond elections to persons who have made available for taxation some real, mixed, or personal property. A three-judge District Court held that this restriction on suffrage did not serve any compelling state interest, and therefore violated the Equal Protection Clause of the Fourteenth Amendment. . . .

The Texas Constitution provides that, in all municipal elections "to determine expenditure of money or assumption of debt," only those who pay taxes on property in the city are eligible to vote. In addition, it directs that, in any election held "for the purpose of issuing bonds or otherwise lending credit, or expending money or assuming any debt," the franchise shall be limited to those qualified voters "who own taxable property in the . . . district . . . where such election is held," and who have "duly rendered the same for taxation." The implementing statutes impose the same requirements, adding that, to qualify for voting, a resident of the district holding the election must have "rendered" his property for taxation to the district during the proper period of the election year, and that he must sign an affidavit indicating that he has done so. The Fort Worth City Charter further provides that the city shall not issue bonds unless they are authorized in an election of the "qualified voters who pay taxes on property situated within the corporate limits of the City of Ft. Worth."

In 1969 . . . the Texas Attorney General de-

vised a "dual box election procedure" to be used in all the State's local bond elections. Under this procedure, all persons owning taxable property rendered for taxation voted in one box, and all other registered voters cast their ballots in a separate box. The results in both boxes were tabulated, and the bond issue would be deemed to have passed only if it was approved by a majority vote both in the "renderers' box" and in the aggregate of both boxes. This scheme ensured that the bonds would be safe from challenge even if the state law restrictions on the franchise were later held unconstitutional.

On April 11, 1972, the city of Fort Worth conducted a tax bond election, using the dual-box system to authorize the sale of bonds to improve the city transportation system and to build a city library. Since the state eligibility restrictions had previously been construed to require only that the prospective voter render some property for taxation, even if he did not actually pay any tax on the property, all those who signed an affidavit indicating that they had rendered some property were permitted to vote in the "renderers' box." . . .

The appellees, three of whom had voted as nonrenderers, then filed this action in the United States District Court for the Northern District of Texas, claiming that the partial disfranchisement of persons not rendering property for taxation denied them equal protection of the laws. A three-judge District Court . . . entered judgment for the appellees. The court declared the relevant provisions of the Texas Constitution, the Texas Election Code, and the Fort Worth City Charter unconstitutional "insofar as they condition the right to vote in bond elections on citizens' rendering property for taxation." Although the court ruled that its decree would not make invalid any bonds already authorized or any bond elections held before the date of the judgment, it ordered the city defendants to count the ballots of those who had voted in the nonrenderers' box, and it enjoined any future restriction of the franchise in state bond elections to those who have rendered property for taxation.

. . .

The basic principle . . . is that, as long as the election in question is not one of special interest, any classification restricting the franchise on grounds other than residence, age, and citizenship cannot stand unless the district or State can demonstrate that the classification serves a compelling state interest.

The appellant's claim that the Fort Worth election was one of special interest, and thus outside the principles of the *Kramer* case, runs afoul of our decision in *City of Phoenix v. Kolodziejski.* . . .

In making the alternative contentions that the "rendering requirement" creates no real "classification," or that the classification created should be upheld as being reasonable, the appellant misconceives the rationale of *Kramer* and its successors. Appellant argues that, since all property is required to be rendered for taxation, and since anyone can vote in a bond election if he renders any property, no matter how little, the Texas scheme does not discriminate on the basis of wealth or property. Our cases, however, have not held or intimated that only property-based classifications are suspect; in an election of general interest, restrictions on the franchise of any character must meet a stringent test of justification. The Texas scheme creates a classification based on rendering, and it, in effect, disfranchises those who have not rendered their property for taxation in the year of the bond election. Mere reasonableness will therefore not suffice to sustain the classification created in this case.

The appellant has sought to justify the State's rendering requirement solely on the ground that

it extends some protection to property owners, who will bear the direct burden of retiring the city's bonded indebtedness. The *Phoenix* case, however, rejected this analysis of the "direct" imposition of costs on property owners. Even under a system in which the responsibility of retiring the bonded indebtedness falls directly on property taxpayers, all members of the community share in the cost in various ways. Moreover, the construction of a library is not likely to be of special interest to a particular, well defined portion of the electorate. Quite apart from the general interest of the library bond election, the appellant's contention that the rendering requirement imposes no real impediment to participation itself undercuts the claim that it serves the purpose of protecting those who will bear the burden of the debt obligations. If anyone can become eligible to vote by rendering property of even negligible value, the rendering requirement can hardly be said to select voters according to the magnitude of their prospective liability for the city's indebtedness.

. . .

In sum, the Texas rendering requirement erects a classification that impermissibly disfranchises persons otherwise qualified to vote, solely because they have not rendered some property for taxation. . . .

In order to avoid the possibility of upsetting previous bond elections in the state, the District Court declined to give retroactive effect to its judgment. We have followed the same course in our prior cases dealing with voting classifications in bond elections, and we agree with the District Court's determination not to give its ruling retroactive effect. Since the portion of the District Court's judgment invalidating the state constitutional and statutory provisions has been in full effect since that time, and since some local bond elections may subsequently have been conducted in reliance on that judgment, we hold that the District Court's ruling should apply only to those bond authorization elections that were not final on the date of the District Court's judgment. As to other jurisdictions that may have restrictive voting classifications similar to those in Texas, we hold that our decision should not apply where the authorization to issue the securities is legally complete as of the date of this decision.

Affirmed.

Briscoe v. Bell
432 U.S. 404 (1977)

At issue in this case is the construction of §4 of the Voting Rights Act of 1965. . . . While the Act has had a dramatic effect in increasing the participation of black citizens in the electoral process, both as voters and elected officials, Congress has not viewed it as an unqualified success. Most recently, as part of the 1975 amendments to the Voting Rights Act, Congress extended the Act's strong protections to cover language minorities— that is, citizens living in environments where the dominant language is not English. Congress concluded after extensive hearings that there was "overwhelming evidence" showing "the ingenuity and prevalence of discriminatory practices that have been used to dilute the voting strength and otherwise affect the voting rights of language minorities." Concern was particularly expressed over the plight of Mexican-American citizens in Texas, a state that had not been covered by the 1965 Act. This case arises out of Texas' efforts to prevent application of the 1975 amendments to it.

Petitioners, the Governor and Secretary of State of Texas, filed suit in the District Court for the District of Columbia against the Attorney General of the United States and the Director of the Census. These officials are responsible for determining whether the preconditions for application of the Act to particular jurisdictions are met. Petitioners sought interlocutory injunctive relief to restrain official publication of respondents' determinations that Texas was covered by the 1975 amendments, and a "declaratory judgment" determining "how and under what circumstances the determinations . . . should be made."

Respondents opposed the motion for a preliminary injunction, and moved to dismiss the suit for failure to state a claim upon which relief could be granted and for lack of jurisdiction to review determinations made under §4(b). . . . The District Court ruled, however, that this apparent preclusion of judicial review was not absolute. It found that there was jurisdiction to consider the "pure legal question" whether the Executive officials had correctly interpreted an Act of Congress. Reaching the merits of petitioners' claims, the District Court rejected them all and granted summary judgment for respondents.

On appeal to the Court of Appeals for the District of Columbia Circuit, respondents discussed, but did not "take issue with," the jurisdictional ruling of the District Court. The Court of Appeals . . . found that respondents had correctly interpreted the Act, and affirmed the judgment of the District Court.

. . .

For the foregoing reasons, we hold that the courts below erred in finding that they had jurisdiction to review petitioners' claims of erroneous application of §4(b). The only procedure available to Texas to seek termination of Voting Rights Act coverage is a bailout suit under the strict limitations of § 4(a). Accordingly, the decision of the Court of Appeals is vacated, and the case is remanded with instructions to direct the District Court to dismiss the complaint.

Ball v. James
451 U.S. 355 (1981)

This appeal concerns the constitutionality of the system for electing the directors of a large water reclamation district in Arizona, a system which, in essence, limits voting eligibility to landowners and apportions voting power according to the amount of land a voter owns. The case requires us to consider whether the peculiarly narrow function of this local governmental body and the special relationship of one class of citizens to that body releases it from the strict demands of the one-person, one-vote principle of the Equal Protection Clause of the Fourteenth Amendment.

. . .

This lawsuit was brought by a class of registered voters who live within the geographic boundaries of the District and who own either no land or less than an acre of land within the District. The complaint alleged that the District enjoys such governmental powers as the power to condemn land, to sell tax-exempt bonds, and to levy taxes on real property. It also alleged that, because the District sells electricity to virtually half the population of Arizona, and because, through its water operations, it can exercise significant influence on flood control and environmental management within its boundaries, the District's policies and actions have a substantial effect on all people who live within the District, regardless of property ownership. Seeking declaratory and injunctive relief, the appellees claimed that the acreage-based scheme for electing directors of the District violates the Equal Protection Clause of the Fourteenth Amendment.

On cross-motions for summary judgment and on stipulated facts, the District Court for the District of Arizona held the District voting scheme constitutional, and dismissed the complaint. A divided panel of the Court of Appeals for the Ninth Circuit reversed. . . .

. . .

The Court of Appeals was correct in conceiving the question in this case to be whether the purpose of the District is sufficiently specialized and narrow, and whether its activities bear on landowners so disproportionately, as to distinguish the District from those public entities whose more general governmental functions demand application of the *Reynolds* principle. We conclude, however, that, in its efforts to distinguish *Salyer* the Court of Appeals did not apply these criteria correctly to the facts of this case.

. . .

The appellees claim, and the Court of Appeals agreed, that the sheer size of the power operations and the great number of people they affect serve to transform the District into an entity of general governmental power. But no matter how great the number of nonvoting residents buying electricity from the District, the relationship between them and the District's power operations is essentially that between consumers and a business enterprise from which they buy. Nothing in the *Avery*, *Hadley*, or *Salyer* cases suggests that the volume of business or the breadth of economic effect of a venture undertaken by a government entity as an incident of its narrow and primary governmental public function can, of its own weight, subject the entity to the one-person, one-vote requirements of the *Reynolds* case.

. . .

As in the *Salyer* case, we conclude that the voting scheme for the District is constitutional because it bears a reasonable relationship to its statutory objectives. Here, according to the stipulation of the parties, the subscriptions of land which made the Association and then the District possible might well have never occurred had not the subscribing landowners been assured a special voice in the conduct of the District's business. Therefore, as in *Salyer*, the State could rationally limit the vote to landowners. Moreover, Arizona could rationally make the weight of their vote dependent upon the number of acres they own, since that number reasonably reflects the relative risks they incurred as landowners and the distribution of the benefits and the burdens of the District's water operations.

The judgment of the Court of Appeals is reversed, and the case is remanded for further proceedings consistent with this opinion.

Hunter v. Underwood
471 U.S. 222 (1985)

We are required in this case to decide the constitutionality of Art. VIII, §182, of the Alabama Constitution of 1901, which provides for the disenfranchisement of persons convicted of, among other offenses, "any crime . . . involving moral turpitude." Appellees Carmen Edwards, a black, and Victor Underwood, a white, have been blocked from the voter rolls pursuant to §182 by the Boards of Registrars for Montgomery and Jefferson Counties, respectively, because they each have been convicted of presenting a worthless check. In determining that the misdemeanor of presenting a worthless check is a crime involving moral turpitude, the Registrars relied on opinions of the Alabama Attorney General.

. . .

On appeal, the Court of Appeals for the Eleventh Circuit reversed. . . .

. . .

Section 182 on its face is racially neutral, applying equally to anyone convicted of one of the enumerated crimes or a crime falling within one of the catchall provisions. Appellee Edwards nonetheless claims that the provision has had a racially discriminatory impact. The District Court made no finding on this claim, but the Court of Appeals implicitly found the evidence of discriminatory impact indisputable. . . .

So far as we can tell, the impact of the provision has not been contested, and we can find no evidence in the record below or in the briefs and oral argument in this Court that would undermine this finding by the Court of Appeals.

. . .

. . . [T]he enactment of §182 violated the Fourteenth Amendment, and the Tenth Amendment cannot save legislation prohibited by the subsequently enacted Fourteenth Amendment. The single remaining question is whether §182 is excepted from the operation of the Equal Protection Clause of §1 of the Fourteenth Amendment by the "other crime" provision of §2 of that Amendment. Without again considering the implicit authorization of §2 to deny the vote to citizens "for participation in rebellion, or other crime," we are confident that §2 was not designed to permit the purposeful racial discrimination attending the enactment and operation of §182 which otherwise violates §1 of the Fourteenth Amendment. . . .

The judgment of the Court of Appeals is affirmed.

City of Pleasant Grove v. United States
479 U.S. 462 (1987)

Appellant, Pleasant Grove, a city in Alabama that until recently had an all-white population, is covered by §5 of the Voting Rights Act of 1965, and accordingly must seek preclearance before instituting any change in a standard, practice, or procedure affecting voting. Appellant unsuccessfully sought preclearance by the Attorney General for the annexation of two parcels of land, one vacant and the other inhabited by a few whites. Appellant also failed to convince a three-judge District Court that the annexations did not have the purpose of abridging or denying the right to vote on account of race. . . .

· · ·

It is quite plausible to see appellant's annexation of the Glasgow and Western Additions as motivated, in part, by the impermissible purpose of minimizing future black voting strength. Common sense teaches that appellant cannot indefinitely stave off the influx of black residents and voters—indeed, the process of integration, long overdue, has already begun. One means of thwarting this process is to provide for the growth of a monolithic white voting block, thereby effectively diluting the black vote in advance. This is just as impermissible a purpose as the dilution of present black voting strength. To hold otherwise would make appellant's extraordinary success in resisting integration thus far a shield for further resistance. Nothing could be further from the purposes of the Voting Rights Act.

In light of the record before us, we are not left with the definite and firm conviction that the District Court was mistaken either in finding that the refusal to annex the Highlands was racially motivated or that there was insufficient proof that the annexation of the Glasgow and Western Additions did not have a purpose forbidden by §5. Those findings are not, therefore, clearly erroneous.

The judgment of the District Court is accordingly affirmed.

Chisom v. Roemer
501 U.S. 380 (1991)

Petitioners in No. 90–757 represent a class of approximately 135,000 black registered voters in Orleans Parish, Louisiana. They brought this action against the Governor and other state officials (respondents) to challenge the method of electing justices of the Louisiana Supreme Court from the New Orleans area. The United States, petitioner in No. 90–1032, intervened to support the claims advanced by the plaintiff class.

The Louisiana Supreme Court consists of seven justices, five of whom are elected from five single-member Supreme Court Districts, and two of whom are elected from one multi-member Supreme Court District. Each of the seven members of the court must be a resident of the district from which he or she is elected and must have resided there for at least two years prior to election. Each of the justices on the Louisiana Supreme Court serves a term of 10 years. The one multi-member district, the First Supreme Court District, consists of the parishes of Orleans, St. Bernard, Plaquemines, and Jefferson. Orleans Parish contains about half of the population of the First Supreme Court District and about half of the registered voters in that district. More than one-half of the registered voters of Orleans Parish are black, whereas more than three-fourths of the registered voters in the other three parishes are white.

· · ·

The District Court granted respondents' motion to dismiss the complaint. It held that the constitutional claims were insufficient because the complaint did not adequately allege a specific intent to discriminate. . . . The court concluded that, because judges are not "representatives," judicial elections are not covered by §2.

The Court of Appeals for the Fifth Circuit reversed. . . .

After the case was remanded to the District Court, the United States filed a complaint in intervention in which it alleged that the use of a multi-member district to elect two members of the Louisiana Supreme Court is a "standard, practice or procedure" that "results in a denial or abridgment of the right to vote on account of race or color in violation of Section 2 of the Voting Rights Act." After a nonjury trial, however, the District Court concluded that the evidence did not establish a violation of §2. . . . The District Court also dismissed the constitutional claims. Petitioners and the United States appealed. While their appeal was pending, the Fifth Circuit, sitting en banc in another case, held that judicial elections were not covered under §2 of the Act. . . .

. . .

Any abridgment of the opportunity of members of a protected class to participate in the political process inevitably impairs their ability to influence the outcome of an election. As the statute is written, however, the inability to elect representatives of their choice is not sufficient to establish a violation unless, under the totality of the circumstances, it can also be said that the members of the protected class have less opportunity to participate in the political process. The statute does not create two separate and distinct rights. Subsection (a) covers every application of a qualification, standard, practice, or procedure that results in a denial or abridgement of "the right" to vote. The singular form is also used in subsection (b) when referring to an injury to members of the protected class who have less "opportunity" than others "to participate in the political process and to elect representatives of their choice." It would distort the plain meaning

of the sentence to substitute the word "or" for the word "and." . . .

. . .

. . . The word "representative" refers to someone who has prevailed in a popular election, whereas the word "candidate" refers to someone who is seeking an office. Thus, a candidate is nominated, not elected. When Congress used "candidate" in other parts of the statute, it did so precisely because it was referring to people who were aspirants for an office.

. . .

The fundamental tension between the ideal character of the judicial office and the real world of electoral politics cannot be resolved by crediting judges with total indifference to the popular will while simultaneously requiring them to run for elected office. When each of several members of a court must be a resident of a separate district, and must be elected by the voters of that district, it seems both reasonable and realistic to characterize the winners as representatives of that district. . . . Louisiana could, of course, exclude its judiciary from the coverage of the Voting Rights Act by changing to a system in which judges are appointed, and in that way, it could enable its judges to be indifferent to popular opinion. . . .

. . .

The judgment of the Court of Appeals is reversed and the case is remanded for further proceedings consistent with this opinion.

Burdick v. Takushi
504 U.S. 428 (1992)

The issue in this case is whether Hawaii's prohibition on write-in voting unreasonably infringes upon its citizens' rights under the First and Fourteenth Amendments. Petitioner contends that the constitution requires Hawaii to provide for the casting, tabulation, and publication of write-in votes. The Court of Appeals for the Ninth Circuit disagreed, holding that the prohibition, taken as part of the state's comprehensive election scheme, does not impermissibly burden the right to vote. . . .

Petitioner is a registered voter in the city and county of Honolulu. In 1986, only one candidate filed nominating papers to run for the seat representing petitioner's district in the Hawaii House of Representatives. Petitioner wrote to state officials inquiring about Hawaii's write-in voting policy, and received a copy of an opinion letter issued by the Hawaii Attorney General's Office stating that the state's election law made no provision for write-in voting.

Petitioner then filed this lawsuit, claiming that he wished to vote in the primary and general elections for a person who had not filed nominating papers, and that he wished to vote in future elections for other persons whose names were not and might not appear on the ballot. The United States District Court for the District of Hawaii concluded that the ban on write-in voting violated petitioner's First Amendment right of expression and association, and entered a preliminary injunction ordering respondents to provide for the casting and tallying of write-in votes in the November 1986 general election. The District Court denied a stay pending appeal.

The Court of Appeals entered the stay and vacated the judgment of the District Court, reasoning that consideration of the federal constitutional question raised by petitioner was premature, because

> neither the plain language of Hawaii statutes nor any definitive judicial interpretation of those statutes establishes that the Hawaii legislature has enacted a ban on write-in voting.

Accordingly, the Court of Appeals ordered the District Court to abstain, until state courts had determined whether Hawaii's election laws permitted write-in voting.

On remand, the District Court certified the following three questions to the Supreme Court of Hawaii:

> (1) Does the Constitution of the State of Hawaii require Hawaii's election officials to permit the casting of write-in votes and require Hawaii's election officials to count and publish write-in votes?
> (2) Do Hawaii's election laws require Hawaii's election officials to permit the casting of write-in votes and require Hawaii's election officials to count and publish write-in votes?
> (3) Do Hawaii's election laws permit, but not require, Hawaii's election officials to allow voters to cast write-in votes and to count and publish write-in votes?

Hawaii's high court answered "No" to all three questions, holding that Hawaii's election laws barred write-in voting, and that these measures were consistent with the state's constitution. The United States District Court then granted petitioner's renewed motion for summary judgment and injunctive relief, but entered a stay pending appeal.

The Court of Appeals again reversed, holding that Hawaii was not required to provide for write-in votes. . . . In so ruling, the Ninth Circuit expressly declined to follow an earlier decision regarding write-in voting by the Court of Appeals for the Fourth Circuit. . . .

. . .

There is no doubt that the Hawaii election laws, like all election regulations, have an impact on the right to vote, but it can hardly be said that the laws at issue here unconstitutionally limit access to the ballot by party or independent candidates or unreasonably interfere with the right of voters to associate and have candidates of their choice placed on the ballot. Indeed, petitioners understandably do not challenge the manner in which the State regulates candidate access to the ballot.

To obtain a position on the November general election ballot, a candidate must participate in Hawaii's open primary, "in which all registered voters may choose in which party primary to vote." The State provides three mechanisms through which a voter's candidate of choice may appear on the primary ballot.

. . .

Although Hawaii makes no provision for write-in voting in its primary or general elections, the system outlined above provides for easy access to the ballot until the cutoff date for the filing of nominating petitions, two months before the primary. Consequently, any burden on voters' freedom of choice and association is borne only by those who fail to identify their candidate of choice until days before the primary. But in *Storer v. Brown*, we gave little weight to "the interest the candidate and his supporters may have in making a late, rather than an early, decision to seek independent ballot status." We think the same reasoning applies here, and therefore conclude that any burden imposed by Hawaii's write-in vote prohibition is a very limited one. . . .

Because he has characterized this as a voting rights, rather than ballot access, case, petitioner submits that the write-in prohibition deprives him of the opportunity to cast a meaningful ballot, conditions his electoral participation upon the waiver of his First Amendment right to remain free from espousing positions that he does not support, and discriminates against him based on the content of

the message he seeks to convey through his vote. At bottom, he claims that he is entitled to cast and Hawaii required to count a "protest vote" for Donald Duck, and that any impediment to this asserted "right" is unconstitutional.

Petitioner's argument is based on two flawed premises. First, in *Bullock v. Carter*, we minimized the extent to which voting rights cases are distinguishable from ballot access cases, stating that "the rights of voters and the rights of candidates do not lend themselves to neat separation." Second, the function of the election process is "to winnow out and finally reject all but the chosen candidates," not to provide a means of giving vent to "short-range political goals, pique, or personal quarrel[s]." Attributing to elections a more generalized expressive function would undermine the ability of states to operate elections fairly and efficiently.

Accordingly, we have repeatedly upheld reasonable, politically neutral regulations that have the effect of channeling expressive activity at the polls. Petitioner offers no persuasive reason to depart from these precedents. Reasonable regulation of elections does not require voters to espouse positions that they do not support; it does require them to act in a timely fashion if they wish to express their views in the voting booth. And there is nothing content-based about a flat ban on all forms of write-in ballots.

. . .

We turn next to the interests asserted by Hawaii to justify the burden imposed by its prohibition of write-in voting. Because we have already concluded that the burden is slight, the State need not establish a compelling interest to tip the constitutional scales in its direction. Here, the State's interests outweigh petitioner's limited interest in waiting until the eleventh hour to choose his preferred candidate.

Hawaii's interest in "avoid[ing] the possibility of unrestrained factionalism at the general election," provides adequate justification for its ban on write-in voting in November. The primary election is "an integral part of the entire election process," and the State is within its rights to reserve "[t]he general election ballot . . . for major struggles . . . [and] not a forum for continuing intraparty feuds." The prohibition on write-in voting is a legitimate means of averting divisive sore-loser candidacies. Hawaii further promotes the two-stage, primary-general election process of winnowing out candidates, by permitting the unopposed victors in certain primaries to be designated office holders. This focuses the attention of voters upon contested races in the general election. This would not be possible, absent the write-in voting ban.

Hawaii also asserts that its ban on write-in voting at the primary stage is necessary to guard against "party raiding." Party raiding is generally defined as "the organized switching of blocs of voters from one party to another in order to manipulate the outcome of the other party's primary election." Petitioner suggests that, because Hawaii conducts an open primary, this is not a cognizable interest. We disagree. While voters may vote on any ticket in Hawaii's primary, the State requires that party candidates be "member[s] of the party," and prohibits candidates from filing "nomination papers both as a party candidate and as a nonpartisan candidate." Hawaii's system could easily be circumvented in a party primary election by mounting a write-in campaign for a person who had not filed in time or who had never intended to run for election. It could also be frustrated at the general election by permitting write-in votes for a loser in a party primary or for an independent who had failed to

get sufficient votes to make the general election ballot. The State has a legitimate interest in preventing these sorts of maneuvers, and the write-in voting ban is a reasonable way of accomplishing this goal.

. . .

. . . We think that Hawaii's prohibition on write-in voting, considered as part of an electoral scheme that provides constitutionally sufficient ballot access, does not impose an unconstitutional burden upon the First and Fourteenth Amendment rights of the State's voters. Accordingly, the judgment of the Court of Appeals is affirmed.

Young v. Fordice
520 U.S. 273 (1997)

In 1993, Congress enacted the National Voter Registration Act of 1993 (NVRA), to take effect for states like Mississippi on January 1, 1995. The NVRA requires states to provide simplified systems for registering to vote in federal elections, i.e., elections for federal officials, such as the President, congressional Representatives, and United States Senators. The states must provide a system for voter registration by mail, a system for voter registration at various state offices (including those that provide "public assistance" and those that provide services to people with disabilities), and, particularly important, a system for voter registration on a driver's license application. The NVRA specifies various details about how these systems must work, including, for example, the type of information that states can require on a voter registration form. It also imposes requirements about just when, and how, states may remove people from the federal voter rolls. The NVRA adds that it does not "supersede, restrict or limit the application of the Voting Rights

Act of 1965," and that it does not "authoriz[e] or requir[e] conduct that is prohibited by the Voting Rights Act of 1965."

. . .

The case before us concerns three different Mississippi voting registration systems: the first system, which we shall call the "Old System," is that used by Mississippi before it tried to comply with the NVRA. The second system, the "Provisional Plan," is a system aimed at NVRA compliance, which Mississippi tried to implement for about six weeks between January 1, 1995, and February 10, 1995. The third system, the "New System," is the system that Mississippi put into place after February 10, 1995, in a further effort to comply with the NVRA. We shall briefly explain the relevant features of each system.

Before 1995, Mississippi administered a voting registration system, which, like the systems of most states, provided for a single registration that allowed the registrant to vote in both federal elections and state elections (i.e., elections for state and local offices). Under Mississippi law, a citizen could register to vote either by appearing personally at a county or municipal clerk's office or at other locations (such as polling places) that the clerk or his deputy visited to register people to vote. Mississippi citizens could also register by obtaining a mail-in registration form available at driver's license agencies, public schools, and public libraries, among other places, and mailing it back to the clerk. The law set forth various details, requiring, for example, that a mail-in application contain the name and address of the voter and that it be attested to by a witness (although there is some dispute between the parties about whether an application could be rejected for failing to have the witness's signature). State law also allowed

county registration officials to purge voters from the rolls if they had not voted in four years.

In late 1994, the Mississippi Secretary of State, with the help of an NVRA implementation committee, prepared a series of voter registration changes designed to ensure compliance with the NVRA. The new voter registration application that was incorporated into the driver's license form, for example, did not require that the registrant repeat his or her address, nor did it require an attesting witness. The Secretary of State provided information and instructions about those changes to voter registration officials and state agency personnel throughout the state. The Secretary of State and the implementing committee assumed—and recommended—that the Mississippi Legislature would change state law insofar as that law might prevent a valid registration under the NVRA's provisions from counting as a valid registration for a state or local election. And, on that assumption at least one official in the Secretary of State's office told state election officials to place the name of any new valid applicant under the NVRA on a list that would permit him or her to vote in state, as well as in federal, elections.

Using this Provisional Plan, at least some Mississippi officials registered as many as 4,000 voters between January 1, 1995, and February 10, 1995. On January 25, however, the state legislature tabled a bill that would have made NVRA registrations valid for all elections in Mississippi (by, for example, allowing applicants at driver's license and other agencies to register on the spot, without having to mail in the application themselves, by eliminating the attesting witness' signature on the mail-in application, and by eliminating the optional four-year purge of nonvoting registrants, replacing it with other methods for maintaining up-to-date voter rolls.) Because of the legislature's failure to change the Old System's requirements for state election registration, the state Attorney General concluded that Provisional Plan registrations that did not meet Old System requirements would not work, under state law, as registration for state elections. State officials notified voter registration officials throughout the state; and they, in turn, were asked to help notify the 4,000 registrants that they were not registered to vote in state or local elections.

On February 10, 1995, Mississippi began to use what we shall call the New System. That system consists of the changes that its Provisional Plan set forth—but as applied only to registration for federal elections. Mississippi maintains the Old System as the only method for registration for state elections, and as one set of methods to register for federal elections. All other states, we are told, have modified their voter registration rules so that NVRA registration registers voters for both federal and state elections.

This case arises out of efforts by Mississippi to preclear, under §5 of the VRA, changes that it made to comply with the NVRA. In December, 1994, Mississippi submitted to the United States Attorney General a list of NVRA-implementing changes that it then intended to make. That submission essentially described what we have called the Provisional Plan. The submission contained numerous administrative changes described in two booklets called *The National Voter Registration Act*, and the *Mississippi Agency Voter Registration Procedures Manual*. It also included the proposed state legislation necessary to make the Provisional Plan work for state elections as well. Mississippi requested preclearance. On February 1, 1995, the Department of Justice wrote to Mississippi that the Attorney General did "not in-

terpose any objection to the specified changes" thereby preclearing Mississippi's submitted changes.

. . . [O]n January 25, about one week before the Attorney General precleared the proposed changes, the state legislature had tabled the proposed legislation needed to make those changes effective for state elections. On February 10, 10 days after the Department precleared the proposed changes, Mississippi officials wrote to voter registration officials around the state, telling them that it "appears unlikely that the Legislature will" revive the tabled bill; that the Provisional Plan's registration would therefore not work for state elections; that they should write—or help the Secretary of State write—to tell those who had registered under that system that they were not registered to vote in state elections; that they should make certain future registrants understand that they would need to register separately to be eligible to vote in state, as well as federal, elections; and that they should develop a system for distinguishing between NVRA and other voters.

On February 16, about two weeks after the Department of Justice sent its preclearance letter, the Department of Justice wrote another letter to Mississippi, which letter made clear that the Department did not believe its earlier preclearance had precleared what it now saw as a new plan. The Department asked the state to submit what it called this new "dual voter registration and purge system" for preclearance. . . .

On April 20, 1995, four private citizens (appellants) brought this lawsuit before a three-judge District Court. They claimed that Mississippi and its officials had implemented changes in its registration system without preclearance in violation of §5. The United States, which is an amicus curiae here, brought a similar lawsuit, and the two actions were consolidated.

The three-judge District Court granted Mississippi's motion for summary judgment. It considered the plaintiffs' basic claim, namely that the differences between the Provisional Plan and the New System amounted to a change in the administration of Mississippi's voting registration practice, which change had not been precleared. The court rejected this argument on the ground that the Provisional Plan was a misapplication of state law, never ratified by the state. Since the differences between the New System and the Provisional Plan were attributable to the state's attempt to correct this misapplication of state law, the court held, those differences were not changes subject to preclearance.

The court also considered a different question, namely, whether the New System differed from the Old System; and whether Mississippi had precleared all the changes that the New System made in the Old. The court held that the Department had (on February 1) precleared the administrative changes needed to implement the NVRA. The court also held that Mississippi did not need to preclear its failure to pass a law that would have permitted NVRA registration to count for state, as well as for federal, elections, as the distinction between state and federal elections was due to the NVRA's own provisions, not to the state's changes in voting practices.

. . .

We hold that Mississippi has not precleared, and must preclear, the "practices and procedures" that it sought to administer on and after February 10, 1995. The decision of the District Court is reversed, and the case remanded with instructions for the District Court to enter an order enjoining further use of Mississippi's unprecleared changes as appropriate. . . .

Rice v. Cayetano
528 U.S. 495 (2000)

. . .

The Hawaiian Constitution limits the right to vote for nine trustees chosen in a statewide election. The trustees compose the governing authority of a state agency known as the Office of Hawaiian Affairs, or OHA. The agency administers programs designed for the benefit of two subclasses of the Hawaiian citizenry. The smaller class comprises those designated as "native Hawaiians," defined by statute, with certain supplementary language later set out in full, as descendants of not less than one-half part of the races inhabiting the Hawaiian Islands prior to 1778. The second, larger class of persons benefited by OHA programs is "Hawaiians," defined to be, with refinements contained in the statute we later quote, those persons who are descendants of people inhabiting the Hawaiian Islands in 1778. The right to vote for trustees is limited to "Hawaiians," the second, larger class of persons, which of course includes the smaller class of "native Hawaiians."

Petitioner Rice, a citizen of Hawaii and thus himself a Hawaiian in a well-accepted sense of the term, does not have the requisite ancestry even for the larger class. He is not, then, a "Hawaiian" in terms of the statute; so he may not vote in the trustee election. The issue presented by this case is whether Rice may be so barred. . . .

. . .

Petitioner Harold Rice is a citizen of Hawaii and a descendant of pre-annexation residents of the islands. He is not . . . a descendant of pre-1778 natives, and so he is neither "native—Hawaiian" nor "Hawaiian" as defined by the statute. Rice applied in March 1996 to vote in the elections for OHA trustees. To register to vote for the office of trustee he was required to attest: "I am also Hawaiian and desire to register to vote in OHA elections." Rice marked through the words "am also Hawaiian and," then checked the form "yes." The State denied his application.

Rice sued Benjamin Cayetano, the Governor of Hawaii, in the United States District Court for the District of Hawaii. (The Governor was sued in his official capacity, and the Attorney General of Hawaii defends the challenged enactments. We refer to the respondent as "the State.") Rice contested his exclusion from voting in elections for OHA trustees and from voting in a special election relating to native Hawaiian sovereignty which was held in August 1996. After the District Court rejected the latter challenge, the parties moved for summary judgment on the claim that the Fourteenth and Fifteenth Amendments to the United States Constitution invalidate the law excluding Rice from the OHA trustee elections.

The District Court granted summary judgment to the State. Surveying the history of the islands and their people, the District Court determined that Congress and the State of Hawaii have recognized a guardian-ward relationship with the native Hawaiians, which the court found analogous to the relationship between the United States and the Indian tribes. On this premise, the court examined the voting qualification with the latitude that we have applied to legislation passed pursuant to Congress' power over Indian affairs. Finding that the electoral scheme was "rationally related to the State's responsibility under the Admission Act to utilize a portion of the proceeds from the §5(b) lands for the betterment of Native Hawaiians," the District Court held that the voting restriction did not violate the Constitution's ban on racial classifications.

The Court of Appeals affirmed. . . .

. . .

The purpose and command of the Fifteenth Amendment are set forth in language both explicit and comprehensive. The national government and the states may not violate a fundamental principle: They may not deny or abridge the right to vote on account of race. Color and previous condition of servitude, too, are forbidden criteria or classifications, though it is unnecessary to consider them in the present case.

. . .

The design of the amendment is to reaffirm the equality of races at the most basic level of the democratic process, the exercise of the voting franchise. A resolve so absolute required language as simple in command as it was comprehensive in reach. Fundamental in purpose and effect and self-executing in operation, the amendment prohibits all provisions denying or abridging the voting franchise of any citizen or class of citizens on the basis of race. "[B]y the inherent power of the Amendment the word white disappeared" from our voting laws, bringing those who had been excluded by reason of race within "the generic grant of suffrage made by the State." The Court has acknowledged the amendment's mandate of neutrality in straightforward terms: "If citizens of one race having certain qualifications are permitted by law to vote, those of another having the same qualifications must be. Previous to this amendment, there was no constitutional guaranty against this discrimination: now there is."

. . .

Hawaii's argument fails on more essential grounds. The State's position rests, in the end, on the demeaning premise that citizens of a particular race are somehow more qualified than others to vote on certain matters. That reasoning attacks the central meaning of the Fifteenth Amendment. The amendment applies to "any election in which

public issues are decided or public officials selected." There is no room under the amendment
for the concept that the right to vote in a particular election can be allocated based on race. Race
cannot qualify some and disqualify others from
full participation in our democracy. All citizens,
regardless of race, have an interest in selecting
officials who make policies on their behalf, even
if those policies will affect some groups more
than others. Under the Fifteenth Amendment voters are treated not as members of a distinct race
but as members of the whole citizenry. Hawaii
may not assume, based on race, that petitioner or
any other of its citizens will not cast a principled
vote. To accept the position advanced by the
State would give rise to the same indignities,
and the same resulting tensions and animosities,
the amendment was designed to eliminate. The
voting restriction under review is prohibited by
the Fifteenth Amendment.

When the culture and way of life of a people
are all but engulfed by a history beyond their
control, their sense of loss may extend down
through generations; and their dismay may be
shared by many members of the larger community. As the State of Hawaii attempts to address
these realities, it must, as always, seek the political consensus that begins with a sense of shared
purpose. One of the necessary beginning points
is this principle: The Constitution of the United
States, too, has become the heritage of all the
citizens of Hawaii.

In this case the Fifteenth Amendment invalidates the electoral qualification based on ancestry. The judgment of the Court of Appeals for the
Ninth Circuit is reversed.

2
Poll Taxes and Literacy Tests

Poll taxes and literacy tests as qualifications for voting were ultimately declared unconstitutional by the Supreme Court.

Breedlove v. Suttles
302 U.S. 277 (1937)

A Georgia statute provides that there shall be levied and collected each year from every inhabitant of the state between the ages of 21 and 60 a poll tax of one dollar, but that the tax shall not be demanded from the blind or from females who do not register for voting. The state constitution declares that to entitle a person to register and vote at any election he shall have paid all poll taxes that he may have had opportunity to pay agreeably to law. The form of oath prescribed to qualify an elector contains a clause declaring compliance with that requirement. Tax collectors may not allow any person to register for voting unless satisfied that his poll taxes have been paid. Appellant brought this suit in the superior court of Fulton county to have the clause of the constitution and the statutory provisions above mentioned declared repugnant to various provisions of the Federal Constitution and to compel appellee to allow him to register for voting without payment of poll taxes. The court dismissed his petition. The state Supreme Court affirmed.

The pertinent facts alleged in the petition are these. [On] March 16, 1936, appellant, a white male citizen 28 years old, applied to appellee to register him for voting for federal and state officers at primary and general elections. He informed appellee he had neither made poll tax returns nor paid any poll taxes and had not registered to vote because a receipt for poll taxes and an oath that he had paid them are prerequisites to registration. He demanded that appellee administer the oath, omitting the part declaring payment of poll taxes, and allow him to register. Appellee refused.

Appellant maintains that the provisions in question are repugnant to the equal protection clause and the privileges and immunities clause of the Fourteenth Amendment and to the Nineteenth Amendment.

. . .

Levy by the poll has long been a familiar form of taxation, much used in some countries and to a considerable extent here, at first in the colonies and later in the states. To prevent burdens deemed grievous and oppressive, the constitutions of some states prohibit or limit poll taxes. That of Georgia prevents more than a dollar a year. Poll taxes are laid upon persons without regard to their occupations or property to raise money for the support of government or some more specific end. The equal protection clause does not require absolute equality. While possible by statutory declaration to levy a poll tax upon every inhabitant of whatsoever sex, age or condition, collection from all would be impossible for always there are many too poor to pay. Attempt equally to en-force such a measure would justify condemna-tion of the tax as harsh and unjust. Collection from minors would be to put the burden upon their fa-thers or others upon whom they depend for sup-port. It is not unreasonable to exclude them from the class taxed.

. . . The burden laid upon appellant is precisely that put upon other men. The rate is a dollar a year, commencing at 21 and ending at 60 years of age.

The tax being upon persons, women may be exempted on the basis of special considerations to which they are naturally entitled. In view of burdens necessarily borne by them for the pres-ervation of the race, the state reasonably may exempt them from poll taxes. The laws of Geor-gia declare the husband to be the head of the fam-ily and the wife to be subject to him. To subject her to the levy would be to add to his burden. Moreover, Georgia poll taxes are laid to raise money for educational purposes, and it is the father's duty to provide for education of the chil-dren. Discrimination in favor of all women be-ing permissible, appellant may not complain because the tax is laid only upon some or object to registration of women without payment of taxes for previous years.

Payment as a prerequisite is not required for the purpose of denying or abridging the privi-lege of voting. . . . Exaction of payment before registration undoubtedly serves to aid collection from electors desiring to vote, but that use of the state's power is not prevented by the Federal Constitution.

To make payment of poll taxes a prerequisite of voting is not to deny any privilege or immu-nity protected by the Fourteenth Amendment. Privilege of voting is not derived from the United States, but is conferred by the state and, save as

restrained by the Fifteenth and Nineteenth Amendments and other provisions of the Federal Constitution, the state may condition suffrage as it deems appropriate. The privileges and immu-nities protected are only those that arise from the Constitution and laws of the United States and not those that spring from other sources.

The Nineteenth Amendment . . . applies to men and women alike and by its own force supersedes inconsistent measures, whether federal or state. Its purpose is not to regulate the levy or collec-tion of taxes. . . . The payment of poll taxes as a prerequisite to voting is a familiar and reason-able regulation long enforced in many states and for more than a century in Georgia. That mea-sure reasonably may be deemed essential to that form of levy. Imposition without enforcement would be futile. Power to levy and power to col-lect are equally necessary. And, by the exaction of payment before registration, the right to vote is neither denied nor abridged on account of sex. It is fanciful to suggest that the Georgia law is a mere disguise under which to deny or abridge the right of men to vote on account of their sex. The challenged enactment is not repugnant to the Nineteenth Amendment.

Affirmed.

Lane v. Wilson
307 U.S. 268 (1939)

The case is here . . . to review the judgment of the Circuit Court of Appeals for the Tenth Cir-cuit affirming that of the United States District Court for the Eastern District of Oklahoma, en-tered upon a directed verdict in favor of the de-fendants. The action was . . . brought under Section 1979 of the Revised Statutes, by a col-ored citizen claiming discriminatory treatment resulting from electoral legislation of Oklahoma, in violation of the Fifteenth Amendment. . . .

The constitution under which Oklahoma was admitted into the Union regulated the suffrage by Article III, whereby its "qualified electors" were to be "citizens of the State . . . who are over the age of twenty-one years" with disqualifications in the case of felons, paupers and lunatics. Soon after its admission the suffrage provisions of the Oklahoma Constitution were radically amended by the addition of a literacy test from which white voters were in effect relieved through the operation of a "grandfather clause." The clause was stricken down by this Court as violative of the prohibition against discrimination "on account of race, color, or previous condition of servitude" of the Fifteenth Amendment. This outlawry occurred on June 21, 1915. In the meantime the Oklahoma general election of 1914 had been based on the offending "grandfather clause." After the invalidation of that clause a special session of the Oklahoma legislature enacted a new scheme for registration as a prerequisite to voting. . . . Those who had voted in the general election of 1914, automatically remained qualified voters. The new registration requirements affected only others. These had to apply for registration between April 30, 1916 and May 11, 1916, if qualified at that time, with an extension to June 30, 1916, given only to those "absent from the county . . . during such period of time, or . . . prevented by sickness or unavoidable misfortune from registering . . . within such time." The crux of the present controversy is the validity of this registration scheme, with its dividing line between white citizens who had voted under the "grandfather clause" immunity . . . and citizens who were outside it, and the not more than 12 days as the normal period of registration for the theretofore proscribed class.

The petitioner, a colored citizen of Oklahoma, who was the plaintiff below and will hereafter be referred to as such, sued three county election officials for declining to register him on October 17, 1934. He was qualified for registration in 1916 but did not then get on the registration list. The evidence is in conflict whether he presented himself in that year for registration and, if so, under what circumstances registration was denied him. The fact is that plaintiff did not get on the register in 1916. Under the terms of the statute he thereby permanently lost the right to register and hence the right to vote. The central claim of plaintiff is that of the unconstitutionality of Section 5654. The defendants joined issue on this claim and further insisted that if there had been illegality in a denial of the plaintiff's right to registration, his proper recourse was to the courts of Oklahoma. The District Court took the case from the jury and its action was affirmed by the Circuit Court of Appeals. It found no proof of discrimination against negroes in the administration of Section 5654 and denied that the legislation was in conflict with the Fifteenth Amendment.

The defendants urge two bars to the plaintiff's recovery, apart from the constitutional validity of Section 5654. They say that on the plaintiff's own assumption of its invalidity, there is no Oklahoma statute under which he could register and therefore no right to registration has been denied. Secondly, they argue that the state procedure for determining claims of discrimination must be employed before invoking a federal judiciary. These contentions will be considered first, for the disposition of a constitutional question must be reserved to the last.

. . .

. . . The Fifteenth Amendment secures freedom from discrimination on account of race in matters affecting the franchise. Whosoever "under color of any statute" subjects another to such discrimination thereby deprives him of what the Fifteenth Amendment secures and, under Section 1979 becomes "liable to the party injured in an action at law." The theory of the plaintiff's action is that the defendants, acting under color of Section 5654, did discriminate against him because that Section inherently operates discriminatorily. If this claim is sustained his right to sue under Section 1979 follows. The basis of this action is inequality of treatment though under color of law, not denial of the right to vote.

. . .

We therefore cannot avoid passing on the merits of plaintiff's constitutional claims. The reach of the Fifteenth Amendment against contrivances by a state to thwart equality in the enjoyment of the right to vote by citizens of the United States regardless of race or color, has been amply expounded by prior decisions. The amendment nullifies sophisticated as well as simple-minded modes of discrimination. It hits onerous procedural requirements which effectively handicap exercise of the franchise by the colored race although the abstract right to vote may remain unrestricted as to race. . . . We are compelled to conclude, however reluctantly, that the legislation of 1916 partakes too much of the infirmity of the "grandfather clause" to be able to survive.

Section 5652 of the Oklahoma statutes makes registration a prerequisite to voting. . . . All citizens who were qualified to vote in 1916 but had not voted in 1914 were required to register, save in the exceptional circumstances, between April 30 and May 11, 1916, and in default of such registration were perpetually disenfranchised. Exemption from this onerous provision was enjoyed by all who had registered in 1914. . . . Unfair discrimination was . . . retained by automatically granting voting privileges for life to the white citizens whom the constitutional "grandfather clause" had sheltered while subjecting colored citizens to a new burden. The practical effect of the 1916 legislation was to accord to the members of the negro race who had been discriminated against in the outlawed registration system of 1914, not more than 12 days within which to reassert constitutional rights. . . . We believe that the opportunity thus given negro voters to free themselves from the effects of discrimination to which they should never have been subjected was too *cabined* and confined. The restrictions imposed must be judged with reference to those for whom they were designed. It must be remembered that we are dealing with a body of citizens lacking the habits and traditions of political independence and otherwise living in circumstances which do not encourage initiative and enterprise. To be sure, in exceptional cases a supplemental period was available. But the narrow basis of the supplemental registration, the very brief normal period of relief for the persons and purposes in question, the practical difficulties, of which the record in this case gives glimpses, inevitable in the administration of such strict registration provisions, leave no escape from the conclusion that the means chosen as substitutes for the invalidated "grandfather clause" were themselves invalid under the Fifteenth Amendment. They operated unfairly against the very class on whose behalf the protection of the Constitution was here successfully invoked.

The judgment of the Circuit Court of Appeals must, therefore, be reversed and the cause remanded to the District Court for further proceedings in accordance with this opinion.

*Lassiter v. Northampton Election
Board*
360 U.S. 45 (1959)

. . . Appellant, a Negro citizen of North Carolina,
sued to have the literacy test for voters prescribed
by that State declared unconstitutional and void.
A three-judge court . . . noted that the literacy
test was part of a provision of the North Carolina
Constitution that also included a grandfather
clause. It said that the grandfather clause plainly
would be unconstitutional. . . . It noted, however,
that the North Carolina statute which enforced
the registration requirements contained in the
state constitution had been superseded by a 1957
Act and that the 1957 Act does not contain the
grandfather clause or any reference to it. But being uncertain as to the significance of the 1957
Act and deeming it wise to have all administrative remedies under that Act exhausted before the
federal court acted, it stayed its action, retaining
jurisdiction for a reasonable time to enable appellant to exhaust her administrative remedies and
obtain from the state courts an interpretation of
the statute in light of the state constitution.

Thereupon the instant case was commenced.
It started as an administrative proceeding. Appellant applied for registration as a voter. Her
registration was denied by the registrar because
she refused to submit to a literacy test as required
by the North Carolina statute. She appealed to
the County Board of Elections. On the de novo
hearing before that Board appellant again refused
to take the literacy test and she was again denied
registration for that reason. She appealed to the
Superior Court which sustained the Board against
the claim that the requirement of the literacy test
violated the Fourteenth, Fifteenth, and Seventeenth Amendments of the Federal Constitution.
Preserving her federal question, she appealed to

the North Carolina Supreme Court which affirmed the lower court. . . .

The literacy test is a part of 4 of Art. VI of the
North Carolina Constitution. That test is contained in the first sentence of 4. The second sentence contains a so-called grandfather clause. The
entire 4 reads as follows:

> Every person presenting himself for registration
> shall be able to read and write any section of the
> Constitution in the English language. But no male
> person who was, on January 1, 1867, or at any time
> prior thereto, entitled to vote under the laws of any
> state in the United States wherein he then resided,
> and no lineal descendant of any such person, shall
> be denied the right to register and vote at any elec-
> tion in this State by reason of his failure to possess
> the educational qualifications herein prescribed:
> Provided, he shall have registered in accordance
> with the terms of this section prior to December 1,
> 1908. The General Assembly shall provide for the
> registration of all persons entitled to vote without
> the educational qualifications herein prescribed,
> and shall, on or before November 1, 1908, provide
> for the making of a permanent record of such reg-
> istration, and all persons so registered shall for-
> ever thereafter have the right to vote in all elections
> by the people in this State, unless disqualified un-
> der section 2 of this article.

Originally Art. VI contained in 5 the following provision:

> That this amendment to the Constitution is pre-
> sented and adopted as one indivisible plan for the
> regulation of the suffrage, with the intent and pur-
> pose to so connect the different parts, and to make
> them so dependent upon each other, that the whole
> shall stand or fall together.

But the North Carolina Supreme Court in the
instant case held that a 1945 amendment to Article
VI freed it of the indivisibility clause. That amendment rephrased 1 of Art. VI to read as follows:

> Every person born in the United States, and every

person who has been naturalized, twenty-one years of age, and possessing the qualifications set out in this article, shall be entitled to vote. . . .

That court said that "one of those qualifications" was the literacy test contained in 4 of Art. VI; and that the 1945 amendment "had the effect of incorporating and adopting anew the provisions as to the qualifications required of a voter as set out in Article VI, freed of the indivisibility clause of the 1902 amendment. And the way was made clear for the General Assembly to act."

In 1957 the Legislature rewrote General Statutes 163–28. . . . Prior to that 1957 amendment 163–28 perpetuated the grandfather clause contained in 4 of Art. VI of the Constitution and 163–32 established a procedure for registration to effectuate it. But the 1957 amendment contained a provision that "All laws and clauses of laws in conflict with this Act are hereby repealed." The federal three-judge court ruled that this 1957 amendment eliminated the grandfather clause from the statute.

The Attorney General of North Carolina, in an amicus brief, agrees that the grandfather clause contained in Art. VI is in conflict with the Fifteenth Amendment. Appellee maintains that the North Carolina Supreme Court ruled that the invalidity of that part of Art. VI does not impair the remainder of Art. VI since the 1945 amendment to Art. VI freed it of its indivisibility clause. Under that view Art. VI would impose the same literacy test as that imposed by the 1957 statute and neither would be linked with the grandfather clause which, though present in print, is separable from the rest and void. We so read the opinion of the North Carolina Supreme Court.

. . .

The states have long been held to have broad powers to determine the conditions under which the right of suffrage may be exercised absent of course the discrimination which the Constitution condemns. Article I, 2 of the Constitution in its provision for the election of members of the House of Representatives and the Seventeenth Amendment in its provision for the election of Senators provide that officials will be chosen "by the People." Each provision goes on to state that "the Electors in each State shall have the Qualifications requisite for Electors of the most numerous Branch of the State Legislature." So while the right of suffrage is established and guaranteed by the Constitution it is subject to the imposition of state standards which are not discriminatory and which do not contravene any restriction that Congress, acting pursuant to its constitutional powers, has imposed. While 2 of the Fourteenth Amendment, which provides for apportionment of Representatives among the states according to their respective numbers counting the whole number of persons in each state (except Indians not taxed), speaks of "the right to vote," the right protected "refers to the right to vote as established by the laws and constitution of the State."

We do not suggest that any standards which a state desires to adopt may be required of voters. But there is wide scope for exercise of its jurisdiction. Residence requirements, age, previous criminal record are obvious examples indicating factors which a state may take into consideration in determining the qualifications of voters. The ability to read and write likewise has some relation to standards designed to promote intelligent use of the ballot. Literacy and illiteracy are neutral on race, creed, color, and sex, as reports around the world show. Literacy and intelligence are obviously not synonymous. Illiterate people may be intelligent voters. Yet in our society where newspapers, periodicals, books, and other printed matter canvass and debate campaign issues, a state might conclude that only those who are literate should exercise the franchise. It was said last century in Massachusetts that a literacy test was designed to insure an "independent and intelligent" exercise of the right of suffrage. North Carolina agrees. We do not sit in judgment on the wisdom of that policy. We cannot say, however, that it is not an allowable one measured by constitutional standards.

Of course a literacy test, fair on its face, may be employed to perpetuate that discrimination which the Fifteenth Amendment was designed to uproot. No such influence is charged here. On the other hand, a literacy test may be unconstitutional on its face. . . . The present requirement, applicable to members of all races, is that the prospective voter "be able to read and write any section of the Constitution of North Carolina in the English language." That seems to us to be one fair way of determining whether a person is literate, not a calculated scheme to lay springes for the citizen. Certainly we cannot condemn it on its face as a device unrelated to the desire of North Carolina to raise the standards for people of all races who cast the ballot.

Affirmed.

Harman v. Forssenius
380 U.S. 528 (1965)

We are called upon in this case to construe, for the first time, the Twenty-fourth Amendment to the Constitution of the United States. . . .

The precise issue is whether §24–17.2 of the Virginia Code—which provides that, in order to qualify to vote in federal elections, one must either pay a poll tax or file a witnessed or notarized certificate of residence—contravenes this command.

Prior to the adoption of the Twenty-fourth Amendment, the Virginia Constitution and statutes established uniform standards for qualification for voting in both federal and state elections. The requirements were: (1) United States citizenship; (2) a minimum age of twenty-one; (3) residence in the State for one year, in the city or county for six months, and in the voting precinct for thirty days; and (4) payment

> at least six months prior to any election . . . to the proper officer all State poll taxes ($1.50 annually) assessed or assessable against him for three years next preceding . . . such election.

The statutes further provided for permanent registration. Once registered, the voters could qualify for elections in subsequent years merely by paying the poll taxes.

In 1963, in anticipation of the promulgation of the Twenty-fourth Amendment, the Governor of Virginia convened a special session of the Virginia General Assembly. On November 21 of that year, the General Assembly enacted two Acts designed

> (1) to enable persons to register and vote in federal elections without the payment of poll tax or other tax, as required by the 24th Amendment to the Constitution of the United States, (2) to continue in effect in all other elections the present registration and voting requirements of the Constitution of Virginia, and (3) to provide methods by which all persons registered to vote in federal or other elections may prove that they meet the residence requirements of § 18 of the Constitution of Virginia.

No changes were made with regard to qualification for voting in state elections. With regard to federal elections, however, the payment of a poll tax as an absolute prerequisite to registration and voting was eliminated, and a provision was added requiring the federal voter to file a certificate of residence in each election year or, at his option, to pay the customary poll taxes. The statute provides that the certificate of residence must be filed no earlier than October 1 of the year immediately preceding that in which the voter desires to vote, and not later than six months prior to the election. The voter must state in the certificate (which must be notarized or witnessed) his present address, that he is currently a resident of Virginia, that he has been a resident since the date of his registration, and that he does not presently intend to remove from the city or county of which he is a resident prior to the next general election. Thus, as a result of the 1963 Acts, a citizen, after registration, may vote in both federal and state elections upon the payment of all assessable poll taxes. If he has not paid such taxes, he cannot vote in state elections, and may vote in federal elections only upon filing a certificate of residence in each election year.

The present appeal originated as two separate class actions, brought by appellees in the United States District Court for the Eastern District of Virginia, attacking the foregoing provisions of the 1963 Virginia legislation as violative of Art. I, §2, of the Constitution of the United States, and the Fourteenth, Seventeenth, and Twenty-fourth Amendments thereto. The complaints, which prayed for declaratory and injunctive relief, named as defendants (appellants here) the three members of the Virginia State Board of Elections and, in one case, the County Treasurer of Roanoke County, Virginia, and, in the other, the Director of Finance of Fairfax County. . . .

The District Court denied the State's motion to stay the proceedings in order to give the Virginia courts an opportunity to resolve the issues and interpret the statutes involved. The court further denied the State's motions to dismiss for failure to join indispensable parties, for failure to state a claim on which relief could be granted,

and for want of a justiciable controversy. On the merits, the District Court held that the certificate of residence requirement was "a distinct qualification," or at least an "increase [in] the quantum of necessary proof of residence" imposed solely on the federal voter, and that it therefore violated Art. I, §2, and the Seventeenth Amendment, which provide that electors choosing a Representative or Senator in the Congress of the United States "shall have the qualifications requisite for electors of the most numerous branch of the State legislature." The court rejected the argument that the residency certificate was merely a method, like the poll tax, of proving the residence qualification which is imposed on both federal and state voters. Accordingly, the District Court entered an order declaring invalid the portions of the 1963 Virginia legislation which required the filing of a certificate of residence and enjoining appellants from requiring compliance by a voter with said portions of the 1963 Acts. . . .

We hold that §24–17.2 is repugnant to the Twenty-fourth Amendment, and affirm the decision of the District Court on that basis. We therefore find it unnecessary to determine whether that section violates Art. I, §2, and the Seventeenth Amendment.

. . .

. . . The District Court was faced with two class actions attacking a statutory scheme allegedly impairing the right to vote in violation of Art. I, § 2, and the Fourteenth, Seventeenth and Twenty-fourth Amendments. . . . In appraising the motion to stay proceedings, the District Court was thus faced with a claimed impairment of the fundamental civil rights of a broad class of citizens. The motion was heard about two months prior to the deadline for meeting the statutory requirements and just eight months before the 1964 general elections. Given the importance and immediacy of the problem, and the delay inherent in referring questions of state law to state tribunals it is evident that the District Court did not abuse its discretion in refusing to abstain.

Reaching the merits, it is important to emphasize that the question presented is not whether it would be within a State's power to abolish entirely the poll tax and require all voters—state and federal—to file annually a certificate of residence. Rather, the issue here is whether the State of Virginia may constitutionally confront the federal voter with a requirement that he either pay the customary poll taxes as required for state elections or file a certificate of residence. We conclude that this requirement constitutes an abridgment of the right to vote in federal elections in contravention of the Twenty-fourth Amendment.

Prior to the proposal of the Twenty-fourth Amendment in 1962, federal legislation to eliminate poll taxes, either by constitutional amendment or statute, had been introduced in every Congress since 1939. The House of Representatives passed anti-poll tax bills on five occasions and the Senate twice proposed constitutional amendments. Even though, in 1962, only five states retained the poll tax as a voting requirement, Congress reflected widespread national concern with the characteristics of the tax. Disenchantment with the poll tax was many-faceted. One of the basic objections to the poll tax was that it exacted a price for the privilege of exercising the franchise. Congressional hearings and debates indicate a general repugnance to the disenfranchisement of the poor occasioned by failure to pay the tax. . . . Another objection to the poll tax raised in the congressional hearings was that the tax usually had to be paid long before the election—at a time when political campaigns were still quiescent—which tended to eliminate

from the franchise a substantial number of voters who did not plan so far ahead. The poll tax was also attacked as a vehicle for fraud which could be manipulated by political machines by financing block payments of the tax. In addition, and of primary concern to many, the poll tax was viewed as a requirement adopted with an eye to the disenfranchisement of Negroes and applied in a discriminatory manner. It is against this background that Congress proposed, and three-fourths of the states ratified, the Twenty-fourth Amendment abolishing the poll tax as a requirement for voting in federal elections.

Upon adoption of the Amendment, of course, no state could condition the federal franchise upon payment of a poll tax. The State of Virginia accordingly removed the poll tax as an absolute prerequisite to qualification for voting in federal elections, but, in its stead substituted a provision whereby the federal voter could qualify either by paying the customary poll tax or by filing a certificate of residence six months before the election.

. . . [T]he Twenty-fourth Amendment does not merely insure that the franchise shall not be "denied" by reason of failure to pay the poll tax; it expressly guarantees that the right to vote shall not be "denied or abridged" for that reason. Thus, like the Fifteenth Amendment, the Twenty-fourth "nullifies sophisticated, as well as simple-minded modes" of impairing the right guaranteed. . . .

Thus, in order to demonstrate the invalidity of §24–17.2 of the Virginia Code, it need only be shown that it imposes a material requirement solely upon those who refuse to surrender their constitutional right to vote in federal elections without paying a poll tax. Section 24–17.2 unquestionably erects a real obstacle to voting in federal elections for those who assert their constitutional exemption from the poll tax. As previously indicated, the requirement for those who wish to participate in federal elections without paying the poll tax is that they file in each election year, within a stated interval ending six months before the election, a notarized or witnessed certificate attesting that they have been continuous residents of the State since the date of registration (which might have been many years before under Virginia's system of permanent registration), and that they do not presently intend to leave the city or county in which they reside prior to the forthcoming election. Unlike the poll tax bill which is sent to the voter's residence, it is not entirely clear how one obtains the necessary certificate. The statutes merely provide for the distribution of the forms to city and county court clerks, and for further distribution to local registrars and election officials. Construing the statutes in the manner least burdensome to the voter, it would seem that the voter could either obtain the certificate of residence from local election officials or prepare personally "a certificate in form substantially" as set forth in the statute. The certificate must then be filed "in person, or otherwise" with the city or county treasurer. This is plainly a cumbersome procedure. In effect, it amounts to annual re-registration, which Virginia officials have sharply contrasted with the "simple" poll tax system. For many, it would probably seem far preferable to mail in the poll tax payment upon receipt of the bill. In addition, the certificate must be filed six months before the election, thus perpetuating one of the disenfranchising characteristics of the poll tax which the Twenty-fourth Amendment was designed to eliminate. We are thus constrained to hold that the requirement imposed upon the voter who refuses to pay the poll tax constitutes an abridgment of his right to vote by reason of failure to pay the poll tax.

The requirement imposed upon those who reject the poll tax method of qualifying would not be saved even if it could be said that it is no more onerous, or even somewhat less onerous, than the poll tax. For federal elections, the poll tax is abolished absolutely as a prerequisite to voting, and no equivalent or milder substitute may be imposed. Any material requirement imposed upon the federal voter solely because of his refusal to waive the constitutional immunity subverts the effectiveness of the Twenty-fourth Amendment, and must fall under its ban.

Nor may the statutory scheme be saved, as the State asserts, on the ground that the certificate is a necessary substitute method of proving residence, serving the same function as the poll tax. As this Court has held in analogous situations, constitutional deprivations may not be justified by some remote administrative benefit to the State. Moreover, in this case the State has not demonstrated that the alternative requirement is in any sense necessary to the proper administration of its election laws. The forty-six States which do not require the payment of poll taxes have apparently found no great administrative burden in insuring that the electorate is limited to bona fide residents. The availability of numerous devices to enforce valid residence requirements—such as registration, use of the criminal sanction, purging of registration lists, challenges and oaths, public scrutiny by candidates and other interested parties—demonstrates quite clearly the lack of necessity for imposing a requirement whereby persons desiring to vote in federal elections must either pay a poll tax or file a certificate of residence six months prior to the election.

. . .

The judgment of the District Court is affirmed.

Harper v. Virginia Board of Elections 383 U.S. 663 (1966)

These are suits by Virginia residents to have declared unconstitutional Virginia's poll tax. The three-judge District Court, feeling bound by our decision in *Breedlove v. Suttles*, dismissed the complaint. . . .

While the right to vote in federal elections is conferred by Art. I, §2, of the Constitution, the right to vote in state elections is nowhere expressly mentioned. It is argued that the right to vote in state elections is implicit, particularly by reason of the First Amendment, and that it may not constitutionally be conditioned upon the payment of a tax or fee. We do not stop to canvass the relation between voting and political expression. For it is enough to say that, once the franchise is granted to the electorate, lines may not be drawn which are inconsistent with the Equal Protection Clause of the Fourteenth Amendment. . . . [T]he *Lassiter* case does not govern the result here, because, unlike a poll tax, the "ability to read and write . . . has some relation to standards designed to promote intelligent use of the ballot."

We conclude that a State violates the Equal Protection Clause of the Fourteenth Amendment whenever it makes the affluence of the voter or payment of any fee an electoral standard. Voter qualifications have no relation to wealth nor to paying or not paying this or any other tax. Our cases demonstrate that the Equal Protection Clause of the Fourteenth Amendment restrains the States from fixing voter qualifications which invidiously discriminate. . . . Previously we had said that neither homesite nor occupation "affords a permissible basis for distinguishing between qualified voters within the State." We think the same must be true of requirements of wealth or affluence or payment of a fee.

. . .

. . . The principle that denies the State the right to dilute a citizen's vote on account of his economic status or other such factors, by analogy, bars a system which excludes those unable to pay a fee to vote or who fail to pay.

It is argued that a State may exact fees from citizens for many different kinds of licenses; that, if it can demand from all an equal fee for a driver's license, it can demand from all an equal poll tax for voting. But we must remember that the interest of the State, when it comes to voting, is limited to the power to fix qualifications. Wealth, like race, creed, or color, is not germane to one's ability to participate intelligently in the electoral process. Lines drawn on the basis of wealth or property, like those of race, are traditionally disfavored. To introduce wealth or payment of a fee as a measure of a voter's qualifications is to introduce a capricious or irrelevant factor. The degree of the discrimination is irrelevant. In this context—that is, as a condition of obtaining a ballot—the requirement of fee paying causes an "invidious" discrimination that runs afoul of the Equal Protection Clause. Levy "by the poll" . . . is an old familiar form of taxation, and we say nothing to impair its validity so long as it is not made a condition to the exercise of the franchise. *Breedlove* sanctioned its use as "a prerequisite of voting." To that extent the *Breedlove* case is overruled.

. . .

. . . Our conclusion, like that, in *Reynolds v. Sims*, is founded not on what we think governmental policy should be, but on what the Equal Protection Clause requires.

. . .

. . . For, to repeat, wealth or fee paying has, in our view, no relation to voting qualifications; the right to vote is too precious, too fundamental to be so burdened or conditioned.

Reversed.

Katzenbach v. Morgan
384 U.S. 641 (1966)

These cases concern the constitutionality of §4(e) of the Voting Rights Act of 1965. That law, in the respects pertinent in these cases, provides that no person who has successfully completed the sixth primary grade in a public school in, or a private school accredited by, the Commonwealth of Puerto Rico in which the language of instruction was other than English shall be denied the right to vote in any election because of his inability to read or write English. Appellees, registered voters in New York City, brought this suit to challenge the constitutionality of §4(e) insofar as it . . . prohibits the enforcement of the election laws of New York requiring an ability to read and write English as a condition of voting. Under these laws, many of the several hundred thousand New York City residents who have migrated there from the Commonwealth of Puerto Rico had previously been denied the right to vote, and appellees attack §4(e) insofar as it would enable many of these citizens to vote. Pursuant to §14(b) of the Voting Rights Act of 1965, appellees commenced this proceeding in the District Court for the District of Columbia seeking a declaration that §4(e) is invalid, and an injunction prohibiting appellants, the Attorney General of the United States and the New York City Board of Elections, from either enforcing or complying with §4(e). A three-judge district court . . . granted the declaratory and injunctive relief appellees sought. The court held that, in enacting §4(e), Congress exceeded the powers granted to it by the Constitution, and therefore usurped powers reserved to the States by the Tenth Amendment. . . .

Under the distribution of powers effected by the Constitution, the States establish qualifications for voting for state officers, and the qualifications established by the States for voting for members of the most numerous branch of the state legislature also determine who may vote for United States Representatives and Senators. But, of course, the States have no power to grant or withhold the franchise on conditions that are forbidden by the Fourteenth Amendment, or any other provision of the Constitution. Such exercises of state power are no more immune to the limitations of the Fourteenth Amendment than any other state action. The Equal Protection Clause itself has been held to forbid some state laws that restrict the right to vote.

. . .

. . . [O]ur task in this case is not to determine whether the New York English literacy requirement, as applied to deny the right to vote to a person who successfully completed the sixth grade in a Puerto Rican school, violates the Equal Protection Clause. Accordingly, our decision in *Lassiter v. Northampton Election Board* sustaining the North Carolina English literacy requirement as not in all circumstances prohibited by the first sections of the Fourteenth and Fifteenth Amendments is inapposite. *Lassiter* did not present the question before us here: without regard to whether the judiciary would find that the Equal Protection Clause itself nullifies New York's English literacy requirement as so applied, could Congress prohibit the enforcement of the state law by legislating under §5 of the Fourteenth Amendment? In answering this question, our task is limited to determining whether such legislation is, as required by §5, appropriate legislation to enforce the Equal Protection Clause.

. . .

We therefore proceed to the consideration whether §4(e) is "appropriate legislation" to enforce the Equal Protection Clause, that is, under the *McCulloch v. Maryland* standard, whether

§4(e) may be regarded as an enactment to enforce the Equal Protection Clause, whether it is "plainly adapted to that end," and whether it is not prohibited by, but is consistent with, "the letter and spirit of the constitution."

There can be no doubt that §4(e) may be regarded as an enactment to enforce the Equal Protection Clause. . . . The persons referred to include those who have migrated from the Commonwealth of Puerto Rico to New York and who have been denied the right to vote because of their inability to read and write English, and the Fourteenth Amendment rights referred to include those emanating from the Equal Protection Clause. More specifically, §4(e) may be viewed as a measure to secure for the Puerto Rican community residing in New York nondiscriminatory treatment by government—both in the imposition of voting qualifications and the provision or administration of governmental services, such as public schools, public housing and law enforcement.

Section 4(e) may be readily seen as "plainly adapted" to furthering these aims of the Equal Protection Clause. The practical effect of §4(e) is to prohibit New York from denying the right to vote to large segments of its Puerto Rican community. Congress has thus prohibited the State from denying to that community the right that is "preservative of all rights." This enhanced political power will be helpful in gaining nondiscriminatory treatment in public services for the entire Puerto Rican community. Section 4(e) thereby enables the Puerto Rican minority better to obtain "perfect equality of civil rights and the equal protection of the laws." It was well within congressional authority to say that this need of the Puerto Rican minority for the vote warranted federal intrusion upon any state interests served by the English literacy requirement. It was for Congress, as the branch that made this judgment,

to assess and weigh the various conflicting considerations—the risk or pervasiveness of the discrimination in governmental services, the effectiveness of eliminating the state restriction on the right to vote as a means of dealing with the evil, the adequacy or availability of alternative remedies, and the nature and significance of the state interests that would be affected by the nullification of the English literacy requirement as applied to residents who have successfully completed the sixth grade in a Puerto Rican school. It is not for us to review the congressional resolution of these factors. It is enough that we be able to perceive a basis upon which the Congress might resolve the conflict as it did. There plainly was such a basis to support §4(e) in the application in question in this case. Any contrary conclusion would require us to be blind to the realities familiar to the legislators.

The result is no different if we confine our inquiry to the question whether §4(e) was merely legislation aimed at the elimination of an invidious discrimination in establishing voter qualifications. We are told that New York's English literacy requirement originated in the desire to provide an incentive for non-English speaking immigrants to learn the English language, and in order to assure the intelligent exercise of the franchise. Yet Congress might well have questioned, in light of the many exemptions provided, and some evidence suggesting that prejudice played a prominent role in the enactment of the requirement, whether these were actually the interests being served. Congress might have also questioned whether denial of a right deemed so precious and fundamental in our society was a necessary or appropriate means of encouraging persons to learn English, or of furthering the goal of an intelligent exercise of the franchise. Finally, Congress might well have concluded that, as a means of furthering the intelligent exercise of the franchise, an ability to read or understand Spanish is as effective as ability to read English for those to whom Spanish language newspapers and Spanish language radio and television programs are available to inform them of election issues and governmental affairs. Since Congress undertook to legislate so as to preclude the enforcement of the state law, and did so in the context of a general appraisal of literacy requirements for voting, to which it brought a specially informed legislative competence, it was Congress's prerogative to weigh these competing considerations. Here again, it is enough that we perceive a basis upon which Congress might predicate a judgment that the application of New York's English literacy requirement to deny the right to vote to a person with a sixth grade education in Puerto Rican schools in which the language of instruction was other than English constituted an invidious discrimination in violation of the Equal Protection Clause.

There remains the question whether the congressional remedies adopted in §4(e) constitute means which are not prohibited by, but are consistent "with the letter and spirit of the constitution." The only respect in which appellees contend that §4(e) fails in this regard is that the section itself works an invidious discrimination in violation of the Fifth Amendment by prohibiting the enforcement of the English literacy requirement only for those educated in American-flag schools (schools located within United States jurisdiction) in which the language of instruction was other than English, and not for those educated in schools beyond the territorial limits of the United States in which the language of instruction was also other than English. This is not a complaint that Congress, in enacting §4(e), has unconstitutionally denied or diluted anyone's right to vote,

but rather that Congress violated the Constitution by not extending the relief effected in §4(e) to those educated in non-American-flag schools. We need not pause to determine whether appellees have a sufficient personal interest to have §4(e) invalidated on this ground, since the argument, in our view, falls on the merits.

Section 4(e) does not restrict or deny the franchise, but, in effect, extends the franchise to persons who otherwise would be denied it by state law. Thus, we need not decide whether a state literacy law conditioning the right to vote on achieving a certain level of education in an American-flag school (regardless of the language of instruction) discriminates invidiously against those educated in non-American-flag schools. We need only decide whether the challenged limitation on the relief effected in §4(e) was permissible. In deciding that question, the principle that calls for the closest scrutiny of distinctions in laws denying fundamental rights, is inapplicable; for the distinction challenged by appellees is presented only as a limitation on a reform measure aimed at eliminating an existing barrier to the exercise of the franchise. Rather, in deciding the constitutional propriety of the limitations in such a reform measure, we are guided by the familiar principles that a "statute is not invalid under the Constitution because it might have gone farther than it did," that a legislature need not "strike at all evils at the same time," and that "reform may take one step at a time, addressing itself to the phase of the problem which seems most acute to the legislative mind."

Guided by these principles, we are satisfied that appellees' challenge to this limitation in §4(e) is without merit. In the context of the case before us, the congressional choice to limit the relief effected in §4(e) may, for example, reflect Congress' greater familiarity with the quality of instruction in American-flag schools, a recognition of the unique historic relationship between the Congress and the Commonwealth of Puerto Rico, an awareness of the federal government's acceptance of the desirability of the use of Spanish as the language of instruction in Commonwealth schools, and the fact that Congress has fostered policies encouraging migration from the Commonwealth to the States. We have no occasion to determine in this case whether such factors would justify a similar distinction embodied in a voting qualification law that denied the franchise to persons educated in non-American-flag schools. We hold only that the limitation on relief effected in §4(e) does not constitute a forbidden discrimination, since these factors might well have been the basis for the decision of Congress to go "no farther than it did."

We therefore conclude that §4(e), in the application challenged in this case, is appropriate legislation to enforce the Equal Protection Clause, and that the judgment of the District Court must be, and hereby is, reversed.

Cardona v. Power
384 U.S. 672 (1966)

. . . In this case, which was adjudicated by the New York courts before the enactment of §4(e), appellant unsuccessfully sought a judicial determination that the New York English literacy requirement, as applied to deny her the right to vote in all elections, violated the Federal Constitution.

Appellant was born and educated in the Commonwealth of Puerto Rico, and has lived in New York City since about 1948. On July 23, 1963, she attempted to register to vote, presenting evidence of United States citizenship, her age and residence; and she represented that, although she was able to read and write Spanish, she could not satisfy New York's English literacy requirement. The New York City Board of Elections refused to register her as a voter solely on the ground that she was not literate in English. Appellant then brought this proceeding in state court against the Board of Elections and its members. She alleged that the New York English literacy requirement, as applied, was invalid under the Federal Constitution, and sought an order directing the Board to register her as a duly qualified voter, or, in the alternative, directing the Board to administer a literacy test in the Spanish language, and, if she passed the test, to register her as a duly qualified voter. The trial court denied the relief prayed for, and the New York Court of Appeals . . . affirmed.

Although appellant's complaint alleges that she attended a school in Puerto Rico, it is not alleged therein, nor have we been clearly informed in any other way whether, as required by §4(e), she successfully completed the sixth grade of a public school in, or a private school accredited by, the Commonwealth. If she had completed the sixth grade in such a school, her failure to satisfy the New York English literacy requirement would no longer be a bar to her registration in light of our decision today in *Katzenbach v. Morgan*. This case might therefore be moot; appellant would not need any relief if §4(e) in terms accomplished the result she sought. Moreover, even if appellant were not specifically covered by §4(e), the New York courts should, in the first instance, determine whether, in light of this federal enactment, those applications of the New York English literacy requirement not, in terms prohibited by §4(e), have continuing validity. We therefore vacate the judgment, without costs to either party in this Court, and remand the cause to the Court of Appeals of New York for such further proceedings as it may deem appropriate.

Gaston County v. United States
395 U.S. 285 (1969)

On March 29, 1966, the Attorney General and the Director of the Census published the necessary determinations with respect to appellant, Gaston County, North Carolina. Use of the State's literacy test within the County was thereby suspended. On August 18, 1966, appellant brought this action in the District Court, making the requisite averments and seeking to reinstate the literacy test.

The United States opposed the granting of relief on the ground, inter alia, that use of the test had "the effect of denying or abridging the right to vote on account of race or color" because it placed a specially onerous burden on the county's Negro citizens for whom the county had maintained separate and inferior schools.

After a full trial on this and other issues, the District Court denied the relief requested, holding that appellant had not met its burden of proving that its use of the literacy test, in the context of its historic maintenance of segregated and unequal schools, did not discriminatorily deprive Negroes of the franchise. . . .

. . .

Appellant contends that the decision of the District Court is erroneous on three scores: first, as a matter of statutory construction and legislative history, the court could not consider Gaston County's practice of educational discrimination in determining whether its literacy test had the effect of discriminatorily denying the franchise; second, on the facts of this case, appellant met its burden of proving that the education it provided had no such effect, and third, whatever may have been the situation in the past, Gaston County has not fostered discrimination in education or voting in recent years. We consider these arguments in turn.

The legislative history of the Voting Rights Act of 1965 discloses that Congress was fully cognizant of the potential effect of unequal educational opportunities upon exercise of the franchise. This causal relationship was, indeed, one of the principal arguments made in support of the Act's test suspension provisions. . . .

. . .

We conclude that, in an action brought under §4(a) of the Voting Rights Act of 1965, it is appropriate for a court to consider whether a literacy or educational requirement has the "effect of denying . . . the right to vote on account of race or color" because the State or subdivision which seeks to impose the requirement has maintained separate and inferior schools for its Negro residents who are now of voting age.

. . .

All persons of voting age in 1966 who attended schools in Gaston County attended racially separate and unequal schools. . . .

. . .

Of those persons over 25 years old at the time of the 1960 census, the proportion of Negroes with no schooling whatever was twice that of whites in Gaston County; the proportion of Negroes with four or less years of education was slightly less than twice that of white.

In 1962, Gaston County changed its system of registration, and required a general reregistration of all voters. North Carolina law provides that "[e]very person presenting himself for registration shall be able to read and write any section of the Constitution in the English language." The State Supreme Court has described this requirement as "relatively high, even after more than a half century of free public schools and universal education," and a Negro minister active in voter registration testified that it placed an especially heavy burden on the county's older Negro citizens. It was publicized throughout the county that the literacy requirement would be enforced. A registrar told a Negro leader not to bring illiterates to register. Some Negroes who attempted to register were, in fact, rejected because they could not pass the test, and others did not attempt to register, knowing that they could not meet the standard.

With this evidence, the government had not only put its contention in issue, but had made out a prima facie case. It is only reasonable to infer that, among black children compelled to endure a segregated and inferior education, fewer will achieve any given degree of literacy than will their better-educated white contemporaries. And, on the government's showing, it was certainly proper to infer that Gaston County's inferior Negro schools provided many of its Negro residents with a subliterate education, and gave many others little inducement to enter or remain in school.

. . .

Appellant urges that it administered the 1962 reregistration in a fair and impartial manner, and that, in recent years, it has made significant strides toward equalizing and integrating its school system. Although we accept these claims as true, they fall wide of the mark. Affording today's Negro youth equal educational opportunities will doubtless prepare them to meet, on equal terms, whatever standards of literacy are required when they reach voting age. It does nothing for their parents, however. From this record, we cannot escape the sad truth that, throughout the years, Gaston County systematically deprived its black citizens of the educational opportunities it granted to its white citizens. "Impartial" administration of the literacy test today would serve only to perpetuate these inequities in a different form. The judgment of the District Court is affirmed.

3

Apportionment and Redistricting

This chapter discusses states' responsibility to draw federal legislative districts. This responsibility has been tempered by the Voting Rights Act of 1965 and in particular the Act's preclearance provision.

Richardson v. McChesney
218 U.S. 487 (1910)

Shortly stated, this is an attack upon the validity of the Kentucky act of March 12, 1898, and certain amendments thereto, apportioning the state into eleven congressional districts. The bill alleges that the districts do not conform to the requirement of the acts of Congress apportioning representatives among the states, which acts require that such districts shall be of contiguous territory, "containing as nearly as practicable an equal number of inhabitants." The averments of the bill are that the districts are grossly and unnecessarily unequal in population.

The bill was filed in an equity court of the state. A demurrer, as not stating a case good in law, was sustained and the bill dismissed. This judgment was affirmed upon an appeal to the court of appeals of Kentucky. The ground upon which the Kentucky court rested its judgment was, in substance, that neither the Constitution of the United States nor of the state contained any provision which vested in the court any authority to annul an apportionment of the state into districts for the election of Congressmen, and that the matter

pertained to the political department of the government, and was subject only to the supervising control of the Congress, if any such power of supervision existed at all.

The bill, in substance, alleges that a congressional election in each of the eleven congressional districts of the state will be held in November 1908. That under the law of Kentucky it is the duty of the defendant McChesney, as secretary of the commonwealth, or his successor in office at the time, to certify, within sixty days prior to said election, the names of the nominees of the Republican and Democratic parties for members of Congress in each district, to clerks of the various county courts of the state, and the duty of such clerks to print the name so certified upon the official ballots to be used in said congressional election.

The complainant's interest in the matter is that he is a citizen of the United States and of the state of Kentucky, and a qualified voter and resident of Hart county, one of the counties of said state, and as such entitled to vote for a Congressman in the district to which that county is lawfully attached....

. . .

Dismiss the writ of error.

Smiley v. Holm
285 U.S. 355 (1932)

Under the reapportionment following the fifteenth decennial census, as provided by the Act of Congress of June 18, 1929, Minnesota is entitled to nine Representatives in Congress, being one less than the number previously allotted. In April 1931, the bill known as House File No. 1456, dividing the state into nine congressional districts and specifying the counties of which they should be composed, was passed by the House of Representatives and the Senate of the state, and was transmitted to the Governor, who returned it without his approval. Thereupon, without further action upon the measure by the House of Representatives and the Senate, and in compliance with a resolution of the House of Representatives, House File No. 1456 was deposited with the secretary of state of Minnesota. This suit was brought by the petitioner as a "citizen, elector and taxpayer" of the state to obtain a judgment declaring invalid all fillings for nomination for the office of Representative in Congress, which should designate a subdivision of the state as a congressional district, and to enjoin the secretary of state from giving notice of the holding of elections for that office in such subdivisions. The petition alleged that House File No. 1456 was a nullity, in that, after the Governor's veto, it was not repassed by the Legislature as required by law, and also in that the proposed congressional districts were not "compact" and did not "contain an equal number of inhabitants as nearly as practicable" in accordance with the Act of Congress of August 8, 1911.

. . . The trial court sustained the demurrer, and its order was affirmed by the Supreme Court of the state. The action was then dismissed upon the merits, and the Supreme Court affirmed the judgment upon its previous opinion. . . .

. . .

The question . . . is whether the provision of the Federal Constitution, thus regarded as determinative, invests the Legislature with a particular authority, and imposes upon it a corresponding duty, the definition of which imports a function different from that of lawgiver, and thus renders inapplicable the conditions which attach to the making of state laws. Much that is urged in argument with regard to the meaning of the term "Legislature" is beside the point. . . . The question here is not with respect to the "body" as thus described but as to the function to be performed. The use in the Federal Constitution of the same term in different relations does not always imply the performance of the same function. The Legislature may act as an electoral body. . . . It may act as a ratifying body. . . . It may act as a consenting body. . . . Wherever the term "legislature" is used in the Constitution, it is necessary to consider the nature of the particular action in view. The primary question now before the Court is whether the function contemplated by article 1, 4, is that of making laws.

. . . The subject-matter is the "times, places and manner of holding elections for senators and representatives." It cannot be doubted that these comprehensive words embrace authority to provide a complete code for congressional elections, not only as to times and places, but in relation to notices, registration, supervision of voting, protection of voters, prevention of fraud and corrupt practices, counting of votes, duties of inspectors and canvassers, and making and publication of election returns; in short, to enact the numerous requirements as to procedure and safeguards which experience shows are necessary in order to enforce the fundamental right involved. And these requirements would be nugatory if they did not have appropriate sanctions in the definition of offenses and punishments. All this is comprised in the subject of "times, places and manner of holding elections," and involves lawmaking in its essential features and most important aspect.

. . .

The term defining the method of action, equally with the nature of the subject matter, aptly points to the making of laws. The state Legislature is authorized to "prescribe" the times, places, and manner of holding elections. Respondent urges that the fact that the words "by law" are found in the clause relating to the action of the Congress, and not in the clause giving authority to the state Legislature, supports the contention that the latter was not to act in the exercise of the lawmaking power. We think that the inference is strongly to the contrary. It is the nature of the function that makes the phrase "by law" apposite. That is the same whether it is performed by state or national Legislature, and the use of the phrase places the intent of the whole provision in a strong light. Prescribing regulations to govern the conduct of the citizen, under the first clause, and making and altering such rules by law, under the second clause, involve action of the same inherent character.

As the authority is conferred for the purpose of making laws for the state, it follows, in the absence of an indication of a contrary intent, that the exercise of the authority must be in accordance with the method which the state has prescribed for legislative enactments. We find no suggestion in the federal constitutional provision of an attempt to endow the Legislature of the state with power to enact laws in any manner other than that in which the constitution of the state has provided that laws shall be enacted. Whether the Governor of the state, through the veto power, shall have a part in the making of state laws, is a matter of state polity. Article 1, 4, of the Federal Constitution, neither requires nor excludes such participation. And provision for it, as a check in the legislative process, cannot be regarded as repugnant to the grant of legislative authority. . . .

The practical construction of article 1, 4, is impressive. General acquiescence cannot justify departure from the law, but long and continuous interpretation in the course of official action under the law may aid in removing doubts as to its meaning. This is especially true in the case of constitutional provisions governing the exercise of political rights, and hence subject to constant and careful scrutiny. . . . The Attorney General of Minnesota, in his argument in the instant case, states: "It is conceded that until 1931 whenever the State of Minnesota was divided into districts for the purpose of congressional elections such action was taken by the legislature in the form of a bill and presented to and approved by the governor." That the constitutional provision contemplates the exercise of the lawmaking power was definitely recognized by the Congress in the Act of August 8, 1911, which expressly provided in section 4 for the election of Representatives in Congress, as stated, "by the districts now prescribed by law until such State shall be redistricted in the manner provided by the laws thereof, and in accordance with the rules enumerated in section three of this Act." The significance of the clause "in the manner provided by the laws thereof" is manifest from its occasion and purpose. It was to recognize the propriety of the referendum in establishing congressional districts where the state had made it a part of the legislative process. . . .

. . .

It clearly follows that there is nothing in article 1, 4, which precludes a state from providing that legislative action in districting the state for congressional elections shall be subject to the veto power of the Governor as in other cases of the exercise of the lawmaking power. Accordingly, in this instance, the validity of House File No. 1456 cannot be sustained by virtue of any authority conferred by the Federal Constitution upon the Legislature of Minnesota to create congressional districts independently of the participation of the Governor as required by the state Constitution with respect to the enactment of laws.

. . .

There are three classes of states with respect to the number of Representatives under the present apportionment pursuant to the act of 1929, (1) where the number remains the same, (2) where it is increased, and (3) where it is decreased. In states where the number of Representatives remains the same, and the districts are unchanged, no question is presented; there is nothing inconsistent with any of the requirements of the Congress in proceeding with the election of Representatives in such states in the same manner as heretofore. Section 4 of the act of 1911 provided that, in case of an increase in the number of Representatives in any state, "such additional Representative or Representatives shall be elected by the State at large and the other Representatives by the districts now prescribed by law" until such state shall be redistricted. The Constitution itself provides in article 1, 2, that "The house of representatives shall be composed of members chosen every second year by the people of the several states," and we are of the opinion that under this provision, in the absence of the creation of new districts, additional Representatives allotted to a state under the present reapportionment would appropriately be elected by the state at large. Such a course, with the election of the other Representatives in the existing districts until a redistricting act was passed, would present no inconsistency with any policy declared in the act of 1911.

Where, as in the case of Minnesota, the number of Representatives has been decreased, there is a different situation, as existing districts are not at all adapted to the new apportionment. It follows that in such a case, unless and until new districts are created, all Representatives allotted to the state must be elected by the state at large. That would be required, in the absence of a redistricting act, in order to afford the representation to which the state is constitutionally entitled, and the general provisions of the act of 1911 cannot be regarded as intended to have a different import.

This conclusion disposes of all the questions properly before the Court. Questions in relation to the application of the standards defined in section 3 of the act of 1911 to a redistricting statute, if such a statute should hereafter be enacted, are wholly abstract. The judgment is reversed, and the cause is remanded for further proceedings not inconsistent with this opinion.

Koenig v. Flynn
285 U.S. 375 (1932)

The petitioners, "citizens and voters" of the state, sought a writ of mandamus to compel the Secretary of State of New York, in issuing certificates for the election of representatives in Congress, to certify that they are to be elected in the congressional districts defined in the concurrent resolution of the senate and assembly of the state, adopted April 10, 1931. The secretary of state, invoking the provisions of Art. I, § 4, of the Constitution of the United States, and those of the Act of Congress of August 8, 1911, and also the requirements of the constitution of the state in relation to the enactment of laws, alleged that the concurrent resolution in question was ineffective, as it had not been submitted to the governor for approval and had not been approved by him. The court of appeals of the state, construing the federal constitutional provision as contemplating the exercise of the lawmaking power, sustained the respondent's defense and affirmed the decision of the lower courts refusing the writ.

The State of New York, under the reapportionment pursuant to the Act of Congress of June 18, 1929, is entitled to forty-five representatives in Congress in place of forty-three, the number allotted under the previous apportionment. The court of appeals decided that, in the absence of a new districting statute dividing the state into forty-five congressional districts, forty-three representatives are to be elected in the existing districts as defined by the state law, and the two additional representatives by the state at large.

For the reasons stated in the opinion *Smiley v. Holm*, the judgment is affirmed.

Carroll v. Becker
285 U.S. 380 (1932)

The State of Missouri, under the reapportionment of representatives in Congress, is entitled to thirteen representatives in place of sixteen as theretofore. The petitioner brought this proceeding to obtain a writ of mandamus to compel the Secretary of State of Missouri to file a declaration of the petitioner's candidacy for the office of representative in Congress in one of the congressional districts alleged to have been created by a bill passed by the House of Representatives and the Senate of Missouri in April 1931. An alternative writ was issued, and respondent, Secretary of State, alleged in his return that the bill in question had been vetoed by the governor, and hence had not become a valid law of the state. The supreme court of the state, in the view that Article I, § 4, of the Federal Constitution, provided for the enactment of laws, upheld the action of the secretary of state and quashed the alternative writ. The court also decided that, "since the number

of representatives for Missouri has been reduced, the former districts no longer exist, and representatives must be elected at large."

The questions are substantially the same as those which were presented in *Smiley v. Holm*, and the judgment is affirmed.

Wood v. Broom
287 U.S. 1 (1932)

Under the reapportionment pursuant to the act of June 18, 1929, Mississippi is entitled to seven Representatives in Congress, instead of eight as theretofore. The Legislature of Mississippi . . . divided the state into seven congressional districts. The complainant, alleging that he was a citizen of Mississippi, a qualified elector under its laws, and also qualified to be a candidate for election as Representative in Congress, brought this suit to have the redistricting act of 1932 declared invalid and the restrain the defendants, state officers, from taking proceedings for an election under its provisions. The alleged grounds of invalidity were that the act violated article 1, 4, and the Fourteenth Amendment, of the Constitution of the United States, and section 3 of the Act of Congress of August 8, 1911. Defendants moved to dismiss the bill (1) for want of equity, (2) for lack of equitable jurisdiction to grant the relief asked, (3) because on the facts alleged the complainant was not entitled to have his name placed upon the election ballot as a candidate from the state at large, and (4) because the decree of the court would be inefficacious. The District Court . . . granted an interlocutory injunction, and, after answer, which admitted the material facts alleged in the bill and set up the same grounds of defense as the motion to dismiss together with a denial of the unconstitutionality of the challenged act, the court on final hearing, on bill and answer, entered a final decree making the injunction permanent as prayed. Defendants appeal to this Court.

The District Court held that the new districts, created by the redistricting act, were not composed of compact and contiguous territory, having as nearly as practicable the same number of inhabitants, and hence failed to comply with the mandatory requirements of section 3 of the Act of August 8, 1911. . . .

. . .

There is thus no ground for the conclusion that the act of 1929 re-enacted or made applicable to new districts the requirements of the act of 1911. That act in this respect was left as it has stood, and the requirements it had contained as to the compactness, contiguity and equality in population of districts did not outlast the apportionment to which they related.

In this view, it is unnecessary to consider the questions raised as to the right of the complainant to relief in equity upon the allegations of the bill of complaint, or as to the justiciability of the controversy, if it were assumed that the requirements invoked by the complainant are still in effect. Upon these questions the Court expresses no opinion.

The decree is reversed and the cause is remanded to the District Court with directions to dismiss the bill of complaint.

Colegrove v. Green
328 U.S. 549 (1946)

This case is appropriately here on direct review of a judgment of the District Court of the Northern District of Illinois . . . dismissing the complaint of these appellants. Petitioners are three qualified voters in Illinois districts which have much larger populations than other Illinois Congressional districts. They brought this suit against the Governor, the Secretary of State, and the Auditor of the State of Illinois, as members ex officio of the Illinois Primary Certifying Board, to restrain them, in effect, from taking proceedings for an election in November 1946, under the provisions of Illinois law governing Congressional districts. Formally, the appellees asked for a decree, with its incidental relief, declaring these provisions to be invalid because they violated various provisions of the United States Constitution and 3 of the Reapportionment Act of August 8, 1911, in that by reason of subsequent changes in population the Congressional districts for the election of Representatives in the Congress created by the Illinois Laws of 1901, lacked compactness of territory and approximate equality of population. The District Court, feeling bound by this Court's opinion in *Wood v. Broom*, dismissed the bill.

The District Court was clearly right in deeming itself bound by *Wood*, and we could also dispose of this case on the authority of *Wood*. . . . Nothing has now been adduced to lead us to overrule what this Court found to be the requirements under the Act of 1929, the more so since seven Congressional elections have been held under the Act of 1929 as construed by this Court. No manifestation has been shown by Congress even to question the correctness of that which seemed compelling to this Court in enforcing the will of Congress in *Wood v. Broom*.

. . .

We are of opinion that the petitioners ask of this Court what is beyond its competence to grant. This is one of those demands on judicial power which cannot be met by verbal fencing about "jurisdiction." It must be resolved by considerations on the basis of which this Court, from time to time, has refused to intervene in controversies. It has refused to do so because due regard for the effective working of our Government revealed this issue to be of a peculiarly political nature and therefore not meet for judicial determination.

... The basis for the suit is not a private wrong, but a wrong suffered by Illinois as a polity. In effect this is an appeal to the federal courts to reconstruct the electoral process of Illinois in order that it may be adequately represented in the councils of the Nation. Because the Illinois legislature has failed to revise its Congressional Representative districts in order to reflect great changes, during more than a generation, in the distribution of its population, we are asked to do this, as it were, for Illinois. Of course no court can affirmatively remap the Illinois districts so as to bring them more in conformity with the standards of fairness for a representative system. At best we could only declare the existing electoral system invalid. The result would be to leave Illinois undistricted and to bring into operation, if the Illinois legislature chose not to act, the choice of members for the House of Representatives on a state-wide ticket. The last stage may be worse than the first. The upshot of judicial action may defeat the vital political principle which led Congress, more than a hundred years ago, to require districting. . . . Nothing is clearer than that this controversy concerns matters that bring courts into immediate and active relations with party contests. From the determination of such issues this Court has traditionally held aloof. It is hostile to a democratic system to involve the judiciary in the politics of the people. And it is not less pernicious if such judicial intervention in an essentially political contest be dressed up in the abstract phrases of the law.

. . .

To sustain this action would cut very deep into the very being of Congress. Courts ought not to enter this political thicket. The remedy for unfairness in districting is to secure State legislatures that will apportion properly, or to invoke the ample powers of Congress. The Constitution has many commands that are not enforceable by courts because they clearly fall outside the conditions and purposes that circumscribe judicial action. Thus, "on Demand of the executive Authority," of a State it is the duty of a sister State to deliver up a fugitive from justice. But the fulfillment of this duty cannot be judicially enforced. The duty to see to it that the laws are faithfully executed cannot be brought under legal compulsion. Violation of the great guaranty of a republican form of government in States cannot be challenged in the courts. The Constitution has left the performance of many duties in our governmental scheme to depend on the fidelity of the executive and legislative action and, ultimately, on the vigilance of the people in exercising their political rights.

Dismissal of the complaint is affirmed.

Gomillion v. Lightfoot
364 U.S. 339 (1960)

This litigation challenges the validity, under the United States Constitution, of Local Act No. 140, passed by the Legislature of Alabama in 1957, redefining the boundaries of the City of Tuskegee. Petitioners, Negro citizens of Alabama who were, at the time of this redistricting measure, residents of the City of Tuskegee, brought an action in the United States District Court for the Middle District of Alabama for a declaratory judgment that Act 140 is unconstitutional, and for an injunction to restrain the Mayor and officers of

Tuskegee and the officials of Macon County, Alabama, from enforcing the Act against them and other Negroes similarly situated. Petitioners' claim is that enforcement of the statute . . . will constitute a discrimination against them in violation of the Due Process and Equal Protection Clauses of the Fourteenth Amendment to the Constitution and will deny them the right to vote in defiance of the Fifteenth Amendment.

The respondents moved for dismissal of the action for failure to state a claim upon which relief could be granted and for lack of jurisdiction of the District Court. The court granted the motion, stating, "This Court has no control over, no supervision over, and no power to change any boundaries of municipal corporations fixed by a duly convened and elected legislative body, acting for the people in the State of Alabama." On appeal, the Court of Appeals for the Fifth Circuit, affirmed the judgment. . . .

. . .

When a State exercises power wholly within the domain of state interest, it is insulated from federal judicial review. But such insulation is not carried over when state power is used as an instrument for circumventing a federally protected right. This principle has had many applications. It has long been recognized in cases which have prohibited a State from exploiting a power acknowledged to be absolute in an isolated context to justify the imposition of an "unconstitutional condition." What the Court has said in those cases is equally applicable here, viz., that "Acts generally lawful may become unlawful when done to accomplish an unlawful end, and a constitutional power cannot be used by way of condition to attain an unconstitutional result." The petitioners are entitled to prove their allegations at trial.

For these reasons, the principal conclusions of the District Court and the Court of Appeals are clearly erroneous and the decision below must be reversed.

Baker v. Carr
369 U.S. 186 (1962)

. . . The complaint, alleging that by means of a 1901 statute of Tennessee apportioning the members of the General Assembly among the State's 95 counties, "these plaintiffs and others similarly situated, are denied the equal protection of the laws accorded them by the Fourteenth Amendment to the Constitution of the United States by virtue of the debasement of their votes," was dismissed by a three-judge court in the Middle District of Tennessee. The court held that it lacked jurisdiction of the subject matter and also that no claim was stated upon which relief could be granted. . . .

. . .

Between 1901 and 1961, Tennessee has experienced substantial growth and redistribution of her population. In 1901 the population was 2,020,616, of whom 487,380 were eligible to vote. The 1960 Federal Census reports the State's population at 3,567,089, of whom 2,092,891 are eligible to vote. The relative standings of the counties in terms of qualified voters have changed significantly. It is primarily the continued application of the 1901 Apportionment Act to this shifted and enlarged voting population which gives rise to the present controversy.

Indeed, the complaint alleges that the 1901 statute, even as of the time of its passage, "made no apportionment of Representatives and Senators in accordance with the constitutional formula . . . but instead arbitrarily and capriciously apportioned representatives in the Senate and House without reference . . . to any logical or reasonable formula whatever." It is further alleged that "because of the population changes since 1900, and the failure of the Legislature to reapportion itself since 1901," the 1901 statute became "unconstitutional and obsolete." Appellants also argue that, because of the composition of the legislature effected by the 1901 Apportionment Act, redress in the form of a state constitutional amendment to change the entire mechanism for reapportioning, or any other change short of that, is difficult or impossible. The complaint concludes that "these plaintiffs and others similarly situated, are denied the equal protection of the laws accorded them by the Fourteenth Amendment to the Constitution of the United States by virtue of the debasement of their votes." They seek a declaration that the 1901 statute is unconstitutional and an injunction restraining the appellees from acting to conduct any further elections under it. They also pray that unless and until the General Assembly enacts a valid reapportionment, the District Court should either decree a reapportionment by mathematical application of the Tennessee constitutional formulae to the most recent Federal Census figures, or direct the appellees to conduct legislative elections, primary and general, at large. They also pray for such other and further relief as may be appropriate.

Because we deal with this case on appeal from an order of dismissal granted on appellees' motions, precise identification of the issues presently confronting us demands clear exposition of the grounds upon which the District Court rested in dismissing the case. The dismissal order recited that the court sustained the appellees' grounds "(1) that the Court lacks jurisdiction of the subject matter, and (2) that the complaint fails to state a claim upon which relief can be granted. . . ."

. . .

. . . Dismissal of the complaint upon the ground

of lack of jurisdiction of the subject matter would . . . be justified only if that claim were "so attenuated and unsubstantial as to be absolutely devoid of merit" or "frivolous." That the claim is unsubstantial must be "very plain." Since the District Court obviously and correctly did not deem the asserted federal constitutional claim unsubstantial and frivolous, it should not have dismissed the complaint for want of jurisdiction of the subject matter. And of course no further consideration of the merits of the claim is relevant to a determination of the court's jurisdiction of the subject matter. . . .

. . .

We hold that the District Court has jurisdiction of the subject matter of the federal constitutional claim asserted in the complaint.

. . . Have the appellants alleged such a personal stake in the outcome of the controversy as to assure that concrete adverseness which sharpens the presentation of issues upon which the court so largely depends for illumination of difficult constitutional questions? This is the gist of the question of standing. It is, of course, a question of federal law.

The complaint was filed by residents of Davidson, Hamilton, Knox, Montgomery, and Shelby Counties. Each is a person allegedly qualified to vote for members of the General Assembly representing his county. These appellants sued "on their own behalf and on behalf of all qualified voters of their respective counties, and further, on behalf of all voters of the State of Tennessee who are similarly situated. . . ." The appellees are the Tennessee Secretary of State, Attorney General, Coordinator of Elections, and members of the State Board of Elections; the members of the State Board are sued in their own right and also as representatives of the County Election Commissioners whom they appoint.

We hold that the appellants do have standing to maintain this suit. . . .

. . .

It would not be necessary to decide whether appellants' allegations of impairment of their votes by the 1901 apportionment will, ultimately, entitle them to any relief, in order to hold that they have standing to seek it. If such impairment does produce a legally cognizable injury, they are among those who have sustained it. . . .

In holding that the subject matter of this suit was not justiciable, the District Court relied on *Colegrove v. Green* and subsequent per curiam cases. . . . We understand the District Court to have read the cited cases as compelling the conclusion that since the appellants sought to have a legislative apportionment held unconstitutional, their suit presented a "political question" and was therefore nonjusticiable. We hold that this challenge to an apportionment presents no nonjusticiable "political question." The cited cases do not hold the contrary.

Of course the mere fact that the suit seeks protection of a political right does not mean it presents a political question. . . . Rather, it is argued that apportionment cases, whatever the actual wording of the complaint, can involve no federal constitutional right except one resting on the guaranty of a republican form of government, and that complaints based on that clause have been held to present political questions which are nonjusticiable.

We hold that the claim pleaded here neither rests upon nor implicates the Guaranty Clause and that its justiciability is therefore not foreclosed by our decisions of cases involving that clause. The District Court misinterpreted *Colegrove* and other decisions of this Court on which it relied. . . .

. . .

We conclude that the complaint's allegations of a denial of equal protection present a justiciable constitutional cause of action upon which appellants are entitled to a trial and a decision. The right asserted is within the reach of judicial protection under the Fourteenth Amendment.

The judgment of the District Court is reversed and the cause is remanded for further proceedings consistent with this opinion.

Wesberry v. Sanders
376 U.S. 1 (1964)

Appellants are citizens and qualified voters of Fulton County, Georgia, and as such are entitled to vote in congressional elections in Georgia's Fifth Congressional District. That district, one of ten created by a 1931 Georgia statute, includes Fulton, DeKalb, and Rockdale Counties, and has a population, according to the 1960 census, of 823,680. The average population of the ten districts is 394,312, less than half that of the Fifth. One district, the Ninth, has only 272,154 people, less than one-third as many as the Fifth. Since there is only one Congressman for each district, this inequality of population means that the Fifth District's Congressman has to represent from two to three times as many people as do Congressmen from some of the other Georgia districts.

Claiming that these population disparities deprived them and voters similarly situated of a right under the Federal Constitution to have their votes for Congressmen given the same weight as the votes of other Georgians, the appellants brought this action . . . asking that the Georgia statute be declared invalid and that the appellees, the Governor and Secretary of State of Georgia, be enjoined from conducting elections under it. The complaint alleged that appellants were deprived of the full benefit of their right to vote, in violation of (1) Art. I, § 2, of the Constitution of the United States . . . (2) the Due Process, Equal Protection, and Privileges and Immunities Clauses of the Fourteenth Amendment, and (3) that part of Section 2 of the Fourteenth Amendment which provides that "Representatives shall be apportioned among the several States according to their respective numbers. . . ."

The case was heard by a three-judge District Court. . . . [A] majority of the court dismissed the complaint. . . .

. . .

. . . We agree with the District Court that the 1931 Georgia apportionment grossly discriminates against voters in the Fifth Congressional District. A single Congressman represents from two to three times as many Fifth District voters as are represented by each of the Congressmen from the other Georgia congressional districts. The apportionment statute thus contracts the value of some votes and expands that of others. If the Federal Constitution intends that, when qualified voters elect members of Congress, each vote be given as much weight as any other vote, then this statute cannot stand.

We hold that, construed in its historical context, the command of Art. I, § 2 that Representatives be chosen "by the People of the several States" means that, as nearly as is practicable, one man's vote in a congressional election is to be worth as much as another's. . . . We do not believe that the Framers of the Constitution intended to permit the same vote-diluting discrimination to be accomplished through the device of districts containing widely varied numbers of inhabitants. To say that a vote is worth more in one district than in another would not only run counter to our fundamental ideas of democratic government, it would cast aside the principle of a House of Representatives elected "by the People," a principle tenaciously fought for and established at the Constitutional Convention. . . .

. . .

While it may not be possible to draw congressional districts with mathematical precision, that is no excuse for ignoring our Constitution's plain objective of making equal representation for equal numbers of people the fundamental goal for the House of Representatives. That is the high standard of justice and common sense which the Founders set for us.

Reversed and remanded.

Wright v. Rockefeller
376 U.S. 52 (1964)

Appellants, citizens and registered voters of New York's Seventeenth, Eighteenth, Nineteenth, and Twentieth Congressional Districts, all in New York County, brought this action in the United States District Court for the Southern District of New York challenging the constitutionality of that part of Chapter 980 of New York's 1961 congressional apportionment statute which defined these four districts. The Governor and several other New York state officials were named as defendants. . . . Appellants charged that the part of the New York Act in question deprived them of rights guaranteed by the Due Process and Equal Protection Clauses of the Fourteenth Amendment and by the Fifteenth Amendment, which provides that "The right of citizens of the United States to vote shall not be denied or abridged by the United States or by any State on account of race, color, or previous condition of servitude." . . .

. . .

A majority of the District Court found that appellants had not made out their case on the crucial factual issues. . . .

. . .

. . . We accept the findings of the majority of the District Court that appellants failed to prove that the New York Legislature was either motivated by racial considerations or in fact drew the districts on racial lines. . . . As the majority below pointed out, the concentration of colored and Puerto Rican voters in one area in the county made it difficult, even assuming it to be permissible, to fix districts so as to have anything like an equal division of these voters among the districts. Undoubtedly some of these voters . . . would prefer a more even distribution of minority groups among the four congressional districts, but others . . . would argue strenuously that the kind of districts for which appellants contended would be undesirable and, because based on race or place of origin, would themselves be unconstitutional.

We accept the District Court's finding that appellants have not shown that the challenged part of the New York Act was the product of a state contrivance to segregate on the basis of race or place of origin. That finding was crucial to appellants' case as they presented it, and for that reason their challenge cannot be sustained. We do not pass on the question which appellants have not presented here, that is, whether the state apportionment is constitutionally invalid because it may fail in its objective to create districts based as nearly as practicable on equal population. Since no such challenge has been urged here, the issues have not been formulated to bring it into focus, and the evidence has not been offered or appraised to decide it, our holding has no bearing on that wholly separate question.

The judgment dismissing the complaint is affirmed.

Reynolds v. Sims
377 U.S. 533 (1964)

Involved in these cases are an appeal and two cross-appeals from a decision of the Federal District Court for the Middle District of Alabama holding invalid, under the Equal Protection Clause of the Federal Constitution, the existing and two legislatively proposed plans for the apportionment of seats in the two houses of the Alabama Legislature, and ordering into effect a temporary reapportionment plan comprised of parts of the proposed but judicially disapproved measures.

On August 26, 1961, the original plaintiffs, residents, taxpayers and voters of Jefferson County, Alabama, filed a complaint in the United States District Court for the Middle District of Alabama, in their own behalf and on behalf of all similarly situated Alabama voters, challenging the apportionment of the Alabama Legislature. Defendants below (appellants in No. 23), sued in their representative capacities, were various state and political party officials charged with the performance of certain duties in connection with state elections. The complaint alleged a deprivation of rights under the Alabama Constitution and under the Equal Protection Clause of the Fourteenth Amendment, and asserted that the District Court had jurisdiction under provisions of the Civil Rights Act.

. . .

The maximum size of the Alabama House was increased from 105 to 106 with the creation of a new county in 1903, pursuant to the constitutional provision which states that, in addition to the prescribed 105 House seats, each county thereafter created shall be entitled to one representative. Article IX, 202 and 203, of the Alabama Constitution established precisely the boundaries of the

State's senatorial and representative districts until the enactment of a new reapportionment plan by the legislature. These 1901 constitutional provisions, specifically describing the composition of the senatorial districts and detailing the number of House seats allocated to each county, were periodically enacted as statutory measures by the Alabama Legislature, as modified only by the creation of an additional county in 1903, and provided the plan of legislative apportionment existing at the time this litigation was commenced.

Plaintiffs below alleged that the last apportionment of the Alabama Legislature was based on the 1900 federal census, despite the requirement of the State Constitution that the legislature be reapportioned decennially. They asserted that, since the population growth in the State from 1900 to 1960 had been uneven, Jefferson and other counties were now victims of serious discrimination with respect to the allocation of legislative representation. As a result of the failure of the legislature to reapportion itself, plaintiffs asserted, they were denied "equal suffrage in free and equal elections . . . and the equal protection of the laws" in violation of the Alabama Constitution and the Fourteenth Amendment to the Federal Constitution. The complaint asserted that plaintiffs had no other adequate remedy, and that they had exhausted all forms of relief other than that available through the federal courts. They alleged that the Alabama Legislature had established a pattern of prolonged inaction from 1911 to the present which "clearly demonstrates that no reapportionment . . . shall be effected"; that representation at any future constitutional convention would be established by the legislature, making it unlikely that the membership of any such convention would be fairly representative; and that, while the Alabama Supreme Court had found that the legislature had not complied with

the State Constitution in failing to reapportion according to population decennially, that court had nevertheless indicated that it would not interfere with matters of legislative reapportionment.

Plaintiffs . . . sought a declaration that the existing constitutional and statutory provisions, establishing the present apportionment of seats in the Alabama Legislature, were unconstitutional under the Alabama and Federal Constitutions, and an injunction against the holding of future elections for legislators until the legislature reapportioned itself in accordance, with the State Constitution. They further requested the issuance of a mandatory injunction, effective until such time as the legislature properly reapportioned, requiring the conducting of the 1962 election for legislators at large over the entire State, and any other relief which "may seem just, equitable and proper."

. . .

On March 29, 1962, just three days after this Court had decided *Baker v. Carr*, plaintiffs moved for a preliminary injunction requiring defendants to conduct at large the May 1962 Democratic primary election and the November 1962 general election for members of the Alabama Legislature. The District Court set the motion for hearing in an order stating its tentative views that an injunction was not required before the May 1962 primary election to protect plaintiffs' constitutional rights, and that the Court should take no action which was not "absolutely essential" for the protection of the asserted constitutional rights before the Alabama Legislature had had a "further reasonable but prompt opportunity to comply with its duty" under the Alabama Constitution.

On April 14, 1962, the District Court, after reiterating the views expressed in its earlier order, reset the case for hearing on July 16, noting that the importance of the case, together with the necessity for effective action within a limited period of time, required an early announcement of its views. . . . It stated that it was taking judicial notice of the facts that there had been population changes in Alabama's counties since 1901, that the present representation in the State Legislature was not on a population basis, and that the legislature had never reapportioned its membership as required by the Alabama Constitution. Continuing, the Court stated that if the legislature complied with the Alabama constitutional provision requiring legislative representation to be based on population there could be no objection on federal constitutional grounds to such an apportionment. The Court further indicated that, if the legislature failed to act, or if its actions did not meet constitutional standards, it would be under a "clear duty" to take some action on the matter prior to the November 1962 general election. The District Court stated that its "present thinking" was to follow an approach suggested by Justice Clark in his concurring opinion in *Baker*— awarding seats released by the consolidation or revamping of existing districts to counties suffering "the most egregious discrimination," thereby releasing the strangle hold on the legislature sufficiently so as to permit the newly elected body to enact a constitutionally valid and permanent reapportionment plan, and allowing eventual dismissal of the case. Subsequently, plaintiffs were permitted to amend their complaint by adding a further prayer for relief, which asked the District Court to reapportion the Alabama Legislature provisionally so that the rural strangle hold would be relaxed enough to permit it to reapportion itself.

On July 12, 1962, an extraordinary session of the Alabama Legislature adopted two reapportionment plans to take effect for the 1966 elections. One was a proposed constitutional amendment, referred to as the "67-Senator Amendment." It provided for a House of Representatives consisting of 106 members, apportioned by giving one seat to each of Alabama's 67 counties and distributing the others according to population by the "equal proportions" method. Using this formula, the constitutional amendment specified the number of representatives allotted to each county until a new apportionment could be made on the basis of the 1970 census. The Senate was to be composed of 67 members, one from each county. The legislation provided that the proposed amendment should be submitted to the voters for ratification at the November 1962 general election.

The other reapportionment plan was embodied in a statutory measure adopted by the legislature and signed into law by the Alabama Governor, and was referred to as the "Crawford-Webb Act." It was enacted as standby legislation to take effect in 1966 if the proposed constitutional amendment should fail of passage by a majority of the State's voters, or should the federal courts refuse to accept the proposed amendment (though not rejected by the voters) as effective action in compliance with the requirements of the Fourteenth Amendment. The act provided for a Senate consisting of 35 members, representing 35 senatorial districts established along county lines, and altered only a few of the former districts. In apportioning the 106 seats in the Alabama House of Representatives, the statutory measure gave each county one seat, and apportioned the remaining 39 on a rough population basis, under a formula requiring increasingly more population for a county to be accorded additional seats. The Crawford-Webb Act also provided that it would be effective "until the legislature is reapportioned according to law," but provided no standards for such a reapportionment. Future apportionments would presumably be based on the existing provisions of the Alabama Constitution which the statute, unlike the proposed constitutional amendment, would not affect.

. . .

On July 21, 1962, the District Court held that the inequality of the existing representation in the Alabama Legislature violated the Equal Protection Clause of the Fourteenth Amendment, a finding which the Court noted had been "generally conceded" by the parties to the litigation, since population growth and shifts had converted the 1901 scheme, as perpetuated some 60 years later, into an invidiously discriminatory plan completely lacking in rationality. . . .

The Court then considered both the proposed constitutional amendment and the Crawford-Webb Act to ascertain whether the legislature had taken effective action to remedy the unconstitutional aspects of the existing apportionment. . . .

The Court stated that the apportionment of one senator to each county, under the proposed constitutional amendment, would "make the discrimination in the Senate even more invidious than at present." . . . Noting that the "only conceivable rationalization" of the senatorial apportionment scheme is that it was based on equal representation of political subdivisions within the State and is thus analogous to the Federal Senate, the District Court rejected the analogy on the ground that Alabama counties are merely involuntary political units of the State created by statute to aid in the administration of state government. . . .

The Court also noted that the senatorial apportionment proposal "may not have complied with the State Constitution," since not only is it explicitly provided that the population basis of legislative representation "shall not be changed by constitutional amendments," but the Alabama Supreme Court had previously indicated that that

requirement could probably be altered only by constitutional convention. The Court concluded, however, that the apportionment of seats in the Alabama House, under the proposed constitutional amendment, was "based upon reason, with a rational regard for known and accepted standards of apportionment." . . .

Turning next to the provisions of the Crawford-Webb Act, the District Court found that its apportionment of the 106 seats in the Alabama House of Representatives, by allocating one seat to each county and distributing the remaining 39 to the more populous counties in diminishing ratio to their populations, was "totally unacceptable." . . . The Court regarded the senatorial apportionment provided in the Crawford-Webb Act as "a step in the right direction, but an extremely short step," and but a "slight improvement over the present system of representation." . . .

. . .

The District Court then directed its concern to the providing of an effective remedy. . . . Stating that it was retaining jurisdiction and deferring any hearing on plaintiffs' motion for a permanent injunction "until the Legislature, as provisionally reapportioned . . . has an opportunity to provide for a true reapportionment of both Houses of the Alabama Legislature," the Court emphasized that its "moderate" action was designed to break the strangle hold by the smaller counties on the Alabama Legislature and would not suffice as a permanent reapportionment. On July 25, 1962, the Court entered its decree in accordance with its previously stated determinations, concluding that "plaintiffs . . . are denied . . . equal protection . . . by virtue of the debasement of their votes since the Legislature of the State of Alabama has failed and continues to fail to reapportion itself as required by law." It enjoined the defendant state officials from holding any future elections under any of the apportionment plans that it had found invalid, and stated that the 1962 election of Alabama legislators could validly be conducted only under the apportionment scheme specified in the Court's order.

After the District Court's decision, new primary elections were held pursuant to legislation enacted in 1962 at the same special session as the proposed constitutional amendment and the Crawford-Webb Act, to be effective in the event the Court itself ordered a particular reapportionment plan into immediate effect. The November 1962 general election was likewise conducted on the basis of the District Court's ordered apportionment of legislative seats. . . . Consequently, the present Alabama Legislature is apportioned in accordance with the temporary plan prescribed by the District Court's decree. . . .

. . .

Notices of appeal to this Court from the District Court's decision were timely filed by defendants below and by two groups of intervenor-plaintiffs. Appellants contend that the District Court erred in holding the existing and the two proposed plans for the apportionment of seats in the Alabama Legislature unconstitutional, and that a federal court lacks the power to affirmatively reapportion seats in a state legislature. Cross-appellants assert that the court below erred in failing to compel reapportionment of the Alabama Senate on a population basis as allegedly required by the Alabama Constitution and the Equal Protection Clause of the Federal Constitution. Cross-appellants contend that the District Court should have required and ordered into effect the apportionment of seats in both houses of the Alabama Legislature on a population basis. . . .

. . .

Legislators represent people, not trees or acres. Legislators are elected by voters, not farms or cities or economic interests. As long as ours is a representative form of government, and our legislatures are those instruments of government elected directly by and directly representative of the people, the right to elect legislators in a free and unimpaired fashion is a bedrock of our political system. It could hardly be gainsaid that a constitutional claim had been asserted by an allegation that certain otherwise qualified voters had been entirely prohibited from voting for members of their state legislature. And, if a State should provide that the votes of citizens in one part of the State should be given two times, or five times, or 10 times the weight of votes of citizens in another part of the State, it could hardly be contended that the right to vote of those residing in the disfavored areas had not been effectively diluted. It would appear extraordinary to suggest that a State could be constitutionally permitted to enact a law providing that certain of the State's voters could vote two, five, or 10 times for their legislative representatives, while voters living elsewhere could vote only once. And it is inconceivable that a state law to the effect that, in counting votes for legislators, the votes of citizens in one part of the State would be multiplied by two, five, or 10, while the votes of persons in another area would be counted only at face value, could be constitutionally sustainable. Of course, the effect of state legislative districting schemes which give the same number of representatives to unequal numbers of constituents is identical. Overweighting and overvaluation of the votes of those living here has the certain effect of dilution and undervaluation of the votes of those living there. The resulting discrimination against those individual voters living in disfavored areas is easily demonstrable mathematically. Their right to vote is simply not the same right to vote as that of those living in a favored part of the State.

Two, five, or 10 of them must vote before the effect of their voting is equivalent to that of their favored neighbor. Weighting the votes of citizens differently, by any method or means, merely because of where they happen to reside, hardly seems justifiable. One must be ever aware that the Constitution forbids "sophisticated as well as simple-minded modes of discrimination." . . .

State legislatures are, historically, the fountainhead of representative government in this country. A number of them have their roots in colonial times, and substantially antedate the creation of our nation and our federal government. In fact, the first formal stirrings of American political independence are to be found, in large part, in the views and actions of several of the colonial legislative bodies. With the birth of our national government, and the adoption and ratification of the Federal Constitution, state legislatures retained a most important place in our nation's governmental structure. But representative government is in essence self-government through the medium of elected representatives of the people, and each and every citizen has an inalienable right to full and effective participation in the political processes of his State's legislative bodies. Most citizens can achieve this participation only as qualified voters through the election of legislators to represent them. Full and effective participation by all citizens in state government requires, therefore, that each citizen have an equally effective voice in the election of members of his state legislature. Modern and viable state government needs, and the Constitution demands, no less.

Logically, in a society ostensibly grounded on representative government, it would seem reasonable that a majority of the people of a State could elect a majority of that State's legislators. To conclude differently, and to sanction minority control of state legislative bodies, would appear to deny majority rights in a way that far surpasses any possible denial of minority rights that might otherwise be thought to result. Since legislatures are responsible for enacting laws by which all citizens are to be governed, they should be bodies which are collectively responsive to the popular will. And the concept of equal protection has been traditionally viewed as requiring the uniform treatment of persons standing in the same relation to the governmental action questioned or challenged. With respect to the allocation of legislative representation, all voters, as citizens of a State, stand in the same relation regardless of where they live. Any suggested criteria for the differentiation of citizens are insufficient to justify any discrimination, as to the weight of their votes, unless relevant to the permissible purposes of legislative apportionment. Since the achieving of fair and effective representation for all citizens is concededly the basic aim of legislative apportionment, we conclude that the Equal Protection Clause guarantees the opportunity for equal participation by all voters in the election of state legislators. Diluting the weight of votes because of place of residence impairs basic constitutional rights under the Fourteenth Amendment just as much as invidious discriminations based upon factors such as race or economic status. Our constitutional system amply provides for the protection of minorities by means other than giving them majority control of state legislatures. And the democratic ideals of equality and majority rule, which have served this Nation so well in the past, are hardly of any less significance for the present and the future.

We are told that the matter of apportioning representation in a state legislature is a complex and many-faceted one. We are advised that States can rationally consider factors other than population in apportioning legislative representation.

We are admonished not to restrict the power of the States to impose differing views as to political philosophy on their citizens. We are cautioned about the dangers of entering into political thickets and mathematical quagmires. Our answer is this: a denial of constitutionally protected rights demands judicial protection; our oath and our office require no less of us.

. . .

To the extent that a citizen's right to vote is debased, he is that much less a citizen. The fact that an individual lives here or there is not a legitimate reason for overweighting or diluting the efficacy of his vote. The complexions of societies and civilizations change, often with amazing rapidity. A nation once primarily rural in character becomes predominantly urban. Representation schemes once fair and equitable become archaic and outdated. But the basic principle of representative government remains, and must remain, unchanged—the weight of a citizen's vote cannot be made to depend on where he lives. Population is, of necessity, the starting point for consideration and the controlling criterion for judgment in legislative apportionment controversies. A citizen, a qualified voter, is no more nor no less so because he lives in the city or on the farm. This is the clear and strong command of our Constitution's Equal Protection Clause. This is an essential part of the concept of a government of laws and not men. . . .

We hold that, as a basic constitutional standard, the Equal Protection Clause requires that the seats in both houses of a bicameral state legislature must be apportioned on a population basis. Simply stated, an individual's right to vote for state legislators is unconstitutionally impaired when its weight is in a substantial fashion diluted when compared with votes of citizens living in other parts of the State. Since, under neither the

existing apportionment provisions nor either of the proposed plans was either of the houses of the Alabama Legislature apportioned on a population basis, the District Court correctly held that all three of these schemes were constitutionally invalid. Furthermore, the existing apportionment, and also to a lesser extent the apportionment under the Crawford-Webb Act, presented little more than crazy quilts, completely lacking in rationality, and could be found invalid on that basis alone.

Although the District Court presumably found the apportionment of the Alabama House of Representatives under the 67–Senator Amendment to be acceptable, we conclude that the deviations from a strict population basis are too egregious to permit us to find that that body, under this proposed plan, was apportioned sufficiently on a population basis so as to permit the arrangement to be constitutionally sustained. . . . While mathematical nicety is not a constitutional requisite, one could hardly conclude that the Alabama House, under the proposed constitutional amendment, had been apportioned sufficiently on a population basis to be sustainable under the requirements of the Equal Protection Clause. And none of the other apportionments of seats in either of the bodies of the Alabama Legislature, under the three plans considered by the District Court, came nearly as close to approaching the required constitutional standard as did that of the House of Representatives under the 67–Senator Amendment.

. . .

. . . [W]e conclude that the plan contained in the 67–Senator Amendment for apportioning seats in the Alabama Legislature cannot be sustained by recourse to the so-called federal analogy. Nor can any other inequitable state legislative apportionment scheme be justified on such an asserted basis. This does not necessarily mean that such a plan is irrational or involves something other than a "republican form of government." We conclude simply that such a plan is impermissible for the States under the Equal Protection Clause, since perforce resulting, in virtually every case, in submergence of the equal-population principle in at least one house of a state legislature.

Since we find the so-called federal analogy inapposite to a consideration of the constitutional validity of state legislative apportionment schemes, we necessarily hold that the Equal Protection Clause requires both houses of a state legislature to be apportioned on a population basis. The right of a citizen to equal representation and to have his vote weighted equally with those of all other citizens in the election of members of one house of a bicameral state legislature would amount to little if States could effectively submerge the equal-population principle in the apportionment of seats in the other house. If such a scheme were permissible, an individual citizen's ability to exercise an effective voice in the only instrument of state government directly representative of the people might be almost as effectively thwarted as if neither house were apportioned on a population basis. Deadlock between the two bodies might result in compromise and concession on some issues. But in all too many cases the more probable result would be frustration of the majority will through minority veto in the house not apportioned on a population basis, stemming directly from the failure to accord adequate overall legislative representation to all of the State's citizens on a nondiscriminatory basis. In summary, we can perceive no constitutional difference, with respect to the geographical distribution of state legislative representation, between the two houses of a bicameral state legislature.

We do not believe that the concept of bicam-

eralism is rendered anachronistic and meaningless when the predominant basis of representation in the two state legislative bodies is required to be the same— population. A prime reason for bicameralism, modernly considered, is to insure mature and deliberate consideration of, and to prevent precipitate action on, proposed legislative measures. Simply because the controlling criterion for apportioning representation is required to be the same in both houses does not mean that there will be no differences in the composition and complexion of the two bodies. Different constituencies can be represented in the two houses. . . . The length of terms of the legislators in the separate bodies could differ. The numerical size of the two bodies could be made to differ, even significantly, and the geographical size of districts from which legislators are elected could also be made to differ. And apportionment in one house could be arranged so as to balance off minor inequities in the representation of certain areas in the other house. . . .

. . .

. . . Somewhat more flexibility may . . . be constitutionally permissible with respect to state legislative apportionment than in congressional districting. Lower courts can and assuredly will work out more concrete and specific standards for evaluating state legislative apportionment schemes in the context of actual litigation. For the present, we deem it expedient not to attempt to spell out any precise constitutional tests. What is marginally permissible in one State may be unsatisfactory in another, depending on the particular circumstances of the case. Developing a body of doctrine on a case-by-case basis appears to us to provide the most satisfactory means of arriving at detailed constitutional requirements in the area of state legislative apportionment. Thus, we proceed to state here only a few rather general considerations which appear to us to be relevant.

A State may legitimately desire to maintain the integrity of various political subdivisions, insofar as possible, and provide for compact districts of contiguous territory in designing a legislative apportionment scheme. Valid considerations may underlie such aims. Indiscriminate districting, without any regard for political subdivision or natural or historical boundary lines, may be little more than an open invitation to partisan gerrymandering. . . . Whatever the means of accomplishment, the overriding objective must be substantial equality of population among the various districts, so that the vote of any citizen is approximately equal in weight to that of any other citizen in the State.

. . . So long as the divergences from a strict population standard are based on legitimate considerations incident to the effectuation of a rational state policy, some deviations from the equal-population principle are constitutionally permissible with respect to the apportionment of seats in either or both of the two houses of a bicameral state legislature. . . .

A consideration that appears to be of more substance in justifying some deviations from population-based representation in state legislatures is that of insuring some voice to political subdivisions, as political subdivisions. Several factors make more than insubstantial claims that a State can rationally consider according political subdivisions some independent representation in at least one body of the state legislature, as long as the basic standard of equality of population among districts is maintained. Local governmental entities are frequently charged with various responsibilities incident to the operation of state government. In many States much of the legislature's activity involves the enactment of so-called local legislation, directed only to the concerns of particular political subdivisions. And a State may legitimately desire to construct districts along political subdivision lines to deter the possibilities of gerrymandering. However, permitting deviations from population-based representation does not mean that each local governmental unit or political subdivision can be given separate representation, regardless of population. Carried too far, a scheme of giving at least one seat in one house to each political subdivision . . . could easily result, in many States, in a total subversion of the equal-population principle in that legislative body. . . . But if, even as a result of a clearly rational state policy of according some legislative representation to political subdivisions, population is submerged as the controlling consideration in the apportionment of seats in the particular legislative body, then the right of all of the State's citizens to cast an effective and adequately weighted vote would be unconstitutionally impaired.

One of the arguments frequently offered as a basis for upholding a State's legislative apportionment arrangement, despite substantial disparities from a population basis in either or both houses, is grounded on congressional approval, incident to admitting States into the Union, of state apportionment plans containing deviations from the equal-population principle. . . . Congress presumably does not assume, in admitting States into the Union, to pass on all constitutional questions relating to the character of state governmental organization. In any event, congressional approval, however well-considered, could hardly validate an unconstitutional state legislative apportionment. Congress simply lacks the constitutional power to insulate States from attack with respect to alleged deprivations of individual constitutional rights.

That the Equal Protection Clause requires that both houses of a state legislature be apportioned on a population basis does not mean that States cannot adopt some reasonable plan for periodic revision of their apportionment schemes. Decennial reapportionment appears to be a rational approach to readjustment of legislative representation in order to take into account population shifts and growth. . . . Limitations on the frequency of reapportionment are justified by the need for stability and continuity in the organization of the legislative system, although undoubtedly reapportioning no more frequently than every 10 years leads to some imbalance in the population of districts toward the end of the decennial period and also to the development of resistance to change on the part of some incumbent legislators. In substance, we do not regard the Equal Protection Clause as requiring daily, monthly, annual or biennial reapportionment, so long as a State has a reasonably conceived plan for periodic readjustment of legislative representation. While we do not intend to indicate that decennial reapportionment is a constitutional requisite, compliance with such an approach would clearly meet the minimal requirements for maintaining a reasonably current scheme of legislative representation. And we do not mean to intimate that more frequent reapportionment would not be constitutionally permissible or practicably desirable. But if reapportionment were accomplished with less frequency, it would assuredly be constitutionally suspect.

. . .

We do not consider here the difficult question of the proper remedial devices which federal courts should utilize in state legislative apportionment cases. Remedial techniques in this new and developing area of the law will probably often differ with the circumstances of the challenged apportionment and a variety of local conditions. It is enough to say now that, once a

State's legislative apportionment scheme has been found to be unconstitutional, it would be the unusual case in which a court would be justified in not taking appropriate action to insure that no further elections are conducted under the invalid plan. However, under certain circumstances, such as where an impending election is imminent and a State's election machinery is already in progress, equitable considerations might justify a court in withholding the granting of immediately effective relief in a legislative apportionment case, even though the existing apportionment scheme was found invalid. In awarding or withholding immediate relief, a court is entitled to and should consider the proximity of a forthcoming election and the mechanics and complexities of state election laws, and should act and rely upon general equitable principles. . . .

We feel that the District Court in this case acted in a most proper and commendable manner. It initially acted wisely in declining to stay the impending primary election in Alabama, and properly refrained from acting further until the Alabama Legislature had been given an opportunity to remedy the admitted discrepancies in the State's legislative apportionment scheme, while initially stating some of its views to provide guidelines for legislative action. And it correctly recognized that legislative reapportionment is primarily a matter for legislative consideration and determination, and that judicial relief becomes appropriate only when a legislature fails to reapportion according to federal constitutional requisites in a timely fashion after having had an adequate opportunity to do so. Additionally, the court below acted with proper judicial restraint, after the Alabama Legislature had failed to act effectively in remedying the constitutional deficiencies in the State's legislative apportionment scheme, in ordering its own temporary reapportionment plan into effect, at a time sufficiently early to permit the holding of elections pursuant to that plan without great difficulty, and in prescribing a plan admittedly provisional in purpose so as not to usurp the primary responsibility for reapportionment which rests with the legislature.

We find, therefore, that the action taken by the District Court in this case, in ordering into effect a reapportionment of both houses of the Alabama Legislature for purposes of the 1962 primary and general elections, by using the best parts of the two proposed plans which it had found, as a whole, to be invalid, was an appropriate and well-considered exercise of judicial power. Admittedly, the lower court's ordered plan was intended only as a temporary and provisional measure and the District Court correctly indicated that the plan was invalid as a permanent apportionment. In retaining jurisdiction while deferring a hearing on the issuance of a final injunction in order to give the provisionally reapportioned legislature an opportunity to act effectively, the court below proceeded in a proper fashion. Since the District Court evinced its realization that its ordered reapportionment could not be sustained as the basis for conducting the 1966 election of Alabama legislators, and avowedly intends to take some further action should the reapportioned Alabama Legislature fail to enact a constitutionally valid, permanent apportionment scheme in the interim, we affirm the judgment below and remand the cases for further proceedings consistent with the views stated in this opinion.

WMCA, Inc. v. Lomenzo
377 U.S. 633 (1964)

Appellants initially brought this action on May 1, 1961, in the Federal District Court for the Southern District of New York. Plaintiffs below included individual citizens and voters residing in five of the six most populous New York counties . . . suing in their own behalf and on behalf of all New York citizens similarly situated. Appellees, sued in their representative capacities, are various state and local officials charged with duties in connection with reapportionment and the conducting of state elections. . . .

Plaintiffs below sought a declaration that those provisions of the state constitution which establish the formulas for apportioning seats in the two houses of the New York Legislature, and the statutes implementing them, are unconstitutional since violative of the Fourteenth Amendment to the Federal Constitution. The complaint further asked the District Court to enjoin defendants from performing any acts or duties in compliance with the allegedly unconstitutional legislative apportionment provisions. Plaintiffs asserted that they had no adequate remedy other than the judicial relief sought, and requested the court to retain jurisdiction until the New York Legislature, "freed from the fetters imposed by the Constitutional provisions invalidated by this Court, provides for such apportionment of the State legislature as will insure to the urban voters of New York State the rights guaranteed them by the Constitution of the United States."

. . .

The complaint asserted that the legislative apportionment provisions of the 1894 New York Constitution, as amended, are not only presently unconstitutional, but also were invalid and violative of the Fourteenth Amendment at the time of their adoption, and that "[t]he population growth in the State of New York and the shifts of population to urban areas have aggravated the violation of Plaintiffs' rights under the XIV Amendment."

. . . The New York City defendants admitted the allegations of the complaint and requested the Court to grant plaintiffs the relief they were seeking. The remaining defendants moved to dismiss. On January 11, 1962, the District Court. . . . held that it had jurisdiction but dismissed the complaint, without reaching the merits, on the ground that it failed to state a claim upon which relief could be granted, since the issues raised were nonjusticiable. . . .

. . .

Plaintiffs appealed to this Court from the District Court's dismissal of their complaint. On June 11, 1962, we vacated the judgment below and remanded for further consideration. . . .

On August 16, 1962, the District Court, after conducting a hearing, dismissed the complaint on the merits, concluding that plaintiffs had not shown by a preponderance of the evidence that there was any invidious discrimination, that the apportionment provisions of the New York Constitution were rational and not arbitrary, that they were of historical origin and contained no improper geographical discrimination, that they could be amended by an electoral majority of the citizens of New York, and that therefore the apportionment of seats in the New York Senate and Assembly was not unconstitutional. Finding no failure by the New York Legislature to comply with the state constitutional provisions requiring and establishing the formulas for periodic reapportionment of Senate and Assembly seats, the court below relied on the presumption of constitutionality attaching to a state constitutional provision and the necessity for a clear violation "before a federal court of equity will lend its power to the disruption of the state election processes. . . ." After postulating a number of "tests" for invidious discrimination, including the "[r]ationality of state policy and whether or not

the system is arbitrary," "[w]hether or not the present complexion of the legislature has a historical basis," whether the electorate has an available political remedy, and "[g]eography, including accessibility of legislative representatives to their electors," the Court concluded that none of the relevant New York constitutional provisions were arbitrary or irrational in giving weight to, in addition to population, "the ingredient of area, accessibility and character of interest." Stating that in New York "the county is a classic unit of governmental organization and administration," the District Court found that the allocation of one Assembly seat to each county was grounded on a historical basis. . . . As a result of the District Court's dismissal of the complaint, the November 1962 election of New York legislators was conducted pursuant to the existing apportionment scheme. . . .

. . .

No adequate political remedy to obtain relief against alleged legislative malapportionment appears to exist in New York. No initiative procedure exists under New York law. A proposal to amend the State Constitution can be submitted to a vote by the State's electorate only after approval by a majority of both houses of two successive sessions of the New York Legislature. A majority vote of both houses of the legislature is also required before the electorate can vote on the calling of a constitutional convention. Additionally, under New York law the question of whether a constitutional convention should be called must be submitted to the electorate every 20 years, commencing in 1957. But even if a constitutional convention were convened, the same alleged discrimination which currently exists in the apportionment of Senate seats against each of the counties having 6 percent or more of a State's citizen population would be perpetuated in the election of convention delegates. And, since the New York Legislature has rather consistently complied with the state constitutional requirement for decennial legislative reapportionment in accordance with the rather explicit constitutional rules, enacting effective apportionment statutes in 1907, 1917, 1943, and 1953, judicial relief in the state courts to remedy the alleged malapportionment was presumably unavailable.

. . .

We have examined the state constitutional formulas governing legislative apportionment in New York in a detailed fashion in order to point out that, as a result of following these provisions, the weight of the votes of those living in populous areas is of necessity substantially diluted in effect. However complicated or sophisticated an apportionment scheme might be, it cannot, consistent with the Equal Protection Clause, result in a significant undervaluation of the weight of the votes of certain of a State's citizens merely because of where they happen to reside. New York's constitutional formulas relating to legislative apportionment demonstrably include a built-in bias against voters living in the State's more populous counties. . . .

We find it inappropriate to discuss questions relating to remedies at the present time, beyond what we said in our opinion in *Reynolds*. Since all members of both houses of the New York Legislature will be elected in November 1964, the court below, acting under equitable principles, must now determine whether, because of the imminence of that election and in order to give the New York Legislature an opportunity to fashion a constitutionally valid legislative apportionment plan, it would be desirable to permit the 1964 election of legislators to be conducted pursuant to the existing provisions, or whether under the circumstances the effectuation of appellants' right

to a properly weighted voice in the election of state legislators should not be delayed beyond the 1964 election. We therefore reverse the decision below and remand the case to the District Court for further proceedings consistent with the views stated here and in our opinion in *Reynolds v. Sims*.

Maryland Committee for Fair Representation v. Tawes
377 U.S. 656 (1964)

Appellants, residents, taxpayers and voters in four populous Maryland counties . . . and the City of Baltimore, and an unincorporated association, originally brought an action in the Circuit Court of Anne Arundel County, in August 1960, challenging the apportionment of the Maryland Legislature. Defendants below, sued in their representative capacities, were various officials charged with duties in connection with state elections. Plaintiffs below alleged that the apportionment of both houses of the Maryland Legislature, pursuant to Art. III, 2 and 5, of the 1867 Maryland Constitution, discriminated against inhabitants of the more populous counties and the City of Baltimore by according these persons substantially less representation than that given to persons residing in other areas of the state. They contended that the alleged legislative malapportionment violated the Equal Protection Clause of the Fourteenth Amendment since that provision prohibits any State from "denying, diluting or restricting the equality of voting rights or privileges among classes of otherwise eligible voters similarly situated," and asserted that there was no political remedy practicably available under Maryland law to obtain the relief sought.

Plaintiffs below sought a declaratory judgment that Art. III, 2 and 5, of the Maryland Constitution deny them and those similarly situated rights protected under the Equal Protection Clause, and that the failure of the Maryland Legislature to reapportion its membership in accordance with a formula which would reasonably reflect present population figures deprived them of their constitutional rights. Plaintiffs also requested a declaration that the failure of the Maryland General Assembly to convene a constitutional convention as approved by a majority of the State's voters in the general election of 1950 violated various provisions of the state constitution.

Plaintiffs requested that, unless the November 1962 election and elections thereafter were conducted on an at-large basis, the court enjoin defendants from performing various election duties until such time as the General Assembly should submit for a referendum vote by eligible state voters an amendment to Art. III, 2 and 5, which would reapportion the membership of the Maryland Legislature on a population basis in conformity with the requirements of the Fourteenth Amendment. Plaintiffs also asked the court to retain jurisdiction of the case until the General Assembly submitted such a constitutional amendment to the state's voters.

On February 21, 1961, the Circuit Court sustained defendants' demurrers to plaintiffs' complaint and dismissed the complaint without leave to amend. On appeal, the Maryland Court of Appeals . . . reversed the order of the Circuit Court and remanded the case for a hearing on the merits. . . .

. . . In remanding to the lower state court to "receive evidence to determine whether or not an invidious discrimination does exist with respect to representation in either or both houses" of the Maryland Legislature, the Court of Appeals stated that, if the Maryland constitutional provisions relating to legislative apportionment were held invalid as to the November 1962 election,

the Circuit Court should "also declare that the Legislature has the power, if called into Special Session by the Governor and such action be deemed appropriate by it, to enact a bill reapportioning its membership for purposes" of that election.

On May 24, 1962, the Circuit Court, after receiving various exhibits and hearing argument, held that the apportionment of the Maryland House of Delegates invidiously discriminated against the people of Baltimore, Montgomery, and Prince George's counties, but not against the people of Baltimore City or Anne Arundel County, and that therefore Art. III, 5, of the Maryland Constitution, which apportions seats in the House of Delegates, violates the Equal Protection Clause of the Fourteenth Amendment. Although stating that the apportionment of the Maryland Senate might be "constitutionally based upon area and geographical location regardless of population or eligible voters," the Circuit Court refrained from formally passing on the validity of the senatorial apportionment. The lower court also stated that the Maryland Legislature had the power to enact a statute providing for the reapportionment of the House of Delegates as well as to propose a constitutional amendment providing for such a reapportionment. It withheld the granting of injunctive relief but retained jurisdiction to do so before the November 1962 election if such became appropriate.

On May 31, 1962, the Maryland Legislature, called into special session by the Governor, enacted temporary "stop-gap" legislation reapportioning seats in the House of Delegates, by allocating 19 added seats to the more populous areas of the State. However, the legislature failed to pass a proposed constitutional amendment reapportioning the Maryland House. The newly enacted apportionment statute expires automatically on January 1, 1966, except that, if a constitutional amendment superseding the statutory provisions is submitted to the voters at the 1964 general election and is rejected, the statute will continue in force until January 1, 1970. The statute further provides that upon its expiration the House of Delegates shall again be apportioned according to Art. III, 5, which the Circuit Court had previously held unconstitutional. No appeal was taken from the Circuit Court's decision holding invalid the existing apportionment of the Maryland House of Delegates.

Following the Circuit Court's failure to rule upon the validity of the senatorial apportionment, plaintiffs appealed this question to the Maryland Court of Appeals. On June 8, 1962, the Court of Appeals ordered the case remanded to the Circuit Court for a prompt decision on whether Art. III, 2, of the Maryland Constitution, apportioning seats in the Senate, was valid or invalid under the Equal Protection Clause. On June 28, 1962, the Circuit Court held that the apportionment of the Maryland Senate did not violate the Federal Constitution because it felt that an apportionment based upon area and geographical location, without regard to population, served to protect minorities, preserve legislative checks and balances, and prevent hasty, though temporarily popular, legislation, and accorded with history, tradition and reason, placing considerable reliance on a comparison of that body of the Maryland Legislature with the Federal Senate.

On July 23, 1962, the Maryland Court of Appeals . . . affirmed the Circuit Court's decision holding valid the apportionment of the Maryland Senate, noting that its reasons would be stated in an opinion to be filed at a later date. Plaintiffs' motion for reargument, calling attention to recent decisions and developments relating to legislative apportionment, was denied by the Maryland Court of Appeals on September 11,

1962. On September 25, 1962, the Court of Appeals filed its opinion. It stated initially that the appeal did not question the apportionment of the Maryland House. Continuing, the Maryland court indicated that it was affirming the decision below and upholding the constitutionality of the senatorial apportionment. . . .

. . .

We applaud the willingness of state courts to assume jurisdiction and render decision in cases involving challenges to state legislative apportionment schemes. However, in determining the validity of a State's apportionment plan, the same federal constitutional standards are applicable whether the matter is litigated in a federal or a state court. Maryland's plan is plainly insufficient under the requirements of the Equal Protection Clause as spelled out in our opinion in *Reynolds.*

For the reasons stated in *Reynolds,* appellees' reliance on the so-called federal analogy as a sustaining principle for the Maryland apportionment scheme, despite significant deviations from population-based representation in both houses of the General Assembly, is clearly misplaced. And considerations of history and tradition, relied upon by appellees, do not, and could not, provide a sufficient justification for the substantial deviations from population-based representation in both houses of the Maryland Legislature.

. . .

Since primary responsibility for legislative apportionment rests with the legislature itself, and since adequate time exists in which the Maryland General Assembly can act, the Maryland courts need feel obliged to take further affirmative action only if the legislature fails to enact a constitutionally valid state legislative apportionment scheme in a timely fashion after being afforded a further opportunity by the courts to do so. However, under no circumstances should the 1966 election of members of the Maryland Legislature be permitted to be conducted pursuant to the existing or any other unconstitutional plan. We therefore reverse the judgment of the Maryland Court of Appeals, and remand the case to that Court for further proceedings not inconsistent with the views stated here and in our opinion in *Reynolds v. Sims*.

Davis v. Mann
377 U.S. 678 (1964)

Plaintiffs below, residents, taxpayers, and qualified voters of Arlington and Fairfax Counties, filed a complaint on April 9, 1962, in the United States District Court for the Eastern District of Virginia, in their own behalf and on behalf of all voters in Virginia similarly situated, challenging the apportionment of the Virginia General Assembly. Defendants, sued in their representative capacities, were various officials charged with duties in connection with state elections. . . .

The complaint alleged that the present statutory provisions apportioning seats in the Virginia Legislature, as amended in 1962, result in invidious discrimination against plaintiffs and "all other voters of the state Senatorial and House districts" in which they reside, since voters in Arlington and Fairfax Counties are given substantially less representation than voters living in other parts of the State. Plaintiffs asserted that the discrimination was violative of the Fourteenth Amendment as well as the Virginia Constitution, and contended that the requirements of the Equal Protection Clause of the Federal Constitution, and of the Virginia Constitution, could be met only by a redistribution of legislative representation among the counties and independent cities of the State "substantially in proportion to their respective populations." Plaintiffs asserted that they "possess an inherent right to vote for members of the General Assembly . . . and to cast votes that are equally effective with the votes of every other citizen" of Virginia, and that this right was being diluted and effectively denied by the discriminatory apportionment of seats in both houses of the Virginia Legislature under the statutory provisions attacked as being unconstitutional. Plaintiffs contended that the alleged inequalities and distortions in the allocation of legislative seats prevented the Virginia Legislature from "being a body representative of the people of the Commonwealth," and resulted in a minority of the people of Virginia controlling the General Assembly.

. . . With respect to relief, plaintiffs sought a declaratory judgment that the statutory scheme of legislative apportionment in Virginia, prior as well as subsequent to the 1962 amendments, contravenes the Equal Protection Clause of the Fourteenth Amendment and is thus unconstitutional and void. Plaintiffs also requested the issuance of a prohibitory injunction restraining defendants from performing their official duties relating to the election of members of the General Assembly pursuant to the present statutory provisions. Plaintiffs further sought a mandatory injunction requiring defendants to conduct the next primary and general elections for legislators on an at-large basis throughout the State.

. . .

On November 28, 1962, the District Court . . . sustained plaintiffs' claim and entered an interlocutory order holding the apportionment of the Virginia Legislature violative of the Federal Constitution. The Court refused to dismiss the case or stay its action on the ground, asserted by defendants, that plaintiffs should be required first to procure the views of the state courts on the validity of the apportionment scheme. Instead, it held that, since neither the 1962 legislation nor the relevant state constitutional provisions were ambiguous, no question of state law necessitating abstention by the Federal District Court was presented. In applying the Equal Protection Clause to the Virginia apportionment scheme, the Court stated that, although population is the predominant consideration, other factors may be of some relevance "in assaying the justness of the apportionment." Stating that the Federal Constitution requires a state legislative apportionment to "accord the citizens of the State substantially equal representation," the Court held that the inequalities found in the statistical information relating to the population of the State's various legislative districts, if unexplained, sufficiently showed an "invidious discrimination" against plaintiffs and those similarly situated. The Court rejected any possibility of different bases of representation being applicable in the two houses of the Virginia Legislature, stating that, in Virginia, each house has "a direct, indeed the same, relation to the people," and that the principal present-day justification for bicameralism in state legislatures is to insure against precipitate action by imposing greater deliberation upon proposed legislation. Because of the gross inequalities in representation among various districts in both houses of the Virginia Legislature, the Court put the burden of explanation on defendants, and found that they had failed to meet it. Consequently, the Court concluded that the discrimination against Arlington and Fairfax Counties and the City of Norfolk was a grave and "constitutionally impermissible" deprivation, violative of the Equal Protection Clause of the Fourteenth Amendment.

With respect to relief, the Court stated that, while it would have preferred that the General Assembly itself correct the unconstitutionality of the 1962 apportionment legislation, it would not defer deciding the case until after the next regular session of the Virginia Legislature in January 1964, because senators elected in November 1963 would hold office until 1968 and delegates elected in 1963 would serve until 1966. Deferring action would thus result in unreasonable delay in correcting the injustices in the apportionment of the Senate and the House of Delegates, concluded the Court.

The District Court's interlocutory order declared that the 1962 apportionment violated the Equal Protection Clause and accordingly was void and of no effect. It also restrained and enjoined defendants from proceeding with the conducting of elections under the 1962 legislation, but stayed the operation of the injunction until January 31, 1963, so that either the General Assembly could act or an appeal could be taken to this Court, provided that, if neither of these steps was taken, plaintiffs might apply to the District Court for further relief. Finally, the court below retained jurisdiction of the case for the entry of such orders as might be required.

. . . On application by appellants, the Chief Justice, on December 15, 1962, granted a stay of the District Court's injunction pending final disposition of the case by this Court. Because of this stay, the November 1963 election of members of the Virginia Legislature was conducted under the existing statutory provisions. . . .

. . .

We reject appellants' argument that the underrepresentation of Arlington, Fairfax and Norfolk is constitutionally justifiable since it allegedly resulted in part from the fact that those areas contain large numbers of military and military-related personnel. Discrimination against a class of individuals, merely because of the nature of their employment, without more being shown, is constitutionally impermissible. Additionally, no showing was made that the Virginia Legislature in fact took such a factor into account in allocating legislative representation. And state policy, as evidenced by Virginia's election laws, actually favors and fosters voting by military and military-related personnel. Furthermore, even if such persons were to be excluded in determining the populations of the various legislative districts, the discrimination against the disfavored areas would hardly be satisfactorily explained, because, after deducting military and military-related personnel, the maximum population-variance ratios would still be 2.22-to-1 in the Senate and 3.53-to-1 in the House.

We also reject appellants' claim that the Virginia apportionment is sustainable as involving an attempt to balance urban and rural power in the legislature. Not only does this explanation lack legal merit, but it also fails to conform to the facts. . . . And, for the reasons stated in *Reynolds*, in rejecting the so-called federal analogy, and in *Gray v. Sanders*, appellants' reliance on an asserted analogy to the deviations from population in the Federal Electoral College is misplaced. The fact that the maximum variances in the populations of various state legislative districts are less than the extreme deviations from a population basis in the composition of the Federal Electoral College fails to provide a constitutionally cognizable basis for sustaining a state apportionment scheme under the Equal Protection Clause.

. . . Since the District Court stated that it was retaining jurisdiction and that plaintiffs could seek further appropriate relief, the court below presumably intends to take further action should the Virginia Legislature fail to act promptly in remedying the constitutional defects in the State's

legislative apportionment plan. We therefore affirm the judgment of the District Court on the merits of this litigation, and remand the case for further proceedings consistent with the views stated here and in our opinion in *Reynolds v. Sims.*

Roman v. Sincock
377 U.S. 695 (1964)

. . . [P]laintiffs below, residents, taxpayers and qualified voters of New Castle County, Delaware, filed a complaint in the United States District Court for the District of Delaware, in their own behalf and on behalf of all persons similarly situated, challenging the apportionment of the Delaware Legislature. Defendants, sued in their representative capacities, were various officials charged with the performance of certain duties in connection with state elections. The complaint alleged deprivation of rights under the Equal Protection Clause of the Fourteenth Amendment.

Plaintiffs below alleged that the apportionment of seats in the Delaware Legislature resulted in an "invidious discrimination as to the inhabitants of New Castle County and the City of Wilmington," operated to deny them the right to cast votes for Delaware legislators "that are of equal effect with that of every other citizen of the State of Delaware," and was arbitrary and capricious in failing to provide a reasonable classification of those voting for members of the Delaware General Assembly. Plaintiffs also asserted that they were without any other adequate remedy since the existing legislative apportionment was frozen into the 1897 Delaware Constitution; that the present legislature was dominated by legislators representing the two less populous counties; that it was, as a practical matter, impossible to amend the state constitution or convene a constitutional convention for the purpose of reapportioning the General Assembly; and that the Delaware Legislature had consistently failed to take, appropriate action with respect to reapportionment.

Plaintiffs below sought a declaration that Art. II, 2, of the Delaware Constitution, which established the apportionment of seats in both houses of the Delaware Legislature, is unconstitutional, and an injunction against defendants to prevent the holding of any further elections under the existing apportionment scheme. Plaintiffs also requested that the District Court either reapportion the Delaware Legislature on a population basis or, alternatively, direct that the November 1962 general election be conducted on an at-large basis. . . .

On July 25, 1962, the District Court entered an order staying the proceedings until August 7, 1962, in order to permit the Delaware Legislature to take "some appropriate action." The court noted that, since publication of any proposed constitutional amendment at least three months prior to the next general election was required under Delaware law, it would serve no useful purpose to grant a stay beyond August 7, 1962.

On July 30, 1962, the General Assembly approved a proposed amendment to the legislative apportionment provisions of the Delaware Constitution, based upon recommendations of a bipartisan reapportionment committee appointed by the Delaware Governor. Under Delaware law this amendment could not, however, become effective unless again approved during the next succeeding session of the General Assembly.

On August 7, 1962, the District Court entered an order refusing to dismiss the suit, and stated that, while it had no desire to substitute its judgment for the collective wisdom of the Delaware General Assembly in matters of legislative apportionment, it had no alternative but to proceed promptly in deciding the case. Some of the de-

fendants applied for a further stay of proceedings so that the General Assembly coming into office in January 1963 would have an opportunity to approve the proposed constitutional amendment. On August 8, 1962, plaintiffs applied for a preliminary injunction against the conducting of the November 1962 general election under the existing apportionment provisions. Plaintiffs were thereafter permitted to amend their complaint to request that the proposed constitutional amendment also be declared unconstitutional and that the court order a provisional reapportionment of the Delaware Legislature.

On October 16, 1962, the District Court denied both the applications for a preliminary injunction and for a further stay. Denial of a preliminary injunction effectively permitted the holding of the November 1962 general election pursuant to the legislative apportionment provisions of the 1897 Delaware Constitution. After extended pretrial proceedings, the court, on November 27, 1962, entered a pretrial order in which the parties agreed to the accuracy of a series of exhibits, statistics and various statistical computations. In early January 1963, the Delaware General Assembly, elected in November 1962, approved the proposed constitutional amendment by the requisite two-thirds vote. As a result, the amendment to the legislative apportionment provisions of Art. II, 2, became effective on January 17, 1963, having been passed by two successive General Assemblies. Trial before the District Court ensued, with the expert testimony of various political scientists being presented.

On April 17, 1963, the District Court . . . held that Art. II, 2, of the Delaware Constitution, both before and after the 1963 amendment, resulted in gross and invidious discrimination against the plaintiffs and others similarly situated, in violation of the Equal Protection Clause of the Fourteenth Amendment. Stating that "the fundamental issue presented for . . . adjudication is whether or not the apportioning of members of the General Assembly of the State of Delaware offends the electors of the State because of an alleged debasement of their voting rights," the court indicated that it would pass upon the constitutional validity of both the provisions of the 1897 Constitution and the provisions of the 1963 constitutional amendment. After considering in detail the apportionment of legislative seats under the provisions of the 1897 Delaware Constitution, the court below concluded that "[t]he uneven growth of the different areas of the State created a condition because of which the numbers of inhabitants in representative and senatorial districts differed not only on an intercounty basis but also on an intracounty basis." After discussing the effect of the 1963 reapportionment amendment, the District Court turned to a consideration of plaintiffs' claim under the Federal Constitution. . . .

After holding that the apportionment of at least one house of a bicameral state legislature must be based substantially on population, the District Court rejected the relevancy of the so-called federal analogy as a justification for departures from a population-based apportionment scheme in the other house of a state legislature. Although finding no rational or reasonable basis for the Delaware apportionment, either as it previously existed or as amended, the court nevertheless concluded that reapportionment was basically a legislative function, and that a further opportunity should be given to the General Assembly to reapportion itself properly in accordance with the requirements of the Fourteenth Amendment. After attempting to delineate some guidelines for the Delaware Legislature to follow in reapportioning, the court below, with an eye toward the impending 1964 elections, gave the General As-

sembly until October 1, 1963, to adopt a constitutionally valid plan. The District Court entered a decree declaring Art. II, 2, of the Delaware Constitution to be unconstitutional, and retained jurisdiction to order injunctive or other relief if it became necessary to do so.

On May 6, 1963, the Supreme Court of Delaware advised the Delaware Governor that, notwithstanding the holding of the District Court, he should proceed according to the provisions of the invalidated 1963 constitutional amendment to proclaim a redistricting plan for House of Representatives seats. The Delaware Supreme Court's opinion was predicated on the view that the District Court's decision was not a final one, since it was appealable and since no injunctive relief had been granted. Acting on this advice, while making reference to the District Court's decision, the Governor, on May 17, 1963, proclaimed a plan providing for the redistricting of certain House districts in accordance with the provisions of the 1963 reapportionment amendment. Under these circumstances, on May 20, 1963, the District Court entered an injunction against the holding of any elections for General Assembly seats under Art. II, 2, of the Delaware Constitution, either as it had previously existed or as amended, and again reserved jurisdiction to make such further orders as it might deem necessary. The District Court denied a motion to stay its injunction pending appeal, but, on application by defendants below, Justice Brennan, on June 27, 1963, stayed the operation of the District Court's injunction pending final disposition of the case by this Court. Notices of appeal from the District Court's final decree, and from its injunction and denial of the motion for a stay, were timely filed by defendants. Pursuant to this Court's Rule 15 (3), both appeals have been treated as a single case. When appellees filed a motion to affirm, appellants countered with a motion to advance. . . .

. . .

For the reasons stated in our opinion in *Reynolds*, appellants' reliance upon the so-called federal analogy to justify the deviations from a population basis in the apportionment of seats in the Delaware Legislature is misplaced. And appellants' argument that the Delaware apportionment scheme should be upheld since Congress has admitted various States into the Union although the apportionment of seats in their legislatures was based on factors other than population is also unconvincing. In giving the Delaware Legislature an opportunity to adopt a constitutionally valid plan of legislative apportionment, and in deferring decision until after the November 1962 general election, because of the imminence of that election and the disruptive effect which its decision might have had, the District Court acted in a wise and temperate manner. And the court below did not err in granting injunctive relief after it had become apparent that, despite its decree holding that the 1963 constitutional amendment reapportioning seats in the Delaware Legislature failed to comply with federal constitutional requirements, no further reapportionment by the Delaware General Assembly was probable.

Our affirmance of the decision below is not meant to indicate approval of the District Court's attempt to state in mathematical language the constitutionally permissible bounds of discretion in deviating from apportionment according to population. In our view the problem does not lend itself to any such uniform formula, and it is neither practicable nor desirable to establish rigid mathematical standards for evaluating the constitutional validity of a state legislative apportionment scheme under the Equal Protection Clause. Rather, the proper judicial approach is to ascertain whether, under the particular circumstances existing in the individual State whose legislative apportionment is at issue, there has been a faithful adherence to a plan of population-based representation, with such minor deviations only as may occur in recognizing certain factors that are free from any taint of arbitrariness or discrimination.

Apart from what we said in *Reynolds*, we express no view on questions relating to remedies at the present time. Regardless of the requirements of the Delaware Constitution and the fact that legislative apportionment has traditionally been considered a constitutional matter in Delaware, the delay inherent in following the state constitutional prescription for approval of constitutional amendments by two successive General Assemblies cannot be allowed to result in an impermissible deprivation of appellees' right to an adequate voice in the election of legislators to represent them. Acting under general equitable principles, the court below must now determine whether it would be advisable, so as to avoid a possible disruption of state election processes and permit additional time for the Delaware Legislature to adopt a constitutionally valid apportionment scheme, to allow the 1964 election of Delaware legislators to be conducted pursuant to the provisions of the 1963 constitutional amendment, or whether those factors are insufficient to justify any further delay in the effectuation of appellees' constitutional rights. We therefore affirm the decisions of the District Court here appealed from, and remand the case for further proceedings consistent with the views stated here and in our opinion in *Reynolds v. Sims*.

Lucas v. Forty-Fourth General Assembly of Colorado
377 U.S. 713 (1964)

Appellants, voters, taxpayers and residents of counties in the Denver metropolitan area, filed two separate actions, consolidated for trial and disposition, on behalf of themselves and all others similarly situated, in March and July 1962, challenging the constitutionality of the apportionment of seats in both houses of the Colorado General Assembly. Defendants below, sued in their representative capacities, included various officials charged with duties in connection with state elections. Plaintiffs below asserted that Art. V, 45, 46, and 47, of the Colorado Constitution, and the statutes implementing those constitutional provisions, result in gross inequalities and disparities with respect to their voting rights. They alleged that "one of the inalienable rights of citizenship . . . is equality of franchise and vote, and that the concept of equal protection of the laws requires that every citizen be equally represented in the legislature of his State." Plaintiffs sought declaratory and injunctive relief, and also requested the Court to order a constitutionally valid apportionment plan into effect for purposes of the 1962 election of Colorado legislators. Proponents of the current apportionment scheme, which was then to be voted upon in a November 1962 referendum as proposed Amendment No. 7 to the Colorado Constitution, were permitted to intervene. . . .

On August 10, 1962, the District Court announced its initial decision. After holding that it had jurisdiction, that the issues presented were justiciable, and that grounds for abstention were lacking, the court below stated that the population disparities among various legislative districts under the existing apportionment "are of sufficient magnitude to make out a prima facie case of invidious discrimination. . . ." However, because of the imminence of the primary and general elections, and since two constitutional amendments, proposed through the initiative procedure and prescribing rather different schemes for legislative apportionment, would be voted upon in the impending election, the District Court continued the cases without further action until after the November 1962 election. Colorado legislators were thus elected in 1962 pursuant to the provisions of the existing apportionment scheme.

At the November 1962 general election, the Colorado electorate adopted proposed Amendment No. 7 by a vote of 305,700 to 172,725, and defeated proposed Amendment No. 8 by a vote of 311,749 to 149,822. Amendment No. 8, rejected by a majority of the voters, prescribed an apportionment plan pursuant to which seats in both houses of the Colorado Legislature would purportedly be apportioned on a population basis. Amendment No. 7, on the other hand, provided for the apportionment of the House of Representatives on the basis of population, but essentially maintained the existing apportionment in the Senate, which was based on a combination of population and various other factors.

After the 1962 election the parties amended their pleadings so that the cases involved solely a challenge to the apportionment scheme established in the newly adopted Amendment No. 7. Plaintiffs below requested a declaration that Amendment No. 7 was unconstitutional under the Fourteenth Amendment since resulting in substantial disparities from population-based representation in the Senate, and asked for a decree reapportioning both houses of the Colorado Legislature on a population basis. After an extended trial, at which a variety of statistical and testimonial evidence regarding legislative apportionment in Colorado, past and present, was introduced, the District Court, on July 16, 1963 . . . concluded that the apportionment scheme prescribed by Amendment No. 7 comported with the requirements of the Equal Protection Clause, and thus dismissed the consolidated actions. In sustaining the validity of the senatorial apportionment provided for in Amendment No. 7, despite deviations from population-based representation, the District Court stated that the Fourteenth Amendment does not require "equality of population within representation districts for each house of a bicameral state legislature." Finding that the disparities from a population basis in the apportionment of Senate seats were based upon rational considerations, the court below stated that the senatorial apportionment under Amendment No. 7 "recognizes population as a prime, but not controlling, factor and gives effect to such important considerations as geography, compactness and contiguity of territory, accessibility, observance of natural boundaries, [and] conformity to historical divisions such as county lines and prior representation districts. . . ." Stressing also that the apportionment plan had been recently adopted by popular vote in a statewide referendum, the Court stated:

> [Plaintiffs'] argument that the apportionment of the Senate by Amendment No. 7 is arbitrary, invidiously discriminatory, and without any rationality [has been answered by the] voters of Colorado. . . . By adopting Amendment No. 7 and by rejecting Amendment No. 8, which proposed to apportion the legislature on a per capita basis, the electorate has made its choice between the conflicting principles.

. . .

Several aspects of this case serve to distinguish it from the other cases involving state legislative apportionment also decided this date. Initially, one house of the Colorado Legislature is at least arguably apportioned substantially on a population basis under Amendment No. 7 and the implementing statutory provisions. Under the apportionment schemes challenged in the other cases, on the other hand, clearly neither of the houses in any of the state legislatures is apportioned sufficiently on a population basis so as to be constitutionally sustainable. Additionally, the Colorado scheme of

legislative apportionment here attacked is one adopted by a majority vote of the Colorado electorate almost contemporaneously with the District Court's decision on the merits in this litigation. Thus, the plan at issue did not result from prolonged legislative inaction. However, the Colorado General Assembly, in spite of the state constitutional mandate for periodic reapportionment, has enacted only one effective legislative apportionment measure in the past 50 years.

As appellees have correctly pointed out, a majority of the voters in every county of the State voted in favor of the apportionment scheme embodied in Amendment No. 7's provisions, in preference to that contained in proposed Amendment No. 8, which, subject to minor deviations, would have based the apportionment of seats in both houses on a population basis. However, the choice presented to the Colorado electorate, in voting on these two proposed constitutional amendments, was hardly as clear-cut as the court below regarded it. One of the most undesirable features of the existing apportionment scheme was the requirement that, in counties given more than one seat in either or both of the houses of the General Assembly, all legislators must be elected at large from the county as a whole. Thus, under the existing plan, each Denver voter was required to vote for 8 senators and 17 representatives. Ballots were long and cumbersome, and an intelligent choice among candidates for seats in the legislature was made quite difficult. No identifiable constituencies within the populous counties resulted, and the residents of those areas had no single member of the Senate or House elected specifically to represent them. Rather, each legislator elected from a multimember county represented the county as a whole. Amendment No. 8, as distinguished from Amendment No. 7, while purportedly basing the apportionment of seats in both houses on a population basis, would have perpetuated, for all practical purposes, this debatable feature of the existing scheme. Under Amendment No. 8, senators were to be elected at large in those counties given more than one Senate seat, and no provision was made for subdistricting within such counties for the purpose of electing senators. Representatives were also to be elected at large in multimember counties pursuant to the provisions of Amendment No. 8, at least initially, although subdistricting for the purpose of electing House members was permitted if the voters of a multimember county specifically approved a representative subdistricting plan for that county. Thus, neither of the proposed plans was, in all probability, wholly acceptable to the voters in the populous counties, and the assumption of the court below that the Colorado voters made a definitive choice between two contrasting alternatives and indicated that "minority process in the Senate is what they want" does not appear to be factually justifiable.

Finally, this case differs from the others decided this date in that the initiative device provides a practicable political remedy to obtain relief against alleged legislative malapportionment in Colorado. An initiated measure proposing a constitutional amendment or a statutory enactment is entitled to be placed on the ballot if the signatures of 8 percent of those voting for the Secretary of State in the last election are obtained. No geographical distribution of petition signers is required. Initiative and referendum has been frequently utilized throughout Colorado's history. Additionally, Colorado courts have traditionally not been hesitant about adjudicating controversies relating to legislative apportionment. However, the Colorado Supreme Court, in its 1962 decision discussed previously in this opinion, refused to consider or pass upon the federal con-

stitutional questions, but instead held only that the Colorado General Assembly was not required to enact a reapportionment statute until the following legislative session.

In *Reynolds v. Sims*, decided also this date, we held that the Equal Protection Clause requires that both houses of a bicameral state legislature must be apportioned substantially on a population basis. Of course, the court below assumed, and the parties apparently conceded, that the Colorado House of Representatives, under the statutory provisions enacted by the Colorado Legislature in early 1963 pursuant to Amendment No. 7's dictate that the legislature should create 65 House districts "as nearly equal in population as may be," is now apportioned sufficiently on a population basis to comport with federal constitutional requisites. We need not pass on this question, since the apportionment of Senate seats, under Amendment No. 7, clearly involves departures from population-based representation too extreme to be constitutionally permissible, and there is no indication that the apportionment of the two houses of the Colorado General Assembly, pursuant to the 1962 constitutional amendment, is severable. We therefore conclude that the District Court erred in holding the legislative apportionment plan embodied in Amendment No. 7 to be constitutionally valid. Under neither Amendment No. 7's plan, nor, of course, the previous statutory scheme, is the overall legislative representation in the two houses of the Colorado Legislature sufficiently grounded on population to be constitutionally sustainable under the Equal Protection Clause.

. . .

Because of the imminence of the November 1962 election, and the fact that two initiated proposals relating to legislative apportionment would be voted on by the State's electorate at that election, the District Court properly stayed its hand and permitted the 1962 election of legislators to be conducted pursuant to the existing statutory scheme. But appellees' argument, accepted by the court below, that the apportionment of the Colorado Senate, under Amendment No. 7, is rational because it takes into account a variety of geographical, historical, topographical and economic considerations fails to provide an adequate justification for the substantial disparities from population-based representation in the allocation of Senate seats to the disfavored populous areas. And any attempted reliance on the so-called federal analogy is factually as well as constitutionally without merit.

Since the apportionment of seats in the Colorado Legislature, under the provisions of Amendment No. 7, fails to comport with the requirements of the Equal Protection Clause, the decision below must be reversed. Beyond what we said in our opinion in *Reynolds*, we express no view on questions relating to remedies at the present time. On remand, the District Court must now determine whether the imminence of the 1964 primary and general elections requires that utilization of the apportionment scheme contained in the constitutional amendment be permitted, for purposes of those elections, or whether the circumstances in Colorado are such that appellants' right to cast adequately weighted votes for members of the State Legislature can practicably be effectuated in 1964. Accordingly, we reverse the decision of the court below and remand the case for further proceedings consistent with the views stated here and in our opinion in *Reynolds v. Sims*.

Parsons v. Buckley
379 U.S. 359 (1965)

The District Court on August 3, 1964, entered a judgment holding invalid under the Fourteenth

Amendment to the United States Constitution, §§ 13 and 18 of Chapter II of the Constitution of Vermont relating to apportionment of the General Assembly of the State of Vermont. . . .

. . .

The cases are removed from the argument list . . . and . . . the judgment of the District Court is modified by vacating Paragraph (3) and substituting in lieu thereof the quoted language of the Stipulation. As so modified, the judgment of the District Court dated August 3, 1964, is affirmed. The judgment of this Court shall issue forthwith.

Fortson v. Dorsey
379 U.S. 433 (1965)

The appellees, registered voters of Georgia, brought this action in the District Court for the Northern District of Georgia against the Secretary of State of Georgia and local election officials seeking a decree that the requirement of county-wide voting in the seven multi-district counties violates the Equal Protection Clause of the Fourteenth Amendment. A three-judge court granted appellees' motion for summary judgment. . . .

. . .

. . . The equal protection argument is focused solely upon the question whether county-wide voting in the seven multi-district counties results in denying the residents therein a vote "approximately equal in weight to that of" voters resident in the single-member constituencies. Contrary to the District Court, we cannot say that it does. . . .

In reversing the District Court we should emphasize that the equal-protection claim below was based upon an alleged infirmity that attaches to the statute on its face. Agreeing with appellees' contention that the multi-member constituency feature of the Georgia scheme was per se bad, the District Court entered the decree on summary judgment. We treat the question as presented in that context, and our opinion is not to be understood to say that in all instances or under all circumstances such a system as Georgia has will comport with the dictates of the Equal Protection Clause. It might well be that, designedly or otherwise, a multi-member constituency apportionment scheme, under the circumstances of a particular case, would operate to minimize or cancel out the voting strength of racial or political elements of the voting population. When this is demonstrated it will be time enough to consider whether the system still passes constitutional muster. . . .

Reversed.

Fortson v. Toombs
379 U.S. 621 (1965)

The District Court, having held that the Georgia Legislature was malapportioned, enjoined appellants, election officials,

> from placing on the ballot to be used in the General Election to be held on November 3, 1964, or at any subsequent election until the General Assembly is reapportioned in accordance with constitutional standards, the question whether a constitutional amendment purporting to amend the present state constitution by substituting an entirely new constitution therefor shall be adopted.

Appellants challenge that provision on the merits. Appellees, while defending it on the merits, suggest alternatively that the issue has become moot.

The situation has changed somewhat since the 1964 election, as both the Senate and the House have new members, and appellees, for whose benefit the challenged provision was added, say it is now highly speculative as to what the 1965 legislature will do, and suggest the paragraph in question be vacated as moot.

We vacate this part of the decree and remand to the District Court, to whom we give a wide range in moulding a decree, for reconsideration of the desirability and need for the ongoing injunction in light of the results of the 1964 election and the representations of appellees.

Scott v. Germano
381 U.S. 407 (1965)

Upon remand of this case, for further proceedings consistent with the views stated in *Reynolds v. Sims*, the District Court, on January 22, 1965, entered a judgment declaring invalid Art. IV, § 6, of the Illinois Constitution and Ill.Rev.Stat., c. 46, §§ 158-1 to 158-5, apportioning the Illinois Senate, directing that all members of the Illinois General Assembly be made parties defendant, and requiring that "any implementation, amendment or substitution of all or part of the said defective portions" of the Illinois Constitution or legislation be submitted to it for approval before the holding of any election thereunder. It further held that, if no such "implementation, amendment or substitution" was submitted, it would order the parties to show cause why all Illinois State Senators should not be elected from the State at large in the 1966 election and every four years thereafter.

In April, 1964, the case of *People ex rel. Engle v. Kerner* was filed in the Circuit Court of Sangamon County, Illinois. It contested the composition of both houses of the General Assembly, but was dismissed by the trial court. Upon appeal, the Supreme Court of Illinois, on February 4, 1965, held the composition of the Illinois Senate invalid; the court expressed confidence that the General Assembly would "successfully perform its duty to enact a constitutionally valid plan during its current session," which expires July 1, 1965. However, the court retained jurisdiction of the case "for the purpose of taking such affirmative action as may be necessary to insure that the 1966 election is pursuant to a constitutionally valid plan."

On February 8, 1965, the appellants here moved that the United States District Court reconsider and vacate its order of January 22, 1965, and stay further proceedings in light of the Supreme Court of Illinois' opinion in *Engle*. This the District Court refused to do. . . .

We believe that the District Court should have stayed its hand. The power of the judiciary of a State to require valid reapportionment or to formulate a valid redistricting plan has not only been recognized by this Court, but appropriate action by the States in such cases has been specifically encouraged.

We therefore vacate the order of the District Court dated May 7, 1965. The case is remanded with directions that the District Court enter an order fixing a reasonable time within which the appropriate agencies of the State of Illinois, including its Supreme Court, may validly redistrict the Illinois State Senate; provided that the same be accomplished within ample time to permit such plan to be utilized in the 1966 election of the members of the State Senate, in accordance with the provisions of the Illinois election laws.

The District Court shall retain jurisdiction of the case, and, in the event a valid reapportionment plan for the State Senate is not timely adopted, it may enter such orders as it deems appropriate, including an order for a valid reapportionment plan for the State Senate or an order directing that its members be elected at large pending a valid reapportionment by the State itself.

Swann v. Adams
383 U.S. 210 (1966)

We previously remanded this case to the District Court for further proceedings in light of *Reynolds v. Sims*, and the other cases relating to legislative reapportionment decided with *Reynolds*. The District Court deferred action until the conclusion of the legislative session which convened on April 6, 1965, stating that it would reconsider its decision should the Florida Legislature fail to effect a valid reapportionment by July 1, 1965.

A reapportionment law was passed by the legislature on June 29, 1965. On July 6, the appellants filed a joint petition asking the District Court to declare the newly enacted plan unconstitutional and proposing an alternative plan. The District Court did not take action until October 5, when it ordered oral argument for November 2, 1965. On December 23, the District Court concluded that the newly passed reapportionment plan failed to "meet the requirements of the Equal Protection Clause of the Federal Constitution as construed and applied in *Reynolds*. . . ."

Although the District Court concluded that the plan did not comport with constitutional requirements, it approved the plan . . . on an interim basis. Its approval was limited to the period ending 60 days after the adjournment of the 1967 session of the Florida Legislature.

We have no occasion to review the District Court's determination that the legislative reapportionment plan fails to meet constitutional standards. Indeed, Florida does not contend that the District Court erred in this regard, having conceded below that the plan was constitutionally deficient. We hold, however, that, in approving the plan on an interim basis, the District Court erred. This litigation was commenced in 1962. The effect of the District Court's decision is to delay effectuation of a valid apportionment in Florida until at least 1969. While recognizing the desirability of permitting the Florida Legislature itself to determine the course of reapportionment, we find no warrant for perpetuating what all concede to be an unconstitutional apportionment for another three years.

We reverse and remand to the District Court so that a valid reapportionment plan will be made effective for the 1966 elections.

Burns v. Richardson
384 U.S. 73 (1966)

This reapportionment case was brought in the District Court of Hawaii by residents and qualified voters of the City and County of Honolulu, appellees in each of the three appeals consolidated here. They alleged that Hawaii's legislative apportionment was unconstitutional under our decisions in *Reynolds v. Sims*, and companion cases. William S. Richardson, Lieutenant Governor of Hawaii, also an appellee in all three appeals, was named defendant in his capacity as the state officer responsible for supervising state elections. John A. Burns, Governor of Hawaii, appellant in No. 318, intervened as a party plaintiff. Members of the State House of Representatives, appellants in No. 323, and members of the State Senate, appellants in No. 409, intervened as parties defendant.

Under the Hawaii Constitution, adopted in 1950 and put into effect upon admission to statehood in 1959, the State is divided into four major counties, referred to in the state constitution as "basic areas." Each county is made up of a group of islands, separated from each of the other counties by wide and deep ocean waters. The principal island of the City and County of Honolulu,

the most populous county, is the island of Oahu. It is the State's industrial center, principal tourist attraction, and site of most of the many federal military establishments located in the State. In 1960, 79 percent of the State's population lived there. The three other counties, primarily rural and agricultural, are Hawaii County, Maui County, and Kauai County.

The apportionment article of the state constitution was framed to assure that the three small counties would choose a controlling majority of the State Senate, and that the population center, Oahu, would control the State House of Representatives. Thus, Art. III, § 2, of the state constitution apportions a 25-member senate among six fixed senatorial districts, assigning a specified number of seats to each. Fifteen senate seats, a controlling majority, are allocated among Hawaii, Kauai and Maui Counties, and 10 seats are assigned to Oahu. Alteration of this apportionment is made very difficult by a provision

> that no constitutional amendment altering . . . the representation from any senatorial district in the senate shall become effective unless it shall also be approved by a majority of the votes tallied upon the question in each of a majority of the counties.

For the State House of Representatives, on the other hand, the state constitution establishes 18 representative districts, 10 of which are on Oahu, and requires the Governor to apportion the 51-member body among these districts on the basis of the number of voters registered in each. The first apportionment occurred in 1959, just prior to statehood, and was based on registration figures for the 1958 territorial election. It produced 13 multimember representative districts and five single member districts, and allocated 36 representatives, a controlling majority, to Oahu. The Governor is required to reapportion the State decennially, a duty which may be enforced by mandamus from the State Supreme Court.

This apportionment scheme was first attacked in the Supreme Court of Hawaii within a month after we decided *Reynolds*. That court refused to pass on the validity of the apportionment at that time. It noted the imminence of the 1964 election, and stated its belief that, consistent with the Hawaii Constitution, judicial proceedings should await legislative proposals for a constitutional amendment or a constitutional convention. A special legislative session was then called by the Governor to consider reapportionment. It failed to act.

This suit was brought on August 13 1964. A three-Judge court was convened. . . . Interim relief was denied in view of the pendency of the 1964 elections, and hearings were set for January 1965. The court published its first decision and order on February 17, 1965. That order declared all provisions of the apportionment plan contained in the Hawaii Constitution valid under the Equal Protection Clause except the mentioned provisions relating to the apportionment of the State Senate. These were affirmatively declared to be invalid and unconstitutional.

In the February 17 order, the District Court decided not to fashion its own reapportionment plan for the senate. Nor did it instruct the legislature to reapportion the senate or to propose constitutional amendments for that purpose. Instead, it directed the legislature to submit to the electorate at an immediate special election the question, "Shall there be a convention to propose a revision of or amendments to the Constitution?" The legislature was also directed to establish the convention procedures according to a timetable the court set. The court retained jurisdiction for all purposes, including that of itself reapportioning the senate in the event of a negative vote on the question, failure of the convention to adopt a suitable amendment, or rejection by the electorate of the amendment adopted by the convention.

The court chose the convention route over the legislative route for two reasons. Under the Hawaii Constitution, all elections necessary to adoption of amendments proposed by a constitutional convention may be held on a special basis. Legislative proposals, on the other hand, may be submitted only at a general election. In starting the machinery necessary for a convention, the court hoped that a valid permanent plan could be presented to the electorate and adopted before the next general election, to be held in 1966. The second reason was that the court doubted that the legislature would be able to agree on an amendment proposal for reapportioning the senate, in view of the failure of the previously called legislative special session to act.

The special elections necessary under the court's order, however, entailed substantial expense. On motion of the intervening legislators, which showed substantial progress towards a legislative proposal for amendment, the court, on March 9, 1965, modified its order. As suggested by the parties, it suspended the February 17 order, and instead required the legislature to enact three separate statutes before turning to regular legislative business. One statute was to propose an interim senate apportionment plan, using registered voters as a basis, to be submitted to the court. If approved, it would be adopted by the court as its plan for use in the 1966 general election. The second statute was to propose a constitutional amendment embodying pertinent provisions of the interim plan, to be submitted to the people for approval at that election. The third statute was to submit the question of calling a constitutional convention to the electorate at the 1966 general election.

Three statutes were enacted. H.B. 987, the only one of these measures before us, proposed an interim plan of apportionment for the senate. The plan followed the pattern for house apportionment. It established eight senatorial districts, five on Oahu. As required by the court's order, the 25 senators were to be apportioned on the basis of registered voters. Using figures derived from registration for the 1964 general elections, Oahu was allocated 19 out of the 25 senators, a controlling majority.

Under the total apportionment scheme which resulted from this enactment, Oahu would not have any single-member districts in either the house or the senate. The distribution of registered voters in Oahu is such that Oahu's 10 representative districts have two to six representatives each, and its five senatorial districts each would have either three or four senators. Hawaii County would be a single senatorial district represented by three senators, and have five representative districts, four choosing a single representative and the fifth electing three. Maui County would be a single senatorial district electing two senators and have two representative districts, one electing four, and the other a single representative. Kauai County would be a single senatorial and a single representative district electing one senator and three representatives. Thus, Oahu, with 79 percent of total population, would elect 76 percent of the senate, 19 of 25 senators, and 71 percent of the house, 36 of 51 representatives.

The new senate apportionment scheme was submitted to the court immediately upon passage. By opinion and order of April 28, 1965, the District Court disapproved it, and reinstated the provision of its earlier order requiring immediate resort to the convention method. It expressly approved the use of the registered voters measure of population. Its disapproval was based on the legislative decision not to create single-member senatorial districts for Oahu, but merely to increase the number of multi-member senatorial districts on that island from two to five. It was not contended that the apportionment failed to meet the standard of *Reynolds* if the use of multimember districts and the use of registered voters as the apportionment base did not offend the Equal Protection Clause.

In May, 1965, the Governor filed a notice of appeal to this Court from certain provisions of the two orders, and thereafter the participating senators and representatives also filed notices of appeal from parts of the orders. . . .

. . . The District Court concluded that, as a matter of state law, the house and senate apportionment plans were severable. . . . The Governor argues that the District Court committed "fundamental error" in preventing the Hawaii Legislature from engaging in such deliberations, and that, for that reason alone, the legislative product was inevitably tinged with constitutional error.

We agree that, once the District Court decided to permit legislative action, it could and should have made clear to the Hawaii Legislature that it could propose modification of the house as well as the senate plan, both as to the interim apportionment to be adopted under court order and as to proposals for permanent reapportionment through constitutional amendment. That approach would have enabled the legislature to channel its efforts to permanent, rather than temporary, change. Indeed, the failure to invite such thoroughgoing consideration was particularly unfortunate in connection with the court's requirement in its order of March 9 that the Hawaii Legislature prepare constitutional amendments for a permanent apportionment plan. By directing that the permanent plan incorporate the interim reapportionment plan, and by restricting the choices available to the legislature in adopting an interim plan, the court put significant restraints on the legislature's deliberations about permanent apportionment. It seemed not only to limit the legislature to consideration of senate apportionment, but also to require that a registered voters basis be used for that apportionment. These constraints, together with the District Court's action in explicitly sustaining the constitutionality of the house apportionment in its order of February 17, may have limited the opportunities of the legislature to construct the total scheme of apportionment best suited to the State's needs. . . .

We are dealing here, however, only with the interim plan. The State remains free to adopt other plans for apportionment, and the present interim plan will remain in effect for no longer time than is necessary to adopt a permanent plan. The 1966 general elections are imminent, and election machinery must be put into operation before further proceedings could be completed. In this context, the question of embarrassment of state legislative deliberations may be put aside. For present purposes, H.B. 987 may be treated together with the existing house apportionment as a new, overall proposal for interim apportionment. The only question for us is whether, viewing the resulting plan in its entirety and without regard to its history, it fall short of federal constitutional standards. We conclude for reasons to be stated that H.B. No. 987 and the existing house apportionment together constitute an interim legislative apportionment which has not been shown to fall short of federal standards. We direct the District Court to enter an order appropriate to adopt the plan as the court's own for legislative apportionment applicable to the 1966 election, and thereafter until a constitutional permanent plan is adopted, constitutional deficiencies in the interim plan are shown or another interim plan for reapportionment of the Hawaii Legislature suggested by the legislature is approved by the court.

. . .

. . . In relying on conjecture as to the effects of multimember districting, rather than demonstrated fact, the court acted in a manner more appropriate to the body responsible for drawing up the districting plan. Speculations do not supply evidence that the multimember districting was designed to have or had the invidious effect necessary to a judgment of the unconstitutionality of the districting. Indeed, while it would have been better had the court not insisted that the legislature "justify" its proposal, except insofar as it thus reserved to itself the ultimate decision of constitutionality vel non, the legislature did assign reasons for its choice. Once the District Court had decided, properly, not to impose its own senate apportionment, but to allow the legislature to frame one, such judgments were exclusively for the legislature to make. They were subject to constitutional challenge only upon a demonstration that the interim apportionment, although made on a proper population basis, was designed to, or would operate to, minimize or cancel out the voting strength of racial or political elements of the voting population.

. . .

. . . The District Court was careful to disclaim any holding that it was a "perfect basis." We agree. It may well be that reapportionment more frequently than every 10 years, perhaps every four or eight years, would better avoid the hazards of its use. Use of presidential election year figures might both assure a high level of participation and reduce the likelihood that varying degrees of local interest in the outcome of the election would produce different patterns of political activity over the State. Other measures, such as a system of permanent personal registration, might also contribute to the stability and accuracy of the registered voters figure as an apportionment basis. Future litigation may reveal infirmities, temporary or permanent, not established by the present record. We hold that, with a view to its interim use, Hawaii's registered voter basis does not, on this record, fall short of constitutional standards.

Our conclusion that the interim apportionment should apply to the 1966 election requires that the provisions of the order of February 17 mandating an immediate special election on the question of calling a constitutional convention should remain inoperative. The imminence of the 1966 elections precludes any further action pending that event. But the question remains what role the District Court has in bringing about a permanent reapportionment as promptly as reasonably may be after that election. We believe it should retain jurisdiction of the case to take such further proceedings as may be appropriate in the event a permanent reapportionment is not made effective. We note that the electorate will vote at the 1966 election on the question whether a constitutional convention should be convened. We see no reason, however, why the newly elected legislature should either be compelled to propose amendments or be precluded from proposing them. The legislature will doubtless find reason enough to act in the fact that the District Court will retain jurisdiction over the cause to take any action that may be appropriate pending the adoption of a permanent reapportionment which complies with constitutional standards. Such action may include further inquiry into the constitutionality of the present plan in its operation, consideration of substitute interim plans for apportioning the house and senate that might be submitted by the legislature in the event of failure of proposals for constitutional amendment, or judicial apportionment if the present plan is shown to be

constitutionally deficient and no acceptable substitute is forthcoming.

The District Court is accordingly directed on remand to enter an appropriate order (1) adopting H.B. No. 987 and the existing house apportionment as an interim legislative apportionment for Hawaii and (2) retaining jurisdiction of the cause for all purposes.

Swann v. Adams
385 U.S. 440 (1967)

This case presents . . . another development in the efforts of the State of Florida to apportion its legislature in accordance with the requirements of the Federal Constitution. . . . The litigation began in 1962. On June 22, 1964, in *Swann v. Adams*, we reversed the judgment of the three-judge District Court upholding the then-current legislative apportionment in Florida and remanded the case for further proceedings, consistent with the Court's opinion in *Reynolds v. Sims*, and its companion cases. The District Court then deferred further action until the conclusion of the legislative session which convened on April 6, 1965. The legislature proceeded to reapportion the State on June 29, 1965. The District Court forthwith held the new plan failed to meet the requirements of the Fourteenth Amendment, but approved the plan on an interim basis, limiting it to the period ending 60 days after the adjournment of the 1967 session of the Florida Legislature. This Court, finding no warrant for perpetuating what all conceded was an unconstitutional apportionment for another three years, reversed the judgment and remanded the case to the District Court so that a valid reapportionment plan would be made effective for the 1966 elections. The Florida Legislature again acted on the matter in March,

1966, by adopting still another reapportionment plan which the appellants promptly attacked in the District Court.

. . .

. . . [T]he plan was held constitutional.

The State would have us dismiss this case for lack of standing on the part of appellants to maintain this appeal because appellants are from Dade County, Florida, which appellants concede has received constitutional treatment under the legislative plan. Appellants, however, had before the District Court their own plan which would have accorded different treatment to Dade County in some respects as compared with the legislative plan, and the alternative plan was rejected by the District Court. Moreover, the District Court has apparently consistently denied intervention to other plaintiffs, seemingly treating the appellants as representing other citizens in the State. The challenge to standing cannot succeed.

. . .

. . . The District Court made no attempt to explain or justify the many variations among the legislative districts. As for the State, all it suggested in either the lower court or here is that its plan comes as close as "practical" to complete population equality and that the State was attempting to follow congressional district lines. There was, however, no attempt to justify any particular deviations, even the larger ones, with respect to either of these considerations. Moreover, the State's brief states only that the legislature followed "in most instances" the congressional boundaries, and, with respect to "practicality," it seems quite obvious that the State could have come much closer to providing districts of equal population than it did. The appellants themselves placed before the court their own plan which revealed much smaller variations between the districts than did the plan approved by the District Court. Further-

more, appellants suggested to the District Court specific amendments to the legislative plan which, if they had been accepted, would have measurably reduced the population differences between many of the districts. Appellants' own plan and their suggested amendments to the legislative plan might have been infirm in other respects but they do demonstrate that a closer approximation to equally populated districts was a feasible undertaking. The State, with admirable candor, states that it offered no evidence in the District Court to explain the challenged variations with respect to either the house or the senate. In its view, however, the plan should be approved on the record as it is.

. . .

Reversed.

Kilgarlin v. Hill
386 U.S. 120 (1967)

Following judicial invalidation of the constitutional and statutory provisions governing the apportionment of the Texas State Legislature, the State Legislature reapportioned both the House and the Senate. Appellants promptly challenged on various grounds the constitutionality of H.B. 195, which reapportioned the House of Representatives in a combination of single-member, multimember and floterial districts. The District Court sustained all aspects of the plan except those provisions respecting the counties included in 11 floterial districts, which were found violative of the equality principles announced in *Reynolds v. Sims*. The court did, however, over appellants' objections, permit the 1966 election to proceed under H.B. 195 with a proviso to the effect that, if the legislature did not adopt corrective legislation by August 1, 1967, the counties in the floterial districts would be reconstituted as multimember districts and all the representatives assigned to those counties would be elected at large.

. . .

The District Court sustained the constitutionality of H.B. 195 on two grounds. First, it held that appellants had the burden not only of demonstrating the degree of variance from the equality principle, but also of "negat[ing] the existence of any state of facts which would sustain the constitutionality of the legislation." This, the court held, appellants had not done. At that time, of course, had not been announced. Under that case, it is quite clear that, unless satisfactorily justified by the court or by the evidence of record, population variances of the size and significance evident here are sufficient to invalidate an apportionment plan. Without such justification, appellants' analysis of H.B. 195 made out a sufficient case under the Fourteenth Amendment.

Second, the District Court, not resting exclusively on its burden of proof ruling, found that the deviations from the equal population principle were amply justified here because they resulted from a bona fide attempt to conform to the state policy requiring legislative apportionment plans to respect county boundaries wherever possible. We are doubtful, however, that the deviations evident here are the kind of "minor" variations which *Reynolds v. Sims* indicated might be justified by local policies counseling the maintenance of established political subdivisions in apportionment plans. But we need not reach that constitutional question, for we are not convinced that the announced policy of the State of Texas necessitated the range of deviations between legislative districts which is evident here. In the first place, Texas policy, as elaborated by the Attorney General and concurred in by the District Court, permits the formation of multimember and floterial

districts and even, where necessary, the violation of county lines in order to surmount undue population variations. In the second place, the District Court did not relate its declared justification to any specific inequalities among the districts, nor demonstrate why or how respect for the integrity of county lines required the particular deviations called for by H.B. 195. Nor did the District Court articulate any satisfactory grounds for rejecting at least two other plans presented to the court, which respected county lines but which produced substantially smaller deviations from the principles of *Reynolds v. Sims*. Similar fault can be found in accepting a general county-line justification for the population deviations that would occur should the present floterial districts be reconstituted as multimember districts. . . .

. . . If other districts cannot be re-formed within county lines in such a way as to afford Dallas and Bexar Counties another representative and at the same time to afford the re-formed districts constitutional representation, we would have to meet the question whether the state policy advanced here justifies the seeming underrepresentation in Dallas and Bexar Counties. . . . But on the record that is now before us, we do not reach this issue, and believe that the District Court should give further consideration to these counties.

. . .

The judgment is reversed in part and the case remanded for further proceedings consistent with this opinion.

Moody v. Flowers
387 U.S. 97 (1967)

In No. 624, appellants attack the validity of an Alabama statute prescribing the apportionment and districting scheme for electing members of the Houston County Board of Revenue and Control. Under the statute, the Board consists of five members, each elected by the qualified electors of the district of which he is a resident. The challenged statute prescribes the areas constituting the various districts. The action is brought against the appellees, including some state officials, seeking a declaration that the statute is invalid and an injunction prohibiting its enforcement, and requesting that the court order at-large elections until the State Legislature redistricts and reapportions the Board on a population basis. The theory is that the apportionment and districting scheme results in the overrepresentation of certain areas and the underrepresentation of others. . . . A three-judge court was convened and the complaint was dismissed. . . .

In No. 491, appellees brought an action against appellants, members of the Suffolk County Board of Supervisors, seeking a declaration that so much of §203 of the Suffolk County Charter as provides that each supervisor shall have one vote as a member of the Suffolk County Board of Supervisors violates the Fourteenth Amendment and an injunction prohibiting the appellants from acting as a Board of Supervisors unless and until a change in their voting strength is made, and requesting the convening of a three-judge court. The 10 towns of Suffolk County, New York, elect, by popular vote, a supervisor every two years. The supervisor is the town's representative on the Suffolk County Board of Supervisors. And, each supervisor is entitled to one vote on the County Board of Supervisors. Pursuant to Art. 9, §§1 and 2, of the New York Constitution, the State Legislature approved a charter for the county containing . . . the above provisions.

Appellees claim that granting each supervisor one vote regardless of the population of the town which elected him results in an overrepresentation

of the towns with small populations and underrepresentation of towns with large populations.

A three-judge court was convened and it declared §203 of the Suffolk County Charter invalid because in conflict with the Equal Protection Clause of the Fourteenth Amendment, and ordered the Board to submit to the county electorate a plan for reconstruction of the Board so as to insure voter equality. . . .

. . .

In No. 624, the constitutional attack was directed to a state statute dealing with matters of local concern—the apportionment and districting for one county's governing board. The statute is not a statute of statewide application, but relates solely to the affairs of one county in the State. The fact that state officers were named as defendants cannot change the result.

It is said that there is enough similarity between this law and the laws governing other Alabama counties as to give this case a statewide interest. It is said that 29 counties having a city of consequence located within their borders have the same "crazy quilt" of malapportionment to insure rural voters' control. It is said that 32 other counties provide for election of county board members at large, but with a local residence requirement which insures rural control. It is said that six rural counties elect their governing bodies on an at-large basis with no local residence requirement. We indicate no views on the merits. But we do suggest that even a variety of different devices, working perhaps to the same end, still leaves any one device local, rather than statewide for purposes of the statutory three-judge court.

In No. 491, the constitutional attack is directed at provisions of a county charter providing that the county governing board shall be composed of the supervisors of the several towns and that each supervisor shall have one vote. The county charter is similar to a local ordinance, a challenge to which cannot support a three-judge court. The fact that the charter was enacted into state law does not change the result. The charter provisions plainly relate only to one county and the statute enacting the charter is similarly limited. It does not remotely resemble a state statute of general, statewide application. It is a statute dealing solely with matters of local concern. Nor was the action brought against "state officers" within the meaning of the statute; it was brought to enjoin local officers acting solely with reference to local matters.

It is argued, however, that the alleged malapportionment reflected in the charter is also reflected in §150 and §153 of the New York County Law, which does have a statewide application, and that the provisions of the charter here challenged are actually interchangeable with §150 and §153 of the County Law. It is also argued that, to get rid of this alleged malapportionment, the Court would have to declare unconstitutional not only the provisions of the charter, but also §150 and §153 of the County Law. The complaint, however, challenges only the charter. It makes no challenge of any statewide law. And the three-judge court considered it as an attack only on the charter.

We therefore do not accept the invitation to get into the niceties of the relationship between the provisions of the charter and the New York County Law, but take the complaint as we find it for purposes of the jurisdictional question, and conclude on the face of the complaint that we have only an alleged malapportionment under a county charter.

Since the "statute" in each of these cases is one of limited application, concerning only a particular county involved in the litigation, a three-judge court was improperly convened. Ap-

peals should, therefore, have been taken to the respective Courts of Appeals, not to this Court. Since the time for perfecting those appeals may have passed, we vacate the judgments and remand the causes to the court which heard each case so that they may enter a fresh decree from which appellants may, if they wish, perfect timely appeals to the respective Courts of Appeals.

Avery v. Midland County
390 U.S. 474 (1968)

Midland County has a population of about 70,000. The Commissioners Court is composed of five members. One, the County Judge, is elected at large from the entire county, and in practice casts a vote only to break a tie. The other four are Commissioners chosen from districts. The population of those districts, according to the 1963 estimates that were relied upon when this case was tried, was respectively 67,906; 852; 414; and 828. This vast imbalance resulted from placing in a single district virtually the entire city of Midland, Midland County's only urban center, in which 95 percent of the county's population resides.

. . .

Petitioner sued the Commissioners Court and its members in the Midland County District Court, alleging that the disparity in district population violated the Fourteenth Amendment and that he had standing as a resident, taxpayer, and voter in the district with the largest population. Three of the four commissioners testified at the trial, all telling the court (as indeed the population statistics for the established districts demonstrated) that population was not a major factor in the districting process. The trial court ruled for petitioner. It made no explicit reference to the Fourteenth Amendment, but said the apportionment plan in effect was not "for the convenience of the people," the apportionment standard established by Art. V, 18, of the Texas Constitution. The court ordered the defendant commissioners to adopt a new plan in which each precinct would have "substantially the same number of people."

The Texas Court of Civil Appeals reversed the judgment of the District Court and entered judgment for the respondents. It held that neither federal nor state law created a requirement that Texas county commissioners courts be districted according to population.

The Texas Supreme Court reversed the Court of Civil Appeals. It held that, under "the requirements of the Texas and the United States Constitutions," the present districting scheme was impermissible "for the reasons stated by the trial court." However, the Supreme Court disagreed with the trial court's conclusion that precincts must have substantially equal populations, stating that such factors as "number of qualified voters, land areas, geography, miles of county roads and taxable values" could be considered. It also decreed that no Texas courts could redistrict the Commissioners Court.

. . .

When the State apportions its legislature, it must have due regard for the Equal Protection Clause. Similarly, when the State delegates lawmaking power to local government and provides for the election of local officials from districts specified by statute, ordinance, or local charter, it must insure that those qualified to vote have the right to an equally effective voice in the election process. If voters residing in oversize districts are denied their constitutional right to participate in the election of state legislators, precisely the same kind of deprivation occurs when the members of a city council, school board, or county governing board are elected from districts

of substantially unequal population. If the five senators representing a city in the state legislature may not be elected from districts ranging in size from 50,000 to 500,000, neither is it permissible to elect the members of the city council from those same districts. In either case, the votes of some residents have greater weight than those of others; in both cases, the equal protection of the laws has been denied.

That the state legislature may itself be properly apportioned does not exempt subdivisions from the Fourteenth Amendment. While state legislatures exercise extensive power over their constituents and over the various units of local government, the States universally leave much policy and decision making to their governmental subdivisions. Legislators enact many laws, but do not attempt to reach those countless matters of local concern necessarily left wholly or partly to those who govern at the local level. What is more, in providing for the governments of their cities, counties, towns, and districts, the States characteristically provide for representative government—for decision making at the local level by representatives elected by the people. And, not infrequently, the delegation of power to local units is contained in constitutional provisions for local home rule which are immune from legislative interference. In a word, institutions of local government have always been a major aspect of our system, and their responsible and responsive operation is today of increasing importance to the quality of life of more and more of our citizens. We therefore see little difference, in terms of the application of the Equal Protection Clause and of the principles of *Reynolds v. Sims*, between the exercise of state power through legislatures and its exercise by elected officials in the cities, towns, and counties.

We are urged to permit unequal districts for

the Midland County Commissioners Court on the ground that the court's functions are not sufficiently "legislative." The parties have devoted much effort to urging that alternative labels—"administrative" versus "legislative"—be applied to the Commissioners Court. . . . The Texas commissioners courts are assigned some tasks which would normally be thought of as "legislative," others typically assigned to "executive" or "administrative" departments, and still others which are "judicial." In this regard, Midland County's Commissioners Court is representative of most of the general governing bodies of American cities, counties, towns, and villages. . . .

. . .

The Equal Protection Clause does not, of course, require that the State never distinguish between citizens, but only that the distinctions that are made not be arbitrary or invidious. The conclusion of *Reynolds v. Sims* was that bases other than population were not acceptable grounds for distinguishing among citizens when determining the size of districts used to elect members of state legislatures. We hold today only that the Constitution permits no substantial variation from equal population in drawing districts for units of local government having general governmental powers over the entire geographic area served by the body.

This Court is aware of the immense pressures facing units of local government, and of the greatly varying problems with which they must deal. The Constitution does not require that a uniform straitjacket bind citizens in devising mechanisms of local government suitable for local needs and efficient in solving local problems. . . .

The *Sailors* and *Dusch* cases demonstrate that the Constitution and this Court are not roadblocks in the path of innovation, experiment, and development among units of local government. . . .

Our decision today is only that the Constitution imposes one ground rule for the development of arrangements of local government: a requirement that units with general governmental powers over an entire geographic area not be apportioned among single member districts of substantially unequal population.

The judgment below is vacated, and the case is remanded for disposition not inconsistent with this opinion.

Kirkpatrick v. Preisler
394 U.S. 526 (1969)

The Missouri congressional redistricting statute challenged in these cases resulted from that State's second attempt at congressional redistricting since *Wesberry* was decided. In 1965, a three-judge District Court for the Western District of Missouri declared that the Missouri congressional districting Act then in effect was unconstitutional under *Wesberry*, but withheld any judicial relief "until the Legislature of the State of Missouri has once more had an opportunity to deal with the problem. . . ." Thereafter, the General Assembly of Missouri enacted a redistricting statute, but this statute too was declared unconstitutional. The District Court, however, retained jurisdiction to review any further plan that might be enacted. In 1967, the General Assembly enacted the statute under attack here, and the Attorney General of Missouri moved in the District Court for a declaration sustaining the Act and an order dismissing the case.

. . .

The District Court found that the General Assembly had not . . . relied on the census figures, but instead had based its plan on less accurate data. In addition, the District Court found that the General Assembly had rejected a redistricting plan submitted to it which provided for districts with smaller population variances among them. Finally, the District Court found that the simple device of switching some counties from one district to another would have produced a plan with markedly reduced variances among districts. Based on these findings, the District Court . . . held that the 1967 Act did not meet the constitutional standard of equal representation for equal numbers of people "as nearly as practicable," and that the State had failed to make any acceptable justification for the variances. . . .

Missouri's primary argument is that the population variances among the districts created by the 1967 Act are so small that they should be considered de minimis, and, for that reason, to satisfy the "as nearly as practicable" limitation and not to require independent justification. Alternatively, Missouri argues that justification for the variances was established in the evidence: it is contended that the General Assembly provided for variances out of legitimate regard for such factors as the representation of distinct interest groups, the integrity of county lines, the compactness of districts, the population trends within the State, the high proportion of military personnel, college students, and other nonvoters in some districts, and the political realities of "legislative interplay."

We reject Missouri's argument that there is a fixed numerical or percentage population variance small enough to be considered de minimis and to satisfy without question the "as nearly as practicable" standard. The whole thrust of the "as nearly as practicable" approach is inconsistent with adoption of fixed numerical standards which excuse population variances without regard to the circumstances of each particular case. The extent to which equality may practicably be achieved may differ from state to state and from district to district. Since "equal representation for equal numbers of people [is] the fundamental goal for the House of Representatives," the "as nearly as practicable" standard requires that the State make a good faith effort to achieve precise mathematical equality. Unless population variances among congressional districts are shown to have resulted despite such effort, the State must justify each variance, no matter how small.

There are other reasons for rejecting the de minimis approach. We can see no nonarbitrary way to pick a cut-off point at which population variances suddenly become de minimis. Moreover, to consider a certain range of variances de minimis would encourage legislators to strive for that range, rather than for equality as nearly as practicable. The District Court found, for example, that, at least one leading Missouri legislator deemed it proper to attempt to achieve a 2 percent level of variance, rather than to seek population equality.

Equal representation for equal numbers of people is a principle designed to prevent debasement of voting power and diminution of access to elected representatives. Toleration of even small deviations detracts from these purposes. . . .

. . . We agree with the District Court that "the rule is one of 'practicability,' rather than political 'practicality.'" Problems created by partisan politics cannot justify an apportionment which does not otherwise pass constitutional muster.

Similarly, we do not find legally acceptable the argument that variances are justified if they necessarily result from a State's attempt to avoid fragmenting political subdivisions by drawing congressional district lines along existing county, municipal, or other political subdivision boundaries. The State's interest in constructing congressional districts in this manner, it is suggested, is to minimize the opportunities for partisan gerry-mandering. But an argument that deviations from equality are justified in order to inhibit legislators from engaging in partisan gerrymandering is no more than a variant of the argument, already rejected, that considerations of practical politics can justify population disparities.

Missouri further contends that certain population variances resulted from the legislature's taking account of the fact that the percentage of eligible voters among the total population differed significantly from district to district—some districts contained disproportionately large numbers of military personnel stationed at bases maintained by the Armed Forces and students in attendance at universities or colleges. There may be a question whether distribution of congressional seats except according to total population can ever be permissible under Art. I, §2. But assuming without deciding that apportionment may be based on eligible voter population, rather than total population, the Missouri plan is still unacceptable. Missouri made no attempt to ascertain the number of eligible voters in each district and to apportion accordingly. At best, it made haphazard adjustments to a scheme based on total population. . . .

Missouri also argues that population disparities between some of its congressional districts result from the legislature's attempt to take into account projected population shifts. We recognize that a congressional districting plan will usually be in effect for at least 10 years and five congressional elections. Situations may arise where substantial population shifts over such a period can be anticipated. Where these shifts can be predicted with a high degree of accuracy, States that are redistricting may properly consider them. By this we mean to open no avenue for subterfuge. Findings as to population trends must be thoroughly documented and applied throughout the State in a systematic, not an ad hoc, manner. Missouri's attempted justification of the substantial underpopulation in the Fourth and Sixth Districts falls far short of this standard. . . .

Finally, Missouri claims that some of the deviations from equality were a consequence of the legislature's attempt to ensure that each congressional district would be geographically compact. . . .

In any event, Missouri's claim of compactness is based solely upon the unaesthetic appearance of the map of congressional boundaries that would result from an attempt to effect some of the changes in district lines which, according to the lower court, would achieve greater equality. A State's preference for pleasingly shaped districts can hardly justify population variances.

Affirmed.

Wells v. Rockefeller
394 U.S. 542 (1969)

. . . Before us here is a judgment of a three-judge District Court for the Southern District of New York which sustained the validity of New York's 1968 congressional districting statute. In 1967, that court had struck down an earlier districting statute apportioning New York's 41 congressional seats and had retained jurisdiction of the case pending action by the New York Legislature to redress the plan's deficiencies. The court recognized that a thorough revision of district lines might not be possible in time for the upcoming 1968 congressional election, but concluded nevertheless that "[t]here are enough changes which can be superimposed on the present districts to cure the most flagrant inequalities."

On February 28, 1968, a month and a half after the New York Legislature reconvened, the districting statute presently under attack was enacted. After a hearing, the three-judge court, on March 20, 1968, sustained the statute, stating that the districting plan afforded New York voters "an opportunity to vote in the 1968 and 1970 elections on a basis of population equality within reasonably comparable districts." . . .

Appellant levels two constitutional attacks against the statute: (1) that the statute violates the equal population principle of *Wesberry v. Sanders*, and (2) that the statute represents a systematic and intentional partisan gerrymander violating Art. I, §2, of the Constitution and the Fourteenth Amendment. . . .

. . .

. . . To accept a scheme such as New York's would permit groups of districts with defined interest orientations to be overrepresented at the expense of districts with different interest orientations. Equality of population among districts in a substate is not a justification for inequality among all the districts in the State.

Nor are the variations in the "North country" districts justified by the fact that these districts are constructed of entire counties.

. . . We . . . reverse the judgment of the District Court insofar as it approved the plan for use in the 1970 election and remand the case for the entry of a new judgment consistent with this opinion.

Hadley v. Junior College District of Metropolitan Kansas City
397 U.S. 50 (1970)

This case involves the extent to which the Fourteenth Amendment and the "one man, one vote" principle apply in the election of local governmental officials. Appellants are residents and taxpayers of the Kansas City School District, one of eight separate school districts that have combined to form the Junior College District of Metropolitan Kansas City. Under Missouri law, separate school districts may vote by referendum to establish a consolidated junior college district and elect six trustees to conduct and manage the necessary affairs of that district. The state law also provides that these trustees shall be apportioned among the separate school districts on the basis of "school enumeration," defined as the number of persons between the ages of six and 20 years who reside in each district. In the case of the Kansas City School District, this apportionment plan results in the election of three trustees, or 50 percent of the total number, from that district. Since that district contains approximately 60 percent of the total school enumeration in the junior college district, appellants brought suit claiming that their right to vote for trustees was being unconstitutionally diluted in violation of the Equal Protection Clause of the Fourteenth Amendment. The Missouri Supreme Court upheld the trial court's dismissal of the suit, stating that the "one man, one vote" principle was not applicable in this case. . . .

. . .

Appellants in this case argue that the junior college trustees exercised general governmental powers over the entire district, and that, under *Avery*, the State was thus required to apportion the trustees according to population on an equal basis, as far as practicable. Appellants argue that, since the trustees can levy and collect taxes, issue bonds with certain restrictions, hire and fire teachers, make contracts, collect fees, supervise and discipline students, pass on petitions to annex school districts, acquire property by condemnation, and in general manage the operations of the junior colleges, their powers are equivalent, for apportionment purposes, to those exercised by the county commissioners in *Avery*. We feel that these powers, while not fully as broad as those of the Midland County Commissioners, certainly show that the trustees perform important governmental functions within the districts, and we think these powers are general enough and have sufficient impact throughout the district to justify the conclusion that the principle which we applied in *Avery* should also be applied here.

This Court has consistently held in a long series of cases that, in situations involving elections, the States are required to insure that each person's vote counts as much, insofar as it is practicable, as any other person's. We have applied this principle in congressional elections, state legislative elections, and local elections. The consistent theme of those decisions is that the right to vote in an election is protected by the United States Constitution against dilution or debasement. While the particular offices involved in these cases have varied, in each case, a constant factor is the decision of the government to have citizens participate individually by ballot in the selection of certain people who carry out governmental functions. Thus, in the case now before us, while the office of junior college trustee differs in certain respects from those offices considered in prior cases, it is exactly the same in the one crucial factor—these officials are elected by popular vote.

When a court is asked to decide whether a State is required by the Constitution to give each qualified voter the same power in an election open to all, there is no discernible valid reason why constitutional distinctions should be drawn on the basis of the purpose of the election. If one person's vote is given less weight through unequal apportionment, his right to equal voting participation is impaired just as much when he votes for a

school board member as when he votes for a state legislator. While there are differences in the powers of different officials, the crucial consideration is the right of each qualified voter to participate on an equal footing in the election process. It should be remembered that, in cases like this one, we are asked by voters to insure that they are given equal treatment, and, from their perspective, the harm from unequal treatment is the same in any election, regardless of the officials selected.

If the purpose of a particular election were to be the determining factor in deciding whether voters are entitled to equal voting power, courts would be faced with the difficult job of distinguishing between various elections. We cannot readily perceive judicially manageable standards to aid in such a task. It might be suggested that equal apportionment is required only in "important" elections, but good judgment and common sense tell us that what might be a vital election to one voter might well be a routine one to another. In some instances, the election of a local sheriff may be far more important than the election of a United States Senator. If there is any way of determining the importance of choosing a particular governmental official, we think the decision of the State to select that official by popular vote is a strong enough indication that the choice is an important one. This is so because, in our country, popular election has traditionally been the method followed when government by the people is most desired.

. . . We . . . hold today that, as a general rule, whenever a state or local government decides to select persons by popular election to perform governmental functions, the Equal Protection Clause of the Fourteenth Amendment requires that each qualified voter must be given an equal opportunity to participate in that election, and when members of an elected body are chosen from separate districts, each district must be established on a basis that will insure, as far as is practicable, that equal numbers of voters can vote for proportionally equal numbers of officials. It is, of course, possible that there might be some case in which a State elects certain functionaries whose duties are so far removed from normal governmental activities and so disproportionately affect different groups that a popular election in compliance with *Reynolds*, might not be required, but certainly we see nothing in the present case that indicates that the activities of these trustees fit in that category. Education has traditionally been a vital governmental function, and these trustees, whose election the State has opened to all qualified voters, are governmental officials in every relevant sense of that term.

. . .

In holding that the guarantee of equal voting strength for each voter applies in all elections of governmental officials, we do not feel that the States will be inhibited in finding ways to insure that legitimate political goals of representation are achieved. We have previously upheld against constitutional challenge an election scheme that required that candidates be residents of certain districts that did not contain equal numbers of people. Since all the officials in that case were elected at large, the right of each voter was given equal treatment. We have also held that, where a State chooses to select members of an official body by appointment, rather than election, and that choice does not itself offend the Constitution, the fact that each official does not "represent" the same number of people does not deny those people equal protection of the laws. And a State may, in certain cases, limit the right to vote to a particular group or class of people. . . .

. . .

For the reasons set forth above, the judgment below is reversed, and the case is remanded to the Missouri Supreme Court for proceedings not inconsistent with this opinion.

Connor v. Johnson
402 U.S. 690 (1971)

On May 14, 1971, a three-judge District Court, convened in the Southern District of Mississippi, invalidated the Mississippi Legislature's latest reapportionment statute as allowing impermissibly large variations among House and Senate districts. The parties were requested by the court to submit suggested plans, and the applicants did so on May 17. All four plans suggested by applicants utilized single member districts exclusively in Hinds County. The following day, May 18, the court issued its own plan, which included single- and multimember districts in each House; Hinds County was constituted as a multimember district electing five senators and 12 representatives. The court expressed some reluctance over use of multi-member districts in counties electing four or more senators or representatives, saying: "[I]t would be ideal if [such counties] could be divided into districts, for the election of one member [from] the district." However, in view of the June 4, 1971, deadline for filing notices of candidacy, the court concluded that:

> [W]ith the time left available it is a matter of sheer impossibility to obtain dependable data, population figures, boundary locations, etc. so as fairly and correctly to divide these counties into districts for the election of single members of the Senate or the House in time for the elections of 1971.

The court promised to appoint a special master in January 1972 to investigate the possibility of single member districts for the general elections of 1975 and 1979.

Applicants moved the District Court to stay its order. The motion was denied on May 24. Applicants have now applied to this Court for a stay of the District Court's order and for an extension of the June 4 filing deadline until the District Court shall have provided single member districts in Hinds County, or until the Attorney General or the District Court for the District of Columbia approves the District Court's apportionment plan under Section 5 of the Voting Rights Act of 1965.

. . .

In failing to devise single member districts, the court was under the belief that insufficient time remained until June 4, the deadline for the filing of notices of candidacy. Yet, at that time, June 4 was 17 days away and, according to an uncontradicted statement in the brief supporting this motion, the applicants were able to formulate and offer to the court four single member district plans for Hinds County in the space of three days. Also according to uncontradicted statements, these plans were based on data which included county maps showing existing political subdivisions, the supervisory districts used by the Census Bureau for the taking of the 1970 census, official 1970 Census Bureau "final population counts," and "computer print-out from Census Bureau official computer tapes showing total and white/Negro population by census enumeration districts." Applicants also assert that no other population figures will subsequently become available.

The District Court's judgment was that single member districting would be "ideal" for Hinds County. We agree that, when district courts are forced to fashion apportionment plans, single member districts are preferable to large multimember districts as a general matter. Furthermore, given the census information apparently available and the dispatch with which the applicants devised suggested plans for the District Court, it is our view that, on this record, the District Court had ample time to devise single member districts for Hinds County prior to the June 4 filing deadline. While meeting the June 4 date is no longer possible, there is nothing before us to suggest any insurmountable barrier to devising such a plan by June 14, 1971. Therefore the motion for stay is granted and the judgment below is stayed until June 14. The District Court is instructed, absent insurmountable difficulties, to devise and put into effect a single-member district plan for Hinds County by that date. In light of this disposition, the District Court is directed to extend the June 4 filing date for legislative candidates from Hinds County to an appropriate date so that those candidates and the State of Mississippi may act in light of the new districts into which Hinds County will be divided.

Ely v. Klahr
403 U.S. 108 (1971)

In April, 1964 . . . suit was filed in the District Court for the District of Arizona attacking the then-existing state districting laws as unconstitutional. Following those decisions, the three-judge District Court ordered all proceedings stayed "until the expiration of a period of 30 days next following adjournment of the next session" of the Arizona Legislature. Nearly a year later, on May 18, 1965, after the legislature had failed to act, the court again deferred trial pending a special legislative session called by the Governor to deal with the necessity of reapportionment. The special session enacted Senate Bill 11, which, among other things, provided one senator for a county of 7,700 and another for a county of

55,000. The session did not undertake to reapportion the House. Trial was had in November 1965, and on February 2, 1966, the court enjoined enforcement of Senate Bill 11, which, it held, "bears evidence of having been thrown together as a result of considerations wholly apart from those laid down as compulsory by the decisions of the Supreme Court." The plan, said the court, was "shot through with invidious discrimination." The court also held that the existing House plan produced disparities of nearly four to one, which was clearly impermissible under our decisions.

Noting that the legislature "has had ample opportunity" to produce a valid reapportionment plan, the court formulated its own plan as a "temporary and provisional reapportionment," designed to govern the impending preparation for the 1966 elections. The plan was to be in effect

> for the 1966 primary and general elections and for such further elections as may follow until such time as the Legislature itself may adopt different and valid plans for districting and reapportionment.

It retained jurisdiction, as it has done since.

Some 16 months later, in June 1967, the Arizona Legislature enacted "Chapter 1, 28th Legislature," which again attempted reapportionment of the State. Within the month, suit was filed charging that this Act also was unconstitutional, but the court deferred action pending the outcome of a referendum scheduled with the November 1968, election for the legislature and Congress. It ordered those elections to be held in accordance with its own 1966 plan, as supplemented. The legislative plan was approved by the voters in the referendum and signed into law by the Governor on January 17, 1969. A hearing on the plan was commenced the same day. The court concluded on July 22, 1969, that the plan, which set up "election districts" based on population and

"legislative" subdistricts based on voter registration, would allow deviations among the legislative subdistricts of up to 40 percent from ideal until 1971, and up to 16 percent thereafter. . . . The court ordered its 1966 plan continued once again "until the Legislature shall have adopted different, valid, and effective plans for redistricting and reapportionment. . . ." It refused to order the 1970 elections to be held at large, since there was "ample time" for the legislature "to meet its obligation" before the machinery for conducting the 1970 elections would be engaged.

The legislature attempted a third time to enact a valid plan. It passed "Chapter 1, House Bill No. 1, 29th Legislature," which was signed into law by the Governor on January 22, 1970, and which is the plan involved in the decision from which this appeal is taken. Appellant challenged the bill, alleging that it "substantially disenfranchises, unreasonably and unnecessarily, a large number of the citizens of the state," and "creates legislative districts that are grossly unequal." . . . Appellant's primary dispute with the new plan was that it substantially misconceived the current population distribution in Arizona. The court agreed that appellant's plan, which utilized 1968 projections of 1960 and 1965 Arizona censuses, could "very likely [result in] a valid reapportionment plan," but it declined to implement the plan, since it was based on census tracts, rather than the existing precinct boundaries, and "the necessary reconstruction of the election precincts could not be accomplished in time" to serve the 1970 election, whose preliminary preparations were to begin in a few weeks. At the same time, the court observed that its 1966 plan had fallen behind contemporary constitutional requirements, due to more recent voter registration data . . . and the intervening decisions of this Court in *Kirkpatrick* and *Wells* and *Burns v. Richardson*.

. . .

Reapportionment history in the State lends some substance to these fears, but, as we have often noted, districting and apportionment are legislative tasks in the first instance, and the court did not err in giving the legislature a reasonable time to act based on the 1970 census figures which the court thought would be available in the summer of 1971. We agree with appellant that the District Court should make very sure that the 1972 elections are held under a constitutionally adequate apportionment plan. But the District Court knows better than we whether the November 1 deadline will afford it ample opportunity to assess the legality of a new apportionment statute if one is forthcoming and to prepare its own plan by June 1, 1972, if the official version proves insufficient. The 1970 census figures, if not now available, will be forthcoming soon; and appellant, if he is so inclined, can begin to assemble the necessary information and witnesses and himself prepare and have ready for submission what he deems to be an adequate apportionment plan. Surely, had a satisfactory substitute for Chapter 1, held unconstitutional by the District Court, been prepared and ready, the court would have ordered the 1970 elections held under that plan, rather than the invalid legislative scheme. And surely if appellant has ready for court use on November 1, 1971, a suitable alternative for an unacceptable legislative effort, or at least makes sure that the essential information is on hand, there is no justifiable ground for thinking the District Court could not, prior to June 1, 1972, complete its hearings and consideration of a new apportionment statute and, if that is rejected, adopt a plan of its own for use in the 1972 elections. Nor do we read the District Court decree as forbidding appellant from petitioning for reopening of the case prior to November 1, 1971,

and presenting to the District Court the problem which it has now raised here but which we prefer at this juncture to leave in the hands of the District Court. The judgment is affirmed.

Whitcomb v. Chavis
403 U.S. 124 (1971)

We have before us in this case the validity under the Equal Protection Clause of the statutes districting and apportioning the State of Indiana for its general assembly elections. The principal issue centers on those provisions constituting Marion County, which includes the city of Indianapolis, a multimember district for electing state senators and representatives.

Indiana has a bicameral general assembly consisting of a house of representatives of 100 members and a senate of 50 members. Eight of the 31 senatorial districts and 25 of the 39 house districts are multimember districts, that is, districts that are represented by 2 or more legislators elected at large by the voters of the district. Under the statutes here challenged, Marion County is a multimember district electing eight senators and 15 members of the house.

On January 9, 1969, six residents of Indiana, five of whom were residents of Marion County, filed a suit described by them as

> attacking the constitutionality of two statutes of the State of Indiana which provide for multi-member districting at large of General Assembly seats in Marion County, Indiana. . . .

Plaintiffs Chavis, Ramsey, and Bryant alleged that the two statutes invidiously diluted the force and effect of the vote of Negroes and poor persons' living within certain Marion County census tracts constituting what was termed "the ghetto area."

Residents of the area were alleged to have particular demographic characteristics rendering them cognizable as a minority interest group with distinctive interests in specific areas of the substantive law. With single member districting, it was said, the ghetto area would elect three members of the house and one senator, whereas, under the present districting, voters in the area "have almost no political force or control over legislators because the effect of their vote is cancelled out by other contrary interest groups" in Marion County. The mechanism of political party organization and the influence of party chairmen in nominating candidates were additional factors alleged to frustrate the exercise of power by residents of the ghetto area.

Plaintiff Walker, a Negro resident of Lake County, also a multimember district, but a smaller one, alleged an invidious discrimination against Lake County Negroes because Marion County Negroes, although no greater in number than Lake County Negroes, had the opportunity to influence the election of more legislators than Lake County Negroes. The claim was that Marion County was one-third larger in population. and thus had approximately one-third more assembly seats than Lake County, but that voter influence does not vary inversely with population, and that permitting Marion County voters to elect 23 assemblymen at large gave them a disproportionate advantage over voters in Lake County. . . .

. . .

The three-judge court filed its opinion containing its findings and conclusions on July 28, 1969, holding for plaintiffs. In sum, it concluded that Marion County's multi-member district must be disestablished, and, because of population disparities not directly related to the phenomena alleged in the complaint, the entire State must be redistricted. . . .

. . .

. . . Judgment was withheld in all respects, however, to give the State until October 1, 1969, to enact legislation remedying the improper districting and malapportionment found to exist by the court. In so doing, the court thought the State "might wish to give consideration to certain principles of legislative apportionment brought out at the trial in these proceedings." . . .

On October 15, the court judicially noticed that the Indiana general assembly had not been called to redistrict and reapportion the State. Following further hearings and examination of various plans submitted by the parties, the court drafted and adopted a plan based on the 1960 census figures. With respect to Marion County, the court followed plaintiffs' suggested scheme, which was said to protect "the legally cognizable racial minority group against dilution of its voting strength." Single member districts were employed throughout the State, county lines were crossed where necessary, judicial notice was taken of the location of the nonwhite population in establishing district lines in metropolitan areas of the State and the court's plan expressly aimed at giving "recognition to the cognizable racial minority group whose grievance lead [sic] to this litigation."

The court enjoined state officials from conducting any elections under the existing apportionment statutes, and ordered that the 1970 elections be held in accordance with the plan prepared by the court. Jurisdiction was retained to pass upon any future claims of unconstitutionality with respect to any future legislative apportionments adopted by the State.

. . .

Plaintiffs level two quite distinct challenges to the Marion County district. The first charge is that any multimember district bestows on its voters several unconstitutional advantages over voters in single member districts or smaller multimember districts. The other allegation is that the Marion County district, on the record of this case, illegally minimizes and cancels out the voting power of a cognizable racial minority in Marion County. The District Court sustained the latter claim and considered the former sufficiently persuasive to be a substantial factor in prescribing uniform, single member districts as the basic scheme of the court's own plan.

. . .

We are not ready . . . to agree that multi-member districts, wherever they exist, overrepresent their voters as compared with voters in single member districts, even if the multimember delegation tends to bloc voting. The theory that plural representation itself unduly enhances a district's power and the influence of its voters remains to be demonstrated in practice and in the day-to-day operation of the legislature. Neither the findings of the trial court nor the record before us sustains it, even where bloc voting is posited.

In fashioning relief, the three-judge court appeared to embrace the idea that each member of a bloc-voting delegation has more influence than legislators from a single-member district. But its findings of fact fail to deal with the actual influence of Marion County's delegation in the Indiana Legislature. Nor did plaintiffs' evidence make such a showing. That bloc voting tended to occur is sustained by the record, and defendants' own witness thought it was advantageous for Marion County's delegation to stick together. But nothing demonstrates that senators and representatives from Marion County counted for more in the legislature than members from single-member districts or from smaller multimember districts. Nor is there anything in the court's findings indicating that what might be true of Marion County is also true of other multi-member districts in Indi-

ana, or is true of multimember districts generally. Moreover, Marion County would have no less advantage, if advantage there is, if it elected from individual districts and the elected representatives demonstrated the same bloc-voting tendency, which may also develop among legislators representing single member districts widely scattered throughout the State. Of course it is advantageous to start with more than one vote for a bill. But nothing before us shows or suggests that any legislative skirmish affecting the State of Indiana or Marion County in particular would have come out differently had Marion County been subdistricted and its delegation elected from single-member districts.

Rather than squarely finding unacceptable discrimination against out-state voters in favor of Marion County voters, the trial court struck down Marion County's multimember district because it found the scheme worked invidiously against a specific segment of the county's voters as compared with others. The court identified an area of the city as a ghetto, found it predominantly inhabited by poor Negroes with distinctive substantive law interests, and thought this group unconstitutionally underrepresented because the proportion of legislators with residences in the ghetto elected from 1960 to 1968 was less than the ghetto's proportion of the population, less than the proportion of legislators elected from Washington Township, a less populous district, and less than the ghetto would likely have elected had the county consisted of single member districts. We find major deficiencies in this approach.

. . .

On the record before us, plaintiffs' position comes to this: that, although they have equal opportunity to participate in and influence the selection of candidates and legislators, and although the ghetto votes predominantly Democratic and that party slates candidates satisfactory to the ghetto, invidious discrimination nevertheless results when the ghetto, along with all other Democrats, suffers the disaster of losing too many elections. But typical American legislative elections are district-oriented, head-on races between candidates of two or more parties. As our system has it, one candidate wins, the others lose. Arguably, the losing candidates' supporters are without representation, since the men they voted for have been defeated; arguably, they have been denied equal protection of the laws, since they have no legislative voice of their own. This is true of both single member and multimember districts. But we have not yet deemed it a denial of equal protection to deny legislative seats to losing candidates, even in those so-called "safe" districts where the same party wins year after year.

Plainly, the District Court saw nothing unlawful about the impact of typical single member district elections. The court's own plan created districts giving both Republicans and Democrats several predictably safe general assembly seats, with political, racial or economic minorities in those districts being "unrepresented" year after year. But similar consequences flowing from Marion County multimember district elections were viewed differently. Conceding that all Marion County voters could fairly be said to be represented by the entire delegation, just as is each voter in a single member district by the winning candidate, the District Court thought the ghetto voters' claim to the partial allegiance of 8 senators and 15 representatives was not equivalent to the undivided allegiance of 1 senator and 2 representatives; nor was the ghetto voters' chance of influencing the election of an entire slate as significant as the guarantee of 1 ghetto senator and 2 ghetto representatives. As the trial court saw it, ghetto voters could not be adequately and

equally represented unless some of Marion County's general assembly seats were reserved for ghetto residents serving the interests of the ghetto majority. But are poor Negroes of the ghetto any more underrepresented than poor ghetto whites who also voted Democratic and lost, or any more discriminated against than other interest groups or voters in Marion County with allegiance to the Democratic Party, or, conversely, any less represented than Republican areas or voters in years of Republican defeat? We think not. The mere fact that one interest group or another concerned with the outcome of Marion County elections has found itself outvoted and without legislative seats of its own provides no basis for invoking constitutional remedies where, as here, there is no indication that this segment of the population is being denied access to the political system.

There is another gap in the trial court's reasoning. As noted by the court, the interest of ghetto residents in certain issues did not measurably differ from that of other voters. Presumably, in these respects, Marion County's assemblymen were satisfactorily representative of the ghetto. As to other matters, ghetto residents had unique interests not necessarily shared by others in the community, and, on these issues, the ghetto residents were invidiously underrepresented absent their own legislative voice to further their own policy views.

Part of the difficulty with this conclusion is that the findings failed to support it. Plaintiffs' evidence purported to show disregard for the ghetto's distinctive interests; defendants claimed quite the contrary. We see nothing in the findings of the District Court indicating recurring poor performance by Marion County's delegation with respect to Center Township ghetto, nothing to show what the ghetto's interests were in particular legislative situations, and nothing to indicate that the outcome would have been any different if the 23 assemblymen had been chosen from single member districts. Moreover, even assuming bloc voting by the delegation contrary to the wishes of the ghetto majority, it would not follow that the Fourteenth Amendment had been violated unless it is invidiously discriminatory for a county to elect its delegation by majority vote based on party or candidate platforms, and so, to some extent, predetermine legislative votes on particular issues. Such tendencies are inherent in government by elected representatives, and surely elections in single member districts visit precisely the same consequences on the supporters of losing candidates whose views are rejected at the polls.

The District Court's holding, although, on the facts of this case, limited to guaranteeing one racial group representation, is not easily contained. It is expressive of the more general proposition that any group with distinctive interests must be represented in legislative halls if it is numerous enough to command at least one seat and represents a majority living in an area sufficiently compact to constitute a single member district. This approach would make it difficult to reject claims of Democrats, Republicans, or members of any political organization in Marion County who live in what would be safe districts in a single member district system but who, in one year or another, or year after year, are submerged in a one-sided multimember district vote. There are also union-oriented workers, the university community, religious or ethnic groups occupying identifiable areas of our heterogeneous cities and urban areas. Indeed, it would be difficult for a great many, if not most, multimember districts to survive analysis under the District Court's view unless combined with some voting arrangement

such as proportional representation or cumulative voting aimed at providing representation for minority parties or interests. At the very least, affirmance of the District Court would spawn endless litigation concerning the multimember district systems now widely employed in this country.

We are not insensitive to the objections long voiced to multimember district plans. Although not as prevalent as they were in our early history, they have been with us since colonial times, and were much in evidence both before and after the adoption of the Fourteenth Amendment. Criticism is rooted in their winner-take-all aspects, their tendency to submerge minorities and to overrepresent the winning party as compared with the party's state-wide electoral position, a general preference for legislatures reflecting community interests as closely as possible and disenchantment with political parties and elections as devices to settle policy differences between contending interests. The chance of winning or significantly influencing intraparty fights and issue-oriented elections has seemed to some inadequate protection to minorities, political, racial, or economic; rather, their voice, it is said, should also be heard in the legislative forum, where public policy is finally fashioned. In our view, however, experience and insight have not yet demonstrated that multimember districts are inherently invidious and violative of the Fourteenth Amendment. Surely the findings of the District Court do not demonstrate it. Moreover, if the problems of multimember districts are unbearable, or even unconstitutional, it is not at all clear that the remedy is a single member district system with its lines carefully drawn to ensure representation to sizable racial, ethnic, economic, or religious groups, and with its own capacity for overrepresenting and underrepresenting parties and interests, and even for permitting a minority of the voters to control the legislature and government of a State. The short of it is that we are unprepared to hold that district-based elections decided by plurality vote are unconstitutional in either single- or multimember districts simply because the supporters of losing candidates have no legislative seats assigned to them. As presently advised, we hold that the District Court misconceived the Equal Protection Clause in applying it to invalidate the Marion County multimember district.

Even if the District Court was correct in finding unconstitutional discrimination against poor inhabitants of the ghetto, it did not explain why it was constitutionally compelled to disestablish the entire county district and to intrude upon state policy any more than necessary to ensure representation of ghetto interests. The court entered judgment without expressly putting aside on supportable grounds the alternative of creating single-member districts in the ghetto and leaving the district otherwise intact, as well as the possibility that the Fourteenth Amendment could be satisfied by a simple requirement that some of the at-large candidates each year must reside in the ghetto.

We are likewise at a loss to understand how, on the court's own findings of fact and conclusions of law, it was justified in eliminating every multimember district in the State of Indiana. It did not forthrightly sustain the theory that multimember districts always overrepresent their voters to the invidious detriment of single-member residents. Nor did it examine any multi-member district aside from Marion County for possible intradistrict discrimination.

The remedial powers of an equity court must be adequate to the task, but they are not unlimited. Here, the District Court erred in so broadly

brushing aside state apportionment policy without solid constitutional or equitable grounds for doing so.

. . .

Nor can we accept defendant's argument that the statutory plan was beyond attack because the District Court had held in 1965 that, at that time, the plan met the "substantial equality" test of *Reynolds*. Defendant does not argue that the 1969 variances were acceptable under the *Reynolds* test, which has been considerably refined since that decision. Rather, he contends that, because *Reynolds* indicated that decennial reapportionment would be a "rational approach" to the problem, a State cannot be compelled to reapportion itself more than once in a 10–year period. Such a reading misconstrues the thrust of *Reynolds* in this respect. Decennial reapportionment was suggested as a presumptively rational method to avoid "daily, monthly, annual or biennial reapportionment" as population shifted throughout the State. Here, the District Court did not order reapportionment as a result of population shifts since the 1965 Stout decision, but only because the disparities among districts which were thought to be permissible at the time of that decision had been shown by intervening decisions of this Court to be excessive.

We therefore reverse the judgment of the District Court and remand the case to that court for further proceedings consistent with this opinion.

Abate v. Mundt
403 U.S. 182 (1971)

For more than 100 years, Rockland County was governed by a board of supervisors consisting of the supervisors of each of the county's five constituent towns. This county legislature was not separately elected; rather, its members held their county offices by virtue of their election as town supervisors—a pattern that typified New York county government. The result has been a local structure in which overlapping public services are provided by the towns and their county working in close cooperation. . . . There is no indication that these joint efforts have declined in importance; in fact, respondents strenuously urge that the county's rapidly expanding population has amplified the need for town and county coordination in the future.

The county's increased population also produced severe malapportionment—so severe that, in 1966, a federal district court required that the county board submit a reapportionment plan to the Rockland County voters. Pursuant to that order, three different plans were devised and submitted to the electorate, but each was rejected at the polls. The present action was brought in 1968 to compel the board to reapportion. After its initial proposal was rejected by the New York courts, the board submitted the plan that is the subject of this decision.

The challenged plan, based on 1969 population figures, provides for a county legislature composed of 18 members chosen from five legislative districts. These districts exactly correspond to the county's five constituent towns. Each district is assigned its legislators according to the district's population in relation to the population of the smallest town. . . . The number of representatives granted the other districts is determined by dividing the population of each by the population of the smallest town. Fractional results of the computation are rounded to the nearest integer, and this need to round off "fractional representatives" produces some variations among districts in terms of population per legislator. . . . Petitioners attack these deviations as unconstitutional.

. . .

The mere absence of a built-in bias is not, of course, justification for a departure from population equality. In this case, however, Rockland County defends its plan by asserting the long history of, and perceived need for, close cooperation between the county and its constituent towns. The need for intergovernmental coordination is often greatest at the local level, and we have already commented on the extensive functional interrelationships between Rockland County and its towns. But because almost all governmental entities are interrelated in numerous ways, we would be hesitant to accept this justification by itself. To us, therefore, it is significant that Rockland County has long recognized the advantages of having the same individuals occupy the governing positions of both the county and its towns. For over 100 years, the five town supervisors were the only members of the county board, a system that necessarily fostered extensive interdependence between the towns and their county government. When population shifts required that some towns receive a greater portion of seats on the county legislature, Rockland County responded with a plan that substantially remedies the malapportionment and that, by preserving an exact correspondence between each town and one of the county legislative districts, continues to encourage town supervisors to serve on the county board.

We emphasize that our decision is based on the long tradition of overlapping functions and dual personnel in Rockland County government and on the fact that the plan before us does not contain a built-in bias tending to favor particular political interests or geographic areas. And nothing we say today should be taken to imply that even these factors could justify substantially greater deviations from population equality. But we are not prepared to hold that the Rockland County reapportionment plan violates the Constitution, and, therefore, we affirm.

Connor v. Williams
404 U.S. 549 (1972)

After determining that the reapportionment plan for the State Senate and House of Representatives, passed by the Mississippi Legislature in January 1971, failed to comply with the Equal Protection Clause because of a total variance of 26 between the largest and the smallest senatorial district (a determination that was not appealed), the District Court fashioned its own plan for the quadrennial elections for both Houses scheduled for 1971, and these elections were held under the court's plan. Appellants now challenge the constitutionality of the court's plan, contending that a total variance of 18.9 percent between the largest and smallest Senate district and one of 19.7 percent between the largest and smallest House district require that the court's districting plan be voided, a new plan instituted, and new elections held.

Appellants rely on our recent cases invalidating congressional redistricting statutes that contained total variations of 5.97 percent and of 13.1 percent, between the largest and the smallest districts. These decisions do not squarely control the instant appeal, since they do not concern state legislative apportionment, but they do raise substantial questions concerning the constitutionality of the District Court's plan as a design for permanent apportionment.

But conceding, arguendo, that the District Court's plan does not precisely square with Fourteenth Amendment requirements, it does not necessarily follow that the 1971 elections must be invalidated and new elections ordered. In the circumstances of this case, we decline to disturb these elections.

The prospective validity of the plan for the 1975 elections, absent legislative action, poses different issues, but we need not decide those questions at the present time. Under the District Court plan, approximately one-fifth of the seats in both Houses were filled by at-large elections from temporary countywide districts in 1971. The District Court retained jurisdiction over these three counties, and ordered that a Special Master be appointed in January, 1972. . . . Pending completion of those proceedings, we deem it inappropriate to give further consideration to this case. If we are to consider the applicability of *Preisler* and *Wells* to state legislative districts, it would be preferable to have before us a final judgment with respect to the entire State. To accomplish this result and to preserve the right to appeal from such a judgment, the judgment of the District Court is vacated except insofar as it applied to the 1971 elections, and the case is remanded to the District Court for further proceedings consistent with this opinion.

Sixty-Seventh Minnesota State Senate v. Beens
406 U.S. 187 (1972)

These two appeals are taken by the Minnesota State Senate from orders of a three-judge Federal District Court reapportioning the Minnesota Legislature. The appeals do not challenge the District Court's conclusion that the legislature is now malapportioned. And, at this point, they are not concerned with population variances or with other issues of the type customarily presented in reapportionment litigation. The controversy focuses, instead, on (a) the District Court's refusal to honor the Minnesota statute fixing the number of the State's legislative districts at 67 and (b) the court's proceeding, over the initial opposition of all parties (but upon the suggestion of two amici, the Lieutenant Governor and a representative), to reduce the number of legislative districts to 35, the number of senators by almost 50 percent, and the number of representatives by nearly 25 percent. . . .

. . .

The 1970 federal census took place in due course. The Minnesota Legislature did not produce a reapportionment act during its regular session in 1971. One was passed on October 29, 1971, during the reconvening of an extra session called that year. The lawmakers adjourned sine die on October 30. The governor, however, vetoed the act on November 1, and this 1971 reapportionment endeavor failed to become law. The Governor has not called the legislature to another extra session for more work on reapportionment, and it is not scheduled to meet again in regular session until January, 1973. The 1972 primary and general elections will take place in the interim. Thus, the 1966 statute remains as the State's last effective legislative apportionment.

. . .

That the three-judge federal court possesses the power to reapportion the State's legislature when the applicable state statutes fall short of constitutional requirements is not questioned. The 1966 Minnesota apportionment legislation, the court found, in the light of the 1970 census figures, no longer provided a constitutionally acceptable apportionment of either house. No one challenges that basic finding here, and we have no reason to rule otherwise. The 1971 legislature had endeavored to reapportion and, thus, to fulfill the requirement imposed upon it by Art. IV,

§23, of the state's constitution. The legislature's efforts in that direction, however, were nullified by the Governor's veto of the Act it passed, an action the executive had the power to take. The net result was the continuing applicability of the 1966 act. Under these circumstances, judicial relief was appropriate.

The three-judge court, however, was not content with devising judicial apportionment within the framework of the existing and otherwise valid statutory structure. Instead of recognizing the provision in Minn.Stat. §2.021 (1969), that the state senate "is composed of 67 members and the house of representatives is composed of 135 members," and the further provision in §2.031 that the senators and representatives "are apportioned throughout the state in 67 legislative districts," the court declared those sections invalid along with §§2.0412.711, the provisions that delineate the boundaries of the specified 67 legislative districts.

We need not review at length the several pronouncements of this Court relating to state legislative reapportionment. The pertinent cases, particularly those of June 15, 1964, and the guidelines they provide, are well known. . . .

It follows from this that a federal reapportionment court should accommodate the relief ordered to the appropriate provisions of state statutes relating to the legislature's size insofar as is possible. We do not have difficulty, as the District Court professed to have, in discerning the State's policy as to the legislature's size. That policy, long in effect in Minnesota and restated no longer than six years ago in §2.021, is for 67 senators and 135 representatives, and, in §2.031, is for 67 legislative districts. These are figures that have been determined by the legislature and approved by the Governor of the State. The present Governor's contrary recommendation, although certainly entitled to thoughtful consideration, represents only the executive's proffered current policy, just as the reapportionment plan he vetoed on November 1, 1971, represented only the legislature's proffered current policy.

We note, in repetition, that the District Court invalidated the entire 1966 Act, despite the fact that the details of the legislative districts' configurations are included only in §§2.041–2.711. Section 2.021 merely specifies the number of senators and representatives; §2.031 calls for the apportionment of those legislators throughout the State in 67 districts; and § 2.712 provided the effective date of the 1966 act, the efficacy of which, for the period prior to the 1970 census, is not at issue here. In the light of the State's policy of statutory severability, and recognizing that this specific number of legislative districts has been in effect in Minnesota since 1913 and through two succeeding reapportionments, we necessarily conclude that the District Court's invalidation of the six-year-old reapportionment law swept too broadly in nullifying statutory sections that are capable of standing alone.

We know of no federal constitutional principle or requirement that authorizes a federal reapportioning court to go as far as the District Court did and, thus, to bypass the State's formal judgment as to the proper size of its legislative bodies. No case decided by this Court has gone that far, and we have found no district court decision that has employed such radical surgery in reapportionment. There are cases where judicial reapportionment has effectuated minor changes in a legislature's size. Nearly all those cases reflect an increase or decrease of only a few seats, and most appear to have been justified by a state constitutional demand, agreement of the parties, the observance of geographical boundaries, or mathematical convenience. We do not disapprove a court-imposed minor variation from a State's prescribed figure when that change is shown to be necessary to meet constitutional requirements. And we would not oppose the District Court's reducing, in this case, the number of representatives in the Minnesota house from 135 to 134, as the parties apparently have been willing to concede. That action would fit exactly the 67-district pattern. But to slash a state senate's size almost in half and a state house's size by nearly one-fourth is to make more than a mere minor variation. If a change of that extent were acceptable, so, too, would be a federal court's cutting or increasing size by 75 percent or 90 percent or, indeed, by prescribing a unicameral legislature for a State that has always followed the bicameral precedent. . . .

. . .

We conclude that the action of the three-judge court in so drastically changing the number of legislative districts and the size of the respective houses of the Minnesota Legislature is not required by the Federal Constitution and is not justified as an exercise of federal judicial power.

Our ruling here, of course, is no expression of opinion on our part as to what is desirable by way of legislative size for the State of Minnesota, or for any other State. It may well be that 67 senators and 135 representatives make a legislature of unwieldy size. That is a matter of state policy. We certainly are not equipped—and it is not our function and task—to effectuate policy of that kind or to evaluate it once it has been determined by the State. Neither is it the function and task of the Federal District Court. Size is for the State to determine in the exercise of its wisdom and in the light of it awareness of the needs and desires of its people.

The orders of the District Court are vacated, and the cases are remanded for further proceedings consistent with this opinion. The District

Court is instructed to give this matter priority, and to act promptly and forthwith so that the State's 1972 electoral process may get under way with assurance as soon as possible. It is already late in the day, but the maintenance of legislative districts long in effect provides a minimum of disruption even now.

Taylor v. McKeithen
407 U.S. 191 (1972)

The 1970 self-reapportionment of the Louisiana Legislature was challenged in this lawsuit on the dual grounds that it offended both the one-man, one-vote principle and the prohibition against voting arrangements designed to dilute the voting strength of racial minorities. After the United States Attorney General interposed an objection to the election law change under §5 of the Voting Rights Act of 1965, the District Court appointed a Special Master to prepare a court-imposed plan. . . .

The Special Master . . . submitted his recommendation to the District Court and, after a hearing, it was adopted by the court.

This dispute involves only four state senate seats affected by the reapportionment. At the hearing held by the District Judge on the Master's proposal, the State Attorney General presented a counterplan which differed from the Master's only with respect to four senatorial districts in the New Orleans area. Although the judge found that both plans satisfied the one-man, one-vote requirement, he found that the two schemes differed in their racial composition of the four districts, as is set out in greater detail in the margin. Under the State Attorney General's scheme, four "safe" white districts were proposed, whereas the Master's design would have created two districts of slight majorities of black voters. Also, under the counterplan, each incumbent would continue to reside in his "own" district, whereas, under the Master's proposal, the residences of the four incumbents would fall evenly between the two districts to be composed primarily of white voters, ensuring defeat for two of the four incumbents.

. . .

Despite the District Court's findings, however, the Court of Appeals reversed without opinion and adopted the Attorney General's alternative division of New Orleans. The petitioners are the original plaintiffs, and they now seek review of this summary reversal.

An examination of the record in this case suggests that the Court of Appeals may have believed that benign districting by federal judges is itself unconstitutional gerrymandering even where (a) it is employed to overcome the residual effects of past state dilution of Negro voting strength and (b) the only alternative is to leave intact the traditional "safe" white districts. If that were, in fact, the reasoning of the lower court, then this petition would present an important federal question of the extent to which the broad equitable powers of a federal court, are limited by the color-blind concept of *Gomillon v. Lightfoot* and *Wright v. Rockefeller.* In reapportionment cases, as Justice Stewart has observed, "the federal courts are often going to be faced with hard remedial problems" in minimizing friction between their remedies and legitimate state policies.

Because this record does not fully inform us of the precise nature of the litigation, and because we have not had the benefit of the insight of the Court of Appeals, we grant the petition for writ of certiorari, vacate the judgment below, and remand the case to the Court of Appeals for proceedings in conformity with this opinion.

Mahan v. Howell
410 U.S. 315 (1973)

Acting pursuant to the mandate of its newly revised state constitution, the Virginia General Assembly enacted statutes apportioning the State for the election of members of its House of Delegates and Senate. Two suits were brought challenging the constitutionality of the House redistricting statute on the grounds that there were impermissible population variances in the districts, that the multimember districts diluted representation, and that the use of multimember districts constituted racial gerrymandering. The Senate redistricting statute was attacked in a separate suit, which alleged that the city of Norfolk was unconstitutionally split into three districts, allocating Navy personnel "home-ported" in Norfolk to one district and isolating Negro voters in one district. . . .

The consolidated District Court entered an interlocutory order that, inter alia, declared the legislative reapportionment statutes unconstitutional and enjoined the holding of elections in electoral districts other than those established by the court's opinion. Appellant, the Secretary of the State Board of Elections and its members and the city of Virginia Beach, have appealed directly to this Court from those portions of the court's order. . . .

The statute apportioning the House provided for a combination of 52 single member, multi-member, and floater delegate districts from which 100 delegates would be elected. As found by the lower court, the ideal district in Virginia consisted of 46,485 persons per delegate, and the maximum percentage variation from that ideal under the Act was 16.4 percent—the 12th district being overrepresented by 6.8 percent and the 16th district being underrepresented by 9.6 percent. The population ratio between these two districts was 1.18 to 1. The average percentage variance under the plan was +3.89 percent, and the minimum population percentage necessary to elect a majority of the House was 49.29 percent. Of the 52 districts, 35 were within 4 percent of perfection and nine exceeded a 6 percent variance from the ideal. With one exception, the delegate districts followed political jurisdictional lines of the counties and cities. That exception, Fairfax County, was allotted 10 delegates but was divided into two five-member districts.

. . . [T]he District Court concluded that the 16.4 percent variation was sufficient to condemn the House statute under the "one person, one vote" doctrine. While it noted that the variances were traceable to the desire of the General Assembly to maintain the integrity of traditional county and city boundaries, and that it was impossible to draft district lines to overcome unconstitutional disparities and still maintain such integrity, it held that the State proved no governmental necessity for strictly adhering to political subdivision lines. Accordingly, it undertook its own redistricting and devised a plan having a percentage variation of slightly over 10 percent from the ideal district, a percentage it believed came "within passable constitutional limits as 'a good faith effort to achieve absolute equality.'"

. . .

Application of the "absolute equality" test of *Kirkpatrick* and *Wells* to state legislative redistricting may impair the normal functioning of state and local governments. Such an effect is readily apparent from an analysis of the District Court's plan in this case. Under Art. VII, §§2 and 3 of Virginia's Constitution, the General Assembly is given extensive power to enact special legislation regarding the organization of, and the exercise of governmental powers by, counties, cities, towns, and other political subdivisions. The statute redistricting the House of Delegates consistently sought to avoid the fragmentation of such subdivisions, assertedly to afford them a voice in Richmond to seek such local legislation.

The court's reapportionment . . . resulted in a maximum deviation of slightly over 10 percent, as compared with the roughly 16 percent maximum variation found in the plan adopted by the legislature. But to achieve even this limit of variation, the court's plan extended single and multimember districts across subdivision lines in 12 instances, substituting population equality for subdivision representation. . . .

. . .

We conclude . . . that the constitutionality of Virginia's legislative redistricting plan was not to be judged by the more stringent standards that *Kirkpatrick* and *Wells* make applicable to congressional reapportionment, but instead by the equal protection test enunciated in *Reynolds v. Sims.* . . .

. . .

We are not prepared to say that the decision of the people of Virginia to grant the General Assembly the power to enact local legislation dealing with the political subdivisions is irrational. And if that be so, the decision of the General Assembly to provide representation to subdivisions qua subdivisions in order to implement that constitutional power is likewise valid when measured against the Equal Protection Clause of the Fourteenth Amendment. The inquiry then becomes whether it can reasonably be said that the state policy urged by Virginia to justify the divergences in the legislative reapportionment plan of the House is, indeed, furthered by the plan adopted by the legislature, and whether, if so justified, the divergences are also within tolerable limits. For a State's policy urged in justification

of disparity in district population, however rational, cannot constitutionally be permitted to emasculate the goal of substantial equality.

There was uncontradicted evidence offered in the District Court to the effect that the legislature's plan, subject to minor qualifications, "produces the minimum deviation above and below the norm, keeping intact political boundaries. . . ." That court itself recognized that equality was impossible if political boundaries were to be kept intact in the process of districting. But it went on to hold that, since the State "proved no governmental necessity for strictly adhering to political subdivision lines," the legislative plan was constitutionally invalid. As we noted above, however, the proper equal protection test is not framed in terms of "governmental necessity," but instead in terms of a claim that a State may "rationally consider."

The District Court intimated that one reason for rejecting the justification for divergences offered by the State was its conclusion that the legislature had not, in fact, implemented its asserted policy, "as witness the division of Fairfax County." But while Fairfax County was divided, it was not fragmented. And had it not been divided, there would have been one ten-member district in Fairfax County, a result that this Court might we'll have been thought to disfavor as a result of its opinion in *Connor v. Johnson.* The State can scarcely be condemned for simultaneously attempting to move toward smaller districts and to maintain the integrity of its political subdivision lines.

Appellees argue that the traditional adherence to such lines is no longer a justification since the Virginia constitutional provision regarding reapportionment, neither specifically provides for apportionment along political subdivision lines nor draws a distinction between the standards for congressional and legislative districting. The standard in each case is described in the "as nearly as is practicable" language used in *Wesberry v. Sanders* and *Reynolds v. Sims*. But, as we have previously indicated, the latitude afforded to States in legislative redistricting is somewhat broader than that afforded to them in congressional redistricting. Virginia was free as a matter of federal constitutional law to construe the mandate of its Constitution more liberally in the case of legislative redistricting than in the case of congressional redistricting, and the plan adopted by the legislature indicates that it has done so.

We also reject the argument that, because the State is not adhering to its tradition of respecting the boundaries of political subdivisions in congressional and State Senate redistricting, it may not do so in the case of redistricting for the House of Delegates. Nothing in the fact that Virginia has followed the constitutional mandate of this Court in the case of congressional redistricting, or that it has chosen in some instances to ignore political subdivision lines in the case of the State Senate, detracts from the validity of its consistently applied policy to have at least one house of its bicameral legislature responsive to voters of political subdivisions as such.

We hold that the legislature's plan for apportionment of the House of Delegates may reasonably be said to advance the rational state policy of respecting the boundaries of political subdivisions. The remaining inquiry is whether the population disparities among the districts that have resulted from the pursuit of this plan exceed constitutional limits. We conclude that they do not.

. . .

Neither courts nor legislatures are furnished any specialized calipers that enable them to extract from the general language of the Equal Protection Clause of the Fourteenth Amendment the

mathematical formula that establishes what range of percentage deviations is permissible, and what is not. The 16-odd percent maximum deviation that the District Court found to exist in the legislative plan for the reapportionment of the House is substantially less than the percentage deviations that have been found invalid in the previous decisions of this Court. While this percentage may well approach tolerable limits, we do not believe it exceeds them. Virginia has not sacrificed substantial equality to justifiable deviations.

The policy of maintaining the integrity of political subdivision lines in the process of reapportioning a state legislature, the policy consistently advanced by Virginia as a justification for disparities in population among districts that elect members to the House of Delegates, is a rational one. It can reasonably be said, upon examination of the legislative plan, that it does in fact, advance that policy. The population disparities that are permitted thereunder result in a maximum percentage deviation that we hold to be within tolerable constitutional limits. We, therefore, hold the General Assembly's plan for the reapportionment of the House of Delegates constitutional and reverse the District Court's conclusion to the contrary. . . .

. . .

Appellants charge that the District Court was not justified in overturning the districts established by the General Assembly, since the Assembly validly used census tracts in apportioning the area and that the imposition by the court of a multimember district contravened the valid legislative policy in favor of single member districts. We conclude that under the unusual, if not unique, circumstances in this case the District Court did not err in declining to accord conclusive weight to the legislative reliance on census figures. That court justifiably found that with respect to the three single member districts in question, the legislative plan resulted in both significant population disparities and the assignment of military personnel to vote in districts in which they admittedly did not reside. Since discriminatory treatment of military personnel in legislative reapportionment is constitutionally impermissible, we hold that the interim relief granted by the District Court as to the State Senate was within the bounds of the discretion confided to it.

. . .

The court below was faced with severe time pressures. The reapportionment plans were first forwarded to the Attorney General on March 1, 1971. By April 7, these three cases had been filed and consolidated. The first hearing was scheduled for May 24, but on May 7, the Attorney General interposed his objections pursuant to the Voting Rights Act. As a result, the May 24 hearing was largely devoted to arguing about the effect of such objections and after that hearing, the court directed the cases to be continued until June 15. It also postponed the primary elections, which had been set for June 8, until September 14. The cases were finally heard on June 16, and the court's interlocutory order was entered on July 2, just two weeks prior to the revised July 16 filing deadline for primary candidates.

Prior to the time the court acted, this Court had handed down *Whitcomb v. Chavis*, recognizing that multimember districts were not per se violative of the Equal Protection Clause. The court conscientiously considered both the legislative policy and this Court's admonition in *Connor v. Johnson*, that in fashioning apportionment remedies, the use of single-member districts is preferred. But it was confronted with plausible evidence of substantial malapportionment with respect to military personnel, the mandate of this Court that voting discrimination against military

personnel is constitutionally impermissible, and the fear that too much delay would have seriously disrupted the fall 1971 elections. Facing as it did this singular combination of unique factors, we cannot say that the District Court abused its discretion in fashioning the interim remedy of combining the three districts into one multimember district. We, therefore, affirm the order of that Court insofar as it dealt with the State Senate.

Affirmed in part, reversed in part.

Salyer Land Co. v. Tulare Lake Basin Water Storage District
410 U.S. 719 (1973)

The particular type of local government unit whose organization is challenged on constitutional grounds in this case is a water storage district, organized pursuant to the California Water Storage District Act. . . .

. . .

Appellee district consists of 193,000 acres of intensively cultivated, highly fertile farm land located in the Tulare Lake Basin. Its population consists of 77 persons, including 18 children, most of whom are employees of one or another of the four corporations that farm 85 percent of the land in the district.

Such districts are authorized to plan projects and execute approved projects "for the acquisition, appropriation, diversion, storage, conservation, and distribution of water. . . ." Incidental to this general power, districts may "acquire, improve, and operate" any necessary works for the storage and distribution of water as well as any drainage or reclamation works connected therewith, and the generation and distribution of hydroelectric power may be provided for. They may fix tolls and charges for the use of water and collect them from all persons receiving the benefit of the water or other services in proportion to the services rendered. The costs of the projects are assessed against district land in accordance with the benefits accruing to each tract held in separate ownership. And land that is not benefited may be withdrawn from the district on petition.

Governance of the districts is undertaken by a board of directors. Each director is elected from one of the divisions within the district, and each must take an official oath and execute a bond. General elections for the directors are to be held in odd-numbered years.

It is the voter qualification for such elections that appellants claim invidiously discriminates against them and persons similarly situated. Appellants are landowners, a landowner-lessee, and residents within the area included in the appellee's water storage district. They brought this action . . . seeking declaratory and injunctive relief in an effort to prevent appellee from giving effect to certain provisions of the California Water Code. They allege that §§ 41000 and 41001 unconstitutionally deny to them the equal protection of the laws guaranteed by the Fourteenth Amendment, in that only landowners are permitted to vote in water storage district general elections, and votes in those elections are apportioned according to the assessed valuation of the land. . . . A majority of the District Court held that both statutes comported with the dictates of the Equal Protection Clause. . . .

. . .

It is first argued that §41000, limiting the vote to district landowners, is unconstitutional since non-landowning residents have as much interest in the operations of a district as landowners who may or may not be residents. Particularly, it is pointed out that the homes of residents may be damaged by floods within the district's bound-aries, and that floods may, as with appellant Ellison, cause them to lose their jobs. Support for this position is said to come from the recent decisions of this Court striking down various state laws that limited voting to landowners.

. . .

We conclude that the appellee water storage district, by reason of its special limited purpose and of the disproportionate effect of its activities on landowners as a group, is the sort of exception to the rule laid down in *Reynolds* which the quoted language from *Hadley* and the decision in *Avery* contemplated.

The appellee district in this case, although vested with some typical governmental powers, has relatively limited authority. Its primary purpose, indeed the reason for its existence, is to provide for the acquisition, storage, and distribution of water for farming in the Tulare Lake Basin. It provides no other general public services such as schools, housing, transportation, utilities, roads, or anything else of the type ordinarily financed by a municipal body. There are no towns, shops, hospitals, or other facilities designed to improve the quality of life within the district boundaries, and it does not have a fire department, police, buses, or trains.

Not only does the district not exercise what might be thought of as "normal governmental" authority, but its actions disproportionately affect landowners. All of the costs of district projects are assessed against land by assessors in proportion to the benefits received. Likewise, charges for services rendered are collectible from persons receiving their benefit in proportion to the services. When such persons are delinquent in payment, just as in the case of delinquency in payments of assessments, such charges become a lien on the land. In short, there is no way that the economic burdens of district operations can fall on residents qua residents, and the operations of the districts primarily affect the land within their boundaries.

Under these circumstances, it is quite understandable that the statutory framework for election of directors of the appellee focuses on the land benefited, rather than on people as such. . . . The franchise is extended to landowners, whether they reside in the district or out of it, and indeed whether or not they are natural persons who would be entitled to vote in a more traditional political election. Appellants do not challenge the enfranchisement of nonresident landowners or of corporate landowners for purposes of election of the directors of appellee. Thus, to sustain their contention that all residents of the district must be accorded a vote would not result merely in the striking down of an exclusion from what was otherwise a delineated class, but would instead engraft onto the statutory scheme a wholly new class of voters in addition to those enfranchised by the statute.

. . .

Appellants assert that, even if residents may be excluded from the vote, lessees who farm the land have interests that are indistinguishable from those of the landowners. Like landowners, they take an interest in increasing the available water for farming and, because the costs of district projects may be passed on to them either by express agreement or by increased rentals, they have an equal interest in the costs.

Lessees undoubtedly do have an interest in the activities of appellee district analogous to that of landowners in many respects. But in the type of special district we now have before us, the question for our determination is not whether or not we would have lumped them together had we been enacting the statute in question, but, instead, whether "if any state of facts reasonably may be conceived to justify" California's decision to deny the franchise to lessees while granting it to landowners.

The term "lessees" may embrace the holders of a wide spectrum of leasehold interests in land, from the month-to-month tenant holding under an oral lease, on the one hand, to the long-term lessee holding under a carefully negotiated written lease, on the other. The system which permitted a lessee for a very short term to vote might easily lend itself to manipulation on the part of large landowners because of the ease with which such landowners could create short-term interests on the part of loyal employees. And, even apart from the fear of such manipulation, California may well have felt that landowners would be unwilling to join in the forming of a water storage district if short-term lessees whose fortunes were not, in the long run, tied to the land were to have a major vote in the affairs of the district.

The administration of a voting system which allowed short-term lessees to vote could also pose significant difficulties. Apparently, assessment rolls as well as state and federal land lists are used by election boards in determining the qualifications of the voters. Such lists, obviously, would not ordinarily disclose either long- or short-term leaseholds. While reference could be made to appropriate conveyancing records to determine the existence of leases which had been recorded, leases for terms less than one year need not be recorded under California law in order to preserve the right of the lessee.

Finally, we note that California has not left the lessee without remedy for his disenfranchised state. Sections 41002 and 41005 of the California Water Code provide for voting in the general election by proxy. To the extent that a lessee entering into a lease of substantial duration, thereby likening his status more to that of a landowner, feels that the right to vote in the election of directors of the district is of sufficient import to him, he may bargain for that right at the time he negotiates his lease. And the longer the term of the lease, and the more the interest of the lessee becomes akin to that of the landowner, presumably the more willing the lessor will be to assign his right. Just as the lessee may by contract be required to reimburse the lessor for the district assessments, so he may by contract acquire the right to vote for district directors.

Under these circumstances, the exclusion of lessees from voting in general elections for the directors of the district does not violate the Equal Protection Clause.

The last claim by appellants is that §41001, which weights the vote according to assessed valuation of the land, is unconstitutional. They point to the fact that several of the smaller landowners have only one vote per person, whereas the J. G. Boswell Company has 37,825 votes, and they place reliance on the various decisions of this Court holding that wealth has no relation to resident-voter qualifications and that equality of voting power may not be evaded.

. . . [A]s the District Court found, "the benefits and burdens to each landowner . . . are in proportion to the assessed value of the land." We cannot say that the California legislative decision to permit voting in the same proportion is not rationally based.

. . . [W]e affirm the judgment of the . . . District Court and hold that the voter qualification statutes for California water storage district elections are rationally based, and therefore do not violate the Equal Protection Clause.

Georgia v. United States
411 U.S. 526 (1973)

The Attorney General of the United States brought this suit under §12(d) of the Voting Rights Act of 1965, to enjoin the State of Georgia from conducting elections for its House of Representatives under the 1972 legislative reapportionment law. A three-judge District Court in the Northern District of Georgia agreed that certain aspects of the reapportionment law came within the ambit of §5 of the Act, and that the State, which is subject to the provisions of §5, had not obtained prior clearance from either the Attorney General or the District Court for the District of Columbia. Accordingly, and without reaching the question whether the reapportionment plan had the purpose or effect of "denying or abridging the right to vote on account of race or color," the District Court issued the requested injunction. The State brought this appeal. . . .

Following the 1970 Census, the Georgia Legislature set out to reapportion its State House of Representatives, State Senate, and federal congressional electoral districts. We are here concerned only with the reapportionment plan for the State House of Representatives. The result of the legislature's deliberations was a plan (hereinafter the 1971 plan) that, as compared with the prior 1968 scheme, decreased the number of districts from 118 to 105 and increased the number of multimember districts from 47 to 49. Whereas the prior apportionment plan had generally preserved county lines, the 1971 plan did not: 31 of the 49 multimember districts and 21 of the 56 single member districts irregularly crossed county boundaries. The boundaries of nearly all districts were changed, and, in many instances, the number of representatives per district was altered. Residents of some 31 counties formerly in single member districts were brought into multimember districts. Under continuing Georgia law, a candidate receiving less than a majority of the votes cast for a position was required to participate in a majority runoff election. And in the multimember districts, each candidate was required to designate the seat for which he was running, referred to as the "numbered post."

Section 5 of the Voting Rights Act forbids States subject to the Act from implementing any change in a "voting qualification or prerequisite to voting, or standard, practice, or procedure with respect to voting" without first obtaining a declaratory judgment from the District Court for the District of Columbia that the proposed change "does not have the purpose and will not have the effect of denying or abridging the right to vote on account of race or color," or submitting the plan to the Attorney General of the United States and receiving no objection within 60 days. Pursuant to this requirement, the State of Georgia submitted the 1971 plan to the Attorney General on November 5, 1971. Two weeks later, a representative of the Department of Justice wrote to the State Attorney General, requesting further information needed to assess the racial impact of the tendered plan. This information was received on January 6, 1972, and on March 3, 1972, the Attorney General of the United States formally objected to the State's plan. The objection letter cited the combination of multimember districts, numbered posts, majority runoff elections, and the extensive departure from the State's prior policy of adhering to county lines. On the basis of these changes, plus particular changes in the structure of potential black majority single member districts, the Attorney General was "unable to conclude that the plan does not have a discriminatory racial effect on voting." The letter stated that the Attorney General therefore felt obligated to "interpose an objection to changes submitted by these reapportionment plans."

The State Legislature immediately enacted a new reapportionment plan and repealed its predecessor. The 1972 plan increased the number of districts from 105 to 128 and decreased the number of multimember districts from 49 to 32. Twenty-two of the multimember districts and 37 of the single member districts still crossed county boundaries.

This 1972 plan was submitted to the Attorney General on March 15, and he objected on March 24. . . .

. . .

When the Georgia Legislature resolved that it would take no further steps to enact a new plan, the Attorney General brought the present lawsuit.

The State of Georgia claims that §5 is inapplicable to the 1972 House plan, both because the Act does not reach "reapportionment" and because the 1972 plan does not constitute a change from procedures "in force or effect on November 1, 1964." If applicable, the Act is claimed to be unconstitutional as applied. The State also challenges two aspects of the Attorney General's conduct of the §5 objection procedure, claiming, first, that the Attorney General cannot object to a state plan without finding that it, in fact, has a discriminatory purpose or effect, and, second, that the Attorney General's objection to the 1971 plan was not made within the 60-day time period allowed for objection under the Act.

Despite the fact that multimember districts, numbered posts, and a majority runoff requirement were features of Georgia election law prior to November 1, 1964, the changes that followed from the 1972 reapportionment are plainly sufficient to invoke §5 if that section of the Act reaches the substance of those changes. Section 5 is not concerned with a simple inventory of voting procedures, but rather with the reality of changed practices as they affect Negro voters. It seems clear that the extensive reorganization of voting districts and the creation of multimember districts in place of single member districts in certain areas amounted to substantial departures from the electoral state of things under previous law. The real question is whether the substance of these changes undertaken as part of the state reapportionment are "standards, practices, or procedures with respect to voting" within the meaning of §5.

. . .

. . . The judgment that the Attorney General must make is a difficult and complex one, and no one would argue that it should be made without adequate information. There is no serious claim in this case that the additional information requested was unnecessary or irrelevant to §5 evaluation of the submitted reapportionment plan. Yet, if the Attorney General were denied the power to suspend the 60-day period until a complete submission were tendered, his only plausible response to an inadequate or incomplete submission would be simply to object to it. He would then leave it to the State to submit adequate information if it wished to take advantage of this means of clearance under §5. This result would only add acrimony to the administration of §5. We conclude, therefore, that this facet of the Attorney General's regulations is wholly reasonable, and consistent with the Act.

For the foregoing reasons, the judgment of the District Court is affirmed. Since, however, elections were conducted under the disputed 1972 plan by reason of this Court's stay order, it would be inequitable to require new elections at this time.

The case is remanded to the District Court with instructions that any future elections under the Georgia House reapportionment plan be enjoined unless and until the State, pursuant to §5 of the Voting Rights Act, tenders to the Attorney General a plan to which he does not object, or obtains a favorable declaratory judgment from the District Court for the District of Columbia.

Gaffney v. Cummings
412 U.S. 735 (1973)

The questions in this case are whether the population variations among the election districts provided by a reapportionment plan for the Connecticut General Assembly, proposed in 1971, made out a prima facie case of invidious discrimination under the Equal Protection Clause and whether an otherwise acceptable reapportionment plan is constitutionally vulnerable where its purpose is to provide districts that would achieve "political fairness" between the political parties.

The reapportionment plan for the Connecticut General Assembly became law when published by Connecticut's Secretary of State in December 1971. Under the state's constitution, the legislature is given the initial opportunity to reapportion itself in the months immediately following the completion of a decennial census of the United States. In the present case, the legislature was unable to agree on a plan by the state constitutional deadline of April 1, 1971. The task was therefore transferred, as required by the constitution, to an eight-member bipartisan commission. The Democratic and Republican Party leaders in the legislature each appointed four commissioners. The commission was given until July 1, 1971, to devise a reapportionment plan, but, although the commission approached agreement, it too was unable to adopt a plan within the deadline. Accordingly, as a final step in the constitutional process, a three-man bipartisan Board was constituted. The Speaker of the House of Representatives, a Democrat, and the Republican Minority Leader of the House each chose a judge of the State Superior Court to be a Board member, and the two judges in turn designated a third Board member, who was a justice of the State Supreme Court.

This Apportionment Board, using the census data available during the summer of 1971, and relying heavily on the legislative commission's tentative plans, filed a reapportionment plan on September 30, 1971. . . .

. . .

In November, 1971, not long after the Board filed the reapportionment plan with the Secretary of the State, an action was brought in federal district court seeking declaratory and injunctive relief against implementation of the plan. . . . The complaint further alleged the plan amounted to a political gerrymander, and contained "a built-in bias in favor of the Republican Party." Appellant Gaffney, the Chairman of the State Republican Party, was permitted to intervene in support of the Board's plan and, after a three-judge court was empaneled, the court heard testimony in March 1972. At the hearing, plaintiff appellees introduced three alternative House apportionment plans that required fewer town-line cuts, although all three plans involved total deviations from population equality in excess of those contained in the Board plan. A fourth plan for the House was submitted with a total maximum deviation from population equality among districts of 2.61 percent, as compared with the Board plan, which contained a 7.83 percent total maximum deviation. This alternative plan, however, was prepared without regard for town lines, which were cut substantially more times than in the Board plan. Considerable evidence was introduced demonstrating the obvious political considerations in the Board's district-making. In late March, the District Court filed its decision invalidating the Board plan and permanently enjoining its use in future elections. . . .

On June 12, 1972, after a motion to expedite consideration of the appeal had been denied this Court granted appellant's motion for a stay of the District Court's judgment. On the basis of that stay, and a subsequent supportive state order, the 1972 fall elections for the State Assembly were held under the Board's reapportionment plan. When this Court convened in October 1972, we noted probable jurisdiction over the appeal. By this time, a Special Master had been appointed by the District Court and had prepared a reapportionment plan.

We think that appellees' showing of numerical deviations from population equality among the Senate and House districts in this case failed to make out a prima facie violation of the Equal Protection Clause of the Fourteenth Amendment, whether those deviations are considered alone or in combination with the additional fact that another plan could be conceived with lower deviations among the State's legislative districts. Put another way, the allegations and proof of population deviations among the districts fail in size and quality to amount to an invidious discrimination under the Fourteenth Amendment which would entitle appellees to relief, absent some countervailing showing by the State.

The requirement of Art. I, §2, of the Constitution, that representatives be chosen "by the People of the several States," mandates that "one man's vote in a congressional election is to be worth as much as another's." This standard "permits only the limited population variances which are unavoidable despite a good faith effort to achieve absolute equality, or for which justification is shown." . . .

. . .

In the case now before us, appellant urges that the population variations among Senate and House districts in the Board plan did not, in and of themselves, demonstrate an equal protection violation, and that the State was not required to justify them absent further proof of invidiousness by appellees. For several reasons, we think the point is well taken, and that the District Court erred in holding to the contrary.

. . .

This very case represents what should not happen in the federal courts. The official state functionaries proposed a plan with a maximum variation among the districts of 7.83 percent in the House and 1.81 percent in the Senate, and with respective average variations of 1.90 percent and .45 percent. Appellees then proposed four alternate plans for the House, three of which involved slightly larger variations among districts but cut fewer town lines. The fourth cut more lines, but had a maximum variation between its largest and smallest district of only 2.6 percent. The District Court thought the state plan involved unacceptably large variations between districts, although, in the House, with districts of about 20,000 people, the average variation involved only 399 people, and the largest variations involved only 1,573 people. But neither did the District Court adopt any of the plans submitted by appellees. Instead, it appointed its own Master to come up with still another scheme. That plan, we are told, involves a total maximum deviation in the House of only 1.16 percent. Was the Master compelled, as a federal constitutional matter, to come up with a plan with smaller variations than were contained in appellees' plans? And what is to happen to the Master's plan if a resourceful mind hits upon a plan better than the Master's by a fraction of a percentage point? Involvements like this must end at some point, but that point constantly recedes if those who litigate need only produce a plan that is marginally "better" when measured against a rigid and unyielding population equality standard.

The point is, that such involvements should never begin. We have repeatedly recognized that state reapportionment is the task of local legislatures or of those organs of state government selected to perform it. Their work should not be invalidated under the Equal Protection Clause when only minor population variations among districts are proved. Here, the proof at trial demonstrated that the House districts under the State Apportionment Board's plan varied in population from one another by a maximum of only about 8 percent, and that the average deviation from the ideal House district was only about 2 percent. The Senate districts had even less variations. On such a showing, we are quite sure that a prima facie case of invidious discrimination under the Fourteenth Amendment was not made out.

State legislative districts may be equal or substantially equal in population and still be vulnerable under the Fourteenth Amendment. A districting statute, otherwise acceptable, may be invalid because it fences out a racial group so as to deprive them of their preexisting municipal vote. A districting plan may create multimember districts perfectly acceptable under equal population standards, but invidiously discriminatory because they are employed "to minimize or cancel out the voting strength of racial or political elements of the voting population." We must, therefore, respond to appellees' claims in this case that, even if acceptable population-wise, the Apportionment Board's plan was invidiously discriminatory because a "political fairness principle" was followed in making up the districts in both the House and Senate.

The record abounds with evidence, and it is frankly admitted by those who prepared the plan, that virtually every Senate and House district line was drawn with the conscious intent to create a districting plan that would achieve a rough approximation of the statewide political strengths of the Democratic and Republican Parties, the only two parties in the State large enough to elect legislators from discernible geographic areas. Appellant insists that the spirit of "political fairness" underlying this plan is not only permissible, but a desirable consideration in laying out districts that otherwise satisfy the population standard of the reapportionment cases. Appellees, on the other hand, label the plan as nothing less than a gigantic political gerrymander, invidiously discriminatory under the Fourteenth Amendment.

We are quite unconvinced that the reapportionment plan offered by the three-member Board violated the Fourteenth Amendment because it attempted to reflect the relative strength of the parties in locating and defining election districts. It would be idle, we think, to contend that any political consideration taken into account in fashioning a reapportionment plan is sufficient to invalidate it. Our cases indicate quite the contrary. The very essence of districting is to produce a different—a more "politically fair"—result than would be reached with elections at large, in which the winning party would take 100 percent of the legislative seats. Politics and political considerations are inseparable from districting and apportionment. The political profile of a State, its party registration, and voting records are available precinct by precinct, ward by ward. These subdivisions may not be identical with census tracts, but, when overlaid on a census map, it requires no special genius to recognize the political consequences of drawing a district line along one street rather than another. It is not only obvious, but absolutely unavoidable, that the location and shape of districts may well determine the political complexion of the area. District lines are rarely neutral phenomena. They can well determine what district will be predominantly Democratic or predominantly Republican, or make a close race likely. Redistricting may pit incumbents against one another or make very difficult the election of the most experienced legislator. The reality is that districting inevitably has and is intended to have substantial political consequences.

It may be suggested that those who redistrict and reapportion should work with census, not political, data, and achieve population equality without regard for political impact. But this politically mindless approach may produce, whether intended or not, the most grossly gerrymandered results; and, in any event, it is most unlikely that the political impact of such a plan would remain undiscovered by the time it was proposed or adopted, in which event the results would be both known and, if not changed, intended.

It is much more plausible to assume that those who redistrict and reapportion work with both political and census data. Within the limits of the population equality standards of the Equal Protection Clause, they seek, through compromise or otherwise, to achieve the political or other ends of the State, its constituents, and its officeholders. What is done in so arranging for elections, or to achieve political ends or allocate political power, is not wholly exempt from judicial scrutiny under the Fourteenth Amendment. As we have indicated, for example, multimember districts may be vulnerable, if racial or political groups have been fenced out of the political process and their voting strength invidiously minimized. Beyond this, we have not ventured far or attempted the impossible task of extirpating politics from what are the essentially political processes of the sovereign States. Even more plainly, judicial interest should be at its lowest ebb when a State purports fairly to allocate political power to the parties in accordance with their voting strength and, within quite tolerable limits, succeeds in doing so. There is no doubt that there may be other reapportionment plans for Connecticut that would have different political consequences, and that would also be constitutional. Perhaps any of appellees' plans would have fallen into this category, as would the court's, had it propounded one. But neither we nor the district courts have a constitutional warrant to invalidate a state plan, otherwise within tolerable population limits, because it undertakes not to minimize or eliminate the political strength of any group or party, but to recognize it and, through districting, provide a rough sort of proportional representation in the legislative halls of the State.

Reversed.

White v. Regester
412 U.S. 755 (1973)

The Texas Constitution requires the state legislature to reapportion the House and Senate at its first regular session following the decennial census. In 1970, the legislature proceeded to reapportion the House of Representatives, but failed to agree on a redistricting plan for the Senate. Litigation was immediately commenced in state court challenging the constitutionality of the House reapportionment. The Texas Supreme Court held that the legislature's plan for the House violated the Texas Constitution. Meanwhile, pursuant to the requirements of the Texas Constitution, a Legislative Redistricting Board had been formed to begin the task of redistricting the Texas Senate. Although the Board initially confined its

work to the reapportionment of the Senate, it was eventually ordered, in light of the judicial invalidation of the House plan, to also reapportion the House.

On October 15, 1971, the Redistricting Board's plan for the reapportionment of the Senate was released, and, on October 22, 1971, the House plan was promulgated. Only the House plan remains at issue in this case. That plan divided the 150-member body among 79 single-member and 11 multimember districts. Four lawsuits, eventually consolidated, were filed challenging the Board's Senate and House plans and asserting with respect to the House plan that it contained impermissible deviations from population equality and that its multimember districts for Bexar County and Dallas County operated to dilute the voting strength of racial and ethnic minorities.

A three-judge District Court sustained the Senate plan, but found the House plan unconstitutional. The House plan was held to contain constitutionally impermissible deviations from population equality, and the multimember districts in Bexar and Dallas Counties were deemed constitutionally invalid. The District Court gave the Texas Legislature until July 1, 1973, to reapportion the House, but the District Court permitted the Board's plan to be used for purposes of the 1972 election, except for requiring that the Dallas County and Bexar County multi-member districts be reconstituted into single member districts for the 1972 election.

Appellants appealed the statewide invalidation of the House plan and the substitution of single member for multimember districts in Dallas County and Bexar County. . . .

. . .

. . . We are unable to conclude from these deviations alone that appellees satisfied the threshold requirement of proving a prima facie case of invidious discrimination under the Equal Protection Clause. Because the District Court had a contrary view, its judgment must be reversed in this respect.

We affirm the District Court's judgment, however, insofar as it invalidated the multimember districts in Dallas and Bexar Counties, and ordered those districts to be redrawn into single member districts. Plainly, under our cases, multimember districts are not per se unconstitutional, nor are they necessarily unconstitutional when used in combination with single member districts in other parts of the State. But we have entertained claims that multimember districts are being used invidiously to cancel out or minimize the voting strength of racial groups. To sustain such claims, it is not enough that the racial group allegedly discriminated against has not had legislative seats in proportion to its voting potential. The plaintiffs' burden is to produce evidence to support findings that the political processes leading to nomination and election were not equally open to participation by the group in question—that its members had less opportunity than did other residents in the district to participate in the political processes and to elect legislators of their choice.

With due regard for these standards, the District Court first referred to the history of official racial discrimination in Texas, which at times touched the right of Negroes to register and vote and to participate in the democratic processes. It referred also to the Texas rule requiring a majority vote as a prerequisite to nomination in a primary election and to the so-called "place" rule limiting candidacy for legislative office from a multimember district to a specified "place" on the ticket, with the result being the election of representatives from the Dallas multimember district reduced to a head-to-head contest for each

position. These characteristics of the Texas electoral system, neither in themselves improper nor invidious, enhanced the opportunity for racial discrimination, the District Court thought. More fundamentally, it found that, since Reconstruction days, there have been only two Negroes in the Dallas County delegation to the Texas House of Representatives, and that these two were the only two Negroes ever slated by the Dallas Committee for Responsible Government (DCRG), a white-dominated organization that is in effective control of Democratic Party candidate slating in Dallas County. That organization, the District Court found, did not need the support of the Negro community to win elections in the county, and it did not therefore exhibit good faith concern for the political and other needs and aspirations of the Negro community. The court found that, as recently as 1970, the DCRG was relying upon "racial campaign tactics in white precincts to defeat candidates who had the overwhelming support of the black community." Based on the evidence before it, the District Court concluded that "the black community has been effectively excluded from participation in the Democratic primary selection process," and was therefore generally not permitted to enter into the political process in a reliable and meaningful manner. These findings and conclusions are sufficient to sustain the District Court's judgment with respect to the Dallas multimember district, and, on this record, we have no reason to disturb them.

. . .

The District Court apparently paid due heed to *Whitcomb v. Chavis*, did not hold that every racial or political group has a constitutional right to be represented in the state legislature, but did, from its own special vantage point, conclude that the multimember district, as designed and operated in Bexar County, invidiously excluded Mexican Americans from effective participation in political life, specifically in the election of representatives to the Texas House of Representatives. On the record before us, we are not inclined to overturn these findings, representing as they do a blend of history and an intensely local appraisal of the design and impact of the Bexar County multimember district in the light of past and present reality, political and otherwise.

Affirmed in part, reversed in part, and remanded.

White v. Weiser
412 U.S. 783 (1973)

On June 17, 1971, the Governor of the State of Texas signed into law Senate Bill One (S.B. 1), providing for the congressional redistricting of the State. S.B. 1 divided the State into 24 congressional districts for the ensuing decennium. Based upon 1970 census figures, absolute population equality among the 24 districts would mean a population of 466,530 in each district. The districts created by S.B. 1 varied from a high of 477,856 in the 13th District to a low of 458,581 in the 15th District. The 13th District exceeded the ideal district by 2.43 percent and the 15th District was smaller by 1.7 percent. The population difference between the two districts was 1,275 persons, and their total percentage deviation was 4.13 percent. The ratio of the 13th District to the 15th was 1.04 to 1. The average deviation of all districts from the ideal district of 466,530 was .745 percent or 3,421 persons.

On October 19, 1971, appellees, residents of the 6th, 13th, 16th, and 19th congressional districts, filed suit in the United States District Court for the Northern District of Texas against appellant, the Secretary of State of Texas and the chief election officer of the State. Appellees alleged

that the reapportionment of the Texas congressional seats, as embodied in S.B. 1, violated their rights under Art. I, §2, and the Equal Protection Clause of the Fourteenth Amendment. They requested an injunction against the use of S.B. 1, an order requiring a new apportionment or the use of a plan submitted with their complaint, or at-large elections. The plan appended to appellees' original complaint, which came to be called Plan B, generally followed the redistricting pattern of S.B. 1. However, the district lines were adjusted where necessary so as to achieve smaller population variances among districts. Plan B created districts varying from 466,930 to 466,234, for a total absolute deviation between the largest and smallest district of 696 persons. District 12 exceeded the ideal by .086 percent and District Four was under the ideal by .063%, for a total percentage deviation of .149 percent. Although the plan followed the district lines of S.B. 1 where possible, in order to achieve maximum population equality, Plan B cut across 18 more county lines than did S.B. 1.

... On January 10, 1972, several days prior to the scheduled hearing of the case, appellees filed an amended complaint suggesting an alternative plan, which came to be called Plan C. Plan C, unlike Plan B, substantially disregarded the configuration of the districts in S.B. 1. Instead, as the authors of the plan frankly admitted and the District Court found, Plan C represented an attempt to attain lower deviations without regard to any consideration other than population. The districts in Plan C varied in population from 467,173 as a high to 465,855 as a low, a difference of 1,318 persons. The largest district was overpopulated by .139 percent, and the smallest underpopulated by .145 percent, the total percentage deviation being .284 percent. Plan C had 14 districts with greater deviations than Plan B, eight districts with deviations equal to those found in Plan B, and two districts with deviations smaller than those in Plan B.

On January 21, 1972, the District Court heard argument and received into evidence various depositions. The next day, the . . . District Court declared S.B. 1 unconstitutional and enjoined appellant from "conducting or permitting any primary or general elections based upon the districts established by S.B. 1." The District Court ordered the adoption of Plan C as "the plan of this Court for the congressional districts of the State of Texas." . . .

This Court, on application of appellant, granted a stay of the order of the District Court. The 1972 congressional elections were therefore conducted under the plan embodied in S.B. 1. . . .

. . .

The percentage deviations now before us in S.B. 1 are smaller than those invalidated in *Kirkpatrick* and *Wells*, but we agree with the District Court that, under the standards of those cases, they were not "unavoidable," and the districts were not as mathematically equal as reasonably possible. Both Plans B and C demonstrate this much, and the State does not really dispute it. . . .

The State asserts that the variances present in S.B. 1 nevertheless represent good faith efforts by the State to promote "constitutency representative relations," a policy frankly aimed at maintaining existing relationships between incumbent congressmen and their constituents and preserving the seniority the members of the State's delegation have achieved in the United States House of Representatives. We do not disparage this interest. . . . But we need not decide whether this state interest is sufficient to justify the deviations at issue here, for Plan B admittedly serves this purpose as well as S.B. 1 while adhering more closely to population equality. S.B. 1 and its popu-

lation variations, therefore, were not necessary to achieve the asserted state goal, and the District Court was correct in rejecting it.

. . .

The District Court properly rejected S.B. 1, but it had before it both Plan B and Plan C, and there remains the question whether the court correctly chose to implement the latter. Plan B adhered to the basic district configurations found in S.B. 1, but adjusted the district lines, where necessary, in order to achieve maximum population equality among districts. Each district in Plan B contained generally the same counties as the equivalent district in S.B. 1. Plan C, on the other hand, was based entirely upon population considerations and made no attempt to adhere to the district configurations found in S.B. 1. Both plans were submitted to the District Court by appellees. After deciding that S.B. 1 was unacceptable, the District Court ordered the implementation of Plan C. . . .

. . . We have adhered to the view that state legislatures have "primary jurisdiction" over legislative reapportionment. Just as a federal district court, in the context of legislative reapportionment, should follow the policies and preferences of the State, as expressed in statutory and constitutional provisions or in the reapportionment plans proposed by the state legislature, whenever adherence to state policy does not detract from the requirements of the Federal Constitution, we hold that a district court should similarly honor state policies in the context of congressional reapportionment. In fashioning a reapportionment plan or in choosing among plans, a district court should not preempt the legislative task, nor "intrude upon state policy any more than necessary."

Here, it is clear that Plan B, to a greater extent than did Plan C, adhered to the desires of the state legislature while attempting to achieve population equality among districts. S.B. 1, a duly enacted statute of the State of Texas, established the State's 24 congressional districts with locations and configurations found appropriate by the duly elected members of the two houses of the Texas Legislature. As we have often noted, reapportionment is a complicated process. Districting inevitably has sharp political impact and inevitably political decisions must be made by those charged with the task. Here those decisions were made by the legislature in pursuit of what were deemed important state interests. Its decisions should not be unnecessarily put aside in the course of fashioning relief appropriate to remedy what were held to be impermissible population variations between congressional districts.

Plan B, as all parties concede, represented an attempt to adhere to the districting preferences of the state legislature while eliminating population variances. Indeed, Plan B achieved the goal of population equality to a greater extent than did Plan C. Despite the existence of Plan B, the District Court ordered implementation of Plan C, which, as conceded by all parties, ignored legislative districting policy and constructed districts solely on the basis of population considerations. The District Court erred in this choice. Given the alternatives, the court should not have imposed Plan C, with its very different political impact, on the State. It should have implemented Plan B, which most clearly approximated the reapportionment plan of the state legislature while satisfying constitutional requirements. The court said only that Plan C is "significantly more compact and contiguous" than Plan B. But both Plan B and Plan C feature contiguous districts, and, even if the districts in Plan C can be called more compact, the District Court's preferences do not override whatever state goals were embodied in S.B. 1 and, derivatively, in Plan B. . . . If there was a good reason for adopting Plan C rather than Plan B, the District Court failed to state it.

Of course, the District Court should defer to state policy in fashioning relief only where that policy is consistent with constitutional norms and is not itself vulnerable to legal challenge. The District Court should not, in the name of state policy, refrain from providing remedies fully adequate to redress constitutional violations which have been adjudicated and must be rectified. But here, the District Court did not suggest or hold that the legislative policy of districting so as to preserve the constituencies of congressional incumbents was unconstitutional or even undesirable. . . . And we note that appellees themselves submitted Plan B to the District Court and defended it on the basis that it adhered to state goals, as embodied in S.B. 1, while eliminating impermissible deviations.

The judgment of the District Court invalidating S.B. 1 is affirmed. The adoption of Plan C is, however, reversed, and the case is remanded for further proceedings consistent with this opinion.

Chapman v. Meier
420 U.S. 1 (1975)

North Dakota's original constitution, adopted at the State's admission into the Union in 1889, is still in effect. It has been amended, of course, from time to time. Since 1918, §25 thereof has read: "The legislative power of this state shall be vested in a legislature consisting of a senate and a house of representatives." That legislative power for 70 years has been subject to the initiative and the referendum. The Constitution has further provided that the State's senate "shall be composed of forty-nine members," elected for a four-year term with one-half thereof elected every two years, and that no one shall be a senator unless he is a qualified elector of the senatorial district, has attained the age of 25 years, and has been a resident of the State for the two years next preceding the election. Since 1960, §29 has read:

> Each existing senatorial district as provided by law at the effective date of this amendment shall permanently constitute a senatorial district. Each senatorial district shall be represented by one senator and no more.

The document also states that the house of representatives "shall be composed of not less than sixty, nor more than one hundred forty members," elected for a two-year term, and that no one shall be a representative unless he is a qualified elector of the district, has attained the age of 21 years, and has been a resident of the State for the two years next preceding the election. Section 35 provides for at least one representative for each senatorial district and for as many representatives as there are counties in the district; states that the Legislative Assembly, after each federal decennial census, shall apportion "the balance of the members of the House of Representatives," and, if the Legislative Assembly fails in its apportionment duty, places the task of apportioning the house in a designated group of officials of the state.

. . . An apportionment effected by Laws . . . was in effect for over 30 years despite the mandate of §35 of the Constitution that apportionment be effected after each federal census.

. . . The State's Legislative Assembly of 1961 had failed to apportion the house following the 1960 census. After *Baker* had been decided at the District Court level, and between the argument and reargument of the case here, the Supreme Court of North Dakota dismissed an original action for a prerogative writ to enjoin its Chief Justice from issuing the apportionment proclamation which would have announced the conclusions of the statutorily designated "apportionment group" that were then anticipated. The petition asserted that the group's plan would apportion the house in an unconstitutional manner and not according to population. The Supreme Court ruled that the function of the group was legislative; that it had not yet completed its work; that it was performing a function the Legislative Assembly should have performed; and that, until the proclamation was issued, the group's action was not subject to challenge in the courts.

Citizens of North Dakota then sought declaratory and injunctive relief in federal court under the Civil Rights Acts. By this time, the State's Chief Justice had issued the proclamation. A three-judge District Court held that the presence of the proclamation eliminated the aspect of prematurity that had characterized the earlier challenge in the state court. But the "basic issues," the court concluded with one dissent, had not been presented to the Supreme Court of North Dakota. "We believe that court should have the opportunity of passing on all questions herein." The court, accordingly, abstained from passing upon those issues; it stayed further proceedings before it, but did not dismiss the action.

The plaintiffs in the federal case promptly took to the Supreme Court of North Dakota their attack upon the plan adopted by the apportionment group. That court assumed jurisdiction. It noted that no question arising under the United States Constitution was presented, and that it was not concerned with the validity of the allotment of one representative to each senatorial district, as prescribed by the first sentence of §35 of the Constitution. The court recognized that there was inherent in a constitutional direction to apportion according to population "a limited discretion to make the apportionment that will approach, as nearly as is reasonably possible, a mathematical equality." It then went on to hold that the apportionment made by the group "violates the constitutional mandate of apportionment according to the population of the several districts and is void," and that the apportionment effected by the 1931 statute continued to be the law until superseded by an apportionment valid under §35 or under a further amendment of the Constitution.

The same plaintiffs then turned again to the federal court. The three-judge court . . . denied the request for injunctive relief on the ground that the only challenge before it was to the apportionment group's plan, and that the 1931 apportionment was not challenged. It noted that the Legislative Assembly would meet the following January, that it had "the mandatory duty" to apportion the house, and that the court would not presume that it would not perform that duty. Jurisdiction was retained, with the observation that, if the Legislative Assembly failed to act, the plaintiffs, upon appropriate amendment of their complaint, might further petition the court for relief.

The 1963 Legislative Assembly did reapportion. . . . A new suit then was instituted in federal court to invalidate North Dakota's entire apportionment system on federal constitutional grounds. Sections 26, 29, and 35 of the Constitution and the 1963 statute were challenged. The three-judge court held that these constitutional and statutory provisions were violative of the Equal Protection Clause. It went on to hold that the 1931 apportionment, being "the last valid apportionment," as described by the North Dakota Supreme Court, and by which the 1963 legislators had been elected, was also invalid. Thus, "there is no constitutionally valid legislative apportionment law in existence in the State of North Dakota at this time." The court encountered difficulty as to an appropriate remedy. It concluded

. . . that adequate time was not available within which to formulate a proper plan for the then forthcoming 1964 elections, that the 1965 Legislative Assembly would have a de facto status; and that that Assembly should promptly devise a constitutional system. Injunctive relief was denied.

The 1965 Legislative Assembly produced a reapportionment act, although it was not approved or disapproved by the Governor.

The North Dakota Secretary of State, defendant in the federal court, then moved to dismiss the federal action on the ground that the 1965 act met constitutional requirements. The three-judge court . . . ruled otherwise. It turned to the question of remedy and concluded that the Legislative Assembly had had its opportunity and that the court now had the duty itself to take affirmative action. It considered several plans that had been introduced in the Assembly and centered its attention on the Smith plan. Although the court found the plan "not perfect" (five multi-member senatorial districts, and county lines violated in 12 instances), it concluded that the plan, if "slightly" modified, would meet constitutional standards ("impressive mathematical exactness," namely, 25 of 39 districts within 5 percent of the average population, 4 slightly over 5 percent, and only 2 exceeding 9 percent). The "slight" modification was made and reapportionment, really the first to be finally effected since 1931, was therefore accomplished in North Dakota by federal court intervention.

Still another original proceeding in the State's Supreme Court was instituted. This one challenged the right of senators from the multi-member districts to hold office. It was claimed that this multiple membership violated §29 of the North Dakota Constitution, which provided that each senatorial district "shall be represented by one senator and no more." The state court held that the 1965 judgment of the federal court was not res judicata as to the then plaintiffs; that the initial or "freezing" portion of §29 was clearly invalid; that the concluding portion, restricting representation of a district to one senator, would not have been desired by the people without the "balance" of the freezing portion; and that §29 as a unit must fall as violative of equal protection. The result was that multimember senatorial districts were not held illegal by the state court.

The 1970 federal census was taken in due course. The 1971 Legislative Assembly failed to reapportion. The present federal action was instituted the following November. The plaintiffs alleged that substantial shifts in population had taken place, and that the court-ordered plan of 1965 no longer complied with the requirements of the Equal Protection Clause. The relief requested was that the court order apportionment upon the 1970 census figures and also provide for single member districts; that the 1965 plan be declared invalid; and that the Secretary of State be restrained from administering the election laws under that plan.

On May 22, 1972, the three-judge court entered an order to the effect that the existing North Dakota apportionment failed to meet federal constitutional standards and that the court would attempt to reapportion. It appointed a commission to formulate and present a plan within 30 days, and it submitted guidelines to the commission. . . .

. . .

On November 8, 1972, immediately after the election that year, the three-judge court suspended its June 30 order until further notice and directed the State's Attorney General promptly to report any action taken by the 1973 Legislative Assembly.

That Assembly not only passed an apportionment Act but overrode its veto by the Governor.

The Act provided for 37 legislative districts, each having one senator and two representatives, except for five multimember senatorial districts. Section 3 thereof specifically recited the population of each district and the population variance . . . from the average of 12,355 per senator.

The effectiveness of the legislative plan, however, promptly was suspended by a referendum petition. By a companion initiative petition, an amendment to the State's Constitution was proposed; this would have created a commission to reapportion the State and, in addition, would have mandated single-member senatorial districts. A special election on these took place December 4, 1973. Both were defeated. The Legislative Assembly's work to reapportion was thus nullified by the people. It could be suggested, and apparently was, that the people also reacted against the elimination of the five multimember districts. In any event, the defendant thereupon moved the federal court to readopt the plan temporarily approved by its order of June 1972. The plaintiffs resisted.

The three-judge District Court . . . then made "permanent" the 1972 Dobson plan, with its five multimember districts providing 18 senators out of a statewide total of 51. . . .

. . .

This Court has refrained from holding that multimember districts in apportionment plans adopted by States for their legislatures are per se unconstitutional. On the contrary, the Court has upheld numerous state-initiated apportionment schemes utilizing multimember districts. . . . the Court has indicated that a State might devise an apportionment plan for a bicameral legislature with one body composed of at least some multimember districts, as long as substantial equality of population per representative is maintained.

Notwithstanding this past acceptance of multimember districting plans, we recognize that there are practical weaknesses inherent in such schemes. First, as the number of legislative seats within the district increases, the difficulty for the voter in making intelligent choices among candidates also increases. Ballots tend to become unwieldy, confusing, and too lengthy to allow thoughtful consideration. Second, when candidates are elected at large, residents of particular areas within the district may feel that they have no representative specially responsible to them. Third, it is possible that bloc voting by delegates from a multimember district may result in undue representation of residents of these districts relative to voters in single member districts.... Criticism of multimember districts has been frequent and widespread. ... Further, there must be more evidence than a simple disproportionality between the voting potential and the legislative seats won by a racial or political group. There must be evidence that the group has been denied access to the political process equal to the access of other groups. Such evidence may be more easily developed where the multimember districts compose a large part of the legislature, where both bodies in a bicameral legislature utilize multimember districts, or where the members' residences are concentrated in one part of the district. Whether such factors are present or not, proof of lessening or cancellation of voting strength must be offered.

This requirement that one challenging a multimember districting plan must prove that the plan minimizes or cancels out the voting power of a racial or political group has been applied in cases involving apportionment schemes adopted by state legislatures....

The standards for evaluating the use of multimember districts thus clearly differ depending on whether a federal court or a state legislature

has initiated the use. ... When the plan is court-ordered, there often is no state policy of multimember districting which might deserve respect or deference. Indeed, if the court is imposing multimember districts upon a State which always has employed single member districts, there is special reason to follow the *Connor* rule favoring the latter type of districting.

Appellants do not contend that any racial or political group has been discriminated against by the multimember districting ordered by the District Court. They only suggest that the District Court has not followed our mandate in *Connor v. Johnson*, and that the court has failed to articulate any reasons for this departure. We agree. Absent particularly pressing features calling for multimember districts, a United States district court should refrain from imposing them upon a State.

The District Court cannot avoid the multimember issue by labeling it, a political issue to be resolved by the State....

. . .

It is true that, in 1973, the voters of North Dakota voted down a proposed constitutional amendment which would have reestablished the State's tradition of single-member senatorial districts. At the same time, the voters also rejected by referendum the Legislative Assembly's 1973 Act which would have continued the multimember format for five districts. We are unable to infer from these simultaneous actions of the electorate any particular attitude toward multimember districts. It simply appears that North Dakota's voters have not been satisfied with any reapportionment proposal, and that they are frustrated by the years of confusion since the obviously impermissible apportionment provisions of the State's Constitution were invalidated.

We are confident that the District Court, with

perhaps the aid of its Special Masters, will be able to reinstitute the use of single member districts while also attaining the necessary goal of substantial population equality. . . . Unless the District Court can articulate such a "singular combination of unique factors" as was found to exist in *Mahan v. Howell,* or unless the 1975 Legislative Assembly appropriately acts, the court should proceed expeditiously to reinstate single member senatorial districts in North Dakota.

The second aspect of the court-ordered reapportionment plan that is challenged by the appellants is the population divergence in the various senatorial districts. . . .

. . .

. . . [W]e have had the opportunity to observe attempts in many state legislative reapportionment plans to achieve the goal of population equality. Although each case must be evaluated on its own facts, and a particular population deviation from the ideal may be permissible in some cases but not in others, certain guidelines have been developed for determining compliance with the basic goal of one person, one vote. . . .

On the other hand, we have acknowledged that some leeway in the equal population requirement should be afforded States in devising their legislative reapportionment plans. As contrasted with congressional districting, where population equality appears now to be the preeminent, if not the sole, criterion on which to adjudge constitutionality, when state legislative districts are at issue we have held that minor population deviations do not establish a prima facie constitutional violation. . . .

. . .

. . . In the present North Dakota case . . . the 20 percent variance is in the plan formulated by the federal court. We believe that a population deviation of that magnitude in a court-ordered plan is constitutionally impermissible in the absence

of significant state policies or other acceptable considerations that require adoption of a plan with so great a variance. The burden is on the District Court to elucidate the reasons necessitating any departure from the goal of population equality, and to articulate clearly the relationship between the variance and the state policy furthered.

The basis for the District Court's allowance of the 20 variance is claimed to lie in the absence of "electorally victimized minorities," in the fact that North Dakota is sparsely populated, in the division of the State caused by the Missouri River, and in the goal of observing geographical boundaries and existing political subdivisions. We find none of these factors persuasive here, and none of them has been explicitly shown to necessitate the substantial population deviation embraced by the plan.

. . .

Examination of the asserted justifications of the court-ordered plan thus plainly demonstrates that it fails to meet the standards established for evaluating variances in plans formulated by State legislatures or other state bodies. . . . A court-ordered plan . . . must be held to higher standards than a State's own plan. With a court plan, any deviation from approximate population equality must be supported by enunciation of historically significant state policy or unique features. We have felt it necessary in this case to clarify the greater responsibility of the District Court, when devising its own reapportionment plan, because of the severe problems occasioned for the citizens of North Dakota during the several years of redistricting confusion.

We hold . . . that, unless there are persuasive justifications, a court-ordered reapportionment plan of a state legislature must avoid use of multimember districts, and, as well, must ordinarily achieve the goal of population equality with little more than de minimis variation. Where important and significant state considerations rationally mandate departure from these standards, it is the reapportioning court's responsibility to articulate precisely why a plan of single member districts with minimal population variance cannot be adopted.

. . .

The judgment of the District Court is reversed, and the case is remanded for further proceedings consistent with this opinion.

Harris County Commissioners v. Moore
420 U.S. 77 (1975)

Under Texas law, the Commissioners Court is the general governing body of each county; one of its duties is to divide the county into precincts for the election of justices of the peace and constables, and to redistrict the precincts when necessary.

In June 1973, the Commissioners Court of Harris County adopted a redistricting plan for the eight justice of the peace precincts in the county. The last redistricting had taken place in 1876, and the enormous population changes in the Houston area had resulted in gross disparities in population among the precincts: the largest precinct contained approximately one million persons, while the smallest had fewer than 7,000.

Under the old plan, one justice of the peace and one constable were assigned to each precinct except the largest, which was allotted two justices and one constable. Because of the apparent discrepancy in the workload of the officials in different precincts, the Commissioners Court adopted a redistricting plan that redrew the precinct lines. Although the proposed new precincts still varied substantially in population size, the disparity was much less than it had been.

Among other changes, the plan consolidated three of the smallest precincts and parts of two others into a single new precinct. As a result, four justices and three constables found themselves residents of a single precinct, which was entitled by law to a maximum of only one constable and two justices of the peace. Pursuant to a Texas statute, the Commissioners Court declared the constable and justice posts for that precinct to be vacant, since there were more officials living in the precinct than positions available. The Commissioners Court then filled the vacancies, appointing one of the displaced constables to the new constable post and one of the displaced justices to one of the two new justice positions. A nonincumbent was appointed to fill the other slot.

The five officeholders, threatened with removal prior to the expiration of their elected terms, resorted to court action in an effort to block implementation of the redistricting plan. One of the constables filed suit in state court, but, when that court denied his application for a temporary injunction, he apparently abandoned the action. Shortly thereafter, the three displaced justices and two constables, along with two voters who had lived in their precincts, brought suit in the United States District Court for the Southern District of Texas, claiming that the redistricting scheme was unconstitutional. Their removal pursuant to Art. 2351 1/2(c) violated the Due Process and Equal Protection Clauses of the Fourteenth Amendment, the officials contended. More specifically, they argued that the redistricting order was constitutionally invalid because it did not meet "one man, one vote" standards, because it denied voters in certain precincts the full effect of their votes, and because the precincts were redrawn along racial lines. . . .

A three-judge court . . . held that the statute, as applied, had discriminated between those who voted for or were entitled to vote for the displaced officials and the voters in other precincts where the elected officials were permitted to serve a full term. Because it found no compelling interest served by redistricting in the middle of plaintiffs' terms, the court held that, to the extent that the redistricting order appointed other persons to plaintiffs' offices and prevented plaintiffs from carrying out their duties and receiving their salaries for the remainder of their elected terms, the order was invalid.

. . .

. . . The proper scope of the order entered by the District Court and the applicability of that order to the plaintiffs' claims depend directly on questions of state law. The court's initial order held Art. 2351 1/2(c) unconstitutional, and enjoined the redistricting plan altogether. In its opinion, the court apparently intended to narrow its order somewhat by holding the statute unconstitutional as applied and by enjoining the redistricting order only to the extent that it removed the appellees from their jobs. Yet even that relief was broader than the court's holding would support. Absent Art. 2351 1/2(c), Texas law may well dictate that, upon redistricting, all the justice and constable positions in the county would be vacated. Since the District Court concluded only that Art. 2351 1/2(c) denied the officeholders and voters equal protection by removing some officials in the county but not others, it should not automatically have imposed one remedy—reinstatement—when Texas law might well call for quite another—removal of all the affected officeholders. Yet if the District Court had limited itself to declaring Art. 2351 1/2(c) unconstitutional, and the Commissioners Court had determined that state law would then require that all the county justice and constable positions be vacated, the appellees would be forced to resort to state court in order to vindicate their claim-

ed right to reinstatement. In short, not only the character of the federal right asserted in this case, but even the availability of the relief sought, turn in large part on the same unsettled state law questions. Because the federal claim in this case is "entangled in a skein of state law that must be untangled before the federal case can proceed," we conclude that the District Court erred in not adopting appellants' suggestion to abstain.

In order to remove any possible obstacles to state court jurisdiction, we direct the District Court to dismiss the complaint. The dismissal should be without prejudice, so that any remaining federal claim may be raised in a federal forum after the Texas courts have been given the opportunity to address the state law questions in this case.

Reversed and remanded.

East Carroll Parish School Board v. Marshall
424 U.S. 636 (1976)

. . . Plaintiff Zimmer, a white resident of East Carroll Parish, Louisiana, brought suit in 1968 alleging that population disparities among the wards of the parish had unconstitutionally denied him the right to cast an effective vote in elections for members of the police jury and the school board. After a hearing the District Court agreed that the wards were unevenly apportioned and adopted a reapportionment plan suggested by the East Carroll police jury calling for the at-large election of members of both the police jury and the school board. The 1969 and 1970 elections were held under this plan.

The proceedings were renewed in 1971 after the District Court . . . instructed the East Carroll police jury and school board to file reapportionment plans revised in accordance with the 1970 census. In response, the jury and board resubmitted the at-large plan. Respondent Marshall was permitted to intervene on behalf of himself and all other black voters in East Carroll. Following a hearing, the District Court again approved the multimember arrangement. The intervenor appealed, contending that at-large elections would tend to dilute the black vote in violation of the Fourteenth and Fifteenth Amendments and the Voting Rights Act of 1965.

. . . [A] panel of the Court of Appeals affirmed, but, on rehearing en banc, the court reversed. It found clearly erroneous the District Court's ruling that at-large elections would not diminish the black voting strength of East Carroll Parish. Relying upon *White v. Regester*, it seemingly held that multimember districts were unconstitutional unless their use would afford a minority greater opportunity for political participation or unless the use of single member districts would infringe protected rights.

. . .

The District Court, in adopting the multimember, at-large reapportionment plan, was silent as to the relative merits of a single-member arrangement. And the Court of Appeals, inexplicably in our view, declined to consider whether the District Court erred under *Connor v. Johnson*, in endorsing a multimember plan, resting its decision instead upon constitutional grounds. We have frequently reaffirmed the rule that, when United States district courts are put to the task of fashioning reapportionment plans to supplant concededly invalid state legislation, single member districts are to be preferred absent unusual circumstances. As the en banc opinion of the Court of Appeals amply demonstrates, no special circumstances here dictate the use of multimember districts. Thus, we hold that, in

shaping remedial relief, the District Court abused its discretion in not initially ordering a single-member reapportionment plan.

On this basis, the judgment is affirmed.

Beer v. United States
425 U.S. 130 (1976)

The city of New Orleans brought this suit under §5 seeking a judgment declaring that a reapportionment of New Orleans' councilmanic districts did not have the purpose or effect of denying or abridging the right to vote on account of race or color. The District Court entered a judgment of dismissal, holding that the new reapportionment plan would have the effect of abridging the voting rights of New Orleans' Negro citizens. The city appealed the judgment to this Court, claiming that the District Court used an incorrect standard in assessing the effect of the reapportionment in this §5 suit. . . .

. . . In 1954, New Orleans adopted a mayor-council form of government. Since that time, the municipal charter has provided that the city council is to consist of seven members, one to be elected from each of five councilmanic districts, and two to be elected by the voters of the city at large. The 1954 charter also requires an adjustment of the boundaries of the five single member councilmanic districts following each decennial census to reflect population shifts among the districts.

In 1961, the city council redistricted the city based on the 1960 census figures. That reapportionment plan established four districts. . . . The fifth district was wedge-shaped, and encompassed the city's downtown area. In one of these councilmanic districts, Negroes constituted a majority of the population, but only about half of the registered voters. In the other four districts, white voters clearly outnumbered Negro voters. No Negro was elected to the New Orleans City Council during the decade from 1960 to 1970.

After receipt of the 1970 census figures, the city council adopted a reapportionment plan (Plan I) that continued the basic north-to-south pattern of councilmanic districts combined with a wedge-shaped, downtown district. Under Plan I, Negroes constituted a majority of the population in two districts, but they did not make up a majority of registered voters in any district. The largest percentage of Negro voters in a single district under Plan I was 45.2 percent. When the city submitted Plan I to the Attorney General pursuant to §5, he objected to it, stating that it appeared to "dilute black voting strength by combining a number of black voters with a larger number of white voters in each of the five districts." He also expressed the view that "the district lines [were not] drawn as they [were] because of any compelling governmental need," and that the district lines did "not reflect numeric population configurations or considerations of district compactness or regularity of shape."

Even before the Attorney General objected to Plan I, the city authorities had commenced work on . . . Plan II. That plan followed the general north-to-south districting pattern common to the 1961 apportionment and Plan I. It produced Negro population majorities in two districts and a Negro voter majority (52.6 percent) in one district. When Plan II was submitted to the Attorney General, he posed the same objections to it that he had raised to Plan I. In addition, he noted that "the predominantly black neighborhoods in the city are located generally in an east to west progression," and pointed out that the use of north-to-south districts in such a situation almost inevitably would have the effect of diluting the

maximum potential impact of the Negro vote. Following the rejection by the Attorney General of Plan II, the city brought this declaratory judgment action in the United States District Court for the District of Columbia.

The District Court concluded that Plan II would have the effect of abridging the right to vote on account of race or color. It calculated that, if Negroes could elect city councilmen in proportion to their share of the city's registered voters, they would be able to choose 2.42 of the city's seven councilmen, and, if in proportion to their share of the city's population, to choose 3.15 councilmen. But, under Plan II, the District Court concluded that, since New Orleans' elections had been marked by bloc voting along racial lines, Negroes would probably be able to elect only one councilman. . . . This difference between mathematical potential and predicted reality was such that "the burden in the case at bar was at least to demonstrate that nothing but the redistricting proposed by Plan II was feasible." . . .

As a separate and independent ground for rejecting Plan II, the District Court held that the failure of the plan to alter the city charter provision establishing two at-large seats had the effect in itself of "abridging the right to vote . . . on account of race or color." . . .

The District Court therefore refused to allow Plan II to go into effect. As a result, there have been no councilmanic elections in New Orleans since 1970, and the councilmen elected at that time (or their appointed successors) have remained in office ever since.

The appellants urge, and the United States on reargument of this case has conceded, that the District Court was mistaken in holding that Plan II could be rejected under §5 solely because it did not eliminate the two at-large councilmanic seats that had existed since 1954. . . .

. . .

The principal argument made by the appellants in this Court is that the District Court erred in concluding that the makeup of the five geographic councilmanic districts under Plan II would have the effect of abridging voting rights on account of race or color. In evaluating this claim, it is important to note at the outset that the question is not one of constitutional law, but of statutory construction. A determination of when a legislative reapportionment has "the effect of denying or abridging the right to vote on account of race or color" must depend, therefore, upon the intent of Congress in enacting the Voting Rights Act, and specifically §5.

. . .

It is . . . apparent that a legislative reapportionment that enhances the position of racial minorities with respect to their effective exercise of the electoral franchise can hardly have the "effect" of diluting or abridging the right to vote on account of race within the meaning of §5. We conclude, therefore, that such an ameliorative new legislative apportionment cannot violate §5 unless the new apportionment itself so discriminates on the basis of race or color as to violate the Constitution.

The application of this standard to the facts of the present case is straightforward. Under the apportionment of 1961, none of the five councilmanic districts had a clear Negro majority of registered voters, and no Negro has been elected to the New Orleans City Council while that apportionment system has been in effect. Under Plan II, by contrast, Negroes will constitute a majority of the population in two of the five districts and a clear majority of the registered voters in one of them. Thus, there is every reason to predict, upon the District Court's hypothesis of bloc voting, that at least one and perhaps two Negroes may well be elected to the council under Plan II.

It was therefore error for the District Court to conclude that Plan II "will . . . have the effect of denying or abridging the right to vote on account of race or color" within the meaning of §5 of the Voting Rights Act.

Accordingly, the judgment of the District Court is vacated, and the case is remanded to that court for further proceedings consistent with this opinion.

Connor v. Coleman
425 U.S. 675 (1976)

Ten years of litigation have not yet resulted in a constitutionally apportioned Mississippi Legislature. The District Court for the Southern District of Mississippi in 1966 invalidated the 1962 apportionment. A legislative apportionment that followed was also declared unconstitutional. Thereupon, the District Court promulgated its own plan for the 1967 elections. Still another legislative plan enacted in 1971 was held unconstitutional by the District Court, and another court-ordered plan, this for the 1971 elections, was formulated. That court-promulgated plan, however, was stayed by this Court with direction that the District Court, "absent insurmountable difficulties," should "devise and put into effect a single member district plan for Hinds County" by June 14, 1971. The District Court did not divide Hinds County into single member districts because the court found that there were insurmountable difficulties.

After the 1971 elections, this Court addressed the constitutionality of the 1971 court-formulated plan. Because the District Court had retained jurisdiction over plans for Hinds, Harrison, and Jackson Counties and had stated its intention to appoint a special master in January, 1972, to consider the subdivision of those counties into single member districts, we vacated the District Court judgment, without disturbing the 1971 elections, and remanded with direction to the District Court that "[s]uch proceedings should go forward and be promptly concluded," declining meanwhile to consider the prospective validity of the court-formulated 1971 plan until the proceedings were completed, and a final judgment was entered respecting the entire State. The District Court did not appoint a special master.

In April 1973, the Mississippi Legislature enacted an apportionment plan. Pending decision by the District Court of objections to that plan, however, the legislature, in April 1975, adopted new legislation that differed from the 1971 court-formulated plan only in that Harrison, Hinds, and Jackson Counties remained multimember districts. The District Court thereupon dismissed the complaint addressed to the 1973 legislative plan and directed the filing of an amended complaint addressing the 1975 legislation. This was done and the District Court entered judgment approving the 1975 law. We reversed, holding that the 1975 legislation could not be effective as law until after clearance in compliance with §5 of the Voting Rights Act of 1965, and holding further that the District Court erred in deciding constitutional challenges to the Mississippi legislation based upon claims of racial discrimination. . . .

Thereafter, Mississippi submitted the 1975 legislation to the Attorney General of the United States in compliance with §5 of the Voting Rights Act. The Attorney General objected, and accordingly the District Court held a hearing to formulate a court plan for the conduct of the 1975 elections. By orders entered in June 1975, the District Court promulgated a "temporary plan for the election of Senators and Representatives for the 1975 elections ONLY," and ordered the parties

to file alternative permanent reapportionment plans. . . . Proposed permanent plans were thereafter submitted by the United States and movants, and on January 26, 1976, the United States moved that a hearing be held on February 10, 1976, on the proposed permanent plans. However, three days later, January 29, 1976, the District Court denied the motion. . . .

. . . There is no occasion for the District Court any longer to postpone the hearing on the proposed permanent plan awaiting this Court's decisions of those cases. . . . The District Court should, in the circumstances, promptly carry out the assurance given in its order of January 29, 1976, to "bring this case to trial forthwith . . ." and schedule a hearing to be held within 30 days on all proposed permanent reapportionment plans to the end of entering a final judgment embodying a permanent plan reapportioning the Mississippi Legislature in accordance with law to be applicable to the election of legislators in the 1979 quadrennial elections, and also ordering any necessary special elections to be held to coincide with the November 1976, presidential and congressional elections, or, in any event, at the earliest practicable date thereafter. . . .

United States v. Board of Supervisors of Warren County, Mississippi
429 U.S. 642 (1977)

In November 1970, the Board of Supervisor of Warren County, Mississippi, submitted a county redistricting plan to the Attorney General for his approval under §5 of the Voting Rights Act of 1965. The new plan was to replace a plan in effect since 1929. After requesting and receiving additional information, the Attorney General entered an objection to the plan. Despite this objection, the Board held elections in 1971 pursuant to the 1970 plan. After the elections, the Board sought reconsideration of the objection. The Attorney General refused to withdraw the objection, and, in 1973, filed a complaint, pursuant to §5, in the District Court for the Southern District of Mississippi. The complaint alleged that the Attorney General's objection to the 1970 redistricting plan rendered that plan unenforceable under §5, and that the election districts in effect prior to the 1970 redistricting were malapportioned under the Fourteenth Amendment. Three forms of relief were requested: (1) a declaration that implementation of the 1970 plan violated §5; (2) an injunction against implementing the 1970 plan or any other new plan until there had been compliance with one of the two procedures required by §5; and (3) an order that a new redistricting plan be developed and implemented after being found acceptable under §5.

A properly convened three-judge court granted the Government's motion for summary judgment. In its later order implementing that judgment, the court found that because the upcoming 1975 County elections could not be held as scheduled "without abridging rights guaranteed by the Fourteenth and Fifteenth Amendments to the Constitution," the elections had to be stayed subject to compliance with the procedure set out in the court's order. The order provided that the County submit a redistricting plan to the Attorney General for §5 review and, if no objection were interposed, that elections then be held in accordance with a stipulated schedule. In the event that the County submitted no plan by a stated deadline, or that the Attorney General objected to a submitted plan, or that a submitted plan contained infirmities with respect to the "one person one vote" requirements of the Fourteenth Amendment, the court would consider plans prepared by both parties and adopt an appropriate redistricting plan to be used in elections held according to the ordered schedule.

The County then informally submitted two plans to the Attorney General for comment and the Attorney General indicated his reservations concerning the validity of the plans. This impasse continued until the deadline in the court's order, after which time the court directed the parties to file their proposed plans for its consideration. After a hearing, the court adopted one of the plans prepared by the County despite the fact that the plan had not been approved pursuant to §5 procedures. The court found that the adopted plan "neither dilutes black voting strength nor is deficient in one-man, one-vote considerations." It ordered that the county's districts be reorganized according to the plan and that elections be held. The United States appealed. . . .

Section 5 provides for two alternative methods by which a State or political subdivision covered by the Act may satisfy the requirement of federal scrutiny of changes in voting procedures. First, the State or political subdivision may institute an action in the District Court for the District of Columbia for a declaratory judgment that the proposed change does not have the purpose or effect of abridging the right to vote on account of race; second, it may submit the proposed change to the Attorney General. No new voting practice or procedure may be enforced unless the State or political subdivision has succeeded in its declaratory judgment action or the Attorney General has declined to object to a proposal submitted to him. Attempts to enforce changes that have not been subjected to §5 scrutiny may be enjoined by any three-judge district court in a suit brought by a voter or by the Attorney General on behalf of the United States.

. . .

Allen, *Perkins*, and *Connor* involved private suits by voters claiming noncompliance with §5 procedures; we now hold that the same limitations on the inquiry of local district courts apply in §5 actions brought by the Attorney General. The limitation inheres in Congress's determination that only the District Court for the District of Columbia has jurisdiction to consider the issue of whether a proposed change actually discriminate on account of race, and that other district courts may consider §5 "coverage" questions.

The District Court in this case twice exceeded the permissible scope of its §5 inquiry. In the order implementing its summary judgment for the United States, the court apparently decided that the 1970 redistricting plan did not comply with the Fifteenth Amendment . . . and then determined that the County plan "will not lessen the opportunity of black citizens of Warren County to participate in the political process and elect officials of their choice." In both instances, the court below erred in deciding the questions of constitutional law; it should have determined only whether Warren County could be enjoined from holding elections under a new redistricting plan because such plan had not been cleared under §5. Accordingly, the judgment is reversed, and the case is remanded for further proceedings consistent with this opinion.

United Jewish Organizations Williamsburgh, Inc. v. Carey 430 U.S. 144 (1977)

Kings County, New York, together with New York (Manhattan) and Bronx Counties, became subject to §§4 and 5 of the Act, by virtue of a determination by the Attorney General that a literacy test was used in these three counties as of November 1, 1968, and a determination by the Director of the Census that fewer than 50 percent of the voting-age residents of these three counties voted in the Presidential election of 1968. Litigation to secure exemption from the Act was unsuccessful, and it became necessary for New York to secure the approval of the Attorney General or of the United States District Court for the District of Columbia for its 1972 reapportionment statute insofar as that statute concerned Kings, New York, and Bronx Counties. On January 31, 1974, the provisions of the statute districting these counties for congressional, state senate, and state assembly seats were submitted to the Attorney General. In accordance with the regulations governing his §5 review, the Attorney General considered submissions from interested parties criticizing and defending the plan. Those submissions included assertions that voting in these counties was racially polarized and that the district lines had been created with the purpose or effect of diluting the voting strength of nonwhites. . . . On April 1, 1974, the Attorney General concluded that, as to certain districts in Kings County covering the Bedford-Stuyvesant area of Brooklyn, the State had not met the burden placed on it by §5 and the regulations thereunder to demonstrate that the redistricting had neither the purpose nor the effect of abridging the right to vote by reason of race or color.

Under §5, the State could have challenged the Attorney General's objections to the redistricting plan by filing a declaratory judgment action in a three-judge court in the District of Columbia. Instead, the State sought to meet what it understood to be the Attorney General's objections and to secure his approval in order that the 1974 primary and general elections could go forward under the 1972 statute. A revised plan, submitted to the Attorney General on May 31, 1974, in its essentials did not change the number of districts with nonwhite majorities, but did change the size of the nonwhite majorities in most of those districts. Under the 1972 plan, Kings County had three state senate districts with nonwhite majorities of approximately 91 percent, 61 percent, and 53 percent; under the revised 1974 plan, there were again three districts with nonwhite majorities, but now all three were between 70 percent and 75 percent nonwhite. As for state assembly districts, both the 1972 and the 1974 plans provided for seven districts with nonwhite majorities. However, under the 1972 plan, there were four between 85 percent and 95 percent nonwhite, and three were approximately 76 percent, 61 percent, and 52 percent, respectively; under the 1974 plan, the two smallest nonwhite majorities were increased to 65 percent and 67.5 percent, and the two largest nonwhite majorities were decreased from greater than 90 percent to between 80 percent and 90 percent The report of the legislative committee on reapportionment stated that these changes were made "to overcome Justice Department objections" by creating more "substantial nonwhite majorities" in two assembly districts and two senate districts.

One of the communities affected by these revisions in the Kings County reapportionment plan was the Williamsburgh area, where about 30,000 Hasidic Jews live. Under the 1972 plan, the Hasidic community was located entirely in one assembly district (61percent nonwhite) and one senate district (37 percent nonwhite); in order to create substantial nonwhite majorities in these districts, the 1974 revisions split the Hasidic community between two senate and two assembly districts. A staff member of the legislative reapportionment committee testified that, in the course of meetings and telephone conversations with Justice Department officials, he "got the feeling . . . that

65 percent would be probably an approved figure" for the nonwhite population in the assembly district in which the Hasidic community was located, a district approximately 61percent nonwhite under the 1972 plan. To attain the 65 percent figure, a portion of the white population, including part of the Hasidic community, was reassigned to an adjoining district.

Shortly after the State submitted this revised redistricting plan for Kings County to the Attorney General, petitioners sued on behalf of the Hasidic Jewish community of Williamsburgh, alleging that the 1974 plan "would dilute the value of each plaintiff's franchise by halving its effectiveness," solely for the purpose of achieving a racial quota, and therefore in violation of the Fourteenth Amendment. Petitioners also alleged that they were assigned to electoral districts solely on the basis of race, and that this racial assignment diluted their voting power in violation of the Fifteenth Amendment. Petitioners sought an injunction restraining New York officials from enforcing the new redistricting plan and a declaratory judgment that the Attorney General of the United States had used unconstitutional and improper standards in objecting to the 1972 plan.

On June 20, 1974, the District Court held a hearing on petitioners' motion for a preliminary injunction. On July 1, 1974, the Attorney General informed the State of New York that he did not object to the implementation of the revised plan. The Attorney General moved to be dismissed as a party on the ground that the relief sought against him could be obtained only in the District Court for the District of Columbia and only by a State or political subdivision subject to the Voting Rights Act; the State and the intervenor NAACP moved to dismiss the complaint on the ground that it failed to state a claim upon which relief could be granted. The District Court granted the motions to dismiss the complaint, reasoning that petitioners enjoyed no constitutional right in reapportionment to separate community recognition as Hasidic Jews, that the redistricting did not disenfranchise petitioners, and that racial considerations were permissible to correct past discrimination.

A divided Court of Appeals affirmed. . . . After agreeing with the District Court that petitioners had no constitutional right to separate community recognition in reapportionment—a holding not challenged by petitioners here—the Court of Appeals went on to address petitioners' claims as white voters that the 1974 plan denied them equal protection of the laws and abridged their right to vote on the basis of race. The court noted that the 1974 plan left approximately 70 percent of the senate and assembly districts in Kings County with white majorities; given that only 65 percent of the population of the county was white, the 1974 plan would not underrepresent the white population, assuming that voting followed racial lines. Petitioners thus could not claim that the plan canceled out the voting strength of whites as a racial group. . . . The court then observed that the case did not present the question whether a legislature, "starting afresh," could draw lines on a racial basis so as to bolster nonwhite voting strength, but rather the "narrower" question whether a State could use racial considerations in drawing lines in an effort to secure the Attorney General's approval under the Voting Rights Act. . . . The court below reasoned that the Act contemplated that the Attorney General and the state legislature would have "to think in racial terms"; because the Act "necessarily deals with race or color, corrective action under it must do the same." . . .

. . .

It is apparent from the face of the Act, from its legislative history, and from our cases that the Act itself was broadly remedial in the sense that it was "designed by Congress to banish the blight of racial discrimination in voting. . . ." It is also plain, however, that, after "repeatedly try[ing] to cope with the problem by facilitating case-by-case litigation against voting discrimination," Congress became dissatisfied with this approach, which required judicial findings of unconstitutional discrimination in specific situations and judicially approved remedies to cure that discrimination. Instead, Congress devised more stringent measures, one of which, §5, required the covered States to seek the approval of either the Attorney General or of a three-judge court in the District of Columbia whenever they sought to implement new voting procedures. Under §4, a State became subject to §5 whenever it was administratively determined that certain conditions which experience had proved were indicative of racial discrimination in voting had existed in the area—in the case of New York, as already indicated, that a literacy test was in use in certain counties in 1968 and that fewer than 50 percent of the voting-age residents in these counties voted in the Presidential election that year. At that point, New York could have escaped coverage by demonstrating to the appropriate court that the test had not been used to discriminate within the past 10 years, which New York was unable to do.

Given this coverage of the counties involved, it is evident that the Act's prohibition against instituting new voting procedures without the approval of the Attorney General or the three-judge District Court is not dependent upon proving past unconstitutional apportionments, and that, in operation, the Act is aimed at preventing the use of new procedures until their capacity for discrimination has been examined by the Attorney General or by a court. Although recognizing that the "stringent new remedies," including §5, were "an uncommon exercise of congressional power," we nevertheless sustained the Act as a "permissibly decisive" response to

> the extraordinary stratagem of contriving new rules of various kinds for the sole purpose of perpetrating voting discrimination in the face of adverse federal court decrees.

It is also clear that, under §5, new or revised reapportionment plans are among those voting procedures, standards, or practices that may not be adopted by a covered State without the Attorney General's or a three-judge court's ruling that the plan "does not have the purpose and will not have the effect of denying or abridging the right to vote on account of race or color." . . . When it renewed the Voting Rights Act in 1970 and again in 1975, Congress was well aware of the application of §5 to redistricting. In its 1970 extension, Congress relied on findings by the United States Commission on Civil Rights that the newly gained voting strength of minorities was in danger of being diluted by redistricting plans that divided minority communities among predominantly white districts. . . . As the Court of Appeals understood the Act and our decision in *Allen*, compliance with the Act in reapportionment cases would often necessitate the use of racial considerations in drawing district lines. That the Court of Appeals correctly read the Act has become clearer from later cases.

. . .

. . . Section 5 and its authorization for racial redistricting where appropriate to avoid abridging the right to vote on account of race or color are constitutional. Contrary to petitioners' first argument, neither the Fourteenth nor the Fifteenth Amendment mandates any per se rule against using racial factors in districting and apportion-

ment. Nor is petitioners' second argument valid. The permissible use of racial criteria is not confined to eliminating the effects of past discriminatory districting or apportionment.

Moreover, in the process of drawing black majority districts in order to comply with §5, the State must decide how substantial those majorities must be in order to satisfy the Voting Rights Act. . . . At a minimum and by definition, a "black majority district" must be more than 50 percent black. But whatever the specific percentage, the State will inevitably arrive at it as a necessary means to ensure the opportunity for the election of a black representative and to obtain approval of its reapportionment plan. Unless we adopted an unconstitutional construction of §5 in *Beer* and *City of Richmond*, a reapportionment cannot violate the Fourteenth or Fifteenth Amendment merely because a State uses specific numerical quotas in establishing a certain number of black majority districts. . . .

. . . we turn to the fourth question, which is whether the racial criteria New York used in this case—the revision of the 1972 plan to create 65 percent nonwhite majorities in two additional senate and two additional assembly districts— were constitutionally infirm. We hold they are not, on two separate grounds.

. . .

It is true that New York deliberately increased the nonwhite majorities in certain districts in order to enhance the opportunity for election of nonwhite representatives from those districts. Nevertheless, there was no fencing out of the white population from participation in the political processes of the county, and the plan did not minimize or unfairly cancel out white voting strength. Petitioners have not objected to the impact of the 1974 plan on the representation of white voters in the county or in the State as a

236 APPORTIONMENT AND REDISTRICTING

whole. As the Court of Appeals observed, the plan left white majorities in approximately 70 percent of the assembly and senate districts in Kings County, which had a countywide population that was 65 percent white. Thus, even if voting in the county occurred strictly according to race, whites would not be underrepresented relative to their share of the population.

In individual districts where nonwhite majorities were increased to approximately 65 percent, it became more likely, given racial bloc voting, that black candidates would be elected instead of their white opponents, and it became less likely that white voters would be represented by a member of their own race; but as long as whites in Kings County, as a group, were provided with fair representation, we cannot conclude that there was a cognizable discrimination against whites or an abridgment of their right to vote on the grounds of race. Furthermore, the individual voter in the district with a nonwhite majority has no constitutional complaint merely because his candidate has lost out at the polls and his district is represented by a person for whom he did not vote. Some candidate, along with his supporters, always loses.

Where it occurs, voting for or against a candidate because of his race is an unfortunate practice. But it is not rare; and in any district where it regularly happens, it is unlikely that any candidate will be elected who is a member of the race that is in the minority in that district. However disagreeable this result may be, there is no authority for the proposition that the candidates who are found racially unacceptable by the majority, and the minority voters supporting those candidates, have had their Fourteenth or Fifteenth Amendment rights infringed by this process. Their position is similar to that of the Democratic or Republican minority that is submerged year after year by the adherents to the majority party

who tend to vote a straight party line.

It does not follow, however, that the State is powerless to minimize the consequences of racial discrimination by voters when it is regularly practiced at the polls. . . .

In this respect, New York's revision of certain district lines is little different in kind from the decision by a State in which a racial minority is unable to elect representatives from multimember districts to change to single-member districting for the purpose of increasing minority representation. This change might substantially increase minority representation at the expense of white voters, who previously elected all of the legislators but who, with single-member districts, could elect no more than their proportional share. If this intentional reduction of white voting power would be constitutionally permissible, as we think it would be, we think it also permissible for a State, employing sound districting principles such as compactness and population equality, to attempt to prevent racial minorities from being repeatedly outvoted by creating districts that will afford fair representation to the members of those racial groups who are sufficiently numerous and whose residential patterns afford the opportunity of creating districts in which they will be in the majority.

As the Court said in *Gaffney*:

> [C]ourts have [no] constitutional warrant to invalidate a state plan, otherwise within tolerable population limits, because it undertakes not to minimize or eliminate the political strength of any group or party, but to recognize it, and, through districting, provide a rough sort of proportional representation in the legislative halls of the State.

New York was well within this rule when, under the circumstances present in Kings County, it amended its 1972 plan.

The judgment is affirmed.

Connor v. Finch
431 U.S. 407 (1977)

The question in this litigation concerns the constitutional validity of a legislative reapportionment plan devised by a three-judge Federal District Court for Mississippi's Senate and House of Representatives. In Nos. 76–777 and 76–935, the appellants are the Mississippi voters who originally brought this class action in the District Court. They challenge the court's entire Senate plan, and aspects of the House plan, as failing to meet the basic one-person, one-vote requirements of the Equal Protection Clause of the Fourteenth Amendment, and particularly the constitutional and equitable requirements of a court-ordered reapportionment plan. In No. 76–934, the appellant is the Government, an intervenor in the District Court. These appellants join in asserting that the District Court's plan works an impermissible dilution of Negro voting strength, and they challenge as well the District Court's decree for its failure to order special elections in all legislative districts where new or significantly stronger Negro voting majorities were created by the District Court's plan. In No. 76–933, the appellants are the state officers who were named as defendants in the District Court. These appellants assert that the District Court should have accorded greater deference to Mississippi's historic policy of respecting county boundaries, and thus should have established multimember legislative districts, and they further assert that the court erred in ordering any special elections at all.

We do not reach all the complicated issues raised by the various appellants, because we have concluded that both the Senate and the House reapportionments ordered by the District Court fail to meet the most elemental requirement of the Equal Protection Clause in this area—that

legislative districts be "as nearly of equal population as is practicable."

The effort to reapportion the Mississippi Legislature in accordance with constitutional requirements has occupied the attention of the federal courts for 12 years. This painfully protracted process of litigation began in the wake of *Reynolds v. Sims*, when the appellants in No. 76–777 challenged in the District Court for the Southern District of Mississippi, the extreme population variances of the legislative apportionment that had been enacted by the state legislature in 1962. The District Court invalidated that plan. After waiting for an ultimately unsuccessful attempt by the legislature to enact a constitutional reapportionment, the District Court then promulgated its own plan for the 1967 quadrennial elections, relying rather extensively on multimember districting in both legislative houses to achieve substantial population equality.

In 1971, the state legislature enacted another apportionment; that legislation was held unconstitutional because the District Court could find no justification for the continuing substantial population variances among the various legislative districts. The court consequently formulated its own plan to govern the 1971 elections, continuing to rely extensively on multimember districts, and failing altogether to formulate a final plan with respect to the State's three largest counties—Hinds, Harrison, and Jackson. Those counties instead were given interim multimember representation. In an interlocutory appeal from that order, this Court pointed out that single-member districts are preferable to large multimember districts in court-ordered reapportionment plans, and accordingly stayed the judgment of the District Court and instructed it, "absent insurmountable difficulties, to devise and put into effect a single member district plan for Hinds County." The District Court found itself confronted by insurmountable difficulties, however, and did not divide Hinds County into single-member districts before the 1971 election.

On direct appeal, after the 1971 elections had taken place pursuant to the District Court's plan, this Court declined to consider the prospective validity of the 1971 plan in the continued absence of a final plan redistricting Hinds, Harrison, and Jackson Counties. . . .

No Special Master was appointed. In anticipation of the 1975 elections, however, the Mississippi Legislature, in April 1973, enacted a new apportionment. A hearing was not held on the plaintiffs' prompt objections to that legislation until February 1975. Before the District Court reached a decision, however, the Mississippi Legislature enacted yet another apportionment almost identical to the 1971 court-ordered plan, but permanently adopting multimember districts for Hinds, Harrison, and Jackson Counties. The District Court ordered the filing of a new complaint addressing the 1975 legislation, and concluded that it was constitutional. We reversed, holding that the legislative apportionment could not be effective as law until it had been submitted and had received clearance under §5 of the Voting Rights Act of 1965, and that the District Court had accordingly erred in considering its constitutional validity.

In compliance with §5 of the Voting Rights Act, Mississippi then submitted the 1975 legislation to the Attorney General of the United States. When he objected to the legislation, the District Court proceeded to formulate another temporary reapportionment plan using multimember districts for the conduct of the 1975 elections. When the District Court delayed consideration of a permanent plan for the 1979 elections, this Court allowed the filing of a petition for a writ of mandamus to compel the District Court to enter a final judg-

ment embodying a permanent reapportionment plan for the Mississippi Legislature. The District Court thereupon held hearings and entered a judgment adopting a final plan. We noted probable jurisdiction of these appeals challenging that judgment.

In approaching the task of devising a reapportionment plan for the 122-member House and 52-member Senate, the District Court announced certain guidelines to structure its analysis, drawn from previous cases in this court and other courts and from Mississippi policy. Population variances were to be as "near de minimis as possible"; districts were to be reasonably contiguous and compact; Negro voting strength would not be minimized or canceled; and every effort would be made to maintain the integrity of county lines. The plaintiffs do not really challenge the criteria enunciated by the District Court, but rather argue that the court failed to abide by its criteria in putting together the reapportionment plans. The defendants, as cross-appellants, argue by contrast that the District Court went too far, and that the Mississippi policy of respecting county lines required the court to continue the utilization of multimember districts.

. . .

Because the practice of multimember districting can contribute to voter confusion, make legislative representatives more remote from their constituents, and tend to submerge electoral minorities and overrepresent electoral majorities, this Court has concluded that single member districts are to be preferred in court-ordered legislative reapportionment plans unless the court can articulate a "singular combination of unique factors" that justifies a different result. In its final plan, and over the defendants' objection, the District Court in the present case accordingly abandoned—albeit reluctantly—its previous adherence to multimember districting. The defendants' unallayed reliance on Mississippi's historic policy against fragmenting counties is insufficient to overcome the strong preference for single member districting that this Court originally announced in this very litigation.

The Equal Protection Clause requires that legislative districts be of nearly equal population, so that each person's vote may be given equal weight in the election of representatives. It was recognition of that fundamental tenet that motivated judicial involvement in the first place in what had been called the "political thicket" of legislative apportionment. The District Court's plan nevertheless departs from that norm in deference to Mississippi's historic respect for the integrity of county boundaries in conjunction with legislative districts. The result, as the District Court itself recognized, was "greater variances in population percentages in some instances than ordinarily would have been preferred."

Given the 1970 Mississippi population of 2,216,912 to be apportioned among 52 Senate districts, the population norm for a Senate seat if absolute population equality were to be achieved would be 42,633. As computed by the District Court, the Senate plan contains a maximum deviation from population equality of 16.5, with the largest variances occurring in District 6 (8.2 percent above the norm) and in District 38 (8.3 percent below the norm). Fourteen of the court's 52 Senate districts have variances from population equality of over 5, plus or minus, and 4 of those have variances of 8 percent or more, plus or minus. In the House plan, with 122 seats, and a population norm of 18,171, there is a maximum deviation of 19.3 percent, with the largest variances occurring in District 5 (9.4 percent over the norm) and District 47 (9.9 percent below the norm). Forty-eight districts vary more than 5 per-

cent either way, and 11 of those districts vary more than 8 percent either way.

Such substantial deviations from population equality simply cannot be tolerated in a court-ordered plan, in the absence of some compelling justification. . . .

The maximum population deviations of 16.5 percent in the Senate districts and 19.3 percent in the House districts can hardly be characterized as de minimis; they substantially exceed the "under-10" deviations the Court has previously considered to be of prima facie constitutional validity only in the context of legislatively enacted apportionments. Hence, even a legislatively crafted apportionment with deviations of this magnitude could be justified only if it were "based on legitimate considerations incident to the effectuation of a rational state policy."

As justification for both the Senate and House plans, the District Court pointed to a fairly consistent state policy of maintaining the borders of its 82 counties when allotting seats in the legislature, and to the fact that this policy is rationalized in part by the lack of legislative powers entrusted to the counties, whose legislative needs must instead be met by reliance on private bills introduced by members of the state legislature. But the District Court itself recognized at an earlier stage in this litigation that the policy against breaking county boundary lines is virtually impossible of accomplishment in a State where population is unevenly distributed among 82 counties, from which 52 Senators and 122 House members are to be elected. Only 11 of 82 counties have enough people to elect a Senator, and only 44 counties have enough people to elect a Representative.

The policy of maintaining the inviolability of county lines in such circumstances, if strictly adhered to, must inevitably collide with the basic equal protection standard of one person, one vote. Indeed, Mississippi's insistent adherence to that policy resulted in the invalidation of three successive legislative apportionments as constitutionally impermissible.

Recognition that a State may properly seek to protect the integrity of political subdivisions or historical boundary lines permits no more than "minor deviations" from the basic requirement that legislative districts must be "as nearly of equal population as is practicable." The question is one of degree. . . . The District Court failed here to identify any such "unique features" of the Mississippi political structure as would permit a judicial protection of county boundaries in the teeth of the judicial duty to "achieve the goal of population equality with little more than de minimis variation."

. . . [T]he plaintiffs in this case submitted to the District Court an alternative Senate plan that served the state policy against fragmenting county boundaries better than did the plan the court ultimately adopted, and also came closer to achieving districts that are "as nearly of equal population as is practicable." The 19 county boundaries cut by the court plan would have been reduced to 15 in the so-called "Modified Henderson Plan" submitted by the plaintiffs; the maximum population deviation in any district would have been reduced from 16.5 percent to 13.66 percent, and the number of districts deviating by more than 5 percent from the population norm, plus or minus, would have been reduced from 15 to 9. . . .

In the absence of a convincing justification for its continued adherence to a plan that even in state policy terms is less efficacious than another plan actually proposed, there can be no alternative but to set aside the District Court's decree for its failure to embody the equitable discretion necessary to effectuate the established standards of the Equal Protection Clause.

Since the District Court's legislative reapportionment decree is invalid under the elementary standards of *Reynolds v. Sims*, we do not reach the more particularized challenges to certain aspects of that reapportionment plan made by the plaintiff challenges based upon claims that the plan's apportionment of some districts impermissibly dilutes Negro voting strength. But since the 1979 elections are on the horizon and a constitutionally permissible legislative reapportionment plan for the State of Mississippi has yet to be drawn, it is appropriate to give some further guidance to the District Court with these challenges in mind.

. . .

Such unexplained departures from the results that might have been expected to flow from the District Court's own neutral guidelines can lead, as they did here, to a charge that the departures are explicable only in terms of a purpose to minimize the voting strength of a minority group. The District Court could have avoided this charge by more carefully abiding by its stated intent of adopting reasonably contiguous and compact districts, and by fully explaining any departures from that goal.

Twelve years have passed since this litigation began, but there is still no constitutionally permissible apportionment plan for the Mississippi Legislature. It is therefore imperative for the District Court, in drawing up a new plan, to make every effort not only to comply with established constitutional standards, but also to allay suspicions and avoid the creation of concerns that might lead to new constitutional challenges. In view of the serious questions raised concerning the purpose and effect of the present decree's unusually shaped legislative districts in areas with concentrations of Negro population, the District Court on remand should either draw legislative districts that are reasonably contiguous and compact, so as to put to rest suspicions that Negro voting strength is being impermissibly diluted, or explain precisely why, in a particular instance, that goal cannot be accomplished.

The task facing the District Court on remand must be approached not only with great care, but with a compelling awareness of the need for its expeditious accomplishment, so that the citizens of Mississippi at long last will be enabled to elect a legislature that properly represents them.

Reversed and remanded.

Morris v. Gressette
432 U.S. 491 (1977)

The events leading up to this litigation date back to November 11, 1971, when South Carolina enacted Act 932 reapportioning the State Senate. South Carolina promptly submitted Act 932 to the Attorney General of the United States for preclearance review pursuant to §5 of the Voting Rights Act. . . . While the Attorney General had Act 932 under review, several suits were filed in the United States District Court for the District of South Carolina challenging that Act as violative of the Fourteenth and Fifteenth Amendments and seeking to enjoin its enforcement until preclearance had been obtained under §5. The cases were consolidated, and a three-judge District Court was convened.

On March 6, 1972, the Attorney General interposed an objection to Act 932. Although the South Carolina District Court as aware of this objection—an objection that, standing alone, would have justified an injunction against enforcement of the Act—the court proceeded to address the constitutional validity of the reapportionment plan. That court rejected the Fifteenth

Amendment claim for lack of evidence that Act 932 was racially motivated, but held that the Act violated the Fourteenth Amendment due to malapportionment. The court retained jurisdiction and allowed South Carolina 30 days to enact an acceptable substitute reapportionment plan.

On May 6, 1972, a new senate reapportionment plan was enacted into law as §2 of Act 1205. This new plan was filed with the District Court, and it was submitted to the Attorney General on May 12 for preclearance review. On May 23, the District Court found the plan constitutional. By letter dated June 30, the Attorney General notified South Carolina that he would not interpose an objection to the new plan. . . . Thus, as of June 30, 1972, §2 of Act 1205 had been declared constitutional by a three-judge District Court, and the Attorney General had declined to interpose an objection under §5 of the Voting Rights Act.

Not content with the Attorney General's decision to defer to the judicial determination of the three-judge District Court, several of the named plaintiffs in the consolidated . . . action commenced another suit in the United States District Court for the District of Columbia on August 10, 1972, in which they challenged the Attorney General's failure to object to the new senate reapportionment plan. On May 16, 1973, that court ordered the Attorney General to make "a reasoned decision in accordance with his statutory responsibility." In response to this order, the Attorney General stated that, in his view, the plan violated the Fifteenth Amendment, but he reaffirmed his refusal to interpose an objection on the ground that he was constrained to defer to the ruling of the District Court. . . . On July 19, 1973, the District of Columbia District Court directed the Attorney General to consider Act 1205 without regard to the decision in *Twiggs v. West*. The next day, the Attorney General interposed an objection because he was "unable to conclude that Act No. 1205 does not have the effect of abridging voting rights on account of race."

On appeal, the United States Court of Appeals for the District of Columbia Circuit affirmed. It held that the Attorney General's decision not to interpose an objection was reviewable under the circumstances of this case, and that §5 requires him to make an independent determination on the merits of §5 issues.

Armed with the decision of the Court of Appeals and the belated objection interposed by the Attorney General, two South Carolina voters filed the present suit in the United States District Court for the District of South Carolina as a class action under §5 of the Voting Rights Act. The plaintiffs, appellants here, sought an injunction against implementation of §2 of Act 1205 on the ground that the Attorney General had interposed an objection and the State had not subsequently obtained a favorable declaratory judgment from the United States District Court for the District of Columbia. . . . [T]he District Court concluded that the failure of the Attorney General to interpose an objection within the applicable 60-day period left South Carolina free to implement the new senate reapportionment plan.

. . .

The ultimate issue in this case concerns the implementation of South Carolina's reapportionment plan for the State Senate. Since that plan has not been declared by the District Court for the District of Columbia to be without racially discriminatory purpose or effect, it can be implemented only if the Attorney General "has not interposed an objection" to the plan within the meaning of §5 of the Voting Rights Act. It conceded that no objection was entered within the 60-day period. . . .

. . .

The nature of the §5 remedy, which this Court has characterized as an "unusual" and "severe" procedure, strongly suggests that Congress did not intend the Attorney General's actions under that provision to be subject to judicial review. Section 5 requires covered jurisdictions to delay implementation of validly enacted state legislation until federal authorities have had an opportunity to determine whether that legislation conforms to the Constitution and to the provisions of the Voting Rights Act. Section 5 establishes two alternative methods by which covered jurisdictions can comply with this severe requirement of federal preclearance review. First, a covered jurisdiction may file a declaratory judgment action in the District Court for the District of Columbia and subsequently may implement the change in voting laws if that court declares that the change "does not have the purpose and will not have the effect of denying or abridging the right to vote on account of race or color." Second, a covered jurisdiction may submit a change in voting laws to the Attorney General and subsequently may enforce the change if "the Attorney General has not interposed an objection within sixty days after such submission."

According to the terms of §5, a covered jurisdiction is in compliance pursuant to the latter alternative once it has (i) filed a complete submission with the Attorney General, and (ii) received no objection from that office within 60 days. This second method of compliance under §5 is unlike the first in that implementation of changes in voting laws is not conditioned on an affirmative statement by the Attorney General that the change is without discriminatory purpose or effect. To the contrary, compliance with §5 is measured solely by the absence, for whatever reason, of a timely objection on the part of the Attorney General. . . .

Although there is no legislative history bearing directly on the issue of reviewability of the Attorney General's actions under §5, the legislative materials do indicate a desire to provide a speedy alternative method of compliance to covered States. Section 8 of the original bill provided for preclearance review only by means of a declaratory judgment action in the District Court for the District of Columbia. Justified concerns arose that the time required to pursue such litigation would unduly delay the implementation of validly enacted, nondiscriminatory state legislation. Cognizant of the problem, Attorney General Katzenbach suggested that the declaratory judgment procedure "could be improved by applying it only to those laws which the Attorney General takes exception to within a given period of time." The legislation was changed to incorporate this suggestion.

In light of the potential severity of the §5 remedy, the statutory language, and the legislative history, we think it clear that Congress intended to provide covered jurisdictions with an expeditious alternative to declaratory judgment actions. The congressional intent is plain: the extraordinary remedy of postponing the implementation of validly enacted state legislation was to come to an end when the Attorney General failed to interpose a timely objection based on a complete submission. Although there was to be no bar to subsequent constitutional challenges to the implemented legislation, there also was to be "no dragging out" of the extraordinary federal remedy beyond the period specified in the statute. Since judicial review of the Attorney General's actions would unavoidably extend this period, it is necessarily precluded.

Our conclusions in this respect are reinforced by the fact that the Attorney General's failure to object is not conclusive with respect to the constitutionality of the submitted state legislation. . . . It is true that it was the perceived inadequacy of private suits under the Fifteenth Amendment that prompted Congress to pass the Voting Rights Act. But it does not follow that Congress did not intend to preclude judicial review of Attorney General actions under §5. The initial alternative requirement of submission to the Attorney General substantially reduces the likelihood that a discriminatory enactment will escape detection by federal authorities. Where the discriminatory character of an enactment is not detected upon review by the Attorney General, it can be challenged in traditional constitutional litigation. But it cannot be questioned in a suit seeking judicial review of the Attorney General's exercise of discretion under §5, or his failure to object within the statutory period.

For these reasons, we hold that the objection interposed by the Attorney General to §2 of Act 1205 . . . is invalid. South Carolina is therefore free to implement its reapportionment plan for the State Senate.

Affirmed.

Wise v. Lipscomb
437 U.S. 535 (1978)

In 1971 respondents, Negro and Mexican-American residents of Dallas, Texas, filed suit in the United States District Court for the Northern District of Texas against petitioners, the Mayor and members of the City Council of Dallas, the city's legislative body, alleging that the at-large system of electing council members unconstitutionally diluted the vote of racial minorities. They sought a declaratory judgment to this effect and an injunction requiring the election of councilmen from single-member districts. The complaint was dismissed for failure to state a claim, but the Court of Appeals for the Fifth Circuit disagreed and remanded.

On January 17, 1975, after certifying a plaintiff class consisting of all Negro citizens of the city of Dallas and, following an evidentiary hearing, the District Court orally declared that the system of at-large elections to the Dallas City Council unconstitutionally diluted the voting strength of Negro citizens. The District Court then "afforded the city an opportunity as a legislative body for the City of Dallas to prepare a plan which would be constitutional."

On January 20, 1975, the City Council passed a resolution which stated that the Council intended to enact an ordinance which would provide for eight Council members to be elected from single-member districts and for the three remaining members, including the Mayor, to be elected at-large. This plan was submitted to the District Court on January 24, 1975. The court then conducted a remedy hearing "to determine the constitutionality of the new proposed plan by the City of Dallas." After an extensive hearing, the court announced in an oral opinion delivered on February 8, 1975, that the city's plan met constitutional guidelines and was acceptable, and that it would issue a written opinion in the near future. Two days later, the City Council formally enacted the promised ordinance, and, on March 25, the court issued a memorandum opinion containing its findings of fact and conclusions of law and again sustaining the city plan as a valid legislative Act.

The Court of Appeals reversed. It held that the District Court erred by evaluating the city's actions only under constitutional standards, rather than also applying the teaching of *East Carroll Parish School Board v. Marshall*, that, absent exceptional circumstances, judicially imposed reapportionment plans should employ only single-member districts. It concluded that no considerations existed in this case which justified a departure from this preference, and remanded with instructions that the District Court require the city to reapportion itself into an appropriate number of single-member districts. . . .

. . .

Texas was not subject to the Voting Rights Act when this case was pending in the District Court. Hence, insofar as federal law was concerned, when the District Court invalidated the provisions of the Dallas City Charter mandating at-large Council elections, the city was not only free, but was expected, to devise a substitute, rather than to leave the matter to the District Court. This duty, the District Court found, was discharged when the city enacted the eight/three plan of electing Council members. Noting that only if "the legislature failed in [its reapportionment] task, would the responsibility fall to the federal courts," and declaring that the plan adopted by the Council was not one "hastily conceived merely for the purposes of this litigation," the District Court proceeded to declare the plan constitutional despite the use of at-large voting for three Council seats. Although there are some indications in the District Court's opinion that it was striving to satisfy those rules governing federal courts when they devise their own reapportionment plans, it seems to us that, on balance, the District Court, as the United States observes in its amicus brief, reviewed the apportionment plan proposed by the Council as a legislatively enacted plan.

The Court of Appeals was not in disagreement in this respect. . . .

Neither did the Court of Appeals disturb the ruling of the District Court that the ordinance was constitutional. It did, however, insist that the plan also satisfy the special preference for single member districts applicable where district courts are themselves put to the task of devising reapportionment plans, and reversed the judgment of the District Court because, in its view, the record did not disclose the presence of those special circumstances that would warrant departure from the rule. This was clearly in error unless there was some convincing reason why the District Court was not entitled to consider the substitute plan under the principles applicable to legislatively adopted reapportionment plans. As we see it, no such reason has been presented.

It is suggested that the city was without power to enact the ordinance, because the at-large system declared unconstitutional was established by the City Charter and because, under the Texas Constitution, and Texas statutory law, the Charter cannot be amended without a vote of the people. But the District Court was of a different view. Although the Council itself had no power to change the at-large system as long as the Charter provision remained intact, once the Charter provision was declared unconstitutional, and, in effect, null and void, the Council was free to exercise its legislative powers, which it did by enacting the eight/three plan. When the City Council reapportioned itself by means of resolution and ordinance, it was not purporting to amend the City Charter, but only to exercise its legislative powers as Dallas's governing body. The Court of Appeals did not disagree with the District Court in this respect, and we are in no position to overturn the District Court's acceptance of the city ordinance as a valid legislative response to the court's declaration of unconstitutionality.

· · ·

. . . After the District Court found that the existing method of electing the City Council was constitutionally defective on January 17, 1975, it "gave the City of Dallas an opportunity to per-

form its duty to enact a constitutionally acceptable plan." The City Council, the legislative body governing Dallas, promptly took advantage of this opportunity, and, on January 24, 1975, passed a resolution which stated

> that it is the intention of the majority of this City Council to pass an ordinance [enacting a plan of eight single member districts with three individuals, including the Mayor, to be elected at-large].

On February 8, 1975, the District Court announced . . . that it was accepting the city's plan, but retained jurisdiction. Two days later, on February 10, the City Council, as promised, enacted an ordinance incorporating the eight/three plan. In a written opinion filed subsequently, the District Court specifically found "that [the city of Dallas] has met [its constitutional] duty in enacting the eight/three plan of electing council members." Here . . . as the Court there viewed it, the body governing Dallas validly met its responsibility of replacing the apportionment provision invalidated by the District Court with one which could survive constitutional scrutiny. The Court of Appeals therefore erred in regarding the plan as court imposed and in subjecting it to a level of scrutiny more stringent than that required by the Constitution.

Finally, it is urged that the Court of Appeals be affirmed because Texas became subject to §5 of the Voting Rights Act while the case was pending on appeal and because, under §5, as amended, Dallas could neither enact nor seek to administer any reapportionment plan different from that in effect on November 1, 1972, without securing the clearance called for by that section. It is urged that the city ordinance of February 1975, relied upon by the District Court and validly enacted prior to §5's becoming applicable to Texas, cannot be considered as effective law until it has secured the necessary approval. The same is said with respect to the Charter amendment approved by the people of Dallas in 1976.

We think it inappropriate, however, to address the §5 issue. Respondents may, of course, seek to sustain the judgment below on grounds not employed by the Court of Appeals; but there is a preliminary question as to whether the §5 issue is open in this Court. Respondents did not cross-petition, and sustaining the §5 submission, even if it would not expand the relief in respondents' favor, would alter the nature of the judgment issued by the Court of Appeals. In any event, however, we are not obligated to address the issue here, particularly where the Court of Appeals did not deal with it one way or another—apparently because it considered the plan to be a judicial product beyond the reach of the section. The impact of the Voting Rights Act on the city ordinance and on the Charter amendment approved by referendum will be open on remand, and we deem it appropriate for the Court of Appeals to deal with these questions.

The judgment of the Court of Appeals is reversed, and the case is remanded to that court for further proceedings.

Connor v. Coleman
440 U.S. 612 (1979)

Petitioners are plaintiffs in a suit seeking reapportionment of the Mississippi Legislature. In the most recent of the Court's decisions in this extended litigation, *Connor v. Finch*, it reversed the Judgment of the District Court and directed that court to draw a new reapportionment plan for the 1979 elections "with a compelling awareness of the need for its expeditious accomplishment."

On remand, and after further proceedings, the parties developed a settlement plan. Negotiations broke down, however, over the wording of a consent decree. In the meantime, the State had adopted a new statutory reapportionment plan fashioned by the legislature. Because the Attorney General of the United States, acting pursuant to the Voting Rights Act of 1965, refused to approve the legislature's plan, the State brought suit under the Act in the United States District Court for the District of Columbia, seeking a declaration that the plan does not have a discriminatory purpose or effect.

Acting on the state defendants' motion, the District Court in this case determined to stay all proceedings until judgment was entered in the District of Columbia litigation. If upheld, the statutory plan would supersede any court-ordered one. Petitioners then submitted this motion for leave to file a petition for a writ of mandamus to require the District Court to adopt a plan. Petitioners contend that some reapportionment scheme must be in effect by June 7, the filing deadline for the 1979 elections. Petitioners argue that the legislature's plan may not be in effect by that date, and that, unless the court files its plan now, time limitations effectively will preclude them from obtaining review of that order in this Court. It is argued in response that immediate filing would be unduly disruptive if the filed plan were supplanted before June 7. The District Court has indicated, however, that, absent the conclusion of the District of Columbia suit, it will order a plan into effect on May 7.

The only issue here, therefore, is whether this Court should require the District Court to file its plan now, rather than on May 7; we do not question the good faith of the District Court. We believe, however, that the better course is to file its plan now. In the unlikely event that a legislative plan should supersede the court plan before May 7, potential candidates would have more than a month to reassess their prospects. If, on the other hand, the legislative plan does not go into effect and the court plan is filed only on May 7, this Court will be faced with requests for emergency review that, if granted, could force changes only days before the June 7 deadline.

Leave to file the petition is therefore granted. The District Court is instructed, forthwith and without further delay, to adopt a final plan for the reapportionment of the Mississippi Legislature. Our consideration of the petition for a writ of mandamus is continued for 30 days.

City of Mobile v. Bolden
446 U.S. 55 (1980)

The city of Mobile, Alabama, has, since 1911, been governed by a City Commission consisting of three members elected by the voters of the city at large. The question in this case is whether this at-large system of municipal elections violates the rights of Mobile's Negro voters in contravention of federal statutory or constitutional law.

The appellees brought this suit in the Federal District Court for the Southern District of Alabama as a class action on behalf of all Negro citizens of Mobile. Named as defendants were the city and its three incumbent Commissioners, who are the appellants before this Court. The complaint alleged that the practice of electing the City Commissioners at large unfairly diluted the voting strength of Negroes in violation of §2 of the Voting Rights Act of 1965, of the Fourteenth Amendment, and of the Fifteenth Amendment. . . . the District Court found that the constitutional rights of the appellees had been violated, entered a judgment in their favor, and ordered that the City Commission be disestablished and replaced

by a municipal government consisting of a Mayor and a City Council with members elected from single-member districts. The Court of Appeals affirmed the judgment in its entirety, agreeing that Mobile's at-large elections operated to discriminate against Negroes in violation of the Fourteenth and Fifteenth Amendments, and finding that the remedy formulated by the District Court was appropriate. . . .

In Alabama, the form of municipal government a city may adopt is governed by state law. Until 1911, cities not covered by specific legislation were limited to governing themselves through a Mayor and City Council. In that year, the Alabama Legislature authorized every large municipality to adopt a commission form of government. Mobile established its City Commission in the same year, and has maintained that basic system of municipal government ever since.

The three Commissioners jointly exercise all legislative, executive, and administrative power in the municipality. They are required after election to designate one of their number as Mayor, a largely ceremonial office, but no formal provision is made for allocating specific executive or administrative duties among the three. As required by the state law enacted in 1911, each candidate for the Mobile City Commission runs for election in the city at large for a term of four years in one of three numbered posts, and may be elected only by a majority of the total vote. This is the same basic electoral system that is followed by literally thousands of municipalities and other local governmental units throughout the Nation.

. . .

The appellees have argued in this Court that *Smith v. Allwright* and *Terry v. Adams* support the conclusion that the at-large system of elections in Mobile is unconstitutional, reasoning that the effect of racially polarized voting in Mobile is the same as that of a racially exclusionary primary. The only characteristic, however, of the exclusionary primaries that offended the Fifteenth Amendment was that Negroes were not permitted to vote in them. The difficult question was whether the "State ha[d] had a hand in" the patent discrimination practiced by a nominally private organization.

The answer to the appellees' argument is that, as the District Court expressly found, their freedom to vote has not been denied or abridged by anyone. The Fifteenth Amendment does not entail the right to have Negro candidates elected, and neither *Smith v. Allwright* nor *Terry v. Adams* contains any implication to the contrary. That Amendment prohibits only purposefully discriminatory denial or abridgment by government of the freedom to vote "on account of race, color, or previous condition of servitude." Having found that Negroes in Mobile "register and vote without hindrance," the District Court and Court of Appeals were in error in believing that the appellants invaded the protection of that Amendment in the present case.

The Court of Appeals also agreed with the District Court that Mobile's at-large electoral system violates the Equal Protection Clause of the Fourteenth Amendment. There remains for consideration, therefore, the validity of its judgment on that score.

The claim that at-large electoral schemes unconstitutionally deny to some persons the equal protection of the laws has been advanced in numerous cases before this Court. That contention has been raised most often with regard to multimember constituencies within a state legislative apportionment system. The constitutional objection to multimember districts is not and cannot be that, as such, they depart from apportionment on a population basis in violation of

Reynolds v. Sims and its progeny. Rather, the focus in such cases has been on the lack of representation multimember districts afford various elements of the voting population in a system of representative legislative democracy. . . .

. . .

We may assume, for present purposes, that an at-large election of city officials with all the legislative, executive, and administrative power of the municipal government is constitutionally indistinguishable from the election of a few members of a state legislative body in multimember districts—although this may be a rash assumption. But even making this assumption, it is clear that the evidence in the present case fell far short of showing that the appellants "conceived or operated [a] purposeful devic[e] to further racial . . . discrimination."

. . .

The fact is that the Court has sternly set its face against the claim, however phrased, that the Constitution somehow guarantees proportional representation.

The judgment is reversed, and the case is remanded to the Court of Appeals for further proceedings.

McDaniel v. Sanchez
452 U.S. 130 (1981)

We granted certiorari to decide whether the preclearance requirement of §5 of the Voting Rights Act . . . applies to a reapportionment plan submitted to a Federal District Court by the legislative body of a covered jurisdiction in response to a judicial determination that the existing apportionment of its electoral districts is unconstitutional. Relying on *East Carroll Parish School Board v. Marshall*, the District Court held that the plan submitted to it in this case was a judicial plan, and thus excepted from the requirements of §5. Relying on *Wise v. Lipscomb*, the Court of Appeals for the Fifth Circuit reversed; it held that, because the plan had been prepared by a legislative body, it was a legislative plan within the coverage of §5. We are persuaded that Congress intended to require compliance with the statutory preclearance procedures under the circumstances of this case. . . .

The covered jurisdiction in this case is Kleberg County, a rural county in Texas. Under Texas law, a Commissioners Court, which is composed of four county commissioners presided over by the county judge, is authorized to govern Kleberg County. The county is divided periodically by the Commissioners Court into four commissioners' precincts, each of which elects a resident to the position of county commissioner. The county judge is elected at large. The county commissioners and the county judge serve 4-year terms.

In January 1978, four Mexican-American residents of Kleberg County brought this class action against various county officials alleging that the apportionment of the four commissioners' precincts denied individual residents of the larger precincts a vote of equal weight, and unconstitutionally diluted the voting strength of the county's substantial Mexican-American population. After a trial, the District Court rejected the plaintiffs' claim that the county's apportionment plan unconstitutionally diluted the voting power of Mexican-Americans as a class, but held that individual voters were denied equal representation because of the substantial disparity in the number of residents in each commissioners' precinct. The District Court therefore directed the county officials to submit a proposed reapportionment plan to the court within six weeks, and scheduled a hearing on the validity of the proposal for four weeks thereafter.

Pursuant to the District Court's order, the Commissioners Court undertook the task of devising a new apportionment plan. The Commissioners Court employed Dr. Robert Nash . . . to prepare a new plan, instructing him to define the commissioners' precincts "on a one-person/one-vote basis." With one insignificant modification, the Commissioners Court officially adopted the plan prepared by Dr. Nash as the plan it would submit to the District Court.

Respondents objected to the proposed plan. They challenged the data used by the Dean, they claimed that the plan diluted the voting strength of Mexican-Americans, and they contended that the Voting Rights Act required the county to obtain preclearance from the Attorney General of the United States or the United States District Court for the District of Columbia before the plan could become effective. After an evidentiary hearing, the District Court rejected both of respondents' factual contentions, and held as a matter of law that the Voting Rights Act did not require preclearance. The court entered an order approving the new plan and authorizing the Commissioners Court to conduct the 1980 primary and general elections under it.

Without expressing any opinion with respect to the constitutionality of the new plan, the Court of Appeals vacated the District Court's order in a per curiam opinion. . . . The court thereafter denied petitioners' application for a stay pending filing and consideration of a petition for writ of certiorari. On August 14, 1980, however, Justice Powell, in his capacity as Circuit Justice, entered an order recalling the mandate and staying the judgment of the Court of Appeals pending disposition of the petition for certiorari. . . .

. . .

In this case, we are concerned only with the question whether the reapportionment plan submitted to the District Court should be considered a legislative plan for purposes of preclearance under §5. We are not presented with any question concerning the substantive acceptability of that plan. Nonetheless, we draw significant guidance from prior cases in which the substantive acceptability of a reapportionment plan, rather than the applicability of §5, was at issue.

In neither of the cases on which the respective parties now place their primary reliance did the Court predicate its decision on the Voting Rights Act. In both of those cases, the question before the Court was whether it was error for the District Court to approve the inclusion of a multimember district in the reapportionment plan under review.

. . .

This is not a case in which the language of the controlling statute unambiguously answers the question presented. The Solicitor General, on behalf of the United States as amicus curiae, contends that a covered jurisdiction "seek[s] to administer" a new voting practice when it submits a redistricting plan to a district court as a proposed remedy for a constitutional violation. This is a plausible, but not an obviously correct, reading of the statutory language. For there is force to the contrary argument that Kleberg County had no intention to administer any new plan until after it was given legal effect by incorporation in a judicial decree. Arguably, therefore, the statute has no application before the District Court enters its decree, and because the Act does not require the District Court to have its decisions precleared, once such a decree is entered, it is too late for the statute to qualify the county's duty to administer the plan as entered by the District Court. We find sufficient ambiguity in the statutory language to make it appropriate to turn to legislative history for guidance.

In 1975, when Congress adopted the amendments that ultimately brought Texas and Kleberg County within the coverage of the Act, it directed special attention to §5 and to the redistricting that would be required after the 1980 census. In its Report on S. 1279, the bill that extended the life of the Voting Rights Act beyond 1975, the Senate Committee on the Judiciary explained "the future need for the Act" by pointing out that redrafting of district lines to correct violations of the one-person, one-vote rule created opportunities to disenfranchise minority voters.

By providing that Section 5 protections not be removed before 1985, S. 1279 would guarantee federal protection of minority voting rights during the years that the post-census redistrictings will take place.

The Committee unambiguously stated that the statutory protections are to be available even when the redistricting is ordered by a federal court to remedy a constitutional violation that has been established in pending federal litigation. . . .

. . . The preclearance procedure is designed to forestall the danger that local decisions to modify voting practices will impair minority access to the electoral process. The federal interest in preventing local jurisdictions from making changes that adversely affect the rights of minority voters is the same whether a change is required to remedy a constitutional violation or is merely the product of a community's perception of the desirability of responding to new social patterns.

It is true, of course, that the federal interest may be protected by the federal district court presiding over voting right litigation, but sound reasons support the Committee's view that the normal §5 preclearance procedures should nevertheless be followed in cases such as this. The procedures contemplated by the statute reflect a congressional choice in favor of specialized review either by the Attorney General of the United States or by the United States District Court for the District of Columbia. Because a large number of voting changes must necessarily undergo the preclearance process, centralized review enhances the likelihood that recurring problems will be resolved in a consistent and expeditious way. Moreover, if covered jurisdictions could avoid the normal preclearance procedure by awaiting litigation challenging a refusal to redistrict after a census is completed, the statute might have the unintended effect of actually encouraging delay in making obviously needed changes in district boundaries. The federal interest in evenhanded review of all changes in covered jurisdictions is furthered by the application of the statute in cases such as this.

The application of the statute is not dependent on a showing that the county's proposed plan is defective in any way. The prophylactic purposes of the §5 remedy are achieved by automatically requiring "review of all voting changes prior to implementation by the covered jurisdictions." It is therefore not material that the plan submitted by the Commissioners Court of Kleberg County in this case was actually prepared by an independent expert. His expertise may facilitate the satisfactory completion of the preclearance process, but it does not obviate the preclearance requirement itself. For just as the reasons for the county's decision to propose a new plan are irrelevant to the statutory preclearance requirement, so also is the particular method that is employed in formulating the plan that is submitted to the court on behalf of the county irrelevant.

The application of the statute also is not dependent upon any showing that the Commissioners Court had authority under state law to enact the apportionment plan at issue in this case. . . . The fact that particular requirements of state law

may not be satisfied before a plan is proposed to a federal court does not alter this essential characteristic. The applicability of §5 to specific remedial plans is a matter of federal law that federal courts should determine pursuant to a uniform federal rule.

As we construe the congressional mandate, it requires that whenever a covered jurisdiction submits a proposal reflecting the policy choices of the elected representatives of the people—no matter what constraints have limited the choices available to them—the preclearance requirement of the Voting Rights Act is applicable. It was therefore error for the District Court to act on the county's proposed plan before it had been submitted to the Attorney General or the United States District Court for the District of Columbia for preclearance.

The judgment of the Court of Appeals is therefore affirmed.

Upham v. Seamon
456 U.S. 37 (1982)

After the 1980 census, Texas' congressional delegation increased from 24 to 27 members. A reapportionment plan, Senate Bill No. 1 (SB1), was enacted on August 14, 1981, and then submitted to the Attorney General for preclearance. While it was pending before him, suit was filed in the Federal District Court for the Eastern District of Texas challenging the constitutionality of SB1 and its validity under §2 of the Voting Rights Act of 1965. A three-judge court . . . delayed any further action until after the Attorney General acted. On January 29, 1982, the Attorney General entered an objection to SB1. Specifically, he objected to the lines drawn for two contiguous districts in south Texas, Districts 15 and 27. He stated that the State "has satisfied its burden of demonstrating that the submitted plan is nondiscriminatory in purpose and effect" with respect to the other 25 districts. In the face of this objection, which made SB1 unenforceable, and the obvious unconstitutionality of the prior apportionment plan, the court ordered the parties to provide written submissions along with maps, plats, and other data to aid the court in reaching a court-ordered reapportionment plan. A hearing was held on February 9. The court then proceeded to resolve the Attorney General's objection to Districts 15 and 27. All other districts of the court's plan, except for those in Dallas County, were identical to those of SB1. The court devised its own districts for Dallas County, and it is that part of the District Court's judgment that is on appeal here. A stay and expedited consideration are requested.

. . .

SB1's treatment of Dallas County failed to meet the test of racial fairness for a court-ordered plan. Under SB1, minority strength in District 5, in Dallas County, would have gone from 29.1 percent to 12.1 percent. Apparently, the minority votes had been shifted to District 24, which increased in minority population from 37.4 percent to 63.8 percent. . . . The court . . . redrew the boundaries of Districts 5 and 24, and the two adjoining Districts, 3 and 26. Under the court-ordered plan, District 5 would have a minority population of 31.87 percent and District 24 would have 45.7 percent.

Appellants, who are Republican Party officials in Texas, contend that the District Court simply substituted its own reapportionment preferences for those of the state legislature. . . . They argue that, in the absence of any objection to the Dallas County districts by the Attorney General, and in the absence of any finding of a constitutional or statutory violation with respect to those districts,

a court must defer to the legislative judgments the plans reflect, even under circumstances in which a court order is required to effect an interim legislative apportionment plan. . . .

. . .

Whenever a district court is faced with entering an interim reapportionment order that will allow elections to go forward, it is faced with the problem of "reconciling the requirements of the Constitution with the goals of state political policy." An appropriate reconciliation of these two goals can only be reached if the district court's modifications of a state plan are limited to those necessary to cure any constitutional or statutory defect. Thus, in the absence of a finding that the Dallas County reapportionment plan offended either the Constitution or the Voting Rights Act, the District Court was not free, and certainly was not required, to disregard the political program of the Texas State Legislature.

Although the District Court erred, it does not necessarily follow that its plan should not serve as an interim plan governing the forthcoming congressional elections. The filing date for candidates, which was initially postponed by the District Court, has now come and gone. The District Court has also adjusted other dates so that the primary elections scheduled for May 1 may be held. The State of Texas, although it disagrees with the judgment of the District Court with respect to Dallas County, urges that the election process should not now be interrupted and a new schedule adopted, even for Dallas County. It is urged that, because the District Court's plan is only an interim plan and is subject to replacement by the legislature in 1983, the injury to appellants, if any, will not be irreparable.

It is true that we have authorized District Courts to order or to permit elections to be held pursuant to apportionment plans that do not in all respects measure up to the legal requirements, even constitutional requirements. Necessity has been the motivating factor in these situations.

Because we are not now as familiar as the District Court with the Texas election laws and the legal and practical factors that may bear on whether the primary elections should be rescheduled, we vacate the District Court judgment and remand the case to that court for further proceedings. Having indicated the legal error of the District Court, we leave it to that court in the first instance to determine whether to modify its judgment and reschedule the primary elections for Dallas County or, in spite of its erroneous refusal to adopt the SB1 districts for Dallas County, to allow the election to go forward in accordance with the present schedule.

The judgment of the Court shall issue forthwith.

Karcher v. Daggett
462 U.S. 725 (1983)

After the results of the 1980 decennial census had been tabulated, the Clerk of the United States House of Representatives notified the Governor of New Jersey that the number of Representatives to which the State was entitled had decreased from 15 to 14. Accordingly, the New Jersey Legislature was required to reapportion the State's congressional districts. The State's 199th Legislature passed two reapportionment bills. One was vetoed by the Governor, and the second, although signed into law, occasioned significant dissatisfaction among those who felt it diluted minority voting strength in the city of Newark. In response, the 200th Legislature returned to the problem of apportioning congressional districts when it convened in January 1982, and it swiftly passed a bill (S-711) . . . which created the apportionment

plan at issue in this case. The bill was signed by the Governor on January 19, 1982, becoming Pub.L.1982, (hereinafter Feldman Plan).

. . .

Almost immediately after the Feldman Plan became law, a group of individuals with varying interests, including all incumbent Republican Members of Congress from New Jersey, sought a declaration that the apportionment plan violated Art. I, §2, of the Constitution and an injunction against proceeding with the primary election for United States Representatives under the plan. . . .

. . . [T]he District Court issued an opinion and order declaring the Feldman Plan unconstitutional. Denying the motions for summary judgment and resolving the case on the record as a whole, the District Court held that the population variances in the Feldman Plan were not "unavoidable despite a good faith effort to achieve absolute equality." The court rejected appellants' argument that a deviation lower than the statistical imprecision of the decennial census was "the functional equivalent of mathematical equality." It also held that appellants had failed to show that the population variances were justified by the legislature's purported goals of preserving minority voting strength and anticipating shifts in population. The District Court enjoined appellants from conducting primary or general elections under the Feldman Plan, but that order was stayed pending appeal to this Court. . . .

. . .

. . . [T]wo basic questions shape litigation over population deviations in state legislation apportioning congressional districts. First, the court must consider whether the population differences among districts could have been reduced or eliminated altogether by a good faith effort to draw districts of equal population. Parties challenging apportionment legislation must bear the burden of proof on this issue, and if they fail to show that the differences could have been avoided, the apportionment scheme must be upheld. If, however, the plaintiffs can establish that the population differences were not the result of a good faith effort to achieve equality, the State must bear the burden of proving that each significant variance between districts was necessary to achieve some legitimate goal.

Appellants' principal argument in this case is addressed to the first question described above. They contend that the Feldman Plan should be regarded per se as the product of a good faith effort to achieve population equality because the maximum population deviation among districts is smaller than the predictable undercount in available census data.

Kirkpatrick squarely rejected a nearly identical argument.

The whole thrust of the "as nearly as practicable" approach is inconsistent with adoption of fixed numerical standards which excuse population variances without regard to the circumstances of each particular case. Adopting any standard other than population equality, using the best census data available, would subtly erode the Constitution's ideal of equal representation. If state legislators knew that a certain de minimis level of population differences was acceptable, they would doubtless strive to achieve that level, rather than equality. Furthermore, choosing a different standard would import a high degree of arbitrariness into the process of reviewing apportionment plans. In this case, appellants argue that a maximum deviation of approximately 0.7 percent should be considered de minimis. If we accept that argument, how are we to regard deviations of 0.8 percent, 0.95 percent, 1 percent, or 1.1 percent?

Any standard, including absolute equality, involves a certain artificiality. As appellants point out, even the census data are not perfect, and the well-known restlessness of the American people means that population counts for particular localities are outdated long before they are completed. Yet problems with the data at hand apply equally to any population-based standard we could choose. As between two standards—equality or something less than equality—only the former reflects the aspirations of Art. I, §2.

To accept the legitimacy of unjustified, though small, population deviations in this case would mean to reject the basic premise of *Kirkpatrick* and *Wesberry*. We decline appellants' invitation to go that far. The unusual rigor of their standard has been noted several times. Because of that rigor, we have required that absolute population equality be the paramount objective of apportionment only in the case of congressional districts, for which the command of Art. I, §2, as regards the National Legislature outweighs the local interests that a State may deem relevant in apportioning districts for representatives to state and local legislatures, but we have not questioned the population equality standard for congressional districts. The principle of population equality for congressional districts has not proved unjust or socially or economically harmful in experience. If anything, this standard should cause less difficulty now for state legislatures than it did when we adopted it in *Wesberry*. The rapid advances in computer technology and education during the last two decades make it relatively simple to draw contiguous districts of equal population and at the same time to further whatever secondary goals the State has. Finally, to abandon unnecessarily a clear and oft-confirmed constitutional interpretation would impair our authority in other cases, would implicitly open the door to a plethora of requests that we reexamine other rules that some may consider burdensome, and would prejudice those who have relied upon the rule of law in seeking an equipopulous congressional apportionment in New Jersey. We thus reaffirm that there are no de minimis population variations which could practicably be avoided but which nonetheless meet the standard of Art. I, without justification.

The sole difference between appellants' theory and the argument we rejected in *Kirkpatrick* is that appellants have proposed a de minimis line that gives the illusion of rationality and predictability: the "inevitable statistical imprecision of the census." . . .

. . .

In essence, appellants' 1 percent benchmark is little more than an attempt to present an attractive de minimis line with a patina of scientific authority. . . . [I]f we accepted appellants' theory that the national undercount level sets a limit on our ability to use census data to tell the difference between the populations of congressional districts, we might well be forced to set that level far above 1 percent when final analyses of the 1980 census are completed.

. . . The undercount in the census affects the accuracy of the deviations between districts only to the extent that the undercount varies from district to district. For a 1 percent undercount to explain a 1 percent deviation between the census populations of two districts, the undercount in the smaller district would have to be approximately three times as large as the undercount in the larger district. It is highly unlikely, of course, that this condition holds true, especially since appellants have utterly failed to introduce evidence showing that the districts were designed to compensate for the probable undercount. . . . Only by bizarre coincidence could the systematic undercount in the census bear some statisti-

cal relationship to the districts drawn by the Feldman Plan.

The census may systematically undercount population, and the rate of undercounting may vary from place to place. Those facts, however, do not render meaningless the differences in population between congressional districts, as determined by uncorrected census counts. To the contrary, the census data provide the only reliable—albeit less than perfect—indication of the districts' "real" relative population levels. Even if one cannot say with certainty that one district is larger than another merely because it has a higher census count, one can say with certainty that the district with a larger census count is more likely to be larger than the other district than it is to be smaller or the same size. That certainty is sufficient for decisionmaking. Furthermore, because the census count represents the "best population data available," it is the only basis for good faith attempts to achieve population equality. Attempts to explain population deviations on the basis of flaws in census data must be supported with a precision not achieved here.

Given that the census-based population deviations in the Feldman Plan reflect real differences among the districts, it is clear that they could have been avoided or significantly reduced with a good faith effort to achieve population equality. For that reason alone, it would be inappropriate to accept the Feldman Plan as "functionally equivalent" to a plan with districts of equal population.

The District Court found that several other plans introduced in the 200th Legislature had smaller maximum deviations than the Feldman Plan. Appellants object that the alternative plans considered by the District Court were not comparable to the Feldman Plan, because their political characters differed profoundly. We have never denied that apportionment is a political process, or that state legislatures could pursue legitimate secondary objectives as long as those objectives were consistent with a good faith effort to achieve population equality at the same time. Nevertheless, the claim that political considerations require population differences among congressional districts belongs more properly to the second level of judicial inquiry in these cases, in which the State bears the burden of justifying the differences with particularity.

In any event, it was unnecessary for the District Court to rest its finding on the existence of alternative plans with radically different political effects. . . . Starting with the Feldman Plan itself and the census data available to the legislature at the time it was enacted, one can reduce the maximum population deviation of the plan merely by shifting a handful of municipalities from one district to another. Thus the District Court did not err in finding that the plaintiffs had met their burden of showing that the Feldman Plan did not come as nearly as practicable to population equality.

By itself, the foregoing discussion does not establish that the Feldman Plan is unconstitutional. Rather, appellees' success in proving that the Feldman Plan was not the product of a good faith effort to achieve population equality means only that the burden shifted to the State to prove that the population deviations in its plan were necessary to achieve some legitimate state objective. . . . Any number of consistently applied legislative policies might justify some variance, including, for instance, making districts compact, respecting municipal boundaries, preserving the cores of prior districts, and avoiding contests between incumbent Representatives. As long as the criteria are nondiscriminatory, these are all legitimate objectives that, on a proper showing, could justify minor population deviations. The

State must, however, show with some specificity that a particular objective required the specific deviations in its plan, rather than simply relying on general assertions. The showing required to justify population deviations is flexible, depending on the size of the deviations, the importance of the State's interests, the consistency with which the plan as a whole reflects those interests, and the availability of alternatives that might substantially vindicate those interests yet approximate population equality more closely. By necessity, whether deviations are justified requires case-by-case attention to these factors.

The possibility that a State could justify small variations in the census-based population of its congressional districts on the basis of some legitimate, consistently applied policy was recognized in *Kirkpatrick* itself. . . . We rejected its arguments not because those factors were impermissible considerations in the apportionment process, but rather because of the size of the resulting deviations and because Missouri "[a]t best . . . made haphazard adjustments to a scheme based on total population," made "no attempt" to account for the same factors in all districts, and generally failed to document its findings thoroughly and apply them "throughout the State in a systematic, not an ad hoc, manner."

The District Court properly found that appellants did not Justify the population deviations in this case. At argument before the District Court and on appeal in this Court, appellants emphasized only one justification for the Feldman Plan's population deviations—preserving the voting strength of racial minority groups. . . .

Under the Feldman Plan, the largest districts are the Fourth and Ninth Districts, and the smallest are the Third and Sixth. None of these districts borders on the Tenth, and only one—the Fourth—is even mentioned in appellants' discussions of preserving minority voting strength. Nowhere do appellants suggest that the large population of the Fourth District was necessary to preserve minority voting strength; in fact, the deviation between the Fourth District and other districts has the effect of diluting the votes of all residents of that district, including members of racial minorities, as compared with other districts with fewer minority voters. The record is completely silent on the relationship between preserving minority voting strength and the small populations of the Third and Sixth Districts. Therefore, the District Court's findings easily pass the "clearly erroneous" test.

The District Court properly applied the two-part test of *Kirkpatrick v. Preisler* to New Jersey's 1982 apportionment of districts for the United States House of Representatives. It correctly held that the population deviations in the plan were not functionally equal as a matter of law, and it found that the plan was not a good faith effort to achieve population equality using the best available census data. It also correctly rejected appellants' attempt to justify the population deviations as not supported by the evidence. The judgment of the District Court, therefore, is affirmed.

Brown v. Thomson
462 U.S. 835 (1983)

Since Wyoming became a State in 1890, its legislature has consisted of a Senate and a House of Representatives. The State's constitution provides that each of the State's counties "shall constitute a senatorial and representative district," and that "[e]ach county shall have at least one senator and one representative." The senators and representatives are required to be "apportioned among the said counties as nearly as may be according to

the number of their inhabitants." The State has had 23 counties since 1922. Because the apportionment of the Wyoming House has been challenged three times in the past 20 years, some background is helpful.

In 1963, voters from the six most populous counties filed suit in the District Court for the district of Wyoming challenging the apportionment of the State's 25 senators and 61 representatives. The three-judge District Court held that the apportionment of the Senate—one senator allocated to each of the State's 23 counties, with the two largest counties having two senators—so far departed from the principle of population equality that it was unconstitutional. But the court upheld the apportionment of the State House of Representatives. The State's constitutional requirement that each county shall have at least one representative had produced deviations from population equality: the average deviation from the ideal number of residents per representative was 16 percent, while the maximum percentage deviation between largest and smallest number of residents per representative was 90 percent. The District Court held that these population disparities were justifiable as the result of an honest attempt, based on legitimate considerations, to effectuate a rational and practical policy for the house of representatives under conditions as they exist in Wyoming.

The 1971 reapportionment of the House was similar to that in 1963, with an average deviation of 15 percent and a maximum deviation of 86 percent. Another constitutional challenge was brought in the District Court. The three-judge court again upheld the apportionment of the House, observing that only "five minimal adjustments" had been made since 1963, with three districts gaining a representative and two districts losing a representative because of population shifts.

The present case is a challenge to Wyoming's 1981 statute reapportioning its House of Representatives in accordance with the requirements of Art. 3, 3, of the state constitution. The 1980 census placed Wyoming's population at 469,557. The statute provided for 64 representatives, meaning that the ideal apportionment would be 7,337 persons per representative. Each county was given one representative, including the six counties the population of which fell below 7,337. The deviations from population equality were similar to those in prior decades, with an average deviation of 16 percent and a maximum deviation of 89 percent.

The issue in this case concerns only Niobrara County, the State's least populous county. Its population of 2,924 is less than half of the ideal district of 7,337. Accordingly, the general statutory formula would have dictated that its population for purposes of representation be rounded down to zero. This would have deprived Niobrara County of its own representative for the first time since it became a county in 1913. The state legislature found, however, that the opportunity for oppression of the people of this state or any of them is greater if any county is deprived a representative in the legislature than if each is guaranteed at least one representative.

It therefore followed the state constitution's requirement and expressly provided that a county would receive a representative even if the statutory formula rounded the county's population to zero. Niobrara County thus was given one seat in a 64-seat House. The legislature also provided that, if this representation for Niobrara County were held unconstitutional, it would be combined with a neighboring county in a single representative district. The House then would consist of 63 representatives.

Appellants, members of the state League of Women Voters and residents of seven counties in which the population per representative is greater than the state average, filed this lawsuit in the District Court for the District of Wyoming. . . . They sought declaratory and injunctive relief that would prevent the State from giving a separate representative to Niobrara County, thus implementing the alternative plan calling for 63 representatives.

The three-judge District Court upheld the constitutionality of the statute. The court noted that the narrow issue presented was the alleged discriminatory effect of a single county's representative, and concluded, citing expert testimony, that "the 'dilution' of the plaintiffs' votes is de minimis when Niobrara County has its own representative." The court also found that Wyoming's policy of granting a representative to each county was rational and, indeed, particularly well-suited to the special needs of Wyoming.

. . .

In this case, there is no question that Niobrara County's deviation from population equality—60 percent below the mean—is more than minor. There also can be no question that Wyoming's constitutional policy—followed since statehood—of using counties as representative districts and ensuring that each county has one representative is supported by substantial and legitimate state concerns. . . .

Moreover, it is undisputed that Wyoming has applied this factor in a manner "free from any taint of arbitrariness or discrimination." The State's policy of preserving county boundaries is based on the state constitution, has been followed for decades, and has been applied consistently throughout the State. As the District Court found, this policy has particular force, given the peculiar size and population of the State and the nature of its governmental structure. In addition, population equality is the sole other criterion used, and the State's apportionment formula ensures that population deviations are no greater than necessary to preserve counties as representative districts. Finally, there is no evidence of "a built-in bias tending to favor particular political interests or geographic areas." . . .

In short, this case presents an unusually strong example of an apportionment plan the population variations of which are entirely the result of the consistent and nondiscriminatory application of a legitimate state policy. This does not mean that population deviations of any magnitude necessarily are acceptable. Even a neutral and consistently applied criterion such as use of counties as representative districts can frustrate *Reynolds'* mandate of fair and effective representation if the population disparities are excessively high. . . . It remains true, however, as the Court in *Reynolds* noted, that consideration must be given "to the character as well as the degree of deviations from a strict population basis." The consistency of application and the neutrality of effect of the nonpopulation criteria must be considered along with the size of the population disparities in determining whether a state legislative apportionment plan contravenes the Equal Protection Clause.

Here we are not required to decide whether Wyoming's nondiscriminatory adherence to county boundaries justifies the population deviations that exist throughout Wyoming's representative districts. Appellants deliberately have limited their challenge to the alleged dilution of their voting power resulting from the one representative given to Niobrara County. The issue therefore is not whether a 16 percent average deviation and an 89 percent maximum deviation, considering the state apportionment plan as a whole, are constitutionally permissible. Rather,

the issue is whether Wyoming's policy of preserving county boundaries justifies the additional deviations from population equality resulting from the provision of representation to Niobrara County.

It scarcely can be denied that, in terms of actual effect on appellants' voting power, it matters little whether the 63-member or 64-member House is used. The District Court noted, for example, that the 7 counties in which appellants reside will elect 28 representatives under either plan. The only difference, therefore, is whether they elect 43.75 percent of the legislature (28 of 64 members) or 44.44 percent of the legislature (28 of 63 members). The District Court aptly described this difference as "de minimis."

We do not suggest that a State is free to create and allocate an additional representative seat in any way it chooses simply because that additional seat will have little or no effect on the remainder of the State's voters. The allocation of a representative to a particular political subdivision still may violate the Equal Protection Clause if it greatly exceeds the population variations existing in the rest of the State and if the State provides no legitimate justifications for the creation of that seat. Here, however, considerable population variations will remain even if Niobrara County's representative is eliminated. Under the 63-member plan, the average deviation per representative would be 13 percent and the maximum deviation would be 66 percent. These statistics make clear that the grant of a representative to Niobrara County is not a significant cause of the population deviations that exist in Wyoming.

Moreover, we believe that the differences between the two plans are justified on the basis of Wyoming's longstanding and legitimate policy of preserving county boundaries. Particularly where there is no "taint of arbitrariness or discrimination," substantial deference is to be accorded the political decisions of the people of a State acting through their elected representatives. Here it is noteworthy that, by enacting the 64-member plan, the State ensured that its policy of preserving county boundaries applies nondiscriminatorily. The effect of the 63-member plan would be to deprive the voters of Niobrara County of their own representative, even though the remainder of the House of Representatives would be constituted so as to facilitate representation of the interests of each county. In these circumstances, we are not persuaded that Wyoming has violated the Fourteenth Amendment by permitting Niobrara County to have its own representative.

The judgment of the District Court is affirmed.

Thornburg v. Gingles
478 U.S. 30 (1986)

In April 1982, the North Carolina General Assembly enacted a legislative redistricting plan for the State's Senate and House of Representatives. Appellees, black citizens of North Carolina who are registered to vote, challenged seven districts, one single-member and six multimember districts, alleging that the redistricting scheme impaired black citizens' ability to elect representatives of their choice in violation of the Fourteenth and Fifteenth Amendments to the United States Constitution and of §2 of the Voting Rights Act.

After appellees brought suit, but before trial, Congress amended §2. The amendment was largely a response to this Court's plurality opinion in *Mobile v. Bolden*, which had declared that, in order to establish a violation either of §2 or of the Fourteenth or Fifteenth Amendments, minority voters must prove that a contested electoral mechanism was intentionally adopted or maintained by state officials for a discriminatory purpose. Congress substantially revised §2 to make clear that a violation could be proved by showing discriminatory effect alone, and to establish as the relevant legal standard the "results test," applied by this Court in *White v. Regester*, and by other federal courts before *Bolden*.

. . .

The District Court applied the "totality of the circumstances" test set forth in §2(b) to appellees' statutory claim, and, relying principally on the factors outlined in the Senate Report, held that the redistricting scheme violated §2 because it resulted in the dilution of black citizens' votes in all seven disputed districts. In light of this conclusion, the court did not reach appellees' constitutional claims.

. . .

. . . [T]he court declared the contested portions of the 1982 redistricting plan violative of §2, and enjoined appellants from conducting elections pursuant to those portions of the plan. Appellants, the Attorney General of North Carolina and others, took a direct appeal to this Court . . . with respect to five of the multimember districts—House Districts 21, 23, 36, and 39, and Senate District 22. . . .

. . .

Having stated the general legal principles relevant to claims that §2 has been violated through the use of multimember districts, we turn to the arguments of appellants and of the United States as amicus curiae addressing racially polarized voting. . . .

. . .

Whether appellants and the United States believe that it is the voter's race or the candidate's race that must be the primary determinant of the voter's choice is unclear; indeed, their catalogs of relevant variables suggest both. Age, religion, income, and education seem most relevant to the voter; incumbency, campaign expenditures, name identification, and media use are pertinent to the candidate; and party affiliation could refer both to the voter and the candidate. In either case, we disagree: for purposes of §2, the legal concept of racially polarized voting incorporates neither causation nor intent. It means simply that the race of voters correlates with the selection of a certain candidate or candidates; that is, it refers to the situation where different races (or minority language groups) vote in blocs for different candidates. . . .

The first reason we reject appellants' argument that racially polarized voting refers to voting patterns that are in some way caused by race, rather than to voting patterns that are merely correlated with the race of the voter, is that the reasons black and white voters vote differently have no relevance to the central inquiry of §2. By contrast, the correlation between race of voter and the selection of certain candidates is crucial to that inquiry.

Both §2 itself and the Senate Report make clear that the critical question in a §2 claim is whether the use of a contested electoral practice or structure results in members of a protected group having less opportunity than other members of the electorate to participate in the political process and to elect representatives of their choice. As we explained, multimember districts may impair the ability of blacks to elect representatives of their choice where blacks vote sufficiently as a bloc as to be able to elect their preferred candidates in a black majority, single-member district and where a white majority votes sufficiently as a bloc usually to defeat the candidates chosen by blacks. It is the difference between the choices made by blacks and whites—not the reasons for that difference—that results in blacks having less opportunity than whites to elect their preferred

representatives. Consequently, we conclude that, under the "results test" of §2, only the correlation between race of voter and selection of certain candidates, not the causes of the correlation, matters.

The irrelevance to a §2 inquiry of the reasons why black and white voters vote differently supports, by itself, our rejection of appellants' theory of racially polarized voting. However, their theory contains other equally serious flaws that merit further attention. . . .

Appellants and the United States contend that the legal concept of "racially polarized voting" refers not to voting patterns that are merely correlated with the voter's race, but to voting patterns that are determined primarily by the voter's race, rather than by the voter's other socioeconomic characteristics.

The first problem with this argument is that it ignores the fact that members of geographically insular racial and ethnic groups frequently share socioeconomic characteristics, such as income level, employment status, amount of education, housing and other living conditions, religion, language, and so forth. Where such characteristics are shared, race or ethnic group not only denotes color or place of origin, it also functions as a shorthand notation for common social and economic characteristics. Appellants' definition of racially polarized voting is even more pernicious where shared characteristics are causally related to race or ethnicity. The opportunity to achieve high employment status and income, for example, is often influenced by the presence or absence of racial or ethnic discrimination. A definition of racially polarized voting which holds that black bloc voting does not exist when black voters' choice of certain candidates is most strongly influenced by the fact that the voters have low incomes and menial jobs—when the reason most of those voters have menial jobs and low incomes is attributable to past or present racial discrimination—runs counter to the Senate Report's instruction to conduct a searching and practical evaluation of past and present reality, and interferes with the purpose of the Voting Rights Act to eliminate the negative effects of past discrimination on the electoral opportunities of minorities.

Furthermore, under appellants' theory of racially polarized voting, even uncontrovertible evidence that candidates strongly preferred by black voters are always defeated by a bloc voting white majority would be dismissed for failure to prove racial polarization whenever the black and white populations could be described in terms of other socioeconomic characteristics.

. . .

According to appellants' theory of racially polarized voting, proof that black and white voters in this hypothetical district regularly choose different candidates, and that the blacks' preferred candidates regularly lose, could be rejected as not probative of racial bloc voting. The basis for the rejection would be that blacks chose a certain candidate not principally because of their race, but principally because this candidate best represented the interests of residents who, because of their low incomes, are particularly interested in government-subsidized health and welfare services; who are generally poorly educated, and thus share an interest in job training programs; who are, to a greater extent than the white community, concerned with rent control issues; and who favor major public transportation expenditures. Similarly, whites would be found to have voted for a different candidate, not principally because of their race, but primarily because that candidate best represented the interests of residents who, due to their education and income levels, and to their property and vehicle ownership, favor gentrification, low residential property

taxes, and extensive expenditures for street and highway improvements.

Congress could not have intended that courts employ this definition of racial bloc voting. First, this definition leads to results that are inconsistent with the effects test adopted by Congress when it amended §2 and with the Senate Report's admonition that courts take a "functional" view of the political process, and conduct a searching and practical evaluation of reality. . . .

Second, appellants' interpretation of "racially polarized voting" creates an irreconcilable tension between their proposed treatment of socioeconomic characteristics in the bloc voting context and the Senate Report's statement that

> the extent to which members of the minority group . . . bear the effects of discrimination in such areas as education, employment and health

may be relevant to a §2 claim. We can find no support in either logic or the legislative history for the anomalous conclusion to which appellants' position leads—that Congress intended, on the one hand, that proof that a minority group is predominately poor, uneducated, and unhealthy should be considered a factor tending to prove a §2 violation, but that Congress intended, on the other hand, that proof that the same socioeconomic characteristics greatly influence black voters' choice of candidates should destroy these voters' ability to establish one of the most important elements of a vote dilution claim.

North Carolina's and the United States' suggestion that racially polarized voting means that voters select or reject candidates principally on the basis of the candidate's race is also misplaced.

First, both the language of §2 and a functional understanding of the phenomenon of vote dilution mandate the conclusion that the race of the candidate per se is irrelevant to racial bloc voting analysis. Section 2(b) states that a violation is established if it can be shown that members of a protected minority group "have less opportunity than other members of the electorate to . . . elect representatives of their choice." Because both minority and majority voters often select members of their own race as their preferred representatives, it will frequently be the case that a black candidate is the choice of blacks, while a white candidate is the choice of whites. Indeed, the facts of this case illustrate that tendency—blacks preferred black candidates, whites preferred white candidates. Thus, as a matter of convenience, we and the District Court may refer to the preferred representative of black voters as the "black candidate" and to the preferred representative of white voters as the "white candidate." Nonetheless, the fact that race of voter and race of candidate is often correlated is not directly pertinent to a §2 inquiry. . . .

. . .

Finally, we reject the suggestion that racially polarized voting refers only to white bloc voting which is caused by white voters' racial hostility toward black candidates. To accept this theory would frustrate the goals Congress sought to achieve by repudiating the intent test of *Mobile v. Bolden*, and would prevent minority voters who have clearly been denied an opportunity to elect representatives of their choice from establishing a critical element of a vote dilution claim.

In amending §2, Congress rejected the requirement announced by this Court in *Bolden* that §2 plaintiffs must prove the discriminatory intent of state or local governments in adopting or maintaining the challenged electoral mechanism. Appellants' suggestion that the discriminatory intent of individual white voters must be proved in order to make out a §2 claim must fail for the very

reasons Congress rejected the intent test with respect to governmental bodies.

. . .

In sum, we would hold that the legal concept of racially polarized voting, as it relates to claims of vote dilution, refers only to the existence of a correlation between the race of voters and the selection of certain candidates. Plaintiffs need not prove causation or intent in order to prove a prima facie case of racial bloc voting, and defendants may not rebut that case with evidence of causation or intent.

. . .

The District Court did err, however, in ignoring the significance of the sustained success black voters have experienced in House District 23. In that district, the last six elections have resulted in proportional representation for black residents. This persistent proportional representation is inconsistent with appellees' allegation that the ability of black voters in District 23 to elect representatives of their choice is not equal to that enjoyed by the white majority.

In some situations, it may be possible for §2 plaintiffs to demonstrate that such sustained success does not accurately reflect the minority group's ability to elect its preferred representatives, but appellees have not done so here. Appellees presented evidence relating to black electoral success in the last three elections; they failed utterly, though, to offer any explanation for the success of black candidates in the previous three elections. Consequently, we believe that the District Court erred, as a matter of law, in ignoring the sustained success black voters have enjoyed in House District 23, and would reverse with respect to that District.

Finally, appellants and the United States dispute the District Court's ultimate conclusion that the multimember districting scheme at issue in

this case deprived black voters of an equal opportunity to participate in the political process
and to elect representatives of their choice.

. . .

The District Court in this case carefully considered the totality of the circumstances and found
that, in each district, racially polarized voting;
the legacy of official discrimination in voting
matters, education, housing, employment, and
health services; and the persistence of campaign
appeals to racial prejudice acted in concert with
the multimember districting scheme to impair the
ability of geographically insular and politically
cohesive groups of black voters to participate
equally in the political process and to elect candidates of their choice. It found that the success a
few black candidates have enjoyed in these districts is too recent, too limited, and, with regard
to the 1982 elections, perhaps too aberrational,
to disprove its conclusion. Excepting House District 23, with respect to which the District Court
committed legal error, we affirm the District
Court's judgment. We cannot say that the District Court, composed of local judges who are well
acquainted with the political realities of the State,
clearly erred in concluding that use of a
multimember electoral structure has caused black
voters in the districts other than House District
23 to have less opportunity than white voters to
elect representatives of their choice.

The judgment of the District Court is affirmed
in part and reversed in part.

Davis v. Bandemer
478 U.S. 109 (1986)

The Indiana Legislature, also known as the "General Assembly," consists of a House of Representatives and a Senate. There are 100 members
of the House of Representatives, and 50 members of the Senate. The members of the House
serve 2-year terms, with elections held for all seats
every two years. The members of the Senate serve
4-year terms, and Senate elections are staggered,
so that half of the seats are up for election every
two years. The members of both Houses are
elected from legislative districts, but, while all
Senate members are elected from single-member districts, House members are elected from a
mixture of single-member and multimember districts. The division of the State into districts is accomplished by legislative enactment, which is
signed by the Governor into law. Reapportionment
is required every 10 years, and is based on the federal decennial census. There is no prohibition
against more frequent reapportionments.

In early 1981, the General Assembly initiated
the process of reapportioning the State's legislative districts pursuant to the 1980 census. At this
time, there were Republican majorities in both
the House and the Senate, and the Governor was
Republican. Bills were introduced in both Houses,
and a reapportionment plan was duly passed and
approved by the Governor. This plan provided
50 single-member districts for the Senate; for the
House, it provided 7 triple-member, 9 double-
member, and 61 single-member districts. In the
Senate plan, the population deviation between
districts was 1.15 percent; in the House plan, the
deviation was 1.05 percent. The multimember
districts generally included the more metropolitan areas of the State, although not every metropolitan area was in a multimember district.
Marion County, which includes Indianapolis, was
combined with portions of its neighboring counties to form five triple-member districts. Fort
Wayne was divided into two parts, and each part
was combined with portions of the surrounding
county or counties to make two triple-member

districts. On the other hand, South Bend was divided and put partly into a double-member district and partly into a single-member district (each part combined with part of the surrounding county or counties). Although county and city lines were not consistently followed, township lines generally were. The two plans, the Senate and the House, were not nested—that is, each Senate district was not divided exactly into two House districts. There appears to have been little relation between the lines drawn in the two plans.

In early 1982, this suit was filed by several Indiana Democrats (here the appellees) against various state officials (here the appellants), alleging that the 1981 reapportionment plans constituted a political gerrymander intended to disadvantage Democrats. Specifically, they contended that the particular district lines that were drawn and the mix of single-member and multimember districts were intended to, and did, violate their right, as Democrats, to equal protection under the Fourteenth Amendment. A three-judge District Court was convened to hear these claims.

In November 1982, before the case went to trial, elections were held under the new districting plan. All of the House seats and half of the Senate seats were up for election. Over all the House races statewide, Democratic candidates received 51.9 percent of the vote. Only 43 Democrats, however, were elected to the House. Over all the Senate races statewide, Democratic candidates received 53.1percent of the vote. Thirteen (of twenty-five) Democrats were elected. In Marion and Allen Counties, both divided into multimember House districts, Democratic candidates drew 46.6 percent of the vote, but only 3 of the 21 House seats were filled by Democrats.

On December 13, 1984, a divided District Court issued a decision declaring the reapportionment to be unconstitutional, enjoining the appellants from holding elections pursuant to the 1981 redistricting, ordering the General Assembly to prepare a new plan, and retaining jurisdiction over the case.

To the District Court majority, the results of the 1982 elections seemed "to support an argument that there is a built-in bias favoring the majority party, the Republicans, which instituted the reapportionment plan." Although the court thought that these figures were unreliable predictors of future elections, it concluded that they warranted further examination of the circumstances surrounding the passage of the reapportionment statute. In the course of this further examination, the court noted the irregular shape of some district lines, the peculiar mix of single-member and multimember districts, and the failure of the district lines to adhere consistently to political subdivision boundaries to define communities of interest. The court also found inadequate the other explanations given for the configuration of the districts, such as adherence to the one person, one vote imperative and the Voting Rights Act's no-retrogression requirement. These factors, concluded the court, evidenced an intentional effort to favor Republican incumbents and candidates and to disadvantage Democratic voters. This was achieved by "stacking" Democrats into districts with large Democratic majorities and "splitting" them in other districts, so as to give Republicans safe but not excessive majorities in those districts. Because the 1982 elections indicated that the plan also had a discriminatory effect, in that the proportionate voting influence of Democratic voters had been adversely affected and because any scheme "which purposely inhibit[s] or prevent[s] proportional representation cannot be tolerated," the District Court invalidated the statute.

The defendants appealed. . . .

. . .

Having determined that the political gerrymandering claim in this case is justiciable, we turn to the question whether the District Court erred in holding that the appellees had alleged and proved a violation of the Equal Protection Clause.

. . .

The typical election for legislative seats in the United States is conducted in described geographical districts, with the candidate receiving the most votes in each district winning the seat allocated to that district. If all or most of the districts are competitive—defined by the District Court in this case as districts in which the anticipated split in the party vote is within the range of 45 percent to 55 percent—even a narrow statewide preference for either party would produce an overwhelming majority for the winning party in the state legislature. This consequence, however, is inherent in winner-take-all, district-based elections, and we cannot hold that such a reapportionment law would violate the Equal Protection Clause because the voters in the losing party do not have representation in the legislature in proportion to the statewide vote received by their party candidates. . . . This is true of a racial, as well as a political, group. It is also true of a statewide claim as well as an individual district claim.

To draw district lines to maximize the representation of each major party would require creating as many safe seats for each party as the demographic and predicted political characteristics of the State would permit. This, in turn, would leave the minority in each safe district without a representative of its choice. We upheld this "political fairness" approach in *Gaffney v. Cummings*, despite its tendency to deny safe district minorities any realistic chance to elect their own representatives. But *Gaffney* in no way suggested that

the Constitution requires the approach that Connecticut had adopted in that case.

In cases involving individual multimember districts, we have required a substantially greater showing of adverse effects than a mere lack of proportional representation to support a finding of unconstitutional vote dilution. Only where there is evidence that excluded groups have "less opportunity to participate in the political processes and to elect candidates of their choice" have we refused to approve the use of multimember districts. In these cases, we have also noted the lack of responsiveness by those elected to the concerns of the relevant groups.

These holdings rest on a conviction that the mere fact that a particular apportionment scheme makes it more difficult for a particular group in a particular district to elect the representatives of its choice does not render that scheme constitutionally infirm. This conviction, in turn, stems from a perception that the power to influence the political process is not limited to winning elections. An individual or a group of individuals who votes for a losing candidate is usually deemed to be adequately represented by the winning candidate, and to have as much opportunity to influence that candidate as other voters in the district. We cannot presume in such a situation, without actual proof to the contrary, that the candidate elected will entirely ignore the interests of those voters. This is true even in a safe district where the losing group loses election after election. Thus, a group's electoral power is not unconstitutionally diminished by the simple fact of an apportionment scheme that makes winning elections more difficult, and a failure of proportional representation alone does not constitute impermissible discrimination under the Equal Protection Clause.

As with individual districts, where unconstitutional vote dilution is alleged in the form of statewide political gerrymandering, the mere lack of proportional representation will not be sufficient to prove unconstitutional discrimination. Again, without specific supporting evidence, a court cannot presume in such a case that those who are elected will disregard the disproportionately underrepresented group. Rather, unconstitutional discrimination occurs only when the electoral system is arranged in a manner that will consistently degrade a voter's or a group of voters' influence on the political process as a whole.

Although this is a somewhat different formulation than we have previously used in describing unconstitutional vote dilution in an individual district, the focus of both of these inquiries is essentially the same. In both contexts, the question is whether a particular group has been unconstitutionally denied its chance to effectively influence the political process. In a challenge to an individual district, this inquiry focuses on the opportunity of members of the group to participate in party deliberations in the slating and nomination of candidates, their opportunity to register and vote, and hence their chance to directly influence the election returns and to secure the attention of the winning candidate. Statewide, however, the inquiry centers on the voters' direct or indirect influence on the elections of the state legislature as a whole. And, as in individual district cases, an equal protection violation may be found only where the electoral system substantially disadvantages certain voters in their opportunity to influence the political process effectively. In this context, such a finding of unconstitutionality must be supported by evidence of continued frustration of the will of a majority of the voters or effective denial to a minority of voters of a fair chance to influence the political process.

Based on these views, we would reject the District Court's apparent holding that any interference with an opportunity to elect a representative of one's choice would be sufficient to allege or make out an equal protection violation, unless justified by some acceptable state interest that the State would be required to demonstrate. In addition to being contrary to the above-described conception of an unconstitutional political gerrymander, such a low threshold for legal action would invite attack on all or almost all reapportionment statutes. District-based elections hardly ever produce a perfect fit between votes and representation. The one person, one vote imperative often mandates departure from this result, as does the no-retrogression rule required by §5 of the Voting Rights Act. Inviting attack on minor departures from some supposed norm would too much embroil the judiciary in second-guessing what has consistently been referred to as a political task for the legislature, a task that should not be monitored too closely unless the express or tacit goal is to effect its removal from legislative halls. We decline to take a major step toward that end which would be so much at odds with our history and experience.

. . .

Relying on a single election to prove unconstitutional discrimination is unsatisfactory. The District Court observed, and the parties do not disagree, that Indiana is a swing State. Voters sometimes prefer Democratic candidates, and sometimes Republican. The District Court did not find that, because of the 1981 Act, the Democrats could not, in one of the next few elections, secure a sufficient vote to take control of the assembly. Indeed, the District Court declined to hold that the 1982 election results were the predictable consequences of the 1981 Act, and expressly refused to hold that those results were a reliable prediction of future ones. The District Court did not ask by what percentage the state-wide Democratic vote would have had to increase to control either the House or the Senate. The appellants argue here, without a persuasive response from the appellees, that, had the Democratic candidates received an additional few percentage points of the votes cast statewide, they would have obtained a majority of the seats in both houses. Nor was there any finding that the 1981 reapportionment would consign the Democrats to a minority status in the Assembly throughout the 1980s, or that the Democrats would have no hope of doing any better in the reapportionment that would occur after the 1990 census. Without findings of this nature, the District Court erred in concluding that the 1981 Act violated the Equal Protection Clause.

The District Court's discussion of the multimember districts created by the 1981 Act does not undermine this conclusion. For the purposes of the statewide political gerrymandering claim, these districts appear indistinguishable from safe Republican and safe Democratic single-member districts. Simply showing that there are multimember districts in the State, and that those districts are constructed so as to be safely Republican or Democratic, in no way bolsters the contention that there has been statewide discrimination against Democratic voters. It could be, were the necessary threshold effect to be shown, that multimember districts could be demonstrated to be suspect on the ground that they are particularly useful in attaining impermissibly discriminatory ends; at this stage of the inquiry, however, the multimember district evidence does not materially aid the appellees' case.

. . .

This participatory approach to the legality of individual multimember districts is not helpful where the claim is that such districts discriminate against Democrats, for it could hardly be said that Democrats, any more than Republicans, are excluded from participating in the affairs of their own party or from the processes by which candidates are nominated and elected. For constitutional purposes, the Democratic claim in this case, insofar as it challenges vel non the legality of the multimember districts in certain counties, is like that of the Negroes in Whitcomb who failed to prove a racial gerrymander, for it boils down to a complaint that they failed to attract a majority of the voters in the challenged multimember districts.

. . .

Moreover, as we discussed above, a mere lack of proportionate results in one election cannot suffice in this regard. We have reached this conclusion in our cases involving challenges to individual multimember districts, and it applies equally here. In the individual multimember district cases, we have found equal protection violations only where a history of disproportionate results appeared in conjunction with strong indicia of lack of political power and the denial of fair representation. In those cases, the racial minorities asserting the successful equal protection claims had essentially been shut out of the political process. In the statewide political gerrymandering context, these prior cases lead to the analogous conclusion that equal protection violations may be found only where a history (actual or projected) of disproportionate results appears in conjunction with similar indicia. The mere lack of control of the General Assembly after a single election does not rise to the requisite level.

. . .

In sum, we decline to adopt the approach enunciated by Justice Powell. In our view, that approach departs from our past cases and invites judicial interference in legislative districting whenever a political party suffers at the polls. We recognize that our own view may be difficult of application. Determining when an electoral system has been "arranged in a manner that will consistently degrade a voter's or a group of voters' influence on the political process as a whole," is of necessity a difficult inquiry. Nevertheless, we believe that it recognizes the delicacy of intruding on this most political of legislative functions, and is at the same time consistent with our prior cases regarding individual multimember districts, which have formulated a parallel standard.

In sum, we hold that political gerrymandering cases are properly justiciable under the Equal Protection Clause. We also conclude, however, that a threshold showing of discriminatory vote dilution is required for a prima facie case of an equal protection violation. In this case, the findings made by the District Court of an adverse effect on the appellees do not surmount the threshold requirement. Consequently, the judgment of the District Court is reversed.

Board of Estimate of City of New York v. Morris
489 U.S. 688 (1989)

Appellees, residents and voters of Brooklyn, New York City's most populous borough, commenced this action against the city in December 1981. They charged that the city's charter sections that govern the composition of the Board of Estimate are inconsistent with the Equal Protection Clause of the Fourteenth Amendment as construed and applied in various decisions of this Court dealing with districting and apportionment for the purpose of electing legislative bodies. The District Court dismissed the complaint on the ground

that the board was not subject to the rule established by *Reynolds v. Sims*, its companion cases, and its progeny, such as *Abate v. Mundt*, because, in its view, the board is a nonelective, nonlegislative body. The Court of Appeals reversed. Because all eight officials on the board ultimately are selected by popular vote, the court concluded that the board's selection process must comply with the so-called "one-person, one-vote" requirement of the reapportionment cases. The court remanded to the District Court to ascertain whether this compliance exists. Bifurcating the proceedings, the District Court determined, first, that applying this Court's methodology in *Abate v. Mundt*, to the disparate borough populations produced a total deviation of 132.9 percent from voter equality among these electorates, and, second, that the city's several explanations for this range neither require nor justify the electoral scheme's gross deviation from equal representation. The court thus found it unnecessary to hold that the deviation it identified was per se unconstitutional.

The Court of Appeals affirmed. Tracing the imperative of each citizen's equal power to elect representatives from *Reynolds* to *Abate* and beyond, the court endorsed the District Court's focus on population per representative. The court held that the presence of the citywide representatives did not warrant departure from the *Abate* approach, and that the District Court's finding of a 132 percent deviation was correct. Without deciding whether this gross deviation could ever be justified in light of the flexibility accorded to local governments in ordering their affairs, the Court of Appeals, agreeing with the District Court, held inadequate the city's justifications for its departure from the equal protection requirement that elective legislative bodies be chosen from districts substantially equal in population, especially since alternative measures could address the city's valid policy concerns and at the same time lessen the discrimination against voters in the more populous districts. . . .

As an initial matter, we reject the city's suggestion that, because the Board of Estimate is a unique body wielding nonlegislative powers, board membership elections are not subject to review under the prevailing reapportionment doctrine. The equal protection guarantee of "one-person, one-vote" extends not only to congressional districting plans, not only to state legislative districting, but also to local government apportionment. Both state and local elections are subject to the general rule of population equality between electoral districts. No distinction between authority exercised by state assemblies and the general governmental powers delegated by these assemblies to local, elected officials, suffices to insulate the latter from the standard of substantial voter equality. . . .

· · ·

We note that no case of ours has indicated that a deviation of some 78 percent could ever be justified. At the very least, the local government seeking to support such a difference between electoral districts would bear a very difficult burden, and we are not prepared to differ with the holding of the courts below that this burden has not been carried. The city presents in this Court nothing that was not considered below, arguing chiefly that the board, as presently structured, is essential to the successful government of a regional entity, the city of New York. The board, it is said, accommodates natural and political boundaries, as well as local interests. Furthermore, because the board has been effective, it should not be disturbed. All of this, the city urges, is supported by the city's history. The courts below, of course, are in a much better position than we to assess the weight of these arguments, and they concluded that the proffered governmental interests

were either invalid or were not sufficient to justify a deviation of 132 percent, in part because the valid interests of the city could be served by alternative ways of constituting the board that would minimize the discrimination in voting power among the five boroughs. Their analysis is equally applicable to a 78 percent deviation, and we conclude that the city's proffered governmental interests do not suffice to justify such a substantial departure from the one-person, one-vote ideal.

Accordingly the judgment of the Court of Appeals is affirmed.

Quinn v. Millsap
491 U.S. 95 (1989)

The constitution of the State of Missouri provides that the governments of the city of St. Louis and St. Louis County may be reorganized by a vote of the electorate of the city and county upon a plan of reorganization drafted by a "board of free-holders." Appellants contend that this provision violates the Equal Protection Clause of the Fourteenth Amendment to the United States Constitution because it requires that every member of this official board own real property. The Supreme Court of Missouri, without disputing appellants' premise that ownership of real property is a prerequisite for appointment to the board of free-holders, ruled that "the Equal Protection Clause has no relevancy here" because the board "exercises no general governmental powers." . . .

In 1987, pursuant to Art. VI, §30, of the Missouri Constitution, a sufficient number of voters signed petitions "to establish a board of St. Louis area property owners (freeholders)" to consider the reorganization of "governmental structures and responsibilities" for the city and county. As a result, under §30, the city's mayor and the county executive were required each to appoint nine members to this board, and the Governor was required to appoint one.

After the mayor had chosen nine individuals based on several criteria, including a history of community service and demonstrated leadership ability, he was informed by the city's counsel that ownership of real property was a prerequisite for board membership. One of the persons selected by the mayor, Reinert, did not own real property. He was removed from the mayor's list and replaced with an appointee who satisfied the real property requirement.

The county executive similarly was told by the county's counsel that real property ownership was a necessary condition for board membership. The Governor also considered real property ownership as a necessary qualification. Thus, all 19 members appointed to the board of freeholders in 1987 owned real property, as was inevitable given the prevailing belief that §30 required this result.

In November 1987, appellants Quinn and Kampsen filed in the United States District Court for the Western District of Missouri a class action complaint on behalf of all Missouri voters who did not own real property. Appellants claimed that §30 violated the Equal Protection Clause of the Fourteenth Amendment on its face, insofar as it required ownership of real property in order to serve on the board that was to consider proposals for reorganizing the St. Louis city and county governments. Appellants also claimed that §30 violated the Equal Protection Clause as applied, because in this instance "appointment to the board [of freeholders] was actually limited to those who were ascertained to be owners of real property." . . .

. . .

Once the property qualification issue became

embroiled in litigation, the official view of §30 changed. Whereas the mayor, the county executive, and the Governor all had assumed during the appointment process that ownership of real property was a prerequisite for board membership, they (together with the other appellees) have argued in court that the use of the term "freeholder" in §30—contrary to its generally accepted meaning—does not entail a condition of property ownership. Because §30(a) states that "a board of freeholders" shall consist of "nine . . . electors of the city and nine electors of the county and one . . . elector of some other county," appellees contend that the only qualification necessary for appointment to a board of freeholders is that one be an "elector" of a relevant jurisdiction.

Based on their contention that the meaning of "freeholder" in §30 is an unsettled question of state law, appellees urged the Federal District Court to abstain from adjudicating the merits of appellants' complaint while the state court proceeding was pending. The District Court refused to abstain, finding appellees' interpretation of the term "freeholder" to be "strained at best" and contrary both to the generally recognized meaning of the term and to its use in Missouri decisional law. Reaching the merits of appellants' constitutional claim, the court agreed with appellants that . . . §30 (construed to contain a property requirement) violates the Equal Protection Clause. The Federal Court of Appeals, after a preliminary order, reversed, holding that the District Court should have abstained.

. . .

The Missouri Supreme Court affirmed this judgment, but relied exclusively on its interpretation of the Equal Protection Clause. The court did not address the argument that §30 does not impose a property ownership requirement, except to say: "We recognize membership on the Board of Freeholders was restricted to owners of real property." . . . Thus, the Missouri Supreme Court rejected both the facial and as-applied challenges to §30 based on its belief that the Equal Protection Clause was inapplicable to the board of freeholders.

Contesting the Missouri Supreme Court's interpretation of the Equal Protection Clause, appellants filed the appeal now before us. . . .

. . .

In holding the board of freeholders exempt from the constraints of the Equal Protection Clause, the Missouri Supreme Court also relied on the fact that the "Board of Freeholders serves only to recommend a plan of reorganization to the voters of St. Louis City and St. Louis County," and does not enact any laws of its own. But this fact cannot immunize the board of freeholders from equal protection scrutiny. . . . Membership on the board of freeholders is a form of public service, even if the board only recommends a proposal to the electorate, and does not enact laws directly. Thus, the Equal Protection Clause protects appellants' right to be considered for appointment to the board without the burden of "invidiously discriminatory disqualifications."

The rationale of the Missouri Supreme Court's contrary decision would render the Equal Protection Clause inapplicable even to a requirement that all members of the board be white males. This result, and the reasoning that leads to it, are obviously untenable. Thus, we conclude that it is incorrect to say, as that court did, that the Equal Protection Clause does not apply to the board of freeholders because the electorate votes on its proposals and it "does not exercise general governmental powers." The board in this case . . . is subject to the constraints of the Equal Protection Clause.

The question, of course, remains whether the land ownership requirement in this particular case passes or fails equal protection scrutiny. . . .

. . .

. . . The purpose of the board of freeholders . . . is not so directly linked with land ownership. Even if the board of freeholders considers land use issues, the scope of its mandate is far more encompassing: it has the power to draft and submit a plan to reorganize the entire governmental structure of St. Louis city and county. The work of the board of freeholders thus affects all citizens of the city and county, regardless of land ownership. Consequently, Missouri cannot entirely exclude from eligibility for appointment to this board all persons who do not own real property, regardless of their other qualifications and their demonstrated commitment to their community.

In sum, we cannot agree with appellees that, under the Equal Protection Clause as previously construed by this Court, landowners alone may be eligible for appointment to a body empowered to propose a wholesale revision of local government. . . .

The judgment of the Missouri Supreme Court is reversed.

Presley v. Etowah County Commission
502 U.S. 491 (1992)

In various Alabama counties, voters elect members of county commissions whose principal function is to supervise and control the maintenance, repair, and construction of the county roads. The consolidated appeals now before us concern certain changes in the decisionmaking authority of the elected members on two different county commissions, and the question to be decided is whether these were changes "with respect to voting" within the meaning of §5 of the

Voting Rights Act. The case has significance well beyond the two county commissions, for the appellants, and the United States as amicus curiae, ask us to adopt a rule embracing the routine actions of state and local governments at all levels. We must interpret the provisions of §5, which require a jurisdiction covered by the Act to obtain either judicial or administrative preclearance before enforcing any new "voting qualification or prerequisite to voting, or standard, practice, or procedure with respect to voting."

. . .

We consider first the Etowah County Commission. On November 1, 1964, commission members were elected at large under a "residency district" system. The entire electorate of Etowah County voted on candidates for each of the five seats. Four of the seats corresponded to the four residency districts of the county. Candidates were required to reside in the appropriate district. The fifth member, the chairman, was not subject to a district residency requirement, though residency in the county itself was a requirement.

. . .

Under a consent decree issued in 1986, the commission is being restructured, so that, after a transition period, there will be a six-member commission, with each of the members elected by the voters of a different district. The changes required by the consent decree were precleared by the Attorney General. For present purposes, it suffices to say that, when this litigation began, the commission consisted of four holdover members who had been on the commission before the entry of the consent decree and two new members elected from new districts. Commissioner Williams, who is white, was elected from new district 6, and Commissioner Presley, who is black, was elected from new district 5. Presley is the principal appellant in the Etowah County case.

His complaint relates . . . to actions taken by the four holdover members when he and Williams first took office.

On August 25, 1987, the commission passed the "Road Supervision Resolution." It provided that each holdover commissioner would continue to control the workers and operations assigned to his respective road shop, which, it must be remembered, accounted for all the road shops the county had. It also gave the four holdovers joint responsibility for overseeing the repair, maintenance, and improvement of all the roads of Etowah County in order to pick up the roads in the districts where the new commissioners resided. The new commissioners, now foreclosed from exercising any authority over roads, were given other functions under the resolution. Presley was to oversee maintenance of the county courthouse and Williams the operation of the engineering department. . . .

The same day the Road Supervision Resolution was passed, the commission passed a second, the so-called "Common Fund Resolution." . . . This had the effect of altering the prior practice of allowing each commissioner full authority to determine how to spend the funds allocated to his own district. The Etowah County Commission did not seek judicial or administrative preclearance of either the Road Supervision Resolution or the Common Fund Resolution. The District Court held that the Road Supervision Resolution was subject to preclearance, but that the Common Fund Resolution was not. No appeal was taken from the first ruling, so only the Common Fund Resolution is before us in the Etowah County case.

. . .

In May 1989, the appellants in both cases now before us filed a single complaint in the District Court for the Middle District of Alabama, alleg-

274 CHAPTER 3: APPORTIONMENT AND REDISTRICTING

ing racial discrimination in the operation of the Etowah and Russell County Commissions in violation of prior court orders, the Constitution, Title VI of the Civil Rights Act of 1964 and §2 of the Voting Rights Act. In a series of amended complaints, the appellants added claims under §5. The §5 claims alleged that Etowah County had violated the Act by failing to obtain preclearance of the 1987 Road Supervision and Common Fund Resolutions, and that Russell County had failed to preclear the 1979 change to the Unit System. . . . [A] three-judge District Court was convened to hear the appellants' §5 claims. . . .

. . .

. . . Innumerable state and local enactments having nothing to do with voting affect the power of elected officials. When a state or local body adopts a new governmental program or modifies an existing one, it will often be the case that it changes the powers of elected officials. So too, when a state or local body alters its internal operating procedures, for example by modifying its subcommittee assignment system, it "implicate[s] an elected official's decisionmaking authority."

. . .

Changes which affect only the distribution of power among officials are not subject to §5, because such changes have no direct relation to, or impact on, voting. The Etowah County Commission's Common Fund Resolution was not subject to the preclearance requirement.

We next consider Russell County's adoption of the Unit System and its concomitant transfer of operations to the county engineer. . . .

The change in Russell County does not prohibit voters "from electing an officer formerly subject to the[ir] approval." Both before and after the change, the citizens of Russell County were able to vote for the members of the Russell County Commission. To be sure, after the 1979

resolution, each commissioner exercised less direct authority over road operations, that authority having been delegated to an official answerable to the commission. But as we concluded with respect to Etowah County, the fact that an enactment alters an elected official's powers does not, in itself, render the enactment a rule governing voting.

It is a routine part of governmental administration for appointive positions to be created or eliminated, and for their powers to be altered. Each time this occurs, the relative balance of authority is altered in some way. The making or unmaking of an appointive post often will result in the erosion or accretion of the powers of some official responsible to the electorate, but it does not follow that those changes are covered by §5. By requiring preclearance of changes with respect to voting, Congress did not mean to subject such routine matters of governance to federal supervision. Were the rule otherwise, neither state nor local governments could exercise power in a responsible manner within a federal system.

The District Court, wrestling with the problem we now face and recognizing the need to draw principled lines, held that Russell County's adoption of the Unit System is not a covered change, because it did not transfer power among officials answerable to different constituencies. Even upon the assumption (the assumption we reject in this case) that some transfers of power among government officials could be changes with respect to voting as that term is used in the Act, we disagree with the District Court's test. The question whether power is shifted among officials answerable to the same or different constituencies is quite distinct from the question whether the power voters exercise over elected officials is affected. Intraconstituency changes may have a large indirect effect on the voters, while interconstituency changes may have a small indirect effect, but in neither case is the effect a change in voting for purposes of the Act. The test adopted by the District Court does not provide the workable rule we seek. In any event, because it proceeds from the faulty premise that reallocations of authority within government can constitute voting changes, we cannot accept its approach.

. . .

. . . The Voting Rights Act is not an all-purpose antidiscrimination statute. The fact that the intrusive mechanisms of the Act do not apply to other forms of pernicious discrimination does not undermine its utility in combating the specific evils it was designed to address.

Our prior cases hold, and we reaffirm today, that every change in rules governing voting must be precleared. . . .

If federalism is to operate as a practical system of governance and not a mere poetic ideal, the States must be allowed both predictability and efficiency in structuring their governments. Constant minor adjustments in the allocation of power among state and local officials serve this elemental purpose.

Covered changes must bear a direct relation to voting itself. That direct relation is absent in both cases now before us. The changes in Etowah and Russell Counties affected only the allocation of power among governmental officials. They had no impact on the substantive question whether a particular office would be elective or the procedural question how an election would be conducted. Neither change involves a new "voting qualification or prerequisite to voting, or standard, practice, or procedure with respect to voting."

The judgment of the District Court is affirmed.

Growe v. Emison
507 U.S. 25 (1993)

In January 1991, a group of Minnesota voters filed a state court action against the Minnesota Secretary of State and other officials responsible for administering elections, claiming that the State's congressional and legislative districts were malapportioned, in violation of the Fourteenth Amendment of the Federal Constitution and Article 4, §2, of the Minnesota Constitution. The plaintiffs asserted that the 1990 federal census results revealed a significant change in the distribution of the State population, and requested that the court declare the current districts unlawful and draw new districts if the Legislature failed to do so. In February, the parties stipulated that, in light of the new census, the challenged districting plans were unconstitutional. The Minnesota Supreme Court appointed a Special Redistricting Panel . . . to preside over the case.

In March, a second group of plaintiffs filed an action in federal court against essentially the same defendants, raising similar challenges to the congressional and legislative districts. The Emison plaintiffs (who include members of various racial minorities) in addition raised objections to the legislative districts under §2 of the Voting Rights Act, alleging that those districts needlessly fragmented two Indian reservations and divided the minority population of Minneapolis. The suit sought declaratory relief and continuing federal jurisdiction over any legislative efforts to develop new districts. . . .

While the federal and state actions were getting underway, the Minnesota Legislature was holding public hearings on, and designing, new legislative districts. In May, it adopted a new legislative districting plan and repealed the prior 1983 apportionment. . . .

Later in August, another group of plaintiffs filed a second action in federal court, again against the Minnesota Secretary of State. The Benson plaintiffs, who include the Republican minority leaders of the Minnesota Senate and House, raised federal and state constitutional challenges to Chapter 246, but no Voting Rights Act allegations. The Benson action was consolidated with the Emison suit; the Cotlow plaintiffs, as well as the Minnesota House of Representatives and State Senate, intervened.

With the Legislature out of session, the committees' proposed curative measures for Chapter 246 pending, and the state court in Cotlow considering many of the same issues, the District Court granted the defendants' motion to defer further proceedings pending action by the Minnesota Legislature. It denied, however, defendants' motion to abstain in light of the Cotlow suit, or to allow the state court first to review any legislative action or, if the Legislature failed to act, to allow the state court first to issue a court-ordered redistricting plan. The District Court set a January 20, 1992, deadline for the state Legislature's action on both redistricting plans, and appointed special masters to develop contingent plans in the event the Legislature failed to correct Chapter 246 or to reapportion Minnesota's eight congressional districts.

Meanwhile, the Cotlow panel concluded . . . that Chapter 246, applied as written (i.e., with its drafting errors), violated both the State and Federal Constitutions, and invited the parties to submit alternative legislative plans based on Chapter 246. It also directed the parties to submit by mid-October written arguments on any Chapter 246 violations of the Voting Rights Act. In late November, the state court issued an order containing its preliminary legislative redistricting plan—essentially Chapter 246 with the technical

corrections . . . contained in Senate File 1596. (Since no party had responded to its order concerning Voting Rights Act violations, the court concluded that Chapter 246 did not run afoul of that Act.) It proposed putting its plan into effect on January 21, 1992, if the Legislature had not acted by then. Two weeks later, after further argument, the Cotlow panel indicated it would release a revised and final version of its legislative redistricting plan in a few days.

In early December, before the state court issued its final plan, the District Court stayed all proceedings in the Cotlow case and enjoined parties to that action. . . . The court explained its action as necessary to prevent the state court from interfering with the Legislature's efforts to redistrict and with the District Court's jurisdiction. It mentioned the Emison Voting Rights Act allegations as grounds for issuing the injunction, which it found necessary in aid of its jurisdiction.

Four days later, the state court issued an order containing its final legislative plan, subject to the District Court's injunction and still conditioned on the Legislature's failure to adopt a lawful plan. The same order provided, again subject to the District Court's injunction, that congressional redistricting plans be submitted by mid-January. The obstacle of the District Court injunction was removed on January 10, 1992, when, upon application of the Cotlow plaintiffs, we vacated the injunction.

When the Legislature reconvened in January, both houses approved the corrections to Chapter 246 contained in Senate File 1596, and also adopted a congressional redistricting plan that legislative committees had drafted the previous October. The Governor, however, vetoed the legislation. On January 30, the state court issued a final order adopting its legislative plan and requiring that to be used for the 1992 primary and general elections. By February 6, pursuant to an order issued shortly after this Court vacated the injunction, the parties had submitted their proposals for congressional redistricting, and, on February 17, the state court held hearings on the competing plans.

Two days later, the District Court issued an order adopting its own legislative and congressional districting plans and permanently enjoining interference with state implementation of those plans. The Emison panel found that the state court's modified version of Chapter 246 "fails to provide the equitable relief necessary to cure the violation of the Voting Rights Act," which, in its view, required at least one "super-majority minority" Senate district, a district in which the minority constitutes a clear majority. The District Court rejected Chapter 246 as a basis for its plan, and instead referred to state policy as expressed in the Minnesota Constitution and in a resolution adopted by both houses of the Legislature. . . . The District Court was unanimous . . . in its adoption of a congressional redistricting plan, after concluding that the preexisting 1982 plan violated Art. I, §2 of the Federal Constitution. Although it had received the same proposed plans submitted to the state court earlier that month, it used instead a congressional plan prepared by its special masters. Finally, the District Court retained jurisdiction to ensure adoption of its reapportionment plans and to enforce the permanent injunction.

In early March, the state court indicated that it was "fully prepared to release a congressional plan," but that the federal injunction prevented it from doing so. In its view, the federal plan reached population equality "without sufficient regard for the preservation of municipal and county boundaries."

Appellants sought a stay of the District Court's February order pending this appeal. Justice Blackmun granted the stay with respect to the legislative redistricting plan. . . .

. . .

. . . [T]he District Court's December injunction of state court proceedings, vacated by this Court in January, was clear error. It seems to have been based upon the mistaken view that federal judges need defer only to the Minnesota Legislature, and not at all to the State's courts. Thus, the January 20 deadline the District Court established was described as a deadline for the Legislature, ignoring the possibility and legitimacy of state judicial redistricting. And the injunction itself treated the state court's provisional legislative redistricting plan as "interfering" in the reapportionment process. . . . The Minnesota Special Redistricting Panel's issuance of its plan . . . far from being a federally enjoinable "interference," was precisely the sort of state judicial supervision of redistricting we have encouraged.

. . .

. . . Our consideration of this appeal, long after the Minnesota primary and final elections have been held, itself reflects the improbability of completing judicial review before the necessary deadline for a new redistricting scheme.

. . .

With respect to the congressional plan, the District Court did not ignore any state court judgment, but only because it had actively prevented such a judgment from issuing. The wrongfully entered December injunction prevented the Special Redistricting Panel from developing a contingent plan for congressional redistricting, as it had for legislative redistricting prior to the injunction. The state court's December order to the parties for mid-January submission of congressional plans was rendered a nullity by the injunction, which was not vacated until January 10. The net effect was a delay of at least a few weeks in the submissions to the state court, and in hearings on those submissions. . . . It would have been appropriate for the District Court to establish a deadline by which, if the Special Redistricting Panel had not acted, the federal court would proceed. But the January 20 deadline that the District Court established here was explicitly directed solely at the Legislature. The state court was never given a time by which it should decide on reapportionment, legislative or congressional, if it wished to avoid federal intervention.

Of course the District Court would have been justified in adopting its own plan if had been apparent that the state court, through no fault of the District Court itself, would not develop a redistricting plan in time for the primaries. . . . The record simply does not support a conclusion that the state court was either unwilling or unable to adopt a congressional plan in time for the elections. What occurred here was not a last-minute federal court rescue of the Minnesota electoral process, but a race to beat the Minnesota Special Redistricting Panel to the finish line. That would have been wrong, even if the Panel had not been tripped earlier in the course. The District Court erred in not deferring to the state court's timely consideration of congressional reapportionment.

. . .

As an initial matter, it is not clear precisely which legislative districting plan produced the vote dilution that necessitated the supermajority remedy. For almost a decade prior to the 1992 election season, the only legislative districting plan that had been in use in Minnesota was the 1983 plan, which all parties agreed was unconstitutional in light of the 1990 census. More importantly, the state court had declared the 1983 plan to be unconstitutional in its final order of January 30. Once that order issued, the Emison

plaintiffs' claims that the 1983 plan violated the Voting Rights Act became moot, unless those claims also related to the superseding plan. But no party to this litigation has ever alleged that either Chapter 246 or the modified version of Chapter 246 adopted by the state court resulted in vote dilution. The District Court did not hold a hearing or request written argument from the parties on the §2 validity of any particular plan; nor does the District Court's discussion focus on any particular plan.

. . . The District Court was of the view . . . that any legislative plan lacking a supermajority minority Senate district in Minneapolis violated §2. . . .

. . .

In the present case, even if we make the dubious assumption that the minority voters were "geographically compact," there was quite obviously a higher-than-usual need for the second of the *Gingles* showings. . . . Since a court may not presume bloc voting within even a single minority group, it made no sense for the District Court to (in effect) indulge that presumption as to bloc voting within an agglomeration of distinct minority groups.

We are satisfied that, in the present case, the *Gingles* preconditions were not only ignored, but were unattainable. As the District Court acknowledged, the record simply "contains no statistical evidence" of minority political cohesion . . . or of majority bloc voting in Minneapolis. . . .

The District Court erred in not deferring to the state court's efforts to redraw Minnesota's state legislative and federal congressional districts. Its conclusion that the state court's legislative districting plan . . . violated §2 of the Voting Rights Act was also erroneous. . . .

The judgment is reversed, and the case is remanded with instructions to dismiss.

Voinovich v. Quilter
507 U.S. 146 (1993)

Under the Ohio Constitution, the state apportionment board must reapportion electoral districts for the state legislature every 10 years. In 1991, the board selected James Tilling to draft a proposed apportionment plan. After conducting public hearings and meeting with members of historically underrepresented groups, Tilling drafted a plan that included eight so-called majority-minority districts—districts in which a majority of the population is a member of a specific minority group. The board adopted the plan with minor amendments by a 3-to-2 vote along party lines. The board's three Republican members voted for the plan; the two Democrats voted against it.

Appellees Barney Quilter and Thomas Ferguson, the two Democratic members of the Board who voted against the plan, and various Democratic electors and legislators filed this lawsuit in the United States District Court for the Northern District of Ohio seeking the plan's invalidation. They alleged that the plan violated §2 of the Voting Rights Act of 1965, and the Fourteenth and Fifteenth Amendments to the United States Constitution. According to appellees, the plan "packed" black voters by creating districts in which they would constitute a disproportionately large majority. This, appellees contended, minimized the total number of districts in which black voters could select their candidate of choice. In appellees' view, the plan should have created a larger number of "influence" districts—districts in which black voters would not constitute a majority, but in which they could, with the help of a predictable number of cross-over votes from white voters, elect their candidates of choice. Appellants, by contrast, argued that the plan actually enhanced the strength of black voters by providing "safe" minority-dominated districts. The plan, they pointed out, compared favorably with the 1981 apportionment and had the backing of the National Association for the Advancement of Colored People, Ohio Conference of Branches (Ohio NAACP).

A three-judge District Court heard the case and held for appellees. . . . The court found that the board had created minority-dominated districts "whenever possible." The District Court rejected appellants' contention that §2 of the Voting Rights Act of 1965, requires that such districts be created wherever possible. It further held that §2 actually prohibits the "wholesale creation of majority-minority districts" unless necessary to "'remedy'" a §2 violation. The District Court therefore ordered the board to draft a new plan or demonstrate that it was remedying a §2 violation.

. . .

The apportionment board responded by creating a record that, in its view, justified the creation of majority-minority districts. The board also adjusted the plan to correct "technical" errors that the Ohio Supreme Court had identified in its independent review of the plan. This revised 1992 plan created only five majority-black districts. The District Court, however, was not satisfied with the board's proof. In an order issued on March 10, 1992, it held that

> the [b]oard fail[ed] once again to justify its wholesale creation of majority-minority districts, thus rendering the plan, as submitted, violative of the Voting Rights Act of 1965.

The court then appointed a special master to prepare a redistricting plan. . . .

. . .

. . . The District Court further concluded that, because the board had applied the 'remedy' intentionally" and for the purpose of political advantage, it had violated not only §2 but the Fifteenth Amendment as well. Finally, the court held that the plan violated the Fourteenth Amendment because it departed from the requirement that all districts be of nearly equal population.

On March 31, 1992, the District Court ordered that the primary elections for Ohio's General Assembly be rescheduled. On April 20, 1992, this Court granted appellants' application for a stay of the District Court's orders. . . .

. . .

This case focuses not on the fragmentation of a minority group among various districts, but on the concentration of minority voters within a district. How such concentration or "packing" may dilute minority voting strength is not difficult to conceptualize. A minority group, for example, might have sufficient numbers to constitute a majority in three districts. So apportioned, the group inevitably will elect three candidates of its choice, assuming the group is sufficiently cohesive. But if the group is packed into two districts in which it constitutes a super-majority, it will be assured only two candidates. . . .

. . .

The practice challenged here, the creation of majority-minority districts, does not invariably minimize or maximize minority voting strength. Instead, it can have either effect or neither. On the one hand, creating majority-black districts necessarily leaves fewer black voters, and therefore diminishes black voter influence in predominantly white districts. On the other hand, the creation of majority-black districts can enhance the influence of black voters. Placing black voters in a district in which they constitute a sizeable and therefore "safe" majority ensures that they are able to elect their candidate of choice. Which effect the practice has, if any at all, de-

pends entirely on the facts and circumstances of each case.

The District Court, however, initially thought it unnecessary to determine the effect of creating majority-black districts under the totality of the circumstances. In fact, the court did not believe it necessary to find vote dilution at all. It instead held that §2 prohibits the creation of majority-minority districts unless such districts are necessary to remedy a statutory violation. We disagree. Section 2 contains no per se prohibitions against particular types of districts: it says nothing about majority-minority districts, districts dominated by certain political parties, or even districts based entirely on partisan political concerns. Instead, §2 focuses exclusively on the consequences of apportionment. Only if the apportionment scheme has the effect of denying a protected class the equal opportunity to elect its candidate of choice does it violate §2; where such an effect has not been demonstrated, §2 simply does not speak to the matter. . . . As a result, the District Court was required to determine the consequences of Ohio's apportionment plan before ruling on its validity; the failure to do so was error.

The District Court's decision was flawed for another reason as well. By requiring appellants to justify the creation of majority-minority districts, the District Court placed the burden of justifying apportionment on the State. Section 2, however, places at least the initial burden of proving an apportionment's invalidity squarely on the plaintiff's shoulders. Section 2(b) specifies that §2(a) is violated if "it is shown" that a state practice has the effect of denying a protected group equal access to the electoral process. The burden of "show[ing]" the prohibited effect, of course, is on the plaintiff; surely Congress could not have intended the State to prove the invalidity of its own apportionment scheme. The District Court relieved appellees of that burden in this case solely because the State had created majority-minority districts. Because that departure from the statutorily required allocation of burdens finds no support in the statute, it was error for the District Court to impose it.

Of course, the federal courts may not order the creation of majority-minority districts unless necessary to remedy a violation of federal law. But that does not mean that the State's powers are similarly limited. Quite the opposite is true: federal courts are barred from intervening in state apportionment in the absence of a violation of federal law precisely because it is the domain of the States, and not the federal courts, to conduct apportionment in the first place. . . .

. . .

In its order of March 19, 1992, the District Court found that the 1992 plan's creation of majority-minority districts "ha[d] a dilutive effect on black votes." Again we disagree.

. . .

Had the District Court employed the *Gingles* test in this case, it would have rejected appellees' §2 claim. Of course, the *Gingles* factors cannot be applied mechanically and without regard to the nature of the claim. . . . The District Court specifically found that Ohio does not suffer from "racially polarized voting." Even appellees agree. . . . The District Court's finding of a §2 violation, therefore, must be reversed.

The District Court also held that the redistricting plan violated the Fifteenth Amendment because the apportionment board intentionally diluted minority voting strength for political reasons. This Court has not decided whether the Fifteenth Amendment applies to vote-dilution claims; in fact, we never have held any legislative apportionment inconsistent with the Fifteenth Amendment. Nonetheless, we need not decide the precise scope of the Fifteenth Amendment's pro-

hibition in this case. Even if we assume that the Fifteenth Amendment speaks to claims like respondents', the District Court's decision still must be reversed: its finding of intentional discrimination was clearly erroneous.

. . .

Finally, the District Court held that the plan violated the Fourteenth Amendment because it created legislative districts of unequal size. The Equal Protection Clause does require that electoral districts be "of nearly equal population, so that each person's vote may be given equal weight in the election of representatives." But the requirement is not an inflexible one. . . . Here, the District Court found that the maximum total deviation from ideal district size exceeded 10 percent. As a result, appellees established a prima facie case of discrimination, and appellants were required to justify the deviation. Appellants attempted to do just that, arguing that the deviation resulted from the State's constitutional policy in favor of preserving county boundaries. . . . Rather than undertaking that inquiry, the District Court simply held that total deviations in excess of 10 percent cannot be justified by a policy of preserving the boundaries of political subdivisions. Our case law is directly to the contrary. On remand, the District Court should consider whether the deviations from the ideal district size are justified using the analysis employed in *Brown* and *Mahan*.

The judgment of the District Court is reversed, and the case is remanded for further proceedings in conformity with this opinion.

Shaw v. Reno
509 U.S. 630 (1993)

. . . As a result of the 1990 census, North Carolina became entitled to a twelfth seat in the United

States House of Representatives. The General Assembly enacted a reapportionment plan that included one majority-black congressional district. After the Attorney General of the United States objected to the plan pursuant to §5 of the Voting Rights Act of 1965, the General Assembly passed new legislation creating a second majority-black district. Appellants allege that the revised plan, which contains district boundary lines of dramatically irregular shape, constitutes an unconstitutional racial gerrymander. . . .

The voting age population of North Carolina is approximately 78 percent white, 20 percent black, and 1 percent Native American; the remaining 1 percent is predominantly Asian. The black population is relatively dispersed; blacks constitute a majority of the general population in only 5 of the State's 100 counties. . . . The largest concentrations of black citizens live in the Coastal Plain, primarily in the northern part. The General Assembly's first redistricting plan contained one majority-black district centered in that area of the State.

Forty of North Carolina's one hundred counties are covered by §5 of the Voting Rights Act of 1965. . . . Because the General Assembly's reapportionment plan affected the covered counties, the parties agree that §5 applied. The State chose to submit its plan to the Attorney General for preclearance.

The Attorney General . . . specifically objected to the configuration of boundary lines drawn in the south-central to southeastern region of the State. In the Attorney General's view, the General Assembly could have created a second majority-minority district "to give effect to black and Native American voting strength in this area" by using boundary lines "no more irregular than [those] found elsewhere in the proposed plan," but failed to do so for "pretextual reasons."

Under §5, the State remained free to seek a declaratory judgment from the District Court for the District of Columbia notwithstanding the Attorney General's objection. It did not do so. Instead, the General Assembly enacted a revised redistricting plan, that included a second majority-black district. The General Assembly located the second district not in the south-central to southeastern part of the State, but in the north-central region. . . .

The first of the two majority-black districts contained in the revised plan, District 1, is somewhat hook shaped. Centered in the northeast portion of the State, it moves southward until it tapers to a narrow band; then, with finger-like extensions, it reaches far into the southern-most part of the State near the South Carolina border. District 1 has been compared to a "Rorschach ink-blot test," and a "bug splattered on a windshield."

The second majority-black district, District 12, is even more unusually shaped. It is approximately 160 miles long and, for much of its length, no wider than the I-86 corridor. It winds in snake-like fashion through tobacco country, financial centers, and manufacturing areas "until it gobbles in enough enclaves of black neighborhoods." Northbound and southbound drivers on I-85 sometimes find themselves in separate districts in one county, only to "trade" districts when they enter the next county. Of the 10 counties through which District 12 passes, five are cut into three different districts; even towns are divided. At one point, the district remains contiguous only because it intersects at a single point with two other districts before crossing over them. One state legislator has remarked that "'[i]f you drove down the interstate with both car doors open, you'd kill most of the people in the district.'" The district even has inspired poetry: "Ask not for whom the line is drawn; it is drawn to avoid thee."

The Attorney General did not object to the General Assembly's revised plan. But numerous North Carolinians did. The North Carolina Republican Party and individual voters brought suit in Federal District Court alleging that the plan constituted an unconstitutional political gerrymander. . . . That claim was dismissed and this Court summarily affirmed.

. . . Appellants alleged . . . that the State had created an unconstitutional racial gerrymander. . . .

. . .

The three-judge District Court granted the federal appellees' motion to dismiss. . . .

. . .

. . . In our view, the District Court properly dismissed appellants' claims against the federal appellees. Our focus is on appellants' claim that the State engaged in unconstitutional racial gerrymandering. That argument strikes a powerful historical chord: it is unsettling how closely the North Carolina plan resembles the most egregious racial gerrymanders of the past.

. . .

Appellants contend that redistricting legislation that is so bizarre on its face that it is "unexplainable on grounds other than race," demands the same close scrutiny that we give other state laws that classify citizens by race. Our voting rights precedents support that conclusion.

. . .

. . . [W]e believe that reapportionment is one area in which appearances do matter. A reapportionment plan that includes in one district individuals who belong to the same race, but who are otherwise widely separated by geographical and political boundaries, and who may have little in common with one another but the color of their skin, bears an uncomfortable resemblance to political apartheid. It reinforces the perception that members of the same racial group—regardless of their age, education, economic status, or the community in which they live—think alike, share the same political interests, and will prefer the same candidates at the polls. We have rejected such perceptions elsewhere as impermissible racial stereotypes. By perpetuating such notions, a racial gerrymander may exacerbate the very patterns of racial bloc voting that majority-minority districting is sometimes said to counteract.

The message that such districting sends to elected representatives is equally pernicious. When a district obviously is created solely to effectuate the perceived common interests of one racial group, elected officials are more likely to believe that their primary obligation is to represent only the members of that group, rather than their constituency as a whole. This is altogether antithetical to our system of representative democracy. . . .

For these reasons, we conclude that a plaintiff challenging a reapportionment statute under the Equal Protection Clause may state a claim by alleging that the legislation, though race-neutral on its face, rationally cannot be understood as anything other than an effort to separate voters into different districts on the basis of race, and that the separation lacks sufficient justification. It is unnecessary for us to decide whether or how a reapportionment plan that, on its face, can be explained in nonracial terms successfully could be challenged. Thus, we express no view as to whether "the intentional creation of majority-minority districts, without more" always gives rise to an equal protection claim. We hold only that, on the facts of this case, plaintiffs have stated a claim sufficient to defeat the state appellees' motion to dismiss.

. . .

Racial classifications of any sort pose the risk of lasting harm to our society. They reinforce the belief, held by too many for too much of our history, that individuals should be judged by the color of their skin. Racial classifications with respect to voting carry particular dangers. Racial gerrymandering, even for remedial purposes, may balkanize us into competing racial factions; it threatens to carry us further from the goal of a political system in which race no longer matters— a goal that the Fourteenth and Fifteenth Amendments embody, and to which the Nation continues to aspire. It is for these reasons that race-based districting by our state legislatures demands close judicial scrutiny.

In this case, the Attorney General suggested that North Carolina could have created a reasonably compact second majority-minority district in the south-central to southeastern part of the State. We express no view as to whether appellants successfully could have challenged such a district under the Fourteenth Amendment. We also do not decide whether appellants' complaint stated a claim under constitutional provisions other than the Fourteenth Amendment. Today we hold only that appellants have stated a claim under the Equal Protection Clause by alleging that the North Carolina General Assembly adopted a reapportionment scheme so irrational on its face that it can be understood only as an effort to segregate voters into separate voting districts because of their race, and that the separation lacks sufficient justification. If the allegation of racial gerrymandering remains uncontradicted, the District Court further must determine whether the North Carolina plan is narrowly tailored to further a compelling governmental interest. Accordingly, we reverse the judgment of the District Court and remand the case for further proceedings consistent with this opinion.

Louisiana v. Hays
515 U.S. 737 (1995)

... Appellees Ray Hays, Edward Adams, Susan Shaw Singleton, and Gary Stokley claim that the State of Louisiana's congressional districting plan is such a "racial gerrymander," and that it violates the Fourteenth Amendment. But appellees do not live in the district that is the primary focus of their racial gerrymandering claim, and they have not otherwise demonstrated that they, personally, have been subjected to a racial classification. For that reason, we conclude that appellees lack standing to bring this lawsuit.

Louisiana has been covered by §4(b) of the Voting Rights Act of 1965 (VRA), since November 1964. . . .

Accordingly, in 1991, Louisiana submitted to the Attorney General for preclearance a districting plan for its Board of Elementary and Secondary Education (BESE). Louisiana's BESE districts historically have paralleled its congressional districts, so the submitted plan contained one majority-minority district (that is, a district "in which a majority of the population is a member of a specific minority group") out of eight, as did Louisiana's congressional districting plan then in force. The Attorney General refused to preclear the plan, claiming that Louisiana had failed to demonstrate that its decision not to create a second majority-minority district was free of racially discriminatory purpose. The Attorney General subsequently precleared a revised BESE plan, which contained two majority-minority districts.

As a result of the 1990 census, Louisiana's congressional delegation was reduced from eight to seven representatives, requiring Louisiana to redraw its district boundaries. Perhaps in part because of its recent experience with the BESE districts, the Louisiana Legislature set out to create a districting plan containing two majority-minority districts. Act 42 of the 1992 Regular Session, passed in May 1992, was such a plan. One of Act 42's majority-minority districts, District 2, was located in the New Orleans area and resembled the majority-minority district in the previous district map. The other, District 4, was "[a] Z-shaped creature" that "zigzag[ged] through all or part of 28 parishes and five of Louisiana's largest cities." The Attorney General precleared Act 42.

Appellees . . . are residents of Lincoln Parish, which is located in the north-central part of Louisiana. According to the complaint, all but Singleton reside in that part of Lincoln Parish that was contained in the majority-minority District 4 of Act 42. In August 1992, appellees filed suit in state court, challenging Act 42 under the state and federal Constitutions, as well as the VRA. The State removed the case to the United States District Court for the Western District of Louisiana, and, as required by the VRA, a three-judge court convened to hear the case. . . . [T]he District Court denied appellees' request for a preliminary injunction, denied the state and federal constitutional claims, and took the VRA claims under advisement. While the case was pending, this Court decided *Shaw v. Reno*, whereupon the District Court revoked its prior rulings and held another . . . hearing. Focusing almost exclusively on the oddly-shaped District 4, the District Court decided that Act 42 violated the Constitution, and enjoined its enforcement.

Louisiana, and the United States as defendant-intervenor, appealed directly to this Court. . . . While the appeal was pending, the Louisiana Legislature repealed Act 42 and enacted a new districting plan, Act 1 of the 1994 Second Extraordinary Session. The Attorney General precleared Act 1. We then vacated the District

Court's judgment and remanded the case "for further consideration in light of Act 1."

Act 1, like Act 42, contains two majority-minority districts, one of which (District 2) is again located in the New Orleans area. The second majority-minority district in Act 1, however, is considerably different from that in Act 42. While Act 42's District 4 ran in a zigzag fashion along the northern and eastern borders of the State, Act 1's District 4 begins in the northwestern part of the State and runs southeast along the Red River until it reaches Baton Rouge. For present purposes, the most significant difference between the two district maps is that in Act 42, part of Lincoln Parish was contained in District 4, while in Act 1, Lincoln Parish is entirely contained in District 5.

On remand, the District Court allowed appellees to amend their complaint to challenge Act 1's constitutionality. It then held another . . . hearing and concluded . . . that Act 1 was unconstitutional. The court enjoined the State from conducting any elections pursuant to Act 1, substituted its own districting plan, and denied the State's motion for a stay of judgment pending appeal. Louisiana and the United States again appealed directly to this Court. . . .

. . .

. . . [A]ppellees have not produced evidence sufficient to carry the burden our standing doctrine imposes upon them. Even assuming . . . that Act 1 causes injury sufficient to invoke strict scrutiny under Shaw, appellees have pointed to no evidence tending to show that they have suffered that injury, and our review of the record has revealed none. Neither Act 1 itself, nor any other evidence in the record indicates that appellees, or any other residents of Lincoln Parish, have been subjected to racially discriminatory treatment. The record does contain evidence tending to show that the legislature was aware of the racial composition of District 5, and of Lincoln Parish. . . . It follows that proof of "[t]hat sort of race consciousness" in the redistricting process is inadequate to establish injury in fact.

Appellees urge that District 5 is a "segregated" voting district, and thus that their position is no different from that of a student in a segregated school district. But even assuming arguendo that the evidence in this case is enough to state a *Shaw* claim with respect to District 4, that does not prove anything about the legislature's intentions with respect to District 5, nor does the record appear to reflect that the legislature intended District 5 to have any particular racial composition. Of course, it may be true that the racial composition of District 5 would have been different if the legislature had drawn District 4 in another way. But an allegation to that effect does not allege a cognizable injury under the Fourteenth Amendment. We have never held that the racial composition of a particular voting district, without more, can violate the Constitution.

Appellees insist that they challenged Act 1 in its entirety, not District 4 in isolation. That is true. It is also irrelevant. The fact that Act 1 affects all Louisiana voters by classifying each of them as a member of a particular congressional district does not mean—even if Act 1 inflicts race-based injury on some Louisiana voters—that every Louisiana voter has standing to challenge Act 1 as a racial classification. Only those citizens able to allege injury "as a direct result of having personally been denied equal treatment," may bring such a challenge, and citizens who do so carry the burden of proving their standing, as well as their case on the merits.

. . .

. . . [A]ppellees' argument that "they do have a right not to be placed into or excluded from a district because of the color of their skin," cannot help them, because they have not established that they have suffered such treatment in this case.

. . .

We conclude that appellees have failed to show that they have suffered the injury our standing doctrine requires. Appellees point us to no authority for the proposition that an equal protection challenge may go forward in federal court absent that showing of individualized harm, and we decline appellees' invitation to approve that proposition in this case. Accordingly, the judgment of the District Court is vacated, and the case is remanded with instructions to dismiss the complaint.

Miller v. Johnson
515 U.S. 900 (1995)

In 1965, the Attorney General designated Georgia a covered jurisdiction under §4(b) of the Voting Rights Act. . . .

Between 1980 and 1990, one of Georgia's 10 congressional districts was a majority-black district, that is, a majority of the district's voters were black. The 1990 Decennial Census indicated that Georgia's population of 6,478,216 persons, 27 percent of whom are black, entitled it to an additional eleventh congressional seat, prompting Georgia's General Assembly to redraw the State's congressional districts. Both the House and the Senate adopted redistricting guidelines which, among other things, required single-member districts of equal population, contiguous geography, nondilution of minority voting strength, fidelity to precinct lines where possible, and compliance with §§2 and 5 of the Act. . . . Only after these requirements were met did the guidelines permit drafters to consider other ends, such as maintaining the integrity of political subdivisions, preserving the core of existing districts, and avoiding contests between incumbents.

A special session opened in August 1991, and the General Assembly submitted a congressional redistricting plan to the Attorney General for preclearance on October 1, 1991. The legislature's plan contained two majority-minority districts, the Fifth and Eleventh, and an additional district, the Second, in which blacks comprised just over 35 percent of the voting age population. Despite the plan's increase in the number of majority-black districts from one to two and the absence of any evidence of an intent to discriminate against minority voters, the Department of Justice refused preclearance on January 21, 1992. The Department's objection letter noted a concern that Georgia had created only two majority-minority districts, and that the proposed plan did not "recognize" certain minority populations by placing them in a majority-black district.

. . . A new plan was enacted and submitted for preclearance. This second attempt assigned the black population in Central Georgia's Baldwin County to the Eleventh District and increased the black populations in the Eleventh, Fifth, and Second Districts. The Justice Department refused preclearance again, relying on alternative plans proposing three majority-minority districts. One of the alternative schemes relied on by the Department was the so-called "max-black" plan, drafted by the American Civil Liberties Union (ACLU) for the General Assembly's black caucus. The key to the ACLU's plan was the "Macon/Savannah trade." The dense black population in the Macon region would be transferred from the Eleventh District to the Second, converting the Second into a majority-black district, and the Eleventh District's loss in black population would be offset by extending the Eleventh to include the black populations in Savannah. Pointing to

the General Assembly's refusal to enact the Macon/Savannah swap into law, the Justice Department concluded that Georgia had "failed to explain adequately" its failure to create a third majority-minority district. The State did not seek a declaratory judgment from the District Court for the District of Columbia.

. . . [T]he General Assembly set out to create three majority-minority districts to gain preclearance. Using the ACLU's "max-black" plan as its benchmark, the General Assembly enacted a plan. . . . The new plan also enacted the Macon/Savannah swap necessary to create a third majority-black district. . . . Georgia's plan included three majority-black districts, though, and received Justice Department preclearance on April 2, 1992.

Elections were held under the new congressional redistricting plan on November 4, 1992, and black candidates were elected to Congress from all three majority-black districts. On January 13, 1994, appellees, five white voters from the Eleventh District, filed this action against various state officials. . . . As residents of the challenged Eleventh District, all appellees had standing. Their suit alleged that Georgia's Eleventh District was a racial gerrymander and so a violation of the Equal Protection Clause. . . .

A majority of the District Court panel agreed that the Eleventh District was invalid. . . . After sharp criticism of the Justice Department for its use of partisan advocates in its dealings with state officials and for its close cooperation with the ACLU's vigorous advocacy of minority district maximization, the majority turned to a careful interpretation of our opinion in *Shaw*. It read *Shaw* to require strict scrutiny whenever race is the "overriding, predominant force" in the redistricting process. Citing much evidence of the legislature's purpose and intent in creating the final plan, as well as the irregular shape of the District ... the court found that race was the overriding and predominant force in the districting determination. The court proceeded to apply strict scrutiny. Though rejecting proportional representation as a compelling interest, it was willing to assume that compliance with the Voting Rights Act would be a compelling interest. As to the latter, however, the court found that the Act did not require three majority-black districts, and that Georgia's plan for that reason was not narrowly tailored to the goal of complying with the Act.

. . .

Finding that the "evidence of the General Assembly's intent to racially gerrymander the Eleventh District is overwhelming, and practically stipulated by the parties involved," the District Court held that race was the predominant, overriding factor in drawing the Eleventh District. Appellants do not take issue with the court's factual finding of this racial motivation. Rather, they contend that evidence of a legislature's deliberate classification of voters on the basis of race cannot alone suffice to state a claim under *Shaw*. They argue that, regardless of the legislature's purposes, a plaintiff must demonstrate that a district's shape is so bizarre that it is unexplainable other than on the basis of race, and that appellees failed to make that showing here. Appellants' conception of the constitutional violation misapprehends our holding in *Shaw* and the Equal Protection precedent upon which *Shaw* relied.

. . . [T]he essence of the equal protection claim recognized in *Shaw* is that the State has used race as a basis for separating voters into districts. Just as the State may not, absent extraordinary justification, segregate citizens on the basis of race in its public parks, buses, golf courses, beaches, and schools, so did we recognize in *Shaw* that it may not separate its citizens into different voting districts on the basis of race. . . . When the State assigns voters on the basis of race, it engages in the offensive and demeaning assumption that voters of a particular race, because of their race, "think alike, share the same political interests, and will prefer the same candidates at the polls." . . . They also cause society serious harm. . . .

Our observation in *Shaw* of the consequences of racial stereotyping was not meant to suggest that a district must be bizarre on its face before there is a constitutional violation. Nor was our conclusion in *Shaw* that in certain instances a district's appearance (or, to be more precise, its appearance in combination with certain demographic evidence) can give rise to an equal protection claim, a holding that bizarreness was a threshold showing, as appellants believe it to be. Our circumspect approach and narrow holding in *Shaw* did not erect an artificial rule barring accepted equal protection analysis in other redistricting cases. Shape is relevant not because bizarreness is a necessary element of the constitutional wrong or a threshold requirement of proof, but because it may be persuasive circumstantial evidence that race for its own sake, and not other districting principles, was the legislature's dominant and controlling rationale in drawing its district lines. The logical implication, as courts applying *Shaw* have recognized, is that parties may rely on evidence other than bizarreness to establish race-based districting.

. . .

Federal court review of districting legislation represents a serious intrusion on the most vital of local functions. It is well settled that "reapportionment is primarily the duty and responsibility of the State." Electoral districting is a most difficult subject for legislatures, and so the States must have discretion to exercise the political judgment necessary to balance competing interests. . . . The courts, in assessing the sufficiency of a challenge to a districting plan, must be sensitive to the complex interplay of forces that enter a legislature's redistricting calculus. Redistricting legislatures will, for example, almost always be aware of racial demographics; but it does not follow that race predominates in the redistricting process. The distinction between being aware of racial considerations and being motivated by them may be difficult to make. This evidentiary difficulty, together with the sensitive nature of redistricting and the presumption of good faith that must be accorded legislative enactments, requires courts to exercise extraordinary caution in adjudicating claims that a state has drawn district lines on the basis of race. The plaintiff's burden is to show, either through circumstantial evidence of a district's shape and demographics or more direct evidence going to legislative purpose, that race was the predominant factor motivating the legislature's decision to place a significant number of voters within or without a particular district. To make this showing, a plaintiff must prove that the legislature subordinated traditional race-neutral districting principles, including but not limited to compactness, contiguity, respect for political subdivisions or communities defined by actual shared interests, to racial considerations. Where these or other race-neutral considerations are the basis for redistricting legislation, and are not subordinated to race, a state can "defeat a claim that a district has been gerrymandered on racial lines." These principles inform the plaintiff's burden of proof at trial. . . .

In our view, the District Court applied the correct analysis, and its finding that race was the predominant factor motivating the drawing of the Eleventh District was not clearly erroneous. The court found it was "exceedingly obvious" from the shape of the Eleventh District, together with the relevant racial demographics, that the drawing of narrow land bridges to incorporate within the District outlying appendages containing nearly 80 percent of the district's total black population was a deliberate attempt to bring black populations into the district. Although by comparison with other districts the geometric shape of the Eleventh District may not seem bizarre on its face, when its shape is considered in conjunction with its racial and population densities, the story of racial gerrymandering seen by the District Court becomes much clearer. Although this evidence is quite compelling, we need not determine whether it was, standing alone, sufficient to establish a *Shaw* claim that the Eleventh District is unexplainable other than by race. The District Court had before it considerable additional evidence showing that the General Assembly was motivated by a predominant, overriding desire to assign black populations to the Eleventh District and thereby permit the creation of a third majority-black district in the Second.

. . .

We do not accept the contention that the State has a compelling interest in complying with whatever preclearance mandates the Justice Department issues. When a state governmental entity seeks to justify race-based remedies to cure the effects of past discrimination, we do not accept the government's mere assertion that the remedial action is required. Rather, we insist on a strong basis in evidence of the harm being remedied. . . . Our presumptive skepticism of all racial classifications, prohibits us as well from accepting on its face the Justice Department's conclusion that racial districting is necessary under the Voting Rights Act. Where a State relies on the Department's determination that race-based districting is necessary to comply with the Voting Rights Act, the judiciary retains an independent obligation in adjudicating consequent equal protection challenges to ensure that the State's actions are narrowly tailored to achieve a compelling interest. Were we to accept the Justice Department's objection itself as a compelling interest adequate to insulate racial districting from constitutional review, we would be surrendering to the Executive Branch our role in enforcing the constitutional limits on race-based official action. We may not do so.

For the same reasons, we think it inappropriate for a court engaged in constitutional scrutiny to accord deference to the Justice Department's interpretation of the Act. Although we have deferred to the Department's interpretation in certain statutory cases, and cases cited therein, we have rejected agency interpretations to which we would otherwise defer where they raise serious constitutional questions. When the Justice Department's interpretation of the Act compels race-based districting, it by definition raises a serious constitutional question, and should not receive deference.

Georgia's drawing of the Eleventh District was not required under the Act, because there was no reasonable basis to believe that Georgia's earlier enacted plans violated §5. . . .

. . .

The Voting Rights Act, and its grant of authority to the federal courts to uncover official efforts to abridge minorities' right to vote, has been of vital importance in eradicating invidious discrimination from the electoral process and enhancing the legitimacy of our political institutions. Only if our political system and our society cleanse themselves of that discrimination will all members of the polity share an equal opportunity to gain public office regardless of race. As a Nation we share both the obligation and the aspiration of working toward this end. The end is neither assured nor

well served, however, by carving electorates into racial blocs. . . . It takes a shortsighted and unauthorized view of the Voting Rights Act to invoke that statute, which has played a decisive role in redressing some of our worst forms of discrimination, to demand the very racial stereotyping the Fourteenth Amendment forbids.

The judgment of the District Court is affirmed, and the case is remanded for further proceedings consistent with this decision.

Shaw v. Hunt
517 U.S. 899 (1995)

This case is here for a second time. In *Shaw v. Reno* . . . we held that plaintiffs whose complaint alleged that the deliberate segregation of voters into separate and bizarre-looking districts on the basis of race stated a claim for relief under the Equal Protection Clause of the Fourteenth Amendment. We remanded the case for further consideration by the District Court. That court held that the North Carolina redistricting plan did classify voters by race, but that the classification survived strict scrutiny, and therefore did not offend the Constitution. We now hold that the North Carolina plan does violate the Equal Protection Clause because the State's reapportionment scheme is not narrowly tailored to serve a compelling state interest.

The facts are set out in detail in our prior opinion. . . .

. . .

Although we have not always provided precise guidance on how closely the means (the racial classification) must serve the end (the justification or compelling interest), we have always expected that the legislative action would substantially address, if not achieve, the avowed purpose. Where, as here, we assume avoidance of §2 liability to be a compelling state interest, we think that the racial classification would have to realize that goal; the legislative action must at a minimum, remedy the anticipated violation or achieve compliance to be narrowly tailored.

District 12 could not remedy any potential §2 violation. . . . No one looking at District 12 could reasonably suggest that the district contains a "geographically compact" population of any race. Therefore where that district sits, "there neither has been a wrong nor can be a remedy."

. . .

. . . [T]he judgment of the District Court is reversed.

Bush v. Vera
517 U.S. 952 (1996)

. . . [T]he Texas Legislature promulgated a redistricting plan that, among other things: created District 30, a new majority African American district in Dallas County; created District 29, a new majority Hispanic district in and around Houston in Harris County; and reconfigured District 18, which is adjacent to District 29, to make it a majority African American district. The Department of Justice precleared that plan under [Voting Rights Act of 1965] VRA §5 in 1991, and it was used in the 1992 congressional elections.

The plaintiffs, six Texas voters, challenged the plan, alleging that 24 of Texas' 30 congressional districts constitute racial gerrymanders in violation of the Fourteenth Amendment. The three-judge United States District Court for the Southern District of Texas held Districts 18, 29, and 30 unconstitutional. The Governor of Texas, private intervenors, and the United States (as intervenor) now appeal. . . .

. . .

Strict scrutiny does not apply merely because redistricting is performed with consciousness of race. Nor does it apply to all cases of intentional creation of majority minority districts. Electoral district lines are "facially race neutral," so a more searching inquiry is necessary before strict scrutiny can be found applicable in redistricting cases than in cases of "classifications based explicitly on race." For strict scrutiny to apply, the plaintiffs must prove that other, legitimate districting principles were "subordinated" to race. By that, we mean that race must be "the predominant factor motivating the legislature's [redistricting] decision." . . .

The present case is a mixed motive case. The appellants concede that one of Texas' goals in creating the three districts at issue was to produce majority minority districts, but they also cite evidence that other goals, particularly incumbency protection . . . also played a role in the drawing of the district lines. The record does not reflect a history of "purely race-based" districting revisions. A careful review is, therefore, necessary to determine whether these districts are subject to strict scrutiny. But review of the District Court's findings of primary fact and the record convinces us that the District Court's determination that race was the "predominant factor" in the drawing of each of the districts must be sustained.

. . .

The judgment of the District Court is affirmed.

Reno v. Bossier Parish School Board
520 U.S. 471 (1997)

Appellee Bossier Parish School Board (Board) is a jurisdiction subject to the preclearance requirements of §5 of the Voting Rights Act of 1965, and must therefore obtain the approval of either the United States Attorney General or the United States district court for the District of Columbia before implementing any changes to a voting "qualification, prerequisite, standard, practice, or procedure." The Board has 12 members who are elected from single member districts by majority vote to serve 4-year terms. When the 1990 census revealed wide population disparities among its districts the Board decided to redraw the districts to equalize the population distribution.

During this process, the Board considered two redistricting plans. It considered, and initially rejected, the redistricting plan that had been recently adopted by the Bossier Parish Police Jury, the parish's primary governing body (the Jury plan), to govern its own elections. Just months before, the Attorney General had precleared the Jury plan, which also contained 12 districts. None of the 12 districts in the Board's existing plan or in the Jury plan contained a majority of black residents. Because the Board's adoption of the Jury plan would have maintained the status quo regarding the number of black-majority districts, the parties stipulated that the Jury plan was not "retrogressive." Appellant George Price, president of the local chapter of the National Association for the Advancement of Colored People (NAACP), presented the Board with a second option—a plan that created two districts each containing not only a majority of black residents, but a majority of voting-age black residents. Over vocal opposition from local residents, black and white alike, the Board voted to adopt the Jury plan as its own, reasoning that the Jury plan would almost certainly be precleared again and that the NAACP plan would require the Board to split 46 electoral precincts.

But the Board's hopes for rapid preclearance were dashed when the Attorney General interposed a formal objection to the Board's plan on the basis of "new information" not available when the Justice Department had precleared the plan for the Police Jury—namely, the NAACP's plan, which demonstrated that "black residents are sufficiently numerous and geographically compact so as to constitute a majority in two single member districts." The objection letter asserted that the Board's plan violated §2 of the Act because it "unnecessarily limit[ed] the opportunity for minority voters to elect their candidates of choice" as compared to the new alternative. . . . [T]he Attorney General concluded that the Board's redistricting plan warranted a denial of preclearance under §5. The Attorney General declined to reconsider the decision.

The Board then filed this action seeking preclearance under §5 in the district court for the District of Columbia. Appellant Price and others intervened as defendants. The three-judge panel granted the Board's request for preclearance, over the dissent of one judge. The district court squarely rejected the appellants' contention that a voting change's alleged failure to satisfy §2 constituted an independent reason to deny preclearance under §5. . . . Given this holding, the district court quite properly expressed no opinion on whether the Jury plan in fact violated §2, and its refusal to reach out and decide the issue in dicta does not require us . . . to "assume that the record discloses a 'clear violation' of §2." That issue has yet to be decided by any court. The district court did, however, reject appellants' related argument that a court "must still consider evidence of a §2 violation as evidence of discriminatory purpose under §5." . . .

. . .

We are unable to determine from the district court's opinion in this action whether it deemed irrelevant all evidence of the dilutive impact of the redistricting plan adopted by the Board. . . .

... [T]he district court gave no indication that it was assuming the plan's dilutive effect, and we hesitate to attribute to the district court a rationale it might not have employed. Because we are not satisfied that the district court considered evidence of the dilutive impact of the Board's redistricting plan, we vacate this aspect of the district court's opinion. . . .

The judgment of the district court is vacated, and the case is remanded for further proceedings consistent with this decision.

Abrams v. Johnson
521 U.S. 74 (1997)

The electoral district lines for Georgia's congressional delegation are before us a second time, appeal now being taken from the trial court's rulings and determinations after our remand in *Miller v. Johnson.* . . .

Given the contorted shape of the district and the undue predominance of race in drawing its lines, it was unlikely the district could be redrawn without changing most or all of Georgia's congressional districts, 11 in total number. The plan being challenged contained three majority-black districts, and after our remand the complaint was amended to challenge another of these, the then Second District. The trial court found this district, too, was improperly drawn under the standards we confirmed in *Miller.*

For the task of drawing a new plan, the court deferred to Georgia's legislature, but the legislature could not reach agreement. The court then drew its own plan; we declined to stay the order, and the 1996 general elections were held under it. The court's plan contained but one majority-black district. The absence of a second, if not a third, majority-black district has become the principal point of contention. Though the elections have been completed, the plan remains in effect until changed by a valid legislative act, and the appellants ask us to set it aside.

The private appellants are various voters, defendant-intervenors below, who contend that the interests of Georgia's black population were not adequately taken into account. The United States, also a defendant-intervenor, joins in the appeal. The state officials, defendants below, do not object to the plan and appeared before us as appellees to defend it. The other set of appellees are the private plaintiffs below, who argued that racial gerrymandering under the previous plan violated their right to equal protection.

. . .

. . . When faced with the necessity of drawing district lines by judicial order, a court, as a general rule, should be guided by the legislative policies underlying the existing plan, to the extent those policies do not lead to violations of the Constitution or the Voting Rights Act. Much of the argument from the parties centers around what legislative redistricting principles the District Court should have acknowledged in drawing its plan. The appellants say the relevant redistricting guideline should be the three majority-black districts of the precleared plan at issue in *Miller v. Johnson*; and, if not, the two majority-black districts in an earlier legislative effort. . . .

. . .

On remand, the district court deferred to the Georgia Legislature, giving it time to draw a new congressional map. The governor called a special session of the General Assembly, which met from August 14 to September 12, 1995. The legislature, however, deadlocked on the congressional reapportionment plan. The Georgia House of Representatives adopted a plan with two majority-black districts, while the Senate adopted a plan with one. On September 13, 1995, defendants notified the district court that the legislature was unable to resolve its differences and had adjourned, leaving the district court to develop a remedy.

Plaintiffs had moved to amend their complaint to challenge the Second District as unconstitutional on the same grounds as the Eleventh District, and the court received additional evidence for the purpose. None of the private defendant-intervenors lived in the Second District and, assuming their lack of standing to defend it, they asked for the addition of other parties. The court disallowed the request, ruling the State could defend this aspect of the plan under review.

The court found that race was the "overriding and predominant factor" in drawing the Second District's borders. The district, the court noted, split 12 of the district's 35 counties, 28 of its precincts, and numerous cities. . . .

. . .

The District Court considered the plans submitted by the various parties and then adopted its own. Noting the Justice Department's thorough "subversion of the redistricting process" since the 1990 census, it based its plan on the State's 1972 and 1982 plans. The court first had to decide where to locate the new Eleventh District, and did so in an area of significant population growth near Atlanta, so as to displace the fewest counties. It then considered Georgia's traditional redistricting principles based on maintaining: district cores, four traditional "corner districts" in the corners of the State, political subdivisions such as counties and cities, and an urban majority-black district in the Atlanta area. Protecting incumbents from contests with each other was another factor, which the court subordinated to the others because it was "inherently more political." The District Court stated that, in

fashioning a remedy, it considered the possibility of creating a second majority-black district but decided doing so would require it to "subordinate Georgia's traditional districting policies and consider race predominantly, to the exclusion of both constitutional norms and common sense." Georgia did not have a black population of sufficient concentration to allow creation of a second majority-black district, the court found, adding that if it had the court "would have included one since Georgia's legislature probably would have done so." The resulting plan contained one majority-black district, the Fifth. The plan split no counties outside the Atlanta area. The District Court rejected potential objections to the plan based on §§2 and 5 of the Voting Rights Act and the constitutional requirement of one person, one vote.

. . .

Interference by the Justice Department, leading the state legislature to act based on an overriding concern with race, disturbed any sound basis to defer to the 1991 unprecleared plan; the unconstitutional predominance of race in the provenance of the Second and Eleventh Districts of the 1992 precleared plan caused them to be improper departure points; and the proposals for either two or three majority-black districts in plans urged upon the trial court in the remedy phase were flawed by evidence of predominant racial motive in their design. In these circumstances, the trial court acted well within its discretion in deciding it could not draw two majority-black districts without itself engaging in racial gerrymandering.

The court-ordered plan is not violative of §2 of the Voting Rights Act. We reject appellants' contrary position, which is premised on impermissible vote dilution in the court's failure to create a second majority-black district. . . . On its

face, §2 does not apply to a court ordered remedial redistricting plan, but we will assume courts
should comply with the section when exercising
their equitable powers to redistrict. . . .

. . .

We do not agree that the District Court's maintenance of the Fifth District as a majority-black
district under §2 indicates its §2 findings in reference to other districts are conflicting and not
entitled to deference. The District Court noted
that maintenance of a majority-black district in
the Atlanta area—created in 1972 for compliance
with the Voting Rights Act—had become a state
districting policy. Further, it is possible, although
we do not express any opinion on the subject,
that changing the racial majority of the district
would have violated §5 retrogression principles.

. . . [N]either our precedents nor the Act require the court to hold a separate hearing on the
adequacy under §2 of a remedial plan. Second,
the private defendant-intervenors had ample
opportunity to present evidence of the need for
a second majority-black district under § 2 at
the remedy hearing, in which they fully participated. The finding that appellants have not
shown the threshold *Gingles* factors for a §2
violation is owed deference, and we find it not
clearly erroneous.

. . .

The question arises whether a court decree is
subject to §5. We have held that "[a] decree of
the United States District Court is not within reach
of Section 5 of the Voting Rights Act" such that
it must be precleared. The exception applies to
judicial plans, devised by the court itself, not to
plans submitted to the court by the legislature of
a covered jurisdiction in response to a determination of unconstitutionality. Here, the District
Court made clear it had devised its own plan, a
proposition not in dispute. . . .

. . .

. . . There are sound reasons for requiring
benchmarks to be plans that have been in effect;
otherwise a myriad of benchmarks would be proposed in every case, with attendant confusion.
This rule is all the more appropriate when one
considers the attempt to use as a benchmark the
State's supposed policy of creating two majority-black districts. And the Justice Department's
proposed benchmark—the 1992 plan shorn of its
constitutional defects—was also never in effect.
Nor can the 1992 plan, constitutional defects and
all, be the benchmark. Section 5 cannot be used
to freeze in place the very aspects of a plan found
unconstitutional.

The appropriate benchmark is, in fact, what
the District Court concluded it would be: the 1982
plan, in effect for a decade. . . .

. . . Court-ordered districts are held to higher
standards of population equality than legislative
ones. A court-ordered plan should "ordinarily
achieve the goal of population equality with little
more than de minimis variation." Here the district
court was not designing districts to remedy a one-
person, one-vote violation, but courts should keep
in mind that "absolute population equality [is] the
paramount objective." Slight deviations are allowed
under certain circumstances.

. . .

The task of redistricting is best left to state legislatures, elected by the people and as capable as the
courts, if not more so, in balancing the myriad factors and traditions in legitimate districting policies.
Here, the legislative process was first distorted
and then unable to reach a solution. The District
Court was left to embark on a delicate task with
limited legislative guidance. The court was careful to take into account traditional state districting
factors, and it remained sensitive to the constitutional requirement of equal protection of the laws.

Lawyer v. Department of Justice
521 U.S. 567 (1997)

After the 1990 Decennial Census, the Florida Legislature adopted a reapportionment plan for Florida's 40 Senate districts and 120 House districts. Following the procedure for reapportionment set forth in the state constitution, the attorney general of Florida petitioned the State Supreme Court for a declaration that the plan comported with state and federal law. That court approved the redistricting plan, while noting that time constraints imposed by the state constitution precluded a full review of objections raised to the plan under §2 of the Voting Rights Act of 1965, as amended. The court retained jurisdiction to entertain further objections to the plan.

Since five Florida counties, including Hillsborough County where the city of Tampa is located, are covered jurisdictions under §5 of the Voting Rights Act of 1965, as amended, the state attorney general submitted the redistricting plan to the United States Department of Justice for preclearance. On June 16, 1992, the Department declined to preclear the proposed State Senate districts, on the grounds that the redistricting plan divided "politically cohesive minority populations" in the Hillsborough county area and failed to create a majority-minority district in that region.

The Supreme Court of Florida then entered an order encouraging the state legislature to adopt a new plan to address the Justice Department's objection, and noting that, if the legislature failed to act, the court itself would adopt a reapportionment plan. The state court was advised that the Governor had no intent to convene the legislature in extraordinary session, and that neither the President of the Senate nor the Speaker of the House of Representatives would convene his respective house. The court concluded that a legis-

lative impasse had occurred and, invoking authority under state law, revised the Senate redistricting plan to address the Justice Department's objection.

The amended plan, known as Plan 330, called for an irregularly shaped Senate District 21, with a voting-age population 45.8 percent black and 9.4 percent Hispanic and comprising portions of four counties in the Tampa Bay area. The district included the central portions of Tampa in Hillsborough County, the eastern shore of Tampa Bay running south to Bradenton in Manatee County, central portions of St. Petersburg in Pinellas County, a narrow projection eastward through parts of Hillsborough and Polk Counties, and a narrow finger running north from St. Petersburg to Clearwater. Although the State Supreme Court acknowledged that the district was "more contorted" than other possible plans and that black residents in different parts of the district might have little in common besides their race, it decided that such concerns "must give way to racial and ethnic fairness." Elections were held under Plan 330 in 1992 and 1994.

On April 14, 1994, appellant and five other residents of Hillsborough County filed this suit in the District Court . . . naming the State of Florida, its attorney general, and the United States Department of Justice as defendants, and alleging that District 21 in Plan 330 violated the Equal Protection Clause. The plaintiffs sought declaratory and injunctive relief, including an order requiring Florida to reconfigure the district. A three-judge District Court . . . permitted intervention by the State Senate, House of Representatives, Secretary of State, District 21 Senator James T. Hargrett, Jr., and a group of black and Hispanic voters residing in District 21.

. . . After the mediator declared an impasse in late October, the parties continued discussions on their own and on November 2, 1995, filed with the District Court a settlement agreement signed on behalf of all parties except appellant. The agreement noted that, while the defendants and defendant intervenors denied the plaintiffs' claims that District 21 was unconstitutional, all parties to the settlement concurred that "there is a reasonable factual and legal basis for the plaintiffs' claim." The agreement proposed revising District 21 under a new plan, called Plan 386, which would be subject to public comment and, if approved by the District Court after a public hearing, would be used in state elections unless Florida adopted a new plan. District 21, as revised in Plan 386, would no longer extend into Polk County or north toward Clearwater, would have a boundary length decreased by 58 percent, and would include a resident black voting age population reduced from 45.0 percent to 36.2 percent. The proposed district would cover portions of three counties instead of four and continue to include land on both sides of Tampa Bay.

At a status conference held the same day, the parties filed the settlement agreement, the District Court sought and received specific assurances from lawyers for the President of the Senate and the Speaker of the House that they were authorized to represent their respective government bodies in the litigation and enter into the settlement proposed. . . .

The District Court scheduled a hearing on the proposed plan for November 20, giving notice in 13 area newspapers and making details of the plan available for review in the clerk's office. Before the hearing, the settling parties submitted evidence including affidavits and declarations addressing the factors considered in revising District 21, and appellant submitted his own remedial plan for a District 21 wholly contained within Hillsborough County. At the hearing, counsel for the

State Senate summarized the prehearing filings submitted by proponents of the settlement and the rationale behind the agreement. The District Court denied appellant's motion for ruling on his motion for summary judgment on the legality of Plan 330. . . . Appellant then argued that District 21, as redrawn in Plan 386, would still be unconstitutional, because only race could explain its contours, and counsel for a former state legislator spoke to the same effect.

On March 19, 1996, the District Court approved the settlement. . . .

The District Court then turned to the merits of Plan 386 to determine whether its formation had been "dominated by the single-minded focus" on race that it understood to be constitutionally forbidden under *Miller*. . . . The Court noted that the new district's percentage of minority residents would approximate the racial features of the region surrounding Tampa Bay better than Plan 330 did, that the district's boundaries would be "less strained and irregular" than those in Plan 330, and that all candidates, regardless of race, would have an opportunity to seek office, with "both a fair chance to win and the usual risk of defeat."

. . .

The substance of what appellant claims as a right to the benefit of political diffusion is nothing other than the rule declared in the cases he cites, that state redistricting responsibility should be accorded primacy to the extent possible when a federal court exercises remedial power. A State should be given the opportunity to make its own redistricting decisions so long as that is practically possible and the State chooses to take the opportunity. When it does take the opportunity, the discretion of the federal court is limited except to the extent that the plan itself runs afoul of federal law.

In this case, the State has selected its opportunity by entering into the settlement agreement, which, for reasons set out below, it had every right to do. And it has availed itself of that opportunity by proposing a plan as embodied in the settlement agreement. There can be no question on the present record that proponents of the plan included counsel authorized to represent the State itself, and there is no reason to suppose that the State's attorney general lacked authority to propose a plan as an incident of his authority to represent the State in this litigation. . . .

. . .

We find no merit . . . in appellant's apparently distinct claim that, regardless of any effect on the State's districting responsibility, the District Court was bound to adjudicate liability before settlement because appellant did not agree to settle. . . .

. . .

The District Court concluded that Plan 386 did not subordinate traditional districting principles to race. That finding is subject to review for clear error, of which we find none. The District Court looked to the shape and composition of District 21 as redrawn in Plan 386 and found them "demonstrably benign and satisfactorily tidy." The district is located entirely in the Tampa Bay area, has an end-to-end distance no greater than that of most Florida Senate districts, and in shape does not stand out as different from numerous other Florida House and Senate districts. While District 21 crosses a body of water and encompasses portions of three counties, evidence submitted showed that both features are common characteristics of Florida legislative districts, being products of the State's geography and the fact that 40 Senate districts are superimposed on 67 counties.

. . . The fact that District 21 under Plan 386 is not a majority black district, the black voting-age population being 36.2 percent, supports the District Court's finding that the district is not a "safe" one for black-preferred candidates, but one that "offers to any candidate, without regard to race, the opportunity" to seek and be elected to office.

Based on these and other considerations, the District Court concluded that traditional districting principles had not been subordinated to race in drawing revised District 21. . . . Since districting can be difficult, after all, just because racial composition varies from place to place, and counties and voting districts do not depend on common principles of size and location, facts about the one do not as such necessarily entail conclusions about the other.

In short, the evidence amply supports the trial court's views that race did not predominate over Florida's traditional districting principles in drawing Plan 386. Appellant has provided nothing that calls that conclusion into question, much less that points to any clear error.

We accordingly affirm the decision of the District Court.

Hunt v. Cromartie
526 U.S. 541 (1999)

This is the third time in six years that litigation over North Carolina's Twelfth Congressional District has come before this Court. The first time around, we held that plaintiffs whose complaint alleged that the State had deliberately segregated voters into districts on the basis of race without compelling justification stated a claim for relief under the Equal Protection Clause of the Fourteenth Amendment. After remand, we affirmed the District Court's finding that North Carolina's District 12 classified voters by race, and further held that the State's reapportionment scheme was not narrowly tailored to serve a compelling interest.

. . .

Appellees believed the new District 12, like the old one, to be the product of an unconstitutional racial gerrymander. They filed suit in the United States District Court for the Eastern District of North Carolina against several state officials in their official capacities, seeking to enjoin elections under the State's 1997 plan. The parties filed competing motions for summary judgment and supporting materials, and the three-judge District Court heard argument on the pending motions, but before either party had conducted discovery and without an evidentiary hearing. . . . [T]he District Court granted appellees' motion and entered the injunction they sought. The majority of the Court explained that "the uncontroverted material facts" showed that "District 12 was drawn to collect precincts with high racial identification rather than political identification," that "more heavily Democratic precincts . . . were bypassed in the drawing of District 12 and included in the surrounding congressional districts," and that "[t]he legislature disregarded traditional districting criteria." From these "uncontroverted material facts," the District Court concluded "the General Assembly, in redistricting, used criteria with respect to District 12 that are facially race driven," and thereby violated the Equal Protection Clause of the Fourteenth Amendment. . . .

The state officials filed a notice of appeal. . . .

Our decisions have established that all laws that classify citizens on the basis of race, including racially gerrymandered districting schemes, are constitutionally suspect, and must be strictly scrutinized. When racial classifications are explicit, no inquiry into legislative purpose is necessary. A facially neutral law, on the other hand,

warrants strict scrutiny only if it can be proved that the law was "motivated by a racial purpose or object," or if it is "unexplainable on grounds other than race." The task of assessing a jurisdiction's motivation, however, is not a simple matter; on the contrary, it is an inherently complex endeavor, one requiring the trial court to perform a "sensitive inquiry into such circumstantial and direct evidence of intent as may be available."

. . .

Viewed in toto, appellees' evidence tends to support an inference that the State drew its district lines with an impermissible racial motive—even though they presented no direct evidence of intent. Summary judgment, however, is appropriate only where there is no genuine issue of material fact and the moving party is entitled to judgment as a matter of law. To be sure, appellants did not contest the evidence of District 12's shape (which hardly could be contested), nor did they claim that appellees' statistical and demographic evidence, most if not all of which appears to have been obtained from the State's own data banks, was untrue.

The District Court nevertheless was only partially correct in stating that the material facts before it were uncontroverted. The legislature's motivation is itself a factual question. . . .

. . .

Outright admissions of impermissible racial motivation are infrequent, and plaintiffs often must rely upon other evidence. Summary judgment in favor of the party with the burden of persuasion, however, is inappropriate when the evidence is susceptible of different interpretations or inferences by the trier of fact. That is not to say that summary judgment in a plaintiff's favor will never be appropriate in a racial gerrymandering case sought to be proved exclusively by circumstantial evidence. We can imagine an instance where the uncontroverted evidence and the reasonable inferences to be drawn in the nonmoving party's favor would not be "significantly probative," so as to create a genuine issue of fact for trial. But this is not that case. And even if the question whether appellants had created a material dispute of fact was a close one, we think that "the sensitive nature of redistricting and the presumption of good faith that must be accorded legislative enactments" would tip the balance in favor of the District Court making findings of fact.

In reaching our decision, we are fully aware that the District Court is more familiar with the evidence than this Court, and is likewise better suited to assess the General Assembly's motivations. Perhaps, after trial, the evidence will support a finding that race was the State's predominant motive, but we express no position as to that question. We decide only that this case was not suited for summary disposition. The judgment of the District Court is reversed.

Reno v. Bossier Parish School Board
528 U.S. 320 (2000)

This is the second time the present cases are before us. . . .

. . .

On remand, the District Court, in a comparatively brief opinion relying on, but clarifying, its extensive earlier opinion, again granted preclearance. First, in response to our invitation to address the existence of a discriminatory but nonretrogressive purpose, the District Court summarily concluded that "the record will not support a conclusion that extends beyond the presence or absence of retrogressive intent." It noted that one could "imagine a set of facts that would establish a 'non-retrogressive, but never-

theless discriminatory, purpose,' but those imagined facts are not present here." The District Court therefore left open the question that we had ourselves left open on remand: namely, whether the §5 purpose inquiry extends beyond the search for retrogressive intent.

Second, the District Court considered, at greater length, how any dilutive impact of the Board's plan bore on the question whether the Board enacted the plan with a retrogressive intent. . . .

. . .

Appellants press the two claims initially raised in their jurisdictional statements: first, that the District Court's factual conclusion that there was no evidence of discriminatory but nonretrogressive intent was clearly erroneous, and second, that §5 of the Voting Rights Act prohibits preclearance of a redistricting plan enacted with a discriminatory but nonretrogressive purpose. Our resolution of the second claim renders it unnecessary to address the first. When considered in light of our longstanding interpretation of the "effect" prong of §5 in its application to vote dilution claims, the language of §5 leads to the conclusion that the "purpose" prong of §5 covers only retrogressive dilution.

. . .

. . . In light of the language of §5 and our prior holding in *Beer*, we hold that §5 does not prohibit preclearance of a redistricting plan enacted with a discriminatory but nonretrogressive purpose. Accordingly, the judgment of the District Court is affirmed.

Sinkfield v. Kelley
531 U.S. 28 (2000)

. . . Appellees, the plaintiffs below, are white Alabama voters who are residents of various majority-white districts. The districts in which appellees reside are adjacent to majority-minority districts. All of the districts were created under a state redistricting plan whose acknowledged purpose was the maximization of the number of majority-minority districts in Alabama. Appellants in No. 00-132 are a group of African-American voters whose initial state lawsuit resulted in the adoption of the redistricting plan at issue. Appellants in No. 00–133 are Alabama state officials.

Appellees brought suit in the United States District Court for the Middle District of Alabama challenging their own districts as the products of unconstitutional racial gerrymandering. . . . The District Court ultimately held that seven of the challenged majority-white districts were the product of unconstitutional racial gerrymandering and enjoined their use in any election. On direct appeal to this Court . . . appellants in both cases contend, among other things, that appellees lack standing to maintain this suit under our decision in *United States v. Hays.* . . .

Hays involved a challenge to Louisiana's districting plan for its Board of Elementary and Secondary Education. The plan contained two majority-minority districts. The appellees lived in a majority-white district that bordered on one of the majority-minority districts. The appellees challenged the entire plan, including their own district, as an unconstitutional racial gerrymander under our decision in *Shaw v. Reno.*

. . .

The shapes of appellees' districts, however, were necessarily influenced by the shapes of the majority-minority districts upon which they border, and appellees have produced no evidence that anything other than the deliberate creation of those majority-minority districts is responsible for the districting lines of which they complain. Appellees' suggestion thus boils down to the claim that an unconstitutional use of race in drawing the boundaries of majority-minority districts necessarily involves an unconstitutional use of race in drawing the boundaries of neighboring majority-white districts. We rejected that argument in *Hays*, explaining that evidence sufficient to support a *Shaw* claim with respect to a majority-minority district did "not prove anything" with respect to a neighboring majority-white district in which the appellees resided.

Accordingly, "an allegation to that effect does not allege a cognizable injury under the Fourteenth Amendment."

The judgment of the District Court is vacated, and the cases are remanded with instructions to dismiss the complaint.

4

The Decennial Census

The census is constitutionally required every ten years. The Supreme Court has frequently ruled on the regulations, execution, and implementation of the census.

United States Department of Commerce v. Montana
503 U.S. 442 (1992)

The 1990 census revealed that the population of certain States, particularly California, Florida, and Texas, had increased more rapidly than the national average. The application of the method of equal proportions to the 1990 census caused 8 States to gain a total of 19 additional seats in the House of Representatives and 13 States to lose an equal number. Montana was one of those States. Its loss of one seat cut its delegation in half and precipitated this litigation.

According to the 1990 census, the population of the 50 States that elect the members of the House of Representatives is 249,022,783. The average size of the 435 congressional districts is 572,466. Montana's population of 803,655 forms a single congressional district that is 231,189 persons larger than the ideal congressional district. If it had retained its two districts, each would have been 170,638 persons smaller than the ideal district. In terms of absolute difference, each of the two districts would have been closer to ideal size than the single congressional district.

The State of Montana, its Governor, Attorney General, and Secretary of State, and the State's two Senators and Representatives (hereinafter collectively referred to as Montana) filed suit against appropriate federal defendants (the Government) in the United States District Court for the District of Montana, asserting that Montana was entitled to retain its two seats. They alleged that the existing apportionment method violates Article I, §2, of the Constitution because it "does not achieve the greatest possible equality in the number of individuals per representative," and also violates Article I, §2, and Article I, §7. . . .

The . . . District Court decided that the principle of equal representation for equal numbers of people that was applied to intrastate districting in *Wesberry v. Sanders*, should also be applied to the apportionment of seats among the States. Under that standard, the only population variances that are acceptable are those that "are unavoidable despite a good faith effort to achieve absolute equality, or for which justification is shown." The District Court held that the variance between the population of Montana's single district and the ideal district could not be justified under that standard. . . . Accordingly, the District Court entered a judgment declaring the statute void and enjoining the Government from effecting any reapportionment of the House of Representatives pursuant to the method of equal proportions.

. . .

If either the method of smallest divisors or the method of the harmonic mean, also known as the "Dean Method," had been used after the

1990 census, Montana would have received a second seat. Under the method of equal proportions, which was actually used, five other States had stronger claims to an additional seat, because Montana's claim to a second seat was the 441st on the equal proportions "priority list." Montana would not have received a second seat under either the method of major fractions or greatest divisors.

. . .

The case before us today is "political" in the same sense that *Baker v. Carr* was a "political case." It raises an issue of great importance to the political branches. The issue has motivated partisan and sectional debate during important portions of our history. Nevertheless, the reasons that supported the justiciability of challenges to state legislative districts, as in *Baker*, as well as state districting decisions relating to the election of Members of Congress, apply with equal force to the issues presented by this litigation. The controversy between Montana and the Government turns on the proper interpretation of the relevant constitutional provisions. As our previous rejection of the political question doctrine in this context should make clear, the interpretation of the apportionment provisions of the Constitution is well within the competence of the Judiciary. The political question doctrine presents no bar to our reaching the merits of this dispute and deciding whether the District Court correctly construed the constitutional provisions at issue.

Our previous apportionment cases concerned States' decisions creating legislative districts; today we review the actions of Congress. Respect for a coordinate branch of Government raises special concerns not present in our prior cases, but those concerns relate to the merits of the controversy, rather than to our power to resolve it. As the issue is properly raised in a case other-

wise unquestionably within our jurisdiction, we must determine whether Congress exercised its apportionment authority within the limits dictated by the Constitution. Without the need for another exploration of the *Baker* factors, it suffices to say that, as in *Baker* itself and the apportionment cases that followed, the political question doctrine does not place this kind of constitutional interpretation outside the proper domain of the Judiciary.

. . .

. . . Montana emphasizes that the Dean method is the best method for minimizing the absolute deviations from ideal district size.

There is some force to the argument that the same historical insights that informed our construction of Article 1, §2 in the context of intrastate districting should apply here as well. As we interpreted the constitutional command that Representatives be chosen "by the People of the several States" to require the States to pursue equality in representation, we might well find that the requirement that Representatives be apportioned among the several States "according to their respective Numbers" would also embody the same principle of equality. Yet it is by no means clear that the facts here establish a violation of the *Wesberry* standard. In cases involving variances within a State, changes in the absolute differences from the ideal produce parallel changes in the relative differences. Within a State, there is no theoretical incompatibility entailed in minimizing both the absolute and the relative differences. In this case, in contrast, the reduction in the absolute difference between the size of Montana's district and the size of the ideal district has the effect of increasing the variance in the relative difference between the ideal and the size of the districts in both Montana and Washington. Moreover, whereas reductions in the variances among districts within a given State bring all of the affected districts closer to the ideal, in this case a change that would bring Montana closer to the ideal pushes the Washington districts away from that ideal.

What is the better measure of inequality—absolute difference in district size, absolute difference in share of a Representative, relative difference in district size or share? Neither mathematical analysis nor constitutional interpretation provides a conclusive answer. In none of these alternative measures of inequality do we find a substantive principle of commanding constitutional significance. The polestar of equal representation does not provide sufficient guidance to allow us to discern a single constitutionally permissible course.

. . .

The District Court suggested that the automatic character of the application of the method of equal proportions was inconsistent with Congress's responsibility to make a fresh legislative decision after each census. We find no merit in this suggestion. Indeed, if a set formula is otherwise constitutional, it seems to us that the use of a procedure that is administered efficiently and that avoids partisan controversy supports the legitimacy of congressional action, rather than undermining it. To the extent that the potentially divisive and complex issues associated with apportionment can be narrowed by the adoption of both procedural and substantive rules that are consistently applied year after year, the public is well served, provided, of course, that any such rule remains open to challenge or change at any time. We see no constitutional obstacle preventing Congress from adopting such a sensible procedure.

The decision to adopt the method of equal proportions was made by Congress after decades of experience, experimentation, and debate about the substance of the constitutional requirement. Independent scholars supported both the basic decision to adopt a regular procedure to be followed after each census and the particular decision to use the method of equal proportions. For a half century, the results of that method have been accepted by the States and the Nation. That history supports our conclusion that Congress had ample power to enact the statutory procedure in 1941 and to apply the method of equal proportions after the 1990 census.

The judgment of the District Court is reversed.

Franklin v. Massachusetts
505 U.S. 788 (1992)

... [A]s a result of the 1990 census and reapportionment, Massachusetts lost a seat in the House of Representatives. Appellees Massachusetts and two of its registered voters brought this action against the President, the Secretary of Commerce (Secretary), Census Bureau officials, and the Clerk of the House of Representatives, challenging, among other things, the method used for counting federal employees serving overseas. In particular, the appellants' allocation of 922,819 overseas military personnel to the State designated in their personnel files as their "home of record" altered the relative state populations enough to shift a Representative from Massachusetts to Washington. A three-judge panel of the United States District Court for the District of Massachusetts held that the decision to allocate military personnel serving overseas to their "homes of record" was arbitrary and capricious. ... [T]he District Court directed the Secretary to eliminate the overseas federal employees from the apportionment counts, directed the President to recalculate the number of Representatives per State and transmit the new calculation to Congress, and directed the Clerk of the House of Representatives to inform the States of the change. The federal officials appealed. . . .

. . .

Under the automatic reapportionment statute, the Secretary of Commerce takes the census, "in such form and content as [s]he may determine." The Secretary is permitted to delegate her authority for establishing census procedures to the Bureau of the Census. . . . After receiving the Secretary's report, the President

> shall transmit to the Congress a statement showing the whole number of persons in each State . . . as ascertained under the . . . decennial census of the population, and the number of Representatives to which each State would be entitled under an apportionment of the then existing number of Representatives by the method known as the method of equal proportions. . . .

. . .

Initially, the Bureau took the position that overseas federal employees would not be included in the 1990 state enumerations. . . . There were, however, stirrings in Congress in favor of including overseas federal employees, especially overseas military, in the state population counts. Several bills requiring the Secretary to include overseas military were introduced but not passed in the 100th and 101st Congresses. In July, 1989, nine months before the census taking was to begin, then-Secretary of Commerce Robert Mosbacher agreed to allocate overseas federal employees to their home States for purposes of congressional apportionment. His decision memorandum cites both the growing congressional support for including overseas employees and the Department of Defense's belief that "its employees should not be excluded from apportionment counts because of temporary and invol-

untary residence overseas." Another factor explaining the Secretary's shift was that the Department of Defense, the largest federal overseas employer, planned to poll its employees to determine, among other things, which State they considered their permanent home. In December, 1989, however, the Defense Department canceled its plans to conduct the survey due to a lack of funds. As an alternative, the Defense Department suggested that it could provide data on its employees' last six months of residence in the United States, information that would be more complete and up-to-date than the home of record data already in the personnel files. This possibility also failed to materialize when the Defense Department informed the Census Bureau that it was not able to assemble the information after all.

In the meantime, two more bills were introduced in Congress, but not passed, which would have required the Census Bureau to apportion members of the overseas military to their home States using the "home of record" data already in their personnel files. In July 1990, six months before the census count was due to be reported to the President, the Census Bureau decided to allocate the Department of Defense's overseas employees to the States based on their "home of record." It chose the home of record designation over other data available, including legal residence and last duty station, because home of record most closely resembled the Census Bureau's standard measure of state affiliation—"usual residence." Legal residence was thought less accurate, because the choice of legal residence may have been affected by state taxation. . . . For similar reasons, last duty station was rejected, because it would provide only a work address, and the employee's last home address might have been in a different State, as with those, for example, who worked in the District of Columbia but lived in Virginia or Maryland. Residence at a "last duty station" may also have been of a very short duration, and may not have reflected the more enduring tie of usual residence. Those military personnel for whom home of record information was not available were allocated based on legal residence or last duty station, in that order.

The Census Bureau invited 40 other federal agencies with overseas employees to submit counts of their employees as well. Of those, only 30 actually submitted counts, and only 20 agencies included dependents in their enumeration. Four of the agencies could not provide a home State for all of their overseas employees.

Appellees challenged the decision to allocate federal overseas employees, and the method used to do so, as inconsistent with the APA and with the constitutional requirement that the apportionment of Representatives be determined by an "actual Enumeration" of persons "in each State." Appellees focused their attack on the Secretary's decision to use "home of record" data for military personnel. The District Court, finding that it had jurisdiction to address the merits of the claims, was "skeptical" of the merits of appellees' constitutional claims, speculating that

> [t]here would appear to be nothing inherently unconstitutional in a properly supported decision to include overseas federal employees in apportionment counts.

The District Court nonetheless held that, on the administrative record before it, the Secretary's decision to allocate the employees and to use home of record data was arbitrary and capricious under the standards of the APA.

Appellees raise claims under both the APA and the Constitution. We address first the statutory basis for our jurisdiction under the APA.

The APA sets forth the procedures by which federal agencies are accountable to the public and their actions subject to review by the courts. The Secretary's report to the President is an unusual candidate for "agency action" within the meaning of the APA, because it is not promulgated to the public in the Federal Register, no official administrative record is generated, and its effect on reapportionment is felt only after the President makes the necessary calculations and reports the result to the Congress. Only after the President reports to Congress do the States have an entitlement to a particular number of Representatives.

The APA provides for judicial review of "final agency action for which there is no other adequate remedy in a court." At issue in this case is whether the "final" action that appellees have challenged is that of an "agency" such that the federal courts may exercise their powers of review under the APA. We hold that the final action complained of is that of the President, and the President is not an agency within the meaning of the Act. Accordingly, there is no final agency action that may be reviewed under the APA standards.

. . . In this case, the action that creates an entitlement to a particular number of Representatives and has a direct effect on the reapportionment is the President's statement to Congress, not the Secretary's report to the President.

Unlike other statutes that expressly require the President to transmit an agency's report directly to Congress . . . Section 2a does not expressly require the President to use the data in the Secretary's report, but, rather, the data from the "decennial census." There is no statute forbidding amendment of the "decennial census" itself after the Secretary submits the report to the President. For potential litigants, therefore, the "decennial census" still presents a moving target, even after the Secretary reports to the President. In this case, the Department of Commerce, in its press release issued the day the Secretary submitted the report to the President, was explicit that the data presented to the President was still subject to correction. Moreover, there is no statute that rules out an instruction by the President to the Secretary to reform the census, even after the data is submitted to him. It is not until the President submits the information to Congress that the target stops moving, because only then are the States entitled by §2a to a particular number of Representatives. Because the Secretary's report to the President carries no direct consequences for the reapportionment, it serves more like a tentative recommendation than a final and binding determination. It is, like "the ruling of a subordinate official," not final, and therefore not subject to review.

. . . Under 13 U.S.C. §141(a) . . . the Secretary's report to the President has no direct effect on reapportionment until the President takes affirmative steps to calculate and transmit the apportionment to Congress.

Appellees claim that, because the President exercises no discretion in calculating the numbers of Representatives, his "role in the statutory scheme was intended to have no substantive content," and the final action is the Secretary's, not the President's. . . .

The admittedly ministerial nature of the apportionment calculation itself does not answer the question whether the apportionment is foreordained by the time the Secretary gives her report to the President. To reiterate, §2 does not curtail the President's authority to direct the Secretary in making policy judgments that result in "the decennial census"; he is not expressly required to adhere to the policy decisions reflected in the Secretary's report. Because it is the President's personal transmittal of the report to Congress that settles the apportionment, until he acts, there is no determinate agency action to challenge. The President, not the Secretary, takes the final action that affects the States.

Indeed, it is clear that Congress thought it was important to involve a constitutional officer in the apportionment process. Congress originally considered a bill requiring the Secretary to report the apportionment calculation directly to Congress. The bill was later amended to require the participation of the President. . . . It is hard to imagine a purpose for involving the President if he is to be prevented from exercising his accustomed supervisory powers over his executive officers. Certainly no purpose to alter the President's usual superintendent role is evident from the text of the statute.

As enacted, 2 U.S.C. §2a provides that the Secretary cannot act alone; she must send her results to the President, who makes the calculations and sends the final apportionment to Congress. That the final act is that of the President is important to the integrity of the process, and bolsters our conclusion that his duties are not merely ceremonial or ministerial. Thus, we can only review the APA claims here if the President, not the Secretary of Commerce, is an "agency" within the meaning of the Act.

. . . The President is not explicitly excluded from the APA's purview, but he is not explicitly included, either. Out of respect for the separation of powers and the unique constitutional position of the President, we find that textual silence is not enough to subject the President to the provisions of the APA. We would require an express statement by Congress before assuming it intended the President's performance of his statutory duties to be reviewed for abuse of discretion.

As the APA does not expressly allow review of the President's actions, we must presume that his actions are not subject to its requirements. Although the President's actions may still be reviewed for constitutionality, we hold that they are not reviewable for abuse of discretion under the APA. The District Court erred in proceeding to determine the merits of the APA.

Although the reapportionment determination is not subject to review under the standards of the APA, that does not dispose of appellees' constitutional claims. Constitutional challenges to apportionment are justiciable.

We first address standing. . . .

To determine whether appellees sufficiently allege and prove causation requires separating out appellees' claims: appellees claim both that the Secretary erred in deciding to allocate overseas employees to various States and that the Secretary erred in using inaccurate data to do so. Appellees have shown that Massachusetts would have had an additional Representative if overseas employees had not been allocated at all. They have neither alleged nor shown, however, that Massachusetts would have had an additional Representative if the allocation had been done using some other source of "more accurate" data. Consequently, even if appellees have standing to challenge the Secretary's decision to allocate, they do not have standing to challenge the accuracy of the data used in making that allocation. We need, then, review only the decision to include overseas federal employees in the state population counts, not the Secretary's choice of information sources.

The thornier standing question is whether the injury is redressable by the relief sought. Tracking the statutory progress of the census data from the Census Bureau, through the President, and to the States, the District Court entered an injunc-

tion against the Secretary of Commerce, the President, and the Clerk of the House. While injunctive relief against executive officials like the Secretary of Commerce is within the courts' power, the District Court's grant of injunctive relief against the President himself is extraordinary, and should have raised judicial eyebrows. . . . [I]n general, "this court has no jurisdiction of a bill to enjoin the President in the performance of his official duties." At the threshold, the District Court should have evaluated whether injunctive relief against the President was available, and, if not, whether appellees' injuries were nonetheless redressable.

For purposes of establishing standing, however, we need not decide whether injunctive relief against the President was appropriate, because we conclude that the injury alleged is likely to be redressed by declaratory relief against the Secretary alone. The Secretary certainly has an interest in defending her policy determinations concerning the census; even though she cannot herself change the reapportionment, she has an interest in litigating its accuracy. . . . [W]e may assume it is substantially likely that the President and other executive and congressional officials would abide by an authoritative interpretation of the census statute and constitutional provision by the District Court, even though they would not be directly bound by such a determination.

On the merits, appellees argue that the Secretary's allocation of overseas federal employees to the States violated the command of Article I, §2, cl. 3, that the number of Representatives per State be determined by an "actual Enumeration" of "their respective Numbers," that is, a count of the persons "in" each State. Appellees point out that the first census conducted in 1790 required that persons be allocated to their place of "usual residence." Because the interpretations of the Constitution by the First Congress are persuasive, appellees argue that the Secretary should have allocated the overseas employees to their overseas stations, because those were their usual residences.

The appellants respond, on the other hand, that the allocation of employees temporarily stationed overseas to their home States is fully compatible with the standard of "usual residence" used in the early censuses. We review the dispute to the extent of determining whether the Secretary's interpretation is consistent with the constitutional language and the constitutional goal of equal representation.

"Usual residence" was the gloss given the constitutional phrase "in each State" by the first enumeration Act, and has been used by the Census Bureau ever since to allocate persons to their home States. The term can mean more than mere physical presence, and has been used broadly enough to include some element of allegiance or enduring tie to a place. . . .

. . .

In this case, the Secretary of Commerce made a judgment, consonant with, though not dictated by, the text and history of the Constitution, that many federal employees temporarily stationed overseas had retained their ties to the States, and could and should be counted toward their States' representation in Congress. . . . The Secretary's judgment does not hamper the underlying constitutional goal of equal representation, but, assuming that employees temporarily stationed abroad have indeed retained their ties to their home States, actually promotes equality. . . . Certainly, appellees have not demonstrated that eliminating overseas employees entirely from the state counts will make representation in Congress more equal. We conclude

that appellees' constitutional challenge fails on the merits.

The District Court's judgment is reversed.

Wisconsin v. City of New York
517 U.S. 1 (1996)

In conducting the 1990 United States Census, the Secretary of Commerce decided not to use a particular statistical adjustment that had been designed to correct an undercount in the initial enumeration. The Court of Appeals for the Second Circuit held that the Secretary's decision was subject to heightened scrutiny because of its effect on the right of individual respondents to have their vote counted equally. . . .

. . .

The Constitution provides that the results of the census shall be used to apportion the Members of the House of Representatives among the States. Because the Constitution provides that the number of Representatives apportioned to each State determines in part the allocation to each State of votes for the election of the President, the decennial census also affects the allocation of members of the electoral college. Today, census data also have important consequences not delineated in the Constitution: the Federal Government considers census data in dispensing funds through federal programs to the States, and the States use the results in drawing intrastate political districts.

There have been 20 decennial censuses in the history of the United States. Although each was designed with the goal of accomplishing an "actual Enumeration" of the population, no census is recognized as having been wholly successful in achieving that goal. Despite consistent efforts to improve the quality of the count, errors persist. Persons who should have been counted are not counted at all or are counted at the wrong location; persons who should not have been counted (whether because they died before or were born after the decennial census date, because they were not a citizen of the country, or because they did not exist) are counted; and persons who should have been counted only once are counted twice. It is thought that these errors have resulted in a net "undercount" of the actual American population in every decennial census. In 1970, for instance, the Census Bureau concluded that the census results were 2.7 percent lower than the actual population.

The undercount is not thought to be spread consistently across the population: some segments of the population are "undercounted" to a greater degree than are others, resulting in a phenomenon termed the "differential undercount." Since at least 1940, the Census Bureau has thought that the undercount affects some racial and ethnic minority groups to a greater extent than it does whites. . . . The problem of the differential undercount has persisted even as the census has come to provide a more numerically accurate count of the population. In the 1980 census, for example, the overall undercount was estimated at 1.2 percent, and the undercount of blacks was estimated at 4.9 percent.

The Census Bureau has recognized the undercount and the differential undercount as significant problems, and in the past has devoted substantial effort toward achieving their reduction. Most recently, in its preparations for the 1990 census, the Bureau initiated an extensive inquiry into various means of overcoming the impact of the undercount and the differential undercount. As part of this effort, the Bureau created two task forces: the Undercount Steering Committee (USC), responsible for planning

undercount research and policy development; and the Undercount Research Staff (URS), which conducted research into various methods of improving the accuracy of the census. In addition, the Bureau consulted with state and local governments and various outside experts and organizations.

Largely as a result of these efforts, the Bureau adopted a wide variety of measures designed to reduce the rate of error in the 1990 enumeration, including an extensive advertising campaign, a more easily completed census questionnaire, and increased use of automation, which among other things facilitated the development of accurate maps and geographic files for the 1990 census. The Bureau also implemented a number of improvements specifically targeted at eliminating the differential undercount; these included advertising campaigns developed by and directed at traditionally undercounted populations and expanded questionnaire assistance operations for non-English speaking residents.

In preparing for the 1990 census, the Bureau and the task forces also looked into the possibility of using large-scale statistical adjustment to compensate for the undercount and differential undercount. Although the Bureau had previously considered that possibility (most recently in 1980), it always had decided instead to rely upon more traditional methodology and the results of the enumeration. In 1985, preliminary investigations by the URS suggested that the most promising method of statistical adjustment was the "capture-recapture" or "dual system estimation" approach.

The particular variations of the "dual system estimation" considered by the Bureau are not important for purposes of this opinion. . . .

In the context of the census, the initial enumeration of the entire population (the "capture") would be followed by the post-enumeration survey (PES) (the "recapture") of certain representative geographical areas. The Bureau would then compare the results of the PES to the results of the initial enumeration for those areas targeted by the PES, in order to determine a rate of error in those areas for the initial enumeration, (i.e., the rate at which the initial enumeration undercounted people in those areas). That rate of error would be extrapolated to the entire population, and thus would be used to statistically adjust the results of the initial enumeration.

The URS thought that the PES also held some promise for correcting the differential undercount. The PES would be conducted through the use of a system called post-stratification. Thus, each person counted through the PES would be placed into one, and only one, of over 1,000 post-strata defined by five categories: geography; age; sex; status of housing unit (rent versus own); and race (including Hispanic versus non-Hispanic origin). By comparing the post-stratified PES data to the results of the initial enumeration, the Bureau would be able to estimate not only an overall undercount rate, but also an undercount rate for each post-strata. Hence, the statistical adjustment of the census could reflect differences in the undercount rate for each post-strata.

Through the mid-1980s, the Bureau conducted a series of field tests and statistical studies designed to measure the utility of the PES as a tool for adjusting the census. The Director of the Bureau decided to adopt a PES-based adjustment, and in June, 1987, he informed his superiors in the Department of Commerce of that decision. The Secretary of Commerce disagreed with the Director's decision to adjust, however, and in October 1987, the Department of Commerce announced that the 1990 Census would not be statistically adjusted.

In November 1988, several plaintiffs (including a number of the respondents in this case) brought suit in the United States District Court for the Eastern District of New York, arguing that the Secretary's decision against statistical adjustment of the 1990 census was unconstitutional and contrary to federal law. The parties entered into an interim stipulation providing, inter alia, that the Secretary would reconsider the possibility of a statistical adjustment.

In July 1991, the Secretary issued his decision not to use the PES to adjust the 1990 census. The Secretary began by noting that large-scale statistical adjustment of the census through the PES would "abandon a two hundred year tradition of how we actually count people." Before taking a "step of that magnitude," he held, it was necessary to be "certain that it would make the census better and the distribution of the population more accurate." Emphasizing that the primary purpose of the census was to apportion political representation among the States, the Secretary concluded that

> the primary criterion for accuracy should be distributive accuracy—that is, getting most nearly correct the proportions of people in different areas.

. . . [T]he Secretary concluded that, although numerical accuracy (at the national level) might be improved through statistical adjustment, he could not be confident that the distributive accuracy of the census—particularly at the state and local level—would be improved by a PES-based adjustment. In particular, the Secretary noted, the adjusted figures became increasingly unreliable as one focused upon smaller and smaller political subdivisions.

The Secretary stated that his decision not to adjust was buttressed by a concern that adjustment of the 1990 census might present significant problems in the future. Because small changes in adjustment methodology would have a large impact upon apportionment—an impact that could be determined before a particular methodology was chosen—the Secretary found that statistical adjustment of the 1990 census might open the door to political tampering in the future. The Secretary also noted that statistical adjustment might diminish the incentive for state and local political leaders to assist in the conduct of the initial enumeration. In conclusion, the Secretary stated that the Bureau would continue its research into the possibility of statistical adjustment of future censuses, and would maintain its efforts to improve the accuracy and inclusiveness of the initial enumeration.

The plaintiffs returned to court. The District Court concluded that the Secretary's decision violated neither the Constitution nor federal law.

Respondents appealed, arguing that the District Court had adopted the wrong standard of review for their constitutional claim, and the Court of Appeals for the Second Circuit reversed by a divided vote. . . . The court remanded for an inquiry into whether the Secretary could show that the decision not to adjust was essential for the achievement of a legitimate governmental objective.

. . .

In its decision in this case, the Court of Appeals found that a standard more strict than that established in *Montana* and *Franklin* should apply to the Secretary's decision not to statistically adjust the census. The court looked to equal protection principles distilled from the same line of state redistricting cases relied upon by the plaintiffs in *Montana*, and found that both the nature of the right asserted by respondents—the right to have one's vote counted equally—and the nature of the affected classes—"certain identifiable mi-

nority groups"—required that the Secretary's decision be given heightened scrutiny. The court drew from the District Court's decision "implicit" findings: that the census did not achieve equality of voting power as nearly as practicable. . . .

The court recognized two significant differences between the intrastate districting cases and the instant case: first, that this case involves the federal, rather than a state government; and second, that constitutional requirements make it impossible to achieve precise equality in voting power nationwide. But it found these differences nondeterminative, deciding that no deference was owed to the Executive Branch on a question of law, and that the "impossibility of achieving precise mathematical equality is no excuse for [the Federal Government] not making [the] mandated good faith effort." The court found that the respondents here had established a prima facie violation of the *Wesberry* standard both by showing that the PES-based adjustment would increase numerical accuracy and by virtue of the fact that "the differential undercount in the 1990 enumeration was plainly foreseeable and foreseen." The court held that the Secretary's decision would have to be vacated as unconstitutional unless, on remand, he could show that the decision not to adjust "(a) furthers a governmental objective that is legitimate, and (b) is essential for the achievement of that objective."

We think that the Court of Appeals erred in holding the "one person-one vote" standard of *Wesberry* and its progeny applicable to the case at hand. For several reasons, the "good faith effort to achieve population equality" required of a State conducting intrastate redistricting does not translate into a requirement that the Federal Government conduct a census that is as accurate as possible. First, we think that the Court of Appeals understated the significance of the two differences that it recognized between state redistricting cases and the instant case. The court failed to recognize that the Secretary's decision was made pursuant to Congress' direct delegation of its broad authority over the census. The court also undervalued the significance of the fact that the Constitution makes it impossible to achieve population equality among interstate districts. As we have noted before, the Constitution provides that "[t]he number of Representatives shall not exceed one for every 30,000 persons; each State shall have at least one Representative; and district boundaries may not cross state lines."

While a court can easily determine whether a State has made the requisite "good faith effort" toward population equality through the application of a simple mathematical formula, we see no way in which a court can apply the *Wesberry* standard to the Federal Government's decisions regarding the conduct of the census. The Court of Appeals found that *Wesberry* required the Secretary to conduct a census that "would achieve population equality," which it understood to mean a census that was as accurate as possible. But, in so doing, the court implicitly found that the Constitution prohibited the Secretary from preferring distributive accuracy to numerical accuracy, and that numerical accuracy—which the court found to be improved by a PES-based adjustment—was constitutionally preferable to distributive accuracy. As in *Montana*, where we could see no constitutional basis upon which to choose between absolute equality and relative equality, so here can we see no ground for preferring numerical accuracy to distributive accuracy, or for preferring gross accuracy to some particular measure of accuracy. The Constitution itself provides no real instruction on this point, and extrapolation from our intrastate districting cases is equally unhelpful. Quite simply, "[t]he polestar of equal

representation does not provide sufficient guidance to allow us to discern a single constitutionally permissible course."

. . . [I]t is difficult to see why or how *Wesberry* would apply to the Federal Government's conduct of the census—a context even further removed from intrastate districting than is congressional apportionment. Congress' conduct of the census, even more than its decision concerning apportionment, "commands far more deference than a state districting decision that is capable of being reviewed under a relatively rigid mathematical standard."

Rather than the standard adopted by the Court of Appeals, we think that it is the standard established by this Court in *Montana* and *Franklin* that applies to the Secretary's decision not to adjust. The text of the Constitution vests Congress with virtually unlimited discretion in conducting the decennial "actual Enumeration," and, notwithstanding the plethora of lawsuits that inevitably accompany each decennial census, there is no basis for thinking that Congress' discretion is more limited than the text of the Constitution provides. Through the Census Act, Congress has delegated its broad authority over the census to the Secretary. Hence, so long as the Secretary's conduct of the census is "consistent with the constitutional language and the constitutional goal of equal representation," it is within the limits of the Constitution. In light of the Constitution's broad grant of authority to Congress, the Secretary's decision not to adjust need bear only a reasonable relationship to the accomplishment of an actual enumeration of the population, keeping in mind the constitutional purpose of the census.

In 1990, the Census Bureau made an extraordinary effort to conduct an accurate enumeration, and was successful in counting 98.4 percent of the population. The Secretary then had to consider whether to adjust the census using statistical data derived from the PES. He based his decision not to adjust the census upon three determinations. First, he held that, in light of the constitutional purpose of the census, its distributive accuracy was more important than its numerical accuracy. Second, he determined that the unadjusted census data would be considered the most distributively accurate absent a showing to the contrary. And finally, after reviewing the results of the PES in light of extensive research and the recommendations of his advisors, the Secretary found that the PES-based adjustment would not improve distributive accuracy. Each of these three determinations is well within the bounds of the Secretary's constitutional discretion.

. . . [T]he Secretary's decision to focus on distributive accuracy is not inconsistent with the Constitution. Indeed, a preference for distributive accuracy (even at the expense of some numerical accuracy) would seem to follow from the constitutional purpose of the census, viz., to determine the apportionment of the Representatives among the States. Respondents do not dispute this point. Rather, they challenge the Secretary's first determination by arguing that he improperly "regarded evidence of superior numeric accuracy as 'not relevant' to the determination of distributive accuracy." In support of this argument, respondents note that an enumeration that results in increased numerical accuracy will also result in increased distributive accuracy.

We think that respondents rest too much upon the statement by the Secretary to which they refer. . . . In his decision, the Secretary found numerical accuracy (in addition to distributive accuracy) to be relevant to his decision whether to adjust. Even if the Secretary had chosen to subordinate numerical accuracy, we are not sure why the fact that distributive and numerical ac-

curacy correlate closely in an improved enumeration would require the Secretary to conclude that they correlate also for a PES-based statistical adjustment.

Turning to the Secretary's second determination . . . the importance of historical practice in this area. Nevertheless, respondents challenge the Secretary's second determination by arguing that his understanding of historical practice is flawed. According to respondents, the Secretary assumed that the census traditionally was conducted via a simple "headcount," thereby ignoring the fact that statistical adjustment had been used in both the 1970 and 1980 census.

We need not tarry long with this argument. The Secretary reasonably recognized that a PES-based statistical adjustment would be a significant change from the traditional method of conducting the census. The statistical adjustments in 1970 and 1980 to which respondents refer were of an entirely different type than the adjustment considered here, and they took place on a dramatically smaller scale. Moreover, the PES-based adjustment would have been the first time in history that the States' apportionment would have been based upon counts in other States. Here, the Secretary's understanding of the traditional method of conducting the census was well founded, as was his establishment of a rebuttable presumption that the traditional method was the most accurate.

The Secretary ultimately determined that the available evidence "tends to support the superior distributive accuracy of the actual enumeration" and it is this determination at which respondents direct the brunt of their attack. . . . According to respondents, we should carefully comb the Secretary's decision in order to review his conclusions de novo.

Respondents' argument fundamentally misapprehends the basis for our deference to the

Secretary's determination that the adjusted census results do not provide a more distributively accurate count of the population. Our deference arises not from the highly technical nature of his decision, but rather from the wide discretion bestowed by the Constitution upon Congress, and by Congress upon the Secretary. Regardless of the Secretary's statistical expertise, it is he to whom Congress has delegated its constitutional authority over the census. For that same reason, the mere fact that the Secretary's decision overruled the views of some of his subordinates is by itself of no moment in any judicial review of his decision.

Turning finally to review the Secretary's conclusion that the PES adjustment would not improve distributive accuracy, we need note only that the Secretary's conclusion is supported by the reasoning of some of his advisors, and was therefore a reasonable choice in an area where technical experts disagree. . . .

The Constitution confers upon Congress the responsibility to conduct an "actual Enumeration" of the American public every 10 years, with the primary purpose of providing a basis for apportioning political representation among the States. Here, the Secretary of Commerce, to whom Congress has delegated its constitutional authority over the census, determined that in light of the constitutional purpose of the census, an "actual Enumeration" would best be achieved without the PES-based statistical adjustment of the results of the initial enumeration. We find that conclusion entirely reasonable. Therefore we hold that the Secretary's decision was well within the constitutional bounds of discretion over the conduct of the census provided to the Federal Government. The judgment of the Court of Appeals is reversed.

Department of Commerce v. House of Representatives
525 U.S. 316 (1999)

The Census Bureau (Bureau) has announced a plan to use two forms of statistical sampling in the 2000 Decennial Census to address a chronic and apparently growing problem of "undercounting" certain identifiable groups of individuals. Two sets of plaintiffs filed separate suits challenging the legality and constitutionality of the Bureau's plan. Convened as three-judge courts, the District Court for the Eastern District of Virginia and the District Court for the District of Columbia each held that the Bureau's plan for the 2000 census violates the Census Act, and both courts permanently enjoined the Bureau's planned use of statistical sampling to determine the population for purposes of congressional apportionment. . . .

. . .

The instant dispute centers on the problem of "undercount" in the decennial census. For the last few decades, the Census Bureau has sent census forms to every household, which it asked residents to complete and return. The Bureau followed up on the mailing by sending enumerators to personally visit all households that did not respond by mail. Despite this comprehensive effort to reach every household, the Bureau has always failed to reach—and has thus failed to count—a portion of the population. This shortfall has been labeled the census "undercount."

. . .

Some identifiable groups—including certain minorities, children, and renters—have historically had substantially higher undercount rates than the population as a whole. Accordingly, in previous censuses, the Bureau sought to increase the number of persons from whom it obtained information. In 1990, for instance, the Bureau attempted to reach out to traditionally under-counted groups by promoting awareness of the census and its importance, providing access to Spanish language forms, and offering a toll-free number for those who had questions about the forms. Indeed, the 1990 census was "better de-signed and executed than any previous census." Nonetheless, it was less accurate than its prede-cessor for the first time since the Bureau began measuring the undercount rate in 1940.

In a further effort to address growing concerns about undercount in the census, Congress passed the Decennial Census Improvement Act of 1991, which instructed the Secretary to contract with the National Academy of Sciences (Academy) to study the "means by which the Government could achieve the most accurate population count pos-sible." . . . Two of the three panels established by the Academy pursuant to this Act concluded that "[d]ifferential undercount cannot be reduced to acceptable levels at acceptable costs without the use of integrated coverage measurement," a sta-tistical sampling procedure that adjusts census results to account for undercount in the initial enumeration, and all three panels recommended including integrated coverage measurement in the 2000 census.

In light of these studies and other research, the Bureau formulated a plan for the 2000 census that uses statistical sampling to supplement data ob-tained through traditional census methods. The Bureau plan provides for two types of sampling that are the subject of the instant challenge. First, appellees challenge the proposed use of sampling in the Nonresponse Followup program (NRFU). Under this program, the Bureau would continue to send census forms to all households, as well as make forms available in post offices and in other public places. The Bureau expects that 67 percent of households will return the forms. The Bureau then plans to divide the population into census tracts of approximately 4,000 people that have "homogenous population characteristics, economic status, and living conditions." The Bu-reau would then visit a randomly selected sample of nonresponding housing units, which would be "statistically representative of all housing units in [a] nonresponding tract." The rate of nonresponse follow-up in a tract would vary with the mail re-sponse rate to ensure that the Bureau obtains cen-sus data from at least 90 percent of the housing units in each census tract. For instance, if a cen-sus tract had 1,000 housing units and 800 units responded by mail, the Bureau would survey 100 out of the 200 nonresponding units to obtain in-formation about 90 percent of the housing units. However, if only 400 of the 1,000 housing units responded by mail, the Bureau would visit 500 of the 600 nonresponding units to achieve the same result. The information gathered from the nonresponding housing units surveyed by the Bu-reau would then be used to estimate the size and characteristics of the nonresponding housing units that the Bureau did not visit. Thus, continuing with the first example, the Bureau would use in-formation about the 100 nonresponding units it visits to estimate the characteristics of the remain-ing 100 nonresponding units on which the Bu-reau has no information.

The second challenged sampling procedure—which would be implemented after the first is completed—is known as Integrated Coverage Measurement (ICM). ICM employs the statisti-cal technique called Dual System Estimation (DSE) to adjust the census results to account for undercount in the initial enumeration. The plan requires the Bureau to begin by classifying each of the country's 7 million blocks into "strata," which are defined by the characteristics of each block, including state, racial, and ethnic composition, and the proportion of homeowners to renters, as revealed in the 1990 census. The Bureau then plans to select blocks at random from each stratum, for a total of 25,000 blocks, or an estimated 750,000 housing units. Enumerators would then conduct interviews at each of those 750,000 units, and if discrepancies were detected between the pre-ICM response and ICM response, a follow-up interview would be conducted to determine the "true" situation in the home. The information gathered during this stage would be used to assign each person to a poststratum—a group of people who have similar chances of being counted in the initial data collection—which would be defined by state geographic subdivision (e.g., rural or urban), owner or renter, age, sex, race, and Hispanic origin.

In the final stage of the census, the Bureau plans to use DSE to obtain the final count and characteristics of the population. The census plan calls for the Bureau to compare the dual systems of information—that is, the data gathered on the sample blocks during the ICM and the data gathered on those same blocks through the initial phase of the census—to produce an estimation factor for each poststratum. The estimation factors would account for the differences between the ICM numbers and the initial enumeration and would be applied to the initial enumeration to estimate the total population and housing units in each poststratum. The totals for the poststrata would then be summed to determine state and national population totals.

The Bureau's announcement of its plan to use statistical sampling in the 2000 census led to a flurry of legislative activity. . . . Congress . . . passed, and the President signed, a bill providing for the creation of a

comprehensive and detailed plan outlining [the Bureau's] proposed methodologies for conducting the 2000 Decennial Census and available methods to conduct an actual enumeration of the population, including an explanation of any statistical methodologies that may be used. Pursuant to this directive, the Commerce Department issued the Census 2000 Report. After receiving the Report, Congress passed the 1998 Departments of Commerce, Justice, and State, the Judiciary, and Related Agencies Appropriations Act, which provides that the Census 2000 Report and the Bureau's Census 2000 Operational Plan "shall be deemed to constitute final agency action regarding the use of statistical methods in the 2000 decennial census." The Act also permits any person aggrieved by the plan to use statistical sampling in the decennial census to bring a legal action and requires that any action brought under the Act be heard by a three-judge district court. It further provides for review by appeal directly to this Court.

The publication of the Bureau's plan for the 2000 census occasioned two separate legal challenges. The first suit, styled *Clinton v. Glavin*, was filed on February 12, 1998, in the District Court for the Eastern District of Virginia by four counties . . . and residents of 13 States . . . who claimed that the Bureau's planned use of statistical sampling to apportion Representatives among the States violates the Census Act and the Census Clause of the Constitution. They sought a declaration that the Bureau's plan is unlawful and/ or unconstitutional and an injunction barring use of the NRFU and ICM sampling procedures in the 2000 census.

The District Court held that the case was ripe for review, that the plaintiffs satisfied the requirements for Article III standing, and that the Census Act prohibited use of the challenged sampling procedures to apportion Representatives. The District Court concluded that, because the statute was clear on its face, the court did not need to reach the constitutional questions presented. It thus denied defendants' motion to dismiss, granted plaintiffs' motion for summary judgment, and permanently enjoined the use of the challenged sampling procedures to determine the population for purposes of congressional apportionment. . . .

The second challenge was filed by the United States House of Representatives on February 20, 1998, in the District Court for the District of Columbia. The House sought a declaration that the Bureau's proposed use of sampling to determine the population for purposes of apportioning Members of the House of Representatives among the several States violates the Census Act and the Constitution. The House also sought a permanent injunction barring use of the challenged sampling procedures in the apportionment aspect of the 2000 census.

The District Court held that the House had Article III standing, the suit was ripe for review, equitable concerns did not warrant dismissal, the suit did not violate separation of powers principles, and the Census Act does not permit the use of the challenged sampling procedures in counting the population for apportionment. Because it held that the Census Act does not allow for the challenged sampling procedures, it declined to reach the House's constitutional challenge under the Census Clause. The District Court denied the defendants' motion to dismiss, granted the plaintiffs' motion for summary judgment, and issued an injunction preventing defendants from using the challenged sampling methods in the apportionment aspect of the 2000 census. The defendants appealed to this Court. . . .

We turn our attention first to the issues presented by *Clinton v. Glavin* and we begin our analysis with the threshold issue of justiciability. . . . [T]he District Court below correctly found that the case is ripe for review, and that determination is not challenged here. Thus, the only open justiciability question in this case is whether appellees satisfy the requirements of Article III standing.

. . . Here, the District Court . . . held that the plaintiffs-appellees, residents from 13 States, had established Article III standing to bring suit challenging the proposed method for conducting the 2000 census. . . . The court did not, however, consider whether there was a genuine issue of material fact as to standing.

Nonetheless, because the record before us amply supports the conclusion that several of the appellees have met their burden of proof regarding their standing to bring this suit, we affirm the District Court's holding. . . .

Appellants have failed to set forth any specific facts showing that there is a genuine issue of standing for trial. . . .

. . . In the context of apportionment, we have held that voters have standing to challenge an apportionment statute because "[t]hey are asserting 'a plain, direct and adequate interest in maintaining the effectiveness of their votes.'" The same distinct interest is at issue here: with one fewer Representative, Indiana residents' votes will be diluted. Moreover, the threat of vote dilution through the use of sampling is "concrete" and "actual or imminent, not 'conjectural' or 'hypothetical.'" It is clear that if the Bureau is going to alter its plan to use sampling in the 2000 census, it must begin doing so by March 1999. And it is certainly not necessary for this Court to wait until the census has been conducted to consider the issues presented here, because such a pause would result in extreme—possibly irremediable—hardship. . . . There is undoubtedly a "traceable" connection between the use of sampling in the decennial census and Indiana's expected loss of a Representative, and there is a substantial likelihood that the requested relief—a permanent injunction against the proposed uses of sampling in the census—will redress the alleged injury.

Appellees have also established standing on the basis of the expected effects of the use of sampling in the 2000 census on intrastate redistricting . . . the appellees who live in the aforementioned counties have a strong claim that they will be injured by the Bureau's plan because their votes will be diluted vis-a-vis residents of counties with larger "undercount" rates. . . .

We accordingly arrive at the dispute over the meaning of the relevant provisions of the Census Act. The District Court below examined the plain text and legislative history of the Act and concluded that the proposed use of statistical sampling to determine population for purposes of apportioning congressional seats among the States violates the Act. . . .

. . .

The current Census Act was enacted into positive law in 1954. It contained substantially the same language as did its predecessor statutes, requiring enumerators to "visit personally each dwelling house in his subdivision" in order to obtain "every item of information and all particulars required for any census or survey" conducted in connection with the census. Indeed, the first departure from the requirement that the enumerators collect all census information through personal visits to every household in the Nation came in 1957 at the behest of the Secretary. The Secretary asked Congress to amend the Act to permit the Bureau to use statistical sampling in gathering some of the census information. In re-

sponse, Congress enacted §195, which provided that,

> [e]xcept for the determination of population for apportionment purposes, the Secretary may, where he deems it appropriate, authorize the use of the statistical method known as "sampling" in carrying out the provisions of this title.

This provision allowed the Secretary to authorize the use of sampling procedures in gathering supplemental, nonapportionment census information regarding population, unemployment, housing, and other matters collected in conjunction with the decennial census—much of which is now collected through what is known as the "long form"—but it did not authorize the use of sampling procedures in connection with apportionment of Representatives.

In 1964, Congress repealed former §25(c) of the Census Act, which had required that each enumerator obtain "every item of information" by personal visit to each household. The repeal of this section permitted the Bureau to replace the personal visit of the enumerator with a form delivered and returned via the Postal Service. Pursuant to this new authority, census officials conducted approximately 60 percent of the census through a new "mailout-mailback" system for the first time in 1970. The Bureau then conducted follow-up visits to homes that failed to return census forms. Thus, although the legislation permitted the Bureau to conduct a portion of the census through the mail, there was no suggestion from any quarter that this change altered the prohibition in §195 on the use of statistical sampling in determining the population for apportionment purposes.

In 1976, the provisions of the Census Act at issue in this case took their present form. Congress revised §141 of the Census Act, which is now entitled "Population and other census information." It amended subsection (a) to authorize the Secretary to

> take a decennial census of population as of the first day of April of such year, which date shall be known as the "decennial census date," in such form and content as he may determine, including the use of sampling procedures and special surveys.

Congress also added several subsections to §141, among them a provision specifying that the term "census of population," as used in §141, "means a census of population, housing, and matters relating to population and housing." Together, these revisions provided a broad statement that in collecting a range of demographic information during the decennial census, the Bureau would be permitted to use sampling procedures and special surveys.

This broad grant of authority given in §141(a) is informed, however, by the narrower and more specific §195, which is revealingly entitled, "Use of Sampling." The §141 authorization to use sampling techniques in the decennial census is not necessarily an authorization to use these techniques in collecting all of the information that is gathered during the decennial census. We look to the remainder of the law to determine what portions of the decennial census the authorization covers. When we do, we discover that, as discussed above, §195 directly prohibits the use of sampling in the determination of population for purposes of apportionment.

When Congress amended §195 in 1976, it did not, in doing so, alter the longstanding prohibition on the use of sampling in matters relating to apportionment. Congress modified the section by changing "apportionment purposes" to "purposes of apportionment of Representative in Congress among the several States" and changing the phrase "may, where he deems it appropriate" to

"shall, if he considers it feasible." The amended section thus reads:

> Except for the determination of population for purposes of apportionment of Representatives in Congress among the several States, the Secretary shall, if he considers it feasible, authorize the use of the statistical method known as "sampling" in carrying out the provisions of this title.

. . . [T]he section now requires the Secretary to use statistical sampling assembling the myriad demographic data that are collected in connection with the decennial census. But the section maintains its prohibition on the use of statistical sampling in calculating population for purposes of apportionment.

Absent any historical context, the language in the amended §195 might reasonably be read as either permissive or prohibitive with regard to the use of sampling for apportionment purposes. Indeed, appellees and appellants each cite numerous examples of the "except/shall" sentence structure that support their respective interpretations of the statute. But these dueling examples only serve to illustrate that the interpretation of the "except/shall" structure depends primarily on the broader context in which that structure appears. Here, the context is provided by over 200 years during which federal statutes have prohibited the use of statistical sampling where apportionment is concerned. In light of this background, there is only one plausible reading of the amended §195: It prohibits the use of sampling in calculating population for purposes of apportionment.

. . .

In holding that the 1976 amendments did not change the prohibition on the use of sampling in determining the population for apportionment purposes, we do not mean to suggest, as Justice Stevens claims in dissent, that the 1976 amendments had no purpose. Rather, the amendments served a very important purpose: they changed a provision that permitted the use of sampling for purposes other than apportionment into one that required that sampling be used for such purposes if "feasible." They also added to the existing delegation of authority to the Secretary to carry out the decennial census a statement indicating that despite the move to mandatory use of sampling in collecting nonapportionment information, the Secretary retained substantial authority to determine the manner in which the decennial census is conducted. Justice Stevens's argument reveals a rather limited conception of the extent and purpose of the decennial census. The decennial census is "the only census that is used for apportionment purposes," but the decennial census is not only used for apportionment purposes. Although originally established for the sole purpose of apportioning Representatives, the decennial census has grown considerably over the past 200 years. It now serves as "a linchpin of the federal statistical system by collecting data on the characteristics of individuals, households, and housing units throughout the country." Thus, to say that the 1976 amendments required the use of sampling in collecting nonapportionment information but had no effect on the way in which the Secretary could determine the population for the purposes of apportionment is to say that they had a purpose—just not the purpose that Justice Stevens imagines.

Justice Breyer's interpretation of §195 is equally unpersuasive. Justice Breyer agrees with the Court that the Census Act prohibits the use of sampling as a substitute for traditional enumeration methods. But he believes that this prohibition does not apply to the use of sampling as a "supplement" to traditional enumeration methods. This distinction is not borne out by the language of the statute. The Census Act provides

that sampling cannot be used "for the determination of population for purposes of apportionment of Representatives in Congress among the several States." Whether used as a "supplement" or as a "substitute," sampling is still used in "determining"—that is, in "the act of deciding definitely and firmly." Under the proposed plan, the population is not "determined," not decided definitely and firmly, until the NRFU and ICM are complete. That the distinction drawn by Justice Breyer is untenable is perhaps best demonstrated by his own inability to apply it consistently. He acknowledges that the NRFU uses statistical sampling "to determine the last 10% of the population in each census tract," yet he nonetheless finds that it is a supplement to the headcount and thus permitted by the Act.

The conclusion that the Census Act prohibits the use of sampling for apportionment purposes finds support in the debate and discussions surrounding the 1976 revisions to the Census Act. At no point during the debates over these amendments did a single Member of Congress suggest that the amendments would so fundamentally change the manner in which the Bureau could calculate the population for purposes of apportionment. This is true despite the fact that such a change would profoundly affect Congress by likely shifting the number of seats apportioned to some States and altering district lines in many others. Indeed, it tests the limits of reason to suggest that despite such silence, Members of Congress voting for those amendments intended to enact what would arguably be the single most significant change in the method of conducting the decennial census since its inception. That the 1976 changes to §§141 and 195 were not the focus of partisan debate is almost certainly due to the fact that the Members of Congress voting on the bill read the text of the statute, as do we, to prohibit the use of sampling in determining the population for apportionment purposes. Moreover, it is hard to imagine that, having explicitly prohibited the use of sampling for apportionment purposes in 1957, Congress would have decided to reverse course on such an important issue by enacting only a subtle change in phraseology.

For the reasons stated, we conclude that the Census Act prohibits the proposed uses of statistical sampling in calculating the population for purposes of apportionment. Because we so conclude, we find it unnecessary to reach the constitutional question presented. Accordingly, we affirm the judgment of the District Court for the Eastern District of Virginia in *Clinton v. Glavin*. As this decision also resolves the substantive issues presented by *Department of Commerce v. United States House of Representatives*, that case no longer presents a substantial federal question. The appeal in that case is therefore dismissed.

5

Seeking Public Office

This chapter is about the rights of candidates and legal procedures involved in running for elective office, including getting on the ballot.

United States v. Thayer
209 U.S. 39 (1908)

This is an indictment for soliciting a contribution of money for political purposes from an employee of the United States in a postoffice building of the United States occupied by the employee in the discharge of his duties. By the civil service act of January 16, 1883, "No person shall, in any room or building occupied in the discharge of official duties by any officer or employee of the United States . . . solicit in any manner whatever, or receive, any contribution of money or any other thing of value for any political purpose whatever." . . . a penalty is imposed of fine, imprisonment, or both. The indictment . . . charges the sending of letters to employees, which were intended to be received and read by them in the building, and were so received and read by them in fact. It is admitted that the defendant was not in the building. There was a demurrer, which was sustained by the district court on the ground that the case was not within the act. The only question argued or intended to be raised is whether the defendant's physical presence in the building was necessary to create the offense.

. . . It appears to us no more open to doubt that the statute prohibits solicitation by writing as well as by spoken words. It forbids all persons to solicit

"in any manner whatever." The purpose is . . . to check a political abuse which is not different in kind whether practised by letter or by word of mouth. The limits of the act, presumably, were due to what was considered the reasonable and possibly the constitutional freedom of citizens, whether officeholders or not, when in private life, and it may be conjectured that it was upon this ground that an amendment of broader scope was rejected. If the writer of the letter in person had handed it to the man addressed, in the building, without a word, and the latter had read it then and there, we suppose that no one would deny that the writer fell within the statute. We can see no distinction between personally delivering the letter and sending it by a servant of the writer. If the solicitation is in the building, the statute does not require personal presence, so that the question is narrowed to whether the solicitation alleged took place in the building or outside.

The solicitation was made at some time, somewhere. The time determines the place. It was not complete when the letter was dropped into the post. If the letter had miscarried or had been burned, the defendant would not have accomplished a solicitation. . . . A relation already existed between the parties, and it is because of that relation that posting the letter made the transaction complete. Here a relation was to be established, just as there is at the first stage of a contract when an offer is to be made. . . . Therefore . . . until after the letter had entered the building, the offense was not complete; but, when it had been read, the case was not affected by the nature of the intended means by which it was put into the hands of the person addressed. Neither can the case be affected by speculations as to what the position would have been if the receiver had put the letter in his pocket and had read it later at home. Offenses usually depend for their completion upon events that are not wholly within the offender's control and that may turn out in different ways.

. . . To sum up, the defendant solicited money for campaign purposes; he did not solicit until his letter actually was received in the building; he did solicit when it was received and read there; and the solicitation was in the place where the letter was received. . . .

. . .

Judgment reversed.

Anderson v. Martin
375 U.S. 399 (1964)

Appellants, residents of East Baton Rouge, Louisiana, are Negroes. Each sought election to the School Board of that parish in the 1962 Democratic Party primary election. Prior to the election they filed this suit against the Secretary of State of Louisiana seeking to enjoin the enforcement of Act 538 of the 1960 Louisiana Legislature, which requires the Secretary to print, in parentheses, the race of each candidate opposite his name on all ballots. Asserting that the statute violated, inter alia, the Fourteenth and Fifteenth Amendments, appellants sought both preliminary and permanent injunctions and a temporary restraining order. A United States district judge denied the motion for a temporary restraining order and a three-judge court was convened. After a hearing on the merits, the preliminary injunction was denied. . . . Thereafter the appellants

sought to amend their complaint so as to show that the primary election had been held and that both appellants had been defeated because of the operation and enforcement of the statute here under attack. . . . [T]he district judge and the three-judge court . . . denied the request for a permanent injunction. . . .

At the outset it is well that we point out what this case does not involve. It has nothing whatever to do with the right of a citizen to cast his vote for whomever he chooses and for whatever reason he pleases or to receive all information concerning a candidate which is necessary to a proper exercise of his franchise. It has to do only with the right of a State to require or encourage its voters to discriminate upon the grounds of race. In the abstract, Louisiana imposes no restriction upon anyone's candidacy nor upon an elector's choice in the casting of his ballot. But by placing a racial label on a candidate at the most crucial stage in the electoral process—the instant before the vote is cast—the State furnishes a vehicle by which racial prejudice may be so aroused as to operate against one group because of race and for another. This is true because by directing the citizen's attention to the single consideration of race or color, the State indicates that a candidate's race or color is an important—perhaps paramount—consideration in the citizen's choice, which may decisively influence the citizen to cast his ballot along racial lines. Hence in a State or voting district where Negroes predominate, that race is likely to be favored by a racial designation on the ballot, while in those communities where other races are in the majority, they may be preferred. The vice lies not in the resulting injury but in the placing of the power of the State behind a racial classification that induces racial prejudice at the polls.

. . .

... We see no relevance in the State's pointing up the race of the candidate as bearing upon his qualifications for office. . . .

The State contends that its Act is nondiscriminatory because the labeling provision applies equally to Negro and white. Obviously, Louisiana may not bar Negro citizens from offering themselves as candidates for public office, nor can it encourage its citizens to vote for a candidate solely on account of race. And that which cannot be done by express statutory prohibition cannot be done by indirection. Therefore, we view the alleged equality as superficial. Race is the factor upon which the statute operates and its involvement promotes the ultimate discrimination which is sufficient to make it invalid. The judgment is therefore reversed.

Moore v. Ogilvie
394 U.S. 814 (1969)

This is a suit for declaratory relief and for an injunction, brought by appellants who are independent candidates for the offices of electors of President and Vice President of the United States from Illinois. The defendants or appellees are members of the Illinois Electoral Board. In 1968, appellants filed with appellees petitions containing the names of 26,500 qualified voters who desired that appellants be nominated. The appellees ruled that appellants could not be certified to the county clerks for the November 1968, election because of a proviso added in 1935 to an Illinois statute requiring that at least 25,000 electors sign a petition to nominate such candidates. . . .

A three-judge District Court . . . dismissed the complaint for failure to state a cause of action. . . .

. . .

. . . When a State makes classifications of voters which favor residents of some counties over residents of other counties, a justiciable controversy is presented.

. . .

It is no answer to the argument under the Equal Protection Clause that this law was designed to require statewide support for launching a new political party, rather than support from a few localities. This law applies a rigid, arbitrary formula to sparsely settled counties and populous counties alike, contrary to the constitutional theme of equality among citizens in the exercise of their political rights. The idea that one group can be granted greater voting strength than another is hostile to the one man, one vote basis of our representative government.

Under this Illinois law, the electorate in 49 of the counties which contain 93.4 percent of the registered voters may not form a new political party and place its candidates on the ballot. Yet 25,000 of the remaining 6.6 percent of registered voters properly distributed among the 53 remaining counties may form a new party to elect candidates to office. This law thus discriminates against the residents of the populous counties of the State in favor of rural sections. It, therefore, lacks the equality to which the exercise of political rights is entitled under the Fourteenth Amendment.

MacDougall v. Green is overruled.

Reversed.

Brockington v. Rhodes
396 U.S. 41 (1969)

The appellant sought to run in the November 1968 election as an independent candidate for the United States House of Representatives from the Twenty-first Congressional District of Ohio. His nominating petition bore the signatures of 899 voters in the congressional district, a little over 15 percent of those in the district who had voted in the gubernatorial contest at the last election. The Board of Elections ruled that the appellant's petition was insufficient to put his name on the November ballot because it did not contain the signatures of 7 percent of the qualified voters, as Ohio law then required. The appellant petitioned the Court of Common Pleas for a writ of mandamus. . . . [H]e sought no declaratory relief.

On August 22, 1968, the Court of Common Pleas denied the writ. . . . On October 1, the Court of Appeals for the Eighth Judicial District affirmed that judgment, and, on October 23, the Supreme Court of Ohio dismissed the appeal for want of a substantial constitutional question. The appellant then appealed to this Court. . . . While the appeal was pending here, Ohio amended the controlling statute, effective October 30, 1969, reducing the signature requirement from 7 percent to 4 percent.

We do not think the recent statutory amendment has rendered this case moot. For the appellant has consistently urged the unconstitutionality of any percentage requirement in excess of the 1 percent that Ohio imposed prior to 1952, and he obtained the signatures of only about 1 percent of the voters in his district. He thus could not have won a place on the ballot even under the statute as currently written.

Rather, in view of the limited nature of the relief sought, we think the case is moot because the congressional election is over. The appellant did not allege that he intended to run for office in any future election. He did not attempt to maintain a class action on behalf of himself and other putative independent candidates, present or future. He did not sue for himself and others similarly situated as independent voters, as he might have under Ohio law. He did not

seek a declaratory judgment, although that avenue too was open to him.

Instead, he sought only a writ of mandamus to compel the appellees to place his name on the ballot as a candidate for a particular office in a particular election on November 5, 1968. In Ohio, mandamus is an extraordinary remedy, available to a petitioner only on a showing of clear legal right. The writ does not lie to review the determination by a Board of Elections that a candidate is ineligible to assume the office he seeks or that his petition is invalid, in the absence of allegations of fraud, corruption, abuse of discretion, or a clear disregard of statutes or applicable legal principles. . . .

It is now impossible to grant the appellant the limited, extraordinary relief he sought in the Ohio courts. Accordingly, the judgment of the Supreme Court of Ohio must be vacated without costs in this Court, and the cause remanded for such proceedings as that court may deem appropriate.

Jenness v. Fortson
403 U.S. 431 (1971)

Under Georgia law, a candidate for elective public office who does not enter and win a political party's primary election can have his name printed on the ballot at the general election only if he has filed a nominating petition signed by at least 5 percent of the number of registered voters at the last general election for the office in question. Georgia law also provides that a candidate for elective public office must pay a filing fee equal to 5 percent of the annual salary of the office he is seeking. This litigation arose when the appellants, who were prospective candidates and registered voters, filed a class action in the United States District Court for the Northern District of

Georgia attacking the constitutionality of these provisions of the Georgia Election Code and seeking declaratory and injunctive relief.

. . . [A]ppellants filed a motion for summary judgment based upon a stipulation as to the relevant facts. The District Court granted the motion and entered an injunction with respect to the filing fee requirement, holding that this requirement operates to deny equal protection of the laws as applied to those prospective candidates who cannot afford to pay the fees. No appeal was taken from that injunctive order. With respect to the nominating petition requirement, the District Court denied the motion and refused to enter an injunction, holding that this statutory provision is constitutionally valid. From that refusal a direct appeal was brought here. . . .

The basic structure of the pertinent provisions of the Georgia Election Code is relatively uncomplicated. Any political organization whose candidate received 20 percent or more of the vote at the most recent gubernatorial or presidential election is a "political party." Any other political organization is a "political body." "Political parties" conduct primary elections, regulated in detail by state law, and only the name of the candidate for each office who wins this primary election is printed on the ballot at the subsequent general election as his party's nominee for the office in question. A nominee of a "political body" or an independent candidate, on the other hand, may have his name printed on the ballot at the general election by filing a nominating petition. This petition must be signed by

a number of electors of not less than five percent. of the total number of electors eligible to vote in the last election for the filling of the office the candidate is seeking. . . . The total time allowed for circulating a nominating petition is 180 days, and it must be filed on the second Wednesday in June,

the same deadline that a candidate filing in a party primary must meet.

It is to be noted that these procedures relate only to the right to have the name of a candidate or the nominee of a "political body" printed on the ballot. There is no limitation whatever, procedural or substantive, on the right of a voter to write in on the ballot the name of the candidate of his choice and to have that write-in vote counted.

In this litigation, the appellants have mounted their attack upon Georgia's nominating petition requirement on two different but related constitutional fronts. First, they say that to require a nonparty candidate to secure the signatures of a certain number of voters before his name may be printed on the ballot is to abridge the freedoms of speech and association guaranteed to that candidate and his supporters by the First and Fourteenth Amendments. Secondly, they say that, when Georgia requires a nonparty candidate to secure the signatures of 5 percent of the voters before printing his name on the ballot, yet prints the names of those candidates who have won nomination in party primaries, it violates the Fourteenth Amendment by denying the nonparty candidate the equal protection of the laws. . . .

. . .

. . . Georgia freely provides for write-in votes. . . . Georgia does not require every candidate to be the nominee of a political party, but fully recognizes independent candidacies. . . . Georgia does not fix an unreasonably early filing deadline for candidates not endorsed by established parties. . . . Georgia does not impose upon a small party or a new party the Procrustean requirement of establishing elaborate primary election machinery. Finally, and in sum, Georgia's election laws . . . do not operate to freeze the political status quo. In this setting, we cannot say that

Georgia's 5 percent petition requirement violates the Constitution.

Anyone who wishes, and who is otherwise eligible, may be an independent candidate for any office in Georgia. Any political organization, however new or however small, is free to endorse any otherwise eligible person as its candidate for whatever elective public office it chooses. So far as the Georgia election laws are concerned, independent candidates and members of small or newly formed political organizations are wholly free to associate, to proselytize, to speak, to write, and to organize campaigns for any school of thought they wish. They may confine themselves to an appeal for write-in votes. Or they may seek, over a six months' period, the signatures of 5 percent of the eligible electorate for the office in question. If they choose the latter course, the way is open. For Georgia imposes no suffocating restrictions whatever upon the free circulation of nominating petitions. A voter may sign a petition even though he has signed others, and a voter who has signed the petition of a nonparty candidate is free thereafter to participate in a party primary. The signer of a petition is not required to state that he intends to vote for that candidate at the election. A person who has previously voted in a party primary is fully eligible to sign a petition, and so, on the other hand, is a person who was not even registered at the time of the previous election. No signature on a nominating petition need be notarized.

The open quality of the Georgia system is far from merely theoretical. For the stipulation of facts in this record informs us that a candidate for Governor in 1966 and a candidate for President in 1968, gained ballot designation by nominating petitions, and each went on to win a plurality of the votes cast at the general election.

In a word, Georgia in no way freezes the status quo, but implicitly recognizes the potential fluidity of American political life. Thus, any political body that wins as much as 20 percent support at an election becomes a "political party" with its attendant ballot position rights and primary election obligations, and any "political party" whose support at the polls falls below that figure reverts to the status of a "political body," with its attendant nominating petition responsibilities and freedom from primary election duties. We can find in this system nothing that abridges the rights of free speech and association secured by the First and Fourteenth Amendments.

The appellants' claim under the Equal Protection Clause of the Fourteenth Amendment fares no better. This claim is necessarily bottomed upon the premise that it is inherently more burdensome for a candidate to gather the signatures of 5 percent of the total eligible electorate than it is to win the votes of a majority in a party primary. That is a premise that cannot be uncritically accepted. Although the number of candidates in a party primary election for any particular office will, of course, vary from election to election, the appellee's brief advises us that, in the most recent election year, there were 12 candidates for the nomination for the office of Governor in the two party primaries. Only two of these 12, of course, won their party primaries and had their names printed on the ballot at the general election. Surely an argument could as well be made on behalf of the 10 who lost that it is they who were denied equal protection vis-a-vis a candidate who could have had his name printed on the ballot simply by filing a nominating petition signed by 5 percent of the total electorate.

The fact is, of course, that, from the point of view of one who aspires to elective public office in Georgia, alternative routes are available to getting his name printed on the ballot. He may enter the primary of a political party, or he may circulate nominating petitions either as an independent candidate or under the sponsorship of a political organization. We cannot see how Georgia has violated the Equal Protection Clause of the Fourteenth Amendment by making available these two alternative paths, neither of which can be assumed to be inherently more burdensome than the other.

Insofar as we deal here with the claims of a "political body," as contrasted with those of an individual aspirant for public office or an individual voter, the situation is somewhat different. For it is true that a "political party" in Georgia is assured of having the name of its nominee—the primary election winner—printed on the ballot, whereas the name of the nominee of a "political body" will be printed only if nominating petitions have been filed that contain the requisite number of signatures. But we can hardly suppose that a small or a new political organization could seriously urge that its interests would be advanced if it were forced by the State to establish all of the elaborate state-wide, county-by-county, organizational paraphernalia required of a "political party" as a condition for conducting a primary election. . . .

The fact is that there are obvious differences in kind between the needs and potentials of a political party with historically established broad support, on the one hand, and a new or small political organization, on the other. Georgia has not been guilty of invidious discrimination in recognizing these differences and providing different routes to the printed ballot. . . .

There is surely an important State interest in requiring some preliminary showing of a significant modicum of support before printing the name of a political organization's candidate on the ballot—the interest, if no other, in avoiding confu-

sion, deception, and even frustration of the democratic process at the general election. The 5 percent figure is, to be sure, apparently somewhat higher than the percentage of support required to be shown in many States as a condition for ballot position, but this is balanced by the fact that Georgia has imposed no arbitrary restrictions whatever upon the eligibility of any registered voter to sign as many nominating petitions as he wishes. Georgia in this case has insulated not a single potential voter from the appeal of new political voices within its borders.

The judgment is affirmed.

Bullock v. Carter
405 U.S. 134 (1972)

Appellee Pate met all qualifications to be a candidate in the May 2, 1970, Democratic primary for the office of County Commissioner of Precinct Four for El Paso County, except that he was unable to pay the $1,424.60 assessment required of candidates in that primary. Appellee Wischkaemper sought to be placed on the Democratic primary ballot as a candidate for County Judge in Tarrant County, but he was unable to pay the $6,300 assessment for candidacy for that office. Appellee Carter wished to be a Democratic candidate for Commissioner of the General Land Office; his application was not accompanied by the required $1,000 filing fee.

After being denied places on the Democratic primary ballots in their respective counties, these appellees instituted separate actions in the District Court challenging the validity of the Texas filing fee system. Their actions were consolidated. . . . Appellee Jenkins was permitted to intervene as a voter on his claimed desire to vote for Wischkaemper, and appellee Guzman and others were permitted to intervene as voters desiring to cast their ballots for Pate. On April 3, 1970, the District Court ordered that Wischkaemper and Pate be permitted to participate in the primary conducted on May 2, 1970, without prepayment of filing fees. Following a hearing on the merits, the three-judge court declared the Texas filing fee scheme unconstitutional, and enjoined its enforcement. A direct appeal was taken. . . .

Under the Texas statute, payment of the filing fee is an absolute prerequisite to a candidate's participation in a primary election. There is no alternative procedure by which a potential candidate who is unable to pay the fee can get on the primary ballot by way of petitioning voters, and write-in votes are not permitted in primary elections for public office. Any person who is willing and able to pay the filing fee and who meets the basic eligibility requirements for holding the office sought can run in a primary.

Candidates for most district, county, and precinct offices must pay their filing fee to the county executive committee of the political party conducting the primary; the committee also determines the amount of the fee. The party committee must make an estimate of the total cost of the primary and apportion it among the various candidates "as in their judgment is just and equitable." The committee's judgment is to be guided by "the importance, emolument, and term of office for which the nomination is to be made." In counties with populations of one million or more, candidates for offices of two-year terms can be assessed up to 10 percent of their aggregate annual salary, and candidates for offices of four-year terms can be assessed up to 15 percent of their aggregate annual salary. In smaller counties, there are no such percentage limitations.

The record shows that the fees required of the candidates in this case are far from exceptional in their magnitude. The size of the filing fees is plainly a natural consequence of a statutory system that places the burden of financing primary elections on candidates, rather than on the governmental unit, and that imposes a particularly heavy burden on candidates for local office. The filing fees required of candidates seeking nomination for state offices and offices involving statewide primaries are more closely regulated by statute, and tend to be appreciably smaller. The filing fees for candidates for State Representative range from $150 to $600, depending on the population of the county from which nomination is sought. Candidates for State Senator are subject to a maximum assessment of $1,000. Candidates for nominations requiring statewide primaries, including candidates for Governor and United States Senator, must pay a filing fee of $1,000 to the chairman of the state executive committee of the party conducting the primary. Candidates for the State Board of Education have a fixed filing fee of $50.

The filing fee requirement is limited to party primary elections, but the mechanism of such elections is the creature of state legislative choice, and hence is "state action" within the meaning of the Fourteenth Amendment. Although we have emphasized on numerous occasions the breadth of power enjoyed by the States in determining voter qualifications and the manner of elections, this power must be exercised in a manner consistent with the Equal Protection Clause of the Fourteenth Amendment. The question presented in this case is whether a state law that prevents potential candidates for public office from seeking the nomination of their party due to their inability to pay a portion of the cost of conducting the primary election is state action that unlawfully discriminates against the candidates so excluded or the voters who wish to support them.

The threshold question to be resolved is whether the filing fee system should be sustained if it can be shown to have some rational basis, or whether it must withstand a more rigid standard of review.

. . .

The initial and direct impact of filing fees is felt by aspirants for office, rather than voters, and the Court has not heretofore attached such fundamental status to candidacy as to invoke a rigorous standard of review. However, the rights of voters and the rights of candidates do not lend themselves to neat separation; laws that affect candidates always have at least some theoretical, correlative effect on voters. Of course, not every limitation or incidental burden on the exercise of voting rights is subject to a stringent standard of review. Texas does not place a condition on the exercise of the right to vote, nor does it quantitatively dilute votes that have been cast. Rather, the Texas system creates barriers to candidate access to the primary ballot, thereby tending to limit the field of candidates from which voters might choose. The existence of such barriers does not, of itself, compel close scrutiny. In approaching candidate restrictions, it is essential to examine in a realistic light the extent and nature of their impact on voters.

Unlike a filing fee requirement that most candidates could be expected to fulfill from their own resources, or at least through modest contributions, the very size of the fees imposed under the Texas system gives it a patently exclusionary character. Many potential office seekers lacking both personal wealth and affluent backers are, in every practical sense, precluded from seeking the nomination of their chosen party, no matter how qualified they might be and no matter how broad or enthusiastic their popular support. The effect of this exclusionary mechanism on voters is nei-ther incidental nor remote. Not only are voters substantially limited in their choice of candidates, but also there is the obvious likelihood that this limitation would fall more heavily on the less affluent segment of the community, whose favorites may be unable to pay the large costs required by the Texas system. To the extent that the system requires candidates to rely on contributions from voters in order to pay the assessments, a phenomenon that can hardly be rare in light of the size of the fees, it tends to deny some voters the opportunity to vote for a candidate of their choosing; at the same time, it gives the affluent the power to place on the ballot their own names or the names of persons they favor. . . .

Because the Texas filing fee scheme has a real and appreciable impact on the exercise of the franchise, and because this impact is related to the resources of the voters supporting a particular candidate, we conclude . . . that the laws must be "closely scrutinized" and found reasonably necessary to the accomplishment of legitimate state objectives in order to pass constitutional muster.

. . .

The Court has recognized that a State has a legitimate interest in regulating the number of candidates on the ballot. In so doing, the State understandably and properly seeks to prevent the clogging of its election machinery, avoid voter confusion, and assure that the winner is the choice of a majority, or at least a strong plurality, of those voting, without the expense and burden of runoff elections. . . . Moreover, a State has an interest, if not a duty, to protect the integrity of its political processes from frivolous or fraudulent candidacies.

. . . [A] State cannot achieve its objectives by totally arbitrary means; the criterion for differing treatment must bear some relevance to the object of the legislation. To say that the filing fee requirement tends to limit the ballot to the more serious candidates is not enough. There may well be some rational relationship between a candidate's willingness to pay a filing fee and the seriousness with which he takes his candidacy, but the candidates in this case affirmatively alleged that they were unable, not simply unwilling, to pay the assessed fees, and there was no contrary evidence. It is uncontested that the filing fees exclude legitimate as well as frivolous candidates. And even assuming that every person paying the large fees required by Texas law takes his own candidacy seriously, that does not make him a "serious candidate" in the popular sense. If the Texas fee requirement is intended to regulate the ballot by weeding out spurious candidates, it is extraordinarily ill-fitted to that goal; other means to protect those valid interests are available.

. . . Appellants have not demonstrated that their present filing fee scheme is a necessary or reasonable tool for regulating the ballot.

. . . [T]he filing fees serve to relieve the State treasury of the cost of conducting the primary elections, and this is a legitimate state objective; in this limited sense, it cannot be said that the fee system lacks a rational basis. But, under the standard of review we consider applicable to this case, there must be a showing of necessity. . . . We are not persuaded that Texas would be faced with an impossible task in distinguishing between political parties for the purpose of financing primaries.

We also reject the theory that, since the candidates are availing themselves of the primary machinery, it is appropriate that they pay that share of the cost that they have occasioned. The force of this argument is diluted by the fact that candidates for offices requiring statewide primaries are generally assessed at a lower rate than candidates for local office, although the statewide primaries undoubtedly involve a greater expense. More importantly, the costs do not arise because candidates decide to enter a primary or because the parties decide to conduct one, but because the State has, as a matter of legislative choice, directed that party primaries be held. The State has presumably chosen this course more to benefit the voters than the candidates.

. . . The financial burden for general elections is carried by all taxpayers, and appellants have not demonstrated a valid basis for distinguishing between these two legitimate costs of the democratic process. It seems appropriate that a primary system designed to give the voters some influence at the nominating stage should spread the cost among all of the voters in an attempt to distribute the influence without regard to wealth. Viewing the myriad governmental functions supported from general revenues, it is difficult to single out any of a higher order than the conduct of elections at all levels to bring forth those persons desired by their fellow citizens to govern. Without making light of the State's interest in husbanding its revenues, we fail to see such an element of necessity in the State's present means of financing primaries as to justify the resulting incursion on the prerogatives of voters.

Since the State has failed to establish the requisite justification for this filing fee system, we hold that it results in a denial of equal protection of the laws. It must be emphasized that nothing herein is intended to cast doubt on the validity of reasonable candidate filing fees or licensing fees in other contexts. By requiring candidates to shoulder the costs of conducting primary elections through filing fees and by providing no reasonable alternative means of access to the ballot, the State of Texas has erected a system that utilizes the criterion of ability to pay as a condition to being on the ballot, thus excluding some candidates otherwise qualified and denying an undetermined number of voters the opportunity to vote for candidates of their choice. These salient features of the Texas system are critical to our determination of constitutional invalidity.

Affirmed.

Brown v. Chote
411 U.S. 452 (1973)

. . . [A]ppellee called into question the constitutionality of those provisions of the California Elections Code which require candidates in a primary election to pay a filing fee prior to having their names listed on the primary ballot. Under these provisions, candidates for the Federal House of Representatives must pay $425 (1 percent of the annual salary of the office); candidates for the Federal Senate must pay $850 (2 percent of the salary of the office). Those wishing to run for statewide offices must pay similar fees ranging in amount from $192 for State Assemblyman (1 percent of the annual salary) to $982 for Governor (2 percent of the annual salary). . . .

Appellee commenced this class action on March 3, 1972. He moved, and was granted permission by, a single district judge, to proceed in forma pauperis and as his own attorney. In his complaint, appellee asserted that he wished to become a candidate for the Federal House of Representatives from the 17th District of California, and had taken the following steps to place his name in nomination in the June 6, 1972, California primary election. On February 17, 1972, appellee called the Registrar of Voters of Santa Clara County, an official designated by state law to dispense those forms necessary to place a name in nomination. Appellee was purportedly told by

the Registrar or a member of his office that he was required to pay $425 in advance in order to secure blank copies of the necessary papers. According to appellee, the Registrar's Office also advised him that the papers would be delivered in exchange for a worthless check.

Appellee proceeded immediately to the Registrar's Office, where he presented a personal check for $425 and requested copies of the necessary forms. Across the face of the check, appellee had typed "Written under protest for filing fee." The Registrar issued the requisite papers to appellee and informed him that his check would be forwarded to the California Secretary of State when his completed papers were submitted. Subsequently, a Deputy Secretary of State informed appellee that his name would not be placed on the ballot if his check was not honored.

. . . In addition to requesting declaratory and permanent injunctive relief, appellee moved the District Court to issue a preliminary injunction so as to allow him to participate as a candidate in the upcoming primary. Under state law, the final date on which appellee could submit nominating papers for that primary was March 10, 1972, one week away.

Because of the impending filing deadline, the District Court proceeded quickly to set the case for argument. On March 3, 1972, the same date on which the suit was filed, the single District Judge to whom the case was assigned entered an order requiring appellant to show cause why interlocutory relief should not be granted. The State was given five days in which to respond. It was not until March 7 that the Chief Judge of the Ninth Circuit was notified of the application for a three-judge court. On March 8, he designated the judges who were to compose the panel. On the same day, the court convened and heard oral argument. Because of the speed with which the case had developed, neither the court nor appellee had an opportunity prior to the hearing to consider appellant's return to the order to show cause, the only paper which the State had been able to prepare.

On March 9, 1972 . . . the District Court granted appellee's motion for a preliminary injunction. . . . Under the terms of the preliminary injunction, the State was required to allow appellee and others similarly situated to place their names on the ballot without paying the required fee, so long as they were otherwise eligible for the applicable state or federal office and had deposited with an appropriate state official an affidavit attesting to their indigency.

The State appealed directly to this Court. . . .

. . .

In reviewing such interlocutory relief, this Court may only consider whether issuance of the injunction constituted an abuse of discretion. In light of the arguments presented by appellee and the fact that appellee's opportunity to be a candidate would have been foreclosed absent some relief, we cannot conclude that the court's action was an abuse of discretion. We therefore affirm the action taken by the District Court in granting interim relief.

. . .

The specific deadline which led the District Court to grant equitable relief has now passed. Nothing precludes appellee from seeking a trial on the merits if he chooses to proceed. The case is therefore remanded to the District Court for further proceedings consistent with this opinion.

Affirmed and remanded.

Lubin v. Panish
415 U.S. 709 (1974)

. . . [P]etitioner's claim that the California statute requiring payment of a filing fee of $701.60 in order to be placed on the ballot in the primary election for nomination to the position of County Supervisor, while providing no alternative means of access to the ballot, deprived him, as an indigent person unable to pay the fee, and others similarly situated, of the equal protection guaranteed by the Fourteenth Amendment and rights of expression and association guaranteed by the First Amendment.

The California Elections Code provides that forms required for nomination and election to congressional, state, and county offices are to be issued to candidates only upon prepayment of a nonrefundable filing fee. Generally, the required fees are fixed at a percentage of the salary for the office sought. The fee for candidates for United States Senator, Governor, and other state offices and some county offices, is 2 percent of the annual salary. Candidates for Representative to Congress, State Senator or Assemblyman, or for judicial office or district attorney, must pay 1 percent. No filing fee is required of candidates in the presidential primary, or for offices which pay either no fixed salary or not more than $600 annually.

Under the California statutes in effect at the time this suit was commenced, the required candidate filing fees ranged from $192 for State Assembly, $425 for Congress, $701.60 for Los Angeles County Board of Supervisors, $850 for United States Senator, to $982 for Governor.

The California statute provides for the counting of write-in votes subject to certain conditions. Write-in votes are not counted, however, unless the person desiring to be a write-in candidate files a statement to that effect with the Registrar-Recorder at least eight days prior to the election and pays the requisite filing fee. . . .

Petitioner commenced this class action on February 17, 1972, by petitioning the Los Angeles

Superior Court for a writ of mandate against the Secretary of State and the Los Angeles County Registrar-Recorder. . . . Petitioner asserted that, on February 15, 1972, he had appeared at the office of James S. Allison, then Registrar-Recorder of the County of Los Angeles, to apply for and secure all necessary nomination papers requisite to his proposed candidacy. Petitioner was denied the requested nomination papers orally and in writing solely because he was unable to pay the $701.60 filing fee required of all would-be candidates for the office of Board of Supervisors.

The Los Angeles Superior Court denied the requested writ of mandate on March 6, 1972. Petitioner alleged that he was a serious candidate, that he was indigent, and that he was unable to pay the $701.60 filing fee; no evidence was taken during the hearing. The Superior Court found the fees to be "reasonable, as a matter of law." Accordingly, the court made no attempt to determine whether the fees charged were necessary to the State's purpose, or whether the fees, in addition to deterring some frivolous candidates, also prohibited serious but indigent candidates from entering their names on the ballot. The Superior Court also rejected the argument that the State was required . . . to provide an alternative means of access to the ballot which did not discriminate on the basis of economic factors.

On March 9, 1972, a second petition for writ of mandate was denied by the Court of Appeal, Second District, and on March 22, 1972, after the deadline for filing nomination papers had passed, the California Supreme Court denied petitioner's third application for a writ of mandate.

. . .

The present case draws these two means of achieving an effective, representative political system into apparent conflict, and presents the question of how to accommodate the desire for increased ballot access with the imperative of protecting the integrity of the electoral system from the recognized dangers of ballots listing so many candidates as to undermine the process of giving expression to the will of the majority. The petitioner stated on oath that he is without assets or income, and cannot pay the $701.60 filing fee although he is otherwise legally eligible to be a candidate on the primary ballot. Since his affidavit of indigency states that he has no resources and earned no income whatever in 1972, it would appear that he would make the same claim whether the filing fee had been fixed at $1, $100, or $700. The State accepts this as true, but defends the statutory fee as necessary to keep the ballot from being overwhelmed with frivolous or otherwise nonserious candidates, arguing that, as to indigents, the filing fee is not intended as a test of his pocketbook, but the extent of his political support, and hence the seriousness of his candidacy.

. . . The role of the primary election process in California is underscored by its importance as a component of the total electoral process and its special function to assure that fragmentation of voter choice is minimized. That function is served, not frustrated, by a procedure that tends to regulate the filing of frivolous candidates. A procedure inviting or permitting every citizen to present himself to the voters on the ballot without some means of measuring the seriousness of the candidate's desire and motivation would make rational voter choices more difficult because of the size of the ballot, and hence would tend to impede the electoral process. That no device can be conjured to eliminate every frivolous candidacy does not undermine the State's effort to eliminate as many such as possible.

That "laundry list" ballots discourage voter participation and confuse and frustrate those who do participate is too obvious to call for extended discussion. The means of testing the seriousness of a given candidacy may be open to debate; the fundamental importance of ballots of reasonable size limited to serious candidates with some prospects of public support is not. Rational results within the framework of our system are not likely to be reached if the ballot for a single office must list a dozen or more aspirants who are relatively unknown or have no prospects of success.

This legitimate state interest, however, must be achieved by a means that does not unfairly or unnecessarily burden either a minority party's or an individual candidate's equally important interest in the continued availability of political opportunity. . . .

. . . Filing fees, however large, do not, in and of themselves, test the genuineness of a candidacy or the extent of the voter support of an aspirant for public office. A large filing fee may serve the legitimate function of keeping ballots manageable but, standing alone, it is not a certain test of whether the candidacy is serious or spurious. A wealthy candidate with not the remotest chance of election may secure a place on the ballot by writing a check. Merchants and other entrepreneurs have been known to run for public office simply to make their names known to the public. We have also noted that prohibitive filing fees . . . can effectively exclude serious candidates. Conversely, if the filing fee is more moderate, as here, impecunious but serious candidates may be prevented from running. Even in this day of high-budget political campaigns, some candidates have demonstrated that direct contact with thousands of voters by "walking tours" is a route to success. Whatever may be the political mood at any given time, our tradition has been one of hospitality toward all candidates, without regard to their economic status.

The absence of any alternative means of gaining access to the ballot inevitably renders the California system exclusionary as to some aspirants. . . . [T]he payment of a fee is an absolute, not an alternative, condition, and failure to meet it is a disqualification from running for office. Thus, California has chosen to achieve the important and legitimate interest of maintaining the integrity of elections by means which can operate to exclude some potentially serious candidates from the ballot without providing them with any alternative means of coming before the voters. Selection of candidates solely on the basis of ability to pay a fixed fee without providing any alternative means is not reasonably necessary to the accomplishment of the State's legitimate election interests. Accordingly, we hold that, in the absence of reasonable alternative means of ballot access, a State may not, consistent with constitutional standards, require from an indigent candidate filing fees he cannot pay.

In so holding, we note that there are obvious and well known means of testing the "seriousness" of a candidacy which do not measure the probability of attracting significant voter support solely by the neutral fact of payment of a filing fee. . . . The point, of course, is that ballot access must be genuinely open to all, subject to reasonable requirements. California's present system has not met this standard.

Reversed and remanded for further consideration not inconsistent with this opinion.

Storer v. Brown
415 U.S. 724 (1974)

The California Elections Code forbids ballot position to an independent candidate for elective public office if he voted in the immediately preceding primary, or if he had a registered affiliation with a qualified political party at any time within one year prior to the immediately preceding primary election. The independent candidate must also file nomination papers signed by voters not less in number than 5 percent nor more than 6 percent of the entire vote cast in the preceding general election in the area for which the candidate seeks to run. All of these signatures must be obtained during a 24-day period following the primary and ending 60 days prior to the general election, and none of the signatures may be gathered from persons who vote at the primary election. The constitutionality of these provisions is challenged here as infringing on rights guaranteed by the First and Fourteenth Amendments and as adding qualifications for the office of United States Congressman, contrary to Art. I, §2, cl. 2, of the Constitution.

Prior to the 1972 elections, appellants Storer, Frommhagen, Hall, and Tyner, along with certain of their supporters, filed their actions to have the above sections of the Elections Code declared unconstitutional and their enforcement enjoined. Storer and Frommhagen each sought ballot status as an independent candidate for Congressman from his district. Both complained about the party disaffiliation requirement . . . and asserted that the combined effects of the provisions were unconstitutional burdens on their First and Fourteenth Amendment rights. Hall and Tyner claimed the right to ballot position as independent candidates for President and Vice President of the United States. They were members of the Communist Party, but that party had not qualified for ballot position in California. They, too, complained of the combined effect of the indicated sections of the Elections Code on their ability to achieve ballot position.

A three-judge District Court concluded that the statutes served a sufficiently important state interest to sustain their constitutionality, and dismissed the complaints. Two separate appeals were taken from the judgment. . . .

We affirm the judgment of the District Court insofar as it refused relief to Storer and Frommhagen with respect to the 1972 general election. Both men were registered Democrats until early in 1972, Storer until January and Frommhagen until March of that year. This affiliation with a qualified political party within a year prior to the 1972 primary disqualified both men . . . and, in our view, the State of California was not prohibited by the United States Constitution from enforcing that provision against these men.

. . .

. . . [W]e have no hesitation in sustaining §6830(d). In California, the independent candidacy route to obtaining ballot position is but a part of the candidate nominating process, an alternative to being nominated in one of the direct party primaries. The independent candidate need not stand for primary election, but must qualify for the ballot by demonstrating substantial public support in another way. Otherwise, the qualifications required of the independent candidate are very similar to, or identical with, those imposed on party candidates. Section 6401 imposes a flat disqualification upon any candidate seeking to run in a party primary if he has been

> registered as affiliated with a political party other than that political party the nomination of which he seeks within 12 months immediately prior to the filing of the declaration.

Moreover, §§6402 and 6611 provide that a candidate who has been defeated in a party primary may not be nominated as an independent or be a candidate of any other party, and no person may file nomination papers for a party nomination and an independent nomination for the same office, or for more than one office at the same election.

The requirement that the independent candidate not have been affiliated with a political party for a year before the primary is expressive of a general state policy aimed at maintaining the integrity of the various routes to the ballot. It involves no discrimination against independents. Indeed, the independent candidate must be clear of political party affiliations for a year before the primary; the party candidate must not have been registered with another party for a year before he files his declaration, which must be done not less than 83 and not more than 113 days prior to the primary.

In *Rosario v. Rockefeller*, there was an 11-month waiting period for voters who wanted to change parties. Here, a person terminating his affiliation with a political party must wait at least 12 months before he can become a candidate in another party's primary or an independent candidate for public office. The State's interests recognized in *Rosario* are very similar to those that undergird the California waiting period, and the extent of the restriction is not significantly different. It is true that a California candidate who desires to run for office as an independent must anticipate his candidacy substantially in advance of his election campaign, but the required foresight is little more than the possible 11 months examined in *Rosario*, and its direct impact is on the candidate, and not voters. In any event, neither Storer nor Frommhagen is in position to complain that the waiting period is one year, for each of them was affiliated with a qualified party no more than six months prior to the primary. As applied to them, §6830(d) is valid.

. . .

Section 6830(d) . . . protects the direct primary process by refusing to recognize independent candidates who do not make early plans to leave a party and take the alternative course to the ballot. It works against independent candidacies prompted by short-range political goals, pique, or personal quarrel. It is also a substantial barrier to a party fielding an "independent" candidate to capture and bleed off votes in the general election that might well go to another party.

A State need not take the course California has, but California apparently believes with the Founding Fathers that splintered parties and unrestrained factionalism may do significant damage to the fabric of government. It appears obvious to us that the one-year disaffiliation provision furthers the State's interest in the stability of its political system. We also consider that interest as not only permissible, but compelling, and as outweighing the interest the candidate and his supporters may have in making a late, rather than an early, decision to seek independent ballot status. Nor do we have reason for concluding that the device California chose was not an essential part of its overall mechanism to achieve its acceptable goals. . . .

We conclude that §6830(d) is not unconstitutional, and Storer and Frommhagen were properly barred from the ballot as a result of its application. Having reached this result, there is no need to examine the constitutionality of the other provisions of the Elections Code as they operate singly or in combination as applied to these candidates. Even if these statutes were wholly or partly unconstitutional, Storer and Frommhagen were still properly barred from having their names placed on the 1972 ballot. . . . The District Court need not have heard a challenge to these other provisions of the California Elections Code by one who did not satisfy the age requirement for becoming a member of Congress, and there was no more reason to consider them at the request of Storer and Frommhagen or at the request of voters who desire to support unqualified candidates.

We come to different conclusions with respect to Hall and Tyner. As to these two men, we vacate the judgment of the District Court and remand the case for further proceedings to determine whether the California election laws place an unconstitutional burden on their access to the ballot.

We start with the proposition that the requirements for an independent's attaining a place on the general election ballot can be unconstitutionally severe. We must therefore inquire as to the nature, extent, and likely impact of the California requirements.

Beyond the one-year party disaffiliation condition and the rule against voting in the primary, both of which Hall apparently satisfied, it was necessary for an independent candidate to file a petition signed by voters not less in number than 5 percent of the total votes cast in California at the last general election. This percentage, as such, does not appear to be excessive, but, to assess realistically whether the law imposes excessively burdensome requirements upon independent candidates it is necessary to know other critical facts which do not appear from the evidentiary record in this case.

It is necessary in the first instance to know the "entire vote" in the last general election. Appellees suggest that 5 percent of that figure, whatever that is, is 325,000. Assuming this to be the correct total signature requirement, we also know that it must be satisfied within a period of 24 days between the primary and the general election. But we do not know the number of qualified voters from which the requirement must be satisfied within this period of time. California law disqualifies from signing the independent's petition all registered voters who voted in the primary. In theory, it could be that voting in the primary was so close to 100 percent of those registered, and new registrations since closing the books before primary day were so low, that eligible signers of an unaffiliated candidate's petition would number less than the total signatures required. This is unlikely, for it is usual that a substantial percentage of those eligible do not vote in the primary, and there were undoubtedly millions of voters qualified to vote in the 1972 primary. But it is not at all unlikely that the available pool of possible signers, after eliminating the total primary vote, will be substantially smaller than the total vote in the last general election, and that it will require substantially more than 5 percent of the eligible pool to produce the necessary 325,000 signatures. This would be in excess, percentage-wise, of anything the Court has approved to date as a precondition to an independent's securing a place on the ballot, and in excess of the 5 percent which we said in *Jenness* was higher than the requirement imposed by most state election codes.

. . .

Because further proceedings are required, we must resolve certain issues that are in dispute in order that the ground rules for the additional factfinding in the District Court will more clearly appear. . . .

. . .

. . . No discernible state interest justified the burdensome and complicated regulations that, in effect made impractical any alternative to the major parties. Similarly, here, we perceive no sufficient state interest in conditioning ballot position for an independent candidate on his forming a new political party as long as the State is free to assure itself that the candidate is a serious contender, truly independent, and with a satisfactory level of community support.

Accordingly, we vacate the judgment in No. 72–812 insofar as it refused relief to Hall and Tyner and remand the case in this respect to the District Court for further proceedings consistent with this opinion. In all other respects, the judgment in No. 72–812 and No. 72–6050 is affirmed.

Hynes v. Mayor of Oradell
425 U.S. 610 (1976)

The Borough of Oradell, N.J., has enacted two ordinances that, together, regulate most forms of door-to-door canvassing and solicitation. . . . The ordinance at issue here, Ordinance No. 598A . . . imposes no permit requirement; it covers persons soliciting for

> a recognized charitable cause, or any person desiring to canvass, solicit or call from house to house for a Federal, State, County or Municipal political campaign or cause.

. . .

Appellants are Edward Hynes, a New Jersey state assemblyman whose district was redrawn in 1973 to include the Borough of Oradell, and three Oradell registered voters. They brought suit in the Superior Court of Bergen County, New Jersey, seeking a declaration that Ordinance No. 598A was unconstitutional and an injunction against its enforcement. Appellant Hynes alleged that he wished to campaign for reelection in Oradell. The other appellants alleged either that they wished to canvass door to door in the borough for political causes or that they wished to speak with candidates who campaigned in Oradell. Each appellant claimed that the ordinance would unconstitutionally restrict such activity.

The Superior Court held the ordinance invalid. . . . The Appellate Division of the Superior Court affirmed. . . .

The Supreme Court of New Jersey reversed. . . . [T]he court held that Ordinance No. 598A was a legitimate exercise of the borough's police power, enacted to prevent crime and to reduce residents' fears about strangers wandering door to door. The ordinance regulated conduct—door-to-door canvassing—as well as speech, and, in doing so, "it could hardly be more clear." The ordinance, the court thought, imposed minimal requirements which did not offend free speech interests. . . .

. . .

There is, of course, no absolute right under the Federal Constitution to enter on the private premises of another and knock on a door for any purpose, and the police power permits reasonable regulation for public safety. We cannot say, and indeed appellants do not argue, that door-to-door canvassing and solicitation are immune from regulation under the State's police power, whether the purpose of the regulation is to protect from danger or to protect the peaceful enjoyment of the home.

. . .

The New Jersey Supreme Court undertook to give the ordinance a limiting construction by suggesting that, since the identification requirement "may be satisfied in writing, . . . resort may be had to the mails," but this construction of the ordinance does not explain either what the law covers or what it requires; for example, it provides no clue as to what is a "recognized charity"; nor is political "cause" defined. Even assuming that a more explicit limiting interpretation of the ordinance could remedy the flaws we have pointed out—a matter on which we intimate no view—we are without power to remedy the defects by giving the ordinance constitutionally precise content.

Accordingly, the judgment is reversed, and the case is remanded to the Supreme Court of New

Jersey for further proceedings not inconsistent with this opinion.

Mandel v. Bradley
432 U.S. 173 (1977)

Appellee Bruce Bradley decided in the spring of 1975 to run as an independent candidate for the United States Senate in 1976, a Presidential election year. Starting in the fall of 1975, Bradley collected signatures on nominating petitions. The requisite number was 51,155. On March 8, 1976, the deadline for filing, Bradley submitted 53,239 signatures and filed a certificate of candidacy for the Senate seat. However, on April 15, 1976, the State Administrative Board of Election Laws determined that only 42,049 of the signatures were valid, and denied him a place on the ballot.

Two weeks later, Bradley and the other appellees—petition signers and other voter supporters of Bradley—filed the instant suit, alleging that the procedures mandated by §7–1 of the Md. Elec.Code constitute an unconstitutional infringement of their associational and voting rights under the First and Fourteenth Amendments. They complained that Maryland's early filing date made it more difficult for Bradley to obtain the requisite number of signatures than for a party member to win a primary and sought, inter alia, an injunction against future enforcement of the offending provision of Maryland's election procedures. A three-judge District Court agreed with the appellees that the early filing deadline of §7–1(i) was an unconstitutional burden on an independent candidate's access to the ballot, and ordered the appellants to give Bradley 53 days after the party primaries to gather the requisite number of signatures.

. . .

The District Court erred in believing that our affirmance in [*Tucker v.*] *Salera* adopted the reasoning as well as the judgment of the three-judge court in that case ad thus required the District Court to conclude that the early filing date is impermissibly burdensome. . . .

. . .

This combination of an early filing deadline and the 21-day limitation on signature gathering is sufficient to distinguish *Salera* from the case now before us, where there is no limitation on the period within which such signatures must be gathered. . . .

. . .

. . . We . . . vacate the judgment, and remand the case for further proceedings consistent with this opinion.

Dougherty County Board of Education v. White
439 U.S. 32 (1978)

. . . At issue in this appeal is whether a county board of education in a covered State must seek approval of a rule requiring its employees to take unpaid leaves of absence while they campaign for elective office. Resolution of this question necessitates two related inquiries: first, whether a rule governing leave for employee candidates is a "standard, practice, or procedure with respect to voting" within the meaning of §5 of the Voting Rights Act; and second, whether a county school board is a "political subdivision" within the purview of the Act.

The facts in this case are not in dispute. Appellee, a Negro, is employed as Assistant Coordinator of Student Personnel Services by appellant Dougherty County Board of Education (Board). In May 1972, he announced his candidacy for the Georgia House of Representatives. Less than a month later, on June 12, 1972, the Board adopted Rule 58 without seeking prior federal approval. Rule 58 provides:

> POLITICAL OFFICE. Any employee of the school system who becomes a candidate for any elective political office will be required to take a leave of absence, without pay, such leave becoming effective upon the qualifying for such elective office and continuing for the duration of such political activity, and during the period of service in such office, if elected thereto.

Appellee qualified as a candidate for the Democratic primary in June 1972, and was compelled by Rule 58 to take a leave of absence without pay. After his defeat in the August primary, appellee was reinstated. Again in June 1974, he qualified as a candidate for the Georgia House and was forced to take leave. He was successful in both the August primary and the November general election. Accordingly, his leave continued through mid-November 1974. Appellee took a third leave of absence in June 1976, when he qualified to run for re-election. When it became clear in September that he would be unopposed in the November 1976, election, appellee was reinstated. As a consequence of those mandatory leaves, appellee lost pay in the amount of $2,810 in 1972, $4,780 in 1974, and $3,750 in 1976.

In June 1976, appellee filed this action in the Middle District of Georgia alleging that Rule 58 was a "standard, practice, or procedure with respect to voting" adopted by a covered entity, and therefore subject to the preclearance requirements of §5 of the Act. Appellee averred that he was the first Negro in recent memory, perhaps since Reconstruction, to run for the Georgia General Assembly from Dougherty County. The Board did not contest this fact, and further acknowledged that it was aware of no individual other than appellee who had run for public office while an employee of the Dougherty County Board of Education.

. . . [T]he three-judge District Court held that Rule 58 should have been submitted for federal approval before implementation. . . .

. . .

. . . [I]n contexts other than candidate qualification, we have interpreted §5 expansively to mandate preclearance for changes in the location of polling places, alterations of municipal boundaries, and reapportionment and redistricting plans.

. . .

Despite these consistently expansive constructions of §5, appellants contend that the Attorney General and District Court erred in treating Rule 58 as a "standard, practice, or procedure with respect to voting," rather than as simply "a means of getting a full days work for a full days pay— nothing more and nothing less." In appellants' view, Congress did not intend to subject all internal personnel measures affecting political activity to federal superintendence.

. . . Rule 58 is not a neutral personnel practice governing all forms of absenteeism. Rather, it specifically addresses the electoral process, singling out candidacy for elective office as a disabling activity. Although not in form a filing fee, the Rule operates in precisely the same fashion. By imposing substantial economic disincentives on employees who wish to seek elective office, the Rule burdens entry into elective campaigns and, concomitantly, limits the choices available to Dougherty County voters. Given the potential loss of thousands of dollars by employees subject to Rule 58, the Board's policy could operate as a more substantial inhibition on entry into the elective process than many of the filing fee changes involving only hundreds of dollars to which the Attorney General has successfully interposed objections. That Congress was well aware of these objections is apparent from the Committee Reports supporting extension of the Act in 1975. . . . The reality here is that Rule 58's impact on elections is no different from that of many of the candidate qualification changes for which we have previously required preclearance. Moreover, as a practical matter, Rule 58 implicates the political process to the same extent as do other modifications that this Court and Congress have recognized §5 to encompass, such as changes in the location of polling places and alterations in the procedures for casting a write-in vote.

We do not, of course, suggest that all constraints on employee political activity affecting voter choice violate §5. Presumably, most regulation of political involvement by public employees would not be found to have an invidious purpose or effect. Yet the same could be said of almost all changes subject to §5. . . .

Without intimating any views on the substantive question of Rule 58's legitimacy as a nonracial personnel measure, we believe that the circumstances surrounding its adoption and its effect on the political process are sufficiently suggestive of the potential for discrimination to demonstrate the need for preclearance. Appellee was the first Negro in recent years to seek election to the General Assembly from Dougherty County, an area with a long history of racial discrimination in voting. Less than a month after appellee announced his candidacy, the Board adopted Rule 58, concededly without any prior experience of absenteeism among employees seeking office. That the Board made its mandatory leave-of-absence requirement contingent on candidacy, rather than on absence during working hours, underscores the Rule's potential for inhibiting participation in the electoral process.

Plainly, Rule 58 erects "increased barriers" to candidacy. . . .

. . .

Because we conclude that Rule 58 is a standard, practice, or procedure with respect to voting enacted by an entity subject to §5, the judgment of the District Court is affirmed.

Clements v. Fashing
457 U.S. 957 (1982)

Appellees in this case challenge two provisions of the Texas Constitution that limit a public official's ability to become a candidate for another public office. The primary question in this appeal is whether these provisions violate the Equal Protection Clause of the Fourteenth Amendment.

Article III, §19, of the Texas Constitution. . . . renders an officeholder ineligible for the Texas Legislature if his current term of office will not expire until after the legislative term to which he aspires begins. Resignation is ineffective . . . if the officeholder's current term of office overlaps the term of the legislature to which he seeks election. In other words, §19 requires an officeholder to complete his current term of office before he may be eligible to serve in the legislature.

Article XVI, §65, is commonly referred to as a "resign-to-run" or "automatic resignation" provision. . . . It provides in relevant part:

> [I]f any of the officers named herein shall announce their candidacy, or shall in fact become a candidate, in any General, Special or Primary Election, for any office of profit or trust under the laws of this State or the United States other than the office then held, at any time when the unexpired term of the office then held shall exceed one year, such announcement or such candidacy shall constitute an automatic resignation of the office then held.

Four of the appellees are officeholders subject to the automatic resignation provision of §65. Fashing is a County Judge, Baca and McGhee are Justices of the Peace, and Ybarra is a Constable. Each officeholder appellee alleged in the complaint that he is qualified under Texas law to be a candidate for higher judicial office, and that the reason he has not and will not announce his candidacy is that such an announcement will constitute an automatic resignation from his current position. Appellee Baca alleged in addition that he could not become a candidate for the legislature because of §19. The remaining appellees are 20 voters who allege that they would vote for the officeholder appellees were they to become candidates.

The District Court for the Western District of Texas held that §19 and §65 denied appellees equal protection. . . . The Court of Appeals for the Fifth Circuit affirmed without opinion. . . .

. . .

Section 19 applies only to candidacy for the Texas Legislature. Of the appellees, only Baca, a Justice of the Peace, alleged that he would run for the Texas Legislature. Of the plaintiffs in this case, only appellee Baca's candidacy for another public office has in any fashion been restricted by §19. The issue in this case, therefore, is whether §19 may be applied to a Justice of the Peace in a manner consistent with the Equal Protection Clause.

Section 19 merely prohibits officeholders from cutting short their current term of office in order to serve in the legislature. In Texas, the term of office for a Justice of the Peace is four years, while legislative elections are held every two years. Therefore, §19 simply requires Baca to complete his 4-year term as Justice of the Peace before he may be eligible for the legislature. At most, therefore, Baca must wait two years—one election cycle—before he may run as a candidate for the legislature.

. . .

In establishing a maximum "waiting period" of two years for candidacy by a Justice of the Peace for the legislature, §19 places a de minimis burden on the political aspirations of a current officeholder. Section 19 discriminates neither on the basis of political affiliation nor on any factor not related to a candidate's qualifications to hold political office. Unlike filing fees or the level of support requirements, §19 in no way burdens access to the political process by those who are outside the "mainstream" of political life. In this case, §19 burdens only a candidate who has successfully been elected to one office, but whose political ambitions lead him to pursue a seat in the Texas Legislature.

. . . We conclude that this sort of insignificant interference with access to the ballot need only rest on a rational predicate in order to survive a challenge under the Equal Protection Clause.

Section 19 clearly rests on a rational predicate. That provision furthers Texas' interests in maintaining the integrity of the State's Justices of the Peace. By prohibiting candidacy for the legislature until completion of one's term of office, §19 seeks to ensure that a Justice of the Peace will neither abuse his position nor neglect his duties because of his aspirations for higher office. The demands of a political campaign may tempt a Justice of the Peace to devote less than his full time and energies to the responsibilities of his office. A campaigning Justice of the Peace might be tempted to render decisions and take actions that might serve more to further his political ambitions than the responsibilities of his office. The State's interests are especially important with regard to judicial officers. It is a serious accusation to charge a judicial officer with making a politically motivated decision. By contrast, it is to be expected that a legislator will vote with due regard to the views of his constituents.

. . .

. . . The burdens that §65 imposes on candidacy are even less substantial than those imposed by §19. The two provisions, of course, serve essentially the same state interests. The District Court found §65 deficient, however, not because of the nature or extent of the provision's restriction on candidacy, but because of the manner in which the offices are classified. According to the District Court, the classification system cannot survive equal protection scrutiny, because Texas has failed to explain sufficiently why some elected public officials are subject to §65 and why others are not. As with the case of §19, we conclude that §65 survives a challenge under the Equal Protection Clause unless appellees can show that there is no rational predicate to the classification scheme.

. . .

. . . The Equal Protection Clause does not forbid Texas to restrict one elected officeholder's candidacy for another elected office unless and until it places similar restrictions on other officeholders. The provision's language and its history belie any notion that §65 serves the invidious purpose of denying access to the political process to identifiable classes of potential candidates.

. . .

. . . Appellees are elected state officeholders who contest restrictions on partisan political activity. Section 19 and §65 represent a far more limited restriction on political activity than this Court has upheld with regard to civil servants. These provisions in no way restrict appellees' ability to participate in the political campaigns of third parties. They limit neither political contributions nor expenditures. They do not preclude appellees from holding an office in a political party. . . .

In this case, §19 operates merely to require appellee Baca to await the conclusion of his 4-year term as Justice of the Peace before he may run for the Texas Legislature. By virtue of §65, appellees in this case will automatically resign their current offices if they announce their candidacy for higher judicial office so long as the unexpired term of their current office exceeds one year. . . .

Neither the Equal Protection Clause nor the First Amendment authorizes this Court to review in cases such as this the manner in which a State has decided to govern itself. Constitutional limitations arise only if the classification scheme is invidious or if the challenged provision significantly impairs interests protected by the First Amendment. Our view of the wisdom of a state constitutional provision may not color our task of constitutional adjudication.

The judgment of the Court of Appeals is reversed.

Anderson v. Celebrezze
460 U.S. 780 (1983)

On April 24, 1980, petitioner John Anderson announced that he was an independent candidate for the office of President of the United States. Thereafter, his supporters—by gathering the signatures of registered voters, filing required documents, and submitting filing fees—were able to meet the substantive requirements for having his name placed on the ballot for the general election in November 1980, in all 50 States and the District of Columbia. On April 24, however, it was already too late for Anderson to qualify for a position on the ballot in Ohio and certain other States because the statutory deadlines for filing a statement of candidacy had already passed. The question presented by this case is whether Ohio's early filing deadline placed an unconstitutional burden on the voting and associational rights of Anderson's supporters.

The facts are not in dispute. On May 16, 1980, Anderson's supporters tendered a nominating petition containing approximately 14,500 signatures and a statement of candidacy to respondent Celebrezze, the Ohio Secretary of State. These documents would have entitled Anderson to a place on the ballot if they had been filed on or before March 20, 1980. Respondent refused to accept the petition solely because it had not been filed within the time required by §3513.25.7 of the Ohio Revised Code. Three days later, Anderson and three voters, two registered in Ohio and one in New Jersey, commenced this action in the United States District Court for the Southern District of Ohio, challenging the constitutionality of Ohio's early filing deadline for independent candidates. The District Court granted petitioners' motion for summary judgment and ordered respondent to place Anderson's name on the general election ballot.

The District Court held that the statutory deadline was unconstitutional on two grounds. It imposed an impermissible burden on the First Amendment rights of Anderson and his Ohio supporters and diluted the potential value of votes that might be cast for him in other States. Moreover, by requiring an independent to declare his candidacy in March without mandating comparable action by the nominee of a political party, the State violated the Equal Protection Clause of the Fourteenth Amendment. The District Court noted that the State did not advance any administrative reasons for the early deadline, and rejected the State's asserted justification that the deadline promoted "political stability." Not only

did that interest have diminished importance in a Presidential campaign; it also was adequately vindicated by another statute prohibiting a defeated candidate in a party primary from running as an independent.

The Secretary of State promptly appealed and unsuccessfully requested expedited review in both the Court of Appeals and this Court, but apparently did not seek to stay the District Court's order. The election was held while the appeal was pending. In Ohio, Anderson received 254,472 votes, or 5.9 percent of the votes cast; nationally, he received 5,720,060 votes or approximately 6.6 percent of the total.

The Court of Appeals reversed. It held that Ohio's early deadline ensures that voters making the important choice of their next president have the opportunity for a careful look at the candidates, a chance to see how they withstand the close scrutiny of a political campaign.

In other litigation brought by Anderson challenging early filing deadlines in Maine and Maryland, the Courts of Appeals for the First and Fourth Circuits affirmed District Court judgments ordering Anderson's name placed on the ballot. . . .

After a date toward the end of March, even if intervening events create unanticipated political opportunities, no independent candidate may enter the Presidential race and seek to place his name on the Ohio general election ballot. Thus, the direct impact of Ohio's early filing deadline falls upon aspirants for office. Nevertheless, as we have recognized, the rights of voters and the rights of candidates do not lend themselves to neat separation; laws that affect candidates always have at least some theoretical, correlative effect on voters. . . .

The impact of candidate eligibility requirements on voters implicates basic constitutional rights. . . . The right to vote is "heavily burdened" if that vote may be cast only for major party candidates at a time when other parties or other candidates are "clamoring for a place on the ballot." The exclusion of candidates also burdens voters' freedom of association, because an election campaign is an effective platform for the expression of views on the issues of the day, and a candidate serves as a rallying point for likeminded citizens.

Although these rights of voters are fundamental, not all restrictions imposed by the States on candidates' eligibility for the ballot impose constitutionally suspect burdens on voters' rights to associate or to choose among candidates. . . . States have enacted comprehensive and sometimes complex election codes. Each provision of these schemes, whether it governs the registration and qualifications of voters, the selection and eligibility of candidates, or the voting process itself, inevitably affects—at least to some degree—the individual's right to vote and his right to associate with others for political ends. Nevertheless, the State's important regulatory interests are generally sufficient to justify reasonable, nondiscriminatory restrictions.

. . .

. . . Ohio's filing deadline prevents persons who wish to be independent candidates from entering the significant political arena established in the State by a Presidential election campaign—and creating new political coalitions of Ohio voters—at any time after mid to late March. At this point, developments in campaigns for the major party nominations have only begun, and the major parties will not adopt their nominees and platforms for another five months. Candidates and supporters within the major parties thus have the political advantage of continued flexibility; for independents, the inflexibility imposed by the March filing deadline is a correlative disadvantage because of the competitive nature of the electoral process.

. . .

Not only does the challenged Ohio statute totally exclude any candidate who makes the decision to run for President as an independent after the March deadline, it also burdens the signature-gathering efforts of independents who decide to run in time to meet the deadline. When the primary campaigns are far in the future and the election itself is even more remote, the obstacles facing an independent candidate's organizing efforts are compounded. Volunteers are more difficult to recruit and retain, media publicity and campaign contributions are more difficult to secure, and voters are less interested in the campaign.

It is clear, then, that the March filing deadline places a particular burden on an identifiable segment of Ohio's independent-minded voters. . . .

A burden that falls unequally on new or small political parties or on independent candidates impinges, by its very nature, on associational choices protected by the First Amendment. It discriminates against those candidates and—of particular importance—against those voters whose political preferences lie outside the existing political parties. By limiting the opportunities of independent-minded voters to associate in the electoral arena to enhance their political effectiveness as a group, such restrictions threaten to reduce diversity and competition in the marketplace of ideas. Historically, political figures outside the two major parties have been fertile sources of new ideas and new programs; many of their challenges to the status quo have, in time, made their way into the political mainstream. . . . Furthermore, in the context of a Presidential election, state-imposed restrictions implicate a uniquely important national interest. For the

President and the Vice President of the United States are the only elected officials who represent all the voters in the Nation. Moreover, the impact of the votes cast in each State is affected by the votes cast for the various candidates in other States. Thus, in a Presidential election, a State's enforcement of more stringent ballot access requirements, including filing deadlines, has an impact beyond its own borders. Similarly, the State has a less important interest in regulating Presidential elections than statewide or local elections, because the outcome of the former will be largely determined by voters beyond the State's boundaries. . . . The Ohio filing deadline challenged in this case does more than burden the associational rights of independent voters and candidates. It places a significant state-imposed restriction on a nationwide electoral process.

. . .

The consequences of failing to meet the statutory deadline are entirely different for party primary participants and independents. The name of the nominees of the Democratic and Republican Parties will appear on the Ohio ballot in November even if they did not decide to run until after Ohio's March deadline had passed, but the independent is simply denied a position on the ballot if he waits too long. Thus, under Ohio's scheme, the major parties may include all events preceding their national conventions in the calculus that produces their respective nominees and campaign platforms, but the independent's judgment must be based on a history that ends in March.

. . .

We conclude that Ohio's March filing deadline for independent candidates for the office of President of the United States cannot be justified by the State's asserted interest in protecting political stability. . . .

We began our inquiry by noting that our primary concern is not the interest of candidate Anderson, but rather, the interests of the voters who chose to associate together to express their support for Anderson's candidacy and the views he espoused. Under any realistic appraisal, the "extent and nature" of the burdens Ohio has placed on the voters' freedom of choice and freedom of association, in an election of nationwide importance, unquestionably outweigh the State's minimal interest in imposing a March deadline.

The judgment of the Court of Appeals is reversed.

Chandler v. Miller
520 U.S. 305 (1997)

Georgia requires candidates for designated state offices to certify that they have taken a drug test and that the test result was negative. . . .

. . . Georgia was the first, and apparently remains the only, State to condition candidacy for state office on a drug test.

Under the Georgia statute, to qualify for a place on the ballot, a candidate must present a certificate from a state-approved laboratory, in a form approved by the Secretary of State, reporting that the candidate submitted to a urinalysis drug test within 30 days prior to qualifying for nomination or election and that the results were negative. . . .

. . .

Petitioners were Libertarian Party nominees in 1994 for state offices subject to the requirements of §21–2–140. The Party nominated Walker L. Chandler for the office of Lieutenant Governor, Sharon T. Harris for the office of Commissioner of Agriculture, and James D. Walker for the office of member of the General Assembly. In May, 1994, about one month before the deadline for submission of the certificates required by §21–2–140, petitioners Chandler, Harris, and Walker filed this action in the United States District Court for the Northern District of Georgia. They asserted . . . that the drug tests required by §21–2–140 violated their rights under the First, Fourth, and Fourteenth Amendments to the United States Constitution. Naming as defendants Governor Zell D. Miller and two other state officials involved in the administration of §21–2–140, petitioners requested declaratory and injunctive relief barring enforcement of the statute.

In June 1994, the District Court denied petitioners' motion for a preliminary injunction. Stressing the importance of the state offices sought and the relative unintrusiveness of the testing procedure, the court found it unlikely that petitioners would prevail on the merits of their claims. Petitioners apparently submitted to the drug tests, obtained the certificates required by §21–2–140, and appeared on the ballot. After the 1994 election, the parties jointly moved for the entry of final judgment on stipulated facts. In January 1995, the District Court entered final judgment for respondents.

A divided Eleventh Circuit panel affirmed. . . .

. . .

. . . [T]he testing method the Georgia statute describes is relatively noninvasive; therefore, if the "special need" showing had been made, the State could not be faulted for excessive intrusion. . . . The State permits a candidate to provide the urine specimen in the office of his or her private physician, and the results of the test are given first to the candidate, who controls further dissemination of the report. Because the State has effectively limited the invasiveness of the testing procedure, we concentrate on the core issue: is the certification requirement warranted by a special need?

Our precedents establish that the proffered special need for drug testing must be substantial— important enough to override the individual's acknowledged privacy interest, sufficiently vital to suppress the Fourth Amendment's normal requirement of individualized suspicion. Georgia has failed to show, in justification of §21-2-140, a special need of that kind.

. . .

Nothing in the record hints that the hazards respondents broadly describe are real, and not simply hypothetical, for Georgia's polity. . . .

. . . Georgia's certification requirement is not well designed to identify candidates who violate anti-drug laws. Nor is the scheme a credible means to deter illicit drug users from seeking election to state office. The test date—to be scheduled by the candidate anytime within 30 days prior to qualifying for a place on the ballot—is no secret. As counsel for respondents acknowledged at oral argument, users of illegal drugs, save for those prohibitively addicted, could abstain for a pre-test period sufficient to avoid detection. Even if we indulged respondents' argument that one purpose of §21–2–140 might be to detect those unable so to abstain, respondents have not shown or argued that such persons are likely to be candidates for public office in Georgia. Moreover, respondents have offered no reason why ordinary law enforcement methods would not suffice to apprehend such addicted individuals, should they appear in the limelight of a public stage. Section 21–2–140, in short, is not needed, and cannot work to ferret out lawbreakers, and respondents barely attempt to support the statute on that ground.

. . .

What is left, after close review of Georgia's scheme, is the image the State seeks to project. By requiring candidates for public office to submit to drug testing, Georgia displays its commitment to the struggle against drug abuse. The suspicionless tests, according to respondents, signify that candidates, if elected, will be fit to serve their constituents free from the influence of illegal drugs. But Georgia asserts no evidence of a drug problem among the State's elected officials, those officials typically do not perform high-risk, safety-sensitive tasks, and the required certification immediately aids no interdiction effort. The need revealed, in short, is symbolic, not "special," as that term draws meaning from our case law.

. . . However well meant, the candidate drug test Georgia has devised diminishes personal privacy for a symbol's sake. The Fourth Amendment shields society against that state action.

. . . Georgia's singular drug test for candidates is not part of a medical examination designed to provide certification of a candidate's general health, and we express no opinion on such examinations. Nor do we touch on financial disclosure requirements, which implicate different concerns and procedures. And we do not speak to drug testing in the private sector, a domain unguarded by Fourth Amendment constraints.

. . .

. . . [T]he judgment of the Court of Appeals for the Eleventh Circuit is reversed.

6

Political Parties

This chapter looks at the liberties and restrictions political parties deal with when supporting candidates for elective office. Independent third parties, the Communist Party, and racial policies are common issues the Court has reviewed.

Nixon v. Condon
286 U.S. 73 (1932)

The petitioner, a Negro, has brought this action against judges of election in Texas to recover damages for their refusal by reason of his race or color to permit him to cast his vote at a primary election.

. . .

. . . [T]he state executive committee of the Democratic party adopted a resolution "that all white democrats who are qualified under the constitution and laws of Texas and who subscribe to the statutory pledge, and none other, be allowed to participate in the primary elections to be held July 28, 1928, and August 25, 1928," and the chairman and secretary were directed to forward copies of the resolution to the committees in the several counties.

On July 28, 1928, the petitioner, a citizen of the United States, and qualified to vote unless disqualified by the foregoing resolution, presented himself at the polls and requested that he be furnished with a ballot. The respondents, the judges of election, declined to furnish the ballot or to permit the vote on the ground that the peti-

tioner was a Negro, and that by force of the resolution of the executive committee only white Democrats were allowed to be voters at the Democratic primary. The refusal was followed by this action for damages. In the District Court there was a judgment of dismissal, which was affirmed by the Circuit Court of Appeals for the Fifth Circuit. . . .

. . .

Whether a political party in Texas has inherent power today without restraint by any law to determine its own membership, we are not required at this time either to affirm or to deny. The argument for the petitioner is that, quite apart from the article in controversy, there are other provisions of the Election Law whereby the privilege of unfettered choice has been withdrawn or abridged; that nomination at a primary is in many circumstances required by the statute if nomination is to be made at all; that parties and their representatives have become the custodians of official power; and that, if heed is to be given to the realities of political life, they are now agencies of the state, the instruments by which government becomes a living thing. In that view, so runs the argument, a party is still free to define for itself the political tenets of its members, but to those who profess its tenets there may be no denial of its privileges.

. . .

We recall at this point the wording of the statute invoked by the respondents. "Every political party in this State through its State Executive

Committee shall have the power to prescribe the qualifications of its own members and shall in its own way determine who shall be qualified to vote or otherwise participate in such political party." Whatever inherent power a state political party has to determine the content of its membership resides in the state convention. There platforms of principles are announced and the tests of party allegiance made known to the world. What is true in that regard of parties generally is true more particularly in Texas, where the statute is explicit in committing to the state convention the formulation of the party faith. The state executive committee, if it is the sovereign organ of the party, is not such by virtue of any powers inherent in its being. It is, as its name imports, a committee and nothing more, a committee to be chosen by the convention and to consist of a chairman and thirty-one members, one from each senatorial district of the state. To this committee the statute here in controversy has attempted to confide authority to determine of its own motion the requisites of party membership and in so doing to speak for the party as a whole. Never has the state convention made declaration of a will to bar Negroes of the state from admission to the party ranks. . . .

. . .

. . . We do not impugn the competence of the Legislature to designate the agencies whereby the party faith shall be declared and the party discipline enforced. The pith of the matter is simply this, that, when those agencies are invested with an authority independent of the will of the association in whose name they undertake to speak, they become to that extent the organs of the state itself, the repositories of official power. They are then the governmental instruments whereby parties are organized and regulated to the end that government itself may be established or contin-

ued. What they do in that relation, they must do in submission to the mandates of equality and liberty that bind officials everywhere. They are not acting in matters of merely private concern like the directors or agents of business corporations. They are acting in matters of high public interest, matters intimately connected with the capacity of government to exercise its functions unbrokenly and smoothly. . . . It is not concluded upon such an inquiry by decisions rendered elsewhere. The test is not whether the members of the executive committee are the representatives of the state in the strict sense in which an agent is the representative of his principal. The test is whether they are to be classified as representatives of the state to such an extent and in such a sense that the great restraints of the Constitution set limits to their action.

. . . Delegates of the state's power have discharged their official functions in such a way as to discriminate invidiously between white citizens and black. The Fourteenth Amendment, adopted as it was with special solicitude for the equal protection of members of the Negro race, lays a duty upon the court to level by its judgment these barriers of color.

The judgment below is reversed, and the cause remanded for further proceedings in conformity with this opinion.

Smith v. Allwright
321 U.S. 649 (1944)

. . . [R]eview a claim for damages in the sum of $5,000 on the part of petitioner, a Negro citizen of the 48th precinct of Harris County, Texas, for the refusal of respondents, election and associate election judges respectively of that precinct, to give petitioner a ballot or to permit him to cast a ballot in the primary election of July 27, 1940, for the nomination of Democratic candidates for the United States Senate and House of Representatives, and Governor and other state officers. The refusal is alleged to have been solely because of the race and color of the proposed voter.

> . . . The suit was filed in the District Court of the United States for the Southern District of Texas.

The District Court denied the relief sought and the Circuit Court of Appeals. . . .

> The State of Texas by its Constitution and statutes provides that every person, if certain other requirements are met which are not here in issue, qualified by residence in the district or county "shall be deemed a qualified elector." Primary elections for United States Senators, Congressmen and state officers are provided for by Chapters Twelve and Thirteen of the statutes. Under these chapters, the Democratic Party was required to hold the primary which was the occasion of the alleged wrong to petitioner. . . . These nominations are to be made by the qualified voters of the party. The Democratic Party of Texas is held by the Supreme Court of that state to be a "voluntary association" protected by Section 27 of the Bill of Rights, Constitution of Texas, from interference by the state. . . .
>
> . . .

Texas is free to conduct her elections and limit her electorate as she may deem wise, save only as her action may be affected by the prohibitions of the United States Constitution or in conflict with powers delegated to and exercised by the National Government. The Fourteenth Amendment forbids a state from making or enforcing any law which abridges the privileges or immunities of citizens of the United States and the Fifteenth Amendment specifically interdicts any denial or abridgement by a state of the right of citizens to vote on account of color. Respondents appeared in the District Court and the Circuit Court of Appeals and defended on the ground that

the Democratic party of Texas is a voluntary organization with members banded together for the purpose of selecting individuals of the group representing the common political beliefs as candidates in the general election. As such a voluntary organization, it was claimed, the Democratic party is free to select its own membership and limit to whites participation in the party primary. Such action, the answer asserted, does not violate the Fourteenth, Fifteenth, or Seventeenth Amendment as officers of government cannot be chosen at primaries and the Amendments are applicable only to general elections where governmental officers are actually elected. Primaries, it is said, are political party affairs, handled by party not governmental officers. . . .

. . .

We are . . . brought to an examination of the qualifications for Democratic primary electors in Texas, to determine whether state action or private action has excluded Negroes from participation. Despite Texas's decision that the exclusion is produced by private or party action, Federal courts must for themselves appraise the facts leading to that conclusion. It is only by the performance of this obligation that a final and uniform interpretation can be given to the Constitution, the "supreme Law of the Land." Texas requires electors in a primary to pay a poll tax. Every person who does so pay and who has the qualifications of age and residence is an acceptable voter for the primary. . . . Texas requires by the law the election of the county officers of a party. These compose the county executive committee. The county chairmen so selected are members of the district executive committee and choose the chairman for the district. Precinct primary election officers are named by the county executive committee. Statutes provide for the election by the voters of precinct delegates to the county convention of a party and the selection of delegates to the district and state conventions by the county convention. The state convention selects the state executive committee. No convention may place in platform or resolution any demand for specific legislation without endorsement of such legislation by the voters in a primary. Texas thus directs the selection of all party officers.

Primary elections are conducted by the party under state statutory authority. The county executive committee selects precinct election officials and the county, district or state executive committees, respectively, canvass the returns. These party committees or the state convention certify the party's candidates to the appropriate officers for inclusion on the official ballot for the general election. No name which has not been so certified may appear upon the ballot for the general election as a candidate of a political party. No other name may be printed on the ballot which has not been placed in nomination by qualified voters who must take oath that they did not participate in a primary for the selection of a candidate for the office for which the nomination is made.

. . .

We think that this statutory system for the selection of party nominees for inclusion on the general election ballot makes the party which is required to follow these legislative directions an agency of the state in so far as it determines the participants in a primary election. The party takes its character as a state agency from the duties imposed upon it by state statutes; the duties do not become matters of private law because they are performed by a political party. The plan of the Texas primary follows substantially that of Louisiana, with the exception that in Louisiana the state pays the cost of the primary while Texas assesses the cost against candidates. In numerous instances, the Texas statutes fix or limit the

fees to be charged. Whether paid directly by the state or through state requirements, it is state action which compels. When primaries become a part of the machinery for choosing officials, state and national, as they have here, the same tests to determine the character of discrimination or abridgement should be applied to the primary as are applied to the general election. If the state requires a certain electoral procedure, prescribes a general election ballot made up of party nominees so chosen and limits the choice of the electorate in general elections for state offices, practically speaking, to those whose names appear on such a ballot, it endorses, adopts and enforces the discrimination against Negroes, practiced by a party entrusted by Texas law with the determination of the qualifications of participants in the primary. This is state action within the meaning of the Fifteenth Amendment.

The United States . . . grants to all citizens a right to participate in the choice of elected officials without restriction by any state because of race. This grant to the people of the opportunity for choice is not to be nullified by a state through casting its electoral process in a form which permits a private organization to practice racial discrimination in the election. Constitutional rights would be of little value if they could be thus indirectly denied.

The privilege of membership in a party may be . . . no concern of a state. But when, as here, that privilege is also the essential qualification for voting in a primary to select nominees for a general election, the state makes the action of the party the action of the state. In reaching this conclusion we are not unmindful of the desirability of continuity of decision in constitutional questions. However, when convinced of former error, this Court has never felt constrained to follow precedent. In constitutional questions, where correction depends upon amendment and not upon legislative action this Court throughout its history has freely exercised its power to reexamine the basis of its constitutional decisions. This has long been accepted practice, and this practice has continued to this day. This is particularly true when the decision believed erroneous is the application of a constitutional principle rather than an interpretation of the Constitution to extract the principle itself. Here we are applying, contrary to the recent decision in *Grovey*, the well established principle of the Fifteenth Amendment, forbidding the abridgement by a state of a citizen's right to vote. *Grovey v. Townsend* is overruled.

Judgment reversed.

MacDougall v. Green
335 U.S. 281 (1948)

This action was brought before a three-judge court convened in the Northern District of Illinois. The object of the action is an injunction against the enforcement of a provision which, in 1935, was added to a statute of Illinois and which requires that a petition to form and to nominate candidates for a new political party be signed by at least 25,000 qualified voters, "Provided, that included in the aggregate total of twenty-five thousand signatures are the signatures of two hundred qualified voters from each of at least fifty counties within the State." Appellants are the "Progressive Party," its nominees for United States Senator, Presidential Electors, and State offices, and several Illinois voters. Appellees are the Governor, the Auditor of Public Accounts, and the Secretary of State of Illinois, members of the Boards of Election Commissioners of various cities, and the County Clerks of various counties. The District Court found want of jurisdiction and denied the injunction. . . .

The action arises from the finding of the State Officers Electoral Board that appellants had not obtained the requisite number of signatures from the requisite number of counties and its consequent ruling that their nominating petition was "not sufficient in law to entitle the said candidates' names to appear on the ballot." The appellants' claim to equitable relief against this ruling is based upon the peculiar distribution of population among Illinois' 102 counties. They allege that 52 percent of the State's registered voters are residents of Cook County alone, 87 percent are residents of the 49 most populous counties, and only 13 percent reside in the 50 least populous counties. Under these circumstances, they say, the Illinois statute is so discriminatory in its application as to amount to a denial of the due-process, equal-protection, and privileges-and-immunities clauses of the Fourteenth Amendment, as well as Article I, 2 and 4, Article II, 1, and the Seventeenth Amendment of the Constitution of the United States.

It is clear that the requirement of 200 signatures from at least 50 counties gives to the voters of the less populous counties of Illinois the power completely to block the nomination of candidates whose support is confined to geographically limited areas. But the State is entitled to deem this power not disproportionate: of 25,000 signatures required, only 9,800, or 39 percent, need be distributed; the remaining 61 percent may be obtained from a single county. And Cook County, the largest, contains not more than 52 percent of the State's voters. It is allowable State policy to require that candidates for statewide office should have support not limited to a concentrated locality. This is not a unique policy. To assume that political power is a function exclusively of numbers is to disregard the practicalities of government. Thus, the Constitution protects the interests of the smaller against the greater by giving in the

Senate entirely unequal representation to populations. It would be strange indeed, and doctrinaire, for this Court, applying such broad constitutional concepts as due process and equal protection of the laws, to deny a State the power to assure a proper diffusion of political initiative as between its thinly populated counties and those having concentrated masses, in view of the fact that the latter have practical opportunities for exerting their political weight at the polls not available to the former. The Constitution—a practical instrument of government—makes no such demands on the States.

On the record before us, we need not pass upon purely local questions, also urged by appellants, having no federal constitutional aspect.

Judgment affirmed.

Ray v. Blair
343 U.S. 214 (1952)

The Supreme Court of Alabama upheld a peremptory writ of mandamus requiring the petitioner, the chairman of that state's Executive Committee of the Democratic Party, to certify respondent Edmund Blair, a member of that party, to the Secretary of State of Alabama as a candidate for Presidential Elector in the Democratic Primary to be held May 6, 1952. Respondent Blair was admittedly qualified as a candidate except that he refused to include the following quoted words in the pledge required of party candidates—a pledge to aid and support "the nominees of the National Convention of the Democratic Party for President and Vice President of the United States." The chairman's refusal of certification was based on that omission.

The mandamus was approved on the sole ground that the above requirement restricted the freedom of a federal elector to vote in his Electoral College for his choice for President. The pledge was held void as unconstitutional under the Twelfth Amendment of the Constitution of the United States. . . .

. . .

The controversy arose under the Alabama laws permitting party primaries. Title 17 of the Code of Alabama, 1940, provides for regular optional primary elections in that state on the first Tuesday in May of even years by any political party, as defined in the chapter, at state cost. They are subject to the same penalties and punishment provisions as regular state elections. Parties may select their own committee in such manner as the governing authority of the party may desire. Section 344 provides that the chairman of the state executive committee shall certify the candidates other than those who are candidates for county offices to the Secretary of State of Alabama. That official, within not less than 30 days prior to the time of holding the primary elections, shall certify these names to the probate judge of any county holding an election.

Every state executive committee is given the power to fix political or other qualifications of its own members. It may determine who shall be entitled and qualified to vote in the primary election or to be a candidate therein. The qualifications of voters and candidates may vary.

Section 348 requires a candidate to file his declaration of candidacy with the executive committee in the form prescribed by the governing body of the party. There is a provision, which reads as follows: "At the bottom of the ballot and after the name of the last candidate shall be printed the following, viz: 'By casting this ballot I do pledge myself to abide by the result of this primary election and to aid and support all the nominees thereof in the ensuing general election.'"

On consideration of these sections in other cases the Supreme Court of Alabama has reached conclusions generally conformable to the current of authority. . . .

. . .

As is well known, political parties in the modern sense were not born with the Republic. They were created by necessity, by the need to organize the rapidly increasing population, scattered over our Land, so as to coordinate efforts to secure needed legislation and oppose that deemed undesirable. The party conventions of locally chosen delegates, from the county to the national level, succeeded the caucuses of self-appointed legislators or other interested individuals. Dissatisfaction with the manipulation of conventions caused that system to be largely superseded by the direct primary. This was particularly true in the South because, with the predominance of the Democratic Party in that section, the nomination was more important than the election. There primaries are generally, as in Alabama, optional. Various tests of party allegiance for candidates in direct primaries are found in a number of states. The requirement of a pledge from the candidate participating in primaries to support the nominee is not unusual. Such a provision protects a party from intrusion by those with adverse political principles. It was under the authority of 347 of the Alabama Code, that the State Democratic Executive Committee of Alabama adopted a resolution on January 26, 1952, requiring candidates in its primary to pledge support to the nominees of the National Convention of the Democratic Party for President and Vice President. It is this provision in the qualifications required by the party under 347 which the Supreme Court of Alabama held unconstitutional in this case.

The opinion of the Supreme Court of Alabama

concluded that the Executive Committee requirement violated the Twelfth Amendment. . . .

. . .

The applicable constitutional provisions on their face furnish no definite answer to the query whether a state may permit a party to require party regularity from its primary candidates for national electors. The presidential electors exercise a federal function in balloting for President and Vice President but they are not federal officers or agents any more than the state elector who votes for congressmen. They act by authority of the state that in turn receives its authority from the Federal Constitution. Neither the language of Art. II, 1, nor that of the Twelfth Amendment forbids a party to require from candidates in its primary a pledge of political conformity with the aims of the party. Unless such a requirement is implicit, certainly neither provision of the Constitution requires a state political party, affiliated with a national party through acceptance of the national call to send state delegates to the national convention, to accept persons as candidates who refuse to agree to abide by the party's requirement.

The argument against the party's power to exclude as candidates in the primary those unwilling to agree to aid and support the national nominees runs as follows: The constitutional method for the selection of the President and Vice President is for states to appoint electors who shall in turn vote for our chief executives. The intention of the Founders was that those electors should exercise their judgment in voting for President and Vice President. Therefore this requirement of a pledge is a restriction in substance, if not in form, that interferes with the performance of this constitutional duty to select the proper persons to head the Nation, according to the best judgment of the elector. This interference with the elector's freedom of balloting for President relates directly to the general election and is not confined to the primary, it is contended, because under *United States v. Classic* and *Smith v. Allwright*, the Alabama primary is an integral part of the general election. Although Alabama, it is pointed out, requires electors to be chosen at the general election by popular vote, the real election takes place in the primary. Limitation as to entering a primary controls the results of the general election.

. . .

In Alabama . . . the primary and general elections are a part of the state-controlled elective process. . . . A state's or a political party's exclusion of candidates from a party primary because they will not pledge to support the party's nominees is a method of securing party candidates in the general election, pledged to the philosophy and leadership of that party. It is an exercise of the state's right to appoint electors in such manner, subject to possible constitutional limitations, as it may choose. The fact that the primary is a part of the election machinery is immaterial unless the requirement of pledge violates some constitutional or statutory provision. It was the violation of a secured right that brought about the *Classic* and *Allwright* decisions. Here they do not apply unless there was a violation of the Twelfth Amendment by the requirement to support the nominees of the National Convention.

. . . [W]e consider the argument that the Twelfth Amendment demands absolute freedom for the elector to vote his own choice, uninhibited by a pledge. It is true that the Amendment says the electors shall vote by ballot. But it is also true that the Amendment does not prohibit an elector's announcing his choice beforehand, pledging himself. The suggestion that in the early elections candidates for electors—contemporaries of the Founders—would have hesitated, because of con-

stitutional limitations, to pledge themselves to support party nominees in the event of their selection as electors is impossible to accept. History teaches that the electors were expected to support the party nominees. Experts in the history of government recognize the long-standing practice. Indeed, more than twenty states do not print the names of the candidates for electors on the general election ballot. Instead, in one form or another, they allow a vote for the presidential candidate of the national conventions to be counted as a vote for his party's nominees for the electoral college. This long-continued practical interpretation of the constitutional propriety of an implied or oral pledge of his ballot by a candidate for elector as to his vote in the electoral college weighs heavily in considering the constitutionality of a pledge, such as the one here required, in the primary.

However, even if such promises of candidates for the electoral college are legally unenforceable because violative of an assumed constitutional freedom of the elector under the Constitution, to vote as he may choose in the electoral college, it would not follow that the requirement of a pledge in the primary is unconstitutional. A candidacy in the primary is a voluntary act of the applicant. He is not barred, discriminatorily, from participating but must comply with the rules of the party. Surely one may voluntarily assume obligations to vote for a certain candidate. The state offers him opportunity to become a candidate for elector on his own terms, although he must file his declaration before the primary. Even though the victory of an independent candidate for elector in Alabama cannot be anticipated, the state does offer the opportunity for the development of other strong political organizations where the need is felt for them by a sizable block of voters. Such parties may leave their electors to their own choice.

We conclude that the Twelfth Amendment does not bar a political party from requiring the pledge to support the nominees of the National Convention. Where a state authorizes a party to choose its nominees for elector in a party primary and to fix the qualifications for the candidates, we see no federal constitutional objection to the requirement of this pledge.

Terry v. Adams
345 U.S. 461 (1953)

. . . This case raises questions concerning the constitutional power of a Texas county political organization called the Jaybird Democratic Association or Jaybird Party to exclude Negroes from its primaries on racial grounds. The Jaybirds deny that their racial exclusions violate the Fifteenth Amendment. They contend that the Amendment applies only to elections or primaries held under state regulation, that their association is not regulated by the state at all, and that it is not a political party but a self-governing voluntary club. The District Court held the Jaybird racial discriminations invalid and entered judgment accordingly. The Court of Appeals reversed, holding that there was no constitutional or congressional bar to the admitted discriminatory exclusion of Negroes because Jaybird's primaries were not to any extent state controlled. . . .

. . .

The Jaybird Association or Party was organized in 1889. Its membership was then and always has been limited to white people; they are automatically members if their names appear on the official list of county voters. It has been run like other political parties with an executive committee named from the county's voting precincts. Expenses of the party are paid by the assessment of candidates for office in its primaries. Candidates for county offices submit their names to the Jaybird Committee in accordance with the normal practice followed by regular political parties all over the country. Advertisements and posters proclaim that these candidates are running subject to the action of the Jaybird primary. While there is no legal compulsion on successful Jaybird candidates to enter Democratic primaries, they have nearly always done so and with few exceptions since 1889 have run and won without opposition in the Democratic primaries and the general elections that followed. Thus the party has been the dominant political group in the county since organization, having endorsed every county-wide official elected since 1889.

It is apparent that Jaybird activities follow a plan purposefully designed to exclude Negroes from voting and at the same time to escape the Fifteenth Amendment's command that the right of citizens to vote shall neither be denied nor abridged on account of race. . . .

. . .

The District Court found that the Jaybird Association was a political organization or party; that the majority of white voters generally abide by the results of its primaries and support in the Democratic primaries the persons endorsed by the Jaybird primaries; and that the chief object of the Association has always been to deny Negroes any voice or part in the election of Fort Bend County officials.

. . .

The Amendment bans racial discrimination in voting by both state and nation. It thus establishes a national policy, obviously applicable to the right of Negroes not to be discriminated against as voters in elections to determine public governmental policies or to select public officials, national, state, or local. . . .

. . .

The Amendment, the congressional enactment and the cases make explicit the rule against racial discrimination in the conduct of elections. Together they show the meaning of "elections." Clearly the Amendment includes any election in which public issues are decided or public officials selected. Just as clearly the Amendment excludes social or business clubs. And the statute shows the congressional mandate against discrimination whether the voting on public issues and officials is conducted in community, state, or nation. Size is not a standard.

It is significant that precisely the same qualifications as those prescribed by Texas entitling electors to vote at county-operated primaries are adopted as the sole qualifications entitling electors to vote at the county-wide Jaybird primaries with a single proviso—Negroes are excluded. Everyone concedes that such a proviso in the county-operated primaries would be unconstitutional. The Jaybird Party thus brings into being and holds precisely the kind of election that the Fifteenth Amendment seeks to prevent. When it produces the equivalent of the prohibited election, the damage has been done.

For a state to permit such a duplication of its election processes is to permit a flagrant abuse of those processes to defeat the purposes of the Fifteenth Amendment. The use of the county-operated primary to ratify the result of the prohibited election merely compounds the offense. It violates the Fifteenth Amendment for a state, by such circumvention, to permit within its borders the use of any device that produces an equivalent of the prohibited election.

The only election that has counted in this Texas county for more than fifty years has been that held by the Jaybirds from which Negroes were excluded. The Democratic primary and the general election have become no more than the perfunctory ratifiers of the choice that has already been made in Jaybird elections from which Negroes have been excluded. It is immaterial that the state does not control that part of this elective process which it leaves for the Jaybirds to manage. The Jaybird primary has become an integral part, indeed the only effective part, of the elective process that determines who shall rule and govern in the county. The effect of the whole procedure, Jaybird primary plus Democratic primary plus general election, is to do precisely that which the Fifteenth Amendment forbids—strip Negroes of every vestige of influence in selecting the officials who control the local county matters that intimately touch the daily lives of citizens.

We reverse the Court of Appeals' judgment reversing that of the District Court. We affirm the District Court's holding that the combined Jaybird-Democratic-general election machinery has deprived these petitioners of their right to vote on account of their race and color. The case is remanded to the District Court to enter such orders and decrees as are necessary and proper under the jurisdiction it has retained. In exercising this jurisdiction, the Court is left free to hold hearings to consider and determine what provisions are essential to afford Negro citizens of Fort Bend County full protection from future discriminatory Jaybird-Democratic-general election practices which deprive citizens of voting rights because of their color.

Communist Party of the United States v. Subversive Activities Control Board
367 U.S. 1 (1961)

. . . On November 22, 1950, the Attorney General petitioned the Subversive Activities Control

Board for an order to require that the Communist Party register as a Communist-action organization. The Party thereupon brought suit in the District Court for the District of Columbia, seeking to have the proceedings of the Board enjoined. A statutory three-judge court denied preliminary relief. . . . After this Court denied a petition for extension of the stay, the Party abandoned the suit. Hearings began on April 23, 1951, and ended on July 1, 1952. . . . On April 20, 1953, the Board issued its . . . report concluding that the Party was a Communist-action organization within the meaning of the Subversive Activities Control Act, and its order requiring that the Party register in the manner prescribed by 7. Pending disposition in the Court of Appeals for the District of Columbia of the Party's petition for review of the registration order, the Party moved in that court, pursuant to 14(a), for leave to adduce additional evidence which it alleged would show that three witnesses for the Attorney General . . . had testified perjuriously before the Board. The Court of Appeals denied the motion and affirmed the order of the Board. . . . Finding that the Party's allegations of perjury had not been denied by the Attorney General, and concluding that the registration order based on a record impugned by a charge of perjurious testimony on the part of three witnesses whose evidence constituted a not insubstantial portion of the Government's case could not stand, this Court remanded to the Board "to make certain that [it] bases its findings upon untainted evidence."

On remand the Party filed several motions with the Board seeking to reopen the record for the introduction of additional evidence. These were denied. A motion in the Court of Appeals for leave to adduce additional evidence was similarly denied, except that the Board was granted permission to entertain a motion concerning the Party's

offer to show that another of the Attorney General's witnesses . . . had committed perjury with regard to a specified aspect of her testimony. The Board granted the Party's motion; hearings were reopened. . . . Motions by the Party for orders requiring the Government to produce certain documents relevant to the matter of her testimony were denied. On December 18, 1956, the Board issued its . . . Modified Report. It . . . reaffirmed its conclusion that the Party was a Communist-action organization and recommended that the Court of Appeals affirm its registration order. That court, while affirming the Board's actions in other regards . . . remanded. . . .

. . . [T]he Board re-examined the record as a whole and issued its Modified Report on Second Remand—its findings of fact consisting principally of the findings contained in its first Modified Report, with a few deletions—again concluding that the Communist Party of the United States was a Communist-action organization, and again recommending that its order to register be affirmed. The same panel of the Court of Appeals affirmed the order. . . .

. . .

The constitutional contentions raised by the Party with respect to the registration requirement of 7 are (A) that that requirement, in the context of the Act, in effect "outlaws" the Party and is in the nature of a bill of attainder; (B) that compelling organizations to register and to list their members on a showing merely that they are foreign-dominated and operate primarily to advance the objectives of the world Communist movement constitutes a restraint on freedom of expression and association in violation of the First Amendment; (C) that requiring Party officers to file registration statements for the Party subjects them to self-incrimination forbidden by the Fifth Amendment; (D) that the Act violates due process by legislative predetermination of facts essential to bring the Communist Party within the definition of a Communist-action organization, and that the evidentiary elements prescribed for consideration by the Board bear no rational relation to that definition; (E) that in several aspects the Act is unconstitutionally vague; and (F) that the Subversive Activities Control Board is so necessarily biased against the Communist Party as to deprive it of a fair hearing.

Our determination that in the present proceeding all questions are premature which regard only the constitutionality of the various particular consequences of a registration order to a registered organization and its members, does not foreclose the Party from arguing—and it does argue—that in light of the cumulative effect of those consequences the registration provisions of §7 are not what they seem, but represent a legislative attempt, by devious means, to "outlaw" the Party. . . .

. . .

The judgment of the Court of Appeals is affirmed.

Scales v. United States
367 U.S. 203 (1961)

. . . Smith Act . . . among other things, makes a felony the acquisition or holding of knowing membership in any organization which advocates the overthrow of the Government of the United States by force or violence. The indictment charged that from January 1946 to the date of its filing, the Communist Party of the United States was such an organization, and that petitioner throughout that period was a member thereof, with knowledge of the Party's illegal purpose and a specific intent to accomplish overthrow "as speedily as circumstances would permit."

. . .

. . . Petitioner would most plainly be correct if the statute under which he was indicted purported to proscribe membership in Communist organizations, as such, and to punish membership per se in an organization engaging in proscribed advocacy. But the membership clause of the Smith Act, on its face, much less as we construe it in this case, does not do this, for it neither proscribes membership in Communist organizations, as such, but only in organizations engaging in advocacy of violent overthrow, nor punishes membership in that kind of organization except as to one "knowing the purposes thereof," and, as we have interpreted the clause, with a specific intent to further those purposes. . . .

. . .

It seems apparent from the foregoing that the language of §4(f), in its natural import and context, should not be taken to immunize members of Communist organizations from the membership clause of the Smith Act, but rather as a mandate to the courts charged with the construction of subsections (a) and (c) "or . . . any other criminal statute" that neither those two named criminal provisions nor any other shall be construed so as to make "membership" in a Communist organization "per se a violation." Indeed, as we read the first sentence of §4(f), even if the membership clause of the Smith Act could be taken as punishing naked Communist Party membership, it would then be our duty under §4(f) to construe it in accordance with that mandate, certainly not to strike it down. Although we think that the membership clause, on its face, goes beyond making mere Party membership a violation, in that it requires a showing both of illegal Party purposes and of a member's knowledge of such purposes, we regard the first sentence of §4(f) as a clear warrant for construing the clause as requiring not only knowing membership, but active and purposive membership, purposive that is as to the organization's criminal ends. . . .

. . .

It will bring the constitutional issues into clearer focus to notice first the premises on which the case was submitted to the jury. The jury was instructed that, in order to convict, it must find that, within the three-year limitations period, (1) the Communist Party advocated the violent overthrow of the Government, in the sense of present "advocacy of action" to accomplish that end as soon as circumstances were propitious, and (2) petitioner was an "active" member of the Party, and not merely "a nominal, passive, inactive or purely technical" member, with knowledge of the Party's illegal advocacy and a specific intent to bring about violent overthrow "as speedily as circumstances would permit."

The constitutional attack upon the membership clause, as thus construed, is that the statute offends (1) the Fifth Amendment, in that it impermissibly imputes guilt to an individual merely on the basis of his associations and sympathies, rather than because of some concrete personal involvement in criminal conduct, and (2) the First Amendment, in that it infringes on free political expression and association. Subsidiarily, it is argued that the statute cannot be interpreted as including a requirement of a specific intent to accomplish violent overthrow, or as requiring that membership in a proscribed organization must be "active" membership, in the absence of both or either of which it is said the statute becomes a fortiori unconstitutional. It is further contended that, even if the adjective "active" may properly be implied as a qualification upon the term "member," petitioner's conviction would nonetheless be unconstitutional because, so construed, the statute would be impermissibly vague under the Fifth and Sixth Amendments, and, so applied, would, in any event, infringe the Sixth Amendment, in that the indictment charged only that Scales was a "member," not an "active" member, of the Communist Party.

. . .

We find hardly greater difficulty in interpreting the membership clause to reach only "active" members. We decline to attribute to Congress a purpose to punish nominal membership, even though accompanied by "knowledge" and "intent," not merely because of the close constitutional questions that such a purpose would raise, but also for two other reasons: it is not to be lightly inferred that Congress intended to visit upon mere passive members the heavy penalties imposed by the Smith Act. Nor can we assume that it was Congress's purpose to allow the quality of the punishable membership to be measured solely by the varying standards of that relationship as subjectively viewed by different organizations. It is more reasonable to believe that Congress contemplated an objective standard fixed by the law itself, thereby assuring an evenhanded application of the statute.

. . .

. . . The indictment was not defective in failing to charge that Scales was an "active" member of the Party, for that factor was not, in itself, a discrete element of the crime, but an inherent quality of the membership element. As such, it was a matter not for the indictment, but for elucidating instructions to the jury on what the term "member" in the statute meant. Nor do we think that the objection on the score of vagueness is a tenable one. The distinction between "active" and "nominal" membership is well understood in common parlance, and the point at which one shades into the other is something that goes not to the sufficiency of the statute, but to the adequacy of the trial court's guidance to the jury by way of instructions in a particular case. . . . For petitioner's actions on behalf of the Communist Party most certainly amounted to active membership by whatever standards one could reasonably anticipate, and he can therefore hardly be considered to have acted unadvisedly on this score.

. . .

. . . It must indeed be recognized that a person who merely becomes a member of an illegal organization, by that "act" alone need be doing nothing more than signifying his assent to its purposes and activities on one hand, and providing, on the other, only the sort of moral encouragement which comes from the knowledge that others believe in what the organization is doing. . . . A member, as distinguished from a conspirator, may indicate his approval of a criminal enterprise by the very fact of his membership without thereby necessarily committing himself to further it by any act or course of conduct whatever.

. . .

. . . We can discern no reason why membership, when it constitutes a purposeful form of complicity in a group engaging in this same forbidden advocacy, should receive any greater degree of protection from the guarantees of that Amendment.

. . . There must be clear proof that a defendant "specifically intend[s] to accomplish [the aims of the organization] by resort to violence." Thus, the member for whom the organization is a vehicle for the advancement of legitimate aims and policies does not fall within the ban of the statute: he lacks the requisite specific intent "to bring about the overthrow of the government as speedily as circumstances would permit." Such a person may be foolish, deluded, or perhaps merely optimistic, but he is not by this statute made a criminal.

. . .

The only other question on this phase of the case is whether such advocacy was sufficiently broadly based to permit its attribution to the Party. We think it was. The advocacy of action was not "sporadic" the instances of it being neither infrequent, remote in time, nor casual. It cannot be said that the jury could not have found that the criminal advocacy was fully authorized and condoned by the Party. . . . All of these factors combine to justify the inference that the illegal individual advocacy as to which testimony was adduced was in truth the expression of Party policy and purpose.

. . .

. . . Scales's "active" membership in the Party is indisputable, and that issue was properly submitted to the jury under instructions that were entirely adequate. The elements of petitioner's "knowledge" and "specific intent" require no further discussion of the evidence beyond that already given as to Scales's utterances and activities. . . .

. . .

The judgment of the Court of Appeals must be affirmed.

Aptheker v. Secretary of State
378 U.S. 500 (1964)

This appeal involves a single question: the constitutionality of §6 of the Subversive Activities Control Act of 1950. Section 6 provides in pertinent part that:

> (a) When a Communist organization . . . is registered, or there is in effect a final order of the Board requiring such organization to register, it shall be unlawful for any member of such organization, with

knowledge or notice that such organization is so registered or that such order has become final—
    (1) to make application for a passport, or the renewal of a passport, to be issued or renewed by or under the authority of the United States; or
    (2) to use or attempt to use any such passport.

Section 6 became effective, with respect to appellants, on October 20, 1961, when a final order of the Subversive Activities Control Board issued directing the Communist Party of the United States to register under §7 of the Subversive Activities Control Act. . . . Prior to issuance of the final registration order, both appellants, who are native-born citizens and residents of the United States, had held valid passports. Subsequently, on January 22, 1962, the Acting Director of the Passport Office notified appellants that their passports were revoked because the Department of State believed that their use of the passports would violate §6. Appellants were also notified of their right to seek administrative review of the revocations under Department of State regulations.

. . . [T]he examiners recommended that the passport revocations be sustained. Both appellants appealed to the Board of Passport Appeals, which recommended affirmance of the revocations. The Secretary of State subsequently approved the recommendations of the Board. . . .

Appellants thereupon filed separate complaints seeking declaratory and injunctive relief in the United States District Court for the District of Columbia. The complaints, which have been considered together, asked that judgments be entered declaring §6 of the Subversive Activities Control Act unconstitutional and ordering the Secretary of State to issue passports to appellants. Each appellant-plaintiff alleged that §6 was unconstitutional as "a deprivation without due process of law of plaintiff's constitutional liberty to travel abroad, in violation of the Fifth Amendment to the Constitution of the United States." Appellants conceded that the Secretary of State had an adequate basis for finding that they were members of the Communist Party of the United States, and that the action revoking their passports was proper if §6 was constitutional. The parties agreed that all administrative remedies had been exhausted, and that it would be futile, and indeed a criminal offense, for either appellant to apply for a passport while remaining a member of the Communist Party.

The three-judge District Court, which was convened to review the constitutional question, rejected appellants' contentions, sustained the constitutionality of §6 of the Control Act, and granted the Secretary's motion for summary judgment. . . .

. . .

We hold, for the reasons stated below, that §6 of the Control Act too broadly and indiscriminately restricts the right to travel, and thereby abridges the liberty guaranteed by the Fifth Amendment.

. . .

Accordingly, the judgment of the three-judge District Court is reversed, and the cause remanded for proceedings in conformity with this opinion.

United States v. Brown
381 U.S. 437 (1965)

In this case, we review for the first time a conviction under §504 of the Labor-Management Reporting and Disclosure Act of 1959, which makes it a crime for a member of the Communist Party to serve as an officer or . . . as an employee of a labor union. Section 504, the purpose of which is to protect the national economy by minimizing the danger of political strikes, was enacted to replace §9(h) of the National Labor Relations Act, which conditioned a union's access to the National Labor Relations Board upon the filing of affidavits by all of the union's officers attesting that they were not members of or affiliated with the Communist Party.

Respondent has been a working longshoreman on the San Francisco docks, and an open and avowed Communist, for more than a quarter of a century. He was elected to the Executive Board of Local 10 of the International Longshoremen's and Warehousemen's Union for consecutive one-year terms in 1959, 1960, and 1961. On May 24, 1961, respondent was charged in a one-count indictment returned in the Northern District of California with . . . wilful violation of . . . Section 504. . . . The jury found respondent guilty, and he was sentenced to six months' imprisonment. The Court of Appeals for the Ninth Circuit, sitting en banc, reversed and remanded with instructions to set aside the conviction and dismiss the indictment, holding that §504 violates the First and Fifth Amendments to the Constitution. . . .

. . .

It is argued . . . that, in §504, Congress . . . promulgated a general rule to the effect that persons possessing characteristics which make them likely to incite political strikes should not hold union office, and simply inserted in place of a list of those characteristics an alternative, shorthand criterion—membership in the Communist Party. Again, we cannot agree. The designation of Communists as those persons likely to cause political strikes is not the substitution of a semantically equivalent phrase; on the contrary, it rests . . . upon an empirical investigation by Congress of the acts, characteristics and propensities of Communist Party members. In a number of decisions, this Court has pointed out the fallacy of the

suggestion that membership in the Communist Party, or any other political organization, can be regarded as an alternative, but equivalent, expression for a list of undesirable characteristics. . . .

. . .

Section 504 . . . disqualifies from the holding of union office not only present members of the Communist Party, but also anyone who has, within the past five years, been a member of the Party. However, even if we make the assumption that the five-year provision was inserted not out of desire to visit retribution, but purely out of a belief that failure to include it would lead to pro forma resignations from the Party which would not decrease the threat of political strikes, it still clearly appears that §504 inflicts "punishment" within the meaning of the Bill of Attainder Clause. It would be archaic to limit the definition of "punishment" to "retribution." Punishment serves several purposes; retributive, rehabilitative, deterrent—and preventive. One of the reasons society imprisons those convicted of crimes is to keep them from inflicting future harm, but that does not make imprisonment any the less punishment.

. . .

The judgment of the Court of Appeals is affirmed.

Albertson v. Subversive Activities Control Board
382 U.S. 70 (1965)

The Communist Party of the United States of America failed to register with the Attorney General as required by the order of the Subversive Activities Control Board. . . . Accordingly, no list of Party members was filed as required by §7(d)(4) of the Subversive Activities Control Act of 1950. Sections 8(a) and (c) of the Act provide that, in that circumstance, each member of the organization must register and file a registration statement; in default thereof, §13(a) authorizes the Attorney General to petition the Board for an order requiring the member to register. The Attorney General invoked §13(a) against petitioners, and the Board, after evidentiary hearings, determined that petitioners were Party members and ordered each of them to register. . . . The Court of Appeals affirmed the orders. . . .

. . .

The risks of incrimination which the petitioners take in registering are obvious. Form IS-52a requires an admission of membership in the Communist Party. Such an admission of membership may be used to prosecute the registrant under the membership clause of the Smith Act, or under §4(a) of the Subversive Activities Control Act, to mention only two federal criminal statutes. Accordingly, we have held that mere association with the Communist Party presents sufficient threat of prosecution to support a claim of privilege. These cases involved questions to witnesses on the witness stand, but if the admission cannot be compelled in oral testimony, we do not see how compulsion in writing makes a difference for constitutional purposes. It follows that the requirement to accomplish registration by completing and filing Form IS-52a is inconsistent with the protection of the Self-Incrimination Clause.

. . .

The judgment of the Court of Appeals is reversed, and the Board's orders are set aside.

United States v. Robel
389 U.S. 258 (1967)

. . . [A]ppellee, a member of the Communist Party, was employed as a machinist at the Seattle, Wash-

ington, shipyard of Todd Shipyards Corporation. On August 20, 1962, the Secretary of Defense, acting under authority delegated by §5(b) of the Act, designated that shipyard a "defense facility." Appellee's continued employment at the shipyard after that date subjected him to prosecution under §5(a)(1)(D), and on May 21, 1963, an indictment was filed charging him with a violation of that section. The indictment alleged in substance that appellee had "unlawfully and willfully engage[d] in employment" at the shipyard with knowledge of the outstanding order against the Party and with knowledge and notice of the shipyard's designation as a defense facility by the Secretary of Defense. The United States District Court for the Western District of Washington granted appellee's motion to dismiss. . . .

We cannot agree with the District Court that §5(a)(1)(D) can be saved from constitutional infirmity by limiting its application to active members of Communist-action organizations who have the specific intent of furthering the unlawful goals of such organizations. . . . It is precisely because that statute sweeps indiscriminately across all types of association with Communist-action groups, without regard to the quality and degree of membership, that it runs afoul of the First Amendment.

. . .

. . . That statute casts its net across a broad range of associational activities, indiscriminately trapping membership which can be constitutionally punished and membership which cannot be so proscribed. It is made irrelevant to the statute's operation that an individual may be a passive or inactive member of a designated organization, that he may be unaware of the organization's unlawful aims, or that he may disagree with those unlawful aims. It is also made irrelevant that an individual who is subject to the penalties of

§5(a)(1)(D) may occupy a nonsensitive position in a defense facility. Thus, §5(a)(1)(D) contains the fatal defect of overbreadth, because it seeks to bar employment both for association which may be proscribed and for association which may not be proscribed consistently with First Amendment rights. This the Constitution will not tolerate.

. . .

Affirmed.

Williams v. Rhodes
393 U.S. 23 (1968)

The State of Ohio, in a series of election laws, has made it virtually impossible for a new political party, even though it has hundreds of thousands of members, or an old party which has a very small number of members, to be placed on the state ballot to choose electors pledged to particular candidates for the Presidency and Vice Presidency of the United States.

Ohio Revised Code, §3517.01, requires a new party to obtain petitions signed by qualified electors totaling 15 percent of the number of ballots cast in the last preceding gubernatorial election. The detailed provisions of other Ohio election laws result in the imposition of substantial additional burdens. . . . Together, these various restrictive provisions make it virtually impossible for any party to qualify on the ballot except the Republican and Democratic Parties. These two Parties face substantially smaller burdens because they are allowed to retain their positions on the ballot simply by obtaining 10 percent of the votes in the last gubernatorial election, and need not obtain any signature petitions. Moreover, Ohio laws make no provision for ballot position for independent candidates, as distinguished from political parties. The State of Ohio claims the power to keep minority parties and independent candidates off the ballot under Art. II, §1, of the Constitution . . .

The Ohio American Independent Party, an appellant in No. 543, and the Socialist Labor Party, an appellant in No. 544, both brought suit to challenge the validity of these Ohio laws as applied to them, on the ground that they deny these Parties and the voters who might wish to vote for them the equal protection of the laws, guaranteed against state abridgment by the Equal Protection Clause of the Fourteenth Amendment. The three-judge District Court . . . ruled these restrictive Ohio election laws unconstitutional, but refused to grant the Parties the full relief they had sought. . . .

The Ohio American Independent Party was formed in January 1968 by Ohio partisans of former Governor George C. Wallace of Alabama. During the following six months, a campaign was conducted for obtaining signatures on petitions to give the Party a place on the ballot, and over 450,000 signatures were eventually obtained, more than the 433,100 required. The State contends, and the Independent Party agrees, that, due to the interaction of several provisions of the Ohio laws, such petitions were required to be filed by February 7, 1968, and so the Secretary of the State of Ohio informed the Party that it would not be given a place on the ballot. Neither in the pleadings, the affidavits before the District Court, the arguments there, nor in our Court has the State denied that the petitions were signed by enough qualified electors of Ohio to meet the 15 percent requirement under Ohio law. Having demonstrated its numerical strength, the Independent Party argued that this and the other burdens, including the early deadline for filing petitions and the requirement of a primary election conforming to detailed and rigorous standards, denied the

Party and certain Ohio voters equal protection of the laws. The three-judge District Court . . . ruled that the State must be required to provide a space for write-in votes. A majority of the District Court refused to hold, however, that the Party's name must be printed on the ballot, on the ground that Wallace and his adherents had been guilty of "laches" by filing their suit too late to allow the Ohio Legislature an opportunity to remedy, in time for the presidential balloting, the defects which the District Court held the law possessed. The appellants in No. 543 then moved. . . .

The Socialist Labor Party, an appellant in No. 544, has all the formal attributes of a regular party. It has conventions and a State Executive Committee, as required by the Ohio law, and it was permitted to have a place on the ballot until 1948. Since then, however, it has not filed petitions with the total signatures required under new Ohio laws for ballot position, and, indeed, it conceded it could not do so this year. The same three-judge panel heard the Party's suit and reached a similar result—write-in space was ordered, but ballot position was denied the Socialist Labor Party. In this case, the District Court assigned both the Party's small membership of 108 and its delay in bringing suit as reasons for refusing to order more complete relief for the 1968 election. A motion to stay the District Court's judgment was presented. . . . The motion was denied principally because of the Socialist Party's failure to move quickly to obtain relief, with the consequent confusion that would be caused by requiring Ohio once again to begin completely reprinting its election ballots, but the case was set by this Court for oral argument, along with the Independent Party case.

. . .

The State also contends that it has absolute power to put any burdens it pleases on the selection of electors because of the First Section of the Second Article of the Constitution, providing that "Each State shall appoint, in such Manner as the Legislature thereof may direct, a Number of Electors . . ." to choose a President and Vice President. There of course can be no question but that this section does grant extensive power to the States to pass laws regulating the selection of electors. But the Constitution is filled with provisions that grant Congress or the States specific power to legislate in certain areas; these granted powers are always subject to the limitation that they may not be exercised in a way that violates other specific provisions of the Constitution. . . . Nor can it be thought that the power to select electors could be exercised in such a way as to violate express constitutional commands that specifically bar States from passing certain kinds of laws. Clearly, the Fifteenth and Nineteenth Amendments were intended to bar the Federal Government and the States from denying the right to vote on grounds of race and sex in presidential elections. And the Twenty-fourth Amendment clearly and literally bars any State from imposing a poll tax on the right to vote "for electors for President or Vice President." Obviously we must reject the notion that Art. II, §1, gives the States power to impose burdens on the right to vote where such burdens are expressly prohibited in other constitutional provisions. We therefore hold that no State can pass a law regulating elections that violates the Fourteenth Amendment's command that "No State shall . . . deny to any person . . . the equal protection of the laws."

We turn then to the question whether the court below properly held that the Ohio laws before us result in a denial of equal protection of the laws. . . . In determining whether or not a state law violates the Equal Protection Clause, we must consider the facts and circumstances behind the law, the interests which the State claims to be protecting, and the interests of those who are disadvantaged by the classification. In the present situation, the state laws place burdens on two different, although overlapping, kinds of rights—the right of individuals to associate for the advancement of political beliefs, and the right of qualified voters, regardless of their political persuasion, to cast their votes effectively. Both of these rights, of course, rank among our most precious freedoms. . . .

No extended discussion is required to establish that the Ohio laws before us give the two old, established parties a decided advantage over any new parties struggling for existence, and thus place substantially unequal burdens on both the right to vote and the right to associate. The right to form a party for the advancement of political goals means little if a party can be kept off the election ballot, and thus denied an equal opportunity to win votes. So also, the right to vote is heavily burdened if that vote may be cast only for one of two parties at a time when other parties are clamoring for a place on the ballot. . . .

The State has here failed to show any "compelling interest" which justifies imposing such heavy burdens on the right to vote and to associate.

. . . [T]he Ohio system does not merely favor a "two-party system"; it favors two particular parties the Republicans and the Democrat—and, in effect, tends to give them a complete monopoly. There is, of course, no reason why two parties should retain a permanent monopoly on the right to have people vote for or against them. Competition in ideas and governmental policies is at the core of our electoral process and of the First Amendment freedoms. New parties struggling for their place must have the time and opportunity to organize in order to meet reasonable requirements for ballot position, just as the old parties have had in the past.

. . .

The State also argues that its requirement of a party structure and an organized primary insures that those who disagree with the major parties and their policies "will be given a choice of leadership, as well as issues," since any leader who attempts to capitalize on the disaffection of such a group is forced to submit to a primary in which other, possibly more attractive, leaders can raise the same issues and compete for the allegiance of the disaffected group. But while this goal may be desirable, Ohio's system cannot achieve it. Since the principal policies of the major parties change to some extent from year to year, and since the identity of the likely major party nominees may not be known until shortly before the election, this disaffected "group" will rarely, if ever, be a cohesive or identifiable group until a few months before the election. Thus, Ohio's burdensome procedures, requiring extensive organization and other election activities by a very early date, operate to prevent such a group from ever getting on the ballot, and the Ohio system thus denies the "disaffected" not only a choice of leadership, but a choice on the issues, as well.

. . . Ohio claims that its highly restrictive provisions are justified because, without them, a large number of parties might qualify for the ballot, and the voters would then be confronted with a choice so confusing that the popular will could be frustrated. But the experience of many States, including that of Ohio prior to 1948, demonstrates that no more than a handful of parties attempts to qualify for ballot positions even when a very low number of signatures, such as 1 percent of the electorate, is required. It is true that the existence of multitudinous fragmentary groups might justify some regulatory control, but, in Ohio at the present time, this danger seems to us no more than "theoretically imaginable." . . .

Of course, the number of voters in favor of a party, along with other circumstances, is relevant in considering whether state laws violate the Equal Protection Clause. And, as we have said, the State is left with broad powers to regulate voting, which may include laws relating to the qualification and functions of electors. But here, the totality of the Ohio restrictive laws, taken as a whole, imposes a burden on voting and associational rights which we hold is an invidious discrimination, in violation of the Equal Protection Clause.

This leaves only the propriety of the judgments of the District Court. That court held that the Socialist Labor Party could get relief to the extent of having the right, despite Ohio laws, to get the advantage of write-in ballots. It restricted the Independent Party to the same relief. The Independent Party went before the District Court, made its challenge, and prayed for broader relief, including a judgment declaring the Ohio laws invalid. It also asked that its name be put on the ballot along with the Democratic and Republican Parties. The Socialist Labor Party also went to the District Court and asked for the same relief. On this record, however, the parties stand in different positions before us. Immediately after the District Court entered its judgment, the new Independent Party brought its case to this Court, where Justice Stewart conducted a hearing. At that hearing, Ohio represented to Justice Stewart that the Independent Party's name could be placed on the ballot without disrupting the state election, but, if there was a long delay, the situation would be different. It was not until several days after that hearing was concluded, and after Justice Stewart had issued his order staying the judgment against the Independent Party, that the Socialist Labor Party asked for similar relief. The State objected on the ground that, at that time, it

was impossible to grant the relief to the Socialist Labor Party without disrupting the process of its elections; accordingly, Justice Stewart denied it relief, and the State now repeats its statement that relief cannot be granted without serious disruption of election process. Certainly, at this late date, it would be extremely difficult, if not impossible, for Ohio to provide still another set of ballots. Moreover, the confusion that would attend such a last-minute change poses a risk of interference with the rights of other Ohio citizens, for example, absentee voters. Under the circumstances, we require Ohio to permit the Independent Party to remain on the ballot, along with its candidates for President and Vice President, subject, of course, to compliance with valid regulatory laws of Ohio, including the law relating to the qualification and functions of electors. We do not require Ohio to place the Socialist Party on the ballot for this election. The District Court's judgment is affirmed with reference to No. 544, the Socialist Labor Party case, but is modified in No. 543, the Independent Party case, with reference to granting that Party the right to have its name printed on the ballot.

Hadnott v. Amos
394 U.S. 358 (1969)

This suit is a class action brought by the National Democratic Party of Alabama (NDPA) and some of its officers and candidates in the 1968 general election against Alabama state officials who had refused to include various NDPA candidates on the ballot for various county and statewide offices. As the complaint sought an injunction against enforcement of Alabama statutes on federal constitutional grounds, a three-judge federal court was impaneled.

The District Court entered a temporary restraining order. Thereafter appellees filed their answer challenging . . . the qualifications of NDPA candidates because of their failure to satisfy certain specified requirements of Alabama law. On October 11, 1968, after a hearing on the merits, the three-judge court . . . dissolved the temporary injunction and upheld on their face and as applied all the challenged Alabama statutes.

. . .

NDPA candidates, mostly Negroes, were elected to various local offices in Etowah, Marengo, and Sumter Counties. But in Greene County the NDPA candidates for local office were left off the ballot except for absentee voters. In Greene County the only candidates appearing on the ballot were the regular Democratic Party nominees for local offices and they received between 1,699 and 1,709 votes each. It appears that NDPA candidates in Greene County would have won had they been on the ballot for 1,938 ballots were marked for the NDPA "straight ticket."

. . .

. . . The Alabama Corrupt Practices Act requires each candidate within five days "after the announcement of his candidacy for any office" to file a statement showing "the name of not less than one nor more than five persons" chosen to receive, expend, audit, and disburse funds for his election.

The disqualification of the NDPA candidates for their alleged failure to satisfy this provision of the Alabama Act implicates Probate Judge Herndon, who was responsible for the preparation of the Greene County ballot which omitted their names.

In this case, the black candidates for Greene County offices designated finance committees in February, 1968, prior to their entry in the Democratic primary. Appellees contend that it was sufficient to justify Judge Herndon's omission of the names that the NDPA candidates did not file a second designation of financial committee after May 7, the date of the primary, and the date on which those candidates were nominated by the NDPA. Appellants contend that disqualification for that reason constituted discriminatory enforcement of the Corrupt Practices Act in violation of the Equal Protection Clause. Since the names of the white candidates who won the May 7 primary were placed on the ballot, although they also did not file a second designation after that date, appellees clearly have the burden of justifying the denial of ballot places to the black NDPA candidates. Appellees have failed to satisfy that burden.

Alabama law requires all candidates for local office, not selected in primaries, to be nominated by mass meeting on the first Tuesday in May of the election year. The certificate of nomination sent to Judge Herndon, probate judge for Greene County, on September 4, stated that NDPA nominees had been selected pursuant to a mass meeting.

On September 18, the District Court temporarily restrained the omission from the ballot of NDPA candidates for state and local office. That restraint was dissolved on October 11. Meanwhile, counsel for the white Greene County candidates, who was the county solicitor, prompted Judge Herndon to file an affidavit in which he stated that, to the "best of [his] knowledge and belief," the NDPA held no local mass meeting on May 7 at which nominations were made, and further that none of the six NDPA candidates "filed or offered to file in [his] office" the designation of financial committee required by the Corrupt Practices Act. Yet, when his deposition was taken on December 27, the judge conceded that the mass meeting might have been held without his hearing about, it and admitted knowledge that the black candidates had filed designations of financial committee in February. He did not say why, in these circumstances, the February filing did not suffice for the general election; the designations refer to candidacies for the general election as well as the primary election. Nor did he offer any explanation why, if the February filings by the white candidates sufficed for the general election, the filings of the black candidates should be treated differently. The record is therefore utterly devoid of any explanation adequate to satisfy appellees' burden. . . .

We deal here with Fifteenth Amendment rights which guarantee the right of people regardless of their race, color, or previous condition of servitude to cast their votes effectively and with First Amendment rights which include the right to band together for the advancement of political beliefs. While the regulation of corrupt practices in state and federal elections is an important governmental function, we refuse to accept a reading of an Act which gives such a loose meaning to words and such discretionary authority to election officials as to cause Fifteenth and First Amendment rights to be subject to disparate treatment. That risk is compounded here where the penalty is the irrevocable striking of candidates from the ballot without notice or an opportunity for contest and correction.

When the Alabama Act is construed as appellants' opponents were allowed to construe it without suffering disqualification, we conclude that appellants met the same requirements. Unequal application of the same law to different racial groups has an especially invidious connotation.

. . . In 1967, Alabama passed the Garrett Act barring from the ballot in a general election a candidate for a state, district, or federal office

> who does not file a declaration of intention to become a candidate for such office with the secretary of state on or before the first day of March of the year in which such general election is held.

The Garrett Act also requires a declaration of the political party whose nomination the candidate seeks; or if he is not a party candidate that he will run as an independent. A like provision bars probate judges from printing on ballots the names of candidates for county offices unless they have filed a declaration of intention on or before the prior March 1. Accordingly, appellees justify their disqualification of NDPA candidates in Etowah, Marengo, and Sumter Counties, and Judge Herndon justifies his omission of those candidates from the Greene County ballot, on the ground that they did not comply with the Garrett Act.

. . . As a result of the Garrett Act, an independent candidate had to decide whether to run at the same time as candidates in the primary made their determination.

The question is whether the Garrett Act is affected by §5 of the Voting Rights Act of 1965, which provides that, whenever States like Alabama seek to administer

> any voting qualification or prerequisite to voting, or standard, practice, or procedure with respect to voting different from that, in force or effect on November 1, 1964,

the State may institute an action in the United States District Court for the District of Columbia for a declaratory judgment that

> such qualification, prerequisite, standard, practice, or procedure does not have the purpose and will not have the effect of denying or abridging the right to vote on account of race or color.

It is further provided in §5 that, unless and until the District of Columbia court enters such judgment, no person shall be denied the right to vote for failure to comply with such qualification, prerequisite, standard, practice, or procedure.

. . .

... The increased barriers placed on independent candidates by Alabama's Garrett Act likewise bring it within the purview of §5 of the Federal Act. The Alabama officials, therefore, acted unlawfully in disqualifying independent candidates in the 1968 election for failure to comply with the Garrett Act.

On the merits, we reverse the District Court and remand the cause with directions (1) to issue an appropriate order requiring the prevailing NDPA candidates in Etowah, Marengo, and Sumter Counties to be treated as duly elected to the offices for which they ran, and (2) to require the state and local officials promptly to conduct a new election in Greene County for the various county offices contested by NDPA candidates, at which election the NDPA candidates for those respective positions shall appear on the ballot.

In re Herndon
394 U.S. 399 (1969)

The appeal in *Hadnott*, decided today, was argued with the motion filed by appellants on November 19, 1968, "for an order to show cause why Judge Herndon should not be held in contempt and for other relief."

On September 18, 1968, the three-judge court entered a temporary restraining order enjoining appropriate Alabama officials from using any ballots at the general election of November 5, 1968 which did not include the names of the candidates of the National Democratic Party of Alabama (NDPA). This order was dissolved on October 11, 1968. ... The appellants sought interim relief from this Court pending appeal, and on October 14, 1968, we entered an order that: "The application for restoration of temporary relief is granted pending oral argument on the

application. ...." Oral argument was heard on October 18, and on October 19 we entered an order that:

> The order entered on October 14, 1968, restoring temporary relief is continued pending action upon the jurisdictional statement which has been filed.

Nevertheless, Judge Herndon, who was responsible for the preparation of the Greene County ballot for local offices, did not place the NDPA candidates for such offices on the ballot.

We conclude that decision on the motion should await timely initiation and completion of appropriate proceedings in the District Court to determine whether Judge Herndon's failure to place NDPA candidates on the ballot constituted contempt of the order of September 18 of the District Court. Decision on the motion is therefore postponed.

Socialist Labor Party v. Gilligan
406 U.S. 583 (1972)

Appellant Socialist Labor Party has engaged in a prolonged legal battle to invalidate various Ohio laws restricting minority party access to the ballot. Concluding that "the totality of the Ohio restrictive laws, taken as a whole," violated the Equal Protection Clause of the Fourteenth Amendment, this Court struck down those laws in *Socialist Labor Party v. Rhodes*. Following that decision, the Ohio Legislature revised the state election code, but the Party was dissatisfied with the revisions, and instituted the present suit in 1970.

The Socialist Labor Party, its officers, and members, joined as plaintiffs in requesting a three-judge District Court to invalidate on constitutional grounds various sections of the revised election laws of Ohio. The plaintiffs specifically challenged provisions of the Ohio election laws requiring that a party either receive a certain percentage of the vote cast in the last preceding election or else file petitions of qualified electors corresponding to the same percentage; provisions relating to the organizational structure of a party; provisions requiring that a political party elect a specified number of delegates and alternates to a state convention; and provisions requiring a party to be part of a national political party that holds national conventions at which delegates elected in state primaries nominate presidential and vice presidential candidates. In addition, they challenged that part of the Ohio election code requiring a political party to file an affidavit under oath stating in substance that the party is not engaged in an attempt to overthrow the government by force or violence, is not associated with a group making such an attempt, and does not carry on a program of sedition or treason as defined by the criminal law.

The case was decided on cross-motions for summary judgment, the three-judge District Court having before it the complaint and answer of the respective parties. . . . The court ruled on the merits in favor of all of appellants' constitutional challenges to the Ohio election laws except that involving the oath requirement, with respect to which it ruled in favor of the appellees. Both sides appealed. . . .

Since then, the posture of this litigation has undergone a significant change. On December 23, 1971, the Ohio Legislature enacted Senate Bill No. 460, which embodied an extensive revision of the state election code. Both sides now agree that the passage of this Act renders moot all but one of the issues decided below. The one challenged provision that remains unamended is the State's requirement that a political party execute the above-described affidavit under oath in order to obtain a position on the ballot.

Appellants' 1970 complaint represented a broadside attack against interrelated and allegedly overly restrictive provisions of the Ohio election laws. The three-judge District Court, in its ruling for the appellants on the issues that have now become moot, stated:

> The 1969 amendments to the election laws merely perpetuate the restrictive laws enacted between 1948 and 1952. The overall effect of these laws is still to deny to plaintiffs their constitutional right of political association.

Thus, appellants, at the time they filed their 1970 action, were fenced out of the political process by a series of restrictive provisions that prevented them from making any progress toward a position on the ballot as a designated political party. Their challenge was necessarily of a somewhat abstract character, since, under their allegations, they were able to comply with very few of the provisions regulating access to the ballot. Now, however, with the enactment of a revised election code, the abstract character of the single remaining challenge to the Ohio election procedures stands out all the more.

Appellants did not, in their action that came here in 1968, challenge the loyalty oath. Their 1970 complaint respecting the loyalty oath is singularly sparse in its factual allegations. There is no suggestion in it that the Socialist Labor Party has ever refused in the past, or will now refuse, to sign the required oath. There is no allegation of injury that the party has suffered or will suffer because of the existence of the oath requirement.

It is fairly inferable that the absence of such allegations is not merely an oversight in the drafting of a pleading. The requirement of the affidavit under oath was enacted in 1941, and has remained continuously in force since that date. The Socialist Labor Party has appeared on the state ballot since the law's passage, and, unless the state officials have ignored what appear to be mandatory oath provisions, it is reasonable to conclude that the party has in the past executed the required affidavit.

It is axiomatic that the federal courts do not decide abstract questions posed by parties who lack "a personal stake in the outcome of the controversy." Appellants argue that the affidavit requirement violates the First and Fourteenth Amendments, but their pleadings fail to allege that the requirement has in any way affected their speech or conduct, or that executing the oath would impair the exercise of any right that they have as a political party or as members of a political party. They contend that to require it of them, but not of the two major political parties, denies them equal protection, but they do not allege any particulars that make the requirement other than a hypothetical burden. Finally, they claim that the required affidavit is impermissibly vague and that its enforcement procedures do not comport with due process. But the record before the three-judge District Court, and now before this Court, is extraordinarily skimpy in the sort of proved or admitted facts that would enable us to adjudicate this claim. Since appellants have previously secured a position on the ballot with no untoward consequences, the gravamen of their claim that it injures them remains quite unclear.

In the usual case in which this Court has passed on the validity of similar oath provisions, the party challenging constitutionality was either unable or unwilling to execute the required oath, and, in the circumstances of the particular case, sustained, or faced the immediate prospect of sustaining, some direct injury as a result of the penalty provisions associated with the oath.

. . . [A]ppellants have apparently signed the oath at previous times, and, so far as this record shows, they have suffered no injury as a result. The State has never questioned the truth of the affidavit, and appellants' conduct and associations have not been constricted as a result of their having executed the affidavit.

The long and the short of the matter is that we know very little more about the operation of the Ohio affidavit procedure as a result of this lawsuit than we would if a prospective plaintiff who had never set foot in Ohio had simply picked this section of the Ohio election laws out of the statute books and filed a complaint in the District Court setting forth the allegedly offending provisions and requesting an injunction against their enforcement. These plaintiffs may well meet the technical requirement of standing, and they may be parties to a case or controversy, but their case has not given any particularity to the effect on them of Ohio's affidavit requirement.

. . .

. . . All issues litigated below have become moot except for one that received scant attention in appellants' complaint and was treated not at all in the affidavits filed in support of the cross-motions for summary judgment. Nothing in the record shows that appellants have suffered any injury thus far, and the law's future effect remains wholly speculative. Notwithstanding the indications that appellants have in the past executed the required affidavit without injury, it is, of course, possible that, at some future time, they may be able to demonstrate some injury as a result of the application of the provision challenged here. Our adjudication of the merits of such a challenge will await that time. This appeal must be dismissed.

O'Brien v. Brown
409 U.S. 1 (1972)

Yesterday, July 6, 1972, the petitioners filed petitions . . . to review judgments of the United States Court of Appeals for the District of Columbia Circuit in actions challenging the recommendations of the Credentials Committee of the 1972 Democratic National Convention regarding the seating of certain delegates to the convention that will meet three days hence.

In No. 72–35, the Credentials Committee recommended unseating 59 uncommitted delegates from Illinois on the ground, among others, that they had been elected in violation of the "slate-making" guideline adopted by the Democratic Party in 1971. A complaint challenging the Credentials Committee action was dismissed by the District Court. The Court of Appeals, on review, rejected the contentions of the unseated delegates that the action of the Committee violated their rights under the Constitution of the United States.

In No. 72–34, the Credentials Committee recommended unseating 151 of 271 delegates from California committed by California law to Senator George McGovern under that State's "winner-take-all" primary system. The Committee concluded that the winner-take-all system violated the mandate of the 1968 Democratic National Convention calling for reform in the party delegate selection process, even though such primaries had not been explicitly prohibited by the rules adopted by the party in 1971 to implement that mandate. A complaint challenging the Credentials Committee action was dismissed by the District Court. On review, the Court of Appeals concluded that the action of the Credentials Committee in this case violated the Constitution of the United States.

Accompanying the petitions . . . were applications to stay the judgments of the Court of Appeals pending disposition of the petitions.

The petitions for certiorari present novel questions of importance to the litigants and to the political system under which national political parties nominate candidates for office and vote on their policies and programs. The particular actions of the Credentials Committee on which the Court of Appeals ruled are recommendations that have yet to be submitted to the National Convention of the Democratic Party. Absent judicial intervention, the Convention could decide to accept or reject, or accept with modification, the proposals of its Credentials Committee.

This Court is now asked to review these novel and important questions and to resolve them within the remaining days prior to the opening sessions of the convention now scheduled to be convened Monday, July 10, 1972.

The Court concludes it cannot in this limited time give to these issues the consideration warranted for final decision on the merits; we therefore take no action on the petitions . . . at this time.

. . .

Absent a stay, the mandate of the Court of Appeals denies to the Democratic National Convention its traditional power to pass on the credentials of the California delegates in question. The grant of a stay, on the other hand, will not foreclose the Convention's giving the respective litigants in both cases the relief they sought in federal courts.

We must also consider the absence of authority supporting the action of the Court of Appeals in intervening in the internal determinations of a national political party, on the eve of its convention, regarding the seating of delegates. No case is cited to us in which any federal court has undertaken to interject itself into the deliberative processes of a national political convention; no holding of this Court up to now gives support for judicial intervention in the circumstances presented here, involving as they do relationships of great delicacy that are essentially political in nature. Judicial intervention in this area traditionally has been approached with great caution and restraint. It has been understood since our national political parties first came into being as voluntary associations of individuals that the convention itself is the proper forum for determining intraparty disputes as to which delegates shall be seated. Thus, these cases involve claims of the power of the federal judiciary to review actions heretofore thought to lie in the control of political parties.

Highly important questions are presented concerning justiciability, whether the action of the Credentials Committee is state action and, if so, the reach of the Due Process Clause in this unique context. Vital rights of association guaranteed by the Constitution are also involved. While the Court is unwilling to undertake final resolution of the important constitutional questions presented without full briefing and argument and adequate opportunity for deliberation, we entertain grave doubts as to the action taken by the Court of Appeals.

In light of the availability of the convention as a forum to review the recommendations of the Credentials Committee, in which process the complaining parties might obtain the relief they have sought from the federal courts, the lack of precedent to support the extraordinary relief granted by the Court of Appeals, and the large public interest in allowing the political processes to function free from judicial supervision, we conclude the judgments of the Court of Appeals must be stayed.

We recognize that a stay of the Court of Appeals' judgments may well preclude any judicial review of the final action of the Democratic National Convention on the recommendation of its Credentials Committee. But, for nearly a century

and a half, the national political parties themselves have determined controversies regarding the seating of delegates to their conventions. If this system is to be altered by federal courts in the exercise of their extraordinary equity powers, it should not be done under the circumstances and time pressures surrounding the actions brought in the District Court, and the expedited review in the Court of Appeals and in this Court.

The applications for stays of the judgments of the Court of Appeals are granted.

Communist Party of Indiana v. Whitcomb
414 U.S. 441 (1974)

. . . The question for decision is whether the First and Fourteenth Amendments are violated by Indiana's requirement, that

> [n]o existing or newly organized political party or organization shall be permitted on or to have the names of its candidates printed on the ballot used at any election until it has filed an affidavit, by its officers, under oath, that it does not advocate the overthrow of local, state or national government by force or violence. . . .

Appellants are the Communist Party of Indiana, a new political party in Indiana, certain of its officers and potential voters, and its candidates for President and Vice President in the 1972 election. Appellees are the Indiana State Election Board and its members. When appellants applied to the Election Board in August, 1972, for a place on Indiana's National Ballot for the 1972 general election without submitting the required oath, the Board, on the advice of the Attorney General of Indiana, rejected the application. Appellants thereupon filed this action in the District Court for the Northern District of Indiana seeking a declaration of the unconstitutionality of §29–3812, and an injunction requiring that the Election Board place the Party on the ballot. A three-judge court was convened, and . . . declared the provision of §29–3812 that is challenged on this appeal constitutional, and issued an order requiring the Election Board to place the Communist Party and its nominees on the National Ballot only "[i]n the event that the Communist Party of Indiana shall submit an affidavit in keeping with this memorandum and order. . . ." The Communist Party submitted an affidavit that, in addition to the statutory language, added the following:

The term "advocate," as used herein, has the meaning given it by the Supreme Court of the United States in *Yates v. United States*, "the advocacy and teaching of concrete action for the forcible overthrow of the government, and not of principles divorced from action."

The Election Board rejected the affidavit, and appellants, on October 3, returned to the District Court, seeking an order directing the Board to accept it. On the same day, the Election Board filed a motion requesting reconsideration of the order of September 28. The District Court, on October 4, denied both motions by order entered that day. Appellants, on October 10, filed a notice of appeal to this Court to enable them to seek emergency relief. That effort was abandoned, and appellants then sought leave of the District Court to withdraw the notice of appeal in order that the District Court might act on a motion of appellants, also filed October 10, that the District Court amend its September 28 order to include a determination that §29–3812 was constitutional "only insofar as it proscribes advocacy directed at promoting unlawful action, as distinguished from advocacy of abstract doctrine." On October 31, the District Court entered an order granting leave to withdraw the notice of appeal of October 10 but denying the motion to amend the September 28 memorandum.

Appellants refiled their notice of appeal on November 29. Appellees moved to dismiss the appeal as jurisdictionally untimely, arguing that the 60-day period for appeal, expired on November 27. . . .

. . .

. . . [B]urdening access to the ballot, rights of association in the political party of one's choice, interests in casting an effective vote and in running for office not because the Party urges others "to do something, now or in the future . . . [but] . . . merely to believe in something," infringe interests certainly as substantial as those in public employment, tax exemption, or the practice of law. For "the right to exercise the franchise in a free and unimpaired manner is preservative of other basic civil and political rights. . . ." "Other rights, even the most basic, are illusory if the right to vote is undermined."

. . .

As we understand appellees, this is an argument that, at least for purposes of determining whether to grant a place on the ballot, any group that advocates violent overthrow as abstract doctrine must be regarded as necessarily advocating unlawful action. We reject that proposition. Its acceptance would only return the law to the "thoroughly discredited" regime of *Whitney v. California*, unanimously overruled by the Court in *Brandenburg v. Ohio*.

Reversed.

American Party of Texas v. White
415 U.S. 767 (1974)

The American Party of Texas sought ballot position at the general election in 1972 for a slate of candidates for various statewide and local officers, including governor and county commissioner. The

New Party of Texas wanted ballot recognition for its candidates for the general election for governor, Congress, state representative and county sheriff. The Socialist Workers Party made similar claims with respect to its candidates for governor, lieutenant governor and United States Senator. Laurel Dunn, a nonpartisan candidate, attempted to run for the United States House of Representatives from the Eleventh Congressional District. In his action, he represented himself and other named independent candidates for state and local offices. Finally, Robert Hainsworth sought election as state representative from District No. 86.

In these actions, it was alleged that, by excluding appellants from the general election ballot, various provisions of the Texas Election Code infringed their First and Fourteenth Amendment right to associate for the advancement of political beliefs and invidiously discriminated against new and minority political parties, as well as independent candidates. Appellants sought to enjoin the enforcement of the challenged provisions in the forthcoming November 1972 general election. They also challenged the failure of the Texas law to require printing minority party and independent candidates on absentee ballots and the exclusion of minority parties from the benefits of the McKool-Stroud Primary Law of 1972. The individual cases involving the parties in No. 72-887 were consolidated, and a statutory three-judge District Court was convened. Following a trial, the District Court denied all relief after holding that, in their totality, the challenged provisions served a compelling state interest and did not suffocate the election process. Hainsworth, appellant in No. 72-942, was also subsequently denied relief on similar grounds. Two separate appeals were taken. . . .

The State of Texas has established a detailed statutory scheme for regulating the conduct of political parties as it relates to qualifying for participation in the electoral process. Under the laws challenged in this case, four methods are provided for nominating candidates to the ballot for the general election.

Candidates of political parties whose gubernatorial candidate polled more than 200,000 votes in the last general election may be nominated by primary election only, and the nominees of these parties automatically appear on the ballot. Texas holds a statewide primary for these major parties or the first Saturday in May, with a runoff primary the first Saturday in June, should no candidate garner a majority.

Candidates of parties whose candidate polled less than 200,000 votes, but more than 2 percent of the total vote cast for governor in the last general election may be nominated, and thereby qualify for the general election ballot, by primary election or nominating conventions. The nominating conventions are held sequentially, with the precinct conventions on the same date as the statewide primaries for the major parties (the first Saturday in May), the county conventions on the following Saturday, and the state convention on the second Saturday in June.

Because their candidates polled less than 2 percent of the total gubernatorial vote in the preceding general election or they did not nominate a candidate for governor, the political parties in this litigation were required to pursue the third method for ballot qualification: precinct nominating conventions, and, if the required support was not evidenced at the conventions, the circulation of petitions for signature.

Finally, unaffiliated nonpartisan or independent candidates such as Dunn and Hainsworth could qualify by filing within a fixed period a written application or petition signed by a specified percentage of the vote cast for governor in the relevant electoral district in the last general election.

We consider first the appeals of the political parties and their supporters. Article 13.45(2) of the Texas Election Code, the validity of which is at issue here, requires that the political parties to which it applies nominate candidates through the process of precinct, county, and state conventions. The party must also evidence support by persons numbering at least 1 percent of the total vote cast for governor at the last preceding general election. In 1972, this number was approximately 22,000 electors. Two opportunities are offered to satisfy the 1 percent signature requirement. At the statutorily mandated precinct nominating conventions, held on the first Saturday in May and the same day as the major party primary, the party must prepare a list of all participants, who must be qualified voters, along with other pertinent information. The list is to be forwarded to the Secretary of State within 20 days after the convention. If it reveals the necessary support and if the party has satisfied the other statutory requirements imposed upon all political parties, the Secretary of State will certify that the party is entitled to be placed on the general election ballot.

Should the party not obtain the requisite 1 percent convention participation, supplemental petitions may be circulated for signature. When these are signed by a sufficient number of qualified voters in addition to the convention lists to make a combined total of the requisite 1 percent, the party qualifies for the ballot. Approximately 55 days after the general primary election in May are allotted for the supplementation process. A voter who has already participated in any other party's primary election or nominating process is ineligible to sign the petition. Furthermore, each signatory must be administered and sign an oath that he is a qualified voter and has not partici-

pated in any other party's nominating or qualification proceedings. The oath must also be notarized.

The American Party of Texas was able to secure only 2,732 signatures at its precinct conventions in May 1972. By the deadline for filing the precinct lists and supplemental petitions, the total had risen to 7,828, far short of the over 22,000 required signatures. The Texas New Party apparently made no effort to comply with the 1 percent requirement. Two relatively small parties, however, which were also plaintiffs in this litigation, La Raza Unida Party and the Socialist Workers Party, complied with the qualification provisions of Art. 13.45(2) and were placed on the general election ballot.

The party appellants challenge various aspects of the Texas ballot qualification system as they interact with each other: the 1 percent support requirement with its precinct conventions and petition apparatus, the pre-primary ban on petition circulation, the disqualification from signing of those voters participating in another party's nominating process, the 55-day limitation on securing signatures, and the notarization requirement. They assert that these preconditions for access to the general election ballot are impermissible burdens on rights secured by the First and Fourteenth Amendments and violate the Equal Protection Clause of the Fourteenth Amendment as invidious discriminations against new or small political parties.

We have concluded that these claims are without merit. We agree with the District Court that whether the qualifications for ballot position are viewed as substantial burdens on the right to associate or as discriminations against parties not polling 2 percent of the last election vote, their validity depends upon whether they are necessary to further compelling state interests. But we also agree with the District Court that the foregoing limitations, whether considered alone or in combination, are constitutionally valid measures, reasonably taken in pursuit of vital state objectives that cannot be served equally well in significantly less burdensome ways.

It is too plain for argument, and it is not contested here, that the State may limit each political party to one candidate for each office on the ballot and may insist that intraparty competition be settled before the general election by primary election or by party convention. Neither can we take seriously the suggestion made here that the State has invidiously discriminated against the smaller parties by insisting that their nominations be by convention, rather than by primary election. We have considered the arguments presented, but we are wholly unpersuaded by the record before us that the convention process is invidiously more burdensome than the primary election, followed by a runoff election where necessary, particularly where the major party, in addition to the elections, must also hold its precinct, county, and state conventions to adopt and promulgate party platforms and to conduct other business. If claiming an equal protection violation, the appellants' burden was to demonstrate in the first instance a discrimination against them of some substance. "Statutes create many classifications which do not deny equal protection; it is only 'invidious discrimination' which offends the Constitution." Appellants' burden is not satisfied by mere assertions that small parties must proceed by convention when major parties are permitted to choose their candidates by primary election. The procedures are different, but the Equal Protection Clause does not necessarily forbid the one in preference to the other.

To obtain ballot position, the parties subject to Art. 13.45(2), as were these appellants, were also required to demonstrate support from electors equal in number to 1 percent of the vote for governor at the last general election. Appellants apparently question whether they must file any list of supporters where the major parties are required to file none. But we think that the State's admittedly vital interests are sufficiently implicated to insist that political parties appearing on the general ballot demonstrate a significant, measurable quantum of community support. So long as the larger parties must demonstrate major support among the electorate at the last election, whereas the smaller parties need not, the latter, without being invidiously treated, may be required to establish their position in some other manner. Of course, what is demanded may not be so excessive or impractical as to be in reality a mere device to always, or almost always, exclude parties with significant support from the ballot. The Constitution requires that access to the electorate be real, not "merely theoretical."

The District Court recognized that any fixed percentage requirement is necessarily arbitrary, but we agree with it that the required measure of support—1 percent of the vote for governor at the last general election, and, in this instance, 22,000 signatures—falls within the outer boundaries of support the State may require before according political parties ballot position. To demonstrate this degree of support does not appear either impossible or impractical, and we are unwilling to assume that the requirement imposes a substantially greater hardship on minority party access to the ballot. Two political parties which were plaintiffs in this very litigation qualified for the ballot under Art. 13.45(2) in the 1972 election. It is not, therefore, immediately obvious that the Article, on its face or as it operates in practice, imposes insurmountable obstacles to fledgling political party efforts to generate support among the electorate and to evidence that support within the time allowed.

The aspiring party is free to campaign before the primary and to compete with the major parties for voter support on primary election and precinct convention day. Any voter, however registered, may attend the new party's precinct convention and be counted toward the necessary 1 percent level. Unlike the independent candidate under Texas law, and his California counterpart, a party qualifying under Art. 13.45(2) need not wait until the primary to crystallize its support among the voters. It is entitled to compete before the primary election and to count noses at its convention on primary day, just as the major parties and their candidates count their primary votes. Furthermore, should they fall short of the magic figure, they have another chance— they may make up the shortage and win ballot position by circulating petitions for signature for a period of 55 days beginning after the primary and ending 120 days prior to the general election.

It is true that, at this juncture, the pool of possible supporters is severely reduced, for anyone voting in the just-completed primary is no longer qualified to sign the petition requesting that the petitioning party and its nominees for public office be listed on the ballot. Appellants attack this restriction, but, as such, it is nothing more than a prohibition against any elector's casting more than one vote in the process of nominating candidates for a particular office. Electors may vote in only one party primary; and it is not apparent to us why the new or smaller party seeking voter support should be entitled to get signatures of those who have already voted in another nominating primary and have already demonstrated their preference for other candidates for the same office the petitioning party seeks to fill. . . .

We have previously held that to protect the integrity of party primary elections, States may establish waiting periods before voters themselves may be permitted to change their registration and participate in another party's primary. Likewise, it seems to us that the State may determine that it is essential to the integrity of the nominating process to confine voters to supporting one party and its candidates in the course of the same nominating process. At least where, as here, the political parties had access to the entire electorate and an opportunity to commit voters on primary day, we see nothing invidious in disqualifying those who have voted at a party primary from signing petitions for another party seeking ballot position for its candidates for the same offices.

Neither do we consider that the 55 days is an unduly short time for circulating supplemental petitions. Given that time span, signatures would have to be obtained only at the rate of 400 per day to secure the entire 22,000, or four signatures per day for each 100 canvassers—only two each per day if half the 22,000 were obtained at the precinct conventions on primary day. A petition procedure may not always be a completely precise or satisfactory barometer of actual community support for a political party, but the Constitution has never required the States to do the impossible. Hard work and sacrifice by dedicated volunteers are the lifeblood of any political organization. Constitutional adjudication and common sense are not at war with each other, and we are thus unimpressed with arguments that burdens like those imposed by Texas are too onerous, especially where two of the original party plaintiffs themselves satisfied these requirements.

Finally, there remains another facet to the signature requirement. Article 13.45(2) provides that all signatures evidencing support for the party, whether originating at the precinct conventions or with supplemental petitions circulated after primary day, must be notarized. The parties object to this requirement, but make little or no effort to demonstrate its impracticability or that it is unusually burdensome. The District Court determined that it was not, indicating that one of the plaintiff political parties had conceded as much. The District Court also found no alternative if the State was to be able to enforce its laws to prevent voters from crossing over or from voting twice for the same office. On the record before us, we are in no position to disagree.

In sum, Texas "in no way freezes the status quo, but implicitly recognizes the potential fluidity of American political life." It affords minority political parties a real and essentially equal opportunity for ballot qualification. Neither the First and Fourteenth Amendments nor the Equal Protection Clause of the Fourteenth Amendment requires any more.

Appellants Dunn and Hainsworth challenged Arts. 13.50 and 13.51, which govern the eligibility of nonpartisan or independent candidates for general election ballot position. Regardless of the office sought, an independent candidate must file, within 30 days after the second or runoff primary election, a written petition signed by a specified number of qualified voters. The signatures required vary with the office sought. Dunn was required to obtain signatures equaling 3 percent of the 1970 vote for governor in the congressional district in which he desired to run; Hainsworth, a candidate for the State House of Representatives, needed 5 percent of the same vote in his locality. Article 13.50, however, states that in no event would candidates for any "district office," as Dunn and Hainsworth were, be required to file more that 500 signatures. The law also provides

that a voter may not sign more than one petition for the same office and is barred from signing any petitions if he voted at either primary election of any party at which a nomination was made for that office. Each voter signing an independent candidate's petition must also subscribe to a notarized oath declaring his nonparticipation in any political party's nominating process.

Dunn and Hainsworth contend that the First and Fourteenth Amendments, including the Equal Protection Clause, forbid the State to impose unduly burdensome conditions on their opportunity to appear on the general election ballot. The principle is unexceptionable, but requiring independent candidates to evidence a "significant modicum of support" is not unconstitutional. Demanding signatures equal in number to 3 percent or 5 percent of the vote in the last election is not invalid on its face, and with a 500-signature limit in any event, the argument that the statute is unduly burdensome approaches the frivolous.

It is true that those who have voted in the party primaries are ineligible to sign an independent candidate's petition. In theory, at least, the consequence of this restriction is that the pool of eligible signers of an independent candidate's petition, calculated by subtracting from all eligible voters in the 1972 primaries all those who voted in the primary and then adding new registrations since the closing of the registration books, could be reduced nearly to zero or to so few qualified electors that securing even 500 of them would be an impractical undertaking. But this likelihood seems remote, to say the least, particularly when it will be very likely that a substantial percentage, perhaps 25 percent, of the total registered voters will not turn out for the primary, and will thus be eligible to sign petitions, along with all new registrants since the losing of the registration books prior to the primary. In any event, nothing in the record before us indicates what the total vote in the last election was in the districts at issue here, nothing showing what the primary vote would be or was in 1972, and nothing suggesting what the size of the pool of eligible signers might be. As the District Court noted, the independent candidates presented "absolutely no factual basis in support of their claims" that Art. 13.50 imposed unduly burdensome requirements. Dunn and Hainsworth relied solely on the minimal 500-signature requirement. This was simply a failure of proof, and, for that reason, we must affirm the District Court's judgments with respect to these appellants.

In response to this Court's decision in *Bullock v. Carter*, invalidating the Texas filing fee requirements, the state legislature enacted as a temporary measure the McKool-Stroud Primary Financing Law of 1972. The statute generally provided for public financing from state revenues for primary elections of only those political parties casting 200,000 or more votes for governor in the last preceding general election. On its face, therefore, the law precluded any payment of state funds to minor political parties to reimburse them for the costs incurred in conducting their nominating and ballot qualification processes. In all, over $3,000,000 was appropriated by the state legislature to the two major political parties to defray their expenses in connection with the 1972 primary elections.

The District Court rejected all constitutional challenges to the law, noting that the statute was designed to compensate for primary election expenses and that

> [t]he convention and petition procedure available for small or new parties carries with it none of the expensive election requirements burdening those parties required to conduct primaries,

The District Court also emphasized that, in response to the State's argument in *Bullock* that state financing of primary elections would necessitate defining those political parties entitled to financial aid and would invite new charges of discrimination, this Court pointed out that, under Texas law, only those parties whose gubernatorial candidates received more than 200,000 votes were required to conduct primaries, and said

> [w]e are not persuaded that Texas would be faced with an impossible task in distinguishing between political parties for the purpose of financing primaries.

We affirm the judgment of the District Court. All political parties who desire ballot position, including the major parties, must hold precinct, county, and state conventions. The State reimburses political parties for none of the expenses in carrying out these procedures. New parties and those with less than 2% of the vote in the last election are permitted to nominate their candidates for office in the course of their convention proceedings. The major parties may not do so, and must conduct separate primary elections. As we understand it, it is the expense of these primaries that the State defrays in whole or in part. As far as the record before us shows, none of these reimbursed primary expenses are incurred by minority parties not required to hold primaries. They must undergo expense, to be sure, in holding their conventions and accumulating the necessary signatures to qualify for the ballot, but we are not persuaded that the State's refusal to reimburse for these expenses is any discrimination at all against the smaller parties, and, if it is, that it is also a denial of the equal protection of the laws within the meaning of the Fourteenth Amendment. We are unconvinced, at least based upon the facts presently available, that this financing law is an "exclusionary mechanism" which "tends to deny some voters the opportunity to vote for a candidate of their choosing," or that it has "a real and appreciable impact on the exercise of the franchise."

We should also point out that the appellant American Party mounts the major challenge to the primary financing law. The party, however, failed to qualify for the general election ballot; and we cannot agree that the State, simply because it defrays the expenses of party primary elections, must also finance the efforts of every nascent political group seeking to organize itself and unsuccessfully attempting to win a place on the general election ballot.

Under Art. 5.05, otherwise qualified voters in Texas may vote absentee in a primary or general election by personal appearance at the county clerk's office or by mail. It is the State's practice, however, to print on the absentee ballot only the names of the two major, established political parties, the Democrats and the Republicans.

The District Court sustained the exclusion of minority parties from the absentee ballot, relying on the presumption of constitutionality of state laws and the rationality of not incurring the expense of printing absentee ballots for parties without substantial voter support. The Socialist Workers Party, however, satisfied the statutory requirement for demonstrating the necessary community support needed to win general ballot position for its candidates, and, with respect to this appellant, the unavailability of the absentee ballot is obviously discriminatory. The State offered no justification for the difference in treatment in the District Court, did not brief the issue here, and had little to say in oral argument to justify the discrimination.

We have twice since *McDonald v. Board of Election Commissioners* dealt with alleged discriminations in the availability of the absentee ballot. From the latter case, it is plain that permitting absentee voting by some classes of voters and denying the privilege to other classes of otherwise qualified voters in similar circumstances, without affording a comparable alternative means to vote, is an arbitrary discrimination violative of the Equal Protection Clause. Plainly, the District Court in this case employed an erroneous standard in judging the Texas absentee voting law as it was applied in this case. We therefore vacate the judgment of the District Court in No. 72–887 in this respect and remand the Socialist Workers Party case to the District Court for further consideration. . . . In all other respects, that judgment is affirmed, as is the judgment in No. 72–942.

Cousins v. Wigoda
419 U.S. 477 (1975)

At the March 1972 Illinois primary election, Chicago's Democratic voters elected the 59 respondents (Wigoda delegates) as delegates to the 1972 Democratic National Convention to be held in July 1972 in Miami, Florida. Some of the 59 petitioners (Cousins delegates) challenged the seating of the Wigoda delegates before the Credentials Committee of the National Democratic Party on the ground, among others, that the slate-making procedures under which the Wigoda delegates were selected violated Party guidelines incorporated in the Call of the Convention. On June 30, 1972, the Credentials Committee sustained the Findings and Report of a Hearing Officer that the Wigoda delegates had been chosen in violation of the guidelines, and also adopted the Hearing Officer's recommendation that the Wigoda delegates be unseated and the Cousins delegates (who had been chosen in June at private caucuses in Chicago) be seated in their stead.

On July 8, 1972, two days before the Convention opened, the Wigoda delegates obtained from the Circuit Court of Cook County, Illinois., an injunction that enjoined each of the 59 petitioners

> from acting or purporting to act as a delegate to the Democratic National Convention . . . [and] from performing the functions of delegates . . . [and] from receiving or accepting any credentials, badges or other indicia of delegate status. . . .

Nevertheless, when the Convention, on July 10, adopted the Credentials Committee's recommendation and seated the Cousins delegates, they took their seats and participated fully as delegates throughout the Convention. In consequence, proceedings to adjudge petitioners in criminal contempt of the July 8 injunction are pending in the Circuit Court awaiting this Court's decision in this case.

The Illinois Appellate Court affirmed the injunction, and the Supreme Court of Illinois, without opinion, on November 29, 1973, denied leave to appeal. . . .

. . .

Respondents argue that Illinois had a compelling interest in protecting the integrity of its electoral processes and the right of its citizens under the State and Federal Constitutions to effective suffrage. They rely on the numerous statements of this Court that the right to vote is a "fundamental political right, because preservative of all rights." But respondents overlook the significant fact that the suffrage was exercised at the primary election to elect delegates to a National Party Convention. Consideration of the special function of delegates to such a Convention militates persuasively against the conclusion that the asserted interest constitutes a compelling state interest. Delegates perform a task of supreme importance to every citizen of the Nation regardless of their State of residence. The vital business of the Convention is the nomination of the Party's candidates for the offices of President and Vice President of the United States. To that end, the state political parties are "affiliated with a national party through acceptance of the national call to send state delegates to the national convention." The States themselves have no constitutionally mandated role in the great task of the selection of Presidential and Vice Presidential candidates. . . . The Convention serves the pervasive national interest in the selection of candidates for national office, and this national interest is greater than any interest of an individual State. . . .

Thus, Illinois' interest in protecting the integrity of its electoral process cannot be deemed compelling in the context of the selection of delegates to the National Party Convention. Whatever the case of action's presenting claims that the Party's delegate selection procedures are not exercised within the confines of the Constitution—and no such claims are made here—this is a case where "the convention itself [was] the proper forum for determining intra-party disputes as to which delegates [should] be seated."

Reversed.

Lefkowitz v. Cunningham
431 U.S. 801 (1977)

Under §22 of the New York Election Law, an officer of a political party may be subpoenaed by a grand jury or other authorized tribunal and required to testify concerning his conduct of the party office he occupies. If the officer refuses to answer any question, or if he declines to waive immunity from the use of his testimony against him in a later prosecution, the statute immediately terminates his party office and prohibits him from holding any other party or public office for a period of five years.

In December 1975, appellee Patrick J. Cunningham (appellee) was subpoenaed pursuant to §22 to appear and testify before a special grand jury authorized to investigate his conduct in the political offices he then held, which consisted of four unsalaried elective positions in the Democratic Party of the State of New York. Appellee moved to quash the subpoena in the state courts, arguing . . . that §22 violated his federal constitutional right to be free of compelled self-incrimination; his motion was denied. On April 12, 1976, he appeared before the grand jury in response to the subpoena. Appellee refused to sign a waiver of immunity form which would have waived his constitutional right not to be compelled to incriminate himself. Because §22 is self-executing, appellee's refusal to waive his constitutional immunity automatically divested him of all his party offices and activated the five-year ban on holding any public or party office.

The following day, appellee commenced this action in the United States District Court for the Southern District of New York. After hearing, the District Judge entered a temporary restraining order against enforcement of §22. A three-judge court was then convened, and that court granted appellee declaratory and permanent injunctive relief against enforcement of §22 on the ground that it violated appellee's Fifth and Fourteenth Amendment rights. . . .

. . .

. . . Appellee's party offices carry substantial prestige and political influence, giving him a powerful voice in recommending or selecting candidates for office and in other political decisions. The threatened loss of such widely sought positions, with their power and perquisites, is inherently coercive. Additionally, compelled forfeiture of these posts diminishes appellee's general reputation in his community.

. . .

Section 22 is coercive for yet another reason: it requires appellee to forfeit one constitutionally protected right as the price for exercising another. As an officer in a private political party, appellee is in a far different position from a government policymaking official holding office at the pleasure of the President or Governor. By depriving appellee of his offices, §22 impinges on his right to participate in private, voluntary political associations. That right is an important aspect of First Amendment freedom which this Court has consistently found entitled to constitutional protection. Appellant argues that even if §22 is violative of Fifth Amendment rights, the State's overriding interest in preserving public confidence in the integrity of its political process justifies the constitutional infringement. We have already rejected the notion that citizens may be forced to incriminate themselves because it serves a governmental need. . . .

. . .

Accordingly, the judgment is affirmed.

Illinois State Board of Elections v. Socialist Workers Party
440 U.S. 173 (1979)

Under the Illinois Election Code, new political parties and independent candidates must obtain the signatures of 25,000 qualified voters in order to appear on the ballot in statewide elections. However, a different standard applies in elections for offices of political subdivisions of the State. The minimum number of signatures required for those elections is 5 percent of the number of persons who voted at the previous election for offices of the particular subdivision. In the city of Chicago, application of this standard has pro-

389 ILLINOIS STATE BOARD OF ELECTIONS V. SOCIALIST WORKERS PARTY

duced the incongruous result that a new party or an independent candidate needs substantially more signatures to gain access to the ballot than a similarly situated party or candidate for state-wide office. The question before us is whether this discrepancy violates the Equal Protection Clause of the Fourteenth Amendment.

In January, 1977, the Chicago City Council ordered a special mayoral election to be held on June 7, 1977, to fill the vacancy created by the death of Mayor Richard J. Daley. Pursuant to that order, the Chicago Board of Election Commissioners (Chicago Board) issued an election calendar that listed the filing dates and signature requirements applicable to independent candidates and new political parties. Independent candidates had to obtain 35,947 valid signatures by February 19, and new political parties were required to file petitions with 63,373 valid signatures by April 4. Subsequently, the Chicago Board and the State Board of Elections (State Board) agreed for purposes of the special election to bring into conformity the requirements for independent candidates and new parties. The filing deadline for independents was extended to April 4, and the signature requirement for new parties was reduced to 35,947.

Because they had received less than 5 percent of the votes cast in the last mayoral election, the Socialist Workers Party and United States Labor Party were new political parties as defined in the Illinois statute. Along with Gerald Rose, a candidate unaffiliated with any party, they were therefore subject to the signature requirements and filing deadlines specified in the election calendar. On January 24, 1977, the Socialist Workers Party and two voters who supported its candidate for Mayor brought this action against the Chicago Board and the State Board to enjoin enforcement of the signature requirements and fil-

ing deadlines for new parties. One week later, Gerald Rose, the United States Labor Party, and four voters sued the Chicago Board, challenging the restrictions on new parties and independent candidates. The State Board intervened as a defendant . . . and the District Court consolidated the two cases for trial.

Plaintiff-appellees contended at trial that the discrepancy between the requirements for state and city elections violated the Equal Protection Clause. They argued further that the restrictions on independent candidates and new parties were unconstitutionally burdensome in the context of a special election because of the short time for collection of signatures between notice of the election and the filing deadline. . . .

. . . [T]he District Court permanently enjoined the enforcement of the 5 percent provision insofar as it mandated more than 25,000 signatures, the number required for statewide elections. The court also declined to dismiss appellees' claim that the April 4 filing deadline, coupled with the signature requirement, impermissibly burdened First and Fourteenth Amendment rights, but it postponed a decision on this issue pending submission of additional evidence to justify the selection of that date.

. . .

The State Board, but not the Chicago Board, appealed from both the March 14 order and the March 17 order. In a per curiam decision rendered six months after the election, the Court of Appeals for the Seventh Circuit adopted the opinion of the District Court. Also, with respect to the March 17 order, the Court of Appeals dismissed as moot the State Board's contention that the Chicago Board lacked authority to conclude a settlement agreement without prior state approval. In so ruling, the court noted that the settlement order applied only to the June 7 election, which had long passed, and held that the question of the Chicago Board's authority for its actions was not "capable of repetition, yet evading review."

. . .

The provisions of the Illinois Election Code at issue incorporate a geographic classification. For purposes of setting the minimum signature requirements, the Code distinguishes state candidates, political parties, and the voters supporting each, from city candidates, parties, and voters. In 1977, an independent candidate or a new political party in Chicago, a city with approximately 718,937 voters eligible to sign nominating petitions for the mayoral election in 1977, had to secure over 10,000 more signatures on nominating petitions than an independent candidate or new party in state elections, who had a pool of approximately 4.5 million eligible voters from which to obtain signatures. That the distinction between state and city elections undoubtedly is valid for some purposes does not resolve whether it is valid as applied here.

. . . The freedom to associate as a political party, a right we have recognized as fundamental, has diminished practical value if the party can be kept off the ballot. Access restrictions also implicate the right to vote because, absent recourse to referendums, "voters can assert their preferences only through candidates or parties or both." By limiting the choices available to voters, the State impairs the voters' ability to express their political preferences. And for reasons too self-evident to warrant amplification here, we have often reiterated that voting is of the most fundamental significance under our constitutional structure.

When such vital individual rights are at stake, a State must establish that its classification is necessary to serve a compelling interest. To be sure, the Court has previously acknowledged that States have a legitimate interest in regulating the number of candidates on the ballot. . . .

However, our previous opinions have also emphasized that, "even when pursuing a legitimate interest, a State may not choose means that unnecessarily restrict constitutionally protected liberty," and we have required that States adopt the least drastic means to achieve their ends. This requirement is particularly important where restrictions on access to the ballot are involved. The States' interest in screening out frivolous candidates must be considered in light of the significant role that third parties have played in the political development of the Nation. Abolitionists, Progressives, and Populists have undeniably had influence, if not always electoral success. As the records of such parties demonstrate, an election campaign is a means of disseminating ideas, as well as attaining political office. Overbroad restrictions on ballot access jeopardize this form of political expression.

The signature requirements for independent candidates and new political parties seeking offices in Chicago are plainly not the least restrictive means of protecting the State's objectives. The Illinois Legislature has determined that its interest in avoiding overloaded ballots in statewide elections is served by the 25,000 signature requirement. Yet appellant has advanced no reason, much less a compelling one, why the State needs a more stringent requirement for Chicago. . . . Not only were independent candidates and new political parties in state elections required to obtain 25,000 signatures, but those signatures also had to meet standards pertaining to geographic distribution. By comparison, candidates and parties in city elections had only to obtain signatures from a flat percentage of the qualified voters. . . . Following *Moore* [*v. Ogilvie*], the Court of Appeals for the Seventh Circuit invalidated a provision in the amended statute which specified that no more than 13,000 signatures on a new party's petition for statewide elections could come from any one county. Thus, appellant noted, the invalidation of the geographic constraints has tied the requirements for both city and state candidates solely to a population standard, giving rise to the anomaly at issue here.

Although this account may explain the anomaly, appellant still has suggested no reasons that justify its continuation. Historical accident, without more, cannot constitute a compelling state interest. We therefore hold that the Illinois Election Code is unconstitutional insofar as it requires independent candidates and new political parties to obtain more than 25,000 signatures in Chicago.

. . .

The judgment of the Court of Appeals is affirmed.

Marchioro v. Chaney
442 U.S. 191 (1979)

Since 1927, a Washington statute has required each major political party to have a State Committee consisting of two persons from each county in the State. The question presented by this appeal is whether the Washington Supreme Court correctly held that this statute does not violate the First Amendment of the United States Constitution.

The powers of the Democratic State Committee are derived from two sources: the authorizing statute and the Charter of the Democratic Party of Washington. The statute gives the State Committee the power to call conventions, to provide for the election of delegates to national conventions and for the nomination of Presidential

electors, and to fill vacancies on the party ticket.

The principal activities performed by the State Committee are authorized by the Charter of the Democratic Party of Washington. The Charter provides that the State Committee shall act as the party's governing body when the Convention is in adjournment. And it gives the State Committee authority to organize and administer the party's administrative apparatus, to raise and distribute funds to candidates, to conduct workshops, to instruct candidates on effective campaign procedures and organization, and generally to further the party's objectives of influencing policy and electing its adherents to public office.

Under both party rules and state law, the State Convention, rather than the State Committee, is the governing body of the party. The Charter explicitly provides that the Convention is "the highest policy-making authority within the State Democratic Party." . . .

In 1976, the State Democratic Convention adopted a Charter amendment directing that the State Committee include members other than those specified by state statute. The Charter amendment provided that, in addition to the two delegates from each of the State's 39 counties, there should be one representative elected from each of the State's 49 legislative districts. Pursuant to this Charter amendment, new legislative district representatives were elected to serve on the State Committee. At the January, 1977, meeting of the State Committee, a motion to seat these newly elected representatives was ruled out of order, apparently in reliance on the statutory definition of the composition of the Committee.

Thereafter, members and officers of the State Democratic Party, including four who had been elected as legislative district representatives, instituted this action for declaratory and injunctive relief in the King County Superior Court. Among their contentions was a claim that the statutory restriction on the composition of the Democratic State Committee violated their rights to freedom of association protected by the First and Fourteenth Amendments.

The Superior Court granted appellants' motion for a partial summary judgment. On appeal, a divided State Supreme Court reversed that part of the trial court's judgment that invalidated the statutory definition of the central Committee. The state court reasoned that, although "substantial burdens" on the right to associate for political purposes are invalid unless "essential to serve a compelling state interest," these appellants failed to establish that this statute had imposed any such burden on their attempts to achieve the objectives of the Democratic Party. Since this initial burden had not been met, the court upheld the constitutionality of the challenged statute.

. . .

The requirement that political parties form central or county committees composed of specified representatives from each district is common in the laws of the States. These laws are part of broader election regulations that recognize the critical role played by political parties in the process of selecting and electing candidates for state and national office. The State's interest in ensuring that this process is conducted in a fair and orderly fashion is unquestionably legitimate. . . . That interest is served by a state statute requiring that a representative central committee be established, and entrusting that committee with authority to perform limited functions, such as filling vacancies on the party ticket, providing for the nomination of Presidential electors and delegates to national conventions, and calling statewide conventions. Such functions are directly related to the orderly participation of the political party in the electoral process.

Appellants have raised no objection to the Committee's performance of these tasks. Rather, it is the Committee's other activities—those involving "purely internal party decisions"—that concern appellants and give rise to their constitutional attack on the statute.

. . .

In short, all of the "internal party decisions" which appellants claim should not be made by a statutorily composed Committee are made not because of anything in the statute, but because of delegations of authority from the Convention itself. Nothing in the statute required the party to authorize such decisionmaking by the Committee; as far as the statutory scheme is concerned, there is no reason why the Convention could not have created an entirely new committee or one, for example, composed of members of the State Committee and such additional membership as might be desired to perform the political functions now performed by the State Committee. The fact that it did not choose such an alternative course is hardly the responsibility of the state legislature.

The answer to appellants' claims of a substantial burden on First Amendment rights, then, turns out to be a simple one. There can be no complaint that the party's right to govern itself has been substantially burdened by statute when the source of the complaint is the party's own decision to confer critical authority on the State Committee. The elected legislative representatives who claim that they have been unable to participate in the internal policymaking of the Committee should address their complaint to the party which has chosen to entrust those tasks to the Committee, rather than to the state legislature. Instead of persuading us that this is a case in which a state statute has imposed substantial burdens on the party's right to govern its affairs, appellants' own statement of the facts establishes that it is the party's exercise of that very right that is the source of whatever burdens they suffer.

The judgment of the Washington Supreme Court is affirmed.

Democratic Party v. Wisconsin ex rel. La Follette
450 U.S. 107 (1981)

The charter of the appellant Democratic Party of the United States (National Party) provides that delegates to its National Convention shall be chosen through procedures in which only Democrats can participate. Consistently with the charter, the National Party's Delegate Selection Rules provide that only those who are willing to affiliate publicly with the Democratic Party may participate in the process of selecting delegates to the Party's National Convention. The question on this appeal is whether Wisconsin may successfully insist that its delegates to the Convention be seated, even though those delegates are chosen through a process that includes a binding state preference primary election in which voters do not declare their party affiliation. The Wisconsin Supreme Court held that the National Convention is bound by the Wisconsin primary election results, and cannot refuse to seat the delegates chosen in accord with Wisconsin law.

Rule 2A of the Democratic Selection Rules for the 1980 National Convention states:

> Participation in the delegate selection process in primaries or caucuses shall be restricted to Democratic voters only who publicly declare their party preference and have that preference publicly recorded.

Under National Party rules, the "delegate selection process" includes any procedure by which delegates to the Convention are bound to vote for the nomination of particular candidates.

The election laws of Wisconsin allow non-Democrats—including members of other parties and independents—to vote in the Democratic primary without regard to party affiliation and without requiring a public declaration of party preference. The voters in Wisconsin's "open" primary express their choice among Presidential candidates for the Democratic Party's nomination; they do not vote for delegates to the National Convention. Delegates to the National Convention are chosen separately, after the primary, at caucuses of persons who have stated their affiliation with the Party. But these delegates, under Wisconsin law, are bound to vote at the National Convention in accord with the results of the open primary election. Accordingly, while Wisconsin's open Presidential preference primary does not itself violate National Party rules, the State's mandate that the results of the primary shall determine the allocation of votes cast by the State's delegates at the National Convention does.

In May 1979 the Democratic Party of Wisconsin (State Party) submitted to the Compliance Review Commission of the National Party its plan for selecting delegates to the 1980 National Convention. The plan incorporated the provisions of the State's open primary laws, and, as a result, the Commission disapproved it as violating Rule 2A. Since compliance with Rule 2A was a condition of participation at the Convention, for which no exception could be made, the National Party indicated that Wisconsin delegates who were bound to vote according to the results of the open primary would not be seated.

The State Attorney General then brought an original action in the Wisconsin Supreme Court on behalf of the State. Named as respondents in the suit were the National Party and the Democratic National Committee, who are the appellants in this Court, and the State Party, an appellee here. The State sought a declaration that the Wisconsin delegate selection system was constitutional as applied to the appellants and that the appellants could not lawfully refuse to seat the Wisconsin delegation at the Convention. The State Party responded by agreeing that state law may validly be applied against it and the National Party, and cross-claimed against the National Party, asking the court to order the National Party to recognize the delegates selected in accord with Wisconsin law. The National Party argued that, under the First and Fourteenth Amendments, it could not be compelled to seat the Wisconsin delegation in violation of Party rules.

The Wisconsin Supreme Court entered a judgment declaring that the State's system of selecting delegates to the Democratic National Convention is constitutional and binding on the appellants. The court assumed that the National Party's freedom of political association, protected by the First and Fourteenth Amendments, gave it the right to restrict participation in the process of choosing Presidential and Vice Presidential candidates to Democrats. It concluded, however, that the State had not impermissibly impaired that right. The court said that the State's primary election laws were themselves intended to permit persons to vote only for the candidates of the party they preferred, and that, as a practical matter, requiring a public declaration of party affiliation would not prevent persons who are not Democrats from voting in the primary. . . .

The court declared that the votes of the state delegation at the National Convention for Presidential and Vice Presidential candidates must be apportioned and cast as prescribed by Wisconsin law, and that the State's delegates could not, for that reason, be disqualified from being seated at the Conven-

tion. The National Party and the Democratic National Committee then brought this appeal. . . .

Wisconsin held its primary on April 1, 1980, in accord with its election laws. Subsequently, the State Party chose delegates to the 1980 Democratic National Convention. . . . This Court . . . stayed the judgment of the Wisconsin Supreme Court. On July 20, 1980, the Credentials Committee of the National Convention decided to seat the delegates from Wisconsin, despite this Court's stay, and despite the delegates' selection in a manner that violated Rule 2A.

. . .

The question in this case is . . . whether, once Wisconsin has opened its Democratic Presidential preference primary to voters who do not publicly declare their party affiliation, it may then bind the National Party to honor the binding primary results, even though those results were reached in a manner contrary to National Party rules.

. . . The issue is whether the State may compel the National Party to seat a delegation chosen in a way that violates the rules of the Party. . . .

. . .

Here, the members of the National Party, speaking through their rules, chose to define their associational rights by limiting those who could participate in the processes leading to the selection of delegates to their National Convention. On several occasions, this Court has recognized that the inclusion of persons unaffiliated with a political party may seriously distort its collective decisions—thus impairing the party's essential functions—and that political parties may accordingly protect themselves "from intrusion by those with adverse political principles." . . .

The Wisconsin Supreme Court recognized these constitutional doctrines in stating that the National Party could exclude persons who are not Democrats from the procedures through which the Party's national candidates are actually chosen. . . .

The State argues that its law places only a minor burden on the National Party. The National Party argues that the burden is substantial, because it prevents the Party from "screen[ing] out those whose affiliation is . . . slight, tenuous, or fleeting," and that such screening is essential to build a more effective and responsible Party. But it is not for the courts to mediate the merits of this dispute. For even if the State were correct, a State, or a court, may not constitutionally substitute its own judgment for that of the Party. A political party's choice among the various ways of determining the makeup of a State's delegation to the party's national convention is protected by the Constitution. And as is true of all expressions of First Amendment freedoms, the courts may not interfere on the ground that they view a particular expression as unwise or irrational.

We must consider, finally, whether the State has compelling interests that justify the imposition of its will upon the appellants. "Neither the right to associate nor the right to participate in political activities is absolute." The State asserts a compelling interest in preserving the overall integrity of the electoral process, providing secrecy of the ballot, increasing voter participation in primaries, and preventing harassment of voters. But all those interests go to the conduct of the Presidential preference primary—not to the imposition of voting requirements upon those who, in a separate process, are eventually selected as delegates. Therefore, the interests advanced by the State do not justify its substantial intrusion into the associational freedom of members of the National Party.

The State has a substantial interest in the manner in which its elections are conducted, and the National Party has a substantial interest in the manner in which the delegates to its National Convention are selected. But these interests are not incompatible, and, to the limited extent they clash in this case, both interests can be preserved. The National Party rules do not forbid Wisconsin to conduct an open primary. But if Wisconsin does open its primary, it cannot require that Wisconsin delegates to the National Party Convention vote there in accordance with the primary results if to do so would violate Party rules. Since the Wisconsin Supreme Court has declared that the National Party cannot disqualify delegates who are bound to vote in accordance with the results of the Wisconsin open primary, its judgment is reversed.

Rodriguez v. Popular Democratic Party
457 U.S. 1 (1982)

The question presented by this appeal is whether Puerto Rico may, by statute, vest in a political party the power to fill an interim vacancy in the Puerto Rico Legislature. The Supreme Court of Puerto Rico held that such a procedure did not violate the United States Constitution. . . .

In the November 4, 1980, Puerto Rico general election, Ramon Muniz, a member of appellee Popular Democratic Party, was elected to the Puerto Rico House of Representatives from District 31. Muniz died on January 28, 1981. The Governor of Puerto Rico, a member of the opposition New Progressive Party, subsequently called for a "by-election"—open to all qualified voters in District 31—to fill the vacancy caused by Muniz's death. The Governor purported to act pursuant to Articles 5.006 and 5.007 of the Electoral Law of Puerto Rico.

On March 3, 1981, the Popular Democratic Party instituted this action in the Superior Court of Puerto Rico, alleging that Articles 5.006 and

5.007 authorized only candidates and electors affiliated with the Party to participate in the by-election. Appellants, 10 qualified electors in District 31 who are not affiliated with the Popular Democratic Party, intervened as defendants. On March 20, 1981, the Superior Court entered judgment for the Popular Democratic Party; it ordered the Governor and General Administrator of Elections to limit participation in the by-election to Party members.

A divided Supreme Court of Puerto Rico modified the Superior Court's judgment. It interpreted Articles 5.006 and 5.007 to require a by-election only in the event that the party of the legislator vacating the seat fails to designate a replacement within 60 days after the vacancy occurred; if the party selects a single candidate within the 60-day period, that candidate is "automatically elected to fill the vacancy," rendering a by-election unnecessary. The court held further that, if the party presents more than one candidate during the 60-day period, a by-election must be conducted in which only party-affiliated candidates may run but in which all qualified electors may vote. In the event no candidate is presented within the 60-day period, candidates affiliated with any party, as well as independent candidates, are permitted to run in the by-election. Because of the delay already occasioned by the litigation, the court permitted appellee Party only 30 days from the entry of judgment, May 8, 1981, to present a "slate" of candidates to the Commonwealth Election Commission. . . .

The court rejected appellants' contention that this procedure violated the United States Constitution. It noted that the Constitution does not expressly require a fixed method for filling vacancies in a state or commonwealth legislature. The court also held that Puerto Rico's party appointment system serves several "compelling

interests," such as ensuring the stability and continuity of the "legislative balance" until the next general election; protecting the "electoral mandate" of the previous election; and reducing "inter-partisan political campaigns to once every four years."

Puerto Rico, in common with many of the States, has adopted means of filling interim vacancies in elective commonwealth offices without the necessity of a full-scale special election. If a vacancy occurs in the office of Governor, it is automatically filled by the Secretary of State, an officer appointed by the Governor. Mayoral vacancies and vacancies in the municipal assemblies are filled by appointment upon the recommendation of the political party to which the incumbent belonged. Similarly, the Commonwealth Constitution provides that vacancies in the posts of at-large senators and representatives, shall be filled "upon recommendation of the political party to which belonged the Senator or Representative causing the vacancy. . . ." Article 5.006 of the Puerto Rico Electoral Law, as interpreted by the Supreme Court of Puerto Rico in this case, likewise confers on a political party the initial opportunity to appoint an interim replacement for one of its members who vacates a position as a district senator or representative. In each case, the appointee serves only until the next regularly scheduled election.

Appellants' challenge to the procedure mandated by Article 5.006 is essentially two-pronged. Appellants first contend that qualified voters have a federal constitutional right to elect their representatives to the Puerto Rico Legislature, and that vacancies in legislative offices therefore must be filled by a special election open to all qualified electors, not by interim appointment of any kind. Alternatively, appellants maintain that, even if legislative vacancies may be filled by an interim appointment of the Governor or some other elected official, Puerto Rico's party appointment mechanism impermissibly infringes upon their right of association under the First Amendment and denies them equal protection of the laws.

. . .

. . . Puerto Rico, like a state, is an autonomous political entity, "sovereign over matters not ruled by the Constitution." The methods by which the people of Puerto Rico and their representatives have chosen to structure the Commonwealth's electoral system are entitled to substantial deference. Moreover, we should accord weight to the Puerto Rico Supreme Court's assessment of the justification and need for particular provisions to fill vacancies caused by the death, resignation, or removal of a member of the legislature. Bearing these considerations in mind, we turn to appellants' constitutional challenges.

No provision of the Federal Constitution expressly mandates the procedures that a state or the Commonwealth of Puerto Rico must follow in filling vacancies in its own legislature. Appellants nevertheless maintain that qualified electors have an absolute constitutional right to vote for the members of a state or commonwealth legislature, even when a special election is required for this purpose. However, this Court has often noted that the Constitution "does not confer the right of suffrage upon any one," and that "the right to vote, per se, is not a constitutionally protected right." Moreover, we have previously rejected claims that the Constitution compels a fixed method of choosing state or local officers or representatives.

. . .

To be sure, when a state or the Commonwealth of Puerto Rico has provided that its representatives be elected, "a citizen has a constitutionally protected right to participate in elections on an equal basis with other citizens in the jurisdiction."

However, the Puerto Rico statute at issue here does not restrict access to the electoral process or afford unequal treatment to different classes of voters or political parties. All qualified voters have an equal opportunity to select a district representative in the general election; and the interim appointment provision applies uniformly to all legislative vacancies, whenever they arise.

. . .

. . . [T]he fact that the Seventeenth Amendment permits a state, if it chooses, to forgo a special election in favor of a temporary appointment to the United States Senate suggests that a state is not constitutionally prohibited from exercising similar latitude with regard to vacancies in its own legislature. We discern nothing in the Federal Constitution that imposes greater constraints on the Commonwealth of Puerto Rico.

The Commonwealth's choice to fill legislative vacancies by appointment, rather than by a full-scale special election, may have some effect on the right of its citizens to elect the members of the Puerto Rico Legislature; however, the effect is minimal, and . . . it does not fall disproportionately on any discrete group of voters, candidates, or political parties. Moreover, the interim appointment system plainly serves the legitimate purpose of ensuring that vacancies are filled promptly, without the necessity of the expense and inconvenience of a special election. The Constitution does not preclude this practical and widely accepted means of addressing an infrequent problem.

Puerto Rico's appointment mechanism is not rendered constitutionally defective by virtue of the fact that the interim appointment power is given to the political party with which the previous incumbent was affiliated. Appellants maintain that the power to make interim appointments must be vested in an elected official, such as the

Governor of the Commonwealth, so that the appointments will have "the legitimacy of derivative voter approval and control." However, that such control may often be largely illusory is illustrated by this case, where the Governor and the incumbent belonged to different parties. The Puerto Rico Legislature could reasonably conclude that appointment by the previous incumbent's political party would more fairly reflect the will of the voters than appointment by the Governor or some other elected official.

The Supreme Court of Puerto Rico held that party appointment was a legitimate mechanism serving to protect the mandate of the preceding election and to preserve the "legislative balance" until the next general election is held. Such protection is particularly important in light of Puerto Rico's special interest in ensuring minority representation in its legislature. It was thus not unreasonable for the Puerto Rico Legislature, in establishing an appointment system for filling legislative vacancies, to make provision for continuity of party representation. Absent some clear constitutional limitation, Puerto Rico is free to structure its political system to meet its "special concerns and political circumstances."

Finally, appellants argue that their rights of association and equal protection of the laws were violated by their exclusion, based solely upon their party affiliation, from the Party-sponsored election held to select Muniz's successor. However, appellants' argument misconceives the nature of the election held in this case. Puerto Rico law authorized the Popular Democratic Party to designate an interim replacement to fill Muniz's seat. The Party was entitled to adopt its own procedures to select this replacement; it was not required to include nonmembers in what can be analogized to a party primary election. Appellants' exclusion from this election did not violate

their rights of association, nor did it deprive them of equal protection of the laws.

We hold that the mechanism adopted by the Puerto Rico Legislature for filling legislative vacancies is not foreclosed by the Federal Constitution. Accordingly, the judgment of the Supreme Court of Puerto Rico is affirmed.

Munro v. Socialist Workers Party
479 U.S. 189 (1986)

The State of Washington requires that a minor party candidate for partisan office receive at least 1 percent of all votes cast for that office in the State's primary election before the candidate's name will be placed on the general election ballot. The question for decision is whether this statutory requirement, as applied to candidates for statewide offices, violates the First and Fourteenth Amendments to the United States Constitution. The Court of Appeals for the Ninth Circuit declared the provision unconstitutional.

. . .

In 1977, the State of Washington enacted amendments to its election laws, changing the manner in which candidates from minor political parties qualify for placement on the general election ballot. Before the amendments, a minor party candidate did not participate in the State's primary elections, but rather sought his or her party's nomination at a party convention held on the same day as the primary election for "major" parties. The convention-nominated, minor party candidate secured a position on the general election ballot upon the filing of a certificate signed by at least 100 registered voters who had participated in the convention and who had not voted in the primary election. The 1977 amendments retained the requirement that a minor party candidate be nominated by convention, but imposed the additional requirement that, as a precondition to general ballot access, the nominee for an office appear on the primary election ballot and receive at least 1 percent of all votes cast for that particular office at the primary election.

Washington conducts a "blanket primary" at which registered voters may vote for any candidate of their choice, irrespective of the candidate's political party affiliation. A candidate seeking placement on the primary election ballot must declare his candidacy no earlier than the last Monday in July, and no later than the following Friday. Minor party nominating conventions are to be held on the Saturday preceding this filing period. The primary election is held on the third Tuesday in September.

The events giving rise to this action occurred in 1983, after the state legislature authorized a special primary election to be held on October 11, 1983, to fill a vacancy in the office of United States Senator. Appellee Dean Peoples qualified to be placed on the primary election ballot as the nominee of appellee Socialist Workers Party (Party). Also appearing on that ballot were 32 other candidates. At the primary, Mr. Peoples received approximately nine one-hundredths of one percent of the total votes cast for the office, and, accordingly, the State did not place his name on the general election ballot.

Appellees (Peoples, the Party, and two registered voters) commenced this action in United States District Court, alleging that §29.18.110 abridged their rights secured by the First and Fourteenth Amendments. The District Court entered judgment denying appellees relief, but the Court of Appeals for the Ninth Circuit reversed, holding that §29.18.110, as applied to candidates for statewide offices, was unconstitutional. . . .

Restrictions upon the access of political par-

ties to the ballot impinge upon the rights of individuals to associate for political purposes, as well as the rights of qualified voters to cast their votes effectively, and may not survive scrutiny under the First and Fourteenth Amendments. . . . These associational rights, however, are not absolute, and are necessarily subject to qualification if elections are to be run fairly and effectively.

While there is no "litmus-paper test" for deciding a case like this, it is now clear that States may condition access to the general election ballot by a minor party or independent candidate upon a showing of a modicum of support among the potential voters for the office. . . .

. . .

We have never required a State to make a particularized showing of the existence of voter confusion, ballot overcrowding, or the presence of frivolous candidacies prior to the imposition of reasonable restrictions on ballot access. . . .

To require States to prove actual voter confusion, ballot overcrowding, or the presence of frivolous candidacies as a predicate to the imposition of reasonable ballot access restrictions would invariably lead to endless court battles over the sufficiency of the "evidence" marshaled by a State to prove the predicate. Such a requirement would necessitate that a State's political system sustain some level of damage before the legislature could take corrective action. Legislatures, we think, should be permitted to respond to potential deficiencies in the electoral process with foresight, rather than reactively, provided that the response is reasonable and does not significantly impinge on constitutionally protected rights.

In any event, the record here suggests that revision of §29.18.110 was, in fact, linked to the state legislature's perception that the general election ballot was becoming cluttered with candidates from minor parties who did not command significant voter support. In 1976, one year prior to revision of §29.18.110, the largest number of minor political parties in Washington's history—twelve—appeared on the general election ballot. The record demonstrates that at least part of the legislative impetus for revision of §29.18.110 was concern about minor parties having such easy access to Washington's general election ballot.

. . . We think that the State can properly reserve the general election ballot "for major struggles," by conditioning access to that ballot on a showing of a modicum of voter support. In this respect, the fact that the State is willing to have a long and complicated ballot at the primary provides no measure of what it may require for access to the general election ballot. The State of Washington was clearly entitled to raise the ante for ballot access, to simplify the general election ballot, and to avoid the possibility of unrestrained factionalism at the general election.

Neither do we agree with the Court of Appeals and appellees that the burdens imposed on appellees' First Amendment rights by the 1977 amendments are far too severe to be justified by the State's interest in restricting access to the general ballot. Much is made of the fact that, prior to 1977, virtually every minor party candidate who sought general election ballot position so qualified, while, since 1977, only 1 out of 12 minor party candidates has appeared on that ballot. Such historical facts are relevant, but they prove very little in this case, other than the fact that §29.18.110 does not provide an insuperable barrier to minor party ballot access. It is hardly a surprise that minor parties appeared on the general election ballot before §29.18.110 was revised, for, until then, there were virtually no restrictions on access. Under our cases, however, Washington was not required to afford such automatic access, and would have been entitled to insist on

a more substantial showing of voter support. Comparing the actual experience before and after 1977 tells us nothing about how minor parties would have fared in those earlier years had Washington conditioned ballot access to the maximum extent permitted by the Constitution.

. . . Because Washington provides a "blanket primary," minor party candidates can campaign among the entire pool of registered voters. Effort and resources that would otherwise be directed at securing petition signatures can instead be channeled into campaigns to "get the vote out," foster candidate name recognition, and educate the electorate. To be sure, candidates must demonstrate, through their ability to secure votes at the primary election, that they enjoy a modicum of community support in order to advance to the general election. But requiring candidates to demonstrate such support is precisely what we have held States are permitted to do.

Appellees argue that voter turnout at primary elections is generally lower than the turnout at general elections, and therefore enactment of §29.18.110 has reduced the pool of potential supporters from which Party candidates can secure 1% of the vote. We perceive no more force to this argument than we would with an argument by a losing candidate that his supporters' constitutional rights were infringed by their failure to participate in the election. Washington has created no impediment to voting at the primary elections; every supporter of the Party in the State is free to cast his or her ballot for the Party's candidates. . . . States are not burdened with a constitutional imperative to reduce voter apathy or to "handicap" an unpopular candidate to increase the likelihood that the candidate will gain access to the general election ballot. As we see it, Washington has done no more than to visit on a candidate a requirement to show a "significant modicum" of voter support, and it was entitled to require that showing in its primary elections.

... Washington has chosen a vehicle by which minor party candidates must demonstrate voter support that serves to promote the very First Amendment values that are threatened by overly burdensome ballot access restrictions. It can hardly be said that Washington's voters are denied freedom of association because they must channel their expressive activity into a campaign at the primary as opposed to the general election. It is true that voters must make choices as they vote at the primary, but there are no state-imposed obstacles impairing voters in the exercise of their choices. Washington simply has not substantially burdened the "availability of political opportunity."

... [B]ecause Washington affords a minor party candidate easy access to the primary election ballot and the opportunity for the candidate to wage a ballot-connected campaign, we conclude that the magnitude of §29.18.110's effect on constitutional rights is slight when compared to the restrictions we upheld in *Jenness* and *American Party*. Accordingly, Washington did not violate the Constitution by denying appellee Peoples a position on the general election ballot on November 8, 1983.

The judgment of the Court of Appeals for the Ninth Circuit is therefore reversed.

Tashjian v. Republican Party of Connecticut
479 U.S. 208 (1986)

Appellee Republican Party of the State of Connecticut (Party) in 1984 adopted a Party rule which permits independent voters—registered voters not affiliated with any political party—to vote in Republican primaries for federal and state-wide offices. Appellant Julia Tashjian, the Secretary of the State of Connecticut, is charged with the administration of the State's election statutes, which include a provision requiring voters in any party primary to be registered members of that party. Appellees, who in addition to the Party include the Party's federal officeholders and the Party's state chairman, challenged this eligibility provision on the ground that it deprives the Party of its First Amendment right to enter into political association with individuals of its own choosing. The District Court granted summary judgment in favor of appellees. The Court of Appeals affirmed. . . .

In 1955, Connecticut adopted its present primary election system. For major parties, the process of candidate selection for federal and statewide offices requires a statewide convention of party delegates; district conventions are held to select candidates for seats in the state legislature. The party convention may certify as the party-endorsed candidate any person receiving more than 20 percent of the votes cast in a rollcall vote at the convention. Any candidate not endorsed by the party who received 20 percent of the vote may challenge the party-endorsed candidate in a primary election, in which the candidate receiving the plurality of votes becomes the party's nominee. Candidates selected by the major parties, whether through convention or primary, are automatically accorded a place on the ballot at the general election. The costs of primary elections are paid out of public funds.

The statute challenged in these proceedings, §9–431, has remained substantially unchanged since the adoption of the State's primary system. In 1976, the statute's constitutionality was upheld by a three-judge District Court against a challenge by an independent voter who sought a declaration of his right to vote in the Republican primary. In that action, the Party opposed the plaintiff's efforts to participate in the Party primary.

Subsequent to the decision in *Nader*, however, the Party changed its views with respect to participation by independent voters in Party primaries. Motivated in part by the demographic importance of independent voters in Connecticut politics, in September, 1983, the Party's Central Committee recommended calling a state convention to consider altering the Party's rules to allow independents to vote in Party primaries. In January, 1984, the state convention adopted the Party rule now at issue, which provides:

> Any elector enrolled as a member of the Republican Party and any elector not enrolled as a member of a party shall be eligible to vote in primaries for nomination of candidates for the offices of United States Senator, United States Representative, Governor, Lieutenant Governor, Secretary of the State, Attorney General, Comptroller and Treasurer.

During the 1984 session, the Republican leadership in the state legislature, in response to the conflict between the newly enacted Party rule and §9–431, proposed to amend the statute to allow independents to vote in primaries when permitted by Party rules. The proposed legislation was defeated, substantially along party lines, in both houses of the legislature, which at that time were controlled by the Democratic Party.

. . .

The Party here contends that §9–431 impermissibly burdens the right of its members to determine for themselves with whom they will associate, and whose support they will seek, in their quest for political success. The Party's attempt to broaden the base of public participation in and support for its activities is conduct undeniably central to the exercise of the right of association. . . .

. . .

Appellant contends that §9–431 is a narrowly tailored regulation which advances the State's compelling interests by ensuring the administrability of the primary system, preventing raiding, avoiding voter confusion, and protecting the responsibility of party government.

Although it was not presented to the Court of Appeals as a basis for the defense of the statute, appellant argues here that the administrative burden imposed by the Party rule is a sufficient ground on which to uphold the constitutionality of §9–481. Appellant contends that the Party's rule would require the purchase of additional voting machines, the training of additional poll workers, and potentially the printing of additional ballot materials specifically intended for independents voting in the Republican primary. In essence, appellant claims that the administration of the system contemplated by the Party rule would simply cost the State too much.

Even assuming the factual accuracy of these contentions, which have not been subjected to any scrutiny by the District Court, the possibility of future increases in the cost of administering the election system is not a sufficient basis here for infringing appellees' First Amendment rights. Costs of administration would likewise increase if a third major party should come into existence in Connecticut, thus requiring the State to fund a third major party primary. Additional voting machines, poll workers, and ballot materials would all be necessary under these circumstances as well. But the State could not forever protect the two existing major parties from competition solely on the ground that two major parties are all the public can afford. While the State is of course entitled to take administrative and financial considerations into account in choosing whether or not to have a primary system at all, it can no more restrain the Republican

Party's freedom of association for reasons of its own administrative convenience than it could on the same ground limit the ballot access of a new major party.

. . . [A] raid on the Republican Party primary by independent voters, a curious concept only distantly related to the type of raiding discussed in *Kusper* and *Rosario*, is not impeded by §9–431; the independent raiders need only register as Republicans and vote in the primary. Indeed, under Conn.Gen.Stat. §9–56 , which permits an independent to affiliate with the Party as late as noon on the business day preceding the primary, the State's election statutes actually assist a "raid" by independents, which could be organized and implemented at the eleventh hour. The State's asserted interest in the prevention of raiding provides no justification for the statute challenged here.

Appellant's next argument in support of §9–431 is that the closed primary system avoids voter confusion. . . . To the extent that party labels provide a shorthand designation of the views of party candidates on matters of public concern, the identification of candidates with particular parties plays a role in the process by which voters inform themselves for the exercise of the franchise. Appellant's argument depends upon the belief that voters can be "misled" by party labels. But "[o]ur cases reflect a greater faith in the ability of individual voters to inform themselves about campaign issues." Moreover, appellant's concern that candidates selected under the Party rule will be the nominees of an "amorphous" group using the Party's name is inconsistent with the facts. The Party is not proposing that independents be allowed to choose the Party's nominee without Party participation; on the contrary, to be listed on the Party's primary ballot continues to require, under a statute not challenged here, that the primary candidate have obtained at least 20 percent

of the vote at a Party convention, which only Party members may attend. If no such candidate seeks to challenge the convention's nominee in a primary, then no primary is held, and the convention nominee becomes the Party's nominee in the general election without any intervention by independent voters. Even assuming, however, that putative candidates defeated at the Party convention will have an increased incentive under the Party's rule to make primary challenges, hoping to attract more substantial support from independents than from Party delegates, the requirement that such challengers garner substantial minority support at the convention greatly attenuates the State's concern that the ultimate nominee will be wedded to the Party in nothing more than a marriage of convenience.

In arguing that the Party rule interferes with educated decisions by voters, appellant also disregards the substantial benefit which the Party rule provides to the Party and its members in seeking to choose successful candidates. Given the numerical strength of independent voters in the State, one of the questions most likely to occur to Connecticut Republicans in selecting candidates for public office is how can the Party most effectively appeal to the independent voter? By inviting independents to assist in the choice at the polls between primary candidates selected at the Party convention, the Party rule is intended to produce the candidate and platform most likely to achieve that goal. The state statute is said to decrease voter confusion, yet it deprives the Party and its members of the opportunity to inform themselves as to the level of support for the Party's candidates among a critical group of electors. . . .

Finally, appellant contends that §9–431 furthers the State's compelling interest in protecting the integrity of the two-party system and the responsibility of party government. Appellant argues vigorously and at length that the closed primary system chosen by the state legislature promotes responsiveness by elected officials and strengthens the effectiveness of the political parties.

The relative merits of closed and open primaries have been the subject of substantial debate since the beginning of this century, and no consensus has as yet emerged. . . . But our role is not to decide whether the state legislature was acting wisely in enacting the closed primary system in 1955, or whether the Republican Party makes a mistake in seeking to depart from the practice of the past thirty years.

. . .

. . . In the present case, the state statute is defended on the ground that it protects the integrity of the Party against the Party itself.

Under these circumstances, the views of the State, which to some extent represent the views of the one political party transiently enjoying majority power, as to the optimum methods for preserving party integrity lose much of their force. The State argues that its statute is well designed to save the Republican Party from undertaking a course of conduct destructive of its own interests. But on this point "even if the State were correct, a State, or a court, may not constitutionally substitute its own judgment for that of the Party." The Party's determination of the boundaries of its own association, and of the structure which best allows it to pursue its political goals, is protected by the Constitution. . . .

We conclude that the State's enforcement, under these circumstances, of its closed primary system burdens the First Amendment rights of the Party. The interests which the appellant adduces in support of the statute are insubstantial, and accordingly the statute, as applied to the Party in this case, is unconstitutional.

. . .

The Court of Appeals rejected appellant's argument, holding that the Qualifications Clause and the parallel provision of the Seventeenth Amendment do not apply to primary elections. The concurring opinion took a different view, reaching the conclusion that these provisions require only that "anyone who is permitted to vote for the most numerous branch of the state legislature has to be permitted to vote" in federal legislative elections. We agree.

. . . The constitutional goal of assuring that the Members of Congress are chosen by the people can only be secured if that principle is applicable to every stage in the selection process. If primaries were not subject to the requirements of the Qualifications Clauses contained in Article I, §2 and the Seventeenth Amendment, the fundamental principle of free electoral choice would be subject to the sort of erosion these prior decisions were intended to prevent.

Accordingly, we hold that the Qualifications Clauses of Article I, §2, and the Seventeenth Amendment are applicable to primary elections in precisely the same fashion that they apply to general congressional elections. Our task is then to discover whether, as appellant contends, those provisions require that voter qualifications, such as party membership, in primaries for federal office must be absolutely symmetrical with those pertaining to primaries for state legislative office.

. . .

. . . We hold that the implementation of the Party rule does not violate the Qualifications Clause or the Seventeenth Amendment because it does not disenfranchise any voter in a federal election who is qualified to vote in a primary or general election for the more numerous house of the state legislature.

We conclude that §9–431 impermissibly burdens the rights of the Party and its members protected by the First and Fourteenth Amendments. The interests asserted by appellant in defense of the statute are insubstantial. The judgment of the Court of Appeals is affirmed.

Eu v. San Francisco Democratic Central Committee
489 U.S. 214 (1989)

The California Elections Code forbids the official governing bodies of political parties from endorsing candidates in party primaries. It also dictates the organization and composition of those bodies, limits the term of office of a party chair, and requires that the chair rotate between residents of northern and southern California. The Court of Appeals for the Ninth Circuit held that these provisions violate the free speech and associational rights of political parties and their members guaranteed by the First and Fourteenth Amendments. . . .

The State of California heavily regulates its political parties. Although the laws vary in extent and detail from party to party, certain requirements apply to all "ballot-qualified" parties. The California Elections Code (Code) provides that the "official governing bodies" for such a party are its "state convention," "state central committee," and "county central committees," and that these bodies are responsible for conducting the party's campaigns. At the same time, the Code provides that the official governing bodies "shall not endorse, support, or oppose, any candidate for nomination by that party for partisan office in the direct primary election." It is a misdemeanor for any primary candidate, or a person on her behalf, to claim that she is the officially endorsed candidate of the party.

Although the official governing bodies of political parties are barred from issuing endorsements, other groups are not. Political clubs affiliated with a party, labor organizations, political action committees, other politically active associations, and newspapers frequently endorse primary candidates. With the official party organizations silenced by the ban, it has been possible for a candidate with views antithetical to those of her party nevertheless to win its primary.

In addition to restricting the primary activities of the official governing bodies of political parties, California also regulates their internal affairs. Separate statutory provisions dictate the size and composition of the state central committees; set forth rules governing the selection and removal of committee members; fix the maximum term of office for the chair of the state central committee; require that the chair rotate between residents of northern and southern California; specify the time and place of committee meetings; and limit the dues parties may impose on members. Violations of these provisions are criminal offenses punishable by fine and imprisonment.

Various county central committees of the Democratic and Republican Parties, the state central committee of the Libertarian Party, members of various state and county central committees, and other groups and individuals active in partisan politics in California brought this action in federal court against state officials responsible for enforcing the Code (State or California). They contended that the ban on primary endorsements and the restrictions on internal party governance deprive political parties and their members of the rights of free speech and free association guaranteed by the First and Fourteenth Amendments of the United States Constitution. The first count of the complaint challenged the ban on endorsements in partisan primary elections; the second count challenged the ban on endorsements in nonpartisan school, county, and municipal elections; and the third count challenged the provisions that prescribe the composition of state central committees, the term of office and eligibility criteria for state central committee chairs, the time and place of state and county central committee meetings, and the dues county committee members must pay.

The plaintiffs moved for summary judgment, in support of which they filed 28 declarations from the chairs of each plaintiff central committee, prominent political scientists, and elected officials from California and other States. The State moved to dismiss, and filed a cross-motion for summary judgment. . . .

The District Court granted summary judgment for the plaintiffs on the first count, ruling that the ban on primary endorsements in §§11702 and 29430 violated the First Amendment as applied to the States through the Fourteenth Amendment. The court stayed all proceedings on the second count. . . . On the third count, the court ruled that the laws prescribing the composition of state central committees, limiting the committee chairs' terms of office, and designating that the chair rotate between residents of northern and southern California violate the First Amendment. The court denied summary judgment with respect to the statutory provisions establishing the time and place of committee meetings and the amount of dues.

The Court of Appeals for the Ninth Circuit affirmed. This Court vacated that decision and remanded for further consideration in light of *Tashjian v. Republican Party of Connecticut.*

After supplemental briefing, the Court of Appeals again affirmed. . . . Turning to the merits, the court characterized the prohibition on primary endorsements as an "outright ban" on political

speech. . . . The court rejected the State's argument that the ban served a compelling state interest in preventing internal party dissension and factionalism. . . . The court noted, moreover, that the State had not shown that banning primary endorsements protects parties from factionalism. The court concluded that the ban was not necessary to protect voters from confusion. . . .

The Court of Appeals also found that California's regulation of internal party affairs "burdens the parties' right to govern themselves as they think best." This interference with the parties' and their members' First Amendment rights was not justified by a compelling state interest, for a State has a legitimate interest "in orderly elections, not orderly parties." In any event, the court noted, the State had failed to submit "'a shred of evidence,'" that the regulations of party internal affairs helped minimize party factionalism. Accordingly, the court held that the challenged provisions were unconstitutional under the First and Fourteenth Amendments.

. . .

We first consider California's prohibition on primary endorsements by the official governing bodies of political parties. California concedes that its ban implicates the First Amendment, but contends that the burden is "miniscule." We disagree. The ban directly affects speech, which "is at the core of our electoral process and of the First Amendment freedoms." We have recognized repeatedly that "debate on the qualifications of candidates [is] integral to the operation of the system of government established by our Constitution." Indeed, the First Amendment "has its fullest and most urgent application" to speech uttered during a campaign for political office. Free discussion about candidates for public office is no less critical before a primary than before a general election. In both instances, the "election campaign is a means of disseminating ideas as well as attaining political office."

California's ban on primary endorsements, however, prevents party governing bodies from stating whether a candidate adheres to the tenets of the party or whether party officials believe that the candidate is qualified for the position sought. This prohibition directly hampers the ability of a party to spread its message, and hamstrings voters seeking to inform themselves about the candidates and the campaign issues. A "highly paternalistic approach" limiting what people may hear is generally suspect, but it is particularly egregious where the State censors the political speech a political party shares with its members.

Barring political parties from endorsing and opposing candidates not only burdens their freedom of speech, but also infringes upon their freedom of association. It is well settled that partisan political organizations enjoy freedom of association protected by the First and Fourteenth Amendments. Freedom of association means not only that an individual voter has the right to associate with the political party of her choice, but also that a political party has a right to "identify the people who constitute the association," and to select a "standardbearer who best represents the party's ideologies and preferences."

Depriving a political party of the power to endorse suffocates this right. The endorsement ban prevents parties from promoting candidates

> at the crucial juncture at which the appeal to common principles may be translated into concerted action, and hence to political power in the community.

Even though individual members of the state central committees and county central committees are free to issue endorsements, imposing limitation

on individuals wishing to band together to advance their views on a ballot measure, while placing none on individuals acting alone, is clearly a restraint on the right of association.

Because the ban burdens appellees' rights to free speech and free association, it can only survive constitutional scrutiny if it serves a compelling governmental interest. The State offers two: stable government and protecting voters from confusion and undue influence. Maintaining a stable political system is, unquestionably, a compelling state interest. California, however, never adequately explains how banning parties from endorsing or opposing primary candidates advances that interest. . . .

The only explanation the State offers is that its compelling interest in stable government embraces a similar interest in party stability. The State relies heavily on *Storer v. Brown*, where we stated that, because "splintered parties and unrestrained factionalism may do significant damage to the fabric of government," States may regulate elections to ensure that "some sort of order, rather than chaos . . . accompan[ies] the democratic processes." Our decision in *Storer*, however, does not stand for the proposition that a State may enact election laws to mitigate intraparty factionalism during a primary campaign. To the contrary, *Storer* recognized that "contending forces within the party employ the primary campaign and the primary election to finally settle their differences." A primary is not hostile to intraparty feuds; rather, it is an ideal forum in which to resolve them. . . .

. . . Presumably a party will be motivated by self-interest, and not engage in acts or speech that run counter to its political success. However, even if a ban on endorsements saves a political party from pursuing self-destructive acts, that would not justify a State substituting its judgment for that of the party. Because preserving party unity during a primary is not a compelling state interest, we must look elsewhere to justify the challenged law.

The State's second justification for the ban on party endorsements and statements of opposition is that it is necessary to protect primary voters from confusion and undue influence. Certainly the State has a legitimate interest in fostering an informed electorate. . . . While a State may regulate the flow of information between political associations and their members when necessary to prevent fraud and corruption, there is no evidence that California's ban on party primary endorsements serves that purpose.

Because the ban on primary endorsements by political parties burdens political speech while serving no compelling governmental interest, we hold that §§11702 and 29430 violate the First and Fourteenth Amendment.

We turn next to California's restrictions on the organization and composition of official governing bodies, the limits on the term of office for state central committee chair, and the requirement that the chair rotate between residents of northern and southern California. These laws directly implicate the associational rights of political parties and their members. . . . Freedom of association also encompasses a political party's decisions about the identity of, and the process for electing, its leaders.

. . . By requiring parties to establish official governing bodies at the county level, California prevents the political parties from governing themselves with the structure they think best. And by specifying who shall be the members of the parties' official governing bodies, California interferes with the parties' choice of leaders. . . .

Each restriction thus limits a political party's discretion in how to organize itself, conduct its

affairs, and select its leaders. Indeed, the associational rights at stake are much stronger than those we credited in *Tashjian*. There, we found that a party's right to free association embraces a right to allow registered voters who are not party members to vote in the party's primary. Here, party members do not seek to associate with nonparty members, but only with one another in freely choosing their party leaders.

Because the challenged laws burden the associational rights of political parties and their members, the question is whether they serve a compelling state interest. A State indisputably has a compelling interest in preserving the integrity of its election process. Toward that end, a State may enact laws that interfere with a party's internal affairs when necessary to ensure that elections are fair and honest. . . . Rather, the infringement on the associational rights of the parties and their members was the indirect consequence of laws necessary to the successful completion of a party's external responsibilities in ensuring the order and fairness of elections.

In the instant case, the State has not shown that its regulation of internal party governance is necessary to the integrity of the electoral process. Instead, it contends that the challenged laws serve a compelling "interest in the 'democratic management of the political party's internal affairs.'" This, however, is not a case where intervention is necessary to prevent the derogation of the civil rights of party adherents. Moreover, as we have observed, the State has no interest in "protect[ing] the integrity of the Party against the Party itself." The State further claims that limiting the term of the state central committee chair and requiring that the chair rotate between residents of northern and southern California helps "prevent regional friction from reaching a 'critical mass.'" However, a State cannot substitute its judgment for that of the party as to the desirability of a particular internal party structure any more than it can tell a party that its proposed communication to party members is unwise.

In sum, a State cannot justify regulating a party's internal affairs without showing that such regulation is necessary to ensure an election that is orderly and fair. Because California has made no such showing here, the challenged laws cannot be upheld.

For the reasons stated above, we hold that the challenged California election laws burden the First Amendment rights of political parties and their members without serving a compelling state interest. Accordingly, the judgment of the Court of Appeals is affirmed.

Renne v. Geary
501 U.S. 312 (1991)

Petitioners seek review of a decision of the United States Court of Appeals for the Ninth Circuit holding that Article II, §6(b) of the California Constitution violates the First and Fourteenth Amendments to the Constitution of the United States. Section 6(b) reads: "No political party or party central committee may endorse, support, or oppose a candidate for nonpartisan office." Its companion provision, provides that "[a]ll judicial, school, county, and city offices shall be nonpartisan."

. . . Petitioners are the City and County of San Francisco, its Board of Supervisors, and certain local officials. The individual respondents are ten registered voters residing in the City and County of San Francisco. They include the chairman and three members of the San Francisco Republican County Central Committee and one member of the San Francisco Democratic County Central Committee. Election Action, an association of

voters, is also a respondent, but it asserts no interest in relation to the issues before us different from that of the individual voters. . . .

Respondents filed this suit in the United States District Court for the Northern District of California. Their third cause of action challenged §6(b) and petitioners' acknowledged policy, based on that provision, of deleting any references to a party endorsement from the candidate statements included in voter pamphlets. As we understand it, petitioners print the pamphlets and pay the postage required to mail them to voters. The voter pamphlets contain statements prepared by candidates for office and arguments submitted by interested persons concerning other measures on the ballot. The complaint sought a declaration that Article II, §6 was unconstitutional, and an injunction preventing petitioners from editing candidate statements to delete references to party endorsements.

The District Court granted summary judgment for respondents on their third cause of action, declaring §6(b) unconstitutional and enjoining petitioners from enforcing it. The court entered judgment on this claim . . . and petitioners appealed. A Ninth Circuit panel reversed, but the en banc Court of Appeals affirmed the District Court's decision.

. . .

The free speech issues argued in the briefs filed here have fundamental and far-reaching import. For that very reason, we cannot decide the case based upon the amorphous and ill-defined factual record presented to us. Rules of justiciability serve to make the judicial process a principled one. Were we to depart from those rules, our disposition of the case would lack the clarity and force which ought to inform the exercise of judicial authority.

The judgment is vacated and the case remanded with instructions to dismiss respondents' third cause of action without prejudice.

Norman v. Reed
502 U.S. 279 (1992)

In these consolidated cases, we review a decision of the Supreme Court of Illinois barring petitioners in No. 90–1126 (petitioners) from appearing under the name of the Harold Washington Party on the November, 1990, ballot for Cook County offices. . . .

Under Illinois law, citizens organizing a new political party must canvass the electoral area in which they wish to field candidates and persuade voters to sign their nominating petitions. Organizers seeking to field candidates for statewide office must collect the signatures of 25,000 eligible voters, and, if they wish to run candidates solely for offices within a large "political subdivision" like Cook County, they need 25,000 signatures from the subdivision. If, however, the subdivision itself comprises large separate districts from which some of its officers are elected, party organizers seeking to fill such offices must collect 25,000 signatures from each district. If the organizers collect enough signatures to place their candidates on the ballot, their organization becomes a "new political party" under Illinois law, and if the party succeeds in gathering 5 percent of the vote in the next election, it becomes an "established political party," freed from the signature requirements of § 10–2. A political party that has not engaged in a statewide election, however, can be "established" only in a political subdivision where it has fielded candidates. A party is not established in Cook County, for example, merely because it has fared well in Chicago's municipal elections.

The Harold Washington Party (HWP or Party), named after the late mayor of Chicago, has been established in the city of Chicago since 1989. Petitioners were the principal organizers of an effort to expand the Party by establishing it in Cook County, and, as candidates for county office, they sought to run under the Party name in the November, 1990, elections.

Cook County comprises two electoral districts: the area corresponding to the city of Chicago (city district) and the rest of the county (suburban district). Although some county officials are elected at large by citizens of the entire county, members of the County Board of Commissioners are elected separately by the citizens of each district to fill county board seats specifically designated for that district. While certain petitioners wished to run for offices filled by election at large, others sought to capture the county board seats representing the city and suburban districts of Cook County.

Because the Party had previously engaged solely in Chicago municipal elections, petitioners were obliged to qualify as a "new party" in Cook County in order to run under the Party name. Accordingly, § 10–2 required them to obtain 25,000 nominating signatures in order to designate candidates for the at-large offices. And since petitioners wished to field candidates for the county board seats allocated to the separate districts, they also had to collect 25,000 signatures from each district. Petitioners gathered 44,000 signatures on the city-district component of their petition, but only 7,800 on the suburban component.

After petitioners filed the petition with the county authorities and presented their slate of candidates for both at-large and district-specific seats, respondent Dorothy Reed and several other interested voters (collectively, Reed) filed objections to the slate with the Cook County Officers Electoral Board (Board or Electoral Board). The Board rejected most of Reed's claims. First, it dismissed her contention that, because there was already an established political party named the "Harold Washington Party" in the city of Chicago, petitioners could not run under that name for the various county offices. Reed relied on the provision of Illinois law that a "new political party," which petitioners sought to form, "shall not bear the same name as, nor include the name of any established political party. . . ." The Board, however, suggested that a literal reading of §10–5 would effectively forbid a political party established in one political subdivision from expanding into others, and held that the provision's true purpose was

> to prevent persons who are not affiliated with a party from "latching on" to the popular party name, thereby promoting voter confusion and denigrating party cohesiveness.

The Board found no such dangers here, as Timothy Evans, the only HWP candidate to run in Chicago's most recent municipal election, had authorized petitioners to use the Party name.

The Board also rejected Reed's claim that petitioners had failed to gather enough nominating signatures to run as a party for any Cook County office. While the Board found that their failure to gather 25,000 signatures from the suburbs disqualified those who wished to run for the suburban district commissioner seats, it held that this failure was no reason under §10–2 to disqualify the candidates running under the Party name for city district and countywide offices. The Board observed that construing the statute to disqualify the entire Cook County slate on this basis would advance no valid state interest, and would raise serious constitutional concerns.

Finally, the Board rejected Reed's claim that, under §10–2, petitioners' failure to designate Party candidates for any of the judicial seats designated for either the city district, the suburban district, or the county at large disqualified the entire slate of candidates running under the Party name for all county offices. It decided, among other things, that §10–2 did not apply because the judgeships at issue were not offices of the same "political subdivision" as nonjudicial offices within Cook County.

On appeal, the Circuit Court of Cook County affirmed the Board's ruling on the use of the "Harold Washington Party" name, but on grounds different from the Board's. It ruled that, while Evans had no statutory power to authorize the use of the Party name, §10–2 implicitly confined the scope of §10–5 to cases where two parties seeking to use the same name coexist in the same political subdivision. Since Cook County and the city of Chicago are separate subdivisions, the Circuit Court found no violation of the Election Code.

The Circuit Court nonetheless held that, under the plain language of §10–2, petitioners' failure to obtain 25,000 signatures for the suburban district candidates doomed the entire slate, and it alternatively held that petitioners' failure to list Party candidates for judicial office compelled the same result. For these two independent reasons, the Circuit Court reversed the Board.

On review, the Supreme Court of Illinois held, in a brief written order, that §10–5 prohibited petitioners from using the "Harold Washington Party" name, and that their failure to gather enough signatures for the candidates in the suburban district races disqualified the entire slate. It expressly declined "to discuss other points raised on the appeal," and thus chose not to address the effect of the petitioners' failure to list candidates for County judgeships. . . .

Petitioners then applied for a stay from Justice Stevens, who, in his capacity as Circuit Justice, ordered the mandate of the Illinois Supreme Court to be "stayed or, if necessary, recalled" pending further review by this Court. On October 25, 1990, the full Court granted petitioners' application for stay pending the filing and disposition of a petition . . . thereby effectively reviving the Electoral Board's decision and permitting petitioners to run under the Party name in the November 6, 1990, Cook County election. According to the undisputed representation of the Board, while none of the HWP candidates was elected, several did receive over 5 percent of the vote, thus fulfilling, if the election stands, a necessary and apparently sufficient condition for the Party's qualification as an "established political party" within all or part of Cook County at the next election.

. . .

We start with respondent Reed's contention that we should treat the controversy as moot because the election is over. We should not. Even if the issue before us were limited to petitioners' eligibility to use the Party name on the 1990 ballot, that issue would be worthy of resolution as "capable of repetition, yet evading review." There would be every reason to expect the same parties to generate a similar, future controversy subject to identical time constraints if we should fail to resolve the constitutional issues that arose in 1990.

The matter before us carries a potential of even greater significance, however. As we have noted, the 1990 electoral results would entitle the HWP to enter the next election as an established party in all or part of Cook County, freed from the petition requirements of §10–2, so long as its candidates were entitled to the places on the ballot

that our stay order effectively gave them. This underscores the vitality of the questions posed, even though the election that gave them life is now behind us.

. . .

Reversing the judgment of the Circuit Court, the State Supreme Court held, under §10–5, that the Cook County candidates could not claim to represent the "Harold Washington Party" because there already was a party by that name in the city of Chicago. The court gave no reasons for so concluding beyond declaring that "petitioner[s'] use of the Harold Washington Party name in their petition . . . violate[d] the provisions of section 10–5," which, the court noted, "prohibits use of the name of an established political party." Thus, the issue on review is not whether the Chicago HWP and the Cook County HWP are in some sense "separate parties," but whether and how candidates running for county office may adopt the name of a party established only in the city.

While the Board based its answer to this question on a determination that the city HWP had authorized petitioners to use the Party name, the State Supreme Court's order seems to exclude the very possibility of authorization, reading the prohibition on the "use of the name of an established political party" so literally as to bar candidates running in one political subdivision from ever using the name of a political party established only in another. . . .

To prevent misrepresentation and electoral confusion, Illinois may, of course, prohibit candidates running for office in one subdivision from adopting the name of a party established in another if they are not in any way affiliated with the party. The State's interest is particularly strong where, as here, the party and its self-described candidates coexist in the same geographical area. But Illinois could avoid these ills merely by requiring the candidates to get formal permission to use the name from the established party they seek to represent, a simple expedient for fostering an informed electorate without suppressing the growth of small parties. Thus, the State Supreme Court's inhospitable reading of §10–5 sweeps broader than necessary to advance electoral order, and accordingly violates the First Amendment right of political association.

. . .

. . . Our review of §10–2 reveals the possibility that Illinois law empowers a newly established party's candidate or candidates (here, Evans) merely to appoint party "committeemen," whose authority to "manage and control the affairs" of the party might include an exclusive right to authorize the use of its name outside the party's original political subdivision. It seems unlikely, however, that the Supreme Court of Illinois had such reasoning in mind. Any limitation on Evans' power to authorize likeminded candidates to use the Party name would have had to arise under §10–2, whereas the order below held simply that petitioners' use of the Party name "violate[d] the provisions of section 10–5." In any event, it is not this Court's role to review a state court decision on the basis of inconclusive and unargued theories of state law that the state court itself found unworthy of mention.

As an alternative basis for prohibiting petitioners from running together under the Party name, the Supreme Court of Illinois invoked the statutory requirement of §10–2 that "[e]ach component of the petition for each district . . . be signed by [25,000] qualified voters of the district. . . ." The court apparently held that disqualification of a party's entire slate of candidates is the appropriate penalty for failing to meet this requirement, and it accordingly treated petitioners' failure to collect enough signatures for their sub-urban district candidates as an adequate ground for disqualifying every candidate running under the HWP name in Cook County.

. . .

Under the interpretation of §10–2 rendered below . . . Illinois law retains the constitutional flaw at issue in *Socialist Workers* by effectively increasing the signature requirement applicable to elections for at least some offices in subdivisions with separate districts. Under that interpretation, the failure of a party's organizers to obtain 25,000 signatures for each district in which they run candidates disqualifies the party's candidates in all races within the subdivision. Thus, a prerequisite to establishing a new political party in such multi-district subdivisions is some multiple of the number of signatures required of new statewide parties. Since petitioners chose to field candidates for the county board seats allocated to the separate districts and, as required by state law, used the "component" (i.e., district-specific) form of nominating petition, the State Supreme Court's construction of §10–2 required petitioners to accumulate 50,000 signatures (25,000 from the city district and another 25,000 from the suburbs) to run any candidates in Cook County elections. The State may not do this in the face of *Socialist Workers*, which forbids it to require petitioners to gather twice as many signatures to field candidates in Cook County as they would need statewide.

Reed nonetheless tries to skirt *Socialist Workers* by advancing what she claims to be a state interest, not addressed by the earlier case, in ensuring that the electoral support for new parties in a multidistrict political subdivision extends to every district. Accepting the legitimacy of the interest claimed would not, however, excuse the requirement's unconstitutional breadth. Illinois might have compelled the organizers of a new party to demonstrate a distribution of support throughout Cook County without, at the same time, raising the overall quantum of needed support above what the State expects of new parties fielding candidates only for statewide office. The State might, for example, have required some minimum number of signatures from each of the component districts, while maintaining the total signature requirement at 25,000. While we express no opinion as to the constitutionality of any such requirement, what we have said demonstrates that Illinois has not chosen the most narrowly tailored means of advancing even the interest that Reed suggests.

. . . Illinois does not require a new party fielding candidates solely for statewide office to apportion its nominating signatures among the various counties or other political subdivisions of the State. Organizers of a new party could therefore win access to the statewide ballot, but not the Cook County ballot, by collecting all 25,000 signatures from the county's city district. But if the State deems it unimportant to ensure that new statewide parties enjoy any distribution of support, it requires elusive logic to demonstrate a serious state interest in demanding such a distribution for new local parties. Thus . . . the State's requirements for access to the statewide ballot become criteria in the first instance for judging whether rules of access to local ballots are narrow enough to pass constitutional muster. Reed has adduced no justification for the disparity here.

. . .

This case presents one final issue, which we are unable to resolve. Some of Cook County's judges are elected by citizens of the entire county, and others by citizens of the separate districts. In responding to Reed's objection that the HWP had not fielded candidates for any elected judicial offices in Cook County, the Circuit Court held that, under §10–2, "the exclusion of judicial can-

didates on the slate was a failure to fulfill the 'complete slate requirement' of the Election Code." The court then overruled the Electoral Board and treated this failure as an alternative ground for invalidating the Party's entire slate.

We decline to consider whether that ruling was constitutional. The Supreme Court of Illinois itself did not address it, and therefore did not decide whether, under Illinois law, the Party's omission of judicial candidates doomed the entire slate. We therefore remand the case to that court for its prompt resolution of this issue.

The judgment of the State Supreme Court is affirmed in part and reversed in part, and the case is remanded for further proceedings not inconsistent with this opinion.

Morse v. Republican Party of Virginia
517 U.S. 186 (1996)

In 1994, all registered voters in Virginia who were willing to declare their intent to support the Republican Party's nominees for public office at the next election could participate in the nomination of the Party's candidate for the office of United States Senator if they paid either a $35 or $45 registration fee. Appellants contend that the imposition of that fee as a condition precedent to participation in the candidate selection process was a poll tax prohibited by the Voting Rights Act of 1965. The questions we must decide are whether §5 of the Act required preclearance of the Party's decision to exact the fee and whether appellants were permitted to challenge it as a poll tax prohibited by §10.

On December 16, 1993, the Republican Party of Virginia (Party) issued a call for a state convention to be held on June 3, 1994, to nominate the Republican candidate for United States Senator. The call invited all registered voters in Virginia to participate in local mass meetings, canvasses, or conventions to be conducted by officials of the Party. Any voter could be certified as a delegate to the state convention by a local political committee upon payment of a registration fee of $35 or $45 depending on the date of certification. Over 14,000 voters paid the fee and took part in the convention.

In response to the call, appellants Bartholomew, Enderson, and Morse sought to become delegates to the convention. As a registered voter in Virginia willing to declare his or her intent to support the Party's nominee, each was eligible to participate upon payment of the registration fee. Bartholomew and Enderson refused to pay the fee, and did not become delegates; Morse paid the fee with funds advanced by supporters of the eventual nominee.

On May 2, 1994, appellants filed a complaint in the United States District Court for the Western District of Virginia alleging that the imposition of the registration fee violated §§5 and 10 of the Voting Rights Act as well as the Equal Protection Clause of the Fourteenth Amendment and the Twenty-fourth Amendment to the Constitution. They sought an injunction preventing the Party from imposing the fee and ordering it to return the fee paid by Morse. As §§5 and 10 require, a three-judge District Court was convened to consider the statutory claims. That court remanded the two constitutional claims to a single-judge District Court, and, after expedited briefing and argument, granted the Party's motion to dismiss the §5 and §10 claims.

After noting "a general rule" that political parties are subject to §5 to the extent that they are empowered to conduct primary elections, the Court gave two reasons for concluding that the rule did not apply to the selection of delegates to a state nominating convention. First, it read a regulation promulgated by the Attorney General as disavowing §5 coverage of political party activities other than the conduct of primary elections. Second, it relied on our summary affirmance of the District Court's holding in *Williams v. Democratic Party of Georgia*, that §5 does not cover a party's decision to change its method of selecting delegates to a national convention. Its dismissal of the §10 claim rested on its view that only the Attorney General has authority to enforce that section of the Act.

. . .

. . . We are satisfied that the Department's interpretation of its own regulation is correct. Accordingly, we conclude that the regulation required preclearance of the Party's delegate filing fee.

. . .

The District Court was therefore incorrect to base its decision on either the Attorney General's regulation or on our summary affirmance in *Williams*. The Party's activities fall directly within the scope of the regulation. . . .

. . .

. . . By limiting the opportunity for voters to participate in the Party's convention, the fee undercuts their influence on the field of candidates whose names will appear on the ballot, and thus weakens the "effectiveness" of their votes cast in the general election itself. . . .

. . . A fee of $45 to cast a vote for the Party nominee is, if anything, a more onerous burden than a mere obligation to include certain public information about oneself next to one's name on a nominating petition. . . .

. . .

The reference to "party office" in §14, which defines the terms "vote" and "voting" as they appear throughout the Act, reinforces this construction of §5. Section 14 specifically recognizes that the selection of persons for "party office" is one type of action that may determine the effectiveness of a vote in the general election. Delegates to a party convention are party officers. The phrase "votes cast with respect to candidates for public or party office" in §14 is broad enough to encompass a variety of methods of voting beyond a formal election. The Party itself recognizes this point, for both in its brief to this Court and in its Plan of Organization, it repeatedly characterizes its own method of selecting these delegates as an "election."

. . . Under the broad sweep of this language, exclusion from a nominating convention would qualify as a violation. Section 2 "adopts the functional view of 'political process'" and applies to "any phase of the electoral process."

. . .

The distinction between a primary and a nominating convention is just another variation in electoral practices that §5 was intended to cover. The imposition of a $45 fee on the privilege of participating in the selection of the Party's nominee for the United States Senate is equally a practice or procedure relating to voting whether the selection is made by primary election or by a "convention" in which every voter willing to pay the fee is eligible to cast a vote. A primary election would not cease to be a practice relating to voting if the Party imposed such a high fee that only 14,000 voters cast ballots; nor should a "convention" performing the same electoral function as a primary avoid coverage because fewer voters participate in the process than normally vote in a primary. . . .

. . .

Appellees advance two practical objections to our interpretation of §5: that it will create an administrative nightmare for political parties as well as the Department of Justice by requiring

preclearance of a multitude of minor changes in party practices, and that it threatens to abridge associational rights protected by the First Amendment. Each of these objections merits a response.

With respect to the first, it is important to emphasize the limitations spelled out in the Attorney General's regulation. To be subject to preclearance, a change must be one "affecting voting." Examples of changes that are not covered include "changes with respect to the recruitment of party members, the conduct of political campaigns, and the drafting of party platforms." The line between changes that are covered and those that are not may be difficult to articulate in the abstract, but, given the fact that the Regulation has been in effect since 1981 and does not appear to have imposed any unmanageable burdens on covered jurisdictions, it seems likely that the administrative concerns described by the Party are more theoretical than practical. Indeed, past cases in which we were required to construe the Act evoked similar protestations that the advocated construction would prove administratively unworkable. Those fears were not borne out, and we think it no more likely that these will either.

With respect to the second argument, we wholeheartedly agree with appellees that the right of association of members of a political party "is a basic constitutional freedom," and that "governmental action that may have the effect of curtailing freedom to associate is subject to the closest scrutiny." Such scrutiny, however, could not justify a major political party's decision to exclude eligible voters from the candidate selection process because of their race; the Fifteenth Amendment and our cases construing its application to political parties foreclose such a possibility.

Moreover, appellees have not argued that the

registration fee at issue in this case—which is challenged because it curtails the freedom of association of eligible voters arguably in conflict with the interests protected by the Twenty-fourth Amendment—is itself protected by the First Amendment. Rather, they have suggested that hypothetical cases unrelated to the facts of this case might implicate First Amendment concerns that would foreclose application of the preclearance requirement. It is sufficient for us now to respond that we find no constitutional impediment to enforcing §5 in the case before us. We leave consideration of hypothetical concerns for another day.

. . .

. . . Even if it mattered whether §10 created rights or remedies, the other provisions of the Act indicate that the anti-poll tax provision established a right to vote without paying a fee.

. . .

Last, appellees argue that §10 does not apply to the Party's nominating convention because a delegate registration fee is not a poll tax. This argument addresses the merits, rather than the right to sue. Without reaching the merits, the District Court dismissed appellants' claim because it held there was no private cause of action under §10. Since we hold that this conclusion is incorrect, we postpone any consideration of the merits until after they have been addressed by the District Court.

The judgment of the District Court is reversed, and the case is remanded for further proceedings consistent with this opinion.

Timmons v. Twin Cities Area New Party
520 U.S. 351 (1997)

Respondent is a chartered chapter of the national New Party. Petitioners are Minnesota election officials. In April 1994, Minnesota State Representative Andy Dawkins was running unopposed in the Minnesota Democratic-Farmer-Labor Party's (DFL) primary. That same month, New Party members chose Dawkins as their candidate for the same office in the November 1994 general election. Neither Dawkins nor the DFL objected, and Dawkins signed the required affidavit of candidacy for the New Party. Minnesota, however, prohibits fusion candidacies. Because Dawkins had already filed as a candidate for the DFL's nomination, local election officials refused to accept the New Party's nominating petition.

The New Party filed suit in United States District Court, contending that Minnesota's anti-fusion laws violated the Party's associational rights under the First and Fourteenth Amendments. The District Court granted summary judgment for the state defendants, concluding that Minnesota's fusion ban was "a valid and nondiscriminatory regulation of the election process," and noting that "issues concerning the mechanics of choosing candidates . . . are, in large part, matters of policy best left to the deliberative bodies themselves."

The Court of Appeals reversed. First, the court determined that Minnesota's fusion ban "unquestionably" and "severe[ly]" burdened the New Party's "freedom to select a standard bearer who best represents the party's ideologies and preferences" and its right to "broaden the base of public participation in and support for [its] activities." The court then decided that Minnesota's absolute ban on multiple party nominations was "broader than necessary to serve the State's asserted interests" in avoiding intraparty discord and party-splintering, maintaining a stable political system, and avoiding voter confusion, and that the State's remaining concerns about multiple party nomination were "simply unjustified in this case." The court noted, however, that the Court of Appeals for the Seventh Circuit had upheld Wisconsin's similar fusion ban. . . . Nonetheless, the court concluded that Minnesota's fusion ban provisions, were unconstitutional because they severely burdened the New Party's associational rights and were not narrowly tailored to advance Minnesota's valid interests. . . .

. . .

The New Party's claim that it has a right to select its own candidate is uncontroversial, so far as it goes. That is, the New Party, and not someone else, has the right to select the New Party's "standard bearer." It does not follow, though, that a party is absolutely entitled to have its nominee appear on the ballot as that party's candidate. A particular candidate might be ineligible for office, unwilling to serve, or, as here, another party's candidate. That a particular individual may not appear on the ballot as a particular party's candidate does not severely burden that party's association rights.

The New Party relies on *Eu v. San Francisco County Democratic Central Committee* and *Tashjian v. Republican Party of Connecticut.* In *Eu,* we struck down California election provisions that prohibited political parties from endorsing candidates in party primaries and regulated parties' internal affairs and structure. And, in *Tashjian,* we held that Connecticut's closed primary statute, which required voters in a party primary to be registered party members, interfered with a party's associational rights by limiting "the group of registered voters whom the Party may invite to participate in the basic function of selecting the Party's candidates." But while *Tashjian* and *Eu* involved regulation of political parties' internal affairs and core associational activities, Minnesota's fusion ban does not. The ban, which applies to major and minor

parties alike, simply precludes one party's candidate from appearing on the ballot, as that party's candidate, if already nominated by another party.

Respondent is free to try to convince Representative Dawkins to be the New Party's, not the DFL's, candidate. Whether the Party still wants to endorse a candidate who, because of the fusion ban, will not appear on the ballot as the Party's candidate, is up to the Party.

The Court of Appeals also held that Minnesota's laws "keep the New Party from developing consensual political alliances, and thus broadening the base of public participation in and support for its activities." . . . In the view of the Court of Appeals, Minnesota's fusion ban forces members of the new party to make a "no-win choice" between voting for "candidates with no realistic chance of winning, defect[ing] from their party and vot[ing] for a candidate who does, or declin[ing] to vote at all."

But Minnesota has not directly precluded minor political parties from developing and organizing. Nor has Minnesota excluded a particular group of citizens, or a political party, from participation in the election process. The New Party remains free to endorse whom it likes, to ally itself with others, to nominate candidates for office, and to spread its message to all who will listen.

The Court of Appeals emphasized its belief that, without fusion-based alliances, minor parties cannot thrive. This is a predictive judgment which is by no means self-evident. But, more importantly, the supposed benefits of fusion to minor parties does not require that Minnesota permit it. Many features of our political system— e.g., single-member districts, "first past the post" elections, and the high costs of campaigning— make it difficult for third parties to succeed in American politics. But the Constitution does not require States to permit fusion any more than it

requires them to move to proportional representation elections or public financing of campaigns.

. . .

It is true that Minnesota's fusion ban prevents
the New Party from using the ballot to communicate to the public that it supports a particular
candidate who is already another party's candidate. In addition, the ban shuts off one possible
avenue a party might use to send a message to its
preferred candidate because, with fusion, a candidate who wins an election on the basis of two
parties' votes will likely know more—if the parties' votes are counted separately—about the particular wishes and ideals of his constituency. We
are unpersuaded, however, by the Party's contention that it has a right to use the ballot itself to
send a particularized message, to its candidate
and to the voters, about the nature of its support
for the candidate. Ballots serve primarily to elect
candidates, not as fora for political expression.
Like all parties in Minnesota, the New Party is able
to use the ballot to communicate information about
itself and its candidate to the voters, so long as that
candidate is not already someone else's candidate.
The Party retains great latitude in its ability to communicate ideas to voters and candidates through its
participation in the campaign, and Party members
may campaign for, endorse, and vote for their preferred candidate even if he is listed on the ballot as
another party's candidate.

In sum, Minnesota's laws do not restrict the
ability of the New Party and its members to endorse, support, or vote for anyone they like. The
laws do not directly limit the Party's access to
the ballot. They are silent on parties' internal
structure, governance, and policymaking. Instead,
these provisions reduce the universe of potential
candidates who may appear on the ballot as the
Party's nominee only by ruling out those few individuals who both have already agreed to be

another party's candidate and also, if forced to
choose, themselves prefer that other party. They
also limit, slightly, the Party's ability to send a
message to the voters and to its preferred candidates. We conclude that the burdens Minnesota
imposes on the Party's First and Fourteenth
Amendment associational rights—though not
trivial—are not severe.

The Court of Appeals determined that Minnesota's fusion ban imposed "severe" burdens on
the New Party's associational rights, and so it
required the State to show that the ban was narrowly tailored to serve compelling state interests.
We disagree; given the burdens imposed, the bar
is not so high. Instead, the State's asserted regulatory interests need only be "sufficiently weighty
to justify the limitation" imposed on the Party's
rights. Nor do we require elaborate, empirical
verification of the weightiness of the State's asserted justifications.

The Court of Appeals acknowledged Minnesota's interests in avoiding voter confusion and
overcrowded ballots, preventing party-splintering
and disruptions of the two party system, and
being able to clearly identify the election winner. Similarly, the Seventh Circuit . . . noted
Wisconsin's "compelling" interests in avoiding
voter confusion, preserving the integrity of the
election process, and maintaining a stable political system. Minnesota argues here that its fusion
ban is justified by its interests in avoiding voter
confusion, promoting candidate competition (by
reserving limited ballot space for opposing candidates), preventing electoral distortions and ballot manipulations, and discouraging party
splintering and "unrestrained factionalism."

States certainly have an interest in protecting
the integrity, fairness, and efficiency of their ballots and election processes as means for electing
public officials. Petitioners contend that a candi-

date or party could easily exploit fusion as a way of associating his or its name with popular slogans and catch phrases.

. . .

Whether or not the putative "fusion" candidates' names appeared on one or four ballot lines, such maneuvering would undermine the ballot's purpose by transforming it from a means of choosing candidates to a billboard for political advertising. The New Party responds to this concern, ironically enough, by insisting that the State could avoid such manipulation by adopting more demanding ballot access standards, rather than prohibiting multiple party nomination. However . . . because the burdens the fusion ban imposes on the Party's associational rights are not severe, the State need not narrowly tailor the means it chooses to promote ballot integrity. The Constitution does not require that Minnesota compromise the policy choices embodied in its ballot access requirements to accommodate the New Party's fusion strategy.

Relatedly, petitioners urge that permitting fusion would undercut Minnesota's ballot access regime by allowing minor parties to capitalize on the popularity of another party's candidate, rather than on their own appeal to the voters, in order to secure access to the ballot. That is, voters who might not sign a minor party's nominating petition based on the party's own views and candidates might do so if they viewed the minor party as just another way of nominating the same person nominated by one of the major parties. Thus, Minnesota fears that fusion would enable minor parties, by nominating a major party's candidate, to bootstrap their way to major party status in the next election and circumvent the State's nominating petition requirement for minor parties. The State surely has a valid interest in making sure that minor and third parties who are granted access to the ballot are bona fide and actu-

ally supported, on their own merits, by those who have provided the statutorily required petition or ballot support.

States also have a strong interest in the stability of their political systems. This interest does not permit a State to completely insulate the two party system from minor parties' or independent candidates' competition and influence, nor is it a paternalistic license for States to protect political parties from the consequences of their own internal disagreements. That said, the States' interest permits them to enact reasonable election regulations that may, in practice, favor the traditional two party system, and that temper the destabilizing effects of party-splintering and excessive factionalism. The Constitution permits the Minnesota Legislature to decide that political stability is best served through a healthy two party system. And while an interest in securing the perceived benefits of a stable two party system will not justify unreasonably exclusionary restrictions, States need not remove all of the many hurdles third parties face in the American political arena today.

. . .

Minnesota's fusion ban is far less burdensome than the disaffiliation rule upheld in *Storer*, and is justified by similarly weighty state interests. . . . Minnesota's fusion ban is not nearly so restrictive; the challenged provisions say nothing about the previous party affiliation of would-be candidates, but only require that, in order to appear on the ballot, a candidate not be the nominee of more than one party. . . . Minnesota's precludes only a handful who freely choose to be so limited. . . . Minnesota's fusion ban only prohibits a candidate from being named twice.

We conclude that the burdens Minnesota's fusion ban imposes on the New Party's associational rights are justified by "correspondingly weighty" valid state interests in ballot integrity and political stability. In deciding that Minnesota's fusion ban does not unconstitutionally burden the New Party's First and Fourteenth Amendment rights, we express no views on the New Party's policy-based arguments concerning the wisdom of fusion. It may well be that, as support for new political parties increases, these arguments will carry the day in some States' legislatures. But the Constitution does not require Minnesota, and the approximately forty other States that do not permit fusion, to allow it. The judgment of the Court of Appeals is reversed.

California Democratic Party v. Jones
530 U.S. ___ (2000)

Under California law, a candidate for public office has two routes to gain access to the general ballot for most state and federal elective offices. He may receive the nomination of a qualified political party by winning its primary, or he may file as an independent by obtaining (for a statewide race) the signatures of 1 percent of the State's electorate or (for other races) the signatures of 3 percent of the voting population of the area represented by the office in contest.

Until 1996, to determine the nominees of qualified parties California held what is known as a "closed" partisan primary, in which only persons who are members of the political party . . . can vote on its nominee. In 1996 the citizens of California adopted by initiative Proposition 198. . . . Proposition 198 changed California's partisan primary from a closed primary to a blanket primary. Under the new system, "[a]ll persons entitled to vote, including those not affiliated with any political party, shall have the right to vote . . . for any candidate regardless of the candidate's

political affiliation." . . . [A]s a result of Proposition 198 each voter's primary ballot now lists every candidate regardless of party affiliation and allows the voter to choose freely among them. It remains the case, however, that the candidate of each party who wins the greatest number of votes "is the nominee of that party at the ensuing general election."

Petitioners in this case are four political parties—the California Democratic Party, the California Republican Party, the Libertarian Party of California, and the Peace and Freedom Party—each of which has a rule prohibiting persons not members of the party from voting in the party's primary. Petitioners brought suit in the United States District Court for the Eastern District of California against respondent California Secretary of State, alleging . . . that California's blanket primary violated their First Amendment rights of association, and seeking declaratory and injunctive relief. The group Californians for an Open Primary, also respondent, intervened as a party defendant. The District Court recognized that the new law would inject into each party's primary substantial numbers of voters unaffiliated with the party. It further recognized that this might result in selection of a nominee different from the one party members would select, or at the least cause the same nominee to commit himself to different positions. Nevertheless, the District Court held that the burden on petitioners' rights of association was not a severe one, and was justified by state interests ultimately reducing to this: "enhanc[ing] the democratic nature of the election process and the representativeness of elected officials." The Ninth Circuit, adopting the District Court's opinion as its own, affirmed. . . .

Respondents rest their defense of the blanket primary upon the proposition that primaries play an integral role in citizens' selection of public officials. As a consequence, they contend, primaries are public rather than private proceedings, and the States may and must play a role in ensuring that they serve the public interest. . . .

. . .

In no area is the political association's right to exclude more important than in the process of selecting its nominee. That process often determines the party's positions on the most significant public policy issues of the day, and even when those positions are predetermined it is the nominee who becomes the party's ambassador to the general electorate in winning it over to the party's views. . . .

Unsurprisingly, our cases vigorously affirm the special place the First Amendment reserves for, and the special protection it accords, the process by which a political party "select[s] a standard bearer who best represents the party's ideologies and preferences." The moment of choosing the party's nominee . . . is "the crucial juncture at which the appeal to common principles may be translated into concerted action, and hence to political power in the community."

. . .

. . . Proposition 198 forces political parties to associate with . . . those who, at best, have refused to affiliate with the party, and, at worst, have expressly affiliated with a rival. In this respect, it is qualitatively different from a closed primary. Under that system, even when it is made quite easy for a voter to change his party affiliation the day of the primary, and thus, in some sense, to "cross over," at least he must formally become a member of the party; and once he does so, he is limited to voting for candidates of that party.

The evidence in this case demonstrates that under California's blanket primary system, the prospect of having a party's nominee determined by adherents of an opposing party is far from re-

mote. . . . The impact of voting by nonparty members is much greater upon minor parties, such as the Libertarian Party and the Peace and Freedom Party. In the first primaries these parties conducted following California's implementation of Proposition 198, the total votes cast for party candidates in some races was more than double the total number of registered party members.

. . .

. . . [T]he deleterious effects of Proposition 198 are not limited to altering the identity of the nominee. Even when the person favored by a majority of the party members prevails, he will have prevailed by taking somewhat different positions–and, should he be elected, will continue to take somewhat different positions in order to be renominated. . . . It encourages candidates— and officeholders who hope to be renominated— to curry favor with persons whose views are more "centrist" than those of the party base. In effect, Proposition 198 has simply moved the general election one step earlier in the process, at the expense of the parties' ability to perform the "basic function" of choosing their own leaders.

Nor can we accept the Court of Appeals' contention that the burden imposed by Proposition 198 is minor because petitioners are free to endorse and financially support the candidate of their choice in the primary. The ability of the party leadership to endorse a candidate is simply no substitute for the party members' ability to choose their own nominee. . . . [T]he ability of the party leadership to endorse a candidate does not assist the party rank and file, who may not themselves agree with the party leadership, but do not want the party's choice decided by outsiders.

We are similarly unconvinced by respondents' claim that the burden is not severe because Proposition 198 does not limit the parties from engaging fully in other traditional party behavior, such as ensuring orderly internal party governance, maintaining party discipline in the legislature, and conducting campaigns. The accuracy of this assertion is highly questionable, at least as to the first two activities. That party nominees will be equally observant of internal party procedures and equally respectful of party discipline when their nomination depends on the general electorate rather than on the party faithful seems to us improbable. Respondents themselves suggest as much when they assert that the blanket primary system "will lead to the election of more representative 'problem solvers' who are less beholden to party officials." In the end, however, the effect of Proposition 198 on these other activities is beside the point. We have consistently refused to overlook an unconstitutional restriction upon some First Amendment activity simply because it leaves other First Amendment activity unimpaired. There is simply no substitute for a party's selecting its own candidates.

In sum, Proposition 198 forces petitioners to adulterate their candidate-selection process . . . by opening it up to persons wholly unaffiliated with the party. Such forced association has the likely outcome . . . of changing the parties' message. We can think of no heavier burden on a political party's associational freedom. Proposition 198 is therefore unconstitutional unless it is narrowly tailored to serve a compelling state interest. . . .

. . .

Respondents' legitimate state interests and petitioners' First Amendment rights are not inherently incompatible. To the extent they are in this case, the State of California has made them so by forcing political parties to associate with those who do not share their beliefs. And it has done this at the "crucial juncture" at which party members traditionally find their collective voice and select their spokesman. The burden Proposition 198 places on petitioners' rights of political association is both severe and unnecessary. The judgment for the Court of Appeals for the Ninth Circuit is reversed.

7

Campaign Contributions, Finance, and Spending

Campaign finance has been a major political issue that has not escaped attention from the Supreme Court. The ongoing debate is how to restrict contributions that might lead to corruption without restricting political rights, free speech, and associational rights.

Newberry v. United States
256 U.S. 232 (1921)

Plaintiffs in error—Truman H. Newberry, Paul H. King, and fifteen others—were found guilty of conspiring to violate the federal Corrupt Practices Act, which provides:

> No candidate for Representative in Congress or for Senator of the United States shall give, contribute, expend, use, or promise, or cause to be given, contributed, expended, used, or promised, in procuring his nomination and election any sum, in the aggregate, in excess of the amount which he may lawfully give, contribute, expend, or promise under the laws of the state in which he resides: Provided, that no candidate for Representative in Congress shall give, contribute, expend, use, or promise any sum, in the aggregate, exceeding five thousand dollars in any campaign for his nomination and election; and no candidate for Senator of the United States shall give, contribute, expend, use, or promise any sum, in the aggregate, exceeding ten thousand dollars in any campaign for his nomination and election:Provided further, that money expended by any such candidate to meet and discharge any assessment, fee, or charge made

> or levied upon candidates by the laws of the state in which he resides, or for his necessary personal expenses, incurred for himself alone, for travel and subsistence, stationery and postage, writing or printing (other than in newspapers), and distributing letters, circulars, and posters, and for telegraph and telephone service, shall not be regarded as an expenditure within the meaning of this section, and shall not be considered any part of the sum herein fixed as the limit of expense and need not be shown in the statements herein required to be filed.

Act No. 109, Sec. I, Michigan Legislature, 1913, prohibits expenditure by or on behalf of a candidate, to be paid by him, in securing his nomination, of any sum exceeding 25 percent of one year's compensation; and puts like limitation upon expenditures to obtain election after nomination.

Taken with the state enactment, the federal statute in effect declares a candidate for the United States Senate punishable by fine and imprisonment, if . . . he gives, contributes, expends, uses, promises or causes to be given, contributed, expended, used, or promised in procuring his nomination and election more than $3,750–one-half of one year's salary. Under the construction of the act urged by the government and adopted by the court below it is not necessary that the inhibited sum be paid, promised or expended by the candidate himself, or be devoted to any secret or immoral purpose. . . .

The indictment charges: That Truman H. Newberry became a candidate for the Republican nomination for United States Senator from Michigan at the primary election held August 27, 1918;

that by reason of selection and nomination therein he became a candidate at the general election, November 5, 1918; that he and 134 others . . . from December 1, 1917, to November 5, 1918, unlawfully and feloniously did conspire, combine, confederate, and agree together to commit the offense on his part of wilfully violating the Act of Congress . . . by giving, contributing, expending, and using and by causing to be given, contributed, expended, and used, in procuring his nomination and election at said primary and general elections, a greater sum than the laws of Michigan permitted and above $10,000, to wit, $100,000, and on the part of the other defendants of aiding, counseling, inducing, and procuring Newberry as such candidate to give, contribute, expend, and use or cause to be given, contributed, expended, and used said large and excessive sum in order to procure his nomination and election. Plaintiffs in error were convicted under count one, set out in the margin. The court below overruled a duly interposed demurrer which challenged the constitutionality of section 8. . . .

Manifestly, this section applies not only to final elections for choosing Senators but also to primaries and conventions of political parties for selection of candidates. Michigan and many other states undertake to control these primaries by statutes and give recognition to their results. And the ultimate question for solution here is whether under the grant of power to regulate "the manner of holding elections" Congress may fix the maximum sum which a candidate therein may spend, or advise or cause to be contributed and spent by others to procure his nomination.

. . .

Undoubtedly elections within the original intendment of section 4 were those wherein Senators should be chosen by Legislatures and Representatives by voters possessing "the qualifications req-

uisite for electors of the most numerous branch of the state Legislature." The Seventeenth Amendment, which directs that Senators be chosen by the people, neither announced nor requires a new meaning of election and the word now has the same general significance as it did when the Constitution came into existence—final choice of an officer by the duly qualified electors. Primaries were then unknown. Moreover, they are in no sense elections for an office but merely methods by which party adherents agree upon candidates whom they intend to offer and support for ultimate choice by all qualified electors. General provisions touching elections in Constitutions or statutes are not necessarily applicable to primaries-the two things are radically different. And this view has been declared by many state courts.

. . .

. . . Our immediate concern is with the clause which grants power by law to regulate the "manner of holding elections for Senators and Representatives"—not broadly to regulate them. As an incident to the grant there is, of course, power to make all laws which shall be necessary and proper for carrying it into effect. Although the Seventeenth Amendment now requires Senators to be chosen by the people, reference to the original plan of selection by the Legislatures may aid in interpretation.

. . .

The judgment of the court below must be reversed, and the cause remanded for further proceedings in conformity with this opinion.

United States v. Norris
300 U.S. 564 (1937)

April 10, 1930, the United States Senate, by resolution, empowered the Vice President to appoint a special committee to investigate campaign expenditures of candidates for the Senate, the committee to sit at such times and places as it should deem proper, to require attendance of witnesses and production of books and papers, and to act by any subcommittee. Failure to obey process of the committee or refusal to answer questions pertinent to the investigation was to be punished according to law. The resolution recited that the Senate desired facts to aid it in enacting remedial legislation and in deciding contests involving senatorial elections. The committee so appointed authorized Senator Nye, the Chairman, to act as a subcommittee and to name a subcommittee of one or more members. Such a subcommittee, consisting of Senators Nye and Dale, met September 22, 1930, at Lincoln, Nebraska. The Nebraska primary election had been held on August 12, 1930; the general election at which the names of senatorial candidates were to appear on the ballots was to be held the following November. Senator George W. Norris of McCook, Nebraska, had filed for the Republican primaries on January 1, 1930, and W. M. Stebbins had, on November 12, 1929, filed his acceptance of Republican nominating petitions in his behalf. The respondent had attempted to file for the same primaries on July 5, 1930, but the Supreme Court of the state had ruled on July 18 that his application was not filed within the time prescribed by law and had ordered the Secretary of State to omit his name from the list of candidates for United States Senator to be certified to county clerks and election commissioners. In the light of these facts the subcommittee summoned the respondent to testify on September 22, 1930. . . .

> After the conclusion of his testimony the subcommittee adjourned until the following day, when several witnesses were examined, amongst whom was one Johnson. The respondent was present and heard Johnson testify. After consulting his counsel, he asked and was granted permission to return to the stand. He then admitted the receipt from Johnson of $50 to be used for his filing fee and a $500 government bond, and stated that he had cashed the bond through his brother at North Platte.

June 23, 1931, the grand jury for the District of Nebraska indicted the respondent for perjury. . . . On his trial the government proved the facts as above outlined and called Johnson as a witness who testified that, pursuant to a plan devised by himself and others, he had approached the respondent on June 30 and requested him not to file as a candidate for Railway Commissioner but to file for United States Senator telling him that if he were willing to do this the Republican Party would support him and $50 would at once be paid him for his filing fee and $500, the estimated amount of his campaign expenses, would also be paid to him. He swore that, on July 2, he gave the respondent $50 and, on the next day, handed him a $500 bond.

The respondent took the witness stand and admitted that he "[knew] at the time of testifying (before the Senate Committee) that he had received $500 and $50 and what he was saying was not true."

. . .

. . . The jury rendered a verdict of guilty, sentence was imposed, and the respondent appealed to the Circuit Court of Appeals which reversed the judgment. . . .

> The respondent insists that reversal of his conviction was right because (1) Congress exceeded its power in adopting Resolution No. 215, since it cannot legislate for the purpose of regulating primary elections; (2) perjury can only be committed if an oath be taken in a case wherein a law of the United States authorizes an oath to be administered, and the committee hearing was not such a case; (3) the false testimony concerned an immaterial matter; and (4) the whole of a witness' evidence must be taken together and, if his testimony be ulti-

mately true, his indictment for perjury cannot be predicated thereon.

. . .

The judgment of the Circuit Court of Appeals must be reversed and that of the District Court affirmed.

McDonald v. Commissioner of Internal Revenue
323 U.S. 57 (1944)

In December 1938, the Governor of Pennsylvania appointed petitioner to serve an unexpired term as Judge of the Court of Common Pleas of Luzerne County. Under Pennsylvania law, such an interim judgeship is filled for a full term at the next election. McDonald accepted this temporary appointment with the understanding that he would contest both the primary and general elections. To obtain the support of his party organization, he was obliged to pay to the party fund an "assessment" made by the party's executive committee against all of the party's candidates. The amounts of such "assessments" were fixed on the basis of the total prospective salaries to be received from the various offices. The salary of a common pleas judge was $12,000 a year for a term of ten years, and the "assessment" against petitioner was fixed at $8,000. The proceeds from these "assessments" went to the general campaign fund in the service of the party's entire ticket. In addition to this political levy, McDonald also spent $5,017.27 for customary campaign expenses —advertising, printing, traveling, etc. The sum of these outlays, $13,017.27, McDonald deducted as a "reelection expense." The Commissioner of Internal Revenue disallowed the item and notified him of a deficiency of $2,506.77.

. . . [T]he Tax Court of the United States . . . sustained the Commissioner, and its decision was affirmed by the Circuit Court of Appeals for the Third Circuit. . . .

. . .

It is not for this Court to initiate policies as to the deduction of campaign expenses. It is for Congress to determine the relation of campaign expenditures to tax deductions by candidates for public office under such circumstances and within such limits as commend themselves to its judgment. But we certainly cannot draw intimations of such a policy from legislation by Congress increasingly restrictive against campaign contributions and political activities by government officials. The relation between money and politics generally, and more particularly the cost of campaigns and contributions by prospective officeholders, especially judges—involves issues of far-reaching importance to a democracy, and is beset with legislative difficulties that even judges can appreciate. But these difficulties can neither be met nor avoided by spurious interpretation of tax provisions dealing with allowable deductions.

To find sanction in existing tax legislation for deduction of petitioner's campaign expenditures would necessarily require allowance of deduction for campaign expenditures by all candidates, whether incumbents seeking reelection or new contenders. To draw a distinction between outlays for reelection and those for election—to allow the former and disallow the latter—is unsupportable in reason. It is even more unsupportable in public policy to derive from what Congress has thus far enacted a handicap against candidates challenging existing officeholders. And so we cannot recognize petitioner's claim on the score that he was a candidate for reelection.

. . .

Affirmed.

Pipefitters Local Union No. 562 v.
United States
407 U.S. 385 (1972)

Petitioners—Pipefitters Local Union No. 562 and three individual officers of the Union—were convicted by a jury in the United States District Court for the Eastern District of Missouri of conspiracy . . . to violate 1 U.S.C. §610. At the time of trial, §610 provided in relevant part:

> It is unlawful . . . for any corporation . . . or . . . labor organization to make a contribution or expenditure in connection with any election at which Presidential and Vice Presidential electors or a Senator or Representative in . . . Congress are to be voted for, or in connection with any primary election or political convention or caucus held to select candidates for any of the foregoing offices. . . .
>
> Every corporation or labor organization which makes any contribution or expenditure in violation of this section shall be fined not more than $5,000; and every officer or director of any corporation, or officer of any labor organization, who consents to any contribution or expenditure by the corporation or labor organization, as the case may be . . . in violation of this section shall be fined not more than $1,000 or imprisoned not more than on year, or both; and if the violation was willful, shall be fined not more than $10,000 or imprisoned not more than two years, or both.
>
> For the purposes of this section "labor organization" means any organization of any kind, or any agency or employee representation committee or plan, in which employees participate and which exist [sic] for the purpose, in whole or in part, of dealing with employers concerning grievances, labor disputes, wages, rates of pay, hours of employment, or conditions of work.

The indictment charged, in essence, that petitioners had conspired from 1963 to May 9, 1968, to establish and maintain a fund that (1) would receive regular and systematic payments from Local 562 members and members of other locals working under the Union's jurisdiction; (2) would have the appearance, but not the reality of being an entity separate from the Union; and (3) would conceal contributions and expenditures by the Union in connection with federal elections in violation of §610.

. . . [I]t was established that, from 1949 through 1962, the Union maintained a political fund to which Union members and others working under the Union's jurisdiction were, in fact, required to contribute, and that the fund was then succeeded in 1963 by the present fund, which was, in form, set up as a separate "voluntary" organization. Yet a principal Union officer assumed the role of director of the present fund, with full and unlimited control over its disbursements. The Union's business manager, petitioner Lawler, became the first director of the fund, and was later succeeded by petitioner Callanan, whom one Local 562 member described as "the Union" in explaining his influence within the local. Moreover, no significant change was made in the regular and systematic method of collection of contributions at a prescribed rate based on hours worked, and Union agents continued to collect donations at jobsites on Union time. In addition, changes in the rate of contributions were tied to changes in the rate of members' assessments. In 1966, for example, when assessments were increased from 2 ½ percent to 3 ¾ percent of gross wages, the contribution rate was decreased from $1 to 50¢ per day worked, with the result that the change did not cause, in the words of the Union's executive board, "one extra penny cost to members of Local Union 562." At the same time, the contribution rate for nonmembers, who were not required to pay the prescribed travel card fee for working under Local 562's jurisdiction, remained the same at $2 per day worked, approximately matching the total assessment and contribution of members. . . .

On the other hand, the evidence also indicated that the political contributions by the fund were made from accounts strictly segregated from Union dues and assessments, and that donations to the fund were not, in fact, necessary for employment or Union membership. The fund generally required contributors to sign authorization cards, which contained a statement that their donations were "voluntary . . . [and] no part of the dues or financial obligations of Local Union No. 562 . . ." and the testimony was overwhelming from both those who contributed and those who did not, as well as from the collectors of contributions, that no specific pressure was exerted, and no reprisals were taken, to obtain donations. Significantly, the Union's attorney who had advised on the organization of the fund testified on cross-examination that his advice had been that payments to the fund could not be made a condition of employment or Local 562 membership, but it was immaterial whether contributions appeared compulsory to those solicited.

Under instructions to determine whether, on this evidence, the fund was in reality a Union fund or the contributors' fund, the jury found each defendant guilty. The jury also found specially that a willful violation of §610 was not contemplated, and the trial court imposed sentence accordingly. The Union was fined $5,000, while the individual defendants were each sentenced to one year's imprisonment and fined $1,000.

On appeal to the Court of Appeals for the Eighth Circuit, petitioners contended that the indictment failed to allege, and the evidence was insufficient to sustain, a conspiracy to violate §610, and that §610, on its face or as construed and applied, abridged their rights under the First, Fifth, Sixth, and Seventeenth Amendments and Art. I, §2, of the Constitution. They argued further that the special finding by the jury that a

willful violation of §610 was not contemplated effectively resulted in acquittal, since such willfulness was an essential element of the conspiracy. . . . The Court of Appeals . . . rejecting each of these claims. . . .

After we heard oral argument, the President, on February 7, 1972, signed into law the Federal Election Campaign Act of 1971, which in §205 amends §610. We accordingly requested the parties to file supplemental briefs addressing the impact of that amendment on this prosecution. Having considered those briefs, we now hold that §205 of the Federal Election Campaign Act merely codifies prior law, with one possible exception pertinent to this case; that the change in the law, if in fact, made, does not, in any event, require this prosecution to abate; but that the judgment below must, nevertheless, be reversed because of erroneous jury instructions. This disposition makes decision of the constitutional issues premature, and we therefore do not decide them.

. . .

We think that neither side fully and accurately portrays the attributes of legitimate political funds. We hold that such a fund must be separate from the sponsoring union only in the sense that there must be a strict segregation of its monies from union dues and assessments. We hold, too, that, although solicitation by union officials is permissible, such solicitation must be conducted under circumstances plainly indicating that donations are for a political purpose, and that those solicited may decline to contribute without loss of job, union membership, or any other reprisal within the union's institutional power. . . .

. . .

Nowhere . . . has Congress required that the political organization be formally or functionally independent of union control or that union officials be barred from soliciting contributions or even precluded from determining how the monies raised will be spent. . . . When Congress prohibited labor organizations from making contributions or expenditures in connection with federal elections, it was, of course, concerned not only to protect minority interests within the union, but to eliminate the effect of aggregated wealth on federal elections. But the aggregated wealth it plainly had in mind was the general union treasury—not the funds donated by union members of their own free and knowing choice. . . . The only conditions for that kind of direct electioneering were that the costs of publication be financed through individual subscriptions, rather than through union dues, and that the newspapers be recognized by the subscribers as political organs that they could refuse to purchase. Neither the absence of even a formally separate organization, the solicitation of subscriptions by the union, nor the method for choosing the candidates to be supported was mentioned as being material. Similarly, the only requirements for permissible political organizations were that they be funded through separate contributions and that they be recognized by the donors as political organizations to which they could refuse support. . . .

. . .

The instant case is controlled by *Reisinger*, rather than by *Hamm*. Section 205 of the Federal Election Campaign Act may, of course, make lawful what was previously unlawful—namely, the financing of the establishment, administration, and solicitation of contributions for voluntary political funds from general union monies. But §205 does not, in any event, "[substitute] a right for a crime." To the contrary, as in *Reisinger* and *Tynen*, it retains the basic offense—contributions or expenditures by labor organizations in connection with federal elections are still forbidden so long

as they are paid for from actual or effective dues or assessments. We therefore hold that, even if there has been an implied repeal of §610, petitioners remain punishable under that provision. . . .

. . .

The judgment of the Court of Appeals as to petitioners Callanan and Lawler is vacated, and the case is remanded to the District Court with directions to dismiss the indictment against them. The judgment of the Court of Appeals as to petitioners Local 562 and Seaton is reversed, and the case is remanded to the District Court for proceedings as to them consistent with this opinion.

Cort v. Ash
422 U.S. 66 (1975)

In August and September, 1972, an advertisement with the caption "I say let's keep the campaign honest. Mobilize 'truth squads'" appeared in various national publications, including Time, Newsweek, and U.S. News and World Report, and in nineteen local newspapers in communities where Bethlehem Steel Corp. (Bethlehem), a Delaware corporation, has plants. Reprints of the advertisement, which consisted mainly of quotations from a speech by petitioner Stewart S. Cort, chairman of the board of directors of Bethlehem, were included with the September 11, 1972, quarterly dividend checks mailed to the stockholders of the corporation. The main text of the advertisement appealed to the electorate to "encourage responsible, honest, and truthful campaigning." It alleged that vigilance was needed because "careless rhetoric and accusations . . . are being thrown around these days—their main target being the business community." In italics, under a picture of Mr. Cort, the advertisement quoted "the following statement made by a political candidate: 'The time has come for a tax system that says to big business—you must pay your fair share.'" It then printed Mr. Cort's rejoinder to this in his speech, including his opinion that to say "large corporations [are] not carrying their fair share of the tax burden" is "baloney." The advertisement concluded with an offer to send, on request, copies of Mr. Cort's entire speech and a folder "telling how to go about activating Truth Squads." These publications could be obtained free from the Public Affairs Department of Bethlehem. It is stipulated that the entire costs of the advertisements and various mailings were paid from Bethlehem's general corporate funds.

Respondent owns fifty shares of Bethlehem stock and was qualified to vote in the 1972 Presidential election. He filed this suit in the United States District Court for the Eastern District of Pennsylvania on September 28, 1972, on behalf of himself and, derivatively, on behalf of Bethlehem. The complaint specified two separate and distinct bases for jurisdiction and relief. . . . Immediate injunctive relief against further corporate expenditures in connection with the 1972 Presidential election or any future campaign was sought, as well as compensatory and punitive damages in favor of the corporation.

The District Court denied a preliminary injunction on October 25, 1972. While the denial was supported on three grounds, it was upheld on appeal to the Court of Appeals for the Third Circuit only on the narrow ground that irreparable harm was not shown.

. . .

The District Court . . . granted petitioners' motion for summary judgment without opinion. The Court of Appeals reversed. The Court of Appeals held that, since the amended complaint sought damages for the corporation for violation

of §610, the controversy was not moot, although the election which occasioned it was past. . . .

. . .

Because injunctive relief is not presently available in light of the Amendments, and because implication of a federal right of damages on behalf of a corporation under §610 would intrude into an area traditionally committed to state law without aiding the main purpose of §610, we reverse.

Buckley v. Valeo
424 U.S. 1 (1976)

These appeals present constitutional challenges to the key provisions of the Federal Election Campaign Act of 1971 (Act), and related provisions of the Internal Revenue Code of 1954.

. . . The statutes at issue, summarized in broad terms, contain the following provisions: (a) individual political contributions are limited to $1,000 to any single candidate per election, with an overall annual limitation of $25,000 by any contributor; independent expenditures by individuals and groups "relative to a clearly identified candidate" are limited to $1,000 a year; campaign spending by candidates for various federal offices and spending for national conventions by political parties are subject to prescribed limits; (b) contributions and expenditures above certain threshold levels must be reported and publicly disclosed; (c) a system for public funding of Presidential campaign activities is established by Subtitle H of the Internal Revenue Code; and (d) a Federal Election Commission is established to administer and enforce the legislation.

This suit was originally filed by appellants in the United States District Court for the District of Columbia. Plaintiffs included a candidate for the Presidency of the United States, a United States Senator who is a candidate for reelection, a potential contributor, the Committee for a Constitutional Presidency—McCarthy '76, the Conservative Party of the State of New York, the Mississippi Republican Party, the Libertarian Party, the New York Civil Liberties Union, Inc., the American Conservative Union, the Conservative Victory Fund, and Human Events, Inc. The defendants included the Secretary of the United States Senate and the Clerk of the United States House of Representatives, both in their official capacities and as ex officio members of the Federal Election Commission. The Commission itself was named as a defendant. Also named were the Attorney General of the United States and the Comptroller General of the United States.

. . . The complaint sought both a declaratory judgment that the major provisions of the Act were unconstitutional and an injunction against enforcement of those provisions. . . . The District Judge denied the application for a three-judge court and directed that the case be transmitted to the Court of Appeals. . . . After considering matters regarding factfinding procedures, the Court of Appeals entered an order en banc remanding the case to the District Court to (1) identify the constitutional issues in the complaint; (2) take whatever evidence was found necessary in addition to the submissions suitably dealt with by way of judicial notice; (3) make findings of fact with reference to those issues; and (4) certify the constitutional questions arising from the foregoing steps to the Court of Appeals. On remand, the District Judge entered a memorandum order adopting extensive findings of fact and transmitting the augmented record back to the Court of Appeals.

On plenary review, a majority of the Court of Appeals rejected, for the most part, appellants'

constitutional attacks. The court found "a clear and compelling interest," in preserving the integrity of the electoral process. On that basis, the court upheld, with one exception, the substantive provisions of the Act with respect to contributions, expenditures, and disclosure. It also sustained the constitutionality of the newly established Federal Election Commission. . . . The provisions for public funding of the three stages of the Presidential selection process were upheld as a valid exercise of congressional power under the General Welfare Clause of the Constitution.

In this Court, appellants argue that the Court of Appeals failed to give this legislation the critical scrutiny demanded under accepted First Amendment and equal protection principles. In appellants' view, limiting the use of money for political purposes constitutes a restriction on communication violative of the First Amendment, since virtually all meaningful political communications in the modern setting involve the expenditure of money. Further, they argue that the reporting and disclosure provisions of the Act unconstitutionally impinge on their right to freedom of association. Appellants also view the federal subsidy provisions of Subtitle H as violative of the General Welfare Clause, and as inconsistent with the First and Fifth Amendments. Finally, appellants renew their attack on the Commission's composition and powers.

. . .

. . . [T]his Court has never suggested that the dependence of a communication on the expenditure of money operates itself to introduce a nonspeech element or to reduce the exacting scrutiny required by the First Amendment. . . .

. . . The interests served by the Act include restricting the voices of people and interest groups who have money to spend and reducing the overall scope of federal election campaigns. Although the Act does not focus on the ideas expressed by persons or groups subject to its regulations, it is aimed in part at equalizing the relative ability of all voters to affect electoral outcomes by placing a ceiling on expenditures for political expression by citizens and groups. . . . It is beyond dispute that the interest in regulating the alleged "conduct" of giving or spending money "arises in some measure because the communication allegedly integral to the conduct is itself thought to be harmful."

. . .

A restriction on the amount of money a person or group can spend on political communication during a campaign necessarily reduces the quantity of expression by restricting the number of issues discussed, the depth of their exploration, and the size of the audience reached. This is because virtually every means of communicating ideas in today's mass society requires the expenditure of money. The distribution of the humblest handbill or leaflet entails printing, paper, and circulation costs. Speeches and rallies generally necessitate hiring a hall and publicizing the event. The electorate's increasing dependence on television, radio, and other mass media for news and information has made these expensive modes of communication indispensable instruments of effective political speech.

The expenditure limitations contained in the Act represent substantial, rather than merely theoretical, restraints on the quantity and diversity of political speech. The $1,000 ceiling on spending "relative to a clearly identified candidate," would appear to exclude all citizens and groups except candidates, political parties, and the institutional press from any significant use of the most effective modes of communication. Although the Act's limitations on expenditures by campaign organizations and political parties provide substantially

greater room for discussion and debate, they would have required restrictions in the scope of a number of past congressional and Presidential campaigns and would operate to constrain campaigning by candidates who raise sums in excess of the spending ceiling.

By contrast with a limitation upon expenditures for political expression, a limitation upon the amount that any one person or group may contribute to a candidate or political committee entails only a marginal restriction upon the contributor's ability to engage in free communication. A contribution serves as a general expression of support for the candidate and his views, but does not communicate the underlying basis for the support. The quantity of communication by the contributor does not increase perceptibly with the size of his contribution, since the expression rests solely on the undifferentiated, symbolic act of contributing. At most, the size of the contribution provides a very rough index of the intensity of the contributor's support for the candidate. A limitation on the amount of money a person may give to a candidate or campaign organization thus involves little direct restraint on his political communication, for it permits the symbolic expression of support evidenced by a contribution but does not in any way infringe the contributor's freedom to discuss candidates and issues. While contributions may result in political expression if spent by a candidate or an association to present views to the voters, the transformation of contributions into political debate involves speech by someone other than the contributor.

Given the important role of contributions in financing political campaigns, contribution restrictions could have a severe impact on political dialogue if the limitations prevented candidates and political committees from amassing the resources necessary for effective advocacy. There is no indication, however, that the contribution limitations imposed by the Act would have any dramatic adverse effect on the funding of campaigns and political associations. The overall effect of the Act's contribution ceilings is merely to require candidates and political committees to raise funds from a greater number of persons and to compel people who would otherwise contribute amounts greater than the statutory limits to expend such funds on direct political expression, rather than to reduce the total amount of money potentially available to promote political expression.

The Act's contribution and expenditure limitations also impinge on protected associational freedoms. Making a contribution, like joining a political party, serves to affiliate a person with a candidate. In addition, it enables like-minded persons to pool their resources in furtherance of common political goals. The Act's contribution ceilings thus limit one important means of associating with a candidate or committee, but leave the contributor free to become a member of any political association and to assist personally in the association's efforts on behalf of candidates. And the Act's contribution limitations permit associations and candidates to aggregate large sums of money to promote effective advocacy. By contrast, the Act's $1,000 limitation on independent expenditures "relative to a clearly identified candidate" precludes most associations from effectively amplifying the voice of their adherents, the original basis for the recognition of First Amendment protection of the freedom of association. The Act's constraints on the ability of independent associations and candidate campaign organizations to expend resources on political expression "is simultaneously an interference with the freedom of [their] adherents."

In sum, although the Act's contribution and expenditure limitations both implicate fundamental First Amendment interests, its expenditure ceilings impose significantly more severe restrictions on protected freedoms of political expression and association than do its limitations on financial contributions.

. . . The $1,000 ceiling applies regardless of whether the contribution is given to the candidate, to a committee authorized in writing by the candidate to accept contributions on his behalf, or indirectly via earmarked gifts passed through an intermediary to the candidate. The restriction applies to aggregate amounts contributed to the candidate for each election—with primaries, run-off elections, and general elections counted separately, and all Presidential primaries held in any calendar year treated together as a single election campaign.

. . .

As the general discussion . . . indicated, the primary First Amendment problem raised by the Act's contribution limitations is their restriction of one aspect of the contributor's freedom of political association. . . .

. . .

It is unnecessary to look beyond the Act's primary purpose—to limit the actuality and appearance of corruption resulting from large individual financial contributions—in order to find a constitutionally sufficient justification for the $1,000 contribution limitation. Under a system of private financing of elections, a candidate lacking immense personal or family wealth must depend on financial contributions from others to provide the resources necessary to conduct a successful campaign. The increasing importance of the communications media and sophisticated mass-mailing and polling operations to effective campaigning make the raising of large sums of money an ever more essential ingredient of an effective candidacy. To the extent that large contributions are given to secure a political quid pro quo from current and potential office holders, the integrity of our system of representative democracy is undermined. . . .

Of almost equal concern as the danger of actual quid pro quo arrangements is the impact of the appearance of corruption stemming from public awareness of the opportunities for abuse inherent in a regime of large individual financial contributions. . . . Congress could legitimately conclude that the avoidance of the appearance of improper influence "is also critical . . . if confidence in the system of representative Government is not to be eroded to a disastrous extent."

. . .

The Act's $1,000 contribution limitation focuses precisely on the problem of large campaign contributions—the narrow aspect of political association where the actuality and potential for corruption have been identified—while leaving persons free to engage in independent political expression, to associate actively through volunteering their services, and to assist to a limited but nonetheless substantial extent in supporting candidates and committees with financial resources. Significantly, the Act's contribution limitations in themselves do not undermine to any material degree the potential for robust and effective discussion of candidates and campaign issues by individual citizens, associations, the institutional press, candidates, and political parties.

We find that, under the rigorous standard of review established by our prior decisions, the weighty interests served by restricting the size of financial contributions to political candidates are sufficient to justify the limited effect upon First Amendment freedoms caused by the $1,000 contribution ceiling.

Appellants' first overbreadth challenge to the contribution ceilings rests on the proposition that most large contributors do not seek improper influence over a candidate's position or an officeholder's action. Although the truth of that proposition may be assumed, it does not undercut the validity of the $1,000 contribution limitation. Not only is it difficult to isolate suspect contributions but, more importantly, Congress was justified in concluding that the interest in safeguarding against the appearance of impropriety requires that the opportunity for abuse inherent in the process of raising large monetary contributions be eliminated.

A second, related overbreadth claim is that the $1,000 restriction is unrealistically low because much more than that amount would still not be enough to enable an unscrupulous contributor to exercise improper influence over a candidate or officeholder, especially in campaigns for statewide or national office. While the contribution limitation provisions might well have been structured to take account of the graduated expenditure limitations for congressional and Presidential campaigns, Congress's failure to engage in such fine tuning does not invalidate the legislation. . . .

. . . [I]t is important at the outset to note that the Act applies the same limitations on contributions to all candidates regardless of their present occupations, ideological views, or party affiliations. Absent record evidence of invidious discrimination against challengers as a class, a court should generally be hesitant to invalidate legislation which on its face imposes evenhanded restrictions.

There is no such evidence to support the claim that the contribution limitations in themselves discriminate against major party challengers to incumbents. . . . [T]o the extent that incumbents generally are more likely than challengers to attract very large contributions, the Act's $1,000 ceiling has the practical effect of benefiting challengers as a class. . . .

The charge of discrimination against minor party and independent candidates is more troubling, but the record provides no basis for concluding that the Act invidiously disadvantages such candidates. . . . [T]he restriction would appear to benefit minor party and independent candidates relative to their major party opponents, because major party candidates receive far more money in large contributions. . . .

In view of these considerations, we conclude that the impact of the Act's $1,000 contribution limitation on major party challengers and on minor party candidates does not render the provision unconstitutional on its face.

Section 608(b)(2) permits certain committees, designated as "political committees," to contribute up to $5,000 to any candidate with respect to any election for federal office. In order to qualify for the higher contribution ceiling, a group must have been registered with the Commission as a political committee . . . for not less than six months, have received contributions from more than 50 persons, and, except for state political party organizations, have contributed to five or more candidates for federal office. Appellants argue that these qualifications unconstitutionally discriminate against ad hoc organizations in favor of established interest groups and impermissibly burden free association. The argument is without merit. Rather than undermining freedom of association, the basic provision enhances the opportunity of bona fide groups to participate in the election process, and the registration, contribution, and candidate conditions serve the permissible purpose of preventing individuals from evading the applicable contribution limitations by labeling themselves committees.

. . . Certain expenses incurred by persons in providing volunteer services to a candidate are exempt from the $1,000 ceiling only to the extent that they do not exceed $500. . . .

If, as we have held, the basic contribution limitations are constitutionally valid, then surely these provisions are a constitutionally acceptable accommodation of Congress's valid interest in encouraging citizen participation in political campaigns while continuing to guard against the corrupting potential of large financial contributions to candidates. The expenditure of resources at the candidate's direction for a fundraising event at a volunteer's residence or the provision of in-kind assistance in the form of food or beverages to be resold to raise funds or consumed by the participants in such an event provides material financial assistance to a candidate. The ultimate effect is the same as if the person had contributed the dollar amount to the candidate and the candidate had then used the contribution to pay for the fundraising event or the food. Similarly, travel undertaken as a volunteer at the direction of the candidate or his staff is an expense of the campaign and may properly be viewed as a contribution if the volunteer absorbs the fare. Treating these expenses as contributions when made to the candidate's campaign or at the direction of the candidate or his staff forecloses an avenue of abuse without limiting actions voluntarily undertaken by citizens independently of a candidate's campaign.

. . . [T]he Act contains an overall $25,000 limitation on total contributions by an individual during any calendar year. A contribution made in connection with an election is considered, for purposes of this subsection, to be made in the year the election is held. Although the constitutionality of this provision was drawn into question by appellants, it has not been separately addressed at length by the parties. The overall $25,000 ceiling does impose an ultimate restriction upon the number of candidates and committees with which an individual may associate himself by means of financial support. But this quite modest restraint upon protected political activity serves to prevent evasion of the $1,000 contribution limitation by a person who might otherwise contribute massive amounts of money to a particular candidate through the use of unearmarked contributions to political committees likely to contribute to that candidate, or huge contributions to the candidate's political party. The limited, additional restriction on associational freedom imposed by the overall ceiling is thus no more than a corollary of the basic individual contribution limitation that we have found to be constitutionally valid.

The Act's expenditure ceilings impose direct and substantial restraints on the quantity of political speech. The most drastic of the limitations restricts individuals and groups, including political parties that fail to place a candidate on the ballot, to an expenditure of $1,000 "relative to a clearly identified candidate during a calendar year." Other expenditure ceilings limit spending by candidates, their campaigns, and political parties in connection with election campaigns. It is clear that a primary effect of these expenditure limitations is to restrict the quantity of campaign speech by individuals, groups, and candidates. The restrictions, while neutral as to the ideas expressed, limit political expression "at the core of our electoral process and of the First Amendment freedoms."

Section 608(e)(1) provides that

> [n]o person may make any expenditure . . . relative to a clearly identified candidate during a calendar year which, when added to all other expenditures made by such person during the

year advocating the election or defeat of such candidate, exceeds $1,000.

The plain effect of §608(e)(1) is to prohibit all individuals, who are neither candidates nor owners of institutional press facilities, and all groups, except political parties and campaign organizations, from voicing their views "relative to a clearly identified candidate" through means that entail aggregate expenditures of more than $1,000 during a calendar year. The provision, for example, would make it a federal criminal offense for a person or association to place a single one-quarter page advertisement "relative to a clearly identified candidate" in a major metropolitan newspaper.

. . .

. . . [T]he distinction between discussion of issues and candidates and advocacy of election or defeat of candidates may often dissolve in practical application. Candidates, especially incumbents, are intimately tied to public issues involving legislative proposals and governmental actions. Not only do candidates campaign on the basis of their positions on various public issues, but campaigns themselves generate issues of public interest. . . .

. . .

We find that the governmental interest in preventing corruption and the appearance of corruption is inadequate to justify §608(e)(1)'s ceiling on independent expenditures. First, assuming, arguendo, that large independent expenditures pose the same dangers of actual or apparent quid pro quo arrangements as do large contributions, §608(e)(1) does not provide an answer that sufficiently relates to the elimination of those dangers. Unlike the contribution limitations' total ban on the giving of large amounts of money to candidates, §608(e)(1) prevents only some large expenditures. So long as persons and groups eschew expenditures that, in express terms advocate the election or defeat of a clearly identified candidate, they are free to spend as much as they want to promote the candidate and his views. The exacting interpretation of the statutory language necessary to avoid unconstitutional vagueness thus undermines the limitation's effectiveness as a loophole-closing provision by facilitating circumvention by those seeking to exert improper influence upon a candidate or officeholder. . . .

Second . . . the independent advocacy restricted by the provision does not presently appear to pose dangers of real or apparent corruption comparable to those identified with large campaign contributions. . . . [Section] 608(e)(1) limits expenditures for express advocacy of candidates made totally independently of the candidate and his campaign. Unlike contributions, such independent expenditures may well provide little assistance to the candidate's campaign, and indeed may prove counterproductive. The absence of prearrangement and coordination of an expenditure with the candidate or his agent not only undermines the value of the expenditure to the candidate, but also alleviates the danger that expenditures will be given as a quid pro quo for improper commitments from the candidate. Rather than preventing circumvention of the contribution limitations, §608(e)(1) severely restricts all independent advocacy despite its substantially diminished potential for abuse.

While the independent expenditure ceiling thus fails to serve any substantial governmental interest in stemming the reality or appearance of corruption in the electoral process, it heavily burdens core First Amendment expression. . . . Advocacy of the election or defeat of candidates for federal office is no less entitled to protection under the First Amendment than the discussion of political policy generally or advocacy of the passage or defeat of legislation. . . . The First Amendment's protection against governmental abridgment of free expression cannot properly be made to depend on a person's financial ability to engage in public discussion.

. . .

. . . [W]e conclude that §608(e)(1)'s independent expenditure limitation is unconstitutional under the First Amendment.

The Act also sets limits on expenditures by a candidate "from his personal funds, or the personal funds of his immediate family, in connection with his campaigns during any calendar year." These ceilings vary from $50,000 for Presidential or Vice Presidential candidates to $35,000 for senatorial candidates, and $25,000 for most candidates for the House of Representatives.

The ceiling on personal expenditures by candidates on their own behalf, like the limitations on independent expenditures contained in §608(e)(1), imposes a substantial restraint on the ability of persons to engage in protected First Amendment expression. The candidate, no less than any other person, has a First Amendment right to engage in the discussion of public issues and vigorously and tirelessly to advocate his own election and the election of other candidates. Indeed, it is of particular importance that candidates have the unfettered opportunity to make their views known so that the electorate may intelligently evaluate the candidates' personal qualities and their positions on vital public issues before choosing among them on election day. . . . Section 608(a)'s ceiling on personal expenditures by a candidate in furtherance of his own candidacy thus clearly and directly interferes with constitutionally protected freedoms.

The primary governmental interest served by the Act—the prevention of actual and apparent corruption of the political process—does not support the limitation on the candidate's expenditure of his own personal funds. . . . Indeed, the use of personal funds reduces the candidate's dependence on outside contributions, and thereby counteracts the coercive pressures and attendant risks of abuse to which the Act's contribution limitations are directed.

The ancillary interest in equalizing the relative financial resources of candidates competing for elective office, therefore, provides the sole relevant rationale for §608(a)'s expenditure ceiling. That interest is clearly not sufficient to justify the provision's infringement of fundamental First Amendment rights. . . . We therefore hold that §608(a)'s restriction on a candidate's personal expenditures is unconstitutional.

Section 608(c) places limitations on overall campaign expenditures by candidates seeking nomination for election and election to federal office. Presidential candidates may spend $10,000,000 in seeking nomination for office, and an additional $20,000,000 in the general election campaign. The ceiling on senatorial campaigns is pegged to the size of the voting-age population of the State, with minimum dollar amounts applicable to campaigns in States with small populations. In senatorial primary elections, the limit is the greater of eight cents multiplied by the voting-age population or $100,000, and, in the general election, the limit is increased to 12 cents multiplied by the voting-age population, or $150,000. The Act imposes blanket $70,000 limitations on both primary campaigns and general election campaigns for the House of Representatives, with the exception that the senatorial ceiling applies to campaigns in States entitled to only one Representative. These ceilings are to be adjusted upwards at the beginning of each calendar year by the average percentage rise in the consumer price index for the 12 preceding months.

No governmental interest that has been suggested is sufficient to justify the restriction on the quantity of political expression imposed by § 608(c)'s campaign expenditure limitations. The major evil associated with rapidly increasing campaign expenditures is the danger of candidate dependence on large contributions. The interest in alleviating the corrupting influence of large contributions is served by the Act's contribution limitations and disclosure provisions, rather than by §608(c)'s campaign expenditure ceilings. . . .

The interest in equalizing the financial resources of candidates competing for federal office is no more convincing a justification for restricting the scope of federal election campaigns. Given the limitation on the size of outside contributions, the financial resources available to a candidate's campaign, like the number of volunteers recruited, will normally vary with the size and intensity of the candidate's support. There is nothing invidious, improper, or unhealthy in permitting such funds to be spent to carry the candidate's message to the electorate. Moreover, the equalization of permissible campaign expenditures might serve not to equalize the opportunities of all candidates, but to handicap a candidate who lacked substantial name recognition or exposure of his views before the start of the campaign.

The campaign expenditure ceilings appear to be designed primarily to serve the governmental interests in reducing the allegedly skyrocketing costs of political campaigns. . . . [T]he mere growth in the cost of federal election campaigns, in and of itself, provides no basis for governmental restrictions on the quantity of campaign spending and the resulting limitation on the scope of federal campaigns. The First Amendment denies government the power to determine that spending to promote one's political views is wasteful, excessive, or unwise. In the free society ordained by our Constitution, it is not the government, but the people—individually, as citizens and candidates, and collectively, as associations and political committees—who must retain control over the quantity and range of debate on public issues in a political campaign.

For these reasons, we hold that §608(c) is constitutionally invalid.

. . .

. . . [T]he disclosure requirements of the Act . . . are not challenged by appellants as per se unconstitutional restrictions on the exercise of First Amendment freedoms of speech and association. . . . The Court of Appeals found no constitutional infirmities in the provisions challenged here. . . .

. . .

Each political committee is required to register with the Commission and to keep detailed records of both contributions and expenditures. These records must include the name and address of everyone making a contribution in excess of $10, along with the date and amount of the contribution. If a person's contributions aggregate more than $100, his occupation and principal place of business are also to be included. These files are subject to periodic audits and field investigations by the Commission.

Each committee and each candidate also is required to file quarterly reports. The reports are to contain detailed financial information, including the full name, mailing address, occupation, and principal place of business of each person who has contributed over $100 in a calendar year, as well as the amount and date of the contributions. They are to be made available by the Commission "for public inspection and copying." Every candidate for federal office is required to designate a "principal campaign committee,"

which is to receive reports of contributions and expenditures made on the candidate's behalf from other political committees and to compile and file these reports, together with its own statements, with the Commission.

Every individual or group, other than a political committee or candidate, who makes "contributions" or "expenditures" of over $100 in a calendar year "other than by contribution to a political committee or candidate" is required to file a statement with the Commission. Any violation of these recordkeeping and reporting provisions is punishable by a fine of not more than $1,000 or a prison term of not more than a year, or both.

. . .

We long have recognized that significant encroachments on First Amendment rights of the sort that compelled disclosure imposes cannot be justified by a mere showing of some legitimate governmental interest. . . . We also have insisted that there be a "relevant correlation" or "substantial relation" between the governmental interest and the information required to be disclosed. This type of scrutiny is necessary even if any deterrent effect on the exercise of First Amendment rights arises not through direct government action, but indirectly, as an unintended but inevitable result of the government's conduct in requiring disclosure.

. . .

The governmental interests sought to be vindicated by the disclosure requirements. . . . fall into three categories. First, disclosure provides the electorate with information "as to where political campaign money comes from and how it is spent by the candidate" in order to aid the voters in evaluating those who seek federal office. It allows voters to place each candidate in the political spectrum more precisely than is often possible solely on the basis of party labels and campaign speeches. The sources of a candidate's financial support also alert the voter to the interests to which a candidate is most likely to be responsive, and thus facilitate predictions of future performance in office.

Second, disclosure requirements deter actual corruption and avoid the appearance of corruption by exposing large contributions and expenditures to the light of publicity. This exposure may discourage those who would use money for improper purposes either before or after the election. A public armed with information about a candidate's most generous supporters is better able to detect any post-election special favors that may be given in return. . . .

Third, and not least significant, recordkeeping, reporting, and disclosure requirements are an essential means of gathering the data necessary to detect violations of the contribution limitations described above.

. . .

It is undoubtedly true that public disclosure of contributions to candidates and political parties will deter some individuals who otherwise might contribute. In some instances, disclosure may even expose contributors to harassment or retaliation. These are not insignificant burdens on individual rights, and they must be weighed carefully against the interests which Congress has sought to promote by this legislation. In this process, we note and agree with appellants' concession that disclosure requirements—certainly in most applications—appear to be the least restrictive means of curbing the evils of campaign ignorance and corruption that Congress found to exist. Appellants argue, however, that the balance tips against disclosure when it is required of contributors to certain parties and candidates. . . .

. . .

Section 434(e) requires "[e]very person (other than a political committee or candidate) who makes contributions or expenditures" aggregating over $100 in a calendar year "other than by contribution to a political committee or candidate" to file a statement with the Commission. Unlike the other disclosure provisions, this section does not seek the contribution list of any association. Instead, it requires direct disclosure of what an individual or group contributes or spends.

. . .

The Court of Appeals upheld §434(e) as necessary to enforce the independent expenditure ceiling imposed by §608(e)(1). . . . We have found that §608(e)(1) unconstitutionally infringes upon First Amendment rights. If the sole function of §434(e) were to aid in the enforcement of that provision, it would no longer serve any governmental purpose.

But the two provisions are not so intimately tied. The legislative history on the function of §434(e) is bare, but it was clearly intended to stand independently of §608(e)(1). . . . Like the other disclosure provisions, §434(e) could play a role in the enforcement of the expanded contribution and expenditure limitations included in the 1974 amendments, but it also has independent functions. Section 434(e) is part of Congress's effort to achieve "total disclosure" by reaching "every kind of political activity" in order to insure that the voters are fully informed and to achieve through publicity the maximum deterrence to corruption and undue influence possible. The provision is responsive to the legitimate fear that efforts would be made, as they had been in the past, to avoid the disclosure requirements by routing financial support of candidates through avenues not explicitly covered by the general provisions of the Act.

In its effort to be all-inclusive, however, the

provision raises serious problems of vagueness, particularly treacherous where, as here, the violation of its terms carries criminal penalties and fear of incurring these sanctions may deter those who seek to exercise protected First Amendment rights.

. . .

. . . [Section] 434(e), as construed, imposes independent reporting requirements on individuals and groups that are not candidates or political committees only in the following circumstances: (1) when they make contributions earmarked for political purposes or authorized or requested by a candidate or his agent, to some person other than a candidate or political committee, and (2) when they make expenditures for communications that expressly advocate the election or defeat of a clearly identified candidate.

. . . [Section] 434(e), as construed, bears a sufficient relationship to a substantial governmental interest. As narrowed, §434(e) . . . does not reach all partisan discussion, for it only requires disclosure of those expenditures that expressly advocate a particular election result. This might have been fatal if the only purpose of §434(e) were to stem corruption or its appearance by closing a loophole in the general disclosure requirements. But the disclosure provisions, including §434(e), serve another, informational interest, and, even as construed, §434(e) increases the fund of information concerning those who support the candidates. It goes beyond the general disclosure requirements to shed the light of publicity on spending that is unambiguously campaign-related, but would not otherwise be reported because it takes the form of independent expenditures or of contributions to an individual or group not itself required to report the names of its contributors. By the same token, it is not fatal that §434(e) encompasses purely independent expenditures uncoordinated with a particular candidate or his agent. The corruption potential of these expenditures may be significantly different, but the informational interest can be as strong as it is in coordinated spending, for disclosure helps voters to define more of the candidates' constituencies.

. . . The burden imposed by §434(e) is no prior restraint, but a reasonable and minimally restrictive method of furthering First Amendment values by opening the basic processes of our federal election system to public view.

Appellants' third contention . . . is that the monetary thresholds in the recordkeeping and reporting provisions lack a substantial nexus with the claimed governmental interests, for the amounts involved are too low even to attract the attention of the candidate, much less have a corrupting influence.

The provisions contain two thresholds. Records are to be kept by political committees of the names and addresses of those who make contributions in excess of $10, and these records are subject to Commission audit. If a person's contributions to a committee or candidate aggregate more than $100, his name and address, as well as his occupation and principal place of business, are to be included in reports filed by committees and candidates with the Commission, and made available for public inspection.

The Court of Appeals rejected appellants' contention that these thresholds are unconstitutional. It found the challenge on First Amendment grounds to the $10 threshold to be premature, for it could "discern no basis in the statute for authorizing disclosure outside the Commission . . . ; and hence no substantial 'inhibitory effect' operating upon" appellants. The $100 threshold was found to be within the "reasonable latitude" given the legislature "as to where to draw the line." . . .

The $10 and $100 thresholds are indeed low. Contributors of relatively small amounts are likely to be especially sensitive to recording or disclosure of their political preferences. These strict requirements may well discourage participation by some citizens in the political process, a result that Congress hardly could have intended. Indeed, there is little in the legislative history to indicate that Congress focused carefully on the appropriate level at which to require recording and disclosure. Rather, it seems merely to have adopted the thresholds existing in similar disclosure laws since 1910. But we cannot require Congress to establish that it has chosen the highest reasonable threshold. The line is necessarily a judgmental decision, best left in the context of this complex legislation to congressional discretion. We cannot say, on this bare record, that the limits designated are wholly without rationality.

We are mindful that disclosure serves informational functions, as well as the prevention of corruption and the enforcement of the contribution limitations. Congress is not required to set a threshold that is tailored only to the latter goals. In addition, the enforcement goal can never be well served if the threshold is so high that disclosure becomes equivalent to admitting violation of the contribution limitations.

The $10 recordkeeping threshold, in a somewhat similar fashion, facilitates the enforcement of the disclosure provisions by making it relatively difficult to aggregate secret contributions in amounts that surpass the $100 limit. We agree with the Court of Appeals that there is no warrant for assuming that public disclosure of contributions between $10 and $100 is authorized by the Act. Accordingly, we do not reach the question whether information concerning gifts of this size can be made available to the public without trespassing impermissibly on First Amendment rights. . . . [W]e find no constitutional infirmities in the recordkeeping, reporting, and disclosure provisions of the Act.

A series of statutes for the public financing of Presidential election campaigns produced the scheme now found in §6096 and Subtitle H of the Internal Revenue Code of 1954. Both the District Court and the Court of Appeals sustained Subtitle H against a constitutional attack. Appellants renew their challenge here, contending that the legislation violates the First and Fifth Amendments. . . .

Section 9006 establishes a Presidential Election Campaign Fund (Fund), financed from general revenues in the aggregate amount designated by individual taxpayers, under §6096, who on their income tax returns may authorize payment to the Fund of one dollar of their tax liability in the case of an individual return or two dollars in the case of a joint return. The Fund consists of three separate accounts to finance (1) party nominating conventions, (2) general election campaigns, and (3) primary campaigns.

. . .

Major parties are entitled to $2,000,000 to defray their national committee Presidential nominating convention expenses, must limit total expenditures to that amount, and may not use any of this money to benefit a particular candidate or delegate. A minor party receives a portion of the major party entitlement determined by the ratio of the votes received by the party's candidate in the last election to the average of the votes received by the major parties' candidates. The amounts given to the parties and the expenditure limit are adjusted for inflation, using 1974 as the base year. No financing is provided for new parties, nor is there any express provision for financing independent candidates or parties not holding a convention.

For expenses in the general election campaign,

§9004(a)(1) entitles each major party candidate to $20,000,000. This amount is also adjusted for inflation. To be eligible for funds the candidate must pledge not to incur expenses in excess of the entitlement under §9004(a)(1) and not to accept private contributions except to the extent that the fund is insufficient to provide the full entitlement. Minor party candidates are also entitled to funding, again based on the ratio of the vote received by the party's candidate in the preceding election to the average of the major party candidates. Minor party candidates must certify that they will not incur campaign expenses in excess of the major party entitlement and that they will accept private contributions only to the extent needed to make up the difference between that amount and the public funding grant. New party candidates receive no money prior to the general election, but any candidate receiving 5 percent or more of the popular vote in the election is entitled to post-election payments according to the formula applicable to minor party candidates. Similarly, minor party candidates are entitled to post-election funds if they receive a greater percentage of the average major party vote than their party's candidate did in the preceding election; the amount of such payments is the difference between the entitlement based on the preceding election and that based on the actual vote in the current election. A further eligibility requirement for minor and new party candidates is that the candidate's name must appear on the ballot, or electors pledged to the candidate must be on the ballot, in at least ten States.

Chapter 96 establishes a third account in the Fund, the Presidential Primary Matching Payment Account. This funding is intended to aid campaigns by candidates seeking Presidential nomination "by a political party," in "primary elections." The threshold eligibility requirement is that the candidate raise at least $5,000 in each of twenty States, counting only the first $250 from each person contributing to the candidate. In addition, the candidate must agree to abide by the spending limits in §9035. Funding is provided according to a matching formula: each qualified candidate is entitled to a sum equal to the total private contributions received, disregarding contributions from any person to the extent that total contributions to the candidate by that person exceed $250. Payments to any candidate under Chapter 96 may not exceed 50 percent of the overall expenditure ceiling accepted by the candidate.

Appellants argue that Subtitle H is invalid (1) as "contrary to the 'general welfare,'" (2) because any scheme of public financing of election campaigns is inconsistent with the First Amendment, and (3) because Subtitle H invidiously discriminates against certain interests in violation of the Due Process Clause of the Fifth Amendment. We find no merit in these contentions.

. . .

. . . [W]e reject appellants' claims that Subtitle H is facially unconstitutional.

. . . We . . . hold Subtitle H severable from those portions of the legislation today held constitutionally infirm.

The 1974 amendments to the Act create an eight-member Federal Election Commission (Commission) and vest in it primary and substantial responsibility for administering and enforcing the Act. The question that we address in this portion of the opinion is whether, in view of the manner in which a majority of its members are appointed, the Commission may, under the Constitution, exercise the powers conferred upon it. . . .

. . .

We hold that these provisions of the Act, vesting in the Commission primary responsibility for conducting civil litigation in the courts of the

United States for vindicating public rights, violate Art. II, §2, cl. 2, of the Constitution. Such functions may be discharged only by persons who are "Officers of the United States" within the language of that section.

All aspects of the Act are brought within the Commission's broad administrative powers: rule making, advisory opinions, and determinations of eligibility for funds and even for federal elective office itself. These functions, exercised free from day-to-day supervision of either Congress or the Executive Branch, are more legislative and judicial in nature than are the Commission's enforcement powers, and are of kinds usually performed by independent regulatory agencies or by some department in the Executive Branch under the direction of an Act of Congress. Congress viewed these broad powers as essential to effective and impartial administration of the entire substantive framework of the Act. Yet each of these functions also represents the performance of a significant governmental duty exercised pursuant to a public law. While the President may not insist that such functions be delegated to an appointee of his removable at will, none of them operates merely in aid of congressional authority to legislate or is sufficiently removed from the administration and enforcement of public law to allow it to be performed by the present Commission. These administrative functions may therefore be exercised only by persons who are "Officers of the United States."

It is also our view that the Commission's inability to exercise certain powers because of the method by which its members have been selected should not affect the validity of the Commission's administrative actions and determinations to this date, including its administration of those provisions, upheld today, authorizing the public financing of federal elections. The past acts of the Commission are therefore accorded de facto validity, just as we have recognized should be the case with respect to legislative acts performed by legislators held to have been elected in accordance with an unconstitutional apportionment plan. We also draw on the Court's practice in the apportionment and voting rights cases and stay, for a period not to exceed thirty days, the Court's judgment insofar as it affects the authority of the Commission to exercise the duties and powers granted it under the Act. This limited stay will afford Congress an opportunity to reconstitute the Commission by law or to adopt other valid enforcement mechanisms without interrupting enforcement of the provisions the Court sustains, allowing the present Commission in the interim to function de facto in accordance with the substantive provisions of the Act.

In summary, we sustain the individual contribution limits, the disclosure and reporting provisions, and the public financing scheme. We conclude, however, that the limitations on campaign expenditures, on independent expenditures by individuals and groups, and on expenditures by a candidate from his personal funds are constitutionally infirm. Finally, we hold that most of the powers conferred by the Act upon the Federal Election Commission can be exercised only by "Officers of the United States," appointed in conformity with Art. II, §2, cl. 2, of the Constitution, and therefore cannot be exercised by the Commission as presently constituted.

In No. 75–436, the judgment of the Court of Appeals is affirmed in part and reversed in part. The judgment of the District Court in No. 75–437 is affirmed. The mandate shall issue forthwith, except that our judgment is stayed, for a period not to exceed thirty days, insofar as it affects the authority of the Commission to exercise the duties and powers granted it under the Act.

Federal Election Commission v. Democratic Senatorial Campaign Committee
454 U.S. 27 (1981)

The Federal Election Campaign Act of 1971, limits the contributions that may be made to candidates or political committees in an election for federal office. One provision of the Act, authorizes limited expenditures by the national and state committees of a political party in connection with a general election campaign for federal office. After authorizing such expenditures, which otherwise would be impermissible, the section specifies the amount a national committee may spend in connection with a Presidential campaign, and limits the amount that national and state committees of a political party may spend in connection with the general election campaign of a candidate for the Senate or the House of Representatives. In this litigation, we examine whether §441a(d)(3) is violated when a state committee of a political party designates the national senatorial campaign committee of that party as its agent for the purpose of making expenditures allowed by the Act.

The National Republican Senatorial Committee (NRSC) is a political committee organized specifically to support Republican candidates in elections for the United States Senate. Although the NRSC is authorized by §441a(h) to contribute up to $17,500 to a candidate for election to the Senate, it is not given authority by §441a(d) to make expenditures on behalf of such candidates, and it is the position of the Federal Election Commission, the agency charged with enforcement of the Act, that the NRSC may not do so on its own account. The Commission, however, has permitted the NRSC to act as the agent of national and state party committees in making expenditures on their behalf.

In February 1977, in response to an inquiry submitted late in 1976, the Commission issued an Advisory Opinion, 1976–108, that it would be consistent with the Act for the NRSC to spend its own funds in support of congressional candidates as the designated agent of the Republican National Committee (RNC). In April 1977, the Commission issued a regulation, which provides that the national party committees may make expenditures in the general election campaign for President "through any designated agent, including state and subordinate party committees." On the basis of this regulatory authority, the National Committee of the Democratic Party entered into an agreement specifying the Democratic Senatorial Campaign Committee (DSCC) as its agent for the expenditure of authorized funds in Senate campaigns. In 1978, certain state Republican Party committees designated the NRSC as their agent for §441a(d)(3) expenditure purposes. Complaints were filed with the Commission challenging this practice as inconsistent with the Act. In dismissing these complaints, the Commission twice ruled . . . that the agency arrangements were not forbidden by the Act. In 1980, certain state committees again designated the NRSC as their agent, and on May 19, the DSCC filed its complaint with the Commission asserting that the NRSC's agreements with the state committees were contrary to §441a(d)(3). The complaint did not challenge the contemporaneous agency agreement under which the NRSC acted as the agent of the RNC in connection with the latter's expenditures under 441a(d). After considering the report of its General Counsel, the Commission unanimously dismissed the complaint, concluding that there was "no reason to believe" that the agreements violated the Act.

The DSCC petitioned for review in the District Court for the District of Columbia pursuant to §437g(a)(8). That court granted the Commission's motion for summary judgment, concluding that the decision of the Commission was not "arbitrary, capricious, an abuse of discretion or otherwise not in accordance with law." On appeal, the Court of Appeals for the District of Columbia Circuit granted the NRSC leave to intervene and reversed the judgment of the District Court after concluding that the "plain language of Section 441a(d)(3) precludes" the agency agreements between state committees and the NRSC. . . .

. . .

. . . [T]he absence of a prohibition on the agency arrangements at issue, the lack of a clearly enunciated legislative purpose to that effect, and indeed, the countervailing existence of a transfer mechanism whose presence is difficult to reconcile with the interpretation urged by the Court of Appeals, prevent us from finding that the Commission's determination was "contrary to law." Therefore, the judgment of the Court of Appeals is reversed.

Brown v. Socialist Workers '74 Campaign Committee
459 U.S. 87 (1982)

This case presents the question whether certain disclosure requirements of the Ohio Campaign Expense Reporting Law, can be constitutionally applied to the Socialist Workers Party, a minor political party which historically has been the object of harassment by government officials and private parties. The Ohio statute requires every political party to report the names and addresses of campaign contributors and recipients of campaign disbursements. . . . [A] three-judge District Court for the Southern District of Ohio held that the Ohio statute is unconstitutional as applied to the Socialist Workers Party. . . .

The Socialist Workers Party (SWP) is a small political party with approximately sixty members in the State of Ohio. The Party states in its constitution that its aim is "the abolition of capitalism and the establishment of a workers' government to achieve socialism." As the District Court found, the SWP does not advocate the use of violence. It seeks instead to achieve social change through the political process, and its members regularly run for public office. The SWP's candidates have had little success at the polls. . . .

In 1974, appellees instituted a class action in the District Court for the Northern District of Ohio challenging the constitutionality of the disclosure provisions of the Ohio Campaign Expense Reporting Law. The Ohio statute requires every candidate for political office to file a statement identifying each contributor and each recipient of a disbursement of campaign funds. The "object or purpose" of each disbursement must also be disclosed. The lists of names and addresses of contributors and recipients are open to public inspection for at least six years. Violations of the disclosure requirements are punishable by fines of up to $1,000 for each day of violation.

On November 6, 1974, the District Court for the Northern District of Ohio entered a temporary restraining order barring the enforcement of the disclosure requirements against the class pending a determination of the merits. The case was then transferred to the District Court for the Southern District of Ohio, which entered an identical temporary restraining order in February 1975. Accordingly, since 1974, appellees have not disclosed the names of contributors and recipients, but have otherwise complied with the statute. . . .

. . .

We reject appellants' unduly narrow view of the minor party exemption recognized in *Buckley*. Appellants' attempt to limit the exemption to laws requiring disclosure of contributors is inconsistent with the rationale for the exemption stated in *Buckley*. The Court concluded that the government interests supporting disclosure are weaker in the case of minor parties, while the threat to First Amendment values is greater. Both of these considerations apply not only to the disclosure of campaign contributors, but also to the disclosure of recipients of campaign disbursements.

Although appellants contend that requiring disclosure of recipients of disbursements is necessary to prevent corruption, this Court recognized in *Buckley* that this concededly legitimate government interest has less force in the context of minor parties. The federal law considered in *Buckley*, like the Ohio law at issue here, required campaign committees to identify both campaign contributors and recipients of campaign disbursements. . . . We concluded, however, that, because minor party candidates are unlikely to win elections, the government's general interest in "deterring the 'buying' of elections" is "reduced" in the case of minor parties.

Moreover, appellants seriously understate the threat to First Amendment rights that would result from requiring minor parties to disclose the recipients of campaign disbursements. Expenditures by a political party often consist of reimbursements, advances, or wages paid to party members, campaign workers, and supporters, whose activities lie at the very core of the First Amendment. Disbursements may also go to persons who choose to express their support for an unpopular cause by providing services rendered scarce by public hostility and suspicion. Should their involvement be publicized, these persons would be as vulnerable to threats, harassment, and reprisals as are contributors whose connection with the party is solely financial. Even individuals who receive disbursements for "merely" commercial transactions may be deterred by the public emnity attending publicity, and those seeking to harass may disrupt commercial activities on the basis of expenditure information. Because an individual who enters into a transaction with a minor party purely for commercial reasons lacks any ideological commitment to the party, such an individual may well be deterred from providing services by even a small risk of harassment. Compelled disclosure of the names of such recipients of expenditures could therefore cripple a minor party's ability to operate effectively, and thereby reduce "the free circulation of ideas both within and without the political arena."

We hold, therefore, that the test announced in *Buckley* for safeguarding the First Amendment interests of minor parties and their members and supporters applies not only to the compelled disclosure of campaign contributors, but also to the compelled disclosure of recipients of campaign disbursements.

The District Court properly applied the *Buckley* test to the facts of this case. The District Court found "substantial evidence of both governmental and private hostility toward and harassment of SWP members and supporters." Appellees introduced proof of specific incidents of private and government hostility toward the SWP and its members. . . .

. . .

The First Amendment prohibits a State from compelling disclosures by a minor party that will subject those persons identified to the reasonable probability of threats, harassment, or reprisals. Such disclosures would infringe the First Amendment rights of the party and its members and supporters. In light of the substantial evidence of past and present hostility from private persons and Government officials against the SWP, Ohio's campaign disclosure requirements cannot be constitutionally applied to the Ohio SWP.

The judgment of the three-judge District Court for the Southern District of Ohio is affirmed.

Federal Election Commission v. National Conservative Political Action Committee
470 U.S. 480 (1985)

The Presidential Election Campaign Fund Act (Fund Act), offers the Presidential candidates of major political parties the option of receiving public financing for their general election campaigns. If a Presidential candidate elects public financing, §9012(f) makes it a criminal offense for independent "political committees," such as appellees National Conservative Political Action Committee (NCPAC) and Fund For A Conservative Majority (FCM), to expend more than $1,000 to further that candidate's election. A three-judge District Court for the Eastern District of Pennsylvania, in companion lawsuits brought respectively by the Federal Election Commission (FEC) and by the Democratic Party of the United States and the Democratic National Committee (DNC), held §9012(f) unconstitutional on its face because it violated the First Amendment to the United States Constitution. These plaintiffs challenge that determination on this appeal, and the FEC also appeals from that part of the judgment holding that the Democratic Party and the DNC have standing . . . to seek a declaratory judgment against appellees upholding the constitutionality of §9012(f). . . .

The present litigation began in May 1983, when the Democratic Party, the DNC, and Edward Mezvinsky, Chairman of the Pennsylvania Democratic State Committee, in his individual capacity as a citizen eligible to vote for President of the United States (collectively, the Democrats), filed suit against NCPAC and FCM (the PACs), who had announced their intention to spend large sums of money to help bring about the reelection of President Ronald Reagan in 1984. Their amended complaint sought a declaration that §9012(f), which they believed would prohibit the PACs' intended expenditures, was constitutional. The FEC intervened for the sole purpose of moving, along with the PACs, to dismiss the complaint for lack of standing.

In June, 1983, the FEC brought a separate action against the same defendants seeking identical declaratory relief. It was referred to the same three-judge District Court, which consolidated the two cases for all purposes. . . . [T]he court issued a comprehensive opinion, holding that the Democrats had standing under §9011(b)(1) and Art. III of the Constitution to seek the requested declaratory relief, but that the Democrats and the FEC were not entitled to a declaration that §9012(f) is constitutional. The court held that §9012(f) abridges First Amendment freedoms of speech and association, that it is substantially overbroad, and that it cannot permissibly be given a narrowing construction to cure the overbreadth. The court did not, however, declare §9012(f) unconstitutional, because the PACs had not filed a counterclaim requesting such a declaration.

. . .

Despite the identity of the relief requested by the FEC and the Democrats, the FEC asks this Court to reverse the District Court's holding that the Democrats also have standing under §9011(b)(1). The Democrats maintain that there is no need to resolve this question, because there is no doubt about the standing of the FEC and the legal issues and relief requested are the same in the two cases. The PACs have declined to renew or brief their jurisdictional challenge in this Court because, in the present procedural posture, they see the standing question as a "turf fight" in which they do not wish to participate.

. . .

The judgment of the District Court is affirmed as to the constitutionality of §9012(f), but is reversed on the issue of the Democrats' standing, with instructions to dismiss their complaint for lack of standing.

Colorado Republican Federal Campaign Committee v. Jones
518 U.S. 604 (1996)

In April 1986, before the Colorado Republican Party had selected its senatorial candidate for the fall's election, that Party's Federal Campaign Committee bought radio advertisements attacking Timothy Wirth, the Democratic Party's likely candidate. The Federal Election Commission (FEC) charged that this "expenditure" exceeded the dollar limits that a provision of the Federal Election Campaign Act of 1971 (FECA) imposes upon political party "expenditure[s] in connection with" a "general election campaign" for congressional office. This case focuses upon the constitutionality of those limits as applied to this case. . . .

. . . That Act sought both to remedy the appearance of a "corrupt" political process (one in which large contributions seem to buy legislative votes) and to level the electoral playing field by reducing campaign costs. It consequently imposed limits upon the amounts that individuals, corporations, "political committees" (such as

political action committees, or PAC's), and political parties could contribute to candidates for federal office, and it also imposed limits upon the amounts that candidates, corporations, labor unions, political committees, and political parties could spend, even on their own, to help a candidate win election.

. . .

FECA . . . has a special provision . . . that governs contributions and expenditures by political parties. . . . [A] party's coordinated expenditures would be subject to the $5,000 limitation.

However, FECA's special provision, which we shall call the "Party Expenditure Provision," creates a general exception from this contribution limitation, and from any other limitation on expenditures. . . . After exempting political parties from the general contribution and expenditure limitations of the statute, the Party Expenditure Provision then imposes a substitute limitation upon party "expenditures" in a senatorial campaign equal to the greater of $20,000 or "2 cents multiplied by the voting age population of the State," adjusted for inflation since 1974. The Provision permitted a political party in Colorado in 1986 to spend about $103,000 in connection with the general election campaign of a candidate for the United States Senate. . . .

In January 1986, Timothy Wirth, then a Democratic Congressman, announced that he would run for an open Senate seat in November. In April, before either the Democratic primary or the Republican convention, the Colorado Republican Federal Campaign Committee (Colorado Party), the petitioner here, bought radio advertisements attacking Congressman Wirth. The State Democratic Party complained to the Federal Election Commission. It pointed out that the Colorado Party had previously assigned its $103,000 general election allotment to the National Republican Senatorial Committee, leaving it without any permissible spending balance. It argued that the purchase of radio time was an "expenditure in connection with the general election campaign of a candidate for Federal office," which, consequently, exceeded the Party Expenditure Provision limits.

The FEC agreed with the Democratic Party. It brought a complaint against the Colorado Republican Party, charging a violation. The Colorado Party defended in part by claiming that the Party Expenditure Provision's expenditure limitations violated the First Amendment—a charge that it repeated in a counterclaim that said the Colorado Party intended to make other "expenditures directly in connection with" senatorial elections, and attacked the constitutionality of the entire Party Expenditure Provision. The Federal District Court interpreted the Provision's words "'in connection with' the general election campaign of a candidate" narrowly, as meaning only expenditures for advertising using "express words of advocacy of election or defeat." As so interpreted, the court held, the provision did not cover the expenditures here. The court entered summary judgment for the Colorado Party and dismissed its counterclaim as moot.

Both sides appealed. The Government, for the FEC, argued for a somewhat broader interpretation of the statute—applying the limits to advertisements containing an "electioneering message" about a "clearly identified candidate"—which, it said, both covered the expenditure and satisfied the Constitution. The Court of Appeals agreed. It found the Party Expenditure Provision applicable, held it constitutional, and ordered judgment in the FEC's favor.

. . .

. . . A political party's independent expression not only reflects its members' views about the philosophical and governmental matters that bind them together, it also seeks to convince others to join those members in a practical democratic task, the task of creating a government that voters can instruct and hold responsible for subsequent success or failure. The independent expression of a political party's views is "core" First Amendment activity no less than is the independent expression of individuals, candidates, or other political committees.

We are not aware of any special dangers of corruption associated with political parties that tip the constitutional balance in a different direction. When this Court considered, and held unconstitutional, limits that FECA had set on certain independent expenditures by political action committees, it reiterated *Buckley*'s observation that "the absence of prearrangement and coordination" does not eliminate, but it does help to "alleviate," any "danger" that a candidate will understand the expenditure as an effort to obtain a "quid pro quo." The same is true of independent party expenditures.

We recognize that FECA permits individuals to contribute more money ($20,000) to a party than to a candidate ($1,000) or to other political committees ($5,000). We also recognize that FECA permits unregulated "soft money" contributions to a party for certain activities, such as electing candidates for state office, or for voter registration and "get out the vote" drives. But the opportunity for corruption posed by these greater opportunities for contributions is, at best, attenuated. Unregulated "soft money" contributions may not be used to influence a federal campaign except when used in the limited, party-building activities specifically designated in the statute. Any contribution to a party that is earmarked for a particular campaign is considered a contribution to the candidate, and is subject to the contribution limitations. A party may not simply channel unlimited amounts of even undesignated contributions to a candidate, since such direct transfers are also considered contributions, and are subject to the contribution limits on a "multi-candidate political committee." The greatest danger of corruption, therefore, appears to be from the ability of donors to give sums up to $20,000 to a party which may be used for independent party expenditures for the benefit of a particular candidate. We could understand how Congress, were it to conclude that the potential for evasion of the individual contribution limits was a serious matter, might decide to change the statute's limitations on contributions to political parties. But we do not believe that the risk of corruption present here could justify the "markedly greater burden on basic freedoms caused by" the statute's limitations on expenditures. Contributors seeking to avoid the effect of the $1,000 contribution limit indirectly by donations to the national party could spend that same amount of money (or more) themselves more directly by making their own independent expenditures promoting the candidate. If anything, an independent expenditure made possible by a $20,000 donation, but controlled and directed by a party rather than the donor, would seem less likely to corrupt than the same (or a much larger) independent expenditure made directly by that donor. In any case, the constitutionally significant fact, present equally in both instances, is the lack of coordination between the candidate and the source of the expenditure. This fact prevents us from assuming, absent convincing evidence to the contrary, that a limitation on political parties' independent expenditures is necessary to combat a substantial danger of corruption of the electoral system.

The Government does not point to record evidence or legislative findings suggesting any special corruption problem in respect to independent party expenditures. To the contrary, this Court's opinions suggest that Congress wrote the Party Expenditure Provision not so much because of a special concern about the potentially "corrupting" effect of party expenditures, but rather for the constitutionally insufficient purpose of reducing what it saw as wasteful and excessive campaign spending. In fact, rather than indicating a special fear of the corruptive influence of political parties, the legislative history demonstrates Congress's general desire to enhance what was seen as an important and legitimate role for political parties in American elections.

. . . We do not see how a Constitution that grants to individuals, candidates, and ordinary political committees the right to make unlimited independent expenditures could deny the same right to political parties. Having concluded this, we need not consider the Party's further claim that the statute's "in connection with" language, and the FEC's interpretation of that language, are unconstitutionally vague.

The Government does not deny the force of the precedent we have discussed. Rather, it argued below, and the lower courts accepted, that the expenditure in this case should be treated under those precedents, not as an "independent expenditure," but rather as a "coordinated expenditure," which those cases have treated as "contributions," and which those cases have held Congress may constitutionally regulate.

While the District Court found that the expenditure in this case was "coordinated," it did not do so based on any factual finding that the Party had consulted with any candidate in the making or planing of the advertising campaign in question. Instead, the District Court accepted the Government's argument that all party expenditures should be treated as if they had been coordinated as a matter of law, "[b]ased on Supreme Court precedent and the Commission's interpretation of the statute." The Court of Appeals agreed with this legal conclusion. Thus, the lower courts' "finding" of coordination does not conflict with our conclusion, that the summary judgment record shows no actual coordination as a matter of fact. The question, instead, is whether the Court of Appeals erred as a legal matter in accepting the Government's conclusive presumption that all party expenditures are "coordinated." We believe it did.

. . .

Finally, we recognize that the FEC may have characterized the expenditures as "coordinated" in light of this Court's constitutional decisions prohibiting regulation of most independent expenditures. But, if so, the characterization cannot help the Government prove its case. An agency's simply calling an independent expenditure a "coordinated expenditure" cannot (for constitutional purposes) make it one.

The Government also argues that the Colorado Party has conceded that the expenditures are "coordinated." But there is no such concession in respect to the underlying facts. . . . The Government has not referred us to any place where the Party conceded away or abandoned its legal claim that Congress may not limit the uncoordinated expenditure at issue here. And, in any event, we are not bound to decide a matter of constitutional law based on a concession by the particular party before the Court as to the proper legal characterization of the facts.

Finally, the Government and supporting amici argue that the expenditure is "coordinated" because a party and its candidate are identical, i.e., the party, in a sense, "is" its candidates. We cannot assume, however, that this is so. Congress chose to treat candidates and their parties quite

differently under the Act, for example, by regulating contributions from one to the other. And we are not certain whether a metaphysical identity would help the Government, for in that case one might argue that the absolute identity of views and interests eliminates any potential for corruption, as would seem to be the case in the relationship between candidates and their campaign committees.

The Colorado Party and supporting amici have argued a broader question than we have decided, for they have claimed that, in the special case of political parties, the First Amendment forbids congressional efforts to limit coordinated expenditures as well as independent expenditures. Because the expenditure before us is an independent expenditure we have not reached this broader question in deciding the Party's "as applied" challenge.

. . .

. . . In our view, given the important competing interests involved in campaign finance issues, we should proceed cautiously, consistent with this precedent, and remand for further proceedings.

For these reasons, the judgment of the Court of Appeals is vacated, and the case is remanded for further proceedings.

Nixon v. Shrink Missouri Government PAC 528 U.S. 377 (2000)

The principal issues in this case are whether *Buckley* is authority for state limits on contributions to state political candidates and whether the federal limits approved in *Buckley*, with or without adjustment for inflation, define the scope of permissible state limitations today. . . .

In 1994, the Legislature of Missouri enacted Senate Bill 650 (SB650) to restrict the permissible amounts of contributions to candidates for state office. Before the statute became effective, however, Missouri voters approved a ballot initiative with even stricter contribution limits, effective immediately. The United States Court of Appeals for the Eighth Circuit then held the initiative's contribution limits unconstitutional under the First Amendment, with the upshot that the previously dormant 1994 statute took effect.

As amended in 1997, that statute imposes contribution limits ranging from $250 to a $1,000, depending on specified state office or size of constituency. . . . The statutory dollar amounts are baselines for an adjustment each even-numbered year, to be made "by multiplying the base year amount by the cumulative consumer price index . . . and rounded to the nearest $25 amount, for all years since January 1, 1995." When this suit was filed, the limits ranged from a high of $1,075 for contributions to candidates for statewide office (including state auditor) and for any office where the population exceeded 250,000, down to $275 for contributions to candidates for state representative or for any office for which there were fewer than 100,000 people represented.

Respondents Shrink Missouri Government PAC, a political action committee, and Zev David Fredman, a candidate for the 1998 Republican nomination for state auditor, sought to enjoin enforcement of the contribution statute as violating their First and Fourteenth Amendment rights. . . . Shrink Missouri gave $1,025 to Fredman's candidate committee in 1997, and another $50 in 1998. Shrink Missouri represented that, without the limitation, it would contribute more to the Fredman campaign. Fredman alleged he could campaign effectively only with more generous contributions than §130.032.1 allowed.

On cross-motions for summary judgment, the District Court sustained the statute. . . . The District Court rejected respondents' contention that inflation since *Buckley*'s approval of a federal $1,000 restriction meant that the state limit of $1,075 for a statewide office could not be constitutional today.

The Court of Appeals for the Eighth Circuit nonetheless enjoined enforcement of the law pending appeal and ultimately reversed the District Court. Finding that *Buckley* had "articulated and applied a strict scrutiny standard of review," the Court of Appeals held that Missouri was bound to demonstrate "that it has a compelling interest and that the contribution limits at issue are narrowly drawn to serve that interest." The appeals court treated Missouri's claim of a compelling interest "in avoiding the corruption or the perception of corruption brought about when candidates for elective office accept large campaign contributions" as insufficient by itself to satisfy strict scrutiny. . . .

. . .

In *Buckley*, we specifically rejected the contention that $1,000, or any other amount, was a constitutional minimum below which legislatures could not regulate. . . . [W]e referred instead to the outer limits of contribution regulation by asking whether there was any showing that the limits were so low as to impede the ability of candidates to "amas[s] the resources necessary for effective advocacy." We asked, in other words, whether the contribution limitation was so radical in effect as to render political association ineffective, drive the sound of a candidate's voice below the level of notice, and render contributions pointless. Such being the test, the issue in later cases cannot be truncated to a narrow question about the power of the dollar, but must go to the power to mount a campaign with all the dollars likely to be forthcoming. . . .

. . .

. . . Shrink and Fredman did not request that *Buckley* be overruled; the furthest reach of their arguments about the law was that subsequent decisions already on the books had enhanced the State's burden of justification beyond what

Buckley required, a proposition we have rejected as mistaken.

There is no reason in logic or evidence to doubt the sufficiency of *Buckley* to govern this case in support of the Missouri statute. The judgment of the Court of Appeals is, accordingly, reversed, and the case is remanded for proceedings consistent with this opinion.

8

Electors, Elections, and Challenges to Electoral Outcomes

The United States does not elect its president and vice president by popular vote. Instead the Constitution relies on the mechanism of the electoral college, which comprises electors selected by state officials. This chapter includes the landmark decision of Bush v. Gore.

McPherson v. Blacker
146 U.S. 1 (1892)

. . .

The manner of the appointment of electors directed by the act of Michigan is the election of an elector and an alternate elector in each of the twelve congressional districts into which the state of Michigan is divided, and of an elector and an alternate elector at large in each of two districts defined by the act. It is insisted that it was not competent for the legislature to direct this manner of appointment, because the state is to appoint as a body politic and corporate, and so must act as a unit, and cannot delegate the authority to subdivisions created for the purpose; and it is argued that the appointment of electors by districts is not an appointment by the state, because all its citizens otherwise qualified are not permitted to vote for all the presidential electors. . . .

If the legislature possesses plenary authority to direct the manner of appointment, and might itself exercise the appointing power by joint ballot or concurrence of the two houses, or according to such mode as designated, it is difficult to perceive why, if the legislature prescribes as a method of appointment choice by vote, it must necessarily be by general ticket, and not by districts. In other words, the act of appointment is none the less the act of the state in its entirety because arrived at by districts, for the act is the act of political agencies duly authorized to speak for the state, and the combined result is the expression of the voice of the state, a result reached by direction of the legislature, to whom the whole subject is committed.

. . .

Although it is thus declared that the people of the several states shall choose the members of Congress . . . the state legislatures, prior to 1842, in prescribing the times, places, and manner of holding elections for representatives, had usually apportioned the state into districts, and assigned to each a representative; and by act of congress of June 25, 1842, it was provided that, where a state was entitled to more than one representative, the election should be by districts. It has never been doubted that representatives in congress thus chosen represented the entire people of the state acting in their sovereign capacity.

By original Clause 3, 1, Art. 2, and by the Twelfth Amendment, which superseded that clause in case of a failure in the election of President by the people the House of Representatives is to choose the President; and "the vote shall be taken by states, the representation from each state having one vote." The state acts as a unit, and its vote is given as a unit, but that vote is arrived at through the votes of its representatives in Congress elected by districts.

The state also acts individually through its electoral college, although, by reason of the power of its legislature over the manner of appointment, the vote of its electors may be divided.

The Constitution does not provide that the appointment of electors shall be by popular vote, nor that the electors shall be voted for upon a general ticket, nor that the majority of those who exercise the elective franchise can alone choose the electors. It recognizes that the people act through their representatives in the legislature, and leaves it to the legislature exclusively to define the method of effecting the object.

. . .

It has been said that the word "appoint" is not the most appropriate word to describe the result of a popular election. Perhaps not; but it is sufficiently comprehensive to cover that mode, and was manifestly used as conveying the broadest power of determination. It was used in Article 5 of the Articles of Confederation, which provided that "delegates shall be annually appointed in such manner as the legislature of each state shall direct"; and in the resolution of Congress of February 21, 1787, which declared it expedient that "a convention of delegates who shall have been appointed by the several states" should be held. The appointment of delegates was, in fact, made by the legislatures directly, but that involved no denial of authority to direct some other mode. . . .

. . .

In short, the appointment and mode of appointment of electors belong exclusively to the states under the Constitution of the United States. . . .

Congress is empowered to determine the time of choosing the electors and the day on which they are to give their votes, which is required to be the same day throughout the United States; but otherwise the power and jurisdiction of the state is exclusive, with the exception of the provisions as to the number of electors and the ineligibility of certain persons, so framed that congressional and federal influence might be excluded.

. . .

It is argued that the district mode of choosing electors, while not obnoxious to constitutional objection, if the operation of the electoral system had conformed to its original object and purpose, had become so in view of the practical working of that system. Doubtless it was supposed that the electors would exercise a reasonable independence and fair judgment in the selection of the chief executive, but experience soon demonstrated that, whether chosen by the legislatures or by popular suffrage on general ticket or in districts, they were so chosen simply to register the will of the appointing power in respect of a particular candidate. In relation, then, to the independence of the electors, the original expectation may be said to have been frustrated. But we can perceive no reason for holding that the power confided to the states by the Constitution has ceased to exist because the operation of the system has not fully realized the hopes of those by whom it was created. . . .

. . .

If, because it happened, at the time of the adoption of the Fourteenth Amendment, that those who exercised the elective franchise in the state of Michigan were entitled to vote for all the presidential electors, this right was rendered permanent by that amendment, then the second clause of Article 2 has been so amended that the states can no longer appoint in such manner as the legislatures thereof may direct; and yet no such result is indicated by the language used, nor are the amendments necessarily inconsistent with that clause. The first section of the Fourteenth Amendment does not refer to the exercise of the elective franchise, though the second provides that if the right to vote is denied or abridged to any male inhabitant of the state having attained majority, and being a citizen of the United States, then the basis of representation to which each state is entitled in the Congress shall be proportionately reduced. Whenever presidential electors are appointed by popular election, then the right to vote cannot be denied or abridged without invoking the penalty; and so of the right to vote for representatives in Congress, the executive and judicial officers of a state, or the members of the legislature thereof. The right to vote intended to be protected refers to the right to vote as established by the laws and constitution of the state. There is no color for the contention that under the amendments every male inhabitant of the state, being a citizen of the United States, has from the time of his majority a right to vote for presidential electors.

The object of the Fourteenth Amendment in respect of citizenship was to preserve equality of rights and to prevent discrimination as between citizens, but not to radically change the whole theory of the relations of the state and federal governments to each other, and of both governments to the people.

. . .

If presidential electors are appointed by the legislatures, no discrimination is made; if they are elected in districts where each citizen has an equal right to vote, the same as any other citizen has, no discrimination is made. Unless the authority vested in the legislatures by the second clause of section 1 of Article 2 has been divested,

and the state has lost its power of appointment, except in one manner, the position taken on behalf of relators is untenable, and it is apparent that neither of these amendments can be given such effect.

The third clause of section 1 of Article 2 of the Constitution is: "The congress may determine the time of choosing the electors, and the day on which they shall give their votes; which day shall be the same throughout the United States."

Under the act of Congress of March 1, 1792, it was provided that the electors should meet and give their votes on the first Wednesday in December at such place in each state as should be directed by the legislature thereof, and by act of Congress of January 23, 1845, that the electors should be appointed in each state on the Tuesday next after the first Monday in the month of November in the year in which they were to be appointed: provided, that each state might by law provide for the filling of any vacancies in its college of electors when such college meets to give its electoral vote: and provided that when any state shall have held an election for the purpose of choosing electors, and has failed to make a choice on the day prescribed, then the electors may be appointed on a subsequent day, in such manner as the state may by law provide. These provisions were carried forward into sections 131, 133, 134, and 135 of the Revised Statutes.

By the act of Congress of February 3, 1887, entitled "An act to fix the day for the meeting of the electors of president and vice president," etc., it was provided that the electors of each state should meet and give their votes on the second Monday in January next following their appointment. The state law in question here fixes the first Wednesday of December as the day for the meeting of the electors, as originally designated by Congress. In this respect it is in conflict with the act of Congress, and must necessarily give way. But this part of the act is not so inseparably connected, in substance, with the other parts as to work the destruction of the whole act. Striking out the day for the meeting, which had already been otherwise determined by the act of Congress, the act remains complete in itself, and capable of being carried out in accordance with the legislative intent. The state law yields only to the extent of the collision. The construction to this effect by the state court is of persuasive force, if not of controlling weight.

We do not think this result affected by the provision in Act No. 50 in relation to a tie vote. Under the constitution of the state of Michigan, in case two or more persons have an equal and the highest number of votes for any office, as canvassed by the board of state canvassers, the legislature in joint convention chooses one of these persons to fill the office. This rule is recognized in this act, which also makes it the duty of the governor in such case to convene the legislature in special session for the purpose of its application, immediately upon the determination by the board of state canvassers.

We entirely agree with the supreme court of Michigan that it cannot be held, as matter of law, that the legislature would not have provided for being convened in special session but for the provision relating to the time of the meeting of the electors contained in the act, and are of opinion that that date may be rejected, and the act be held to remain otherwise complete and valid.

And as the state is fully empowered to fill any vacancy which may occur in its electoral college, when it meets to give its electoral vote, we find nothing in the mode provided for anticipating such an exigency which operates to invalidate the law. We repeat that the main question arising for consideration is one of power, and not of policy,

and we are unable to arrive at any other conclusion than that the act of the legislature of Michigan of May 1, 1891, is not void as in contravention of the Constitution of the United States, for want of power in its enactment.

The judgment of the supreme court of Michigan must be affirmed.

Taylor v. Beckham
178 U.S. 548 (1900)

It is obviously essential to the independence of the states, and to their peace and tranquillity, that their power to prescribe the qualifications of their own officers, the tenure of their offices, the manner of their election, and the grounds on which, the tribunals before which, and the mode in which, such elections may be contested, should be exclusive and free from external interference, except so far as plainly provided by the Constitution of the United States.

And where controversies over the election of state officers have reached the state courts in the manner provided by, and been there determined in accordance with, the state constitutions and laws, the cases must necessarily be rare in which the interference of this court can properly be invoked.

. . .

For more than a hundred years the Constitution of Kentucky has provided that contested elections for governor and lieutenant governor shall be determined by the general assembly. In 1799, by a committee, "to be selected from both houses of the general assembly, and formed and regulated in such manner as shall be directed by law"; since 1850, "by both houses of the general assembly, according to such regulations as may be established by law."

The highest court of the state has often held, and, in the present case has again declared, that under these constitutional provisions the power of the general assembly to determine the result is exclusive, and that its decision is not open to judicial review. . . .

. . .

Our system of elections was unknown to the common law, and the whole subject is regulated by constitutions and statutes passed thereunder. In the view of the court of appeals the mode of contesting elections was part of the machinery for ascertaining the result of the election, and hence the rights of the officer who held the certificate of the state board of canvassers "were provisional or temporary until the determination of the result of the election as provided in the Constitution, and upon that determination, if adverse to him, they ceased altogether." In fact, the statute provided that when the "incumbent is adjudged not to be entitled his powers shall immediately cease," and under the Constitution the holder of the certificate manifestly held it for the time being subject to the issue of a contest if initiated.

It is clear that the judgment of the court of appeals, in declining to go behind the decision of the tribunal vested by the state constitution and laws with the ultimate determination of the right to these offices, denied no right secured by the Fourteenth Amendment.

. . .

. . . The commonwealth of Kentucky is in full possession of its faculties as a member of the Union, and no exigency has arisen requiring the interference of the general government to enforce the guaranties of the Constitution, or to repel invasion, or to put down domestic violence. In the eye of the Constitution, the legislative, executive, and judicial departments of the state are peace-fully operating by the orderly and settled methods prescribed by its fundamental law, notwithstanding there may be difficulties and disturbances arising from the pendency and determination of these contests. This very case shows that this is so, for those who assert that they were aggrieved by the action of the general assembly properly accepted the only appropriate remedy which, under the law, was within the reach of the parties. That this proved ineffectual as to them, even though their grounds of complaint may have been in fact well founded, was the result of the Constitution and laws under which they lived and by which they were bound. Any remedy beside that is to be found in the august tribunal of the people, which is continually sitting, and over whose judgments on the conduct of public functionaries the courts exercise no control.

We must decline to take jurisdiction on the ground of deprivation of rights embraced by the Fourteenth Amendment, without due process of law, or of the violation of the guaranty of a republican form of government by reason of similar deprivation.

. . .

Writ of error dismissed.

Reed v. County Commissioners of Delaware County, Pennsylvania
277 U.S. 376 (1928)

The petitioners brought this suit in the United States court for the Eastern District of Pennsylvania. The court held it was without jurisdiction and dismissed the case. The Circuit of Appeals adopted its opinion, and affirmed the decree.

. . .

Petitioners, other than South, are United States Senators, and constitute a special committee created by Senate Resolution, to make investigation of means used to influence the nomination of candidates for the Senate. The Resolution empowered the committee "to require by subpoena or otherwise the attendance of witnesses, the production of books, papers, and documents, and to do such other acts as may be necessary in the matter of said investigation."

At a general election held in Pennsylvania November 2, 1926, William S. Vare and William B. Wilson were opposing candidates for the United States Senate. Vare was given the certificate of election, and Wilson initiated a contest. Thereafter January 11, 1927, the Senate passed Resolution 324. It recites that Wilson charges fraudulent and unlawful practices in connection with Vare's nomination and the election, and declares that, unless preserved for the use of the Senate, evidence relating to the election will be lost or destroyed. The Resolution empowers the special committee "to take . . . and preserve all ballot boxes . . . ballots, return sheets . . . and other records, books and documents used in said senatorial election. . . . "It confers on the committee "all powers of procedure with respect to the subject-matter of this resolution that said committee possesses under Resolution numbered 195 . . . with respect to the subject-matter of that resolution'; and it requires the Sergeant at Arms of the Senate to attend and execute the directions of the committee.

The Chairman of the Committee on Audit and Control of Contingent Expenditures having refused to approve the special committee's vouchers for expenses after the expiration of that Congress, the Sergeant at Arms refused to execute its orders. Thereupon the special committee directed the petitioner South, as its representative, to take possession of the boxes, ballots, and other things referred to in Resolution 324.

Respondents are the commissioners. . . . They are authorized custodians of boxes, ballots, and other things used in connection with the election. These were demanded by South in behalf of the committee. Respondents declined to give them up, and this suit was brought to obtain possession of them.

Petitioners do not claim that any act of Congress authorizes the committee or its members, collectively or separately, to sue. Of course, South's authority is no greater than that of the committee which he represents. The suit cannot be maintained unless the committee or its members were authorized to sue by Resolutions 195 and 324, even if it be assumed that the Senate alone may give that authority. The power is not specifically granted by either resolution. Petitioners rely on the general language in Resolution 195, which follows the express authorization of the committee to use its own process to require the production of evidence. The words are, "and to do such other acts as may be necessary in the matter of said investigation." The resolutions are to be construed having regard to the power possessed and customarily exerted by the Senate. It is the judge of the elections, returns, and qualifications of its members. It is fully empowered, and may determine such matters without the aid of the House of Representatives or the executive or judicial department. That power carries with it authority to take such steps as may be appropriate and necessary to secure information upon which to decide concerning elections. It has been customary for the Senate—and the House as well—to rely on its own power to compel attendance of witnesses and production of evidence in investigations made by it or through its committees. By means of its own process or that of its committee, the Senate is empowered to obtain evidence relating to the matters committed to it by the Constitution. And Congress has passed laws calculated to facilitate such investigations. Petitioners have not called attention to any action of the Senate, and we know of none, that supports the construction for which they contend. In the absence of some definite indication of that purpose, the Senate may not reasonably be held to have intended to depart from its established usage. Authority to exert the powers of the Senate to compel production of evidence differs widely from authority to invoke judicial power for that purpose. The phrase, "such other acts as may be necessary," may not be taken to include everything that under any circumstances might be covered by its words. The meaning of the general language employed is to be confined to acts belonging to the same general class as those specifically authorized. The context, the established practice of the Senate to rely on its own powers, and the attending circumstances, oppose the construction for which petitioners contend, and show that the Senate did not intend to authorize the committee, or anticipate that there might be need, to invoke the power of the Judicial Department. Petitioners are not "authorized by law to sue."

Decree affirmed.

Barry v. United States ex rel Cunningham
279 U.S. 597 (1929)

The questions here presented for determination grow out of an inquiry instituted by the United States Senate in respect of the validity of the election of a United States Senator from Pennsylvania in November 1926. The inquiry began before the election, immediately after the conclusion of the primaries, by the adoption of a resolution appointing a special committee to investigate expenditures, promises, etc., made to influence the nomination of any person as a candidate or promote the election of any person as a member of the Senate at the general election to be held in November 1926.

After the Pennsylvania primaries, Cunningham was subpoenaed and appeared before this committee. Among other things, he testified that he was a member of an organization which supported William. S. Vare for Senator at the primary election; that he had given to the chairman of the organization $50,000 in two installments of $25,000 each prior to the holding of the primaries. . . .

Mr. Vare was nominated and elected at the succeeding November election. The special committee thereafter submitted a partial report in respect of Cunningham's refusal to testify. In January 1927, Vare's election having been contested by William B. Wilson upon the ground of fraud and unlawful practices in connection with the nomination and election, the Senate adopted a resolution further authorizing the special committee to take possession of ballot boxes, tally sheets, etc., and to preserve evidence in respect of the charges made by Wilson. In February 1927, Cunningham was recalled, and, questions previously put to him having been repeated, he again refused to give the information called for, as he had done at the first hearing.

At the opening of Congress in December 1927, the Senate adopted an additional resolution, reciting among other things, that there were numerous instances of fraud and corruption in behalf of Vare's candidacy, and that there had been expended in his behalf at the primary election a sum exceeding $785,000. . . . [I]t was resolved, Vare should be denied a seat in the Senate. By a subsequent resolution, the committee on privileges and elections was directed to hear and determine the contest between Vare and Wilson.

... The Senate ... passed a resolution reciting Cunningham's contumacy and instructing the President to issue his warrant commanding the sergeant-at-arms or his deputy to take the body of Cunningham into custody, and to bring him before the bar of the Senate, "then and there or elsewhere, as it may direct, to answer such questions pertinent to the matter under inquiry as the Senate, through its said committee, or the President of the Senate, may propound, and to keep the said Thomas W. Cunningham in custody to await further order of the Senate." The warrant was issued and executed, and thereupon Cunningham brought a habeas corpus proceeding in the federal District Court for the Eastern District of Pennsylvania.

. . .

The District Court ... entered an order discharging the writ and remanding Cunningham to the custody of the sergeant-at-arms. . . .

Upon appeal, the Circuit Court of Appeals reversed the District Court, holding that the arrest was in reality one for contempt, but, if it should be regarded as an arrest to procure Cunningham's attendance as a witness, it was void, because a subpoena to attend at the bar of the Senate had not previously been served upon him, and that this was a necessary prerequisite to the issue of an attachment. . . .

. . . The Senate resolution, after a recital of Cunningham's refusal to answer certain questions, directs that he be attached and brought before the bar of the Senate, not to show cause why he should not be punished for contempt, but "to answer such questions pertinent to the matter under inquiry as the Senate through its said committee or the President of the Senate may propound. . . . "We must accept this unequivocal language as expressing the purpose of the Senate to elicit testimony in response to questions to be propounded at the bar of the Senate, and the question whether the information sought to be elicited from Cunningham by the committee was pertinent to the inquiry which the committee had been directed to make may be put aside as immaterial.

. . .

Generally, the Senate is a legislative body, exercising in connection with the House only the power to make laws. But it has had conferred upon it by the Constitution certain powers, which are not legislative, but judicial, in character. Among these is the power to judge of the elections, returns, and qualifications of its own members. "That power carries with it authority to take such steps as may be appropriate and necessary to secure information upon which to decide concerning elections." Exercise of the power necessarily involves the ascertainment of facts, the attendance of witnesses, the examination of such witnesses, with the power to compel them to answer pertinent questions, to determine the facts and apply the appropriate rules of law, and, finally, to render a judgment which is beyond the authority of any other tribunal to review. . . .

. . . When a candidate is elected to either house, he of course is elected a member of the body; and when that body determines, upon presentation of his credentials, without first giving him his seat, that the election is void, there would seem to be no real substance in a claim that the election of a "member" has not been adjudged. To hold otherwise would be to interpret the word "member" with a strictness in no way required by the obvious purpose of the constitutional provision, or necessary to its effective enforcement in accordance with such purpose, which, so far as the present case is concerned, was to vest the Senate with authority to exclude persons asserting membership, who either had not been elected or, what amounts to the same thing, had been elected by resort to fraud, bribery, corruption, or other sinister methods having the effect of vitiating the election.

Nor is there merit in the suggestion that the effect of the refusal of the Senate to seat Vare pending investigation was to deprive the state of its equal representation in the Senate. . . . The temporary deprivation of equal representation which results from the refusal of the Senate to seat a member pending inquiry as to his election or qualifications is the necessary consequence of the exercise of a constitutional power, and no more deprives the state of its "equal suffrage" in the constitutional sense than would a vote of the Senate vacating the seat of a sitting member or a vote of expulsion.

In exercising the power to judge of the elections, returns, and qualifications of its members, the Senate acts as a judicial tribunal, and the authority to require the attendance of witnesses is a necessary incident of the power to adjudge, in no wise inferior under like circumstances to that exercised by a court of justice. That this includes the power in some cases to issue a warrant of arrest to compel such attendance, as was done here, does not admit of doubt. That case dealt with the power of the Senate thus to compel a witness to appear to give testimony necessary to enable that body efficiently to exercise a legislative function; but the principle is equally, if not a fortiori, applicable where the Senate is exercising a judicial function.

The real question is not whether the Senate had power to issue the warrant of arrest, but whether it could do so under the circumstances disclosed by the record. The decision of the Circuit Court of Appeals is that, as a necessary prerequisite to the issue of a warrant of arrest, a subpoena first should have been issued, served, and disobeyed. And undoubtedly the courts rec-

ognize this as the practice generally to be followed. But undoubtedly, also, a court has power in the exercise of a sound discretion to issue a warrant of arrest without a previous subpoena, when there is good reason to believe that otherwise the witness will not be forthcoming. A statute of the United States provides that any federal judge, on application of the district attorney, and being satisfied by proof that any person is a competent and necessary witness in a criminal proceeding in which the United States is a party or interested, may have such person brought before him by a warrant of arrest, to give recognizance, and that such person may be confined until removed for the purpose of giving his testimony, or until he gives the recognizance required by said judge. The constitutionality of this statute apparently has never been doubted. Similar statutes exist in many of the states and have been enforced without question.

. . .

Here the question under consideration concerns the exercise by the Senate of an indubitable power; and if judicial interference can be successfully invoked, it can only be upon a clear showing of such arbitrary and improvident use of the power as will constitute a denial of due process of law. That condition we are unable to find in the present case.

Judgment reversed.

Fortson v. Morris
385 U.S. 231 (1966)

Since 1824, a provision of the constitution of the State of Georgia, now Art. V, § I, IV, has provided that its Governor shall be selected (1) by a majority of votes cast in a general election, and (2) if no candidate receives a majority of votes at such election, then a majority of the members of the Georgia General Assembly shall elect the Governor "from the two persons having the highest number of votes. . . ." At the State's general election, held Tuesday, November 8, 1966, no single candidate received a majority of the votes cast. A Georgia three-judge federal district court has in this case enjoined the State Assembly from electing one of the two highest candidates as Governor on the ground that this method of election, required by Article V of the Georgia Constitution, would deny Georgia voters equal protection of the laws in violation of the Fourteenth Amendment. . . .

. . .

The language of Article V of the state constitution struck down by the District Court has been a part of Georgia's state constitution since 1824, and was readopted by the people in 1945. . . . There is no provision of the United States Constitution or any of its amendments which either expressly or impliedly dictates the method a State must use to select its Governor. A method which would be valid if initially employed is equally valid when employed as an alternative. It would be surprising to conclude that, after a State has already held two primaries and one general election to try to elect by a majority, the United States Constitution compels it to continue to hold elections in a futile effort to obtain a majority for some particular candidate. Statewide elections cost time and money, and it is not strange that Georgia's people decided to avoid repeated elections. The method they chose for this purpose was not unique, but was well known and frequently utilized before and since the Revolutionary War. Georgia Governors were selected by the State Legislature, not the people, until 1824. At that time, a new constitution provided for popular election, but with the provision that, upon the

failure of any one candidate to receive a majority, the General Assembly should elect.

. . . Thirty-eight States of the Union which today provide for election of their governors by a plurality also provide that, in case of a tie vote, the State Legislatures shall elect.

. . . The District Court below treated Article V of the Georgia Constitution as the valid law of the State except as it thought itself compelled to strike it down because of *Gray v. Sanders*. The *Gray* case, however, did no more than to require the State to eliminate the county unit machinery from its election system. The State did this in an election that resulted in the election of no candidate. Its duty now, under Article V of its constitution, is to proceed to have the General Assembly elect its Governor from the two highest candidates in the election unless, as some of the parties contend, the entire legislative body is incapable of performing its responsibility of electing a Governor because it is malapportioned. But this is not correct. In *Toombs v. Fortson*, we held that, with certain exceptions not here material, the Georgia Assembly could continue to function until May 1, 1968. Consequently, the Georgia Assembly is not disqualified to elect a Governor as required by Article V of the state's constitution. Neither is it disqualified by the fact that its Democratic members had obligated themselves to support the Democratic nominee in the general election on November 8, 1966. That election is over, and with it terminated any promises by the Democratic legislators to support the Democratic nominee.

Article V of Georgia's Constitution provides a method for selecting the Governor which is as old as the Nation itself. Georgia does not violate the Equal Protection Clause by following this article as it was written.

Reversed.

Sailors v. Board of Education of the County of Kent
387 U.S. 105 (1967)

Appellants, qualified and registered electors of Kent County, Michigan, brought this suit in the Federal District Court to enjoin the Board of Education of Kent County from detaching certain schools from the city of Grand Rapids and attaching them to Kent County, to declare the county board to be unconstitutionally constituted, and to enjoin further elections until the electoral system is redesigned. Attack is also made on the adequacy of the statutory standards governing decisions of the county board in light of the requirements of due process. We need not bother with the intricate problems of state law involved in the dispute. For the federal posture of the case is a very limited one. The people of Michigan (qualified school electors) elect the local school boards. No constitutional question is presented as respects those elections. The alleged constitutional questions arise when it comes to the county school board. It is chosen not by the electors of the county, but by delegates from the local boards. Each board sends a delegate to a biennial meeting, and those delegates elect a county board of five members, who need not be members of the local boards, from candidates nominated by school electors. It is argued that this system of choosing county board members parallels the county unit system which we invalidated under the Equal Protection Clause of the Fourteenth Amendment in *Gray v. Sanders*, and violates the principle of "one man, one vote" which we held in that case and in *Reynolds v. Sims*, was constitutionally required in state elections. . . . A three-judge court was convened, and it held by a divided vote that the method of constitution of the county board did not violate the Fourteenth Amendment. . . .

. . .

We find no constitutional reason why state or local officers of the nonlegislative character involved here may not be chosen by the governor, by the legislature, or by some other appointive means, rather than by an election. Our cases have, in the main, dealt with elections for United States Senator or Congressman or for state officers or for state legislators.

They were all cases where elections had been provided and cast no light on when a State must provide for the election of local officials.

A State cannot, of course, manipulate its political subdivisions so as to defeat a federally protected right, as for example, by realigning political subdivisions so as to deny a person his vote because of race. . . .

. . .

The Michigan system for selecting members of the county school board is basically appointive, rather than elective. We need not decide at the present time whether a State may constitute a local legislative body through the appointive, rather than the elective, process. . . .

Viable local governments may need many innovations, numerous combinations of old and new devices, great flexibility in municipal arrangements to meet changing urban conditions. We see nothing in the Constitution to prevent experimentation. At least as respects nonlegislative officers, a State can appoint local officials or elect them or combine the elective and appointive systems as was done here. If we assume arguendo, that, where a State provides for an election of a local official or agency—whether administrative, legislative, or judicial—the requirements of *Gray* and *Reynolds* must be met, no question of that character is presented. For while there was an election here for the local school board, no constitutional complaint is raised respecting that election. Since the choice of members of the county school board did not involve an election, and since none was required for these nonlegislative offices, the principle of "one man, one vote" has no relevancy.

Affirmed.

Roudebush v. Hartke
405 U.S. 15 (1972)

The 1970 election for the office of United States Senator was the closest in Indiana history. The incumbent, Senator R. Vance Hartke (Hartke), was declared the winner by a plurality of 4,383 votes—a margin of approximately one vote per state precinct. On November 16, 1970, 13 days after the election, the Indiana Secretary of State certified to the Governor that Hartke had been reelected. On the following day, candidate Richard L. Roudebush (Roudebush) filed in the Superior Court of Marion County a timely petition for recount. Hartke moved in that court to dismiss the petition, arguing that the state recount procedure conflicted with the Indiana and Federal Constitutions. On December 1, the state court denied the motion to dismiss and granted the petition for a recount. It appointed a three-man recount commission and directed it to begin its task on December 8.

Hartke then filed a complaint in the United States District Court for the Southern District of Indiana asking for an injunction against the recount. He . . . claimed that the recount was prohibited by Art. I, §5, of the Constitution of the United States, which delegates to the Senate the power to judge the elections, returns, and qualifications of its members. A single district judge issued an order temporarily restraining the recount pending decision by a three-judge district

court. The Attorney General of Indiana then moved successfully to intervene as a defendant, and a three-judge court was . . . ruled in Hartke's favor and issued an interlocutory injunction. Roudebush and the Attorney General both brought direct appeals to this Court.

On January 21, 1971, shortly after the jurisdictional statements were filed, the Senate administered the oath of office to Hartke, who had been issued a certificate of election by the Governor. . . . Following the Senate's decision to seat him, Hartke moved to dismiss the appeals as moot. . . .

We consider first the claim that these appeals are moot. This claim is based upon the proposition, as stated in appellee Hartke's brief, that the "basic issue" before the Court is "whether appellee Hartke or appellant Roudebush is entitled to the office of United States Senator from Indiana." Since the Senate has now seated Hartke, and since this Court is without power to alter the Senate's judgment, it follows, the argument goes, that the cause is moot.

The difficulty with this argument is that it is based on an erroneous statement of the "basic issue." Which candidate is entitled to be seated in the Senate is, to be sure, a nonjusticiable political question—a question that would not have been the business of this Court even before the Senate acted. The actual question before us, however, is a different one. It is whether an Indiana recount of the votes in the 1970 election is a valid exercise of the State's power, under Art. I, §4, to prescribe the times, places, and manner of holding elections, or is a forbidden infringement upon the Senate's power under Art. I, §5.

That question is not moot, because the Senate has postponed making a final determination of who is entitled to the office of Senator pending the outcome of this lawsuit. Once this case is resolved and the Senate is assured that it has received the final Indiana tally, the Senate will be free to make an unconditional and final judgment under Art. I, §5. Until that judgment is made, this controversy remains alive, and we are obliged to consider it.

It is the position of the appellants that, quite apart from the merits of the controversy, the three-judge District Court was barred from issuing an injunction. . . . This argument has weight, of course, only if the Indiana statutory recount procedure is a "proceeding in a State court." . . .

. . .

. . . The state courts' duties in connection with a recount may be characterized as ministerial, or perhaps administrative, but they clearly do not fall within this definition of a "judicial inquiry." The process of determining that the recount petition is correct as to form—that it contains the proper information, such as the names and addresses of all candidates, and is timely filed—is clearly not a judicial proceeding. Nonjudicial functionaries continually make similar determination in the processing of all kinds of applications.

And finally, Hartke's complaint in this cause did not ask the three-judge federal court to restrain the action of the Indiana court as such. It did not seek to enjoin the state court from ruling on the formal correctness of the petition; it did not even seek to enjoin the state court's appointive function. It sought, rather, to enjoin the recount commission from proceeding after the court had appointed the members of the commission.

We conclude that the three-judge District Court was not prohibited . . . from issuing, and had power . . . to issue, an injunction in this cause.
. . . The Indiana Election Code calls for the vote to be initially counted, in each precinct, by an election board. After recording the voting machine totals, the board seals the machines. Paper ballots, including absentee ballots, are then counted and tallied. Counted ballots are placed in a bag and sealed. Ballots that bear distinguishing marks or are mutilated or do not clearly reveal the voter's choice are not counted. These rejected ballots are sealed in a separate bag. Both bags are preserved for six months, and may not be opened except in the case of a recount.

If a recount is conducted in any county, the voting machine tallies are checked and the sealed bags containing the paper ballots are opened. The recount commission may make new and independent determinations as to which ballots shall be counted. In other words, it may reject ballots initially counted and count ballots initially rejected. Disputes within the commission are settled by a majority vote. When the commission finishes its task, it seals the ballots it counted in one bag, and the ballots it rejected in another. Once the recount is completed, all previous returns are superseded.

The District Court held these procedures to be contrary to the Constitution in two ways. First, the court found that, in making judgments as to which ballots to count, the recount commission would be judging the qualifications of a member of the Senate. It held this would be a usurpation of a power that only the Senate could exercise. Second, it found that the Indiana ballots and other election paraphernalia would be essential evidence that the Senate might need to consider in judging Hartke's qualifications. The court feared that the recount might endanger the integrity of those materials and increase the hazard of their accidental destruction. Thus, the court held that, even if the commission would not be usurping the Senate's exclusive power, it would be hindering the Senate's exercise of that power.

We cannot agree with the District Court on either ground. Unless Congress acts, Art. I, §4, empowers the States to regulate the conduct of senatorial elections. . . .

Indiana has found, along with many other States, that one procedure necessary to guard against irregularity and error in the tabulation of votes is the availability of a recount. Despite the fact that a certificate of election may be issued to the leading candidate within 30 days after the election, the results are not final if a candidate's option to compel a recount is exercised. A recount is an integral part of the Indiana electoral process, and is within the ambit of the broad powers delegated to the States by Art. I, §4.

It is true that a State's verification of the accuracy of election results pursuant to its Art. I, §4, powers is not totally separable from the Senate's power to judge elections and returns. But a recount can be said to "usurp" the Senate's function only if it frustrates the Senate's ability to make an independent final judgment. A recount does not prevent the Senate from independently evaluating the election any more than the initial count does. The Senate is free to accept or reject the apparent winner in either count, and, if it chooses, to conduct its own recount.

It would be no more than speculation to assume that the Indiana recount procedure would impair such an independent evaluation by the Senate. The District Court's holding was based on a finding that a recount would increase the probability of election fraud and accidental destruction of ballots. But there is no reason to suppose that a court-appointed recount commission would be less honest or conscientious in the performance of its duties than the precinct election boards that initially counted the ballots.

For the reasons expressed, we conclude that Art. I, §5, of the Constitution does not prohibit Indiana from conducting a recount of the 1970 election ballots for United States Senator. Accordingly, the judgment of the District Court is reversed.

Dallas County v. Reese
421 U.S. 477 (1975)

Appellees are residents of the city of Selma, Alabama, who brought this action to challenge the system by which members of the Dallas County, Alabama, Commission are elected. The system, which is established by a state statute, provides for countywide balloting for each of the four commission members, but requires that a member be elected from each of four residency districts. Appellees' constitutional claim was premised on the fact that the populations of the four districts vary widely, with the result that only one resident of the city of Selma can be a member of the commission, although the city contains about one-half of the county's population.

After extensive discovery, the United States District Court for the Southern District of Alabama entered summary judgment for appellants, Dallas County and the members of the Dallas County Commission. . . .

The Court of Appeals for the Fifth Circuit . . . reversed. The majority concluded that the unequal residency districts diluted the votes of city residents, and that the resulting discrimination was invidious. . . .

. . .

. . . [T]he judgment of the Court of Appeals must be reversed, and the cause is remanded for further proceedings not inconsistent with this opinion.

Hathorn v. Lovorn
457 U.S. 255 (1982)

Since 1960, the Louisville School District has been coextensive with Winston County, Mississippi. Until last December, the Louisville mayor and city aldermen appointed three of the five members of the District's Board of Trustees, and Winston County voters residing outside Louisville elected the other two members.

In 1964, the Mississippi Legislature enacted a statute providing in part:

> The boards of trustees of all municipal separate school districts, either with or without added territory, shall consist of five (5) members, each to be chosen for a term of five (5) years, but so chosen that the term of office of one (1) member shall expire each year. . . . [I]n any county in which a municipal separate school district embraces the entire county in which Highways 14 and 15 intersect, one (1) trustee shall be elected from each supervisors district.

Winston County is the only Mississippi county in which Highways 14 and 15 intersect. Officials in that county never implemented §37-7-203(1), because they believed the statute's reference to Highways 14 and 15 violated a state constitutional prohibition against local, private, or special legislation.

In 1975, five Winston County voters filed an action in the Chancery Court of Winston County, seeking to enforce the neglected 1964 state statute. These plaintiffs, respondents here, named numerous Louisville and Winston County officials as defendants. The Chancery Court dismissed respondents' complaint, holding that the statute violated Mississippi's constitutional bar against local legislation. The Mississippi Supreme Court reversed, striking only the specific reference to Highways 14 and 15 and upholding the remaining requirement that, "in any county in which a municipal separate school district embraces the entire county," each supervisors district must elect one trustee. The court then "remanded to the chancery court for further proceedings not inconsistent with [its] opinion."

The local officials, petitioners here, filed a petition for rehearing, in which they argued for the first time that the Chancery Court could not implement the reformed statute until the change had been precleared under §5 of the Voting Rights Act. The Mississippi Supreme Court denied the petition without comment, and this Court denied a petition for a writ of certiorari.

On remand, the Chancery Court ordered an election pursuant to the redacted statute. . . . The court derived the latter requirement from Miss.Code Ann. §37-7-217, which mandates runoffs in elections conducted under §37-7-203(1). The Chancery Court also agreed with petitioners' claim that the changes in election procedure fell within §5 of the Voting Rights Act, and directed petitioners to submit the election plan to the United States Attorney General for preclearance.

Upon review of petitioners' submission, the Attorney General objected to the proposed change in election procedure "insofar as it incorporate[d] a majority vote requirement." Because of the substantial black population in Winston County, an apparent pattern of racially polarized voting in the county, and the historical absence of blacks from various local governing boards, the Attorney General concluded that the runoff procedure could have a discriminatory effect.

. . .

Failing to obtain an election from the Chancery Court, respondents once again appealed to the Mississippi Supreme Court. That court observed that its "prior decision, which the United States Supreme Court declined to reverse or alter in any respect, became and is the law of the case." The court explained that, because the prior decision upheld a statute referring to the statute requiring runoffs, and because both parties had agreed during oral argument to abide by the runoff procedure, the Chancery Court properly enforced the law requiring runoffs and improperly conditioned the election on compliance with the Voting Rights Act. Accordingly, the Mississippi Supreme Court reversed the portion of the Chancery Court's decree referring to the Voting Rights Act and "remanded with directions for the lower court to call and require the holding of an election." . . .

. . .

Our holding mandates reversal of the lower court judgment. Under our analysis, the change in election procedure is subject to §5, and the Mississippi courts may not further implement that change until the parties comply with §5. At this time, however, we need not decide whether petitioners are entitled to any additional relief. The United States has initiated a federal suit challenging the change at issue here, and we agree with the Solicitor General that the District Court entertaining that suit should address the problem of relief in the first instance. . . . In this case, the District Court for the Northern District of Mississippi will be better able to decide whether a special election is necessary, whether a more moderate form of interim relief will satisfy §5, or whether new elections are so imminent that special relief is inappropriate. We hold only that the Mississippi courts must withhold further implementation of the disputed change in election procedures until the parties demonstrate compliance with §5. Accordingly, the judgment of the Mississippi Supreme Court is reversed, and the case is remanded for further proceedings not inconsistent with this opinion.

Rogers v. Lodge
458 U.S. 613 (1982)

The issue in this case is whether the at-large system of elections in Burke County, Georgia, violates the Fourteenth Amendment rights of Burke County's black citizens.

Burke County is a large, predominately rural county located in eastern Georgia. Eight hundred and thirty-one square miles in area, it is approximately two-thirds the size of the State of Rhode Island. According to the 1980 census, Burke County had a total population of 19,349, of whom 10,385, or 53.6 percent, were black. The average age of blacks living there is lower than the average age of whites, and therefore whites constitute a slight majority of the voting age population. As of 1978, 6,373 persons were registered to vote in Burke County, of whom 38 percent were black.

The Burke County Board of Commissioners governs the county. It was created in 1911, and consists of five members elected at large to concurrent 4-year terms by all qualified voters in the county. The county has never been divided into districts, either for the purpose of imposing a residency requirement on candidates or for the purpose of requiring candidates to be elected by voters residing in a district. In order to be nominated or elected, a candidate must receive a majority of the votes cast in the primary or general election, and a runoff must be held if no candidate receives a majority in the first primary or general election. Each candidate must run for a specific seat on the Board, and a voter may vote only once for any candidate. No Negro has ever been elected to the Burke County Board of Commissioners.

Appellees, eight black citizens of Burke County, filed this suit in 1976 in the United States District Court for the Southern District of Georgia. The suit was brought on behalf of all black citizens in Burke County. The class was certified in 1977. The complaint alleged that the county's system of at-large elections violates appellees' First, Thirteenth, Fourteenth, and Fifteenth

Amendment rights, as well as their rights under 42 U.S.C. §§1971, 1973, and 1983, by diluting the voting power of black citizens. . . . [T]he court issued an order on September 29, 1978, stating that appellees were entitled to prevail and ordering that Burke County be divided into five districts for purposes of electing County Commissioners. The court later issued detailed findings of fact and conclusions of law in which it stated that, while the present method of electing County Commissioners was "racially neutral when adopted, [it] is being maintained for invidious purposes" in violation of appellees' Fourteenth and Fifteenth Amendment rights.

The Court of Appeals affirmed. . . .

At-large voting schemes and multimember districts tend to minimize the voting strength of minority groups by permitting the political majority to elect all representatives of the district. A distinct minority, whether it be a racial, ethnic, economic, or political group, may be unable to elect any representatives in an at-large election, yet may be able to elect several representatives if the political unit is divided into single-member districts. The minority's voting power in a multimember district is particularly diluted when bloc voting occurs and ballots are cast along strict majority-minority lines. While multimember districts have been challenged for "their winner-take-all aspects, their tendency to submerge minorities and to overrepresent the winning party," this Court has repeatedly held that they are not unconstitutional per se. The Court has recognized, however, that multimember districts violate the Fourteenth Amendment if "conceived or operated as purposeful devices to further racial discrimination" by minimizing, canceling out or diluting the voting strength of racial elements in the voting population. Cases charging that multimember districts

unconstitutionally dilute the voting strength of racial minorities are thus subject to the standard of proof generally applicable to Equal Protection Clause cases. . . .

. . .

The District Court found that blacks have always made up a substantial majority of the population in Burke County, but that they are a distinct minority of the registered voters. There was also overwhelming evidence of bloc voting along racial lines. Hence, although there had been black candidates, no black had ever been elected to the Burke County Commission. These facts bear heavily on the issue of purposeful discrimination. Voting along racial lines allows those elected to ignore black interests without fear of political consequences, and, without bloc voting, the minority candidates would not lose elections solely because of their race. Because it is sensible to expect that at least some blacks would have been elected in Burke County, the fact that none have ever been elected is important evidence of purposeful exclusion.

Under our cases, however, such facts are insufficient in themselves to prove purposeful discrimination absent other evidence such as proof that blacks have less opportunity to participate in the political processes and to elect candidates of their choice. Both the District Court and the Court of Appeals thought the supporting proof in this case was sufficient to support an inference of intentional discrimination. . . .

. . .

Although finding that the state policy behind the at-large electoral system in Burke County was "neutral in origin," the District Court concluded that the policy "has been subverted to invidious purposes." As a practical matter, maintenance of the state statute providing for at-large elections in Burke County is determined by Burke County's state representatives, for the legislature defers to their wishes on matters of purely local application. The court found that Burke County's state representatives "have retained a system which has minimized the ability of Burke County Blacks to participate in the political system."

. . .

None of the District Court's findings underlying its ultimate finding of intentional discrimination appears to us to be clearly erroneous, and as we have said, we decline to overturn the essential finding of the District Court, agreed to by the Court of Appeals, that the at-large system in Burke County has been maintained for the purpose of denying blacks equal access to the political processes in the county. . . .

We also find no reason to overturn the relief ordered by the District Court. Neither the District Court nor the Court of Appeals discerned any special circumstances that would militate against utilizing single-member districts. . . .

The judgment of the Court of Appeals is affirmed.

Foster v. Love
522 U.S. 67 (1997)

Under 2 U.S.C. §§1 and 7, the Tuesday after the first Monday in November in an even-numbered year "is established" as the date for federal congressional elections. Louisiana's "open primary" statute provides an opportunity to fill the offices of United States Senator and Representative during the previous month, without any action to be taken on federal election day. The issue before us is whether such an ostensible election runs afoul of the federal statute. . . .

The Elections Clause of the Constitution, Art. I, §4, cl. 1, provides that

> [t]he Times, Places and Manner of holding Elections for Senators and Representatives, shall be prescribed in each State by the Legislature thereof; but the Congress may at any time by Law make or alter such Regulations.

The Clause is a default provision; it invests the States with responsibility for the mechanics of congressional elections, but only so far as Congress declines to preempt state legislative choices. Thus, it is well settled that the Elections Clause grants Congress "the power to override state regulations" by establishing uniform rules for federal elections, binding on the States. . . .

One congressional rule adopted under the Elections Clause (and its counterpart for the Executive Branch, Art. II, §1, cl. 3) sets the date of the biennial election for federal offices. . . . This provision, along with 2 U.S.C. §1 (setting the same rule for electing Senators under the Seventeenth Amendment) and 3 U.S.C. §1 (doing the same for selecting presidential electors), mandates holding all elections for Congress and the Presidency on a single day throughout the Union.

In 1975, Louisiana adopted a new statutory scheme for electing United States Senators and Representatives. In October of a federal election year, the State holds what is popularly known as an "open primary" for congressional offices, in which all candidates, regardless of party, appear on the same ballot, and all voters, with like disregard of party, are entitled to vote. If no candidate for a given office receives a majority, the State holds a run-off (dubbed a "general election") between the top two vote-getters the following month on federal election day. But if one such candidate does get a majority in October, that candidate "is elected," and no further act is done on federal election day to fill the office in question. Since this system went into effect in 1978, over 80 percent of the contested congressional elections in Louisiana have ended as a matter of law with the open primary.

Respondents are Louisiana voters who sued petitioners, the State's Governor and secretary of state, challenging the open primary as a violation of federal law. The District Court granted summary judgment to petitioners, finding no conflict between the state and federal statutes, whereas a divided panel of the Fifth Circuit reversed, concluding that Louisiana's system squarely "conflicts with the federal statutes that establish a uniform federal election day." . . .

The Fifth Circuit's conception of the issue here as a narrow one turning entirely on the meaning of the state and federal statutes is exactly right. For all of petitioners' invocations of state sovereignty, there is no colorable argument that §7 goes beyond the ample limits of the Elections Clause's grant of authority to Congress. When the federal statutes speak of "the election" of a Senator or Representative, they plainly refer to the combined actions of voters and officials meant to make a final selection of an officeholder. By establishing a particular day as "the day" on which these actions must take place, the statutes simply regulate the time of the election, a matter on which the Constitution explicitly gives Congress the final say.

While true that there is room for argument about just what may constitute the final act of selection within the meaning of the law, our decision does not turn on any nicety in isolating precisely what acts a State must cause to be done on federal election day (and not before it) in order to satisfy the statute. Without paring the term "election" in §7 down to the definitional bone, it is enough to resolve this case to say that a contested selection of candidates for a congressional office that is concluded as a matter of law before the federal election day, with no act in law or in fact to take place on the date chosen by Congress, clearly violates §7.

. . .

While the conclusion that Louisiana's open primary system conflicts with 2 U.S.C. §7 does not depend on discerning the intent behind the federal statute, our judgment is buttressed by an appreciation of Congress's object "to remedy more than one evil arising from the election of members of Congress occurring at different times in the different States." . . . The Louisiana open primary has tended to foster both evils, having had the effect of conclusively electing more than 80% of the State's Senators and Representatives before the election day elsewhere, and, in presidential election years, having forced voters to turn out for two potentially conclusive federal elections.

When Louisiana's statute is applied to select from among congressional candidates in October, it conflicts with federal law, and to that extent is void. The judgment below is affirmed.

Gutierrez v. Ada
528 U.S. 250 (2000)

The question here is whether the statute governing elections for Governor and Lieutenant Governor of the Territory of Guam compels a runoff election when a candidate slate has received a majority of the votes cast for Governor and Lieutenant Governor, but not a majority of the number of ballots cast in the simultaneous general election. . . .

In the November 3, 1998, Guam general election, petitioners Carl T. C. Gutierrez and Madeleine Z. Bordallo were candidates running on one slate for Governor and Lieutenant Governor, opposed by the slate of respondents Joseph F. Ada and Felix P. Camacho. Gutierrez received

24,250 votes, as against 21,200 for Ada. One thousand and two hundred ninety-four voted for write-in candidates; 1,313 persons who cast ballots did not vote for either slate or any write-in candidate; and 609 voted for both slates. The total number of ballots cast in the general election was thus 48,666, and the Gutierrez slate's votes represented 49.83 percent of that total. The Guam Election Commission certified the Gutierrez slate as the winner, finding it had received 51.21 percent of the vote, as calculated by deducting the 1,313 ballots left blank as to the gubernatorial election from the total number of ballots cast. Respondents Ada and Camacho sued in the United States District Court for a writ of mandamus ordering a runoff election, contending that Gutierrez and Bordallo had not received a majority of the votes cast, as required by the Organic Act of Guam.

. . . Respondents' position boils down to the claim that the phrase "majority of the votes cast in any election" requires that a slate of candidates for Governor and Lieutenant Governor receive a majority of the total number of ballots cast in the general election, regardless of the number of votes for all gubernatorial slates by those casting ballots. If this is the correct reading of the phrase, the parties agree that a runoff was required. If, however, the phrase refers only to votes cast for gubernatorial slates, no runoff was in order, and petitioners were elected Governor and Lieutenant Governor.

The United States District Court for the District of Guam read the statute to require a majority of the total number of voters casting ballots in the general election and so ruled that the Gutierrez slate had not received "a majority of the votes cast in any election." The court accordingly issued a writ of mandamus for a runoff election to be held on December 19, 1998.

Although the Court of Appeals for the Ninth Circuit issued an emergency stay of the District Court's order pending appeal, it ultimately affirmed. The Court of Appeals understood the reference to "majority of the votes cast" as meaning "all votes cast at the general election, for Congress presumably would not have included the phrase 'in any election,' if it meant to refer only to the votes cast in the single election for governor and lieutenant governor." The court thought that any other reading would render the phrase "in any election" a "nullity." The Court of Appeals also relied on a comparison of §1422, with 48 U.S.C. §1712 which provides that a candidate for Guam's Delegate to Congress must receive "a majority of the votes cast for the office of Delegate" in order to be elected. The Ninth Circuit reasoned that Congress could have used similar language of limitation if it had intended the election of a Governor and Lieutenant Governor to require only a majority of votes cast for gubernatorial slates. The Ninth Circuit stayed its mandate pending disposition of petitioners' petition for a writ of certiorari.

. . .

The key to understanding what the phrase "in any election" means is also the most salient feature of the provision in which it occurs. The section contains six express references to an election for Governor and Lieutenant Governor. . . . The reference to "any election" is preceded by two references to gubernatorial election and followed by four. With "any election" so surrounded, what could it refer to except an election for Governor and Lieutenant Governor, the subject of such relentless repetition? To ask the question is merely to apply an interpretive rule as familiar outside the law as it is within, for words and people are known by their companions.

Other clues confirm that Congress did not shift

its attention when it used "any election" un-adorned by a gubernatorial reference or other definite modifier. . . .

It would be equally odd to think that after repeatedly using "votes" or "vote" to mean an expression of choice for the gubernatorial slate, Congress suddenly used "votes cast in any election" to mean "ballots cast." And yet that is just what would be required if we were to treat the phrase respondents' way, for they read "votes cast in any election" as referring to "ballots containing a vote for any office." Surely a Congress that meant to refer to ballots, midway through a statute repeatedly referring to "votes" for gubernatorial slates, would have said "ballots." To argue otherwise is to tag Congress with an extravagant preference for the opaque when the use of a clear adjective or noun would have worked nicely. But even aside from that, Congress has shown that it recognizes the difference between ballots and votes in the very context of Guamanian elections. . . .

. . .

The judgment of the Court of Appeals is reversed, and the case is remanded for proceedings consistent with this opinion.

Bush v. Palm Beach County Canvassing Board
531 U. S. 70 (2000)

The Supreme Court of the State of Florida interpreted its elections statutes in proceedings brought to require manual recounts of ballots, and the certification of the recount results, for votes cast in the quadrennial Presidential election held on November 7, 2000. Governor George W. Bush, Republican candidate for the Presidency, filed a petition for certiorari to review the Florida Supreme Court decision. . . .

On November 8, 2000, the day following the Presidential election, the Florida Division of Elections reported that Governor Bush had received 2,909,135 votes, and respondent Democrat Vice President Albert Gore, Jr., had received 2,907,351, a margin of 1,784 in Governor Bush's favor. Under Fla. Stat. §102.141(4), because the margin of victory was equal to or less than one-half of one percent of the votes cast, an automatic machine recount occurred. The recount resulted in a much smaller margin of victory for Governor Bush. Vice President Gore then exercised his statutory right to submit written requests for manual recounts to the canvassing board of any county. He requested recounts in four counties: Volusia, Palm Beach, Broward, and Miami-Dade. The parties urged conflicting interpretations of the Florida Election Code respecting the authority of the canvassing boards, the Secretary of State (hereinafter Secretary), and the Elections Canvassing Commission. On November 14, in an action brought by Volusia County, and joined by the Palm Beach County Canvassing Board, Vice President Gore, and the Florida Democratic Party, the Florida Circuit Court ruled that the statutory seven-day deadline was mandatory, but that the Volusia board could amend its returns at a later date. The court further ruled that the Secretary, after "considering all attendant facts and circumstances," could exercise her discretion in deciding whether to include the late amended returns in the statewide certification.

The Secretary responded by issuing a set of criteria by which she would decide whether to allow a late filing. The Secretary ordered that, by 2 P.M. the following day, November 15, any county desiring to forward late returns submit a written statement of the facts and circumstances justifying a later filing. Four counties submitted statements and, after reviewing the submissions, the

Secretary determined that none justified an extension of the filing deadline. On November 16, the Florida Democratic Party and Vice President Gore filed an emergency motion in the state court, arguing that the Secretary had acted arbitrarily and in contempt of the court's earlier ruling. The following day, the court denied the motion, ruling that the Secretary had not acted arbitrarily and had exercised her discretion in a reasonable manner consistent with the court's earlier ruling. The Democratic Party and Vice President Gore appealed to the First District Court of Appeal, which certified the matter to the Florida Supreme Court. That court . . . entered an order enjoining the Secretary and the Elections Canvassing Commission from finally certifying the results of the election and declaring a winner until further order of that court.

The Supreme Court, with the expedition requisite for the controversy, issued its decision on November 21. As the court saw the matter, there were two principal questions: whether a discrepancy between an original machine return and a sample manual recount resulting from the way a ballot has been marked or punched is an "error in vote tabulation" justifying a full manual recount; and how to reconcile what it spoke of as two conflicts in Florida's election laws: (a) between the time frame for conducting a manual recount under Fla. Stat. §102.166 and the time frame for submitting county returns under §§102.111 and 102.112, and (b) between §102.111, which provides that the Secretary "shall . . . ignor[e]" late election returns, and §102.112, which provides that she "may . . . ignor[e]" such returns.

With regard to the first issue, the court held that, under the plain text of the statute, a discrepancy between a sample manual recount and machine returns due to the way in which a ballot was punched or marked did constitute an "error

in vote tabulation" sufficient to trigger the statutory provisions for a full manual recount.

With regard to the second issue, the court held that the "shall . . . ignor[e]" provision of §102.111 conflicts with the "may . . . ignor[e]" provision of §102.112, and that the "may . . . ignor[e]" provision controlled. The court turned to the questions whether and when the Secretary may ignore late manual recounts. The court relied in part upon the right to vote set forth in the Declaration of Rights of the Florida Constitution in concluding that late manual recounts could be rejected only under limited circumstances. The court then stated: "[B]ecause of our reluctance to rewrite the Florida Election Code, we conclude that we must invoke the equitable powers of this Court to fashion a remedy. . . ." The court thus imposed a deadline of November 26, at 5 P.M., for a return of ballot counts. The 7-day deadline of §102.111, assuming it would have applied, was effectively extended by 12 days. The court further directed the Secretary to accept manual counts submitted prior to that deadline.

As a general rule, this Court defers to a state court's interpretation of a state statute. But in the case of a law enacted by a state legislature applicable not only to elections to state offices, but also to the selection of Presidential electors, the legislature is not acting solely under the authority given it by the people of the State, but by virtue of a direct grant of authority made under Art. II, §1, cl. 2, of the United States Constitution. . . . Although we did not address the same question petitioner raises here, in *McPherson v. Blacker*, we said:

> [Art. II, §1, cl. 2] does not read that the people or the citizens shall appoint, but that each State shall; and if the words "in such manner as the legislature thereof may direct," had been omitted, it would seem that the legislative power of appointment

could not have been successfully questioned in the absence of any provision in the state constitution in that regard. Hence the insertion of those words, while operating as a limitation upon the State in respect of any attempt to circumscribe the legislative power, cannot be held to operate as a limitation on that power itself.

There are expressions in the opinion of the Supreme Court of Florida that may be read to indicate that it construed the Florida Election Code without regard to the extent to which the Florida Constitution could, consistent with Art. II, §1, cl. 2, "circumscribe the legislative power." The opinion states, for example, that "[t]o the extent that the Legislature may enact laws regulating the electoral process, those laws are valid only if they impose no 'unreasonable or unnecessary' restraints on the right of suffrage" guaranteed by the state constitution. The opinion also states that "[b]ecause election laws are intended to facilitate the right of suffrage, such laws must be liberally construed in favor of the citizens' right to vote. . . ."

In addition, 3 U.S.C. §5 provides in pertinent part:

> If any State shall have provided, by laws enacted prior to the day fixed for the appointment of the electors, for its final determination of any controversy or contest concerning the appointment of all or any of the electors of such State, by judicial or other methods or procedures, and such determination shall have been made at least six days before the time fixed for the meeting of the electors, such determination made pursuant to such law so existing on said day, and made at least six days prior to said time of meeting of the electors, shall be conclusive, and shall govern in the counting of the electoral votes as provided in the Constitution, and as hereinafter regulated, so far as the ascertainment of the electors appointed by such State is concerned.

The parties before us agree that whatever else may be the effect of this section, it creates a "safe harbor" for a State insofar as congressional consideration of its electoral votes is concerned. If the state legislature has provided for final determination of contests or controversies by a law made prior to election day, that determination shall be conclusive if made at least six days prior to said time of meeting of the electors. The Florida Supreme Court cited 3 U.S.C. §§1-10 in a footnote . . . but did not discuss §5. Since §5 contains a principle of federal law that would assure finality of the State's determination if made pursuant to a state law in effect before the election, a legislative wish to take advantage of the "safe harbor" would counsel against any construction of the Election Code that Congress might deem to be a change in the law.

After reviewing the opinion of the Florida Supreme Court, we find "that there is considerable uncertainty as to the precise grounds for the decision." This is sufficient reason for us to decline at this time to review the federal questions asserted to be present. . . .

Specifically, we are unclear as to the extent to which the Florida Supreme Court saw the Florida Constitution as circumscribing the legislature's authority under Art. II, §1, cl. 2. We are also unclear as to the consideration the Florida Supreme Court accorded to 3 U.S.C. §5. The judgment of the Supreme Court of Florida is therefore vacated, and the case is remanded for further proceedings not inconsistent with this opinion.

Bush v. Gore
531 U.S. 98 (2000)

On December 8, 2000, the Supreme Court of Florida ordered that the Circuit Court of Leon County tabulate by hand 9,000 ballots in Miami-

Dade County. It also ordered the inclusion in the certified vote totals of 215 votes identified in Palm Beach County and 168 votes identified in Miami-Dade County for Vice President Albert Gore, Jr., and Senator Joseph Lieberman, Democratic Candidates for President and Vice President. The Supreme Court noted that petitioner, Governor George W. Bush asserted that the net gain for Vice President Gore in Palm Beach County was 176 votes, and directed the Circuit Court to resolve that dispute on remand. The court further held that relief would require manual recounts in all Florida counties where so-called "undervotes" had not been subject to manual tabulation. The court ordered all manual recounts to begin at once. Governor Bush and Richard Cheney, Republican Candidates for the Presidency and Vice Presidency, filed an emergency application for a stay of this mandate. On December 9, we granted the application, treated application as a petition for a writ of certiorari, and granted certiorari.

The proceedings leading to the present controversy are discussed in some detail in our opinion in *Bush v. Palm Beach County Canvassing Board* (Bush I). On November 8, 2000, the day following the Presidential election, the Florida Division of Elections reported that petitioner, Governor Bush, had received 2,909,135 votes, and respondent, Vice President Gore, had received 2,907,351 votes, a margin of 1,784 for Governor Bush. Because Governor Bush's margin of victory was less than "one-half of a percent . . . of the votes cast," an automatic machine recount was conducted under §102.141(4) of the election code, the results of which showed Governor Bush still winning the race but by a diminished margin. Vice President Gore then sought manual recounts in Volusia, Palm Beach, Broward, and Miami-Dade Counties, pursuant to

Florida's election protest provisions. A dispute arose concerning the deadline for local county canvassing boards to submit their returns to the Secretary of State (Secretary). The Secretary declined to waive the November 14 deadline imposed by statute. The Florida Supreme Court, however, set the deadline at November 26. We granted certiorari and vacated the Florida Supreme Court's decision, finding considerable uncertainty as to the grounds on which it was based. On December 11, the Florida Supreme Court issued a decision on remand reinstating that date.

On November 26, the Florida Elections Canvassing Commission certified the results of the election and declared Governor Bush the winner of Florida's 25 electoral votes. On November 27, Vice President Gore, pursuant to Florida's contest provisions, filed a complaint in Leon County Circuit Court contesting the certification. He sought relief pursuant to §102.168(3)(c), which provides that "[r]eceipt of a number of illegal votes or rejection of a number of legal votes sufficient to change or place in doubt the result of the election" shall be grounds for a contest. The Circuit Court denied relief, stating that Vice President Gore failed to meet his burden of proof. He appealed to the First District Court of Appeal, which certified the matter to the Florida Supreme Court.

Accepting jurisdiction, the Florida Supreme Court affirmed in part and reversed in part. The court held that the Circuit Court had been correct to reject Vice President Gore's challenge to the results certified in Nassau County and his challenge to the Palm Beach County Canvassing Board's determination that 3,300 ballots cast in that county were not, in the statutory phrase, "legal votes."

The Supreme Court held that Vice President Gore had satisfied his burden of proof under §102.168(3)(c) with respect to his challenge to

Miami-Dade County's failure to tabulate, by manual count, 9,000 ballots on which the machines had failed to detect a vote for President ("undervotes"). Noting the closeness of the election, the Court explained that "[o]n this record, there can be no question that there are legal votes within the 9,000 uncounted votes sufficient to place the results of this election in doubt." A "legal vote," as determined by the Supreme Court, is "one in which there is a 'clear indication of the intent of the voter.'" The court therefore ordered a hand recount of the 9,000 ballots in Miami-Dade County. Observing that the contest provisions vest broad discretion in the circuit judge to "provide any relief appropriate under such circumstances," the Supreme Court further held that the Circuit Court could order "the Supervisor of Elections and the Canvassing Boards, as well as the necessary public officials, in all counties that have not conducted a manual recount or tabulation of the undervotes . . . to do so forthwith, said tabulation to take place in the individual counties where the ballots are located."

The Supreme Court also determined that both Palm Beach County and Miami-Dade County, in their earlier manual recounts, had identified a net gain of 215 and 168 legal votes for Vice President Gore. Rejecting the Circuit Court's conclusion that Palm Beach County lacked the authority to include the 215 net votes submitted past the November 26 deadline, the Supreme Court explained that the deadline was not intended to exclude votes identified after that date through ongoing manual recounts. As to Miami-Dade County, the Court concluded that although the 168 votes identified were the result of a partial recount, they were "legal votes [that] could change the outcome of the election." The Supreme Court therefore directed the Circuit Court to include those totals in the certified results, sub-

ject to resolution of the actual vote total from the Miami-Dade partial recount.

The petition presents the following questions: whether the Florida Supreme Court established new standards for resolving Presidential election contests, thereby violating Art. II, §1, cl. 2, of the United States Constitution and failing to comply with 3 U.S.C. §5 and whether the use of standardless manual recounts violates the Equal Protection and Due Process Clauses. . . .

. . .

The individual citizen has no federal constitutional right to vote for electors for the President of the United States unless and until the state legislature chooses a statewide election as the means to implement its power to appoint members of the Electoral College. This is the source for the statement in *McPherson v. Blacker*, that the State legislature's power to select the manner for appointing electors is plenary; it may, if it so chooses, select the electors itself, which indeed was the manner used by State legislatures in several States for many years after the Framing of our Constitution. History has now favored the voter, and in each of the several States the citizens themselves vote for Presidential electors. When the state legislature vests the right to vote for President in its people, the right to vote as the legislature has prescribed is fundamental; and one source of its fundamental nature lies in the equal weight accorded to each vote and the equal dignity owed to each voter. The State, of course, after granting the franchise in the special context of Article II, can take back the power to appoint electors.

The right to vote is protected in more than' the initial allocation of the franchise. Equal protection applies as well to the manner of its exercise. Having once granted the right to vote on equal terms, the State may not, by later arbitrary and disparate treatment, value one person's vote over that of another. It must be remembered that "the right of suffrage can be denied by a debasement or dilution of the weight of a citizen's vote just as effectively as by wholly prohibiting the free exercise of the franchise."

There is no difference between the two sides of the present controversy on these basic propositions. Respondents say that the very purpose of vindicating the right to vote justifies the recount procedures now at issue. The question before us, however, is whether the recount procedures the Florida Supreme Court has adopted are consistent with its obligation to avoid arbitrary and disparate treatment of the members of its electorate.

Much of the controversy seems to revolve around ballot cards designed to be perforated by a stylus but which, either through error or deliberate omission, have not been perforated with sufficient precision for a machine to count them. In some cases a piece of the card–a chad–is hanging, say by two corners. In other cases there is no separation at all, just an indentation.

The Florida Supreme Court has ordered that the intent of the voter be discerned from such ballots. For purposes of resolving the equal protection challenge, it is not necessary to decide whether the Florida Supreme Court had the authority under the legislative scheme for resolving election disputes to define what a legal vote is and to mandate a manual recount implementing that definition. The recount mechanisms implemented in response to the decisions of the Florida Supreme Court do not satisfy the minimum requirement for non-arbitrary treatment of voters necessary to secure the fundamental right. Florida's basic command for the count of legally cast votes is to consider the "intent of the voter." This is unobjectionable as an abstract proposition and a starting principle. The problem inheres in the absence of specific standards to ensure its equal application. The formulation of uniform rules to determine intent based on these recurring circumstances is practicable and, we conclude, necessary.

The law does not refrain from searching for the intent of the actor in a multitude of circumstances; and in some cases the general command to ascertain intent is not susceptible to much further refinement. In this instance, however, the question is not whether to believe a witness but how to interpret the marks or holes or scratches on an inanimate object, a piece of cardboard or paper which, it is said, might not have registered as a vote during the machine count. The factfinder confronts a thing, not a person. The search for intent can be confined by specific rules designed to ensure uniform treatment.

The want of those rules here has led to unequal evaluation of ballots in various respects. As seems to have been acknowledged at oral argument, the standards for accepting or rejecting contested ballots might vary not only from county to county but indeed within a single county from one recount team to another.

The record provides some examples. A monitor in Miami-Dade County testified at trial that he observed that three members of the county canvassing board applied different standards in defining a legal vote. And testimony at trial also revealed that at least one county changed its evaluative standards during the counting process. Palm Beach County, for example, began the process with a 1990 guideline which precluded counting completely attached chads, switched to a rule that considered a vote to be legal if any light could be seen through a chad, changed back to the 1990 rule, and then abandoned any pretense of a per se rule, only to have a court order that the county consider dimpled chads legal. This is not a process with sufficient guarantees of equal treatment.

An early case in our one person, one vote jurisprudence arose when a State accorded arbitrary and disparate treatment to voters in its different counties. The Court found a constitutional violation. We relied on these principles in the context of the Presidential selection process in *Moore v. Ogilvie*, where we invalidated a county-based procedure that diluted the influence of citizens in larger counties in the nominating process. There we observed that "[t]he idea that one group can be granted greater voting strength than another is hostile to the one man, one vote basis of our representative government."

The State Supreme Court ratified this uneven treatment. It mandated that the recount totals from two counties, Miami-Dade and Palm Beach, be included in the certified total. The court also appeared to hold sub silentio that the recount totals from Broward County, which were not completed until after the original November 14 certification by the Secretary of State, were to be considered part of the new certified vote totals even though the county certification was not contested by Vice President Gore. Yet each of the counties used varying standards to determine what was a legal vote. Broward County used a more forgiving standard than Palm Beach County, and uncovered almost three times as many new votes, a result markedly disproportionate to the difference in population between the counties.

In addition, the recounts in these three counties were not limited to so-called undervotes but extended to all of the ballots. The distinction has real consequences. A manual recount of all ballots identifies not only those ballots which show no vote but also those which contain more than one, the so-called overvotes. Neither category will be counted by the machine. This is not a trivial concern. At oral argument, respondents estimated there are as many as 110,000 overvotes statewide. As a result, the citizen whose ballot was not read by a machine because he failed to vote for a candidate in a way readable by a machine may still have his vote counted in a manual recount; on the other hand, the citizen who marks two candidates in a way discernable by the machine will not have the same opportunity to have his vote count, even if a manual examination of the ballot would reveal the requisite indicia of intent. Furthermore, the citizen who marks two candidates, only one of which is discernable by the machine, will have his vote counted even though it should have been read as an invalid ballot. The State Supreme Court's inclusion of vote counts based on these variant standards exemplifies concerns with the remedial processes that were under way.

That brings the analysis to yet a further equal protection problem. The votes certified by the court included a partial total from one county, Miami-Dade. The Florida Supreme Court's decision thus gives no assurance that the recounts included in a final certification must be complete. Indeed, it is respondent's submission that it would be consistent with the rules of the recount procedures to include whatever partial counts are done by the time of final certification, and we interpret the Florida Supreme Court's decision to permit this. This accommodation no doubt results from the truncated contest period established by the Florida Supreme Court in Bush I, at respondents' own urging. The press of time does not diminish the constitutional concern. A desire for speed is not a general excuse for ignoring equal protection guarantees.

In addition to these difficulties the actual process by which the votes were to be counted under the Florida Supreme Court's decision raises further concerns. That order did not specify who would recount the ballots. The county canvassing boards were forced to pull together ad hoc teams comprised of judges from various Circuits who had no previous training in handling and interpreting ballots. Furthermore, while others were permitted to observe, they were prohibited from objecting during the recount.

The recount process, in its features here described, is inconsistent with the minimum procedures necessary to protect the fundamental right of each voter in the special instance of a statewide recount under the authority of a single state judicial officer. Our consideration is limited to the present circumstances, for the problem of equal protection in election processes generally presents many complexities.

The question before the Court is not whether local entities, in the exercise of their expertise, may develop different systems for implementing elections. Instead, we are presented with a situation where a state court with the power to assure uniformity has ordered a statewide recount with minimal procedural safeguards. When a court orders a statewide remedy, there must be at least some assurance that the rudimentary requirements of equal treatment and fundamental fairness are satisfied.

Given the Court's assessment that the recount process underway was probably being conducted in an unconstitutional manner, the Court stayed the order directing the recount so it could hear this case and render an expedited decision. The contest provision, as it was mandated by the State Supreme Court, is not well calculated to sustain the confidence that all citizens must have in the outcome of elections. The State has not shown that its procedures include the necessary safeguards. The problem, for instance, of the estimated 110,000 overvotes has not been addressed. . . .

Upon due consideration of the difficulties identified to this point, it is obvious that the recount cannot be conducted in compliance with the requirements of equal protection and due process without substantial additional work. It would require not only the adoption (after opportunity for argument) of adequate statewide standards for determining what is a legal vote, and practicable procedures to implement them, but also orderly judicial review of any disputed matters that might arise. In addition, the Secretary of State has advised that the recount of only a portion of the ballots requires that the vote tabulation equipment be used to screen out undervotes, a function for which the machines were not designed. If a recount of overvotes were also required, perhaps even a second screening would be necessary. Use of the equipment for this purpose, and any new software developed for it, would have to be evaluated for accuracy by the Secretary of State, as required by Fla. Stat. §101.015 (2000).

The Supreme Court of Florida has said that the legislature intended the State's electors to "participat[e] fully in the federal electoral process," as provided in 3 U.S.C. §5. That statute, in turn, requires that any controversy or contest that is designed to lead to a conclusive selection of electors be completed by December 12. That date is upon us, and there is no recount procedure in place under the State Supreme Court's order that comports with minimal constitutional standards. Because it is evident that any recount seeking to meet the December 12 date will be unconstitutional for the reasons we have discussed, we reverse the judgment of the Supreme Court of Florida ordering a recount to proceed.

Seven Justices of the Court agree that there are constitutional problems with the recount ordered by the Florida Supreme Court that demand a remedy. The only disagreement is as to the remedy. . . .

None are more conscious of the vital limits on judicial authority than are the members of this Court, and none stand more in admiration of the Constitution's design to leave the selection of the President to the people, through their legislatures, and to the political sphere. When contending parties invoke the process of the courts, however, it becomes our unsought responsibility to resolve the federal and constitutional issues the judicial system has been forced to confront.

The judgment of the Supreme Court of Florida is reversed, and the case is remanded for further proceedings not inconsistent with this opinion.

9

Election Judges, Inspectors, and Canvassing Boards

To ensure that the casting of votes is done fairly and legally, election officials spread out across the country. This chapter demonstrates that although these officials have considerable authority, it is not absolute.

United States v. Reese
92 U.S. 214 (1875)

... [P]resents an indictment containing four counts, under sects. 3 and 4 of the act of May 31, 1870, against two of the inspectors of a municipal election in the State of Kentucky, for refusing to receive and count at such election the vote of William Garner, a citizen of the United States of African descent. All the questions presented by the certificate of division arose upon general demurrers to the several counts of the indictment. In this court the United States abandon the first and third counts, and expressly waive the consideration of all claims not arising out of the enforcement of the Fifteenth Amendment of the Constitution.

After this concession, the principal question left for consideration is whether the act under which the indictment is found can be made effective for the punishment of inspectors of elections who refuse to receive and count the votes of citizens of the United States, having all the qualifications of voters, because of their race, color, or previous condition of servitude.

. . .

Looking . . . to this statute, we find that its first section provides that all citizens of the United States, who are or shall be otherwise qualified by law to vote at any election, etc., shall be entitled and allowed to vote thereat, without distinction of race, color, or previous condition of servitude, any constitution, etc., of the State to the contrary notwithstanding. This simply declares a right, without providing a punishment for its violation.

The second section provides for the punishment of any officer charged with the duty of furnishing to citizens an opportunity to perform any act, which, by the constitution or laws of any State, is made a prerequisite or qualification of voting, who shall omit to give all citizens of the United States the same and equal opportunity to perform such prerequisite, and become qualified on account of the race, color, or previous condition of servitude, of the applicant. This does not apply to or include the inspectors of an election, whose only duty it is to receive and count the votes of citizens, designated by law as voters, who have already become qualified to vote at the election.

The third section is to the effect, that, whenever by or under the constitution or laws of any State, etc., any act is or shall be required to be done by any citizen as a prerequisite to qualify or entitle him to vote, the offer of such citizen to perform the act required to be done "as aforesaid" shall, if it fail to be carried into execution by reason of the wrongful act or omission "aforesaid" of the person or officer charged with the duty of receiving or permitting such performance, or offer to perform, or acting thereon, be deemed and held as a performance in law of such act; and the person so offering and failing as aforesaid, and being otherwise qualified, shall be entitled to vote in the same manner, and to the same extent, as if he had, in fact, performed such act; and any judge, inspector, or other officer of election, whose duty it is to receive, count, etc., or give effect to, the vote of any such citizen, who shall wrongfully refuse or omit to receive, count, etc., the vote of such citizen, upon the presentation by him of his affidavit stating such offer, and the time and place thereof, and the name of the person or officer whose duty it was to act thereon, and that he was wrongfully prevented by such person or officer from performing such act, shall, for every such offence, forfeit and pay, etc.

The fourth section provides for the punishment of any person who shall, by force, bribery, threats, intimidation, or other unlawful means, hinder, delay, etc., or shall combine with others to hinder, delay, prevent, or obstruct, any citizen from doing any act required to be done to qualify him to vote, or from voting, at any election.

The second count in the indictment is based upon the fourth section of this act, and the fourth upon the third section.

. . .

The Fifteenth Amendment does not confer the right of suffrage upon any one. It prevents the States, or the United States, however, from giving preference, in this particular, to one citizen of the United States over another on account of race, color, or previous condition of servitude. Before its adoption, this could be done. It was as much within the power of a State to exclude citizens of the United States from voting on account of race, etc., as it was on account of age, property, or education. Now it is not. If citizens of one race having certain qualifications are permitted by law to vote, those of another having the same qualifications must be. Previous to this amendment, there was no constitutional guaranty against this discrimination: now there is. It follows that the amendment has invested the citizens of the United States with a new constitutional right which is within the protecting power of Congress. That right is exemption from discrimination in the exercise of the elective franchise on account of race, color, or previous condition of servitude. This, under the express provisions of the second section of the amendment, Congress may enforce by "appropriate legislation."

This leads us to inquire whether the act now under consideration is "appropriate legislation" for that purpose. The power of Congress to legislate at all upon the subject of voting at State elections rests upon this amendment. . . . It has not been contended, nor can it be, that the amendment confers authority to impose penalties for every wrongful refusal to receive the vote of a qualified elector at State elections. It is only when the wrongful refusal at such an election is because of race, color, or previous condition of servitude, that Congress can interfere, and provide for its punishment. If, therefore, the third and fourth sections of the act are beyond that limit, they are unauthorized.

The third section does not in express terms limit the offence of an inspector of elections, for which the punishment is provided, to a wrongful discrimination on account of race, etc. This is conceded; but it is urged, that when this section is construed with those which precede it, and to which, as is claimed, it refers, it is so limited. The argument is, that the only wrongful act, on the part of the officer whose duty it is to receive or permit the requisite qualification, which can dispense with actual qualification under the State laws, and substitute the prescribed affidavit therefor, is that mentioned and prohibited in section 2, —to wit, discrimination on account of race, etc.; and that, consequently, section 3 is confined in its operation to the same wrongful discrimination. This is a penal statute, and must be construed strictly; not so strictly, indeed, as to defeat the clear intention of Congress, but the words employed must be understood in the sense they were obviously used. If, taking the whole statute together, it is apparent that it was not the intention of Congress thus to limit the operation of the act, we cannot give it that effect.

The statute contemplates a most important change in the election laws. Previous to its adoption, the States, as a general rule, regulated in their own way all the details of all elections. They prescribed the qualifications of voters, and the manner in which those offering to vote at an election should make known their qualifications to the officers in charge. This act interferes with this practice, and prescribes rules not provided by the laws of the States. It substitutes, under certain circumstances, performance wrongfully prevented for performance itself. If the elector makes and presents his affidavit in the form and to the effect prescribed, the inspectors are to treat this as the equivalent of the specified requirement of the State law. This is a radical change in the practice, and the statute which creates it should be explicit in its terms. Nothing should be left to construction, if it can be avoided. The law ought not to be in such a condition that the elector may act upon one idea of its meaning, and the inspector upon another.

The elector, under the provisions of the statute, is only required to state in his affidavit that he has been wrongfully prevented by the officer from qualifying. There are no words of limitation in this part of the section. In a case like this, if an affidavit is in the language of the statute, it ought to be sufficient both for the voter and the inspector. Laws which prohibit the doing of things, and provide a punishment for their violation, should have no double meaning. A citizen should not unnecessarily be placed where, by an honest error in the construction of a penal statute, he may be subjected to a prosecution for a false oath; and an inspector of elections should not be put in jeopardy because he, with equal honesty, entertains an opposite opinion. If this statute limits the wrongful act which will justify the affidavit to discrimination on account of race, etc., then a citizen who makes an affidavit that he has been wrongfully prevented by the officer, which is true in the ordinary sense of that term, subjects himself to indictment and trial, if not to conviction, because it is not true that he has been prevented by such a wrongful act as the statute contemplated; and if there is no such limitation, but any wrongful act of exclusion will justify the affidavit, and give the right to vote without the actual performance of the prerequisite, then the inspector who rejects the vote because he reads the law in its limited sense, and thinks it is confined to a wrongful discrimination on account of race, etc., subjects himself to prosecution, if not to punishment, because he has misconstrued the law. Penal statutes ought not to be expressed in language so uncertain. If the legislature undertakes to define by statute a new offence, and provide for its punishment, it should express its will in language that need not deceive the common mind. Every man should be able to know with certainty when he is committing a crime.

But when we go beyond the third section, and read the fourth, we find there no words of limitation, or reference even, that can be construed as manifesting any intention to confine its provisions to the terms of the Fifteenth Amendment. That section has for its object the punishment of all persons, who, by force, bribery, etc., hinder, delay, etc., any person from qualifying or voting. In view of all these facts, we feel compelled to say, that, in our opinion, the language of the third and fourth sections does not confine their operation to unlawful discriminations on account of race, etc. If Congress had the power to provide generally for the punishment of those who unlawfully interfere to prevent the exercise of the elective franchise without regard to such discrimination, the language of these sections would be broad enough for that purpose.

It remains now to consider whether a statute, so general as this in its provisions, can be made available for the punishment of those who may be guilty of unlawful discrimination against citizens of the United States, while exercising the elective franchise, on account of their race, etc.

There is no attempt in the sections now under consideration to provide specifically for such an offence. If the case is provided for at all, it is because it comes under the general prohibition against any wrongful act or unlawful obstruction in this particular. We are, therefore, directly called upon to decide whether a penal statute enacted by Congress, with its limited powers, which is in general language broad enough to cover wrongful acts without as well as within the constitutional jurisdiction, can be limited by judicial construction so as to make it operate only on that which Congress may rightfully prohibit and punish. For this purpose, we must take these sections of the statute as they are. We are not able to reject a part which is unconstitutional, and retain the remainder, because it is not possible to separate that which is unconstitutional, if there be any

such, from that which is not. The proposed effect is not to be attained by striking out or disregarding words that are in the section, but by inserting those that are not now there. Each of the sections must stand as a whole, or fall altogether. The language is plain. There is no room for construction, unless it be as to the effect of the Constitution. . . .

. . .

We must, therefore, decide that Congress has not as yet provided by "appropriate legislation" for the punishment of the offence charged in the indictment; and that the Circuit Court properly sustained the demurrers, and gave judgment for the defendants.

This makes it unnecessary to answer any of the other questions certified. Since the law which gives the presiding judge the casting vote in cases of division, and authorizes a judgment in accordance with his opinion, if we find that the judgment as rendered is correct, we need not do more than affirm. If, however, we reverse, all questions certified, which may be considered in the final determination of the case according to the opinion we express, should be answered.

Judgment affirmed.

Ex parte Siebold
100 U.S. 371 (1879)

The petitioners in this case, Albert Siebold, Walter Tucker, Martin C. Burns, Lewis Coleman, and Henry Bowers, were judges of election at different voting precincts in the city of Baltimore at the election held in that city, and in the State of Maryland, on the fifth day of November, 1878, at which representatives to the Forty-sixth Congress were voted for.

At the November Term of the Circuit Court of

the United States for the District of Maryland, an indictment against each of the petitioners was found in said court for offences alleged to have been committed by them respectively at their respective precincts whilst being such judges of election, upon which indictments they were severally tried, convicted, and sentenced by said court to fine and imprisonment. They now apply to this court for a writ of habeas corpus to be relieved from imprisonment.

. . .

The indictments commence with an introductory statement that, on the fifth of November, 1878, at the Fourth [or other] Congressional District of the State of Maryland, a lawful election was held whereat a representative for that congressional district in the Forty-sixth Congress of the United States was voted for; that a certain person [naming him] was then and there a supervisor of election of the United States, duly appointed by the Circuit Court aforesaid, pursuant to sect. 2012 of the Revised Statutes, for the third [or other] voting precinct of the fifteenth [or other] ward of the city of Baltimore, in the said congressional district, for and in respect of the election aforesaid, thereat; that a certain person [naming him] was then and there a special deputy marshal of the United States, duly appointed by the United States marshal for the Maryland district pursuant to section 201 of the Revised Statutes and assigned for such duty as is provided by that and the following section to the said precinct of said ward of said city at the congressional election aforesaid, thereat. . . .

. . .

In our judgment, Congress had the power to vest the appointment of the supervisors in question in the circuit courts.

The doctrine laid down at the close of counsel's brief, that the State and national governments are coordinate and altogether equal, on which their whole argument, indeed, is based, is only partially true.

The true doctrine, as we conceive, is this that, whilst the States are really sovereign as to all matters which have not been granted to the jurisdiction and control of the United States, the Constitution and constitutional laws of the latter are, as we have already said, the supreme law of the land, and, when they conflict with the laws of the States, they are of paramount authority and obligation. This is the fundamental principle on which the authority of the Constitution is based, and unless it be conceded in practice, as well as theory, the fabric of our institutions, as it was contemplated by its founders, cannot stand. The questions involved have respect not more to the autonomy and existence of the States than to the continued existence of the United States as a government to which every American citizen may look for security and protection in every part of the land.

We think that the cause of commitment in these cases was lawful, and that the application for the writ of habeas corpus must be denied.

Ex parte Clarke
100 U.S. 399 (1879)

This case comes before us on the return to a writ of habeas corpus, issued by order of one of the justices of this court. The petition for a habeas corpus was addressed to the judges of the Supreme Court of the United States by Augustus F. Clarke, who states therein that he is a member of the city council of Cincinnati, and, as such, one of the judges of election of precinct A in said city; in which capacity he acted at the State, congressional, county, and municipal elections held in said city in October 1878. That on the twenty-fourth of October, 1878, he was indicted in the Circuit Court of the United States for the Southern District of Ohio for unlawfully neglecting to perform the duty required of him as such judge of election by the laws of the State of Ohio in regard to said election, in this, that having accepted one of the poll books of said election, sealed and directed according to law, for the purpose of conveying the same to the clerk of the Court of Common Pleas of Hamilton County, in said State, at his office, he neglected to do so; and, in another count, that he permitted the said poll books, sealed and directed for the purpose aforesaid, to be broken open before he conveyed the same to said clerk; that a motion to quash said indictment, and a demurrer thereto, having been successively overruled, he pleaded not guilty, and at the February Term, 1879, was tried and found guilty; and having unsuccessfully moved for a new trial, and in arrest of judgment, he was sentenced by said court to be imprisoned in the jail of Hamilton County for twelve months, and to pay a fine of $200 and the cost of prosecution; that in pursuance of said sentence he had been arrested and imprisoned, and is now imprisoned and restrained from his liberty by the marshal of the United States for said district. The petition then asserts that the said Circuit Court had no jurisdiction in the premises, and that its acts were wholly void and his imprisonment unlawful. He, therefore, prays a habeas corpus to the said marshal, and a certiorari to the clerk of said court, if necessary, and that he may be discharged from custody. A certified copy of the indictment, proceedings, and judgment in the Circuit Court is annexed to the petition, from which it appears that the first count charged that the petitioner on the ninth of October 1878, in the county of Hamilton, in the

State of Ohio, being an officer of election at which a representative in Congress was voted for, to wit, a judge of said election at precinct A of the eighth ward of Cincinnati, and being duly appointed such judge of election under the laws of Ohio, did unlawfully neglect to perform a duty required of him by the laws of said State in regard to said election, specifying said neglect, to wit, that he neglected to convey the poll book to the county clerk, which had been sealed up by the judges and delivered to him for that purpose; contrary to the form of the statute and against the peace and dignity of the United States. The second count charged that the petitioner, as such judge of election, violated a duty required of him by the laws of said State in regard to said election, specifying the violation, namely, that having received the poll book in the manner and for the purpose aforesaid, he permitted it to be broken open before he conveyed it to the county clerk, contrary to the form of the statute, etc.

. . .

On the thirty-first day of July 1879, the said petition was presented to Justice Strong, and a writ of habeas corpus was allowed by him, returnable forthwith before himself, at the Catskill Mountain House, in the State of New York. On the eleventh of August 1879, return being made of the body of the petitioner according to the command of the writ, with a copy of the judgment of the Circuit Court, and the warrant of commitment issued thereon, Justice Strong made an order postponing the hearing of the cause into this court, to be heard upon the second Tuesday of October 1879 (being the first day of the present term), and admitted the petitioner to bail in the sum of $5,000 to abide the rule of the Supreme Court in the premises.

The case was argued at the same time with

Ex parte Siebold; and most of the questions involved have been considered in that case.

. . .

As to the merits of the case, there can be no serious question that the indictment charges an offence specified in the act of Congress. Any defect of form in making the charge would be at most an error, of which this court could not take cognizance on habeas corpus. The principal question is, whether Congress had constitutional power to enact a law for punishing a State officer of election for the violation of his duty under a State statute in reference to an election of a representative to Congress. As this question has been fully considered in the previous case, it is unnecessary to add any thing further on the subject. Our opinion is, that Congress had constitutional power to enact the law; and that the cause of commitment was lawful and sufficient.

The petitioner, therefore, must be remanded to the custody of the marshal for the Southern District of Ohio; and it is so ordered.

United States v. Gale
109 U.S. 65 (1883)

The indictment against the defendants in this case was for misconduct as election officers at an election held in Florida for a representative to congress, in stuffing the ballot box with fraudulent tickets, and abstracting tickets which had been voted. In impaneling the grand jury which found the indictment, four persons, otherwise competent, were excluded from the panel for the causes mentioned in section 820 of the Revised Statutes, which grounds are, in substance, voluntarily taking part in the rebellion, and giving aid and comfort thereto. The exclusion of these persons for this cause appears by an amendment of the record . . . showing what took place; but no objection was taken to the indictment or proceedings on that account until after a plea of not guilty, and a conviction, when the objection was first taken on motion in arrest of judgment. The indictment was founded upon sections 5512 and 5515 of the Revised Statutes, and the constitutionality of those sections was called in question, as well as that of section 820. The judges having disagreed upon the motion in arrest of judgment, certified up the following questions for the determination of this court, namely:

(1) Whether sections 5512 and 5515 of the Revised Statutes of the United States, on which such indictment was founded, are repugnant to and in violation of the constitution of the United States; (2) whether section 820 of the Revised Statutes of the United States is repugnant to and in violation of the constitution of the United States; (3) whether judgment of this court could be rendered against the defendants on an indictment found by a grand jury impaneled and sworn under the section aforesaid; and (4) whether the indictment aforesaid charges any offense for which judgment could be rendered against the defendants in this court under the constitution and laws of the United States.

The question of the validity of sections 5512 and 5515 has already been decided by this court in the cases of *Siebold* and *Clarke*, and was determined in favor of their validity. As to those sections, therefore, the answer must be in the negative, namely, that they are not repugnant to, nor in violation of, the constitution of the United States.

. . .

In conclusion, to the third and fourth questions, certified by the court below, the answer will be in the affirmative; and it is so ordered.

Ex parte Coy
127 US 731 (1888)

The essence of this indictment is that, whereas by the law of the state of Indiana it was the duty of these inspectors to take the certified lists of the voters, with the return of the judges, and safely keep them until they delivered them to the county clerk or to the board of canvassers who were to examine and count the votes of all the precincts in the county, they were persuaded by the defendants, who influenced them in various ways, to deliver up the certificates, poll-lists, and tally-papers to other persons who had no authority to take charge of them, and who thus had an opportunity of opening, examining, and falsifying those documents. It is the omission of this duty, which was imposed upon these inspectors by the law of Indiana, of safely keeping these papers confided to their care, that constitutes the foundation of this proceeding. . . .

. . .

. . . [W]e do not doubt that the indictment sets forth a conspiracy by the parties to this appeal to induce the inspectors of election in Indianapolis to omit the discharge of their duty, and to fail to safely keep and guard the poll-lists, tally-papers, and certificates committed to their care for the precincts at which they each presided. Nor do we doubt that the statute of Indiana imposed such a duty upon those inspectors, which they were induced to violate by the persuasion and influence of the parties to this conspiracy. . . . [W]hile we have attempted to answer the main argument of prisoners' counsel, that congress had no power to punish an act not specifically intended to affect the election of a member of congress, though the act was done with a felonious intent, and that if it had such power it has not exercised it, we thought it not necessary . . . to inquire into the

sufficiency of the allegation of the more minute details of the offense as charged in the indictment. . . . We cannot better close this opinion than by a further extract from that of the court in *Ex parte Yarbrough:* "In a republican government, like ours, where political power is reposed in representatives of the entire body of the people, chosen at short intervals by popular elections, the temptations to control these elections by violence and by corruption is a constant source of danger. Such has been the history of all republics, and, though ours has been comparatively free from both these evils in the past, no lover of his country can shut his eyes to the fear of future danger from both sources." The judgment of the circuit court, denying the writ of habeas corpus, is affirmed.

Sherman v. United States
155 U.S. 673 (1895)

The object of the statutes concerning the elective franchise, now embodied in title 26 of the Revised Statutes, was, as declared in the title to the act of May 31, 1870, "to enforce the rights of citizens of the United States to vote in the several states of this Union, and for other purposes," among which was, undoubtedly, the preservation of the purity of elections, and the obtaining of an honest expression of opinion from each individual voter. For this purpose the judge of the circuit court was required, upon the petition of a certain number of citizens of any city or town having upwards of 20,000 inhabitants, or of any county or parish in any congressional district, making known their desire to have the registration or election guarded and scrutinized, to open the circuit court at the most convenient point in the circuit; to appoint and commission, from day to day, two citizens from each voting precinct, to be known and designated as "supervisors of elections," who were required to attend at the registration of the voters, to challenge voters and supervise the registry, to make lists of the voters when required, to attend at the election, to supervise the manner in which the voting was done, to canvass each ballot, and, generally, to see that the election and canvass were fairly conducted, and to make return of their doings to the chief supervisor. . . .

. . .

. . . [I]t is evident that no permanent system for the carrying on of congressional elections was intended to be established. The act was to be operative only in particular cases, when, upon petition filed by the required number of citizens, the circuit court was authorized to appoint supervisors, who attended that election. . . . No system for the permanent registration of voters was contemplated, simply because the exigencies which dictated the appointment of supervisors for a particular election might not exist at the next or any subsequent election. No permanent official is provided for, except a chief supervisor in each judicial district, who served without regular salary, and acted only when the electoral machinery was put in motion, prior to any election, by the petition of the requisite number of voters. No permanent records were contemplated, and, without a system of registration like that obtaining in many of the states, none would be of any value, since persons who are disqualified at one election, by reason of minority, alienage, nonresidence, or other cause, might, when the next election took place, become legal and competent voters. So, those who are this year qualified may next year, either by removal from their present residence, by insanity, conviction of crime, or other cause, become disqualified the next year. The laws of the several states usually recognize

the fact that a person, whose name appears upon the registry of a certain precinct, is presumed to be qualified at the next election in that precinct. But even if a complete registration of voters were made by the chief supervisor, no such presumption would follow, since it is the state, and not the general government, which prescribes the qualification of voters. It was never the design of the act that congress should determine who should vote at any election, or interfere with laws of the state in that regard, but only to protect those who were entitled to vote by the laws of the state in the exercise of the elective franchise. . . .

So, too, a registry of voters, to be of any value, must be kept at the polling places in each precinct, in order that, as each voter presents himself, reference may instantly be made to the list to ascertain his qualifications. Hence the list made by the claimant, to serve any useful purpose, would have to be either printed or copied for use in each precinct; involving, of course, an enormous expense. But even this would have been of little value, since each precinct is concerned only with its own voters, and a list of 61,282 folios, containing the names of probably double that number of voters, would be so long as to be practically useless for ready and immediate reference. Add to this the fact, that thousands of changes are made at each election, and that the services in question were not completed until July 1892, nearly four years after the election took place, and it will be seen that the list made by the claimant could have been of no possible value to the government—of no more value than a city directory published four years after the compilation of names is made. The index, so prepared by him after the election of 1888, was not in fact made until after the congressional election of 1890, and was never used until the election of 1892. . . .

It is claimed, however, that, if the statute requires or authorizes the work to be done, the claimant ought not to be held responsible for the fact that the transcript was of no value, or to lose his compensation for that reason. Assuming that section 2026 vests him with a discretion to require of the supervisors lists of the voters when, in his opinion, it is necessary, and that section 2031 authorizes, and perhaps requires, him to file and care for such lists, there is certainly no requirement that he make a copy of such lists. The entering and indexing the records of his office, for which he is entitled to recover 15 cents per folio, would evidently be complied with by his filing such returns, and indexing them in the name of the supervisor making the return; and, even if the services performed by him in copying and rearranging the names upon these returns could be construed as "entering and indexing" them, it was a service of such manifestly disproportionate value to the cost thereby incurred that we think it could never have been contemplated by the statute. The claimant should have recognized this fact, and, before putting the government to the very large expense of this transcript, he should have been able to point to some statute requiring it to be done in language free from ambiguity.

The very magnitude of the expense incurred should have put the claimant upon inquiry as to the propriety of the service. He has no right to plunge the government into an expense of some $10,000 upon a doubtful interpretation of the law, especially when he is apprised of the fact that the service performed must have been of little or no value to the government. The index which he prepared for the election of 1890, and for which he was paid, covered every possible use for which the index he now charges for could have been made available. It is of no more value than a directory for a certain year issued after a directory for a subsequent year has been published and put upon the market. We do not wish to be understood as imputing any bad faith to the plaintiff in this particular, as there are undoubtedly decisions even of the court of claims, which uphold charges of this description, and the department seems to have paid many of these accounts without question since these decisions. We are, however, clear in our opinion that the service is not one within the spirit or the letter of the statute; that the circuit judge was right in refusing to approve the account; and that the allowance of other accounts of a similar nature works no estoppel upon the government. If there be any estoppel at all, it is against the claimant, who has already been paid for a similar service performed since the transcript in question was made.

The judgment of the court of claims is therefore affirmed.

Dennison v. United States
168 U.S. 241 (1897)

The duties of chief supervisors are prescribed by statute. Their fees are also fixed by statute. To entitle a supervisor to a valid claim against the government, he must make it appear that the services performed were required by the letter of the former sections, or were such as were actually and necessarily performed in the proper execution of the duties therein prescribed. It must also appear that his charges therefor are covered by the latter section, or, if they are not fixed in the very words of that section, that, by analogy to some other service, he is entitled to make a corresponding charge. If the services are only performed for his own convenience, or are manifestly unnecessary or useless—even if they be such as he judges proper himself—they cannot be made the basis of a claim against the government. The petitioner in this case made a claim for his services in the general elections of 1890 and 1892 in the aggregate sum of $35,611.73, of which but $4,265.13 appear to have been for disbursements. Of this very large amount there was disallowed but $5,334.35, an amount which was further reduced by the judgment in his favor of $678.10 to $4,656.25, which is the amount in dispute here.

If the petitioner be entitled by law to the further sum claimed for what are in the main clerical services, he must receive judgment for them; but, as the dates of the approval of his accounts show that his services did not extend over a period of more than six months, he has at least no reason to complain of the illiberality of the government.

The approval of the district court goes only to the facts that the services were rendered as stated in the accounts, and that, in certain matters of discretion, the discretion was properly exercised. Neither of these cases requires the allowance of charges obviously unnecessary.

. . .

. . . While we think the judgment of the court of claims was correct with respect to all the items involved in this case, with the exception of two, the aggregate amount of which is $97.50, for its error in respect to those two the judgment will have to be varied by increasing the same from $678.10 to $775.60, and subject to such increase it is, in all other respects, affirmed.

Love v. Griffith
266 U.S. 32 (1924)

This is a bill in equity alleging that the plaintiffs are qualified electors residing in Houston, Texas, and of the Democratic political faith; that on January 27, 1921, the City Democratic Executive Committee of Houston made and published a rule that negroes would not be allowed to vote in the Democratic City Primary Election to be held on February 9, 1921; that the Committee and Judges of Election threatened to enforce the rule, contrary to the Constitution of the United States; and praying an injunction to restrain the Committee and Judges of Election from carrying out their threats. The bill was filed on February 3, 1921. On February 5, 1921, it was demurred to generally, the demurrer maintaining that the rule did not infringe the Fifteenth Amendment. On February 7, 1921, the demurrer was sustained and the bill was dismissed. . . . The plaintiffs appealed to the Court of Civil Appeals, but that Court held that at the date of its decision, months after the election, the cause of action had ceased to exist and that the appeal would not be entertained on the question of costs alone. It therefore dismissed the appeal with costs. Error is assigned here on the ground that the Fifteenth Amendment prohibits the discrimination which was made the basis of the complaint, and that the decision denied the plaintiffs their constitutional rights.

. . . The rule promulgated by the Democratic Executive Committee was for a single election only that had taken place long before the decision of the Appellate Court. No constitutional rights of the plaintiffs in error were infringed by holding that the cause of action had ceased to exist. The bill was for an injunction that could not be granted at that time. There was no constitutional obligation to extend the remedy beyond what was prayed.

Decree affirmed.

Nixon v. Herndon
273 U.S. 536 (1927)

This is an action against the Judges of Elections for refusing to permit the plaintiff to vote at a primary election in Texas. It lays the damages at

$5,000. The petition alleges that the plaintiff is a negro, a citizen of the United States and of Texas and a resident of El Paso, and in every way qualified to vote, as set forth in detail, except that the statute to be mentioned interferes with his right; that on July 26, 1924, a primary election was held at El Paso for the nomination of candidates for a senator and representatives in Congress and State and other offices, upon the Democratic ticket; that the plaintiff, being a member of the Democratic party, sought to vote but was denied the right by defendants; that the denial was based upon a statute of Texas enacted in May, 1923, and designated article 3093a, by the words of which "in no event shall a negro be eligible to participate in a Democratic party primary election held in the State of Texas," etc., and that this statute is contrary to the Fourteenth and Fifteenth Amendments to the Constitution of the United States. The defendants moved to dismiss upon the ground that the subject matter of the suit was political and not within the jurisdiction of the Court and that no violation of the Amendments was shown. The suit was dismissed and a writ of error was taken directly to this Court. Here no argument was made on behalf of the defendants but a brief was allowed to be filed by the Attorney General of the State.

. . .

. . . We find it unnecessary to consider the Fifteenth Amendment, because it seems to us hard to imagine a more direct and obvious infringement of the Fourteenth. That Amendment, while it applies to all, was passed, as we know, with a special intent to protect the blacks from discrimination against them. That Amendment "not only gave citizenship and the privileges of citizenship to persons of color, but it denied to any State the power to withhold from them the equal protection of the laws. . . . What is this but declaring that the law in the States shall be the same for the black as for the white; that all persons, whether colored or white, shall stand equal before the laws of the States, and, in regard to the colored race, for whose protection the amendment was primarily designed, that no discrimination shall be made against them by law because of their color?" The statute of Texas in the teeth of the prohibitions referred to assumes to forbid negroes to take part in a primary election the importance of which we have indicated, discriminating against them by the distinction of color alone. States may do a good deal of classifying that it is difficult to believe rational, but there are limits, and it is too clear for extended argument that color cannot be made the basis of a statutory classification affecting the right set up in this case.

Judgment reversed.

United States v. Classic
313 U.S. 299 (1941)

Two counts of an indictment found in a federal district court charged that appellees, Commissioners of Elections, conducting a primary election under Louisiana law, to nominate a candidate of the Democratic Party for representative in Congress, willfully altered and falsely counted and certified the ballots of voters cast in the primary election. The questions for decision are whether the right of qualified voters to vote in the Louisiana primary and to have their ballots counted is a right "secured . . . by the Constitution" within the meaning of 19 and 20 of the Criminal Code, and whether the acts of appellees charged in the indictment violate those sections.

On September 25, 1940, appellees were indicted in the District Court for Eastern Louisiana for violations of 19 and 20 of the Criminal Code.

The first count of the indictment alleged that a primary election was held on September 10, 1940, for the purpose of nominating a candidate of the Democratic Party for the office of Representative in Congress for the Second Congressional District of Louisiana, to be chosen at an election to be held on November 10; that in that district nomination as a candidate of the Democratic Party is and always has been equivalent to an election; that appellees were Commissioners of Election, selected in accordance with the Louisiana law to conduct the primary in the Second Precinct of the Tenth Ward of New Orleans, in which there were 537 citizens and qualified voters.

The charge based on these allegations, was that the appellees conspired with each other and with others unknown, to injure and oppress citizens in the free exercise and enjoyment of rights and privileges secured to them by the Constitution and Laws of the United States, namely, (1) the right of qualified voters who cast their ballots in the primary election to have their ballots counted as cast for the candidate of their choice, and (2) the right of the candidates to run for the office of Congressman and to have the votes in favor of their nomination counted as cast. The overt acts alleged were that the appellees altered eighty-three ballots cast for one candidate and fourteen cast for another, marking and counting them as votes for a third candidate, and that they falsely certified the number of votes cast for the respective candidates to the chairman of the Second Congressional District Committee.

The second count, repeating the allegations of fact already detailed, charged that the appellees, as Commissioners of Election willfully and under color of law subjected registered voters at the primary who were inhabitants of Louisiana to the deprivation of rights, privileges and immunities secured and protected by the Constitution and Laws of the United States, namely their right to cast their votes for the candidates of their choice and to have their votes counted as cast. It further charged that this deprivation was effected by the willful failure and refusal of defendants to count the votes as cast, by their alteration of the ballots, and by their false certification of the number of votes cast for the respective candidates in the manner already indicated.

The District Court sustained a demurrer to counts 1 and 2 on the ground that 19 and 20 of the Criminal Code under which the indictment was drawn do not apply to the state of facts disclosed by the indictment and that, if applied to those facts, 19 and 20 are without constitutional sanction. The case comes here on direct appeal from the District Court under the provisions of the Criminal Appeals Act, Judicial Code, which authorize an appeal by the United States from a decision or judgment sustaining a demurrer to an indictment where the decision or judgment is "based upon the invalidity, or construction of the statute upon which the indictment is founded."

Upon such an appeal our review is confined to the questions of statutory construction and validity decided by the District Court. Hence, we do not pass upon various arguments advanced by appellees as to the sufficiency and construction of the indictment.

Section 19 of the Criminal Code condemns as a criminal offense any conspiracy to injure a citizen in the exercise "of any right or privilege secured to him by the Constitution or laws of the United States." Section 20 makes it a penal offense for anyone who, "acting under color of any law" 'willfully subjects, or causes to be subjected, any inhabitant of any State' . . . to the deprivation of any rights, privileges, or immunities secured or protected by the Constitution and laws of the United States." The Government argues that the right of a qualified voter in a Louisiana congressional primary election to have his vote counted as cast is a right secured by Article I, 2 and 4 of the Constitution, and that a conspiracy to deprive the citizen of that right is a violation of 19, and also that the willful action of appellees as state officials, in falsely counting the ballots at the primary election and in falsely certifying the count, deprived qualified voters of that right and of the equal protection of the laws guaranteed by the Fourteenth Amendment, all in violation of 20 of the Criminal Code.

. . .

We look then to the statutes of Louisiana here involved to ascertain the nature of the right which under the constitutional mandate they define and confer on the voter and the effect upon its exercise of the acts with which appellees are charged, all with the view to determining, first, whether the right or privilege is one secured by the Constitution of the United States, second, whether the effect under the state statute of appellee's alleged acts is such that they operate to injure or oppress citizens in the exercise of that right within the meaning of 19 and to deprive inhabitants of the state of that right within the meaning of 20, and finally, whether 19 and 20 respectively are in other respects applicable to the alleged acts of appellees.

. . . [T]he states are given, and in fact exercise a wide discretion in the formulation of a system for the choice by the people of representatives in Congress. In common with many other states Louisiana has exercised that discretion by setting up machinery for the effective choice of party candidates for representative in Congress by primary elections and by its laws it eliminates or seriously restricts the candidacy at the general election of all those who are defeated at the primary. All political parties, which are defined as those that have cast at least 5 percent of the total vote at specified preceding elections, are required to nominate their candidates for representative by direct primary elections.

The primary is conducted by the state at public expense. The primary, as is the general election, is subject to numerous statutory regulations as to the time, place, and manner of conducting the election, including provisions to insure that the ballots cast at the primary are correctly counted, and the results of the count correctly recorded and certified to the Secretary of State, whose duty it is to place the names of the successful candidates of each party on the official ballot. The Secretary of State is prohibited from placing on the official ballot the name of any person as a candidate for any political party not nominated in accordance with the provisions of the Act.

One whose name does not appear on the primary ballot, if otherwise eligible to become a candidate at the general election, may do so in either of two ways, by filing nomination papers with the requisite number of signatures or by having his name "written in" on the ballot on the final election. . . .

Section 15 of Article VIII of the Constitution of Louisiana as amended by Act 80 of 1934, provides that "no person whose name is not authorized to be printed on the official ballot, as the nominee of a political party or as an independent candidate, shall be considered a candidate," unless he shall file in the appropriate office at least ten days before the general election a statement containing the correct name under which he is to be voted for and containing the further statement that he is willing and consents to be voted for that office. The article also provides that "no commissioners of election shall count a ballot as cast for any person whose name is not printed on the ballot or who does not become a candidate in the foregoing manner." Applying these provisions the Louisiana Court of Appeals for the Parish of Orleans has held . . . an unsuccessful candidate at the primary may not offer himself as a candidate at a general election, and that votes for him may not lawfully be written into the ballot or counted at such an election.

The right to vote for a representative in Congress at the general election is, as a matter of law, thus restricted to the successful party candidate at the primary, to those not candidates at the primary who file nomination papers, and those whose names may be lawfully written into the ballot by the electors. Even if, as appellees argue . . . voters may lawfully write into their ballots, cast at the general election, the name of a candidate rejected at the primary and have their ballots counted, the practical operation of the primary law in otherwise excluding from the ballot on the general election the names of candidates rejected at the primary is such as to impose serious restrictions upon the choice of candidates by the voters save by voting at the primary election. In fact, as alleged in the indictment, the practical operation of the primary in Louisiana, is and has been since the primary election was established in 1900 to secure the election of the Democratic primary nominee for the Second Congressional District of Louisiana.

Interference with the right to vote in the Congressional primary in the Second Congressional District for the choice of Democratic candidate for Congress is thus as a matter of law and in fact an interference with the effective choice of the voters at the only stage of the election procedure when their choice is of significance, since it is at the only stage when such interference could have any practical effect on the ultimate result, the choice of the Congressman to represent the district. The primary in Louisiana is an integral part of the procedure for the popular choice of Congressman. The right of qualified voters to vote at the Congressional primary in Louisiana and to have their ballots counted is thus the right to participate in that choice.

. . . While, in a loose sense, the right to vote for representatives in Congress is sometimes spoken of as a right derived from the states, this statement is true only in the sense that the states are authorized by the Constitution, to legislate on the subject as provided by 2 of Art. I, to the extent that Congress has not restricted state action by the exercise of its powers to regulate elections under 4 and its more general power under Article I, 8, clause 18 of the Constitution "To make all Laws which shall be necessary and proper for carrying into Execution the foregoing Powers."

Obviously included within the right to choose, secured by the Constitution, is the right of qualified voters within a state to cast their ballots and have them counted at Congressional elections. This Court has consistently held that this is a right secured by the Constitution. . . .

But we are now concerned with the question whether the right to choose at a primary election, a candidate for election as representative, is embraced in the right to choose representatives secured by Article I, 2. We may assume that the framers of the Constitution in adopting that section, did not have specifically in mind the selection and elimination of candidates for Congress by the direct primary any more than they contemplated the application of the commerce clause to interstate telephone, telegraph, and wireless communication which are concededly within it. But in determining whether a provision of the Constitution applies to a new subject matter, it is of little significance that it is one with which the framers were not familiar. . . .

That the free choice by the people of representatives in Congress, subject only to the restrictions to be found in 2 and 4 of Article I and elsewhere in the Constitution, was one of the great purposes of our Constitutional scheme of government cannot be doubted. We cannot regard it as any the less the constitutional purpose or its words as any the less guarantying the integrity of that choice when a state, exercising its privilege in the absence of Congressional action, changes the mode of choice from a single step, a general election, to two, of which the first is the choice at a primary of those candidates from whom, as a second step, the representative in Congress is to be chosen at the election.

Nor can we say that that choice which the Constitution protects is restricted to the second step because 4 of Article I, as a means of securing a free choice of representatives by the people, has authorized Congress to regulate the manner of elections, without making any mention of primary elections. For we think that the authority of Congress, given by 4, includes the authority to regulate primary elections when, as in this case, they are a step in the exercise by the people of their choice of representatives in Congress. . . .

. . .

. . . There is no historical warrant for supposing that the framers were under the illusion that the method of effecting the choice of the electors would never change or that if it did, the change was for that reason to be permitted to defeat the right of the people to choose representatives for Congress which the Constitution had guaranteed. The right to participate in the choice of representatives for Congress includes, as we have said, the right to cast a ballot and to have it counted at the general election whether for the successful candidate or not. Where the state law has made the primary an integral part of the procedure of choice, or where in fact the primary effectively controls the choice, the right of the elector to have his ballot counted at the primary, is likewise included in the right protected by Article I, 2. And this right of participation is protected just as is the right to vote at the election, where the primary is by law made an integral part of the election machinery, whether the voter exercises his right in a party primary which invariably, sometimes or never determines the ultimate choice of the representative. Here, even apart from the circumstance that the Louisiana primary is made by law an integral part of the procedure of choice, the right to choose a representative is in fact controlled by the primary because, as is alleged in the indictment, the choice of candidates at the Democratic primary determines the choice of the elected representative. Moreover, we cannot close our eyes to the fact already mentioned that the practical influence of the choice of candidates at the primary may be so great as to affect profoundly the choice at the general election even though there is no effective legal prohibition upon the rejection at the election of the choice made at the primary and may thus operate to deprive the voter of his constitutional right of choice. . . .

Unless the constitutional protection of the integrity of "elections" extends to primary elections, Congress is left powerless to effect the constitutional purpose, and the popular choice of representatives is stripped of its constitutional protection save only as Congress, by taking over the control of state elections, may exclude from them the influence of the state primaries. Such an expedient would end that state autonomy with respect to elections which the Constitution contemplated that Congress should be free to leave undisturbed, subject only to such minimum regulation as it should find necessary to insure the freedom and integrity of the choice. . . . The words of 2 and 4 of Article I, read in the sense which is plainly permissible and in the light of the constitutional purpose, require us to hold that a primary election which involves a necessary step in the choice of candidates for election as representatives in Congress, and which in the circumstances of this case controls that choice, is an election within the meaning of the constitutional provision and is subject to congressional regulation as to the manner of holding it.

. . .

There remains the question whether 19 and 20 are an exercise of the congressional authority applicable to the acts with which appellees are charged in the indictment. Section 19 makes it a crime to conspire to "injure" or "oppress" any citizen "in the free exercise . . . of any right or privilege secured to him by the Constitution." . . .

The suggestion that 19, concededly applicable to conspiracies to deprive electors of their votes at congressional elections, is not sufficiently specific to be deemed applicable to primary elections, will hardly bear examination. Section 19 speaks neither of elections nor of primaries. In unambiguous language it protects "any right or privilege secured . . . by the Constitution," a phrase which as we have seen extends to the right of the voter to have his vote counted in both the general election and in the primary election, where the latter is a part of the election machinery, as well as to numerous other constitutional rights which are wholly unrelated to the choice of a representative in Congress.

. . . [T]he right to participate through the primary in the choice of representatives in Congress— a right clearly secured by the Constitution—is within the words and purpose of 19 in the same manner and to the same extent as the right to vote at the general election. It is no extension of the

criminal statute . . . to find a violation of it in a new method of interference with the right which its words protect. For it is the constitutional right, regardless of the method of interference, which is the subject of the statute and which in precise terms it protects from injury and oppression.

It is hardly the performance of the judicial function to construe a statute, which in terms protects a right secured by the Constitution, here the right to choose a representative in Congress, as applying to an election whose only function is to ratify a choice already made at the primary but as having no application to the primary which is the only effective means of choice. . . .

If a right secured by the Constitution may be infringed by the corrupt failure to include the vote at a primary in the official count, it is not significant that the primary, like the voting machine, was unknown when 19 was adopted. Abuse of either may infringe the right and therefore violate 19. Nor does the fact that in circumstances not here present there may be difficulty in determining whether the primary so affects the right of the choice as to bring it within the constitutional protection, afford any ground for doubting the construction and application of the statute once the constitutional question is resolved. That difficulty is inherent in the judicial administration of every federal criminal statute, for none, whatever its terms, can be applied beyond the reach of the congressional power which the Constitution confers.

The right of the voters at the primary to have their votes counted is, as we have stated, a right or privilege secured by the Constitution, and to this 20 also gives protection. The alleged acts of appellees were committed in the course of their performance of duties under the Louisiana statute requiring them to count the ballots, to record the result of the count, and to certify the result of the election. Misuse of power, possessed by virtue of state law and made possible only because the wrongdoer is clothed with the authority of state law, is action taken "under color of" state law. Here the acts of appellees infringed the constitutional right and deprived the voters of the benefit of it within the meaning of 20, unless by its terms its application is restricted to deprivations 'on account of (an) inhabitant being an alien, or by reason of his color, or race."

The last clause of 20 protects inhabitants of a state from being subjected to different punishments, pains or penalties by reason of alienage, color or race, than are prescribed for the punishment of citizens. That the qualification with respect to alienage, color and race, refers only to differences in punishment and not to deprivations of any rights or privileges secured by the Constitution, is evidenced by the structure of the section and the necessities of the practical application of its provisions. The qualification as to alienage, color and race, is a parenthetical phrase in the clause penalizing different punishments "than are prescribed for . . . citizens" and in the common use of language could refer only to the subject matter of the clause and not to that of the earlier one relating to the deprivation of rights to which it makes no reference in terms.

. . . We think that 20 authorizes the punishment of two different offenses. The one is willfully subjecting any inhabitant to the deprivation of rights secured by the Constitution; the other is willfully subjecting any inhabitant to different punishments on account of his color or race, than are prescribed for the punishment of citizens. The meager legislative history of the section supports this conclusion. So interpreted 20 applies to deprivation of the constitutional rights of qualified voters to choose representatives in Congress. The generality of the section made applicable as it is

to deprivations of any constitutional right, does not obscure its meaning or impair its force within the scope of its application, which is restricted by its terms to deprivations which are willfully inflicted by those acting under color of any law, statute and the like.

We do not discuss the application of 20 to deprivations of the right to equal protection of the laws guaranteed by the Fourteenth Amendment, a point apparently raised and discussed for the first time in the Government's brief in this Court. The point was not specially considered or decided by the court below, and has not been assigned as error by the Government. Since the indictment on its face does not purport to charge a deprivation of equal protection to voters or candidates, we are not called upon to construe the indictment in order to raise a question of statutory validity or construction which we are alone authorized to review upon this appeal. Reversed.

Snowden v. Hughes
321 U.S. 1 (1944)

. . . Petitioner was one of several candidates at the April 9, 1940, Republican primary election held in the Third Senatorial District of Illinois for nominees for the office of representative in the Illinois General Assembly. By reason of appropriate action taken respectively by the Republican and Democratic Senatorial Committees of the Third Senatorial District in conformity to the scheme of proportional representation, two candidates for representative in the General Assembly were to be nominated on the Republican ticket and one on the Democratic ticket. Since three representatives were to be elected, and only three were to be nominated by the primary election, election at the primary as one of the two Republican nominees was, so the complaint alleges, tantamount to election to the office of representative.

The votes cast at the primary election were duly canvassed by the Canvassing Board of Cook County, certified and forwarded to the Secretary of State a tabulation showing the results of the primary election in the Third Senatorial District. By this tabulation the Board certified that petitioner and another had received respectively the second highest and highest number of votes for the Republican nominations. [State law] requires that the candidates receiving the highest votes shall be declared nominated.

Respondents Hughes and Lewis and Henry Horner whose executors were joined as defendants and are respondents here, constituted the State Primary Canvassing Board for the election year 1940. By Ill. Rev. Stat., it was made their duty to receive the certified tabulated statements of votes cast, including that prepared by the Canvassing Board of Cook County, to canvass the returns, to proclaim the results and to issue certificates of nomination to the successful candidates. Such a certificate is a prerequisite to the inclusion of a candidate's name on the ballot. Acting in their official capacity as State Primary Canvassing Board they issued, on April 29, 1940, their official proclamation which designated only one nominee for the office of representative in the General Assembly from the Third Senatorial District on the Republican ticket and excluded from the nomination petitioner, who had received the second highest number of votes for the Republican nomination.

After setting out these facts the complaint alleges that Horner and respondents Hughes and Lewis, "willfully, maliciously and arbitrarily" failed and refused to file with the Secretary of State a correct certificate showing that petitioner

was one of the Republican nominees, that they conspired and confederated together for that purpose, and that their action constituted "an unequal, unjust and oppressive administration" of the laws of Illinois. It alleges that Horner, Hughes and Lewis, acting as state officials under color of the laws of Illinois, thereby deprived petitioner of the Republican nomination for representative in the General Assembly and of election to that office . . . and by so doing deprived petitioner . . . of rights, privileges and immunities secured to him as a citizen of the United States, and of the equal protection of the laws, both guaranteed to him by the Fourteenth Amendment. The District Court granted motions by respondents to strike the complaint and dismiss the suit upon the grounds, among others, that the facts alleged did not show that the plaintiff had been deprived of any right, privilege or immunity secured to him by the Constitution or laws of the United States, and that, the alleged cause of action being predicated solely upon a claim that state officers had failed to perform duties imposed upon them by state law, their failure was not state action to which the prohibitions of the Fourteenth Amendment are alone directed, and hence was not sufficient to establish an infringement of rights secured to petitioner by the Fourteenth Amendment. The Court of Appeals for the Seventh Circuit affirmed holding . . . that the action of the members of the State Board, being contrary to state law, was not state action and was therefore not within the prohibitions of the Fourteenth Amendment.

In substance petitioner's alleged cause of action is that the members of the State Primary Canvassing Board, acting as such but in violation of state law, have by their false certificate or proclamation and by their refusal to file a true certificate deprived petitioner of nomination and election as representative in the state assembly. To establish a cause of action arising under the Constitution and laws of the United States within the jurisdiction of the District Court, he relies particularly on the provisions of the Fourteenth Amendment supplemented by two sections of the Civil Rights Act of 1871. Section 43 provides that: "Every person who, under color of any statute, ordinance, regulation, custom, or usage, of any State . . . subjects, or causes to be subjected, any citizen of the United States or other person . . . to the deprivation of any rights, privileges, or immunities secured by the Constitution and laws, shall be liable to the party injured in an action at law . . . for redress." Section 47(3), so far as now relevant, gives an action for damages to any person "injured in his person or property, or deprived of having and exercising any right or privilege of a citizen of the United States," by reason of a conspiracy of two or more persons entered into "for the purpose of depriving . . . any person . . . of the equal protection of the laws, or of equal privileges and immunities under the laws." It is the contention of petitioner that the right conferred on him by state law to become a candidate for and to be elected to the office of representative upon receipt of the requisite number of votes in the primary and general elections, is a right secured to him by the Fourteenth Amendment, and that the action of the State Primary Canvassing Board deprived him of that right and of the equal protection of the laws for which deprivation the Civil Rights Act authorizes his suit for damages.

. . .

The protection extended to citizens of the United States by the privileges and immunities clause includes those rights and privileges which, under the laws and Constitution of the United States, are incident to citizenship of the United States, but does not include rights pertaining to state citizenship and derived solely from the relationship of the citizen and his state established by state law. The right to become a candidate for state office, like the right to vote for the election of state officers is a right or privilege of state citizenship, not of national citizenship which alone is protected by the privileges and immunities clause.

. . .

Nor can we conclude that the action of the State Primary Canvassing Board, even though it be regarded as state action within the prohibitions of the Fourteenth Amendment, was a denial of the equal protection of the laws. The denial alleged is of the right of petitioner to be a candidate for and to be elected to public office upon receiving a sufficient number of votes. The right is one secured to him by state statute and the deprivation of right is alleged to result solely from the Board's failure to obey state law. There is no contention that the statutes of the state are in any respect inconsistent with the guarantees of the Fourteenth Amendment. There is no allegation of any facts tending to show that in refusing to certify petitioner as a nominee, the Board was making any intentional or purposeful discrimination between persons or classes. On the argument before us petitioner disclaimed any contention that class or racial discrimination is involved. The insistence is rather that the Board, merely by failing to certify petitioner as a duly elected nominee, has denied to him a right conferred by state law and has thereby denied to him the equal protection of the laws secured by the Fourteenth Amendment.

. . . Where, as here, a statute requires official action discriminating between a successful and an unsuccessful candidate, the required action is not a denial of equal protection since the distinction between the successful and the unsuccessful candidate is based on a permissible classification. And where the official action purports to be in conformity to the statutory classification, an erroneous or mistaken performance of the statutory duty, although a violation of the statute, is not without more a denial of the equal protection of the laws.

The unlawful administration by state officers of a state statute fair on its face, resulting in its unequal application to those who are entitled to be treated alike, is not a denial of equal protection unless there is shown to be present in it an element of intentional or purposeful discrimination. This may appear on the face of the action taken with respect to a particular class or person, or it may only be shown by extrinsic evidence showing a discriminatory design to favor one individual or class over another not to be inferred from the action itself. But a discriminatory purpose is not presumed; there must be a showing of "clear and intentional discrimination." . . .

. . .

The lack of any allegations in the complaint here, tending to show a purposeful discrimination between persons or classes of persons is not supplied by the opprobrious epithets "willful" and "malicious" applied to the Board's failure to certify petitioner as a successful candidate, or by characterizing that failure as an unequal, unjust, and oppressive administration of the laws of Illinois. These epithets disclose nothing as to the purpose or consequence of the failure to certify, other than that petitioner has been deprived of the nomination and election, and therefore add nothing to the bare fact of an intentional deprivation of petitioner's right to be certified to a nomination to which no other has been certified. So far as appears the Board's failure to certify petitioner was unaffected by and unrelated to the certification of any other nominee. Such allegations are insufficient under our decisions to raise any issue of equal protection of the laws or to call upon a federal court to try questions of state law in order to discover a purposeful discrimination in the administration of the laws of Illinois which is not alleged. Indeed on the allegations of the complaint, the one Republican nominee certified by the Board was entitled to be certified as the nominee receiving the highest number of votes, and the Board's failure to certify petitioner, so far as appears, was unaffected by and unrelated to the certification of the other, successful nominee. While the failure to certify petitioner for one nomination and the certification of another for a different nomination may have involved a violation of state law, we fail to see in this a denial of the equal protection of the laws more than if the Illinois statutes themselves had provided that one candidate should be certified and no other. If the action of the Board is official action it is subject to constitutional infirmity to the same but no greater extent than if the action were taken by the state legislature. Its illegality under the state statute can neither add to nor subtract from its constitutional validity. Mere violation of a state statute does not infringe the federal Constitution. And state action, even though illegal under state law, can be no more and no less constitutional under the Fourteenth Amendment than if it were sanctioned by the state legislature. A state statute which provided that one nominee rather than two should be certified in a particular election district would not be unconstitutional on its face and would be open to attack only if it were shown, as it is not here, that the exclusion of one and the election of another were invidious and purposely discriminatory.

Where discrimination is sufficiently shown, the right to relief under the equal protection clause is not diminished by the fact that the discrimination relates to political rights. But the necessity of a showing of purposeful discrimination is no less in a case involving political rights than in any other. It was not intended by the Fourteenth Amendment and the Civil Rights Acts that all matters formerly within the exclusive cognizance of the states should become matters of national concern.

. . .

As we conclude that the right asserted by petitioner is not one secured by the Fourteenth Amendment and affords no basis for a suit brought under the sections of the Civil Rights Acts relied upon, we find it unnecessary to consider whether the action by the State Board of which petitioner complains is state action within the meaning of the Fourteenth Amendment. . . .

The judgment is accordingly affirmed for failure of the complaint to state a cause of action within the jurisdiction of the District Court.

United States v. Raines
362 U.S. 17 (1960)

The United States brought this action in the United States District Court for the Middle District of Georgia against the members of the Board of Registrars and certain Deputy Registrars of Terrell County, Georgia. Its complaint charged that the defendants had through various devices, in the administration of their offices, discriminated on racial grounds against Negroes who desired to register to vote in elections conducted in the State. The complaint sought an injunction against the continuation of these discriminatory practices, and other relief.

The action was founded upon R.S. 2004, as amended by 131 of the Civil Rights Act of 1957.

Subsections (a) and (c), which are directly involved, provide:

> (a) All citizens of the United States who are otherwise qualified by law to vote at any election by the people in any State, Territory, district, county, city, parish, township, school district, municipality, or other territorial subdivision, shall be entitled and allowed to vote at all such elections, without distinction of race, color, or previous condition of servitude; any constitution, law, custom, usage, or regulation of any State or Territory, or by or under its authority, to the contrary notwithstanding.
>
> . . .
>
> (c) Whenever any person has engaged or there are reasonable grounds to believe that any person is about to engage in any act or practice which would deprive any other person of any right or privilege secured by subsection (a) . . . , the Attorney General may institute for the United States, or in the name of the United States, a civil action or other proper proceeding for preventive relief, including an application for a permanent or temporary injunction, restraining order, or other order. . . .

On the defendants' motion, the District Court dismissed the complaint, holding that subsection (c) was unconstitutional. . . .

. . .

. . . We need not define the scope of the discretion of a District Court in proceedings of this nature, because, exercising a traditional equity discretion, the court below declined to dismiss the complaint on that ground, and we do not discern any basis in the present posture of the case for any contention that it has abused its discretion. Questions as to the relief sought by the United States are posed, but remedial issues are hardly properly presented at this stage in the litigation.

The parties have engaged in much discussion concerning the ultimate scope in which Congress intended this legislation to apply, and concerning its constitutionality under the Fifteenth Amendment in these various applications. We shall not compound the error we have found in the District Court's judgment by intimating any views on either matter.

Reversed.

Foreman v. Dallas County
521 U.S. 979 (1997)

Texas, by statute, authorizes counties to appoint election judges, one for each precinct, who supervise voting at the polls on election days. In 1983 and several times thereafter, Dallas County changed its procedures for selecting these officials. Each of the new methods used party affiliation formulas of one sort or another. After the most recent change in 1996, appellants sued the County and others in the United States District Court, claiming that §5 of the Voting Rights Act, required that the changes be precleared.

A three-judge court held that preclearance was not required because the County was simply exercising, under the state statute, its "discretion to adjust [the procedure for appointing election judges] according to party power." The court apparently concluded that this "discretionary" use of political power meant that the various methods for selecting election judges were not covered changes under §5. The court also concluded that the Justice Department's preclearance of a 1985 submission from the State—the recodification of its entire election code—operated to preclear the County's use of partisan considerations in selecting election judges. The court denied injunctive relief, and later dismissed appellant's complaint pursuant to Fed. Rule Civ. Proc. 12(b)(6). . . .

We believe that the decision of the District Court is inconsistent with our precedents. . . . [T]he fact that the County here was exercising its "discretion" pursuant to a state statute does not shield its actions from §5. The question is simply whether the County, by its actions, whether taken pursuant to a statute or not, "enact[ed] or [sought] to administer any . . . standard, practice, or procedure with respect to voting different from" the one in place on November 1, 1972. The fact that the County's new procedures used political party affiliation as the selection criteria does not mean that the methods were exempt from preclearance.

Second, the State's 1985 submission . . . indicated that the only change being made to the statute concerning election judges was a change to "the beginning date and duration of [their] appointment." Thus, neither the recodified statute nor the State's explanations said anything about the use of specific, partisan affiliation methods for selecting election judges. This submission was clearly insufficient under our precedents to put the Justice Department on notice that the State was seeking preclearance of the use of partisan affiliations in selecting election judges.

Because the parties agree that the record is silent as to the procedure used by Dallas County for appointing election judges as of November 1, 1972, the date on which Texas became a covered jurisdiction under the Voting Rights Act, we cannot make a final determination here as to whether preclearance is in fact required. We therefore vacate the judgment of the District Court in No. 96–1389, dismiss the appeal from the District Court's interlocutory judgment in No. 96–987, and remand for further proceedings.

10

Accountability and Holding Legislative Elective Office

This chapter discusses the rights and restrictions of federal, state, and local legislators. The Supreme Court has ruled on the qualifications of legislators, the Speech and Debate Clause, and the extent of a legislative body's authority over the discipline of its members.

Anderson v. Dunn
19 U.S. 204 (1821)

... The pleadings have narrowed them down to the simple inquiry, whether the House of Representatives can take cognisance of contempts committed against themselves, under any circumstances? The duress complained of was sustained under a warrant issued to compel the party's appearance. ... Yet it cannot be denied, that the power to institute a prosecution must be dependent upon the power to punish. If the House of Representatives possessed no authority to punish for contempt, the initiating process issued in the assertion of that authority must have been illegal. ...

It is certainly true, that there is no power given by the constitution to either House to punish for contempts, except when committed by their own members. Nor does the judicial or criminal power given to the United States, in any part, expressly extend to the infliction of punishment for contempt of either House, or any one co-ordinate branch of the government. ...

. . .

It is true, that the Courts of justice of the United States are vested, by express statute provision, with power to fine and imprison for contempts; but it does not follow, from this circumstance, that they would not have exercised that power without the aid of the statute, or not, in cases, if such should occur, to which such statute provision may not extend; on the contrary, it is a legislative assertion of this right, as incidental to a grant of judicial power, and can only be considered either as an instance of abundant caution, or a legislative declaration, that the power of punishing for contempt shall not extend beyond its known and acknowledged limits of fine and imprisonment.

But it is contended, that if this power in the House of Representatives is to be asserted on the plea of necessity, the ground is too broad, and the result too indefinite; that the executive, and every co-ordinate, and even subordinate, branch of the government, may resort to the same justification, and the whole assume to themselves, in the exercise of this power, the most tyrannical licentiousness.

. . .

But what is the alternative? The argument obviously leads to the total annihilation of the power of the House of Representatives to guard itself from contempts, and leaves it exposed to every indignity and interruption that rudeness, caprice, or even conspiracy, may meditate against it. This result is fraught with too much absurdity not to bring into doubt the soundness of any argument from which it is derived. That a deliberate assembly, clothed with the majesty of the people, and charged with the care of all that is dear to them; composed of the most distinguished citizens, selected and drawn together from every quarter of a great nation; whose deliberations are required by public opinion to be conducted under the eye of the public, and whose decisions must be clothed with all that sanctity which unlimited confidence in their wisdom and purity can inspire; that such an assembly should not possess the power to suppress rudeness, or repel insult, is a supposition too wild to be suggested. And, accordingly, to avoid the pressure of these considerations, it has been argued, that the right of the respective Houses to exclude from their presence, and their absolute control within their own walls, carry with them the right to punish contempts committed in their presence; while the absolute legislative power given to Congress within this District, enables them to provide by law against all other insults against which there is any necessity for providing.

. . .

. . . [W]hy should the House be at liberty to exercise an ungranted, an unlimited, and undefined power within their walls, any more than without them? . . .

. . .

. . . [T]here is nothing on the face of this record from which it can appear on what evidence this warrant was issued. And we are not to presume that the House of Representatives would have issued it without duly establishing the fact charged on the individual. . . . If the inconvenience be urged, the reply is obvious: there is no

difficulty in observing that respectful deportment which will render all apprehension chimerical.

Judgment affirmed.

In re Sawyer
124 U.S. 200 (1888)

The original ordinance of the city council of Lincoln, made part of the record, appears to have been framed with the object that the rules established by statute for conducting proceedings for the removal of county officers should be substantially followed in the removal of city officers elected by the people. After ordaining that whenever any such officer 'shall be guilty of any willful misconduct or malfeasance in office, he may be removed by a vote of two-thirds of all the members elected to the council,' it provides that no such officer shall be removed unless 'charges in writing, specifying the misconduct or nature of the malfeasance, signed by the complainant, and giving the name of at least one witness besides the complainant, to support such charges, shall be filed with the city clerk, president of the council, or mayor,' and be read at a regular meeting of the council; and a certified copy thereof, with a notice to show cause against the removal, be served upon the officer five days before the next meeting; that if he does not then appear, and file a denial in writing, 'the said charge and specifications shall be taken as true, and the council shall declare the office vacant;' but, if he does, the council shall adjourn to some day for his trial; 'and if, upon the trial of said officer, said council shall be satisfied that he is guilty of any misconduct willfully, or malfeasance in office, they shall cause such finding to be entered upon their minutes, and shall declare said office vacant, and shall proceed at once to fill such vacancy in the manner provided by statute and ordinance; and that all proceedings and notices in the matter of such charges may be served by the city marshal or by a policeman, and the 'service and return shall be in the manner provided by law for the service of summonses in justice's courts.' The only material change made in that ordinance by the ordinance of August 24th is that the trial of the officer, and the finding of his guilt, may be either by the whole council, or by a 'committee of the council to whom such charges shall have been referred.' In either case the finding is to be entered upon the minutes of the council, 'and the council shall declare the said office vacant and the said officer removed therefrom,' and certify the fact to the mayor, whereupon the vacancy shall be filled by appointment by the mayor, with the assent of the council.

The whole object of the bill in equity filed by Parsons, the police judge of the city of Lincoln, against the mayor and councilmen of the city, upon which the circuit court of the United States made the order for the disregard of which they are in custody, is to prevent his removal from the office of police judge. No question of property is suggested in the allegations of matters of fact in the bill, or would be involved in any decree that the court could make thereon. The case stated in the bill is that charges in writing against Parsons for appropriating to his own use moneys of the city were filed, as required by the original ordinance, by Sheedy and Saunders, (Hyatt, not otherwise named in those charges, would seem to have signed them as the additional witness required by that ordinance;) that the charges were referred by the mayor to a committee of three members of the council; that upon notice to the accused, and his appearance before that committee, he objected that the committee had no authority to try the charges, and the committee so

reported to the council; that thereupon Sheedy and Saunders procured the passage of the amended ordinance, giving a committee, instead of the whole council, power to try the charges, and report its finding to the council; that after the passage of this ordinance, and against his protest, the committee resumed the trial, and, in order to favor and protect his accusers, and fraudulently to obtain his removal from office, made a report to the city council, falsely stating that they reported all the evidence, and fraudulently suppressing a book which he had offered in evidence, and finding him guilty, and recommending that his office be declared vacant, and be filled by the appointment of some other person; and that the mayor and city council set the matter down for final vote at a future day named, and threatened and declared that they would then, without hearing or reading the evidence taken before the committee, declare the office vacant, and appoint another person to fill it. The bill prays for an injunction to restrain the mayor and councilmen of the city of Lincoln from proceeding any further with the charges against Parsons, or taking any vote on the report of the committee, or declaring the office of police judge vacant, or appointing any person to fill that office.

. . . If the ordinances and proceedings of the city council are in the nature of civil, as distinguished from criminal, proceedings, the only possible ground, therefore, for the interposition of the courts of the United States in any form is that Parsons, if removed from the office of police judge, will be deprived by the state of life, liberty, or property without due process of law, in violation of the fourteenth amendment to the constitution, or that the state has denied him the equal protection of the laws, secured by that amendment.

. . .

. . . [T]he ground of our conclusion is, that whether the proceedings of the city council of Lincoln for the removal of the police judge, upon charges of misappropriating moneys belonging to the city, are to be regarded as in their nature criminal or civil, judicial or merely administrative, they relate to a subject which the circuit court of the United States, sitting in equity, has no jurisdiction or power over, and can neither try and determine for itself, nor restrain by injunction the tribunals and officers of the state and city from trying and determining. . . .

The circuit court being without jurisdiction to entertain the bill in equity for an injunction, all its proceedings in the exercise of the jurisdiction which it assumed are null and void. The restraining order, in the nature of an injunction it had no power to make. The adjudication that the defendants were guilty of a contempt in disregarding that order is equally void, their detention by the marshal under that adjudication is without authority of law, and they are entitled to be discharged. Writ of habeas corpus to issue.

Albright v. Territory of New Mexico ex rel Sandoval
200 U.S. 9 (1906)

This was a proceeding . . . brought in the district court of Bernalillo County, New Mexico, July 20, 1903, by the territory on the relation of Jesus M. Sandoval against George F. Albright, it being alleged that Sandoval was duly elected to the office of assessor of Bernalillo county for the term of two years from the first day of January, 1903; that he duly qualified and entered on the discharge of the duties of the office; and that he had never resigned, vacated, or abandoned the office, and ever since his election and qualification had

continued to discharge the duties thereof. It was further alleged that on March 23, 1903, respondent, Albright, without authority of law, unlawfully usurped the office, and took possession of the assessor's room in the courthouse, and of the books and papers, and other insignia of office, claiming office by virtue of a pretended appointment by the board of county commissioners of Bernalillo county, made under the authority of an act of the legislative assembly of the territory of New Mexico. . . .

Judgment was rendered by the district court in favor of Albright, August 3, 1903, and carried to the supreme court of the territory, which reversed the judgment, and remanded the cause with directions to the court below to reinstate it and proceed in accordance with the views expressed in its opinion. The mandate was filed below October 19, 1904, and on the 19th of November the district court entered judgment. . . .

The case was again carried to the supreme court and heard upon a motion to dismiss and on the merits, and February 24, 1904, the court denied the motion to dismiss. . . . The case comes before us on a motion to dismiss.

. . .

The term of office had expired before the rendition of judgment by the territorial supreme court, and as to the effect of the judgment of ouster in a suit to recover emoluments for the past, that is collateral, even though the judgment might be conclusive in such subsequent action.

Appeal dismissed.

Burton v. United States
202 U.S. 344 (1906)

This criminal prosecution is founded upon the following sections of the Revised Statutes:

...

Sec. 1782. No Senator, Representative, or Delegate, after his election and during his continuance in office, and no head of a department, or other officer or clerk in the employ of the government, shall receive or agree to receive any compensation whatever, directly or indirectly, for any services rendered, or to be rendered, to any person, either by himself or another, in relation to any proceeding, contract, claim, controversy, charge, accusation, arrest, or other matter or thing in which the United States is a party, or directly or indirectly interested, before any department, court-martial, bureau, officer, or any civil, military, or naval commission whatever. Every person offending against this section shall be deemed guilty of a misdemeanor, and shall be imprisoned not more than two years, and fined not more than ten thousand dollars, and shall, moreover, by conviction therefor, be rendered forever thereafter incapable of holding any office of honor, trust, or profit under the government of the United States.

The plaintiff in error was indicted in the district court of the United States for the eastern district of Missouri for a violation of 1782, the offense being alleged to have been committed at St. Louis. The accused was found guilty, and, on writ of error, the judgment was reversed by this court, and a new trial ordered, upon the ground, among others, that, according to the facts disclosed in that case, the offense charged was not committed in the state of Missouri, where the accused was tried.

Subsequently, the defendant was tried under a new indictment (the present one) charging him with certain violations of 1782. The indictment contained eight counts. Stating the case now only in a general way, the first, second, fourth, sixth, and eighth counts charged, in substance, that the defendant, a Senator of the United States, had agreed to receive compensation, namely, the sum of $2,500, for services to be rendered by him for the Rialto Grain & Securities Company ... in re-

lation to a proceeding, matter, and thing, in which the United States was interested, before the Postoffice Department, those counts differing only as to the nature of the interest which the United States had in such proceeding, matter, and thing; some of the counts alleging that the United States was directly, others that it was indirectly, interested in such proceeding, matter, and thing. The third, fifth, and seventh counts charged that the defendant did receive compensation to the amount of $500 for the services alleged to have been so rendered by him, those three counts differing only as to the nature of the interest, whether direct or indirect, which the United States had in the alleged proceeding, matter, and thing before the Postoffice Department. The defendant demurred to each count. The government, at that stage of the prosecution, dismissed the indictment as to the fourth and fifth counts and the court overruled the demurrer as to all the other counts. The accused filed a plea in bar to the third and seventh counts. To that plea the government filed an answer, to which we will advert hereafter. A demurrer to that answer was overruled, and, defendant declining to plead further, the plea in bar was denied. He was then arraigned, tried, and found guilty on the first, second, third, sixth, seventh, and eighth counts. No judgment or sentence was pronounced on the first, second, and eighth counts, because they covered the transaction and offense mentioned in the sixth count. And as the third count covered the transaction and offense embraced by the seventh count, no judgment or sentence was pronounced on it.

...

The first question to be considered is whether 1782 is repugnant to the Constitution of the United States. . . . We cannot doubt the authority of Congress by legislation to make it an offense against the United States for a senator, after his election and during his continuance in office, to agree to receive or to receive compensation for services to be rendered or rendered to any person, before a department of the government, in relation to a proceeding, matter, or thing in which the United States is a party or directly or indirectly interested.

...

It is said that the statute interferes, or, by its necessary operation, will interfere, with the legitimate authority of the Senate over its members, in that a judgment of conviction under it may exclude a Senator from the Senate before his constitutional term expires; whereas, under the Constitution, a Senator is elected to serve a specified number of years, and the Senate is made by that instrument the sole judge of the qualifications of its members, and, with the concurrence of two thirds, may expel a Senator from that body. In our judgment there in no necessary connection between the conviction of a Senator of a public offense prescribed by statute and the authority of the Senate in the particulars named. While the framers of the Constitution intended that each department should keep within its appointed sphere of public action, it was never contemplated that the authority of the Senate to admit to a seat in its body one who had been duly elected as a Senator, or its power to expel him after being admitted, should, in any degree, limit or restrict the authority of Congress to enact such statutes, not forbidden by the Constitution, as the public interests required for carrying into effect the powers granted to it. In order to promote the efficiency of the public service and enforce integrity in the conduct of such public affairs as are committed to the several departments, Congress, having a choice of means, may prescribe such regulations to those ends as its wisdom may suggest, if they be not forbidden by the fundamental law. It possesses the entire legislative authority of the United States. By the provision in the Constitution that 'all legislative powers herein granted shall be vested in a Congress of the United States,' it is meant that Congress-keeping within the limits of its powers and observing the restrictions imposed by the Constitution-may, in its discretion, enact any statute appropriate to accomplish the objects for which the national government was established. A statute like the one before us has direct relation to those objects, and can be executed without in any degree impinging upon the rightful authority of the Senate over its members or interfering with the discharge of the legitimate duties of a Senator. The proper discharge of those duties does not require a Senator to appear before an executive department in order to enforce his particular views, or the views of others, in respect of matters committed to that department for determination. He may often do so without impropriety, and, so far as existing law is concerned, may do so whenever he chooses, provided he neither agrees to receive nor receives compensation for such services. Congress, when passing this statute, knew, as, indeed, everybody may know, that executive officers are apt, and not unnaturally, to attach great, sometimes, perhaps, undue, weight to the wishes of Senators and Representatives. Evidently the statute has for its main object to secure the integrity of executive action against undue influence upon the part of members of that branch of the government, whose favor may have much to do with the appointment to, or retention in, public position of those whose official action it is sought to control or direct. The evils attending such a situation are apparent and are increased when those seeking to influence executive officers are spurred to action by hopes of pecuniary reward. There can be no reason why the government may not, by legislation, protect each department against such evils, indeed, against everything from whatever source it proceeds, that tends or may tend to corruption or inefficiency in the management of public affairs. A Senator cannot claim immunity from legislation directed to that end, simply because he is a member of a body which does not owe its existence to Congress, and with whose constitutional functions there can be no interference. If that which is enacted in the form of a statute is within the general sphere of legitimate legislative, as distinguished from executive and judicial, action, and not forbidden by the Constitution, it is the supreme law of the land,-supreme over all in public stations as well as over all the people. . . . The enforcement of that rule will not impair or disturb those relations or cripple the power of Senators, Representatives, or Delegates to meet all rightful or appropriate demands made upon them as public servants.

Allusion has been made to that part of the judgment declaring that the accused, by his conviction, 'is rendered forever hereafter incapable of holding any office of honor, trust, or profit under the government of the United States.' That judgment, it is argued, in inconsistent with the constitutional rights of a Senator to hold his place for the full term for which he was elected, and operates of its own force to exclude a convicted Senator from the Senate, although that body alone has the power to expel its members. We answer that the above words, in the concluding part of the judgment of conviction, do nothing more than declare or recite what, in the opinion of the trial court, is the legal effect attending or following a conviction under the statute. . . . The final judgment of conviction did not operate ... to vacate the seat of the convicted Senator, nor compel the Senate to expel him or to regard him as expelled

by force alone of the judgment. The seat into which he was originally inducted as a Senator from Kansas could only become vacant by his death, or by expiration of his term of office, or by some direct action on the part of the Senate in the exercise of its constitutional powers. This must be so for the further reason that the declaration in 1782, that anyone convicted under its provisions shall be incapable of holding any office of honor, trust, or profit 'under the government of the United States,' refers only to offices created by, or existing under the direct authority of, the national government, as organized under the Constitution, and not to offices the appointments to which are made by the states, acting separately, albeit proceeding, in respect of such appointments, under the sanction of that instrument. While the Senate, as a branch of the legislative department, owes its existence to the Constitution, and participates in passing laws that concern the entire country, its members are chosen by state legislatures, and cannot properly be said to hold their places 'under the government of the United States.'

We are of opinion that 1782 does not, by its necessary operation, impinge upon the authority or powers of the Senate of the United States, nor interfere with the legitimate functions, privileges, or rights of Senators.

. . .

Judgment affirmed.

Williamson v. United States
207 U.S. 425 (1908)

On February 11, 1905, Williamson, plaintiff in error, while a member of the House of Representatives of the United States, was indicted, with two other persons, for alleged violations of conspiring to commit the crime of subornation of perjury in proceedings for the purchase of public land under the authority of the law commonly known as the timber and stone act. The defendants were found guilty in the month of September 1905. On October 14, 1905, when the court was about to pronounce sentence, Williamson— whose term of office as a member of the House of Representatives did not expire until March 4, 1907—protested against the court passing sentence upon him, and especially to any sentence of imprisonment, on the ground that thereby he would be deprived of his constitutional right to go to, attend at, and return from the ensuing session of Congress. The objection was overruled, and Williamson was sentenced to pay a fine and to imprisonment for ten months. Exceptions were taken both to the overruling of the preliminary objection and to the sentence of imprisonment. Upon these exceptions, assignments of error are based, which, it is asserted, present a question as to the scope and meaning of that portion of article 1, 6, clause 1, of the Constitution, relating to the privilege of senators and representatives from arrest during their attendance on the session of their respective houses, and in going to and returning from the same.

. . .

We . . . consider the clause of the Constitution relied upon, in order to determine whether the accused, because he was a member of Congress, was privileged from arrest and trial for the crime in question, or, upon conviction, was in any event privileged from sentence which would prevent his attendance at an existing or approaching session of Congress.

The full text of the 1st clause of 6, article 1, of the Constitution, is this:

> Sec. 6. The Senators and Representatives shall receive a Compensation for their Services, to be as-

certained by Law, and paid out of the Treasury of the United States. They shall in all Cases, except Treason, Felony, and Breach of the Peace, be privileged from Arrest during their Attendance at the Session of their respective Houses, and in going to and returning from the same; and for any Speech or Debate in either House they shall not be questioned in any other Place.

If the words extending the privilege to all cases were unqualified, and therefore embraced the arrest of a member of Congress for the commission of any crime, we think, as we have previously said, they would not only include such an arrest as operated to prevent the member from going to and returning from a pending session, but would also extend to prohibiting a court during an interim of a session of Congress from imposing a sentence of imprisonment which would prevent him from attending a session of Congress in the future. But the question is not, What would be the scope of the words "all cases" if those words embraced all crimes? but is, What is the scope of the qualifying clause? . . .

. . .

Reversed and remanded.

Newman v. United States ex rel Frizzell
238 U.S. 537 (1915)

. . .

In 1902 Congress adopted a District Code. . . . It was made available to test the right to exercise a public franchise, or to hold an office in a private corporation. . . .

The District Code still treats usurpation of office as a public wrong which can be corrected only by proceeding in the name of the government itself. It permits those proceedings to be instituted by the Attorney General of the United States and by the attorney for the District of

Columbia. By virtue of their position, they, at their discretion, and acting under the sense of official responsibility, can institute such proceedings in any case they deem proper. But there are so many reasons of public policy against permitting a public officer to be harassed with litigation over his right to hold office, that the Code not only does not authorize a private citizen, on his own motion, to attack the incumbent's title, but it throws obstacles in the way of all such private attacks. It recognizes, however, that there might be instances in which it would be proper to allow such proceedings to be instituted by a third person, but it provides that such "third person" must not only secure the consent of the law officers of the government, but the consent of the supreme court of the District of Columbia, before he can use the name of the government in quo warranto proceedings.

The Code-making a distinction between a "third person" and an "interested person"—recognizes also that there might be instances in which a person might have such an interest in the matter as to entitle him to a hearing, even where he had failed to secure the consent of the Attorney General or district attorney to use the name of the United States. Section 1540 deals with that case and provides that where these law officers have refused the request of a "person interested," he may apply to the court by a verified petition for leave to have said writ issue. If, in the opinion of the court, his reasons are sufficient in law, the said writ shall be allowed to be issued in the name of the United States on the relation of said interested person on his giving security for costs.

If the question of Frizzell's "interest" here had depended upon a matter about which the evidence was in conflict, the finding of the supreme court might not be subject to review. But if the established facts show that, as a matter of law, he was not an "interested person," the court had no authority to grant him permission to use the name of the government, and the case must be dismissed. So that the fundamental question is whether the law of force in the District permitted him, as a private citizen, without the consent of the law officers, to test Newman's title to the public office of civil commissioner.

Frizzell does not allege that he had been an incumbent of that office and had been unlawfully ousted before his term expired. He does not set up any claim to the office. And, of course, if he, as a citizen and a taxpayer, has the right to institute these proceedings, any other citizen and taxpayer has a similar right to institute proceedings against Newman and all others. . . .

. . . [G]eneral public interest is not sufficient to authorize a private citizen to institute such proceedings; for if it was, then every citizen and every taxpayer would have the same interest and the same right to institute such proceedings, and a public officer might, from the beginning to the end of his term, be harassed with proceedings to try his title.

. . .

Frizzell applied to the Attorney General for permission to institute the proceedings. Failing to secure that consent, he then applied to the supreme court claiming that the fact that he was a citizen and a taxpayer made him an "interested person," entitled to the use of the writ. But such a construction would practically nullify the requirement to obtain the consent of the Attorney General and the district attorney. . . .

. . .

The conclusion that the relator must have a personal interest in the office before he can sue in the name of the United States is strengthened by the fact that the courts of the District not only have jurisdiction to issued quo warranto against officers of the District, but against all those, attached to the seat of government, who held a statutory office. For, if a private citizen and taxpayer could institute quo warranto proceedings to test the title to the office of civil commissioner of the District, he could, under the same claim of right, institute like proceedings against any of those statutory officers of the United States who, in the District, exercise many important functions which affect persons and things throughout the entire country.

. . . The Code provides that the supreme court shall have jurisdiction to grant quo warranto "against a person who unlawfully holds or exercises within the District a . . . public office, civil or military." It was probably because of this fact that national officers might be involved, that the Attorney General of the United States was given power to institute such proceedings, instead of leaving that power to the district attorney alone, as would probably have been the case if only District officers were referred to in the Code.

Manifestly, Congress did not intend that all these officers attached to the executive branch of the government at Washington should be subject to attacks by persons who had no claim on the office, no right in the office, and no interest which was different from that of every other citizen and taxpayer of the United States.

This fact also shows that 1538–1540 of the District Code, in proper cases, instituted by proper officers or persons, may be enforceable against national officers of the United States. The sections are therefore to be treated as general laws of the United States, not as mere local laws of the District. Being a law of general operation, it can be reviewed on writ of error from this Court.

It follows that the motion to dismiss is denied; the application for a writ of certiorari is refused;

the judgment is reversed; and the case remanded with instructions to dismiss the quo warranto proceedings.

Reversed.

Lamar v. United States
241 U.S. 103 (1916)

Charged in the trial court by an indictment containing two counts, with violating 32 of the Penal Code, the petitioner was convicted and on December 3, 1914, sentenced to two years' imprisonment in the penitentiary. The trial was presided over by the district judge of the western district of Michigan, assigned to duty in the district conformable to the provisions of 18 of the Judicial Code, as amended by the act of Congress of October 3, 1913. To the conviction and sentence in January following error was directly prosecuted from this court, the assignments of error assuming that there was involved not only a question of the jurisdiction of the court as a Federal court, but also constitutional questions. For the purpose of the writ one of the district judges of the southern district of New York gave a certificate as to the existence and character of the question of jurisdiction, evidently with the intention of conforming to 238 of the Judicial Code.

After the record on this writ had been filed in this court, a writ of error to the conviction was prosecuted in May 1915, from the court below. In September following that court, acting on a motion to dismiss such writ of error on the ground that its prosecution was inconsistent with the writ sued out from this court, entered an order providing for dismissal unless the plaintiff in error within ten days elected which of the two writs of error he would rely upon, and subsequently, before the expiration of the time stated, the court declined to comply with the request of the plaintiff in error that the questions at issue be certified to this court. On October 29, 1915, the election required of the plaintiff in error not having been made, the writ of error was dismissed.

On January 31, 1916, the writ of error prosecuted from this court came under consideration as the result of a motion to dismiss, and finding that there was no question concerning the jurisdiction of the trial court within the intendment of the statute and no constitutional question, the writ was dismissed for want of jurisdiction. Thereupon the plaintiff in error in the court below asked that the cause be reinstated and heard, and, upon the refusal of the request, an application was made to this court for leave to file a petition for mandamus to compel such action, and, if not, for the allowance of a certiorari, and although the former application was denied, the case is here because of the allowance of the latter remedy.

. . .

The section of the Penal Code charged to have been violated punishes anyone who, "with intent to defraud either the United States or any person, shall falsely assume or pretend to be an officer or employee acting under the authority of the United States, or any Department, or any officer of the government thereof, and shall take upon himself to act as such, or shall in such pretended character demand or obtain from any person or from the United States, or any Department, or any officer of the government thereof any money, paper, document, or other valuable thing," etc. The indictment charged that at a stated time the petitioner "unlawfully, knowingly and feloniously did falsely assume and pretend to be an officer of the Government of the United States, to wit, a member of the House of Representatives of the Congress of the United States of America, that is to say, A. Mitchell Palmer, a member of Congress representing the twenty-sixth district of the state of Pennsylvania, with the intent, then and there, to defraud Lewis Cass Ledyard," and other persons who were named and others to the grand jury unknown, "and the said defendant, then and there, with the intent and purpose aforesaid, did take upon himself to act as such member of Congress; against the peace," etc., etc.

. . . It is insisted that no offense under the statute was stated in the indictment because a member of the House of Representatives of the United States is not an officer acting under the authority of the United States within the meaning of the provision of the Penal Code upon which the indictment was based. This contention is supported by reference to what is assumed to be the significance in one or more provisions of the Constitution of the words "civil officers." . . .

. . . [W]hen the relations of members of the House of Representatives to the government of the United States are borne in mind, and the nature and character of their duties and responsibilities are considered, we are clearly of the opinion that such members are embraced by the comprehensive terms of the statute. If, however, considered from the face of the statute alone, the question was susceptible of obscurity or doubt—which we think is not the case—all ground for doubt would be removed by the following considerations: (a) Because prior to and at the time of the original enactment in question the common understanding that a member of the House of Representatives was a legislative officer of the United States was clearly expressed in the ordinary, as well as legal, dictionaries. (b) Because at or before the same period in the Senate of the United States . . . it was concluded that a member of Congress was a civil officer of the United States within the purview of the law requiring the taking of an oath of office. (c) Because also in various general statutes of the United States at the time of the enactment in question a member of Congress was assumed to be a civil officer of the United States. (d) Because that conclusion is the necessary result of prior decisions of this court, and harmonizes with the settled conception of the position of members of state legislative bodies as expressed in many state decisions.

. . . [W]hen rightly construed, the operation of the clause is to prohibit and punish the falsely assuming or pretending, with intent to defraud the United States or any person, to be an officer or employee of the United States as defined in the clause, and the doing in the falsely assumed character any overt act, whether it would have been legally authorized had the assumed capacity existed or not, to carry out the fraudulent intent. Briefly stated, we conclude this to be the meaning of the clause for the following reasons: (a) Because the words "acting under the authority of the United States" are words designating the character of the officer or employee whose personation the clause prohibits, since, if the words are thus applied, the clause becomes coherent and free from difficulty, while if, on the other hand, they are applied only as limiting and defining the character of the overt act from which criminality is to arise, confusion and uncertainty as to the officer or employee whose fraudulent simulation is prohibited necessarily results. (b) Because the consequence of a contrary construction would be obviously to limit the application of the clause as shown by its general language and as manifested by the remedial purpose which led to its enactment. (c) Because to adopt a contrary view would be absolutely inharmonious with the context, since it would bring into play a conflict impossible of reconciliation. To make this clear it is to be observed that the last clause of the section makes criminal the

demanding or obtaining in the assumed capacity which the first clause prohibits, "from any person or from the United States . . . any money, paper, document, or other valuable thing. . . ." We say which the first clause prohibits because there is no re-expression of the prohibition against assuming or pretending contained in the first clause except as that prohibition is carried over and made applicable to the second by the words "or shall in such pretended character demand," etc. . . .

. . .

Affirmed.

Alejandrino v. Quezon
271 U.S. 528 (1926)

This proceeding was an original action in the Supreme Court of the Philippines, brought by Jose Alejandrino, a Senator appointed by the Governor General, seeking a mandamus and an injunction against the 22 elected members of the Senate, including its president, its secretary, its sergeant at arms, and its paymaster. The occasion for the proceeding was a resolution of the Senate, passed February 5, 1924. . . .

Jose Alejandrino was appointed under the Philippine Autonomy Act by the Governor General as Senator to represent the twelfth district, a district composed of non-Christian tribes in the northern part of Luzon and the Moros in the department of Mindanao and Sulu. At the time he took his seat in the Senate, another Senator, Vicente de Vera, made a speech on the credentials of Senator Alejandrino, in which he said some things which Alejandrino resented. At night, and after the session of the Senate concluded, and away from the Senate chamber, Alejandrino assaulted de Vera because of his remarks made in the Senate. The resolution complained of was because of this assault.

By section 12 of the Autonomy Act, the general legislative powers in the Philippines, with certain exceptions, are vested in a Legislature consisting of two Houses, the Senate and the House. . . . The Senate is composed of 24 members from 12 Senate districts; 22 of them are elected, and one, the twelfth district, already referred to, has 2 Senators, appointed by the Governor General. By section 17, a Senator appointed by the Governor General holds office until removed by the Governor General. Section 18 provides that the Senate and House respectively shall be the sole judges of the elections, returns and qualifications of their elective members, and each house may determine the rules of its proceedings, punish its members for disorderly behavior, and with the concurrence of two-thirds expel an elective member. The Senators and Representatives shall receive an annual compensation for their services to be ascertained by law and paid out of the treasury of the Philippine Islands. Senators and Representatives shall in all cases, except treason, felony, and breach of the peace, be privileged from arrest during their attendance at the session of their respective houses and in going to and returning from the same, and for any speech or debate in either house they shall not be questioned in any other place.

. . .

. . . Alejandrino is now exercising his functions as a member of the Senate. It is therefore in this court a moot question whether or not he could be suspended in the way in which he was. Equally so is the still more important question whether the Supreme Court of the Philippines had any jurisdiction by extraordinary writ of mandamus or injunction to require the Senate, a part of the Island Legislature, and a separate branch of the government, to rescind its resolution and to readmit Alejandrino to the Senate as an active member.

. . . [T]here still remains a right on his part to the recovery of his emoluments, which were withheld during his suspension, and that we ought to retain the case for the purpose of determining whether he may not have a mandamus for this purpose. . . .

We must assume, in view of the injunction of Congress in the Autonomy Act, that Senators shall receive an annual compensation to be fixed by law, that there is some official or board charged with the executive and ministerial duty of paying the senatorial salaries against whom a Senator entitled might procure a mandamus to compel payment. But the averments of the petition do not set out with sufficient clearness who that official or set of officials may be. Were that set out, the remedy of the Senator would seem to be by mandamus to compel such official in the discharge of his ministerial duty to pay him the salary due, and the presence of the Senate as a party would be unnecessary. Should that official rely upon the resolution of the Senate as a reason for refusing to comply with his duty to pay Senators, the validity of such a defense and the validity of the resolution might become a judicial question affecting the personal right of the complaining Senator properly to be disposed of in such action, but not requiring the presence of the Senate as a party for its adjudication. The right of the petitioner to his salary does not therefore involve the very serious issue raised in this petition as to the power of the Philippine Supreme Court to compel by mandamus one of the two legislative bodies constituting the legislative branch of the government to rescind a resolution adopted by it in asserted lawful discipline of one of its members for disorder and breach of privilege. We think, now that the main question as to the validity of the suspension has become moot, the incidental issue as to the remedy which the suspended Senator may have in recovery of his emoluments if illegally withheld, should properly be tried in a separate proceeding against an executive officer or officers as described. . . .

The case having become moot as respects its main features, and the other feature being incidental and not in itself a proper subject for determination as now presented, further steps looking to an adjudication of the cause can neither be had here nor in the court below. In this situation, we must, following the established practice of this court, vacate the judgment below and remand the cause, with directions to dismiss the petition, without costs to either party.

Judgment vacated, with directions to dismiss petition. . . .

United States v. Wurzbach
280 U.S. 396 (1930)

The respondent was indicted under the Federal Corrupt Practices Act, 1925, on charges that being a representative in Congress he received and was concerned in receiving specified sums of money from named officers and employees of the United States for the political purpose of promoting his nomination as Republican candidate for representative at certain Republican primaries. Upon motion of the defendant the District Court quashed the indictment on the ground that the statute should not be construed to include the political purpose alleged, and, construed to include it, probably would be unconstitutional. The United States appealed.

The section of the statute is as follows:

It is unlawful for any Senator or Representative in, or Delegate or Resident Commissioner, to, Congress, or any candidate for, or individual elected as, Senator, Representative, Delegate, or Resident Commissioner, or any officer or employee of the United States, or any person receiving any salary or compensation for services from money derived from the Treasury of the United States, to directly or indirectly solicit, receive, or be in any manner concerned in soliciting or receiving, any assessment, subscription, or contribution for any political purpose whatever, from any other such officer, employee, or person.

. . .

The doubt of the District Court seems to have come from the assumption that the source of power is to be found in article 1, 4, of the Constitution concerning the time, place and manner of holding elections, etc.; and from the decision that the control of party primaries is purely a State affair. But the power of Congress over the conduct of officers and employees of the Government no more depends upon authority over the ultimate purposes of that conduct than its power to punish a use of the mails for a fraudulent purpose is limited by its inability to punish the intended fraud. It hardly needs argument to show that Congress may provide that its officers and employees neither shall exercise nor be subjected to pressure for money for political purposes, upon or by others of their kind, while they retain their office or employment. . . . Neither the Constitution nor the nature of the abuse to be checked requires us to confine the all embracing words of the Act to political purposes within the control of the United States.

. . .

It is said to be uncertain which of several sections imposes the penalty and therefore uncertain what the punishment is. That question can be raised when a punishment is to be applied. The elaborate argument against the constitutionality of the Act if interpreted as we read it, in accordance with its obvious meaning does not need an elaborate answer. The validity of the Act seems to us free from doubt.

Long v. Ansell
293 U.S. 76 (1934)

On March 27, 1933, Samuel T. Ansell, a resident of the District of Columbia, brought in the Supreme Court of the District, an action for libel against Huey P. Long of Louisiana. The summons was served on the defendant within the District. It directed him to answer and show cause why the plaintiff should not have judgment for the cause of action stated in his declaration. The defendant, appearing specially, and solely for the purpose, filed on April 25, 1933, a motion to quash the summons and the service thereof. . . .

On May 9, 1933, the Supreme Court of the District denied the motion, but stayed further proceedings . . . pending application to the Court of Appeals of the District for a special appeal. That court allowed the appeal. On February 5, 1934, it affirmed the order denying the motion to quash. . . .

Senator Long contends that article 1, 6, cl. 1 of the Constitution, confers upon every member of Congress, while in attendance within the District, immunity in civil cases not only from arrest, but also from service of process. Neither the Senate, nor the House of Representatives, has ever asserted such a claim in behalf of its members. Clause 1 defines the extent of the immunity. Its language is exact and leaves no room for a construction which would extend the privilege beyond the terms of the grant. . . .

. . .

The constitutional privilege here asserted must not be confused with the common-law rule that witnesses, suitors, and their attorneys, while in attendance in connection with the conduct of one suit, are immune from service in another. That rule of practice is founded upon the needs of the court, not upon the convenience or preference of the individuals concerned. And the immunity conferred by the court is extended or withheld as judicial necessities require.

Affirmed.

United States v. Johnson
383 U.S. 169 (1966)

Respondent Johnson, a former United States Congressman, was indicted and convicted on seven counts of violating the federal conflict of interest statute, and on one count of conspiring to defraud the United States. The Court of Appeals for the Fourth Circuit set aside the conviction on the conspiracy count, holding that the Government's allegation that Johnson had conspired to make a speech for compensation on the floor of the House of Representatives was barred by Art. I, §6, of the Federal Constitution, which provides that, "for any Speech or Debate in either House, they [Senators and Representatives] shall not be questioned in any other Place." The Court of Appeals ordered a new trial on the other counts, having found that the evidence adduced under the unconstitutional aspects of the conspiracy count had infected the entire prosecution.

The conspiracy of which Johnson and his three codefendants were found guilty consisted, in broad outline, of an agreement among Johnson, Congressman Frank Boykin of Alabama, and J. Kenneth Edlin and William L. Robinson, who were connected with a Maryland savings and loan institution, whereby the two Congressmen would exert influence on the Department of Justice to obtain the dismissal of pending indictments of the loan company and its officers on mail fraud charges. It was further claimed that, as a part of this general scheme, Johnson read a speech favorable to independent savings and loan associations in the House, and that the company distributed copies to allay apprehensions of potential depositors. The two Congressmen approached the Attorney General and the Assistant Attorney General in charge of the Criminal Division and urged them "to review" the indictment. For these services, Johnson received substantial sums in the form of a "campaign contribution" and "legal fees." The Government contended, and presumably the jury found, that these payments were never disclosed to the Department of Justice, and that the payments were not bona fide campaign contributions or legal fees, but were made simply to "buy" the Congressman.

The bulk of the evidence submitted as to Johnson dealt with his financial transactions with the other conspirators, and with his activities in the Department of Justice. As to these aspects of the substantive counts and the conspiracy count, no substantial question is before us. . . . No argument is made, nor do we think that it could be successfully contended, that the Speech or Debate Clause reaches conduct, such as was involved in the attempt to influence the Department of Justice, that is in no wise related to the due functioning of the legislative process. It is the application of this broad conspiracy statute to an improperly motivated speech that raises the constitutional problem with which we deal.

The language of the Speech or Debate Clause clearly proscribes at least some of the evidence taken during trial. Extensive questioning went on concerning how much of the speech was written by Johnson himself, how much by his administrative assistant, and how much by outsiders representing the loan company. The government attorney asked Johnson specifically about certain sentences in the speech, the reasons for their inclusion and his personal knowledge of the factual material supporting those statements. In closing argument, the theory of the prosecution was very clearly dependent upon the wording of the speech. In addition to questioning the manner of preparation and the precise ingredients of the speech, the Government inquired into the motives for giving it.

The constitutional infirmity infecting this prosecution is not merely a matter of the introduction of inadmissible evidence. The attention given to the speech's substance and motivation was not an incidental part of the Government's case, which might have been avoided by omitting certain lines of questioning or excluding certain evidence. The conspiracy theory depended upon a showing that the speech was made solely or primarily to serve private interests, and that Johnson, in making it, was not acting in good faith, that is, that he did not prepare or deliver the speech in the way an ordinary Congressman prepares or delivers an ordinary speech. Johnson's defense quite naturally was that his remarks were no different from the usual congressional speech, and, to rebut the prosecution's case, he introduced speeches of several other Congressmen speaking to the same general subject, argued that his talk was occasioned by an unfair attack upon savings and loan associations in a Washington, D.C., newspaper, and asserted that the subject matter of the speech dealt with a topic of concern to his State and to his constituents. We see no escape from the conclusion that such an intensive judicial inquiry, made in the course of a prosecution by the Executive Branch under a general conspiracy statute, violates the express language of the Constitution and the policies which underlie it.

. . .

In part because the tradition of legislative privilege is so well established in our polity, there is very little judicial illumination of this clause. Clearly no precedent controls the decision in the case before us. . . .

. . .

We hold that a prosecution under a general criminal statute dependent on such inquiries necessarily contravenes the Speech or Debate Clause. We emphasize that our holding is limited to prosecutions involving circumstances such as those presented in the case before us. Our decision does not touch a prosecution which, though as here founded on a criminal statute of general application, does not draw in question the legislative acts of the defendant member of Congress or his motives for performing them. . . . [W]e expressly leave open for consideration when the case arises a prosecution which, though possibly entailing inquiry into legislative acts or motivations, is founded upon a narrowly drawn statute passed by Congress in the exercise of its legislative power to regulate the conduct of its members.

The Court of Appeals' opinion can be read as dismissing the conspiracy count in its entirety. The making of the speech, however, was only a part of the conspiracy charge. With all references to this aspect of the conspiracy eliminated, we think the Government should not be precluded from a new trial on this count, thus wholly purged of elements offensive to the Speech or Debate Clause.

. . .

. . . [W]e affirm the judgment of the Court of Appeals and remand the case to the District Court for further proceedings consistent with this opinion.

Bond v. Floyd
385 U.S. 116 (1966)

The question presented in this case is whether the Georgia House of Representatives may constitutionally exclude appellant Bond, a duly elected Representative, from membership because of his statements, and statements to which he subscribed, criticizing the policy of the Federal Government in Vietnam and the operation of the Selective Service laws. An understanding of the circumstances of the litigation requires a complete presentation of the events and statements which led to this appeal.

Bond, a Negro, was elected on June 15, 1965, as the Representative to the Georgia House of Representatives from the 136th House District. . . .

. . .

Before January 10, 1966, when the Georgia House of Representatives was scheduled to convene, petitions challenging Bond's right to be seated were filed by 75 House members. These petitions charged that Bond's statements gave aid and comfort to the enemies of the United States and Georgia, violated the Selective Service laws, and tended to bring discredit and disrespect on the House. . . . [T]he petitions asserted that Bond could not take an oath to support the Constitution of the United States. When Bond appeared at the House on January 10 to be sworn in, the clerk refused to administer the oath to him until the issues raised in the challenge petitions had been decided.

Bond filed a response to the challenge petitions in which he stated his willingness to take the oath and argued that he was not unable to do so in good faith. He further argued that the challenge against his seating had been filed to deprive him of his First Amendment rights, and that the challenge was racially motivated. A special committee was appointed to report on the challenge, and a hearing was held to determine exactly what Bond had said and the intentions with which he had said it.

. . .

. . . [T]he House adopted the committee report without findings and without further elaborating Bond's lack of qualifications, and resolved by a vote of 184 to 12 that

> Bond shall not be allowed to take the oath of office as a member of the House of Representatives and that Representative-Elect Julian Bond shall not be seated as a member of the House of Representatives.

Bond then instituted an action in the District Court for the Northern District of Georgia for injunctive relief and a declaratory judgment that the House action was unauthorized by the Georgia Constitution and violated Bond's rights under the First Amendment. . . . [T]he District Court held that the court had jurisdiction to decide the constitutionality of the House action because Bond had asserted substantial First Amendment rights. . . .

. . .

Bond appealed directly to this Court. . . . While this appeal was pending, the Governor of Georgia called a special election to fill the vacancy caused by Bond's exclusion. Bond entered this election and won overwhelmingly. . . . [H]e was again prevented from taking the oath of office, and the seat has remained vacant. Bond again sought the seat from the 136th District in the regular 1966 election, and he won the Democratic primary in September 1966, and won an overwhelming majority in the election of November 8, 1966.

The Georgia Constitution sets out a number of specific provisions dealing with the qualifications and eligibility of state legislators. . . .

. . .

The State argues that the exclusion does not violate the First Amendment because the State has a right, under Article VI of the United States Constitution, to insist on loyalty to the Constitution as a condition of office. A legislator, of course, can be required to swear to support the Constitution of the United States as a condition of holding office, but that is not the issue in this case, as the record is uncontradicted that Bond has repeatedly expressed his willingness to swear to the oaths provided for in the State and Federal Constitutions. Nor is this a case where a legislator swears to an oath pro forma while declaring or manifesting his disagreement with or indifference to the oath. Thus, we do not quarrel with the State's contention that the oath provisions of the United States and Georgia Constitutions do not violate the First Amendment. . . . The State declines to argue that Bond's statements would violate any law if made by a private citizen, but it does argue that, even though such a citizen might be protected by his First Amendment rights, the State may nonetheless apply a stricter standard to its legislators. . . .

. . .

. . . The interest of the public in hearing all sides of a public issue is hardly advanced by extending more protection to citizen critics than to legislators. Legislators have an obligation to take positions on controversial political questions so that their constituents can be fully informed by them, and be better able to assess their qualifications for office; also so they may be represented in governmental debates by the person they have elected to represent them. We therefore hold that the disqualification of Bond from membership in the Georgia House because of his statements violated Bond's right of free expression under the First Amendment. Because of our disposition of the case on First Amendment grounds, we need not decide the other issues advanced by Bond and the amici.

The judgment of the District Court is reversed.

Powell v. McCormack
395 U.S. 486 (1969)

During the 89th Congress, a Special Subcommittee on Contracts of the Committee on House Administration conducted an investigation into the expenditures of the Committee on Education and Labor, of which petitioner Adam Clayton Powell, Jr., was chairman. The Special Subcommittee issued a report concluding that Powell and certain staff employees had deceived the House authorities as to travel expenses. The report also indicated there was strong evidence that certain illegal salary payments had been made to Powell's wife at his direction. No formal action was taken during the 89th Congress. However, prior to the organization of the 90th Congress, the Democratic members-elect met in caucus and voted to remove Powell as chairman of the Committee on Education and Labor.

When the 90th Congress met to organize in January 1967, Powell was asked to step aside while the oath was administered to the other members-elect. Following the administration of the oath to the remaining members, the House discussed the procedure to be followed in determining whether Powell was eligible to take his seat. After some debate, by a vote of 363 to 65, the House adopted House Resolution No. 1, which provided that the Speaker appoint a Select Committee to determine Powell's eligibility. Although the resolution prohibited Powell from taking his seat until the House acted on the Select Committee's report, it did provide that he should receive all the pay and allowances due a member during the period.

. . .

. . . [O]n February 23, 1967, the Committee issued its report, finding that Powell met the standing qualifications of Art. I, §2. However, the Committee further reported that Powell had asserted an unwarranted privilege and immunity from the processes of the courts of New York; that he had wrongfully diverted House funds for the use of others and himself, and that he had made false reports on expenditures of foreign currency to the Committee on House Administration. The Committee recommended that Powell be sworn and seated as a member of the 90th Congress, but that he be censured by the House, fined $40,000, and be deprived of his seniority.

. . . [T]he House debated the Select Committee's proposed resolution. At the conclusion of the debate, by a vote of 222 to 202 the House rejected a motion to bring the resolution to a vote. An amendment to the resolution was then offered; it called for the exclusion of Powell and a declaration that his seat was vacant. The Speaker ruled that a majority vote of the House would be sufficient to pass the resolution if it were so amended. After further debate, the amendment was adopted by a vote of 248 to 176. Then the House adopted by a vote of 307 to 116 House Resolution No. 278 in its amended form, thereby excluding Powell and directing that the Speaker notify the Governor of New York that the seat was vacant.

Powell and 13 voters of the 18th Congressional District of New York subsequently instituted this suit in the United States District Court for the District of Columbia. . . . The complaint alleged that House Resolution No. 278 violated the Constitution, specifically Art. I, §2, cl. 1, because the resolution was inconsistent with the mandate that the members of the House shall be elected by the people of each State, and Art. I, §2, cl. 2, which, petitioners alleged, sets forth the exclusive qualifications for membership. . . .

Petitioners asked . . . that the District Court grant a permanent injunction restraining respondents from executing the House Resolution, and enjoining the Speaker from refusing to administer the oath, the Clerk from refusing to perform the duties due a Representative, the Sergeant at Arms from refusing to pay Powell his salary, and the Doorkeeper from refusing to admit Powell to the Chamber. The complaint also requested a declaratory judgment that Powell's exclusion was unconstitutional.

The District Court granted respondents' motion to dismiss the complaint. . . . The Court of Appeals for the District of Columbia Circuit affirmed. . . . While the case was pending on our docket, the 90th Congress officially terminated, and the 91st Congress was seated. In November, 1968, Powell was again elected as the representative of the 18th Congressional District of New York, and he was seated by the 91st Congress. The resolution seating Powell also fined him $25,000. . . .

. . .

The resolution excluding petitioner Powell was adopted by a vote in excess of two-thirds of the 434 Members of Congress. Article I, §5, grants the House authority to expel a member "with the Concurrence of two thirds." Respondents assert that the House may expel a member for any reason whatsoever, and that, since a two-thirds vote was obtained, the procedure by which Powell was denied his seat in the 90th Congress should be regarded as an expulsion, not an exclusion. . . .

Although respondents repeatedly urge this Court not to speculate as to the reasons for Powell's exclusion, their attempt to equate exclusion with expulsion would require a similar

speculation that the House would have voted to expel Powell had it been faced with that question. Powell had not been seated at the time House Resolution No. 278 was debated and passed. After a motion to bring the Select Committee's proposed resolution to an immediate vote had been defeated, an amendment was offered which mandated Powell's exclusion. Mr. Celler, chairman of the Select Committee, then posed a parliamentary inquiry to determine whether a two-thirds vote was necessary to pass the resolution if so amended "in the sense that it might amount to an expulsion." The Speaker replied that "action by a majority vote would be in accordance with the rules." Had the amendment been regarded as an attempt to expel Powell, a two-thirds vote would have been constitutionally required. The Speaker ruled that the House was voting to exclude Powell, and we will not speculate what the result might have been if Powell had been seated and expulsion proceedings subsequently instituted.

Nor is the distinction between exclusion and expulsion merely one of form. The misconduct for which Powell was charged occurred prior to the convening of the 90th Congress. On several occasions, the House has debated whether a member can be expelled for actions taken during a prior Congress, and the House's own manual of procedure applicable in the 90th Congress states that "both Houses have distrusted their power to punish in such cases." . . . [W]e will not assume that two-thirds of its members would have expelled Powell for his prior conduct had the Speaker announced that House Resolution No. 278 was for expulsion, rather than exclusion.

. . . We must reject respondents' suggestion that we overrule the Speaker, and hold that, although the House manifested an intent to exclude Powell, its action should be tested by whatever standards may govern an expulsion.

. . .

. . . [W]e must . . . determine what power the Constitution confers upon the House through Art. I, §5, before we can determine to what extent, if any, the exercise of that power is subject to judicial review. Respondents maintain that the House has broad power under §5, and, they argue, the House may determine which are the qualifications necessary for membership. On the other hand, petitioners allege that the Constitution provides that an elected representative may be denied his seat only if the House finds he does not meet one of the standing qualifications expressly prescribed by the Constitution.

If examination of §5 disclosed that the Constitution gives the House judicially unreviewable power to set qualifications for membership and to judge whether prospective members meet those qualifications, further review of the House determination might well be barred by the political question doctrine. On the other hand, if the Constitution gives the House power to judge only whether elected members possess the three standing qualifications set forth in the Constitution, further consideration would be necessary to determine whether any of the other formulations of the political question doctrine are "inextricable from the case at bar."

. . .

. . . Our examination of the relevant historical materials leads us to the conclusion that . . . the Constitution leaves the House without authority to exclude any person, duly elected by his constituents, who meets all the requirements for membership expressly prescribed in the Constitution.

. . .

. . . [W]e hold that, since Adam Clayton Powell, Jr., was duly elected by the voters of the 18th Congressional District of New York and was not ineligible to serve under any provision of the Constitution, the House was without power to exclude him from its membership.

. . . [A]s to respondents McCormack, Albert, Ford, Celler, and Moore, the judgment of the Court of Appeals for the District of Columbia Circuit is affirmed. As to respondents Jennings, Johnson, and Miller, the judgment of the Court of Appeals for the District of Columbia Circuit is reversed, and the case is remanded to the United States District Court for the District of Columbia with instructions to enter a declaratory judgment and for further proceedings consistent with this opinion.

United States v. Brewster
408 U.S. 501 (1972)

This direct appeal from the District Court presents the question whether a Member of Congress may be prosecuted under 18 U.S.C. §§201(c)(1), 201(g), for accepting a bribe in exchange for a promise relating to an official act. Appellee, a former United States Senator, was charged in five counts of a 10–count indictment. . . .

Before a trial date was set, the appellee moved to dismiss the indictment on the ground of immunity under the Speech or Debate Clause. . . . After hearing argument, the District Court ruled from the bench:

> It is the opinion of this Court that the immunity under the Speech and [sic] Debate Clause of the Constitution, particularly in view of the interpretation given that Clause by the Supreme Court in Johnson, shields Senator Brewster, constitutionally shields him from any prosecution for alleged bribery to perform a legislative act.
>
> I will, therefore, dismiss the odd counts of the indictment, 1, 3, 5, 7 and 9, as they apply to Senator Brewster.

The United States filed a direct appeal to this Court. . . .

. . .

The immunities of the Speech or Debate Clause were not written into the Constitution simply for the personal or private benefit of Members of Congress, but to protect the integrity of the legislative process by insuring the independence of individual legislators. . . .

. . .

It is well known, of course, that Members of the Congress engage in many activities other than the purely legislative activities protected by the Speech or Debate Clause. These include a wide range of legitimate "errands" performed for constituents, the making of appointments with Government agencies, assistance in securing Government contracts, preparing so-called "news letters" to constituents, news releases, and speeches delivered outside the Congress. The range of these related activities has grown over the years. They are performed in part because they have come to be expected by constituents, and because they are a means of developing continuing support for future elections. Although these are entirely legitimate activities, they are political in nature, rather than legislative, in the sense that term has been used by the Court in prior cases. But it has never been seriously contended that these political matters, however appropriate, have the protection afforded by the Speech or Debate Clause. Careful examination of the decided cases reveals that the Court has regarded the protection as reaching only those things "generally done in a session of the House by one of its members in relation to the business before it," or things "said or done by him, as a representative, in the exercise of the functions of that office."

. . .

In no case has this Court ever treated the Clause as protecting all conduct relating to the legislative process. In every case thus far before this Court, the Speech or Debate Clause has been limited to an act which was clearly a part of the legislative process—the due functioning of the process. Appellee's contention for a broader interpretation of the privilege draws essentially on the flavor of the rhetoric and the sweep of the language used by courts, not on the precise words used in any prior case, and surely not on the sense of those cases, fairly read.

We would not think it sound or wise, simply out of an abundance of caution to doubly insure legislative independence, to extend the privilege beyond its intended scope, its literal language, and its history, to include all thing in any way related to the legislative process. Given such a sweeping reading, we have no doubt that there are few activities in which a legislator engages that he would be unable somehow to "relate" to the legislative process. Admittedly, the Speech or Debate Clause must be read broadly to effectuate its purpose of protecting the independence of the Legislative Branch, but no more than the statutes we apply, was its purpose to make Members of Congress super-citizens, immune from criminal responsibility. In its narrowest scope, the Clause is a very large, albeit essential, grant of privilege. It has enabled reckless men to slander and even destroy others with impunity, but that was the conscious choice of the Framers.

. . .

It is also suggested that, even if we interpreted the Clause broadly so as to exempt from inquiry all matters having any relationship to the legislative process, misconduct of Members would not necessarily go unpunished because each House is empowered to discipline its Members. Article I, §5, does indeed empower each House to "determine the Rules of its Proceedings, punish its Members for disorderly Behavior, and, with the Concurrence of two-thirds, expel a Member," but Congress is ill-equipped to investigate, try, and punish its Members for a wide range of behavior that is loosely and incidentally related to the legislative process. . . .

. . .

. . . Congress has shown little inclination to exert itself in this area. Moreover, if Congress did lay aside its normal activities and take on itself the responsibility to police and prosecute the myriad activities of its Members related to but not directly a part of the legislative function, the independence of individual Members might actually be impaired.

The process of disciplining a Member in the Congress is not without countervailing risks of abuse, since it is not surrounded with the panoply of protective shields that are present in a criminal case. An accused Member is judged by no specifically articulated standards, and is at the mercy of an almost unbridled discretion of the charging body that functions at once as accuser, prosecutor, judge, and jury from whose decision there is no established right of review. In short, a Member would be compelled to defend in what would be comparable to a criminal prosecution without the safeguards provided by the Constitution. Moreover, it would be somewhat naive to assume that the triers would be wholly objective and free from considerations of party and politics and the passions of the moment. Strong arguments can be made that trials conducted in a Congress with an entrenched majority from one political party could result in far greater harassment than a conventional criminal trial with the wide range of procedural protections for the accused, including indictment by grand jury, trial by jury under strict standards

of proof with fixed rules of evidence, and extensive appellate review.

Finally, the jurisdiction of Congress to punish its Members is not all-embracing. For instance, it is unclear to what extent Congress would have jurisdiction over a case such as this, in which the alleged illegal activity occurred outside the chamber, while the appellee was a Member, but was undiscovered or not brought before a grand jury until after he left office.

The sweeping claims of appellee would render Members of Congress virtually immune from a wide range of crimes simply because the acts in question were peripherally related to their holding office. Such claims are inconsistent with the reading this Court has given not only to the Speech or Debate Clause, but also to the other legislative privileges embodied in Art. I, §6. . . .

. . .

We would be closing our eyes to the realities of the American political system if we failed to acknowledge that many non-legislative activities are an established and accepted part of the role of a Member, and are indeed "related" to the legislative process. But if the Executive may prosecute a Member's attempt . . . to influence another branch of the Government in return for a bribe, its power to harass is not greatly enhanced if it can prosecute for a promise relating to a legislative act in return for a bribe. We therefore see no substantial increase in the power of the Executive and Judicial Branches over the Legislative Branch resulting from our holding today. If we underestimate the potential for harassment, the Congress, of course, is free to exempt its Members from the ambit of federal bribery laws, but it has deliberately allowed the instant statute to remain on the books for over a century.

. . .

Taking a bribe is, obviously, no part of the legislative process or function; it is not a legislative act. It is not, by any conceivable interpretation, an act performed as a part of or even incidental to the role of a legislator. It is not an "act resulting from the nature, and in the execution, of the office." Nor is it a "thing said or done by him, as a representative, in the exercise of the functions of that office." Nor is inquiry into a legislative act or the motivation for a legislative act necessary to a prosecution under this statute or this indictment. When a bribe is taken, it does not matter whether the promise for which the bribe was given was for the performance of a legislative act . . . or . . . for use of a Congressman's influence with the Executive Branch. And an inquiry into the purpose of a bribe "does not draw in question the legislative acts of the defendant member of Congress or his motives for performing them."

. . . [T]he Government need not show any act of appellee subsequent to the corrupt promise for payment, for it is taking the bribe, not performance of the illicit compact, that is a criminal act. . . .

. . .

We hold that, under these statutes and this indictment, prosecution of appellee is not prohibited by the Speech or Debate Clause. Accordingly, the judgment of the District Court is reversed, and the case is remanded for further proceedings consistent with this opinion.

Gravel v. United States
408 U.S. 606 (1972)

Among the witnesses subpoenaed were Leonard S. Rodberg, an assistant to Senator Mike Gravel of Alaska and a resident fellow at the Institute of Policy Studies, and Howard Webber, Director of M.I.T. Press. Senator Gravel, as intervenor, filed motions to quash the subpoenas and to require the Government to specify the particular questions to be addressed to Rodberg. He asserted that requiring these witnesses to appear and testify would violate his privilege under the Speech or Debate Clause of the United States Constitution, Art. I, §6, cl. 1.

It appeared that, on the night of June 29, 1971, Senator Gravel, as Chairman of the Subcommittee on Buildings and Grounds of the Senate Public Works Committee, convened a meeting of the subcommittee and there read extensively from a copy of the Pentagon Papers. He then placed the entire 47 volumes of the study in the public record. Rodberg had been added to the Senator's staff earlier in the day and assisted Gravel in preparing for and conducting the hearing. Some weeks later there were press reports that Gravel had arranged for the papers to be published by Beacon Press and that members of Gravel's staff had talked with Webber as editor of M.I.T. Press.

The District Court overruled the motions to quash and to specify questions but entered an order proscribing certain categories of questions. . . . The trial court . . . held the private publication of the documents was not privileged by the Speech or Debate Clause.

The Court of Appeals affirmed the denial of the motions to quash but modified the protective order to reflect its own views of the scope of the congressional privilege. Agreeing that Senator and aide were one for the purposes of the Speech or Debate Clause, and that the Clause foreclosed inquiry of both Senator and aide with respect to legislative acts, the Court of Appeals also viewed the privilege as barring direct inquiry of the Senator or his aide, but not of third parties, as to the sources of the Senator's information used in performing legislative duties. . . .

. . .

Because the claim is that a Member's aide shares the Member's constitutional privilege, we consider first whether and to what extent Senator Gravel himself is exempt from process or inquiry by a grand jury investigating the commission of a crime. Our frame of reference is Art. I, §6, cl. 1, of the Constitution. . . .

The last sentence of the Clause provides Members of Congress with two distinct privileges. Except in cases of "Treason, Felony and Breach of the Peace," the Clause shields Members from arrest while attending or traveling to and from a session of their House. History reveals, and prior cases so hold, that this part of the Clause exempts Members from arrest in civil cases only. . . . Nor does freedom from arrest confer immunity on a Member from service of process as a defendant in civil matters, or as a witness in a criminal case. . . . It is, therefore, sufficiently plain that the constitutional freedom from arrest does not exempt Members of Congress from the operation of the ordinary criminal laws, even though imprisonment may prevent or interfere with the performance of their duties as Members. . . .

In recognition, no doubt, of the force of this part of §6, Senator Gravel disavows any assertion of general immunity from the criminal law. But he points out that the last portion of §6 affords Members of Congress another vital privilege they may not be questioned in any other place for any speech or debate in either House. The claim is not that, while one part of §6 generally permits prosecutions for treason, felony, and breach of the peace, another part nevertheless broadly forbids them. Rather, his insistence is that the Speech or Debate Clause, at the very least, protects him from criminal or civil liability and from questioning elsewhere than in the Senate, with respect to the events occurring at the sub-committee hearing at which the Pentagon Papers were introduced into the public record. To us this claim is incontrovertible. The Speech or Debate Clause was designed to assure a co-equal branch of the government wide freedom of speech, debate, and deliberation without intimidation or threats from the Executive Branch. It thus protects Members against prosecutions that directly impinge upon or threaten the legislative process. We have no doubt that Senator Gravel may not be made to answer either in terms of questions or in terms of defending himself from prosecution— for the events that occurred at the subcommittee meeting. Our decision is made easier by the fact that the United States appears to have abandoned whatever position it took to the contrary in the lower court.

Even so, the United States strongly urges that, because the Speech or Debate Clause confers a privilege only upon "Senators and Representatives," Rodberg himself has no valid claim to constitutional immunity from grand jury inquiry. In our view, both courts below correctly rejected this position. We agree with the Court of Appeals that, for the purpose of construing the privilege a Member and his aide are to be "treated as one.". . .

. . .

The United States fears the abuses that history reveals have occurred when legislators are invested with the power to relieve others from the operation of otherwise valid civil and criminal laws. But these abuses, it seems to us, are for the most part obviated if the privilege applicable to the aide is viewed, as it must be, as the privilege of the Senator, and invocable only by the Senator or by the aide on the Senator's behalf, and if, in all events, the privilege available to the aide is confined to those services that would be immune legislative conduct if performed by the Senator himself. This view places beyond the Speech or Debate Clause a variety of services characteristically performed by aides for Members of Congress, even though within the scope of their employment. It likewise provides no protection for criminal conduct threatening the security of the person or property of others, whether performed at the direction of the Senator in preparation for or in execution of a legislative act or done without his knowledge or direction. Neither does it immunize Senator or aide from testifying at trials or grand jury proceedings involving third-party crimes where the questions do not require testimony about or impugn a legislative act. Thus, our refusal to distinguish between Senator and aide in applying the Speech or Debate Clause does not mean that Rodberg is for all purposes exempt from grand jury questioning.

We are convinced also that the Court of Appeals correctly determined that Senator Gravel's alleged arrangement with Beacon Press to publish the Pentagon Papers was not protected speech or debate within the meaning of Art. I, §6, cl. 1, of the Constitution.

. . .

. . . That Senators generally perform certain acts in their official capacity as Senators does not necessarily make all such acts legislative in nature Members of Congress are constantly in touch with the Executive Branch of the Government and with administrative agencies—they may cajole, and exhort with respect to the administration of a federal statute—but such conduct, though generally done, is not protected legislative activity. . . .

Legislative acts are not all-encompassing. The heart of the Clause is speech or debate in either House. Insofar as the Clause is construed to reach other matters, they must be an integral part of the deliberative and communicative processes by which Members participate in committee and House proceedings with respect to the consideration and passage or rejection of proposed legislation or with respect to other matters which the Constitution places within the jurisdiction of either House. As the Court of Appeals put it, the courts have extended the privilege to matters beyond pure speech or debate in either House, but "only when necessary to prevent indirect impairment of such deliberations."

Here, private publication by Senator Gravel through the cooperation of Beacon Press was in no way essential to the deliberations of the Senate; nor does questioning as to private publication threaten the integrity or independence of the Senate by impermissibly exposing its deliberations to executive influence. The Senator had conducted his hearings; the record and any report that was forthcoming were available both to his committee and the Senate. Insofar as we are advised, neither Congress nor the full committee ordered or authorized the publications. We cannot but conclude that the Senator's arrangements with beacon Press were not part and parcel of the legislative process.

. . . Article I, §6, cl. 1, as we have emphasized, does not purport to confer a general exemption upon Members of Congress from liability or process in criminal cases. Quite the contrary is true. While the Speech or Debate Clause recognizes speech, voting, and other legislative acts as exempt from liability that might otherwise attach, it does not privilege either Senator or aide to violate an otherwise valid criminal law in preparing for or implementing legislative acts. If republication of these classified papers would be a crime under an Act of Congress, it would not be entitled to immunity under the Speech or Debate Clause. It also appears that the grand jury was pursuing this very subject in the normal course of a valid investigation. The Speech or Debate

Clause does not, in our view, extend immunity to Rodberg, as a Senator's aide, from testifying before the grand jury about the arrangement between Senator Gravel and Beacon Press or about his own participation, if any, in the alleged transaction, so long as legislative acts of the Senator are not impugned.

Similar considerations lead us to disagree with the Court of Appeals insofar as it fashioned, tentatively at least, a nonconstitutional testimonial privilege protecting Rodberg from any questioning by the grand jury concerning the matter of republication of the Pentagon Papers. . . . The so-called executive privilege has never been applied to shield executive officers from prosecution for crime, the Court of Appeals was quite sure that third parties were neither immune from liability nor from testifying about the republication matter, and we perceive no basis for conferring a testimonial privilege on Rodberg as the Court of Appeals seemed to do.

. . .

The judgment of the Court of Appeals is vacated, and the cases are remanded to that court for further proceedings consistent with this opinion.

Doe v. McMillan
412 U.S. 306 (1973)

By resolution adopted February 5, 1969, the House of Representatives authorized the Committee on the District of Columbia or its subcommittee

> to conduct a full and complete investigation and study of . . . the organization, management, operation, and administration

of any department or agency of the government of the District of Columbia or of any independent agency or instrumentality of government operating solely within the District of Columbia. The Committee was given subpoena power. . . . On December 8, 1970, a Special Select Subcommittee of the Committee on the District of Columbia submitted to the Speaker of the House a report, represented to be a summary of the Subcommittee's investigation and hearings devoted to the public school system of the District of Columbia. On the same day, the report was referred to the Committee of the Whole House on the State of the Union. . . .

The 450-page report included among its supporting data some 45 pages that are the gravamen of petitioners' suit. . . .

On January 8, 1971, petitioners, under pseudonyms, brought an action in the United States District Court for the District of Columbia on behalf of themselves, their children, and all other children and parents similarly situated. The named defendants were (1) the Chairman and members of the House Committee on the District of Columbia; (2) the Clerk, Staff Director, and Counsel of the Committee; (3) a consultant and an investigator for the Committee; (4) the Superintendent of Documents and the Public Printer; (5) the President and members of the Board of Education of the District of Columbia; (6) the Superintendent of Public Schools of the District of Columbia; (7) the principal of Jefferson Junior High School and one of the teachers at that school; and (8) the United States of America.

Petitioners alleged that, by disclosing, disseminating, and publishing the information contained in the report, the defendants had violated the petitioners' and their children's statutory, constitutional, and common law rights to privacy, and that such publication had caused and would cause grave damage to the children's mental and physical health and to their reputations, good names, and future careers. Petitioners also alleged various violations of local law. Petitioners further charged that, "unless restrained, defendants will continue to distribute and publish information concerning plaintiffs, their children and other students." The complaint prayed for an order enjoining the defendants from further publication, dissemination, and distribution of any report containing the objectionable material, and for an order recalling the reports to the extent practicable and deleting the objectionable material from the reports already in circulation. Petitioners also asked for compensatory and punitive damages.

The District Court, after a hearing on motions for a temporary restraining order and for an order against further distribution of the report, dismissed the action against the individual defendants on the ground that the conduct complained of was absolutely privileged. A divided panel of the United States Court of Appeals for the District of Columbia Circuit affirmed. . . .

To "prevent intimidation of legislators by the Executive and accountability before a possibly hostile judiciary," Art. I, §6, cl. 1, of the Constitution provides that "for any Speech or Debate in either House, they [Members of Congress] shall not be questioned in any other Place." . . .

Without belaboring the matter further, it is plain to us that the complaint in this case was barred by the Speech or Debate Clause insofar as it sought relief from the Congressmen Committee members, from the Committee staff, from the consultant, or from the investigator, for introducing material at Committee hearings that identified particular individuals, for referring the report that included the material to the Speaker of the House, and for voting for publication of the report. Doubtless, also, a published report may, without losing Speech or Debate Clause protection, be distributed to and used for legislative purposes by Members of Congress, congressional committees, and institutional or individual legislative functionaries. At least in these respects, the actions upon which petitioners sought to predicate liability were "legislative acts," and, as such, were immune from suit.

. . . Although we might disagree with the Committee as to whether it was necessary, or even remotely useful, to include the names of individual children in the evidence submitted to the Committee and in the Committee Report, we have no authority to oversee the judgment of the Committee in this respect or to impose liability on its Members if we disagree with their legislative judgment. The acts of authorizing an investigation pursuant to which the subject materials were gathered, holding hearings where the materials were presented, preparing a report where they were reproduced, and authorizing the publication and distribution of that report. . . .

. . .

The proper scope of our inquiry . . . is whether the Speech or Debate Clause affords absolute immunity from private suit to persons who, with authorization from Congress, distribute materials which allegedly infringe upon the rights of individuals. The respondents insist that such public distributions are protected, that the Clause immunizes not only publication for the information and use of Members in the performance of their legislative duties, but also must be held to protect "publications to the public through the facilities of Congress." Public dissemination, it is argued, will serve "the important legislative function of informing the public concerning matters pending before Congress. . . ."

We do not doubt the importance of informing the public about the business of Congress. However, the question remains whether the act of doing so, simply because authorized by Congress, must always be considered "an integral part of the deliberative and communicative processes by which Members participate in committee and House proceedings" with respect to legislative or other matters before the House. . . . [O]thers, such as the Superintendent of Documents or the Public Printer or legislative personnel, who participate in distribution of actionable material beyond the reasonable bounds of the legislative task, enjoy no Speech or Debate Clause immunity.

Members of Congress are themselves immune for ordering or voting for a publication going beyond the reasonable requirements of the legislative function, but the Speech or Debate Clause no more insulates legislative functionaries carrying out such nonlegislative directives. . . . Neither, we think, does it immunize those who publish and distribute otherwise actionable materials beyond the reasonable requirements of the legislative function.

. . . We cannot believe that the purpose of the Clause—"to prevent intimidation of legislators by the Executive and accountability before a possibly hostile judiciary"—will suffer in the slightest if it is held that those who, at the direction of Congress or otherwise, distribute actionable material to the public at large have no automatic immunity under the Speech or Debate Clause, but must respond to private suits to the extent that others must respond in light of the Constitution and applicable laws. To hold otherwise would be to invite gratuitous injury to citizens for little if any public purpose. We are unwilling to sanction such a result, at least absent more substantial evidence that, in order to perform its legislative function, Congress must not only inform the public about the fundamentals of its business, but also must distribute to the public generally materials otherwise actionable under local law.

. . .

In response to these latter allegations, the Court of Appeals, after receiving sufficient assurances from the respondents that they had no intention of seeking a republication or carrying out further distribution of the report, concluded that there was no basis for injunctive relief. But this left the question whether any part of the previous publication and public distribution by respondents other than the Members of Congress and Committee personnel went beyond the limits of the legislative immunity provided by the Speech or Debate Clause of the Constitution. Until that question was resolved, the complaint should not have been dismissed on threshold immunity grounds, unless the Court of Appeals was correct in ruling that the action against the other respondents was foreclosed by the doctrine of official immunity, a question to which we now turn.

. . .

Because the Court has not fashioned a fixed, invariable rule of immunity, but has advised a discerning inquiry into whether the contributions of immunity to elective government in particular contexts outweigh the perhaps recurring harm to individual citizens, there is no ready-made answer as to whether the remaining federal respondents —the Public Printer and the Superintendent of Documents—should be accorded absolute immunity in this case. Of course, to the extent that they serve legislative functions, the performance of which would be immune conduct if done by Congressmen, these officials enjoy the protection of the Speech or Debate Clause. Our inquiry here, however, is whether, if they participate in publication and distribution beyond the legislative sphere, and thus beyond the protection of the Speech or Debate Clause, they are nevertheless protected by the doctrine of official immunity. . . .

. . .

It is apparent that under . . . statutory framework, the printing of documents and their general distribution to the public would be "within the outer perimeter" of the statutory duties of the Public Printer and the Superintendent of Documents. Thus, if official immunity automatically attaches to any conduct expressly or impliedly authorized by law, the Court of Appeals correctly dismissed the complaint against these officials. This, however, is not the governing rule.

. . .

Congress has conferred no express statutory immunity on the Public Printer or the Superintendent of Documents. Congress has not provided that these officials should be immune for printing and distributing materials where those who author the materials would not be. We thus face no statutory or constitutional problems in interpreting this doctrine of "judicial making." . . . We conclude that, for the purposes of the judicially fashioned doctrine of immunity, the Public Printer and the Superintendent of Documents are no more free from suit in the case before us than would be a legislative aide who made copies of the materials at issue and distributed them to the public at the direction of his superiors. The scope of inquiry becomes equivalent to the inquiry in the context of the Speech or Debate Clause, and the answer is the same. The business of Congress is to legislate; Congressmen and aides are absolutely immune when they are legislating. But when they act outside the "sphere of legitimate legislative activity," they enjoy no special immunity from local laws protecting the good name or the reputation of the ordinary citizen.

Because we think the Court of Appeals applied the immunities of the Speech or Debate Clause and of the doctrine of official immunity too broadly, we must reverse its judgment and remand the case for appropriate further proceedings. . . .

. . .

The judgment of the Court of Appeals is reversed in part and affirmed in part, and the case is remanded to the Court of Appeals for further proceedings consistent with this opinion.

Schlesinger v. Reservists Committee to Stop the War
418 U.S. 208 (1974)

Respondents, the Reservists Committee to Stop the War and certain named members thereof, challenged the Reserve membership of Members of Congress as being in violation of the Incompatibility Clause. They commenced a class action in the District Court against petitioners, the Secretary of Defense and the three Service Secretaries, seeking (1) an order in the nature of mandamus directed to petitioners requiring them to strike from the roll of the Reserves all Members of Congress presently thereon, to discharge any member of the Reserves who subsequently became a Member of Congress, and to seek to reclaim from Members and former Members of Congress any Reserve pay said Members received while serving as Members of Congress, (2) a permanent injunction preventing petitioners from placing on the rolls of the Reserves any Member of Congress while serving in Congress, and (3) a declaration that membership in the Reserves is an office under the United States prohibited to Members of Congress by Art. I, §6, cl. 2, and incompatible with membership in the Congress.

Respondents sought the above relief on behalf of four classes of persons. The Committee and the individual respondents sought to represent the interests of (1) all persons opposed to United States military involvement in Vietnam and purporting to use lawful means, including communication with and persuasion of Members of Congress, to end that involvement. The individual respondents alone sought to represent the interests of (2) all officers and enlisted members of the Reserves who were not Members of Congress, (3) all taxpayers of the United States, and (4) all citizens of the United States. The interests of these four classes were alleged to be adversely affected by the Reserve membership of Members of Congress in various ways.

. . .

Petitioners filed a motion to dismiss respondents' complaint on the ground that respondents lacked standing to bring the action, and because the complaint failed to state a cause of action upon which relief could be granted. . . .

. . .

Having resolved the issues of standing and political question in favor of respondents, the District Court held on the merits that a commission in the Reserves is an "Office under the United States" within the meaning of the Incompatibility Clause. On the basis of the foregoing, the court, in its final order, granted partial summary judgment for respondents by declaring that the Incompatibility Clause renders a Member of Congress ineligible, during his continuance in office, to hold a Reserve "commission"; the court denied such parts of respondents' motion for summary judgment which sought a permanent injunction and relief in the nature of mandamus.

The Court of Appeals affirmed the judgment of the District Court. . . .

. . .

Consideration of whether respondents have standing to sue as taxpayers raises a different question from whether they may sue as citizens. . . .

. . . [T]he District Court . . . denied respondents' standing as taxpayers for failure to satisfy the nexus test. We agree with that conclusion,

since respondents did not challenge an enactment under Art. I, §8, but rather the action of the Executive Branch in permitting Members of Congress to maintain their Reserve status.

Accordingly, the judgment of the Court of Appeals is reversed, and the case is remanded to the District Court for further proceedings consistent with this opinion.

Davis v. Passman
442 U.S. 228 (1979)

. . . [R]espondent Otto E. Passman was a United States Congressman from the Fifth Congressional District of Louisiana. On February 1, 1974, Passman hired petitioner Shirley Davis as a deputy administrative assistant. Passman subsequently terminated her employment, effective July 31, 1974, writing Davis that, although she was "able, energetic and a very hard worker," he had concluded "that it was essential that the understudy to my Administrative Assistant be a man."

Davis brought suit in the United States District Court for the Western District of Louisiana, alleging that Passman's conduct discriminated against her "on the basis of sex in violation of the United States Constitution and the Fifth Amendment thereto." Davis sought damages in the form of backpay. . . .

Passman moved to dismiss Davis' action for failure to state a claim upon which relief can be granted. . . . The District Court accepted this argument. . . . A panel of the Court of Appeals for the Fifth Circuit reversed. . . .

The Court of Appeals for the Fifth Circuit, sitting en banc, reversed the decision of the panel. The en banc court did not reach the merits, nor did it discuss the application of the Speech or Debate Clause. . . .

. . .

. . . [A]lthough a suit against a Congressman for putatively unconstitutional actions taken in the course of his official conduct does raise special concerns counseling hesitation, we hold that these concerns are coextensive with the protections afforded by the Speech or Debate Clause. If respondent's actions are not shielded by the Clause, we apply the principle that "legislators ought . . . generally to be bound by [the law] as are ordinary persons." . . .

. . .

We hold today that the Court of Appeals for the Fifth Circuit, en banc, must be reversed because petitioner has a cause of action under the Fifth Amendment, and because her injury may be redressed by a damages remedy. The Court of Appeals did not consider, however, whether respondent's conduct was shielded by the Speech or Debate Clause of the Constitution. Accordingly, we do not reach this question. And, of course, we express no opinion as to the merits of petitioner's complaint.

The judgment of the Court of Appeals is reversed, and the case is remanded for further proceedings consistent with this opinion.

United States v. Helstoski
442 U.S. 477 (1979)

Respondent Helstoski is a former Member of the United States House of Representatives from New Jersey. In 1974, while Helstoski was a Member of the House, the Department of Justice began investigating reported political corruption, including allegations that aliens had paid money for the introduction of private bills which would suspend the application of the immigration laws so as to allow them to remain in this country.

. . .

Helstoski appeared voluntarily before grand juries on 10 occasions between April 1974 and May 1976. Each time he appeared, he was told that he had certain constitutional rights. . . .

. . .

Helstoski testified as to his practices in introducing private immigration bills, and he produced his files on numerous private bills. Included in the files were correspondence with a former legislative aide and with individuals for whom bills were introduced. He also provided copies of 169 bills introduced on behalf of various aliens.

Beginning with his fourth appearance before a grand jury, in October 1975, Helstoski objected to the burden imposed by the requests for information. The requests, he claimed, violated his own right of privacy and that of his constituents. In that appearance, he also stated that there were "some serious Constitutional questions" raised by the failure of the United States Attorney to return tax records which Helstoski had voluntarily delivered. He did not, however, assert a privilege against producing documents until the seventh appearance, on December 12, 1975. Then he declined to answer questions, complaining that the United States Attorney had stated to the District Court that the grand jury had concluded that Helstoski had misapplied campaign funds. He asserted a general invocation of rights under the Constitution and specifically listed the Fourth, Fifth, Sixth, Ninth, and Fourteenth Amendments.

At the next, and eighth, appearance on December 29, 1975, he repeated his objections to the conduct of the United States Attorney. After answering questions about campaign financing, personal loans, and other topics, he declined to answer questions about the receipt of a sum of money. That action was based upon his privilege under the Fifth Amendment "and on further grounds that to answer that question would violate my rights under the Constitution."

Because the grand jury considered that Helstoski's invocation of constitutional privileges was too general to be acceptable, it adjourned and reconvened before the District Judge to seek a ruling on Helstoski's claim of privilege "under the Constitution." After questioning Helstoski, the judge stated that the privilege against compulsory self-incrimination was the only privilege available to Helstoski. The judge assisted Helstoski in wording a statement invoking the privilege that was satisfactory to the grand jury. Thereafter, Helstoski invoked his Fifth Amendment privilege in refusing to answer further questions, including a series of questions about private immigration bills.

Not until his ninth, and penultimate, appearance before a grand jury did Helstoski assert any privilege under the Speech or Debate Clause. On May 7, 1976, Helstoski asked if he was a target of the investigation. The prosecutor declined to answer the question, stating "it would be inappropriate for this Grand Jury or indeed for me to say that you are a target." Helstoski then invoked his privilege against compulsory self-incrimination, and declined to answer further questions or to produce documents. . . .

Although that was the first instance which can even remotely be characterized as reliance upon the Speech or Debate Clause, Helstoski earlier had indicated an awareness of another aspect of the constitutional privileges afforded Congressmen. During his fourth appearance before a grand jury, in October 1975, Helstoski complained that he had been served with a subpoena directing him to appear before a grand jury on a day that Congress was in session.

At his tenth, and final, appearance before a grand jury, Helstoski invoked his Fifth Amend-

ment privilege. But he also referred repeatedly to "other constitutional privileges which prevail." Nevertheless, he continued to promise to produce campaign and personal financial records as requested by the grand jury and directed by the District Judge.

In June 1976, a grand jury returned a multiple-count indictment charging Helstoski and others with various criminal acts. Helstoski moved to dismiss the indictment, contending that the grand jury process had been abused and that the indictment violated the Speech or Debate Clause.

The District Judge denied the motion after examining a transcript of the evidence presented to the indicting grand jury. He held that the Speech or Debate Clause did not require dismissal. He also ruled that the Government would not be allowed to offer evidence of the actual performance of any legislative acts. That ruling prompted the Government to file a motion requesting that the judge pass on the admissibility of twenty-three categories of evidence. The Government urged that a ruling was necessary to avoid the possibility of a mistrial. Helstoski opposed the motion, arguing that the witnesses would not testify as the Government indicated in its proffer.

The District Judge declined to rule separately on each of the categories. . . .

. . .

The Court of Appeals affirmed the District Court's evidentiary ruling. . . .

Turning to the merits of the Government's appeal, the Court of Appeals rejected both of the Government's arguments: (a) that legislative acts could be introduced to show motive; and (b) that legislative acts could be introduced because Helstoski had waived his privilege by testifying before the grand juries. . . .

In holding Helstoski had not waived the protection of the Speech or Debate Clause, the Court of Appeals did not decide whether the protection could be waived. Rather, it assumed that a Member of Congress could waive the privilege, but held that any waiver must be "express and for the specific purpose for which the evidence of legislative acts is sought to be used against the member." Any lesser standard, the court reasoned, would frustrate the purpose of the Clause. Having found on the record before it that no waiver was shown, it affirmed the District Court order under which the Government is precluded from introducing evidence of past legislative acts in any form.

In seeking review of the judgment of the Court of Appeals, the Government contends that the Speech or Debate Clause does not bar the introduction of all evidence referring to legislative acts. It concedes that, absent a waiver, it may not introduce the bills themselves. But the Government argues that the Clause does not prohibit it from introducing evidence of discussions and correspondence which describe and refer to legislative acts if the discussions and correspondence did not occur during the legislative process. The Government contends that it seeks to introduce such evidence to show Helstoski's motive for taking money, not to show his motive for introducing the bills. Alternatively, the Government contends that Helstoski waived his protection under the Speech or Debate Clause when he voluntarily presented evidence to the grand juries. Volunteered evidence, the Government argues, is admissible at trial regardless of its content.

Finally, the Government argues . . . Congress has shared its authority with the Executive and the Judiciary by express delegation authorizing the indictment and trial of Members who violate that section—in short, an institutional decision to waive the privilege of the Clause.

. . .

. . . [T]he Speech or Debate Clause was designed to preclude prosecution of Members for legislative acts. The Clause protects "against inquiry into acts that occur in the regular course of the legislative process and into the motivation for those acts." It "precludes any showing of how [a legislator] acted, voted, or decided." Promises by a Member to perform an act in the future are not legislative acts. . . .

We therefore agree with the Court of Appeals that references to past legislative acts of a Member cannot be admitted without undermining the values protected by the Clause. . . .

. . .

As to what restrictions the Clause places on the admission of evidence, our concern is not with the "specificity" of the reference. Instead, our concern is whether there is mention of a legislative act. To effectuate the intent of the Clause, the Court has construed it to protect other "legislative acts" such as utterances in committee hearings and reports. But it is clear from the language of the Clause that protection extends only to an act that has already been performed. A promise to deliver a speech, to vote, or to solicit other votes at some future date is not "speech or debate." Likewise, a promise to introduce a bill is not a legislative act. Thus . . . the District Court order prohibiting the introduction of evidence "of the performance of a past legislative act" was redundant.

. . .

Like the District Court and the Court of Appeals, we perceive no reason to decide whether an individual Member may waive the Speech or Debate Clause's protection against being prosecuted for a legislative act. Assuming that is possible, we hold that waiver can be found only after explicit and unequivocal renunciation of the protection. The ordinary rules for determining the appropriate standard of waiver do not apply in this setting.

The Speech or Debate Clause was designed neither to assure fair trials nor to avoid coercion. Rather, its purpose was to preserve the constitutional structure of separate, coequal, and independent branches of government. . . .

. . .

On the record before us, Helstoski's words and conduct cannot be seen as an explicit and unequivocal waiver of his immunity from prosecution for legislative acts—assuming such a waiver can be made. The exchanges between Helstoski and the various United States Attorneys indeed indicate a willingness to waive the protection of the Fifth Amendment; but the Speech or Debate Clause provides a separate, and distinct, protection which calls for at least as clear and unambiguous an expression of waiver. No such showing appears on this record.

The Government also argues that there has been a sort of institutional waiver by Congress in enacting §201. According to the Government, §201 represents a collective decision to enlist the aid of the Executive Branch and the courts in the exercise of Congress's powers under Art. I, §5, to discipline its Members. This Court has twice declined to decide whether a Congressman could, consistent with the Clause, be prosecuted for a legislative act as such, provided the prosecution were "founded upon a narrowly drawn statute passed by Congress in the exercise of its legislative power to regulate the conduct of its members." We see no occasion to resolve that important question. We hold only that §201 does not amount to a congressional waiver of the protection of the Clause for individual Members.

. . .

Assuming, arguendo, that the Congress could constitutionally waive the protection of the Clause for individual Members, such waiver could be shown only by an explicit and unequivocal expression. There is no evidence of such a waiver in the language or the legislative history of §201 or any of its predecessors.

We conclude that there was neither individual nor institutional waiver, and that the evidentiary barriers erected by the Speech or Debate Clause must stand. Accordingly, the judgment of the Court of Appeals is affirmed.

United States v. Helstoski
442 U.S. 500 (1979)

The question in this case is whether mandamus is an appropriate means of challenging the validity of an indictment of a Member of Congress on the ground that it violates the Speech or Debate Clause of the Constitution. The Court of Appeals declined to issue the writ. . . .

. . .

Each count charged that Helstoski, acting through his legislative aide, had solicited money from aliens in return for "being influenced in the performance of official acts, to wit: the introduction of private bills in the United States House of Representatives on behalf of" the aliens. . . .

Each count also charged that Helstoski, again acting through his aide, had accepted a bribe in return for his being influenced in the performance of official acts, to-wit: the introduction of private bills in the United States House of Representatives on behalf of the aliens. Finally, each count charged that a private bill had been introduced on a particular date.

. . .

Helstoski moved to dismiss the indictment, contending that the grand jury process had been abused and that the indictment violated the Speech or Debate Clause. . . .

. . .

. . . [I]n June, 1977, Helstoski petitioned the Court of Appeals for a writ of mandamus directing the District Court to dismiss the indictment.

The Court of Appeals declined to issue the writ of mandamus. . . .

In seeking reversal here of the Court of Appeals holding, Helstoski argues that the extraordinary remedy of mandamus is appropriate in this case to protect the constitutional command of separation of powers. He contends that the Speech or Debate Clause assigns exclusive jurisdiction over all legislative acts to Congress. The indictment itself, he urges, is a violation of that Clause, because it represents an impermissible assertion of jurisdiction over the legislative function by the grand jury and the federal courts. He challenges the validity of the indictment on two grounds. First, the indictment itself refers to legislative acts. Any attempt at restricting the proof at trial, as approved by the Court of Appeals, will amount to an amendment of the indictment, thereby violating a Fifth Amendment right to be tried only on an indictment in precisely the form issued by a grand jury. Second, he contends the Speech or Debate Clause was violated when the grand jury was allowed to consider evidence of his legislative acts notwithstanding that such evidence and testimony was presented by him.

. . .

. . . We hold that, if Helstoski wished to challenge the District Court's denial of his motion to dismiss the indictment, direct appeal to the Court of Appeals was the proper course. . . .

Affirmed.

Hutchinson v. Proxmire
443 U.S. 111 (1979)

Ronald Hutchinson, a research behavioral scientist, sued respondents, William Proxmire, a United States Senator, and his legislative assistant, Morton Schwartz, for defamation arising out of Proxmire's giving what he called his "Golden Fleece" award. The "award" went to federal agencies that had sponsored Hutchinson's research. Hutchinson alleged that, in making the award and publicizing it nationwide, respondents had libeled him, damaging him in his professional and academic standing, and had interfered with his contractual relations. The District Court granted summary judgment for respondents, and the Court of Appeals affirmed.

. . .

Respondent Proxmire is a United States Senator from Wisconsin. In March 1975, he initiated the "Golden Fleece of the Month Award" to publicize what he perceived to be the most egregious examples of wasteful governmental spending. The second such award, in April 1975, went to the National Science Foundation, the National Aeronautics and Space Administration, and the Office of Naval Research, for spending almost half a million dollars during the preceding seven years to fund Hutchinson's research. At the time of the award, Hutchinson was director of research at the Kalamazoo State Mental Hospital. Before that, he had held a similar position at the Ft. Custer State Home. Both the hospital and the home are operated by the Michigan State Department of Mental Health; he was therefore a state employee in both positions. During most of the period in question he was also an adjunct professor at Western Michigan University. When the research department at Kalamazoo State Mental Hospital was closed in June 1975, Hutchinson became research director of the Foundation for Behavioral Research, a nonprofit organization. The research funding was transferred from the hospital to the foundation.

The bulk of Hutchinson's research was devoted to the study of emotional behavior. In particular, he sought an objective measure of aggression, concentrating upon the behavior patterns of certain animals, such as the clenching of jaws when they were exposed to various aggravating stressful stimuli. The National Aeronautics and Space Agency and the Navy were interested in the potential of this research for resolving problems associated with confining humans in close quarters for extended periods of time in space and undersea exploration.

The Golden Fleece Award to the agencies that had sponsored Hutchinson's research was based upon research done for Proxmire by Schwartz. While seeking evidence of wasteful governmental spending, Schwartz read copies of reports that Hutchinson had prepared under grants from NASA. Those reports revealed that Hutchinson had received grants from the Office of Naval Research, the National Science Foundation, and the Michigan State Department of Mental Health. Schwartz also learned that other federal agencies had funded Hutchinson's research. After contacting a number of federal and state agencies, Schwartz helped to prepare a speech for Proxmire to present in the Senate on April 18, 1975; the text was then incorporated into an advance press release, with only the addition of introductory and concluding sentences. Copies were sent to a mailing list of 275 members of the news media throughout the United States and abroad.

Schwartz telephoned Hutchinson before releasing the speech to tell him of the award; Hutchinson protested that the release contained an inaccurate and incomplete summary of his research. Schwartz replied that he thought the summary was fair.

In the speech, Proxmire described the federal grants for Hutchinson's research. . . .

In May 1975, Proxmire referred to his Golden Fleece Awards in a newsletter sent to about 100,000 people whose names were on a mailing list that included constituents in Wisconsin as well as persons in other states. The newsletter repeated the essence of the speech and the press release. Later in 1975, Proxmire appeared on a television interview program where he referred to Hutchinson's research, though he did not mention Hutchinson by name.

. . .

After the award was announced, Schwartz, acting on behalf of Proxmire, contacted a number of the federal agencies that had sponsored the research. In his deposition he stated that he did not attempt to dissuade them from continuing to fund the research, but merely discussed the subject. Hutchinson, by contrast, contends that these calls were intended to persuade the agencies to terminate his grants and contracts.

On April 16, 1976, Hutchinson filed this suit in United States District Court in Wisconsin. In Count I, he alleges that, as a result of the actions of Proxmire and Schwartz, he has "suffered a loss of respect in his profession, has suffered injury to his feelings, has been humiliated, held up to public scorn, suffered extreme mental anguish and physical illness and pain to his person. Further, he has suffered a loss of income and ability to earn income in the future." Count II alleges that the respondents' conduct has interfered with Hutchinson's contractual relationships with supporters of his research. He later amended the complaint to add an allegation that his rights of privacy and peace and tranquility have been infringed.

Respondents moved for a change of venue and for summary judgment. In their motion for summary judgment, they asserted that all of their acts and utterances were protected by the Speech or Debate Clause. In addition, they asserted that their criticism of the spending of public funds was privileged under the Free Speech Clause of the First Amendment. They argued that Hutchinson was both a public figure and a public official, and therefore would be obliged to prove the existence of "actual malice." Respondents contended that the facts of this case would not support a finding of actual malice.

Without ruling on venue, the District Court granted respondents' motion for summary judgment. . . .

. . .

The Court of Appeals affirmed, holding that the Speech or Debate Clause protected the statements made in the press release and in the newsletters. . . .

. . .

The purpose of the Speech or Debate Clause is to protect Members of Congress "not only from the consequences of litigation's results, but also from the burden of defending themselves." If the respondents have immunity under the Clause, no other questions need be considered, for they may "not be questioned in any other Place."

. . .

Whatever imprecision there may be in the term "legislative activities," it is clear that nothing in history or in the explicit language of the Clause suggests any intention to create an absolute privilege from liability or suit for defamatory statements made outside the Chamber. . . .

. . .

. . . A speech by Proxmire in the Senate would be wholly immune, and would be available to other Members of Congress and the public in the Congressional Record. But neither the newsletters nor the press release was "essential to the deliberations of the Senate," and neither was part of the deliberative process.

Respondents, however, argue that newsletters and press releases are essential to the functioning of the Senate; without them, they assert, a Senator cannot have a significant impact on the other Senators. We may assume that a Member's published statements exert some influence on other votes in the Congress, and therefore have a relationship to the legislative and deliberative process. . . .

. . . We are unable to discern any "conscious choice" to grant immunity for defamatory statements scattered far and wide by mail, press, and the electronic media.

Respondents also argue that newsletters and press releases are privileged as part of the "informing function" of Congress. . . .

. . .

It is not contended that Hutchinson attained such prominence that he is a public figure for all purposes. Instead, respondents have argued that the District Court and the Court of Appeals were correct in holding that Hutchinson is a public figure for the limited purpose of comment on his receipt of federal funds for research projects. That conclusion was based upon two factors: first, Hutchinson's successful application for federal funds and the reports in local newspapers of the federal grants; second, Hutchinson's access to the media, as demonstrated by the fact that some newspapers and wire services reported his response to the announcement of the Golden Fleece Award. Neither of those factors demonstrates that Hutchinson was a public figure prior to the controversy engendered by the Golden Fleece Award; his access, such as it was, came after the alleged libel.

. . .

We therefore reverse the judgment of the Court of Appeals and remand the case to the Court of Appeals for further proceedings consistent with this opinion.

United States v. Gillock
445 U.S. 360 (1980)

Respondent Edgar H. Gillock was indicted on August 12, 1976, in the Western District of Tennessee on five counts of obtaining money under color of official right. . , one count of using an interstate facility to distribute a bribe. . , and one count of participating in an enterprise through a pattern of racketeering activity. . . . The indictment charged Gillock, then a Tennessee state senator and practicing attorney, with accepting money as a fee for using his public office to block the extradition of a defendant from Tennessee to Illinois, and for agreeing to introduce in the State General Assembly legislation which would enable four persons to obtain master electricians' licenses they had been unable to obtain by way of existing examination processes.

Before trial, Gillock moved to suppress all evidence relating to his legislative activities. The District Court granted his motion, holding that, as a state senator, Gillock had an evidentiary privilege. . . . This privilege, deemed by the District Court to be equivalent to that granted Members of both Houses of Congress under the Speech or Debate Clause was limited to prohibiting the introduction of evidence of Gillock's legislative acts and his underlying motivations. . . .

The Government appealed the pretrial suppression order to the United States Court of Appeals for the Sixth Circuit, which vacated the order and remanded for additional consideration. The Court

of Appeals noted that, although the District Court had expressed its willingness to recognize a legislative privilege, it had not applied the principle to particularize items of evidence.

On remand, the Government submitted a formal offer of proof and requested a ruling on the applicability of the legislative privilege to fifteen specifically described items of evidence. The offer first detailed the evidence the Government proposed to introduce at trial in support of the count of the indictment charging Gillock with soliciting money from one Ruth Howard in exchange for using his influence as a state senator to block the extradition of Howard's brother, James Michael Williams. Williams had been arrested in Tennessee in November 1974, and was being held as a fugitive from Illinois. According to the offer of proof, in January 1975 Howard met in Memphis with her brother's attorney, John Hundley, who allegedly told her that he had a "friend" who could help her brother. A meeting between Gillock and Howard was arranged by Hundley, and Gillock agreed to exercise his influence to block the extradition for a fee.

The Government declared its intention to prove that, on March 6, 1975, Gillock appeared at Williams' extradition hearing. Although he denied that he was attending the hearing either as an attorney or in his capacity as a state senator, Gillock reviewed the extradition papers and questioned the hearing officer about the propriety of extradition on a misdemeanor charge. Later that day, Gillock requested an official opinion from the Tennessee Attorney General concerning "Extradition on a Misdemeanor."

In addition, the Government stated it intended to introduce at trial the transcript of a telephone call Gillock made to Howard on March 25, 1975. During that conversation, Gillock allegedly advised Howard that he had delayed the extradition proceedings, and could have blocked them entirely, by exerting pressure on the extradition hearing officer who had appeared before Gillock's senate judiciary committee on a budgetary matter. To corroborate that conversation, the Government indicated it would prove that, on March 19, 1975, Gillock attended a meeting of the senate judiciary committee where the same extradition hearing officer who conducted Williams' extradition hearing presented his department's budget request.

Next, the Government recited the evidence it proposed to introduce showing that Gillock used his influence as a member of the Tennessee State Senate to assist four individuals in obtaining master electricians' licenses valid in Shelby County, Tennessee According to the offer of proof, the four contacted Gillock in early 1972. Two weeks later, Gillock advised them that he could get legislation enacted by the General Assembly which would provide for reciprocity in licensing. Under his proposal, a person who received a license in another county could be admitted without a test in Shelby County. The prosecution represented it would offer evidence that Gillock fixed a contingent fee of $5,000 per person, to be refunded if the legislation was not passed.

The Government also represented that it would offer evidence that Gillock introduced reciprocity legislation in the senate, and that he arranged for the introduction of a similar bill in the house. The Government further proposed to introduce statements made by Gillock on the floor of the senate in support of the bill. After the bill was passed by both branches of the legislature and forwarded to the Governor, several private persons, including union representatives, allegedly met with Gillock and voiced their opposition to the legislation. The Government intended to prove that Gillock replied that he could not financially afford to withdraw the legislation because he had already accepted "fees" for introducing it. Finally, the Government intended to prove that, on April 13, 1972, Gillock moved to override the Governor's veto of the legislation, and stated that it would introduce into evidence any and all statements made by Gillock on the floor of the senate in support of his motion to override.

Based on this offer of proof, the District Court granted Gillock's renewed motion to exclude evidence of his legislative acts. . . . It ruled inadmissible Gillock's official request for an opinion from the Attorney General regarding extradition and the answer to that request, and Gillock's statements to Howard that he could exert pressure on the extradition hearing officer to block the extradition because the hearing officer had appeared before Gillock's legislative committee. Similarly, the court ruled that all evidence regarding Gillock's introduction and support of the electricians' reciprocal licensing bill, his conversation with the private individuals who opposed the legislation, and the Governor's veto letter would be inadmissible.

The Government again appealed the District Court's suppression order. The Court of Appeals . . . held that "the long history and the felt need for protection of legislative speech or debate and the repeated and strong recognition of that history in the cases . . . from the Supreme Court, fully justify our affirming [the District Court] in [its] protection of the privilege in this case." Turning to the scope of the privilege, the court affirmed the suppression of evidence of Gillock's request for a formal opinion from the Attorney General, his participation in the senate judiciary committee, his introduction of the reciprocity legislation, his motion on the floor of the senate to override the Governor's veto, and all the statements he made on the floor of the senate. The other items of evidence were considered to be insufficiently related to the legislative process to be protected by the privilege.

Gillock urges that we construct an evidentiary privilege barring the introduction of evidence of legislative acts in federal criminal prosecutions against state legislators. He argues first that a speech or debate type privilege for state legislators in federal criminal cases is an established part of the federal common law. . . . Second, he contends that . . . a legislative speech or debate privilege is compelled by principles of federalism rooted in our constitutional structure.

. . .

Gillock argues that the historical antecedents and policy considerations which inspired the Speech or Debate Clause of the Federal Constitution should lead this Court to recognize a comparable evidentiary privilege for state legislators in federal prosecutions. . . .

. . .

In the absence of a constitutional limitation on the power of Congress to make state officials, like all other persons, subject to federal criminal sanctions, we discern no basis in these circumstances for a judicially created limitation that handicaps proof of the relevant facts. Accordingly, the judgment of the Court of Appeals for the Sixth Circuit is reversed.

McCormick v. United States
500 U.S. 257 (1991)

Petitioner Robert L. McCormick was a member of the West Virginia House of Delegates in 1984. He represented a district that had long suffered from a shortage of medical doctors. For several years, West Virginia had allowed foreign medical school graduates to practice under temporary permits while studying for the state licensing exams. Under this program, some doctors were allowed to practice under temporary permits for years, even though they repeatedly failed the state exams. McCormick was a leading advocate and supporter of this program.

In the early 1980s, following a move in the House of Delegates to end the temporary permit program, several of the temporarily licensed doctors formed an organization to press their interests in Charleston. The organization hired a lobbyist, John Vandergrift, who in 1984 worked for legislation that would extend the expiration date of the temporary permit program. McCormick sponsored the House version of the proposed legislation, and a bill was passed extending the program for another year. Shortly thereafter, Vandergrift and McCormick discussed the possibility of introducing legislation during the 1985 session that would grant the doctors a permanent medical license by virtue of their years of experience. McCormick agreed to sponsor such legislation.

During his 1984 reelection campaign, McCormick informed Vandergrift that his campaign was expensive, that he had paid considerable sums out of his own pocket, and that he had not heard anything from the foreign doctors. Vandergrift told McCormick that he would contact the doctors and see what he could do. Vandergrift contacted one of the foreign doctors and later received from the doctors $1,200 in cash. Vandergrift delivered an envelope containing nine $100 bills to McCormick. Later the same day, a second delivery of $2,000 in cash was made to McCormick. During the fall of 1984, McCormick received two more cash payments from the doctors. McCormick did not list any of these payments as campaign contributions, nor did he report the money as income on his 1984 federal income tax return. And although the doctors' organization kept detailed books of its expenditures, the cash payments were not listed as campaign contributions. Rather, the entries for the payments were accompanied only by initials or other codes signifying that the money was for McCormick.

In the spring of 1985, McCormick sponsored legislation permitting experienced doctors to be permanently licensed without passing the state licensing exams. McCormick spoke at length in favor of the bill during floor debate, and the bill ultimately was enacted into law. Two weeks after the legislation was enacted, McCormick received another cash payment from the foreign doctors.

Following an investigation, a federal grand jury returned an indictment charging McCormick with five counts of violating the Hobbs Act, by extorting payments under color of official right, and with one count of filing a false income tax return . . . by failing to report as income the cash payments he received from the foreign doctors. . . .

. . .

The jury convicted McCormick of the first Hobbs Act count (charging him with receiving the initial $900 cash payment) and the income tax violation, but could not reach verdicts on the remaining four Hobbs Act counts. The District Court declared a mistrial on those four counts.

The Court of Appeals affirmed. . . .

. . .

We agree with the Court of Appeals that, in a case like this, it is proper to inquire whether payments made to an elected official are, in fact, campaign contributions, and we agree that the intention of the parties is a relevant consideration in pursuing this inquiry. But we cannot accept the Court of Appeals' approach to distinguishing between legal and illegal campaign contributions. The Court of Appeals stated that payments to elected officials could violate the Hobbs Act without proof of an explicit quid pro quo by proving

that the payments "were never intended to be legitimate campaign contributions." This issue, as we read the Court of Appeals' opinion, actually involved two inquiries, for, after applying the factors the Court of Appeals considered relevant, it arrived at two conclusions: first, that McCormick was extorting money for his continued support of the 1985 legislation, and "[f]urther" that the money was never intended by the parties to be a campaign contribution at all. The first conclusion, especially when considered in light of the second, asserts that the campaign contributions were illegitimate, extortionate payments.

. . .

Serving constituents and supporting legislation that will benefit the district and individuals and groups therein is the everyday business of a legislator. It is also true that campaigns must be run and financed. Money is constantly being solicited on behalf of candidates, who run on platforms and who claim support on the basis of their views and what they intend to do or have done. Whatever ethical considerations and appearances may indicate, to hold that legislators commit the federal crime of extortion when they act for the benefit of constituents or support legislation furthering the interests of some of their constituents, shortly before or after campaign contributions are solicited and received from those beneficiaries, is an unrealistic assessment of what Congress could have meant by making it a crime to obtain property from another, with his consent, "under color of official right." To hold otherwise would open to prosecution not only conduct that has long been thought to be well within the law, but also conduct that, in a very real sense, is unavoidable so long as election campaigns are financed by private contributions or expenditures, as they have been from the beginning of the Nation. It would require statutory language more explicit than the Hobbs Act contains to justify a contrary conclusion.

This is not to say that it is impossible for an elected official to commit extortion in the course of financing an election campaign. Political contributions are, of course, vulnerable if induced by the use of force, violence, or fear. The receipt of such contributions is also vulnerable under the Act as having been taken under color of official right, but only if the payments are made in return for an explicit promise or undertaking by the official to perform or not to perform an official act. In such situations, the official asserts that his official conduct will be controlled by the terms of the promise or undertaking. This is the receipt of money by an elected official under color of official right within the meaning of the Hobbs Act.

. . .

We . . . disagree with the Court of Appeals' holding in this case that a quid pro quo is not necessary for conviction under the Hobbs Act when an official receives a campaign contribution. . . .

. . .

Accordingly we reverse the judgment of the Court of Appeals and remand for further proceedings consistent with this opinion.

Bogan v. Scott-Harris
523 U.S. 44 (1998)

Respondent Janet Scott-Harris was administrator of the Department of Health and Human Services (DHHS) for the city of Fall River, Massachusetts, from 1987 to 1991. In 1990, respondent received a complaint that Dorothy Biltcliffe, an employee serving temporarily under her supervision, had made repeated racial and ethnic slurs about her colleagues. After

respondent prepared termination charges against Biltcliffe, Biltcliffe used her political connections to press her case with several state and local officials, including petitioner Marilyn Roderick, the vice president of the Fall River City Council. The city council held a hearing on the charges against Biltcliffe and ultimately accepted a settlement proposal under which Biltcliffe would be suspended without pay for 60 days. Petitioner Daniel Bogan, the mayor of Fall River, thereafter substantially reduced the punishment.

While the charges against Biltcliffe were pending, Mayor Bogan prepared his budget proposal for the 1992 fiscal year. . . . Bogan proposed freezing the salaries of all municipal employees. . . . Bogan called for the elimination of DHHS, of which respondent was the sole employee. The City Council Ordinance Committee, which was chaired by Roderick, approved an ordinance eliminating DHHS. The city council thereafter adopted the ordinance . . . with petitioner Roderick among those voting in favor. Bogan signed the ordinance into law.

Respondent then filed suit under Rev.Stat. §1979, against the city, Bogan, Roderick, and several other city officials. She alleged that the elimination of her position was motivated by racial animus and a desire to retaliate against her for exercising her First Amendment rights in filing the complaint against Biltcliffe. The District Court denied Bogan's and Roderick's motions to dismiss on the ground of legislative immunity, and the case proceeded to trial.

The jury returned a verdict in favor of all defendants on the racial discrimination charge, but found the city, Bogan, and Roderick liable on respondent's First Amendment claim, concluding that respondent's constitutionally protected speech was a substantial or motivating factor in the elimination of her position. On a motion for judgment notwithstanding the verdict, the District Court again denied Bogan's and Roderick's claims of absolute legislative immunity. . . .

The United States Court of Appeals for the First Circuit set aside the verdict against the city, but affirmed the judgments against Roderick and Bogan. Although the court concluded that petitioners have "absolute immunity from civil liability for damages arising out of their performance of legitimate legislative activities," it held that their challenged conduct was not "legislative." . . .

. . .

Absolute immunity for local legislators under §1983 finds support not only in history, but also in reason. The rationales for according absolute immunity to federal, state, and regional legislators apply with equal force to local legislators. Regardless of the level of government, the exercise of legislative discretion should not be inhibited by judicial interference or distorted by the fear of personal liability. Furthermore, the time and energy required to defend against a lawsuit are of particular concern at the local level, where the part-time citizen legislator remains commonplace. And the threat of liability may significantly deter service in local government, where prestige and pecuniary rewards may pale in comparison to the threat of civil liability.

Moreover, certain deterrents to legislative abuse may be greater at the local level than at other levels of government. Municipalities themselves can be held liable for constitutional violations, whereas States and the Federal Government are often protected by sovereign immunity. And, of course, the ultimate check on legislative abuse—the electoral process—applies with equal force at the local level, where legislators are often more closely responsible to the electorate.

. . .

Whether an act is legislative turns on the nature of the act, rather than on the motive or intent of the official performing it. . . . Furthermore, it simply is "not consonant with our scheme of government for a court to inquire into the motives of legislators." . . .

This leaves us with the question whether, stripped of all considerations of intent and motive, petitioners' actions were legislative. We have little trouble concluding that they were. Most evidently, petitioner Roderick's acts of voting for an ordinance were, in form, quintessentially legislative. Petitioner Bogan's introduction of a budget and signing into law an ordinance also were formally legislative, even though he was an executive official. We have recognized that officials outside the legislative branch are entitled to legislative immunity when they perform legislative functions, Bogan's actions were legislative because they were integral steps in the legislative process.

. . .

. . . [T]he judgment of the Court of Appeals is reversed.

11

First Amendment Implications

This chapter covers the scope of political libel, the use and restrictions of the media in campaigns, and the requirements to the media for fairness in political races.

Farmers Educational & Cooperative Union v. WDAY
360 U.S. 525 (1959)

This suit for libel arose as a result of a speech made over the radio and television facilities of respondent, WDAY, Inc., by A. C. Townley—a legally qualified candidate in the 1956 United States senatorial race in North Dakota. Because it felt compelled to do so by the requirements of §315, WDAY permitted Townley to broadcast his speech, uncensored in any respect, as a reply to previous speeches made over WDAY by two other senatorial candidates. Townley's speech, in substance, accused his opponents, together with petitioner, Farmers Educational and Cooperative Union of America, of conspiring to "establish a Communist Farmers Union Soviet right here in North Dakota." Farmers Union then sued Townley and WDAY for libel in a North Dakota State District Court. That court dismissed the complaint against WDAY on the ground that §315 rendered the station immune from liability for the defamation alleged. The Supreme Court of North Dakota affirmed. . . .

. . .

We are aware that causes of action for libel are widely recognized throughout the States. But we have not hesitated to abrogate state law where satisfied that its enforcement would stand "as an obstacle to the accomplishment and execution of the full purposes and objectives of Congress." Here, petitioner is asking us to attribute to §315 a meaning which would either frustrate the underlying purposes for which it was enacted, or alternatively impose unreasonable burdens on the parties governed by that legislation. In the absence of clear expression by Congress we will not assume that it desired such a result. Agreeing with the state courts of North Dakota that §315 grants a licensee an immunity from liability for libelous material it broadcasts, we merely read §315 in accordance with what we believe to be its underlying purpose.

Affirmed.

New York Times Co. v. Sullivan
376 U.S. 254 (1964)

Respondent L. B. Sullivan is one of the three elected Commissioners of the City of Montgomery, Alabama. . . . He brought this civil libel action against the four individual petitioners, who are Negroes and Alabama clergymen, and against petitioner the New York Times Company, a New York corporation which publishes the *New York Times*, a daily newspaper. A jury in the Circuit Court of Montgomery County awarded him damages of $500,000, the full amount claimed, against all the petitioners, and the Supreme Court of Alabama affirmed.

Respondent's complaint alleged that he had been libeled by statements in a full-page advertisement that was carried in the *New York Times* on March 29, 1960. . . .

. . .

Alabama law denies a public officer recovery of punitive damages in a libel action brought on account of a publication concerning his official conduct unless he first makes a written demand for a public retraction and the defendant fails or refuses to comply. Respondent served such a demand upon each of the petitioners. None of the individual petitioners responded to the demand, primarily because each took the position that he had not authorized the use of his name on the advertisement, and therefore had not published the statements that respondent alleged had libeled him. The *Times* did not publish a retraction in response to the demand. . . . Respondent filed this suit a few days later without answering the letter. The *Times* did, however, subsequently publish a retraction of the advertisement upon the demand of Governor John Patterson of Alabama. . . .

. . .

In affirming the judgment, the Supreme Court of Alabama sustained the trial judge's rulings and instructions in all respects. . . . In sustaining the trial court's determination that the verdict was not excessive, the court said that malice could be inferred from the *Times'* "irresponsibility" in printing the advertisement. . . .

. . .

Injury to official reputation affords no more warrant for repressing speech that would otherwise be free than does factual error. Where judicial officers are involved, this Court has held that concern for the dignity and reputation of the courts does not justify the punishment as criminal contempt of criticism of the judge or his decision. This is true even though the utterance contains "half-truths" and "misinformation." Such repression can be justified, if at all, only by a clear and present danger of the obstruction of justice. If judges are to be treated as "men of fortitude, able to thrive in a hardy climate," surely the same must be true of other government officials, such as elected city commissioners. Criticism of their official conduct does not lose its constitutional protection merely because it is effective criticism, and hence diminishes their official reputations.

If neither factual error nor defamatory content suffices to remove the constitutional shield from criticism of official conduct, the combination of the two elements is no less inadequate. . . .

. . .

We hold today that the Constitution delimits a State's power to award damages for libel in actions brought by public officials against critics of their official conduct. Since this is such an action, the rule requiring proof of actual malice is applicable. While Alabama law apparently requires proof of actual malice for an award of punitive damages, where general damages are concerned malice is "presumed." Such a presumption is inconsistent with the federal rule. "The power to create presumptions is not a means of escape from constitutional restrictions," "the showing of malice required for the forfeiture of the privilege is not presumed but is a matter for proof by the plaintiff. . . ." Since the trial judge did not instruct the jury to differentiate between general and punitive damages, it may be that the verdict was wholly an award of one or the other. But it is impossible to know, in view of the general verdict returned. Because of this uncertainty, the judgment must be reversed and the case remanded.

. . .

The judgment of the Supreme Court of Alabama is reversed, and the case is remanded to that court for further proceedings not inconsistent with this opinion.

Mills v. Alabama
384 U.S. 214 (1966)

On November 6, 1962, Birmingham, Alabama, held an election for the people to decide whether they preferred to keep their existing city commission form of government or replace it with a mayor-council government. On election day, the *Birmingham Post-Herald*, a daily newspaper, carried an editorial written by its editor, appellant, James E. Mills, which strongly urged the people to adopt the mayor-council form of government. Mills was later arrested on a complaint charging that, by publishing the editorial on election day, he had violated §285 of the Alabama Corrupt Practices Act. . . . The trial court sustained demurrers to the complaint on the grounds that the state statute abridged freedom of speech and press in violation of the Alabama Constitution and the First and Fourteenth Amendments to the United States Constitution. On appeal by the State, the Alabama Supreme Court held that publication of the editorial on election day undoubtedly violated the state law, and then went on to reverse the trial court by holding that the state statute, as applied, did not unconstitutionally abridge freedom of speech or press. Recognizing that the state law did limit and restrict both speech and press, the State Supreme Court nevertheless sustained it as a valid exercise of the State's police power chiefly because, as that court said, the press "restriction, everything considered, is within the field of reasonableness,"

and "not an unreasonable limitation upon free speech, which includes free press." . . .

. . .

. . . The question here is whether it abridges freedom of the press for a State to punish a newspaper editor for doing no more than publishing an editorial on election day urging people to vote a particular way in the election. . . . The sole reason for the charge that Mills violated the law is that he wrote and published an editorial on election day urging Birmingham voters to cast their votes in favor of changing their form of government.

Whatever differences may exist about interpretations of the First Amendment, there is practically universal agreement that a major purpose of that Amendment was to protect the free discussion of governmental affairs. This, of course, includes discussions of candidates, structures and forms of government, the manner in which government is operated or should be operated, and all such matters relating to political processes. The Constitution specifically selected the press, which includes not only newspapers, books, and magazines, but also humble leaflets and circulars, to play an important role in the discussion of public affairs. Thus, the press serves and was designed to serve as a powerful antidote to any abuses of power by governmental officials, and as a constitutionally chosen means for keeping officials elected by the people responsible to all the people whom they were selected to serve. Suppression of the right of the press to praise or criticize governmental agents and to clamor and contend for or against change, which is all that this editorial did, muzzles one of the very agencies the Framers of our Constitution thoughtfully and deliberately selected to improve our society and keep it free. The Alabama

Corrupt Practices Act, by providing criminal penalties for publishing editorials such as the one here, silences the press at a time when it can be most effective. It is difficult to conceive of a more obvious and flagrant abridgment of the constitutionally guaranteed freedom of the press.

Admitting that the state law restricted a newspaper editor's freedom to publish editorials on election day, the Alabama Supreme Court nevertheless sustained the constitutionality of the law on the ground that the restrictions on the press were only "reasonable restrictions" or at least "within the field of reasonableness." The court reached this conclusion because it thought the law imposed only a minor limitation on the press—restricting it only on election days—and because the court thought the law served a good purpose. ... This argument, even if it were relevant to the constitutionality of the law, has a fatal flaw. The state statute leaves people free to hurl their campaign charges up to the last minute of the day before election. The law held valid by the Alabama Supreme Court then goes on to make it a crime to answer those "last-minute" charges on election day, the only time they can be effectively answered. Because the law prevents any adequate reply to these charges, it is wholly ineffective in protecting the electorate "from confusive last-minute charges and countercharges." We hold that no test of reasonableness can save a state law from invalidation as a violation of the First Amendment when that law makes it a crime for a newspaper editor to do no more than urge people to vote one way or another in a publicly held election.

The judgment of the Supreme Court of Alabama is reversed, and the case is remanded for further proceedings not inconsistent with this opinion.

St. Amant v. Thompson
390 U.S. 727 (1968)

On June 27, 1962, petitioner St. Amant, a candidate for public office, made a televised speech in Baton Rouge, Louisiana. In the course of this speech, St. Amant read a series of questions which he had put to J. D. Albin, a member of a Teamsters Union local, and Albin's answers to those questions. The exchange concerned the allegedly nefarious activities of E. G. Partin, the president of the local, and the alleged relationship between Partin and St. Amant's political opponent. One of Albin's answers concerned his efforts to prevent Partin from secreting union records; in this answer, Albin referred to Herman A. Thompson, an East Baton Rouge Parish deputy sheriff and respondent here. ...

Thompson promptly brought suit for defamation, claiming that the publication had "impute[d] ... gross misconduct" and "infer[red] conduct of the most nefarious nature." ... The trial judge ruled in Thompson's favor and awarded $5,000 in damages. ... The Louisiana Court of Appeal reversed because the record failed to show that St. Amant had acted with actual malice. ... The Supreme Court of Louisiana reversed the intermediate appellate court. In its view, there was sufficient evidence that St. Amant recklessly disregarded whether the statements about Thompson were true or false. ...

. . .

... [T]he Louisiana Supreme Court ruled that St. Amant had broadcast false information about Thompson recklessly, though not knowingly. Several reasons were given for this conclusion. St. Amant had no personal knowledge of Thompson's activities; he relied solely on Albin's affidavit, although the record was silent as to Albin's reputation for veracity; he failed to verify the information with those in the union office who might have known the facts; he gave no consideration to whether or not the statements defamed Thompson, and went ahead heedless of the consequences, and he mistakenly believed he had no responsibility for the broadcast because he was merely quoting Albin's words.

· · ·

. . . Neither lies nor false communications serve the ends of the First Amendment, and no one suggests their desirability or further proliferation. But to insure the ascertainment and publication of the truth about public affairs, it is essential that the First Amendment protect some erroneous publications, as well as true ones. . . .

· · ·

Because the state court misunderstood and misapplied the actual malice standard which must be observed in a public official's defamation action, the judgment is reversed and the case remanded for further proceedings not inconsistent with this opinion.

Red Lion Broadcasting Co., Inc. v. Federal Communications Commission
395 U.S. 367 (1969)

The Federal Communications Commission has for many years imposed on radio and television broadcasters the requirement that discussion of public issues be presented on broadcast stations, and that each side of those issues must be given fair coverage. This is known as the fairness doctrine, which originated very early in the history of broadcasting and has maintained its present outlines for some time. It is an obligation whose content has been defined in a long series of FCC rulings in particular cases, and which is distinct from the statutory requirement of §315 of the Communications Act that equal time be allotted all qualified candidates for public office. Two aspects of the fairness doctrine, relating to personal attacks in the context of controversial public issues and to political editorializing, were codified more precisely in the form of FCC regulations in 1967. The two cases before us now, which were decided separately below, challenge the constitutional and statutory bases of the doctrine and component rules. Red Lion involves the application of the fairness doctrine to a particular broadcast, and RTNDA [Radio Television News Director Association] arises as an action to review the FCC's 1967 promulgation of the personal attack and political editorializing regulations, which were laid down after the Red Lion litigation had begun.

The Red Lion Broadcasting Company is licensed to operate a Pennsylvania radio station, WGCB. On November 27, 1964, WGCB carried a 15-minute broadcast by the Reverend Billy James Hargis as part of a "Christian Crusade" series. A book by Fred J. Cook entitled "Goldwater—Extremist on the Right" was discussed by Hargis, who said that Cook had been fired by a newspaper for making false charges against city officials; that Cook had then worked for a Communist-affiliated publication; that he had defended Alger Hiss and attacked J. Edgar Hoover and the Central Intelligence Agency, and that he had now written a "book to smear and destroy Barry Goldwater." When Cook heard of the broadcast, he concluded that he had been personally attacked and demanded free reply time, which the station refused. After an exchange of letters among Cook, Red Lion, and the FCC, the FCC declared that the Hargis broadcast constituted a personal attack on Cook; that Red Lion had failed to meet its obligation under the fairness doctrine as expressed in Times-Mirror Broadcasting Co., to send a tape, transcript, or summary of the broadcast to Cook and offer him reply time, and that the station must provide reply time whether or not Cook would pay for it. On review in the Court of Appeals for the District of Columbia Circuit, the FCC's position was upheld as constitutional and otherwise proper.

. . .

The history of the emergence of the fairness doctrine and of the related legislation shows that the Commission's action in the Red Lion case did not exceed its authority, and that, in adopting the new regulations, the Commission was implementing congressional policy, rather than embarking on a frolic of its own.

. . .

The objectives of §315 themselves could readily be circumvented but for the complementary fairness doctrine ratified by §315. The section applies only to campaign appearances by candidates, and not by family, friends, campaign managers, or other supporters. Without the fairness doctrine, then, a licensee could ban all campaign appearances by candidates themselves from the air and proceed to deliver over his station entirely to the supporters of one slate of candidates, to the exclusion of all others. In this way, the broadcaster could have a far greater impact on the favored candidacy than he could by simply allowing a spot appearance by the candidate himself. It is the fairness doctrine as an aspect of the obligation to operate in the public interest, rather than §315, which prohibits the broadcaster from taking such a step.

. . .

The broadcasters challenge the fairness doctrine and its specific manifestations in the personal attack and political editorial rules on conventional First Amendment grounds, alleging that the rules abridge their freedom of speech and press. Their contention is that the First Amendment protects their desire to use their allotted frequencies continuously to broadcast whatever they choose, and to exclude whomever they choose from ever using that frequency. No man may be prevented from saying or publishing what he thinks, or from refusing in his speech or other utterances to give equal weight to the views of his opponents. This right, they say, applies equally to broadcasters.

. . .

In terms of constitutional principle, and as enforced sharing of a scarce resource, the personal attack and political editorial rules are indistinguishable from the equal time provision of §315, a specific enactment of Congress requiring stations to set aside reply time under specified circumstances and to which the fairness doctrine and these constituent regulations are important complements. That provision, which has been part of the law since 1927, has been held valid by this Court as an obligation of the licensee relieving him of any power in any way to prevent or censor the broadcast, and thus insulating him from liability for defamation. The constitutionality of the statute under the First Amendment was unquestioned.

Nor can we say that it is inconsistent with the First Amendment goal of producing an informed public capable of conducting its own affairs to require a broadcaster to permit answers to personal attacks occurring in the course of discussing controversial issues, or to require that the political opponents of those endorsed by the station be given a chance to communicate with the public. Otherwise, station owners and a few networks would have unfettered power to make time available only to the highest bidders, to communicate only their own views on public issues, people and candidates, and to permit on the air only those with whom they agreed. There is no sanctuary in the First Amendment for unlimited private censorship operating in a medium not open to all. . . .

It is strenuously argued, however, that, if political editorials or personal attacks will trigger an obligation in broadcasters to afford the opportunity for expression to speakers who need not pay for time and whose views are unpalatable to the licensees, then broadcasters will be irresistibly forced to self-censorship, and their coverage of controversial public issues will be eliminated, or at least rendered wholly ineffective. Such a result would indeed be a serious matter, for, should licensees actually eliminate their coverage of controversial issues, the purposes of the doctrine would be stifled.

At this point, however, as the Federal Communications Commission has indicated, that possibility is, at best, speculative. The communications industry, and, in particular, the networks, have taken pains to present controversial issues in the past, and even now they do not assert that they intend to abandon their efforts in this regard. It would be better if the FCC's encouragement were never necessary to induce the broadcasters to meet their responsibility. And if experience with the administration of these doctrines indicates that they have the net effect of reducing, rather than enhancing, the volume and quality of coverage, there will be time enough to reconsider the constitutional implications. The fairness doctrine in the past has had no such overall effect.

That this will occur now seems unlikely, however, since, if present licensees should suddenly prove timorous, the Commission is not powerless to insist that they give adequate and fair attention to public issues. It does not violate the First Amendment to treat licensees given the privilege of using scarce radio frequencies as proxies for the entire community, obligated to give suitable time and attention to matters of great public concern. To condition the granting or renewal of licenses on a willingness to present representative community views on controversial issues is consistent with the ends and purposes of those constitutional provisions forbidding the abridgment of freedom of speech and freedom of the press. Congress need not stand idly by and permit those with licenses to ignore the problems which beset the people or to exclude from the airways anything but their own views of fundamental questions. The statute, long administrative practice, and cases are to this effect.

Licenses to broadcast do not confer ownership of designated frequencies, but only the temporary privilege of using them. Unless renewed, they expire within three years. The statute mandates the issuance of licenses if the "public convenience, interest, or necessity will be served thereby." In applying this standard, the Commission for 40 years has been choosing licensees based in part on their program proposals. . . .

. . .

. . . [W]e do hold that the Congress and the Commission do not violate the First Amendment when they require a radio or television station to give reply time to answer personal attacks and political editorials.

. . .

. . . The judgment of the Court of Appeals in Red Lion is affirmed and that in RTNDA reversed, and the causes remanded for proceedings consistent with this opinion.

Monitor Patriot Co. v. Roy
401 U.S. 265 (1971)

On September 10, 1960, three days before the New Hampshire Democratic Party's primary election of candidates for the United States Senate, the Concord Monitor, a daily newspaper in Concord, New Hampshire, published a syndicated "D.C. Merry-Go-Round" column discussing the forthcoming election. The column spoke of political maneuvering in the primary campaign, referred to the criminal records of several of the candidates, and characterized Alphonse Roy, one of the candidates, as a "former small-time bootlegger." Roy was not elected in the primary, and he subsequently sued the Monitor Patriot Co. and the North American Newspaper Alliance (NANA), the distributor of the column, for libel.

. . .

The jury in this case returned verdicts against both the newspaper and NANA. . . .

. . .

Given the realities of our political life, it is by no means easy to see what statements about a candidate might be altogether without relevance to his fitness for the office he seeks. The clash of reputations is the staple of election campaigns, and damage to reputation is, of course, the essence of libel. But whether there remains some exiguous area of defamation against which a candidate may have full recourse is a question we need not decide in this case. . . .

. . . A community that imposed legal liability on all statements in a political campaign deemed "unreasonable" by a jury would have abandoned the First Amendment as we know it. . . .

. . .

. . . [T]he judgment must be reversed and the case remanded for further proceedings not inconsistent with this opinion.

Ocala Star-Banner Co. v. Damron
401 U.S. 295 (1971)

The Ocala Star-Banner Co., a petitioner in this case, publishes a small daily newspaper serving four counties in rural Florida. On April 18, 1966, the *Star-Banner* printed a story to the effect that the respondent, Leonard Damron, then the mayor of Crystal River in Citrus County and a candidate for the office of county tax assessor, had been charged in a federal court with perjury, and that his case had been held over until the following term of that court. This story was false. The respondent had not been charged with any crime in federal court, nor had any case involving him been held over, but the story was substantially accurate as to his brother, James Damron. Two weeks later, the respondent was defeated in the election for county tax assessor.

He filed the present suit against the *Star-Banner* in the Circuit Court of Marion County, Florida, alleging that the article was "libelous per se," and that it had caused him "irreparable damages to his reputation, as an individual, public officer, candidate for public office and as a businessman." He asked $50,000 as compensatory damages and $500,000 as punitive damages. At the trial, the newspaper did not deny that the story was wholly false as to the respondent, and explained the error as the result of a "mental aberration" by one of the paper's area editors. The area editor had been working for the paper for a little more than a month. He testified that he had run several stories about the political activities of the respondent, but had never heard of his brother James. When a local reporter telephoned in the story, correctly identifying the protagonist as James Damron, he inadvertently changed the name. The respondent presented evidence tending to cast doubt on this explanation.

. . . [T]he respondent moved for a directed verdict on the issue of liability, and the trial judge granted the motion. . . . The jury awarded Damron compensatory damages of $22,000, but failed to award any punitive damages.

The *Star-Banner* moved for a new trial, arguing that the case should have been sent to the jury under the "actual malice" test laid down by this Court in *New York Times Co. v. Sullivan.* The trial judge denied the motion. . . . The Florida District Court of Appeal affirmed the judgment. . . . The Supreme Court of Florida refused to review the judgment. . . .

. . .

. . . Public discussion about the qualifications of a candidate for elective office presents what is probably the strongest possible case for application of the *New York Times* rule. And under any test we can conceive, the charge that a local mayor and candidate for a county elective post has been indicted for perjury in a civil rights suit is relevant to his fitness for office.

The First and Fourteenth Amendments require reversal of the judgment. The case is remanded for further proceedings not inconsistent with this opinion.

Columbia Broadcasting System, Inc. v. Democratic National Committee
412 U.S. 94 (1973)

The complainants in these actions are the Democratic National Committee (DNC) and the Business Executives' Move for Vietnam Peace (BEM), a national organization of businessmen opposed to United States involvement in the Vietnam conflict. In January 1970, BEM filed a complaint with the Commission charging that radio station WTOP in Washington, D.C., had refused to sell it time to broadcast a series of one-minute spot announcements expressing BEM views on Vietnam. WTOP, in common with many, but not all, broadcasters, followed a policy of refusing to sell time for spot announcements to individuals and groups who wished to expound their views on controversial issues. WTOP took the position that, since it presented full and fair coverage of important public questions, including the Vietnam conflict, it was justified in refusing to accept editorial advertisements. WTOP also submitted evidence showing that the station had aired the views of critics of our Vietnam policy on numerous occasions. BEM challenged the fairness of WTOP's coverage of criticism of that policy, but it presented no evidence in support of that claim.

. . . [I]n May 1970, DNC filed with the Commission a request for a declaratory ruling. . . .

In two separate opinions, the Commission rejected respondents' claims that "responsible" individuals and groups have a right to purchase advertising time to comment on public issues without regard to whether the broadcaster has complied with the Fairness Doctrine. The Commission viewed the issue as one of major significance in administering the regulatory scheme relating to the electronic media, one going "to the heart of the system of broadcasting which has developed in this country. . . ." After reviewing the legislative history of the Communications Act, the provisions of the Act itself, the Commission's decisions under the Act, and the difficult problems inherent in administering a right of access, the Commission rejected the demands of BEM and DNC.

The Commission also rejected BEM's claim that WTOP had violated the Fairness Doctrine by failing to air views such as those held by members of BEM; the Commission pointed out that BEM had made only a "general allegation" of unfairness in WTOP's coverage of the Vietnam conflict, and that the station had adequately rebutted the charge by affidavit. The Commission did, however, uphold DNC's position that the statute recognized a right of political parties to purchase broadcast time for the purpose of soliciting funds. The Commission noted that Congress has accorded special consideration for access by political parties and that solicitation of funds by political parties is both feasible and appropriate in the short space of time generally allotted to spot advertisements.

. . . [T]he Court of Appeals reversed the Commission. . . .

. . .

Subsequent developments in broadcast regulation illustrate how this regulatory scheme has evolved. Of particular importance, in light of Congress's flat refusal to impose a "common carrier" right of access for all persons wishing to speak out on public issues, is the Commission's "Fairness Doctrine," which evolved gradually over the years spanning federal regulation of the broadcast media. Formulated under the Commission's power to issue regulations consistent with the "public interest," the doctrine imposes two affirmative responsibilities on the broadcaster: coverage of issues of public importance must be adequate, and must fairly reflect differing viewpoints. In fulfilling the Fairness Doctrine obligations, the broadcaster must provide free time for the presentation of opposing views if a paid sponsor is unavailable, and must initiate programming on public issues if no one else seeks to do so.

Since it is physically impossible to provide time for all viewpoints, however, the right to exercise editorial judgment was granted to the broadcaster. The broadcaster, therefore, is allowed significant journalistic discretion in deciding how best to fulfill the Fairness Doctrine obligations, although that discretion is bounded by rules designed to assure that the public interest in fairness is furthered. . . .

Thus, under the Fairness Doctrine broadcasters are responsible for providing the listening and viewing public with access to a balanced presentation of information on issues of public importance. . . . Consistent with that philosophy, the Commission on several occasions has ruled that no private individual or group has a right to command the use of broadcast facilities. Congress has not yet seen fit to alter that policy. . . .

. . .

The Commission was justified in concluding that the public interest in providing access to the marketplace of "ideas and experiences" would scarcely be served by a system so heavily weighted in favor of the financially affluent, or those with access to wealth. Even under a first come, first served system proposed by the dissenting Commissioner in these cases, the views of the affluent could well prevail over those of others, since they would have it within their power to purchase time more frequently. Moreover, there is the substantial danger, as the Court of Appeals acknowledged, that the time allotted for editorial advertising could be monopolized by those of one political persuasion.

These problems would not necessarily be solved by applying the Fairness Doctrine . . . to editorial advertising. If broadcasters were required to provide time, free when necessary, for the discussion of the various shades of opinion on the issue discussed in the advertisement, the affluent could still determine in large part the issues to be discussed. Thus, the very premise of the Court of Appeals' holding—that a right of access is necessary to allow individuals and groups the opportunity for self-initiated speech—would have little meaning to those who could not afford to purchase time in the first instance.

If the Fairness Doctrine were applied to editorial advertising, there is also the substantial danger that the effective operation of that doctrine would be jeopardized. To minimize financial hardship and to comply fully with its public responsibilities, a broadcaster might well be forced to make regular programming time available to those holding a view different from that expressed in an editorial advertisement; indeed, BEM has suggested as much in its brief. The result would be a further erosion of the journalistic discretion of broadcasters in the coverage of public issues, and a transfer of control over the treatment of public issues from the licensees, who are accountable for broadcast performance to private individuals, who are not. The public interest would no longer be "paramount," but, rather, subordinate to private whim, especially since, under the Court of Appeals' decision, a broadcaster would be largely precluded from rejecting editorial advertisements that dealt with matters trivial or insignificant or already fairly covered by the broadcaster. If the Fairness Doctrine and the Cullman doctrine were suspended to alleviate these problems, as respondents suggest might be appropriate, the question arises whether we would have abandoned more than we have gained. Under such a regime, the congressional objective of balanced coverage of public issues would be seriously threatened.

Nor can we accept the Court of Appeals' view that every potential speaker is "the best judge" of what the listening public ought to hear or indeed the best judge of the merits of his or her views. All journalistic tradition and experience is to the contrary. For better or worse, editing is what editors are for, and editing is selection and choice of material. That editors—newspaper or broadcast—can and do abuse this power is beyond doubt, but that is no reason to deny the discretion Congress provided. Calculated risks of abuse are taken in order to preserve higher values. . . .

It was reasonable for Congress to conclude that the public interest in being informed requires periodic accountability on the part of those who are entrusted with the use of broadcast frequencies, scarce as they are. In the delicate balancing historically followed in the regulation of broadcasting, Congress and the Commission could appropriately conclude that the allocation of journalistic priorities should be concentrated in the licensee, rather than diffused among many. This policy gives the public some assurance that the broadcaster will be answerable if he fails to meet its legitimate needs. No such accountability attaches to the private individual, whose only qualifications for using the broadcast facility may be abundant funds and a point of view. To agree that debate on public issues should be "robust, and wide-open" does not mean that we should exchange "public trustee" broadcasting, with all its limitations, for a system of self-appointed editorial commentators.

The Court of Appeals discounted those difficulties by stressing that it was merely mandating a "modest reform," requiring only that broadcasters be required to accept some editorial advertising. The court suggested that broadcasters could place an "outside limit on the total amount of editorial advertising they will sell," and that the Commission and the broadcasters could develop "'reasonable regulations' designed to prevent domination by a few groups or a few viewpoints." If the Commission decided to apply the Fairness Doctrine to editorial advertisements, and, as a result, broadcasters suffered financial harm, the court thought the "Commission could make necessary adjustments." Thus, without providing any specific answers to the substantial objections raised by the Commission and the broadcasters, other than to express repeatedly its "confidence" in the Commission's ability to overcome any difficulties, the court remanded the cases to the Commission for the development of regulations to implement a constitutional right of access.

By minimizing the difficult problems involved in implementing such a right of access, the Court of Appeals failed to come to grips with another problem of critical importance to broadcast regulation and the First Amendment—the risk of an enlargement of Government control over the content of broadcast discussion of public issues. This risk is inherent in the Court of Appeals' remand requiring regulations and procedures to sort out requests to be heard—a process involving the very editing that licensees now perform as to regular programming. Although the use of a public resource by the broadcast media permits a limited degree of Government surveillance, as is not true with respect to private media, the Government's power over licensees, as we have noted, is by no means absolute, and is carefully circumscribed by the Act itself.

. . .

The opinion of the Court of Appeals asserted that the Fairness Doctrine, insofar as it allows broadcasters to exercise certain journalistic judgments over the discussion of public issues, is inadequate to meet the public's interest in being informed. . . .

We reject the suggestion that the Fairness Doctrine permits broadcasters to preside over a "paternalistic" regime. That doctrine admittedly has not always brought to the public perfect or, indeed, even consistently high-quality treatment of all public events and issues; but the remedy does not lie in diluting licensee responsibility. The Commission stressed that, while the licensee has discretion in fulfilling its obligations under the Fairness Doctrine, it is required to "present representative community views and voices on controversial issues which are of importance to [its] listeners," and it is prohibited from "excluding

partisan voices and always itself presenting views in a bland, inoffensive manner. . . ." A broadcaster neglects that obligation only at the risk of losing his license.

. . .

The judgment of the Court of Appeals is reversed.

Miami Herald Publishing Co. v. Tornillo
418 U.S. 241 (1974)

In the fall of 1972, appellee, Executive Director of the Classroom Teachers Association, apparently a teachers' collective bargaining agent, was a candidate for the Florida House of Representatives. On September 20, 1972, and again on September 29, 1972, appellant printed editorials critical of appellee's candidacy. In response to these editorials, appellee demanded that appellant print verbatim his replies, defending the role of the Classroom Teachers Association and the organization's accomplishments for the citizens of Dade County. Appellant declined to print the appellee's replies, and appellee brought suit in Circuit Court, Dade County, seeking declaratory and injunctive relief and actual and punitive damages in excess of $5,000. The action was premised on Florida Statute §104.38, a "right of reply" statute which provides that, if a candidate for nomination or election is assailed regarding his personal character or official record by any newspaper, the candidate has the right to demand that the newspaper print, free of cost to the candidate, any reply the candidate may make to the newspaper's charges. The reply must appear in as conspicuous a place and in the same kind of type as the charges which prompted the reply, provided it does not take up more space than the charges. Failure to comply with the statute constitutes a first-degree misdemeanor.

Appellant sought a declaration that §104.38 was unconstitutional. . . . [T]he Circuit Court . . . held that § 104.38 was unconstitutional as an infringement on the freedom of the press under the First and Fourteenth Amendments to the Constitution. . . .

On direct appeal, the Florida Supreme Court reversed, holding that § 104.38 did not violate constitutional guarantees. . . .

. . .

. . . Compelling editors or publishers to publish that which "'reason' tells them should not be published" is what is at issue in this case. . . .

. . .

Even if a newspaper would face no additional costs to comply with a compulsory access law and would not be forced to forgo publication of news or opinion by the inclusion of a reply, the Florida statute fails to clear the barriers of the First Amendment because of its intrusion into the function of editors. A newspaper is more than a passive receptacle or conduit for news, comment, and advertising. The choice of material to go into a newspaper, and the decisions made as to limitations on the size and content of the paper, and treatment of public issues and public official— whether fair or unfair—constitute the exercise of editorial control and judgment. It has yet to be demonstrated how governmental regulation of this crucial process can be exercised consistent with First Amendment guarantees of a free press as they have evolved to this time. Accordingly, the judgment of the Supreme Court of Florida is reversed.

Lehman v. City of Shaker Heights
418 U.S. 298 (1974)

In 1970, petitioner Harry J. Lehman was a candidate for the office of State Representative to the Ohio General Assembly. . . . On July 3, 1970, petitioner sought to promote his candidacy by purchasing car card space on the Shaker Heights Rapid Transit System for the months of August, September, and October. The general election was scheduled for November 3. . . .

Advertising space on the city's transit system is managed by respondent Metromedia, Inc., as exclusive agent under contract with the city. . . .

When petitioner applied for space, he as informed by Metromedia that, although space was then available, the management agreement with the city did not permit political advertising. The system, however, accepted ads from cigarette companies, banks, savings and loan associations, liquor companies, retail and service establishments, churches, and civic and public service oriented groups. There was uncontradicted testimony at the trial that, during the 26 years of public operation, the Shaker Heights system, pursuant to city council action, had not accepted or permitted any political or public issue advertising on its vehicles.

When petitioner did not succeed in his effort to have his copy accepted, he sought declaratory and injunctive relief in the state courts of Ohio without success. . . . There was no equal protection violation, the court said, because, "[a]s a class, all candidates for political office are treated alike under the Shaker Heights Rapid Transit System's commercial advertising policy." . . .

. . .

No First Amendment forum is here to be found. The city consciously has limited access to its transit system advertising space in order to minimize chances of abuse, the appearance of favoritism, and the risk of imposing upon a captive audience. These are reasonable legislative objectives advanced by the city in a proprietary capacity. In these circumstances, there is no First or Fourteenth Amendment violation.

The judgment of the Supreme Court of Ohio is affirmed.

Greer v. Spock
424 U.S. 828 (1976)

The Fort Dix Military Reservation is a United States Army post located in a predominantly rural area of central New Jersey. . . .

Civilian speakers occasionally have been invited to the base to address military personnel. The subjects of their talks have ranged from business management to drug abuse. Visiting clergymen have, by invitation, participated in religious services at the base chapel. Theatrical exhibitions and musical productions have also been presented on the base. Speeches and demonstrations of a partisan political nature, however, are banned by Fort Dix Reg. . . . The regulation has been rigidly enforced: prior to this litigation, no political campaign speech had ever been given at Fort Dix. Restrictions are also placed on another type of expressive activity. Fort Dix Reg. 210–27 provides that

> [t]he distribution or posting of any publication, including newspapers, magazines, handbills, flyers, circulars, pamphlets or other writings, issued, published or otherwise prepared by any person, persons, agency or agencies . . . is prohibited on the Fort Dix Military Reservation without prior written approval of the Adjutant General, this headquarters.

In 1972, the respondents Benjamin Spock and Julius Hobson were the candidates of the People's Party for the offices of President and Vice President of the United States, and Linda Jenness and Andrew Pulley were the candidates of the So-

cialist Workers Party for the same offices. On September 9, 1972, Spock, Hobson, Jenness, and Pulley wrote a joint letter to Major General Bert A. David, then commanding officer of Fort Dix, informing him of their intention to enter the reservation on September 23, 1972, for the purpose of distributing campaign literature and holding a meeting to discuss election issues with service personnel and their dependents. On September 18, 1972, General David rejected the candidates' request, relying on Fort Dix Regs. Four of the other respondents, Ginaven, Misch, Hardy, and Stanton, were evicted from Fort Dix on various occasions between 1968 and 1972 for distributing literature not previously approved pursuant to Fort Dix Reg. 210–27. Each was barred from reentering Fort Dix and advised that reentry could result in criminal prosecution.

On September 29, 1972, the respondents filed this suit in the United States District Court for the District of New Jersey to enjoin the enforcement of the Fort Dix regulations governing political campaigning and the distribution of literature, upon the ground that the regulations violated the First and Fifth Amendments of the Constitution. The District Court denied a preliminary injunction, but the Court of Appeals reversed that order and directed that preliminary injunctive relief be granted to the respondents Spock, Hobson, Jenness, and Pulley. . . . The District Court subsequently issued a permanent injunction prohibiting the military authorities from interfering with the making of political speeches or the distribution of leaflets in areas of Fort Dix open to the general public, and the Court of Appeals affirmed this final judgment. . . .

. . .

The Court of Appeals . . . did not find, and the respondents do not contend, that the Fort Dix authorities had abandoned any claim of special

interest in regulating the distribution of unauthorized leaflets or the delivery of campaign
speeches for political candidates within the confines of the military reservation. The record is, in
fact, indisputably to the contrary. . . .

. . .

One of the very purposes for which the Constitution was ordained and established was to
"provide for the common defence," and this Court
over the years has on countless occasions recognized the special constitutional function of the
military in our national life, a function both explicit and indispensable. In short, it is "the primary business of armies and navies to fight or be
ready to fight wars should the occasion arise."
And it is consequently the business of a military
installation like Fort Dix to train soldiers, not to
provide a public forum.

. . .

The respondents, therefore, had no generalized
constitutional right to make political speeches or
distribute leaflets at Fort Dix, and it follows that
Fort Dix Regs. 210–26 and 210–27 are not constitutionally invalid on their face. These regulations, moreover, were not unconstitutionally
applied in the circumstances disclosed by the
record in the present case.

. . .

For the reasons set out in this opinion the judgment is reversed.

Columbia Broadcasting System, Inc. v.
Federal Communications Commission
453 U.S. 367 (1981)

On October 11, 1979, Gerald M. Rafshoon, President of the Carter-Mondale Presidential Committee, requested each of the three major television
networks to provide time for a 30-minute pro-

gram between 8 P.M. and 10:30 P.M. on either the
4th, 5th, 6th, or 7th of December, 1979. The Committee intended to present, in conjunction with
President Carter's formal announcement of his
candidacy, a documentary outlining the record
of his administration.

The networks declined to make the requested
time available. Petitioner CBS emphasized the
large number of candidates for the Republican
and Democratic Presidential nominations and the
potential disruption of regular programming to
accommodate requests for equal treatment, but
it offered to sell two 5-minute segments to the
Committee, one at 10:55 P.M. on December 8 and
one in the daytime. Petitioner American Broadcasting Company replied that it had not yet decided when it would begin selling political time
for the 1980 Presidential campaign, but subsequently indicated that it would allow such sales
in January 1980. Petitioner National Broadcasting Company, noting the number of potential requests for time from Presidential candidates,
stated that it was not prepared to sell time for
political programs as early as December 1979.

On October 29, 1979, the Carter-Mondale
Presidential Committee filed a complaint with the
Federal Communications Commission, charging
that the networks had violated their obligation to
provide "reasonable access" under §312(a)(7) of
the Communications Act of 1934. . . . on November 20, 1979, the Commission . . . ruled that
the networks had violated §312(a)(7). . . .

Petitioners sought reconsideration of the
FCC's decision. The reconsideration petitions
were denied. . . .

The networks . . . then petitioned for review of
the Commission's orders in the United States Court
of Appeals for the District of Columbia Circuit. . . .

. . .

The Court of Appeals affirmed. . . .

Section 312(a)(7) represents an effort by Congress to assure that an important resource—the airwaves—will be used in the public interest. We hold that the statutory right of access, as defined by the Commission and applied in these cases, properly balances the First Amendment rights of federal candidates, the public, and broadcasters.

The judgment of the Court of Appeals is affirmed.

Brown v. Hartlage
456 U.S. 45 (1982)

This case involves a challenge to an application of the Kentucky Corrupt Practices Act. The parties were opposing candidates in the 1979 general election for the office of Jefferson County Commissioner. . . . Petitioner, Carl Brown, was the challenger; respondent, Earl Hartlage, was the incumbent. On August 15, 1979, in the course of the campaign, Brown held a televised press conference together with Bill Creech . . . candidate on the same party ticket. Brown charged his opponent with complicity in a form of fiscal abuse. . . .

. . .

Shortly after the press conference, Brown and Creech learned that their commitment to lower their salaries arguably violated the Kentucky Corrupt Practices Act. On August 19, 1979, they issued a joint statement retracting their earlier pledge. . . . In the November 6, 1979, election, Brown defeated Hartlage. . . . Creech was defeated.

Hartlage then filed this action in the Jefferson Circuit Court, alleging that Brown had violated the Corrupt Practices Act and seeking to have the election declared void and the office of Jefferson County Commissioner . . . vacated by Brown. . . .

. . . [T]he trial court found that Brown's

prospective salary had been fixed by law, and that . . . Brown's promise violated the Act. Nevertheless, the court concluded that, in light of Brown's retraction, the defeat of his running mate, who had joined in the pledge, and the presumption that the will of the people had been revealed through the election process, Brown had been "fairly elected." It thus declined to order a new election.

The Kentucky Court of Appeals reversed. . . .

. . .

We begin our analysis . . . by acknowledging that the States have a legitimate interest in preserving the integrity of their electoral processes. Just as a State may take steps to ensure that its governing political institutions and officials properly discharge public responsibilities and maintain public trust and confidence, a State has a legitimate interest in upholding the integrity of the electoral process itself. But when a State seeks to uphold that interest by restricting speech, the limitations on state authority imposed by the First Amendment are manifestly implicated.

. . .

When a State seeks to restrict directly the offer of ideas by a candidate to the voters, the First Amendment surely requires that the restriction be demonstrably supported by not only a legitimate state interest, but a compelling one, and that the restriction operate without unnecessarily circumscribing protected expression.

On its face, §121.055 prohibits a candidate from offering material benefits to voters in consideration for their votes, and, conversely, prohibits candidates from accepting payments in consideration for the manner in which they serve their public function. . . .

The first sentence of §121.055 prohibits a political candidate from giving, or promising to give, anything of value to a voter in exchange for his vote or support. In many of its possible applications, this provision would appear to present little constitutional difficulty, for a State may surely prohibit a candidate from buying votes. No body politic worthy of being called a democracy entrusts the selection of leaders to a process of auction or barter. And as a State may prohibit the giving of money or other things of value to a voter in exchange for his support, it may also declare unlawful an agreement embodying the intention to make such an exchange. Although agreements to engage in illegal conduct undoubtedly possess some element of association, the State may ban such illegal agreements without trenching on any right of association protected by the First Amendment. The fact that such an agreement necessarily takes the form of words does not confer upon it, or upon the underlying conduct, the constitutional immunities that the First Amendment extends to speech. Finally, while a solicitation to enter into an agreement arguably crosses the sometimes hazy line distinguishing conduct from pure speech, such a solicitation, even though it may have an impact in the political arena, remains, in essence, an invitation to engage in an illegal exchange for private profit, and may properly be prohibited.

It is thus plain that some kinds of promises made by a candidate to voters, and some kinds of promises elicited by voters from candidates, may be declared illegal without constitutional difficulty. But it is equally plain that there are constitutional limits on the State's power to prohibit candidates from making promises in the course of an election campaign. Some promises are universally acknowledged as legitimate, indeed, "indispensable to decisionmaking in a democracy.". . . Candidate commitments enhance the accountability of government officials to the people whom they represent, and assist the voters in predicting the effect of their vote. The fact that some voters may find their self-interest reflected in a candidate's commitment does not place that commitment beyond the reach of the First Amendment. We have never insisted that the franchise be exercised without taint of individual benefit; indeed, our tradition of political pluralism is partly predicated on the expectation that voters will pursue their individual good through the political process, and that the summation of these individual pursuits will further the collective welfare. So long as the hoped-for personal benefit is to be achieved through the normal processes of government, and not through some private arrangement, it has always been, and remains, a reputable basis upon which to cast one's ballot.

. . .

In sum, Brown did not offer some private payment or donation in exchange for voter support; Brown's statement can only be construed as an expression of his intention to exercise public power in a manner that he believed might be acceptable to some class of citizens. If Brown's expressed intention had an individualized appeal to some taxpayers who felt themselves the likely beneficiaries of his form of fiscal restraint, that fact is of little constitutional significance. The benefits of most public policy changes accrue not only to the undifferentiated "public," but more directly to particular individuals or groups. Like a promise to lower taxes, to increase efficiency in government, or indeed to increase taxes in order to provide some group with a desired public benefit or public service, Brown's promise to reduce his salary cannot be deemed beyond the reach of the First Amendment, or considered as inviting the kind of corrupt arrangement the appearance of which a State may have a compelling interest in avoiding.

A State may insist that candidates seeking the approval of the electorate work within the frame-

approval of the electorate work within the framework of our democratic institutions, and base their appeal on assertions of fitness for office and statements respecting the means by which they intend to further the public welfare. But a candidate's promise to confer some ultimate benefit on the voter, qua taxpayer, citizen, or member of the general public, does not lie beyond the pale of First Amendment protection.

. . . In barring certain public statements with respect to this issue, the State ban runs directly contrary to the fundamental premises underlying the First Amendment as the guardian of our democracy. That Amendment embodies our trust in the free exchange of ideas as the means by which the people are to choose between good ideas and bad, and between candidates for political office. The State's fear that voters might make an ill-advised choice does not provide the State with a compelling justification for limiting speech. It is simply not the function of government to "select which issues are worth discussing or debating," in the course of a political campaign.

. . .

. . . The chilling effect of such absolute accountability for factual misstatements in the course of political debate is incompatible with the atmosphere of free discussion contemplated by the First Amendment in the context of political campaigns. Although the state interest in protecting the political process from distortions caused by untrue and inaccurate speech is somewhat different from the state interest in protecting individuals from defamatory falsehoods, the principles underlying the First Amendment remain paramount. . . . In a political campaign, a candidate's factual blunder is unlikely to escape the notice of, and correction by, the erring candidate's political opponent. . . . Moreover,

petitioner retracted the statement promptly after discovering that it might have been false. Under these circumstances, nullifying petitioner's election victory was inconsistent with the atmosphere of robust political debate protected by the First Amendment.

Because we conclude that §121.055 has been applied in this case to limit speech in violation of the First Amendment, we reverse the judgment of the Kentucky Court of Appeals and remand for proceedings not inconsistent with this opinion.

Cohen v. Cowles Media Company
501 U.S. 663 (1991)

During the closing days of the 1982 Minnesota gubernatorial race, Dan Cohen, an active Republican associated with Wheelock Whitney's Independent-Republican gubernatorial campaign, approached reporters from the *St. Paul Pioneer Press Dispatch* (*Pioneer Press*) and the *Minneapolis Star and Tribune* (*Star Tribune*) and offered to provide documents relating to a candidate in the upcoming election. Cohen made clear to the reporters that he would provide the information only if he was given a promise of confidentiality. Reporters from both papers promised to keep Cohen's identity anonymous, and Cohen turned over copies of two public court records concerning Marlene Johnson, the Democratic-Farmer-Labor candidate for Lieutenant Governor. The first record indicated that Johnson had been charged in 1969 with three counts of unlawful assembly, and the second that she had been convicted in 1970 of petit theft. Both newspapers interviewed Johnson for her explanation, and one reporter tracked down the person who had found the records for Cohen. As it turned out, the unlawful assembly charges arose out of Johnson's participation in a protest of an alleged failure to hire minority workers on municipal construction projects, and the charges were eventually dismissed. The petit theft conviction was for leaving a store without paying for $6.00 worth of sewing materials. The incident apparently occurred at a time during which Johnson was emotionally distraught, and the conviction was later vacated.

After consultation and debate, the editorial staffs of the two newspapers independently decided to publish Cohen's name as part of their stories concerning Johnson. In their stories, both papers identified Cohen as the source of the court records, indicated his connection to the Whitney campaign, and included denials by Whitney campaign officials of any role in the matter. The same day the stories appeared, Cohen was fired by his employer.

Cohen sued respondents, the publishers of the *Pioneer Press* and *Star Tribune*, in Minnesota state court, alleging fraudulent misrepresentation and breach of contract. The trial court rejected respondents' argument that the First Amendment barred Cohen's lawsuit. A jury returned a verdict in Cohen's favor, awarding him $200,000 in compensatory damages and $500,000 in punitive damages. The Minnesota Court of Appeals . . . reversed the award of punitive damages after concluding that Cohen had failed to establish a fraud claim, the only claim which would support such an award. However, the court upheld the finding of liability for breach of contract and the $200,000 compensatory damage award. . . . Minnesota Supreme Court reversed the compensatory damages award. . . .

. . .

. . . [T]he judgment of the Minnesota Supreme Court is reversed, and the case is remanded for further proceedings not inconsistent with this opinion.

Arkansas Educational Television Commission v. Forbes
523 U.S. 666 (1998)

Petitioner, the Arkansas Educational Television Commission (AETC), is an Arkansas state agency owning and operating a network of five noncommercial television stations (Arkansas Educational Television Network or AETN). The eight members of AETC are appointed by the Governor for 8-year terms, and are removable only for good cause. AETC members are barred from holding any other state or federal office, with the exception of teaching positions. To insulate its programming decisions from political pressure, AETC employs an Executive Director and professional staff who exercise broad editorial discretion in planning the network's programming. AETC has also adopted the Statement of Principles of Editorial Integrity in Public Broadcasting, which counsel adherence to "generally accepted broadcasting industry standards, so that the programming service is free from pressure from political or financial supporters."

In the spring of 1992, AETC staff began planning a series of debates between candidates for federal office in the November 1992 elections. AETC decided to televise a total of five debates, scheduling one for the Senate election and one for each of the four congressional elections in Arkansas. Working in close consultation with Bill Simmons, Arkansas Bureau Chief for the Associated Press, AETC staff developed a debate format allowing about 53 minutes during each 1–hour debate for questions to and answers by the candidates. Given the time constraint, the staff and Simmons "decided to limit participation in the debates to the major party candidates or any other candidate who had strong popular support."

On June 17, 1992, AETC invited the Republican and Democratic candidates for Arkansas' Third Congressional District to participate in the AETC debate for that seat. Two months later, after obtaining the 2,000 signatures required by Arkansas law, respondent Ralph Forbes was certified as an independent candidate qualified to appear on the ballot for the seat. Forbes was a perennial candidate who had sought, without success, a number of elected offices in Arkansas. On August 24, 1992, he wrote to AETC requesting permission to participate in the debate for his district, scheduled for October 22, 1992. On September 4, AETC Executive Director Susan Howarth denied Forbes' request, explaining that AETC had "made a bona fide journalistic judgment that our viewers would be best served by limiting the debate" to the candidates already invited.

On October 19, 1992, Forbes filed suit against AETC, seeking injunctive and declaratory relief as well as damages. Forbes claimed he was entitled to participate in the debate under both the First Amendment and 47 U.S.C. §315, which affords political candidates a limited right of access to television air time. Forbes requested a preliminary injunction mandating his inclusion in the debate. The District Court denied the request, as did the United States Court of Appeals for the Eighth Circuit. The District Court later dismissed Forbes' action for failure to state a claim.

Sitting en banc, the Court of Appeals affirmed the dismissal of Forbes' statutory claim, holding that he had failed to exhaust his administrative remedies. The court reversed, however, the dismissal of Forbes' First Amendment claim. . . .

On remand, the District Court found as a matter of law that the debate was a nonpublic forum, and the issue became whether Forbes' views were the reason for his exclusion. . . . The District Court entered judgment for AETC.

The Court of Appeals again reversed. . . .

. . .

The broadcaster's decision to exclude Forbes was a reasonable, viewpoint-neutral exercise of journalistic discretion consistent with the First Amendment. The judgment of the Court of Appeals is reversed.

12

Initiatives, Referenda, and the Right of Political Advocacy

This chapter involves the role of the right of citizens to preserve self-destination as far as political rights and governance are concerned.

Pacific States Telephone and Telegraph Company v. Oregon
223 U.S. 118 (1912)

. . . [I]n 1902, Oregon amended its constitution. This amendment, while retaining an existing clause vesting the exclusive legislative power in a General Assembly consisting of a senate and house of representatives, added to that provision the following:

> But the people reserve to themselves power to propose laws and amendments to the constitution and to enact or reject the same at the polls, independent of the legislative assembly, and also reserve power at their own option to approve or reject at the polls any act of the legislative assembly.

Specific means for the exercise of the power thus reserved was contained in further clauses authorizing both the amendment of the constitution and the enactment of laws to be accomplished by the method known as the initiative and that commonly referred to as the referendum. . . .

. . .

By resort to the initiative in 1906 a law taxing certain classes of corporations was submitted, voted on and promulgated by the Governor in 1906 as having been duly adopted. By this law, telephone and telegraph companies were taxed, by what was qualified as an annual license, 2 percent upon their gross revenue derived from business done within the State. . . .

The Pacific States Telephone and Telegraph Company, an Oregon corporation engaged in business in that State, made a return of its gross receipts as required by the statute and was accordingly assessed 2 percent upon the amount of such return. The suit which is now before us was commenced by the State to enforce payment of this assessment and the statutory penalties for delinquency. . . .

. . .

The assignments of error . . . are all based upon the single contention that the creation by a State of the power to legislate by the initiative and referendum causes the prior lawful state government to be bereft of its lawful character as the result of the provisions of §4 of Art. IV of the Constitution. . . .

The initiative and the tax measure in question are repugnant to the provisions of section 1 of the Fourteenth Amendment to the Constitution of the United States which forbids a State to deny to any person within its jurisdiction the equal protection of the law.

The initiative amendment and the tax in question, levied pursuant to a measure, passed by authority of the initiative amendment, violate the right to a republican form of government which is guaranteed by section 4, article IV, of the Federal Constitution.

Taxation by the initiative method violates fundamental rights, and is not in accordance with "the law of the land."

The initiative is in contravention of a republican form of government. Government by the people directly is the attribute of a pure democracy, and is subversive of the principles upon which the republic is founded. Direct legislation is, therefore, repugnant to that form of government with which alone Congress could admit a State to the Union and which the State is bound to maintain.

. . . [T]he legislature, is destroyed by the initiative.

The provision in the Oregon constitution for direct legislation violates the provisions of the act of Congress admitting Oregon to the Union.

. . .

As the issues presented, in their very essence, are, and have long since by this court been, definitely determined to be political and governmental, and embraced within the scope of the powers conferred upon Congress, and not therefore within the reach of judicial power, it follows that the case presented is not within our jurisdiction, and the writ of error or must therefore be, and it is, dismissed for want of jurisdiction.

State of Ohio ex rel Davis v. Hildebrant
241 U.S. 565 (1916)

By an amendment to the Constitution of Ohio, adopted September 3, 1912, the legislative power was expressly declared to be vested not only in the senate and house of representatives of the state, constituting the general assembly, but in the people, in whom a right was reserved by way of referendum to approve or disapprove by popular vote any law enacted by the general assembly. And by other constitutional provisions the machinery to carry out the referendum was created. Briefly they were this: Within a certain time after the enactment of a law by the senate and house of representatives, and its approval by the governor, upon petition of 6 percent of the voters, the question of whether the law should become operative was to be submitted to a vote of the people, and, if approved, the law should be operative; and, if not approved, it should have no effect whatever.

In May 1915, the general assembly of Ohio passed an act redistricting the state for the purpose of congressional elections, by which act twenty-two congressional districts were created, in some respects differing from the previously established districts, and this act, after approval by the governor, was filed in the office of the secretary of state. The requisite number of electors under the referendum provision having petitioned for a submission of the law to a popular vote, such vote was taken and the law was disapproved. Thereupon, in the supreme court of the state, the suit before us was begun against state election officers for the purpose of procuring a mandamus, directing them to disregard the vote of the people on the referendum, disapproving the law, and to proceed to discharge their duties as such officers in the next congressional election, upon the assumption that the action by way of referendum was void, and that the law which was disapproved was subsisting and valid. The right to this relief was based upon the charge that the referendum vote was not and could not be a part of the legislative authority of the state, and therefore could have no influence on the subject of the law creating congressional districts for the purpose of representation in Congress. Indeed, it was in substance charged that both from the point of view of the state Constitution and laws and from that of the Constitution of the United States, especially 4 of article 1, providing that "the times, places and manner of holding elections for Senators and Representatives, shall be prescribed in each state by the legislature thereof; but the Congress may at any time by law, make or alter such regulations, except as to the places of choosing Senators"; and also from that of the provisions of the controlling act of Congress of August 8, 1911, apportioning representation among the states, the attempt to make the referendum a component part of the legislative authority empowered to deal with the election of members of Congress was absolutely void. The court below adversely disposed of these contentions, and held that the provisions as to referendum were a part of the legislative power of the state, made so by the Constitution, and that nothing in the act of Congress of 1911, or in the constitutional provision, operated to the contrary, and that therefore the disapproved law had no existence and was not entitled to be enforced by mandamus.

. . .

To the extent that the contention urges that to include the referendum within state legislative power for the purpose of apportionment is repugnant to 4 of article 1 of the Constitution and hence void, even if sanctioned by Congress, because beyond the constitutional authority of that body, and hence that it is the duty of the judicial power so to declare, we again think the contention is plainly without substance, for the following reasons: It must rest upon the assumption that to include the referendum in the scope of the legislative power is to introduce a virus which destroys that power, which in effect annihilates

representative government, and causes a state where such condition exists to be not republican in form, in violation of the guaranty of the Constitution. But the proposition and the argument disregard the settled rule that the question of whether that guaranty of the Constitution has been disregarded presents no justiciable controversy, but involves the exercise by Congress of the authority vested in it by the Constitution. In so far as the proposition challenges the power of Congress, as manifested by the clause in the act of 1911, treating the referendum as a part of the legislative power for the purpose of apportionment, where so ordained by the state Constitutions and laws, the argument but asserts, on the one hand, that Congress had no power to do that which, from the point of view of 4 of article 1, previously considered, the Constitution expressly gave the right to do. In so far as the proposition may be considered as asserting, on the other hand, that any attempt by Congress to recognize the referendum as a part of the legislative authority of a state is obnoxious to a republican form of government as provided by 4 of article 4, the contention necessarily but reasserts the proposition on that subject previously adversely disposed of. And that this is the inevitable result of the contention is plainly manifest, since at best the proposition comes to the assertion that because Congress, upon whom the Constitution has conferred the exclusive authority to uphold the guaranty of a republican form of government, has done something which it is deemed is repugnant to that guaranty, therefore there was automatically created judicial authority to go beyond the limits of judicial power, and, in doing so, to usurp congressional power, on the ground that Congress had mistakenly dealt with a subject which was within its exclusive control, free from judicial interference.

... [W]e are of opinion ... the decree proper to be rendered is one of affirmance, and such a decree is therefore ordered.

Smith v. Interstate Commerce Commission
245 U.S. 33 (1917)

The fundamental contention of appellant is that the Interstate Commerce Commission has no power to ask the questions in controversy and in emphasis of this he asserts "the inquiry was confined exclusively to supposed political activities and efforts to suppress competition." And these, it is further asserted, are not matters which the Commission "is legally entitled to investigate." The contention is attempted to be supported by the insistence that the investigation was provoked and prosecuted solely in obedience to the Senate resolution and neither in exercise of the judgment of the Commission nor in pursuance of a complaint made to it. And the twelfth paragraph of the resolution is dwelt upon as directing and controlling the inquiry as to what amount, if any, the railroads "have subscribed, expended or contributed for the purpose of preventing other railroads from entering any of the territory served by any of these railroads, for maintaining political or legislative agents, for contributing to political campaigns, for creating sentiment in favor of any of the plans of any of said railroads."

. . .

Abstractly speaking, we are not disposed to say that a carrier may not attempt to mold or enlighten public opinion, but we are quite clear that its conduct and the expenditures of its funds are open to inquiry. If it may not rest inactive and suffer injustice, it may not on the other hand use its funds and its power in opposition to the policies of government. Beyond this generality it is not necessary to go. The questions in the case are not of broad extent. They are quite special, and we regard them, as the learned judge of the court below regarded them, as but incident to the amount of expenditures and to the manner of their charge upon the books of the companies. This, we repeat, is within the power of the Commission. The purpose of an investigation is the penetration of disguises or to form a definite estimate of any conduct of the carriers that may in any way affect their relation to the public. We cannot assume that an investigation will be instituted or conducted for any other purpose or in mere wanton meddling.

Order affirmed.

Hawke v. Smith
253 U.S. 221 (1920)

Plaintiff . . . filed a petition for an injunction in the court of common pleas of Franklin County, Ohio, seeking to enjoin the secretary of state of Ohio from spending the public money in preparing and printing forms of ballot for submission of a referendum to the electors of that state on the question of the ratification which the General Assembly had made of the proposed Eighteenth Amendment to the federal Constitution. A demurrer to the petition was sustained in the court of common pleas. Its judgment was affirmed by the Court of Appeals of Franklin County, which judgment was affirmed by the Supreme Court of Ohio. . . .

A joint resolution proposing to the states this amendment to the Constitution of the United States was adopted on the third day of December, 1917. The amendment prohibits the manufacture, sale or transportation of intoxicating liquors within, the importation thereof into, or the exportation thereof from, the United States and all territory subject to the jurisdiction thereof for beverage purposes. The several states were given concurrent power to enforce the amendment by appropriate legislation. The resolution provided that the amendment should be inoperative unless ratified as an amendment of the Constitution by the Legislatures of the several states, as provide in the Constitution, within seven years from the date of the submission thereof to the states. The Senate and House of Representatives of the state of Ohio adopted a resolution ratifying the proposed amendment by the General Assembly of the state of Ohio, and ordered that certified copies of the joint resolution of ratification be forwarded by the Governor to the Secretary of State at Washington and to the presiding officer of each House of Congress. This resolution was adopted on January 7, 1919; on January 27, 1919, the Governor of Ohio complied with the resolution. On January 29, 1919, the Secretary of State of the United States proclaimed the ratification of the amendment, naming 36 states as having ratified the same, among them the state of Ohio.

The question for our consideration is: Whether the provision of the Ohio Constitution, adopted at the general election, November, 1918, extending the referendum to the ratification by the General Assembly of proposed amendments to the federal Constitution is in conflict with article 5 of the Constitution of the United States. . . .

. . .

The Constitution of the United States was ordained by the people, and, when duly ratified, it became the Constitution of the people of the United States. The states surrendered to the general government the powers specifically conferred upon the nation, and the Constitution and the laws of the United States are the supreme law of the land.

The framers of the Constitution realized that it might in the progress of time and the development of new conditions require changes, and they intended to provide an orderly manner in which these could be accomplished; to that end they adopted the fifth article.

This article makes provision for the proposal of amendments either by two-thirds of both houses of Congress, or on application of the Legislatures of two-thirds of the states; thus securing deliberation and consideration before any change can be proposed. The proposed change can only become effective by the ratification of the Legislatures of three-fourths of the states, or by conventions in a like number of states. The method of ratification is left to the choice of Congress. Both methods of ratification, by Legislatures or conventions, call for action by deliberative assemblages representative of the people, which it was assumed would voice the will of the people.

The fifth article is a grant of authority by the people to Congress. The determination of the method of ratification is the exercise of a national power specifically granted by the Constitution; that power is conferred upon Congress, and is limited to two methods, by action of the Legislatures of three-fourths of the states, or conventions in a like number of states. The framers of the Constitution might have adopted a different method. Ratification might have been left to a vote of the people, or to some authority of government other than that selected. The language of the article is plain, and admits of no doubt in its interpretation. It is not the function of courts or legislative bodies, national or state, to alter the method which the Constitution has fixed.

. . .

The constitution of Ohio in its present form, although making provision for a referendum, vests the legislative power primarily in a General Assembly, consisting of a Senate and House of Representatives. Article 2, section 1, provides:

> The legislative power of the state shall be vested in a General Assembly consisting of a Senate and House of Representatives, but the people reserve to themselves the power to propose to the General Assembly laws and amendments to the Constitution, and to adopt or reject the same at the polls on a referendum vote as hereinafter provided.

The argument to support the power of the state to require the approval by the people of the state of the ratification of amendments to the federal Constitution through . . . a referendum rests upon the proposition that the federal Constitution requires ratification by the legislative action of the states through the medium provided at the time of the proposed approval of an amendment. This argument is fallacious in this-ratification by a state of a constitutional amendment is not an act of legislation within the proper sense of the word. It is but the expression of the assent of the state to a proposed amendment.

. . .

. . . [T]he court erred in holding that the state had authority to require the submission of the ratification to a referendum under the state Constitution, and its judgment is reversed and the cause remanded for further proceedings not inconsistent with this opinion.

Burroughs & Cannon v. United States
290 U.S. 534 (1934)

An indictment returned by a grand jury sitting in the District of Columbia charges petitioners, in ten counts, with violations of the Federal Corrupt Practices Act of February 28, 1925. The pertinent provisions of the act defines the term, "political committee," as including any organization which accepts contributions for the purpose of influencing or attempting to influence the election of presidential and vice presidential electors in two or more states. Every political committee is required to have a chairman and a treasurer before any contribution may be accepted. One of the duties of the treasurer is to keep a detailed and exact account of all contributions made to or for the committee. Every person who receives a contribution for a political committee is required to render to the treasurer a detailed account thereof, with specified particulars. By section 244, the treasurer is required to file with the clerk of the House of Representatives, at designated times, a statement containing the name and address of each contributor, date and amount of each contribution, and other particulars, complete as of the day next preceding the date of filing. By section 252(a), penalties of fine and imprisonment are imposed upon any person who violates any of the provisions of the chapter; and, by subdivision (b), increased penalties are imposed upon any person who willfully violates any of those provisions.

The first eight counts of the indictment purport to charge petitioners with substantive violations of the act, and the ninth and tenth counts, with conspiracy to violate it—four of the eight counts charging willful violations; the other four merely charging violations, that is to say, unlawful violations.

In the Supreme Court of the District, a demurrer was interposed to the indictment on the grounds (1) that each count of the indictment failed to allege facts sufficient to constitute an offense against the United States, and (2) that the

Federal Corrupt Practices Act contravenes section 1, art. 2, of the Federal Constitution, providing for the appointment by each state of electors. The District Supreme Court sustained the demurrer upon the first ground, rendering unnecessary any ruling as to the second. Upon appeal to the District Court of Appeals the judgment was reversed. That court ruled each of the ten counts sufficient, and upheld the constitutionality of the act. . . .

. . .

The congressional act under review seeks to preserve the purity of presidential and vice presidential elections. Neither in purpose nor in effect does it interfere with the power of a state to appoint electors or the manner in which their appointment shall be made. It deals with political committees organized for the purpose of influencing elections in two or more states, and with branches or subsidiaries of national committees, and excludes from its operation state or local committees. Its operation, therefore, is confined to situations which, if not beyond the power of the state to deal with at all, are beyond its power to deal with adequately. It in no sense invades any exclusive state power.

While presidential electors are not officers or agents of the federal government, they exercise federal functions under, and discharge duties in virtue of authority conferred by, the Constitution of the United States. The President is vested with the executive power of the nation. The importance of his election and the vital character of its relationship to and effect upon the welfare and safety of the whole people cannot be too strongly stated. To say that Congress is without power to pass appropriate legislation to safeguard such an election from the improper use of money to influence the result is to deny to the nation in a vital particular the power of self-protection. Congress, undoubtedly, possesses that power, as it possesses every other power essential to preserve the departments and institutions of the general government from impairment or destruction, whether threatened by force or by corruption.

. . .

The power of Congress to protect the election of President and Vice President from corruption being clear, the choice of means to that end presents a question primarily addressed to the judgment of Congress. If it can be seen that the means adopted are really calculated to attain the end, the degree of their necessity, the extent to which they conduce to the end, the closeness of the relationship between the means adopted, and the end to be attained, are matters for congressional determination alone. Congress reached the conclusion that public disclosure of political contributions, together with the names of contributors and other details, would tend to prevent the corrupt use of money to affect elections. The verity of this conclusion reasonably cannot be denied. When to this is added the requirement contained in section 244, that the treasurer's statement shall include full particulars in respect of expenditures, it seems plain that the statute as a whole is calculated to discourage the making and use of contributions for purposes of corruption.

The judgment of the court below will be affirmed in respect of the ninth and tenth counts or the indictment only, and the cause remanded to the Supreme Court of the District for further proceedings in conformity with this opinion.

United Public Workers v. Mitchell
330 U.S. 75 (1947)

The Hatch Act, enacted in 1940, declares unlawful certain specified political activities of federal employees. Section 9 forbids officers and employees in the executive branch of the Federal Government, with exceptions, from taking "any active part in political management or in political campaigns." Section 15 declares that the activities theretofore determined by the United States Civil Service Commission to be prohibited to employees in the classified civil service of the United States by the civil service rules shall be deemed to be prohibited to federal employees covered by the Hatch Act. These sections of the Act cover all federal officers and employees whether in the classified civil service or not and a penalty of dismissal from employment is imposed for violation. There is no designation of a single governmental agency for its enforcement.

For many years before the Hatch Act the Congress had authorized the exclusion of federal employees in the competitive classified service from active participation in political management and political campaigns. In June 1938, the Congressional authorization for exclusion had been made more effective by a Civil Service Commission disciplinary rule. That power to discipline members of the competitive classified civil service continues in the Commission under the Hatch Act by virtue of the present applicability of the Executive Order No. 8705, March 5, 1941. The only change in the Civil Service Rules relating to political activity, caused by the Hatch Act legislation, that is of significance in this case is the elimination on March 5, 1941, of the word "privately" from the phrase "to express privately their opinions." This limitation to private expression had regulated classified personnel since 1907.

The present appellants sought an injunction before a statutory three judge district court of the District of Columbia against appellees, members of the United States Civil Service Commission to prohibit them from enforcing against petition-

ers the provisions of the second sentence of 9(a) of the Hatch Act for the reason that the sentence is repugnant to the Constitution of the United States. A declaratory judgment of the unconstitutionality of the sentence was also sought. . . .

. . .

. . . Defendants moved to dismiss the complaint for lack of a justiciable case or controversy. The District Court determined that each of these individual appellants had an interest in their claimed privilege of engaging in political activities, sufficient to give them a right to maintain this suit. The District Court further determined that the questioned provision of the Hatch Act was valid and that the complaint therefore failed to state a cause of action. It accordingly dismissed the complaint and granted summary judgment to defendants.

. . .

This brings us to consider the narrow but important point involved in Poole's situation. Poole's stated offense is taking an "active part in political management or in political campaigns." He was a ward executive committeeman of a political party and was politically active on election day as a worker at the polls and a paymaster for the services of other party workers. The issue for decision and the only one we decide is whether such a breach of the Hatch Act and Rule 1 of the Commission can, without violating the Constitution, be made the basis for disciplinary action.

When the issue is thus narrowed, the interference with free expression is seen in better proportion as compared with the requirements of orderly management of administrative personnel. Only while the employee is politically active, in the sense of Rule 1, must he withhold expression of opinion on public subjects. We assume that Mr. Poole would be expected to comment publicly as committeeman on political matters, so that indirectly there is an attenuated interference. We accept appellant's contention that the nature of political rights reserved to the people by the Ninth and Tenth Amendments are involved. The right claimed as inviolate may be stated as the right of a citizen to act as a party official or worker to further his own political views. Thus we have a measure of interference by the Hatch Act and the Rules with what otherwise would be the freedom of the civil servant under the First, Ninth, and Tenth Amendments. And, if we look upon due process as a guarantee of freedom in those fields, there is a corresponding impairment of that right under the Fifth Amendment. Appellants' objections under the Amendments are basically the same.

We do not find persuasion in appellants' argument that such activities during free time are not subject to regulation even though admittedly political activities cannot be indulged in during working hours. The influence of political activity by government employees, if evil in its effects on the service, the employees or people dealing with them, is hardly less so because that activity takes place after hours. Of course, the question of the need for this regulation is for other branches of government rather than the courts. Our duty in this case ends if the Hatch Act provision under examination is constitutional.

. . .

Another Congress may determine that on the whole, limitations on active political management by federal personnel are unwise. The teaching of experience has evidently led Congress to enact the Hatch Act provisions. They declare that the present supposed evils of political activity are beyond the power of Congress to redress would leave the nation impotent to deal with what many sincere men believe is a material threat to the democratic system. Congress is not politically

naive or regardless of public welfare or that of the employees. It leaves untouched full participation by employees in political decisions at the ballot box and forbids only the partisan activity of federal personnel deemed offensive to efficiency. With that limitation only, employees may make their contributions to public affairs or protect their own interests, as before the passage of the act. The argument that political neutrality is not indispensable to a merit system for federal employees may be accepted. But because it is not indispensable does not mean that it is not desirable or permissible. Modern American politics involves organized political parties. Many classifications of Government employees have been accustomed to work in politics—national, state and local—as a matter of principle or to assure their tenure. Congress may reasonably desire to limit party activity of federal employees so as to avoid a tendency toward a one-party system. It may have considered that parties would be more truly devoted to the public welfare if public servants were not over active politically.

. . . A reading of the Act and Rule 1, together with the Commission's determination shows the wide range of public activities with which there is no interference by the legislation. It is only partisan political activity that is interdicted. It is active participation in political management and political campaigns. Expressions, public or private, on public affairs, personalities and matters of public interest, not an objective of party action, are unrestricted by law so long as the Government employee does not direct his activities toward party success.

It is urged, however, that Congress has gone further than necessary in prohibiting political activity to all types of classified employees. It is pointed out by appellants "that the impartiality of many of these is a matter of complete indifference to the effective performance" of their duties. Mr. Poole would appear to be a good illustration for appellants' argument. The complaint states that he is a roller in the Mint. We take it this is a job calling for the qualities of a skilled mechanic and that it does not involve contact with the public. Nevertheless, if in free time he is engaged in political activity, Congress may have concluded that the activity may promote or retard his advancement or preferment with his superiors. Congress may have thought that Government employees are handy elements for leaders in political policy to use in building a political machine. For regulation of employees it is not necessary that the act regulated be anything more than an act reasonably deemed by Congress to interfere with the efficiency of the public service. There are hundreds of thousands of United States employees with positions no more influential upon policy determination than that of Mr. Poole. Evidently what Congress feared was the cumulative effect on employee morale of political activity by all employees who could be induced to participate actively. It does not seem to us an unconstitutional basis for legislation. There is a suggestion that administrative workers may be barred, constitutionally, from political management and political campaigns while the industrial workers may not be barred, constitutionally, without an act "narrowly drawn to define and punish specific conduct." A ready answer, it seems to us, lies in the fact that the prohibition of 9(a) of the Hatch Act "applies without discrimination to all employees whether industrial or administrative" and that the Civil Service Rules, by 15 made a part of the Hatch Act, makes clear that industrial workers are covered in the prohibition against political activity. Congress has determined that the presence of government employees, whether industrial or administrative, in

the ranks of political party workers is bad. Whatever differences there may be between administrative employees of the Government and industrial workers in its employ are differences in detail so far as the constitutional power under review is concerned. Whether there are such differences and what weight to attach to them, are all matters of detail for Congress. We do not know whether the number of federal employees will expand or contract; whether the need for regulation of their political activities will increase or diminish. The use of the constitutional power of regulation is for Congress, not for the courts.

. . . The regulation of such activities as Poole carried on has the approval of long practice by the Commission, court decisions upon similar problems and a large body of informed public opinion. Congress and the administrative agencies have authority over the discipline and efficiency of the public service. When actions of civil servants in the judgment of Congress menace the integrity and the competency of the service, legislation to forestall such danger and adequate to maintain its usefulness is required. The Hatch Act is the answer of Congress to this need. We cannot say with such a background that these restrictions are unconstitutional.

Section 15 of the Hatch Act defines an active part in political management or political campaigns as the same activities that the United States Civil Service Commission has determined to be prohibited to classified civil service employees by the provisions of the Civil Service rules when 15 took effect July 19, 1940. The activities of Mr. Poole, as ward executive committeeman and a worker at the polls, obviously fall within the prohibitions of 9 of the Hatch Act against taking an active part in political management and political campaigns. They are also covered by the prior determinations of the Commission. We need to examine no further at this time into the validity of the definition of political activity and 15.

The judgment of the District Court is accordingly affirmed.

State of Oklahoma v. United States Civil Service Commission
330 U.S. 127 (1947)

This proceeding brings to this Court another phase of the Hatch Act. The petitioner, the State of Oklahoma, objects to the enforcement by the United States Civil Service Commission of 12(a) of the act. France Paris has been a member of the State Highway Commission of Oklahoma since January 14, 1943. He was elected chairman of the Democratic State Central Committee for Oklahoma for his third term in February 1942 and he occupied such position continuously until October 18, 1943, when he resigned. On October 12, 1943, the Civil Service Commission issued its letter of charges in the matter of France Paris and the State of Oklahoma, in which it notified Mr. Paris and Oklahoma that information which the Civil Service Commission had received warranted an investigation into an alleged improper political activity on the part of France Paris under the provisions of 12 of the Hatch Act. The charge was that since January 14, 1943, Mr. Paris had been an officer of Oklahoma whose principal employment was and is in connection with an activity financed in whole or in part by loans and grants from a Federal agency of the United States and that during such time Mr. Paris also held a political party office, to it, the chairmanship of the State Central Committee above referred to. It later developed that no general election occurred in Oklahoma in 1943. The State Democratic Headquarters had been closed on

January 4, 1943, by Mr. Paris and were later reopened during the year under the direct charge of the vice chairman of that committee, we assume prior to Mr. Paris' resignation on October 18, 1943. On June 14 the committee sponsored a "Victory Dinner" in Oklahoma City. . . .

Pursuant to 12(c) of the State of Oklahoma, after having received notice of the Civil Service Commission's determination, instituted these proceedings for the review of the order in the proper district court of the United States. That court upheld the action of the Civil Service Commission and this action was affirmed by the Circuit Court of Appeals for the Tenth Circuit. . . .

. . .

Judgment affirmed.

United States v. Congress of Industrial Organizations
335 U.S. 106 (1948)

This appeal presents a problem as to the constitutionality of 313 of the Federal Corrupt Practices Act of 1925. An indictment was returned at the January 1948 term in the District Court of the United States for the District of Columbia on two counts charging in count I the Congress of Industrial Organizations and in count II its President, Philip Murray, with violation of 313 of the Federal Corrupt Practices Act because of the publication and distribution in the District of Columbia of an issue, Vol. 10, No. 28, under date of July 14, 1947, of *The CIO News*, a weekly periodical owned and published by the CIO at the expense and from the funds of the CIO and with the consent of its President, Mr. Murray. The number of *The CIO News* in question carried upon its front page a statement by Mr. Murray as President of the CIO, urging all members of the CIO to vote for Judge Ed Garmatz, then a candidate for Congress in Maryland at a special election to be held July 15, 1947. The statement said it was made despite 313 in the belief that the section was unconstitutional because it abridged rights of free speech, free press, and free assemblage, guaranteed by the Bill or Rights.

The defendants moved to dismiss the indictment on the ground that 313 as construed and applied and upon its face abridged as to the CIO and its members and Mr. Murray freedom of speech, press, and assembly and the right to petition the government for a redress of grievances in violation of the Constitution; that the classification of labor organizations was arbitrary and the provisions vague in contravention of the Bill of Rights; and that the terms of the section were an invasion of the rights of defendants, protected by the Ninth and Tenth Amendments. The District Court sustained the motion to dismiss on the ground that as "no clear and present danger to the public interest can be found in the circumstances surrounding the enactment of this legislation" the asserted abridgment of the freedoms of the First Amendment was unjustified. . . .

. . .

Our conclusion leads us to affirm the order of dismissal upon the ground herein announced. It is so ordered.

Affirmed.

United States v. Hood
343 U.S. 148 (1952)

The defendants were charged in the District Court for the Southern District of Mississippi with a conspiracy to violate 18 U.S.C. 215 and numerous substantive violations of the same section. The law provides:

Whoever solicits or receives, either as a political contribution, or for personal emolument, any money or thing of value, in consideration of the promise of support or use of influence in obtaining for any person any appointive office or place under the United States, shall be fined not more than $1,000 or imprisoned not more than one year, or both.

The indictment charged a conspiracy to solicit contributions to the Mississippi Democratic Committee and to the defendants personally in return for promises to use influence to obtain for the contributors appointments in the Post Office Department and in the Office of Price Stabilization. Other counts of the indictment charged substantive violations. Material here are counts 31, 32, and 33 charging the solicitation by two of the defendants of three $300 political contributions from named individuals in return for the promise of support and influence on behalf of the contributors to secure for them appointments as Chairmen of the County Ration Boards of Pike, Amite, and Lawrence Counties, respectively. It is stipulated that no such offices were in existence at the time of the solicitation or at any time thereafter up to the return of the indictment. Authority to create such offices, however, had been granted to the President, well before the violations charged, by the Defense Production Act of 1950.

Defendants successfully moved to dismiss these portions of the indictment on the ground that the statute did not make criminal the sale of non-existent offices or of influence in connection with appointments to them. The District Court also ordered stricken the references in the conspiracy count to the offices of Chairmen of County Ration Boards. The order of dismissal was appealed by the Government under the Criminal Appeals Act. . . .

. . .

The evil at which the statute is directed is the operation of purchased, and thus improper, influence in determining the occupants of federal office. But in attacking that evil, Congress outlawed not the use of such influence, but the solicitation of its purchase, the peddling of the forbidden wares. As is not uncommon in criminal legislation, Congress, in order to strike at the root, made the scope of the statute wider than the immediate evil. Even judges need not be blind to the fact of political life that it helps in influencing political appointments to be forehanded with a recommendation before an office is formally created. Certainly it was not unreal for Congress to believe that the sale of influence in anticipation of jobs was equally damaging to the proper operation of the federal service and to take steps to prevent it. It did so in this Act. Nothing has been suggested, either by the sparse legislative history or by prior judicial construction, to restrain us from giving effect to the obvious, ordinary reading of the statute. It is pressed upon us that criminal statutes are to be strictly construed. But this does not mean that such legislation "must be construed by some artificial and conventional rule." We should not read such laws so as to put in what is not readily found there. But equally we should not read out what as a matter of ordinary English speech is in.

This Act penalized corruption. It is no less corrupt to sell an office one may never be able to deliver than to sell one he can. Dealing in futures also discredits the processes of government. There is no indication that this statute punishes delivery of the fruit of the forbidden transaction— it forbids the sale. The sale is what is here alleged. Whether the corrupt transaction would or could ever be performed is immaterial. We find no basis for allowing a breach of warranty to be a defense to corruption.

. . .

The judgment below is reversed and the case remanded for further proceedings.

United States v. Rumely
345 U.S. 41 (1953)

The respondent Rumely was Secretary of an organization known as the Committee for Constitutional Government, which, among other things, engaged in the sale of books of a particular political tendentiousness. He refused to disclose to the House Select Committee on Lobbying Activities the names of those who made bulk purchases of these books for further distribution, and was convicted under R.S. 102, which provides penalties for refusal to give testimony or to produce relevant papers "upon any matter" under congressional inquiry. The Court of Appeals reversed. . . .

. . .

. . . If "lobbying" was to cover all activities of anyone intending to influence, encourage, promote or retard legislation, why did Congress differentiate between "lobbying activities" and other "activities . . . intended to influence"? Had Congress wished to authorize so extensive an investigation of the influences that form public opinion, would it not have used language at least as explicit as it employed in the very resolution in question in authorizing investigation of government agencies? Certainly it does no violence to the phrase "lobbying activities" to give it a more restricted scope. To give such meaning is not barred by intellectual honesty. So to interpret is in the candid service of avoiding a serious constitutional doubt. "Words have been strained more than they need to be strained here in order to avoid that doubt." With a view to observing this principle of wisdom and duty, the Court very recently strained words more than they need be strained here. The considerations which prevailed in that case should prevail in this.

Only a word need be said about the debate in Congress after the committee reported that Rumely had refused to produce the information which he had a right to refuse under the restricted meaning of the phrase "lobbying activities." The view taken at that time by the committee and by the Congress that the committee was authorized to ask Rumely for the information he withheld is not legislative history defining the scope of a congressional measure. . . . In any event, Rumely's duty to answer must be judged as of the time of his refusal. The scope of the resolution defining that duty is therefore to be ascertained as of that time and cannot be enlarged by subsequent action of Congress.

Grave constitutional questions are matters properly to be decided by this Court but only when they inescapably come before us for adjudication. Until then it is our duty to abstain from marking the boundaries of congressional power or delimiting the protection guaranteed by the First Amendment. Only by such self-restraint will we avoid the mischief which has followed occasional departures from the principles which we profess.

The judgment below should be affirmed.

United States v. Harriss
347 U.S. 612 (1954)

The appellees were charged by information with violation of the Federal Regulation of Lobbying Act. . . . [T]he District Court dismissed the information on the ground that the Act is unconstitutional. . . .

Seven counts of the information are laid un-der 305, which requires designated reports to Congress from every person "receiving any contributions or expending any money" for the purpose of influencing the passage or defeat of any legislation by Congress. One such count charges the National Farm Committee, a Texas corporation, with failure to report the solicitation and receipt of contributions to influence the passage of legislation which would cause a rise in the price of agricultural commodities and commodity futures and the defeat of legislation which would cause a decline in those prices. The remaining six counts under 305 charge defendants Moore and Harriss with failure to report expenditures having the same single purpose. Some of the alleged expenditures consist of the payment of compensation to others to communicate face-to-face with members of Congress, at public functions and committee hearings, concerning legislation, affecting agricultural prices; the other alleged expenditures relate largely to the costs of a campaign to induce various interested groups and individuals to communicate by letter with members of Congress on such legislation.

The other two counts in the information are laid under 308, which requires any person "who shall engage himself for pay or for any consideration for the purpose of attempting to influence the passage or defeat of any legislation" to register with Congress and to make specified disclosures. These two counts allege in considerable detail that defendants Moore and Linder were hired to express certain views to Congress as to agricultural prices or to cause others to do so, for the purpose of attempting to influence the passage of legislation which would cause a rise in the price of agricultural commodities and commodity futures and a defeat of legislation which would cause a decline in such prices; and that pursuant to this undertaking, without having registered as required by 308, they arranged to have members of Congress contacted on behalf of these views, either directly by their own emissaries or through an artificially stimulated letter campaign.

We are not concerned here with the sufficiency of the information as a criminal pleading. Our review under the Criminal Appeals Act is limited to a decision on the alleged "invalidity" of the statute on which the information is based. In making this decision, we judge the statute on its face. The "invalidity" of the Lobbying Act is asserted on three grounds: (1) that 305, 307, and 308 are too vague and indefinite to meet the requirements of due process; (2) that 305 and 308 violate the First Amendment guarantees of freedom of speech, freedom of the press, and the right to petition the Government; (3) that the penalty provision of 310(b) violates the right of the people under the First Amendment to petition the Government.

. . .

To summarize, therefore, there are three prerequisites to coverage under 307: (1) the "person" must have solicited, collected, or received contributions; (2) one of the main purposes of such "person," or one of the main purposes of such contributions, must have been to influence the passage or defeat of legislation by Congress; (3) the intended method of accomplishing this purpose must have been through direct communication with members of Congress. And since 307 modifies the substantive provisions of the Act, our construction of 307 will of necessity also narrow the scope of 305 and 308, the substantive provisions underlying the information in this case. Thus 305 is limited to those persons who are covered by 307; and when so covered, they must report all contributions and expenditures having the purpose of attempting to influence legislation through direct communication with Congress. Similarly, 308 is limited to those persons (with

the stated exceptions) who are covered by 307 and who, in addition, engage themselves for pay or for any other valuable consideration for the purpose of attempting to influence legislation through direct communication with Congress. Construed in this way, the Lobbying Act meets the constitutional requirement of definiteness.

Thus construed, 305 and 308 also do not violate the freedoms guaranteed by the First Amendment—freedom to speak, publish, and petition the Government.

Present-day legislative complexities are such that individual members of Congress cannot be expected to explore the myriad pressures to which they are regularly subjected. Yet full realization of the American ideal of government by elected representatives depends to no small extent on their ability to properly evaluate such pressures. Otherwise the voice of the people may all too easily be drowned out by the voice of special interest groups seeking favored treatment while masquerading as proponents of the public weal. This is the evil which the Lobbying Act was designed to help prevent.

Toward that end, Congress has not sought to prohibit these pressures. It has merely provided for a modicum of information from those who for hire attempt to influence legislation or who collect or spend funds for that purpose. It wants only to know who is being hired, who is putting up the money, and how much. It acted in the same spirit and for a similar purpose in passing the Federal Corrupt Practices Act—to maintain the integrity of a basic governmental process.

Under these circumstances, we believe that Congress, at least within the bounds of the Act as we have construed it, is not constitutionally forbidden to require the disclosure of lobbying activities. To do so would be to deny Congress in large measure the power of self-protection. And here Congress has used that power in a manner restricted to its appropriate end. We conclude that 305 and 308, as applied to persons defined in 307, do not offend the First Amendment.

It is suggested, however, that the Lobbying Act, with respect to persons other than those defined in 307, may as a practical matter act as a deterrent to their exercise of First Amendment rights. Hypothetical borderline situations are conjured up in which such persons choose to remain silent because of fear of possible prosecution for failure to comply with the Act. Our narrow construction of the Act, precluding as it does reasonable fears, is calculated to avoid such restraint. But, even assuming some such deterrent effect, the restraint is at most an indirect one resulting from self-censorship, comparable in many ways to the restraint resulting from criminal libel laws. The hazard of such restraint is too remote to require striking down a statute which on its face is otherwise plainly within the area of congressional power and is designed to safeguard a vital national interest.

. . .

The judgment below is reversed and the cause is remanded to the District Court for further proceedings not inconsistent with this opinion.

Reversed.

United States v. Automobile Workers
352 U.S. 567 (1957)

The issues tendered in this case are the construction and, ultimately, the constitutionality of an Act of Congress that prohibits corporations and labor organizations from making "a contribution or expenditure in connection with" any election for federal office. This is a direct appeal by the Government from a judgment of the District Court for the Eastern District of Michigan dismissing a four-count indictment that charged appellee, a labor organization, with having made expenditures in violation of that law. Appellee had moved to dismiss the indictment on the grounds (1) that it failed to state an offense under the statute and (2) that the provisions of the statute "on their face and as construed and applied" are unconstitutional. The district judge held that the indictment did not allege a statutory offense and that he was therefore not required to rule upon the constitutional questions presented. . . .

. . .

. . . Because the District Court's erroneous interpretation of the statute led it to stop the prosecution prematurely, its judgment must be reversed and the case must be remanded to it for further proceedings not inconsistent with this opinion.

Cammarano v. United States
358 U.S. 498 (1959)

. . . The issues involve the interpretation and validity of Treas. Reg. 111, as applied by the courts below to deny deduction as "ordinary and necessary" business expenses under §23(a)(1)(A) of the Internal Revenue Code of 1939 to sums expended by the respective taxpayer petitioners in furtherance of publicity programs designed to help secure the defeat of initiative measures then pending before the voters of the States of Washington and Arkansas.

. . .

No. 29: In 1948, petitioners William and Louise Cammarano, husband and wife, jointly owned a one-fourth interest in a partnership engaged in the distribution of beer at wholesale in the State of Washington. The partnership was a member of the Washington Beer Wholesalers

Association. In December 1947, the Association had established a trust fund as a repository for assessments collected from its members to help finance a statewide publicity program urging the defeat of "Initiative to the Legislature No. 13," a measure to be submitted to the electorate at the general election of November 2, 1948, which would have placed the retail sale of wine and beer in Washington exclusively in the hands of the State. During 1948, petitioners' partnership paid to the trust fund $3,545.15, of which petitioners' pro rata share was $886.29. The trust fund collected a total of $53,500, which was turned over to an Industry Advisory Committee organized by wholesale and retail wine and beer dealers, which, in turn, expended it as part of contributions totaling $231,257.10 for various kinds of advertising directed to the public, none of which referred to petitioners' wares as such and all of which urged defeat of Initiative No. 13. The initiative was defeated.

In preparing their joint income tax return for 1948, petitioners deducted as a business expense the $886.29 paid to the Association's trust fund as their share of the partnership assessment. The deduction was disallowed by the Commissioner, and petitioners paid under protest the additional sum thus due, and sued in the District Court for refund. That court ruled that the payments made to the trust fund were "expended for . . . the . . . defeat of legislation" within the meaning of Treas. Reg. 111, and were therefore not deductible as ordinary and necessary business expenses under §23(a)(1)(A) of the Internal Revenue Code of 1939. The Court of Appeals affirmed, holding the Regulation applicable and valid as applied.

No. 50: Petitioner F. Strauss & Son, Inc., is a corporation engaged in the wholesale liquor business in Arkansas. In 1950, an initiative calling for an election on statewide prohibition was placed on the ballot to be voted on in the state general election on November 7, 1950. In May of that year, Strauss, together with eight other Arkansas liquor wholesalers, organized Arkansas Legal Control Associates, Inc., as a means of coordinating their efforts to persuade the voters of Arkansas to vote against the proposed prohibition measure. Between May 30 and November 30, 1950, Arkansas Legal Control Associates collected a total of $126,265.84, which was disbursed for various forms of publicity concerning the proposed Act. Strauss' contribution amounted to $9,252.67.

The initiative measure was defeated in the November election. On its 1950 income tax return, Strauss deducted the $9,252.67 as a business expense. The Commissioner disallowed the deduction, and Strauss filed a timely petition in the Tax Court seeking a redetermination of the deficiency asserted. That court upheld the action of the Commissioner in disallowing the claimed deduction, and the Court of Appeals unanimously affirmed.

. . .

. . . [I]t appears to us to express a determination by Congress that, since purchased publicity can influence the fate of legislation which will affect, directly or indirectly, all in the community, everyone in the community should stand on the same footing as regards its purchase so far as the Treasury of the United States is concerned.

Affirmed.

United States v. Shirey
359 U.S. 255 (1959)

The information alleged that appellee had offered S. Walter Stauffer, a member of Congress from Pennsylvania, to contribute $1,000 a year to the

Republican Party in consideration of Stauffer's use of influence to procure for appellee the postmastership of York, Pennsylvania. The District Court granted a motion to dismiss for failure to state facts sufficient to constitute an offense against the United States. The Government appealed directly to this Court. . . .

. . .

. . . The evil which Congress sought to check and the mischief wrought by what it proscribed are the same when the transaction is triangular as when only two parties are involved. It is incredible to suppose that Congress meant to prohibit Shirey from giving $1,000 to Stauffer, to be passed on by the latter to the Party fund, but that Shirey was outside the congressional prohibition for securing the same influence by a promise to deposit $1,000 directly in the Party's fund. That is not the kind of finessing by which this Court has heretofore allowed penal legislation to be construed.

The judgment is reversed.

Eastern R. Conf. v. Noerr Motors
365 U.S. 127 (1961)

The case was commenced by a complaint filed in the United States District Court in Pennsylvania on behalf of forty-one Pennsylvania truck operators and their trade association, the Pennsylvania Motor Truck Association. This complaint, which named as defendants twenty-four Eastern railroads, an association of the presidents of those railroads known as the Eastern Railroad Presidents Conference, and a public relations firm, Carl Byoir & Associates, Inc., charged that the defendants had conspired to restrain trade in and monopolize the long-distance freight business in violation of 1 and 2 of the Sherman Act.

The gist of the conspiracy alleged was that the railroads had engaged Byoir to conduct a publicity campaign against the truckers designed to foster the adoption and retention of laws and law enforcement practices destructive of the trucking business, to create an atmosphere of distaste for the truckers among the general public, and to impair the relationships existing between the truckers and their customers. . . . The complaint then went on to supplement these more or less general allegations with specific charges as to particular instances in which the railroads had attempted to influence legislation by means of their publicity campaign. One of several such charges was that the defendants had succeeded in persuading the Governor of Pennsylvania to veto a measure known as the "Fair Truck Bill," which would have permitted truckers to carry heavier loads over Pennsylvania roads.

. . .

. . . [T]he trial court entered a judgment . . . that the railroads' publicity campaign had violated the Sherman Act while that of the truckers had not. In reaching this conclusion, the trial court expressly disclaimed any purpose to condemn as illegal mere efforts on the part of the railroads to influence the passage of new legislation or the enforcement of existing law. . . .

. . .

. . . The Court of Appeals for the Third Circuit . . . upheld the judgment of the District Court. . . .

. . .

In the first place, such a holding would substantially impair the power of government to take actions through its legislature and executive that operate to restrain trade. In a representative democracy such as this, these branches of government act on behalf of the people and, to a very large extent, the whole concept of representation depends upon the ability of the people to make their wishes known to their representatives. To hold that the government retains the power to act in this representative capacity and yet hold, at the same time, that the people cannot freely inform the government of their wishes would impute to the Sherman Act a purpose to regulate, not business activity, but political activity, a purpose which would have no basis whatever in the legislative history of that Act.

Secondly, and of at least equal significance, such a construction of the Sherman Act would raise important constitutional questions. The right of petition is one of the freedoms protected by the Bill of Rights, and we cannot, of course, lightly impute to Congress an intent to invade these freedoms. Indeed, such an imputation would be particularly unjustified in this case in view of all the countervailing considerations enumerated above. For these reasons, we think it clear that the Sherman Act does not apply to the activities of the railroads at least insofar as those activities comprised mere solicitation of governmental action with respect to the passage and enforcement of laws. We are thus called upon to consider whether the courts below were correct in holding that, notwithstanding this principle, the Act was violated here because of the presence in the railroads' publicity campaign of additional factors sufficient to take the case out of the area in which the principle is controlling.

The first such factor relied upon was the fact, established by the finding of the District Court, that the railroads' sole purpose in seeking to influence the passage and enforcement of laws was to destroy the truckers as competitors for the long-distance freight business. But we do not see how this fact, even if adequately supported in the record, could transform conduct otherwise lawful into a violation of the Sherman Act. . . . The right of the people to inform their representatives

in government of their desires with respect to the passage or enforcement of laws cannot properly be made to depend upon their intent in doing so. It is neither unusual nor illegal for people to seek action on laws in the hope that they may bring about an advantage to themselves and a disadvantage to their competitors. . . . A construction of the Sherman Act that would disqualify people from taking a public position on matters in which they are financially interested would thus deprive the government of a valuable source of information and, at the same time, deprive the people of their right to petition in the very instances in which that right may be of the most importance to them. We reject such a construction of the Act and hold that, at least insofar as the railroads' campaign was directed toward obtaining governmental action, its legality was not at all affected by any anticompetitive purpose it may have had.

. . . Insofar as that Act sets up a code of ethics at all, it is a code that condemns trade restraints, not political activity, and, as we have already pointed out, a publicity campaign to influence governmental action falls clearly into the category of political activity. The proscriptions of the Act, tailored as they are for the business world, are not at all appropriate for application in the political arena. Congress has traditionally exercised extreme caution in legislating with respect to problems relating to the conduct of political activities, a caution which has been reflected in the decisions of this Court interpreting such legislation. All of this caution would go for naught if we permitted an extension of the Sherman Act to regulate activities of that nature simply because those activities have a commercial impact and involve conduct that can be termed unethical.

. . .

. . . [W]e are here concerned only with those parts of the judgments below holding the railroads and Byoir liable for violations of the Sherman Act. And it follows from what we have said that those parts of the judgments below are wrong. They must be and are reversed.

Zwickler v. Koota
389 U.S. 241 (1967)

Section 781–b of the New York Penal Law makes it a crime to distribute in quantity, among other things, any handbill for another which contains any statement concerning any candidate in connection with any election of public officers, without also printing thereon the name and post office address of the printer thereof and of the person at whose instance such handbill is so distributed. Appellant was convicted of violating the statute by distributing anonymous handbills critical of the record of a United States Congressman seeking reelection at the 1964 elections. The conviction was reversed, on state law grounds, by the New York Supreme Court, Appellate Term, and the New York Court of Appeals affirmed without opinion. . . . A three-judge court . . . applied the doctrine of abstention and dismissed the complaint. . . .

. . .

The judgment of the District Court is reversed and the case is remanded for further proceedings consistent with this opinion.

Pickering v. Board of Education of Township High School District 205, Will County
391 U.S. 563 (1968)

Appellant Marvin L. Pickering, a teacher in Township High School District 205, Will County,

Illinois, was dismissed from his position by the appellee Board of Education for sending a letter to a local newspaper in connection with a recently proposed tax increase that was critical of the way in which the Board and the district superintendent of schools had handled past proposals to raise new revenue for the schools. Appellant's dismissal resulted from a determination by the Board, after a full hearing, that the publication of the letter was "detrimental to the efficient operation and administration of the schools of the district" and hence, under the relevant Illinois statute . . . that "interests of the school require[d] [his dismissal]."

Appellant's claim that his writing of the letter was protected by the First and Fourteenth Amendments was rejected. Appellant then sought review of the Board's action in the Circuit Court . . . which affirmed his dismissal on the ground that the determination that appellant's letter was detrimental to the interests of the school system . . . overrode appellant's First Amendment rights. On appeal, the Supreme Court of Illinois . . . affirmed the judgment of the Circuit Court. . . .

In February of 1961, the appellee Board of Education asked the voters of the school district to approve a bond issue to raise $4,875,000 to erect two new schools. The proposal was defeated. Then, in December of 1961, the Board submitted another bond proposal to the voters which called for the raising of $5,500,000 to build two new schools. This second proposal passed, and the schools were built with the money raised by the bond sales. In May of 1964, a proposed increase in the tax rate to be used for educational purposes was submitted to the voters by the Board and was defeated. Finally, on September 19, 1964, a second proposal to increase the tax rate was submitted by the Board, and was likewise defeated. It was in connection with this last proposal of the School Board that appellant wrote the letter to the editor. . . .

Prior to the vote on the second tax increase proposal, a variety of articles attributed to the District 205 Teachers' Organization appeared in the local paper. These articles urged passage of the tax increase and stated that failure to pass the increase would result in a decline in the quality of education afforded children in the district's schools. A letter from the superintendent of schools making the same point was published in the paper two days before the election and submitted to the voters in mimeographed form the following day. It was in response to the foregoing material, together with the failure of the tax increase to pass, that appellant submitted the letter in question to the editor of the local paper.

The letter constituted, basically, an attack on the School Board's handling of the 1961 bond issue proposals and its subsequent allocation of financial resources between the schools' educational and athletic programs. It also charged the superintendent of schools with attempting to prevent teachers in the district from opposing or criticizing the proposed bond issue.

The Board dismissed Pickering for writing and publishing the letter. . . . The Board was then required to hold a hearing on the dismissal. . . .

The Illinois courts reviewed the proceedings solely to determine whether the Board's findings were supported by substantial evidence and whether, on the facts as found, the Board could reasonably conclude that appellant's publication of the letter was "detrimental to the best interests of the schools." Pickering's claim that his letter was protected by the First Amendment was rejected on the ground that his acceptance of a teaching position in the public schools obliged him to refrain from making statements about the operation of the schools "which in the absence

of such position he would have an undoubted right to engage in." . . .

. . .

An examination of the statements in appellant's letter objected to by the Board reveals that they, like the letter as a whole, consist essentially of criticism of the Board's allocation of school funds between educational and athletic programs, and of both the Board's and the superintendent's methods of informing, or preventing the informing of, the district's taxpayers of the real reasons why additional tax revenues were being sought for the schools. The statements are in no way directed towards any person with whom appellant would normally be in contact in the course of his daily work as a teacher. Thus, no question of maintaining either discipline by immediate superiors or harmony among coworkers is presented here. . . .

. . . The Board's original charges included allegations that the publication of the letter damaged the professional reputations of the Board and the superintendent and would foment controversy and conflict among the Board, teachers, administrators, and the residents of the district. However, no evidence to support these allegations was introduced at the hearing. . . .

. . . Certainly an accusation that too much money is being spent on athletics by the administrators of the school system . . . cannot reasonably be regarded as per se detrimental to the district's schools. Such an accusation reflects rather a difference of opinion between Pickering and the Board as to the preferable manner of operating the school system, a difference of opinion that clearly concerns an issue of general public interest.

. . . Pickering's letter was written after the defeat at the polls of the second proposed tax increase. It could, therefore, have had no effect on the ability of the school district to raise necessary revenue, since there was no showing that there was any proposal to increase taxes pending when the letter was written.

More importantly, the question whether a school system requires additional funds is a matter of legitimate public concern on which the judgment of the school administration, including the School Board, cannot, in a society that leaves such questions to popular vote, be taken as conclusive. On such a question free and open debate is vital to informed decisionmaking by the electorate. Teachers are, as a class, the members of a community most likely to have informed and definite opinions as to how funds allotted to the operation of the schools should be spent. Accordingly, it is essential that they be able to speak out freely on such questions without fear of retaliatory dismissal.

. . . The Board could easily have rebutted appellant's errors by publishing the accurate figures itself, either via a letter to the same newspaper or otherwise. . . .

. . . [W]e conclude that the interest of the school administration in limiting teachers' opportunities to contribute to public debate is not significantly greater than its interest in limiting a similar contribution by any member of the general public.

. . .

. . . [I]t is apparent that the threat of dismissal from public employment is nonetheless a potent means of inhibiting speech. . . . in a case such as the present one, in which the fact of employment is only tangentially and insubstantially involved in the subject matter of the public communication made by a teacher, we conclude that it is necessary to regard the teacher as the member of the general public he seeks to be.

. . . [H]is dismissal for writing it cannot be upheld and the judgment of the Illinois Supreme Court must, accordingly, be reversed and the case remanded for further proceedings not inconsistent with this opinion.

Golden v. Zwickler
394 U.S. 103 (1969)

This case was here before as *Zwickler v. Koota*. We there held that the three-judge District Court for the Eastern District of New York erred in abstaining from deciding whether Zwickler, appellee in the instant case, was entitled to a declaratory judgment respecting the constitutionality of New York Penal Law §781–b, now New York Election Law §457, and we remanded to the District Court for a determination of that question. . . .

. . .

The District Court . . . held that the prerequisites of a declaratory judgment had been established by the facts alleged in the complaint, and that the fact that the Congressman who was the original target of the handbills would not again stand for reelection did not affect the question. . . .

. . .

We think that, under all the circumstances of the case, the fact that it was most unlikely that the Congressman would again be a candidate for Congress precluded a finding that there was "sufficient immediacy and reality" here. The allegations of the complaint focus upon the then forthcoming 1966 election, when, it was alleged, the Congressman would again stand for reelection. The anonymous handbills which the complaint identified as to be distributed in the 1966 and subsequent elections were the 1964 handbill and "similar anonymous leaflets." On the record, therefore, the only supportable conclusion was that Zwickler's sole concern was literature relating to the Congressman and his record. Since the New York statute's prohibition of anonymous handbills applies only to handbills directly pertaining to election campaigns, and the prospect was neither real nor immediate of a campaign involving the Congressman, it was wholly conjectural that another occasion might arise when Zwickler might be prosecuted for distributing the handbills referred to in the complaint. His assertion in his brief that the former Congressman can be "a candidate for Congress again" is hardly a substitute for evidence that this is a prospect of "immediacy and reality." . . .

. . .

We conclude that Zwickler did not establish the existence at the time of the hearing on the remand of the elements governing the issuance of a declaratory judgment, and therefore that the District Court should have dismissed his complaint. We accordingly intimate no view upon the correctness of the District Court's holding as to the constitutionality of the New York statute. The judgment of the District Court is reversed, and the case is remanded with direction to enter a new judgment dismissing the complaint.

James v. Valtierra
402 U.S. 137 (1971)

These cases raise but a single issue. It grows out of the United States Housing Act of 1937, which established a federal housing agency authorized to make loans and grants to state agencies for slum clearance and low-rent housing projects. In response, the California Legislature created in each county and city a public housing authority to take advantage of the financing made available by the federal Housing Act. At the time the federal legislation was passed, the California Constitution had for many years reserved to the State's people the power to initiate legislation and to reject or approve by referendum any Act passed by the state legislature. The same section reserved to the electors of counties and cities the power of initiative and referendum over acts of local government bodies. In 1950, however, the State Supreme Court held that local authorities' decisions on seeking federal aid for public housing projects were "executive" and "administrative," not "legislative," and therefore the state constitution's referendum provisions did not apply to these actions. Within six months of that decision, the California voters adopted Article XXXIV of the state constitution to bring public housing decisions under the State's referendum policy. The Article provided that no low-rent housing project should be developed, constructed, or acquired in any manner by a state public body until the project was approved by a majority of those voting at a community election.

The present suits were brought by citizens of San Jose, California, and San Mateo County, localities where housing authorities could not apply for federal funds because low-cost housing proposals had been defeated in referendums. The plaintiffs, who are eligible for low-cost public housing, sought a declaration that Article XXXIV was unconstitutional because its referendum requirement violated: (1) the Supremacy Clause of the United States Constitution; (2) the Privileges and Immunities Clause; and (3) the Equal Protection Clause. A three-judge court held that Article XXXIV denied the plaintiffs equal protection of the laws, and it enjoined its enforcement. Two appeals were taken from the judgment, one by the San Jose City Council and the other by a single member of the council. . . .

The three-judge court found the Supremacy

Clause argument unpersuasive, and we agree. . . . We also find the privileges and immunities argument without merit.

. . .

California's entire history demonstrates the repeated use of referendums to give citizens a voice on questions of public policy. A referendum provision was included in the first state constitution, and referendums have been a commonplace occurrence in the State's active political life. Provisions for referendums demonstrate devotion to democracy, not to bias, discrimination, or prejudice. Nonetheless, appellees contend that Article XXXIV denies them equal protection because it demands a mandatory referendum, while many other referendums only take place upon citizen initiative. They suggest that the mandatory nature of the Article XXXIV referendum constitutes unconstitutional discrimination, because it hampers persons desiring public housing from achieving their objective when no such roadblock faces other groups seeking to influence other public decisions to their advantage. But, of course, a lawmaking procedure that "disadvantages" a particular group does not always deny equal protection. Under any such holding, presumably a State would not be able to require referendums on any subject unless referendums were required on all, because they would always disadvantage some group. And this Court would be required to analyze governmental structures to determine whether a gubernatorial veto provision or a filibuster rule is likely to "disadvantage" any of the diverse and shifting groups that make up the American people.

Furthermore, an examination of California law reveals that persons advocating low income housing have not been singled out for mandatory referendums while no other group must face that obstacle. Mandatory referendums are required for approval of state constitutional amendments, for the issuance of general obligation long-term bonds by local governments, and for certain municipal territorial annexations. California statute books contain much legislation first enacted by voter initiative, and no such law can be repealed or amended except by referendum. Some California cities have wisely provided that their public parks may not be alienated without mandatory referendums.

The people of California have also decided by their own vote to require referendum approval of low-rent public housing projects. This procedure ensures that all the people of a community will have a voice in a decision which may lead to large expenditures of local governmental funds for increased public services and to lower tax revenues. It gives them a voice in decisions that will affect the future development of their own community. This procedure for democratic decisionmaking does not violate the constitutional command that no State shall deny to any person "the equal protection of the laws."

The judgment of the three-judge court is reversed, and the cases are remanded for dismissal of the complaint.

Laird v. Tatum
408 U.S. 1 (1972)

Respondents brought this class action in the District Court seeking declaratory and injunctive relief on their claim that their rights were being invaded by the Department of the Army's alleged "surveillance of lawful and peaceful civilian political activity." . . . In connection with respondents' motion for a preliminary injunction and petitioners' motion to dismiss the complaint, both parties filed a number of affidavits with the District Court and presented their oral arguments at a hearing on the two motions. . . . [T]he District Court granted petitioners' motion to dismiss, holding that there was no justiciable claim for relief.

. . . [A] divided Court of Appeals reversed, and ordered the case remanded. . . .

. . .

The President is authorized by 10 U.S.C. §331 to make use of the armed forces to quell insurrection and other domestic violence if and when the conditions described in that section obtain within one of the States. Pursuant to those provisions, President Johnson ordered federal troops to assist local authorities at the time of the civil disorders in Detroit, Michigan, in the summer of 1967 and during the disturbances that followed the assassination of Dr. Martin Luther King. Prior to the Detroit disorders, the Army had a general contingency plan for providing such assistance to local authorities, but the 1967 experience led Army authorities to believe that more attention should be given to such preparatory planning. The data-gathering system here involved is said to have been established in connection with the development of more detailed and specific contingency planning designed to permit the Army, when called upon to assist local authorities, to be able to respond effectively with a minimum of force. . . .

The system put into operation as a result of the Army's 1967 experience consisted essentially of the collection of information about public activities that were thought to have at least some potential for civil disorder, the reporting of that information to Army Intelligence headquarters at Fort Holabird, Maryland, the dissemination of these reports from headquarters to major Army posts around the country, and the storage of the reported information in a computer data bank located at Fort Holabird. The information itself

was collected by a variety of means, but it is significant that the principal sources of information were the news media and publications in general circulation. Some of the information came from Army Intelligence agents who attended meetings that were open to the public and who wrote field reports describing the meetings, giving such data as the name of the sponsoring organization, the identity of speakers, the approximate number of persons in attendance, and an indication of whether any disorder occurred. And still other information was provided to the Army by civilian law enforcement agencies.

. . .

By early 1970, Congress became concerned with the scope of the Army's domestic surveillance system; hearings on the matter were held before the Subcommittee on Constitutional Rights of the Senate Committee on the Judiciary. . . .

. . .

. . . It was the view of the District Court that respondents failed to allege any action on the part of the Army that was unlawful in itself, and further failed to allege any injury or any realistic threats to their rights growing out of the Army's actions.

In reversing, the Court of Appeals noted that respondents "have some difficulty in establishing visible injury." . . .

. . .

. . . The respondents . . . disagree with the judgments made by the Executive Branch with respect to the type and amount of information the Army needs, and that the very existence of the Army's data-gathering system produces a constitutionally impermissible chilling effect upon the exercise of their First Amendment rights. That alleged "chilling" effect may perhaps be seen as arising from respondents' very perception of the system as inappropriate to the Army's role under our form of government, or as arising from respondents' beliefs that it is inherently dangerous for the military to be concerned with activities in the civilian sector, or as arising from respondents' less generalized yet speculative apprehensiveness that the Army may at some future date misuse the information in some way that would cause direct harm to respondents. Allegations of a subjective "chill" are not an adequate substitute for a claim of specific present objective harm or a threat of specific future harm; "the federal courts established pursuant to Article III of the Constitution do not render advisory opinions."

Stripped to its essentials, what respondents appear to be seeking is a broad-scale investigation, conducted by themselves as private parties armed with the subpoena power of a federal district court and the power of cross-examination, to probe into the Army's intelligence gathering activities, with the district court determining at the conclusion of that investigation the extent to which those activities may or may not be appropriate to the Army's mission. . . .

Carried to its logical end, this approach would have the federal courts as virtually continuing monitors of the wisdom and soundness of Executive action; such a role is appropriate for the Congress acting through its committees and the "power of the purse"; it is not the role of the judiciary, absent actual present or immediately threatened injury resulting from unlawful governmental action.

. . .

. . . Indeed, when presented with claims of judicially cognizable injury resulting from military intrusion into the civilian sector, federal courts are fully empowered to consider claims of those asserting such injury; there is nothing in our Nation's history or in this Court's decided cases, including our holding today, that can properly be seen as giving any indication that actual or threatened injury by reason of unlawful activities of the military would go unnoticed or unremedied.

Reversed.

United States Civil Service Commission v. National Association of Letter Carriers
413 U.S. 548 (1973)

. . . Section 7324(a) provides:

> An employee in an Executive agency or an individual employed by the government of the District of Columbia may not—
> (1) use his official authority or influence for the purpose of interfering with or affecting the result of an election; or
> (2) take an active part in political management or in political campaigns.

. . . A divided three-judge court sitting in the District of Columbia had held the section unconstitutional. . . .

The case began when the National Association of Letter Carriers, six individual federal employees and certain local Democratic and Republican political committees filed a complaint, asserting on behalf of themselves and all federal employees that §7324(a)(2) was unconstitutional on its face and seeking an injunction against its enforcement.

. . .

. . . The District Court then ruled that §7324(a)(2) was unconstitutional on its face and enjoined its enforcement. . . . The District Court ruled, however, that *United Public Workers v. Mitchell*, left open the constitutionality of the statutory definition of "political activity," and proceeded to hold that definition to be both vague and overbroad, and therefore unconstitutional and unenforceable against the plaintiffs in any respect. . . .

. . .

We unhesitatingly reaffirm the *Mitchell* holding that Congress had, and has, the power to prevent Mr. Poole and others like him from holding a party office, working at the polls, and acting as party paymaster for other party workers. An Act of Congress going no farther would, in our view, unquestionably be valid. So would it be if, in plain and understandable language, the statute forbade activities such as organizing a political party or club; actively participating in fund-raising activities for a partisan candidate or political party; becoming a partisan candidate for, or campaigning for, an elective public office; actively managing the campaign of a partisan candidate for public office; initiating or circulating a partisan nominating petition or soliciting votes for a partisan candidate for public office; or serving as a delegate, alternate or proxy to a political party convention. Our judgment is that neither the First Amendment nor any other provision of the Constitution invalidates a law barring this kind of partisan political conduct by federal employees. Such decision on our part would no more than confirm the judgment of history, a judgment made by this country over the last century that it is in the best interest of the country, indeed essential, that federal service should depend upon meritorious performance rather than political service, and that the political influence of federal employees on others and on the electoral process should be limited. That this judgment eventuated is indisputable, and the major steps in reaching it may be simply and briefly set down.

. . .

It seems fundamental in the first place that employees in the Executive Branch of the Government, or those working for any of its agencies, should administer the law in accordance with the will of Congress, rather than in accordance with their own or the will of a political party. They are expected to enforce the law and execute the programs of the Government without bias or favoritism for or against any political party or group or the members thereof. A major thesis of the Hatch Act is that to serve this great end of Government—the impartial execution of the laws—it is essential that federal employees, for example, not take formal positions in political parties, not undertake to play substantial roles in partisan political campaigns, and not run for office on partisan political tickets. Forbidding activities like these will reduce the hazards to fair and effective government.

There is another consideration in this judgment: it is not only important that the Government and its employees in fact, avoid practicing political justice, but it is also critical that they appear to the public to be avoiding it, if confidence in the system of representative Government is not to be eroded to a disastrous extent.

. . .

A related concern, and this remains as important as any other, was to further serve the goal that employment and advancement in the Government service not depend on political performance, and, at the same time, to make sure that Government employees would be free from pressure and from express or tacit invitation to vote in a certain way or perform political chores in order to curry favor with their superiors, rather than to act out their own beliefs. It may be urged that prohibitions against coercion are sufficient protection; but, for many years, the joint judgment of the Executive and Congress has been that, to protect the rights of federal employees with respect to their jobs and their political acts and beliefs, it is not enough merely to forbid one employee to attempt to influence or coerce an-other. . . . Perhaps Congress at some time will come to a different view of the realities of politi-cal life and Government service; but that is its current view of the matter, and we are not now in any position to dispute it. Nor, in our view, does the Constitution forbid it.

Neither the right to associate nor the right to participate in political activities is absolute in any event. Nor are the management, financing, and conduct of political campaigns wholly free from governmental regulation. . . .

. . .

Even if the provisions forbidding partisan cam-paign endorsements and speechmaking were to be considered, in some respects, unconstitutionally overbroad, we would not invalidate the entire stat-ute as the District Court did. The remainder of the statute, as we have said, covers a whole range of easily identifiable and constitutionally proscribable partisan conduct on the part of federal employees, and the extent to which pure expression is imper-missibly threatened, if at all, by §§733.122(a)(10) and (12), does not, in our view, make the statute substantially overbroad, and so invalid on its face.

For the foregoing reasons, the judgment of the District Court is reversed.

Broadrick v. Oklahoma
413 U.S. 601 (1973)

Section 818 of Oklahoma's Merit System of Per-sonnel Administration Act, restricts the political activities of the State's classified civil servants in much the same manner that the Hatch Act pro-scribes partisan political activities of federal employees. Three employees of the Oklahoma Corporation Commission who are subject to the proscriptions of §818 seek to have two of its para-graphs declared unconstitutional on their face and enjoined because of asserted vagueness and over-breadth. After a hearing, the District Court up-held the provisions and denied relief. . . .

. . . The section serves roughly the same func-tion as the analogous provisions of the other 49 States, and is patterned on §9(a) of the Hatch Act. Without question, a broad range of political activi-ties and conduct is proscribed by the section. . . . Violation of §818 results in dismissal from em-ployment and possible criminal sanctions and limited state employment ineligibility.

. . . [A]ppellants maintain that however per-missible, even commendable, the goals of §818 may be, its language is unconstitutionally vague and its prohibitions too broad in their sweep, failing to dis-tinguish between conduct that may be proscribed and conduct that must be permitted. . . .

We have held today that the Hatch Act is not impermissibly vague. We have little doubt that §818 is similarly not so vague that "men of com-mon intelligence must necessarily guess at its meaning." Whatever other problems there are with §818, it is all but frivolous to suggest that the section fails to give adequate warning of what ac-tivities it proscribes or fails to set out "explicit stan-dards" for those who must apply it. In the plainest language, it prohibits any state classified em-ployee from being "an officer or member" of a "partisan political club" or a candidate for "any paid public office." It forbids solicitation of contribu-tions "for any political organization, candidacy or other political purpose" and taking part "in the management or affairs of any political party or in any political campaign." Words inevitably contain germs of uncertainty and, as with the Hatch Act, there may be disputes over the meaning of such terms in §818 as "partisan," or "take part in," or "affairs of" political parties. . . . [E]ven if the outer-most boundaries of §818 may be imprecise, any such uncertainty has little relevance here, where appellants' conduct falls squarely within the "hard core" of the statute's proscriptions and appellants concede as much.

. . .

The judgment of the District Court is affirmed.

Town of Lockport v. Citizens for Community Action at the Local Level, Inc.
430 U.S. 259 (1977)

New York law provides that a new county charter will go into effect only if it is approved in a referendum election by separate majorities of the voters who live in the cities within the county, and of those who live outside the cities. A three-judge Federal District Court held that these requirements violate the Equal Protection Clause of the Fourteenth Amendment. . . .

County government in New York has traditionally taken the form of a single-branch legislature, exercising general governmental powers. General governmental powers are also exercised by the county's constituent cities, villages, and towns. The allocation of powers among these subdivisions can be changed, and a new form of county government adopted, pursuant to referendum procedures specified in Art. IX of the New York Constitution and implemented by §33 of the Municipal Home Rule Law. Under those procedures, a county board of supervisors may submit a proposed charter to the voters for approval. If a majority of the voting city dwellers and a majority of the voting noncity dwellers both approve, the charter is adopted.

In November 1972, a proposed charter for the county of Niagara was put to referendum. The charter created the new offices of County Executive and County Comptroller, and continued the county's existing power to establish tax rates, equalize assessments, issue bonds, maintain roads, and administer health and public welfare services. No explicit provision for redistribution of governmental powers from the cities or towns to the county government was made. The city voters approved the charter by a vote of 18,220 to 14,914. The noncity voters disapproved the charter by a vote of 11,594 to 10,665. A majority of those voting in the entire county thus favored the charter.

The appellees, a group of Niagara County voters, filed suit . . . in the United States District Court for the Western District of New York, seeking a declaration that the New York constitutional and statutory provisions governing adoption of the charter form of county government are unconstitutional, and an order directing the appropriate New York officials to file the Niagara County charter as a duly enacted local law. A three-judge court was convened. Before its decision was announced, however, another new charter was put to referendum in Niagara County in November, 1974. Again a majority of the city dwellers who voted approved the charter, a majority of the noncity voters disapproved it, and an aggregate majority of all those in the county who voted approved it. The District Court subsequently found the concurrent majority requirements of the New York Constitution and the New York Municipal Home Rule Law violative of the Equal Protection Clause of the Fourteenth Amendment, and ordered implementation of the 1972 Charter. On appeal, this Court vacated that judgment and remanded the cause "for reconsideration in light of the provisions of [the] new charter adopted by Niagara County in 1974." In subsequent proceedings on remand, the District Court found that there was "no substantial difference between the two Charters," and that the

1974 County Charter had superseded the 1972 Charter. Pursuant to its previous constitutional adjudication, the court decreed that the 1974 Charter "is in full force and effect as the instrument defining the form of local government for Niagara County."

. . .

The equal protection principles applicable in gauging the fairness of an election involving the choice of legislative representatives are of limited relevance, however, in analyzing the propriety of recognizing distinctive voter interests in a "single-shot" referendum. In a referendum, the expression of voter will is direct, and there is no need to assure that the voters' views will be adequately represented through their representatives in the legislature. The policy impact of a referendum is also different in kind from the impact of choosing representatives—instead of sending legislators off to the state capitol to vote on a multitude of issues, the referendum puts one discrete issue to the voters. That issue is capable, at least, of being analyzed to determine whether its adoption or rejection will have a disproportionate impact on an identifiable group of voters. If it is found to have such a disproportionate impact, the question then is whether a State can recognize that impact either by limiting the franchise to those voters specially affected or by giving their votes a special weight. This question has been confronted by the Court in two types of cases: those dealing with elections involving "special-interest" governmental bodies of limited jurisdiction, and those dealing with bond referenda.

. . .

The argument that the provisions of New York law in question here are unconstitutional rests primarily on the premise that all voters in a New York county have identical interests in the adoption or rejection of a new charter, and that any distinction, therefore, between voters drawn on the basis of residence and working to the detriment of an identifiable class is an invidious discrimination. If the major premise were demonstrably correct—if it were clear that all voters in Niagara County have substantially identical interests in the adoption of a new county charter, regardless of where they reside within the county—the District Court's judgment would have to be affirmed under our prior cases. That major premise, however, simply cannot be accepted. To the contrary, it appears that the challenged provisions of New York law rest on the State's identification of the distinctive interests of the residents of the cities and towns within a county, rather than their interests as residents of the county as a homogeneous unit. This identification is based in the realities of the distribution of governmental powers in New York, and is consistent with our cases that recognize both the wide discretion the States have in forming and allocating governmental tasks to local subdivisions and the discrete interests that such local governmental units may have qua units.

. . .

. . . [I]n terms of recognizing constituencies with separate and potentially opposing interests, the structural decision to annex or consolidate is similar in impact to the decision to restructure county government in New York. In each case, separate voter approval requirements are based on the perception that the real and long-term impact of a restructuring of local government is felt quite differently by the different county constituent units that, in a sense, compete to provide similar governmental services. Voters in these constituent units are directly and differentially affected by the restructuring of county government, which may make the provider of public services more remote and less subject to the voters' individual influence.

The provisions of New York law here in question no more than recognize the realities of these substantially differing electoral interests. Granting to these provisions the presumption of constitutionality to which every duly enacted state and federal law is entitled, we are unable to conclude that they violate the Equal Protection Clause of the Fourteenth Amendment.

For the reasons stated in this opinion, the judgment is reversed.

First National Bank of Boston v. Bellotti
435 U.S. 765 (1978)

In sustaining a state criminal statute that forbids certain expenditures by banks and business corporations for the purpose of influencing the vote on referendum proposals, the Massachusetts Supreme Judicial Court held that the First Amendment rights of a corporation are limited to issues that materially affect its business, property, or assets. The court rejected appellants' claim that the statute abridges freedom of speech in violation of the First and Fourteenth Amendments. . . .

. . .

Section 8 permits a corporation to communicate to the public its views on certain referendum subjects—those materially affecting its business—but not others. It also singles out one kind of ballot question—individual taxation—as a subject about which corporations may never make their ideas public. The legislature has drawn the line between permissible and impermissible speech according to whether there is a sufficient

nexus, as defined by the legislature, between the issue presented to the voters and the business interests of the speaker.

In the realm of protected speech, the legislature is constitutionally disqualified from dictating the subjects about which persons may speak and the speakers who may address a public issue. If a legislature may direct business corporations to "stick to business," it also may limit other corporations—religious, charitable, or civic—to their respective "business" when addressing the public. Such power in government to channel the expression of views is unacceptable under the First Amendment. Especially where, as here, the legislature's suppression of speech suggests an attempt to give one side of a debatable public question an advantage in expressing its views to the people, the First Amendment is plainly offended. Yet the State contends that its action is necessitated by governmental interests of the highest order. . . .

. . .

. . . Referenda are held on issues, not candidates for public office. The risk of corruption perceived in cases involving candidate elections, simply is not present in a popular vote on a public issue. . . .

. . .

The overinclusiveness of the statute is demonstrated by the fact that §8 would prohibit a corporation from supporting or opposing a referendum proposal even if its shareholders unanimously authorized the contribution or expenditure. Ultimately shareholders may decide, through the procedures of corporate democracy, whether their corporation should engage in debate on public issues. . . .

. . .

Because that portion of §8 challenged by appellants prohibits protected speech in a manner unjustified by a compelling state interest, it must be invalidated. The judgment of the Supreme Judicial Court is reversed.

Brown v. Glines
444 U.S. 348 (1980)

Albert Glines was a captain in the Air Force Reserves. While on active duty at the Travis Air Force Base in California, he drafted petitions to several Members of Congress and to the Secretary of Defense complaining about the Air Force's grooming standards. Aware that he needed command approval in order to solicit signatures within a base, Glines at first circulated the petitions outside his base. During a routine training flight through the Anderson Air Force Base in Guam, however, Glines gave the petitions to an Air Force sergeant without seeking approval from the base commander. The sergeant gathered eight signatures before military authorities halted the unauthorized distribution. Glines' commander promptly removed him from active duty, determined that he had failed to meet the professional standards expected of an officer, and reassigned him to the standby reserves. Glines then brought suit in the United States District Court for the Northern District of California claiming that the Air Force regulations requiring prior approval for the circulation of petitions violated the First Amendment and 10 U.S.C. §1034. The court granted Glines' motion for summary judgment and declared the regulations facially invalid.

The Court of Appeals for the Ninth Circuit affirmed. . . .

. . .

The only novel question in this case is whether 10 U.S.C. §1034 bars military regulations that require prior command approval for the circula-

tion within a military base of petitions to Members of Congress. The statute says that

> [n]o person may restrict any member of an armed force in communicating with a member of Congress, unless the communication is unlawful or violates a regulation necessary to the security of the United States.

Glines contends that this law protects the circulation of his collective petitions as well as the forwarding of individual communications. We find his contention unpersuasive.

. . .

We conclude that neither the First Amendment nor 10 U.S.C. §1034 prevents the Air Force from requiring members of the service to secure approval from the base commander before distributing petitions within a military base. We therefore hold that the regulations at issue in this case are not invalid on their face. Accordingly, the judgment of the Court of Appeals is reversed.

Secretary of the Navy v. Huff
444 U.S. 453 (1980)

In 1974, Frank L. Huff, Robert A. Falatine, and Robert E. Gabrielson were serving in the Marine Corps at the United States Marine Corps Air Station in Iwakuni, Japan. On separate occasions, each of them sought the base commander's permission to circulate a petition addressed to a Member of Congress. The petitions dealt with the use of military forces in labor disputes within the United States, amnesty for men who resisted the draft or deserted the Armed Forces during the Vietnam war, and United States support for the Government of South Korea. The first two requests proposed circulation within the base; the last proposed circulation both within and without the base. The commander denied the first two requests, but he allowed the petition about South Korea to circulate within the base.

On another occasion, Huff and Falatine each asked to distribute a leaflet annotating the Declaration of Independence and the First Amendment with commentary critical of military commanders who restrict petitioning. The base commander denied Falatine's request on the ground that the commentary was disrespectful and contemptuous, but on the same day, and without explanation, he granted Huff leave to distribute the same material. Finally, respondents Huff and Falatine were arrested for circulating outside the base a petition to a Member of Congress that objected to American support for the Government of South Korea. They were charged with violating regulations because they had circulated the petition without requesting command approval. Huff was convicted and sentenced to confinement, forfeiture of half-pay, and reduction in grade. The charges against Falatine were dismissed for lack of evidence.

The respondents then brought a class action in the United States District Court for the District of Columbia, seeking declaratory and injunctive relief against future enforcement of four Navy and Marine Corps regulations. . . .

The respondents contended that this requirement violated 10 U.S.C. §1034 and the First Amendment. . . .

On cross-motions for summary judgment, the court declared the regulations invalid with respect to materials distributed within the base during off-duty hours and away from restricted or work areas. The court upheld the regulations with respect to distributions outside the base. . . . The petitioners appealed, but the respondents did not cross-appeal.

The Court of Appeals for the District of Columbia Circuit affirmed in part and vacated in part. It concluded that the only real controversy between the parties concerned the application of the challenged regulations to petitions addressing Members of Congress. The court therefore considered only the validity of the regulations as they affect circulation within the base of petitions to Congress. It held that requiring prior command approval for the circulation of such petitions violated 10 U.S.C. §1034. . . .

. . .

. . . In *Glines* . . . we held that §1034 does not invalidate regulations requiring members of the Armed Forces to secure command approval before circulating petitions within a military base.

Since the Court of Appeals reached a contrary conclusion in this case, its judgment is reversed.

California Medical Association v. Federal Elections Commission
453 U.S. 182 (1981)

The California Medical Association (CMA) is a not-for-profit unincorporated association of approximately 25,000 doctors residing in California. In 1976, CMA formed the California Medical Political Action Committee (CALPAC). CALPAC is registered as a political committee with the Federal Election Commission, and is subject to the provisions of the Federal Election Campaign Act relating to multicandidate political committees. One such provision prohibits individuals and unincorporated associations such as CMA from contributing more than $5,000 per calendar year to any multicandidate political committee such as CALPAC. A related provision of the Act makes it unlawful for political committees such as CALPAC knowingly to accept contributions exceeding this limit.

In October, 1978, the Federal Election Commission found "reason to believe" that CMA had violated the Act by making annual contributions to CALPAC in excess of $5,000, and that CALPAC had unlawfully accepted such contributions. When informal conciliation efforts failed, the Commission, in April 1979 authorized its staff to institute a civil enforcement action against CMA and CALPAC to secure compliance with the contribution limitations of the Act. In early May, 1979, after receiving formal notification of the Commission's impending enforcement action, CMA and CALPAC, together with two individual members of these organizations, filed this declaratory judgment action in the United States District Court for the Northern District of California challenging the constitutionality of the statutory contribution limitations upon which the Commission's enforcement action was to be based. Several weeks later, the Commission filed its enforcement action in the same District Court. In this second suit, CMA and CALPAC pleaded as affirmative defenses the same constitutional claims raised in their declaratory judgment action.

. . . [T]he District Court certified the constitutional questions raised in appellants' declaratory judgment action to the Court of Appeals for the Ninth Circuit. . . . In May 1980, a divided Court of Appeals, sitting en banc, rejected appellants' constitutional claims and upheld the $5,000 limit on annual contributions by unincorporated associations to multicandidate political committees. . . .

. . .

Appellants' First Amendment claim is based largely on . . . *Buckley v. Valeo*. . . .

. . .

. . . The type of expenditures that this Court in *Buckley* considered constitutionally pro-

tected were those made independently by a candidate, individual, or group in order to engage directly in political speech. Nothing in §441a(a)(1)(C) limits the amount CMA or any of its members may independently expend in order to advocate political views; rather, the statute restrains only the amount that CMA may contribute to CALPAC. Appellants nonetheless insist that CMA's contributions to CALPAC should receive the same constitutional protection as independent expenditures because, according to appellants, this is the manner in which CMA has chosen to engage in political speech.

We would naturally be hesitant to conclude that CMA's determination to fund CALPAC rather than to engage directly in political advocacy is entirely unprotected by the First Amendment. Nonetheless, the "speech by proxy" that CMA seeks to achieve through its contributions to CALPAC is not the sort of political advocacy that this Court in *Buckley* found entitled to full First Amendment protection. CALPAC, as a multicandidate political committee, receives contributions from more than fifty persons during a calendar year. Thus, appellants' claim that CALPAC is merely the mouthpiece of CMA is untenable. CALPAC, instead, is a separate legal entity that receives funds from multiple sources and that engages in independent political advocacy. Of course, CMA would probably not contribute to CALPAC unless it agreed with the views espoused by CALPAC, but this sympathy of interests alone does not convert CALPAC's speech into that of CMA.

. . .

. . . If the First Amendment rights of a contributor are not infringed by limitations on the amount he may contribute to a campaign organization which advocates the views and candidacy of a particular candidate, the rights of a contributor are similarly not impaired by limits on the amount he may give to a multicandidate political committee. . . .

We also disagree with appellants' claim that the contribution restriction challenged here does not further the governmental interest in preventing the actual or apparent corruption of the political process. Congress enacted §441a(a)(1)(C) in part to prevent circumvention of the very limitations on contributions that this Court upheld in *Buckley*. Under the Act, individuals and unincorporated associations such as CMA may not contribute more than $1,000 to any single candidate in any calendar year. Moreover, individuals may not make more than $25,000 in aggregate annual political contributions. If appellants' position— that Congress cannot prohibit individuals and unincorporated associations from making unlimited contributions to multicandidate political committees—is accepted, then both these contribution limitations could be easily evaded. Since multicandidate political committees may contribute up to $5,000 per year to any candidate, an individual or association seeking to evade the $1,000 limit on contributions to candidates could do so by channelling funds through a multicandidate political committee. Similarly, individuals could evade the $25,000 limit on aggregate annual contributions to candidates if they were allowed to give unlimited sums to multicandidate political committees, since such committees are not limited in the aggregate amount they may contribute in any year. These concerns prompted Congress to enact §441a(a)(1)(C), and it is clear that this provision is an appropriate means by which Congress could seek to protect the integrity of the contribution restrictions upheld by this Court in *Buckley*.

. . .

. . . Appellants' claim of unfair treatment ignores the plain fact that the statute as a whole imposes far fewer restrictions on individuals and unincorporated associations than it does on corporations and unions. Persons subject to the restrictions of §441a(a)(1)(C) may make unlimited expenditures on political speech; corporations and unions, however, may make only the limited contributions authorized by §441b(b)(2). Furthermore, individuals and unincorporated associations may contribute to candidates, to candidates' committees, to national party committees and to all other political committees, while corporations and unions are absolutely barred from making any such contributions. In addition, multicandidate political committees are generally unrestricted in the manner and scope of their solicitations; the segregated funds that unions and corporations may establish pursuant to §441b(b)(2)(C) are carefully limited in this regard. The differing restrictions placed on individuals and unincorporated associations, on the one hand, and on unions and corporations, on the other, reflect a judgment by Congress that these entities have differing structures and purposes, and that they therefore may require different forms of regulation in order to protect the integrity of the electoral process. Appellants do not challenge any of the restrictions on the corporate and union political activity, yet these restrictions entirely undermine appellants' claim that, because of §441a(a)(1)(C), the Act discriminates against individuals and unincorporated associations in the exercise of their First Amendment rights.

Accordingly, we conclude that the $5,000 limitation on the amount that persons may contribute to multicandidate political committees violates neither the First nor the Fifth Amendment. The judgment of the Court of Appeals is therefore affirmed.

Citizens Against Rent Control/Coalition for Fair Housing v. City of Berkeley, California
454 U.S. 290 (1981)

The voters of Berkeley, California, adopted the Election Reform Act of 1974, by initiative. The campaign ordinance so enacted placed limits on expenditures and contributions in campaigns involving both candidates and ballot measures. Section 602 of the ordinance provides:

> No person shall make, and no campaign treasurer shall solicit or accept, any contribution which will cause the total amount contributed by such person with respect to a single election in support of or in opposition to a measure to exceed two hundred and fifty dollars ($250).

Appellant Citizens Against Rent Control is an unincorporated association formed to oppose a ballot measure at issue in the April 19, 1977, election. The ballot measure would have imposed rent control on many of Berkeley's rental units. To make its views on the ballot measure known, Citizens Against Rent Control raised more than $108,000 from approximately 1,300 contributors. It accepted nine contributions over the $250 limit. Those nine contributions totaled $20,850, or $18,600 more than if none of the contributions exceeded $250. Pursuant to §604 of the ordinance, appellee Berkeley Fair Campaign Practices Commission, 20 days before the election, ordered appellant Citizens Against Rent Control to pay $18,600 into the city treasury.

Two weeks before the election, Citizens Against Rent Control sought and obtained a temporary restraining order prohibiting enforcement of §§602 and 604. The ballot measure relating to rent control was defeated. The Superior Court subsequently granted Citizens Against Rent Control's motion for summary judgment, declaring that §602 was invalid on its face because it violated the First Amendment of the United States Constitution and Art. I, §2, of the California Constitution. A panel of the California Court of Appeal unanimously affirmed that conclusion.

The California Supreme Court . . . reversed. . . .

. . .

The Court has long viewed the First Amendment as protecting a marketplace for the clash of different views and conflicting ideas. That concept has been stated and restated almost since the Constitution was drafted. The voters of the city of Berkeley adopted the challenged ordinance which places restrictions on that marketplace. It is irrelevant that the voters, rather than a legislative body, enacted §602, because the voters may no more violate the Constitution by enacting a ballot measure than a legislative body may do so by enacting legislation.

. . .

. . . Under the Berkeley ordinance, an affluent person can, acting alone, spend without limit to advocate individual views on a ballot measure. It is only when contributions are made in concert with one or more others in the exercise of the right of association that they are restricted by §602.

. . .

. . . [T]he city of Berkeley argues that §602 is necessary as a prophylactic measure to make known the identity of supporters and opponents of ballot measures. It is true that, when individuals or corporations speak through committees, they often adopt seductive names that may tend to conceal the true identity of the source. Here, there is no risk that the Berkeley voters will be in doubt as to the identity of those whose money supports or opposes a given ballot measure, since contributors must make their identities known under §112 of the ordinance, which requires publication of lists of contributors in advance of the voting.

Contributions by individuals to support concerted action by a committee advocating a position on a ballot measure is, beyond question, a very significant form of political expression. . . . The public interest allegedly advanced by §602—identifying the sources of support for and opposition to ballot measures—is insubstantial, because voters may identify those sources under the provisions of §112. In addition, the record in this case does not support the California Supreme Court's conclusion that §602 is needed to preserve voters' confidence in the ballot measure process. It is clear, therefore, that §602 does not advance a legitimate governmental interest significant enough to justify its infringement of First Amendment rights.

. . . As we have noted, an individual may make expenditures without limit under §602 on a ballot measure, but may not contribute beyond the $250 limit when joining with others to advocate common views. The contribution limit thus automatically affects expenditures, and limits on expenditures operate as a direct restraint on freedom of expression of a group or committee desiring to engage in political dialogue concerning a ballot measure.

Whatever may be the state interest or degree of that interest in regulating and limiting contributions to or expenditures of a candidate or a candidate's committees, there is no significant state or public interest in curtailing debate and discussion of a ballot measure. Placing limits on contributions, which, in turn, limits expenditures, plainly impairs freedom of expression. The integrity of the political system will be adequately protected if contributors are identified in a public filing revealing the amounts contributed; if it

is thought wise, legislation can outlaw anonymous contributions.

A limit on contributions in this setting need not be analyzed exclusively in terms of the right of association or the right of expression. The two rights overlap and blend; to limit the right of association places an impermissible restraint on the right of expression. The restraint imposed by the Berkeley ordinance on rights of association and, in turn, on individual and collective rights of expression plainly contravenes both the right of association and the speech guarantees of the First Amendment. Accordingly, the judgment of the California Supreme Court is reversed, and the case is remanded for proceedings not inconsistent with this opinion.

Federal Election Commission v. National Right to Work Committee
459 U.S. 197 (1982)

The question in the case ultimately comes down to whether respondent National Right to Work Committee (NRWC or respondent) limited its solicitation of funds to "members" within the meaning of 2 U.S.C. §441b(b)(4)(C).

In April 1977, petitioner Federal Election Commission (Commission) determined that there was probable cause to believe that NRWC had violated the above-cited provisions of the Act by soliciting contributions from persons who were not its "members." Shortly thereafter, respondent filed a complaint in the United States District Court for the Eastern District of Virginia seeking injunctive and declaratory relief against the Commission. . . . [T]he Commission filed an enforcement proceeding against respondent in the United States District Court for the District of Columbia. . . . The actions were consolidated in the latter court, which granted summary judgment in favor of the Commission. . . . The judgment of the District Court was reversed by the Court of Appeals for the District of Columbia Circuit. . . .

Respondent NRWC is a nonprofit corporation without capital stock organized under the laws of the Commonwealth of Virginia. . . . In 1975, respondent's predecessor and another corporation merged; the articles of merger filed in the District of Columbia by the successor corporation stated that NRWC "shall not have members." A similar statement is contained in the articles of incorporation of NRWC that are presently filed in Virginia. Likewise, respondent's bylaws make no reference to members or to membership in the corporation. . . .

In late 1975, in order to comply with §441b, NRWC established a separate segregated fund "to receive and make contributions on behalf of federal candidates." The fund was denominated the "Employees Rights Campaign Committee" (ERCC); its operation was completely subsidized from the NRWC treasury, which paid all the expenses of establishing and administering the fund, and of soliciting contributions. During part of 1976, NRWC sent letters to some 267,000 individuals, who had at one time contributed to it, soliciting contributions to ERCC. As a result of these solicitations, the fund received some $77,000 in contributions.

In October, 1976, another lobbying group, the Committee for an Effective Congress, filed a complaint against ERCC with the Commission, alleging violation of 2 U.S.C. §441b(b)(4). The complaint asserted that NRWC had violated this section of the Act by using corporate funds to solicit contributions to ERCC from persons who were not NRWC's stockholders, executive or administrative personnel, or their families.

NRWC did not deny these assertions, but took the position that the recipients of its solicitation letters were "members" of NRWC within the proviso set forth in §441b(b)(4)(C). The Commission found probable cause to believe that a violation had occurred, and after completing the investigative procedures set out in the statute and unsuccessfully attempting to resolve the matter through conciliation, it authorized the filing of a civil enforcement suit. . . .

Essential to the proper resolution of the case is the interpretation of §441b(b)(4)(C)'s statement that the prohibition against corporate solicitation contained in §441b(b)(4)(A) shall not prevent

> a . . . corporation without capital stock . . . from soliciting contributions to [a separate segregated fund established by a corporation without capital stock] from members of such . . . corporation. . . .

The Court of Appeals rejected the Commission's contentions regarding the meaning of "member," and went on to hold that the term "embraces at least those individuals whom NRWC describes as its active and supporting members." . . .

The statutory purpose of §441b . . . is to prohibit contributions or expenditures by corporations or labor organizations in connection with federal elections. The section, however, permits some participation of unions and corporations in the federal electoral process by allowing them to establish and pay the administrative expenses of "separate segregated fund[s]," which may be "utilized for political purposes." . . . Finally . . . the section just quoted has its own proviso, which states in pertinent part that

> [t]his paragraph shall not prevent a . . . corporation without capital stock, or a separate segregated fund established by a . . . corporation without capital stock, from soliciting contributions to such a fund from members of the sponsoring corporation. The

effect of this proviso is to limit solicitation by non-profit corporations to those persons attached in some way to it by its corporate structure.

The Court of Appeals . . . construed the term "member" in §441b to embrace "at least those individuals whom NRWC describes as its active and supporting members." . . .

. . .

. . . The Court of Appeals' determination that NRWC's "members" include anyone who has responded to one of the corporation's essentially random mass mailings would, we think, open the door to all but unlimited corporate solicitation, and thereby render meaningless the statutory limitation to "members."

. . .

Applying the statutory language . . . we think Congress did not intend to allow the 267,000 individuals solicited by NRWC during 1976 to come within the exclusion for "members" in 2 U.S.C. §441b(b)(4)(C). Although membership cards are ultimately sent to those who either contribute or respond in some other way to respondent's mailings, the solicitation letters themselves make no reference to members. Members play no part in the operation or administration of the corporation; they elect no corporate officials, and indeed there are apparently no membership meetings. There is no indication that NRWC's asserted members exercise any control over the expenditure of their contributions. Moreover, as previously noted, NRWC's own articles of incorporation and other publicly filed documents explicitly disclaimed the existence of members. We think that, under these circumstances, those solicited were insufficiently attached to the corporate structure of NRWC to qualify as "members" under the statutory proviso.

. . .

. . . [W]e conclude that the associational rights

asserted by respondent may be and are overborne by the interests Congress has sought to protect in enacting §441b.

. . .

To accept the view that a solicitation limited only to those who have in the past proved "philosophically compatible" to the views of the corporation must be permitted under the statute in order for the prohibition to be constitutional would ignore the teachings of our earlier decisions. The governmental interest in preventing both actual corruption and the appearance of corruption of elected representatives has long been recognized, and there is no reason why it may not in this case be accomplished by treating unions, corporations, and similar organizations differently from individuals.

. . . There may be more than one way under the statute to go about determining who are "members" of a nonprofit corporation, and the statute may leave room for uncertainty at the periphery of its exception for solicitation of "members." However, on this record, we are satisfied that NRWC's activities extended in large part, if not in toto, to people who would not be members under any reasonable interpretation of the statute.

The judgment of the Court of Appeals is reversed.

Regan v. Taxation With Representation of Washington
461 U.S. 540 (1983)

Appellee Taxation With Representation of Washington (TWR) is a nonprofit corporation organized to promote what it conceives to be the "public interest" in the area of federal taxation. It proposes to advocate its point of view before Congress, the Executive Branch, and the Judiciary. This case began when TWR applied for tax-exempt status under §501(c)(3) of the Internal Revenue Code. The Internal Revenue Service denied the application because it appeared that a substantial part of TWR's activities would consist of attempting to influence legislation, which is not permitted by §501(c)(3).

TWR then brought this suit in District Court against the appellants, the Commissioner of Internal Revenue, the Secretary of the Treasury, and the United States, seeking a declaratory judgment that it qualifies for the exemption granted by §501(c)(3). It claimed the prohibition against substantial lobbying is unconstitutional under the First Amendment and the equal protection component of the Fifth Amendment's Due Process Clause. The District Court granted summary judgment for appellants. On appeal, the en banc Court of Appeals for the District of Columbia Circuit reversed, holding that §501(c)(3) does not violate the First Amendment but does violate the Fifth Amendment. . . .

TWR was formed to take over the operations of two other nonprofit corporations. One, Taxation With Representation Fund, was organized to promote TWR's goals by publishing a journal and engaging in litigation; it had tax-exempt status under §501(c)(3). The other, Taxation With Representation, attempted to promote the same goals by influencing legislation; it had tax-exempt status under §501(c)(4). Neither predecessor organization was required to pay federal income taxes. For purposes of our analysis, there are two principal differences between §501(c)(3) organizations and §501(c)(4) organizations. Taxpayers who contribute to §501(c)(3) organizations are permitted by §170(c)(2) to deduct the amount of their contributions on their federal income tax returns, while contributions to §501(c)(4) organizations are not deductible. Section 501(c)(4) organizations, but not §501(c)(3) organizations,

are permitted to engage in substantial lobbying to advance their exempt purposes.

In these cases, TWR is attacking the prohibition against substantial lobbying in §501(c)(3) because it wants to use tax deductible contributions to support substantial lobbying activities. To evaluate TWR's claims, it is necessary to understand the effect of the tax exemption system enacted by Congress.

Both tax exemptions and tax deductibility are a form of subsidy that is administered through the tax system. A tax exemption has much the same effect as a cash grant to the organization of the amount of tax it would have to pay on its income. Deductible contributions are similar to cash grants of the amount of a portion of the individual's contributions. The system Congress has enacted provides this kind of subsidy to nonprofit civic welfare organizations generally, and an additional subsidy to those charitable organizations that do not engage in substantial lobbying. In short, Congress chose not to subsidize lobbying as extensively as it chose to subsidize other activities that nonprofit organizations undertake to promote the public welfare.

It appears that TWR could still qualify for a tax exemption under §501(c)(4). It also appears that TWR can obtain tax-deductible contributions for its nonlobbying activity by returning to the dual structure it used in the past, with a §501(c)(3) organization for nonlobbying activities and a §501(c)(4) organization for lobbying. TWR would, of course, have to ensure that the §501(c)(3) organization did not subsidize the §501(c)(4) organization; otherwise, public funds might be spent on an activity Congress chose not to subsidize.

TWR contends that Congress' decision not to subsidize its lobbying violates the First Amendment. . . .

... The Code does not deny TWR the right to receive deductible contributions to support its nonlobbying activity, nor does it deny TWR any independent benefit on account of its intention to lobby. Congress has merely refused to pay for the lobbying out of public moneys. This Court has never held that Congress must grant a benefit such as TWR claims here to a person who wishes to exercise a constitutional right.

. . .

TWR also contends that the equal protection component of the Fifth Amendment renders the prohibition against substantial lobbying invalid. TWR points out that §170(c)(3) permits taxpayers to deduct contributions to veterans' organizations that qualify for tax exemption under §501(c)(19). Qualifying veterans' organizations are permitted to lobby as much as they want in furtherance of their exempt purposes. TWR argues that, because Congress has chosen to subsidize the substantial lobbying activities of veterans' organizations, it must also subsidize the lobbying of §501(c)(3) organizations.

Generally, statutory classifications are valid if they bear a rational relation to a legitimate governmental purpose. Statutes are subjected to a higher level of scrutiny if they interfere with the exercise of a fundamental right, such as freedom of speech, or employ a suspect classification, such as race. Legislatures have especially broad latitude in creating classifications and distinctions in tax statutes. . . .

. . .

... [T]he veterans' organizations that qualify under §501(c)(19) are entitled to receive tax-deductible contributions regardless of the content of any speech they may use, including lobbying. We find no indication that the statute was intended to suppress any ideas, or any demonstration that it has had that effect. The sections of the Internal Revenue Code here at issue do not employ any suspect classification. The distinction between veterans' organizations and other charitable organizations is not at all like distinctions based on race or national origin.

. . .

We have no doubt but that this statute is within Congress' broad power in this area. TWR contends that §501(c)(3) organizations could better advance their charitable purposes if they were permitted to engage in substantial lobbying. This may well be true. But Congress—not TWR or this Court—has the authority to determine whether the advantage the public would receive from additional lobbying by charities is worth the money the public would pay to subsidize that lobbying, and other disadvantages that might accompany that lobbying. It appears that Congress was concerned that exempt organizations might use tax-deductible contributions to lobby to promote the private interests of their members. It is not irrational for Congress to decide that tax-exempt charities such as TWR should not further benefit at the expense of taxpayers at large by obtaining a further subsidy for lobbying.

It is also not irrational for Congress to decide that, even though it will not subsidize substantial lobbying by charities generally, it will subsidize lobbying by veterans' organizations. Veterans have "been obliged to drop their own affairs to take up the burdens of the nation," "subjecting themselves to the mental and physical hazards as well as the economic and family detriments which are peculiar to military service and which do not exist in normal civil life." . . .

The issue in these cases is not whether TWR must be permitted to lobby, but whether Congress is required to provide it with public money with which to lobby. For the reasons stated above, we hold that it is not. Accordingly, the judgment of the Court of Appeals is reversed.

Members of the City Council of the City of Los Angeles v. Taxpayers for Vincent
466 U.S. 789 (1984)

Section 28.04 of the Los Angeles Municipal Code prohibits the posting of signs on public property. . . . In March 1979, Roland Vincent was a candidate for election to the Los Angeles City Council. A group of his supporters known as Taxpayers for Vincent (Taxpayers) entered into a contract with a political sign service company known as Candidates' Outdoor Graphics Service (COGS) to fabricate and post signs with Vincent's name on them. COGS produced 15- by 44-inch cardboard signs and attached them to utility poles at various locations by draping them over crosswires which support the poles and stapling the cardboard together at the bottom. The signs' message was: "Roland Vincent—City Council."

Acting under the authority of §28.04 of the Municipal Code, employees of the city's Bureau of Street Maintenance routinely removed all posters attached to utility poles and similar objects covered by the ordinance, including the COGS signs. The weekly sign removal report covering the period March 1–March 7, 1979, indicated that among the 1,207 signs removed from public property during that week, 48 were identified as "Roland Vincent" signs. Most of the other signs identified in that report were apparently commercial in character.

On March 12, 1979, Taxpayers and COGS filed this action in the United States District Court for the Central District of California, naming the city, the Director of the Bureau of Street Maintenance, and members of the City Council as defendants.

They sought an injunction against enforcement of the ordinance, as well as compensatory and punitive damages. After engaging in discovery, the parties filed cross-motions for summary judgment on the issue of liability. The District Court entered findings of fact, concluded that the ordinance was constitutional, and granted the City's motion.

. . .

In addition, the District Court found that placing signs on utility poles creates a potential safety hazard, and that other violations of §28.04 "block views and otherwise cause traffic hazards." . . .

In its conclusions of law, the District Court characterized the esthetic and economic interests in improving the beauty of the City "by eliminating clutter and visual blight" as "legitimate and compelling." Those interests, together with the interest in protecting the safety of workmen who must scale utility poles and the interest in eliminating traffic hazards, adequately supported the sign prohibition as a reasonable regulation affecting the time, place, and manner of expression.

The Court of Appeals did not question any of the District Court's findings of fact, but it rejected some of its conclusions of law. The Court of Appeals reasoned that the ordinance was presumptively unconstitutional because significant First Amendment interests were involved. . . . The Court of Appeals held that the City had failed to make a sufficient showing that its asserted interests in esthetics and preventing visual clutter were substantial, because it had not offered to demonstrate that the City was engaged in a comprehensive effort to remove other contributions to an unattractive environment in commercial and industrial areas. The City's interest in minimizing traffic hazards was rejected because it was readily apparent that no substantial traffic problems would result from permitting the posting of certain kinds of signs on many of the publicly owned objects covered by the ordinance. Finally, while acknowledging that a flat prohibition against signs on certain objects such as fire hydrants and traffic signals would be a permissible method of preventing interference with the intended use of public property, and that regulation of the size, design, and construction of posters, or of the method of removing them, might be reasonable, the Court of Appeals concluded that the City had not justified its total ban.

. . .

The Court of Appeals concluded that the ordinance was vulnerable to an overbreadth challenge because it was an "overinclusive" response to traffic concerns, and not the "least drastic means" of preventing interference with the normal use of public property. This conclusion rested on an evaluation of the assumed effect of the ordinance on third parties, rather than on any specific consideration of the impact of the ordinance on the parties before the court. This is not, however, an appropriate case to entertain a facial challenge based on overbreadth. For we have found nothing in the record to indicate that the ordinance will have any different impact on any third parties' interests in free speech than it has on Taxpayers and COGS.

. . .

It is well settled that the state may legitimately exercise its police powers to advance esthetic values. . . .

. . .

. . . Here, the substantive evil—visual blight— is not merely a possible byproduct of the activity, but is created by the medium of expression itself. . . . [T]herefore, the application of the ordinance in this case responds precisely to the substantive problem which legitimately concerns the City. The ordinance curtails no more speech than is necessary to accomplish its purpose.

. . .

. . . The Los Angeles ordinance does not affect any individual's freedom to exercise the right to speak and to distribute literature in the same place where the posting of signs on public property is prohibited. To the extent that the posting of signs on public property has advantages over these forms of expression, there is no reason to believe that these same advantages cannot be obtained through other means. To the contrary, the findings of the District Court indicate that there are ample alternative modes of communication in Los Angeles. Notwithstanding appellees' general assertions in their brief concerning the utility of political posters, nothing in the findings indicates that the posting of political posters on public property is a uniquely valuable or important mode of communication, or that appellees' ability to communicate effectively is threatened by ever-increasing restrictions on expression.

. . .

. . . [T]he esthetic interests that are implicated by temporary signs are presumptively at work in all parts of the city, including those where appellees posted their signs, and there is no basis in the record in this case upon which to rebut that presumption. These interests are both psychological and economic. The character of the environment affects the quality of life and the value of property in both residential and commercial areas. We hold that, on this record, these interests are sufficiently substantial to justify this content-neutral, impartially administered prohibition against the posting of appellees' temporary signs on public property, and that such an application of the ordinance does not create an unacceptable threat to the "profound national commitment to the principle that debate on public issues should be uninhibited, robust, and wide-open."

The judgment of the Court of Appeals is reversed, and the case is remanded to that Court.

Pacific Gas & Electric Co. v. Public
Utilities Commission of California
475 U.S. 1 (1986)

For the past sixty-two years, appellant Pacific Gas and Electric Company has distributed a newsletter in its monthly billing envelope. Appellant's newsletter, called Progress, reaches over three million customers. It has included political editorials, feature stories on matters of public interest, tips on energy conservation, and straightforward information about utility services and bills.

In 1980, appellee Toward Utility Rate Normalization (TURN), an intervenor in a ratemaking proceeding before California's Public Utilities Commission, another appellee, urged the Commission to forbid appellant to use the billing envelopes to distribute political editorials, on the ground that appellant's customers should not bear the expense of appellant's own political speech. The Commission decided that the envelope space that appellant had used to disseminate Progress is the property of the ratepayers. . . .

. . .

Appellant appealed the Commission's order to the California Supreme Court, arguing that it has a First Amendment right not to help spread a message with which it disagrees, and that the Commission's order infringes that right. The California Supreme Court denied discretionary review. . . .

. . .

. . . The order does not simply award access to the public at large; rather, it discriminates on the basis of the viewpoints of the selected speakers. Two of the acknowledged purposes of the access order are to offer the public a greater variety of views in appellant's billing envelope and to assist groups (such as TURN) that challenge appellant in the Commission's

ratemaking proceedings in raising funds. Access to the envelopes thus is not content-neutral. The variety of views that the Commission seeks to foster cannot be obtained by including speakers whose speech agrees with appellant's. Similarly, the perceived need to raise funds to finance participation in ratemaking proceedings exists only where the relevant groups represent interests that diverge from appellant's interests. Access is limited to persons or groups—such as TURN—who disagree with appellant's views as expressed in Progress, and who oppose appellant in Commission proceedings.

. . .

. . . Where, as in this case, the danger is one that arises from a content-based grant of access to private property, it is a danger that the government may not impose absent a compelling interest.

The Commission has emphasized that appellant's customers own the "extra space" in the billing envelopes. According to appellees, it follows that appellant cannot have a constitutionally protected interest in restricting access to the envelopes. This argument misperceives both the relevant property rights and the nature of the State's First Amendment violation.

The Commission expressly declined to hold that, under California law, appellant's customers own the entire billing envelopes and everything contained therein. It decided only that the ratepayers own the "extra space" in the envelope, defined as that space left over after including the bill and required notices, up to a weight of one ounce. The envelopes themselves, the bills, and Progress all remain appellant's property. The Commission's access order thus clearly requires appellant to use its property as a vehicle for spreading a message with which it disagrees. . . . [T]he Commission's order requires appellant to use its property—the billing envelopes—to distribute the message of another. This is so whoever is deemed to own the "extra space."

. . .

We conclude that the Commission's order impermissibly burdens appellant's First Amendment rights because it forces appellant to associate with the views of other speakers, and because it selects the other speakers on the basis of their viewpoints. The order is not a narrowly tailored means of furthering a compelling state interest, and it is not a valid time, place, or manner regulation.

For these reasons, the decision of the California Public Utilities Commission must be vacated. The case is remanded to the California Supreme Court for further proceedings not inconsistent with this opinion.

Federal Election Commission v. Massachusetts Citizens for Life, Inc. 479 U.S. 238 (1986)

The questions for decision here arise under §316 of the Federal Election Campaign Act (FECA or Act), as renumbered and amended. The first question is whether appellee Massachusetts Citizens for Life, Inc. (MCFL), a nonprofit, nonstock corporation, by financing certain activity with its treasury funds, has violated the restriction on independent spending contained in §441b. That section prohibits corporations from using treasury funds to make an expenditure "in connection with" any federal election, and requires that any expenditure for such purpose be financed by voluntary contributions to a separate segregated fund. If appellee has violated §441b, the next question is whether application of that section to MCFL's conduct is constitutional. . . .

MCFL was incorporated in January 1973, as a nonprofit, nonstock corporation under Massachusetts law. . . . MCFL does not accept contributions from business corporations or unions. Its resources come from voluntary donations from "members," and from various fundraising activities such as garage sales, bake sales, dances, raffles, and picnics. The corporation considers its "members" those persons who have either contributed to the organization in the past or indicated support for its activities.

. . .

MCFL began publishing a newsletter in January 1973. It was distributed as a matter of course to contributors, and, when funds permitted, to noncontributors who had expressed support for the organization. The total distribution of any one issue has never exceeded 6,000. The newsletter was published irregularly from 1973 through 1978. . . . Each of the newsletters bore a masthead identifying it as the "Massachusetts Citizens for Life Newsletter," as well as a volume and issue number. The publication typically contained appeals for volunteers and contributions and information on MCFL activities, as well as on matters such as the results of hearings on bills and constitutional amendments, the status of particular legislation, and the outcome of referenda, court decisions, and administrative hearings. Newsletter recipients were usually urged to contact the relevant decisionmakers and express their opinion.

In September 1978, MCFL prepared and distributed a "Special Edition" prior to the September 1978 primary elections. While the May 1978 newsletter had been mailed to 2,109 people, and the October 1978 newsletter to 3,119 people, more than 100,000 copies of the "Special Edition" were printed for distribution. The front page of the publication was headlined "EVERYTHING YOU NEED TO KNOW TO VOTE PRO-LIFE," and readers were admonished that "[n]o pro-life candidate can win in November without your vote in September." "VOTE PRO-LIFE" was printed in large bold-faced letters on the back page, and a coupon was provided to be clipped and taken to the polls to remind voters of the name of the "pro-life" candidates. Next to the exhortation to vote "pro-life" was a disclaimer: "This special election edition does not represent an endorsement of any particular candidate."

. . .

The "Special Edition" was edited by an officer of MCFL who was not part of the staff that prepared the MCFL newsletters. The "Special Edition" was mailed free of charge and without request to 5,986 contributors, and to 50,674 others whom MCFL regarded as sympathetic to the organization's purposes. The Commission asserts that the remainder of the 100,000 issues were placed in public areas for general distribution, but MCFL insists that no copies were made available to the general public. The "Special Edition" was not identified on its masthead as a special edition of the regular newsletter, although the MCFL logotype did appear at its top. . . . The corporation spent $9,812.76 to publish and circulate the "Special Edition," all of which was taken from its general treasury funds.

A complaint was filed with the Commission alleging that the "Special Edition" was a violation of §441b. The complaint maintained that the Edition represented an expenditure of funds from a corporate treasury to distribute to the general public a campaign flyer on behalf of certain political candidates. The FEC found reason to believe that such a violation had occurred, initiated an investigation, and determined that probable cause existed to believe that MCFL had violated the Act. After conciliation efforts failed, the Commission filed a complaint in the District Court

under §437g(a)(6)(A), seeking a civil penalty and other appropriate relief.

Both parties moved for summary judgment. The District Court granted MCFL's motion, holding that: (1) the election publications could not be regarded as "expenditures" under §441b(b)(2); (2) the "Special Edition" was exempt from the statutory prohibition by virtue of §431(9)(B)(i), which in general exempts news commentary distributed by a periodical publication unaffiliated with any candidate or political party; and (3) if the statute applied to MCFL, it was unconstitutional as a violation of the First Amendment.

On appeal, the Court of Appeals for the First Circuit held that the statute was applicable to MCFL, but affirmed the District Court's holding that the statute, as so applied, was unconstitutional. . . .

We agree with the Court of Appeals that the "Special Edition" is not outside the reach of §441b. First, we find no merit in appellee's contention that preparation and distribution of the "Special Edition" does not fall within that section's definition of "expenditure." Section 441b(b)(2) defines "contribution or expenditure" as the provision of various things of value "to any candidate, campaign committee, or political party or organization, in connection with any election. . . ." MCFL contends that, since it supplied nothing to any candidate or organization, the publication is not within §441b. However, the general definitions section of the Act contains a broader definition of "expenditure." . . .

. . .

. . . We . . . hold that an expenditure must constitute "express advocacy" in order to be subject to the prohibition of §441b. We also hold, however, that the publication of the "Special Edition" constitutes "express advocacy."

Buckley adopted the "express advocacy" requirement to distinguish discussion of issues and candidates from more pointed exhortations to vote for particular persons. We therefore concluded in that case that a finding of "express advocacy" depended upon the use of language such as "vote for," "elect," "support," etc. Just such an exhortation appears in the "Special Edition." The publication not only urges voters to vote for "pro-life" candidates, but also identifies and provides photographs of specific candidates fitting that description. The Edition cannot be regarded as a mere discussion of public issues that by their nature raise the names of certain politicians. Rather, it provides, in effect, an explicit directive: vote for these (named) candidates. The fact that this message is marginally less direct than "Vote for Smith" does not change its essential nature. The Edition goes beyond issue discussion to express electoral advocacy. The disclaimer of endorsement cannot negate this fact. The "Special Edition" thus falls squarely within §441b, for it represents express advocacy of the election of particular candidates distributed to members of the general public.

. . .

MCFL maintains that its regular newsletter is a "periodical publication" . . . and that the "Special Edition" should be regarded as just another issue in the continuing newsletter series. . . . We need not decide whether the regular MCFL newsletter is exempt under this provision, because, even assuming that it is, the "Special Edition" cannot be considered comparable to any single issue of the newsletter. It was not published through the facilities of the regular newsletter, but by a staff which prepared no previous or subsequent newsletters. It was not distributed to the newsletter's regular audience, but to a group 20 times the size of that audience, most of whom were members of the public who had never received the

newsletter. No characteristic of the Edition associated it in any way with the normal MCFL publication. The MCFL masthead did not appear on the flyer, and, despite an apparent belated attempt to make it appear otherwise, the Edition contained no volume and issue number identifying it as one in a continuing series of issues.

MCFL protests that determining the scope of the press exemption by reference to such factors inappropriately focuses on superficial considerations of form. However, it is precisely such factors that, in combination, permit the distinction of campaign flyers from regular publications. We regard such an inquiry as essential, since we cannot accept the notion that the distribution of such flyers by entities that happen to publish newsletters automatically entitles such organizations to the press exemption. . . .

. . .

The FEC minimizes the impact of the legislation upon MCFL's First Amendment rights by emphasizing that the corporation remains free to establish a separate segregated fund, composed of contributions earmarked for that purpose by the donors, that may be used for unlimited campaign spending. However, the corporation is not free to use its general funds for campaign advocacy purposes. While that is not an absolute restriction on speech, it is a substantial one. Moreover, even to speak through a segregated fund, MCFL must make very significant efforts.

. . .

Because it is incorporated . . . MCFL must establish a "separate segregated fund" if it wishes to engage in any independent spending whatsoever. Since such a fund is considered a "political committee" under the Act, all MCFL independent expenditure activity is, as a result, regulated as though the organization's major purpose is to further the election of candidates. This means that

MCFL must comply with several requirements in addition to those mentioned. . . .

. . .

It is evident from this survey that MCFL is subject to more extensive requirements and more stringent restrictions than it would be if it were not incorporated. These additional regulations may create a disincentive for such organizations to engage in political speech. Detailed record-keeping and disclosure obligations, along with the duty to appoint a treasurer and custodian of the records, impose administrative costs that many small entities may be unable to bear. Furthermore, such duties require a far more complex and formalized organization than many small groups could manage. Restriction of solicitation of contributions to "members" vastly reduces the sources of funding for organizations with either few or no formal members, directly limiting the ability of such organizations to engage in core political speech. It is not unreasonable to suppose that, as in this case, an incorporated group of like-minded persons might seek donations to support the dissemination of their political ideas and their occasional endorsement of political candidates, by means of garage sales, bake sales, and raffles. Such persons might well be turned away by the prospect of complying with all the requirements imposed by the Act. Faced with the need to assume a more sophisticated organizational form, to adopt specific accounting procedures, to file periodic detailed reports, and to monitor garage sales lest nonmembers take a fancy to the merchandise on display, it would not be surprising if at least some groups decided that the contemplated political activity was simply not worth it.

Thus, while §441b does not remove all opportunities for independent spending by organizations such as MCFL, the avenue it leaves open is more burdensome than the one it forecloses. The fact that the statute's practical effect may be to discourage protected speech is sufficient to characterize §441b as an infringement on First Amendment activities. . . .

. . .

Direct corporate spending on political activity raises the prospect that resources amassed in the economic marketplace may be used to provide an unfair advantage in the political marketplace. Political "free trade" does not necessarily require that all who participate in the political marketplace do so with exactly equal resources. Relative availability of funds is, after all, a rough barometer of public support. The resources in the treasury of a business corporation, however, are not an indication of popular support for the corporation's political ideas. They reflect instead the economically motivated decisions of investors and customers. The availability of these resources may make a corporation a formidable political presence, even though the power of the corporation may be no reflection of the power of its ideas.

By requiring that corporate independent expenditures be financed through a political committee expressly established to engage in campaign spending, §441b seeks to prevent this threat to the political marketplace. The resources available to this fund, as opposed to the corporate treasury, in fact reflect popular support for the political positions of the committee. . . . The expenditure restrictions of §441b are thus meant to ensure that competition among actors in the political arena is truly competition among ideas.

. . .

. . . [I]ndividuals contribute to a political organization in part because they regard such a contribution as a more effective means of advocacy than spending the money under their own personal direction. Any contribution therefore necessarily involves at least some degree of delegation of authority to use such funds in a manner that best serves the shared political purposes of the organization and contributor. . . . [A] contributor dissatisfied with how funds are used can simply stop contributing.

. . .

Finally, the FEC maintains that the inapplicability of §441b to MCFL would open the door to massive undisclosed political spending by similar entities, and to their use as conduits for undisclosed spending by business corporations and unions. We see no such danger. Even if §441b is inapplicable, an independent expenditure of as little as $250 by MCFL will trigger the disclosure provisions of §434(c). As a result, MCFL will be required to identify all contributors who annually provide in the aggregate $200 in funds intended to influence elections, will have to specify all recipients of independent spending amounting to more than $200, and will be bound to identify all persons making contributions over $200 who request that the money be used for independent expenditures. These reporting obligations provide precisely the information necessary to monitor MCFL's independent spending activity and its receipt of contributions. The state interest in disclosure therefore can be met in a manner less restrictive than imposing the full panoply of regulations that accompany status as a political committee under the Act.

Furthermore, should MCFL's independent spending become so extensive that the organization's major purpose may be regarded as campaign activity, the corporation would be classified as a political committee. As such, it would automatically be subject to the obligations and restrictions applicable to those groups whose primary objective is to influence political campaigns. In sum, there is no need for the sake of disclosure

to treat MCFL any differently than other organizations that only occasionally engage in independent spending on behalf of candidates.

. . . Voluntary political associations do not suddenly present the specter of corruption merely by assuming the corporate form. . . .

. . .

. . . Some corporations have features more akin to voluntary political associations than business firms, and therefore should not have to bear burdens on independent spending solely because of their incorporated status.

. . .

. . . Where at all possible, government must curtail speech only to the degree necessary to meet the particular problem at hand, and must avoid infringing on speech that does not pose the danger that has prompted regulation. In enacting the provision at issue in this case, Congress has chosen too blunt an instrument for such a delicate task.

The judgment of the Court of Appeals is affirmed.

Meyer v. Grant
486 U.S. 414 (1988)

In Colorado, the proponents of a new law, or an amendment to the State Constitution, may have their proposal placed on the ballot at a general election if they can obtain enough signatures of qualified voters on an "initiative petition" within a 6-month period. One section of the state law regulating the initiative process makes it a felony to pay petition circulators. The question in this case is whether that provision is unconstitutional. The Court of Appeals for the Tenth Circuit, sitting en banc, held that the statute abridged appellees' right to engage in political speech, and therefore violated the First and Fourteenth Amendments to the Federal Constitution. . . .

. . .

State law requires that the persons who circulate the approved drafts of the petitions for signature be registered voters. Before the signed petitions are filed with the Secretary of State, the circulators must sign affidavits attesting that each signature is the signature of the person whose name it purports to be and that, to the best of their knowledge and belief, each person signing the petition is a registered voter. The payment of petition circulators is punished as a felony.

Appellees are proponents of an amendment to the Colorado Constitution that would remove motor carriers from the jurisdiction of the Colorado Public Utilities Commission. In early 1984, they obtained approval of a title, submission clause, and summary for a measure proposing the amendment, and began the process of obtaining the 46,737 signatures necessary to have the proposal appear on the November 1984 ballot. Based on their own experience as petition circulators, as well as that of other unpaid circulators, appellees concluded that they would need the assistance of paid personnel to obtain the required number of signatures within the allotted time. They then brought this action . . . against the Secretary of State and the Attorney General of Colorado, seeking a declaration that the statutory prohibition against the use of paid circulators violates their rights under the First Amendment.

. . . [T]he District Judge entered judgment upholding the statute on alternative grounds. . . .

. . . [T]he Court of Appeals affirmed for the reasons stated by the District Court. After granting rehearing en banc, however, the court reversed. . . .

. . .

The circulation of an initiative petition of necessity involves both the expression of a desire for political change and a discussion of the merits of the proposed change. Although a petition circulator may not have to persuade potential signatories that a particular proposal should prevail to capture their signatures, he or she will at least have to persuade them that the matter is one deserving of the public scrutiny and debate that would attend its consideration by the whole electorate. This will in almost every case involve an explanation of the nature of the proposal and why its advocates support it. Thus, the circulation of a petition involves the type of interactive communication concerning political change that is appropriately described as "core political speech."

The refusal to permit appellees to pay petition circulators restricts political expression in two ways: First, it limits the number of voices who will convey appellees' message and the hours they can speak and, therefore, limits the size of the audience they can reach. Second, it makes it less likely that appellees will garner the number of signatures necessary to place the matter on the ballot, thus limiting their ability to make the matter the focus of statewide discussion. The Colorado Supreme Court has itself recognized that the prohibition against the use of paid circulators has the inevitable effect of reducing the total quantum of speech on a public issue. . . .

. . .

. . . Colorado's prohibition of paid petition circulators restricts access to the most effective, fundamental, and perhaps economical avenue of political discourse, direct one-on-one communication. That it leaves open "more burdensome" avenues of communication, does not relieve its burden on First Amendment expression. The First Amendment protects appellees' right not only to advocate their cause, but also to select what they believe to be the most effective means for so doing.

. . .

We are not persuaded by the State's arguments that the prohibition is justified by its interest in making sure that an initiative has sufficient grass roots support to be placed on the ballot, or by its interest in protecting the integrity of the initiative process. As the Court of Appeals correctly held, the former interest is adequately protected by the requirement that no initiative proposal may be placed on the ballot unless the required number of signatures has been obtained.

The State's interest in protecting the integrity of the initiative process does not justify the prohibition because the State has failed to demonstrate that it is necessary to burden appellees' ability to communicate their message in order to meet its concerns. The Attorney General has argued that the petition circulator has the duty to verify the authenticity of signatures on the petition and that compensation might provide the circulator with a temptation to disregard that duty. No evidence has been offered to support that speculation, however, and we are not prepared to assume that a professional circulator—whose qualifications for similar future assignments may well depend on a reputation for competence and integrity—is any more likely to accept false signatures than a volunteer who is motivated entirely by an interest in having the proposition placed on the ballot.

Other provisions of the Colorado statute deal expressly with the potential danger that circulators might be tempted to pad their petitions with false signatures. It is a crime to forge a signature on a petition, to make false or misleading statements relating to a petition, or to pay someone to sign a petition. Further, the top of each page of the petition must bear a statement printed in red ink warning potential signatories that it is a felony to forge a signature on a petition or to sign the petition when not qualified to vote and admonishing signatories not to sign the petition unless

they have read and understand the proposed initiative. These provisions seem adequate to the task of minimizing the risk of improper conduct in the circulation of a petition, especially since the risk of fraud or corruption, or the appearance thereof, is more remote at the petition stage of an initiative than at the time of balloting. . . .

. . . The Colorado statute prohibiting the payment of petition circulators imposes a burden on political expression that the State has failed to justify. The Court of Appeals correctly held that the statute violates the First and Fourteenth Amendments. Its judgment is therefore affirmed.

Austin v. Michigan Chamber of Commerce
494 U.S. 652 (1990)

In this appeal, we must determine whether §54(1) of the Michigan Campaign Finance Act violates either the First or the Fourteenth Amendment to the Constitution. Section 54(1) prohibits corporations from using corporate treasury funds for independent expenditures in support of or in opposition to any candidate in elections for state office. Corporations are allowed, however, to make such expenditures from segregated funds used solely for political purposes. In response to a challenge brought by the Michigan State Chamber of Commerce, the Sixth Circuit held that §54(1) could not be applied to the Chamber, a Michigan nonprofit corporation, without violating the First Amendment. . . .

Section 54(1) of the Michigan Campaign Finance Act prohibits corporations from making contributions and independent expenditures in connection with state candidate elections. The issue before us is only the constitutionality of the State's ban on independent expenditures. . . .

The Michigan State Chamber of Commerce, a nonprofit Michigan corporation, challenges the constitutionality of this statutory scheme. The Chamber comprises more than 8,000 members, three-quarters of whom are for-profit corporations. The Chamber's general treasury is funded through annual dues required of all members. . . .

In June 1985, Michigan scheduled a special election to fill a vacancy in the Michigan House of Representatives. Although the Chamber had established and funded a separate political fund, it sought to use its general treasury funds to place in a local newspaper an advertisement supporting a specific candidate. As the Act made such an expenditure punishable as a felony, the Chamber brought suit in District Court for injunctive relief against enforcement of the Act, arguing that the restriction on expenditures is unconstitutional under both the First and the Fourteenth Amendments.

The District Court upheld the statute. The Sixth Circuit reversed, reasoning that the expenditure restrictions, as applied to the Chamber, violated the First Amendment. . . .

To determine whether Michigan's restrictions on corporate political expenditures may constitutionally be applied to the Chamber, we must ascertain whether they burden the exercise of political speech and, if they do, whether they are narrowly tailored to serve a compelling state interest. Certainly, the use of funds to support a political candidate is "speech" independent campaign expenditures constitute "political expression 'at the core of our electoral process and of the First Amendment freedoms.'" The mere fact that the Chamber is a corporation does not remove its speech from the ambit of the First Amendment.

. . .

Despite the Chamber's success in adminis-

tering its separate political fund, Michigan's segregated fund requirement still burdens the Chamber's exercise of expression because "the corporation is not free to use its general funds for campaign advocacy purposes." . . . [A] nonprofit corporation like the Chamber may solicit contributions to its political fund only from members, stockholders of members, officers or directors of members, and the spouses of any of these persons. Although these requirements do not stifle corporate speech entirely, they do burden expressive activity. . . .

. . .

The Chamber argues that this concern about corporate domination of the political process is insufficient to justify restrictions on independent expenditures. Although this Court has distinguished these expenditures from direct contributions in the context of federal laws regulating individual donors, it has also recognized that a legislature might demonstrate a danger of real or apparent corruption posed by such expenditures when made by corporations to influence candidate elections. Regardless of whether this danger of "financial quid pro quo" corruption, may be sufficient to justify a restriction on independent expenditures, Michigan's regulation aims at a different type of corruption in the political arena: the corrosive and distorting effects of immense aggregations of wealth that are accumulated with the help of the corporate form and that have little or no correlation to the public's support for the corporation's political ideas. The Act does not attempt "to equalize the relative influence of speakers on elections," rather, it ensures that expenditures reflect actual public support for the political ideas espoused by corporations. We emphasize that the mere fact that corporations may accumulate large amounts of wealth is not the justification for §54; rather, the unique state-conferred corporate structure that facilitates the amassing of large treasuries warrants the limit on independent expenditures. Corporate wealth can unfairly influence elections when it is deployed in the form of independent expenditures, just as it can when it assumes the guise of political contributions. We therefore hold that the State has articulated a sufficiently compelling rationale to support its restriction on independent expenditures by corporations.

We next turn to the question whether the Act is sufficiently narrowly tailored to achieve its goal. We find that the Act is precisely targeted to eliminate the distortion caused by corporate spending while also allowing corporations to express their political views. . . . [T]he Act does not impose an absolute ban on all forms of corporate political spending, but permits corporations to make independent political expenditures through separate segregated funds. Because persons contributing to such funds understand that their money will be used solely for political purposes, the speech generated accurately reflects contributors' support for the corporation's political views.

. . .

Because the right to engage in political expression is fundamental to our constitutional system, statutory classifications impinging upon that right must be narrowly tailored to serve a compelling governmental interest. We find that, even under such strict scrutiny, the statute's classifications pass muster under the Equal Protection Clause. As we explained in the context of our discussions of whether the statute was overinclusive or underinclusive, the State's decision to regulate only corporations is precisely tailored to serve the compelling state interest of eliminating from the political process the corrosive effect of political "war chests" amassed with the aid of the legal advantages given to corporations.

. . .

. . . We . . . hold that the Act does not violate the Equal Protection Clause.

Michigan identified as a serious danger the significant possibility that corporate political expenditures will undermine the integrity of the political process, and it has implemented a narrowly tailored solution to that problem. By requiring corporations to make all independent political expenditures through a separate fund made up of money solicited expressly for political purposes, the Michigan Campaign Finance Act reduces the threat that huge corporate treasuries amassed with the aid of favorable state laws will be used to influence unfairly the outcome of elections. The Michigan Chamber of Commerce does not exhibit the characteristics identified in *MCFL* that would require the State to exempt it from generally applicable restrictions on independent corporate expenditures. We therefore reverse the decision of the Court of Appeals.

Burson v. Freeman
504 U.S. 191 (1992)

The State of Tennessee has carved out an election day "campaign-free zone" through §2-7-111(b) of its election code. That section reads in pertinent part:

> Within the appropriate boundary as established in subsection (a) [100 feet from the entrances], and the building in which the polling place is located, the display of campaign posters, signs or other campaign materials, distribution of campaign materials, and solicitation of votes for or against any person or political party or position on a question are prohibited.

Violation of §2-7-111(b) is a Class C misdemeanor punishable by a term of imprisonment not greater than 30 days or a fine not to exceed $50, or both.

Respondent Mary Rebecca Freeman has been a candidate for office in Tennessee, has managed local campaigns, and has worked actively in state-wide elections. In 1987, she was the treasurer for the campaign of a city council candidate in Metropolitan Nashville-Davidson County.

Asserting that §§2-7-111(b) and 2-19-119 limited her ability to communicate with voters, respondent brought a facial challenge to these statutes in Davidson County Chancery Court. She sought a declaratory judgment that the provisions were unconstitutional under both the United States and the Tennessee Constitutions. She also sought a permanent injunction against their enforcement.

The Chancellor ruled that the statutes did not violate the United States or Tennessee Constitutions, and dismissed respondent's suit. He determined that §2-7-111(b) was a content-neutral and reasonable time, place, and manner restriction; that the 100-foot boundary served a compelling state interest in protecting voters from interference, harassment, and intimidation during the voting process; and that there was an alternative channel for respondent to exercise her free speech rights outside the 100-foot boundary.

The Tennessee Supreme Court . . . reversed. . . .

. . .

The Tennessee statute implicates three central concerns in our First Amendment jurisprudence: regulation of political speech, regulation of speech in a public forum, and regulation based on the content of the speech. The speech restricted by §2-7-111(b) obviously is political speech. . . .

The second important feature of §2-7-111(b) is that it bars speech in quintessential public forums. These forums include those places "which by long tradition or by government fiat have been devoted to assembly and debate," such as parks, streets, and sidewalks. . . .

The Tennessee restriction under consideration, however, is not a facially content-neutral time, place, or manner restriction. Whether individuals may exercise their free speech rights near polling places depends entirely on whether their speech is related to a political campaign. The statute does not reach other categories of speech, such as commercial solicitation, distribution, and display. This Court has held that the First Amendment's hostility to content-based regulation extends not only to a restriction on a particular viewpoint, but also to a prohibition of public discussion of an entire topic.

As a facially content-based restriction on political speech in a public forum, §2-7-111(b) must be subjected to exacting scrutiny: the State must show that the "regulation is necessary to serve a compelling state interest and that it is narrowly drawn to achieve that end."

. . . This case presents us with a particularly difficult reconciliation: the accommodation of the right to engage in political discourse with the right to vote—a right at the heart of our democracy.

Tennessee asserts that its campaign-free zone serves two compelling interests. First, the State argues that its regulation serves its compelling interest in protecting the right of its citizens to vote freely for the candidates of their choice. Second, Tennessee argues that its restriction protects the right to vote in an election conducted with integrity and reliability.

. . .

. . . [T]his Court has concluded that a State has a compelling interest in protecting voters from confusion and undue influence.

The Court also has recognized that a State "indisputably has a compelling interest in preserving the integrity of its election process." . . .

To survive strict scrutiny, however, a State must do more than assert a compelling state interest—it must demonstrate that its law is necessary to serve the asserted interest. . . .

. . .

. . . [A]n examination of the history of election regulation in this country reveals a persistent battle against two evils: voter intimidation and election fraud. After an unsuccessful experiment with an unofficial ballot system, all 50 States, together with numerous other Western democracies, settled on the same solution: a secret ballot secured in part by a restricted zone around the voting compartments. We find that this widespread and time-tested consensus demonstrates that some restricted zone is necessary in order to serve the States' compelling interest in preventing voter intimidation and election fraud.

. . . Intimidation and interference laws fall short of serving a State's compelling interests, because they "deal with only the most blatant and specific attempts" to impede elections. Moreover, because law enforcement officers generally are barred from the vicinity of the polls to avoid any appearance of coercion in the electoral process, many acts of interference would go undetected. These undetected or less than blatant acts may nonetheless drive the voter away before remedial action can be taken.

. . . We agree that distinguishing among types of speech requires that the statute be subjected to strict scrutiny. We do not, however, agree that the failure to regulate all speech renders the statute fatally underinclusive. . . .

. . . [T]he link between ballot secrecy and some restricted zone surrounding the voting area is not merely timing—it is common sense. The only way to preserve the secrecy of the ballot is to limit access to the area around the voter. Accord-

ingly, we hold that some restricted zone around the voting area is necessary to secure the State's compelling interest.

The real question then is how large a restricted zone is permissible or sufficiently tailored. . . .

. . .

. . . [W]e simply do not view the question whether the 100-foot boundary line could be somewhat tighter as a question of "constitutional dimension." Reducing the boundary to 25 feet, as suggested by the Tennessee Supreme Court is a difference only in degree, not a less restrictive alternative in kind. . . . We do not find that this is an unconstitutional choice.

. . .

. . . Here, the State, as recognized administrator of elections, has asserted that the exercise of free speech rights conflicts with another fundamental right, the right to cast a ballot in an election free from the taint of intimidation and fraud. A long history, a substantial consensus, and simple common sense show that some restricted zone around polling places is necessary to protect that fundamental right. Given the conflict between these two rights, we hold that requiring solicitors to stand 100 feet from the entrances to polling places does not constitute an unconstitutional compromise.

The judgment of the Tennessee Supreme Court is reversed, and the case is remanded for further proceedings not inconsistent with this opinion.

McIntyre v. Ohio Elections Commission
514 U.S. 334 (1995)

On April 27, 1988, Margaret McIntyre distributed leaflets to persons attending a public meeting at the Blendon Middle School in Westerville, Ohio. At this meeting, the superintendent of schools planned to discuss an imminent referendum on a proposed school tax levy. The leaflets expressed Mrs. McIntyre's opposition to the levy. There is no suggestion that the text of her message was false, misleading, or libelous. She had composed and printed it on her home computer and had paid a professional printer to make additional copies. Some of the handbills identified her as the author; others merely purported to express the views of "CONCERNED PARENTS AND TAXPAYERS." Except for the help provided by her son and a friend, who placed some of the leaflets on car windshields in the school parking lot, Mrs. McIntyre acted independently.

While Mrs. McIntyre distributed her handbills, an official of the school district, who supported the tax proposal, advised her that the unsigned leaflets did not conform to the Ohio election laws. Undeterred, Mrs. McIntyre appeared at another meeting on the next evening and handed out more of the handbills.

The proposed school levy was defeated at the next two elections, but it finally passed on its third try in November, 1988. Five months later, the same school official filed a complaint with the Ohio Elections Commission charging that Mrs. McIntyre's distribution of unsigned leaflets violated §3599.09(A) of the Ohio Code. The Commission agreed, and imposed a fine of $100.

The Franklin County Court of Common Pleas reversed. Finding that Mrs. McIntyre did not "mislead the public nor act in a surreptitious manner," the court concluded that the statute was unconstitutional as applied to her conduct. The Ohio Court of Appeals . . . reinstated the fine. . . .

The Ohio Supreme Court affirmed. . . . The Ohio court believed that such a law should be upheld if the burdens imposed on the First Amendment rights of voters are "reasonable" and "nondiscriminatory."

. . .

Mrs. McIntyre passed away during the pendency of this litigation. Even though the amount in controversy is only $100, petitioner, as the executor of her estate, has pursued her claim in this Court. . . .

Ohio maintains that the statute under review is a reasonable regulation of the electoral process. The State does not suggest that all anonymous publications are pernicious or that a statute totally excluding them from the marketplace of ideas would be valid. This is a wise (albeit implicit) concession, for the anonymity of an author is not ordinarily a sufficient reason to exclude her work product from the protections of the First Amendment.

. . .

. . . [Section] 3599.09(A) of the Ohio Code does not control the mechanics of the electoral process. It is a regulation of pure speech. Moreover, even though this provision applies evenhandedly to advocates of differing viewpoints, it is a direct regulation of the content of speech. Every written document covered by the statute must contain "the name and residence or business address of the chairman, treasurer, or secretary of the organization issuing the same, or the person who issues, makes, or is responsible therefor." Furthermore, the category of covered documents is defined by their content-only those publications containing speech designed to influence the voters in an election need bear the required markings. Consequently, we are not faced with an ordinary election restriction; this case "involves a limitation on political expression subject to exacting scrutiny."

. . .

Of course, core political speech need not center on a candidate for office. The principles enunciated in *Buckley* extend equally to issue-based elections such as the school tax referendum that Mrs. McIntyre sought to influence through her handbills. Indeed, the speech in which Mrs. McIntyre engaged—handing out leaflets in the advocacy of a politically controversial viewpoint—is the essence of First Amendment expression. That this advocacy occurred in the heat of a controversial referendum vote only strengthens the protection afforded to Ms. McIntyre's expression: urgent, important, and effective speech can be no less protected than impotent speech, lest the right to speak be relegated to those instances when it is least needed. No form of speech is entitled to greater constitutional protection than Mrs. McIntyre's.

When a law burdens core political speech, we apply "exacting scrutiny," and we uphold the restriction only if it is narrowly tailored to serve an overriding state interest. Our precedents thus make abundantly clear that the Ohio Supreme Court applied a significantly more lenient standard than is appropriate in a case of this kind.

. . . Ohio judges its interest in preventing fraudulent and libelous statements and its interest in providing the electorate with relevant information to be sufficiently compelling to justify the anonymous speech ban. These two interests necessarily overlap to some extent, but it is useful to discuss them separately.

Insofar as the interest in informing the electorate means nothing more than the provision of additional information that may either buttress or undermine the argument in a document, we think the identity of the speaker is no different from other components of the document's content that the author is free to include or exclude. . . . The simple interest in providing voters with additional relevant information does not justify a state requirement that a writer make statements or disclosures she would otherwise omit. Moreover, in the case of a handbill written by a private citizen who is not known to the recipient, the name and address of the author adds little, if anything, to the reader's ability to evaluate the document's message. Thus, Ohio's informational interest is plainly insufficient to support the constitutionality of its disclosure requirement.

The state interest in preventing fraud and libel stands on a different footing. We agree with Ohio's submission that this interest carries special weight during election campaigns when false statements, if credited, may have serious adverse consequences for the public at large. Ohio does not, however, rely solely on §3599.09(A) to protect that interest. Its Election Code includes detailed and specific prohibitions against making or disseminating false statements during political campaigns. These regulations apply both to candidate elections and to issue-driven ballot measures. Thus, Ohio's prohibition of anonymous leaflets plainly is not its principal weapon against fraud. Rather, it serves as an aid to enforcement of the specific prohibitions and as a deterrent to the making of false statements by unscrupulous prevaricators. Although these ancillary benefits are assuredly legitimate, we are not persuaded that they justify §3599.09(A)'s extremely broad prohibition.

As this case demonstrates, the prohibition encompasses documents that are not even arguably false or misleading. It applies not only to the activities of candidates and their organized supporters, but also to individuals acting independently and using only their own modest resources. It applies not only to elections of public officers, but also to ballot issues that present neither a substantial risk of libel nor any potential appearance of corrupt advantage. It applies not only to leaflets distributed on the eve of an election, when the opportunity for reply is limited, but also to those distributed months in advance. It applies no matter what the character or strength of the author's interest in anonymity. Moreover, as this case also demonstrates, the absence of the author's name on a document does not necessarily protect either that person or a distributor of a forbidden document from being held responsible for compliance with the election code. Nor has the State explained why it can more easily enforce the direct bans on disseminating false documents against anonymous authors and distributors than against wrongdoers who might use false names and addresses in an attempt to avoid detection. We recognize that a State's enforcement interest might justify a more limited identification requirement, but Ohio has shown scant cause for inhibiting the leafletting at issue here.

. . .

True, in another portion of the *Buckley* opinion, we expressed approval of a requirement that even "independent expenditures" in excess of a threshold level be reported to the Federal Election Commission. But that requirement entailed nothing more than an identification to the Commission of the amount and use of money expended in support of a candidate. Though such mandatory reporting undeniably impedes protected First Amendment activity, the intrusion is a far cry from compelled self-identification on all election-related writings. A written election-related document—particularly a leaflet—is often a personally crafted statement of a political viewpoint. Mrs. McIntyre's handbills surely fit that description. As such, identification of the author against her will is particularly intrusive; it reveals unmistakably the content of her thoughts on a controversial issue. Disclosure of an expenditure and its use, without more, reveals far less information. It may be information that a person prefers to keep secret, and undoubtedly it often gives away something about the spender's

political views. Nonetheless, even though money may "talk," its speech is less specific, less personal, and less provocative than a handbill—and, as a result, when money supports an unpopular viewpoint, it is less likely to precipitate retaliation.

Not only is the Ohio statute's infringement on speech more intrusive than the *Buckley* disclosure requirement, but it rests on different and less powerful state interests. The Federal Election Campaign Act of 1971, at issue in *Buckley*, regulates only candidate elections, not referenda or other issue-based ballot measures; and we construed "independent expenditures" to mean only those expenditures that "expressly advocate the election or defeat of a clearly identified candidate." In candidate elections, the Government can identify a compelling state interest in avoiding the corruption that might result from campaign expenditures. Disclosure of expenditures lessens the risk that individuals will spend money to support a candidate as a quid pro quo for special treatment after the candidate is in office. Curriers of favor will be deterred by the knowledge that all expenditures will be scrutinized by the Federal Election Commission and by the public for just this sort of abuse. Moreover, the federal Act contains numerous legitimate disclosure requirements for campaign organizations; the similar requirements for independent expenditures serve to ensure that a campaign organization will not seek to evade disclosure by routing its expenditures through individual supporters. . . .

. . . The right to remain anonymous may be abused when it shields fraudulent conduct. But political speech, by its nature, will sometimes have unpalatable consequences, and, in general, our society accords greater weight to the value of free speech than to the dangers of its misuse. Ohio has not shown that its interest in preventing the misuse of anonymous election-related speech justifies a prohibition of all uses of that speech. The State may, and does, punish fraud directly. But it cannot seek to punish fraud indirectly by indiscriminately outlawing a category of speech, based on its content, with no necessary relationship to the danger sought to be prevented. One would be hard pressed to think of a better example of the pitfalls of Ohio's blunderbuss approach than the facts of the case before us.

The judgment of the Ohio Supreme Court is reversed.

Federal Election Commission v. Akins
524 U.S. 11 (1998)

The Federal Election Commission (FEC) has determined that the American Israel Public Affairs Committee (AIPAC) is not a "political committee" as defined by the Federal Election Campaign Act of 1971 . . . (FECA), and, for that reason, the Commission has refused to require AIPAC to make disclosures regarding its membership, contributions, and expenditures that FECA would otherwise require. . . .

. . .

This case arises out of an effort by respondents, a group of voters with views often opposed to those of AIPAC, to persuade the FEC to treat AIPAC as a "political committee." Respondents filed a complaint with the FEC, stating that AIPAC had made more than $1,000 in qualifying "expenditures" per year, and thereby became a "political committee." They added that AIPAC had violated the FEC provisions requiring "political committee[s]" to register and to make public the information about members, contributions,

and expenditures to which we have just referred. Respondents also claimed that AIPAC had violated §441b of FECA, which prohibits corporate campaign "contribution[s]" and "expenditure[s]." They asked the FEC to find that AIPAC had violated the Act, and, among other things, to order AIPAC to make public the information that FECA demands of a "political committee."

AIPAC asked the FEC to dismiss the complaint. AIPAC described itself as an issue-oriented organization that seeks to maintain friendship and promote goodwill between the United States and Israel. AIPAC conceded that it lobbies elected officials and disseminates information about candidates for public office. But, in responding to the §441b charge, AIPAC denied that it had made the kinds of "expenditures" that matter for FECA purposes (i.e., the kinds of election-related expenditures that corporations cannot make, and which count as the kind of expenditures that, when they exceed $1,000, qualify a group as a "political committee").

To put the matter more specifically: AIPAC focused on certain "expenditures" that respondents had claimed were election-related, such as the costs of meetings with candidates, the introduction of AIPAC members to candidates, and the distribution of candidate position papers. AIPAC said that its spending on such activities, even if election-related, fell within a relevant exception. They amounted, said AIPAC, to communications by a membership organization with its members, which the Act exempts from its definition of "expenditures." In AIPAC's view, these communications therefore did not violate §441b's corporate expenditure prohibition. And, if AIPAC was right, those expenditures would not count towards the $1,000 ceiling on "expenditures" that might transform an ordinary issue-related group into a "political committee."

The FEC's General Counsel concluded that, between 1983 and 1988, AIPAC had indeed funded communications of the sort described. The General Counsel said that those expenditures were campaign-related, in that they amounted to advocating the election or defeat of particular candidates. He added that these expenditures were "likely to have crossed the $1,000 threshold." At the same time, the FEC closed the door to AIPAC's invocation of the "communications" exception. The FEC said that, although it was a "close question," these expenditures were not membership communications, because that exception applies to a membership organization's communications with its members, and most of the persons who belonged to AIPAC did not qualify as "members" for purposes of the Act. Still, given the closeness of the issue, the FEC exercised its discretion and decided not to proceed further with respect to the claimed "corporate contribution" violation.

The FEC's determination that many of the persons who belonged to AIPAC were not "members" effectively foreclosed any claim that AIPAC's communications did not count as "expenditures" for purposes of determining whether it was a "political committee." Since AIPAC's activities fell outside the "membership communications" exception, AIPAC could not invoke that exception as a way of escaping the scope of the Act's term "political committee" and the Act's disclosure provisions, which that definition triggers.

The FEC nonetheless held that AIPAC was not subject to the disclosure requirements, but for a different reason. In the FEC's view, the Act's definition of "political committee" includes only those organizations that have as a "major purpose" the nomination or election of candidates. AIPAC, it added, was fundamentally an issue-oriented lobbying organization, not a campaign-

related organization, and hence AIPAC fell outside the definition of a "political committee" regardless. The FEC consequently dismissed respondents' complaint.

Respondents filed a petition in Federal District Court seeking review of the FEC's determination dismissing their complaint. The District Court granted summary judgment for the FEC, and a . . . panel of the Court of Appeals affirmed. The en banc Court of Appeals reversed, however, on the ground that the FEC's "major purpose" test improperly interpreted the Act's definition of a "political committee." . . .

. . .

. . . [R]espondents, as voters, have satisfied both prudential and constitutional standing requirements. They may bring this petition for a declaration that the FEC's dismissal of their complaint was unlawful.

The second question presented in the FEC's petition for certiorari is whether an organization that otherwise satisfies the Act's definition of a "political committee," and thus is subject to its disclosure requirements, nonetheless falls outside that definition because "its major purpose" is not "the nomination or election of candidates." . . .

The FEC here interpreted this language as narrowing the scope of the statutory term "political committee," wherever applied. And, as we have said, the FEC's General Counsel found that AIPAC fell outside that definition because the nomination or election of a candidate was not AIPAC's "major purpose."

. . . The Court of Appeals concluded that the language in this Court's prior decisions narrowing the definition of "political committee" did not apply where the special First Amendment "independent expenditure" problem did not exist.

The Solicitor General argues that this Court's narrowing definition of "political committee" applies not simply in the context of independent expenditures, but across the board. We cannot squarely address that matter, however, because of the unusual and complex circumstances in which this case arises. As we previously mentioned, the FEC considered a related question—namely, whether AIPAC was exempt from §441b's prohibition of corporate campaign expenditures on the ground that the so-called "expenditures" involved only AIPAC's communications with its members. The FEC held that the statute's exception to the "expenditure" definition for communications by a "membership organization" did not apply because many of the persons who belonged to AIPAC were not "members" as defined by FEC regulation. The FEC acknowledged, however, that this was a "close question." In particular, the FEC thought that many of the persons who belonged to AIPAC lacked sufficient control of the organization's policies to qualify as "members" for purposes of the Act.

A few months later, however, the Court of Appeals overturned the FEC's regulations defining "members," in part because that court thought the regulations defined membership organizations too narrowly in light of an organization's "First Amendment right to communicate with its 'members.'" The FEC has subsequently issued proposed rules redefining "members." Under these rules, it is quite possible that many of the persons who belong to AIPAC would be considered "members." If so, the communications here at issue apparently would not count as the kind of "expenditures" that can turn an organization into a "political committee," and AIPAC would fall outside the definition for that reason, rather than because of the "major purpose" test.

. . . If the Court of Appeals is right in saying that this Court's narrowing interpretation of "po-litical committee" in *Buckley* reflected First Amendment concerns, then whether the "membership communications" exception is interpreted broadly or narrowly could affect our evaluation of the Court of Appeals claim that there is no constitutionally driven need to apply *Buckley*'s narrowing interpretation in this context. The scope of the "membership communications" exception could also affect our evaluation of the Solicitor General's related argument that First Amendment concerns (reflected in *Buckley*'s narrowing interpretation) are present whenever the Act requires disclosure. . . .

. . . In our view, the FEC should proceed to determine whether or not AIPAC's expenditures qualify as "membership communications," and thereby fall outside the scope of "expenditures" that could qualify it as a "political committee." If the FEC decides that, despite its new rules, the communications here do not qualify for this exception, then the lower courts, in reconsidering respondents' arguments, can still evaluate the significance of the communicative context in which the case arises. If, on the other hand, the FEC decides that AIPAC's activities fall within the "membership communications" exception, the matter will become moot.

For these reasons, the decision of the Court of Appeals is vacated, and the case is remanded for further proceedings consistent with this opinion.

Buckley v. American Constitutional Law Foundation
525 U.S. 182 (1999)

The complaint in this action was filed in 1993 in the United States District Court for the District of Colorado. . . ; it challenged six of Colorado's many controls on the initiative petition process.

Plaintiffs, now respondents, included American Constitutional Law Foundation, Inc., a nonprofit, public interest organization that supports direct democracy, and several individual participants in Colorado's initiative process. In this opinion, we refer to plaintiffs-respondents, collectively, as ACLF. ACLF charged that the following prescriptions of Colorado's law governing initiative petitions violate the First Amendment's freedom of speech guarantee: (1) the requirement that petition circulators be at least 18 years old; (2) the further requirement that they be registered voters; (3) the limitation of the petition circulation period to six months; (4) the requirement that petition circulators wear identification badges stating their names, their status as "VOLUNTEER" or "PAID," and, if the latter, the name and telephone number of their employer; (5) the requirement that circulators attach to each petition section an affidavit containing, inter alia, the circulator's name and address and a statement that "he or she has read and understands the laws governing the circulation of petitions"; and (6) the requirements that initiative proponents disclose (a) at the time they file their petition, the name, address, and county of voter registration of all paid circulators, the amount of money proponents paid per petition signature, and the total amount paid to each circulator, and (b) on a monthly basis, the names of the proponents, the name and address of each paid circulator, the name of the proposed ballot measure, and the amount of money paid and owed to each circulator during the month.

The District Court, after a bench trial, struck down the badge requirement and portions of the disclosure requirements, but upheld the age and affidavit requirements and the six-month limit on petition circulation. The District Court also found that the registration requirement "limits the number of persons available to cir-

culate . . . and, accordingly, restricts core political speech." Nevertheless, that court upheld the registration requirement. In 1980, the District Court noted, the registration requirement had been adopted by Colorado's voters as a constitutional amendment. . . .

The Court of Appeals affirmed in part and reversed in part. That court properly sought guidance from our recent decisions on ballot access and on handbill distribution. Initiative petition circulators, the Tenth Circuit recognized, resemble handbill distributors, in that both seek to promote public support for a particular issue or position. Initiative petition circulators also resemble candidate petition signature gatherers, however, for both seek ballot access. In common with the District Court, the Tenth Circuit upheld, as reasonable regulations of the ballot initiative process, the age restriction, the six-month limit on petition circulation, and the affidavit requirement. The Court of Appeals struck down the requirement that petition circulators be registered voters, and also held portions of the badge and disclosure requirements invalid as trenching unnecessarily and improperly on political expression.

As the Tenth Circuit recognized in upholding the age restriction, the six-month limit on circulation, and the affidavit requirement, States allowing ballot initiatives have considerable leeway to protect the integrity and reliability of the initiative process, as they have with respect to election processes generally. . . .

. . .

The Tenth Circuit reasoned that the registration requirement placed on Colorado's voter-eligible population produces a speech diminution of the very kind produced by the ban on paid circulators at issue in *Meyer*. We agree. The requirement that circulators be not merely voter eligible, but registered voters, it is scarcely debatable given the uncontested numbers, decreases the pool of potential circulators as certainly as that pool is decreased by the prohibition of payment to circulators. Both provisions "limi[t] the number of voices who will convey [the initiative proponents'] message" and, consequently, cut down "the size of the audience [proponents] can reach." In this case, as in *Meyer*, the requirement "imposes a burden on political expression that the State has failed to justify."

Colorado acknowledges that the registration requirement limits speech, but not severely, the State asserts, because "it is exceptionally easy to register to vote." The ease with which qualified voters may register to vote, however, does not lift the burden on speech at petition circulation time. Of course, there are individuals who fail to register out of ignorance or apathy. But there are also individuals for whom, as the trial record shows, the choice not to register implicates political thought and expression. . . .

The State's dominant justification appears to be its strong interest in policing lawbreakers among petition circulators. Colorado seeks to ensure that circulators will be amenable to the Secretary of State's subpoena power, which in these matters does not extend beyond the State's borders. The interest in reaching law violators, however, is served by the requirement, upheld below, that each circulator submit an affidavit setting out, among several particulars, the "address at which he or she resides, including the street name and number, the city or town, [and] the county." . . . The attestation is made at the time a petition section is submitted; a voter's registration may lack that currency.

. . . Colorado maintains that it is more difficult to determine who is a state resident than it is to determine who is a registered voter. The force of that argument is diminished, however, by the af-

fidavit attesting to residence that each circulator must submit with each petition section.

. . .

Colorado enacted the provision requiring initiative petition circulators to wear identification badges in 1993, five years after our decision in *Meyer*. The Tenth Circuit held the badge requirement invalid insofar as it requires circulators to display their names. The Court of Appeals did not rule on the constitutionality of other elements of the badge provision—namely the "requirements that the badge disclose whether the circulator is paid or a volunteer, and if paid, by whom." Nor do we.

. . .

The injury to speech is heightened for the petition circulator because the badge requirement compels personal name identification at the precise moment when the circulator's interest in anonymity is greatest. For this very reason, the name badge requirement does not qualify for inclusion among the "more limited [election process] identification requirement[s]" to which we alluded in *McIntyre*. In contrast, the affidavit requirement upheld by the District Court and Court of Appeals, which must be met only after circulators have completed their conversations with electors, exemplifies the type of regulation for which *McIntyre* left room.

. . . [I]n its final observation, the Court of Appeals noted that ACLF's "arguments and evidence focus[ed] entirely on [the circulator identification] requirement"; therefore, that court expressed no opinion whether the additional requirements—that the badge disclose the circulator's paid or volunteer status, and if paid, by whom—"would pass constitutional muster standing alone." We similarly confine our decision.

. . . Colorado's disclosure provisions were enacted post-*Meyer* in 1993. The Tenth Circuit trimmed these provisions. Colorado requires ballot initiative proponents who pay circulators to file both a final report when the initiative petition is submitted to the Secretary of State, and monthly reports during the circulation period. The Tenth Circuit invalidated the final report provision only insofar as it compels disclosure of information specific to each paid circulator, in particular, the circulators' names and addresses and the total amount paid to each circulator. . . .

The Court of Appeals next addressed Colorado's provision demanding "detailed monthly disclosures." In a concise paragraph, the court rejected compelled disclosure of the name and addresses (residential and business) of each paid circulator, and the amount of money paid and owed to each circulator, during the month in question. The Court of Appeals identified no infirmity in the required reporting of petition proponents' names, or in the call for disclosure of proposed ballot measures for which paid circulators were engaged. We express no opinion whether these monthly report prescriptions, standing alone, would survive review.

In ruling on Colorado's disclosure requirements for paid circulations, the Court of Appeals looked primarily to our decision in *Buckley v. Valeo.* In that decision, we stated that "exacting scrutiny" is necessary when compelled disclosure of campaign-related payments is at issue. We nevertheless upheld, as substantially related to important governmental interests, the recordkeeping, reporting, and disclosure provisions of the Federal Election Campaign Act of 1971, as amended. We explained in *Buckley,* that disclosure provides the electorate with information "as to where political campaign money comes from and how it is spent," thereby aiding electors in evaluat-

ing those who seek their vote. We further observed that disclosure requirements "deter actual corruption and avoid the appearance of corruption by exposing large contributions and expenditures to the light of publicity."

Mindful of *Buckley,* the Tenth Circuit did not upset Colorado's disclosure requirements "as a whole." Notably, the Court of Appeals upheld the State's requirements for disclosure of payors, in particular, proponents' names and the total amount they have spent to collect signatures for their petitions. In this regard, the State and supporting amici stress the importance of disclosure as a control or check on domination of the initiative process by affluent special interest groups. Disclosure of the names of initiative sponsors, and of the amounts they have spent gathering support for their initiatives, responds to that substantial state interest.

. . . [R]evealing the names of paid circulators and amounts paid to each circulator, the lower courts fairly determined from the record as a whole, is hardly apparent and has not been demonstrated.

. . .

Through less problematic measures, Colorado can and does meet the State's substantial interests in regulating the ballot initiative process. Colorado aims to protect the integrity of the initiative process—specifically, to deter fraud and diminish corruption. To serve that important interest, as we observed in *Meyer,* Colorado retains an arsenal of safeguards. To inform the public "where [the] money comes from" we reiterate, the State legitimately requires sponsors of ballot initiatives to disclose who pays petition circulators, and how much.

To ensure grass roots support, Colorado conditions placement of an initiative proposal on the ballot on the proponent's submission of valid signatures representing five percent of the total votes cast for all candidates for Secretary of State at the previous general election. Furthermore, in aid of efficiency, veracity, or clarity, Colorado has provided for an array of process measures not contested here by ACLF. These measures prescribe, inter alia, a single subject per initiative limitation, a signature verification method, a large, plain-English notice alerting potential signers of petitions to the law's requirements, and the text of the affidavit to which all circulators must subscribe.

For the reasons stated, we conclude that the Tenth Circuit correctly separated necessary or proper ballot access controls from restrictions that unjustifiably inhibit the circulation of ballot initiative petitions. Therefore, the judgment of the Court of Appeals is affirmed.

13

Legislative Inquiries and Political Rights

This chapter is not about a failure or refusal to testify in front of Congress or about nominal legislative activities and procedures, but rather it involves cases that center on legislative activities relative to political affiliation, subversive activities, questions of loyalty, or a general refusal to testify in a legislative forum for political reasons.

In re Chapman
166 U.S. 661 (1897)

Sections 102, 103, and 104 and section 859 of the Revised Statutes are as follows:

> Sec. 102. Every person who having been summoned as a witness by the authority of either house of congress, to give testimony or to produce papers upon any matter under inquiry before either house, or any committee of either house of congress, wilfully makes default, or who, having appeared, refuses to answer any question pertinent to the question under inquiry, shall be deemed guilty of a misdemeanor, punishable by a fine of not more than one thousand dollars nor less than one hundred dollars, and imprisonment in a common jail for not less than one month nor more than twelve months.

> Sec. 103. No witness is privileged to refuse to testify to any fact, or to produce any paper, respecting which he shall be examined by either house of congress, or by any committee of either house, upon the ground that his testimony to such fact or his production of such paper may tend to disgrace him or otherwise render him infamous.

> Sec. 104. Whenever a witness summoned as

mentioned in section one hundred and two fails to testify, and the facts are reported to either house, the president of the senate or the speaker of the house, as the case may be, shall certify the fact under the seal of the senate or house to the district attorney for the District of Columbia, whose duty it shall be to bring the matter before the grand jury for their action.

> Sec. 859. No testimony given by a witness before either house, or before any committee of either house of congress, shall be used as evidence in any criminal proceeding against him in any court, except in a prosecution for perjury committed in giving such testimony. But an official paper or record produced by him is not within the said privilege.

. . .

From the record of the proceedings on the trial, accompanying and made part of the petition, it appears that petitioner, in declining to answer the questions propounded, expressly stated that he did not do so on the ground that to answer might expose him, or tend to expose him, to criminal prosecution; nor did he object that his answers might tend to disgrace him. Section 103 had in fact no bearing on the controversy in regard to this witness, and it is difficult to see how he can properly raise the question as to its constitutionality, notwithstanding section 859. And we cannot concur in the view that sections 102 and 103 are so inseparably connected that it can be reasonably concluded that, if section 103 were not sustainable, section 102 would therefore be invalid. . . . it was provided that when a person summoned as a witness by either house to give testimony or produce papers, upon any matter under inquiry before either house, or any committee of either house, willfully fails to appear, or, appearing, refuses to answer 'any question pertinent to the question under inquiry,' he shall be deemed guilty of a misdemeanor. . . .

. . .

According to the preamble and resolutions, the integrity and purity of members of the senate had been questioned in a manner calculated to destroy public confidence in the body, and in such respects as might subject members to censure or expulsion. The senate, by the action taken, signifying its judgment that it was called upon to vindicate itself from aspersion, and to deal with such of its members as might have been guilty of misbehavior, and brought reproach upon it, obviously had jurisdiction of the subject-matter of the inquiry it directed, and power to compel the attendance of witnesses, and to require them to answer any question pertinent thereto. And the pursuit of such inquiry by the questions propounded in this instance was not, in our judgment, in violation of the security against unreasonable searches and seizures protected by the fourth amendment.

. . . Specific charges publicly made against senators had been brought to the attention of the senate, and the senate had determined that investigation was necessary. The subject-matter as affecting the senate was within the jurisdiction of the senate. The questions were not intrusions into the affairs of the citizen. They did not seek to ascertain any facts as to the conduct, methods, extent, or details of the business of the firm in question, but only whether that firm, confessedly engaged in buying and selling stocks, and the particular stock named, was employed by any senator to buy or sell for him any of that stock, whose market price might be affected by the senate's action. We cannot regard these questions as amounting to an unreasonable search into the private affairs of the witness simply because he may have been in some degree connected with the alleged transactions, and, as investigations of this sort are within the power of either of the two houses, they cannot be defeated on purely sentimental grounds.

The questions were undoubtedly pertinent to the subject-matter of the inquiry. The resolutions directed the committee to inquire 'whether any senator had been, or is, speculating in what are known as 'sugar stocks' during the consideration of the tariff bill now before the senate.' What the senate might or might not do upon the facts when ascertained, we cannot say; nor are we called upon to inquire whether such ventures might be defensible, as contended in argument; but it is plain that negative answers would have cleared that body of what the senate regarded as offensive imputations, while affirmative answers might have led to further action on the part of the senate within its constitutional powers.

. . .

In our opinion, the law is not open to constitutional objection, and the record does not exhibit a case in which, on any ground, it can be held that the supreme court of the District, sitting as a criminal court, had no jurisdiction to render judgment.

Writ denied.

Christoffel v. United States
338 U.S. 84 (1949)

In March of 1947, the committee on Education and Labor was . . . a standing committee of the House of Representatives. . . . On March 1, 1947, petitioner appeared as a witness before the committee, under oath, and in the course of the proceedings was asked a series of questions directed to his political affiliations and associations. In his answers he unequivocally denied that he was a Communist or that he endorsed, supported or participated in Communist programs. As a result of these answers he was indicted for perjury and after a trial by jury was convicted. The Court of Appeals affirmed the conviction. . . .

. . . Petitioner's main contention is that the committee was not a "competent tribunal" within the meaning of the statute, in that a quorum of the committee was not present at the time of the incident on which the indictment was based. . . .

. . .

. . . A tribunal that is not competent is no tribunal, and it is unthinkable that such a body can be the instrument of criminal conviction. The Court of Appeals erred in affirming so much of the instructions to the jury as allowed them to find a quorum present without reference to the facts at the time of the alleged perjurious testimony, and its judgment is reversed.

United States v. Bryan
339 U.S. 323 (1950)

Respondent is the executive secretary of an organization known as the Joint Anti-Fascist Refugee Committee (association) and as such has custody of its records. Prior to April 4, 1946, the Committee on Un-American Activities of the House of Representatives, which was conducting an investigation into the activities of the association, had attempted without success to procure these records from respondent and from the chairman of the association's executive board, Dr. Edward K. Barsky. On March 29, 1946, the Committee issued subpoenas to each of the known members of the executive board summoning them to . . . testify and produce certain specified records of the association, and an identical subpoena directed to the association by name was served upon respondent Bryan in her official capacity.

Bryan and the members of the executive board appeared before the Committee at the date and time set out in the subpoenas and in response thereto. Each person so summoned failed to produce any of the records specified in the subpoenas. The members of the executive board made identical statements in which each declared that he or she did not have possession, custody or control of the records; that Miss Bryan, the executive secretary, did. Respondent admitted that the records were in her possession but refused to comply with the subpoena because "after consulting with counsel [she] came to the conclusion that the subpoena was not valid" because the Committee had no constitutional right to demand the books and records. Asked whether the executive board supported her action, she refused to answer because she did not think the question pertinent.

The Committee . . . then submitted its report and resolution to the House. . . .

The resolution directing the Speaker to certify the Committee's report to the United States Attorney for the District of Columbia for legal action was approved by the full House after debate.

Respondent was indicted for violation of R.S. 102, in that she had failed to produce the records called for in the subpoenas and had thereby wilfully made default. At the trial she contended, inter alia, that she was not guilty of wilful default because a quorum of the Committee on Un-American Activities had not been present when she appeared on the return day. However, the trial court withdrew that issue from the jury's consideration by instructing the jury "as a matter of law, that the Committee on Un-American Activities of the House of Representatives was a validly constituted committee of the Congress, and was at the time of the defendant's appearance." Respondent was found guilty, but the Court of Appeals for the District of Columbia Circuit . . . reversed the judgment on the ground that the presence of a quorum of the Committee at the hearing on April 4, 1946, was a material question of fact in the alleged offense and should have been submitted to the jury. . . .

. . .

Respondent advances several contentions which were not passed upon by the Court of Appeals. We do not decide them at this time. The judgment of the Court of Appeals is reversed.

United States v. Fleischman
339 U.S. 349 (1950)

Respondent Fleischman is a member of the executive board of an organization known as the Joint Anti-Fascist Refugee Committee (association), which, during 1945 and 1946, was under investigation by the House Committee on Un-American Activities. In furtherance of its investigation, the Committee issued subpoenas on March 29, 1946, to each of the members of the executive board and to Helen R. Bryan, the executive secretary of the association, demanding that they produce certain of the association's records in the Committee's chamber on April 4, 1946. Fleischman and the other members of the board appeared on that date in response to the subpoenas but did not produce the records. The Committee thereupon reported to the House that the members of the executive board were in contempt of that body. . . . [T]he House voted to direct the Speaker to certify the Committee's report to the United States District Attorney for legal action.

Respondent and the other members of the executive board were jointly indicted for wilful default under R.S. 102, but Fleischman was tried separately from the others. Her defense . . . consisted in part in the contention that she could not be guilty of wilful default because a quorum of the Committee had not been present when she appeared in response to the subpoena. The trial court withdrew that issue from the jury, holding "as a matter of law, that the Committee on Un-American Activities of the House of Representatives was a validly constituted committee of Congress, and was at the time of the defendant's appearance." The Court of Appeals for the District of Columbia reversed . . . on the ground that presence of a quorum of the Committee at the time of respondent's appearance was a material question of fact for the jury. . . .

. . .

Respondent advances a number of contentions which were not passed upon by the Court of Appeals. We do not decide them at this time. The judgment of the Court of Appeals is reversed.

Tenney v. Brandhove
341 U.S. 367 (1951)

William Brandhove brought this action in the United States District Court for the Northern District of California, alleging that he had been deprived of rights guaranteed by the Federal Constitution. The defendants are Jack B. Tenney and other members of a committee of the California Legislature, the Senate Fact-Finding Committee on Un-American Activities, colloquially known as the Tenney Committee. Also named as defendants are the Committee and Elmer E. Robinson, Mayor of San Francisco.

. . .

. . . The Tenney Committee was constituted by a resolution of the California Senate on June 20, 1947. On January 28, 1949, Brandhove circulated a petition among members of the State Legislature. He alleges that it was circulated in order to persuade the Legislature not to appropriate further funds for the Committee. The petition charged that the Committee had used Brandhove as a tool in order "to smear Congressman Franck R. Havenner as a 'Red' when he was a candidate for Mayor of San Francisco in 1947; and that the Republican machine in San Francisco and the campaign management of Elmer E. Robinson, Franck Havenner's opponent, conspired with the Tenney Committee to this end." In view of the conflict between this petition and evidence previously given by Brandhove, the Committee asked local prosecuting officials to institute criminal proceedings against him. The Committee also summoned Brandhove to appear before them at a hearing held on January 29. Testimony was there taken from the Mayor of San Francisco, allegedly a member of the conspiracy. The plaintiff appeared with counsel, but refused to give testimony. For this, he was prosecuted for contempt in the State courts. Upon the jury's failure to return a verdict this prosecution was dropped. After Brandhove refused to testify, the Chairman quoted testimony given by Brandhove at prior hearings. The Chairman also read into the record a statement concerning an alleged criminal record of Brandhove, a newspaper article denying the truth of his charges, and a denial by the Committee's counsel—who was absent—that Brandhove's charges were true.

Brandhove alleges that the January 29 hearing "was not held for a legislative purpose," but was designed "to intimidate and silence plaintiff and deter and prevent him from effectively exercising his constitutional rights of free speech and to petition the Legislature for redress of grievances, and also to deprive him of the equal protection of the laws, due process of law, and of the

enjoyment of equal privileges and immunities as a citizen of the United States under the law, and so did intimidate, silence, deter, and prevent and deprive plaintiff." Damages of $10,000 were asked "for legal counsel, traveling, hotel accommodations, and other matters pertaining and necessary to his defense" in the contempt proceeding arising out of the Committee hearings. The plaintiff also asked for punitive damages.

The action was dismissed without opinion by the District Judge. The Court of Appeals for the Ninth Circuit held, however, that the complaint stated a cause of action against the Committee and its members. . . .

. . .

. . . Legislators are immune from deterrents to the uninhibited discharge of their legislative duty, not for their private indulgence but for the public good. One must not expect uncommon courage even in legislators. . . .

Investigations, whether by standing or special committees, are an established part of representative government. Legislative committees have been charged with losing sight of their duty of disinterestedness. In times of political passion, dishonest or vindictive motives are readily attributed to legislative conduct and as readily believed. . . . To find that a committee's investigation has exceeded the bounds of legislative power it must be obvious that there was a usurpation of functions exclusively vested in the Judiciary or the Executive. The present case does not present such a situation. Brandhove indicated that evidence previously given by him to the committee was false, and he raised serious charges concerning the work of a committee investigating a problem within legislative concern. The Committee was entitled to assert a right to call the plaintiff before it and examine him.

It should be noted that this is a case in which the

642   CHAPTER 13: LEGISLATIVE INQUIRIES AND POLITICAL RIGHTS

defendants are members of a legislature. Legislative privilege in such a case deserves greater respect than where an official acting on behalf of the legislature is sued or the legislature seeks the affirmative aid of the courts to assert a privilege. . . .

. . . We conclude only that here the individual defendants and the legislative committee were acting in a field where legislators traditionally have power to act, and that the statute of 1871 does not create civil liability for such conduct.

The judgment of the Court of Appeals is reversed and that of the District Court affirmed.

Quinn v. United States
349 U.S. 155 (1955)

Petitioner was convicted of contempt of Congress in the District Court for the District of Columbia. Section 192 provides for the punishment of any witness before a congressional committee "who . . . refuses to answer any question pertinent to the question under inquiry. . . ." On appeal, the Court of Appeals for the District of Columbia Circuit reversed the conviction and remanded the case for a new trial. Claiming that the Court of Appeals should have directed an acquittal, petitioner applied to this Court for certiorari. . . .

Pursuant to subpoena, petitioner appeared on August 10, 1949, before a subcommittee of the Committee on Un-American Activities of the House of Representatives. Petitioner was then a member and field representative of the United Electrical, Radio and Machine Workers of America. Also subpoenaed to appear on that day were Thomas J. Fitzpatrick and Frank Panzino, two officers of the same union. At the outset of the hearings, counsel for the committee announced that the purpose of the investigation was to inquire into "the question of Communist af-

filiation or association of certain members" of the union and "the advisability of tightening present security requirements in industrial plants working on certain Government contracts." All three witnesses were asked questions concerning alleged membership in the Communist Party. All three declined to answer.

Fitzpatrick was the first to be called to testify. He based his refusal to answer on "the first and fifth amendments" as well as "the first amendment to the Constitution, supplemented by the fifth amendment." Immediately following Fitzpatrick's testimony, Panzino was called to the stand. In response to the identical questions put to Fitzpatrick, Panzino specifically adopted as his own the grounds relied upon by Fitzpatrick. In addition, at one point in his testimony, Panzino stated that "I think again, Mr. Chairman, under the fifth amendment, that is my own personal belief." On the following day, petitioner, unaccompanied by counsel, was called to the stand and was also asked whether he had ever been a member of the Communist Party. Like Panzino before him, he declined to answer, specifically adopting as his own the grounds relied upon by Fitzpatrick.

On November 20, 1950, all three witnesses were indicted under 192 for their refusals to answer. The three cases were tried before different judges, each sitting without a jury. Fitzpatrick and Panzino were acquitted. In Fitzpatrick's case, it was held that his references to "the first and fifth amendments" and "the first amendment to the Constitution, supplemented by the fifth amendment" constituted an adequate means of invoking the Self-Incrimination Clause of the Fifth Amendment. Similarly, in Panzino's case, it was held that his reference to "the fifth amendment" was sufficient to plead the privilege. In petitioner's case, however, the District Court held that a witness may not incorporate the position of another witness and rejected petitioner's defense based on the Self-Incrimination Clause. Petitioner was accordingly convicted and sentenced to a term of six months in jail and a fine of $500.

In reversing this conviction, the Court of Appeals, sitting en banc, held that "No formula or specific term or expression is required" in order to plead the privilege and that a witness may adopt as his own a plea made by a previous witness. Thus the Court of Appeals viewed the principal issue in the case as "whether Fitzpatrick did or did not claim the privilege." On this issue, a majority of the Court of Appeals expressed no view. They agreed that a reversal without more would be in order if they "were of clear opinion that Fitzpatrick, and therefore Quinn, did claim the privilege." But they were "not of that clear opinion." The Court of Appeals therefore ordered a new trial for determination of the issue by the District Court. The Court of Appeals also directed the District Court on retrial to determine whether petitioner "was aware of the intention of his inquirer that answers were required despite his objections." In that regard, however, it rejected petitioner's contention that a witness cannot be convicted under 192 for a refusal to answer unless the committee overruled his objections and specifically directed him to answer.

. . .

In the instant case petitioner was convicted for refusing to answer the committee's question as to his alleged membership in the Communist Party. Clearly an answer to the question might have tended to incriminate him. As a consequence, petitioner was entitled to claim the privilege. The principal issue here is whether or not he did.

It is agreed by all that a claim of the privilege does not require any special combination of words. Plainly a witness need not have the skill

of a lawyer to invoke the protection of the Self-Incrimination Clause. If an objection to a question is made in any language that a committee may reasonably be expected to understand as an attempt to invoke the privilege, it must be respected both by the committee and by a court in a prosecution under 192.

Here petitioner, by adopting the grounds relied upon by Fitzpatrick, based his refusal to answer on "the first and fifth amendments" and "the first amendment to the Constitution, supplemented by the fifth amendment." The Government concedes—as we think it must—that a witness may invoke the privilege by stating "I refuse to testify on the ground of the Fifth Amendment." Surely, in popular parlance and even in legal literature, the term "Fifth Amendment" in the context of our time is commonly regarded as being synonymous with the privilege against self-incrimination. The Government argues, however, that the references to the Fifth Amendment in the instant case were inadequate to invoke the privilege because Fitzpatrick's statements are more reasonably understood as invoking rights under the First Amendment. We find the Government's argument untenable. The mere fact that Fitzpatrick and petitioner also relied on the First Amendment does not preclude their reliance on the Fifth Amendment as well. If a witness urges two constitutional objections to a committee's line of questioning, he is not bound at his peril to choose between them. By pressing both objections, he does not lose a privilege which would have been valid if he had only relied on one.

. . .

. . . [T]he committee made no attempt to have petitioner particularize his objection. Under these circumstances, we must hold that petitioner's references to the Fifth Amendment were sufficient to invoke the privilege and that the court below erred in failing to direct a judgment of acquittal.

. . .

The judgment below is reversed and the case remanded to the District Court with directions to enter a judgment of acquittal.

Emspak v. United States
349 U.S. 190 (1955)

This is a companion case to *Quinn v. United States*. . . .

Pursuant to subpoena, petitioner appeared on December 5, 1949, before a subcommittee of the Committee on Un-American Activities. The subcommittee consisted of a single member, Rep. Morgan M. Moulder. Petitioner was then the General Secretary-Treasurer of the United Electrical, Radio & Machine Workers of America as well as Editor of the *UE News*, the union's official publication. The subcommittee's hearings had previously been announced as concerning "the question of Communist affiliation or association of certain members" of the union and "the advisability of tightening present security requirements in industrial plants working on certain Government contracts."

Petitioner was asked a total of 239 questions. . . . He declined, however, to answer 68 of the 239 questions. These 68 questions dealt exclusively with petitioner's associations and affiliations. He based his refusal on "primarily the first amendment, supplemented by the fifth." Of the 68 questions, 58 asked in substance that he state whether or not he was acquainted with certain named individuals and whether or not those individuals had ever held official positions in the union. Two of the questions concerned petitioner's alleged

membership in the National Federation for Constitutional Liberties and the Civil Rights Congress. Eight questions concerned petitioner's alleged membership and activity in the Communist Party.

On November 20, 1950, petitioner was indicted under 192 for his refusal to answer the 68 questions. Sitting without a jury, the District Court held that petitioner's references to "primarily the first amendment, supplemented by the fifth" were insufficient to invoke the Fifth Amendment's privilege against self-incrimination. The District Court accordingly found petitioner guilty on all 68 counts and sentenced him to a term of six months and a fine of $500. The Court of Appeals for the District of Columbia Circuit . . . affirmed en banc. . . .

. . .

. . . [L]ess than two months prior to petitioner's appearance before the committee, eleven principal leaders of the Communist Party in this country had been convicted under the Smith Act for conspiring to teach and advocate the violent overthrow of the United States. Petitioner was identified at their trial as a Communist and an associate of the defendants. It was reported that Smith Act indictments against other Communist leaders were being prepared. . . . [T]wo weeks prior to petitioner's appearance, newspapers carried the story that the Department of Justice "within thirty days" would take "an important step" toward the criminal prosecution of petitioner in connection with his non-Communist affidavit filed with the National Labor Relations Board.

Under these circumstances, it seems clear that answers to the 58 questions concerning petitioner's associations "might be dangerous because injurious disclosure could result." To reveal knowledge about the named individuals—all of them having been previously charged with Communist affiliations—could well have furnished "a link in the chain" of evidence needed to prosecute petitioner for a federal crime, ranging from conspiracy to violate the Smith Act to the filing of a false non-Communist affidavit under the Taft-Hartley Act. That being so, it is immaterial that some of the questions sought information about associations that petitioner might have been able to explain away on some innocent basis unrelated to Communism. If an answer to a question may tend to be incriminatory, a witness is not deprived of the protection of the privilege merely because the witness if subsequently prosecuted could perhaps refute any inference of guilt arising from the answer.

. . .

Our disposition of the case makes it unnecessary to pass on petitioner's other contentions as to the First Amendment and the grand jury. The judgment below is reversed and the case remanded to the District Court with directions to enter a judgment of acquittal.

Bart v. United States
349 U.S. 219 (1955)

On November 20, 1950, the petitioner was indicted for refusing to answer thirty-two questions put to him by a subcommittee of the Committee on Un-American Activities of the House of Representatives. During the trial in the District Court for the District of Columbia, the Government abandoned twenty-four of these counts. The District Judge, sitting without a jury, found Bart guilty of the remaining eight charges. On appeal, the Court of Appeals for the District of Columbia Circuit reversed the judgment upon three of the counts and . . . affirmed as to the others. . . .

In response to a subpoena, petitioner appeared before the subcommittee on June 21, 1950. He was then general manager both of Freedom of the Press Co., Inc., which publishes the *Daily Worker*, and of the *Daily Worker* itself. During the course of the interrogation, members of the committee and the committee counsel posed various questions dealing with Bart's background, his activities, and alleged associates. Among these were the five questions which, because of petitioner's refusal to answer, led to the convictions now under scrutiny. The particular inquiries involve petitioner's name when he came to this country as a child, his name before it was changed years ago to Philip Bart pursuant to a New York court order, his father's name, and the identity of officials of the Ohio section of the Communist Party in 1936. To the questions concerning name or family background, he raised objections of pertinency; to the other, he unequivocally pleaded the privilege against self-incrimination.

In finding petitioner guilty, the trial court rejected these defenses as without merit. Before the Court of Appeals, petitioner abandoned his defense as to lack of pertinency. The majority thought that this abandonment in effect erased petitioner's objections from the committee record and that they were thus faced with "naked refusals to answer" which did not require affirmative rulings from the committee. We cannot agree. The objections were in fact made before the committee and the witness was entitled to a clear-cut ruling at that time, even though the claims were later abandoned or found to be invalid. Without such a ruling, evidence of the requisite criminal intent is lacking. . . .

At no time did the committee directly overrule petitioner's claims of self-incrimination or lack of pertinency. Nor was petitioner indirectly informed of the committee's position through a specific direction to answer. . . .

. . .

Because of the consistent failure to advise the witness of the committee's position as to his objections, petitioner was left to speculate about the risk of possible prosecution for contempt; he was not given a clear choice between standing on his objection and compliance with a committee ruling. Because of this defect in laying the necessary foundation for a prosecution, petitioner's conviction cannot stand under the criteria set forth more fully in *Quinn*.

Our disposition of the case makes it unnecessary to consider petitioner's other contentions. The judgment below is reversed and the case remanded to the District Court with directions to enter a judgment of acquittal.

Watkins v. United States
354 U.S. 178 (1957)

On April 29, 1954, petitioner appeared as a witness in compliance with a subpoena issued by a Subcommittee of the Committee on Un-American Activities of the House of Representatives. The Subcommittee elicited from petitioner a description of his background in labor union activities. He had been an employee of the International Harvester Company between 1935 and 1953. During the last eleven of those years, he had been on leave of absence to serve as an official of the Farm Equipment Workers International Union, later merged into the United Electrical, Radio and Machine Workers. He rose to the position of President of District No. 2 of the Farm Equipment Workers, a district defined geographically to include generally Canton and Rock Falls, Illinois, and Dubuque, Iowa. In 1953, petitioner joined the United Automobile Workers International Union as a labor organizer.

Petitioner's name had been mentioned by two witnesses who testified before the Committee at prior hearings. In September 1952, one Donald O. Spencer admitted having been a Communist from 1943 to 1946. He declared that he had been recruited into the Party with the endorsement and prior approval of petitioner, whom he identified as the then District Vice-President of the Farm Equipment Workers. Spencer also mentioned that petitioner had attended meetings at which only card-carrying Communists were admitted. A month before petitioner testified, one Walter Rumsey stated that he had been recruited into the Party by petitioner. Rumsey added that he had paid Party dues to, and later collected dues from, petitioner, who had assumed the name, Sam Brown. Rumsey told the Committee that he left the Party in 1944.

Petitioner answered these allegations freely and without reservation. . . .

. . .

The Subcommittee . . . was apparently satisfied with petitioner's disclosures. After some further discussion elaborating on the statement, counsel for the Committee turned to another aspect of Rumsey's testimony. Rumsey had identified a group of persons whom he had known as members of the Communist Party, and counsel began to read this list of names to petitioner. Petitioner stated that he did not know several of the persons. Of those whom he did know, he refused to tell whether he knew them to have been members of the Communist Party. . . .

The Chairman of the Committee submitted a report of petitioner's refusal to answer questions to the House of Representatives. The House directed the Speaker to certify the Committee's report to the United States Attorney for initiation of criminal prosecution. A seven-count indictment was returned. Petitioner waived his right to jury trial and was found guilty on all counts by the court. The sentence, a fine of $100 and one year in prison, was suspended, and petitioner was placed on probation.

An appeal was taken to the Court of Appeals for the District of Columbia. The conviction was reversed by a three-judge panel. . . . Upon rehearing en banc, the full bench affirmed the conviction. . . .

. . .

. . . *Rumely* makes it plain that the mere semblance of legislative purpose would not justify an inquiry in the face of the Bill of Rights. The critical element is the existence of, and the weight to be ascribed to, the interest of the Congress in demanding disclosures from an unwilling witness. We cannot simply assume, however, that every congressional investigation is justified by a public need that overbalances any private rights affected. To do so would be to abdicate the responsibility placed by the Constitution upon the judiciary to insure that the Congress does not unjustifiably encroach upon an individual's right to privacy nor abridge his liberty of speech, press, religion or assembly.

. . .

We have no doubt that there is no congressional power to expose for the sake of exposure. . . .

. . .

The members of the Committee have clearly demonstrated that they did not feel themselves restricted in any way to propaganda in the narrow sense of the word. Unquestionably the Committee conceived of its task in the grand view of its name. Un-American activities were its target, no matter how or where manifested. Notwithstanding the broad purview of the Committee's experience, the House of Representatives repeatedly approved its continuation. Five times it extended the life of the special committee. Then it made the group a standing committee of the

House. A year later, the Committee's charter was embodied in the Legislative Reorganization Act. On five occasions, at the beginning of sessions of Congress, it has made the authorizing resolution part of the rules of the House. On innumerable occasions, it has passed appropriation bills to allow the Committee to continue its efforts.

Combining the language of the resolution with the construction it has been given, it is evident that the preliminary control of the Committee exercised by the House of Representatives is slight or nonexistent. No one could reasonably deduce from the charter the kind of investigation that the Committee was directed to make. As a result, we are asked to engage in a process of retroactive rationalization. Looking backward from the events that transpired, we are asked to uphold the Committee's actions unless it appears that they were clearly not authorized by the charter. . . .

The Government contends that the public interest at the core of the investigations of the Un-American Activities Committee is the need by the Congress to be informed of efforts to overthrow the Government by force and violence so that adequate legislative safeguards can be erected. From this core, however, the Committee can radiate outward infinitely to any topic thought to be related in some way to armed insurrection. The outer reaches of this domain are known only by the content of "un-American activities." Remoteness of subject can be aggravated by a probe for a depth of detail even farther removed from any basis of legislative action. A third dimension is added when the investigators turn their attention to the past to collect minutiae on remote topics, on the hypothesis that the past may reflect upon the present.

. . .

. . . An excessively broad charter, like that of the House Un-American Activities Committee, places the courts in an untenable position if they are to strike a balance between the public need for a particular interrogation and the right of citizens to carry on their affairs free from unnecessary governmental interference. It is impossible in such a situation to ascertain whether any legislative purpose justifies the disclosures sought and, if so, the importance of that information to the Congress in furtherance of its legislative function. The reason no court can make this critical judgment is that the House of Representatives itself has never made it. Only the legislative assembly initiating an investigation can assay the relative necessity of specific disclosures.

. . .

Having exhausted the several possible indicia of the "question under inquiry," we remain unenlightened as to the subject to which the questions asked petitioner were pertinent. Certainly, if the point is that obscure after trial and appeal, it was not adequately revealed to petitioner when he had to decide at his peril whether or not to answer. Fundamental fairness demands that no witness be compelled to make such a determination with so little guidance. Unless the subject matter has been made to appear with undisputable clarity, it is the duty of the investigative body, upon objection of the witness on grounds of pertinency, to state for the record the subject under inquiry at that time and the manner in which the propounded questions are pertinent thereto. To be meaningful, the explanation must describe what the topic under inquiry is and the connective reasoning whereby the precise questions asked relate to it.

The statement of the Committee Chairman in this case, in response to petitioner's protest, was woefully inadequate to convey sufficient information as to the pertinency of the questions to the subject under inquiry. Petitioner was thus not accorded a fair opportunity to determine whether he was within his rights in refusing to answer, and his conviction is necessarily invalid under the Due Process Clause of the Fifth Amendment.

. . . The conclusions we have reached in this case will not prevent the Congress, through its committees, from obtaining any information it needs for the proper fulfillment of its role in our scheme of government. The legislature is free to determine the kinds of data that should be collected. It is only those investigations that are conducted by use of compulsory process that give rise to a need to protect the rights of individuals against illegal encroachment. That protection can be readily achieved through procedures which prevent the separation of power from responsibility and which provide the constitutional requisites of fairness for witnesses. A measure of added care on the part of the House and the Senate in authorizing the use of compulsory process and by their committees in exercising that power would suffice. That is a small price to pay if it serves to uphold the principles of limited, constitutional government without constricting the power of the Congress to inform itself.

The judgment of the Court of Appeals is reversed, and the case is remanded to the District Court with instructions to dismiss the indictment.

Sweezy v. New Hampshire
354 U.S. 234 (1957)

The investigation in which petitioner was summoned to testify had its origins in a statute passed by the New Hampshire legislature in 1951. It was a comprehensive scheme of regulation of subversive activities. There was a section defining criminal conduct in the nature of sedition. "Subversive organizations" were declared unlawful and ordered dissolved. "Subversive persons" were made ineligible for employment by the state government. Included in the disability were those employed as teachers or in other capacities by any public educational institution. A loyalty program was instituted to eliminate "subversive persons" among government personnel. All present employees, as well as candidates for elective office in the future, were required to make sworn statements that they were not "subversive persons."

In 1953, the legislature adopted a "Joint Resolution Relating to the Investigation of Subversive Activities." . . .

Under state law, this was construed to constitute the Attorney General as a one-man legislative committee. He was given the authority to delegate any part of the investigation to any member of his staff. The legislature conferred upon the Attorney General the further authority to subpoena witnesses or documents. He did not have power to hold witnesses in contempt, however. In the event that coercive or punitive sanctions were needed, the Attorney General could invoke the aid of a State Superior Court which could find recalcitrant witnesses in contempt of court.

Petitioner was summoned to appear before the Attorney General on two separate occasions. On January 5, 1954, petitioner testified at length upon his past conduct and associations. He denied that he had ever been a member of the Communist Party or that he had ever been part of any program to overthrow the government by force or violence. The interrogation ranged over many matters, from petitioner's World War II military service with the Office of Strategic Services to his sponsorship, in 1949, of the Scientific and Cultural Conference for World Peace, at which he spoke.

During the course of the inquiry, petitioner declined to answer several questions. His rea-

sons for doing so were given in a statement he read to the Committee at the outset of the hearing. He declared he would not answer those questions which were not pertinent to the subject under inquiry as well as those which transgress the limitations of the First Amendment. In keeping with this stand, he refused to disclose his knowledge of the Progressive Party in New Hampshire or of persons with whom he was acquainted in that organization. No action was taken by the Attorney General to compel answers to these questions.

The Attorney General again summoned petitioner to testify on June 3, 1954. There was more interrogation about the witness' prior contacts with Communists. The Attorney General lays great stress upon an article which petitioner had co-authored. . . . Petitioner affirmed that he styled himself a "classical Marxist" and a "socialist" and that the article expressed his continuing opinion.

Again, at the second hearing, the Attorney General asked, and petitioner refused to answer, questions concerning the Progressive Party, and its predecessor, the Progressive Citizens of America. . . .

. . .

Petitioner adhered in this second proceeding to the same reasons for not answering he had given in his statement at the first hearing. He maintained that the questions were not pertinent to the matter under inquiry and that they infringed upon an area protected under the First Amendment.

Following the hearings, the Attorney General petitioned the Superior Court of Merrimack County, New Hampshire, setting forth the circumstances of petitioner's appearance before the Committee and his refusal to answer certain questions. . . . [T]he court ruled that the questions . . .

were pertinent. Petitioner was called as a witness by the court and persisted in his refusal to answer for constitutional reasons. The court adjudged him in contempt and ordered him committed to the county jail until purged of the contempt.

The New Hampshire Supreme Court affirmed. . . .

. . .

. . . [H]ere, as in *Wieman*, the program for the rooting out of subversion is drawn without regard to the presence or absence of guilty knowledge in those affected.

. . .

. . . Merely to summon a witness and compel him, against his will, to disclose the nature of his past expressions and associations is a measure of governmental interference in these matters. These are rights which are safeguarded by the Bill of Rights and the Fourteenth Amendment. We believe that there unquestionably was an invasion of petitioner's liberties in the areas of academic freedom and political expression—areas in which government should be extremely reticent to tread.

. . .

Equally manifest as a fundamental principle of a democratic society is political freedom of the individual. Our form of government is built on the premise that every citizen shall have the right to engage in political expression and association. . . . Exercise of these basic freedoms in America has traditionally been through the media of political associations. Any interference with the freedom of a party is simultaneously an interference with the freedom of its adherents. All political ideas cannot and should not be channeled into the programs of our two major parties. History has amply proved the virtue of political activity by minority, dissident groups, who innumerable times have been in the vanguard of democratic thought and whose programs were ultimately accepted. Mere unorthodoxy or dis-

sent from the prevailing mores is not to be condemned. The absence of such voices would be a symptom of grave illness in our society.

. . .

. . . [I]f the Attorney General's interrogation of petitioner were in fact wholly unrelated to the object of the legislature in authorizing the inquiry, the Due Process Clause would preclude the endangering of constitutional liberties. We believe that an equivalent situation is presented in this case. The lack of any indications that the legislature wanted the information the Attorney General attempted to elicit from petitioner must be treated as the absence of authority. It follows that the use of the contempt power, notwithstanding the interference with constitutional rights, was not in accordance with the due process requirements of the Fourteenth Amendment.

. . . We accept the finding of the State Supreme Court that the employment of the Attorney General as the investigating committee does not alter the legislative nature of the proceedings. Moreover, this Court has held that the concept of separation of powers embodied in the United States Constitution is not mandatory in state governments. . . .

The judgment of the Supreme Court of New Hampshire is reversed.

Sacher v. United States
356 U.S. 576 (1958)

. . . Charged in a three-count indictment for failure to answer three questions put to him by a subcommittee of the Internal Security Subcommittee of the Senate Committee on the Judiciary, the petitioner, having waived trial by jury, was found guilty on all counts and sentenced to six months' imprisonment and to pay a fine of $1,000. After the sentence was sustained by the Court of Appeals, this Court, having granted a petition for certiorari, remanded the case, to the Court of Appeals for reconsideration in light of *Watkins*. On reargument before the Court of Appeals sitting en banc, a divided court again affirmed the conviction.

The broad scope of authority vested in Congress to conduct investigations as an incident to the "legislative Powers" granted by the Constitution is not questioned. But when Congress seeks to enforce its investigating authority through the criminal process administered by the federal judiciary, the safeguards of criminal justice become operative. The subject matter of inquiry before the subcommittee at which petitioner appeared as a witness concerned the recantation of prior testimony by a witness named Matusow. In the course of the hearing, the questioning of petitioner entered upon a "brief excursion," into proposed legislation barring Communists from practice at the federal bar, a subject not within the subcommittee's scope of inquiry as authorized by its parent committee. Inasmuch as petitioner's refusal to answer related to questions not clearly pertinent to the subject on which the two-member subcommittee conducting the hearing had been authorized to take testimony, the conditions necessary to sustain a conviction for deliberately refusing to answer questions pertinent to the authorized subject matter of a congressional hearing are wanting. The judgment of the Court of Appeals is therefore reversed and the cause remanded to the District Court with directions to dismiss the indictment.

Flaxer v. United States
358 U.S. 147 (1958)

Petitioner was found guilty, after jury trial, of failure to produce, pursuant to a subpoena duces tecum issued by a Subcommittee of a Senate Committee, records of a union showing the names and addresses of members of that organization who were employed either by the United States or by any state, county, or municipal government in the country. The District Court denied a motion for acquittal or new trial. The Court of Appeals, sitting en banc, affirmed. . . On petition for a writ of certiorari, we vacated and remanded for consideration in light of *Watkins*. . . . The Court of Appeals, sitting en banc, once more affirmed by a divided vote. . . .

The Senate Committee on the Judiciary or a duly authorized Subcommittee was authorized to investigate the administration, operation, and enforcement of the Internal Security Act of 1950. The Committee created a Subcommittee which adopted a resolution to the effect that a single member would constitute a quorum for the purpose of taking testimony.

Petitioner was head of the union under investigation. The Chairman issued a subpoena duces tecum directing him to produce, inter alia, the names and addresses of the union members mentioned above. Petitioner appeared before Senator Watkins, sitting as the Subcommittee, and produced some of the records of the union, but he failed to produce the membership lists. He made several objections to disclosure of them, maintaining that they were protected by a right of privacy. He did not maintain that the lists were unavailable to him. Indeed, he responded to further interrogation, giving the approximate number of members and indicating that about 5 percent were in the employ of the Federal Government, the balance being in state, county, and municipal governments. He also named the federal agencies where the bulk of the 5 percent were employed. But he persisted in his refusal to produce the lists. . . .

. . .

Giving a witness a fair apprisal of the committee's ruling on an objection recognizes the legitimate interests of both the witness and the committee. Just as the witness need not use any particular form of words to present his objection, so also the committee is not required to resort to any fixed verbal formula to indicate its disposition of the objection. So long as the witness is not forced to guess the committee's ruling, he has no cause to complain. And adherence to this traditional practice can neither inflict hardship upon the committee nor abridge the proper scope of legislative investigation.

On this record, the District Court should have directed an acquittal. Reversed.

Scull v. Virginia
359 U.S. 344 (1959)

David H. Scull was convicted of contempt in the Circuit Court of Arlington County, Virginia, for refusing to obey a decision of that court ordering him to answer a number of questions put to him by a Legislative Investigative Committee of the Virginia General Assembly. On appeal the Virginia Supreme Court of Appeals affirmed without opinion. Scull contended at the Committee hearings, in the courts below, and in this Court that the Virginia statute authorizing the investigation, both on its face and as applied, violated the Fourteenth Amendment to the United States Constitution. He claimed, among other things, that: (1) The Committee was "established and given investigative authority, as part of a legislative program of 'massive resistance' to the United States Constitution and the Supreme Court's desegregation decisions, in order to harass, vilify, and publicly embarrass members of the NAACP

and others who are attempting to secure integrated public schooling in Virginia." (2) The questions asked him violated his rights of free speech, assembly and petition by constituting an unjustified restraint upon his associations with others in "legal and laudable political and humanitarian causes." (3) "The information sought from [him] was neither intended to, nor could reasonably be expected to, assist the Legislature in any proper legislative function." (4) Despite his requests, repeated at every stage of the proceedings, the Committee failed to inform him "in what respect its questions were pertinent to the subject under inquiry. . . ."

. . .

Scull is a printer and calendar publisher in Annandale, Virginia, where he has been a longtime resident active in religious, civic and welfare groups. . . . In December of 1954, Scull and a group of other citizens met at a church in Alexandria to consider and discuss "the part which concerned and conscientious citizens can best play in helping to achieve the community adjustments necessary to protect the educational and constitutional rights of all citizens as recently defined and interpreted by the Supreme Court of the United States." The group decided to prepare and publish through a "Citizens Clearing House On Public Education" information about the Virginia educational program and to report on the progress made by various Parent-Teacher Associations in Northern Virginia in developing programs for "orderly integration."

One of the newsletters published by the Clearing House was obtained by the Fairfax Citizens' Council, a group which vigorously opposed any desegregation of Virginia schools. The Council republished a large part of the letter in a pamphlet entitled "The Shocking

Truth!" It called attention to the fact that the newsletter was being "disseminated through Box 218, Annandale, Va. (David Scull)," and stated that "communications with the N.A.A.C.P., Southern Regional Council, Clearing House, B'nai B'rith, Council on Human Relations, American Friends and many other pro-integration groups are funneled through Box 218, Annandale, Va., and membership is encouraged if not actually suggested by the P.T.A. Federation."

The pamphlet came to the attention of Delegate James M. Thomson, Chairman of the Virginia Committee on Law Reform and Racial Activities, who promptly subpoenaed Scull to appear and testify. This group, commonly called the "Thomson Committee," was established a few months after the Virginia General Assembly adopted a resolution attacking the Brown decision and pledging that the Legislature would take all constitutionally available measures to resist desegregation in the public schools. The bill setting up the "Thomson Committee" was one of a series relating to segregation passed on the same day. Among these were bills establishing a pupil-assignment plan, providing for the withdrawal of state funds from integrated schools and forbidding barratry, champerty and maintenance. . . .

Scull appeared before the Thomson Committee, as ordered. He answered several questions about his publishing business, and then was asked whether he belonged "to an organization known as The Fairfax County Council on Human Relations." He replied that "on advice of counsel I wish to state that the language of the subpoena delivered to me was so broad and vague . . . that before going further I wish to ask you to tell me the specific subject of your inquiry today, so that I may judge which of your questions are pertinent." Chairman

Thomson told him that the general subjects under inquiry were "threefold": (1) the tax status of racial organizations and of contributions to them; (2) the effect of integration or its threat on the public schools of Virginia and on the State's general welfare; and (3) the violation of certain statutes against "champerty, barratry, and maintenance, or the unauthorized practice of the law." He told Scull, however, that several of these subjects "primarily do not deal with you." Scull then filed a statement of his objections to the questioning and emphasized that he had not been "properly informed of the subject of inquiry." Without clarifying Chairman Thomson's ambiguous statement or specifying which of the "several" subjects did not apply to Scull, the Committee proceeded to ask 31 questions. . . .

It is difficult to see how some of these questions have any relationship to the subjects the Committee was authorized to investigate, or how Scull could possibly discover any such relationship from the Chairman's statement. . . .

. . .

The judge who ordered Scull to answer the questions made no clearer statement of their pertinence to the investigation or to basic state interests than had the Committee Chairman. . . . He at no time analyzed the individual questions asked, nor explained to Scull what it was that the Committee wanted from him and how the questions put to him related to these desires.

. . . [T]he record shows that the purposes of the inquiry, as announced by the Chairman, were so unclear, in fact conflicting, that Scull did not have an opportunity of understanding the basis for the questions or any justification on the part of the Committee for seeking the information he refused to give. To sustain his conviction for contempt under these circumstances would be to send him to jail for a crime he could not with reasonable certainty know he was committing. . . . The information given to Scull was far too wavering, confused, and cloudy to sustain his conviction.

The case is reversed and remanded to the Virginia Supreme Court of Appeals for further proceedings not inconsistent with this opinion.

Uphaus v. Wyman
360 U.S. 72 (1959)

This case is here again on appeal from a judgment of civil contempt entered against appellant by the Merrimack County Court and affirmed by the Supreme Court of New Hampshire. It arises out of appellant's refusal to produce certain documents before a New Hampshire legislative investigating committee which was authorized and directed to determine, inter alia, whether there were subversive persons or organizations present in the State of New Hampshire. Upon the first appeal from the New Hampshire court, we vacated the judgment and remanded the case to it, for consideration in the light of *Sweezy v. New Hampshire*. That court reaffirmed its former decision, deeming *Sweezy* not to control the issues in the instant case. . . .

. . . [T]he Attorney General of New Hampshire, who had been constituted a one-man legislative investigating committee by Joint Resolution of the Legislature, was conducting a probe of subversive activities in the State. In the course of his investigation the Attorney General called appellant, Executive Director of World Fellowship, Inc., a voluntary corporation organized under the laws of New Hampshire and maintaining a summer camp in the State. Appellant testified concerning his own activities, but refused to comply with two subpoenas duces tecum which called for the production of certain corporate records for the years 1954 and 1955. . . . Met with appellant's refusal, the Attorney General, in accordance with state procedure, petitioned the Merrimack County Court to call appellant before it and require compliance with the subpoenas.

In court, appellant again refused to produce the information. . . .

The Merrimack County Court sustained appellant's objection to the production of the names of the nonprofessional employees. The Attorney General took no appeal from that ruling, and it is not before us. . . . We now pass to a consideration of the sole question before us, namely, the validity of the order of contempt for refusal to produce the list of guests at World Fellowship, Inc., during the summer seasons of 1954 and 1955. In addition to the arguments appellant made to the trial court, he urges here that the "indefinite sentence" imposed upon him constitutes such cruel and unusual punishment as to be a denial of due process.

. . .

The nexus between World Fellowship and subversive activities disclosed by the record furnished adequate justification for the investigation we here review. The Attorney General sought to learn if subversive persons were in the State because of the legislative determination that such persons, statutorily defined with a view toward the Communist Party, posed a serious threat to the security of the State. The investigation was, therefore, undertaken in the interest of self-preservation, "the ultimate value of any society." This governmental interest outweighs individual rights in an associational privacy which, however real in other circumstances, were here tenuous at best. The camp was operating as a public one, furnishing both board and lodging to persons applying therefor. As to them, New Hampshire law requires that World Fellowship, Inc., maintain a register, open to inspection of sheriffs and police officers. It is contended that the list might be "circulated throughout the states and the Attorney Generals throughout the states have cross-indexed files, so that any guest whose name is mentioned in that kind of proceeding immediately becomes suspect, even in his own place of residence." The record before us, however, only reveals a report to the Legislature of New Hampshire made by the Attorney General in accordance with the requirements of the resolution. We recognize, of course, that compliance with the subpoena will result in exposing the fact that the persons therein named were guests at World Fellowship. But so long as a committee must report to its legislative parent, exposure—in the sense of disclosure—is an inescapable incident of an investigation into the presence of subversive persons within a State. And the governmental interest in self-preservation is sufficiently compelling to subordinate the interest in associational privacy of persons who, at least to the extent of the guest registration statute, made public at the inception the association they now wish to keep private. In the light of such a record we conclude that the State's interest has not been "pressed, in this instance, to a point where it has come into fatal collision with the overriding" constitutionally protected rights of appellant and those he may represent.

. . .

We have concluded that the committee's demand for the documents was a legitimate one; it follows that the judgment of contempt for refusal to produce them is valid. We do not impugn appellant's good faith in the assertion of what he believed to be his rights. But three

courts have disagreed with him in interpreting those rights. If appellant chooses to abide by the result of the adjudication and obey the order of New Hampshire's courts, he need not face jail. If, however, he continues to disobey, we find on this record no constitutional objection to the exercise of the traditional remedy of contempt to secure compliance.

Affirmed.

Barenblatt v. United States
360 U.S. 109 (1959)

We here review petitioner's conviction for contempt of Congress, arising from his refusal to answer certain questions put to him by a Subcommittee of the House Committee on Un-American Activities during the course of an inquiry concerning alleged Communist infiltration into the field of education.

The case is before us for the second time. Petitioner's conviction was originally affirmed in 1957 by a unanimous panel of the Court of Appeals. This Court granted certiorari, vacated the judgment of the Court of Appeals, and remanded the case to that court for further consideration in light of *Watkins*. . . . [T]he Court of Appeals, sitting en banc, reaffirmed the conviction. . . .

Pursuant to a subpoena, and accompanied by counsel, petitioner on June 28, 1954, appeared as a witness before this congressional Subcommittee. After answering a few preliminary questions and testifying that he had been a graduate student and teaching fellow at the University of Michigan from 1947 to 1950 and an instructor in psychology at Vassar College from 1950 to shortly before his appearance before the Subcommittee, petitioner objected generally to the right of the Subcommittee to inquire into his "political" and "religious" beliefs or any "other personal and private affairs" or "associational activities," upon grounds set forth in a previously prepared memorandum which he was allowed to file with the Subcommittee. Thereafter petitioner specifically declined to answer each of the following five questions. . . .

In each instance the grounds of refusal were those set forth in the prepared statement. Petitioner expressly disclaimed reliance upon "the Fifth Amendment."

Following receipt of the Subcommittee's report of these occurrences the House duly certified the matter to the District of Columbia United States Attorney for contempt proceedings. An indictment in five Counts. . . . With the consent of both sides the case was tried to the court without a jury, and upon conviction under all Counts a general sentence of six months' imprisonment and a fine of $250 was imposed.

. . .

The precise constitutional issue confronting us is whether the Subcommittee's inquiry into petitioner's past or present membership in the Communist Party transgressed the provisions of the First Amendment, which of course reach and limit congressional investigations.

. . .

The first question is whether this investigation was related to a valid legislative purpose. . . .

That Congress has wide power to legislate in the field of Communist activity in this Country, and to conduct appropriate investigations in aid thereof, is hardly debatable. . . .

On these premises, this Court in its constitutional adjudications has consistently refused to view the Communist Party as an ordinary political party, and has upheld federal legislation aimed at the Communist problem which in a different context would certainly have raised constitutional

issues of the gravest character. On the same premises this Court has upheld under the Fourteenth Amendment state legislation requiring those occupying or seeking public office to disclaim knowing membership in any organization advocating overthrow of the Government by force and violence, which legislation none can avoid seeing was aimed at membership in the Communist Party. Similarly, in other areas, this Court has recognized the close nexus between the Communist Party and violent overthrow of government. To suggest that because the Communist Party may also sponsor peaceable political reforms the constitutional issues before us should now be judged as if that Party were just an ordinary political party from the standpoint of national security, is to ask this Court to blind itself to world affairs which have determined the whole course of our national policy since the close of World War II. . . .

. . .

We conclude that the balance between the individual and the governmental interests here at stake must be struck in favor of the latter, and that therefore the provisions of the First Amendment have not been offended.

We hold that petitioner's conviction for contempt of Congress discloses no infirmity, and that the judgment of the Court of Appeals must be affirmed.

Raley v. Ohio
360 U.S. 423 (1959)

These two appeals involve convictions of four appellants for refusal to answer certain questions put to them at sessions of the "Un-American Activities Commission" of the State of Ohio, established in the legislative branch of the Ohio Government. The appellants had claimed the privilege against self-incrimination in refusing to answer each of the questions. The cases are before us for the second time; on prior appeals the judgments below were vacated and the causes remanded for reconsideration in the light of *Sweezy* and *Watkins*. The remand resulted in a reaffirmance of the prior judgment without discussion. . . .

. . .

Mrs. Morgan was summoned before the Commission and interrogated mainly in regard to Communist Party activities. She appeared without counsel. To each question put she answered, "I regret that I cannot answer your question under the Fifth Amendment of the Constitution, because to do so would give your Committee an opportunity to incriminate me," or some more abbreviated form of words to the same effect. Such responses were given to virtually all the questions and in almost every case the Commission proceeded directly to ask its next question after receiving the response. In no case did the Commission direct that she answer its question. . . .

Raley, Stern, and Brown appeared before the Commission successively on another occasion, about six months later. They were interrogated about subversive activities in the labor movement. Raley answered some questions, but to most of them asserted the privilege against self-incrimination of the Federal and Ohio Constitutions. Most of his assertions of the privilege, including his initial ones, were not made the subject of comment or question by the Commission, the next question in the inquiry being put at once. On some few occasions, when Raley claimed the privilege, the Commission members indicated their doubts whether any answer to a specific question put could be incriminating. On one occasion, the Commission asked Raley as to whether he recollected a certain interview. . . .

Stern was the next person to appear at the in-

quiry. . . . On Stern's continued refusal to answer, the Chairman directed an answer to the question, which was refused. To most subsequent questions, Stern again claimed the privilege against self-incrimination, and on the great majority of questions, the Commission simply passed on to the next question. . . .

Brown then was subjected to inquiry. He claimed the privilege as to self-incrimination to most of the questions put to him. While the Chairman never told him in so many words (as he had told the other three appellants) that the privilege was available, Brown and the Chairman engaged in long colloquies in an attempt by the Chairman to clarify that by using a certain form of words Brown was claiming the privilege. . . . He was on a couple of occasions directed to answer a question when he was engaging in a colloquy with the Commission without either having answered it directly or having claimed the privilege; upon his claim of the privilege, the next question was at once put.

. . .

Indictments were found against the four appellants for failure to answer various of the questions put to them at the inquiry. In the cases of Raley, Stern, and Brown—who were indicted at the same time and tried together, but in a different court from Mrs. Morgan—only a few of the questions were made the subject of the indictment. There appears to have been some effort to restrict their indictments to those questions to which the prosecution thought no answer could have been incriminating. On the other hand, virtually every question asked Mrs. Morgan was made the subject of her indictment.

A jury was waived by Raley, Stern, and Brown, and they were found guilty on each of the relatively few counts found against them, the trial court filing no opinion or conclusions of law. The Court of Appeals affirmed the convictions on some of the counts as to Raley, on one of the two counts as to Stern, and on all the counts as to Brown, and reversed the convictions on some of the counts as to Raley and on one count as to Stern. . . .

A jury was also waived by Mrs. Morgan and she too was found guilty by a trial judge. The judge acquitted her on a few counts as to questions found not pertinent to the inquiry or duplicative of other questions. But as to the remaining counts, he ruled that her plea of self-incrimination was not valid, because she had referred solely to the Fifth Amendment and not to the appropriate provision of the Ohio Constitution guaranteeing freedom from compulsory self-incrimination. . . . The Court of Appeals— a different one from that which passed on the appeal of Raley, Stern, and Brown—affirmed the judgment for the reasons stated in the trial court's opinion.

On appeal, the Supreme Court of Ohio, though affirming the convictions, abandoned reliance on the theories under which the appellants were found guilty by the courts below. It ruled that a fair reference to the privilege against self-incrimination of the United States Constitution was adequate to invoke the privilege under the Ohio Constitution, finding such reference made. . . .

. . .

On writs of certiorari, judgments reversed as to Raley, Brown and Morgan; judgment affirmed as to Stern by an equally divided Court.

McPhaul v. United States
364 U.S. 372 (1960)

. . . Having knowledge that the Civil Rights Congress had been declared a subversive organiza-

tion by the Attorney General—indeed, having itself earlier found that organization to be a subversive one—and having reason to believe that petitioner was its Executive Secretary, the House Committee on Un-American Activities caused a subpoena of the House of Representatives to be issued and served upon petitioner commanding him to appear before its Committee on Un-American Activities, or a subcommittee thereof, at a stated time and place in Detroit, Michigan, on February 26, 1952, and there to produce "all records, correspondence and memoranda pertaining to the organization of, the affiliation with other organizations and all monies received or expended by the Civil Rights Congress . . . [and] then and there to testify touching matters of inquiry committed to said Committee. . . ."

. . .

Following receipt of the Subcommittee's report of these occurrences, the House certified the matter to the United States Attorney for the Eastern District of Michigan for initiation of contempt proceedings against petitioner, and he was indicted on July 29, 1954. After denial of his motion to dismiss the indictment, petitioner entered a plea of not guilty and the case was put to trial before a jury. . . .

. . .

The jury found petitioner guilty, and he was fined the sum of $500 and sentenced to imprisonment for a period of nine months. The Court of Appeals affirmed. . . .

. . .

. . . [W]e cannot say that the breadth of the subpoena was such as to violate the Fourth Amendment.

Affirmed.

Wilkinson v. United States
365 U.S. 399 (1961)

The petitioner was convicted for having unlaw-fully refused to answer a question pertinent to a matter under inquiry before a subcommittee of the House Committee on Un-American Activities at a hearing in Atlanta, Georgia, on July 30, 1958. His conviction was affirmed by the Court of Appeals, which held that our decision in *Barenblatt* was "controlling." . . .

. . .

. . . After being sworn and stating his name he declined to give his residence address, stating that, "As a matter of conscience and personal respon-sibility, I refuse to answer any questions of this committee." . . .

. . .

The subsequent indictment and conviction of the petitioner were based upon his refusal . . . to answer the single question "Are you now a mem-ber of the Communist Party?"

The judgment affirming the petitioner's con-viction is attacked here from several different directions. . . .

. . .

The petitioner argues, however, that the sub-committee was inspired to interrogate him by reason of his opposition to the existence of the Un-American Activities Committee itself, and that its purpose was unauthorized harassment and exposure. He points to the Chairman's opening statement which mentioned activity against the Committee, to the fact that he was subpoenaed to appear before the subcommittee soon after he arrived in Atlanta to stir up opposition to the Committee's activities, and to the statement of the Staff Director indicating the subcommittee's awareness of his efforts to develop a "hostile sen-timent" to the Committee and to "bring pressure

upon the United States Congress to preclude these particular hearings."

. . . [W]e can find nothing to indicate that it was the intent of Congress to immunize from in-terrogation all those (and there are many) who are opposed to the existence of the Un-American Activities Committee.

. . .

. . . As we have noted, a prime purpose of the hearings was to investigate Communist propa-ganda activities in the South. It therefore was entirely logical for the subcommittee to subpoena the petitioner after he had arrived at the site of the hearings, had registered as a member of a group which the subcommittee believed to be Communist dominated, and had conducted a pub-lic campaign against the subcommittee. The fact that the petitioner might not have been summoned to appear had he not come to Atlanta illustrates the very point, for in that event he might not have been thought to have been connected with a sub-ject under inquiry—Communist Party propa-ganda activities in that area of the country.

. . .

The petitioner's claim that the question he re-fused to answer was not pertinent to a subject under inquiry merits no extended discussion. In-deed, it is difficult to imagine a preliminary question more pertinent to the topics under in-vestigation than whether petitioner was in fact a member of the Communist Party. . . .

. . .

The subcommittee's legitimate legislative in-terest was not the activity in which the petitioner might have happened at the time to be engaged, but in the manipulation and infiltration of activi-ties and organizations by persons advocating overthrow of the Government. . . .

We conclude that the First Amendment claims pressed here are indistinguishable from those considered in *Barenblatt*, and that upon the reasoning and the authority of that case they cannot prevail.

Affirmed.

Braden v. United States
365 U.S. 431 (1961)

This case is a companion to *Wilkinson v. United States*, decided today. The petitioner was the witness immediately preceding Wilkinson at the hearing of a subcommittee of the House Un-American Activities Committee, in Atlanta, Georgia, on July 30, 1958. He refused to answer many of the questions directed to him, basing his refusal upon the grounds that the questions were not pertinent to a question under inquiry by the subcommittee and that the interrogation invaded his First Amendment rights. He was subsequently indicted and, after a jury trial, convicted for . . . refusing to answer six specific questions which had been put to him by the subcommittee. The Court of Appeals affirmed. . . .

. . .

Here . . . the refusal to answer was deliberate and intentional. Affirmed.

Slagle v. Ohio
366 U.S. 259 (1961)

Pursuing its statutory powers and duties to investigate subversive activities in Ohio, the Ohio Un-American Activities Commission scheduled a hearing to commence at the Stark County Courthouse on the morning of October 21, 1953, and subpoenaed these five appellants to appear and testify before it at that time and place. Each appeared with counsel, was sworn and examined.

Though having both constructive and actual knowledge of Ohio's immunity statute, each objected to most of the questions propounded on the ground that an answer would compel him to be a witness against himself, in violation of the Ohio Constitution and of the Fifth Amendment to the United States Constitution. Appellants were not, in most instances, directed to answer, but in a few instances some of them (Perry, Cooper, and Mladajan) were directed to answer the question, yet flatly refused to do so.

Acting pursuant to Ohio Rev. Code 103.35, the members of the Commission who sat at the hearing authorized the chairman to cause contempt proceedings to be initiated against appellants under Ohio Rev. Code 2705.02 to 2705.09, and on December 24, 1953, each appellant was separately indicted in the court of common pleas of Stark County on 10 counts—each count charging willful failure, in violation of 2705.02, to answer a question propounded by the Commission. Upon a joint trial to the court, each appellant was convicted and sentenced on some of the counts. On consolidated appeals, the Stark County Court of Appeals affirmed, the Supreme Court of Ohio, finding no debatable constitutional question presented, dismissed appellants' appeals. . . .

. . .

. . . [J]udgments reversed as to Slagle and Bohus; judgments reversed in part and affirmed, by an equally divided Court, in part as to Perry, Cooper and Mladajan.

Deutch v. United States
367 U.S. 456 (1961)

. . . The petitioner was brought to trial in the District Court for the District of Columbia upon an indictment . . . by refusing to answer five questions "which were pertinent to the question then under inquiry" by the subcommittee. He waived a jury and was convicted upon four of the five counts of the indictment. The judgment was affirmed by the Court of Appeals. . . .

. . .

The petitioner answered, "under protest," that he had indeed been a member of the Communist Party while at Cornell. He then testified freely and without further objection as to his own activities and associations. He stated that "from the age of 13 or 14 I had read many books on Marxism and at that time was very much impressed with trying to solve certain of the injustices we have nowadays." He said that when he got to college "I felt if I had ideas I shouldn't be half pregnant about them, so when I came to college I was approached and joined." . . .

. . . Many of his answers indicated a lack of awareness of the details of Communist activities at Cornell. The petitioner testified that as of the time of the hearings he was no longer a member of the Communist Party, but he volunteered the information that "[t]o a great extent it is only fair to say I am a Marxist today—I don't want to deny that."

. . . [He] refused to answer five questions he was asked concerning other people. He declined to give the names of the faculty member who had been a Communist, of the friend who had made the $100 contribution, of the student who had originally approached him about joining the Communist Party, and of the owners of the house where the meetings had been held. He also declined to say whether he was acquainted with one Homer Owen. For his refusal to answer these questions he was indicted, tried, and convicted.

. . .

It is also evident . . . that the thoughts which the petitioner voiced in refusing to answer the questions about other people can hardly be considered as the equivalent of an objection upon the grounds of pertinency. Although he did indicate doubt as to the importance of the questions, the petitioner's main concern was clearly his own conscientious unwillingness to act as an informer. . . .

. . . [I]n any event, it is clear that the Government at the trial failed to carry its burden of proving the pertinence of the questions. . . .

. . .

. . . It was incumbent upon the prosecution in this case to prove that the petitioner had committed the offense for which he was indicted. One element of that offense was the pertinence to the subject matter under inquiry of the questions the petitioner refused to answer. We hold, as a matter of law, that there was a failure of such proof in this case.

. . .

Reversed.

Russell v. United States
369 U.S. 749 (1962)

In these six cases we review judgments of the Court of Appeals for the District of Columbia, which affirmed convictions obtained in the District Court. Each of the petitioners was convicted for refusing to answer certain questions when summoned before a congressional subcommittee. . . .

. . .

In No. 12, *Price v. United States*, the petitioner refused to answer a number of questions put to him by the Internal Security Subcommittee of the Senate Judiciary Committee. . . . [W]hen Price was called to testify before the subcommittee no one offered even to attempt to inform him of what subject the subcommittee did have under inquiry.

At the trial the Government took the position that the subject under inquiry had been Communist activities generally. The district judge before whom the case was tried found that "the questions put were pertinent to the matter under inquiry" without indicating what he thought the subject under inquiry was. The Court of Appeals, in affirming the conviction, likewise omitted to state what it thought the subject under inquiry had been. In this Court the Government contends that the subject under inquiry at the time the petitioner was called to testify was "Communist activity in news media."

It is difficult to imagine a case in which an indictment's insufficiency resulted so clearly in the indictment's failure to fulfill its primary office—to inform the defendant of the nature of the accusation against him. . . . Price was put to trial and convicted upon an indictment which did not even purport to inform him in any way of the identity of the topic under subcommittee inquiry. At every stage in the ensuing criminal proceeding Price was met with a different theory, or by no theory at all, as to what the topic had been. Far from informing Price of the nature of the accusation against him, the indictment instead left the prosecution free to roam at large— to shift its theory of criminality so as to take advantage of each passing vicissitude of the trial and appeal. Yet Price could be guilty of no criminal offense unless the questions he refused to answer were in fact pertinent to a specific topic under subcommittee inquiry at the time he was interrogated.

. . .

For these reasons we conclude that an indictment under 2 U.S.C. 192 must state the question under congressional committee inquiry as found by the grand jury. . . .

Reversed.

Gibson v. Florida Legislative Commission
372 U.S. 539 (1963)

The origins of the controversy date from 1956, when a committee of the Florida Legislature commenced an investigation of the N.A.A.C.P. Upon expiration of this committee's authority, a new committee was established to pursue the inquiry. The new committee, created in 1957, held hearings and sought by subpoena to obtain the entire membership list of the Miami branch of the N.A.A.C.P.; production was refused and the committee obtained a court order requiring that the list be submitted. On appeal, the Florida Supreme Court held that the committee could not require production and disclosure of the entire membership list of the organization, but that it could compel the custodian of the records to bring them to the hearings and to refer to them to determine whether specific individuals, otherwise identified as, or "suspected of being," Communists, were N.A.A.C.P. members.

Because of the impending expiration of the authority of the 1957 committee, the Florida Legislature in 1959 established the respondent Legislative Investigation Committee to resume the investigation of the N.A.A.C.P. . . .

The petitioner, then president of the Miami branch of the N.A.A.C.P., was ordered to appear before the respondent Committee on November 4, 1959, and, in accordance with the prior decision of the Florida Supreme Court, to bring with him records of the association which were in his possession or custody and which pertained to the identity of members of, and contributors to, the Miami and state N.A.A.C.P. organizations. Prior to interrogation of any witnesses the Committee chairman read the text of the statute creating the Committee and declared that the hearings would be "concerned with the activities of various organizations which have been or are presently operating in this State in the fields of, first, race relations; second, the coercive reform of social and educational practices and mores by litigation and pressured administrative action; third, of labor; fourth, of education; fifth, and other vital phases of life in this State." The chairman also stated that the inquiry would be directed to Communists and Communist activities, including infiltration of Communists into organizations operating in the described fields.

Upon being called to the stand, the petitioner admitted that he was custodian of his organization's membership records and testified that the local group had about 1,000 members, that individual membership was renewed annually, and that the only membership lists maintained were those for the then current year.

The petitioner told the Committee that he had not brought these records with him to the hearing and announced that he would not produce them for the purpose of answering questions concerning membership in the N.A.A.C.P. He did, however, volunteer to answer such questions on the basis of his own personal knowledge; when given the names and shown photographs of 14 persons previously identified as Communists or members of Communist front of affiliated organizations, the petitioner said that he could associate none of them with the N.A.A.C.P.

The petitioner's refusal to produce his organization's membership lists was based on the ground that to bring the lists to the hearing and to utilize them as the basis of his testimony would interfere with the free exercise of Fourteenth Amendment associational rights of members and prospective members of the N.A.A.C.P.

In accordance with Florida procedure, the petitioner was brought before a state court and . . .

adjudged in contempt, and sentenced to six months' imprisonment and fined $1,200, or, in default in payment thereof, sentenced to an additional six months' imprisonment. The Florida Supreme Court sustained the judgment. . . .

. . .

. . . It is apparent that the necessary preponderating governmental interest and, in fact, the very result in those cases were founded on the holding that the Communist Party is not an ordinary or legitimate political party, as known in this country, and that, because of its particular nature, membership therein is itself a permissible subject of regulation and legislative scrutiny. Assuming the correctness of the premises on which those cases were decided, no further demonstration of compelling governmental interest was deemed necessary, since the direct object of the challenged questions there was discovery of membership in the Communist Party, a matter held pertinent to a proper subject then under inquiry.

Here, however, it is not alleged Communists who are the witnesses before the Committee and it is not discovery of their membership in that party which is the object of the challenged inquiries. Rather, it is the N.A.A.C.P. itself which is the subject of the investigation, and it is its local president, the petitioner, who was called before the Committee and held in contempt because he refused to divulge the contents of its membership records. There is no suggestion that the Miami branch of the N.A.A.C.P. or the national organization with which it is affiliated was, or is, itself a subversive organization. Nor is there any indication that the activities or policies of the N.A.A.C.P. were either Communist dominated or influenced. In fact, this very record indicates that the association was and is against communism and has voluntarily taken steps to keep Communists from being members. . . .

. . . Compelling such an organization, engaged in the exercise of First and Fourteenth Amendment rights, to disclose its membership presents . . . a question wholly different from compelling the Communist Party to disclose its own membership. . . .

. . .

We do not know from . . . ambiguous testimony how many of the 14 were supposed to have been N.A.A.C.P. members. . . .

It also appears that a number of the 14 persons . . . were no longer even residents of Florida; as to these people, it is difficult to see any basis for supposing that they would be current—much less influential—members of the Miami branch of the N.A.A.C.P., and no other pertinent reason for the inquiry as to them could be found because, as the petitioner testified, the only membership records available related to the then current year.

. . .

Nor does the fact that the N.A.A.C.P. has demonstrated its antipathy to communism and an awareness of its threat by passage of annual antisubversion resolutions carry with it any permissible inference that it has, in fact, been infiltrated, influenced, or in any way dominated or used by Communists. Indeed, given the gross improbability of a Communist dominated or influenced organization denouncing communism, the more reasonable inference would seem to be to the contrary.

. . .

. . . The respondent Committee has failed to demonstrate the compelling and subordinating governmental interest essential to support direct inquiry into the membership records of the N.A.A.C.P.

Nothing we say here impairs or denies the existence of the underlying legislative right to investigate or legislate with respect to subversive activities by Communists or anyone else; our decision today deals only with the manner in which such power may be exercised and we hold simply that groups which themselves are neither engaged in subversive or other illegal or improper activities nor demonstrated to have any substantial connections with such activities are to be protected in their rights of free and private association. . . .

. . .

The judgment below must be and is reversed.

Wheeldin v. Wheeler
373 U.S. 647 (1963)

Petitioner Dawson was served with a subpoena to appear before the House Un-American Activities Committee. He alleges that the subpoena was signed in blank by the Committee Chairman and that respondent Wheeler, an investigator for the Committee, filled in Dawson's name without authorization of the Committee. We read the complaint, as does the Solicitor General, most favorably to Dawson, and conclude that the complaint alleges that no member of the Committee even attempted to delegate the Committee's subpoena power to Wheeler. The complaint also alleges that Wheeler intended to subject petitioner, when he appeared as a witness before the Committee, to public shame, disgrace, ridicule, stigma, scorn, and obloquy, and falsely place upon him the stain of disloyalty without any opportunity of fair defense, to petitioner's irreparable injury. The complaint alleges not only the lack of authority of respondent Wheeler to fill in the blank subpoena, but also the unconstitutionality of the House Resolution and the Act of Congress authorizing the Committee to act and to subpoena witnesses. The complaint alleges that the mere service of the subpoena on Dawson cost him his job, and that Wheeler caused service to be made while petitioner was at work, knowing that loss of employment would result. It prays that the subpoena be declared void and of no force or effect, and asks for damages and for an injunction.

The District Court denied declaratory and injunctive relief, holding that, since Dawson's appearance did not seem imminent, the case was not ripe for equitable intervention, and that the mere apprehension that a federal right might be infringed at some future time did not warrant declaratory or injunctive relief at the present time. The District Court . . . dismissed the complaint for lack of jurisdiction over the subject matter. The Court of Appeals held that declaratory relief, being within the District Court's discretion, was properly denied, and that the claim for injunctive relief had become moot. . . . On remand, the District Court dismissed the action without opinion. The Court of Appeals affirmed. . . .

. . .

We hold on the conceded facts that no federal cause of action was stated, and that the judgment must be and is affirmed.

Yellin v. United States
374 U.S. 109 (1963)

Petitioner Edward Yellin was indicted in the Northern District of Indiana on five counts of willfully refusing to answer questions put to him by a Subcommittee of the House Committee on Un-American Activities (Committee) at a public hearing. He was convicted of contempt of Congress on four counts. He was sentenced to four concurrent terms of imprisonment, each for one year, and fined $250. The Court of Appeals for the Seventh Circuit affirmed. . . .

. . . Having information that petitioner was a Communist, the Committee decided to call Yellin

and question him in a public rather than an executive session. The Committee then subpoenaed petitioner on January 23, 1958. His attorney, Mr. Rabinowitz, sent a telegram to the Committee's general counsel, Mr. Tavenner, on Thursday, February 6, 1958. The telegram asked for an executive session because "testimony needed for legislative . . . purposes can be secured in executive session without exposing witnesses to publicity." Since the Committee and Mr. Tavenner had left Washington, D.C., for Gary, the telegram was answered by the Committee's Staff Director. . . .

. . .

Petitioner's counsel also sought to bring the matter to the Committee's attention when it commenced its public hearing the following Monday, February 10, 1958. His efforts to have the telegrams read into the record were cut short. . . .

It is against this background that the Committee's failure to comply with its own rules must be judged. It has been long settled, of course, that rules of Congress and its committees are judicially cognizable. . . .

. . .

The rule is quite explicit in requiring that injury to a witness' reputation be considered, along with danger to the national security and injury to the reputation of third parties, in deciding whether to hold an executive session.

. . .

. . . When reading a copy of the Committee's rules, which must be distributed to every witness under Rule XVII, the witness' reasonable expectation is that the Committee actually does what it purports to do, adhere to its own rules. To foreclose a defense based upon those rules, simply because the witness was deceived by the Committee's appearance of regularity, is not fair. The Committee prepared the groundwork for prosecution in Yellin's case meticulously. It is not too exacting to require that the Committee be equally meticulous in obeying its own rules.

Reversed.

DeGregory v. Attorney General
383 U.S. 825 (1966)

This is the third time that the constitutional rights of appellant challenged in investigations by New Hampshire into subversion have been brought to us. The present case stems from an investigation by the Attorney General of the State under Rev.Stat.Ann. §588:8-a. . . .

. . .

Appellant was willing to answer questions concerning his relationship with and knowledge of Communist activities since 1957, and in fact he did answer them. But he refused to answer a series of questions put him concerning earlier periods. His refusal, not being based on the Fifth Amendment, raised important questions under the First Amendment, made applicable to the States by the Fourteenth Amendment. He was committed to jail for a period of one year or until he purged himself of contempt. That judgment was affirmed by the New Hampshire Supreme Court. . . .

. . .

. . . Lawmaking at the investigatory stage may properly probe historic events for any light that may be thrown on present conditions and problems. But the First Amendment prevents use of the power to investigate enforced by the contempt power to probe at will and without relation to existing need. The present record is devoid of any evidence that there is any Communist movement in New Hampshire. . . . There is no showing whatsoever of present danger of sedition against the State itself, the only area to which the authority of the State extends. . . . New Hampshire's inter-

est on this record is too remote and conjectural to override the guarantee of the First Amendment that a person can speak or not, as he chooses, free of all governmental compulsion.

Reversed.

Gojack v. United States
384 U.S. 702 (1966)

Petitioner appeared before a Subcommittee of the House Committee on Un-American Activities on February 28 and March 1, 1955. He answered certain questions, but refused to answer others concerning his affiliation with the Communist Party, the affiliation of others, and his connection with a "Peace Crusade." He had challenged the jurisdiction of the Committee and the Subcommittee, the authorization of each, and the constitutionality of the inquiry in general and with specific reference to the questions which he declined to answer. He did not and does not invoke the Fifth Amendment.

He was indicted for contempt of Congress under Rev. Stat. §102, as a result of his refusals to answer. He was convicted. In *Russell v. United States*, this Court reversed, holding that the indictment was defective because it did not allege the "subject under inquiry." The Court noted that, under §192, specification of the subject of the inquiry is fundamental to a charge of violating its provisions. Absent an allegation of the subject matter of the inquiry, this Court held, there is no way in which it can be determined whether the factual recitals of the indictment charged a crime under §192—that is, a refusal to answer questions "pertinent to the inquiry," and within the legislative competence of Congress.

Petitioner was thereafter reindicted. . . . Petitioner was again convicted and given a general sentence of three months' imprisonment and a $200 fine. The Court of Appeals for the District of Columbia Circuit affirmed per curiam. . . .

. . .

. . . We are not here dealing with the justification for an investigation by a committee of the Congress as a matter of congressional administration. That is a legislative matter. We are here concerned with a criminal proceeding. It is clear as a matter of law that the usual standards of the criminal law must be observed, including proper allegation and proof of all the essential elements of the offense. Moreover, the Congress, in enacting §192, specifically indicated that it relied upon the courts to apply the exacting standards of criminal jurisprudence to charges of contempt of Congress in order to assure that the congressional investigative power, when enforced by penal sanctions, would not be abused.

. . .

On November 19, 1954, about a month and a half before appointment of the Subcommittee, the Chairman of the Committee was reported as having announced that "large public hearings in industrial communities" would be held to expose active Communists as part of "a new plan for driving Reds out of important industries."

On February 14, when a representative of petitioner's union appeared to request a postponement, the Chairman of the Committee stated that "all of us are interested in seeing your union go out of business." A similar statement by the Chairman of the Subcommittee was reported in the press on February 15.

On February 21, the record shows that a newspaper in St. Joseph, Michigan, reported a statement of the Committee Chairman that the hearing would expose petitioner and another subpoenaed

witness as "card carrying Communists," and that "The rest is up to the community." The story noted that the rescheduled hearing would precede by three days a representation election, involving the union at St. Joseph.

Near the close of the testimony of the first witness at the hearing, the Chairman and other members of the Subcommittee disavowed any effort "to break or bust unions," but added that the Committee's purpose was to expose and break up Communist control of unions.

At one point in the hearing, the member of the Subcommittee who was then presiding stated that the purpose of the hearing was to consider testimony relating to Communist Party activities within the field of labor, but went on to refer to other purposes. . . .

. . .

. . . Absent proof of a clear delegation to the subcommittee of authority to conduct an inquiry into a designated subject, the subcommittee was without authority which can be vindicated by criminal sanctions under §192, nor was there an authoritative specification of the "subject matter of the inquiry" necessary for the determination of pertinency required by the section.

For the foregoing reasons, the judgment below is reversed.

Dombrowski v. Eastland
387 U.S. 82 (1967)

The Court of Appeals for the District of Columbia Circuit sustained the order granting summary judgment to the respondents who are, respectively, the Chairman and counsel of the Internal Security Subcommittee of the Judiciary Committee of the United States Senate. Petitioners' claim is essentially that respondents tortiously entered into and participated in a conspiracy and concert of action with Louisiana officials to seize property and records of petitioners by unlawful means in violation of petitioners' Fourth Amendment rights. . . . In a civil suit by these same petitioners against the Louisiana officials allegedly involved in the conspiracy, the Court of Appeals for the Fifth Circuit reversing a summary judgment in favor of third-party defendants. . . .

. . . [T]he court below recognized "considerable difficulty" in reaching the conclusion that, on the basis of the affidavits of the parties, there were no disputed issues of fact with respect to petitioners' claim. It nevertheless upheld summary dismissal of the action. . . .

. . . [W]e affirm the order of the Court of Appeals as to respondent Eastland and reverse and remand to the District Court as to respondent Sourwine for further proceedings in accordance with this opinion.

14

Loyalty Tests and Oaths
of Political Allegiance

This chapter is about mandatory oaths of allegiance and compulsory proclamations of loyalty to the Constitution and the United States for purposes of employment, receipt of governmental benefits, and education. Although the Supreme Court has considered several controversies of a similar nature relative to immigration and deportation, these cases are not included in this chapter.

Cummings v. Missouri
71 U.S. 277 (1867)

. . . The plaintiff in error is a priest of the Roman Catholic Church, and was indicted and convicted in one of the circuit courts of the State of the crime of teaching and preaching as a priest and minister of that religious denomination without having first taken the oath, and was sentenced to pay a fine of $500, and to be committed to jail until the same was paid. On appeal to the Supreme Court of the State, the judgment was affirmed.

The oath prescribed by the constitution, divided into its separable parts, embraces more than thirty distinct affirmations or tests. . . . It requires the affiant to deny not only that he has ever "been in armed hostility to the United States, or to the lawful authorities thereof," but, among other things, that he has ever, "by act or word," manifested his adherence to the cause of the enemies

of the United States, foreign or domestic, or his desire for their triumph over the arms of the United States, or his sympathy with those engaged in rebellion, or has ever harbored or aided any person engaged in guerrilla warfare against the loyal inhabitants of the United States, or has ever entered or left the State for the purpose of avoiding enrollment or draft in the military service of the United States; or, to escape the performance of duty in the militia of the United States, has ever indicated, in any terms, his disaffection to the government of the United States in its contest with the Rebellion.

Every person who is unable to take this oath is declared incapable of holding, in the State, any office of honor, trust, or profit under its authority, or of being an officer, councilman, director, or trustee, or other manager of any corporation, public or private, now existing or hereafter established by its authority, or of acting as a professor or teacher in any educational institution, or in any common or other school, or of holding any real estate or other property in trust for the use of any church, religious society, or congregation.

And every person holding, at the time the constitution takes effect, any of the offices, trusts, or positions mentioned is required, within sixty days thereafter, to take the oath, and, if he fail to comply with this requirement, it is declared that his office, trust, or position shall ipso facto become vacant.

No person, after the expiration of the sixty days, is permitted, without taking the oath, to practice as an attorney or counselor at law, nor after that period can any person be competent, as a bishop, priest, deacon, minister, elder, or other clergyman, of any religious persuasion, sect, or denomination, to teach, or preach, or solemnize marriages.

Fine and imprisonment are prescribed as a punishment for holding or exercising any of "the offices, positions, trusts, professions, or functions" specified, without having taken the oath, and false swearing or affirmation in taking it is declared to be perjury, punishable by imprisonment in the penitentiary.

. . .

. . . There can be no connection between the fact that Mr. Cummings entered or left the State of Missouri to avoid enrollment or draft in the military service of the United States and his fitness to teach the doctrines or administer the sacraments of his church; nor can a fact of this kind or the expression of words of sympathy with some of the persons drawn into the Rebellion constitute any evidence of the unfitness of the attorney or counselor to practice his profession, or of the professor to teach the ordinary branches of education, or of the want of business knowledge or business capacity in the manager of a corporation, or in any director or trustee. It is manifest upon the simple statement of many of the acts and of the professions and pursuits that there is no such relation between them as to render a denial of the commission of the acts at all appropriate as a condition of allowing the exercise of the professions and pursuits. The oath could not, therefore, have been required as a means of ascertaining whether parties were qualified or not for their respective callings or the trusts with which they were charged. It was required in order to reach the person, not the calling. It was exacted not from any notion that the several acts designated indicated

unfitness for the callings, but because it was thought that the several acts deserved punishment, and that, for many of them, there was no way to inflict punishment except by depriving the parties who had committed them of some of the rights and privileges of the citizen.

. . .

If the clauses of the second article of the Constitution of Missouri to which we have referred had in terms declared that Mr. Cummings was guilty, or should be held guilty, of having been in armed hostility to the United States, or of having entered that State to avoid being enrolled or drafted into the military service of the United States, and, therefore, should be deprived of the right to preach as a priest of the Catholic Church, or to teach in any institution of learning, there could be no question that the clauses would constitute a bill of attainder within the meaning of the Federal Constitution. If these clauses, instead of mentioning his name, had declared that all priests and clergymen within the State of Missouri were guilty of these acts, or should be held guilty of them, and hence be subjected to the like deprivation, the clauses would be equally open to objection. And further, if these clauses had declared that all such priests and clergymen should be so held guilty, and be thus deprived, provided they did not, by a day designated, do certain specified acts, they would be no less within the inhibition of the Federal Constitution.

. . .

. . . The existing clauses presume the guilt of the priests and clergymen, and adjudge the deprivation of their right to preach or teach unless the presumption be first removed by their expurgatory oath—in other words, they assume the guilt and adjudge the punishment conditionally. The clauses supposed differ only in that they declare the guilt instead of assuming it. . . .

. . .

The clauses in the Missouri Constitution which are the subject of consideration do not, in terms, define any crimes or declare that any punishment shall be inflicted, but they produce the same result upon the parties against whom they are directed as though the crimes were defined and the punishment was declared. They assume that there are persons in Missouri who are guilty of some of the acts designated. They would have no meaning in the constitution were not such the fact. They are aimed at past acts, and not future acts. They were intended especially to operate upon parties who, in some form or manner, by action or words, directly or indirectly, had aided or countenanced the Rebellion, or sympathized with parties engaged in the Rebellion, or had endeavored to escape the proper responsibilities and duties of a citizen in time of war, and they were intended to operate by depriving such persons of the right to hold certain offices and trusts, and to pursue their ordinary and regular avocations. This deprivation is punishment, nor is it any less so because a way is opened for escape from it by the expurgatory oath. The framers of the constitution of Missouri knew at the time that whole classes of individuals would be unable to take the oath prescribed. To them there is no escape provided; to them the deprivation was intended to be, and is, absolute and perpetual. To make the enjoyment of a right dependent upon an impossible condition is equivalent to an absolute denial of the right under any condition, and such denial, enforced for a past act, is nothing less than punishment imposed for that act. It is a misapplication of terms to call it anything else.

. . .

The provisions of the constitution of Missouri accomplish precisely what enactments like those supposed would have accomplished. They impose the same penalty, without the formality of a judicial trial and conviction, for the parties embraced by the supposed enactments would be incapable of taking the oath prescribed; to them, its requirement would be an impossible condition. . . .

. . .

The judgment of the Supreme Court of Missouri must be reversed, and the cause remanded with directions to enter a judgment reversing the judgment of the Circuit Court, and directing that court to discharge the defendant from imprisonment, and suffer him to depart without day.

Ex parte Garland
71 U.S. 333 (1867)

On the second of July, 1862, Congress passed an act prescribing an oath to be taken by every person elected or appointed to any office of honor or profit under the government of the United States, either in the civil, military, or naval departments of the public service, except the President, before entering upon the duties of his office, and before being entitled to its salary, or other emoluments. On the 24th of January, 1865, Congress, by a supplementary act, extended its provisions so as to embrace attorneys and counselors of the courts of the United States. This latter act provides that, after its passage, no person shall be admitted as an attorney and counselor to the bar of the Supreme Court, and, after the fourth of March, 1865, to the bar of any Circuit or District Court of the United States, or of the Court of Claims, or be allowed to appear and be heard by virtue of any previous admission, or any special power of attorney, unless he shall have first taken and subscribed the oath prescribed by the act of July 2, 1862. It also provides that the oath shall be preserved among the files of the court, and if any person take it falsely, he shall be guilty of perjury and, upon conviction, shall be subject to the pains and penalties of that offence.

At the December Term, 1860, the petitioner was admitted as an attorney and counselor of this court, and took and subscribed the oath then required. By the second rule, as it then existed, it was only requisite to the admission of attorneys and counselors of this court that they should have been such officers for the three previous years in the highest courts of the States to which they respectively belonged, and that their private and professional character should appear to be fair.

In March 1865, this rule was changed by the addition of a clause requiring the administration of the oath in conformity with the act of Congress.

In May 1861, the State of Arkansas, of which the petitioner was a citizen, passed an ordinance of secession which purported to withdraw the State from the Union, and afterwards, in the same year, by another ordinance, attached herself to the so-called Confederate States, and by act of the congress of that confederacy was received as one of its members.

The petitioner followed the State, and was one of her representatives—first in the lower house and afterwards in the senate of the congress of that confederacy, and was a member of the senate at the time of the surrender of the Confederate forces to the armies of the United States.

In July 1865, he received from the President of the United States a full pardon for all offences committed by his participation, direct or implied, in the Rebellion. He now produces his pardon, and asks permission to continue to practise as an attorney and counselor of the court without taking the oath required by the act of January 24,

1865, and the rule of the court, which he is unable to take by reason of the offices he held under the Confederate government. . . .

. . .

The statute is directed against parties who have offended in any of the particulars embraced by these clauses. And its object is to exclude them from the profession of the law, or at least from its practice in the courts of the United States. As the oath prescribed cannot be taken by these parties, the act, as against them, operates as a legislative decree of perpetual exclusion. And exclusion from any of the professions or any of the ordinary avocations of life for past conduct can be regarded in no other light than as punishment for such conduct. . . .

In the exclusion which the statute adjudges, it imposes a punishment for some of the acts specified which were not punishable at the time they were committed, and, for other of the acts, it adds a new punishment to that before prescribed, and it is thus brought within the further inhibition of the Constitution against the passage of an ex post facto law. . . .

. . .

This view is strengthened by a consideration of the effect of the pardon produced by the petitioner, and the nature of the pardoning power of the President.

. . .

The power thus conferred is unlimited, with the exception stated. It extends to every offence known to the law, and may be exercised at any time after its commission, either before legal proceedings are taken or during their pendency or after conviction and judgment. This power of the President is not subject to legislative control. Congress can neither limit the effect of his pardon nor exclude from its exercise any class of offenders. The benign prerogative of mercy reposed in him cannot be fettered by any legislative restrictions.

. . .

The pardon produced by the petitioner is a full pardon "for all offences by him committed, arising from participation, direct or implied, in the Rebellion," and is subject to certain conditions which have been complied with. The effect of this pardon is to relieve the petitioner from all penalties and disabilities attached to the offence of treason, committed by his participation in the Rebellion. So far as that offence is concerned, he is thus placed beyond the reach of punishment of any kind. But to exclude him, by reason of that offence, from continuing in the enjoyment of a previously acquired right is to enforce a punishment for that offence notwithstanding the pardon. If such exclusion can be effected by the exaction of an expurgatory oath covering the offence, the pardon may be avoided, and that accomplished indirectly which cannot be reached by direct legislation. It is not within the constitutional power of Congress thus to inflict punishment beyond the reach of executive clemency. From the petitioner, therefore, the oath required by the act of January 24, 1865, could not be exacted even if that act were not subject to any other objection than the one thus stated.

. . .

And the amendment of the second rule of the court, which requires the oath prescribed by the act of January 24, 1865, to be taken by attorneys and counselors, having been unadvisedly adopted, must be rescinded.

Minersville School District v. Gobitis
310 U.S. 586 (1940)

Lillian Gobitis, aged twelve, and her brother William, aged ten, were expelled from the public schools of Minersville, Pennsylvania, for refusing to salute the national flag as part of a daily school exercise. The local Board of Education required both teachers and pupils to participate in this ceremony. The ceremony is a familiar one. The right hand is placed on the breast and the following pledge recited in unison: "I pledge allegiance to my flag, and to the Republic for which it stands; one nation indivisible, with liberty and justice for all." While the words are spoken, teachers and pupils extend their right hands in salute to the flag. The Gobitis family are affiliated with "Jehovah's Witnesses," for whom the Bible as the Word of God is the supreme authority. The children had been brought up conscientiously to believe that such a gesture of respect for the flag was forbidden by command of Scripture.

The Gobitis children were of an age for which Pennsylvania makes school attendance compulsory. Thus, they were denied a free education, and their parents had to put them into private schools. To be relieved of the financial burden thereby entailed, their father, on behalf of the children and in his own behalf, brought this suit. He sought to enjoin the authorities from continuing to exact participation in the flag salute ceremony as a condition of his children's attendance at the Minersville school. After trial of the issues, Judge Maris gave relief in the District Court, on the basis of a thoughtful opinion at a preliminary stage of the litigation; his decree was affirmed by the Circuit Court of Appeals. . . .

. . .

. . . National unity is the basis of national security. To deny the legislature the right to select appropriate means for its attainment presents a totally different order of problem from that of the propriety of subordinating the possible ugliness of littered streets to the free expression of opinion through distribution of handbills.

. . .

. . . The ultimate foundation of a free society is the binding tie of cohesive sentiment. Such a sentiment is fostered by all those agencies of the mind and spirit which may serve to gather up the traditions of a people, transmit them from generation to generation, and thereby create that continuity of a treasured common life which constitutes a civilization. "We live by symbols." The flag is the symbol of our national unity, transcending all internal differences, however large, within the framework of the Constitution. . . .

. . . To stigmatize legislative judgment in providing for this universal gesture of respect for the symbol of our national life in the setting of the common school as a lawless inroad on that freedom of conscience which the Constitution protects, would amount to no less than the pronouncement of pedagogical and psychological dogma in a field where courts possess no marked and certainly no controlling competence. The influences which help toward a common feeling for the common country are manifold. Some may seem harsh, and others no doubt are foolish. Surely, however, the end is legitimate. And the effective means for its attainment are still so uncertain and so unauthenticated by science as to preclude us from putting the widely prevalent belief in flag saluting beyond the pale of legislative power. It mocks reason and denies our whole history to find in the allowance of a requirement to salute our flag on fitting occasions the seeds of sanction for obeisance to a leader.

The wisdom of training children in patriotic impulses by those compulsions which necessarily pervade so much of the educational process is not for our independent judgment. . . . For ourselves, we might be tempted to say that the deepest patriotism is best engendered by giving unfettered scope to the most crochety beliefs. . . . It is not our province to choose among competing considerations in the subtle process of securing effective loyalty to the traditional ideals of democracy, while respecting at the same time individual idiosyncracies among a people so diversified in racial origins and religious allegiances. . . .

. . .

Reversed.

West Virginia State Board of Education v. Barnette
319 U.S. 624 (1943)

The Board of Education on January 9, 1942, adopted a resolution containing recitals taken largely from the Court's *Gobitis* opinion and ordering that the salute to the flag become "a regular part of the program of activities in the public schools." . . .

. . .

Failure to conform is "insubordination," dealt with by expulsion. Readmission is denied by statute until compliance. Meanwhile, the expelled child is "unlawfully absent," and may be proceeded against as a delinquent. His parents or guardians are liable to prosecution, and, if convicted, are subject to fine not exceeding $50 and Jail term not exceeding thirty days.

Appellees, citizens of the United States and of West Virginia, brought suit in the United States District Court for themselves and others similarly situated asking its injunction to restrain enforcement of these laws and regulations against Jehovah's Witnesses. The Witnesses are an unincorporated body teaching that the obligation imposed by law of God is superior to that of laws enacted by temporal government. . . . They consider that the flag is an "image" within this command. For this reason, they refuse to salute it.

. . .

The Board of Education moved to dismiss the complaint. . . . The cause was submitted . . . to a District Court of three judges. It restrained enforcement as to the plaintiffs and those of that class. . . .

. . .

. . . Symbolism is a primitive but effective way of communicating ideas. The use of an emblem or flag to symbolize some system, idea, institution, or personality is a short-cut from mind to mind. Causes and nations, political parties, lodges, and ecclesiastical groups seek to knit the loyalty of their followings to a flag or banner, a color or design. . . . A person gets from a symbol the meaning he puts into it, and what is one man's comfort and inspiration is another's jest and scorn.

. . .

National unity, as an end which officials may foster by persuasion and example, is not in question. The problem is whether, under our Constitution, compulsion as here employed is a permissible means for its achievement.

Struggles to coerce uniformity of sentiment in support of some end thought essential to their time and country have been waged by many good, as well as by evil, men. Nationalism is a relatively recent phenomenon, but, at other times and places, the ends have been racial or territorial security, support of a dynasty or regime, and particular plans for saving souls. As first and moderate methods to attain unity have failed, those bent on its accomplishment must resort to an ever-increasing severity. As governmental pressure toward unity becomes greater, so strife becomes more bitter as to whose unity it shall be. Probably no deeper division of our people could proceed from any provocation than from finding it necessary to choose what doctrine and whose program public educational officials shall compel youth to unite in embracing. . . . Those

who begin coercive elimination of dissent soon find themselves exterminating dissenters. Compulsory unification of opinion achieves only the unanimity of the graveyard.

. . .

. . . To believe that patriotism will not flourish if patriotic ceremonies are voluntary and spontaneous, instead of a compulsory routine, is to make an unflattering estimate of the appeal of our institutions to free minds. We can have intellectual individualism and the rich cultural diversities that we owe to exceptional minds only at the price of occasional eccentricity and abnormal attitudes. When they are so harmless to others or to the State as those we deal with here, the price is not too great. But freedom to differ is not limited to things that do not matter much. That would be a mere shadow of freedom. The test of its substance is the right to differ as to things that touch the heart of the existing order.

. . .

We think the action of the local authorities in compelling the flag salute and pledge transcends constitutional limitations on their power, and invades the sphere of intellect and spirit which it is the purpose of the First Amendment to our Constitution to reserve from all official control.

The decision of this Court in *Minersville School District v. Gobitis*, and the holdings of those few per curiam decisions which preceded and foreshadowed it, are overruled, and the judgment enjoining enforcement of the West Virginia Regulation is affirmed.

Parker v. County of Los Angeles
338 U.S. 327 (1949)

In No. 49, twenty-five classified civil servants of the County of Los Angeles brought an action in the Superior Court of that County, and in No. 50, suit was brought by one such employee. The respective plaintiffs sought relief against enforcement by the County and its officials of what is colloquially known as a loyalty test, and they did so for themselves and "in a representative capacity . . . on behalf of 20,000 employees of Los Angeles County similarly situated."

The plaintiffs, petitioners here, alleged that, on August 26, 1947, the Board of Supervisors of the County of Los Angeles adopted as part of its "Loyalty Check" program the requirement that all County employees execute a prescribed affidavit. . . . By Part A, each employee is required to support the Constitution of the United States, and the Constitution and laws of the California; by Part B, he forswears that, since December 7, 1941, he has been a member of any organization advocating the forcible overthrow of the Government of the United States or of the California or of the County of Los Angeles, that he now advocates such overthrow, or that he will in the future so advocate directly or through an organization; by Part C, he is required to list his aliases, and by Part D, he is asked to indicate whether he has ever been "a member of, or directly or indirectly supported or followed" any of an enumerated list of 145 organizations. Asserting fear of penalizing consequences from the loyalty program, and claiming that the law of California and the Constitution of the United States barred coercive measures by the County to secure obedience to the alleged affidavit requirement, petitioners brought these actions. Demurrers to the complaints were sustained by the Superior Court, and its judgments were affirmed by the District Court of Appeal for the Second Appellate District. . . . [T]he Supreme Court of California denied discretionary review. . . .

To begin with, the California decision under review does not tell us unambiguously what compulsion, if any, the loyalty order of August 26, 1947, carried. It is unequivocally clear that the lower court refused to decide whether an employee who discloses his so-called "subversive" activities or connections may, for that reason, be discharged. It is not clear, however, whether, as petitioners contend, the lower court meant to hold that the Board of Supervisors may discharge an employee who refuses to file an affidavit. . . .

. . . [N]oncomplying employees were advised that the Board of Supervisors had adopted an order providing (1) that, unless they had executed Parts A, B, and C of the affidavit by July 26, they would be discharged, and (2) that, unless they had executed Part D by that time, they would be discharged. . . .

. . . By July 26, the entire affidavit had been executed by all but 45 employees. Of these, 29 had executed only Parts A, B, and C. Sixteen stood their ground against any compliance. They invoked their administrative remedy of review before the Civil Service Commission, which decided against them. On June 24 of this year, these sixteen discharged employees sought a writ of mandate from the Superior Court of the County of Los Angeles to review the decision of the Civil Service Commission, with a prayer for reinstatement and back pay. We are advised that this litigation is now pending in the Superior Court. The petitioners here, except one in No. 49, signed Parts A, B, and C, and that petitioner is a party in the case before the Superior Court.

. . .

Due regard for our Federal system requires that this Court stay its hand until the opportunities afforded by State courts have exhausted claims of litigants under State law. . . .

Dismissed.

Garner v. Board of Public Works of Los Angeles
341 U.S. 716 (1951)

In 1941, the California Legislature amended the Charter of the City of Los Angeles to provide in part as follows:

> ... [N]o person shall hold or retain or be eligible for any public office or employment in the service of the City of Los Angeles, in any office or department thereof, either elective or appointive, who has within five years prior to the effective date of this section advised, advocated or taught, or who may, after this section becomes effective [April 28, 1941], advise, advocate or teach, or who is now or has been within five years prior to the effective date of this section, or who may, after this section becomes effective, become a member of or affiliated with any group, society, association, organization or party which advises, advocates or teaches, or has, within said period of five years, advised, advocated or taught the overthrow by force or violence of the government of the United States of America or of the State of California.
>
> Insofar as this section may be held by any court of competent jurisdiction not to be self-executing, the City Council is hereby given power and authority to adopt appropriate legislation for the purpose of effectuating the objects hereof.

Pursuant to the authority thus conferred, the City of Los Angeles, in 1948, passed ordinance No. 94,004, requiring every person who held an office or position in the service of the city to take an oath prior to January 6, 1949. ...

The ordinance also required every employee to execute an affidavit. ...

On the final date for filing of the oath and affidavit, petitioners were civil service employees of the City of Los Angeles. Petitioners Pacifico and Schwartz took the oath, but refused to execute the affidavit. The remaining fifteen petitioners refused to do either. All were discharged

for such cause. ... The District Court of Appeal denied relief. ...

...

The affidavit raises the issue whether the City of Los Angeles is constitutionally forbidden to require that its employees disclose their past or present membership in the Communist Party or the Communist Political Association. Not before us is the question whether the city may determine that an employee's disclosure of such political affiliation justifies his discharge.

We think that a municipal employer is not disabled because it is an agency of the State from inquiring of its employees as to matters that may prove relevant to their fitness and suitability for the public service. Past conduct may well relate to present fitness; past loyalty may have a reasonable relationship to present and future trust. Both are commonly inquired into in determining fitness for both high and low positions in private industry, and are not less relevant in public employment. The affidavit requirement is valid.

In our view, the validity of the oath turns upon the nature of the Charter amendment (1941) and the relation of the ordinance (1948) to this amendment. ... We assume that, under the Federal Constitution, the Charter amendment is valid to the extent that it bars from the city's public service persons who, subsequent to its adoption in 1941, advise, advocate, or teach the violent overthrow of the Government or who are or become affiliated with any group doing so. ...

...

... We have no reason to suppose that the oath is or will be construed by the City of Los Angeles or by California courts as affecting adversely those persons who, during their affiliation with a proscribed organization, were innocent of its purpose, or those who severed their relations with any such organization when its character became apparent, or those who were affiliated with organizations which, at one time or another during the period covered by the ordinance, were engaged in proscribed activity, but not at the time of affiant's affiliation. We assume that scienter is implicit in each clause of the oath. As the city has done nothing to negative this interpretation, we take for granted that the ordinance will be so read to avoid raising difficult constitutional problems which any other application would present. . . . We assume that, if our interpretation of the oath is correct, the City of Los Angeles will give those petitioners who heretofore refused to take the oath an opportunity to take it as interpreted, and resume their employment.

The judgment as to Pacifico and Schwartz is affirmed. The judgment as to the remaining petitioners is affirmed on the basis of the interpretation of the ordinance which we have felt justified in assuming.

Wieman v. Updegraff
344 U.S. 183 (1952)

This is an appeal from a decision of the Supreme Court of Oklahoma upholding the validity of a loyalty oath prescribed by Oklahoma statute for all state officers and employees. Appellants, employed by the state as members of the faculty and staff of Oklahoma Agricultural and Mechanical College, failed, within the thirty days permitted, to take the oath required by the Act. Appellee Updegraff . . . brought this suit in the District Court of Oklahoma County to enjoin the necessary state officials from paying further compensation to employees who had not subscribed to the oath. The appellants, who were permitted to inter-

vene, attacked the validity of the Act on the grounds, among others, that it was a bill of attainder; an ex post facto law; impaired the obligation of their contracts with the State, and violated the Due Process Clause of the Fourteenth Amendment. They also sought a mandatory injunction directing the state officers to pay their salaries regardless of their failure to take the oath. Their objections centered largely on the following clauses of the oath. . . .

The court upheld the Act and enjoined the state officers from making further salary payments to appellants. The Supreme Court of Oklahoma affirmed. . . .

. . .

The purpose of the Act, we are told, "was to make loyalty a qualification to hold public office or be employed by the State." During periods of international stress, the extent of legislation with such objectives accentuates our traditional concern about the relation of government to the individual in a free society. The perennial problem of defining that relationship becomes acute when disloyalty is screened by ideological patterns and techniques of disguise that make it difficult to identify. Democratic government is not powerless to meet this threat, but it must do so without infringing the freedoms that are the ultimate values of all democratic living. . . .

. . .

. . . [M]embership may be innocent. A state servant may have joined a proscribed organization unaware of its activities and purposes. In recent years, many completely loyal persons have severed organizational ties after learning for the first time of the character of groups to which they had belonged. . . .

At the time of affiliation, a group itself may be innocent, only later coming under the influence of those who would turn it toward illegitimate ends. Conversely, an organization formerly subversive, and therefore designated as such, may have subsequently freed itself from the influences which originally led to its listing.

There can be do dispute about the consequences visited upon a person excluded from public employment on disloyalty grounds. In the view of the community, the stain is a deep one; indeed, it has become a badge of infamy. . . . [U]nder the Oklahoma Act, the fact of association alone determines disloyalty and disqualification; it matters not whether association existed innocently or knowingly. To thus inhibit individual freedom of movement is to stifle the flow of democratic expression and controversy at one of its chief sources. . . . Indiscriminate classification of innocent with knowing activity must fall as an assertion of arbitrary power. The oath offends due process.

. . . We need not pause to consider whether an abstract right to public employment exists. It is sufficient to say that constitutional protection does extend to the public servant whose exclusion pursuant to a statute is patently arbitrary or discriminatory.

Because of this disposition, we do not pass on the serious questions raised as to whether the Act, in proscribing those "communist front or subversive organizations" designated as such on lists of the Attorney General of the United States, gave fair notice to those affected, in view of the fact that those listings have never included a designation of "communist fronts," and have in some cases designated organizations without classifying them. Nor need we consider the significance of the differing standards employed in the preparation of those lists and their limited evidentiary use under the Federal Loyalty Program.

Reversed.

Barsky v. Board of Regents of the University of the State of New York
347 U.S. 442 (1954)

In 1945, the Committee of the United States House of Representatives, known as the Committee on Un-American Activities, was authorized to make investigations of "the extent, character, and objects of un-American propaganda activities in the United States." In 1946, in the course of that investigation, the committee subpoenaed Dr. Edward K. Barsky, appellant herein, who was then the national chairman and a member of the executive board of the Joint Anti-Fascist Refugee Committee. . . . Similar subpoenas were served on the executive secretary and the other members of the executive board of the Refugee Committee. Appellant appeared before the Congressional Committee, but, pursuant to advice of counsel and the action of his executive board, he and the other officers of the Refugee Committee failed and refused to produce the subpoenaed papers.

In 1947, appellant, the executive secretary, and several members of the executive board of the Refugee Committee were convicted by a jury, in the United States District Court for the District of Columbia, of violating R.S. §102, by failing to produce the subpoenaed papers. Appellant was sentenced to serve six months in jail and pay $500. In 1948, this judgment was affirmed by the Court of Appeals, and certiorari was denied. In 1950, a rehearing was denied. . . . Appellant served his sentence, being actually confined five months.

Appellant was a physician who practiced his profession in New York under a license issued in 1919. However, in 1948, following the affirmance of his . . . conviction, charges were filed against him with the Department of Education of the State of New York by an inspector of that department. This was done under §6515 of the Education Law, seeking disciplinary action pursuant to subdivision 2(b) of §6514 of that law. . . .

In 1951, after filing an amended answer, appellant was given an extended hearing before a subcommittee of the Department's Medical Committee on Grievances. The three doctors constituting the subcommittee made a written report of their findings, determination, and recommendation, expressly taking into consideration the five months during which appellant had been separated from his practice while confined in jail, and also the testimony and letters submitted in support of his character. They recommended finding him guilty as charged and suspending him from practice for three months. The ten doctors constituting the full Grievance Committee unanimously found appellant guilty as charged. They also adopted the findings, determination and recommendation of their subcommittee, except that . . . they fixed appellant's suspension at six months. Promptly thereafter, the Committee on Discipline of the Board of Regents of the University of the State of New York held a further hearing at which appellant appeared in person and by counsel. This committee consisted of two lawyers and one doctor. After reviewing the facts and issues, it filed a detailed report recommending that, while appellant was guilty as charged, his license be not suspended, and that he merely be censured and reprimanded. The Board of Regents, however, returned to and sustained the determination of the Medical Committee on Grievances, and suspended appellant's license for six months.

Appellant sought a review of this determination, under §6515 of the Education Law and Article 78 of the New York Civil Practice Act. The proceeding was instituted in the Supreme Court for the County of Albany and transferred to the Appellate Division, Third Department. That court confirmed the order of the Board of Regents. The Court of Appeals affirmed. . . .

. . .

That appellant was convicted of a violation of R.S. §102, in a court of competent jurisdiction is settled. In the New York courts, appellant argued that a violation of that section of the federal statutes was not a crime under the law of New York and that, accordingly, it was not a "crime" within the meaning of §6514 of the New York Education Law. He argued that his conviction, therefore, did not afford the New York Board of Regents the required basis for suspending his license. That issue was settled adversely to him by the Court of Appeals of New York, and that court's interpretation of the state statute is conclusive here.

. . .

The Court has considered the other points raised by appellant, but finds no substantial federal constitutional objection in them, even assuming that they are before us as having been considered by the Court of Appeals, although not mentioned in its opinion or the amendment to its remittitur.

The judgment of the Court of Appeals of the State of New York, accordingly, is affirmed.

Slochower v. Board of Higher Education of New York City
350 U.S. 551 (1956)

This appeal brings into question the constitutionality of §903 of the Charter of the City of New York. That section provides that whenever an employee of the City utilizes the privilege against self-incrimination to avoid answering a question relating to his official conduct, his term or tenure of office or employment shall terminate and such office or employment shall be vacant, and he shall not be eligible to election or appointment to any office or employment under the city or any agency.

Appellant Slochower invoked the privilege against self-incrimination under the Fifth Amendment before an investigating committee of the United States Senate, and was summarily discharged from his position as associate professor at Brooklyn College, an institution maintained by the City of New York. He now claims that the charter provision, as applied to him, violates both the Due Process and Privileges and Immunities Clauses of the Fourteenth Amendment.

On September 24, 1952, the Internal Security Subcommittee of the Committee on the Judiciary of the United States Senate held open hearings in New York City. The investigation, conducted on a national scale, related to subversive influences in the American educational system. . . . Professor Slochower, when called to testify, stated that he was not a member of the Communist Party, and indicated complete willingness to answer all questions about his associations or political beliefs since 1941. But he refused to answer questions concerning his membership during 1940 and 1941 on the ground that his answers might tend to incriminate him. The Chairman of the Senate Subcommittee accepted Slochower's claim as a valid assertion of an admitted constitutional right.

. . .

Shortly after testifying before the Internal Security Subcommittee, Slochower was notified that he was suspended from his position at the College; three days later, his position was declared vacant "pursuant to the provisions of Section 903 of the New York City charter."

Slochower had 27 years' experience as a college teacher, and was entitled to tenure under state law. Under this statute, appellant may be discharged only for cause, and after notice, hearing, and appeal. The Court of Appeals of New York, however, has authoritatively interpreted §903 to mean that "The assertion of the privilege against self-incrimination is equivalent to a resignation." Dismissal under this provision is therefore automatic, and there is no right to charges, notice, hearing, or opportunity to explain.

The Supreme Court of New York, County of Kings, concluded that appellant's behavior fell within the scope of §903, and upheld its application here. The Appellate Division . . . and the Court of Appeals . . . affirmed. . . .

Slochower argues that §903 abridges a privilege or immunity of a citizen of the United States, since it, in effect, imposes a penalty on the exercise of a federally guaranteed right in a federal proceeding. It also violates due process, he argues, because the mere claim of privilege under the Fifth Amendment does not provide a reasonable basis for the State to terminate his employment. Appellee insists that no question of "privileges or immunities" was raised or passed on below, and therefore directs its argument solely to the proposition that §903 does not operate in an arbitrary or capricious manner. We do not decide whether a claim under the "privileges or immunities" clause was considered below, since we conclude the summary dismissal of appellant in the circumstances of this case violates due process of law.

. . .

Here, the Board, in support of its position, contends that only two possible inferences flow from appellant's claim of self-incrimination: (1) that the answering of the question would tend to prove him guilty of a crime in some way connected with his official conduct; or (2) that, in order to avoid answering the question, he falsely invoked the privilege by stating that the answer would tend to incriminate him, and thus committed perjury. Either inference, it insists, is sufficient to justify the termination of his employment. The Court of Appeals, however, accepted the Committee's determination that the privilege had been properly invoked, and it further held that no inference of Communist Party membership could be drawn from such a refusal to testify. It found the statute to impose merely a condition on public employment, and affirmed the summary action taken in the case....

At the outset, we must condemn the practice of imputing a sinister meaning to the exercise of a person's constitutional right under the Fifth Amendment....

. . .

It is one thing for the city authorities themselves to inquire into Slochower's fitness, but quite another for his discharge to be based entirely on events occurring before a federal committee whose inquiry was announced as not directed at "the property, affairs, or government of the city, or . . . official conduct of city employees."... Here, the Board had possessed the pertinent information for 12 years, and the questions which Professor Slochower refused to answer were admittedly asked for a purpose wholly unrelated to his college functions. On such a record, the Board cannot claim that its action was part of a bona fide attempt to gain needed and relevant information.

... [T]he Board seized upon his claim of privilege before the federal committee and converted it through the use of §903 into a conclusive presumption of guilt. Since no inference of guilt was possible from the claim before the federal committee, the discharge falls of its own weight as wholly without support....

This is not to say that Slochower has a consti-

tutional right to be an associate professor of German at Brooklyn College. The State has broad powers in the selection and discharge of its employees, and it may be that proper inquiry would show Slochower's continued employment to be inconsistent with a real interest of the State. But there has been no such inquiry here. We hold that the summary dismissal of appellant violates due process of law.

The judgment is reversed, and the cause is remanded for further proceedings not inconsistent with this opinion.

Jencks v. United States
353 U.S. 657 (1957)

On April 28, 1950, the petitioner, as president of Amalgamated Bayard District Union, Local 890, International Union of Mine, Mill & Smelter Workers, filed an "Affidavit of Non-Communist Union Officer" with the National Labor Relations Board, pursuant to §9(h) of the National Labor Relations Act. He has been convicted under a two-count indictment charging that he violated 18 U.S.C. §1001 by falsely swearing in that affidavit that he was not, on April 28, 1950, a member of the Communist Party or affiliated with such Party. The Court of Appeals for the Fifth Circuit affirmed the conviction, and also an order of the District Court denying the petitioner's motion for a new trial....

. . .

Both the trial court and the Court of Appeals erred. We hold that the petitioner was not required to lay a preliminary foundation of inconsistency, because a sufficient foundation was established by the testimony of Matusow and Ford that their reports were of the events and activities related in their testimony.

. . .

It is unquestionably true that the protection of vital national interests may militate against public disclosure of documents in the Government's possession. This has been recognized in decisions of this Court in civil causes where the Court has considered the statutory authority conferred upon the departments of government to adopt regulations "not inconsistent with law, for . . . use . . . of the records, papers . . . appertaining" to his department. The Attorney General has adopted regulations pursuant to this authority declaring all Justice Department records confidential, and that no disclosure, including disclosure in response to subpoena, may be made without his permission.

. . .

We hold that the criminal action must be dismissed when the Government, on the ground of privilege, elects not to comply with an order to produce, for the accused's inspection and for admission in evidence, relevant statements or reports in its possession of government witnesses touching the subject matter of their testimony at the trial. The burden is the Government's, not to be shifted to the trial judge, to decide whether the public prejudice of allowing the crime to go unpunished is greater than that attendant upon the possible disclosure of state secrets and other confidential information in the Government's possession.

Reversed.

Beilan v. Board of Education, School District of Philadelphia
357 U.S. 399 (1958)

On June 25, 1952, Herman A. Beilan, the petitioner, who had been a teacher for about 22 years in the Philadelphia Public School System, presented himself at his Superintendent's office in response to the latter's request. The Superintendent said he had information which reflected adversely on petitioner's loyalty, and he wanted to determine its truth or falsity. In response to petitioner's suggestion that the Superintendent do the questioning, the latter said he would ask one question, and petitioner could then determine whether he would answer it and others of that type. The Superintendent, accordingly, asked petitioner whether or not he had been the Press Director of the Professional Section of the Communist Political Association in 1944. Petitioner asked permission to consult counsel before answering, and the Superintendent granted his request.

On October 14, 1952, in response to a similar request, petitioner again presented himself at the Superintendent's office. Petitioner stated that he had consulted counsel and that he declined to answer the question as to his activities in 1944. He announced he would also decline to answer any other "questions similar to it," "questions of this type," or "questions about political and religious beliefs. . . ." The Superintendent warned petitioner that this "was a very serious and a very important matter, and that failure to answer the questions might lead to his dismissal." The Superintendent made it clear that he was investigating "a real question of fitness for [petitioner] to be a teacher or to continue in the teaching work." These interviews were given no publicity, and were attended only by petitioner, his Superintendent, and the Assistant Solicitor of the Board.

On November 25, 1953, the Board instituted dismissal proceedings against petitioner under §1127 of the Pennsylvania Public School Code of 1949. The only specification which we need consider charged that petitioner's refusal to answer his Superintendent's questions constituted "incompetency" under §1122 of that Code. The Board conducted a formal hearing on the charge.

Petitioner was present with counsel, but did not testify. Counsel for each side agreed that petitioner's loyalty was not in issue, and that evidence as to his disloyalty would be irrelevant. On January 7, 1954, the Board found that the charge of incompetency had been sustained, and . . . discharged petitioner from his employment as a teacher.

On an administrative appeal, the Superintendent of Public Instruction of Pennsylvania sustained the local Board. However, on petitioner's appeal to the County Court of Common Pleas, that court set aside petitioner's discharge and held that the Board should have followed the procedure specified by the Pennsylvania Loyalty Act, rather than the Public School Code. . . . [T]he Supreme Court of Pennsylvania . . . reversed the Court of Common Pleas and reinstated petitioner's discharge.

. . . The only question before us is whether the Federal Constitution prohibits petitioner's discharge for statutory "incompetency" based on his refusal to answer the Superintendent's questions.

By engaging in teaching in the public schools, petitioner did not give up his right to freedom of belief, speech or association. He did, however, undertake obligations of frankness, candor and cooperation in answering inquiries made of him by his employing Board examining into his fitness to serve it as a public school teacher. . . .

. . .

The question asked of petitioner by his Superintendent was relevant to the issue of petitioner's fitness and suitability to serve as a teacher. Petitioner is not in a position to challenge his dismissal merely because of the remoteness in time of the 1944 activities. It was apparent from the circumstances of the two interviews that the Superintendent had other questions to ask. Petitioner's refusal to answer was not based on the remoteness of his 1944 activities. He made it clear that he would not answer any question of the same type as the one asked. Petitioner blocked from the beginning any inquiry into his Communist activities, however relevant to his present loyalty. The Board based its dismissal upon petitioner's refusal to answer any inquiry about his relevant activities—not upon those activities themselves. It took care to charge petitioner with incompetency, and not with disloyalty. It found him insubordinate and lacking in frankness and candor—it made no finding as to his loyalty.

We find no requirement in the Federal Constitution that a teacher's classroom conduct be the sole basis for determining his fitness. Fitness for teaching depends on a broad range of factors. The Pennsylvania tenure provision specifies several disqualifying grounds, including immorality, intemperance, cruelty, mental derangement, and persistent and willful violation of the school laws, as well as "incompetency." However, the Pennsylvania statute, unlike those of many other States, contains no catch-all phrase, such as "conduct unbecoming a teacher," to cover disqualifying conduct not included within the more specific provisions. Consequently, the Pennsylvania courts have given "incompetency" a broad interpretation. . . .

In the instant case, the Pennsylvania Supreme Court has held that "incompetency" includes petitioner's

> deliberate and insubordinate refusal to answer the questions of his administrative superior in a vitally important matter pertaining to his fitness.

This interpretation is not inconsistent with the Federal Constitution.

. . .

Inasmuch as petitioner's dismissal did not violate the Federal Constitution, the judgment of the Supreme Court of Pennsylvania is affirmed.

Lerner v. Casey
357 U.S. 468 (1958)

In November 1953, the Commission determined the New York City Transit Authority, which the appellees in this case constitute, to be a "security agency," and in March 1954, it listed the Communist Party of the United States as a "subversive group," adopting, as contemplated by the Security Risk Law. . . . In September 1954, appellant was summoned to the office of the Commissioner of Investigation of the City of New York in the course of an investigation being conducted under the Security Risk Law. Appellant, who had been sworn, was asked whether he was then a member of the Communist Party, but he refused to answer and claimed his privilege against self-incrimination under the Fifth Amendment to the Federal Constitution. After he had been advised of the provisions of the Security Risk Law and given time to reconsider his refusal and to engage counsel, appellant, accompanied by counsel, made two further appearances in September and October before the Department of Investigation, on each of which he adhered to his initial position.

Appellees, informed of these events, thereupon adopted a resolution suspending appellant without pay, and sent him a copy of the resolution with a covering letter. This letter notified appellant that his suspension followed a finding under §5 of the Security Risk Law " . . . that, upon all the evidence, reasonable grounds exist for belief that, because of his doubtful trust and reliability . . . " appellant's continued employment would endanger national and state security. . . . Appellant was also advised, pursuant to §5 of the Security Risk Law, that he had thirty days within which to submit statements or affidavits showing why he should be reinstated. At the expiration of this period, appellees, hav-

ing heard nothing further from appellant, dismissed him from his position by a resolution which confirmed the previous "suspension" findings.

. . . The State Supreme Court . . . upheld the Security Risk Law and its application to appellant as constitutional, ruled adversely to appellant's state law contentions, and dismissed the proceeding. The Appellate Division, 2d Dept. and the Court of Appeals both affirmed. . . .

. . .

We come then to what we consider appellant's major constitutional claim, which goes to the manner in which the Security Risk Law was applied to him. It is contended that the administrative finding of reasonable grounds for belief that he was "of doubtful trust and reliability," and therefore a security risk, offends due process. The contention is (1) that the finding rests on an inference, that appellant was a member of the Communist Party, which was drawn from appellant's invocation of the Fifth Amendment, and that this inference lacked any rational connection with appellant's refusal to answer based on the exercise of this constitutional privilege; and (2) that the drawing of such an inference was, in any event, in derogation of the policy behind the Fifth Amendment privilege and contrary to the teaching of this Court's decision in *Slochower*. . . .

. . . [W]e read the court's opinion as meaning that a finding of doubtful trust and reliability could justifiably be based on appellant's lack of frankness, just as if he had refused to give any other information about himself which might be relevant to his employment. It was this lack of candor which provided the evidence of appellant's doubtful trust and reliability which, under the New York statutory scheme, constituted him a security risk. The Court of Appeals went on to reason that, had appellant refused, without more, to answer the question, the finding of "doubtful trust and reliability" would have undoubtedly been permissible, and that the basis for such a finding in appellant's refusal to answer was not destroyed by the claim of the Fifth Amendment privilege, because the Commissioner was not required to accept that claim as an adequate explanation of the refusal.

. . . [W]e are not faced here with the question whether party membership may rationally be inferred from a refusal to answer a question directed to present membership where the refusal rests on the belief that an answer might incriminate or with the question whether membership in the Communist Party which might be "innocent" can be relied upon as a ground for denial of state employment.

. . .

We hold that appellant's discharge was not in violation of rights assured him by the Federal Constitution.

Affirmed.

Speiser v. Randall
357 U.S. 513 (1958)

The appellants are honorably discharged veterans of World War II who claimed the veterans' property tax exemption provided by Art. XIII, §1¼, of the California Constitution. Under California law, applicants for such exemption must annually complete a standard form of application and file it with the local assessor. The form was revised in 1954 to add an oath by the applicant:

> I do not advocate the overthrow of the Government of the United States or of the State of California by force or violence or other unlawful means, nor advocate the support of a foreign Government against the United States in event of hostilities.

Each refused to subscribe the oath and struck it from the form which he executed and filed for the tax year 1954–1955. Each contended that the exaction of the oath as a condition of obtaining a tax exemption was forbidden by the Federal Constitution. The respective assessors denied the exemption solely for the refusal to execute the oath. The Supreme Court of California sustained the assessors' actions against the appellants' claims of constitutional invalidity. . . .

Article XX, §19, of the California Constitution, adopted at the general election of November 4, 1952, provides as follows:

> Notwithstanding any other provision of this Constitution, no person or organization which advocates the overthrow of the Government of the United States or the State by force or violence or other unlawful means or who advocates the support of a foreign government against the United States in the event of hostilities shall:
>
> . . .
>
> (b) Receive any exemption from any tax imposed by this State or any county, city or county, city, district, political subdivision, authority, board, bureau, commission or other public agency of this State.

. . .

To effectuate this constitutional amendment, the California Legislature enacted §32 of the Revenue and Taxation Code, which requires the claimant, as a prerequisite to qualification for any property tax exemption, to sign a statement on his tax return declaring that he does not engage in the activities described in the constitutional amendment. . . . The declaration, while intended to provide a means of determining whether a claimant qualifies for the exemption under the constitutional amendment, is not conclusive evidence of eligibility. The assessor has the duty of investigating the facts underlying all tax liabilities, and is empowered by §454 of the Code to subpoena taxpayers for the purpose of questioning them about statements they have furnished. . . .

. . .

. . . It is settled that speech can be effectively limited by the exercise of the taxing power. To deny an exemption to claimants who engage in certain forms of speech is, in effect, to penalize them for such speech. Its deterrent effect is the same as if the State were to fine them for this speech. The appellees are plainly mistaken in their argument that, because a tax exemption is a "privilege" or "bounty," its denial may not infringe speech. . . .

. . .

. . . The present legislation . . . purports to deal directly with speech and the expression of political ideas. "Encouragement to loyalty to our institutions . . . [is a doctrine] which the state has plainly promulgated and intends to foster." The State argues that veterans as a class occupy a position of special trust and influence in the community, and therefore any veteran who engages in the proscribed advocacy constitutes a special danger to the State. But while a union official or public employee may be deprived of his position, and thereby removed from the place of special danger, the State is powerless to erase the service which the veteran has rendered his country; though he be denied a tax exemption, he remains a veteran. The State, consequently, can act against the veteran only as it can act against any other citizen, by imposing penalties to deter the unlawful conduct.

. . . In the present case . . . it is clear that the declaration may be accepted or rejected on the basis of incompetent information or no information at all. It is only a step in a process throughout which the taxpayer must bear the burden of proof.

. . . Since the entire statutory procedure, by placing the burden of proof on the claimants,

violated the requirements of due process, appellants were not obliged to take the first step in such a procedure.

The judgments are reversed and the causes are remanded for further proceedings not inconsistent with this opinion.

First Unitarian Church of Los Angeles v. County of Los Angeles
357 U.S. 545 (1958)

. . . The petitioners claimed the property tax exemption provided by Art. XIII, §1 1/2, of the California Constitution for real property and buildings used solely and exclusively for religious worship. The Los Angeles assessor denied the exemptions because each petitioner refused to subscribe, and struck from the prescribed application form, the oath that they did not advocate the overthrow of the Government of the United States and of the State of California by force or violence or other unlawful means, nor advocate the support of a foreign government against the United States in the event of hostilities. Each petitioner sued in the Superior Court in and for the County of Los Angeles to recover taxes paid under protest and for declaratory relief. Both contended that the exaction of the oath pursuant to §19 of Art. XX of the State Constitution and §32 of the California Revenue and Taxation Code was forbidden by the Federal Constitution. The court upheld the validity of the provisions in the action brought by petitioner First Unitarian Church of Los Angeles, and the Supreme Court of California affirmed. . . . The Superior Court in the action brought by petitioner Valley Unitarian-Universalist Church, Inc., upheld the validity of the provisions under the Federal Constitution, but held that §32 of the Revenue and Taxation Code violated the California

Constitution because it excluded or exempted householders from the requirement. The Supreme Court of California reversed. . . .

In addition to the contentions advanced by the appellants in *Speiser*, the petitioners argue that the provisions are invalid under the Fourteenth Amendment as abridgments of religious freedom and as violations of the principle of separation of church and state. Our disposition of the cases, however, makes consideration of these questions unnecessary. For the reasons expressed in *Speiser*, we hold that the enforcement of §19 of Art. XX of the State Constitution through procedures which place the burdens of proof and persuasion of the taxpayer is a violation of due process.

The judgments are reversed, and the causes remanded for proceedings not inconsistent with this opinion.

Nelson v. Los Angeles County
362 U.S. 1 (1960)

Petitioners, when employees of the County of Los Angeles, California, were subpoenaed by and appeared before a Subcommittee of the House Un-American Activities Committee, but refused to answer certain questions concerning subversion. Previously, each petitioner had been ordered by the County Board of Supervisors to answer any questions asked by the Subcommittee relating to his subversive activity, and 1028.1 of the Government Code of the State of California made it the duty of any public employee to give testimony relating to such activity on pain of discharge "in the manner provided by law." Thereafter the County discharged petitioners on the ground of insubordination and violation of 1028.1 of the Code. Nelson, a permanent social

worker employed by the County's Department of Charities, was, upon his request, given a Civil Service Commission hearing which resulted in a confirmation of his discharge. Globe was a temporary employee of the same department and was denied a hearing on his discharge on the ground that, as such, he was not entitled to a hearing under the Civil Service Rules adopted pursuant to the County Charter. Petitioners then filed these petitions for mandates seeking reinstatement, contending that the California statute and their discharges violated the Due Process Clause of the Fourteenth Amendment. Nelson's discharge was affirmed by the District Court of Appeal, and Globe's summary dismissal was likewise affirmed. A petition for review in each of the cases was denied without opinion by the Supreme Court of California. . . .

On April 6, 1956, Globe was served with a subpoena to appear before the Subcommittee at Los Angeles. On the same date, he was served with a copy of an order of the County Board of Supervisors, originally issued February 19, 1952, concerning appearances before the Subcommittee. This order provided, among other things, that it was the duty of any employee to appear before the Subcommittee when so ordered or subpoenaed, and to answer questions concerning subversion. The order specifically stated that any "employee who disobeys the declaration of this duty and order will be considered to have been insubordinate . . . and that such insubordination shall constitute grounds for discharge. . . ." At the appointed time, Globe appeared before the Subcommittee and was interrogated by its counsel concerning his familiarity with the John Reid Club. He claimed that this was a matter which was entirely his "own business," and, upon being pressed for an answer, he stated that the question was "completely out of line as far as my rights as a citizen are concerned, [and] I refuse to answer this question under the First and Fifth Amendments of the Constitution of the United States." On the same grounds he refused to answer further questions concerning the Club, including one relating to his own membership. . . . He refused to testify whether he was "a member of the Communist Party now" "on the same grounds" and "as previously stated for previous reasons." On May 2, by letter, Globe was discharged, "without further notice," on "the grounds that [he had] been guilty of insubordination and of violation of Section 1028.1 of the Government Code of the State of California. . . ."

. . .

. . . Globe contends that, despite his temporary status, his summary discharge was arbitrary and unreasonable and, therefore, violative of due process. . . . California law in this regard, as declared by its court, is that Globe "has no vested right to county employment and may therefore be discharged summarily." We take this interpretation of California law as binding upon us.

We, therefore, reach Globe's contention that his summary discharge was nevertheless arbitrary and unreasonable. In this regard he places his reliance on *Slochower v. Board of Education*. However, the New York statute under which Slochower was discharged specifically operated "to discharge every city employee who invokes the Fifth Amendment. In practical effect the questions asked are taken as confessed and made the basis of the discharge." This "built-in" inference of guilt, derived solely from a Fifth Amendment claim, we held to be arbitrary and unreasonable. But the test here, rather than being the invocation of any constitutional privilege, is the failure of the employee to answer. California has not predicated dis-

charge on any "built-in" inference of guilt in its statute, but solely on employee insubordination for failure to give information which we have held that the State has a legitimate interest in securing. Moreover it must be remembered that here—unlike *Slochower*—the Board had specifically ordered its employees to appear and answer.

. . . Globe had been ordered by his employer as well as by California's law to appear and answer questions before the federal Subcommittee. These mandates made no reference to Fifth Amendment privileges. If Globe had simply refused, without more, to answer the Subcommittee's questions, we think that under the principles of *Beilan* and *Lerner* California could certainly have discharged him. The fact that he chose to place his refusal on a Fifth Amendment claim puts the matter in no different posture, for as in *Lerner*, California did not employ that claim as the basis for drawing an inference of guilt. Nor do we think that this discharge is vitiated by any deterrent effect that California's law might have had on Globe's exercise of his federal claim of privilege. The State may nevertheless legitimately predicate discharge on refusal to give information touching on the field of security. Likewise, we cannot say as a matter of due process that the State's choice of securing such information by means of testimony before a federal body can be denied. Finally, we do not believe that California's grounds for discharge constituted an arbitrary classification. We conclude that the order of the County Board was not invalid under the Due Process Clause of the Fourteenth Amendment.

. . . Having found that on the record here the discharge for "insubordination" was not arbitrary, we need go no further.

. . . The judgments are affirmed.

Killian v. United States
368 U.S. 231 (1961)

For the purpose of enabling a labor union of which he was then an officer to comply with §9(h) of the National Labor Relations Act, and hence to use the processes of the National Labor Relations Board, petitioner made on December 9, and caused to be filed with the Board on December 11, 1952, an affidavit reciting, "I am not a member of the Communist Party or affiliated with such Party." Upon receipt of that affidavit and like ones of all other officers of the union, the Board advised the union that it had complied with §9(h) and could make use of the Board's processes.

In November 1955, an indictment in two counts was returned against petitioner in the United States District Court for the Northern District of Illinois. The first count charged that . . . petitioner had falsely sworn, in the affidavit, that he was not a member of the Communist Party, and the second charged that, in violation of the same statute, he had also falsely sworn in that affidavit that he was not affiliated with the Communist Party. A jury trial was had which resulted in a verdict of guilty on both counts, and the court sentenced petitioner to imprisonment. On appeal, the United States Court of Appeals for the Seventh Circuit originally affirmed, but . . . granted the motion for rehearing, reversed the judgment and remanded the case for a new trial. A new trial was had. It also resulted in a verdict of guilty on both counts, and petitioner was sentenced to imprisonment for five years on Count I, and for three years on Count II, the sentences to run concurrently. On appeal, the United States Court of Appeals for the Seventh Circuit affirmed. . . .

. . .

. . . [W]e vacate the judgment and remand the cause to the District Court for a hearing confined to the issues raised by the Solicitor General's representations as stated in this opinion. The District Court shall make findings of fact on those issues. If the District Court finds that the Solicitor General's representations are true in all material respects, it shall enter a new final judgment based upon the record as supplemented by its findings, thereby preserving to petitioner the right to appeal to the Court of Appeals. If, on the other hand, the District Court finds that the Solicitor General's representations are untrue in any material respect, it shall grant petitioner a new trial.

. . .

Petitioner, and the amici curiae, contend that §5 of the Communist Control Act of 1954 is constitutionally invalid in that it violates the First Amendment of the Constitution and denies due process because it permits a jury to base its finding of membership upon statements and acts that are protected by the First Amendment. They then argue that, because the challenged instruction substantially adopted 12 of the 14 criteria mentioned in that section this instruction, too, was violative of the First Amendment and denied due process. We have no occasion here to consider the constitutionality of §5 of the Communist Control Act of 1954 because, as we have said, the indicia which the challenged instruction told the jury to consider as circumstances bearing upon the issue of membership did rationally tend to show, and were sufficient, if believed, to enable the jury rationally and logically to find, the ultimate subjective fact of membership, wholly apart from and independently of §5 of the Communist Control Act of 1954. To petitioner's argument that the submitted criteria permitted the jury to find membership from statements and acts that were wholly innocent in themselves or even' protected by the First Amendment, it is enough to recall that nothing in §9(h) or elsewhere in the

National Labor Relations Act makes or purports to make criminal either membership in or affiliation with the Communist Party, and that petitioner was not charged with criminality for being a member of or affiliated with the Communist Party, nor with participating in any criminal activities of or for the Communist Party, but only with having made and submitted to the Government an affidavit falsely swearing that he was not a member of or affiliated with the Communist Party in violation of 18 U.S.C. §1001. It would be strange doctrine, indeed, to say that membership in the Communist Party—when, as here, a lawful status—cannot be proved by evidence of lawful acts and statements, but only by evidence of unlawful acts and statements.

. . .

. . . It is true that one may be "affiliated with" the Communist Party through membership in an organization that is affiliated with the Communist Party, but that is not to say one may not do so directly, and every decision that has considered the meaning of "affiliated with," as used in §9(h), has held that one may be directly affiliated with the Communist Party.

In a manner similar to his attack upon the court's instruction defining membership, petitioner contends that the instruction in question erroneously defined the phrase "affiliated with" only in subjective terms, and without objective criteria. However, just as with regard to membership, affiliation, in relation to Count II in this case, is necessarily subjective. But the ultimate fact of affiliation, though subjective, may be proved by evidence of objective facts and circumstances having a rational tendency to show, and from which the jury may rationally and logically find, the ultimate fact of affiliation. It cannot be disputed here that there was such evidence at the trial. . . .

. . .

Petitioner, quite understandably, would require instructions as specific as mathematical formulas. But such specificity often is impossible. The phrases "member of" and "affiliated with," especially when applied to the relationship between persons and organizations that conceal their connection, cannot be defined in absolute terms. The most that is possible, and hence all that can be expected, is that the trial court shall give the jury a fair statement of the issues—i.e., whether petitioner was a member of or affiliated with the Communist Party on the date of his affidavit—give a reasonable definition of the terms and outline the various criteria, shown in the evidence, which the jury may consider in determining the ultimate issues. We believe that the instructions in this case, which are consistent with all the judicial precedents under §9(h), adequately met those tests.

Accordingly, the judgment is vacated, and the case is remanded to the District Court for further proceedings consistent with this opinion.

Cramp v. Board of Public Instruction of Orange County
368 U.S. 278 (1961)

A Florida statute requires each employee of the State or its subdivisions to execute a written oath in which he must swear that, among other things, he has never lent his "aid, support, advice, counsel or influence to the Communist Party." Failure to subscribe to this oath results under the law in the employee's immediate discharge.

After the appellant had been employed for more than nine years as a public school teacher in Orange County, Florida, it was discovered in 1959 that he had never been required to execute this statutory oath. When requested to do so, he refused. He then brought an action in the state circuit court asking for a judgment declaring the oath requirement unconstitutional, and for an injunction forbidding the appellee, the Orange County Board of Public Instruction, from requiring him to execute the oath and from discharging him for his failure to do so. The circuit court held the statute valid and denied the prayer for an injunction. The Supreme Court of Florida affirmed. . . .

. . .

The issue to be decided . . . is whether a State can constitutionally compel those in its service to swear that they have never "knowingly lent their aid, support, advice, counsel, or influence to the Communist Party." More precisely, can Florida consistently with the Due Process Clause of the Fourteenth Amendment force an employee either to take such an oath at the risk of subsequent prosecution for perjury, or face immediate dismissal from public service?

The provision of the oath here in question, it is to be noted, says nothing of advocacy of violent overthrow of state or federal government. It says nothing of membership or affiliation with the Communist Party, past or present. The provision is completely lacking in these or any other terms susceptible of objective measurement. Those who take this oath must swear, rather, that they have not in the unending past ever knowingly lent their "aid," or "support," or "advice," or "counsel" or "influence" to the Communist Party. What do these phrases mean? In the not too distant past, Communist Party candidates appeared regularly and legally on the ballot in many state and local elections. Elsewhere, the Communist Party has on occasion endorsed or supported candidates nominated by others. Could one who had ever cast his vote for such a candidate safely subscribe to this legislative oath?

Could a lawyer who had ever represented the Communist Party or its members swear with either confidence or honesty that he had never knowingly lent his "counsel" to the Party? Could a journalist who had ever defended the constitutional rights of the Communist Party conscientiously take an oath that he had never lent the Party his "support"? Indeed, could anyone honestly subscribe to this oath who had ever supported any cause with contemporaneous knowledge that the Communist Party also supported it?

The very absurdity of these possibilities brings into focus the extraordinary ambiguity of the statutory language. With such vagaries in mind, it is not unrealistic to suggest that the compulsion of this oath provision might weigh most heavily upon those whose conscientious scruples were the most sensitive. . . .

. . .

. . . It is not the penalty itself that is invalid, but the exaction of obedience to a rule or standard that is so vague and indefinite as to be really no rule or standard at all.

. . .

. . . The fact . . . that a person is not compelled to hold public office cannot possibly be an excuse for barring him from office by state-imposed criteria forbidden by the Constitution.

Reversed.

Baggett v. Bullitt
377 U.S. 360 (1964)

Appellants, approximately 64 in number, are members of the faculty, staff and student body of the University of Washington who brought this class action asking for a judgment declaring unconstitutional two Washington statutes requiring the execution of two different oaths by state employees and for an injunction against the enforcement of these statutes by appellees, the President of the University, members of the Washington State Board of Regents and the State Attorney General.

The statutes under attack are Chapter 377 and Chapter 103, both of which require employees of the State of Washington to take the oaths prescribed in the statutes as a condition of their employment. . . .

On May 28, 1962 . . . the University President, acting pursuant to directions of the Board of Regents, issued a memorandum to all University employees notifying them that they would be required to take an oath. Oath Form A requires all teaching personnel to swear to the oath of allegiance . . . to aver that they have read, are familiar with and understand the provisions defining "subversive person" in the Subversive Activities Act of 1951, and to disclaim being a subversive person and membership in the Communist Party or any other subversive or foreign subversive organization. Oath Form B requires other state employees to subscribe to all. . . . Both forms provide that the oath and statements pertinent thereto are made subject to the penalties of perjury.

. . . [A] three-judge District Court was convened, and a trial was had. That court determined that the 1955 oath and underlying statutory provisions did not infringe upon any First and Fourteenth Amendment freedoms and were not unduly vague. In respect to the claims that the 1931 oath was unconstitutionally vague on its face, the court held that, although the challenge raised a substantial constitutional issue, adjudication was not proper in the absence of proceedings in the state courts which might resolve or avoid the constitutional issue. The action was dismissed. . . .

. . .

. . . A teacher must swear that he is not a subversive person: that he is not one who commits an act or who advises, teaches, abets or advocates by any means another person to commit or aid in the commission of any act intended to overthrow or alter, or to assist the overthrow or alteration, of the constitutional form of government by revolution, force or violence. A subversive organization is defined as one which engages in or assists activities intended to alter or overthrow the Government by force or violence or which has as a purpose the commission of such acts. The Communist Party is declared in the statute to be a subversive organization, that is, it is presumed that the Party does and will engage in activities intended to overthrow the Government. Persons required to swear they understand this oath may quite reasonably conclude that any person who aids the Communist Party or teaches or advises known members of the Party is a subversive person because such teaching or advice may now or at some future date aid the activities of the Party. Teaching and advising are clearly acts, and one cannot confidently assert that his counsel, aid, influence or support which adds to the resources, rights and knowledge of the Communist Party or its members does not aid the Party in its activities, activities which the statute tells us are all in furtherance of the stated purpose of overthrowing the Government by revolution, force, or violence. . . .

. . . A person is subversive not only if he himself commits the specified acts, but if he abets or advises another in aiding a third person to commit an act which will assist yet a fourth person in the overthrow or alteration of constitutional government. The Washington Supreme Court has said that knowledge is to be read into every provision, and we accept this construction. But what is it that the Washington professor must "know"?

Must he know that his aid or teaching will be used by another, and that the person aided has the requisite guilty intent, or is it sufficient that he knows that his aid or teaching would or might be useful to others in the commission of acts intended to overthrow the Government? Is it subversive activity, for example, to attend and participate in international conventions of mathematicians and exchange views with scholars from Communist countries? What about the editor of a scholarly journal who analyzes and criticizes the manuscripts of Communist scholars submitted for publication? Is selecting outstanding scholars from Communist countries as visiting professors and advising, teaching, or consulting with them at the University of Washington a subversive activity if such scholars are known to be Communists, or, regardless of their affiliations, regularly teach students who are members of the Communist Party, which, by statutory definition, is subversive and dedicated to the overthrow of the Government?

The Washington oath goes beyond overthrow or alteration by force or violence. It extends to alteration by "revolution" which, unless wholly redundant and its ordinary meaning distorted, includes any rapid or fundamental change. Would, therefore, any organization or any person supporting, advocating or teaching peaceful but far-reaching constitutional amendments be engaged in subversive activity? Could one support the repeal of the Twenty-second Amendment or participation by this country in a world government?

We also conclude that the 1931 oath offends due process because of vagueness. The oath exacts a promise that the affiant will, by precept and example, promote respect for the flag and the institutions of the United States and State of Washington. The range of activities which are or might be deemed inconsistent with the required promise is very wide indeed. The teacher who refused to salute the flag or advocated refusal because of religious beliefs might well be accused of breaching his promise. Even criticism of the design or color scheme of the state flag or unfavorable comparison of it with that of a sister State or foreign country could be deemed disrespectful, and therefore violative of the oath. And what are "institutions" for the purposes of this oath? Is it every "practice, law, custom, etc., which is a material and persistent element in the life or culture of an organized social group," or every "established society or corporation," every "establishment, esp[ecially] one of a public character?" The oath may prevent a professor from criticizing his state judicial system or the Supreme Court or the institution of judicial review. Or it might be deemed to proscribe advocating the abolition, for example, of the Civil Rights Commission, the House Committee on Un-American Activities, or foreign aid.

It is likewise difficult to ascertain what might be done without transgressing the promise to "promote . . . undivided allegiance to the government of the United States." It would not be unreasonable for the serious-minded oath-taker to conclude that he should dispense with lectures voicing far-reaching criticism of any old or new policy followed by the Government of the United States. He could find it questionable under this language to ally himself with any interest group dedicated to opposing any current public policy or law of the Federal Government, for if he did, he might well be accused of placing loyalty to the group above allegiance to the United States.

. . .

. . . We are dealing with indefinite statutes whose terms, even narrowly construed, abut upon sensitive areas of basic First Amendment freedoms. The uncertain meanings of the oaths require the oath-taker teachers and public servants to "steer far wider of the unlawful zone," than if the boundaries of the forbidden areas were clearly marked. Those with a conscientious regard for what they solemnly swear or affirm, sensitive to the perils posed by the oath's indefinite language, avoid the risk of loss of employment, and perhaps profession, only by restricting their conduct to that which is unquestionably safe. Free speech may not be so inhibited.

. . .

. . . The challenged oath is not open to one or a few interpretations, but to an indefinite number. There is no uncertainty that the oath applies to the appellants, and the issue they raise is not whether the oath permits them to engage in certain definable activities. Rather, their complaint is that they, about 64 in number, cannot understand the required promise, cannot define the range of activities in which they might engage in the future, and do not want to forswear doing all that is literally or arguably within the purview of the vague terms. In these circumstances, it is difficult to see how an abstract construction of the challenged terms, such as precept, example, allegiance, institutions, and the like, in a declaratory judgment action could eliminate the vagueness from these terms. . . .

. . .

. . . But measures which purport to define disloyalty must allow public servants to know what is and is not disloyal. . . .

Reversed.

Elfbrandt v. Russell
384 U.S. 11 (1966)

. . . One who subscribes to this Arizona oath and who is, or thereafter becomes, a knowing member of an organization which has as "one of its purposes" the violent overthrow of the government is subject to immediate discharge and criminal penalties. Nothing in the oath, the statutory gloss, or the construction of the oath and statutes given by the Arizona Supreme Court purports to exclude association by one who does not subscribe to the organization's unlawful ends. . . . People often label as "communist" ideas which they oppose; and they often make up our juries. . . . Would a teacher be safe and secure in going to a Pugwash Conference? Would it be legal to join a seminar group predominantly Communist, and therefore subject to control by those who are said to believe in the overthrow of the Government by force and violence? Juries might convict though the teacher did not subscribe to the wrongful aims of the organization. And there is apparently no machinery provided for getting clearance in advance.

Those who join an organization but do not share its unlawful purposes, and who do not participate in its unlawful activities, surely pose no threat, either as citizens or as public employees. Laws such as this which are not restricted in scope to those who join with the "specific intent" to further illegal action impose, in effect, a conclusive presumption that the member shares the unlawful aims of the organization. The unconstitutionality of this Act follows a fortiori from *Speiser*, where we held that a State may not even place on an applicant for a tax exemption the burden of proving that he has not engaged in criminal advocacy.

This Act threatens the cherished freedom of association protected by the First Amendment, made applicable to the States through the Fourteenth Amendment. And, as a committee of the Arizona Legislature which urged adoption of this law itself recognized, public employees of character and integrity may well forgo their calling rather than risk prosecution for perjury or compromise their commitment to intellectual and political freedom. . . .

. . . A law which applies to membership without the "specific intent" to further the illegal aims of the organization infringes unnecessarily on protected freedoms. It rests on the doctrine of "guilt by association," which has no place here. Such a law cannot stand.

Reversed.

Keyishian v. Board of Regents
385 U.S. 589 (1967)

Appellants were members of the faculty of the privately owned and operated University of Buffalo, and became state employees when the University was merged in 1962 into the State University of New York, an institution of higher education owned and operated by the State of New York. As faculty members of the State University, their continued employment was conditioned upon their compliance with a New York plan, formulated partly in statutes and partly in administrative regulations, which the State utilizes to prevent the appointment or retention of "subversive" persons in state employment.

Appellants Hochfield and Maud were Assistant Professors of English, appellant Keyishian an instructor in English, and appellant Garver, a lecturer in philosophy. Each of them refused to sign, as regulations then in effect required, a certificate that he was not a Communist, and that, if he had ever been a Communist, he had communicated that fact to the President of the State University of New York. Each was notified that his failure to sign the certificate would require his dismissal. Keyishian's one-year-term contract was not renewed, because of his failure to sign

the certificate. Hochfield and Garver, whose contracts still had time to run, continue to teach, but subject to proceedings for their dismissal if the constitutionality of the New York plan is sustained. Maud has voluntarily resigned, and therefore no longer has standing in this suit.

Appellant Starbuck was a non-faculty library employee and part-time lecturer in English. Personnel in that classification were not required to sign a certificate, but were required to answer in writing under oath. . . . Starbuck refused to answer the question, and, as a result, was dismissed.

Appellants brought this action for declaratory and injunctive relief, alleging that the state program violated the Federal Constitution in various respects. A three-judge federal court held that the program was constitutional. . . .

. . .

We therefore hold that Civil Service Law §105, subd. 1(c), and Education Law §3022, subd. 2, are invalid insofar as they proscribe mere knowing membership, without any showing of specific intent to further the unlawful aims of the Communist Party of the United States or of the State of New York.

The judgment of the District Court is reversed, and the case is remanded for further proceedings consistent with this opinion.

Whitehill v. Elkins
389 U.S. 54 (1967)

This suit for declaratory relief that a Maryland teacher's oath required of appellant was unconstitutional was heard by a three-judge court and dismissed. . . .

Appellant, who was offered a teaching position with the University of Maryland, refused to take the . . . oath. . . .

The question is whether the oath is to be read in isolation or in connection with the Ober Act, which, by §§1 and 13, defines a "subversive" as

> ... any person who commits, attempts to commit, or aids in the commission, or advocates, abets, advises or teaches by any means any person to commit, attempt to commit, or aid in the commission of any act intended to overthrow, destroy or alter, or to assist in the overthrow, destruction or alteration of, the constitutional form of the government of the United States, or of the State of Maryland, or any political subdivision of either of them, by revolution, force, or violence; or who is a member of a subversive organization or a foreign subversive organization, as more fully defined in this article.

Section 1 defines the latter terms: "subversive organization" meaning a group that would "alter" the form of government "by revolution, force, or violence"; "foreign subversive organization" is such a group directed, dominated, or controlled by a foreign government which engages in such activities.

The oath was prepared by the Attorney General and approved by the Board of Regents that has exclusive management of the university. It is conceded that the Board had authority to provide an oath, as §11 of the Act directs every agency of the State which appoints, employs, or supervises officials or employees to establish procedures designed to ascertain before a person is appointed or employed that he or she "is not a subversive person." And that term is, as noted, defined by §1 and 13. . . .

If the Federal Constitution is our guide, a person who might wish to "alter" our form of government may not be cast into the outer darkness. For the Constitution prescribes the method of "alteration" by the amending process in Article V, and while the procedure for amending it is restricted, there is no restraint on the kind of amendment that may be offered. Moreover, the First Amendment, which protects a controversial as well as a conventional dialogue, is as applicable to the States as it is to the Federal Government, and it extends to petitions for redress of grievances as well as to advocacy and debate. So if §§1 and 13 of the Ober Act are the frame of reference in which the challenged oath is to be adjudged, we have important questions to resolve.

. . .

Like the other oath cases mentioned, we have another classic example of the need for "narrowly drawn" legislation in this sensitive and important First Amendment area.

Reversed.

Law Students Civil Rights Research Council v. Wadmond
401 U.S. 154 (1971)

An applicant for admission to the Bar of New York must be a citizen of the United States, have lived in the State for at least six months, and pass a written examination conducted by the State Board of Law Examiners. In addition, New York requires that the Appellate Division of the State Supreme Court in the judicial department where an applicant resides must "be satisfied that such person possesses the character and general fitness requisite for an attorney and counselor at law." . . .

This case involves a broad attack, primarily on First Amendment vagueness and overbreadth grounds, upon this system for screening applicants for admission to the New York Bar. . . .

. . . [T]he court considered the appellants' claims and found certain items on the questionnaires as they then stood to be so vague, overbroad, and intrusive upon applicants' private lives as to be of doubtful constitutional validity. It granted the partial relief. . . . It upheld the statutes and rules as valid on their face, and, with the exceptions noted, sustained the validity of New York's system. . . .

. . .

. . . Rule 9406 of the New York Civil Practice Law and Rules directs the Committees on Character and Fitness not to certify an applicant for admission "unless he shall furnish satisfactory proof to the effect" that he is a citizen of the United States, has resided in New York for at least six months, has complied with the applicable statutes and rules, and "believes in the form of the government of the United States and is loyal to such government."

. . .

If all we had before us were the language of Rule 9406, which seems to require an applicant to furnish proof of his belief in the form of the Government of the United States and of his loyalty to the Government, this would be a different case. For the language of the Rule lends itself to a construction that could raise substantial constitutional questions, both as to the burden of proof permissible in such a context under the Due Process Clause of the Fourteenth Amendment and as to the permissible scope of inquiry into an applicant's political beliefs under the First and Fourteenth Amendments. But this case comes before us in a significant and unusual posture: the appellees are the very state authorities entrusted with the definitive interpretation of the language of the Rule. We therefore accept their interpretation, however we might construe that language were it left for us to do so. . . .

The appellees have made it abundantly clear that their construction of the Rule is both extremely narrow, and fully cognizant of protected constitutional freedoms. There are three key elements to this construction. First, the Rule places upon applicants no burden of proof. Second, "the form of the government of the United States" and the "government" refer solely to the Constitution, which is all that the oath mentions. Third, "belief" and "loyalty" mean no more than willingness to take the constitutional oath and ability to do so in good faith.

Accepting this construction, we find no constitutional invalidity in Rule 9406. There is "no showing of an intent to penalize political beliefs." . . .

. . .

. . . We are not persuaded that careful administration of such a system as New York's need result in chilling effects upon the exercise of constitutional freedoms. Consequently, the choice between systems like New York's and approaches like that urged by the appellants rests with the legislatures and other policymaking bodies of the individual States. New York has made its choice. To disturb it would be beyond the power of this Court.

The judgment is affirmed.

Cole v. Richardson
405 U.S. 676 (1972)

The appellee, Richardson, was hired as a research sociologist by the Boston State Hospital. Cole is superintendent of the hospital. Soon after she entered on duty, Mrs. Richardson was asked to subscribe to the oath required of all public employees in Massachusetts. . . .

Mrs. Richardson informed the hospital's personnel department that she could not take the oath as ordered because of her belief that it was in violation of the United States Constitution. Approximately 10 days later, appellant Cole personally informed Mrs. Richardson that, under state law, she could not continue as an employee of the Boston State Hospital unless she subscribed to the oath. Again she refused. On November 25, 1968, Mrs. Richardson's employment was terminated, and she was paid through that date.

In March, 1969, Mrs. Richardson filed a complaint in the United States District Court for the District of Massachusetts. The complaint alleged the unconstitutionality of the statute, sought damages and an injunction against its continued enforcement. . . .

A three-judge District Court held the oath statute unconstitutional and enjoined the appellants from applying the statute to prohibit Mrs. Richardson from working for Boston State Hospital. . . . The court granted the requested injunction, but denied the claim for damages.

. . . We remanded for consideration of whether the case was moot in light of a suggestion that Mrs. Richardson's job had been filled in the in-

terim. On remand, the District Court concluded that Mrs. Richardson's position had not been filled, and that the hospital stood ready to hire her for the continuing research project except for the problem of the oath. . . . [I]t concluded that the case was not moot, and reinstated its earlier judgment. . . .

. . .

Since there is no constitutionally protected right to overthrow a government by force, violence, or illegal or unconstitutional means, no constitutional right is infringed by an oath to abide by the constitutional system in the future. Therefore, there is no requirement that one who refuses to take the Massachusetts oath be granted a hearing for the determination of some other fact before being discharged.

The judgment of the District Court is reversed, and the case is remanded for further proceedings consistent with this opinion.

15

Forms of Government

This chapter involves a multitude of issues (some of which were also part of Chapters 1 and 3) about how governments are organized and their impact on political rights. Topics include the Voting Rights Act's preclearance requirements.

Dusch v. Davis
387 U.S. 112 (1967)

In 1963 the City of Virginia Beach, Virginia, consolidated with adjoining Princess Anne County, which was both rural and urban, and a borough form of government was adopted. There are seven boroughs, one corresponding to the boundaries of the former city and six corresponding to the boundaries of the six magisterial districts. The consolidation plan was effected pursuant to Virginia law, and the charter embodied in the plan was approved by the legislature.

Three boroughs—Bayside, Kempsville, and Lynnhaven—are primarily urban. Three—Blackwater, Princess Anne, and Pungo—are primarily rural. The borough of Virginia Beach, centering around its famous ocean beach and bay, is primarily tourist.

Electors of five boroughs, having exhausted attempts to obtain relief in the state courts, instituted this suit against local and state officials claiming that the consolidation plan in its distribution of voting rights violated the principle of *Reynolds v. Sims.* . . .

The District Court held the original allocation invalid as denying voter equality and stayed further proceedings to allow the city an opportunity to seek a charter amendment at the 1966 session of the State Legislature. The charter was amended to provide for the Seven-Four Plan now being challenged. Under the amended charter, the council is composed of eleven members. Four members are elected at large without regard to residence. Seven are elected by the voters of the entire city, one being required to reside in each of the seven boroughs. Pursuant to leave of the District Court, appellees filed an amended complaint challenging the validity of the Seven-Four Plan. The District Court approved this plan. The Court of Appeals reversed. . . .

. . .

The Seven-Four Plan makes no distinction on the basis of race, creed, or economic status or location. Each of the eleven councilmen is elected by a vote of all the electors in the city. The fact that each of the seven councilmen must be a resident of the borough from which he is elected, is not fatal. . . .

. . .

The Seven-Four Plan seems to reflect a detente between urban and rural communities that may be important in resolving the complex problems of the modern megalopolis in relation to the city, the suburbia, and the rural countryside. Finding no invidious discrimination we conclude that the judgment of the Court of Appeals must be and is reversed.

Associated Enterprises v. Toltec Watershed Improvement District
410 U.S. 743 (1973)

. . . Appellee Toltec Watershed Improvement District was established after referendum held pursuant to Wyoming's Watershed Improvement District Act. After formation, appellee sought a right of entry onto lands owned by appellant Associated Enterprises, Inc., and leased by Johnston Fuel Liners, for the purpose of carrying out studies to determine the feasibility of constructing a dam and reservoir. When Associated Enterprises resisted, the district sought to enforce its right in state court. Arguing that the statutes authorizing the referendum violated the Equal Protection Clause, since, under §41–354.9, only landowners are entitled to vote, and under §41–354.10, a watershed improvement district cannot be determined to be administratively practicable and feasible unless a majority of the votes cast, representing a majority of the acreage in the district, favor its creation, appellants maintained that the district was illegally formed. The trial court agreed that, had the district been formed in violation of the Equal Protection Clause, appellants would have a good defense under state law to the asserted right of entry, but it held against them on the merits. The Wyoming Supreme Court affirmed.

. . .

. . . The statute authorizing the establishment of improvement districts was enacted by a legislature in which all of the State's electors have the unquestioned right to be fairly represented. Under the act, districts may be formed only as subdivisions of soil and water conservation districts. And a precondition to their formation referendum is a determination by a board of supervisors of the affected conservation district, popularly elected by both occupiers and owners of land within the district, that the watershed improvement district is both necessary and administratively practicable. . . . [W]e hold that the State could rationally conclude that landowners are primarily burdened and benefited by the establishment and operation of watershed districts, and that it may condition the vote accordingly. The judgment appealed from is, therefore, affirmed.

City of Richmond v. United States
422 U.S. 358 (1975)

. . . Here, the city of Richmond annexed land formerly in Chesterfield County, and the issue is whether the city, in its declaratory judgment action brought in the District Court for the District of Columbia, has carried its burden of proof of demonstrating that the annexation had neither the purpose nor the effect of denying or abridging the right to vote of the Richmond Negro community on account of its race or color.

The controlling Virginia statutes permit cities to annex only after obtaining a favorable judgment from a specially constituted three-judge annexation court. In 1962, the city sought judicial approval of two annexation ordinances, one seeking to annex approximately 150 square miles of Henrico County and the other approximately 51 square miles of Chesterfield County. The Henrico case, which was protracted, proceeded first. In 1965, the annexation court authorized the annexation of 16 square miles of Henrico County, but because of a $55 million financial obligation which, as it turned out, annexation would entail, the city council determined that the annexation was not in the city's best interest. The Henrico case was accordingly dismissed.

The city then proceeded with the Chesterfield

case. In May, 1969, a compromise line was approved by the city and Chesterfield County and incorporated in a decree of July 12, 1969, which awarded the city approximately 23 square miles of land adjacent to the city in Chesterfield County. The pre-annexation population of the city as of 1970 was 202,359, of which 104,207 or 52 percent were black citizens. The annexation added to the city 47,262 people, of whom 1,557 were black and 45,705 were nonblack. The post-annexation population of the city was therefore 249,621, of which 105,764 or 42 percent were Negroes. The annexation became effective on January 1, 1970, and the city has exercised jurisdiction over the area since that time.

Before and immediately after annexation, the city had a nine-man council, which was elected at large. In 1968, three candidates endorsed by the Crusade for Voters of Richmond, a black civic organization, were elected to the council. In the post-annexation, at-large election in 1970, three of the nine members elected had also received the endorsement of the Crusade.

On January 14, 1971, a divided Court in *Perkins v. Matthews*, held that §5 of the Voting Rights Act applied to city annexations. On January 28, 1971, the city of Richmond sought the Attorney General's approval of the Chesterfield annexation. On May 7, 1971, after requesting and receiving additional materials from the city, the Attorney General declined to approve the voting change, which he deemed the annexation to represent, saying that the annexation substantially increased the proportion of whites and decreased the proportion of blacks in the city, and that the annexation "inevitably tends to dilute the voting strength of black voters." . . . Following reversal by this Court of the District Court's judgment in *Chavis v. Whitcomb*, a decision on which the Attorney General had relied in disapproving the

Chesterfield annexation, the city's request for reconsideration was denied by the Attorney General on September 30, 1971, again with the suggestion that "single member, non-racially drawn councilmanic districts" would be "one means of minimizing the racial effect of the annexation. . . ."

Meanwhile on February 4, 1971, respondent Curtis Holt brought an action (Holt I) in the United States District Court for the Eastern District of Virginia, asserting that the annexation denied Richmond Negroes their rights under the Fifteenth Amendment. In November, 1971, the District Court ruled in that suit that the annexation had had an illegal racial purpose, and ordered a new election of the city council, seven councilmen to be elected at large from the old city and two primarily from the annexed area. The Court of Appeals for the Fourth Circuit, sitting en banc, reversed on May 3, 1972, holding that no Fifteenth Amendment rights were violated, that the city had valid reasons for seeking to annex in 1962, and that the record would support no finding that the 1969 annexation was not motivated by the same considerations.

. . .

. . . Richmond developed and submitted to the Attorney General various plans for establishing councilmanic districts in the city. With some modification, to which the city council agreed, the Attorney General indicated approval of one of these plans. This was a nine-ward proposal under which four of the wards would have substantial black majorities, four wards substantial white majorities, and the ninth a racial division of approximately 59 percent white and 41 percent black. The city and the Attorney General submitted this plan to the District Court for the District of Columbia in the form of a consent judgment. The intervenors opposed it, and the District Court referred the case to a Special Master for hearings and recommendations. The Special Master submitted recommended findings of fact and conclusions of law. Based on the statements of various officials of the city and other events which he found to have taken place, the Master concluded that the city had not met its burden of proving that the annexation did not have the purpose of diluting the right of black persons to vote, and that the ward plan did not cure the discriminatory racial purpose accompanying the annexation. In addition, he concluded that, in any event, the diluting effect of the annexation had not been dissipated to the greatest extent reasonably possible, that the city had not demonstrated any acceptable counterbalancing economic and administrative benefits, and that deannexation was the only acceptable remedy for the violations of §5 which had been found.

The District Court, essentially accepted the findings and conclusions of the Special Master except for his recommendation with respect to deannexation. . . .

The District Court . . . declined to order deannexation. . . .

. . .

We cannot accept the position that such a single-member ward system would nevertheless have the effect of denying or abridging the right to vote because Negroes would constitute a lesser proportion of the population after the annexation than before, and, given racial bloc voting, would have fewer seats on the city council. If a city having a ward system for the election of a nine-man council annexes a largely white area, the wards are fairly redrawn, and, as a result, Negroes have only two, rather than the four seats they had before, these facts alone do not demonstrate that the annexation has the effect of denying or abridging the right to vote. As long as the ward system fairly reflects the strength of the Negro commu-

nity as it exists after the annexation, we cannot hold, without more specific legislative directions, that such an annexation is nevertheless barred by §5. It is true that the black community, if there is racial bloc voting, will command fewer seats on the city council; and the annexation will have effected a decline in the Negroes' relative influence in the city. But a different city council and an enlarged city are involved after the annexation. Furthermore, Negro power in the new city is not undervalued, and Negroes will not be underrepresented on the council.

As long as this is true, we cannot hold that the effect of the annexation is to deny or abridge the right to vote. To hold otherwise would be either to forbid all such annexations or to require, as the price for approval of the annexation, that the black community be assigned the same proportion of council seats as before, hence perhaps permanently overrepresenting them and underrepresenting other elements in the community, including the nonblack citizens in the annexed area. We are unwilling to hold that Congress intended either consequence in enacting §5.

We are also convinced that the annexation now before us, in the context of the ward system of election finally proposed by the city and then agreed to by the United States, does not have the effect prohibited by §5. The findings on which this case was decided and is presented to us were that the post-annexation population of the city was 42 percent Negro, as compared with 52 percent prior to annexation. The nine-ward system finally submitted by the city included four wards each of which had a greater than a 64 percent black majority. Four wards were heavily white. The ninth had a black population of 40.9 percent. In our view, such a plan does not undervalue the black strength in the community after annexation, and we hold that the annexation in this context does not have the effect of denying or abridging the right to vote within the meaning of §5. To the extent that the District Court rested on a different view, its judgment cannot stand.

The foregoing principles should govern the application of §5 insofar as it forbids changes in voting procedures having the effect of denying or abridging the right to vote on the grounds of race or color. But the section also proscribes changes that are made with the purpose of denying the right to vote on such grounds. . . .

The requirement that the city allocate to the Negro community in the larger city the voting power or the seats on the city council in excess of its proportion in the new community, and thus permanently to underrepresent other elements in the community, is fundamentally at odds with the position we have expressed earlier in this opinion, and we cannot approve treating the failure to satisfy it as evidence of any purpose proscribed by §5.

Accepting the findings of the Master in the District Court that the annexation, as it went forward in 1969, was infected by the impermissible purpose of denying the right to vote based on race through perpetuating white majority power to exclude Negroes from office through at-large elections, we are nevertheless persuaded that, if verifiable reasons are now demonstrable in support of the annexation, and the ward plan proposed is fairly designed, the city need do no more to satisfy the requirements of §5. We are also convinced that, if the annexation cannot be sustained on sound, nondiscriminatory grounds, it would be only in the most extraordinary circumstances that the annexation should be permitted on condition that the Negro community be permanently overrepresented in the governing councils of the enlarged city. We are very doubtful that those circumstances exist in this case, for, as

far as this record is concerned, Chesterfield County was and still is quite ready to receive back the annexed area, to compensate the city for its capital improvements, and to resume governance of the area. . . .

. . .

We have held that an annexation reducing the relative political strength of the minority race in the enlarged city as compared with what it was before the annexation is not a statutory violation as long as the post-annexation electoral system fairly recognizes the minority's political potential. If this is so, it may be asked how it could be forbidden by §5 to have the purpose and intent of achieving only what is a perfectly legal result under that section, and why we need remand for further proceedings with respect to purpose alone. The answer is plain, and we need not labor it. An official action, whether an annexation or otherwise, taken for the purpose of discriminating against Negroes on account of their race has no legitimacy at all under our Constitution or under the statute. Section 5 forbids voting changes taken with the purpose of denying the vote on the grounds of race or color. Congress surely has the power to prevent such gross racial slurs, the only point of which is "to despoil colored citizens, and only colored citizens, of their theretofore enjoyed voting rights." Annexations animated by such a purpose have no credentials whatsoever, for "[a]cts generally lawful may become unlawful when done to accomplish an unlawful end. . . ." An annexation proved to be of this kind and not proved to have a justifiable basis is forbidden by §5, whatever its actual effect may have been or may be.

The judgment of the District Court is vacated, and the case is remanded to that court for further proceedings consistent with this opinion.

United States v. Board of Commissioners of Sheffield, Alabama
435 U.S. 110 (1978)

The city of Sheffield, Alabama (City or Sheffield), was incorporated in 1885 by the Alabama Legislature. As incorporated, the City was governed by a mayor and eight councilmen, two councilmen being elected directly from each of the City's four wards. Sheffield retained this mayor-council government until 1912, when it adopted a system in which three commissioners, elected by the City at large, ran the City. This commission form of government was in effect in Sheffield on November 1, 1964.

Sometime prior to March 20, 1975, Sheffield decided to put to a referendum the question whether the City should return to a mayor-council form of government. On that date, the president of the Board of Commissioners of Sheffield wrote the Attorney General of the United States to

> give notice of the proposal of submitting to the qualified voters of the City, whether the present commission form of government shall be abandoned in favor of the Mayor and Alderman form of government.

On May 13, 1975, before the Attorney General replied, the referendum occurred, and the voters of Sheffield approved the change.

On May 23, the Attorney General formally responded to Sheffield that he did "not interpose an objection to the holding of the referendum," but that, "[s]ince voters in the City of Sheffield elected to adopt the mayor-council form of government on May 13, 1975, the change is also subject to the preclearance requirements of Section 5." The Attorney General's letter also stated that, in the event the City should elect to seek preclearance of the change from the Attorney

General, it should submit detailed information concerning the change. . .

Thereafter the City informed the Attorney General that the proposed change would divide the City into four wards of substantially equal population, that each ward would have two council seats, that councilmen from each ward would be elected at large, and that candidates would run for numbered places. Subsequently the City furnished a detailed map showing ward boundaries, data concerning the population distribution by race for each ward, and a history of black candidacy for city and county offices since 1965. The City's submission was completed on May 5, 1976.

. . .

Notwithstanding the Attorney General's objection, the City scheduled an at-large council election for August 10, 1976. On August 9, the United States instituted this suit in the District Court for the Northern District of Alabama to enforce its §5 objection. A temporary restraining order was denied. After the election was held, a three-judge court was convened and that court dismissed the suit. The District Court unanimously held that Sheffield was not covered by §5, because it is not a "political subdivision" as that term is defined in §14(c)(2) of the Act. . . .

. . .

. . . [T]he legislative background of the enactment and reenactments compels the conclusion that, as the purposes of the Act and its terms suggest, §5 of the Act covers all political units within designated jurisdictions like Alabama. Accordingly, we hold that the District Court erred in concluding that §5 does not apply to Sheffield.

. . .

Under the circumstances, it is irrelevant that the Attorney General might have been on notice that, if the referendum passed, Sheffield would have been required by state law to adopt an at-large system of councilmanic elections. Although the City could have easily placed the request for preclearance of the change in the form of government before the Attorney General—i.e., by taking all action necessary for the completion of the change before submitting it, and by stating in its letter that it desired preclearance of the change itself—it did not, so the Attorney General, quite properly, treated Sheffield as having sought prior clearance only of the referendum. Accordingly, the District Court erred in concluding that the Attorney General has to be understood as having approved the adoption of an at-large system of election.

Since we conclude that Sheffield is covered by §5 of the Act and that the Attorney General did not clear the City's decision to adopt a system of government in which councilmen are elected at large, the judgment of the District Court is reversed.

Berry v. Doles
438 U.S. 190 (1978)

In 1968, the State of Georgia enacted a statute intended to stagger the terms of the three members of the Peach County Board of Commissioners of Roads and Revenues. The then-existing statute, adopted in 1964, provided that all three posts were to be filled at four-year intervals. By operation of the 1968 amendment, the single at-large member was to be elected to a two-year term in 1968 and to a four-year term at subsequent general elections. Appellees concede, and the three-judge court found, that the 1968 statute constituted a change in voting procedures subject to the provisions of §5, and that the change had been implemented without first having been submitted for approval either to the United States

District Court for the District of Columbia or to the Attorney General as required by §5.

Four days prior to the August 10, 1976, primary election for the two seats on the Board not including the at-large post, appellants filed this action to enforce the requirements of §5. Appellants' requests for declaratory and injunctive relief were not acted upon until after the scheduled 1976 primary and general elections.

On February 28, 1977, the three-judge court, without a hearing, enjoined further enforcement of the 1968 statute until such time as appellees effected compliance with §5. However, the District Court refused appellants' request to set aside the 1976 elections. . . .

On April 26, 1977, the three-judge court denied appellants' motion for reconsideration.

. . .

The judgment of the District Court is affirmed insofar as it holds that appellees have violated the approval provisions of §5 of the Voting Rights Act; the judgment is reversed insofar as it denies affirmative relief, and the case is remanded to the District Court with instructions to issue an order allowing appellees 30 days within which to apply for approval of the 1968 voting change under §5, and for further proceedings consistent with this opinion.

Holt Civic Club v. City of Tuscaloosa
439 U.S. 60 (1978)

Holt is a small, largely rural, unincorporated community located on the northeastern outskirts of Tuscaloosa, the fifth largest city in Alabama. Because the community is within the three-mile police jurisdiction circumscribing Tuscaloosa's corporate limits, its residents are subject to the city's "police [and] sanitary regulations." Holt residents are also subject to the criminal jurisdiction of the city's court and to the city's power to license businesses, trades, and professions. Tuscaloosa, however, may collect from businesses in the police jurisdiction only one-half of the license fee chargeable to similar businesses conducted within the corporate limits.

In 1973, appellants, an unincorporated civic association and seven individual residents of Holt, brought this statewide class action in the United States District Court for the Northern District of Alabama challenging the constitutionality of these Alabama statutes. They claimed that the city's extraterritorial exercise of police powers over Holt residents, without a concomitant extension of the franchise on an equal footing with those residing within the corporate limits, denies residents of the police jurisdiction rights secured by the Due Process and Equal Protection Clauses of the Fourteenth Amendment. The District Court denied appellants' request to convene a three-judge court . . . and dismissed the complaint for failure to state a claim upon which relief could be granted. Characterizing the Alabama statutes as enabling Acts, the District Court held that the statutes lack the requisite statewide application necessary to convene a three-judge District Court. On appeal, the Court of Appeals for the Fifth Circuit ordered the convening of a three-judge court, finding that the police jurisdiction statute embodies "a policy of statewide concern."

A three-judge District Court was convened, but appellants' constitutional claims fared no better on the merits. Noting that appellants sought a declaration that extraterritorial regulation is unconstitutional per se, rather than an extension of the franchise to police jurisdiction residents, the District Court held simply that "[e]qual protection has not been extended to cover such contention." The court rejected appellants' due process

claim without comment. Accordingly, appellees' motion to dismiss was granted.

. . .

. . . [A] common characteristic emerges: the challenged statute in each case denied the franchise to individuals who were physically resident within the geographic boundaries of the governmental entity concerned. No decision of this Court has extended the "one man, one vote" principle to individuals residing beyond the geographic confines of the governmental entity concerned, be it the State or its political subdivisions. On the contrary, our cases have uniformly recognized that a government unit may legitimately restrict the right to participate in its political processes to those who reside within its borders. Bona fide residence alone, however, does not automatically confer the right to vote on all matters, for at least in the context of special interest elections the State may constitutionally disfranchise residents who lack the required special interest in the subject matter of the election.

Appellants' argument that extraterritorial extension of municipal powers requires concomitant extraterritorial extension of the franchise proves too much. The imaginary line defining a city's corporate limits cannot corral the influence of municipal actions. A city's decisions inescapably affect individuals living immediately outside its borders. The granting of building permits for high rise apartments, industrial plants, and the like on the city's fringe unavoidably contributes to problems of traffic congestion, school districting, and law enforcement immediately outside the city. . . . [T]he indirect extraterritorial effects of many purely internal municipal actions could conceivably have a heavier impact on surrounding environs than the direct regulation contemplated by Alabama's police jurisdiction statutes. Yet no one would suggest that nonresidents likely to be affected by this sort of municipal action have a constitutional right to participate in the political processes bringing it about. . . .

Given this country's tradition of popular sovereignty, appellants' claimed right to vote in Tuscaloosa elections is not without some logical appeal. . . .

. . .

. . . [W]e conclude that Alabama's police jurisdiction statutes violate neither the Equal Protection Clause nor the Due Process Clause of the Fourteenth Amendment. Accordingly, the judgment of the District Court is affirmed.

City of Rome v. United States
446 U.S. 156 (1980)

This is a declaratory judgment action brought by appellant city of Rome, a municipality in northwestern Georgia, under the Voting Rights Act of 1965. In 1970, the city had a population of 30,759, the racial composition of which was 76.6 percent white and 23.4 percent Negro. The voting-age population in 1970 was 79.4 percent white and 20.6 percent Negro.

The governmental structure of the city is established by a charter enacted in 1918 by the General Assembly of Georgia. Before the amendments at issue in this case, Rome's city charter provided for a nine-member City Commission and a five-member Board of Education to be elected concurrently on an at-large basis by a plurality of the vote. The city was divided into nine wards, with one city commissioner from each ward to be chosen in the city-wide election. There was no residency requirement for Board of Education candidates.

In 1966, the General Assembly of Georgia passed several laws of local application that ex-

tensively amended the electoral provisions of the city's charter. These enactments altered the Rome electoral scheme in the following ways:

(1) the number of wards was reduced from nine to three;

(2) each of the nine commissioners would henceforth be elected at-large to one of three numbered posts established within each ward;

(3) each commissioner would be elected by majority, rather than plurality, vote, and if no candidate for a particular position received a majority, a runoff election would be held between the two candidates who had received the largest number of votes;

(4) the terms of the three commissioners from each ward would be staggered;

(5) the Board of Education was expanded from five to six members;

(6) each Board member would be elected at large, by majority vote, for one of two numbered posts created in each of the three wards, with runoff procedures identical to those applicable to City Commission elections;

(7) Board members would be required to reside in the wards from which they were elected;

(8) the terms of the two members from each ward would be staggered.

. . .

It is not disputed that the 1966 changes in Rome's electoral system were within the purview of the Act. Nonetheless, the city failed to seek preclearance for them. In addition, the city did not seek preclearance for 60 annexations made between November 1, 1964, and February 10, 1975, even though required to do so because an annexation constitutes a change in a "standard, practice, or procedure with respect to voting" under the Act.

In June 1974, the city did submit one annexation to the Attorney General for preclearance.

The Attorney General discovered that other annexations had occurred, and, in response to his inquiries, the city submitted all the annexations and the 1966 electoral changes for preclearance. The Attorney General declined to preclear the provisions for majority vote, numbered posts, and staggered terms for City Commission and Board of Education elections, as well as the residency requirement for Board elections. He concluded that, in a city such as Rome, in which the population is predominately white and racial bloc voting has been common, these electoral changes would deprive Negro voters of the opportunity to elect a candidate of their choice. The Attorney General also refused to preclear 13 of the 60 annexations in question. He found that the disapproved annexations either contained predominately white populations of significant size or were near predominately white areas and were zoned for residential subdivision development. Considering these factors in light of Rome's at-large electoral scheme and history of racial bloc voting, he determined that the city had not carried its burden of proving that the annexations would not dilute the Negro vote.

In response to the city's motion for reconsideration, the Attorney General agreed to clear the 13 annexations for School Board elections. He reasoned that his disapproval of the 1966 voting changes had resurrected the preexisting electoral scheme, and that the revivified scheme passed muster under the Act. At the same time, he refused to clear the annexations for City Commission elections because, in his view, the residency requirement for City Commission contained in the preexisting electoral procedures could have a discriminatory effect.

The city and two of its officials then filed this action, seeking relief from the Act based on a variety of claims. A three-judge court . . . rejected the city's arguments and granted summary judgment for the defendants. . . .

. . .

We conclude that the District Court did not clearly err in finding that the city had failed to prove that the 1966 electoral changes would not dilute the effectiveness of the Negro vote in Rome. The District Court determined that racial bloc voting existed in Rome. It found that the electoral changes from plurality-win to majority-win elections, numbered posts, and staggered terms, when combined with the presence of racial bloc voting and Rome's majority white population and at-large electoral system, would dilute Negro voting strength. The District Court recognized that, under the preexisting plurality-win system, a Negro candidate would have a fair opportunity to be elected by a plurality of the vote if white citizens split their votes among several white candidates and Negroes engage in "single-shot voting" in his favor. . . .

. . .

Because Rome's failure to preclear any of these annexations caused a delay in federal review and placed the annexations before the District Court as a group, the court was correct in concluding that the cumulative effect of the 13 annexations must be examined from the perspective of the most current available population data. . . .

. . .

The District Court properly concluded that these annexations must be scrutinized under the Voting Rights Act. By substantially enlarging the city's number of white eligible voters without creating a corresponding increase in the number of Negroes, the annexations reduced the importance of the votes of Negro citizens who resided within the pre-annexation boundaries of the city. In these circumstances, the city bore the burden of proving that its electoral system "fairly reflects the strength of the Negro community as it exists after the annexation[s]." The District Court's determination that the city failed to meet this burden of proof for City Commission elections was based on the presence of three vote-dilutive factors: the at-large electoral system, the residency requirement for officeholders, and the high degree of racial bloc voting. Particularly in light of the inadequate evidence introduced by the city, this determination cannot be considered to be clearly erroneous.

The judgment of the District Court is affirmed.

Blanding v. DuBose
454 U.S. 393 (1982)

Appellants, citizens of Sumter County, South Carolina have taken an appeal from a summary judgment entered against them . . . by the United States District Court for the District of South Carolina. The three-judge District Court concluded that Sumter County, in June 1979, had made a preclearance submission under §5 of the Voting Rights Act of 1965, when it wrote the United States Attorney General informing him that a referendum had approved at-large County Council elections. Because the Attorney General failed to object within 60 days to the claimed preclearance submission, the District Court permitted Sumter County to proceed with at-large elections for its County Council. . . .

. . .

On November 1, 1964, Sumter County was governed by its South Carolina General Assembly delegation acting through a County Board of Supervisors. In 1967, the General Assembly enacted a local bill that established a new form of government for Sumter County, namely, a seven-member County Commission elected at-large.

Although this change required preclearance under §5 of the Voting Rights Act, no steps were taken to obtain preclearance, and at-large elections were held in 1968, 1970, 1972, and 1974.

In 1975, the General Assembly passed, and the Governor approved, the State's Home Rule Act. The Act permitted a South Carolina county to hold a referendum to select a form of local government and to choose between at-large and single-member district elections. The Act specifically provided that, if Sumter County did not hold a referendum, it would be assigned, effective July 1, 1976, the council-administrator form of government with council members elected at-large.

The Home Rule Act was submitted to the Attorney General of the United States for preclearance. The Attorney General did not interpose an objection to the Act, as such, but he indicated that the outcomes of Home Rule Act referenda or assignments of forms of government under the Act would be subject to preclearance.

Sumter County chose not to hold a referendum. Accordingly, it was assigned the council-administrator form of government with at-large elections. The County Council passed a resolution and ordinance adopting that form of government and method of election.

On August 13, 1976, the County Administrator submitted the Sumter County Home Rule Ordinance and the 1967 Act to the Attorney General for preclearance. On December 3, after having obtained necessary additional information, the Attorney General made a timely objection to the at-large method of election of the Council. He interposed no objection to the council-administrator form of government.

The county requested the Attorney General to reconsider his objection to at-large elections, and the county and the Attorney General continued to correspond during 1977 and 1978. In early

1978, the county asked whether the Attorney General would withdraw his objection if a county referendum endorsed the at-large method of election. On April 28 of that year, the Attorney General declined to withdraw the objection and advised the county that a favorable referendum result, by itself, would not cause him to change his mind.

A Council election was scheduled for June 13, 1978. After the Attorney General refused to withdraw his objection, private parties and the United States brought separate federal suits to prevent elections under the at-large system. The two suits were consolidated. A single judge issued a temporary restraining order, and on June 21, 1978, a three-judge District Court permanently enjoined County Council elections until the requirements of the Voting Rights Act were fulfilled.

In November 1978, Sumter County went ahead with its referendum in which voters were asked whether they preferred that Council members be elected at-large or from single-member districts. The majority endorsed the at-large method. Because Council members already were being elected under the at-large system, the county did not enact any resolution or ordinance to adopt the results of the referendum.

. . . On June 4, 1979, the Attorney General received a letter, dated June 1, from the county advising him of the referendum results. The letter expressed doubt as to whether it was a new preclearance submission of the at-large method, or a request that the Attorney General reconsider his earlier objection to at-large elections. Subsequently, on July 23, a conference was held . . . between county officials and representatives of the Department of Justice. Fifteen days later, on August 7, the Attorney General, referring to the county's letter as a "request for reconsideration," refused to withdraw the objection to at-large elec-

tions, but advised the county that the Department of Justice had not yet completed its review. On September 27, the Attorney General, for a second time, refused to withdraw his objection.

Thereafter, the defendant-appellees moved the District Court for summary judgment. . . . Section 5, the appellees noted, requires the Attorney General to object within 60 days of a preclearance submission. They asserted that, since the Attorney General did not interpose an objection by August 3, the county was free under §5 to proceed with at-large elections.

A three-judge District Court was again convened. It agreed with appellees. Referring to §5 of the Voting Rights Act, the court observed that the 1978 referendum approved a method of electing county officials different from that in effect on November 1, 1964. The letter received June 4, 1979, according to the District Court, was the required preclearance submission. . . .

. . .

. . . [W]e have frequently stated that courts should grant deference to the interpretation given statutes and regulations by the officials charged with their administration. In this case, the Attorney General employed reasonable definitions of a preclearance submission and of a reconsideration request when he treated the June letter as in the latter category. Indeed, the Attorney General followed the more sensible course.

The judgment of the District Court is reversed.

City of Port Arthur v. United States
459 U.S. 159 (1982)

. . . The question in this case is whether the District Court for the District of Columbia correctly held that the electoral plan for the Port Arthur, Texas, City Council could not be approved under §5 because it insufficiently neutralized the adverse impact upon minority voting strength that resulted from the expansion of the city's borders by two consolidations and an annexation.

In December 1977, the city of Port Arthur, Texas, consolidated with the neighboring cities of Pear Ridge and Lake View. Six months later, the city annexed Sabine Pass, an incorporated area. As a result of these expansions of the city's borders, the percentage of the black population in Port Arthur decreased from 45.21 percent to 40.56 percent. Blacks of voting age constituted 35 percent of the population of the enlarged city.

Prior to the expansions, the city was governed by a seven-member Council, including a mayor, each member being elected at large by majority vote. Each member except the mayor was required to reside in a specific district of the city. Members were elected for staggered terms. Following the two consolidations, the City Council passed an ordinance adding an eighth member to the Council, while retaining the at-large system with residency requirements. After the annexation of Sabine Pass, the city further proposed that the Council be expanded to nine members, with at-large elections as before. The two consolidations and the annexation, together with the proposed changes in the governing system, were submitted to the Attorney General for preclearance pursuant to §5 of the Voting Rights Act. The Attorney General refused preclearance, suggesting, however, that he would reconsider if the Council members were elected from fairly drawn single-member districts.

As §5 permitted it to do, the city then filed suit in the United States District Court for the District of Columbia seeking a declaratory judgment that the expansions and the nine-member plan did not have the purpose or effect of denying or abridging the right to vote on account of color or race within the meaning of §5. While that suit was pending, the city approved by referendum the "4-4-1" plan, calling for four members to be elected from single-member districts, four to be elected at large from residency districts identical to the single-member districts, and the ninth member, the mayor, to be elected at large without any residency requirement. That plan, like the previous plans, required a majority vote to elect each Council member. The city then moved to amend its complaint so as to seek a declaratory judgment as to the legality of the 4-4-1 plan.

The District Court concluded that, because there were legitimate purposes behind the annexation and the consolidations . . . could not be denied preclearance as discriminatory in purpose. Because the expansions had substantially reduced the relative political strength of the black population, however, it was necessary for preclearance that the post-expansion electoral system be found to satisfy the requirements of §5. The District Court held that neither the first nine-member plan nor the 4-1-1 plan measured up, not only because each was adopted with a discriminatory purpose but also because, in the context of the severe racial bloc voting characteristic of the recent past in the city, neither plan adequately reflected the minority's potential political strength in the enlarged community. . . .

Soon after this decision, the city and the United States jointly submitted to the court for approval the "4-2-3" electoral plan. Under this scheme, the city would be divided into four single-member districts, Districts 1 through 4. District 5, comprising Districts 1 and 4, would elect another member, as would District 6, which combined Districts 2 and 3. Three additional members would be elected at large, one each from Districts 5 and 6, the third at-large seat to be occupied by the mayor, and to have no residency requirement. All Council seats would be governed by the majority vote rule, that is, runoffs would be required if none of the candidates voted on received a majority of the votes cast. Blacks constituted a majority in Districts 1 and 4, 79 percent and 62.78 percent respectively, as well as a 70.83 percent majority of the fifth district combining the two majority black districts. The sixth district was 10.98 percent black. Although the United States expressed reservations about the at-large and majority vote features, its position was that neither of these aspects of the plan warranted a denial of preclearance.

. . .

. . . This appeal followed, the basic submission being that, under §5 and the controlling cases the District Court exceeded its authority in conditioning clearance of the 4-2-3 plan on the elimination of the majority vote requirement. . . .

. . .

. . . Port Arthur was a party to two consolidations and an annexation. Because the areas taken into the city were predominantly white, the relative percentage of blacks in the enlarged city was substantially less than it was before the expansions. The District Court refused preclearance because, in its view, the post-expansion electoral system did not sufficiently dispel the adverse impact of the expansions on the relative political strength of the black community in Port Arthur. . . .

. . .

First, whether the 4-2-3 plan adequately reflected the political strength of the black minority in the enlarged city is not an issue that is determinable with mathematical precision. Because reasonable minds could differ on the question, and because the District Court was sitting as a court of equity seeking to devise a remedy for what otherwise might be a statutory violation, we should not rush to overturn its judgment.

Second, the 4-2-3 plan undervalued to some extent the political strength of the black community: one-third of the Council seats was to be elected from black majority districts, but blacks constituted 40.56 percent of the population of the enlarged city and 35 percent of the voting age population. In light of this fact, eliminating the majority vote requirement was an understandable adjustment. As the District Court well understood, the majority vote rule, which forbade election by a plurality, would always require the black candidate in an at-large election, if he survived the initial round, to run against one white candidate. In the context of racial bloc voting prevalent in Port Arthur, the rule would permanently foreclose a black candidate from being elected to an at-large seat. Removal of the requirement, on the other hand, might enhance the chances of blacks to be elected to the two at-large seats affected by the District Court's conditional order, but surely would not guarantee that result. Only if there were two or more white candidates running in a district would a black have any chance of winning election under a plurality system. We cannot say that insisting on eliminating the majority vote rule in the two at-large districts would either overvalue black voting strength in Port Arthur or be inconsistent with Richmond.

Third, even if the 4-3 electoral scheme might otherwise be said to reflect the political strength of the minority community, the plan would nevertheless be invalid if adopted for racially discriminatory purposes, i.e., if the majority vote requirement in the two at-large districts had been imposed for the purpose of excluding blacks from any realistic opportunity to represent those districts or to exercise any influence on Council members elected to those positions. The District

Court made no finding that the 4-2-3 plan was tainted by an impermissible purpose, but it had found that the two preceding plans, the first nine-member plan and the 4-1-1 plan, had been adopted for the illicit purpose of preventing black candidates from winning election. The court had also found that the majority vote requirement was a major means of effectuating this discriminatory end. When it was then presented with the 4-2-3 plan retaining the requirement for the two nonmayoral at-large seats, the Court conditioned approval on eliminating the majority vote element. It seems to us that, in light of the prior findings of discriminatory purpose, such action was a reasonable hedge against the possibility that the 4-2-3 scheme contained a purposefully discriminatory element. On balance, we cannot fault the judgment of the District Court.

The judgment of the District Court is accordingly affirmed.

City of Lockhart v. United States
460 U.S. 125 (1983)

The City of Lockhart is a community of just under 8,000 people in Caldwell County, Texas, 30 miles south of Austin. According to the most recent census figures, almost 47 percent of the city's population are Mexican-American. As of 1977, however, fewer than 30 percent of the city's registered voters were Mexican-American.

Before 1973, Lockhart was a "general law" city. Under Texas law, general-law cities have only those powers that the State specifically permits them to possess. As authorized by state law, Lockhart was governed by a commission consisting of a mayor and two commissioners, all serving the same 2-year terms. These offices were filled in April of even-numbered years through

at-large elections using a "numbered post" system. Under this system, the two commissioner posts were designated by number, and each candidate for commissioner specified the post for which he or she sought election. Thus, each race was effectively a separate election for a separate office.

In 1973, Lockhart adopted a new charter and became a "home rule" city. In contrast to a general-law city, a home rule city has authority to do whatever is not specifically prohibited by the State. This includes discretion to define the form of city government and to establish the procedures for city elections. As part of its new charter, Lockhart chose to be governed by a city council consisting of a mayor and four councilmen serving staggered 2-year terms. The mayor and two of the councilmen are elected in April of even-numbered years through at-large elections using the numbered-post system. The other two councilmen are similarly elected in odd-numbered years.

. . .

In 1977, four Mexican-Americans, including appellee Alfred Cano, challenged the constitutionality of Lockhart's election procedures under the 1973 charter. In the course of that suit, the plaintiffs discovered that Lockhart had never obtained approval under §5 for the changes instituted in 1973. A second suit then was brought to enjoin the city from using the new election procedures pending §5 preclearance. The United States District Court for the Western District of Texas granted injunctive relief.

Once future elections were enjoined pending §5 approval, Lockhart sought preclearance. The Attorney General, however, interposed an objection to the election procedures under the 1973 charter to the extent that they incorporate at-large elections, the numbered-post system, and staggered terms for councilmen. Lockhart then filed the present suit for a declaratory judgment in the United States District Court for the District of Columbia. Cano intervened as a defendant. As required by §5, a three-judge court was convened to decide the case.

. . .

We consider first the scope of §5's coverage in the circumstances of this case. Lockhart concedes that §5 applies to its electoral changes, and that the addition of two seats to its governing body and the introduction of staggered terms are covered changes. It contends, however, that §5 does not apply to the "continuation" of the two old seats and the continued use of numbered posts. We conclude that there has been a change with respect to all of the council seats and to the use of numbered places.

In moving from a three-member commission to a five-member council, Lockhart has changed the nature of the seats at issue. Council posts one and two are not identical to the old commission posts one and two. For example, they now constitute only 40 percent of the council, rather than 67 percent of the commission. Moreover, one cannot view these seats in isolation, for they are an integral part of the council. The possible discriminatory purpose or effect of the new seats, admittedly subject to §5, cannot be determined in isolation from the "preexisting" elements of the council. Similarly, the numbered-post system is an integral part of the new election plan. The impact of any of the seats cannot be evaluated without considering the fact that they are all filled in elections using numbered posts. We therefore hold that the entire system introduced in the 1973 charter is subject to preclearance.

. . .

The use of staggered terms also may have a discriminatory effect under some circumstances,

since it, too, might reduce the opportunity for single-shot voting or tend to highlight individual races. But the introduction of staggered terms has not diminished the voting strength of Lockhart's minorities. Under the old system, the voters faced two at-large elections with numbered posts every two years. Now they face two at-large elections with numbered posts every year. The inability to use single-shot voting is identical. The degree of highlighting of individual races is identical. Minorities are in the same position every year that they used to be in every other year. Although there may have been no improvement in their voting strength, there has been no retrogression, either.

Cano argues that the increased frequency of elections made necessary by staggered terms has resulted in retrogression. The more frequent elections are said to reduce voter turnout, and this has a disproportionate impact on minority voters. In support of this argument, he cites figures from the April, 1975, election. That year, when voter turnout was unusually low, only 5.7 percent of the voters were Mexican-Americans. In other years since 1973, the percentage of Mexican-American voters has been three to six times as great. These figures, however, are misleading. In the April, 1975, election, both council candidates were running unopposed, and neither candidate was Mexican-American. This undoubtedly explains both the lower overall turnout and the lower turnout among Mexican-Americans. For other elections since 1973, the overall turnout and the Mexican-American turnout were consistently higher than they were before the new charter, despite the fact that the population increased only slightly. In 1978, a Mexican-American candidate was elected in Lockhart for the first time in its history, after five years of annual elections. The record, therefore, contradicts Cano's argument.

The District Court erred in finding that the introduction of staggered terms has had a retrogressive effect on minority voting strength.

. . . [W]e conclude that the election changes introduced by the 1973 Lockhart City Charter will not have the effect of denying or abridging the right to vote on account of race, color, or membership in a language minority group. The District Court's findings to the contrary were clearly erroneous. We accordingly vacate the District Court's judgment and remand the case for further proceedings consistent with this opinion.

McCain v. Lybrand
465 U.S. 236 (1984)

As of November 1, 1964, local political authority in Edgefield County, South Carolina, was vested in a County Supervisor and a Board of County Commissioners. The County Supervisor, the chairman of the three-member Board, was elected at-large for a 4-year term. The County Supervisor had jurisdiction over public roads, matters relating to county taxes and expenditures, and certain other matters. The other two seats on the Board were appointed offices. These two commissioners were appointed by the Governor, also for 4-year terms, upon the recommendation of a majority of the county's delegation in the state legislature after a countywide straw vote on prospective appointees. There were no residency requirements for commissioners. The Board had limited administrative and ministerial powers.

On June 1, 1966, the South Carolina General Assembly enacted Act No. 1104, which was effective as a matter of state law when it was signed by the Governor on June 7, 1966. The Act cre-

ated a new form of government for Edgefield County, altering the county's election practices. The office of County Supervisor and the Board of County Commissioners were abolished upon expiration of the incumbents' terms. A three-member County Council with broad legislative and administrative powers was created, and the county was divided into three residency districts for purposes of electing Council members. To qualify as a candidate for a seat on the Council under the Act, an individual must be a qualified voter in one of the three districts, and is required to register as a candidate from that district. The Council members, however, are elected at-large: voters throughout the county cast votes for a candidate from each district, and the candidate in each district with the largest number of votes occupies that district's seat on the Council. Council members are elected for 2–year terms, and the members themselves annually elect a chairman.

The 1966 Act was . . . by Act No. 521. . . . The 1971 amendment increased the number of residency districts, and thus the number of Council members, from three to five. Necessarily, the change in the number of districts resulted in new district boundaries. Otherwise, the 1971 amendment did not alter the 1966 Act.

. . .

The appellants, black voters residing in Edgefield County, South Carolina, commenced a class action in 1974 in the United States District Court for the District of South Carolina challenging the county's election practices on constitutional grounds. Specifically, they alleged in their complaint against appellees, various county officials, including the County Council members, that the county's at-large method of electing the County Council diluted the voting strength of black voters, and that the county's residency districts were malapportioned. The

District Court entered judgment in favor of appellants on the malapportionment claim, but that judgment was reversed on appeal. After years of litigation and unsuccessful settlement negotiations, the District Court entered judgment in favor of appellants on their constitutional claim challenging the method of electing the Council at-large from residency districts, and enjoined further elections for the County Council until adoption of a new method of election. A few months later, the District Court vacated the judgment and ordered further proceedings in light of this Court's intervening decision in *City of Mobile.*

. . .

Edgefield County is admittedly a political subdivision of South Carolina subject to the provisions of the Voting Rights Act, and it is conceded that the 1966 Act was subject to the preclearance requirement of §5 of the Act. It is also undisputed that the 1966 Act was never submitted to the Attorney General or the United States District Court for the District of Columbia for §5 review. Accordingly, unless the preclearance of the 1971 amendment can be deemed to ratify the changes embodied in the 1966 Act, §5 of the Voting Rights Act plainly invalidates those changes and the District Court must fashion appropriate relief.

. . . [T]he preclearance procedures mandated by §5 of the Voting Rights Act focus entirely on changes in election practices. The title of the 1971 amendment unambiguously identified the changes in election practices which it effected—an increase in the number of Council members and residency districts—and served to define the scope of the preclearance request. An examination of the correspondence concerning the 1971 submission, plainly shows that only the 1971 amendment was being considered for preclearance, and further indicates that the request for preclearance was viewed as limited to the change in elections practices effected by it.

Thus South Carolina's submission of the 1971 amendment increasing the size of the Edgefield County Council apparently required the Attorney General to determine whether either the change in the district boundaries or the change in the number of districts had a discriminatory purpose or effect, but would not appear to have required him to pass on the question whether the 1966 changes represented a setback for minority voters in Edgefield County. The jurisdiction has never submitted that question to the Attorney General, and has never attempted to shoulder its burden of demonstrating that the 1966 changes were nondiscriminatory.

. . .

. . . In this case, the 1971 submission failed to inform the Attorney General that the provisions of the 1971 amendment which merely recodified various practices contained in the 1966 Act were themselves changes that might give rise to an inference of discrimination.

. . .

. . . [T]o the extent the judgment below may be interpreted as resting upon a factual finding that the Attorney General actually considered and approved the changes made by the 1966 Act in the course of the submission of the 1971 amendment, after reviewing the evidence ourselves, we are "left with the definite and firm conviction that a mistake has been committed," and we thus overturn that finding as clearly erroneous. The District Court erred as a matter of law in concluding that the lack of objection to the 1971 submission rendered the failure to preclear the 1966 Act moot.

Accordingly, we reverse the District Court's judgment and remand to the District Court for proceedings consistent with this opinion.

Escambia County v. McMillan
466 U.S. 48 (1984)

Appellees, black voters of Escambia County, Florida, filed suit in the District Court, alleging that the at-large system for electing the five members of the Board of County Commissioners violated appellees' rights under the First, Thirteenth, Fourteenth, and Fifteenth Amendments, the Civil Rights Act of 1957, and the Voting Rights Act of 1965. Appellees contended that the at-large system operated to "dilute" their voting strength.

The District Court entered judgment for appellees. That court found that the at-large system used by the county discriminated against black voters and had been retained at least in part for discriminatory purposes. The court concluded that the system violated appellees' rights under the Fourteenth and Fifteenth Amendments and the Voting Rights Act. The District Court ordered that the five commissioners be elected from single-member districts.

The Court of Appeals affirmed the District Court's judgment, concluding that the at-large election system violated the Fourteenth Amendment, and that the District Court's remedy was appropriate. As the finding of a Fourteenth Amendment violation was adequate to support the District Court's judgment, the Court of Appeals did not review the District Court's conclusion that the at-large system also violated the Fifteenth Amendment and the Voting Rights Act.

. . .

This appeal presents the question whether the evidence of discriminatory intent in the record before the District Court was adequate to support the finding that the at-large system violated the Fourteenth Amendment. We decline to decide this question. As the Court of Appeals noted, the District Court's judgment rested alternatively upon the Voting Rights Act. Moreover, the 1982 amendments to that Act, were not before the Court of Appeals. Affirmance on the statutory ground would moot the constitutional issues presented by the case. It is a well-established principle governing the prudent exercise of this Court's jurisdiction that normally the Court will not decide a constitutional question if there is some other ground upon which to dispose of the case.

The parties have not briefed the statutory question, and, in any event, that question should be decided in the first instance by the Court of Appeals. We conclude, therefore, that the proper course is to vacate the judgment of the Court of Appeals, and remand the case to that court for consideration of the question whether the Voting Rights Act provides grounds for affirmance of the District Court's judgment.

National Association for the Advancement of Colored People v. Hampton County Election Commission
470 U.S. 166 (1985)

This appeal challenges a three-judge District Court's construction and application of §5 of the Voting Rights Act. That section provides that certain jurisdictions, including the one in which this case arose, may not implement any election practices different from those in force on November 1, 1964, without first obtaining approval from the United States District Court for the District of Columbia or, alternatively, from the Attorney General. The statute further provides that, once a proposed change has been submitted to the Attorney General, he has 60 days in which to object. If an objection is interposed, the submitting authority may request reconsideration. Such a request triggers another 60-day period for the

Attorney General to decide whether to continue or withdraw his objection. The District Court held that §5 did not require the changes in election practices involved here to be cleared by the Attorney General prior to their implementation. . . .

As of November 1, 1964, the Hampton County, South Carolina, public schools were governed by appointed officials and an elected Superintendent of Education. The county comprises two school districts, School District No. 1, where the vast majority of white students live, and School District No. 2, which is predominantly black. Each District was governed by a separate six-member Board of Trustees. These trustees were appointed by a six-member County Board of Education, which in turn was appointed by the county legislative delegation.

On February 18, 1982, apparently in an attempt to facilitate consolidation of these two School Districts, the South Carolina General Assembly enacted Act No. 547. This statute provided that, beginning in 1983, the six members of the County Board of Education were to be elected at large rather than appointed. The first election for the new Board was to be held simultaneously with the general election in November 1982, and prospective candidates were required to file with the Election Commission at least 45 days before the election. Pursuant to §5 of the Voting Rights Act, the State submitted Act No. 547 for the approval of the Attorney General, who received it on February 27. On April 28, the Attorney General informed the State that he had no objection to the change in question.

On April 9, however, before the Attorney General had approved Act No. 547, the Governor of South Carolina signed Act No. 549, which was designed to supersede Act No. 547. Act No. 549 abolished the County Board of Education and the County Superintendent, devolving their duties upon the District Boards of Trustees, which were to be elected separately by each District. Like Act No. 547, Act No. 549 scheduled the first trustee election to coincide with the November 1982, general election. Candidates were required to file between August 16 and August 31. Implementation of the Act was made contingent upon approval in a referendum to be held in May, 1982.

The State did not submit Act No. 549 to the Attorney General for clearance until June 16, 1982, 22 days after it was approved in the referendum and 68 days after it had been enacted. As of August 16—the opening date of the filing period under Act No. 549—no response had yet been received from the Attorney General. Nevertheless, the County Election Commission began accepting filings for elections to be held under Act No. 549. On August 23, the Attorney General interposed an objection. He informed the State that it had not sustained its burden of showing that the proposal to eliminate the County Board of Education did not have a discriminatory purpose or effect. . . .

Because the State was contemplating requesting the Attorney General to reconsider this objection, the County Election Commission continued to accept filings under Act No. 549 through the end of the designated filing period, August 31. On that date, the State officially requested reconsideration. At the same time, the Election Commission began accepting filings under Act No. 547, in case the Attorney General refused to withdraw his objection to Act No. 549. On November 2, the date of the general election, the Attorney General had not yet responded to the request for reconsideration, and elections for County Board members were held pursuant to Act No. 547. No elections were held pursuant to Act No. 549.

On November 19, the Attorney General withdrew his objection to Act No. 549. The objection had been based primarily on the possibility that the County Board, which the Act would abolish, might have consolidated the two School Districts, but, upon reappraising South Carolina law, the Attorney General concluded that the Board lacked authority to approve such a consolidation. Therefore, its elimination would not have a potentially discriminatory impact.

The effect of the Attorney General's clearance of Act No. 549 was to render Act No. 547—and the November elections held pursuant to it—null and void. In response to a request for advice, the South Carolina Attorney General informed the County Election Commission in January that Act No. 549 was now in effect and that an election for school district trustees should be held "as soon as possible." The State Attorney General further opined that there was no reason to reopen the filing period, "as only the date of the election has changed." Accordingly, the Commission set March 15, 1983, as election day.

On March 11, appellants, two civil rights organizations and several residents of Hampton County, filed suit in the United States District Court for the District of South Carolina seeking to enjoin the election as illegal under §5 of the Voting Rights Act. The defendants were the County Election Commission, the two School Districts, and various county officials. The complaint identified a number of alleged "changes" in election procedure, including the scheduling of an election at a time other than that specified in the statute, and the use of the August filing period for the March election. A preliminary injunction was denied, and the election took place as scheduled. Subsequently, a three-judge panel denied a permanent injunction and declaratory relief, holding that no violation of §5 of the Vot-

ing Rights Act had occurred. The court reasoned that, although Act No. 549 itself was a "change" under the Act, the scheduling of the election and the filing period were simply "ministerial acts necessary to accomplish the statute's purpose . . . , and thus did not require preclearance." In the alternative, the court held that, even if these acts did constitute "changes," they had now been "precleared along with the remaining provisions of Act No. 549." That this "preclearance" did not occur until after the filing period had been held was not considered dispositive. . . .

Appellants contend that the opening of the August filing period before preclearance, and the scheduling of an election in March after the Attorney General had approved only a November election date, are changes that come within the scope of §5. Appellees, echoing the rationale of the District Court, maintain that opening the filing period as required by Act No. 549—albeit before the Act had been approved—was merely a preliminary step in its implementation. If the Attorney General had ultimately disapproved Act No. 549, the county would not have held an election under it, and the filing period would have become a nullity. Because Act No. 549 was in fact cleared, the filing period it specified was necessarily cleared as well. The alteration of the date of the election, according to appellees, was merely an "unfreezing" of a process that had been temporarily suspended by the operation of the Voting Rights Act. Although appellees concede that a legislatively enacted change in the date of an election is covered by the Act, they distinguish the change at issue here because it was required only by the Attorney General's failure to approve Act No. 549 before the scheduled election date, and because it was undertaken only to effect the initial implementation of the statute.

We need not decide whether a jurisdiction covered by §5 may ever open a filing period under a statute that has not yet been precleared. In this case, Hampton County not only opened the filing period for School District trustees before preclearance, but it also scheduled the election for a date four months later than that approved by the Attorney General. Thus, the county effectively altered the filing deadline from a date approximately two months before the election to one that was almost six months before the election.

These changes cannot fairly be characterized as "ministerial" in light of the sweeping objectives of the Act. . . .

. . .

Appellees' use of an August filing period in conjunction with a March election, and the setting of the March election date itself, were changes that should have been submitted to the Attorney General under §5. These changes cannot be said to have been approved along with Act No. 549. As in *Berry v. Doles*, it is appropriate in these circumstances for the District Court to enter an order allowing appellees 30 days in which to submit these changes to the Attorney General for approval. If appellees fail to seek this approval, or if approval is not forthcoming, the results of the March 1983 election should be set aside. If, however, the Attorney General determines that the changes had no discriminatory purpose or effect, the District Court should determine, in the exercise of its equitable discretion, whether the results of the election may stand.

We therefore reverse the District Court's judgment that §5 was not violated by appellees' failure to secure approval of these changes, and remand for further proceedings consistent with this opinion.

Clark v. Roemer
500 U.S. 646 (1991)

Appellants are black registered voters and a voting rights organization in Louisiana. They filed this suit in 1986 under §§2 and 5 of the Voting Rights Act, challenging the validity of Louisiana's multimember, at-large electoral scheme for certain appellate, district, and family court judges. Under §2, appellants alleged that Louisiana's electoral scheme diluted minority voting strength. In an amended complaint filed in July, 1987, appellants also alleged that Louisiana violated §5 by failing to submit for preclearance a number of statutory and constitutional voting changes, many of them adopted in the late 1960's and 1970's. The §2 portion of the case was assigned to a single District Court Judge; the §5 allegations were heard by a three-judge District Court.

In response to the appellants' §5 allegations, Louisiana submitted all of the unprecleared voting changes for administrative preclearance. In September 1988, and May 1989, the Attorney General granted preclearance for some of the changes, but objected to others. On June 18 and 20, 1990, Louisiana asked the Attorney General to reconsider his denial of preclearance for these seats, and proceeded with plans to hold elections for them in the fall of 1990. On July 23, 1990, petitioners filed a motion asking the three-judge District Court to enjoin the elections for the unprecleared seats.

On August 15, 1990, the District Court presiding over the §2 case enjoined the State from holding elections in 11 judicial districts which it determined violated §2. Some of these judicial districts were also at issue in the §5 portion of the case. On September 28, 1990, the three-judge District Court presiding over the §5 case denied appellants' motion to enjoin the State from holding elections for the seats not blocked by the §2 injunction. The three-judge panel, however, did enjoin the winning candidates from taking office pending its further orders.

Also on September 28, 1990, the United States Court of Appeals for the Fifth Circuit, sitting en banc, held that judges are not representatives for purposes of §2 of the Voting Rights Act. Based on this precedent, the District Court Judge presiding over the §2 aspect of the case dissolved the §2 injunction on October 2 and ordered that elections for the 11 districts be held on November 6 and December 8, 1990. On the same day, the three-judge District Court presiding over the §5 case refused to enjoin the elections for the unprecleared seats, but it again enjoined the winning candidates from taking office pending its further orders. As of October 2, 1990, then, Louisiana had scheduled elections for all of the judgeships to which the Attorney General had interposed objections.

In an October 22 order and an October 31 opinion, the three-judge District Court made its final pronouncement on the status of the unprecleared judgeships. The court divided the unprecleared electoral changes into two categories. Category one involved at-large judgeships in districts where, for the most part, the State had obtained administrative preclearance for later-created judgeships. The three-judge District Court held that, despite his current objections, the Attorney General had precleared the earlier judgeships when he precleared the later, or related, voting changes. . . . Louisiana submitted and obtained approval for Divisions E, G, H, and I. Division F was not submitted for approval when it was created in 1973; rather, it was submitted and objected to in 1988. The three-judge District Court held, however, that, when the Attorney General precleared Divisions G, H, and I, he also precleared Division F. The court reasoned that, be-cause the legislation creating Divisions G, H, and I added to the number of prior judgeships in Caddo Parish, including Division F, approval of the legislation constituted approval of Division F.

Category two under the court's ruling involved judgeships subject to valid objections by the Attorney General. Yet despite its holding that these unprecleared judgeships violated §5, the court refused to enjoin the elections. . . .

It allowed the election to proceed under the following conditions. The winning candidates could take office if, within 90 days, Louisiana filed a judicial preclearance action in the United States District Court for the District of Columbia or persuaded the Attorney General to withdraw his objections. The winners of the election could remain in office pending judicial preclearance, and could retain office for the remainder of their terms if the State obtained judicial preclearance. If the State failed to obtain judicial preclearance, the installed candidates could remain in office only 150 days after final judgment by the District Court.

On October 29, 1990, appellants filed an emergency application in this Court to enjoin the November 6 and December 8 elections pending appeal. . . .

. . .[T]he State sought judicial preclearance for the electoral changes that the three-judge District Court found to be uncleared. . . .

. . .

The judgment is reversed, and the case is remanded for further proceedings consistent with this opinion.

Houston Lawyers' Association v. Attorney General of Texas 501 U.S. 419 (1991)

Petitioners in No. 90–974 are local chapters of the League of United Latin American Citizens, a statewide organization composed of both Mexican-American and African-American residents of the State of Texas, and various individuals. They brought this action against the Attorney General of Texas and other officials (respondents) to challenge the existing at-large, countywide method of electing state district judges. Although the original challenge encompassed the entire State, and relied on both constitutional and statutory grounds, the issues were later narrowed to include only a statutory challenge to the voting methods in just 10 counties. Petitioners in No. 90–813 are the Houston Lawyers' Association, an organization of African-American attorneys who are registered voters in Harris County, and certain individuals; they are intervenors, supporting the position of the original plaintiffs. Because all of the petitioners have the same interest in the threshold issue of statutory construction that is now before us, we shall refer to them collectively as "petitioners."

Texas district courts are the State's trial courts of general jurisdiction. Electoral districts for Texas district judges consist of one or more entire counties. Eight of the districts included in this case include a single county; the other district includes two counties. The number of district judges in each district at issue varies from the 59 that sit in the Harris County district to the 3 that sit in the Midland County district. Each judge is elected by the voters in the district in which he or she sits pursuant to an at-large, district-wide electoral scheme, and must be a resident of that district. Although several judicial candidates in the same district may be running in the same election, each runs for a separately numbered position. Thus, for example, if there are 25 vacancies in the Harris County district in a particular year, there are 25 district-wide races for 25 separately numbered positions. In the primary

elections, the winner must receive a majority of votes, but in the general election, the candidate with the highest number of votes for a particular numbered position is elected.

Petitioners challenged the at-large, district-wide electoral scheme as diluting the voting strength of African American and Hispanic voters. They cited the example of Harris County, which has a population that is 20 percent African American but has only 3 of 59 district judges that are African American. The petitioners alleged that alternative electoral schemes using electoral subdistricts or modified at-large structures could remedy the dilution of minority votes in district judge elections.

. . . [T]he District Court ruled in favor of petitioners on their statutory vote dilution claim. . . . the District Court granted interim relief (to be used solely for the 1990 election of district judges in the nine districts) that included the creation of electoral subdistricts and a prohibition against the use of partisan elections for district judges. Respondents appealed.

A three-judge panel of the Fifth Circuit reversed the judgment of the District Court, and petitioners' motion for rehearing en banc was granted. The en banc majority held that the results test in §2 of the Voting Rights Act of 1965, is inapplicable to judicial elections. In essence, the majority concluded that Congress' reference to the voters' opportunity to elect "representatives" of their choice evidenced a deliberate decision to exclude the election of judges from scrutiny under the newly enacted test. For reasons stated in our opinion in *Chisom*, we reject that conclusion.

. . .

Because the results test in §2 of the Voting Rights Act applies to claims of vote dilution in judicial elections . . . we reverse the judgment of the Court of Appeals and remand the case for further proceedings consistent with this opinion.

Holder v. Hall
512 U.S. 874 (1994)

The State of Georgia has 159 counties, one of which is Bleckley County, a rural county in central Georgia. Black persons make up nearly 20 percent of the eligible voting population in Bleckley County. Since its creation in 1912, the county has had a single commissioner form of government for the exercise of "county governing authority." Under this system, the Bleckley County Commissioner performs all of the executive and legislative functions of the county government, including the levying of general and special taxes, the directing and controlling of all county property, and the settling of all claims. In addition to Bleckley County, about 10 other Georgia counties use the single commissioner system; the rest have multimember commissions.

In 1985, the Georgia Legislature authorized Bleckley County to adopt a multimember commission consisting of five commissioners elected from single-member districts and a single chairman elected at large. In a referendum held in 1986, however, the electorate did not adopt the change to a multimember commission. . . .

In 1985, respondents (six black registered voters from Bleckley County and the Cochran/ Bleckley County Chapter of the National Association for the Advancement of Colored People) challenged the single commissioner system in a suit filed against petitioners (Jackie Holder, the incumbent county commissioner, and Probate Judge Robert Johnson, the superintendent of elections). . . .

. . .

The Court of Appeals for the Eleventh Circuit reversed on the statutory claim. . . .

. . .

With respect to challenges to the size of a governing authority, respondents fail to explain where the search for reasonable alternative benchmarks should begin and end, and they provide no acceptable principles for deciding future cases. The wide range of possibilities makes the choice "inherently standardless," and we therefore conclude that a plaintiff cannot maintain a §2 challenge to the size of a government body, such as the Bleckley County Commission. The judgment of the Court of Appeals is reversed, and the case is remanded for consideration of respondents' constitutional claim.

Johnson v. DeGrandy
512 U.S. 997 (1994)

On the first day of Florida's 1992 legislative session, a group of Hispanic voters including Miguel De Grandy (De Grandy plaintiffs) complained in the United States District Court against the speaker of Florida's House of Representatives, the president of its Senate, the Governor, and other state officials (State). The complainants alleged that the districts from which Florida voters had chosen their state senators and representatives since 1982 were malapportioned, failing to reflect changes in the State's population during the ensuing decade. The State Conference of NAACP Branches and individual black voters (NAACP plaintiffs) filed a similar suit, which the three-judge District Court consolidated with the De Grandy case.

Several months after the first complaint was filed, on April 10, 1992, the state legislature adopted Senate Joint Resolution 2–G (SJR 2–G), providing the reapportionment plan currently at issue. The plan called for dividing Florida into 40 single-member Senate, and 120 single-member House, districts based on population data from the 1990 census. As the Constitution of Florida required, the state attorney general then petitioned the Supreme Court of Florida for a declaratory judgment that the legislature's apportionment plan was valid under federal and state law. The court so declared, while acknowledging that state constitutional time constraints precluded full review for conformity with §2 of the Voting Rights Act and recognizing the right of any interested party to bring a §2 challenge to the plan in the Supreme Court of Florida.

The De Grandy and NAACP plaintiffs responded to SJR 2–G by amending their federal complaints to charge the new reapportionment plan with violating §2. . . .

The Department of Justice filed a similar complaint, naming the State of Florida and several elected officials as defendants and claiming that SJR 2–G diluted the voting strength of blacks and Hispanics in two parts of the State in violation of §2. The Government alleged that SJR 2–G diluted the votes of the Hispanic population in an area largely covered by Dade County (including Miami) and the black population in an area covering much of Escambia County (including Pensacola). The District Court consolidated this action with the other two. . . .

. . . [T]he District Court ruled . . . the plan's provisions for state House districts to be in violation of §2 because "more than [SJR 2–G's] nine Hispanic districts may be drawn without having or creating a regressive effect upon black voters," and it imposed a remedial plan offered by the De Grandy plaintiffs calling for 11 majority-Hispanic House districts. As to the Senate, the court found that a fourth majority-Hispanic district could be drawn in addition to the three provided by SJR 2–G, but only at the expense of black voters in the area. . . . [I]t ordered elections to be held using SJR 2–G's senatorial districts.

. . .

In sum, the District Court's finding of dilution did not address the statutory standard of unequal political and electoral opportunity, and reflected instead a misconstruction of §2 that equated dilution with failure to maximize the number of reasonably compact majority-minority districts. Because the ultimate finding of dilution in districting for the Florida House was based on a misreading of the governing law, we hold it to be clearly erroneous.

. . . Because the court did not modify the State's plan, however, we hold the ultimate result correct in this instance.

. . .

We affirm the District Court's decision to leave the State's plan for Florida State Senate districts undisturbed. As in the case of the House districts, the totality of circumstances appears not to support a finding of vote dilution here, where both minority groups constitute effective voting majorities in a number of state Senate districts substantially proportional to their share in the population, and where plaintiffs have not produced evidence otherwise indicating that under SJR 2–G voters in either minority group have "less opportunity than other members of the electorate to participate in the political process and to elect representatives of their choice."

There being no violation of the Voting Rights Act shown, we have no occasion to review the District Court's decisions going to remedy. The judgment of the District Court is accordingly affirmed in part and reversed in part.

Lopez v. Monterey County
519 U.S. 9 (1996)

The State of California has 58 counties, one of which is Monterey County (hereinafter County). In 1971, the Attorney General designated the County a covered jurisdiction under §4(b) of the Voting Rights Act of 1965. . . . As a jurisdiction covered by §5, Monterey County must obtain federal preclearance—either administrative or judicial—of any voting practice different from the practices in effect on November 1, 1968. . . .

On November 1, 1968, the County had nine inferior court districts. Two of these districts were municipal court districts, each served by two judges, and the other seven were justice court districts, each served by a single judge. Both municipal and justice courts were trial courts of limited jurisdiction. Municipal courts served districts with populations exceeding 40,000, and justice courts served those districts with smaller populations. The justice courts differed from the municipal courts in other respects. They were not courts of record and were served by judges who often worked part time and did not have to be members of the bar. A few years later, California voters eliminated justice courts altogether.

Each of the municipal and justice courts operated separately and independently. Judges for each court were elected at large by the voters of their respective districts, and they served only the judicial district in which they were elected. The municipal and justice court districts varied widely in population and judicial workloads. For example, a 1972 survey showed that the Monterey-Carmel Municipal Court District had a population of 106,700, with more than enough work for two full-time judges. By contrast, the San Ardo Justice Court District had a population of 3,500, with a caseload that required less than a quarter of one judge's time.

Between 1972 and 1983, the County adopted six ordinances, which ultimately merged the seven justice court districts and the two municipal court districts into a single, county-wide municipal court, served by nine judges whom County residents elected at large. (At present, 10 judges serve on the municipal court.) Each judge was elected to serve for a term of six years. Judicial elections were conducted under various interim schemes in 1974, 1976, 1978, and 1982. Additionally, the County conducted at-large, county-wide judicial elections in 1986, 1988, and 1990.

. . .

Although it was subject to §5 preclearance requirements, the County did not submit any of the consolidation ordinances for federal preclearance under §5. The State, however, in 1983 submitted for administrative preclearance a state law, that mentioned Monterey County's prospective consolidation of the last two justice court districts with the remaining municipal court district. The Department of Justice requested additional information concerning this aspect of the state legislation. In its response, the State included the last of the County's six consolidation ordinances, which was adopted in 1983. The Attorney General interposed no objection to the 1983 state law. The State's submission may well have served to preclear the 1983 county ordinance. The United States points out, however, that the 1983 submission to the Department of Justice did not identify or describe any of the County's previous consolidation ordinances. The State does not contest this point. Thus, under our precedent, these previous consolidation ordinances do not appear to have received federal preclearance approval.

On September 6, 1991, appellants, five Hispanic voters residing in the County, sued the County in the United States District Court for the Northern District of California, alleging that the County had violated §5 by failing to obtain federal preclearance of the six judicial district consolidation ordinances it had adopted between 1972 and 1983. They raised no claim under §2 of the Voting Rights Act or constitutional challenge. A three-judge District Court was convened. On March 31, 1993, the District Court ruled that the challenged ordinances were election changes subject to §5 and consequently unenforceable without federal preclearance. The District Court directed the County to submit the ordinances to federal officials for preclearance. . . .

In August 1993, the County filed a declaratory judgment action in the United States District Court for the District of Columbia, seeking judicial preclearance of the challenged ordinances. Appellants intervened. But before that court made any findings, the County voluntarily dismissed its action, without prejudice. . . .

. . . In late 1993 and early 1994, the County and appellants jointly proposed two plans to the District Court. Each plan divided the County into different election areas, with judges from each area to serve on the county-wide municipal court. The State objected to these schemes on the ground that they contravened California law, including the constitutional requirements that a judge's jurisdictional and electoral bases be coextensive, and that cities not be split into more than one judicial district. Appellants and the County acknowledged these conflicts, but asked the District Court to suspend operation of these state constitutional provisions in the County.

. . .

In June 1994, the District Court decided to give appellants, the County, the State, and the United States, which had at this point weighed in as amicus curiae, another chance to develop a work-able solution. It enjoined the upcoming 1994 elections. It directed the County to attempt to obtain changes in state law that would permit the implementation of a judicial election plan that complied with §5 requirements. It asked the State to assist the County in creating an acceptable judicial election plan. Nevertheless, in late 1994, the parties were back in court, still without a satisfactory plan. The County had sought amendments to the state constitution and statutes, but was unsuccessful.

In a December 20, 1994, order, the District Court concluded that it had to devise a remedy that would permit judicial elections to take place, pending implementation of a permanent, federally precleared voting plan. Otherwise, voters would be deprived of their right to elect judges. The District Court recognized that neither appellants nor the County thought feasible a return to the election scheme in effect on November 1, 1968. Instead, it decided to adopt one of the plans the County and appellants previously had proposed. Under this scheme, the County was divided into four election districts. Voters in three of the districts, in which Hispanics constituted a majority, would each elect one judge. Voters in the fourth district would elect the other seven judges. Judges elected under the plan would serve for 18-month terms, until January, 1997. All 10 judges would serve on the county-wide municipal court. The District Court acknowledged that the interim plan was inconsistent with state law, but reasoned that the intrusion on state interests was minimal. The County submitted the interim plan to the Attorney General for preclearance, and it was precleared on March 6, 1995. In a special election conducted on June 6, 1995, seven judges were elected. . . .

. . . [T]he District Court . . . denied the County's

request to extend the terms of judges elected in the 1995 special election, concerned that such an extension would be "inappropriate" in light of the possible constitutional infirmity of the interim plan. A return to the judicial election system in existence before the adoption of the consolidation ordinances was not "legal, feasible or desired." . . .

. . .

. . . The at-large, county-wide system under which the District Court ordered the County to conduct elections undoubtedly "reflect[ed] the policy choices" of the County; it was the same system that the County had adopted in the first place. It was, therefore, error for the District Court to order elections under that system before it had been precleared by either the Attorney General or the United States District Court for the District of Columbia.

. . .

The County has not discharged its obligation to submit its voting changes to either of the forums designated by Congress. The requirement of federal scrutiny should be satisfied without further delay. The State appears willing to assist the County in pursuing the issue before either the Attorney General or the District Court for the District of Columbia, and its effort will doubtless be of assistance.

The judgment is reversed, and the case is remanded for further proceedings consistent with this opinion.

City of Monroe v. United States
522 U.S. 34 (1997)

The United States claims the city of Monroe, Georgia did not seek preclearance for majority voting in mayoral elections, as required by §5 of the Voting Rights Act of 1965, as amended. The Government seeks to enjoin majority voting and to require Monroe to return to the plurality system it had once used. A three-judge District Court for the Middle District of Georgia agreed with the Government and granted summary judgment. The District Court rejected Monroe's claim that the Attorney General's preclearance of a 1968 statewide law encompassed Monroe's adoption of a majority system. . . .

The parties agree upon the facts. Until 1966, Monroe's city charter did not specify whether a candidate needed a plurality or a majority vote to win a mayoral election. In practice, the city used plurality voting in its elections until 1966 and majority voting thereafter.

In 1966, the General Assembly of Georgia amended the city's charter to require majority voting in mayoral elections. Because Monroe is a jurisdiction covered by §5 of the Voting Rights Act, the change had to be precleared. Georgia or Monroe could have sought preclearance by submitting the change to the Attorney General or seeking a declaratory judgment from the United States District Court for the District of Columbia. Neither did, so the 1966 charter amendment was not precleared.

In 1968, the General Assembly passed a comprehensive Municipal Election Code (the 1968 code), which is still in force today. The statute applies to Monroe and all other municipalities in Georgia. . . .

Georgia submitted the 1968 code to the Attorney General for preclearance. . . .

In 1971, the General Assembly passed a comprehensive revision of Monroe's charter. The 1971 charter made explicit provision for majority voting. Neither Georgia nor Monroe sought to preclear the revisions to the charter.

In 1990, the General Assembly once again

amended Monroe's charter and carried forward the majority vote requirement. This time, Monroe sent the 1990 charter to the Attorney General for preclearance, but the cover letter did not mention the majority vote provision. The Attorney General objected to it nevertheless, interpreting the submission as effecting a change from plurality to majority voting. The Government filed suit against Monroe and city officials in 1994, and prevailed in the District Court.

. . .

Because the 1968 code disposes of the case on this undisputed factual record, the Court need not address appellants' other contentions. The judgment of the District Court is reversed.

16

Other Cases Related to Political Rights

This final chapter looks at Supreme Court opinions that do not neatly fit into the other chapters. For example, there are political rights decisions within the criminal justice, patronage, and judicial orders to a legislative branch.

Neal v. Delaware
103 U.S. 370 (1880)

The Constitution of Delaware, adopted in 1831 (the words of which upon the subject of suffrage had not been changed when the petition for removal was filed, nor since), restricts the right of suffrage at general elections to free white male citizens, of the age of twenty-two years and upwards, who had resided in the State one year next before the election, and the last month thereof in the county where he offers to vote, and who, within two years next before the election, had paid a county tax, which shall have been assessed at least six months before such election—the prerequisite of a payment of tax being dispensed with in the case of free white male citizens between twenty-one and twenty-two years of age, having the prescribed residence in the State and county. The only persons excluded by that Constitution from suffrage are those in the military, naval, or marine service of the United States stationed in Delaware, idiots, insane persons, paupers, and those convicted of felonies.

The statute of Delaware, adopted in 1848 and in force at the trial of this case, provides for an annual selection by the Levy Court of the county of persons to serve as grand and petit jurors, and, from those so selected, the prothonotary and clerk of the peace are required to draw the names of such as shall serve for that year, if summoned. It further provides that all qualified to vote at the general election, being "sober and judicious persons," shall be liable to serve as jurors, except public officers of the State or of the United States, counselors and attorneys at law, ordained ministers of the gospel, officers of colleges, teachers of public schools, practicing physicians and surgeons regularly licensed, cashiers of incorporated banks, and all persons over seventy years of age.

It is thus seen that the statute, by its reference to the constitutional qualifications of voters, apparently restricts the selection of jurors to white male citizens being voters and sober and judicious persons. And although it only declares that such citizens shall be liable to serve as jurors, the settled construction of the State court, prior to the adoption of the Fifteenth Amendment, was that no citizen of the African race was competent under the law to serve on a jury.

Now the argument on behalf of the accused is that, since the statute adopted the standard of voters as the standard for jurors, and since Delaware has never, by any separate or official action of its own, changed the language of its Constitution in reference to the class who may exercise the elective franchise, the State is to be regarded, in the sense of the amendment and of the laws enacted for its enforcement, as denying to the colored race within its limits, to this day, the right, upon equal terms with the white race, to participate as jurors in the administration of justice— and this notwithstanding the adoption of the Fifteenth Amendment and its admitted legal effect upon the constitutions and laws of all the States of the Union.

But to this argument, when urged in the court below, the State court replied, as does the Attorney General of the State here, that although the State had never, by a convention or popular vote, formally abrogated the provision in its State Constitution restricting suffrage to white citizens, that result had necessarily followed as matter of law from the incorporation of the Fourteenth and Fifteenth Amendments into the fundamental law of the nation; that, since the adoption of the latter amendment, neither the legislative, executive, nor judicial authorities of the State had in any mode recognized as an existing part of its Constitution that provision which, in words, discriminates against citizens of the African race in the matter of suffrage; and consequently that the statute prescribing the qualification of jurors by reference to the qualifications for voters should be construed as referring to the State Constitution as modified or affected by the Fifteenth Amendment. . . . [U]pon the fullest consideration we have been able to give the subject, our conclusion is that the alleged discrimination in the State of Delaware against citizens of the African race in the matter of service on juries does not result from her Constitution and laws.

Beyond question, the adoption of the Fifteenth Amendment had the effect in law to remove from the State Constitution or render inoperative that provision which restricts the right of suffrage to the white race. Thenceforward, the statute which prescribed the qualifications of jurors was itself enlarged in its operation so as to embrace all who by the State Constitution, as modified by the supreme law of the land, were qualified to vote at a general election. . . .

. . .

The judgment of the Court of Oyer and Terminer will be reversed, with directions to set aside the judgment and verdict, as well as the order denying the motion to quash the indictment and panels of jurors, and for such proceedings, upon a further hearing of those motions, as may be consistent with the principles of this opinion; and it is so ordered.

Franklin v. State of South Carolina
218 U.S. 161 (1910)

The plaintiff in error, Pink Franklin, a citizen of the Negro race, was convicted, in the court of general sessions for the county of Orangeburg, South Carolina, of the crime of murder by the shooting of one H. E. Valentine; thereupon he was sentenced to suffer the death penalty, and upon appeal to the supreme court of South Carolina the judgment of the court of general sessions was affirmed. The case is here upon a writ of error to the supreme court of South Carolina.

. . .

We will proceed, then, to examine the errors assigned which may be fairly said to raise Federal questions reviewable here. A motion was made to quash the indictment because of the disqualification of the grand jury which returned it. The argument being that the Federal act of June 25, 1868, provides that the Constitutions of certain states, including South Carolina, should never be amended or changed so as to deprive any citizen or class of citizens of the United States, of the right to vote in said state, given to them by the Constitution thereof, named in the act, except for the punishment for crimes such as are now felonies at common law, whereof they shall have been duly convicted under laws equally applicable to all the states. The necessary qualifications of voters in South Carolina at that time were defined in 2, article 8, of the Constitution of South Carolina of 1868, and were:

> Every male citizen of the United States of the age of twenty-one years and upwards, not laboring under the disabilities named in this Constitution, without distinction of race, color, or former condition, who shall be a resident of this state at the time of the adoption of this Constitution, or who shall thereafter reside in this state one year and in the county in which he offers to vote sixty days next preceding any election, shall be entitled to vote for all officers that are now or hereafter may be elected by the people, and upon all questions submitted to the electors at any elections: Provided, that no person shall be allowed to vote or hold office who is now or hereafter may be disqualified therefor by the Constitution of the United States until such disqualification shall be removed by the Congress of the United States: Provided further, that no person, while kept in any almshouse or asylum, or of unsound mind, or confined in any public prison, shall be allowed to vote or hold office.

These qualifications for voters were changed by the Constitution of 1895, and now are:

> Art. 2, 4. The qualifications for suffrage shall be as follows: (a) residence in the state for two years, in the county one year, in the polling precinct in which the elector offers to vote, four months, and the payment, six months before any election, of any poll tax then due and payable; . . . (d) Any person who shall apply for registration after January 1st, 1898, if otherwise qualified, shall be registered: Provided, that he can both read and write any section of this Constitution submitted to him by the registration

officer, or can show that he owns and has paid all taxes collectible during the previous year on property in this state assessed at three hundred dollars ($300) or more.

This change in the qualification for voters, it is said, worked a deprivation of the rights of the accused, because the qualification of grand jurors under the constitution of 1895, they being required to be electors of the state, made eligible different persons than those who were qualified to be electors under the Constitution of 1868. As to this contention, the South Carolina supreme court held that the Constitution of 1895 laid no restriction on color or previous condition to entitle one to be an elector; that the act of Congress of 1868 had no reference to the selection of jurors, and that it was inapplicable to the Constitution of the state in regard to juries.

If it could be held that the act of Congress restricted the state of South Carolina in fixing the qualifications for suffrage, it is unnecessary to decide the point in this case, as there is nothing in the record to show that the grand jury, as actually impaneled, contained any person who was not qualified as an elector under the Constitution of 1868, nor is there anything to show that the grand jury was so made up as to prevent citizens of the race of the plaintiff in error from sitting thereon. There was no allegation in the motion to quash upon this ground, or offer of proof in the case to show that persons of the African race were excluded because of their race or color from serving as grand jurors in the criminal prosecution of a person of that race. . . . Moreover, if the restriction upon the right to fix qualifications for suffrage in the Federal act could have the effect contended for as to subsequent state action, there was nothing in the act to prevent the selection of grand jurors having the qualifications prescribed for electors in the Constitution of 1895, in the absence of a showing that such legislation operated to exclude citizens from such juries on account of race. . . .

. . .

After giving this case the examination its importance deserves, in view of its gravity, we are unable to find in the record anything which worked a deprivation of Federal rights, warranting this court in disturbing the judgment of the Supreme Court of South Carolina, and the judgment is affirmed.

Affirmed.

Marshall v. Dye
231 U.S. 250 (1913)

The case originated in a complaint filed in the circuit court of Marion County, Indiana, by John Dye, in which he alleged that he brought the suit for himself and other electors and taxpayers of the state of Indiana, the object of the suit being to enjoin the defendants, Thomas Marshall, governor, Muter Bachelder, and Charles Roemler, jointly composing the state board of election commissioners, and Lew Ellingham, secretary of state, from taking the steps required by statute to certify and transmit to the clerks of the several counties in the state a new Constitution proposed by the legislature of the state, and from printing and publishing a statement to be printed upon the ballots in such manner that the electors might indicate their choice as to such new Constitution. Upon trial in the circuit court, an injunction was granted. Upon appeal to the supreme court of the state of Indiana the judgment of the circuit court was affirmed. . . .

. . .

The statute under which it was proposed to submit the new Constitution of the state, provided

for its submission at the general election in November 1912, and required the election officials and other officers to perform like duties to those required at general elections, with a view to the submission of such questions. The supreme court sustained the contention that the act was void under the state Constitution, holding in substance that the act of 1911 was unconstitutional for want of authority in the legislature to submit an entire Constitution to the electors of the state for adoption or rejection, and that, if the instrument could be construed to be a series of amendments, it could not be submitted as such for the reason that article 16 of the Constitution of the state requires that all amendments to the state Constitution shall, before being submitted to the electors, receive the approval of two general assemblies, which was not the case here, and that article 16 further provides that while an amendment or amendments to the Constitution, which have been agreed upon by one general assembly, are awaiting the action of a succeeding general assembly or of the electors, no additional amendment or amendments shall be proposed, and that, as a matter of fact, another amendment was still awaiting the action of the electors.

The contention mainly urged by the plaintiffs in error of the denial of Federal rights is that the judgment below is in contravention of article 4, 4, of the Constitution of the United States, which provides that the United States shall guarantee to every state in the Union a republican form of government. . . .

. . .

In the present case the supreme court of the state has enjoined the plaintiff in error, as officers of the state, from taking steps to submit the proposed Constitution to the electors of the state, because in its judgment the act of the legislature of the state, requiring such submission, was in

734 CHAPTER 16: OTHER CASES RELATED TO POLITICAL RIGHTS

violation of the state Constitution. Whether this duty shall or shall not be performed concerns the plaintiffs in error in their official capacity only. The requirement that they refrain from taking such steps concerns their official, and not their personal, rights. Applying the rule established by the previous decisions of this court, it follows the judgment of the state supreme court is not reviewable here, as it is not alleged to violate rights of a personal nature, secured by the Federal Constitution or laws.

It therefore follows that this writ of error must be dismissed.

Blair v. United States
250 U.S. 273 (1919)

It appears that in October 1918, the federal grand jury of the Southern district of New York was making inquiry concerning supposed violations of section 125 of the Criminal Code (relating to perjury) and of the so-called Corrupt Practices Act of June 25, 1910, in connection with the verification and filing in that district of reports to the Secretary of the Senate of the United States made by a candidate for nomination as Senator at a primary election held in the state of Michigan on August 27, 1918. Phillips was served with a subpoena requiring him to appear and testify before this grand jury. Blair and Templeton were subpoenaed to appear and testify and also to produce certain records, correspondence, and other documentary evidence. All were served in the state of Michigan. They appeared before the grand jury in response to the subpoenas, were severally sworn, and were examined by counsel for the United States. Each witness, after answering preliminary questions, asked that he be informed of the object and purpose of the inquiry and against

whom it was directed, whereupon he was informed by counsel for the United States that the inquiry was not directed against him (the witness). After this each witness read to and left with the grand jury a typewritten statement to the effect that upon advice of counsel he refused to answer any questions pertaining to the matter under inquiry, for the reason that the grand jury and the court were without jurisdiction to inquire into the conduct of a campaign in Michigan for the primary election of a United States Senator; that the federal Corrupt Practices Act as amended was unconstitutional; and that no federal court or grand jury in any state had constitutional authority to conduct an inquiry regarding a primary election for United States Senator. Thereupon each witness was asked by counsel for the United States whether he refused to testify for the reason that to do so would incriminate him, to which he made no other answer than to refer to the reasons for his refusal as set forth in his statement.

. . .

The principal contention is that the Act of June 25, 1910, and its amendments are unconstitutional in so far as they attempt to regulate and control the selection by political parties at primary elections of candidates for United States Senator to be voted for at the general elections: it being insisted that the authority of Congress under section 4 of article 1 of the Constitution extends only to the definitive general election, and not to pre-election arrangements or devices such as nominating conventions and primaries.

It is maintained further that, because of the invalidity of these statutes, neither the United States District Court nor the federal grand jury has jurisdiction to inquire into primary elections or to indict or try any person for an offense based upon the statutes, and therefore the order committing appellants is null and void.

. . .

. . . [W]e are of opinion that appellants were not entitled to raise any question about the constitutionality of the statutes under which the grand jury's investigation was conducted.

Final orders affirmed.

De Jonge v. Oregon
299 U.S. 353 (1937)

Appellant, Dirk De Jonge, was indicted in Multnomah County, Oregon, for violation of the Criminal Syndicalism Law of that State. The Act . . . defines "criminal syndicalism" as

> the doctrine which advocates crime, physical violence, sabotage or any unlawful acts or methods as a means of accomplishing or effecting industrial or political change or revolution.

With this preliminary definition, the Act proceeds to describe a number of offenses, embracing the teaching of criminal syndicalism, the printing or distribution of books, pamphlets, etc., advocating that doctrine, the organization of a society or assemblage which advocates it, and presiding at or assisting in conducting a meeting of such an organization, society or group. The prohibited acts are made felonies, punishable by imprisonment for not less than one year nor more than ten years, or by a fine of not more than $1,000, or by both.

. . .

. . . Appellant was found guilty as charged, and was sentenced to imprisonment for seven years. The Judgment was affirmed by the Supreme Court of the State, which considered the constitutional question and sustained the statute as thus applied. . . .

. . .

. . . It thus appears that, while defendant was a member of the Communist Party, he was not indicted for participating in its organization, or for joining it, or for soliciting members or for distributing its literature. He was not charged with teaching or advocating criminal syndicalism or sabotage or any unlawful acts, either at the meeting or elsewhere. He was accordingly deprived of the benefit of evidence as to the orderly and lawful conduct of the meeting and that it was not called or used for the advocacy of criminal syndicalism or sabotage or any unlawful action. His sole offense as charged, and for which he was convicted and sentenced to imprisonment for seven years, was that he had assisted in the conduct of a public meeting, albeit otherwise lawful, which was held under the auspices of the Communist Party.

The broad reach of the statute as thus applied is plain. While defendant was a member of the Communist Party, that membership was not necessary to conviction on such a charge. . . . However innocuous the object of the meeting, however lawful the subjects and tenor of the addresses, however reasonable and timely the discussion, all those assisting in the conduct of the meeting would be subject to imprisonment as felons if the meeting were held by the Communist Party. . . . Thus, if the Communist Party had called a public meeting in Portland to discuss the tariff, or the foreign policy of the Government, or taxation, or relief, or candidacies for the offices of President, members of Congress, Governor, or state legislators, every speaker who assisted in the conduct of the meeting would be equally guilty with the defendant in this case, upon the charge as here defined and sustained. The list of illustrations might be indefinitely extended to every variety of meetings under the auspices of the Communist Party, although held for the discussion of political issues or to adopt protests and pass resolutions of an entirely innocent and proper character.

While the States are entitled to protect themselves from the abuse of the privileges of our institutions through an attempted substitution of force and violence in the place of peaceful political action in order to effect revolutionary changes in government, none of our decisions goes to the length of sustaining such a curtailment of the right of free speech and assembly as the Oregon statute demands in its present application. . . .

. . .

. . . [P]eaceable assembly for lawful discussion cannot be made a crime. The holding of meetings for peaceable political action cannot be proscribed. Those who assist in the conduct of such meetings cannot be branded as criminals on that score. The question, if the rights of free speech and peaceable assembly are to be preserved, is not as to the auspices under which the meeting is held, but as to its purpose; not as to the relations of the speakers, but whether their utterances transcend the bounds of the freedom of speech which the Constitution protects. If the persons assembling have committed crimes elsewhere, if they have formed or are engaged in a conspiracy against the public peace and order, they may be prosecuted for their conspiracy or other violation of valid laws. But it is a different matter when the State, instead of prosecuting them for such offenses, seizes upon mere participation in a peaceable assembly and a lawful public discussion as the basis for a criminal charge.

We are not called upon to review the findings of the state court as to the objectives of the Communist Party. Notwithstanding those objectives, the defendant still enjoyed his personal right of free speech and to take part in a peaceable assembly having a lawful purpose, although called by that Party. The defendant was nonetheless entitled to discuss the public issues of the day, and thus, in a lawful manner, without incitement to violence or crime, to seek redress of alleged grievances. That was of the essence of his guaranteed personal liberty.

We hold that the Oregon statute, as applied to the particular charge as defined by the state court, is repugnant to the due process clause of the Fourteenth Amendment. The judgment of conviction is reversed, and the cause is remanded for further proceedings not inconsistent with this opinion.

Yates v. United States
356 U.S. 363 (1958)

The trial under the conspiracy indictment began on February 5, 1952. Testifying in her own defense, petitioner, on cross-examination on June 26, refused to answer four questions about Communist membership of other persons; she was adjudged guilty of civil contempt and committed to jail until the contempt had been purged. On June 30 she refused to answer eleven questions about Communist membership of other persons; the court announced its intention to treat these refusals as criminal contempt. At the conclusion of the trial, petitioner was found guilty of conspiracy to violate the Smith Act and was sentenced to serve five years' imprisonment and to pay a $10,000 fine. The District Court denied bail pending appeal of the conspiracy conviction; on application to the Court of Appeals to fix bail, the case was remanded to the District Court, which again denied bail. The Court of Appeals then fixed bail at $20,000, and, on August 30, petitioner, upon furnishing that amount, was released from custody, having been in jail since June 26. The conspiracy conviction was later affirmed by the

Court of Appeals, but reversed by this Court. The indictment was eventually dismissed on motion of the Government.

Petitioner had, in the meantime, on August 8, 1952, been adjudged guilty of eleven criminal contempts for her eleven refusals to answer on June 30, and she was sentenced by the District Court to eleven one-year terms of imprisonment, to run concurrently and to commence upon the completion of petitioner's imprisonment for the conspiracy. It is as to this sentence that review is sought here today.

On September 3, 1952, four days after petitioner's release from custody, the District Court ordered her recommitted on the civil contempt arising out of the four refusals to answer on June 26. The District Court denied her application for bail pending appeal, but the Court of Appeals granted it, and she was released two days after her commitment; the Court of Appeals subsequently reversed the recommitment order of the District Court on the ground that petitioner should not have been reconfined for civil contempt after the close of the main trial. Two days after her release on bail, on September 8, petitioner was adjudged guilty of criminal contempt for the four June 26 refusals and sentenced to four three-year terms of imprisonment, to run concurrently. Petitioner was then reconfined; the District Court denied her bail pending appeal, but the Court of Appeals granted it, and she was released on bail three days after her recommitment. The Court of Appeals subsequently reversed this contempt judgment because of the District Court's failure to give any notice that it intended to regard the June 26 refusals as criminal contempts.

Petitioner appealed her conviction of criminal contempt for the eleven refusals to answer on June 30; the Court of Appeals affirmed. This Court held that there was but one contempt, not eleven, and that a sentence for only one offense could be imposed. Accordingly, we vacated the one-year sentence for that one conviction and remanded the case to the District Court for determination of a new sentence appropriate in view of our setting aside of the punishment for eleven offenses when in fact only one was legally established. On remand, the District Court, after hearing, resentenced petitioner to one year's imprisonment. The court denied petitioner bail pending appeal; the Court of Appeals ordered her admitted to bail in the amount of $5,000, and she was released after fifteen days' confinement. The Court of Appeals affirmed the judgment of the District Court, noting that the sentence was "severe."

Reversing a judgment for contempt because of errors of substantive law may naturally call for a reduction of the sentence based on an extent of wrongdoing found unsustainable in law. Such reduction of the sentence, however, normally ought not be made by this Court. It should be left, on remand, to the sentencing court. And so, when this Court found that only a single offense was committed by petitioner, and not eleven offenses, it chose not to reduce the sentence, but to leave this task, with gentle intimations of the necessity for such action, to the District Court. However, when, in a situation like this, the District Court appears not to have exercised its discretion in the light of the reversal of the judgment but, in effect, to have sought merely to justify the original sentence, this Court has no alternative except to exercise its supervisory power over the administration of justice in the lower federal courts by setting aside the sentence of the District Court.

Although petitioner's conviction under the Smith Act, the substantive offense out of which this subsidiary matter arose, was reversed on appeal, and the indictment itself dismissed on motion of the Government, she has, in fact, spent seven months in jail in the course of these proceedings. Not unmindful of petitioner's offense, this Court is of the view, exercising the judgment that we are now called upon to exercise, that the time that petitioner has already served in jail is an adequate punishment for her offense in refusing to answer questions, and is to be deemed in satisfaction of the new sentence herein ordered formally to be imposed. Accordingly, the writ of certiorari is granted, and the judgment of the Court of Appeals is vacated and the cause remanded to the District Court with directions to reduce the sentence to the time petitioner has already been confined in the course of these proceedings.

Hannah v. Larche
363 U.S. 420 (1960)

These cases involve the validity of certain Rules of Procedure adopted by the Commission on Civil Rights. which was established by Congress in 1957. They arise out of the Commission's investigation of alleged Negro voting deprivations in the State of Louisiana. The appellees in No. 549 are registrars of voters in the State of Louisiana, and the respondents in No. 550 are private citizens of Louisiana. After having been summoned to appear before a hearing which the Commission proposed to conduct in Shreveport, Louisiana, these registrars and private citizens requested the United States District Court for the Western District of Louisiana to enjoin the Commission from holding its anticipated hearing. It was alleged, among other things, that the Commission's Rules of Procedure governing the conduct of its investigations were unconstitutional. The specific rules challenged are those which provide that the identity of persons submitting complaints to the

Commission need not be disclosed, and that those summoned to testify before the Commission, including persons against whom complaints have been filed, may not cross-examine other witnesses called by the Commission. The District Court held that the Commission was not authorized to adopt the Rules of Procedure here in question, and therefore issued an injunction which prohibits the Commission from holding any hearings in the Western District of Louisiana as long as the challenged procedures remain in force. The Commission requested this Court to review the District Court's decision. . . .

. . .

A description of the events leading up to this litigation is necessary not only to place the legal questions in their proper factual context, but also to indicate the significance of the Commission's proposed Shreveport hearing. During the months prior to its decision to convene the hearing, the Commission had received some sixty-seven complaints from individual Negroes who alleged that they had been discriminatorily deprived of their right to vote. Based upon these complaints, and pursuant to its statutory mandate to "investigate allegations in writing under oath or affirmation that certain citizens of the United States are being deprived of their right to vote and have that vote counted by reason of their color, race, religion, or national origin," the Commission began its investigation into the Louisiana voting situation by making several ex parte attempts to acquire information. Thus, in March 1959, a member of the Commission's staff interviewed the Voting Registrars of Claiborne, Caddo, and Webster Parishes, but obtained little relevant information. During one of these interviews the staff member is alleged to have informed Mrs. Lannie Linton, the Registrar of Claiborne Parish, that the Commission had on file four sworn statements charging her with depriving Negroes of their voting rights solely because of their race. Subsequent to this interview, Mr. W. M. Shaw, Mrs. Linton's personal attorney, wrote a letter to Mr. Gordon M. Tiffany, the Staff Director of the Commission, in which it was asserted that Mrs. Linton knew the sworn complaints lodged against her to be false. The letter also indicated that Mrs. Linton wished to prefer perjury charges against the affiants, and Mr. Shaw therefore demanded that the Commission forward to him copies of the affidavits so that a proper presentment could be made to the grand jury. On April 14, 1959, Mr. Tiffany replied to Mr. Shaw's letter and indicated that the Commission had denied the request for copies of the sworn affidavits. Mr. Shaw was also informed of the following official statement adopted by the Commission. . . .

A copy of Mr. Tiffany's letter was sent to Mr. Jack Gremillion, the Attorney General of Louisiana, who had previously informed the Commission that under Louisiana law the Attorney General is the legal adviser for all voting registrars in any hearing or investigation before a federal commission.

Another attempt to obtain information occurred on May 13, 1959, when Mr. Tiffany, upon Commission authorization, sent a list of 315 written interrogatories to Mr. Gremillion. These interrogatories requested very detailed and specific information, and were to be answered by the voting registrars of nineteen Louisiana parishes. Although Mr. Gremillion and the Governor of Louisiana had previously assented to the idea of written interrogatories, on May 28, 1959, Mr. Gremillion sent a letter to Mr. Tiffany indicating that the voting registrars refused to answer the interrogatories. The reasons given for the refusal were that many of the questions seemed unrelated to the functions of voting registrars, that the

questions were neither accompanied by specific complaints nor related to specific complaints, and that the time and research required to answer the questions placed an unreasonable burden upon the voting registrars.

In response to this refusal, on May 29, 1959, Mr. Tiffany sent a telegram to Mr. Gremillion, informing the latter that the interrogatories were based upon specific allegations received by the Commission, and reaffirming the Commission's position that the identity of specific complainants would not be disclosed. Mr. Tiffany's letter contained a further request that the interrogatories be answered and sent to the Commission by June 5, 1959. On June 2, 1959, Mr. Gremillion wrote a letter to Mr. Tiffany reiterating the registrars' refusal, and again requesting that the names of complainants be disclosed.

Finally, as a result of this exchange of correspondence, and because the Commission's attempts to obtain information ex parte had been frustrated, the Commission, acting pursuant to Section 105(f) of the Civil Rights Act of 1957, decided to hold the Shreveport hearing commencing on July 13, 1959.

Notice of the scheduled hearing was sent to Mr. Gremillion, and between June 29 and July 6, subpoenas duces tecum were served on the respondents in No. 549, ordering them to appear at the hearing and to bring with them various voting and registration records within their custody and control. Subpoenas were also served upon the respondents in No. 550. These private citizens were apparently summoned to explain their activities with regard to alleged deprivations of Negro voting rights.

On July 8, 1959, Mr. Tiffany wrote to Mr. Gremillion, enclosing copies of the Civil Rights Act and of the Commission's Rules of Procedure. Mr. Gremillion's attention was also drawn to Section 102(h) of the Civil Rights Act, which permits witnesses to submit, subject to the discretion of the Commission, brief and pertinent sworn statements for inclusion in the record.

Two days later, on July 10, 1959, the respondents in No. 549 and No. 550 filed two separate complaints in the District Court for the Western District of Louisiana. Both complaints alleged that the respondents would suffer irreparable harm by virtue of the Commission's refusal to furnish the names of persons who had filed allegations of voting deprivations, as well as the contents of the allegations, and by its further refusal to permit the respondents to confront and cross-examine the persons making such allegations. In addition, both complaints alleged that the Commission's refusals not only violated numerous provisions of the Federal Constitution, but also constituted "ultra vires" acts not authorized either by Congress or the Chief Executive. The respondents in No. 549 also alleged that they could not comply with the subpoenas duces tecum because Louisiana law prohibited voting registrars from removing their voting records except "upon an order of a competent court," and because the Commission was not such a "court." Finally, the complaint in No. 549 alleged that the Civil Rights Act was unconstitutional because it did not constitute "appropriate legislation within the meaning of Section (2) of the XV Amendment."

. . .

On the day that the complaints were filed, the district judge held a combined hearing on the prayers for temporary restraining orders. On July 12, 1959, he found that the respondents would suffer irreparable harm if the hearings were held as scheduled, and he therefore issued the requested temporary restraining orders and rules to show cause why a preliminary injunction should not be granted. The order prohibited the Commission

from holding any hearings which concerned the respondents or others similarly situated until a determination was made on the motion for a preliminary injunction.

Inasmuch as the complaint in No. 549 attacked the constitutionality of the Civil Rights Act, a three-judge court was convened. Since the complaint in No. 550 did not challenge the constitutionality of the Civil Rights Act of 1957, that case was scheduled to be heard by a single district judge. That district judge was also a member of the three-judge panel in No. 549, and a combined hearing was therefore held on both cases on August 7, 1959.

On October 7, 1959, a divided three-judge District Court filed an opinion in No. 549. The court held that the Civil Rights Act of 1957 was constitutional since it "very definitely constitutes appropriate legislation" authorized by the Fourteenth and Fifteenth Amendments and Article I, Section 2, of the Federal Constitution. . . . The single district judge rendered a decision in No. 550 incorporating by reference the opinion of the three-judge District Court, and an injunction, identical in substance to that entered in No. 549, was issued.

. . .

. . . [I]t is obvious that the District Court erred in both cases in enjoining the Commission from holding its Shreveport hearing. The court's judgments are accordingly reversed, and the cases are remanded with direction to vacate the injunctions.

Wood v. Georgia
370 U.S. 375 (1962)

On June 6, 1960, a judge of the Bibb Superior Court issued a charge to a regularly impaneled grand jury, giving it special instructions to conduct an investigation into a political situation which had allegedly arisen in the county. The jury was advised that there appeared to be "an inane and inexplicable pattern of Negro bloc voting" in Bibb County, and that "rumors and accusations" had been made which indicated candidates for public office had paid large sums of money in an effort to gain favor and to obtain the Negro vote. The charge explained that certain Negro leaders, after having met and endorsed a candidate, had switched their support to an opposing candidate who put up a large sum of money, and that this "create[d] an unhealthy, dangerous, and unlawful situation [which] tend[ed] to corrupt public office holders and some candidates for public office." The charge continued by indicating the violations of law which would be involved should the grand jury find the charges to be founded in truth. In addition, certain questions were posed to the jury which it was to investigate in inquiring into the charges of election law violations. The instructions were given in the midst of a local political campaign and the judge, in order to publicize the investigation, requested reporters for all local news media to be present in the courtroom when the charge was delivered.

The following day, while the grand jury was in session investigating the matters set forth in the instructions delivered by the court, the petitioner issued to the local press a written statement in which he criticized the judges' action and in which he urged the citizenry to take notice when their highest judicial officers threatened political intimidation and persecution of voters in the county under the guise of law enforcement. . . .

. . .

At a hearing before the trial judge, certain facts were stipulated: that the petitioner's statements were made while the grand jury was in session investigating matters suggested in the charge by the court; that the grand jury had before it the vot-

ing tabulations and other documents, including endorsements by certain political groups relating to primaries and elections in which the petitioner participated as a candidate and as an active supporter for other candidates; and that the members of the grand jury and the judges themselves had seen and read the press releases issued by the petitioner. In addition, it was stipulated that the petitioner's sworn response be admitted as evidence. The allegations in this response, which must be considered as true in the absence of contrary evidence and in the absence of findings of fact by the trial judge, included the verification that the statements were made by petitioner in his capacity as a private citizen and not as sheriff of the county; that petitioner was directly and personally interested in the outcome of the current primary election not only as a private citizen but also as an announced candidate for public office in the general election to be held the following November, and in which election the petitioner would be running against the contestant who prevailed in the democratic primary; that he believed the language employed in the charge was of such a nature that it tended to create or emphasize issues likely to have a drastic impact upon the outcome of the primary; that his purpose in issuing the statements was simply to inform the public of what he sincerely believed to be the other side of the issue created by the charge; and that the statements were not intended to be contemptuous of the court or to hinder the investigation. The petitioner also asserted that he adopted the same method of distributing his views to the general public as did the court in disseminating the grand jury charge. No witnesses were presented at the hearing and no evidence was introduced to show that the publications resulted in any actual interference or obstruction of the court or the work of the grand jury. The gravamen of the contempt citation, and of the State's case against the petitioner, was that the mere publishing of the news release and defense statement constituted a contempt of court, and in and of itself was a clear and present danger to the administration of justice.

The trial court, without making any findings and without giving any reasons, adjudged petitioner guilty on all counts and imposed concurrent sentences of 20 days and separate fines of $200 on each. On writ of error to the Court of Appeals the convictions on counts one and three were affirmed and the conviction on count two, based on the open letter to the grand jury, was reversed.... the Georgia Supreme Court ... declined to review the convictions on the first and third counts....

. . .

... [D]iscussion serves as a corrective force to political, economic and other influences which are inevitably present in matters of grave importance. The charge given to the jury indicated that the motivation for it was founded on rumor, but that the situation had existed for several years. Yet the charge was directed primarily against one group in the community and was given at the height of the highly important Democratic primary, in which, because of their elected positions, both the judges and the petitioner were interested personally and apart from their official status. The First Amendment envisions that persons be given the opportunity to inform the community of both sides of the issue under such circumstances....

Moreover, it is difficult to imagine how the voting problem may be alleviated by an abridgment of talk and comment regarding its solution. This problem is important not only to an individual or some isolated group or to individual litigants in a particular lawsuit, but affects the entire Nation. When the grand jury is performing its investigatory function into a general problem area, without specific regard to indicting a particular individual, society's interest is best served by a thorough and extensive investigation, and a greater degree of disinterestedness and impartiality is assured by allowing free expression of contrary opinion. Consistent suppression of discussion likely to affect pending investigations would mean that some continuing public grievances could never be discussed at all, or at least not at the moment when public discussion is most needed. The conviction here produces its "restrictive results at the precise time when public interest in the matters discussed would naturally be at its height," and "[n]o suggestion can be found in the Constitution that the freedom there guaranteed for speech and the press bears an inverse ratio to the timeliness and importance of the ideas seeking expression." Thus, in the absence of any showing of an actual interference with the undertakings of the grand jury, this record lacks persuasion in illustrating the serious degree of harm to the administration of law necessary to justify exercise of the contempt power.

Finally, we are told by the respondent that, because the petitioner is sheriff of Bibb County and thereby owes a special duty and responsibility to the court and its judges, his right to freedom of expression must be more severely curtailed than that of an average citizen. Under the circumstances of this case, this argument must be rejected.

. . .

The petitioner was an elected official and had the right to enter the field of political controversy, particularly where his political life was at stake. The role that elected officials play in our society makes it all the more imperative that they be allowed freely to express themselves on matters of current public importance.

Our examination of the content of petitioner's

statements and the circumstances under which they were published leads us to conclude that they did not present a danger to the administration of justice that should vitiate his freedom to express his opinions in the manner chosen.

The judgment is reversed.

Gordon v. Lance
403 U.S. 1 (1971)

On April 29, 1968, the Board of Education of Roane County, West Virginia, submitted to the voters of Roane County a proposal calling for the issuance of general obligation bonds in the amount of $1,830,000 for the purpose of constructing new school buildings and improving existing educational facilities. At the same election, by separate ballot, the voters were asked to authorize the Board of Education to levy additional taxes to support current expenditures and capital improvements. Of the total votes cast, 51.55 percent favored the bond issues and 51.51 percent favored the tax levy. Having failed to obtain the requisite 60 percent affirmative vote, the proposals were declared defeated.

Following the election, respondents appeared before the Board of Education on behalf of themselves and other persons who had voted in favor of the proposals and demanded that the Board authorize the bonds and the additional taxes. The Board refused.

Respondents then brought this action, seeking a declaratory judgment that the 60 percent requirements were unconstitutional as violative of the Fourteenth Amendment. In their complaint, they alleged that the Roane County schools had been basically unimproved since 1946, and fell far below the state average, both in classroom size and facilities. They further alleged that four similar proposals had been previously defeated, although each had received majorities of affirmative votes ranging from 52.51 percent to 55.84 percent. The West Virginia trial court dismissed the complaint. On appeal, the West Virginia Supreme Court of Appeals reversed, holding that the state constitutional and statutory 60 percent requirements violated the Equal Protection Clause of the Fourteenth Amendment. . . .

. . . [T]he state court concluded that West Virginia's requirement was constitutionally defective because the votes of those who favored the issuance of the bonds had a proportionately smaller impact on the outcome of the election than the votes of those who opposed issuance of the bonds.

. . .

Unlike the restrictions in our previous cases, the West Virginia Constitution singles out no "discrete and insular minority" for special treatment. The three-fifths requirement applies equally to all bond issues for any purpose, whether for schools, sewers, or highways. . . .

. . . [W]e can discern no independently identifiable group or category that favors bonded indebtedness over other forms of financing. Consequently, no sector of the population may be said to be "fenced out" from the franchise because of the way they will vote.

Although West Virginia has not denied any group access to the ballot, it has indeed made it more difficult for some kinds of governmental actions to be taken. Certainly any departure from strict majority rule gives disproportionate power to the minority. But there is nothing in the language of the Constitution, our history, or our cases that requires that a majority always prevail on every issue. On the contrary, while we have recognized that state officials are normally chosen by a vote of the majority of the electorate, we have found no constitutional barrier to the selection of a Governor by a state legislature after no candidate received a majority of the popular vote.

. . .

Wisely or not, the people of the State of West Virginia have long since resolved to remove from a simple majority vote the choice on certain decisions as to what indebtedness may be incurred and what taxes their children will bear.

We conclude that, so long as such provisions do not discriminate against or authorize discrimination against any identifiable class, they do not violate the Equal Protection Clause. We see no meaningful distinction between such absolute provisions on debt, changeable only by constitutional amendment, and provisions that legislative decisions on the same issues require more than a majority vote in the legislature. On the contrary, these latter provisions may, in practice, be less burdensome than the amendment process. Moreover, the same considerations apply when the ultimate power, rather than being delegated to the legislature, remains with the people, by way of a referendum. Indeed, we see no constitutional distinction between the 60 percent requirement in the present case and a state requirement that a given issue be approved by a majority of all registered voters.

That West Virginia has adopted a rule of decision, applicable to all bond referenda, by which the strong consensus of three-fifths is required before indebtedness is authorized does not violate the Equal Protection Clause or any other provision of the Constitution.

Reversed.

Elrod v. Burns
427 U.S. 347 (1976)

Respondents brought this suit in the United States District Court for the Northern District of Illi-

nois against petitioners, Richard Elrod, Richard Daley, the Democratic Organization of Cook County, and the Democratic County Central Committee of Cook County. Their complaint alleged that they were discharged or threatened with discharge solely for the reason that they were not affiliated with or sponsored by the Democratic Party. They sought declaratory, injunctive, and other relief for violations of the First and Fourteenth Amendments and 42 U.S.C. §§1983, 1985, 1986, 1988. Finding that the respondents failed to make an adequate showing of irreparable injury, the District Court denied their motion for a preliminary injunction and ultimately dismissed their complaint for failure to state a claim upon which relief could be granted. The United States Court of Appeals for the Seventh Circuit . . . reversed and remanded, holding that respondents' complaint stated a legally cognizable claim. . . .

In December 1970, the Sheriff of Cook County, a Republican, was replaced by Richard Elrod, a Democrat. At that time, respondents, all Republicans, were employees of the Cook County Sheriff's Office. They were non-civil service employees and, therefore, not covered by any statute, ordinance, or regulation protecting them from arbitrary discharge. One respondent, John Burns, was Chief Deputy of the Process Division, and supervised all departments of the Sheriff's Office working on the seventh floor of the building housing that office. Frank Vargas was a bailiff and security guard at the Juvenile Court of Cook County. Fred Buckle was employed as a process server in the office. Joseph Dennard was an employee in the office.

It has been the practice of the Sheriff of Cook County, when he assumes office from a Sheriff of a different political party, to replace non-civil service employees of the Sheriff's Office with members of his own party when the existing employees lack or fail to obtain requisite support from, or fail to affiliate with, that party. Consequently, subsequent to Sheriff Elrod's assumption of office, respondents, with the exception of Buckley, were discharged from their employment solely because they did not support and were not members of the Democratic Party and had failed to obtain the sponsorship of one of its leaders. Buckley is in imminent danger of being discharged solely for the same reasons. Respondents allege that the discharges were ordered by Sheriff Elrod under the direction of the codefendants in this suit.

. . .

Patronage practice falls squarely within the prohibitions of *Keyishian* and *Perry*. Under that practice, public employees hold their jobs on the condition that they provide, in some acceptable manner, support for the favored political party. The threat of dismissal for failure to provide that support unquestionably inhibits protected belief and association, and dismissal for failure to provide support only penalizes its exercise. The belief and association which government may not ordain directly are achieved by indirection. And regardless of how evenhandedly these restraints may operate in the long run, after political office has changed hands several times, protected interests are still infringed and thus the violation remains.

Although the practice of patronage dismissals clearly infringes First Amendment interests, our inquiry is not at an end, for the prohibition on encroachment of First Amendment protections is not an absolute. . . .

. . .

One interest which has been offered in justification of patronage is the need to insure effective government and the efficiency of public employees. It is argued that employees of political persuasions not the same as that of the party in control of public office will not have the incentive to work effectively, and may even be motivated to subvert the incumbent administration's efforts to govern effectively. We are not persuaded. The inefficiency resulting from the wholesale replacement of large numbers of public employees every time political office changes hands belies this justification. And the prospect of dismissal after an election in which the incumbent party has lost is only a disincentive to good work. Further, it is not clear that dismissal in order to make room for a patronage appointment will result in replacement by a person more qualified to do the job, since appointment often occurs in exchange for the delivery of votes, or other party service, not job capability. More fundamentally, however, the argument does not succeed because it is doubtful that the mere difference of political persuasion motivates poor performance; nor do we think it legitimately may be used as a basis for imputing such behavior. The Court has consistently recognized that mere political association is an inadequate basis for imputing disposition to ill-willed conduct. . . .

. . .

The lack of any justification for patronage dismissals as a means of furthering government effectiveness and efficiency distinguishes this case from *CSC v. Letter Carriers* and *United Public Workers v. Mitchell*. In both of those cases, legislative restraints on political management and campaigning by public employees were upheld despite their encroachment on First Amendment rights because . . . they did serve in a necessary manner to foster and protect efficient and effective government. Interestingly, the activities that were restrained by the legislation involved in those cases are characteristic of patronage practices. . . .

A second interest advanced in support of patronage is the need for political loyalty of employees, not to the end that effectiveness and efficiency be insured, but to the end that representative government not be undercut by tactics obstructing the implementation of policies of the new administration, policies presumably sanctioned by the electorate. The justification is not without force, but is nevertheless inadequate to validate patronage wholesale. Limiting patronage dismissals to policymaking positions is sufficient to achieve this governmental end. Nonpolicymaking individuals usually have only limited responsibility and are therefore not in a position to thwart the goals of the in-party.

No clear line can be drawn between policymaking and nonpolicymaking positions. While nonpolicymaking individuals usually have limited responsibility, that is not to say that one with a number of responsibilities is necessarily in a policymaking position. The nature of the responsibilities is critical. Employee supervisors, for example, may have many responsibilities, but those responsibilities may have only limited and well defined objectives. An employee with responsibilities that are not well defined or are of broad scope more likely functions in a policymaking position. In determining whether an employee occupies a policymaking position, consideration should also be given to whether the employee acts as an adviser or formulates plans for the implementation of broad goals. Thus, the political loyalty "justification is a matter of proof, or at least argument, directed at particular kinds of jobs." Since, as we have noted, it is the government's burden to demonstrate an overriding interest in order to validate an encroachment on protected interests, the burden of establishing this justification as to any particular respondent will rest on the petitioners on remand, cases of

doubt being resolved in favor of the particular respondent.

It is argued that a third interest supporting patronage dismissals is the preservation of the democratic process. . . .

Preservation of the democratic process is certainly an interest protection of which may in some instances justify limitations on First Amendment freedoms. But however important preservation of the two-party system or any system involving a fixed number of parties may or may not be, we are not persuaded that the elimination of patronage practice or, as is specifically involved here, the interdiction of patronage dismissals, will bring about the demise of party politics. . . .

Patronage dismissals thus are not the least restrictive alternative to achieving the contribution they may make to the democratic process. The process functions as well without the practice, perhaps even better, for patronage dismissals clearly also retard that process. Patronage can result in the entrenchment of one or a few parties to the exclusion of others. And most indisputably, as we recognized at the outset, patronage is a very effective impediment to the associational and speech freedoms which are essential to a meaningful system of democratic government. Thus, if patronage contributes at all to the elective process, that contribution is diminished by the practice's impairment of the same. Indeed, unlike the gain to representative government provided by the Hatch Act . . . the gain to representative government provided by the practice of patronage, if any, would be insufficient to justify its sacrifice of First Amendment rights.

. . . Today, we hold that subordination of other First Amendment activity, that is, patronage dismissals, not only is permissible, but also is mandated by the First Amendment. And since patronage dismissals fall within the category of political campaigning and management, this conclusion irresistibly flows from *Mitchell* and *Letter Carriers*. For if the First Amendment did not place individual belief and association above political campaigning and management, at least in the setting of public employment, the restraints on those latter activities could not have been judged permissible in *Mitchell* and *Letter Carriers*.

. . . Our decision in obedience to the guidance of that source does not outlaw political parties or political campaigning and management. Parties are free to exist and their concomitant activities are free to continue. We require only that the rights of every citizen to believe as he will and to act and associate according to his beliefs be free to continue as well.

. . . We hold . . . that the practice of patronage dismissals is unconstitutional under the First and Fourteenth Amendments, and that respondents thus stated a valid claim for relief.

. . .

The judgment of the Court of Appeals is affirmed.

Branti v. Finkel
445 U.S. 507 (1980)

Respondents, Aaron Finkel and Alan Tabakman, commenced this action in the United States District Court for the Southern District of New York in order to preserve their positions as assistant public defenders in Rockland County, New York. On January 4, 1978, on the basis of a showing that the petitioner public defender was about to discharge them solely because they were Republicans, the District Court entered a temporary restraining order preserving the status quo. After hearing evidence for eight days, the District Court entered detailed findings of fact and permanently enjoined petitioner from terminating or attempting to terminate respondents' employment "upon the sole grounds of their political beliefs."

. . . The Rockland County Public Defender is appointed by the County Legislature for a term of six years. He in turn appoints nine assistants who serve at his pleasure. The two respondents have served as assistants since their respective appointments in March 1971, and September 1975; they are both Republicans.

Petitioner Branti's predecessor, a Republican, was appointed in 1972 by a Republican-dominated County Legislature. By 1977, control of the legislature had shifted to the Democrats and petitioner, also a Democrat, was appointed to replace the incumbent when his term expired. As soon as petitioner was formally appointed on January 3, 1978, he began executing termination notices for six of the nine assistants then in office. Respondents were among those who were to be terminated. With one possible exception, the nine who were to be appointed or retained were all Democrats, and were all selected by Democratic legislators or Democratic town chairmen on a basis that had been determined by the Democratic caucus.

The District Court found that Finkel and Tabakman had been selected for termination solely because they were Republicans, and thus did not have the necessary Democratic sponsors. . . . The court rejected petitioner's belated attempt to justify the dismissals on nonpolitical grounds. . . .

. . .

. . . On appeal, a panel of the Second Circuit affirmed, specifically holding that the District Court's findings of fact were adequately supported by the record. That court also expressed "no doubt" that the District Court "was correct in concluding that an assistant public defender was neither a policymaker nor a confidential employee." . . .

. . .

Petitioner argues that *Elrod v. Burns* should be read to prohibit only dismissals resulting from an employee's failure to capitulate to political coercion. Thus, he argues that, so long as an employee is not asked to change his political affiliation or to contribute to or work for the party's candidates, he may be dismissed with impunity even though he would not have been dismissed if he had had the proper political sponsorship and even though the sole reason for dismissing him was to replace him with a person who did have such sponsorship. Such an interpretation would surely emasculate the principles set forth in *Elrod*. While it would perhaps eliminate the more blatant forms of coercion described in *Elrod*, it would not eliminate the coercion of belief that necessarily flows from the knowledge that one must have a sponsor in the dominant party in order to retain one's job. . . .

. . .

. . . [I]t is manifest that the continued employment of an assistant public defender cannot properly be conditioned upon his allegiance to the political party in control of the county government. The primary, if not the only, responsibility of an assistant public defender is to represent individual citizen in controversy with the State. . . .

Thus, whatever policymaking occurs in the public defender's office must relate to the needs of individual clients, and not to any partisan political interests. Similarly, although an assistant is bound to obtain access to confidential information arising out of various attorney-client relationships, that information has no bearing whatsoever on partisan political concerns. Under these circumstances, it would undermine, rather than promote, the effective performance of an assistant public defender's office to make his tenure dependent on his allegiance to the dominant political party.

Accordingly, the entry of an injunction against termination of respondents' employment on purely political grounds was appropriate, and the judgment of the Court of Appeals is affirmed.

Bread Political Action Committee v. Federal Election Commission
455 U.S. 577 (1982)

The appellants are two trade associations and three political action committees (PACs): the National Restaurant Association and its associated PAC, the Restauranteurs Political Action Committee, the National Lumber and Building Material Dealers Association and its associated PAC, the Lumber Dealers Political Action Committee, and the Bread Political Action Committee, the PAC associated with the American Bakers Association. In order to challenge the validity of 2 U.S.C. §441b(b)(4)(D), which has the effect of limiting the extent to which trade associations and their PACs may solicit funds for political purposes, the appellants filed an action in the United States District Court for the Northern District of Illinois, seeking expedited consideration of their suit under the procedures set forth in §437h. The District Court denied certification under §437h on the ground that the plaintiff trade associations and PACs do not belong to any of the three categories of plaintiffs listed in §437h(a) as eligible to invoke its expedited procedures. . . . [A] panel of the Court of Appeals reversed, holding that §437h(a) is available for use by plaintiffs whether they belong to an enumerated category or not. On remand, the District Court, as required by §437h, first made findings of fact and then certified the case back to the Court of Appeals sitting en banc for a determination on the constitutional questions raised by the appellants. The en banc court declined to overrule the earlier panel decision regarding the reach of §437h(a), and proceeded to the merits of the appellants' claims, upholding the constitutionality of the challenged provisions. . . .

. . .

. . . [W]e reverse and remand for proceedings consistent with this opinion.

Spallone v. United States
493 U.S. 265 (1990)

This case is the most recent episode of a lengthy lawsuit in which the city of Yonkers was held liable for intentionally enhancing racial segregation in housing in Yonkers. The issue here is whether it was a proper exercise of judicial power for the District Court to hold petitioners, four Yonkers city councilmembers, in contempt for refusing to vote in favor of legislation implementing a consent decree earlier approved by the city. We hold that, in the circumstances of this case, the District Court abused its discretion.

In 1980, the United States filed a complaint alleging, inter alia, that the two named defendants—the city of Yonkers and the Yonkers Community Development Agency—had intentionally engaged in a pattern and practice of housing discrimination, in violation of Title VIII of the Civil Rights Act of 1968 and the Equal Protection Clause of the Fourteenth Amendment. The Government and plaintiff-intervenor National Association for the Advancement of Colored People (NAACP) asserted that the city had, over a period of three decades, selected sites for subsidized housing in order to perpetuate residential racial segregation. The plaintiffs' theory was that the city had equated subsidized housing for families with minority housing, and thus disproportionately

restricted new family housing projects to areas of the city—particularly southwest Yonkers—already predominately populated by minorities.

The District Court found the two named defendants liable, concluding that the segregative effect of the city's actions had been "consistent and extreme.". . . The District Court in its remedial decree enjoined "the City of Yonkers, its officers, agents, employees, successors and all persons in active concert or participation with any of them" from, inter alia, intentionally promoting racial residential segregation in Yonkers, taking any action intended to deny or make unavailable housing to any person on account of race or national origin, and from blocking or limiting the availability of public or subsidized housing in east or northwest Yonkers on the basis of race or national origin. Other parts of the remedial order were directed only to the city. They required affirmative steps to disperse public housing throughout Yonkers. Part IV of the order noted that the city previously had committed itself to provide acceptable sites for 200 units of public housing as a condition for receiving 1983 Community Development Block Grant funds from the Federal Government, but had failed to do so. Consequently, it required the city to designate sites for 200 units of public housing in East Yonkers, and to submit to the Department of Housing and Urban Development an acceptable Housing Assistance Plan for 1984–1985 and other documentation. Part VI directed the city to develop by November 1986, a long-term plan "for the creation of additional subsidized family housing units . . . in existing residential areas in east or northwest Yonkers." The court did not mandate specific details of the plan such as how many subsidized units must be developed, where they should be constructed, or how the city should provide for the units.

Under the Charter of the city of Yonkers, all legislative powers are vested in the city council, which consists of an elected mayor and six councilmembers, including petitioners. The city, for all practical purposes, therefore, acts through the city council when it comes to the enactment of legislation. Pending appeal of the District Court's liability and remedial orders, however, the city did not comply with Parts IV and VI of the remedial order. The city failed to propose sites for the public housing, and in November 1986, informed the District Court that it would not present a long-term plan in compliance with Part VI. The United States and the NAACP then moved for an adjudication of civil contempt and the imposition of coercive sanctions, but the District Court declined to take that action. Instead, it secured an agreement from the city to appoint an outside housing advisor to identify sites for the 200 units of public housing and to draft a long-term plan.

In December 1987, the Court of Appeals for the Second Circuit affirmed the District Court's judgment in all respects, and we subsequently denied certiorari. Shortly after the Court of Appeals' decision, in January 1988, the parties agreed to a consent decree that set forth "certain actions which the City of Yonkers [would] take in connection with a consensual implementation of Parts IV and VI" of the housing remedy order. The decree was approved by the city council in a 5-to-2 vote (petitioners Spallone and Chema voting no), and entered by the District Court as a consent judgment on January 28, 1988. Sections 12 through 18 of the decree established the framework for the long-term plan, and are the underlying bases for the contempt orders at issue in this case. Perhaps most significant was §17, in which the city agreed to adopt, within 90 days, legislation conditioning the construction of all multi-family housing on the inclusion of at least 20 percent assisted units, granting tax abatements and density bonuses to developers, and providing for zoning changes to allow the placement of housing developments.

For several more months, however, the city continued to delay action toward implementing the long-term plan. The city was loath to enact the plan because it wished to exhaust its remedies on appeal, but it had not obtained any stay of the District Court's order. As a result of the city's intransigence, the United States and the NAACP moved the court for the entry of a Long Term Plan Order based on a draft that had been prepared by the city's lawyers during negotiations between January and April, 1988. On June 13, following a hearing and changes in the draft, the District Court entered the Long Term Plan Order, which provided greater detail for the legislation prescribed by §17 of the decree. After several weeks of further delay, the court, after a hearing held on July 26, 1988, entered an order requiring the city of Yonkers to enact on or before August 1, 1988, the "legislative package" described in a section of the earlier consent decree; the second paragraph provided:

> It is further ORDERED that, in the event the City of Yonkers fails to enact the legislative package on or before August 1, 1988, the City of Yonkers shall be required to show cause at a hearing before this Court at 10:00 a.m. on August 2, 1988, why it should not be held in contempt, and each individual City Council member shall be required to show cause at a hearing before this court at 10:00 a.m. on August 2, 1988, why he should not be held in contempt.

Further provisions of the order specified escalating daily amounts of fines in the event of contempt, and provided that, if the legislation were not enacted before August 10, 1988, any councilmember who remained in contempt should be committed to the custody of the United States Marshal for imprisonment. The specified daily fines for the city were $100 for the first day, to be doubled for each consecutive day of noncompliance; the specified daily fine for members of the city council was $500 per day.

Notwithstanding the threat of substantial sanctions, on August 1, the city council defeated a resolution of intent to adopt the legislative package, known as the Affordable Housing Ordinance, by a vote of 4 to 3 (petitioners constituting the majority). On August 2, the District Court held a hearing to afford the city and the councilmembers an opportunity to show cause why they should not be adjudicated in contempt. It rejected the city's arguments, held the city in contempt, and imposed the coercive sanctions set forth in the July 26 order. After questioning the individual council members as to the reasons for their negative votes, the court also held each of the petitioners in contempt and imposed sanctions. It refused to accept the contention that the proper subject of the contempt sanctions was the city of Yonkers alone and overruled the objection that the court lacked the power to direct councilmembers how to vote, because, in light of the consent judgment, it thought the city council's adoption of the Affordable Housing Ordinance would be "in the nature of a ministerial act."

On August 17, the Court of Appeals stayed the contempt sanctions pending appeal. Shortly thereafter, the court affirmed the adjudications of contempt against both the city and the councilmembers, but limited the fines against the city so that they would not exceed $1 million per day. The Court of Appeals refused to accept the councilmembers' argument that the District Court abused its discretion in selecting its method of enforcing the consent judgment. While recogniz-

ing that "a court is obliged to use the 'least possible power adequate to the end proposed,'" it concluded that the District Court's choice of coercive contempt sanctions against the councilmembers could not be an abuse of discretion, because the city council had approved the consent judgment and thereby agreed to implement the legislation described in Section 17 of the decree. The Court of Appeals also rejected petitioners' invocation of the federal common law of legislative immunity. . . .

Both the city and the councilmembers requested this Court to stay imposition of sanctions pending filing and disposition of petitions for certiorari. We granted a stay as to petitioners, but denied the city's request. . . .

. . .

This sort of individual sanction effects a much greater perversion of the normal legislative process than does the imposition of sanctions on the city for the failure of these same legislators to enact an ordinance. In that case, the legislator is only encouraged to vote in favor of an ordinance that he would not otherwise favor by reason of the adverse sanctions imposed on the city. A councilman who felt that his constituents would rather have the city enact the Affordable Housing Ordinance than pay a "bankrupting fine" would be motivated to vote in favor of such an ordinance because the sanctions were a threat to the fiscal solvency of the city for whose welfare he was in part responsible. This is the sort of calculus in which legislators engage regularly.

We hold that the District Court, in view of the "extraordinary" nature of the imposition of sanctions against the individual councilmen, should have proceeded with such contempt sanctions first against the city alone in order to secure compliance with the remedial orders. Only if that approach failed to produce compliance within a reasonable time should the question of imposing contempt sanctions against petitioners even have been considered. . . .

Reversed.

Rutan v. Republican Party of Illinois
497 U.S. 62 (1990)

To the victor belong only those spoils that may be constitutionally obtained. . . . Today we are asked to decide the constitutionality of several related political patronage practices—whether promotion, transfer, recall, and hiring decisions involving low-level public employees may be constitutionally based on party affiliation and support. . . .

The petition and cross-petition before us arise from a lawsuit protesting certain employment policies and practices instituted by Governor James Thompson of Illinois. On November 12, 1980, the Governor issued an executive order proclaiming a hiring freeze for every agency, bureau, board, or commission subject to his control. The order prohibits state officials from hiring any employee, filling any vacancy, creating any new position, or taking any similar action. It affects approximately 60,000 state positions. More than 5,000 of these become available each year as a result of resignations, retirements, deaths, expansion, and reorganizations. The order proclaims that "no exceptions" are permitted without the Governor's "express permission after submission of appropriate requests to [his] office."

Requests for the Governor's "express permission" have allegedly become routine. Permission has been granted or withheld through an agency expressly created for this purpose, the Governor's Office of Personnel (Governor's Office). Agencies have been screening applicants under Illinois' civil service system, making their personnel

choices, and submitting them as requests to be approved or disapproved by the Governor's Office. Among the employment decisions for which approvals have been required are new hires, promotions, transfers, and recalls after layoffs.

By means of the freeze, according to petitioners, the Governor has been using the Governor's Office to operate a political patronage system to limit state employment and beneficial employment-related decisions to those who are supported by the Republican Party. In reviewing an agency's request that a particular applicant be approved for a particular position, the Governor's Office has looked at whether the applicant voted in Republican primaries in past election years, whether the applicant has provided financial or other support to the Republican Party and its candidates, whether the applicant has promised to join and work for the Republican Party in the future, and whether the applicant has the support of Republican Party officials at state or local levels.

Five people (including the three petitioners) brought suit against various Illinois and Republican Party officials in the United States District Court for the Central District of Illinois. They alleged that they had suffered discrimination with respect to state employment because they had not been supporters of the State's Republican Party and that this discrimination violates the First Amendment. Cynthia Rutan has been working for the State since 1974 as a rehabilitation counselor. She claims that, since 1981, she has been repeatedly denied promotions to supervisory positions for which she was qualified because she had not worked for or supported the Republican Party. Franklin Taylor, who operates road equipment for the Illinois Department of Transportation, claims that he was denied a promotion in 1983 because he did not have the support of the local Republican Party. Taylor also maintains that he was denied a transfer to an office nearer to his home because of opposition from the Republican Party chairmen in the counties in which he worked and to which he requested a transfer. James Moore claims that he has been repeatedly denied state employment as a prison guard because he did not have the support of Republican Party officials.

The two other plaintiffs, before the Court as cross-respondents, allege that they were not recalled after layoffs because they lacked Republican credentials. Ricky Standefer was a state garage worker who claims that he was not recalled, although his fellow employees were, because he had voted in a Democratic primary and did not have the support of the Republican Party. Dan O'Brien, formerly a dietary manager with the mental health department, contends that he was not recalled after a layoff because of his party affiliation, and that he later obtained a lower-paying position with the corrections department only after receiving support from the chairman of the local Republican Party.

The District Court dismissed the complaint with prejudice. . . . The United States Court of Appeals for the Seventh Circuit initially issued a panel opinion, but then reheard the appeal en banc. The court affirmed the District Court's decision in part and reversed in part. . . .

. . .

Whether the four employees were in fact denied promotions, transfers, or rehire for failure to affiliate with and support the Republican Party is for the District Court to decide in the first instance. What we decide today is that such denials are irreconcilable with the Constitution, and that the allegations of the four employees state claims under 42 U.S.C. §1983 for violations of the First and Fourteenth Amendments. Therefore, although we affirm the Seventh Circuit's judgment to reverse the District Court's dismissal of

these claims and remand them for further proceedings, we do not adopt the Seventh Circuit's reasoning.

. . .

We hold that the rule of *Elrod* and *Branti* extends to promotion, transfer, recall, and hiring decisions based on party affiliation and support, and that all of the petitioners and cross-respondents have stated claims upon which relief may be granted. We affirm the Seventh Circuit insofar as it remanded Rutan's, Taylor's, Standefer's, and O'Brien's claims. However, we reverse the Circuit Court's decision to uphold the dismissal of Moore's claim. All five claims are remanded for proceedings consistent with this opinion.

Kay v. Ehrler
499 U.S. 432 (1991)

Petitioner is licensed to practice law in Florida. In 1980, he requested the Kentucky Board of Elections (Board) to place his name on the Democratic Party's primary ballot for the office of President of the United States. Because the members of the Board concluded that he was not a candidate who was "generally advocated and nationally recognized" within the meaning of the controlling Kentucky statute, the Board refused his request.

Petitioner filed a successful action on his own behalf in the District Court, challenging the constitutionality of the Kentucky statute. The District Court held that the statute was invalid, and entered an injunction requiring that petitioner's name appear on the ballot. Two years later, the Kentucky General Assembly repealed the statute. In 1986, however, it enacted an identically worded statute. In 1987, petitioner again requested that his name appear on the primary ballot, and when the Board initially refused his request, petitioner again brought suit in the District Court, and prevailed. This time, however, he requested a fee award under 42 U.S.C. §1988.

The District Court denied petitioner's request for attorney's fees under §1988. . . . The United States Court of Appeals for the Sixth Circuit affirmed. . . .

. . .

The judgment of the Court of Appeals is affirmed.

Federal Election Commission v. NRA Political Victory Fund
513 U.S. 88 (1994)

We granted certiorari in this case to review a judgment of the Court of Appeals for the District of Columbia Circuit holding that the congressionally mandated composition of petitioner Federal Election Commission (FEC), including as it did representatives of the Senate and House as nonvoting members, violated the separation of powers principle embodied in the Constitution. . . .

. . .

We hold that the FEC may not independently file a petition for certiorari in this Court under §437d(a)(6), and that the Solicitor General's "after-the-fact" authorization does not relate back to the date of the FEC's unauthorized filing so as to make it timely. We therefore dismiss the petition for certiorari for want of jurisdiction.

U.S. Term Limits, Inc. v. Thornton
514 U.S. 779 (1995)

. . .

At the general election on November 3, 1992, the voters of Arkansas adopted Amendment 73 to their State Constitution. Proposed as a "Term Limitation Amendment," its preamble stated:

"The people of Arkansas find and declare that elected officials who remain in office too long become preoccupied with reelection and ignore their duties as representatives of the people. Entrenched incumbency has reduced voter participation and has led to an electoral system that is less free, less competitive, and less representative than the system established by the Founding Fathers. Therefore, the people of Arkansas, exercising their reserved powers, herein limit the terms of the elected officials."

The limitations in Amendment 73 apply to three categories of elected officials. Section 1 provides that no elected official in the executive branch of the state government may serve more than two 4-year terms. Section 2 applies to the legislative branch of the state government; it provides that no member of the Arkansas House of Representatives may serve more than three 2-year terms and no member of the Arkansas Senate may serve more than two 4-year terms. Section 3, the provision at issue in these cases, applies to the Arkansas Congressional Delegation. . . .

. . .

On cross-motions for summary judgment, the Circuit Court held that 3 of Amendment 73 violated Article I of the Federal Constitution.

. . .

. . . [P]etitioners argue that whatever the constitutionality of additional qualifications for membership imposed by Congress, the historical and textual materials discussed in *Powell* do not support the conclusion that the Constitution prohibits additional qualifications imposed by States. In the absence of such a constitutional prohibition, petitioners argue, the Tenth Amendment and the principle of reserved powers require that States be allowed to add such qualifications.

Petitioners argue that the Constitution contains no express prohibition against state-added qualifications, and that Amendment 73 is therefore an appropriate exercise of a State's reserved power to place additional restrictions on the choices that its own voters may make. We disagree for two independent reasons. First, we conclude that the power to add qualifications is not within the "original powers" of the States, and thus is not reserved to the States by the Tenth Amendment. Second, even if States possessed some original power in this area, we conclude that the Framers intended the Constitution to be the exclusive source of qualifications for members of Congress, and that the Framers thereby "divested" States of any power to add qualifications.

. . .

Contrary to petitioners' assertions, the power to add qualifications is not part of the original powers of sovereignty that the Tenth Amendment reserved to the States. Petitioners' Tenth Amendment argument misconceives the nature of the right at issue because that Amendment could only "reserve" that which existed before. . . .

With respect to setting qualifications for service in Congress, no such right existed before the Constitution was ratified. . . .

. . .

. . . [A]s the Framers recognized, electing representatives to the National Legislature was a new right, arising from the Constitution itself. The Tenth Amendment thus provides no basis for concluding that the States possess reserved power to add qualifications to those that are fixed in the Constitution. Instead, any state power to set the qualifications for membership in Congress must derive not from the reserved powers of state sovereignty, but rather from the delegated powers of national sovereignty. In the absence of any constitutional delegation to the States of power to add qualifications to those enumerated in the Constitution, such a power does not exist.

Even if we believed that States possessed as part of their original powers some control over congressional qualifications, the text and structure of the Constitution, the relevant historical materials, and, most importantly, the "basic principles of our democratic system" all demonstrate that the Qualifications Clauses were intended to preclude the States from exercising any such power and to fix as exclusive the qualifications in the Constitution.

. . .

In light of the Framers' evident concern that States would try to undermine the National Government, they could not have intended States to have the power to set qualifications. Indeed, one of the more anomalous consequences of petitioners' argument is that it accepts federal supremacy over the procedural aspects of determining the times, places, and manner of elections while allowing the states carte blanche with respect to the substantive qualifications for membership in Congress.

The dissent nevertheless contends that the Framers' distrust of the States with respect to elections does not preclude the people of the States from adopting eligibility requirements to help narrow their own choices. As the dissent concedes, however, the Framers were unquestionably concerned that the States would simply not hold elections for federal officers, and therefore the Framers gave Congress the power to "make or alter" state election regulations. Yet under the dissent's approach, the States could achieve exactly the same result by simply setting qualifications for federal office sufficiently high that no one could meet those qualifications. In our view, it is inconceivable that the Framers would provide a specific constitutional provision to ensure that federal elections would be held while at the same time allowing States to render those elections meaningless by simply ensuring that no candidate could be qualified for office. Given the Framers' wariness over the potential for state abuse, we must conclude that the specification of fixed qualifications in the constitutional text was intended to prescribe uniform rules that would preclude modification by either Congress or the States.

. . .

. . . The Constitution's provision for each House to be the judge of its own qualifications . . . provides further evidence that the Framers believed that the primary source of those qualifications would be federal law.

We also find compelling the complete absence in the ratification debates of any assertion that States had the power to add qualifications. In those debates, the question whether to require term limits, or "rotation," was a major source of controversy. . . . Even proponents of ratification expressed concern about the "abandonment in every instance of the necessity of rotation in office." At several ratification conventions, participants proposed amendments that would have required rotation.

. . .

. . . [W]e believe that state-imposed qualifications, as much as congressionally imposed qualifications, would undermine the second critical idea recognized in *Powell*: that an aspect of sovereignty is the right of the people to vote for whom they wish. Again, the source of the qualification is of little moment in assessing the qualification's restrictive impact.

Finally, state-imposed restrictions, unlike the congressionally imposed restrictions at issue in

Powell, violate a third idea central to this basic principle: that the right to choose representatives belongs not to the States, but to the people. . . .

. . .

Petitioners argue that, even if States may not add qualifications, Amendment 73 is constitutional because it is not such a qualification, and because Amendment 73 is a permissible exercise of state power to regulate the "Times, Places and Manner of Holding Elections." We reject these contentions.

Unlike 1 and 2 of Amendment 73, which create absolute bars to service for long-term incumbents running for state office, 3 merely provides that certain Senators and Representatives shall not be certified as candidates and shall not have their names appear on the ballot. They may run as write-in candidates and, if elected, they may serve. Petitioners contend that only a legal bar to service creates an impermissible qualification, and that Amendment 73 is therefore consistent with the Constitution.

. . .

In our view, Amendment 73 is an indirect attempt to accomplish what the Constitution prohibits Arkansas from accomplishing directly. As the plurality opinion of the Arkansas Supreme Court recognized, Amendment 73 is an "effort to dress eligibility to stand for Congress in ballot access clothing," because the "intent and the effect of Amendment 73 are to disqualify congressional incumbents from further service." . . .

. . .

Petitioners make the . . . argument that Amendment 73 merely regulates the "Manner" of elections, and that the Amendment is therefore a permissible exercise of state power under Article I, 4, cl. 1 (the Elections Clause) to regulate the "Times, Places and Manner" of elections. We cannot agree.

A necessary consequence of petitioners' argument is that Congress itself would have the power to "make or alter" a measure such as Amendment 73. That the Framers would have approved of such a result is unfathomable. As our decision in *Powell* and our discussion above make clear, the Framers were particularly concerned that a grant to Congress of the authority to set its own qualifications would lead inevitably to congressional self-aggrandizement and the upsetting of the delicate constitutional balance. Petitioners would have us believe, however, that even as the Framers carefully circumscribed congressional power to set qualifications, they intended to allow Congress to achieve the same result by simply formulating the regulation as a ballot access restriction under the Elections Clause. We refuse to adopt an interpretation of the Elections Clause that would so cavalierly disregard what the Framers intended to be a fundamental constitutional safeguard.

Moreover, petitioners' broad construction of the Elections Clause is fundamentally inconsistent with the Framers' view of that Clause. The Framers intended the Elections Clause to grant States authority to create procedural regulations, not to provide States with license to exclude classes of candidates from federal office. . . .

. . .

. . . [T]he Framers understood the Elections Clause as a grant of authority to issue procedural regulations, and not as a source of power to dictate electoral outcomes, to favor or disfavor a class of candidates, or to evade important constitutional restraints.

Our cases interpreting state power under the Elections Clause reflect the same understanding. The Elections Clause gives States authority "to enact the numerous requirements as to procedure and safeguards which experience shows are necessary in order to enforce the fundamental right involved." However, "[t]he power to regulate the time, place, and manner of elections does not justify, without more, the abridgement of fundamental rights." States are thus entitled to adopt "generally applicable and evenhanded restrictions that protect the integrity and reliability of the electoral process itself." . . . In so doing, we emphasized the States' interest in having orderly, fair, and honest elections "rather than chaos." We also recognized the "States' strong interest in maintaining the integrity of the political process by preventing interparty raiding," and explained that the specific requirements applicable to independents were "expressive of a general state policy aimed at maintaining the integrity of the various routes to the ballot." In other cases, we have approved the States' interests in avoiding "voter confusion, ballot overcrowding, or the presence of frivolous candidacies" in "seeking to assure that elections are operated equitably and efficiently," and in "guard[ing] against irregularity and error in the tabulation of votes." . . .

. . .

The merits of term limits, or "rotation," have been the subject of debate since the formation of our Constitution, when the Framers unanimously rejected a proposal to add such limits to the Constitution. The cogent arguments on both sides of the question that were articulated during the process of ratification largely retain their force today. Over half the States have adopted measures that impose such limits on some offices either directly or indirectly, and the Nation as a whole, notably by constitutional amendment, has imposed a limit on the number of terms that the President may serve. Term limits, like any other qualification for office, unquestionably restrict the ability of voters to vote for whom they wish. On the other hand, such limits may provide for the infusion of fresh ideas and new perspectives, and may decrease the likelihood that representatives will lose touch with their constituents. It is not our province to resolve this longstanding debate.

We are, however, firmly convinced that allowing the several States to adopt term limits for congressional service would effect a fundamental change in the constitutional framework. Any such change must come not by legislation adopted either by Congress or by an individual State, but rather - as have other important changes in the electoral process- through the Amendment procedures set forth in Article V. The Framers decided that the qualifications for service in the Congress of the United States be fixed in the Constitution and be uniform throughout the Nation. That decision reflects the Framers' understanding that Members of Congress are chosen by separate constituencies, but that they become, when elected, servants of the people of the United States. They are not merely delegates appointed by separate, sovereign States; they occupy offices that are integral and essential components of a single National Government. In the absence of a properly passed constitutional amendment, allowing individual States to craft their own qualifications for Congress would thus erode the structure envisioned by the Framers, a structure that was designed, in the words of the Preamble to our Constitution, to form a "more perfect Union."

The judgment is affirmed.

O'Hare Truck Service, Inc. v.
City of Northlake
518 U.S. 712 (1996)

Government officials may not discharge public employees for refusing to support a political party or its candidates, unless political affiliation is a reasonably appropriate requirement for the job in question. We must decide whether the protections of *Elrod* and *Branti* extend to an independent contractor, who, in retaliation for refusing to comply with demands for political support, has a government contract terminated or is removed from an official list of contractors authorized to perform public services. . . .

The suit having been dismissed by the District Court for failure to state a claim, the complaint's factual allegations are taken as true. John Gratzianna is the owner and operator of O'Hare Truck Service, which provides towing services in Cook and DuPage Counties, Illinois. Gratzianna and his company are petitioners here, and we sometimes refer to them as O'Hare.

The city of Northlake, a respondent in this Court, coordinates towing services through its police department and for at least 30 years has maintained a rotation list of available towing companies. When the police receive a tow request, they call the company next on the list to provide the service. Until the events recounted here, the city's policy had been to remove a tow truck operator from the rotation list only for cause. O'Hare had been on the list since 1965, performing towing services at the city's request. O'Hare and the city's former Mayor, Gene Doyle, had a mutual understanding that the city would maintain O'Hare's place on the rotation list so long as O'Hare provided good service. In 1989, soon after being elected Northlake's new Mayor, respondent Reid Paxson told Gratzianna he was pleased with O'Hare's work and would continue using and referring its services.

Four years later, when Paxson ran for reelection, his campaign committee asked Gratzianna for a contribution, which Gratzianna refused to make. Gratzianna instead supported the campaign of Paxson's opponent and displayed the opponent's campaign posters at O'Hare's place of business. Soon after, O'Hare was removed from the rotation list. We shall assume, as the complaint alleges, that the removal was in retaliation for Gratzianna's stance in the campaign. Petitioners allege the retaliation caused them to lose substantial income.

O'Hare and Gratzianna sued in the United States District Court for the Northern District of Illinois, alleging infringement of First Amendment rights. . . . In conformity with binding Seventh Circuit precedent . . . the District Court dismissed the complaint. The Court of Appeals affirmed. . . .

. . .

There is no doubt that if Gratzianna had been a public employee whose job was to perform tow truck operations, the city could not have discharged him for refusing to contribute to Paxson's campaign or for supporting his opponent. . . .

. . . Had Paxson or his backers solicited the contribution as a quid pro quo for not terminating O'Hare's arrangement with the city, they might well have violated criminal bribery statutes. That Paxson may have steered clear of criminal liability, however, does little to diminish the attempted coercion of Gratzianna's political association, enforced by a tangible punishment. Our cases make clear that the government may not coerce support in this manner, unless it has some justification beyond dislike of the individual's political association.

. . . A rigid rule "giv[ing] the government carte blanche to terminate independent contractors for exercising First Amendment rights . . . would leave [those] rights unduly dependent on whether state law labels a government service provider's contract as a contract of employment or a contract for services, a distinction which is at best a very poor proxy for the interests at stake." . . .

. . .

The absolute right to enforce a patronage scheme, insisted upon by respondents as a means of retaining control over independent contractors and satisfying government officials' concerns about reliability, has not been shown to be a necessary part of a legitimate political system in all instances. This was the determination controlling our decisions in *Elrod* and *Branti*, and we see no basis for rejecting that reasoning in this context. We decline to draw a line excluding independent contractors from the First Amendment safeguards of political association afforded to employees.

. . .

The judgment of the Court of Appeals is reversed, and the case is remanded for further proceedings consistent with this opinion.

Cook v. Gralike
531 U.S. 510 (2001)

In *U.S. Term Limits, Inc. v. Thornton*, we reviewed a challenge to an Arkansas law that prohibited the name of an otherwise eligible candidate for the United States Congress from appearing on the general election ballot if he or she had already served three terms in the House of Representatives or two terms in the Senate. We held that the ballot restriction was an indirect attempt to impose term limits on congressional incumbents that violated the Qualifications Clauses in Article I of the Constitution rather than a permissible exercise of the State's power to regulate the "Times, Places and Manner of holding Elections for Senators and Representatives" within the meaning of Article I, §4, cl. 1.

In response to that decision, the voters of Missouri adopted in 1996 an amendment to Article VIII of their State Constitution designed to lead to the adoption of a specified "Congressional Term Limits Amendment" to the Federal Constitution. At issue in this case is the constitutionality of Article VIII.

Article VIII "instruct[s]" each Member of Missouri's congressional delegation "to use all of his or her delegated powers to pass the Congressional Term Limits Amendment" set forth in §16 of the Article. Mo. Const., Art. VIII, §17(1). That proposed amendment would limit service in the United States Congress to three terms in the House of Representatives and two terms in the Senate.

Three provisions in Article VIII combine to advance its purpose. Section 17 prescribes that the statement "DISREGARDED VOTERS' INSTRUCTION ON TERM LIMITS" be printed on all primary and general ballots adjacent to the name of a Senator or Representative who fails to take any one of eight legislative acts in support of the proposed amendment. Section 18 provides that the statement "DECLINED TO PLEDGE TO SUPPORT TERM LIMITS" be printed on all primary and general election ballots next to the name of every nonincumbent congressional candidate who refuses to take a "Term Limit" pledge that commits the candidate, if elected, to performing the legislative acts enumerated in §17. And §19 directs the Missouri Secretary of State to determine and declare, pursuant to §§17 and 18, whether either statement should be printed alongside the name of each candidate for Congress.

Respondent Don Gralike was a nonincumbent candidate for election in 1998 to the United States House of Representatives from Missouri's Third Congressional District. A month after Article VIII was amended, respondent brought suit in the United States District Court for the Western District of Missouri to enjoin petitioner, the Secretary of State of Missouri, from implementing the

Article, which the complaint alleges violates several provisions of the Federal Constitution.

The District Court decided the case on the pleadings, granting Gralike's motion for summary judgment. The court first held that Article VIII contravened the Qualifications Clauses of Article I of the Federal Constitution because it "has the sole purpose of creating additional qualifications for Congress indirectly and has the likely effect of handicapping a class of candidates for Congress." The court further held that Article VIII places an impermissible burden on the candidates' First Amendment right to speak freely on the issue of term limits by "punish[ing] candidates for speaking out against term limits" through putting "negative words next to their names on the ballot," and by "us[ing] the threat of being disadvantaged in the election to coerce candidates into taking a position on the term limits issue." Lastly, the court found Article VIII to be an indirect and unconstitutional attempt by the people of Missouri to interject themselves into the amending process authorized by Article V of the Federal Constitution. In doing so, the court endorsed the reasoning of other decisions invalidating provisions similar to Article VIII on the ground that negative ballot designations "place an undue influence on the legislator to vote in favor of term limits rather than exercise his or her own independent judgment as is contemplated by Article V." Accordingly, the court permanently enjoined petitioner from enforcing §§15 through 19 of Article VIII.

The United States Court of Appeals for the Eighth Circuit affirmed. . . .

. . .

Article VIII furthers the State's interest in adding a term limits amendment to the Federal Constitution in two ways. It encourages Missouri's congressional delegation to support such an amendment in order to avoid an unfavorable ballot designation when running for reelection. And it encourages the election of representatives who favor such an amendment. Petitioner argues that Article VIII is an exercise of the "right of the people to instruct" their representatives reserved by the Tenth Amendment, and that it is a permissible regulation of the "manner" of electing federal legislators within the authority delegated to the States by the Elections Clause, Art. I, §4, cl. 1. Because these two arguments rely on different sources of state power, it is appropriate at the outset to review the distinction in kind between powers reserved to the States and those delegated to the States by the Constitution.

. . .

The federal offices at stake "aris[e] from the Constitution itself." Because any state authority to regulate election to those offices could not precede their very creation by the Constitution, such power "had to be delegated to, rather than reserved by, the States." Through the Elections Clause, the Constitution delegated to the States the power to regulate the "Times, Places and Manner of holding Elections for Senators and Representatives," subject to a grant of authority to Congress to "make or alter such Regulations." No other constitutional provision gives the States authority over congressional elections, and no such authority could be reserved under the Tenth Amendment. By process of elimination, the States may regulate the incidents of such elections, including balloting, only within the exclusive delegation of power under the Elections Clause.

With respect to the Elections Clause, petitioner argues that Article VIII "merely regulates the manner in which elections are held by disclosing information about congressional candidates." As such, petitioner concludes, Article VIII is a valid exercise of Missouri's delegated power.

. . . To be sure, the Elections Clause grants to the States "broad power" to prescribe the procedural mechanisms for holding congressional elections. Nevertheless, Article VIII falls outside of that grant of authority. As we made clear in *U.S. Term Limits*, "the Framers understood the Elections Clause as a grant of authority to issue procedural regulations, and not as a source of power to dictate electoral outcomes, to favor or disfavor a class of candidates, or to evade important constitutional restraints." Article VIII is not a procedural regulation. It does not regulate the time of elections; it does not regulate the place of elections; nor, we believe, does it regulate the manner of elections. As to the last point, Article VIII bears no relation to the "manner" of elections as we understand it, for in our commonsense view that term encompasses matters like "notices, registration, supervision of voting, protection of voters, prevention of fraud and corrupt practices, counting of votes, duties of inspectors and canvassers, and making and publication of election returns." In short, Article VIII is not among "the numerous requirements as to procedure and safeguards which experience shows are necessary in order to enforce the fundamental right involved," ensuring that elections are "fair and honest," and that "some sort of order, rather than chaos, is to accompany the democratic process."

Rather, Article VIII is plainly designed to favor candidates who are willing to support the particular form of a term limits amendment set forth in its text and to disfavor those who either oppose term limits entirely or would prefer a different proposal. As noted, the state provision does not just "instruct" each member of Missouri's congressional delegation to promote in certain ways the passage of the specified term limits amendment. It also attaches a concrete consequence to noncompliance—the printing of the statement "DISREGARDED VOTERS' IN-STRUCTIONS ON TERM LIMITS" by the candidate's name on all primary and general election ballots. Likewise, a nonincumbent candidate who does not pledge to follow the instruction receives the ballot designation "DECLINED TO PLEDGE TO SUPPORT TERM LIMITS."

In describing the two labels, the courts below have employed terms such as "pejorative," "negative," "derogatory," "intentionally intimidating," "particularly harmful," "politically damaging," "a serious sanction," "a penalty," and "official denunciation." The general counsel to petitioner's office, no less, has denominated the labels as "the Scarlet Letter." We agree with the sense of these descriptions. They convey the substantial political risk the ballot labels impose on current and prospective congressional members who, for one reason or another, fail to comply with the conditions set forth in Article VIII for passing its term limits amendment. Although petitioner now claims that the labels "merely" inform Missouri voters about a candidate's compliance with Article VIII, she has acknowledged under oath that the ballot designations would handicap candidates for the United States Congress. To us, that is exactly the intended effect of Article VIII.

Indeed, it seems clear that the adverse labels handicap candidates "at the most crucial stage in the election process–the instant before the vote is cast." At the same time, "by directing the citizen's attention to the single consideration" of the candidates' fidelity to term limits, the labels imply that the issue "is an important–perhaps paramount–consideration in the citizen's choice, which may decisively influence the citizen to cast his ballot" against candidates branded as unfaithful. While the precise damage the labels may exact on candidates is disputed between the parties, the labels surely place their targets at a political

disadvantage to unmarked candidates for congressional office. Thus, far from regulating the procedural mechanisms of elections, Article VIII attempts to "dictate electoral outcomes." Such "regulation" of congressional elections simply is not authorized by the Elections Clause.

Accordingly, the judgment of the Court of Appeals is affirmed.

Hunt v. Cromartie
532 U.S. 234 (2001)

. . .

This racial districting litigation is before us for the fourth time. Our first two holdings addressed North Carolina's *former* Congressional District 12, one of two North Carolina congressional districts drawn in 1992 that contained a majority of African-American voters.

. . .

The issue in this case is evidentiary. We must determine whether there is adequate support for the District Courts key findings, particularly the ultimate finding that the legislatures motive was predominantly racial, not political. . . .

. . .

. . . The basic question is whether the legislature drew District 12s boundaries because of race *rather than* because of political behavior (coupled with traditional, nonracial districting considerations). It is not, as the dissent contends, whether a legislature may defend its districting decisions based on a stereotype about African-American voting behavior. And given the fact that the party attacking the legislatures decision bears the burden of proving that racial considerations are dominant and controlling . . . and given the sensitivity, the extraordinary caution, that district courts must show to avoid treading upon legislative prerogatives, the attacking party has not successfully shown that race, rather than politics, predominantly accounts for the result. . . .

. . . In a case such as this one where majority-minority districts (or the approximate equivalent) are at issue and where racial identification correlates highly with political affiliation, the party attacking the legislatively drawn boundaries must show at the least that the legislature could have achieved its legitimate political objectives in alternative ways that are comparably consistent with traditional districting principles. That party must also show that those districting alternatives would have brought about significantly greater racial balance. Appellees failed to make any such showing here. We conclude that the District Courts contrary findings are clearly erroneous. . . .

The judgment of the District Court is reversed.

Federal Election Commission v. Colorado Republican Federal Campaign Committee
533 U.S. ___ (2001)

In *Colorado Republican Federal Campaign Comm. v. Federal Election Commn, (Colorado I)*, we held that spending limits set by the Federal Election Campaign Act were unconstitutional as applied to the Colorado Republican Party's independent expenditures in connection with a senatorial campaign. . . .

. . .

The Party's broader claim remained: that although prior decisions of this Court had upheld the constitutionality of limits on coordinated expenditures by political speakers other than parties, the congressional campaign expenditure limitations on parties themselves are facially unconstitutional, and so are incapable of reaching

party spending even when coordinated with a candidate. We remanded that facial challenge. . . . On remand the District Court held for the Party and a divided panel of the Court of Appeals for the Tenth Circuit affirmed. . . .

. . .

The First Amendment line between spending and donating is easy to draw when it falls between independent expenditures by individuals or political action committees (PACs) without any candidates approval (or wink or nod), and contributions in the form of cash gifts to candidates. But facts speak less clearly once the independence of the spending cannot be taken for granted, and money spent by an individual or PAC according to an arrangement with a candidate is therefore harder to classify. As already seen, Congress drew a functional, not a formal, line between contributions and expenditures when it provided that coordinated expenditures by individuals and non-party groups are subject to the Acts contribution limits. . . .

. . .

But that still left the question whether the First Amendment allows coordinated election expenditures by parties to be treated functionally as contributions, the way coordinated expenditures by other entities are treated. *Colorado I* found no justification for placing parties at a disadvantage when spending independently; but was there a case for leaving them entirely free to coordinate unlimited spending with candidates when others could not? . . . Coordinated spending by a party. . . covers a spectrum of activity, as does coordinated spending by other political actors. The issue in this case is, accordingly, whether a party is otherwise in a different position from other political speakers, giving it a claim to demand a generally higher standard of scrutiny before its coordinated spending can be limited. The issue is posed by two questions: does limiting coordinated spending impose a unique burden on parties, and is there reason to think that coordinated spending by a party would raise the risk of corruption posed when others spend in coordination with a candidate? The issue is best viewed through the positions developed by the Party and the Government in this case.

. . .

. . . Our evaluation of the arguments . . . leads us to reject the Party's claim to suffer a burden unique in any way that should make a categorical difference under the First Amendment. On the other side, the Government's contentions are ultimately borne out by evidence, entitling it to prevail in its characterization of party coordinated spending as the functional equivalent of contributions.

. . .

The assertion that the party is so joined at the hip to candidates that most of its spending must necessarily be coordinated spending is a statement at odds with the history of nearly 30 years under the Act. It is well to remember that ever since the Act was amended in 1974, coordinated spending by a party committee in a given race has been limited by the provision challenged here (or its predecessor). It was not until 1996 and the decision in *Colorado I* that any spending was allowed above that amount, and since then only independent spending has been unlimited. As a consequence, the Party's claim that coordinated spending beyond the limit imposed by the Act is essential to its very function as a party amounts implicitly to saying that for almost three decades political parties have not been functional or have been functioning in systematic violation of the law. The Party, of course, does not in terms make either statement, and we cannot accept either implication. There is no question about the closeness of candidates to parties and no doubt that

the Act affected parties roles and their exercise of power. . . . There is little evidence to suggest that coordinated party spending limits adopted by Congress have frustrated the ability of political parties to exercise their First Amendment rights to support their candidates, and that [i]n reality, political parties are dominant players, second only to the candidates themselves, in federal elections. For the Party to claim after all these years of strictly limited coordinated spending that unlimited coordinated spending is essential to the nature and functioning of parties is in reality to assert just that metaphysical identity between freespending party and candidate that we could not accept in *Colorado I*.

. . . The fault here is not so much metaphysics as myopia, a refusal to see how the power of money actually works in the political structure.

When we look directly at a party's function in getting and spending money, it would ignore reality to think that the party role is adequately described by speaking generally of electing particular candidates. The money parties spend comes from contributors with their own personal interests. PACs, for example, are frequent party contributors who . . . do not pursue the same objectives in electoral politics, that parties do. PACs are most concerned with advancing their narrow interest[s] and therefore provide support to candidates who share their views, regardless of party affiliation. . . . Parties are thus necessarily the instruments of some contributors whose object is not to support the party's message or to elect party candidates across the board, but rather to support a specific candidate for the sake of a position on one, narrow issue, or even to support any candidate who will be obliged to the contributors.

Parties thus perform functions more complex than simply electing candidates; whether they like it or not, they act as agents for spending on behalf of those who seek to produce obligated officeholders. It is this party role, which functionally unites parties with other self-interested political actors, that the Party Expenditure Provision targets. This party role, accordingly, provides good reason to view limits on coordinated spending by parties through the same lens applied to such spending by donors, like PACs, that can use parties as conduits for contributions meant to place candidates under obligation.

Insofar as the Party suggests that its strong working relationship with candidates and its unique ability to speak in coordination with them should be taken into account in the First Amendment analysis, we agree. It is the accepted understanding that a party combines its members power to speak by aggregating contributions and broadcasting messages more widely than individual contributors generally could afford to do, and the party marshals this power with greater sophistication than individuals generally could, using such mechanisms as speech coordinated with a candidate. In other words, the party is efficient in generating large sums to spend and in pinpointing effective ways to spend them.

. . . [W]hat the Party calls an unusual burden imposed by regulating its spending is not a simple premise for arguing for tighter scrutiny of limits on a party; it is the premise for a question pointing in the opposite direction. If the coordinated spending of other, less efficient and perhaps less practiced political actors can be limited consistently with the Constitution, why would the Constitution forbid regulation aimed at a party whose very efficiency in channeling benefits to candidates threatens to undermine the contribution (and hence coordinated spending) limits to which those others are unquestionably subject?

. . .

A party is not . . . in a unique position. It is in the same position as some individuals and PACs, as to whom coordinated spending limits have already been held valid, and, indeed, a party is better off, for a party has the special privilege the others do not enjoy, of making coordinated expenditures up to the limit of the Party Expenditure Provision.

. . . Despite decades of limitation on coordinated spending, parties have not been rendered useless. In reality, parties continue to organize to elect candidates, and also function for the benefit of donors whose object is to place candidates under obligation, a fact that parties cannot escape. Indeed, parties capacity to concentrate power to elect is the very capacity that apparently opens them to exploitation as channels for circumventing contribution and coordinated spending limits binding on other political players. And some of these players could marshal the same power and sophistication for the same electoral objectives as political parties themselves.

We accordingly apply to a party's coordinated spending limitation the same scrutiny we have applied to the other political actors, that is, scrutiny appropriate for a contribution limit, enquiring whether the restriction is closely drawn to match what we have recognized as the sufficiently important government interest in combating political corruption. . . .

. . . Despite years of enforcement of the challenged limits, substantial evidence demonstrates how candidates, donors, and parties test the limits of the current law, and it shows beyond serious doubt how contribution limits would be eroded if inducement to circumvent them were enhanced by declaring parties coordinated spending wide open.

. . . Donors give to the party with the tacit understanding that the favored candidate will benefit.

. . .

. . . If suddenly every dollar of spending could be coordinated with the candidate, the inducement to circumvent would almost certainly intensify. Indeed, if a candidate could be assured that donations through a party could result in funds passed through to him for spending on virtually identical items as his own campaign funds, a candidate enjoying the patronage of affluent contributors would have a strong incentive not merely to direct donors to his party, but to promote circumvention as a step toward reducing the number of donors requiring time-consuming cultivation. . . .

. . .

. . . There is no significant functional difference between a party's coordinated expenditure and a direct party contribution to the candidate, and there is good reason to expect that a party's right of unlimited coordinated spending would attract increased contributions to parties to finance exactly that kind of spending. Coordinated expenditures of money donated to a party are tailor-made to undermine contribution limits. Therefore the choice here is not, as in *Buckley* and *Colorado I*, between a limit on pure contributions and pure expenditures. The choice is between limiting contributions and limiting expenditures whose special value as expenditures is also the source of their power to corrupt. Congress is entitled to its choice.

We hold that a party's coordinated expenditures, unlike expenditures truly independent, may be restricted to minimize circumvention of contribution limits. We therefore reject the Party's facial challenge and, accordingly, reverse the judgment of the United States Court of Appeals for the Tenth Circuit.

Appendix A

The Constitution of the United States of America

Preamble

We the People of the United States, in Order to form a more perfect Union, establish Justice, insure domestic Tranquillity, provide for the common defence, promote the general Welfare, and secure the Blessings of Liberty to ourselves and our Posterity, do ordain and establish this Constitution for the United States of America.

Article I

Section 1

All legislative Powers herein granted shall be vested in a Congress of the United States, which shall consist of a Senate and House of Representatives.

Section 2

The House of Representatives shall be composed of Members chosen every second Year by the People of the several States, and the Electors in each State shall have the Qualifications requisite for Electors of the most numerous Branch of the State Legislature.

No Person shall be a Representative who shall not have attained to the age of twenty five Years, and been seven Years a Citizen of the United States, and who shall not, when elected, be an Inhabitant of that State in which he shall be chosen.

Representatives and direct Taxes shall be apportioned among the several States which may be included within this Union, according to their respective Numbers, which shall be determined by adding to the whole Number of free Persons, including those bound to Service for a Term of Years, and excluding Indians not taxed, three fifths of all other Persons. The actual Enumeration shall be made within three Years after the first Meeting of the Congress of the United States, and within every subsequent Term of ten Years, in such Manner as they shall by Law direct. The Number of Representatives shall not exceed one for every thirty Thousand, but each State shall have at Least one Representative; and until such enumeration shall be made, the State of New Hampshire shall be entitled to chuse three, Massachusetts eight, Rhode-Island and Providence Plantations one, Connecticut five, New-York six, New Jersey four, Pennsylvania eight, Delaware one, Maryland six, Virginia ten, North Carolina five, South Carolina five, and Georgia three.

When vacancies happen in the Representation from any State, the Executive Authority thereof shall issue Writs of Election to fill such Vacancies.

The House of Representatives shall chuse their

Speaker and other Officers; and shall have the sole Power of Impeachment.

Section 3

The Senate of the United States shall be composed of two Senators from each State, chosen by the Legislature thereof, for six Years; and each Senator shall have one Vote.

Immediately after they shall be assembled in Consequence of the first Election, they shall be divided as equally as may be into three Classes. The Seats of the Senators of the first Class shall be vacated at the Expiration of the second Year, of the second Class at the Expiration of the fourth Year, and of the third Class at the Expiration of the sixth Year, so that one third may be chosen every second Year; and if Vacancies happen by Resignation, or otherwise, during the Recess of the Legislature of any State, the Executive thereof may make temporary Appointments until the next Meeting of the Legislature, which shall then fill such Vacancies.

No Person shall be a Senator who shall not have attained to the Age of thirty Years, and been nine Years a Citizen of the United States, and who shall not, when elected, be an Inhabitant of that State for which he shall be chosen.

The Vice President of the United States shall be President of the Senate but shall have no Vote, unless they be equally divided.

The Senate shall chuse their other Officers, and also a President pro tempore, in the Absence of the Vice President, or when he shall exercise the Office of President of the United States.

The Senate shall have the sole Power to try all Impeachments. When sitting for that Purpose, they shall be on Oath or Affirmation. When the President of the United States is tried the Chief Justice shall preside: And no Person shall be convicted without the Concurrence of two thirds of the Members present.

Judgment in Cases of Impeachment shall not extend further than to removal from Office, and disqualification to hold and enjoy any Office of honor, Trust or Profit under the United States: but the Party convicted shall nevertheless be liable and subject to Indictment, Trial, Judgment and Punishment, according to Law.

Section 4

The Times, Places and Manner of holding Elections for Senators and Representatives, shall be prescribed in each State by the Legislature thereof; but the Congress may at any time by Law make or alter such Regulations, except as to the Places of chusing Senators.

The Congress shall assemble at least once in every Year, and such Meeting shall be on the first Monday in December, unless they shall by Law appoint a different Day.

Section 5

Each House shall be the Judge of the Elections, Returns and Qualifications of its own Members, and a Majority of each shall constitute a Quorum to do Business; but a smaller Number may adjourn from day to day, and may be authorized to compel the Attendance of absent Members, in such Manner, and under such Penalties as each House may provide.

Each House may determine the Rules of its Proceedings, punish its Members for disorderly Behaviour, and, with the Concurrence of two thirds, expel a Member.

Each House shall keep a Journal of its Proceedings, and from time to time publish the same, excepting such Parts as may in their Judgment require Secrecy; and the Yeas and Nays of the Members of either House on any question shall, at the Desire of one fifth of those Present, be entered on the Journal.

Neither House, during the Session of Congress, shall, without the Consent of the other, adjourn for more than three days, nor to any other Place than that in which the two Houses shall be sitting.

Section 6

The Senators and Representatives shall receive a Compensation for their Services, to be ascertained by Law, and paid out of the Treasury of the United States. They shall in all Cases, except Treason, Felony and Breach of the Peace, be privileged from Arrest during their Attendance at the Session of their respective Houses, and in going to and returning from the same; and for any Speech or Debate in either House, they shall not be questioned in any other Place.

No Senator or Representative shall, during the Time for which he was elected, be appointed to any civil Office under the Authority of the United States, which shall have been created, or the Emoluments whereof shall have been encreased during such time; and no Person holding any Office under the United States, shall be a Member of either House during his Continuance in Office.

Section 7

All Bills for raising Revenue shall originate in the House of Representatives; but the Senate may propose or concur with amendments as on other Bills.

Every Bill which shall have passed the House of Representatives and the Senate, shall, before it become a law, be presented to the President of the United States: If he approve he shall sign it, but if not he shall return it, with his Objections to that House in which it shall have originated, who shall enter the Objections at large on their Journal, and proceed to reconsider it. If after such Reconsideration two thirds of that House shall agree to pass the Bill, it shall be sent, together with the Objections, to the other House, by which it shall likewise be reconsidered, and if approved by two thirds of that House, it shall become a Law. But in all such Cases the Votes of both Houses shall be determined by Yeas and Nays, and the Names of the Persons voting for and against the Bill shall be entered on the Journal of each House respectively. If any Bill shall not be returned by the President within ten Days (Sundays excepted) after it shall have been presented to him, the Same shall be a Law, in like Manner as if he had signed it, unless the Congress by their Adjournment prevent its Return, in which Case it shall not be a Law.

Every Order, Resolution, or Vote to which the Concurrence of the Senate and House of Representatives may be necessary (except on a question of Adjournment) shall be presented to the President of the United States; and before the Same shall take Effect, shall be approved by him, or being disapproved by him, shall be repassed by two thirds of the Senate and House of Representatives, according to the Rules and Limitations prescribed in the Case of a Bill.

Section 8

The Congress shall have Power To lay and collect Taxes, Duties, Imposts and Excises, to pay the Debts and provide for the common Defence and general Welfare of the United States; but all Duties, Imposts and Excises shall be uniform throughout the United States;

To borrow Money on the credit of the United States;

To regulate Commerce with foreign Nations, and among the several States, and with the Indian Tribes;

To establish an uniform Rule of Naturalization, and uniform Laws on the subject of Bankruptcies throughout the United States;

To coin Money, regulate the Value thereof, and of foreign Coin, and fix the Standard of Weights and Measures;

To provide for the Punishment of counterfeiting the Securities and current Coin of the United States;

To establish Post Offices and post Roads;

To promote the Progress of Science and useful Arts, by securing for limited Times to Authors and Inventors the exclusive Right to their respective Writings and Discoveries;

To constitute Tribunals inferior to the supreme Court;

To define and punish Piracies and Felonies committed on the high Seas, and Offences against the Law of Nations;

To declare War, grant Letters of Marque and Reprisal, and make Rules concerning Captures on Land and Water;

To raise and support Armies, but no Appropriation of Money to that Use shall be for a longer Term than two Years;

To provide and maintain a Navy;

To make Rules for the Government and Regulation of the land and naval Forces;

To provide for calling forth the Militia to execute the Laws of the Union, suppress Insurrections and repeal Invasions;

To provide for organizing, arming, and disciplining, the Militia, and for governing such Part of them as may be employed in the Service of the United States, reserving to the States respectively, the Appointment of the Officers, and the Authority of training the Militia according to the discipline prescribed by Congress;

To exercise exclusive Legislation in all Cases whatsoever, over such District (not exceeding ten Miles square) as may, by Cession of Particular States, and the Acceptance of Congress, become the Seat of the Government of the United States, and to exercise like Authority over all Places purchased by the Consent of the Legislature of the State in which the Same shall be, for the Erection of Forts, Magazines, Arsenals, dock-Yards and other needful Buildings; And

To make all Laws which shall be necessary and

proper for carrying into Execution the foregoing Powers and all other Powers vested by this Constitution in the Government of the United States, or in any Department or Officer thereof.

Section 9

The Migration or Importation of such Persons as any of the States now existing shall think proper to admit, shall not be prohibited by the Congress prior to the Year one thousand eight hundred and eight, but a Tax or duty may be imposed on such Importation, not exceeding ten dollars for each Person.

The Privilege of the Writ of Habeas Corpus shall not be suspended, unless when in Cases or Rebellion or Invasion the public Safety may require it.

No Bill of Attainder or ex post facto Law shall be passed.

No Capitation, or other direct, Tax shall be laid, unless in Proportion to the Census of Enumeration herein before directed to be taken.

No Tax or Duty shall be laid on Articles exported from any State.

No Preference shall be given by any Regulation of Commerce or Revenue to the Ports of one State over those of another: nor shall Vessels bound to, or from, one State, be obliged to enter, clear or pay Duties in another.

No Money shall be drawn from the Treasury, but in Consequence of Appropriations made by Law; and a regular Statement and Account of the Receipts and Expenditures of all public Money shall be published from time to time.

No Title of Nobility shall be granted by the United States: And no Person holding any Office of Profit or Trust under them, shall, without the Consent of the Congress, accept of any present, Emolument, Office, or Title, of any kind whatever, from any King, Prince or foreign State.

Section 10

No State shall enter into any Treaty, Alliance, or Confederation; grant Letters of Marque and Reprisal; coin Money; emit Bills of Credit; make any Thing but gold and silver Coin a Tender in Payment of Debts; pass any Bill of Attainder, ex post facto Law, or Law impairing the Obligation of Contracts, or grant any Title of Nobility.

No State shall, without the Consent of the Congress, lay any Imposts or Duties on Imports or Exports, except what may be absolutely necessary for executing it's inspection Laws: and the net Produce of all Duties and Imposts, laid by any State on Imports or Exports, shall be for the Use of the Treasury of the United States; and all such Laws shall be subject to the Revision and Controul of the Congress.

No State shall, without the Consent of Congress, lay any Duty of Tonnage, keep Troops, or Ships of War in time of Peace, enter into any Agreement or Compact with another State, or with a foreign Power, or engage in War, unless actually invaded, or in such imminent Danger as will not admit of delay.

Article II

Section 1

The executive Power shall be vested in a President of the United States of America. He shall hold his Office during the Term of four Years, and, together with the Vice President, chosen for the same Term, be elected, as follows:

Each State shall appoint, in such Manner as the Legislature thereof may direct, a Number of Electors, equal to the whole Number of Senators and Representatives to which the State may be entitled in the Congress: but no Senator or Representative, or Person holding an Office of Trust or Profit under the United States, shall be appointed an Elector.

The Electors shall meet in their respective States, and vote by Ballot for two Persons, of whom one at least shall not be an Inhabitant of the same State with themselves. And they shall make a List of all the Persons voted for, and of the Number of Votes for each; which List they shall sign and certify, and transmit sealed to the Seat of the Government of the United States, directed to the President of the Senate. The President of the Senate shall, in the Presence of the Senate and House of Representatives, open all the Certificates, and the Votes shall then be counted. The Person having the greatest Number of Votes shall be the President, if such Number be a Majority of the whole Number of Electors appointed; and if there be more than one who have such Majority, and have an equal Number of Votes, then the House of Representatives shall immediately chuse by Ballot one of them for President; and if no Person have a Majority, then from the five highest on the List the said House shall in like Manner chuse the President. But in chusing the President, the Votes shall be taken by States, the Representatives from each State having one Vote; a quorum for this Purpose shall consist of a Member or Members from two thirds of the States, and a Majority of all the States shall be necessary to a

Choice. In every Case, after the Choice of the President, the Person having the greatest Number of Votes of the Electors shall be the Vice President. But if there should remain two or more who have equal Votes, the Senate shall chuse from them by Ballot the Vice President.

The Congress may determine the Time of chusing the Electors, and the Day on which they shall give their Votes; which Day shall be the same throughout the United States.

No Person except a natural born Citizen, or a Citizen of the United States, at the time of the Adoption of this Constitution, shall be eligible to the Office of President; neither shall any person be eligible to that Office who shall not have attained to the Age of thirty five Years, and been fourteen Years a Resident within the United States.

In Case of the Removal of the President from Office, or of his Death, Resignation, or Inability to discharge the Powers and Duties of the said Office, the Same shall devolve on the Vice President, and the Congress may by Law provide for the Case of Removal, Death, Resignation or Inability, both of the President and Vice President, declaring what Officer shall then act as President, and such Officer shall act accordingly, until the Disability be removed, or a President shall be elected.

The President shall, at stated Times, receive for his Services, a Compensation, which shall neither be encreased nor diminished during the Period for which he shall have been elected, and he shall not receive within that Period any other Emolument from the United States, or any of them.

Before he enter on the Execution of his Office, he shall take the following Oath or Affirmation:—"I do solemnly swear (or affirm) that I will faithfully execute the Office of President of the United States, and will to the best of my Ability, preserve, protect and defend the Constitution of the United States."

Section 2

The President shall be Commander in Chief of the Army and Navy of the United States, and of the Militia of the several States, when called into the actual Service of the United States; he may require the Opinion, in writing, of the principal Officer in each of the executive Departments, upon any Subject relating to the Duties of their respective Offices, and he shall have Power to Grant Reprieves and Pardons for Offences against the United States, except in Cases of Impeachment.

He shall have Power, by and with the Advice and Consent of the Senate, to make Treaties, provided two thirds of the Senators present concur; and he shall nominate, and by and with the Advice and Consent of the Senate, shall appoint Ambassadors, other public Ministers and Consuls, Judges of the supreme Court, and all other Officers of the United States, whose Appointments are not herein otherwise provided for, and which shall be established by Law: but the Congress may by Law vest the Appointment of such inferior Officers, as they think proper, in the President alone, in the Courts of Law, or in the Heads of Departments.

The President shall have Power to fill up all Vacancies that may happen during the Recess of the Senate, by granting Commissions which shall expire at the End of their next Session.

Section 3

He shall from time to time give to the Congress Information on the State of the Union, and recommend to their Consideration such Measures as he shall judge necessary and expedient; he may, on extraordinary Occasions, convene both Houses, or either of them, and in Case of Disagreement between them, with Respect to the Time of Adjournment, he may adjourn them to such Time as he shall think proper; he shall receive Ambassadors and other public Ministers; he shall take Care that the Laws be faithfully executed, and shall Commission all the Officers of the United States.

Section 4

The President, Vice President and all Civil Officers of the United States, shall be removed from Office on Impeachment for and Conviction of, Treason, Bribery, or other high Crimes and Misdemeanors.

Article III

Section 1

The judicial Power of the United States, shall be vested in one supreme Court, and in such inferior Courts as the Congress may from time to time ordain and establish. The Judges, both of the supreme and inferior Courts, shall hold their Offices during good Behaviour, and shall, at stated Times, receive for their Services, a Compensation, which shall not be diminished during their Continuance in Office.

Section 2

The judicial Power shall extend to all Cases, in Law and Equity, arising under this Constitution, the Laws of the United States, and Treaties made, or which shall be made, under their Authority; to all Cases affecting Ambassadors, other public ministers and Consuls; to all Cases of admiralty and maritime Jurisdiction; to Controversies to which the United States shall be a Party; to Controversies between two or more States; between a State and Citizens of another State; between Citizens of different States; between Citizens of the same State claiming Lands under Grants of different States, and between a State, or the Citizens thereof, and foreign States, Citizens or Subjects.

In all Cases affecting Ambassadors, other public Ministers and Consuls, and those in which a State shall be Party, the supreme Court shall have original Jurisdiction. In all the other Cases before mentioned, the supreme Court shall have appellate Jurisdiction, both as to Law and Fact, with such Exceptions, and under such Regulations as the Congress shall make.

The Trial of all Crimes, except in Cases of Impeachment, shall be by Jury; and such Trial shall be held in the State where the said Crimes shall have been committed; but when not committed within any State, the Trial shall be at such Place or Places as the Congress may by Law have directed.

Section 3

Treason against the United States, shall consist only in levying War against them, or in adhering to their Enemies, giving them Aid and Comfort. No Person shall be convicted of Treason unless on the Testimony of two Witnesses to the same overt Act, or on Confession in open Court.

The Congress shall have Power to declare the Punishment of Treason, but no Attainder of Trea-

son shall work Corruption of Blood, or Forfeiture except during the Life of the Person attainted.

Article IV

Section 1

Full Faith and Credit shall be given in each State to the public Acts, Records, and judicial Proceedings of every other State. And the Congress may by general Laws prescribe the Manner in which such Acts, Records and Proceedings shall be proved, and the Effect thereof.

Section 2

The Citizens of each State shall be entitled to all Privileges and Immunities of Citizens in the several States.

A Person charged in any State with Treason, Felony, or other Crime, who shall flee from Justice, and be found in another State, shall on Demand of the executive Authority of the State from which he fled, be delivered up, to be removed to the State having Jurisdiction of the Crime.

No Person held to Service or Labour in one State, under the Laws thereof, escaping into another, shall, in Consequence of any Law or Regulation therein, be discharged from such Service or Labour, but shall be delivered up on Claim of the Party to whom such Service or Labour may be due.

Section 3

New States may be admitted by the Congress into this Union; but no new State shall be formed or erected within the Jurisdiction of any other State; nor any State be formed by the Junction of two or more States, or Parts of States, without the Consent of the Legislatures of the States concerned as well as of the Congress.

The Congress shall have Power to dispose of and make all needful Rules and Regulations respecting the Territory or other Property belonging to the United States; and nothing in this Constitution shall be so construed as to Prejudice any Claims of the United States, or of any particular State.

Section 4

The United States shall guarantee to every State in this Union a Republican Form of Government, and shall protect each of them against Invasion; and on Application of the Legislature, or of the Executive (when the Legislature cannot be convened) against domestic Violence.

Article V

The Congress, whenever two thirds of both Houses shall deem it necessary, shall propose Amendments to this Constitution, or, on the Application of the Legislatures of two thirds of the several States, shall call a Convention for proposing Amendments, which, in either Case, shall be valid to all Intents and Purposes, as Part of this Constitution, when ratified by the Legislatures of three fourths of the several States, or by Conventions in three fourths thereof, as the one or the other Mode of Ratification may be proposed by the Congress; Provided that no Amendment which may be made prior to the Year One thousand eight hundred and eight shall in any Manner affect the first and fourth Clauses in the Ninth Section of the first Article; and that no State, without its Consent, shall be deprived of its equal Suffrage in the Senate.

Article VI

All Debts contracted and Engagements entered into, before the Adoption of this Constitution, shall be as valid against the United States under this Constitution, as under the Confederation.

This Constitution, and the Laws of the United States which shall be made in Pursuance thereof; and all Treaties made, or which shall be made, under the Authority of the United States, shall be the supreme Law of the Land; and the Judges in every State shall be bound thereby, any Thing in the Constitution or Laws of any state to the Contrary notwithstanding.

The Senators and Representatives before mentioned, and the Members of the several State Legislatures, and all executive and judicial Officers, both of the United States and of the several States, shall be bound by Oath or Affirmation, to support this Constitution; but no religious Test shall ever be required as a Qualification to any Office or public Trust under the United States.

Article VII

The Ratification of the Conventions of nine States, shall be sufficient for the Establishment of this Constitution between the States so ratifying the same.

Amendment I

Congress shall make no law respecting an establishment of religion, or prohibiting the free exercise thereof; or abridging the freedom of speech, or of the press; or the right of the people peaceably to assemble, and to petition the Government for a redress of grievances.

Amendment II

A well regulated Militia, being necessary to the security of a free State, the right of the people to keep and bear Arms, shall not be infringed.

Amendment III

No Soldier shall, in time of peace be quartered in any house, without the consent of the Owner, nor in time of war, but in a manner to be prescribed by law.

Amendment IV

The right of the people to be secure in their persons, houses, papers, and effects, against unreasonable searches and seizures, shall not be violated, and no Warrants shall issue, but upon probable cause, supported by Oath or affirmation, and particularly describing the place to be searched, and the persons or things to be seized.

Amendment V

No person shall be held to answer for a capital, or otherwise infamous crime, unless on a presentment or indictment of a Grand Jury, except in cases arising in the land or naval forces, or in the Militia, when in actual service in time of War or public danger; nor shall any person be subject for the same offence to be twice put in jeopardy of life or limb; nor shall be compelled in any criminal case to be a witness against himself, nor be deprived of life, liberty, or property, without due process of law; nor shall private property be taken for public use, without just compensation.

Amendment VI

In all criminal prosecutions, the accused shall enjoy the right to a speedy and public trial, by an impartial jury of the State and district wherein the crime shall have been committed, which district shall have been previously ascertained by law, and to be informed of the nature and cause of the accusation; to be confronted with the witnesses against him; to have compulsory process for obtaining witnesses in his favor, and to have the Assistance of Counsel for his defence.

Amendment VII

In Suits at common law, where the value in controversy shall exceed twenty dollars, the right of trial by jury shall be preserved, and no fact tried by a jury, shall be otherwise re-examined in any Court of the United States, than according to the rules of the common law.

Amendment VIII

Excessive bail shall not be required, nor excessive fines imposed, nor cruel and unusual punishments inflicted.

Amendment IX

The enumeration in the Constitution, of certain rights, shall not be construed to deny or disparage others retained by the people.

Amendment X

The powers not delegated to the United States by the Constitution, nor prohibited by it to the States, are reserved to the States respectively, or to the people.

Amendment XI

The Judicial power of the United States shall not be construed to extend to any suit in law or equity, commenced or prosecuted against one on the United States by Citizens of another State, or by Citizens or Subjects of any Foreign State.

Amendment XII

The Electors shall meet in their respective states and vote by ballot for President and Vice-President, one of whom, at least, shall not be an inhabitant of the same state with themselves; they shall name in their ballots the person voted for as President, and in distinct ballots the person voted for as Vice-President, and they shall make distinct lists of all persons voted for as President, and of all persons voted for as Vice-President, and of the number of votes for each, which lists they shall sign and certify, and transmit sealed to the seat of the government of the United States, directed to the President of the Senate;—The President of the Senate shall, in the presence of the Senate and House of Representatives, open all the certificates and the votes shall then be counted;—The person having the greatest Number of votes for President, shall be the President, if such number be a majority of the whole number of Electors appointed; and if no person have such majority, then from the persons having the highest numbers not exceeding three on the list of those voted for as President, the House of Representatives shall choose immediately, by ballot, the President. But in choosing the President, the votes shall be taken by states, the representation from each state having one vote; a quorum for this purpose shall consist of a member or members from two-thirds of the states, and a majority of all the states shall be necessary to a choice. And if the House of Representatives shall not choose a President whenever the right of choice shall devolve upon them, before the fourth day of March next following, then the Vice- President shall act as President, as in the case of the death or other constitutional disability of the President—The person having the greatest number of votes as Vice-President, shall be the Vice-President, if such number be a majority of the whole number of Electors appointed, and if no person have a majority, then from the two highest numbers on the list, the Senate shall choose the Vice-President; a quorum for the purpose shall consist of two-thirds of the whole number of Senators, and a majority of the whole number shall be necessary to a choice. But no person constitutionally ineligible to the office of President shall be eligible to that of Vice-President of the United States.

Amendment XIII

Section 1

Neither slavery nor involuntary servitude, except as a punishment for crime whereof the party shall have been duly convicted, shall exist within the United States, or any place subject to their jurisdiction.

Section 2

Congress shall have power to enforce this article by appropriate legislation.

Amendment XIV

Section 1

All persons born or naturalized in the United States and subject to the jurisdiction thereof, are citizens of the United States and of the State wherein they reside. No State shall make or enforce any law which shall abridge the privileges or immunities of citizens of the United States;

nor shall any State deprive any person of life, liberty, or property, without due process of law; nor deny to any person within its jurisdiction the equal protection of the laws.

Section 2

Representatives shall be apportioned among the several States according to their respective numbers, counting the whole number of persons in each State, excluding Indians not taxed. But when the right to vote at any election for the choice of electors for President and Vice President of the United States, Representatives in Congress, the Executive and Judicial officers of a State, or the members of the Legislature thereof, is denied to any of the male inhabitants of such State, being twenty-one years of age, and citizens of the United States, or in any way abridged, except for participation in rebellion, or other crime, the basis of representation therein shall be reduced in the proportion which the number of such male citizens shall bear to the whole number of male citizens twenty-one years of age in such State.

Section 3

No person shall be a Senator or Representative in Congress, or elector of President and Vice President, or hold any office, civil or military, under the United States, or under any State, who, having previously taken an oath, as a member of Congress, or as an officer of the United States, or as a member of any State legislature, or as an executive or judicial officer of any State, to support the Constitution of the United States, shall have engaged in insurrection or rebellion against the same, or given aid or comfort to the enemies thereof. But Congress may by a vote of two-thirds of each House, remove such disability.

Section 4

The validity of the public debt of the United States, authorized by law, including debts incurred for payment of pensions and bounties for services in suppressing insurrection or rebellion, shall not be questioned. But neither the United States nor any State shall assume or pay any debt or obligation incurred in aid of insurrection or rebellion against the United States, or any claim for the loss or emancipation of any slave; but all such debts, obligations and claims shall be held illegal and void.

Section 5

The Congress shall have power to enforce, by appropriate legislation, the provisions of this article.

Amendment XV

Section 1

The right of citizens of the United States to vote shall not be denied or abridged by the United States or by any State on account of race, color, or previous condition of servitude.

Section 2

The Congress shall have power to enforce this article by appropriate legislation.

Amendment XVI

The Congress shall have power to lay and collect taxes on incomes, from whatever source derived, without apportionment among the several States, and without regard to any census or enumeration.

Amendment XVII

The Senate of the United States shall be composed of two Senators from each State, elected by the people thereof, for six years; and each Senator shall have one vote. The electors in each State shall have the qualifications requisite for electors of the most numerous branch of the State legislatures.

When vacancies happen in the representation of any State in the Senate, the executive authority of such State shall issue writs of election to fill such vacancies: Provided, That the legislature of any State may empower the executive thereof to make temporary appointments until the people fill the vacancies by election as the legislature may direct.

This amendment shall not be so construed as to affect the election or term of any Senator chosen before it becomes valid as part of the Constitution.

Amendment XVIII

Section 1

After one year from the ratification of this article the manufacture, sale, or transportation of intoxicating liquors within, the importation thereof into, or the exportation thereof from the United States and all territory subject to the jurisdiction thereof for beverage purposes is hereby prohibited.

Section 2

The Congress and the several States shall have concurrent power to enforce this article by appropriate legislation.

Section 3

This article shall be inoperative unless it shall have been ratified as an amendment to the Constitution by the legislatures of the several States, as provided in the Constitution, within seven years from the date of the submission hereof to the States by the Congress.

Amendment XIX

The right of citizens of the United States to vote shall not be denied or abridged by the United States or by any State on account of sex. Congress shall have power to enforce this article by appropriate legislation.

Amendment XX

Section 1

The terms of the President and Vice President shall end at noon on the 20th day of January, and the terms of Senators and Representatives at noon on the 3d day of January, of the years in which such terms would have ended if this article had not been ratified; and the terms of their successors shall then begin.

Section 2

The Congress shall assemble at least once in every year, and such meeting shall begin at noon on the 3d day of January, unless they shall by law appoint a different day.

Section 3

If, at the time fixed for the beginning of the term of the President, the President elect shall have died, the Vice President elect shall become President. If a President shall not have been chosen before the time fixed for the beginning of his term, or if the President elect shall have failed to qualify, then the Vice President elect shall act as President until a President shall have qualified; and the Congress may by law provide for the case wherein neither a President elect nor a Vice President elect shall have qualified, declaring who shall then act as President, or the manner in which one who is to act shall be selected, and such person shall act accordingly until a President or Vice President shall have qualified.

Section 4

The Congress may by law provide for the case of the death of any of the persons from whom the House of Representatives may choose a President whenever the right of choice shall have devolved upon them, and for the case of the death of any of the persons from whom the Senate may choose a Vice President whenever the right of choice shall have devolved upon them.

Section 5

Sections 1 and 2 shall take effect on the 15th day of October following the ratification of this article.

Section 6

This article shall be inoperative unless it shall have been ratified as an amendment to the Constitution by the legislatures of three-fourths of the several States within seven years from the date of its submission.

Amendment XXI

Section 1

The eighteenth article of amendment to the Constitution of the United States is hereby repealed.

Section 2

The transportation or importation into any State, Territory, or possession of the United States for delivery or use therein of intoxicating liquors, in violation of the laws thereof, is hereby prohibited.

Section 3

This article shall be inoperative unless it shall have been ratified as an amendment to the Constitution by conventions in the several States, as provided in the Constitution, within seven years from the date of the submission hereof to the States by the Congress.

Twenty-Second Amendment XXII

Section 1

No person shall be elected to the office of the President more than twice, and no person who has held the office of President, or acted as President, for more than two years of a term to which some other person was elected President shall be elected to the office of the President more than once. But this Article shall not apply to any person holding the office of President, when this Article was proposed by the Congress, and shall not prevent any person who may be holding the office of President, or acting as President, during the term within which this Article becomes operative from holding the office of President or acting as President during the remainder of such term.

Section 2

This article shall be inoperative unless it shall have been ratified as an amendment to the Constitution by the legislatures of three-fourths of the several States within seven years from the date of its submission to the States by the Congress.

Amendment XXIII

Section 1

The District constituting the seat of Government of the United States shall appoint in such manner as the Congress may direct: A number of electors of President and Vice President equal to the whole number of Senators and Representatives in Congress to which the District would be entitled if it were a State, but in no event more than the least populous State; they shall be in addition to those appointed by the States, but they shall be considered, for the purposes of the election of President and Vice President, to be electors appointed by a State; and they shall meet in the District and perform such duties as provided by the twelfth article of amendment.

Section 2

The Congress shall have power to enforce this article by appropriate legislation.

Amendment XXIV

Section 1

The right of citizens of the United States to vote in any primary or other election for President or Vice President, for electors for President or Vice President, or for Senator or Representative in Congress, shall not be denied or abridged by the United States or any State by reason of failure to pay any poll tax or other tax.

Section 2

The Congress shall have power to enforce this article by appropriate legislation.

Amendment XXV

Section 1

In case of the removal of the President from office or of his death or resignation, the Vice President shall become President.

Section 2

Whenever there is a vacancy in the office of the Vice President, the President shall nominate a Vice President who shall take office upon confirmation by a majority vote of both Houses of Congress.

Section 3

Whenever the President transmits to the President pro tempore of the Senate and the Speaker of the House of Representatives has written declaration that he is unable to discharge the powers and duties of his office, and until he transmits to them a written declaration to the contrary, such powers and duties shall be discharged by the Vice President as Acting President.

Section 4

Whenever the Vice President and a majority of either the principal officers of the executive departments or of such other body as Congress may by law provide, transmit to the President pro tempore of the Senate and the Speaker of the House of Representatives their written declaration that the President is unable to discharge the powers and duties of his office, the Vice President shall immediately assume the powers and duties of the office as Acting President.

Thereafter, when the President transmits to the President pro tempore of the Senate and the Speaker of the House of Representatives has written declaration that no inability exists, he shall resume the powers and duties of his office unless the Vice President and a majority of either the principal officers of the executive department or of such other body as Congress may by law provide, transmit within four days to the President pro tempore of the Senate and the Speaker of the House of Representatives their written declaration that the President is unable to discharge the powers and duties of his office. Thereupon Congress shall decide the issue, assembling within forty-eight hours for that purpose if not in session. If the Congress, within twenty-one days after receipt of the latter written declaration, or, if Congress is not in session, within twenty-one days after

Congress is required to assemble, determines by two-thirds vote of both Houses that the President is unable to discharge the powers and duties of his office, the Vice President shall continue to discharge the same as Acting President; otherwise, the President shall resume the powers and duties of his office.

Amendment XXVI

Section 1

The right of citizens of the United States, who are eighteen years of age or older, to vote shall not be denied or abridged by the United States or by any State on account of age.

Section 2

The Congress shall have power to enforce this article by appropriate legislation.

Amendment XXVII

No law varying the compensation for the services of the Senators and Representatives shall take effect, until an election of Representatives shall have intervened.

Appendix B
Table of Cases

Appendix C
Bibliography

Aldrich, John H. *Why Parties?: The Origin and Transformation of Political Parties in America.* Chicago: The University of Chicago Press, 1995.

Allard, Scott, et al. "Representing Urban Interests: The Local Politics of State Legislatures," 12 *Studies in American Political Development* 267–302 (Fall 1998).

Allswang, John M. *The Initiative and Referendum in California, 1898–1998,* Stanford: Stanford University Press, 2000.

Ansolabehere, Stephen and James M. Snyder, Jr. "Soft Money, Hard Money, Strong Parties," 100 *Colum. L. Rev.* 598 (2000).

Askin, Frank. "Political Money and Freedom of Speech: Kathleen Sullivan's Seven Deadly Sins — An Antitoxin," 31:4 *U.C. Davis Law Review* (Summer 1998).

Baker, C. Edwin. "Campaign Expenditures and Free Speech," 33:1 *Harv. C.R.-C.L. L. Rev.* (Winter 1998).

Bowler, Shaun, Todd Donovan, and Caroline J. Tolbert (eds.). *Citizens as Legislators: Direct Democracy in the United States.* Columbus: Ohio State University Press, 1998.

Briffault, Richard. "Ballot Propositions and Campaign Finance Reform." 1:1 *New York University Journal of Legislation and Public Policy* (1997).

Briffault, Richard. "The Political Parties and Campaign Finance Reform," 100:3 *Colum. L. R.* 620 (April 2000).

Brittain, John C. "Direct Democracy by the Majority Can Jeopardize the Civil Rights of Minority or Other Powerless Groups." 1:1 *New York University Journal of Legislation and Public Policy* (1997).

Brockington, David, et al. "Minority Representation under Cumulative and Limited Voting," 60 *Journal of Politics* 1108–25 (Nov. 1998).

Brown, Clifford W., Jr., Linda W. Powell, and Clyde Wilcox. *Serious Money: Fundraising and Contributing in Presidential Nominating Campaigns.* New York: Cambridge University Press, 1995.

Burke, Christopher. *The Appearance of Equality: Racial Gerrymandering, Redistricting, and the Supreme Court.* Westport, CT: Greenwood Press, 1999.

Bybee, Keith J. *Mistaken Identity: The Supreme Court and the Politics of Minority Representation.* Princeton: Princeton University Press, 1998.

Canon, David T. *Race, Redistricting, and Representation: The Unintended Consequences of Black Majority Districts.* Chicago: University of Chicago Press, 1999.

Carey, John M. Richard G. Niemi, and Lynda W. Powell. *Term Limits in State Legislatures.* Ann Arbor: University of Michigan Press, 2000.

Cates, Cynthia L. "Splitting the Atom of Sovereignty: Terms Limits, Inc.'s Conflicting Views of Popular Autonomy in a Federal Republic," 26:3 *Publius: The Journal of Federalism* (Summer 1996).

Clawson, Dan, Alan Neustadtl, and Mark Weller. *Dollars and Votes: How Business Campaign Contributions Subvert Democracy.* Philadelphia: Temple University Press, 1998.

Clayton, Dewey M. *African Americans and the Politics of Congressional Redistricting.* New York: Garland, 2000.

Clayton, Dewey. "Black Congressional Districts in the South: Making the Case for Majority Black Districts," 28 *Black Scholar* 36–46 (Summer 1998).

Cofsky, Kevin. "Pruning the Political Thicket: The Case for Strict Scrutiny of State Ballot Access Restrictions," 145:2 *University of Pennsylvania Law Review* 353 (Dec. 1996).

Corrado, Anthony. "Giving, Spending and 'Soft Money,'" 6 *J. L. & Pol'y* 45 (1997).

Crain, W. Mark. "The Constitutionality of Race-Conscious Redistricting: An Empirical Analysis." 30:1 *The Journal of Legal Studies* 193 (2001).

Dinkin, Robert J. *Before Equal Suffrage: Women in Partisan Politics from Colonial Times to 1920.* Westport, CT: Greenwood Press, 1995.

Donley, Dave. "The Case for a U.S. Constitutional Amendment to Allow Campaign Spending Limits," 70:2 *Spectrum: The Journal of State Government* 32 (Spring 1997).

Dubois, Philip L. and Floyd Feeney. *Lawmaking by Initiative: Issues, Options, and Comparisons.* New York: Agathon Press, 1998.

"Elections: The Scope of Congressional Authority in Election Administration." GAO-01–470. (March 2001).

Eisenberg, Arthur N. "Buckley, Rupert Murdoch, and the Pursuit of Equality in the Conduct of Elections." 1:1 *New York University Journal of Legislation and Public Policy* (1997).

Ely, John Hart. "Standing to Challenge Pro-Minority Gerrymanders," 111:2 *Harvard Law Review* 576 (Dec. 1997).

Epstein, David and Sharyn O'Halloran. *Race, Redistricting, and Representation.* Princeton: Princeton University Press, 2001.

Finnegan, Margaret. *Selling Suffrage: Consumer Culture and Votes for Women.* New York: Columbia University Press, 1999.

Fisher, Jeffrey L. "The Unwelcome Judicial Obligation to Respect Politics in Racial Gerrymandering Remedies," 95:5 *Michigan Law Review* 1404 (March 1997).

Fiss, Owen M. "Money and Politics," 97 *Colum. L. Rev.* 2470 (1997).

Frickey, Philip P. "Interpretation on the Borderline: Constitution, Canons, Direct Democracy." 1:1 *New York University Journal of Legislation and Public Policy* (1997).

Gais, Thomas. *Improper Influence: Campaign Finance Law, Political Interest Groups, and the Problem of Equality.* Ann Arbor: University of Michigan Press, 1996.

Gavin, Jennifer. "Redistricting." 11:6 *The CQ Researcher* 113–128 (February 16, 2001).

Gerard, Jules B. "Election Signs and Time Limits," 3 *J. L. & Pol'y* 379 (2000).

Goldman, Robert Michael. *Reconstruction and Black Suffrage: Losing the Vote in Reese and Cruikshank.* Lawrence: University Press of Kansas, 2001.

Goldstein, Thomas C. "Corporate Influence in Referenda: A Comment About the Prescription." 1:1 *New York University Journal of Legislation and Public Policy* (1997).

Gordon, Ann D. et al. (eds.). *African American Women and the Vote, 1837–1965.*

Graham, Sara Hunter. *Woman Suffrage and the New Democracy.* Amherst: University of Massachusetts Press, 1997.

Grofman, Bernard. *Race and Redistricting in the 1990's.* New York: Agathon Press, 1998.

Gross, Donald A. and Robert K. Goidel. "The Impact Of State Campaign Finance Laws." 1:2 *State Politics & Policy Quarterly* (Summer 2001).

Harvey, Anna L. *Votes Without Leverage: Women in American Electoral Politics, 1920–1970.* New York: Cambridge University Press, 1998.

Hasen, Richard L. "Parties Take the Initiative (and Vice Versa)," 100 *Colum. L. Rev.* 731 (2000).

Hasen, Richard L. "Shrink Missouri, Campaign Finance and 'The Thing That Wouldn't Leave.'" Paper prepared for delivery at the 2000 Annual Meeting of the American Political Science Association, Washington, D.C., August 31–September 3, 2000.

Hasen, Richard L. "Vote Buying," 88 *Calif. L. Rev.* 1323 (2000).

Hayden, Grant M. "The Limits of Social Choice Theory: A Defense of the Voting Rights Act." 74:1 *Tulane Law Review* (November 1999).

Hudson, David Michael. *Along Racial Lines: Consequences of the 1965 Voting Rights Act.* New York: Peter Lang Publishing, 1998.

Issacharoff, Samuel and Pamela S. Karlan. "Standing and Misunderstanding in Voting Rights Law," 111 *Harvard Law Review* 576 (1997).

Issacharoff, Samuel. "The Constitutional Contours of Race and Politics," *Supreme Court Review* 45 (Annual 1995).

James, Scott C. and Brian L. Lawson. "The Political Economy of Voting Rights Enforcement in America's Gilded Age: Electoral College Competition, Partisan Commitment, and the Federal Election Law," 93 *American Political Science Review* 115–31 (March 1999).

Johnson-Cartee, Karen S. and Gary A. Copeland. *The Manipulation of the American Voter: Political Campaign Commercials.* Westport, CT: Praeger, 1997.

Keene, David. "Campaign Finance: Life as a Political Consultant," 6 *J. L. & Pol'y* 57 (1997).

Keyssar, Alexander. *The Right to Vote: The Contested History of Democracy in the United States.* New York: Basic Books, 2000.

Kirschner, William R. "Fusion and the Associational Rights of Minor Political Parties," 95:3 *Colum. L. R.* 683 (April 1995).

Kobach, Kris W. "May 'We the People' Speak?: The Forgotten Role of Constituent Instruction in Amending the Constitution," 33:1 *U.C. Davis Law Review* (Fall 1999).

Kousser, J. Morgan. "Colorblind Injustice: Minority Voting Rights and the Undoing of the Second Reconstruction," 47:2 *Cleveland State Law Review* (1999).

Kousser, J. Morgan. *Colorblind Injustice: Minority Voting Rights and the Undoing of the Second Reconstruction.* Chapel Hill: University of North Carolina Press, 1999.

La Pierre, D. Bruce. "Raising a New First Amendment Hurdle for Campaign Finance 'Reform.'" 76 *Wash. U.L.Q.* 217 (Spring 1998).

La Pierre, D. Bruce. "Campaign Contribution Limits: Pandering to Public Fears About 'Big Money' and Protecting Incumbents." 52 *Admin. L. Rev.* 687 (2000).

Leffel, Michael D. "A More Sensible Approach to Regulating Independent Expenditures: Defending the Constitutionality of the FEC's New Express Advocacy Standard," 95:3 *Michigan Law Review* 686 (Dec. 1996).

Linde, Hans A. "Practicing Theory: The Forgotten Law of Initiative Lawmaking," 45:6 *UCLA Law Review* (August 1998).

Littlewood, Thomas B. *Calling Elections: The Politics of Horse-Race Journalism.* Notre Dame, IN: University of Notre Dame Press, 1998.

Lubin, David and D. Stephen Voss. "Racial Redistricting and Realignment in Southern State Legislatures," *American Journal of Political Science* (October 2000).

Lublin, David. *The Paradox of Representation: Racial Gerrymandering and Minority Interests in Congress.* Princeton: Princeton University Press, 1997.

Lumsden, Linda J. *Rampant Women: Suffragists and the Right of Assembly.* Knoxville: University of Tennessee Press, 1997.

Maisel, L. Sandy and John F. Bibby. "Election Laws and Party Rules: Contributions to a Strong Party Role?." Paper prepared for delivery at the 2000 Annual Meeting of the American Political Science Association, Washington, D.C., August 31–September 3, 2000.

Marilley, Suzanne M. *Woman Suffrage and the Origins of Liberal Feminism in the United States, 1820–1920.* Cambridge: Harvard University Press, 1996.

Marshall, Susan E. *Splintered Sisterhood: Gender and Class in the Campaign Against Woman Suffrage.* Madison: University of Wisconsin Press, 1997.

Mayer, William G. (ed.). *In Pursuit of the White House: How We Choose Our Presidential Nominees.* New York: Chatham House Publishers, 2000.

McWilliams, Wilson Carey. *The Politics of Disappointment: American Elections 1976–1994.* Chatham, NJ: Chatham House Publishers, 1995.

Menifield, Charles E. "Redistricting and the Future of African American Representation." Paper prepared for delivery at the 2000 Annual Meeting of the American Political Science Association, Washington, D.C., August 31–September 3, 2000.

Monmonier, Mark S. *Bushmanders and Bullwinkles: How Politicians Manipulate Electronic Maps and Census Data to Win Elections.* Chicago: University of Chicago Press, 2001.

Morrison, Allan B. "Watch What You Wish For: The Perils of Reversing *Buckley v. Valeo,*" 36 *The American Prospect* 38 (Jan–Feb 1998).

Mulroy, Steven J. "The Way Out: A Legal Standard For Imposing Alternative Electoral Systems as Voting Rights Remedies," 33:2 *Harv. C.R.-C.L. L. Rev.* (Summer 1998).

Nagle, John Copeland. "Direct Democracy and Hastily Enacted Statutes." 1:1 *New York University Journal of Legislation and Public Policy* (1997).

Nagel, Mark S. "Constitutional Limits on Racial Redistricting: *Miller v. Johnson,*" 19:1 *Harvard Journal of Law & Public Policy* 188 (Fall 1995).

Neuborne, Burt. "Buckley's Analytical Flaws," 6 *J. L. & Pol'y* 111 (1997).

Nixon, Jeremiah W. Nixon and Paul R. Maguffee. "Money Talks: In Defense of Common-sense Approach to Judicial Review of Campaign Contribution Limits," 52:2 *Administrative Law Review* 661 (Spring 2000).

Persily, Nathaniel and Bruce E. Cain. "The Legal Status of Political Parties: A Reassessment of Competing Paradigms," 100:3 *Colum. L. Rev.* 775 (April 2000).

Persily, Nathaniel. "The Legal Regulation of Party Nomination Methods: *California Democratic Party v. Jones,* John McCain and Beyond." Paper prepared for delivery at the 2000 Annual Meeting of the American Political Science Association, Washington, D.C., August 31–September 3, 2000.

Persily, Nathaniel. "Color by Numbers: Race, Redistricting and the 2000 Census," 85 *Minn. L. Rev.* 899–947 (2001).

Pierre-Louis, Stanley. "The Politics of Influence: Recognizing Influence Dilution Claims Under §2 of the Voting Rights Act," 62:3 *University of Chicago Law Review* 1215 (Summer 1995).

Podolefsky, Ronnie L. "The Illusion of Suffrage: Female Voting Rights and the Women's Poll Tax Repeal Movement After the Nineteenth Amendment," 7:2 *Columbia Journal of Gender and Law* 185–237 (1998).

Post, Robert and Michael Rogin (eds.). *Race and Representation: Affirmative Action.* New York: Zone Books, 1998.

Raskin, Jamin B. "Direct Democracy, Corporate Power, and Judicial Review of Popularly-Enacted Campaign Finance Reform," 1:1 *New York University Journal of Legislation and Public Policy* (1997).

Raskin, Jamin B. "Is This America? The District of Columbia and the Right to Vote," 34:1 *Harv. C.R.-C.L. L. Rev.,* (Winter 1999).

Raskin, Jamin B. "A Complicated and Indirect Encroachment": Is the Federal Election Commission Unconstitutionally Composed?," 52:2 *Administrative Law Review* 609 (Spring 2000).

Rogers, Catherine and David L. Faigman. "And to the Republic For Which It Stands: Guaranteeing a Republican Form of Government," 23:4 *Hastings Constitutional Law Quarterly* 1057 (Summer 1996).

Rosenkranz, E. Joshua (ed.). *If Buckley Fell: A First Amendment Blueprint for Regulating Money in Politics.* Washington: Brookings Institution Press, 2000.

Rosenkranz, E. Joshua, Andrew L. Shapiro, and Alan B. Morrison. "Should Buckley Be Overturned?," 37 *The American Prospect* 78 (March–April 1998).

Rush, Mark E. "From 'Shaw v. Reno' to 'Miller v. Johnson': Minority Representation and State Compliance with the Voting Rights Act," 25:3 *Publius* 155 (Summer 1995).

Rush, Mark E. (ed.). *Voting Rights and Redistricting in the United States.* Westport, CT: Greenwood. 1998.

Rush, Mark E. and Richard Lee Engstrom. *Fair and Effective Representation: Debating Electoral Reform and Minority Rights.* Lanham, MD: Rowman & Littlefield, 2001.

Ryden, David K. (ed.). *The U.S. Supreme Court and the Electoral Process.* Washington: Georgetown University Press, 2000.

Scher, Richard K., Jon L. Mills, and John J. Hatoling. *Voting Rights & Democracy: The Law and Politics of Districting.* Chicago: Nelson-Hall, 1997.

Schotland, Roy A. "And for the Student? The Seven Striking Strengths of 'Ballots, Bucks, Maps & the Law' (Election Law as Its Own Field of Study)," 32 *Loy. L.A. L. Rev.* 1227 (1999).

Skerry, Peter. *Counting on the Census? Race, Group Identity, and the Evasion of Politics.* Washington: Brookings Institution Press, 2000.

Smith, Bradley A. "Faulty Assumptions and Undemocratic Consequences of Campaign Finance Reform," 105 *Yale L.J.* 1049, 1053–55 (1996).

Smith, Bradley A. "The Siren's Song: Campaign Finance Regulation and the First Amendment," 6 *J. L. & Pol'y* 1 (1997).

Smith, Daniel A. "Homeward Bound?: Micro-Level Legislative Responsiveness to Ballot Initiatives," 1:1 *State Politics & Policy Quarterly* (Spring 2001).

Smith, Eric Ledell. "The End of Black Voting Rights in Pennsylvania: African Americans and the Pennsylvania Constitutional Convention of 1837–1838," 65 *Pennsylvania History* 279–99 (Summer 1998).

Smith, George Bundy. "State Courts and Democracy: The Role of State Courts in the Battle for Inclusive Participation in the Electoral Process," 74:4 *New York University Law Review* 937 (Oct. 1999).

Snyder, James M., Jr. and Stephen Ansolabehere. "Soft Money, Hard Money, Strong Parties," 100:3 *Colum. L. Rev.* 598 (April 2000).

Spiro, Peter J. "Dual Nationality and the Meaning of Citizenship," 46:4 *Emory Law Journal* (Fall 1997).

Sullivan, Kathleen M. "Political Money and Freedom of Speech: A Reply to Frank Askin," 31:4 *U.C. Davis Law Review* (Summer 1998).

Szarawarski, Alan E. "Do 'Appearances Matter'? Minority Representation and the Misplaced Focus of *Shaw v. Reno.*" Paper prepared for delivery at the 2000 Annual Meeting of the American Political Science Association, Washington, D.C., August 31–September 3, 2000.

Taylor, Christopher M. "Vote Dilution and the Census Undercount: A State-by-State Remedy," 94:4 *Michigan Law Review* 1098 (Feb 1996).

Terborg-Penn, Rosalyn. *African American Women in the Struggle for the Vote, 1850–1920.* Bloomington: Indiana University Press, 1998.

Theriault, Sean M. "Patronage, the Pendleton Act, and the Power of the People." Paper prepared for delivery at the 2000 Annual Meeting of the American Political Science Association, Washington, D.C., August 31–September 3, 2000.

Thomas, Scott E. and Jeffrey H. Bowman. "Obstacles to Effective Enforcement of the Federal Election Campaign Act," 52:2 *Administrative Law Review* 575 (Spring 2000).

Thomas, Sue and Clyde Wilcox (eds.). *Women and Elective Office: Past, Present, and Future.* New York: Oxford University Press, 1998.

Tushnet, Mark. "Fear of Voting: Differential Standards of Judicial Review of Direct Legislation," 1:1 *New York University Journal of Legislation and Public Policy* (1997).

Viator, James Étienne. "The Losers Know Best the Meaning of the Game: What the Anti-Federalists Can Teach Us About Race-based Congressional Districts," 1 *Loy. J. Pub. Int. L.* 1–48 (2000).

Voss-Hubbard, Mark. "The 'Third Party Tradition' Reconsidered: Third Parties and American Public Life, 1830–1900," 86:1 *The Journal of American History* (June 1999).

West, Darrell M. and Burdett A. Loomis. *The Sound of Money: How Political Interests Get What They Want.* New York: W.W. Norton, 1999.

Wigton, Robert C. "American Political Parties Under the First Amendment," 7 *J. L. & Pol'y* 411 (1999).

Winkler, Adam. "Voters' Rights and Parties' Wrongs: Early Political Party Regulation in the State Courts, 1886–1915," 100 *Colum. L. Rev.* 873 (2000).

Winter, Ralph K. "The History and Theory of *Buckley v. Valeo*," 6 *J. L. & Pol'y* 93 (1997).

Yang, Elizabeth M. "Balancing Campaign Finance Reform Against the First Amendment," 64:5 *Social Education* 320 (September 2000).

Appendix D
Index

About the Editor

Christopher A. Anzalone is the editor of *Encyclopedia of Supreme Court Quotations* (M.E. Sharpe, 2000) and *Supreme Court Cases on Gender and Sexual Equality, 1787–2001* (M.E. Sharpe, 2002). He resides in Germantown, MD.